T

For Reference

Not to be taken from this room

Not to be taken from this room

AVOTAYNU
GUIDE TO
Jewish
Genealogy

Edited by Sallyann Amdur Sack & Gary Mokotoff

Avotaynu
Bergenfield, New Jersey
2004

Requests for permission to make copies of any part of this publication should be addressed to:

Avotaynu, Inc.
155 N. Washington Ave.
Bergenfield, NJ 07621

Printed in the United States of America

Credits:
Cover illustration: Caroline Guillot
Cover design: Kim Griswold Gardiner
The German, Polish and Russian alphabets in Appendix A are from *Following the Paper Trail* by Jonathan D. Shea and William F. Hoffman, Teaneck, N.J.: Avotaynu, 1994. The Hebrew and Yiddish alphabets are from *Jewish Roots in Ukraine and Moldova: Pages from the Past and Archival Inventories* by Miriam Weiner, Secaucus, N.J.: Routes to Routes Foundation, 1999.
Photo credits are provided in the caption of pictures where appropriate. Photos of Jewish life circa beginning of the 20th century are from *The Jewish Encyclopedia,* edited by Isadore Singer. New York and London: Funk and Wagnalls, 1901-1906

Guide to Jewish genealogy.
  Avotaynu guide to Jewish genealogy / edited by Sallyann Amdur Sack and
Gary Mokotoff.
     p. cm.
Includes bibliographical references.
  ISBN 1-886223-17-3
  1. Jews-Genealogy-Handbooks, manuals, etc. I. Sack, Sallyann Amdur,
1936- II. Mokotoff, Gary. III. Title.

CS21.G85 2003
929'.1'072-dc22

                                                                    2003022930

In years past, rabbis customarily began their books with a listing of their lineages. We dedicate this book to our parents, spouses and descendants.

Max Amdur=Frances Steinsnider
    Sallyann Amdur=Lawrence C. Sack
        Robert I. Sack=MaryAnn Mannes
            Benjamin Meyer Sack
            Daniel Amdur Sack
            Matthew Philip Sack
        Elizabeth Sack=Daniel Felber
            Emily Rose Felber
            Adam Samuel Felber
        Kathryn Sack=Gregory Solomon
            Julia Rachel Solomon
            Jacob Louis Solomon

Jack Mokotoff=Sylvia Friedberg
    Gary Mokotoff=Ruth Lois Auerbach
        Alexis Laraine Mokotoff=Jon Shapiro
            Kayla Mills Shapiro
            Amanda Rose Shapiro
        Jessica Lynn Mokotoff=Mark Gollin
            Tyler Joseph Gollin
        Gregory Scott Mokotoff=Heather Paul

Contents

Maps

Foreword:
Genealogy As a Spiritual Pilgrimage

by Arthur Kurzweil

I am thinking about the mitzvahs that we do as genealogists. It seems to me that every step of the way when we pursue our genealogical research, we are involved in mitzvahs. Who more than we honor the elderly? Who more than we reach out to the elderly people in our family and our communities and make them feel like we need them—because we do. And what is that but a mitzvah, to honor the elderly.

Who more than we ask questions? The Talmud consists of questions, thousands of ways of asking different questions. Did you ever ask the question, "Where did you get that information from?" Well, there is a little code word in the Talmud for the question, "Where did you get that question from?" And who has perfected the art of asking questions more than we have? Who has perfected the art of being humble, that personality trait of Moses that we say was his great trait of humility? What greater act of humility can there be than to go to someone and say, "I don't know something you know that I need to know. Let me ask you a question?"

Who like we genealogists performs the mitzvah of *ahavat Yisrael*, the love of the people of Israel, which really means tolerance. What Jews in the world are more tolerant than Jewish genealogists? Why are we tolerant? We are tolerant because we learn that on this branch of the family there are Galicianers, and on this branch there are Litvaks, and on this branch there are assimilated Jews and on this branch there are intermarriages! And we see that each of our families really is everybody, and in the process we become tolerant.

Rabbi Adin Steinsaltz wrote a guidebook for newly observant Jews, a book called *Tesuvah* (published by Free Press). This is a book written by an orthodox rabbi about how to become more religious. Chapter 10 in that book is on doing your genealogy as the tool to get more connected to your heritage. Who more than we have discovered that?

Who more than we have discovered that the older people in our neighborhoods and in our families are the people we need—when we ask them to translate something for us, when we ask them any kind of question? What a beautiful mitzvah it is—that act of kindness to tell somebody, "I need you;" to tell somebody, "You can help me; you are important to me."

How about cemeteries? How many of us have gone to cemeteries that nobody has been in for years and years and years, and you get there and have that sense that the reason that people chipped away at those stones and wrote those letters and words is because you were going to get there one day, and you were going to read that inscription and perform the mitzvah of honoring the dead. Who more than we have performed that mitzvah of going to those cemeteries and honoring our deceased and our past?

Who more than we understand what Maimonides meant in the *Mishnah Torah,* when he asked if you only have enough money to teach yourself or your children, who do you teach first? The answer is that you teach yourself first. You don't send your kids to Hebrew School. You go, and then you teach your children. Who more than we are involved with adult Jewish education—involved with it ourselves and pursuing our own Jewish education independently as adults and doing what Maimonides said centuries ago: You don't first give somebody else the opportunity to educate themselves Jewishly; you take that opportunity yourself. And you perform the mitzvah of Jewish education, participating yourself.

Who more than we have performed the mitzvah of remembering? Just of remembering. Twice a day Jews say the *Shema*. And when we say the *Shema* in the morning and the evening, one of the things we are supposed to have in our minds is to perform the mitzvah of remembering. To fulfill the mitzvah of saying the *Shema* is not just to say a bunch of words. It is also to consciously remember. Who more than we have been perfecting the art of remembering, which, of course, is a mitzvah in itself. How many of us know that in the Passover haggadah, it says that we should feel as if we—we ourselves—came out of Egypt? I want every moment of Jewish history to be a moment of my history. I want to participate in every moment of Jewish history. Who more than we have been participating in that mitzvah of remembering?

I have had the experience countless times that I go to a relative, that I contact somebody I know is a relative, and they say to me, "Who are you?" And I say, "I am Arthur Kurzweil," and it means nothing to them. "Yeah, but who *are* you?" And when I say, "I am Zalman Leib's grandson," "You are Zalman Leib's grandson!?" Suddenly they know—"You mean your great-grandmother was...?" Suddenly they know who you are, and they welcome you. It's, "Oh! You're Zalman Leib's grandson! Come on in." Three times a day we Jews say a set of prayers, the *Shemonah Esrei*—19 blessings. We stand up straight with our feet together and in silence we imagine that we are in the inner chamber of the King of Kings of Kings. That's the psychodrama that we participate in three times a day, to stand before God Himself and feel as if we are speaking directly to God. The first blessing of those 19 blessings is a genealogical blessing: "*Barukh Atah Hashem Elokeinu Velokei Avoteinu Elokei Abraham, Elokei Yitschak, Velokei Yaakov....*" It is as if you are going into the chamber of the palace of the King of Kings of Kings, and what are you saying? "You know who I am? I am a descendant of Abraham, Isaac and Jacob. Now you know who I am?" "Yeah, sure. Come on in." If I had just started praying.... "Who are you Kurzweil?" But when I say that I am the *einicle* (grandson) of so-and-so, suddenly it is "Sure, come on in," and I feel much more welcome.

There is another mitzvah that is our mitzvah. One of the mitzvot, the obligation of each Jew, is something that almost nobody does—the mitzvah of writing the Torah. Each of us is actually supposed to write our own *Sefer Torah*. Many authorities today tell us that not only is that impractical, but it is not even necessary. Really, the spirit of the mitzvah of each person writing our own *Sefer Torah* is really to maintain a Jewish library, to bring Jewish books into our lives and into our homes. And who more than we has personified that act of bringing Jewish books into our homes, of bringing Jewish books into our lives, filling our shelves with Jewish source material?

Mitzvah after mitzvah after mitzvah after mitzvah. Isn't it strange that sometimes they think that what we are doing is just putting names and dates on pieces of paper? They don't see that that has very little to do with what we are involved with. What we are involved with is mitzvah work—on a personal level, on a family level, on a community level, on a world level. Every step of the way, what we do has to do with mitzvot.

Who more than we understand the mystery and the importance in Jewish tradition of the power of names, of not just to jumble everybody together, but that everybody is important? The fact of six million Jews being killed during the Holocaust is unfathomable to us, but we have specific names of the people in our families. I don't know what to do with the Holocaust. Most people in the world don't know what to do with the Holocaust. But I think we genealogists have found out what to do with the Holocaust. We remember names.

When the Nazis rounded up our relatives, they took away their names and gave them numbers. What we genealogists are involved with is taking away the numbers and giving them back their names.

Another mitzvah that we are involved with is the mitzvah of *shalom bayit*—peace in the house. It is a mitzvah in Jewish tradition to make peace in the household. I have spoken to lots of people whom nobody spoke to in 40 years because there was some kind of a fight, and no one even remembers what the fight was anymore. And who cares what the fight is about? It ends up that you are the one who made the bridge; you are the one who helped to heal the family; you are the one who helped to bring about that sense of *shalom bayit*.

Who has helped the libraries and archives to understand what they themselves have but we genealogists? How many times have we pointed out to the archivists and the librarians what kinds of collections they themselves have that are important to us? I used to go to YIVO in New York years ago when Moshe Laub was the director. When I arrived in the lobby, Moshe Laub would run out of his office and say, "Kurzweil, you're the one who is giving us all the trouble." One day, Moshe Laub heard from a friend of mine who works at YIVO that I was going to Poland, to the city of Przemsyl. The next time I was in the building, he ran out of his office, and I said, "I know. I am giving you all the trouble." And he said, "No, no, no. Come into my office." He took out his wallet, and from it he took a piece of paper that must have been 60 years old that had the address of the house in

Przemsyl where he was born. He said to me, "You are going to Przemsyl; will you take a picture of the house for me?" And I said, "I thought I was the one who was giving you all the trouble." Suddenly he realized that I wasn't giving him so much trouble any more. He was a convert now. He saw. He said, "Oh, I want to give pictures to my children." And I smiled and I said, "Yes, that's what we genealogists have been doing, bothering you and your librarians all these years. We want to give things to our children. We don't want it to cut off. And you have a gold mine and we need it," and we have gotten it.

Perhaps you have read the book by the late Paul Cowen. Paul wrote a book called *An Orphan in History*, which was about Paul's own genealogical search and his reconnection with his own Jewish roots. Paul and I were neighbors on the Upper West Side in New York when he was writing that book. We bumped into each other on the sidewalk one day, and he said, "Kurzweil, you are just the person I wanted to see! I want to find out where my grandfather was born. How do I find out?" I said, "Well, where did he die?" He said, "Chicago." I said, "Get his death certificate. Often on a death certificate it will give you, if anybody knew, the place of birth." "Thank you very much." He left. I left.

A couple of months later, I went to the YIVO Institute to the fifth floor to visit my good friend Dr. Lucien Dobroszycki. I walked into Dr. Dobroszycki's office, and who was sitting there but Paul Cowen. He says, "Kurzweil, you are just the person I wanted to see! I took your advice, I sent to Chicago for the death certificate. You are right. It does give the place of birth, and we are trying to find it on this map of Lithuania. We can't seem to find it." There was this big map sprawled out on the table, and Dr. Dobroszycki and Paul Cowen are looking at this map and they say, "Maybe you can help us. We have been looking for three hours to find this town. It looks to us to be something like Unkanowen." I looked at the certificate and I said, "Paul, it isn't Unkanowen; it's *unknown*!" UNKNOWN—Unkanowen! My one genealogical tip of the evening is, if you come from Unkanowen also, you might be related to Paul Cowen!

Some of you have known me for a long time, and you know that I had the beard long before it meant anything Jewish to me. Some of you knew me long before I put the yarmulke on my head or long before a lot of changes happened in my life. I would say without a shadow of a doubt that it was my genealogical research that affected me like Kafka's Metamorphosis— you know, one morning you wake up and you're a cockroach! I hated those Orthodox Jews, and one morning I woke up and I realized that I was part of them.

One of the things that my family and I did was to move to Brooklyn, and I spent a good number of years *davening* (praying) with the Hasidic community in Borough Park, the Bobover Hasidim. It happens that the Bobover rebbe is Rabbi Halberstam, and I went to see him every Shabbos and danced with the Hasidim and celebrated Shabbos with them week after week after week. One of my friends said to me that I ought to go and speak to the rabbi one night. I said, "Well, how do you do it?" And he said, "Well, you get on line and you eventually get in to see him." I went there early, and I was the second person in line.

As some of you might know from some of the things I have written, it happens that my great-great-great-grandfather was a Hasidic rebbe. He wrote a book, and the introduction to the book was written by the great-grandfather of the Bobover rebbe. Before I went in to see him, a friend of mine who is a Bobover Hasid said, "You don't just go in there to shmooze; you have to have something on your mind, so maybe you should think of something to talk to him about." So I thought about it, and I had three questions that I wanted to ask him.

I walked into the rebbe's office, and I had a piece of paper with my children's names on it because I wanted him to make a blessing for the children. I gave him the paper, and the Bobover rebbe was holding my hand; he was sitting and I was standing, and my first question to him was going to be, "Why am I here in your office? Why am I in your office and not somebody else's office? There are so many rebbes; why am I here?" I didn't get a word out of my mouth. He looked at me and he said, "So you are wondering why you are here. You are wondering why you are in my office and not somebody else's office." He said to me, "I want to tell you something very important." This 80-something-year-old man with piercing eyes—beautiful man, his face shines with light—said to me, "I want to tell you something very important. There is no such thing as a coincidence."

He let go of my hand, and he pulled out the five books of Moses, the *Chumash*, and he flipped through until he came to where it tells about Abraham sending his servant Eleazar to find a bride for his son. And the Bobover rebbe showed me in the commentary that if you read the sentence a certain way, it reads, "They planned to meet by chance." The rebbe looked at me and he said, "How could they plan to meet by chance? Either they planned to meet, or it's a chance." He said, "That's the point. You think you wandered into this rebbe and not another. There is no such thing as a coincidence." Any of you, by the way, who believe that there is such a thing as coincidence haven't been doing much genealogical research, because they happen so often that after a while, you just don't believe that it is a coincidence anymore.

The second question that I wanted to ask him was, "What do I do with my sins?" As a Jew who is learning more and more, I realize every day what I did wrong yesterday. I am accumulating all this knowledge of what I did wrong yesterday, so I wanted to say to the rebbe, "What do I do with my sins?"

I didn't get a word out of my mouth. He looked at me and he said, "And stop worrying about your sins." Honestly, this happened! He said, "Don't worry about your past and don't worry about your future. Just worry about your mitzvahs in the present. Mitzvahs in the present are going to take care of your past, and they are going to take care of your future."

The third question I was going to ask him was if he had any advice for me. I didn't get a word out of my mouth, and he said to me, "I'd like to give you some advice." And then he gave me some advice.

For some of us, this is a path that leads us closer to Jewish tradition. And in Brooklyn, as our children began arriving, we realized that the apartment was too small and we had to move. I said to my wife, "I don't care where we move as long as we stay on the F train," because the F train was, at that time, the best subway line there was. The air conditioning usually worked in the summertime, and if you took the F train from Brooklyn to Manhattan every morning and returned every evening, you could have a minyan on every car. There are men studying Talmud, and there are women reading psalms. It's like Jewish Disneyland, and I liked being among them. My first Talmud teacher taught me that it says in the Talmud that you are not supposed to go two cubits—which is from the tip of your elbow to the tip of your fingers—with a fellow Jew without talking Torah. And here I am, sitting every morning and every evening in the subway not talking to anybody, because in the New York City subway system, the etiquette is that you don't talk to anybody. There I am every morning and every evening with all these fellow Jews, and nobody is talking to anybody, and I'm thinking about the Talmud telling me that I've got to talk to people—and I can't get up the courage to do it.

Well, every morning and every evening on the subway I spent my time reading my favorite book in the world. It's called *The Thirteen-Petalled Rose* (Jason Aronson), a 180-page book about Jewish thought, written by Rabbi Adin Steinsaltz. One evening going back to Brooklyn, I am reading this book, and a Hasid is sitting next to me, about 70 years old, with the whole get-up—and he is reading the *New York Post*. The *New York Post* is a rag. When you read the headline in the *New York Post*, you are sure that didn't happen.

I am feeling very good about myself, because I am this assimilated kid from Long Island who didn't have much of a Jewish education, and I am reading this interesting book on Jewish theology by the great Rabbi Steinsaltz of Jerusalem, and here's this Hasid reading the *Post*! I wanted to talk to this Jew. I finally got up the nerve and I said, "Excuse me. Did you ever see this book?" He looked at the beginning of the book, and he said, "I don't look at books unless they have at least two *haskamahs* (approbations)."

Those of you who have done genealogical research on rabbinical lines know that a *haskamah* is a genealogical tool. In the old country and in this country, if you write a book, you want to get someone to say, "This is a kosher book." In most rabbinic books, you have at least two haskamahs. The reason why they are genealogical tools is because they usually say "So-and-so, who is the author of this book, is the son of So-and-so, the grandson of So-and-so, who came from this town," so I knew haskamahs from genealogical research.

When this Hasid said, "I don't look at books unless they have two haskamahs," I wanted to say to him, "Where is the haskamah on the *New York Post* thank you very much?" But then he surprised me when he said, "But you know, it isn't really that important. What is the book about?" I said, "It is a basic introduction to Jewish thought," and I opened to the table of contents and I said, "There is a chapter called Torah and one called Mitzvot and a chapter called Holiness. In fact, I have a question for you." I said, "Could I ask you a question?" And this Hasid put down his *Post* and said, "Yes." I said, "I would like to read a passage from this book to you"—on the F train winding its way to Brooklyn. Steinsaltz writes: It has been said that each of the letters of the Torah has some corresponding soul. That is to say, every soul is a letter in the entire Torah and has its own part to play. The soul that has fulfilled its task, the soul that has done what it needs to do in terms of repairing or creating its own part of the world, this soul can wait after death for the perfection of the world as a whole, but, he says, not all souls are so privileged. Many souls stray for one reason or another. Sometimes a person does not do all of the proper things. Sometimes he misuses forces and spoils his portion, spoils the portion of others. In such a case, the soul does not complete its task and may even itself be damaged by contact with the world. It has not managed to complete that portion of reality which only this particular soul can complete and, therefore, after the death of the body the soul returns and is reincarnated in the body of another person and again must try and complete what it failed to correct or it injured in the past. I said to this Hasid, "Do we believe in this?" He said, "Sure." I said, "Jews believe in reincarnation? I never heard of it." He said to me, "Well, where did you get your Jewish education?" And I told him that I didn't get much of a Jewish education, and I began to tell him about the kind of a household that I grew up in and about the struggles that I have had personally in connecting myself back to Jewish tradition, and he looked at me as if to say, "So now you are asking me why you never heard of this?" He said, "Yes, this is truly part of Jewish tradition."

We began to talk more as the train went into Brooklyn, and I was telling him more about my troubles and more about my problems. At a certain point, this Hasid looked at me and said, "You know, you are luckier than I am." I said, "I am luckier than you are? I just got finished telling you all my troubles. I just got finished telling you that I didn't receive a Jewish education as a kid, and you're telling me that I am luckier than you are? How is it possible?"

And he said, "Every Jew, every person, is connected to God by a rope." He was talking metaphorically. He said, "Sometimes that rope breaks, as in your case, but when you take that broken rope and you tie it together, you are closer than you were had the rope not broken. So you are closer than I'll ever be."

I learned a couple of things from that episode. Number one, my Talmud teacher is right; you shouldn't go two cubits without talking Torah with somebody else. The second thing that I learned from him sums up the whole of my genealogical experience. It's been a process of grabbing hold of those two pieces of broken rope and somehow tying them together again.

The Talmud says that when the Temple in Jerusalem was destroyed, the survivors of that cataclysm had to say to themselves, "What are we going to do? Is this the end, or do we rebuild?" The Talmud says that when the Temple in Jerusalem was destroyed, then the Jews did their family trees. Now as a student of Talmud and a student of Jewish genealogy, I was quite intrigued to see that it says that when the Temple in Jerusalem was destroyed, the Jews did their family trees. A commentator makes the observation, as we know so well, that sometimes if you want to go forward, you first have to go backward. You see where you are coming from, and you know where you are going.

Thank God we are here today as Jews, because our ancestors who survived that cataclysm did their family trees. I believe, as I am sure you do, that we are in that same kind of situation today. We are a rebuilding generation. We come after two of the worst moments of Jewish history—one, of course, the Holocaust when a third of our people were murdered and two, the mass migration of Jews when our families were torn apart. There is probably not a family here this evening that if you go back two or three generations, you will not see that family torn apart—brothers and sisters never saw each other again, husbands and wives, grandparents and grandchildren. And I believe that in the same way that the Talmud says that when the Temple was destroyed, they rebuilt by doing their family trees, in our generation we have the same task. As a rebuilding generation, we are doing our family trees to rebuild, to put the pieces back together again, to take that shattered people and to bring them back together again. Our work is mitzvah work. I think we are doing a good job.

Rabbi Malcolm H. Stern
(1915–1994)
Father of Jewish-American genealogy.

A Guide to Using This Book

by Sallyann Amdur Sack

The *Wall Street Journal* carried a front-page story in March 2003 reporting that 60 percent of all Americans were actively engaged in researching their family histories. Genealogy has joined the mainstream, and Jews all over the world—not just in the United States—are participating. Gone are the days when a family member asked (with apparent sincerity) if genealogists traced their dead relatives because they didn't have any living friends!

Ever since I began my own genealogical research a generation ago, many have asked how they could do this, too. Advice was simple in the early years: "Read Rottenberg and Kurzweil and join (or form) a Jewish genealogy society." A little later we pioneers added: "Subscribe to AVOTAYNU, read all the back issues, check the Consolidated Jewish Surname Index, and attend the annual Jewish genealogical seminars." By the mid- to late-1990s, the advice included: "Read the JewishGen Digest, register your research on its Family Finder and on the Family Tree of the Jewish People, and join a Special Interest Group (SIG)."

By now the body of knowledge about Jewish genealogy has grown so large and is expanding so rapidly that the list of initial instructions can be bewilderingly extensive and complex.

For years I have wanted to have one book to place into a novice's hands with the advice to "read this and do everything it recommends." In part, this *Guide* is the fulfillment of that wish—and much more. It represents the efforts of 52 leading Jewish genealogists to survey the field, extract the essence, and present it in what we hope is a manageable, user-friendly package. This book is designed to be both a beginner's guide and a basic reference book for everyone researching their Jewish roots.

Until the publication of *Finding Our Fathers*, by Dan Rottenberg in 1977, and *From Generation to Generation*, by Arthur Kurzweil in 1980, most late 20th-century Jews thought it was impossible to trace Jewish family history. I almost never thought about genealogy when growing up in the U.S. Midwest, but the few times I heard the term "family trees," I assumed that they were akin to Christmas trees and Easter egg hunts—something Christians had—not for Jews.

On the few occasions when I asked my mother about the grandmother after whom I am named, she replied that my grandmother had come from the "Old Country" (wherever that was) and that Hitler had killed everyone; no one was left to ask anything. Others of my generation heard that "the name was changed at Ellis Island" and there was no way to learn more. We knew that the Jewish religion (and Jews) began with the patriarch Abraham more than 5,000 years ago, but in a strange way, many of us felt as if we Jews were essentially rootless.

Rottenberg and Kurzweil effectively dispelled these discouraging beliefs. Like a match to tinder, their books ignited a passion of latent interest in Jewish roots that, more than 25 years later, continues to blaze ever more strongly and shows no sign of dissipating. We have discovered that it is possible to trace our Jewish roots. In the process, the body of knowledge and the Jewish genealogical community have grown exponentially.

Soon after we began our genealogical research, we learned another basic truth. It is not possible simply to join a local, nonsectarian genealogical society and hope to learn much about tracing a Jewish family. Facts of Jewish history, religion, and culture are sufficiently different from those of our non-Jewish neighbors that to find the documents and traces left by our ancestors, we must immerse ourselves in their worlds (see Jewish Religion, Culture and Tradition). To help educate ourselves about our ancestors' lives, we have needed to develop the world of Jewish genealogy, with our own genealogical societies, conferences, publications, and special interest groups (see Organized Jewish Genealogy). Jewish genealogical research and activities have burgeoned during these past 25-plus years.

How This Book is Organized

This *Guide* features four sections. The first section deals with the basics of Jewish genealogical research; the second section is devoted to several special topics; research in the United States is the subject of the third section. The fourth and largest portion of the book includes a chapter on virtually every country (or region) in the world where a significant number of Jews live today or have lived within the past 200 years. With two exceptions described below, countries are defined according to present-day boundaries.

Authors were asked to imagine that they had just learned of relatives who once lived (or still live) in a specific country. The researcher, seeking to learn more about these relatives' lives, needs to know what resources are available and how to access them. In addition, each chapter has a brief history of Jewish life in the country, addresses of institutions mentioned and a bibliography for further reading. Beyond that, each expert developed his or her chapters as each saw fit. The results reflect the truth (told by Eileen Polakoff in her Methodology chapter) that genealogical research is an art, not a science. Each author approached the topic somewhat differently. Our intent is that the result be a canvas that conveys some of the subtleties and nuances of the various approaches to our topic.

Important Instructions

At the beginning of several country chapters is the advice to read one or another "empire" chapter first. This is important. Until the end of World War I, only four empires dominated the regions where most Jews lived. They were the German, Austrian (later, Austro-Hungarian) Empire, Ottoman Empire, and Czarist Russian Empire. Many countries were created upon the dissolution of these empires, but while they existed, each created laws that applied across the empire, some specific to Jews. To conserve space in a book that is already larger than we prefer, we elected to describe the laws only once, rather than repeat the information with each country. Sometimes, especially in the Austro-Hungarian Empire, variations existed in the application of the laws. These are noted, where relevant, within the country chapter. Most of the laws of the German Empire apply only to Germany today, so we found it unnecessary to include a chapter on the German Empire.

Poland, home to the single largest European Jewish population, ceased to exist as a sovereign country at the end of the 18th century and was not reconstituted until the end of World War I. We have divided information on Poland into three chapters to reflect the governance of that country when most of our ancestors lived on its soil. To a somewhat lesser extent we have done the same with the former Yugoslavia.

Asterisks and "See" References

Two conventions are intended to help the reader. Within a chapter, whenever the name of a resource repository or institution is followed by an asterisk, contact information for that location is cited in the address section at the end of that chapter. "See" references followed by the title of another chapter written in SMALL CAPITAL LETTERS points to additional information elsewhere in the book. Sometimes (as above) only the title of the chapter is given (in small capitals).

Miscellaneous Tips

Over time most genealogists develop their own pet list of favorite tips. Following are some of mine that do not appear elsewhere in the book.

The Centrality of Israel. Given its size and the size of its Jewish population, it seemed obvious that an entire section of the book had to be devoted to U.S. research. For a while, we considered treating Israel the same way, making it a fifth section. In the end, we decided to include Israel with the other countries, but all serious researchers should read the Israel chapter—even if they do not think they have or had any relatives there. In reality, every Jew undoubtedly has some relatives in Israel, just as we all had family members who died in the Holocaust. It all depends on how you define family. Do you consider your grandparents' brothers and sisters (your great-aunts and great-uncles) to be members of your family? What about their children, your second cousins? What about your grandparents' parents, your great-grandparents? Were their siblings part of your family?

Obviously not all Jews left Europe in the great migration at the turn of the 20th century. Left behind were the parents, grandparents, brothers and sisters, aunts and uncles, and cousins of those who emigrated—those who became the six million murdered during the *Shoah*. Most of those who survived initially settled in Israel—individuals a generation closer to the "old country" homes left behind by the emigrants of 1900. Some are your second and third cousins.

Others are *landsmen*, individuals from your ancestral town. Find these individuals and, at a minimum, you will learn about the community your European ancestors left behind; often you will find someone who knew members of your family. *Olim* societies, organizations of immigrants from various countries that exist for nearly every immigrant group in Israel, are valuable sources of information.

Good U.S. Resources. If your turn-of-the-20th-century immigrant relatives to the United States did not settle in New York, check the Industrial Removal Organization (IRO) records held by the American Jewish Historical Society (AJHS). The IRO settled many immigrants all across the United States, and its files are filled with personal information. Don't overlook the Hebrew Immigrant Aid Society (HIAS) records at YIVO. Orphanage records are another often overlooked resource. AJHS holds substantial records. Also check the JewishGen Digest archives (see JEWISHGEN) for a reference to an Internet site on the topic.

Alliance Israélite Universelle. Nearly every chapter about a Muslim country mentions the schools operated by the Alliance Israélite Universelle at the end of the 19th and early 20th centuries. Files and reports generated by these schools are held today at the Alliance headquarters in Paris. Philip and Laurence Abensur, editors of *Etsi: The Sephardi Genealogical and Historical Review*, have mined this resource extensively. See their Internet site at WWW.GEOCITIES.COM/ETSI-SEFARAD for details.

Jewish Travel Guide, international edition, published yearly by the *London Jewish Chronicle*, includes contact information and brief historical bits about virtually every place in the world where Jews live today. It is an easy way to find what communities exist in every country and how to reach them.

Why We Do This: Some Thoughts on "Jewishness"

Newcomers to Jewish genealogy often are struck by the intensity with which the pursuit grips them. We speak of being "bitten by the genealogy bug" as if it were a contagion of some sort. Many, myself included, have tried to understand the mysterious power this hobby holds. We also wonder about the way it causes us to "feel more Jewish."

Seth Jacobson, a Jewish genealogist who lives in Jerusalem, tells about a distant relative who asked at the end of an interview with her, "What good is all this collection of information?" A *haredi* (ultra-Orthodox) woman who lives in Jerusalem's Mea Shearim quarter, she did not cooperate easily with Jacobson. Jacobson writes:

> The perception that genealogy is a hobby or *stam* (Yiddish for "just like that"), documenting data about people who may be your relatives (and previously unknown to you) was, in her eyes, not an issue worthy of *bitul Torah* (avoiding the study of Torah). Many ultra-Orthodox Jews believe that *limud Torah* (study of Torah) is the only activity a man should pursue, except for certain existential activities. The best answer I could think to tell her was to explain that we Jews are called to remember generations gone, especially

those who died for *Kiddush Hashem* (sanctification of the Name), such as relatives murdered by the Nazis in the Holocaust. She accepted my answer and cooperated.

Yitzhak Navon, fifth president of Israel and keynote speaker at the 1994 Jewish genealogical conference in Jerusalem, talked about genealogy and Jewishness this way. Navon brought "props" to his talk—three sets of Israelis, all of whom were descendants of prominent Jews who had lived in Spain in 1492 and who, under pressure from the Edict of Expulsion, had converted to Christianity. Some generations later, their descendants returned to Judaism—and today the descendants of those who returned are citizens of Israel.

As Navon explained it, we do not choose to be Jews; God chose us to carry out his purposes on Earth. We may observe God's commandments and live as observant Jews, or we may ignore them. In either case, says Navon, we are still Jews—because the choice was not ours in the first place. Even when we seek to escape our Jewishness entirely and convert to another religion, it often happens (as Navon demonstrated) that some of our descendants later return to the Jewish people.

Mark Twain and others have speculated about the mysterious endurance of the Jews. In 1899 in his article "Concerning the Jews" (*Harper's New Monthly Magazine*), Twain wrote:

> If the statistics are right, the Jews constitute but one percent of the human race. It suggests a nebulous, dim puff of stardust lost in the blaze of the Milky Way. Properly the Jew ought hardly to be heard of, but he is heard of, has always been heard of. He is as prominent on the planet as any other people, and his commercial importance is extravagantly out of proportion to the smallness of his bulk. His contributions to the world's list of great names in literature, science, art, music, finance, medicine and abstruse learning are also way out of proportion to the smallness of his numbers. He has made a marvelous flight in this world, in all the ages, and has done it with his hands tied behind him. He could be vain of himself and be excused for it.

> The Egyptians, the Babylonians and the Persians rose, filled the planet with sound and splendor, then faded to dream-stuff and passed away; the Greeks and Romans followed and made a vast noise, and they are gone; other peoples have sprung up and held their torch high for a time, but it burned out, and they sit in twilight now or have vanished. The Jew saw them all, beat them all, and is now what he always was, exhibiting no decadence, no infirmities of age, no weakening of his parts, no slowing of his energies, no dulling of his alert and aggressive mind. All things are mortal, but the Jews, all other forces pass, but he remains. What is the secret of his immortality?

All three—the *haredi* woman in Mea Shearim, Yitzhak Navon, and Mark Twain—as well as many of us who have engaged in the compelling pursuit of Jewish genealogy, have felt the power of Jewishness—whatever its reason, whatever its source, we come to feel and to understand that we are indeed a people, an enormous extended family, and that Judaism is an all-encompassing way of life. We became a people at Mount Sinai when God presented the Ten Commandments to the Jewish people through Moses. Whether we individual Jews observe the *mitzvot* or ignore them (or don't know what they are), we remain Jews.

An intelligent, middle-aged professor, once commented to me that she envied us Jews because, she said, "You don't have to do anything (like be baptized, christened, or make an affirmation) to be Jews; you are simply born Jewish. That must confer a marvelous sense of belonging."

Some of us are Jews by choice (conversion). Most of us are Jews because our parents were Jews. We were born this way in the same way that we were born male or female, blue-eyed or brown-eyed, blonde or brunette. In Jewish tradition we all stand at Mount Sinai—all the Jews who came before us and all who will come after. And although we Jews do not proselytize, the Book of Ruth illustrates also that whoever becomes Jewish by choice is as fully one who stood at Sinai as a Jew who was born into our peoplehood.

Whatever the reason for the strangely intense attraction of Jewish genealogy, most of us writing this book have felt it. It seems to have something basic to do with a sense of belonging, but beyond that, it is hard to say.

So for those readers who are picking up this book as a preparation to delve into their roots, we say welcome to the wonderful world of Jewish genealogy and to the thrilling adventure on which you are about to embark. Be aware that it may become habit forming.

Part I

The Essentials of
Jewish Genealogical Research

Methodology: How to Be a Genealogist

by Eileen Polakoff

Family history research is about questions—and finding the answers to questions. The first questions are: "What should I do first? How or where should I begin?" This chapter addresses these questions.

Although some basic principles exist, researching one's genealogy is nothing like following a cookbook recipe. Genealogical research is not guided by a recipe with steps that must be followed in sequence lest the cake collapse in the oven. Genealogical research is a process of exploring, learning, analyzing, and redoing interviews and research based upon additional information. Every family history is different, and to some extent every researcher follows a different path to knowledge.

The succeeding chapters in this book elaborate on the topics described here. In general, the more a researcher knows about available resources, the best able he or she will be to devise strategies to obtain information.

Research Process

Genealogical research is an art, not a science. Some have compared it to a jigsaw puzzle, because you can work in many directions at the same time. Piece by piece, a picture of the family begins to emerge. You may work in many different directions and make many side trips—but always with the goal of gaining more information or understanding about a person or a family.

This research does not employ simple linear thinking; rather, it's a more eclectic process. No one path exists to learn everything about a family. Instead, you will jump around between interviews, documents, books, and so on. It may be helpful to think of the process as akin to a search for information on the Web. You go to one site and learn something. While exploring that site, you see a link to something else of interest, so you go there, and so on.

Layer each new fact or clue onto the family tree. Review previous information and compare it with newly acquired data. Does the new information shed light on older facts and point to a new direction for research? Periodically review everything you know about an individual or family. As you learn more about the family, the records, and the research process, you will realize that there were hidden clues waiting to be discovered.

Preliminary Steps

Begin by buying a large notebook and several dividers or a set of file folders. Right from the start you need a place to put every letter and scrap of paper that comes your way—and plan to keep track of all your sources (see Organize Your Material below). You also may decide to buy a genealogy software program—but this step (discussed below) can be deferred for a while. Decide which family line or lines you want to trace. Are you interested in a snapshot of the immediate family at a certain time and place, or do you want to learn about its everyday life and work too? Do you want to record all individuals related to you or just your immediate forebears? Pursue many paths at once. You never know in advance whether or not you will find a desired vital record or naturalization certificate. What might be a family secret in one branch may be an oft-told story in another.

Your sources will be people and paper. Start with people first; the paper will be there when you get to it. People may not be.

Interview Yourself First

The basic elements of genealogy are names, dates, and places. Write down what you know about all members of your family. Start with yourself and systematically move back in time generation by generation, recording what you learn (and where you learned it and when), using that information to move back yet another generation. Write down everything you know about yourself, your children, your parents, and your grandparents. Most genealogists find it convenient either to use standardized genealogy forms, which help organize the information you have and identify information you need (described below), or to enter data directly into a genealogy software program. If you have decided to include aunts, uncles, and cousins, write down that information as well. Don't worry if you have gaps in your knowledge. Your research will enable you to fill in the gaps in the puzzle—and this book teaches you how.

Interview Others to Fill in the Blanks

To plug the gaps in your knowledge, interview the oldest living members (preferably using audio or videotape) of the family and record what they tell you about each person or event in the family. Where they exist, also interview old family friends. Sometimes they know more than some family members.

After transcribing the interviews, arrange the information in one or more of a number of standard ways: a hand-drawn family tree with notations in the margins, a family group sheet, a narrative summary of the interviews, a pedigree chart, or some other inventive method. Do whatever is easiest—but use a technique that encourages you to cite a source and date for each new clue or fact.

You may use a combination of methods. For example, if you understand a graphic family tree best for basic information and relationships, you can also create a narrative to accompany it in which you cite your sources. If an interview with Great-aunt Sarah produces information about an unknown family branch, document the source of this information (who, when, and where), so future research can confirm (or contradict) the basic data.

After you have completed initial interviews with the eldest family members and close friends, and have recorded the pertinent facts, it is time to undertake a new set of interviews. Now interview all other family members, regardless of age or knowledge. Don't restrict yourself to direct ancestors only. Collect as much information as possible about aunts, uncles, cousins, great-aunts, great-uncles, and their close friends. Distant relatives often know a crucial fact—such as a maiden name—that your own grandparents or parents have forgotten (see INTERVIEWS).

Once you have created a basic outline of the family based on your own knowledge and interviews with relatives and family friends, you may decide to re-interview the older family members based on new clues gleaned from the others.

Often your goal is more than a series of names and dates. Your family was part of a community, and you may want to learn about it as well.

Check to See if Others Have Done Your Research

After you have completed your initial interviews and are ready to start looking for documents to substantiate what you have been told, consider the possibility that someone else may have compiled your family history already. There is no point in reinventing the wheel!

As interest in Jewish genealogical research continues to grow exponentially, increasing numbers of family trees are becoming publicly available. Look for your family surname, ancestral town, or actual family in the following places: the Family Tree of the Jewish People (see JEWISHGEN), the JewishGen Family Finder (see JEWISHGEN), *Sourcebook for Jewish Genealogies and Family Histories*, by Zubatsky and Berent (see COMPILED GENEALOGIES), catalogue of the U.S. Library of Congress (see LIBRARY OF CONGRESS), an Internet search engine for surnames (see INTERNET), the LDS (Mormon) Family History Library (see LDS).

If you find your family surname and/or ancestral town in this search, gather the information as you would any other data. Analyze what you have found in terms of what you already know about your family. Investigate those areas that appear most important. If at all possible, review the original source material. Proceed as if this information were just additional clues to be evaluated. Just because it was found in a book or on the Internet does not mean that information is factual.

Two Indispensable Bits of Data

Most Jews today do not live where their families lived 150 or 200 years ago. Massive migration (see MIGRATION) is one of the two (along with the Holocaust [see HOLOCAUST]) major upheavals of Jewish life of the past two centuries. In tracing your family backward in time, it will not be long for many before the trail takes you to another continent—most often Central or Eastern Europe or North Africa. In order to continue tracing, it is essential to know where the family lived a century or more ago.

Among the most important questions to ask everyone early in the interview process is where the family lived before emigration. Ask the relatives and friends to pronounce the town name as best they can remember. Write the name

phonetically and then consult Mokotoff and Sack's *Where Once We Walked* to determine the current and past spellings of the town name. Sometimes it is not easy to determine the previous town of residence. For further details on how to pursue that information, see SHTETL GEOGRAPHY.

Immigrants commonly changed their last names to sound more like names in their new country of residence—but in order to find traces of them in the "old country," it is necessary to know what the name was before emigration. Be sure to query your informants on that as well. Consult LAST NAMES and NATURALIZATION for additional information on how to track down this often-elusive information.

Migration patterns are equally important in many families that never left their continents. Odds are that *some* branch of the family picked up roots and crossed an ocean sooner or later. And you'll want to discover and learn about that branch, too.

Unusual Last Names

Contrary to popular belief, most Jewish names are not Cohen, Goldberg, or Schwartz! If the family name is unusual, it probably is worthwhile to collect any and all documents and references to *everyone* with that name. As additional information is acquired, relationships can be noted, and individuals with this surname can be combined into family groups. Later, when your knowledge of the family has been extended, you may discover relationships to people you originally thought were unrelated to you.

One strategy for finding occurrences of an unusual surname is to search major databases of names, including Avotaynu's Consolidated Jewish Surname Index (see AVOTAYNU), the U.S. Social Security Death Index on the Internet, the U.S. World War I draft registration (see U.S. WORLD WAR I DRAFT RECORDS), Pages of Testimony at Yad Vashem (see HOLOCAUST), the All-Country Databases or the JRI-Poland indexes (see JEWISHGEN), or the U.S. census (see U.S. CENSUS RECORDS). A number of databases in Israel are extremely valuable but not yet computerized (see ISRAEL). You may begin to notice patterns in searching these databases. Maybe family members tended to live in certain locations, or you might notice name variants within a family in census records that lead to a modern spelling of the name.

Location, Location, Location

In nearly all situations, genealogical research requires knowledge of a location—and not only the last residence abroad. The location may be the last place the family lived before emigration, the first place they lived in America or South Africa, the port from which they left Europe, the location of records of the ancestral towns, or the location of information about research. It is not possible to search for an Abraham Schwartz born in 1875 "in Russia," married to a Sarah Cohen born in 1888 "in Austria." More information is needed. For example, where did they marry? Was Sarah born in the Austro-Hungarian Empire? If yes, in which part? Where did they live in America? Where were they buried? Where were their children born?

Get the Documents

Once you have created a basic outline of the family based on your own knowledge and interviews with relatives and family friends, it may be time to seek documents that confirm what you have been told. Usually the first documents we find about our family are considered "basic" by many researchers; these may be the most easily found. Among basic records are vital records (birth, marriage and death), census returns, passenger arrival manifests, citizenship documents, court records (business, civil, criminal, divorce, name change and probate), city and telephon directories. These supply information about your family—but many more documents can lead to additional knowledge.

Seek out also newspaper articles, obituaries, U.S. Social Security applications, military records, histories of your ancestral town or area, Holocaust documents, Internet sources, voter registrations, and insurance records. In addition to documents, search for family papers and photographs. Not only are they nice to have, but they often also provide additional clues.

If the family lived in same community for many years, a search for vital records, probate, and cemetery records may confirm or supplement specifics on individuals that can lead to a more developed picture of the family as a whole (see VITAL RECORDS, PROBATE, CEMETERY RESEARCH.) If the family moved from location to location every generation or more often, it may be more difficult to gather basic documents. This does not mean that the task is impossible—only that it will take more time and effort. Add the new documentary information to your family tree and narrative—and add the new sources to your research log (see below).

At this point you may have noticed that some of the facts and clues you have collected contradict the information on your preliminary family tree. You may have redone the tree two or three times by now or pasted on so many additional pages that you are lost before beginning. It may be time to stop and regroup. Develop a system to organize the information and paper you are accumulating (see Organizing below). This also may be a good time to computerize your information.

Keep a Research Log

The most common mistake novice genealogists make is to think that they will always remember how or where they found a specific piece of information. "Surely, I will never forget how I found that great-grandmother's maiden name," we think. But after months or years of doing research, you will have gathered so much information that you will no longer remember sources. A good research strategy is to begin from day one to record both every source you consult and the result of that search. Genealogists call this a research log. Actually you create two lists: one of all sources investigated for information and the results and a citation linked to the source for that fact. Sources that produced no information are just as important to record as those that produced data used on your family tree. You will not want to waste time years from now looking again for information that you learned did not exist in that archive.

Part of your research log should include what you sought in a specific source. For instance, if you have searched the 1900 U.S. census for a family, be sure to include your search criteria. A notation may read:

> 1900 U.S. Census for Massachusetts. Search for individuals named Tartotsky with first names beginning with A through G living in Suffolk County. Results: Found three families. Made copies of records. Note research date.

If you return to this source of information at a later date, you will be able to review what you had already done and found, so you need not repeat that search. In keeping track of

Research Calendar

Ancestry.com.

Family _____   Researcher _____

Date	Repository / Call #/Microfilm #	Description of Source	Time Period/ Names Searched	Results

Form # F102   http://www.ancestry.com/save/charts/researchcal.htm   ©MyFamily.com, Inc. 1998-2000

The most common mistake novice genealogists make is to think that they will always remember how or where they found a specific piece of information. A research log helps solve this problem. Form courtesy of Ancestry.com.

sources, be sure to list all variant names you searched for. You may find a new spelling of the name and consider returning to that source at a later date.

Citations should be clear and lead back to the original source. Use standard formats such as those found in style manuals such as the *Chicago Manual of Style* or *Evidence!* by Elizabeth Shown Mills.

It is relatively easy to keep track of all sources on a computer. One method is to use a genealogical software program that permits source citation. If a program does not have a citation feature, create a text file about the person or family and record sources in that file. Create your own research log in a word processing or other computer program. The ability to search for specifics of previous research will save time and money that can be used better on new research.

What to Collect

Soon after starting to trace their family history, most genealogists realize that they already are buried in paper and/or electronic files. Two major questions arise: When do I have enough information about a person? How can I keep track of all this paper? Experienced genealogists obtain every possible document or bit of data known to exist about a person. Each additional document may provide nothing new, conflicting information, or considerable new data. We and our ancestors have gone through life generating scads of paper about ourselves. Each new document may open a door to something we never suspected about our family. Don't ignore anything. Every clue or piece of paper is potentially important.

For example, you already may have determined the birth date of your great-great-grandfather and see no reason to find his World War I draft registration. But when you do find that registration card and it confirms the date you have, you also learn for whom he was working at the time, which opens a door to a lost branch of the family. The same applies to wills, other probate records, and just about every other category of record that you can imagine. Here is another example. Professional genealogist Nancy Arbeiter was stumped trying to learn the European birth place of a mid-19th century German-speaking Jewish immigrant to the United States. Arbeiter knew that although the U.S. did not require passports until the 20th century, some travelers acquired them anyway. To be thorough, Arbeiter searched to see if her immigrant ever had applied for a passport—and was amply rewarded. He had—in the mid-1870s. On the passport was the name of the town in Germany he intended to visit. Further research proved that this was the long-sought town of his birth.

In the course of your research you will come to learn a good deal about family members and the communities in which they lived. In the course of learning about the family, you also will want to keep track of information about related topics. A filing system should include a section about ancestral towns, including maps from various time periods. An article about the Jews of Poland in 1820 may help place the family in context. Save it in your files. Background information on the ancestral towns, occupations, history of surnames in your

family, etymology of given names, migration patterns, locations for research—all should be part of your resources.

Organize Your Material

Once we have begun to learn the methods of genealogical research and are collecting facts, documents, interviews, photographs, and other memorabilia, we are faced with what to do with all this information and paper. This is where that notebook and dividers or file folders come in. Notebooks also are useful for taking notes when doing research or interviewing relatives. The binder can be divided into sections for each major branch of a family. Alternatively, a filing system can be used in the same way for loose papers.

Soon you acquire piles and piles of paper—notes from interviews; correspondence to and from relatives; answers to questionnaires sent to relatives; photocopies of documents and non-paper items such as photographs, computer disks, and CD-ROMs; audio and video tapes; memorabilia; and lists of things to do to find more information. This material grows and grows—each time you find another bit of information about someone in your family, another piece of paper is added to the pile—sometimes more than one piece of paper.

Organize Files by Family. If you are researching the families of your four grandparents, start with four files, file pockets, or binders, even though some may have only one or two documents while others may have hundreds. If a document concerns more than one family, make duplicate copies (if possible), one for each family file. If a file or binder becomes too thick, divide it into subfamilies, even down to the person level.

Organize by Type. Also organize files by type. Ideally make duplicate copies of the most important documents to use in a work file. You may decide to keep a file of copies of all census records found regardless of family, since more than one family may be on the same census page. An alternate plan is to make a separate list of all records found. Such a list is best kept in a searchable computer file and can serve double duty, both as a research log of all work done and also as a summary of the result.

Standard Genealogy Forms. Standard genealogy forms have evolved over many years and are recognizable to most genealogists at a glance. Again there is no need to reinvent the wheel. The basic charts found either in paper form or in a genealogical software program are family group sheets, pedigree/ancestry charts, descendants charts, and "drop" charts (similar to an organizational chart). In addition to the basic forms, you may come across forms that help keep track of persons to whom you have written (correspondence logs), what you have done (research logs), what you have found (abstracts), and others. Books containing forms and charts may be purchased, or you can create your own forms on your computer. As genealogy has developed into a hobby pursued by millions, countless articles and books have been written about keeping track of information. Look in local libraries for examples. Various computer software programs created for this purpose also may be helpful. Cyndi's List on the

Family Group Record

Prepared By _____ Relationship to Preparer _____

Address _____ Date _____ Ancestral Chart # _____ Family Unit # _____

Husband		Occupation(s)			Religion	

	Date —Day, Month, Year	City	County	State or Country	
Born					
Christened					Name of Church
Married					Name of Church
Died					Cause of Death
Buried		Cem/Place			Date Will Written/Proved
Father		Other Wives			
Mother					

Wife maiden name		Occupation(s)			Religion	

		City	County	State or Country	
Born					
Christened					Name of Church
Died					Cause of Death
Buried		Cem/Place			Date Will Written/Proved
Father		Other Husbands			
Mother					

*	Sex M/F	Children Given Names	Birth Day	Month	Year	Birthplace City	County	St./Ctry.	Date of first marriage/Place Name of Spouse	Date of Death/Cause City	County	State/Country	Computer I.D. #
		1											
		2											
		3											
		4											
		5											
		6											
		7											
		8											
		9											
		10											
		11											
		12											

NOTE: *=Direct Ancestor   Form # F106   http://www.ancestry.com/save/charts/familysheet.htm   ©MyFamily.com, Inc. 1998-2000

Prior to the days of genealogical software programs, the Family Group Sheet was the mainstay documentation in genealogy. It shows all known information about each family unit: husband, wife and children. Form courtesy of Ancestry.com.

Internet will lead you to dozens of downloadable forms on the Internet. They can be linked to at WWW.CYNDISLIST.COM/SUPPLIES.HTM#ONLINE.

Data Management. Genealogy and family history research involves much more than names, dates, and places—and all of this additional information requires considerable paper and space. This section deals briefly with the management of information. Ultimately a computer may be the best means of dealing with information retrieval and management (see "Using computers" below).

Many genealogists have developed information systems. The best system for one person may be cumbersome for another. Every genealogist devises the system that works best for him or her. Following are some issues to consider when developing your own system. You may find it advantageous to alter the system as your research and the amount of information you collect grows. Be flexible. Don't lock yourself into a complex system that is difficult to maintain. Don't be too compulsive about filing systems: Don't allow yourself to be controlled by them. The joy of genealogy lies in the pursuit of new information, not in sorting paper. Be uniform.

Use the same size pages all the time. Small pieces of paper are lost easily and large pieces can be unwieldy. Photocopy odd-sized documents so that they become your standard size. To reduce the chance of disastrous loss, keep original documents and important photocopies in a separate location away from active research files. Send copies of your computer files to a friend or relative. Make photocopies or abstracts of information in original documents and keep the copies in your active research files. Whenever possible, cross-reference your material, either manually or via a computerized system—and don't forget to document all sources. Most genealogists eventually alter their organizational system as their experience with genealogy grows. Many speak of the "80/20 Rule" of paper management, which says that we use 20 percent of what we have 80 percent of the time. Plan your system with the understanding that a small portion of it will be used often, while other parts will be used rarely. Thin out files that you don't use often. Plan to review everything about once a year and discard items that have not been used for a long time—especially if these are things you can find somewhere else when you need them.

Using Computers

Maintaining information about a family's history can become overwhelming. As more individuals are located and documented, the volume of material being kept can become cumbersome to manage. While much of it is accurate and you will keep it as a permanent record, other items are guesses or speculations that must be corrected when additional facts are gathered. It is good to have a system that allows changes to be made easily—and that is one of the major things that computers do. At the beginning of the 21st century, it is rare to find anyone without access to a computer—and using computers to assist you in your research is now as common as notebooks and pencils were 10 years ago.

Only a short while after you have used a computer for your genealogical research, you will wonder how anyone did family history without one. A computer offers many advantages. It creates orderliness out of disorder; easily allows us to revise our charts, lists, and other representations as new information is obtained; easily presents information in a variety of sequences and formats; permits large volumes of information to be accessed and maintained with ease; and can search large collections of data rapidly.

When evaluating genealogical software consider the following five major questions. The significance of each depends on the individual.

- Ease of learning. Are you a beginner in the use of computer software? If so, the quality of the documentation supplied with the software is important.
- Ease of use. Is it easy to add information to the files? How easy is it to change, locate, and delete records? How forgiving is the software? If you make a mistake, will the software tell you (e.g., entering children without parents, marriages with only one spouse)?
- Capability. What features exist in the system? Will they satisfy your needs as a genealogist? Does it support GEDCOM which is the ability to transfer data to and from another genealogical software program.
- Flexibility. What options exist in the system? How much can you customize the system to meet your particular needs?
- "Jewishness." Some needs are specific to Jewish genealogy. Can you record the person named after, *yahrzeit* date, and religious name?

In addition to using a computer and software for your personal genealogical pursuits, a computer now is indispensable for a number of other functions within genealogy. Computerized databases are available for searching on the Internet (see INTERNET and JEWISHGEN). Learning about sources of information is much easier with a computer. Searching across many languages and disciplines is possible with powerful search engines. Specialty sites for genealogy, especially Jewish genealogy, are easily found. Electronic mail makes communication with other genealogists worldwide rapid and inexpensive.

How to Analyze a Problem

When you start to work on a specific genealogical problem, first outline or summarize everything you know about the individual or family. Determine where you might find new information and which sources are most likely to provide the sought-after data. In the summary include an analysis of the reliability of the information that you already have and the source(s) from which it came. It cannot be repeated often enough: When gathering information about an individual or family, *always* record the source of the information. If the information came from oral history interviews or from a letter written by a relative, write that down. If the information was from a census record or a naturalization record, recall all the details of the research. Each of these types of sources may be more or less reliable than another source. Each case is different. No matter how difficult a specific genealogical problem, a systematic approach, combined with extensive knowledge of potential sources, eventually almost always produces at least one or two avenues to pursue for potential solutions.

Every genealogist must weigh evidence and—on the basis of his or her experience as a researcher—decide which facts are most likely to be true. Evaluate new data in light of what has been learned previously. Sometimes it is helpful to write oneself a memo (include the date) to the file about the evidence and why you have concluded what you have concluded at this time. The note need not be long, but it can help in the future when additional evidence is found. Here is an example:

> Death certificate of Abraham Schwartz from New York City on January 15, 1918, indicates that he was born in March 1871, but his tombstone says April 10, 1872. 1900 census also indicates 1872. (memo written May 15, 2002).

Evaluating Information

Evaluation of information is one of the most important steps in research. In order to determine a record's accuracy, it is important to know why the record was created, when it was created, who reported the data, and if it was contemporaneous with the event recorded. When learning about sources of data, be sure to learn all you can about the source. It is important to weigh the information against a number of criteria.

Consider how to evaluate death certificates. A death certificate was completed by one or more individuals—but not, obviously, by the subject of the certificate (i.e., the decedent). This means that the information on a death certificate must be evaluated item by item in order to estimate how accurate it may be.

The dates and places of death and burial probably are accurate, but the birth date of the decedent usually was supplied by someone not present at the birth. It may be wrong. Other information on a death certificate may have been supplied by the decedent for another record and re-recorded in this document. For example, if the person were admitted to a hospital prior to death, he or she may have been questioned about such items as date of birth. Note that the person supplying the information for the death certificate may have been a family member under stress because of the recent demise of a loved one. When asked for the names of the parents of the decedent, informants may say that they do not remember—even though they actually do know the information. At the time when they are questioned, the maiden name of the decedent's mother probably is one of the last things on their minds.

Evidence

Not all documents or sources are equal in value and reliability. In some cases the source—a spouse—may be reliable, but spouses are not necessarily well versed in all aspects of their partners' life facts. Each genealogist must make this determination. Careful genealogists distinguish between original (primary) and derivative (secondary) sources, and between primary (original) and secondary (derivative) evidence. Even within these categories of sources, there may be varying degrees of good evidence. Nothing is cut and dried; genealogy is an art, not a science.

Original and Derivative Sources. An original source usually, but not necessarily, is a better source of accurate data than a secondary source. An original source is a specific document created for a specific purpose. Examples are vital records created at the time of birth, marriage, or death in order to record the event; census records created so that a government may learn about its population; petitions for naturalization created during the process of becoming a citizen; passenger arrival manifests created when an individual boarded a ship to sail to a new country, used in the case of the United States to determine who would and who would not be admitted into the U.S.; World War I U.S. draft registrations created when an individual registered for military conscription; and deeds created when parties bought, sold, or transferred property. All of these documents may be considered original sources—but that does not ensure that all of the information included is accurate.

A derivative source is created after an event or for an alternative purpose, but may be useful for genealogical purposes. Examples are city directories (see DIRECTORIES) created by publishing companies for marketing purposes, obituaries (often a paid insert in a newspaper published after a person has died; written by a relative or a reporter), online computer vital record indexes (created for a variety of reasons) and a book of will extracts (created by people interested in specific wills from a specific courthouse for a specific time period).

Derivative sources may be valuable and, in some instances, may be the only source of information available. Whenever possible, however, this type of data should be used only as clues to further avenues of research. Secondary sources are rife with human error, inconsistencies, and poorly documented information.

Primary and Secondary Evidence. Locate as many original sources as possible, but remember that not all data in a primary resource is factual. While some data in a primary source probably is fact, some may be fiction—some inadvertent, some intentional. The goal is to identify and extract the factual data and to use the possibly fictional data to help locate other primary records. Data based on first-hand knowledge is called primary evidence. Data from a second-hand source is called secondary evidence. Secondary evidence may be information that has passed through one or more media. An index to records is secondary because it

passed through at least one media (the transcriber or indexer) as it was being created. Any single document can include primary, secondary or even tertiary evidence. (Tertiary evidence is data from a source based on secondary evidence.) Every fact in a source must be evaluated. To determine what is primary evidence and what is secondary, ask the following "five W" questions of each document located:

- Who created the document or source? Who provided the information? Did the informant offer proof of the information provided? Was the document created because of a governmental decree, or for something like a burial society?
- What type of information does it contain? Is the information in a standard format (such as post-1906 naturalization records), or is it a clue in a diary?
- Why was the document or resource created? Was a law passed mandating the record?
- Where was the document created? Was it created at the place of the event or by an indexer far away?
- When was the document created—at the time of the event, soon thereafter, or many months or years after the event?

Reliability of Documents. Genealogical information comes from many sources with varying degrees of reliability. Throughout history, documents have been created about events in a person's life. Most people are familiar with birth, marriage, and death certificates, but few wonder how accurate the information is on any given document. A good rule of thumb is to consider who created the document, when it was written, and for what purpose. A modern birth certificate completed by a doctor at the time of birth probably accurately records the date, place of birth and gender of the child. Other information typically found on birth certificates—such as the mother's maiden name—probably was reported to the hospital or to the doctor, who undoubtedly did not ask for proof.

Older birth records may present additional issues, such as compliance with regulations regarding the registration of a birth or any other records. Regulations may have required the registration of a birth, but that does not mean that everyone observed the regulation. For various reasons, an event may have been registered long after the actual date or never reported at all.

Because information on a marriage license usually is provided by the individuals getting married, such data may be considered reliable, but not always truthful. The individuals reporting the information should know their ages, but they may have decided to report a different age for reasons known only to them. Death certificates are filled out at a stressful time for the family member who provides the information. Moreover, the informant may not know accurate information about the deceased. For these reasons, death certificates typically are unreliable sources of information about such items as the birth date of the deceased.

Other documents that can provide information about an individual may have been collected by a clerk instructed to fill out a form or questionnaire. In the United States, a census of the population is taken every 10 years. If the enumerator came to the household and asked questions about members of the family, it is possible that the respondent did not offer totally correct facts; or the enumerator had difficulty understanding the heavily accented English of the respondent; or the enumerator had poor handwriting. The name David easily can be misread as Daniel on handwritten forms. For these reasons experienced genealogists view census and similar documents as clues that may lead to other documents that may confirm the data.

Strategies

Strategies for discovering missing information about a family may have many aspects. First, attempt to determine what information is missing, and then learn if it can be discovered. Depending on what you are seeking and what sources are available, you may devise different approaches. If searching for the original surname of an immigrant family, it does not make sense to look only at present-day documents, which probably uniformly use the "new" name. Documents that predate the name change are much more likely to contain clues. Did the family arrive in America or elsewhere at a time when passenger manifests asked the name of a family member in the country of origin? If so, these manifests may offer a clue. If not, there is no reason to find the manifests to learn the surname—though it might be worthwhile to seek the manifests to learn other additional information.

You might also weigh the time used to search for a document against the usefulness of the information that document might provide. Consider how many sources may contain the information you are seeking, and then determine which might provide additional clues that make them more desirable.

In the beginning you may have had only a few names, a city where these individuals lived, and a guess about the years during which they lived there. This seemingly simple set of clues may lead to many new sources of information if analyzed properly. Consider which records existed for the time and place of interest. Which could have had information about your family? Was a census compiled by the government? Does an index to the census exist, or must you learn more about where the family lived in order to find the family at its home? What information does the census record have? How will finding the census record of your family help you learn more about your family?

Consider, for example, the 1890 police census of the residents of Manhattan (New York City). It includes the address of residence, name, gender, and age—but no relationships, no year of immigration, and no hint to the number of years married. If you already have found your family in the 1880 and/or 1900 census, this 1890 census probably will not add much.

Indexes

Searches for many types of documents require two steps. First, one must locate a name of interest in an index. After the name is located, the next step is to find the actual records.

Indexes come in various styles. Among the most common are alphabetical or soundex. Soundex is a method of converting the name of a person or place to a series of letters and/or numbers based upon the sound of the word, regardless of the actual spelling. Genealogists are likely to encounter two major soundex systems: the Russell system used by the U.S. government for census records and the Daitch-Mokotoff system used by Jewish genealogists for a variety of records (see DAITCH-MOKOTOFF SOUNDEX).

Alphabetical systems come in a number of formats. Most common are strictly alphabetical or those arranged in more or less alphabetical order. In some systems, all surnames that begin with a single letter are grouped together. In other systems, the groupings may be semi-alphabetical within a single letter (i.e., all the Sa's together, followed by the Se's, the Si's, the Sk's and so on). Always take the time to determined the method used before proceeding further and wasting time because you initially misunderstood the system. If the index was created manually (i.e., not computerized), remember to look after the letter Z or at the end of the index for additional entries. If the index was compiled from cards, it sometimes happens that a card was dislodged from its original place in the series and was refiled at the very end. If a page was full, a new page was started at the end of a bound book. Remember also that some alphabets (such as the Polish and Czech alphabets) use Roman letters with diacritical marks that alter the order familiar to those using the English alphabet.

Although some indexes are actually abstracts of the information in a document, always complete the search by acquiring a copy of the full record or document. It is good genealogical research practice always to look at a record itself and not merely the index or abstract, in case errors or omissions have occurred.

Second-Round Issues

About the time that you are collecting your first round of family documents, other issues probably will come to your attention. This includes the issue of family legends—especially a tradition of descent from a famous individual—name variants, and the issue of collateral research.

Family Legends. Genealogists have learned that every family legend usually includes at least a grain of truth, no matter how farfetched it seems at first. Consider the following. The Schwartz family had a legend about triplets dying in a fire, but no one knew which branch or when it had happened. The story, found eventually in the *Brooklyn Eagle* newspaper, told about a family with five children, all of whom died in a fire—but none were triplets or even twins. After finding the story about the fire and the sadness of the parents who survived, the researcher learned that one year after the fire, the wife bore triplets, and the family considered the babies to be God's gift to the family. So, there was a fire and there were triplets, and it was all the same family—but the details had become scrambled over time.

Listen to all family stories and write them down. Whenever possible look for a fact or clue that pertains to the tale and see where the trail takes you. It doesn't matter if you cannot work it all out at once; eventually you probably will piece together some version of the family legend.

Pay close attention to all family traditions and tales. Details often are confused, but experience has shown that many are based on some facts.

Famous Relatives. What path should you follow if you believe that you are related to a famous person? How should you connect to a famous rabbinic line? If family legend indicates that you are descended from a famous person or family, the first thing to do is to review what has been published about that person or family. If you do not find an obvious connection, then it is best to return to the basics of genealogical research: Begin with what you know and systematically work backward in time, generation by generation. Eventually, if the legend is true, you will find the connection.

Those who have heard that they descend from, say, the Vilna Gaon, are understandably eager to establish the exact relationship. Much time may be lost, however, if you attempt to connect yourself by beginning with the famous person or family. In order to make a connection in that way, you would need to research all descendants of that person or family, maybe to discover in the end that you are not related at all—but descend from a sister of the Vilna Gaon or from one of his disciples. The same is true of non-Jews who have heard that some ancestor was Jewish. If one has a Jewish forebear, step-by-step research back in time eventually reveals that ancestor—or not.

Name Variants. Consistent spelling of surnames is a relatively recent occurrence in human history (see FAMILY NAMES). Be sure to note all variant spellings you find for both first and last names and the geographical area, source material or book where the variants are found. While checking indexes or lists of names, remember to look for all possible name variants. Think phonetically. For example, the *off* ending in Polakoff also can be *ow, ov* or *of*. In some cases, consonants are added to or deleted from names (e.g., Kelner versus Kellner). Spelling variants of given names seldom create much confusion, but major problems are possible when dealing with Hebrew first names, Yiddish variants, nicknames, Americanized/Anglicized names, and "modern" names. For example, an immigrant Hungarian grandmother named Roche Leah may have become Rosalie after emigration to the United States.

Collateral Research. Collateral research is a fancy term for doing research on the whole family, not just on direct ancestors. Many people are interested in only one family line, such as, for example, their father's direct ancestors. If you take that approach, it usually means that information about your father's sister, grandfather's uncle, and cousins is not collected. By limiting research to blood relatives only, you miss the opportunity to learn more about the family as a whole. If you concentrate on finding information about a single ancestor and hit a brick wall, you will miss the chance to learn more about the family. Most Jewish genealogists think that collateral research is preferable to single-line, direct-ascendancy research. Collateral relatives are related to your direct ancestors in some way. The challenge is to determine exactly how—and in the process, you will learn more

about your direct line as well. For example, a first cousin's records may include information about your mutual grandparents found nowhere else. Many researchers eventually expand their scope to include community research on the theory that in the 1880s, a shtetl of 500 Jewish people had many interrelated families.

"Maybe Relatives." In the course of researching your family, you will find documents for individuals who may be related but whom, at this time, you cannot connect to your tree. These are "maybe relatives," individuals whose documents you have collected, who perhaps are related to you, but whom you cannot connect to your family at this time. Unless the collection of such documents becomes onerous, it is probably worthwhile to keep it in a separate file for future reference. As you discover additional information, "maybe relatives" often are shown to be actual relatives.

Brick Walls

Eventually we all come up against what appears to be the end of the line on information (i.e., we have "hit a brick wall"). In some cases this obstacle exists because the genealogist has not learned yet about records that exist or about a technique that will breach the wall. Unlike the act of, say, hooking a rug or knitting a sweater, genealogical research is a continuing, ongoing venture, a hobby that can, and often does, last a lifetime. One never "finishes" family history research. As we become more familiar with the techniques of research, we should periodically revisit our brick walls to see where we can remove another brick. Even if you have traced your family backward in time as far as you can go with existing records, you always will have new branches on the tree (the new generations). And new records may come to light or become accessible. As you learn more about your ancestors, you probably will want to understand their lives in more detail than just names, dates, and places alone provide. Learning about the social history and the life of your family is a great part of the experience.

If you hit a brick wall, avoid becoming fixated on the problem. Research other aspects of your family history instead. Perhaps when you return to the problem, you will see it in a new light—or new clues (or new resources) may have surfaced that will enable you to solve the problem. Regularly review information learned earlier in light of new facts you learned in the interim. Do not overlook the possibility of using DNA testing, the newest resource in the Jewish genealogist's bag of tools; see JEWISHGEN for information on how to contact a company that specializes in Jewish DNA testing.[1]

Preservation of Material

In addition to finding original documents relating to your family, you may find other original or antique items that you want to preserve for future generations. With today's technology, it is possible to preserve photographs by scanning and to create CDs or a website that can be shared with relatives. The most permanent way to preserve information, however, is on acid-free paper in a scrapbook. For items such as prayer books, *ketubot* (marriage contracts), prayer shawls, and similar objects, purchase preservation materials to ensure that they will survive to be shared with your descendants.

Sharing Your Findings

Most genealogists eventually want to compile a report about their findings. The report can take one of many forms— a classic book, a collection of family group sheets or family trees, a webpage, or a CD-ROM. To make the project more manageable, write reports to yourself that can be used later as the basis for a book. The ideal may be to use a genealogical software program for the basic data and source citations. Scan all photographs and documents and link them electronically to a person or a couple. Compose abstracts or transcripts of the documents in a word processing program. It is easier to search for key words than to read photocopied old documents over and over again. Type verbatim transcripts of interviews. Make videos of oral history interviews. List names, postal and e-mail addresses, and telephone numbers—all pulled together in a narrative of the family story. All of this can be duplicated on a CD-ROM and given to family members at a reunion.

Where to Learn More

A wealth of sources exists to help you learn about doing research and all the related aspects of uncovering your family history. No one source can teach everything you need to know, but among the best are:

- Information files. FAQs (frequently asked questions) on the web at JewishGen (see JEWISHGEN) and other websites often provide valuable introductions to a subject.
- Articles in newsletters and journals. For nearly 25 years individuals interested in learning about Jewish genealogy have referred to a wealth of written sources. Among these are (and were) *Toledot*, the first modern Jewish genealogy journal (no longer in publication), and *AVOTAYNU: The International Review of Jewish Genealogy* (see AVOTAYNU), Jewish genealogy society newsletters, and publications of special interest groups (see ORGANIZED GENEALOGY) such as *Gesher Galicia, Kielce-Radom, Landsman,* and *Stammbaum.*
- Books. Dozens of books have been written to help Jewish genealogists learn. First were Rottenberg's *Finding Our Fathers* and Kurzweil's *From Generation to Generation.* Others are Blatt and Mokotoff's *Getting Started in Jewish Genealogy* and such specialized books as Mokotoff and Sack's *Where Once We Walked* and Alexander Beider's *Dictionary of Jewish Surnames from the Russian Empire* and *Dictionary of Jewish Surnames from the Kingdom of Poland.* Avotaynu's list of recommended books for a Jewish genealogy library (available at WWW.AVOTAYNU.COM) is another good source, as is its yearly catalogue. Don't restrict yourself to books for Jewish genealogy only, but check out general genealogy books as well.
- Bibliographies. See the references listed at the ends of the chapters in this guide. Read or review as many as possible.

- Genealogy society meetings and annual conferences. These meetings are wonderful resources for learning and exchanging ideas. Plan to attend local genealogical society meetings regularly and the annual conference as often as possible (see ORGANIZED GENEALOGY). Lectures at these events often lead to new sources of information. Network with others interested in genealogy and you are likely to find new cousins and *landsmen.* Audio tapes of lectures are additional sources of information. Since 1991 Repeat Performance* has tape recorded major U.S. genealogical conferences and at least one conference in Jerusalem. Some local Jewish genealogical societies also record speakers and circulate the tapes. The basic idea is to learn from the experience of others.

Climb on the Jewish genealogy grapevine. Jewish genealogy has burgeoned in the past 25 years. This has been a time of great discovery and change as resources in formerly communist Europe have opened up and the creation of the Internet has made the exchange of information so quick and easy. Join a Jewish genealogy society and special interest group, subscribe to *AVOTAYNU* and read the JewishGen digest. Use your imagination to determine what records may exist that will help you document your family. Think about all of the times you have filled out a form or given information to some governmental agency. In this respect, life was not so different one or two hundred years ago.

Address

Repeat Performances, 2911 Crabapple Lane, Hobart, Indiana; website: WWW.AUDIOTAPES.COM.

Bibliography

Beider, Alexander. *A Dictionary of Jewish Surnames from the Russian Empire.* Teaneck, N.J.: Avotaynu, 1993.
———. *A Dictionary of Jewish Surnames from the Kingdom of Poland.* Teaneck, N.J.: Avotaynu, 1996.
Blatt, Warren and Gary Mokotoff. *Getting Started in Jewish Genealogy.* Bergenfield, N.J.: Avotaynu, 2000
Chicago Manual of Style. 14th edition. Chicago: University of Chicago Press, 1993
Kurzweil, Arthur. *From Generation to Generation,* rev. ed. New York: Harper Collins, 1994.
Meshenberg, Michael J. *Documents of Our Ancestors: A Selection of Reproducible Genealogy Forms and Tips for Using Them.* Teaneck, N.J.: Avotaynu, 1996.
Mills, Elizabeth Shown. *Evidence!* Baltimore: Genealogical Publishing, 1997.
Mokotoff, Gary and Sallyann Amdur Sack with Alexander Sharon. *Where Once We Walked,* rev. ed. Bergenfield, N.J.: Avotaynu, 2002.
Rottenberg, Dan. *Finding Our Fathers.* New York: Random House, 1977.
Zubatsky, David S. and Irwin M. Berent. *Sourcebook for Jewish Genealogies and Family Histories.* Teaneck, N.J.: Avotaynu, 1996.

Note

1. Kim Phillips, "Genealogy: The Great Paper Chase." *AVOTAYNU* 16, no. 1 (Spring 2000): 35.

The Art of the Interview

by Bill Gladstone

My great-aunt Sophie was 90 years old the first time I called her, out of the blue. She was the youngest and only sibling remaining of 13 children; Sophie had been a sister of my grandmother, Dora, who had died years earlier. Delighted to have found her, I was eager to pose some questions to her about the family tree. She admitted her memory wasn't good, but said she would try to answer my questions as best she could.

There was much that Sophie didn't know, I learned. She couldn't tell me her Hebrew name, for instance, or identify who she was named after. She couldn't name her siblings in order of their ages. And her memory was far from reliable at times. She said she had come to Canada with her family at the age of three in 1904, but I had already found records indicating that her parents had brought her here from Bristol, England, about 1911.

At first she couldn't tell me much about her father, David, who had died in 1929. I suspected that he had been born in Russia-Poland, but the earliest document I had for him pertained to his 1880 marriage in London. Sophie eventually offered some startling revelations:

"Dad came from Scotland, you know."

"You're certain?"

"Oh, yes. Dad was from Scotland. He told me so."

"Before he was married, in other words."

"Probably...."

She was struggling for more words to describe her father. She told me he was a lovely person, kind and patient. "He was a good Jew but he wasn't *like* a Jew, if you know what I mean."

I said that I wasn't sure what she meant.

"He was more of an English guy," she said. "He was *different*."

"You mean he had Scottish mannerisms?"

"You see, he had—," she began, stopping because her words were evidently failing her. "Oh, I'm going back years and years now."

"Oh, please do."

"He was a Jew, and he went to *shul* on Shabbos and Rosh Hashanah. But he was more like an English guy."

It occurred to me that she was not alluding to well-established biographical facts, but rather to less obvious social clues related to the way a person presents himself in public.

"Did he speak with an accent?"

"Yeah."

"What kind of accent?"

"Scot."

"Really? A Scottish accent?"

"Yeah."

"There was no Polish? no Russian?"

"Oh God, no."

"Nothing like that?"

"No way. He was very Scottish. He wore the Fraser tartan."

"Your father wore a kilt?"

"Yes, sometimes he did."

This conversation forever shattered my notion that my great-grandfather had been a typical Yiddish-accented Zayde. Although I had evidence that suggested he was born in Russia-Poland, I gathered from this and like conversations that he most likely came to Glasgow at an early age and probably spent most of his childhood there. (This new information, naturally, dispatched me on whole new avenues of investigation; only this year, accessing the UK 1901 census via the Internet, I discovered that David was actually born in Berlin, Germany.)

Over time, Sophie imparted numerous other genealogical gold nuggets to me, always when I least expected them. In all likelihood, I could not have uncovered such details from anyone else.

Each time we spoke she seemed to remember more things about the dim, dark past. She told me her mother had been born in Hungary, had cherished a German-language Bible, had a brother named Joseph. She divulged the unhappy fate of two nephews of hers, cousins of my father who had mysteriously disappeared from the family. (They had been given to a Christian agency for adoption.) And sister Sarah, who had "married out" and been disowned, had married a Toronto postman whose name Sophie also remembered. (The information has not yet been confirmed).

Sophie died in 1997, may she rest in peace. I doubt there's another living soul anywhere who could have told me some of the things I learned from her.

Do Not Delay Interviewing Elderly Relatives

It is a truism of family tree research that you can visit libraries and archives any time you like, either now or next year, but you must not delay interviewing elderly relatives about your family history, because they will not be around forever.

The greatest regret of many genealogists is that they didn't ask the right people the right questions at the right time. Tombstones often have stories to tell, but they're usually not nearly as articulate as living people.

"Why didn't I ask him (or her) that question while I had the chance?" is a sad but common refrain among genealogists.

The interview is the first and possibly the most important stage of doing genealogical research. Many historians assert that first-person eyewitness testimony outweighs documentary evidence as a significant historical source.

One may exhaust the materials in a given archives or library, but it's almost impossible to exhaust the human resources on one's family tree. Usually, there are always more distant relatives to be discovered, with valuable family information to impart. Good interviewing skills are essential to unlocking the secrets and mysteries usually contained on a family tree.

Old photographs can jog people's memories about people and events of the past. The author's great-aunt Sophie was delighted to receive this photograph of her family from the author. "You have made an old woman very happy," she said, as she began recounting numerous family stories. Taken in Bristol, England, about 1905, the photo shows the six younger siblings with their oldest nephew Joey, who would soon mysteriously disappear from the family. Nearly 90 years later, Sophie would resolve the mystery by explaining what happened to him.

As a journalist, I've been conducting interviews for more than two decades, almost as long as I've been an active genealogist. But as far as interview protocol is concerned, I haven't hit upon one good technique or formula applicable in all situations. Each interview is different and depends upon the person being interviewed. You must be flexible enough to adapt your style to the needs of the moment.

Probably the first and most fundamental question you face is: Whom shall I interview? Some researchers attempt to speak with everyone in a family, but this approach is not necessary and certainly not practical in particularly large and extended families. Sometimes a family friend can also be a fount of information.

Your first choice, therefore, is to determine the right subject or subjects to interview. The ideal subject is a raconteur with a sharp and honest memory, who is old enough to remember important family events of long ago. Not everyone, of course, is a fount of knowledge on family matters. Talk to a potential subject first by telephone to determine how much they might be able to tell you and how willing they may be to go into the details of family history with you.

Jewish genealogists often don't have the luxury of picking and choosing among a multitude of relatives for the best interview subjects. Families of Holocaust survivors are not the only ones in which it may seem that "there's no one left to interview."

By no means should you give up your investigations on this account. Genealogists sometimes surprise themselves by finding very elderly persons, sometimes even 100 years or older, whom they'd wrongly assumed had died decades earlier. Don't seek and you won't find.

In deciding whom to interview, you must also examine the nature of your project and the type of information you wish to acquire. Are you interested in a rich oral history, involving as many sources and points of view as possible? If so, you may wish to interview as many living relatives as possible.

Alternately, you may wish to hone in on specific questions, such as the quality of life your ancestors experienced in the Old Country and the process by which they came to America or elsewhere. In that case, focus on your immigrant relatives.

Many genealogists have certain persistent mysteries they wish to solve, such as identifying the name of an ancestral town. In such cases, one's chances of success will increase by "triangulating" one's research efforts and choosing elderly interview subjects from distant family branches.

Prepare your questions before the interview. Effective oral history cannot occur by asking questions on the spur of the moment, without forethought. Always be ready, however, to follow some new lead or conversational tangent when you feel it might bear some fruit.

Here are 10 sample areas of questioning, suitable for a relative born in the Old Country:

1. What towns did the family come from in Europe? What do you remember of your life in these places? (Write down the town names phonetically, as they sound to your ear, and look them up later in *Where Once We Walked* to find them on a map and determine their past and present spellings.)
2. Please tell me about your parents, grandparents and great-grandparents. (Ask about each individual separately, and try to establish the time and place of all births, marriages, deaths, and so forth.)
3. Who came from Europe to Canada (the United States, South Africa, elsewhere)? In what order?
4. Why did they leave?
5. When and how did they get here? If by ship, what do you remember of the voyage?
6. On what vessel? Where did the ship dock?
7. Who was the first person in the family to come to Canada/America/elsewhere?
8. Where did family members settle in Canada/America/ elsewhere? In what cities and on what streets?
9. Did contact continue with relatives in the Old Country? With whom and for how long?
10. Can you tell or show any stories, traditions, observances, recipes, photographs, documents or other objects from the Old Country? (Ask about each separately.)

If your name is Gladstone but your grandfather crossed the ocean under the surname Glickstein and the parents he left behind in the Old Country were named Glicenstein, for example, it's obviously important that you determine as best as possible what names were used when and where, and by whom, and try to get accurate spellings and any other known variants (i.e. Gluckstein) that might help you discover other lost family branches.

Other lists of questions, in greater detail, may be found in the very useful book *Record and Remember: Tracing Your Roots Through Oral History*, by Ellen Robinson Epstein and Rona Mendelsohn. Another good sourcebook on oral histories is the classic text on Jewish genealogy, *From Generation to Generation*, by Arthur Kurzweil.

"The Art of the Interview" is also the title of a nice talk that Sam Eneman gave at the Salt Lake City conference in July 2000; a taped copy is available from Repeat Performance, 2911 Crabtree Lane, Hobart, Indiana 46342; telephone: (291) 465-1234; website: WWW.AUDIOTAPES.COM.

The Art of the Interview

Interviewing involves some technological practicalities. Many genealogists use cassette tape recorders, which ideally allow them to participate more freely in the conversation. If you're using a tape recorder, make sure it is working properly as you begin the interview, and check it intermittently. Too many interviews are lost because the tape jams, an incorrect button is pushed, the microphone connection is faulty or the batteries go dead. Don't let a technological mishap foil your noble intent to preserve your family history. For complete security, take notes as a backup.

When you're doing an interview, remember to be a good listener: let your subject do most of the talking. Don't interrupt a good story by asking for minor details that can be attained later. Use your notepad to jot down intended follow-up questions.

Getting people to open up and share information can sometimes be difficult. Family photographs and other items are often effective in prodding a person's memory. Many Holocaust survivors, in particular, are reluctant to talk about their experiences during the Shoah. In such cases, you may wish to emphasize the importance of preserving family history for the benefit of future generations.

A genealogical interview with a newfound relative can be an intense, even bewildering experience. Avoid tiring an elderly person by asking too many questions in one visit. Talk for an hour or so, then arrange to come back another time.

If you promise to send photographs, send photographs. If you promise to keep in touch, keep in touch.

In cases where distant relatives hesitate to share details of their close family members, it may be easier for them to fill out a blank family form instead. People are naturally protective of personal family information and may be reluctant to share such details even with a newfound relative.

If you've taped an interview, listen to the tape afterwards, analyze the information it contains, and draft a list of follow-up questions to present either in person or by telephone. Also, make sure to document the time, place and participants, and label the tape accordingly.

If time and energy permit, produce a written transcript of the interview; at the very least, write down the essential points on a dated sheet of paper for your files. This will help ensure that the information is preserved even if the tape should corrode or break.

Shtetl Geography

by Gary Mokotoff

The political upheavals of the 1990s in Central and Eastern Europe—the collapse of the Soviet Union and the break-up of both Czechoslovakia and Yugoslavia—are not the only major geopolitical events to have taken place in this geographic area. Frequent boundary changes have been a feature of European geography for the past 250 years. This has led to changes in town names and country names as the incoming political forces sought to divorce themselves from the cultural aspects of past systems. This evolution of place names poses a challenge to genealogists who are confronted with either oral history or documents from prior eras that mention town names that were changed or even country names no longer in use.

Remarkably some people are living today who were born in Lemberg, Austria; bar mitzvahed in Lwów, Poland; married in L'vov, Soviet Union; and reside today in L'viv, Ukraine, but who have never left their home town. The names Lemberg, Lwów, L'vov and L'viv have been used for the same city in western Ukraine during the past 85 years.

Following is an overview of the historical geography of Central and Eastern Europe.

Europe Before World War I

If your family emigrated from Central or Eastern Europe before World War I, the four least genealogically useful statements are:

- My family came from Russia.
- My family came from Germany.
- My family came from Austria.
- My family came from Hungary.

This is true because prior to World War I almost all of the territory within the contemporary boundaries of these four countries lay within only three sovereignties: the German Empire, Russian Empire and Austro-Hungarian Empire. (See map of "Central & Eastern Europe Before World War I" at the end of this chapter.) Poland did not exist; it had been divided and separate parts annexed by Prussia, Russia and Austro-Hungary at the end of the 18th century; neither did Belarus, Czechoslovakia, Estonia, Latvia, Lithuania, Moldova or Ukraine. Therefore, if family tradition or documents say your ancestors came from Austria, Germany, Hungary or Russia, you must investigate further their true, more detailed geographical origins.

Europe Between the World Wars

What happened to Europe after World War I? Historically, when a country loses a war, it loses territory. This is what happened to the three great empires of the 19th century. (See map of "Central & Eastern Europe Between the Wars" at the end of this chapter.)

Russian Empire. Russia lost territory as a result of the Bolshevik Revolution and World War I. From the former Russian Empire, the Baltic states of Estonia, Latvia and Lithuania emerged as independent countries, and Poland reappeared on the world map with Russia returning Polish land acquired in 1795 (often called Russia-Poland). The Bolsheviks considered their country to be a union of Soviet socialist republics and created entities that were states of the Soviet Union with distinct names. This included the Ukrainian, Byelorussian and Moldavian Socialist Republics.

German Empire. The German Empire was carved up along ethnic grounds. The League of Nations combined the lands of the Bohemians, Moravians and Slovakians, and a new country, Czechoslovakia was created. Land acquired from Poland in 1795 was returned to Poland. Because the League of Nations tried to keep ethnic groups together, a portion of the former northeastern German Empire, East Prussia, remained with Germany, isolated from the major portion of Germany by what became know as the Danzig Corridor, a small piece of newly recreated Poland that separated the two parts of the new Germany.

Austro-Hungarian Empire. This empire was also carved up along ethnic lines. Today's Austria and Hungary were created after World War I. The portion of Hungary whose majority was ethnically Romanian was given to a vastly enlarged Romania. In the Balkan peninsula of southern Europe, Yugoslavia emerged as a nation comprised of Slovenians, Croatians, Bosnians and Macedonians.

Europe After World War II

The Soviet dictator Josef Stalin was the major influence in redrawing the borders of Europe at the close of World War II. (See map of "Central & Eastern Europe After World War II" at the end of this chapter.) Stalin annexed the independent countries of Estonia, Latvia and Lithuania and declared them to be Soviet socialist states. He declared that the eastern tip of Czechoslovakia, known as Carpathia-Ruthenia, was ethnically Ukrainian and annexed it to the Ukrainian Soviet Socialist Republic. Stalin occupied the entire eastern portion of interwar Poland and divided that area, annexing parts to the Byelorussian, Lithuanian and Ukrainian Soviet Socialist Republics. Germany also suffered dismemberment. To appease Poland for its loss of land to the Soviets, Poland annexed the eastern portion of Germany; the allies divided the remainder of Germany into West Germany and East Germany. Thousands of ethnic Germans fled to East Germany.

Europe in the Decade of the 1990s

European geography underwent four major changes during the last decade of the 20th century. (See map of "Central & Eastern Europe Today" at the end of this chapter.)

- East and West Germany unified to become Germany.
- The Soviet Union collapsed and all the Soviet Socialist

Republics became independent countries. Byelorussia became Belarus, Moldavia became Moldova and the republics of Ukraine, Lithuania, Latvia and Estonia each became independent.

- Czechoslovakia peacefully divided into two countries, the Czech Republic and the Slovak Republic.
- Yugoslavia collapsed as a single entity. It divided into five sovereign states along its ancient geographical lines: Bosnia-Herzegovina, Croatia, Macedonia, Serbia and Slovenia.

Changes in Town Names

One of the frequent consequences of the change to new political regimes or the redefining of boundaries is that town names change. The changes fall into four major categories.

Phonetic. Phonetic name changes are the most common type of name change. In fact, they are not name changes at all. The new power retains the town name, but spells it according to the rules of its own language. Incoming political powers did not bother to change the names of the thousands of existing towns. They simply changed the spelling.

Examples of Town Name Changes That Are Phonetic

Former Name	New Name
Allenstein, Germany	Olsztyn, Poland
Corjeva, Romania	Korzhevo, Moldova
Dziatlowicze, Poland	Dyatlovichi, Belarus
Gerend, Hungary	Grind, Romania
Horodnica, Poland	Gorodnitsa, Ukraine
Szaniszlo, Hungary	Sanislau, Romania
Velky Berezny, Czech.	Velikiy Bereznyy, Ukraine

Translation. Town names with specific meanings in one language keep the meaning, but the town names are translated into the language of the new rulers.

Examples of Town Name Changes by Translation
Former Name—*New Name*—Meaning

Kaltwasser, Germany—*Zimna Voda, Ukraine*—Cold water
Neuhof, Germany—*Nowy Dwor, Poland*—New place
Fantana Alba, Romania—*Belaya Krinitsa, Ukraine*—White fountain
Grunberg, Austro-Hungary—*Zelen Hora, Czechoslovakia*—Green mountain
Weisswasser, Austro-Hungary—*Bila Voda, Czechoslovakia*—White water

Total Change. When a town name clearly represented the outgoing power, or in cases where ethnic groups had deep contempt for the outgoing group, all reference to the outgoing power was obliterated, even at the small town level. Examples include Romanian names for some former Hungarian towns.

Examples of Total Change of Town Name
Former Name—*New Name*
Magyarfrata, Austro-Hungary—*Frata, Romania*

Pressburg, Austro-Hungary—*Bratislava, Czechoslovakia*
Friedrichstadt, Germany—*Jaunjelgava, Latvia*
Chemnitz, Germany—*Karl-Marx-Stadt, East Germany*
Karl-Marx-Stadt, East Germany—*Chemnitz, Germany*
St.Petersburg, Russia—*Leningrad, USSR*
Leningrad, USSR—*St. Petersburg, Russia*
Varna, Bulgaria—*Stalin, Bulgaria*
Stalin, Bulgaria—*Varna, Bulgaria*

To understand how this process works, pretend that Poland invaded North America and conquered the United States and Canada. Town names would change. The city of Chicago might be changed to Szikago, because *chicago* is pronounced *kikago* in Polish but Szikago is pronounced *shikagoh*. This is an example of a phonetic change. New York would likely become Nowy Jork, *nowy* being the Polish word for *new* and Jork being phonetically closer in Polish to the pronouncing of that word. This is a mixture of translation and phonetic change. Montreal, Quebec might have its name changed to Góra Krowlewski. Montreal means "royal mountain" in French; Góra Krowlewski means "royal mountain" in Polish—a translation change. Finally, Washington, D.C., would likely have its name changed to Wałęsa, to honor the famous Polish statesman and remove the name of the hero of the losing political system.

This is the process that has been occurring in Europe for the past two centuries.

Strategies for Locating Town of Ancestry

Atlases. Try to find the town in an atlas. If it cannot be found, consider the source of your family information. If the source is oral tradition, you may be spelling the town name phonetically rather than by its correct spelling. If the source is a document, question whether the document was created in the country where the town is located today. A Polish passport will spell accurately a Polish town of birth—it was created in Poland. An application for citizenship in another country may show the town of birth based on how the clerk thought it sounded—or perhaps it was spelled phonetically for the clerk by the immigrant himself.

Passenger emigration and immigration lists, and documents from the country of origin usually spell town names accurately. Marriage and death records, census records, applications for naturalization and documents written in Yiddish or translated from Yiddish are all examples of records in which town names may be spelled phonetically.

Where Once We Walked: Revised Edition[1] (*WOWW*) was designed primarily to help genealogists to locate their towns of ancestry in Central and Eastern Europe. This gazetteer lists some 23,500 towns in Central and Eastern Europe where Jews lived before the Holocaust. It also includes more than 17,500 alternate names for the towns. These alternate names include 19th and early 20th century names for the towns, phonetic spellings and Yiddish names.

An important feature of the book is a phonetic index that uses the Daitch-Mokotoff Soundex System that aids the researcher in locating the town even if the spelling is uncertain.

(For a detailed description of this system, see Appendix D.) Because more than one town in a country often shares the same name, the authors of WOWW researched the many possibilities and determined which was the town where the Jews lived.

The following example of a listing in WOWW shows the current name of the town, Alba Iulia, Romania. In parentheses are five alternate names and spellings for the town. This information is followed by the town's Jewish population between the wars, its location relative to a major city in Romania—in this case, Cluj—its exact latitude and longitude, and a list of abbreviations representing eight different sources that have information about the Jews of the town.

> Alba Iulia, Rom. (Alba Julia, Albaiulia, Carlosburg, Gyulafehervar, Karlsburg); pop. 1,558; 82 km S of Cluj; 46°04'/23°35'; AMG, EJ, GUM3, GUM4, GUM6, JGFF, LDL, PHR1.

Although town names in the following example of a soundex entry in WOWW are spelled differently, they appear together in the soundex index.

> 459400—Siegritz, Skaros, Skorcz, Skurcze, Sykorice, Szekeres, Zagorz, Zagorze, Zagorzh, Zagurzhe, Zakrocz, Zakrzyze, Zgaritza, Zgerzh, Zgierz, Zguritsa

Where Once We Walked is widely distributed and is likely to be found in local libraries. If it is not available, request the librarian to obtain a copy using interlibrary loan. If you cannot find your town in *Where Once We Walked,* any library should have at least one good-quality, detailed, indexed atlas of the world.

Shtetl Seeker. A valuable site on the Internet that can be helpful in locating towns is called Shtetl Seeker at WWW.JEWISHGEN.ORG/SHTETLSEEKER. Its principal advantage is that it lists every city, town and hamlet in Central and Eastern Europe showing the exact latitude/longitude based on the U.S. Board on Geographic Names gazetteer. The fact that Shtetl Seeker shows every town in the region can be a disadvantage because many towns have the same name, and Shtetl Seeker does not distinguish between them. For example, 100 towns in Poland are named Dabrowa, and three European locations are called Berlin. Shtetl Seeker is helpful if the location is known of a town within 30 miles of a specific location.

Case Study

Consider the case of a researcher who was looking for the ancestral town of his grandfather. The grandfather's naturalization papers stated he was from a town named Mosiska. The passenger list showing his arrival in the U.S. stated that he was Ruthenian, the area where Hungary, the Slovak Republic and Ukraine meet. The researcher was also looking for

the village of Dobrjan, Poland, because a person with the same name as the grandfather came from that town.

Where Once We Walked identified no town named "Mosiska." The source of the information was U.S. naturalization papers which were created by a clerk writing down the information provided by the immigrant. Clerks often misspelled town names because they wrote what they heard. This is one reason why the Daitch-Mokotoff Soundex Index in *WOWW* is useful. Using the tables provided with the Soundex Index yields a soundex code for Mosiska of 644500. The index shows the following possibilities for towns whose names sound like Mosiska: Machocice, Mezoseg, Miedzyrzec, Miescisko, Mosciska, Moshatzik, Moshschisk and Moshtchisk. Going into the alphabetical listing of towns in *WOWW*, Machocice, Mezoseg, Miedzyrzec, Miescisko and Moshatzik are rejected because they are not it the Ruthenia region of Europe. Moshschisk and Moshtchisk are alternate spellings for the town of Mostishche which is in Ruthenia. There are three references to Mosciska. One states it is an alternate name for Mostiska, also in Ruthenia.

Which town is it: Mostishche or Mostiska? When there is a choice and there is no other evidence available, assume it is the town with the larger Jewish population, especially if significantly larger. Mostishche, listed in *WOWW*, was found in only one source. Its Jewish population is not shown. On the other hand, Mostiska had 2,328 Jews between World War I and II. Furthermore, references to the town were found in 15 different sources. The conclusion is that it is highly likely this is the town being sought.

But we have another clue. It is near the town of Dobrjan, Poland. Dobrjan is not listed in *WOWW*. The soundex code for the town is 379600. None of the listings in *WOWW* with this soundex number is a town in Ruthenia. Because WOWW is not helpful in this case, turn to the Shtetl Seeker. Anticipating that Dobrjan is near Mostiska, we entered the latitude/longitude of Mostiska (49°48'/23°09') and requested a listing for all towns within 30 miles of Mostiska that start with the letter *D*. Shtetl Seeker identified 87 towns within 30 miles of Mostiska that start with the letter *D* (three of them named Dabrowa), but only one is phonetically similar to Dobrjan: Dobzhany, Ukraine, located at 49°45'/23°31', about 20 miles north of Mostiska.

We have found our two towns. Both Mostiska and Dobrjan were under Polish jurisdiction between the two world wars; today both are in Ukraine.

Internet Resources
See chapter on HOLISTIC GEOGRAPHY for Internet resources.

Bibliography
See chapter on HOLISTIC GEOGRAPHY for bibliography.

Note
1. Mokotoff, Gary and Sallyann Amdur Sack with Alexander Sharon. *Where Once We Walked: Revised Edition.* Bergenfield, N.J.: Avotaynu, 2002.

CENTRAL & EASTERN EUROPE
BEFORE WORLD WAR I

RUSSIAN EMPIRE

St. Petersburg

Reval

Dorpat

o Pskov

Tver

Riga

Moskva

Velikiye Luki

Shavli

Dvinsk

Kovno

Vitebsk

Smolensk

Vilna

Minsk

Bryansk

GERMANY

Rostock

Danzig

Königsberg

Hamburg

Stettin

Belostok

Gomel

Kursk

Voronezh

Hannover

Posen

Warszawa

Pinsk

Konotop

Berlin

Köln

Leipzig

Lodz

Lublin

Kiev

Breslau

Chenstokhov

Rovno

Kharkov

Frankfurt-am-Main

Prague

Cracow

Przemysl

Lemberg

Yekaterinoslav

Nürnberg

Vinnitsa

Stuttgart

Brünn

Kaschau

Munkacs

Czernowitz

o Uman

München

Wien

o Pressburg

o Miskolcz

Salzburg

Budapest

Jassy

Kishinev

Odessa

Innsbruck

Graz

Koloszvar

Nagykanizsa

Szeged

Simferopol

Agram

AUSTRIA-HUNGARY

RUMANIA

Bucharest

Belgrade

SERBIA

BULGARIA

Varna

MONTE-NEGRO

Skoplje

Sofia

ALBANIA

Salonika

Janina

GREECE

Athens

Copyright 2002, Avotaynu, Inc.
All Rights Reserved

Shtetl Geography • 19

CENTRAL & EASTERN EUROPE

BETWEEN THE WARS

Leningrad

ESTONIA
Tallinn
Tartu

Pskov

Kalinin

Moskva

LATVIA
Riga

Velikiye Luki

U.S.S.R.

Siauliai
Daugavpils

LITHUANIA
Kovno

Vitebsk
Smolensk

Rostock
Danzig
Königsberg
(GERMANY)

Wilno

Minsk

Bryansk

Voronezh

Hamburg
Stettin

BYELORUSSIA
S.S.R.
Gomel

Kursk

Hannover

GERMANY
Berlin

Bialystok

Poznan
Warszawa

Pinsk

Konotop

Köln

Leipzig

Lodz

POLAND

Lublin

Kiyev

Kharkov

Frankfurt-am-Main

Breslau
Czestochowa

Rowne

UKRAINE
S.S.R.

Dnepropetrovsk

Nürnberg

Stuttgart

Praha

Lwow

Vinnitsa

Krakow
Przemysl

Uman

CZECHOSLOVAKIA

München

Brno

Kosice
Mukachevo

Cernauti

Salzburg
Wien

Bratislava

Miskolc

Iasi

Chisinau

Odessa

Innsbruck

AUSTRIA
Graz

Budapest

HUNGARY
Nagykanizsa
Szeged

Cluj

Simferopol

Zagreb

RUMANIA

Beograd

Bucharest

YUGOSLAVIA

BULGARIA
Varna

Skoplje

Sofija

ALBANIA

Thessaloniki

Ioannina

GREECE

Athens

CENTRAL & EASTERN EUROPE

1991

Leningrad

Tallinn

ESTONIA

Tartu

Pskov

Kalinin

LATVIA

Riga

Moskva

Velikiye Luki

U. S. S. R.

Siauliai

Daugavpils

LITHUANIA

Vitebsk

Smolensk

Kaunas

Minsk

Bryansk

Vilnius

R.S.F.S.R.

Rostock

Gdansk

Kaliningrad

BYELORUSSIA

Gomel

Voronezh

Hamburg

Szczecin

Bialystok

Pinsk

Kursk

Hannover

POLAND

Berlin

Poznan

Warszawa

Konotop

GERMANY

Köln

Leipzig

Lodz

Kiyev

Kharkov

Wroclaw

Lublin

Rovno

Frankfurt-am-Main

Czestochowa

UKRAINE

Nürnberg

Praha

Krakow

Przemysl

Lvov

Dnepropetrovsk

Stuttgart

CZECHOSLOVAKIA

Vinnitsa

München

Brno

Kosice

Mukachevo

Chernovtsy

Uman

Salzburg

Wien

Bratislava

Miskolc

MOLDAVIA

Innsbruck

AUSTRIA

Graz

Budapest

Iasi

Kishinev

Odessa

HUNGARY

Cluj

Simferopol

Nagykanizsa

Szeged

Zagreb

ROMANIA

YUGOSLAVIA

Beograd

Bucuresti

Varna

BULGARIA

Skopje

Sofija

ALBANIA

Thessaloniki

GREECE

Ioannina

Athens

CENTRAL &
EASTERN EUROPE

TODAY

St. Petersburg

Tallinn
ESTONIA
Tartu

Pskov

Tver

LATVIA
Rīga

Moskva

Velíkiye Luki

Liepāja

Daugavpils

Šiauliai

Smolensk

LITHUANIA
Kaunas

Vitsyebsk

RUSSIA

Vilnius

RUSSIA

Minsk

Bryansk

Rostock

Gdańsk

Kaliningrad

BELARUS

Hamburg

Szczecin

POLAND

Białystok

Homyel

Kursk

Hannover

Berlin

Poznań

Warszawa

Pinsk

Konotop

Köln

Leipzig

Łódź

Lublin

Rivne

Kyyiv

Kharkiv

GERMANY

Wrocław

Częstochowa

L'viv

Frankfurt am Main

Nürnberg

Praha

Kraków

Przemyśl

UKRAINE

Dnipropetrovs'k

Stuttgart

CZECH REPUBLIC

Vinnytsya

Uman

Kirovohrad

Brno

SLOVAK
REPUBLIC

Košice

Chernivtsi

München

Wien

Bratislava

Miskolc

MOLDOVA

Salzburg

Iaşi

Chişinău

Odesa

Innsbruck

AUSTRIA

Budapest

Gráz

HUNGARY

Cluj-Napoca

Simferopol'

SLOVENIA

Nagykanizsa

Szeged

Ljubljana

Zagreb

ROMANIA

CROATIA

Timişoara

BOSNIA &
HERZEGO-
VINA

Beograd

Bucureşti

Sarajevo

SERBIA

BULGARIA

Varna

MONTE-
NEGRO

Sofija

Podgorica

Skopje

ALBANIA

MACEDONIA

Thessaloníki

Ioánnina

GREECE

Athínai

Copyright 2002, Avotaynu, Inc.
All Rights Reserved

Holistic Geography
by Randy Daitch

One of the milestone achievements for many family historians is the discovery of an ancestor's immigration or citizenship record. To the Jewish genealogist, this is the Rosetta Stone that points the way to identifying the ancestral *shtetl*. Frequently, however, what these documents deliver is not illumination, but frustration. Squinting in puzzlement at the entry for "Place of Birth," many a researcher finds that a name that was supposed to reveal an ancestor's place of birth or origin instead becomes a locality that eludes verification.

There are many possible causes for this frustration:

1. The town is listed by its Yiddish name. Determining how that name is represented on an official map can be a challenge because the attempt to spell it was often mangled by the transcribing clerk. A classic case was the naturalization petition for one of my cousins, which listed his place of birth as *Balguis*, Poland. Only by letting my imagination distort the word's original form was I able to deduce that his birthplace was actually Bildzhuis (pronounced bill-jew-iss), the Yiddish name for a locality in northern Vilna province called *Bildyugi* in Russian and *Bildziugi* in Polish.

2. The place name given is a historical variant no longer in use. For example, a passenger manifest of an immigrant with an unusual surname indicated he came from the town of Bodružal, Czechoslovakia (formerly Austria-Hungary). Another immigrant with that surname on a different document had his birthplace listed as *Rozsadomb*, Hungary. Only much later did I discover in an interwar Czechoslovakian gazetteer that Rozsadomb was the Hungarian name for Bodružal.

3. The name of the town resembles the name of a better-known place. For example, one Russian Jew's naturalization record listed his birthplace as *Bresslow*, Russia. This led to the puzzling question of how a Russian Jew could have been born in a place that sounded like a German city (Breslau). It turned out that his birthplace was *Braslav*, a small town in Belorussia.

4. Ambiguous handwriting leads to a misread place name. A U.S. Declaration of Intent to Become a Citizen listed an individual's birthplace as *Koone*, Russia. A closer look at the handwriting revealed that the second *o* was actually a *v*; thus, Koone became *Kovne* or *Kovna*, the name of both a *guberniya* (province) and a city in Czarist Russia that today is Kaunas, Lithuania.

5. A typographical error occurs in an otherwise accurate entry. An example is *Tadgoszcz*, a misspelling of *Radgoszcz*.

6. The entry is written in phonetic English rather than the unfamiliar spelling of the native language, for example, *Dombrova* instead of *Dąbrowa*.

7. The locality is listed by its root name rather than its full name, for example, *Pohost*, short for *Nowy Pohost* (New Pohost), and *Apša*, short for *Vyšní Apša* (Upper Apsha).

Problems of this type can be solved by inserting the foreign-language equivalent for new, old, upper, lower, big, small, in front of the root word.

An effective way to meet these challenges is through an approach that I call holistic geography. When we encounter a foreign place name in a public record, the first question to ask is not "Where on a map can I find an exact match for this name?" but rather, "How does this name fit into the big picture?"

For Eastern European Jewish research, the big picture includes six major components:

1. Changing national boundaries in Europe during the 20th century
2. The administrative district (*guberniya, oblast, powiat,* etc.) to which a locality belonged
3. The locality's many possible misspellings
4. The locality's historical names and Yiddish names
5. The locality's position on a map relative to the birth places of other foreign-born members of the same extended family.

Many documents can be misleading because the locality cited may not be the immigrant's place of birth, but the name of the district in which he lived. This often is a place name identical to the capital city of the district (e.g. Vilna, Vitebsk, Minsk), which can sometimes be more than a hundred kilometers from the ancestor's actual birthplace. By browsing through the pre-World War I map in *Where Once We Walked: Revised Edition* (p. xxix), which includes the names of many district capitals, the researcher can spot handwriting and spelling errors and identify place names that would otherwise leave him clueless: e.g.: Koone (Kovne) and Widepsk (Vitebsk).

Sometimes it may be necessary to do a wild card or soundex search to identify an incorrectly spelled name. For example, one way to identify *Charkochina* would be to use the wild card feature on the Internet search engine *GEOnet Names Server* and type in %arko%china. The use of the percent signs (%) allow the query engine to search all the localities that begin with any letter or group of letters plus *arko* plus any letter or group of letters plus *china*. The result of this search would be the Belorussian town of *Sharkovshchina*. To identify the Polish town of *Kshepitsa*, using the soundex feature on JewishGen ShtetlSeeker yields the town of *Krzepice*. The two approaches complement each other and, together, should catch most errors, other than those caused by misread handwriting.

Occasionally, the only way a locality can be identified is through a source that cites both its Yiddish name and its official name. A person whose grandfather was born in *Amshinov* will not find this name in any standard gazetteer, but can locate it in two resources that include Yiddish place names: *Where Once we Walked* and *Hebrew Subscription*

Lists. There, the researcher will learn that the town's official Polish name was *Mszczonów*.

Knowing a locality's Jewish population before World War II can be crucial in correctly identifying a town. Suppose an immigrant's ship manifest states that he was born in *Teresif*, Hungary, and that his last foreign residence was *Taèovo*, Czechoslovakia. Since Taèovo was a former Hungarian town in the sub-Carpathian region of Czechoslovakia, we can start with the working hypothesis that Teresif was also in this region. Indeed, a pre-war gazetteer of Czechoslovakia, *Místopisný Slovnik Èeskoslovenské Republiky*, indicates that, while there was no place in that country called Teresif, there were two towns in Taèovo county with similar sounding names: Teresva, with 471 Jews, and Teresova, with no Jews at all. Armed with the right research tool, *Teresif's* true identity was obvious.

Sometimes the best way to zero in on an obscure place is by collecting information from a number of public records (birth, marriage, death, naturalization, ship manifests, World War I draft records, etc.) of every known member of the extended family, noting all European place names that can be identified and highlighting them on a map. This creates a context within which the correct place can be identified. Suppose that we have the following information about the extended family of an immigrant who arrived in the United States in 1922:

1. The immigrant's Declaration of Intent to Become a Citizen states that he was born in *Loza*, Czechoslovakia.
2. The birth record of the American-born son of his first cousin states that the father and mother were born in *Ilosva*, Hungary.
3. The ship manifest of the immigrant's uncle, who arrived in the United States in 1901, states that his last foreign residence was *Munkács*, Hungary.

Mistopisny Slovnik Èeskoslovenské Republiky indicates that *Ilosva* and *Munkács* were the Hungarian names for *Iršava* and *Mukačevo*. Since the names referred to were counties as well as towns in pre-war Czechoslovakia, they can be located easily and highlighted on a modern map, despite the change of national boundaries, by using Shtetl Seeker and its link to MapQuest. (The towns are now known as *Irshava* and *Mukacheve*, Ukraine.) Once the larger towns have been identified, the challenge narrows from a needle in a haystack to a needle in a pin box. We can then return to our Czechoslovakian gazetteer, where we will find two places named *Loza*—one in Bohemia and the other in Iršava county, not far from Mukaèevo.

Following is a list of sources that are essential for the Jewish genealogist:

CD-ROMs

Encarta Interactive World Atlas is a CD-ROM which is part of *Microsoft Encarta Reference Library*. Its detail is remarkable, pinpointing close to two million populated localities throughout the world including, in Eastern Europe, villages that never had more than a handful of Jews. The atlas features a soundex-style search engine, a zoom-in/zoom-out tool, a

latitude/longitude sensor, a virtual "measuring tape" to determine distances between locations, and digital "push pins" to highlight places of interest. For more information, see SHOP.MICROSOFT.COM.

Microsoft AutoRoute, a CD-ROM resource for much of Europe, lists virtually every locality in Germany, Lithuania, Poland, Hungary, Slovakia, and the Balkans, including even some farms. It includes many of the same features as *Encarta Interactive World Atlas*. For more information, see the "Mapping CD-ROMs" link at WWW.ELSTEAD.CO.UK.

Online Resources

Shtetl Seeker at WWW.JEWISHGEN.ORG/SHTETLSEEKER/LOCTOWN.HTM is the mother of all geographic search engines for Central and Eastern Europe. It includes options to search by Daitch-Mokotoff soundex, exact name or beginning of a name. Each "hit" includes a link to an online map from MapQuest.

MSN Maps and Directions at MAPPOINT.MSN.COM is the free, online version of *Encarta Interactive World Atlas*.

GEOnet Names Server at GNSWWW.NIMA.MIL/GEONAMES/GNS/INDEX.JSP contains data on every locality in the world outside the United States. Information includes latitude and longitude, administrative district (province, oblast, etc.), and names of mountains, forests, lakes, streams, and railroad stations. Many former Polish localities, today in Belarus and Ukraine, are cross-referenced under their historical names.

International Jewish Cemetery Project at WWW.JEWISHGEN.ORG/CEMETERY/E-EUROPE lists Jewish cemeteries throughout the world, but is most useful for its entries on communities in Europe, especially Ukraine.

Yizkor Book Database at WWW.JEWISHGEN.ORG/YIZKOR/DATABASE.HTML is an excellent source, not only for *yizkor* books, but also for pinpointing a locality when only the Yiddish name is known. It is searchable by soundex, and many of the entries include links to *yizkor* book translations.

Shtetl Links at SHTETLINKS.JEWISHGEN.ORG is the single most important website for historical data on Jewish communities in Europe. Many of the communities documented on this site have links to maps, encyclopedia entries, *yizkor* book translations, community records, testimonies on the Holocaust, portraits of individuals, business directories, family photos, and a necrology of people who perished.

Hungarian Village Finder and Gazetteer for the Kingdom of Hungary at WWW.HUNGARIANVILLAGEFINDER.COM includes Czech and Romanian variants of localities that belonged to the Kingdom of Hungary before World War I. Access is by paid subscription.

Ostrák-Magyar Monarchia vármegyéi at LAZARUS.ELTE.HU/HUN/MAPS/1910/VMLISTA.HTM is a detailed and well-designed map series, organized by county, of the entire Kingdom of Hungary in 1910. This resource, unavailable even at the Library of Congress, can be accessed free on the internet.

Ukraine 1:100,000 Topographic Maps: http://WWW.LIB.BERKELEY.EDU/EART/X-USSR/UKRAINE.HTML

Austria-Hungary 1:200,000 Topographic Maps: HTTP://LAZARUS.ELTE.HU/HUN/DIGKONYV/TOPO/3FELMERES.HTM

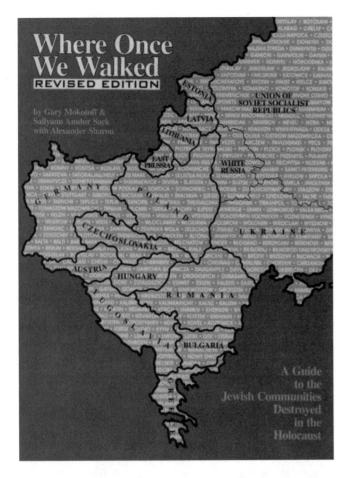

Where Once We Walked: Revised Edition (Avotaynu, 2002) includes entries for more than 23,000 towns in Central and Eastern Europe where Jews lived before the Holocaust. Also included are more than 17,000 alternate names for these towns as well as former names and Yiddish variants.

1929 Polish Business Directory Project at WWW.JEWISHGEN.ORG/JRI-PL/BIZDIR/BD1929.HTM includes a database of approximately 30,000 towns and villages in interwar Poland. Each entry provides a link to scanned pages, organized by occupation, of individuals from that town who advertised in the directory.

Jewish Records Indexing–Poland at WWW.JEWISHGEN.ORG/JRI-PL/JRIPLWEB.HTM has developed a database of close to 2,000,000 records from nearly 300 Polish towns. If an ancestor has a rare surname but his origins have not been determined, this resource can be particularly useful. For example, a document listed an individual named "Skopicki" from "Gawoshicz." The JRI-P database revealed that the only person in the database with this surname came from *Dzialoszyce* (pronounced *Dzhawoshits* in Polish).

Ukraine 1:100,000 topographic maps at WWW.LIB.BERKELEY.EDU/EART/x-USSR/UKRAINE.HTML is an extremely detailed map series of the entire Ukraine, published between 1972-2000 in Cyrillic by the Soviet Union Generalnyi shtab. Each region included in this series can be accessed through a clickable grid sheet. The significance of these maps is that they document an area that is poorly covered by most online

sources, and contain a level of detail that is found, in hard copy, in only a few libraries in North America.

Közép-Európa általános földrajzi térképének szelvénybeosztása at LAZARUS.ELTE.HU/HUN/DIGKONYV/TOPO/3FELMERES.HTM is a 1:200,000 map series, published around 1910, covering most of the Austro-Hungarian Empire. Accessible through a clickable grid sheet, these maps provide detailed coverage of Moravia, Silesia, Slovakia, Ruthenia, Transylvania, Bukovina, and most of Galicia.

Printed Resources

Except where noted, the following resources can be found at the U.S. Library of Congress or one of the major university libraries and can often be accessed through interlibrary loan at a local public library:

Where Once We Walked: Revised Edition (Bergenfield, N.J.: Avotaynu, 2002). A pioneering gazetteer of Jewish communities in Eastern and Central Europe, it includes entries for more than 23,000 towns along with figures for latitude/longitude and Jewish population. There are an additional 17,500 variant names for towns including Yiddish, pre-World War I and interwar names. The revised 2002 edition adds 800 towns and includes an improved soundex that solves some of the spelling problems described in this article. The book can be ordered on Avotaynu's website, WWW.AVOTAYNU.COM.

Blackbook of Localities Whose Jewish Population Was Destroyed by the Nazis (Jerusalem: Yad Vashem, 1964). The single most important source for *Where Once We Walked*, it includes administrative data and Jewish population figures for 32,000 towns and villages in Europe. An alphabetized version is available on microfiche at Avotaynu's website.

Deutsches Ortsverzeichnis (Berlin: 1930, Dr. H. Höpker, reprinted Frankfurt a.M., 1978). This post-World War I gazetteer of Germany and the Free State of Danzig lists approximately 72,000 towns and includes an appendix of about 11,000 towns which became part of Poland after the First World War. It is available at the Family History Library in Salt Lake City

Das Ortsbuch Für Das Deutsche Reich (Berlin, 1938). This massive, 2,000 page German gazetteer has close to 130,000 entries, including a comprehensive list of former German localities in Poland. It may be the only complete gazetteer of Germany published before World War II that uses non-gothic lettering, accessible to the English reader. The only known edition of this work in North America is at the Survivors of the Shoah Visual History Foundation in Los Angeles.

Amtliches Gemeinde- und Ortsnamenverzeichnis der Deutschen Ostgebiete unter fremder Verwaltung (Remagen: Bundesanstalt für Landeskunde, 1955). This is a comprehensive list of every populated locality in the territories of Germany that were annexed by Poland and the USSR after World War II. The work consists of a German-Polish volume and a Polish-German volume. The former lists localities alphabetically by their German names, followed by the German district, the Polish or Russian name, and the post-war Polish or Soviet district.

Distribution of the Jewish Population of the USSR, 1939. Mordechai Altschuler, ed. (Jerusalem: Hebrew University,

Centre for Research and Documentation of Eastern European Jewry, 1993). This volume includes the Jewish population of localities not listed in Yad Vashem's *Blackbook*.

Kontorkarte der Tschechoslowakischen Republic (Vienna: Freytag & Berndt, 1938). This detailed map (1:600,000 scale) of Czechoslovakia before World War II is accompanied by a map index of Czech towns and villages that identifies each place by province.

Magyar Helysegnev-Azonosito Szotar, by Gyorgy Leikes (Budapest: Talma Konyvkiado, 1992). A gazetteer of every populated locality in greater historical Hungary (including Slovakia, Subcarpathian Ruthenia, Transylvania, and much of Yugoslavia), the main section is an alphabetical list of places, according to their Hungarian name. Each entry includes (1) county to which it belonged during the Austro-Hungarian period; (2) German, Hungarian, Latin, Russian, Serbo-Croatian, and Ukrainian place name variants; (3) name of locality and the country to which it belonged in 1992. At the back of the book is an appendix that lists localities by their non-Hungarian names. This section is subdivided into the languages of the variants mentioned in the main section. The book's one significant omission is that, for localities in Subcarpathian Ruthenia, it lists only the old Hungarian names and the modern Russian and Ukrainian names; missing are the interwar Czechoslovakian names. To a lesser extent, this problem applies to Slovakia and Romania, where the modern place names are occasionally different from the interwar name.

Místopisný Slovnik Èeskoslovenské Republiky, by Bretislav Chromec (Prague, 1935). This gazetteer lists alphabetically every populated locality in interwar Czechoslovakia, along with German and Hungarian cross-references. Each entry includes the name of the county and province of the locality, along with ethnic population figures (including two different ways of counting Jews!)

Sefer Shefer harere kedem, by Shelomoh Rozman (Brooklyn, 1991). An essential reference for finding the Yiddish names of towns in the Carpathian-Maramaros region of pre-World War II Czechoslovakia and Romania, it includes a Yiddish-language map showing the approximate latitude and longitude of each town.

Polska, by E. Romer (1929), is an exceptionally detailed four-sheet map of pre-World War II Poland (1:600,000 scale), with an accompanying map index of 30,000 Polish towns and villages.

Postal Place Names in Poland, by George K. Kay (Edinburgh, 1992), includes virtually all Polish localities larger than a village, cross-referenced by their variant names. This source is particularly valuable for finding Polish towns that once belonged to Germany or Austria-Hungary. Among the types of variant names listed are German names from the Austro-Hungarian, World War I, and World War II periods, Polish names at different points in history, and the post-World War II names of territories annexed by the Soviet Union. Also cited are the names of the counties and provinces in which the town was located at different points in the 20th century.

Skorowidz Miejscowosci Rzeczypospolitej Polskiej (Index of places in the Polish Republic) (Glowny Urząd Statystyczny Rzeczypospolitej Polskiej. Warsawa, 1923–1926. 16 volumes) This work was the basis for the statistics listed in the Polish section of Yad Vashem's *Blackbook*. Organized by *voivodship* (province), it includes ethnic population figures for every locality in interwar Poland, except for Silesia and two counties in Vilna *voivodship*. Even farms and estates are listed!

Indicatorul Statistic al Satelor °i unitāþilor Administrative din România (Publicatia Directiei Recensāmântului General al Populatiei din Ministerul Muncii, Bucharest, 1932). Based on a 1930 national census, this gazetteer lists alphabetically by its official Romanian name, every populated locality in interwar Romania. Each entry includes the name of the county in which the locality is situated. For the official spellings of Romanian place names during the interwar period, this source is more reliable than either the Blackbook or Pinkas Hakehillot Romania.

Words Associated with Geographic Place Names

English	German	Hungarian	Romanian	Czech / Slovak	Polish	Russian
region	gebiet, bezirk	vidék	regiune	rajón, oblast, kraj	okrąg, okolica	okrug
state	land, staat	állapot	stat	štát		gubernya
province	provinz	tartomány, vidék	provincie	provincie, venkov	wojewodztwo (woj.)	oblast
county	kreis	vármegye, megye	judet	okres	powiat (pow.)	rayon, raion
district	gemeinde	jaras	plasa	obec	gmina (gm.)	volost
township		köszég				
City	Stadt	Nagyváros, Város	Oraş, Cetate	Mesto	Miasto (m-to.)	Gorod, Grad
Town	Stadt	Város, Köszég	Oraş	Mestsky	Miasteczko (m-tko.)	Mestechko, Gorod
Townlet					Osada Miejska (os.m.)	
Village	Dorf	Falva, Falu, Közég	Comună, Sat	Ves, Obec	Wies	Derevnya, Selo
Colony	Kolonie	Kolónia, Gyarmat	Colonie	Kolonie, Kolónia	Kolonia (kol.)	Koloniya
Settlement	Siedlung	Település	Colonie	Osada	Osada (os.)	Osadka
Settlement (factory)					Osada fabryczyna (os.fabr.)	
Settlement (mill)					Osada młynarska (os.ml.)	
Hamlet	Kleines Dorf				Futor (fut.)	
Farm		Tanya				
Manor Farm					Folwark (folw.)	
Estate					Obszar Dworski (ob. dw.)	
Place	Ort, Platz	Hely	Loc	Místo, Miesto	Miejsce	Mesto
Market	Markt	Vásár	Târg, Tîrg		Targ	
Marketplace		Vásárhely	Târgul, Tîrgu			
Square	Hof					
castle	burg	vár		zamek, hrad	zamek, grad	zamek, dvorets
manor house	schloss	kastély	costeiu		dwór	
small house					buda, budy	
house / house of	hausen	ház, háza				
houses						
Old	Alt	O	Vechi, Vechiul	Stary	Stary	Stariy
New	Neu	Uj	Nou	Novy	Nowy	Noviy
Great / Big	Gross	Nagy	Mare, Gros	Velký, Veľký, Veliký	Wielki	Vel'ky, Velikiy, Bol'shoy
Small	Klein	Kis	Mic	Malý	Mały	Malyy
Upper	Ober	Felsö	de-Sus	Vyšní, Horní, Vrchný	Górny	Verkhniy, Vyshniy
Lower	Unter	Alsó	de-Jos	Nižní, Dolní, Dolný	Dolny	Nizhniy
Middle	Mittel	Közép	de-Mijloc	Střední, Stredný	Srednia	Sredniy

English	German	Hungarian	Romanian	Czech / Slovak	Polish	Russian
below / under	unter			pod	pod (p.)	pod, po
above / over	über			nad, na	nad (n.)	nad, na
on / on the	an, am, auf				nad (n.)	
in / in the	in, im				kolo (k.)	
near	bei					
North / Northern	Nord, Nordisch	Eszaki	Nordic, de Nord	Severní, Severný	Północny	Severniy
South / Southern	Süd, Südlich	Déli	Sudic, de Sud	Jižní, Južný	Pohudniowy	Yuzhniy
East / Eastern	Ost, Ostlich	Keleti	Estic, de Est	Východní, Východný	Wschodni	Vostochniy
West / Western	West, Westlich	Nyugati	Vestic, Occidental	Západní, Západný	Zachodni	Zapadniy
Black	Schwarz	Fekete, Néger	Negru	Cerný, Cierny	Czarny	Chorniy
White	Weiss	Fehér	Alba	Biely	Bialy	Bely
Grey	Grau	Szürke	Gri, Cenuşiu	Sivý, Sedý, Sedivý	Siwy, Szary	Sedoy, Seriy
Brown	Braun	Barna	Brun	Hnědý, Hnedý	Brązowy	Korichevniy
Red	Roth, Rot	Piros, Vörös	Roşu	Cervený, rudý	Czerwony	Krasniy
Rose	Rosen	Rozsa	Roz	Ružový	Różany	Rozovy
Green	Grün, Gruen	Zöld	Verde	Zelený	Zielony	Zeleniy
Gold	Gold, Golden	Arany	Aur	Zlatý	Złoty	Zolotoy
Silver	Silber, Silbern	Ezüst	Argint	Stříbrný, Strieborný	Srebrny	Serebrianiy
Lake	See	Tó, Lakk	Lac	Jezero, Jazero, Rybník	Jezioro	Ozero
River	Fluss	Folyó	Râu, Rîu	Reka, Rieka	Rzeka	Reka
Stream / Brook	Strom, Bach	Folyam, Patak	Potoc	Potok, Rička, Riečka	Potok, Rzeczka, Rzeki	Potok, Ruchey
Spring / Well	Born	Forrás	Izvor	Zřídlo, Zriedlo, Lázně	Zródło	Ictochnik
Bath / Spa	Bad	Gyógyfurdö	Izvor	Zriedlo, Lázně	Zdrój	Banya, Kurort
Water	Wasser	Víz	Apă	Voda	Woda	Voda
Wilderness	Wüste, Wildnis	Vadon, Pusztaság			Puszcza	
Forest / Woods	Wald	Erdö	Padurea		Puszcza, Bór, Las	
Marsh / Moor	Sumpf, Marsh	Mocsár, Láp			Moczary	
Glade	Lichtung, Schneis	Tisztás, Irtás	Poiană, Luminiş	Cistina, Paseka, Palouk	Polana	Polyana
Mountain	Berg	Hegy	Munte	Hora, Kopec, Vrch	Góra	Gora
Hill	Höhe	Domb	Colină	Pahorek, Pahorok	Pagórek, Wzgórze	Kholm, Gorka
Upland					Wyżyna, Górsky	
Peak						
Meadow	Wiese	Rét, Mezö	Luncă	Louka, Lúka	Łąka	Lug
Valley	Tal	Völgy	Vale	Dolina, Udolí, Udolie	Dolina	Dolina
Plains / Prairie	Prärie	Puszta	Prerie	Prérie, Préria	Preria	Preriya, Step'
Field	Feld, Acker	Mezö	Câmp, Cîmp	Pole	Pole	Pole, Lug

English	German	Hungarian	Romanian	Czech / Slovak	Polish	Russian
Mine / Quarry	Mine, Bergwerk	Bánya, Akna	Mină, Ocna	Mina, Mína, Baňa	Kopalnia	Shakhta
Iron works					Huta	Guta
Iron ore					Ruda	
Stone	Stein					
German	Deutsch	Német	German	Německý, Nemecký	Niemiecki, Germański	Nemetskiy
Prussian	Preussisch	Porosz	Prusian	Pruský	Prusacki, Pruski	Prusskiy
Silesia	Schlesien	Slezsko			Śląsk	
Upper Silesia	Oberschlesien				Śląsk, Opole	
Lower Silesia	Niederschlesien				Dolnośląsk	
Polish	Polnisch	Lengyel	Polon	Polský, Poľský	Polski	Pol'skiy
Galicia	Galizien				Galicia	
Lithuanian	Litauisch	Litván	Lituanian	Litevský	Litewski	Litovskiy
Russian	Russisch	Orosz	Rus	Ruský	Ruski, Rosyjski	Russkiy
Belorussian		Belorusz	Bielorus	Běloruský	Białoruski	Belorusskiy
Ukrainian		Ukrán	Ucrainean		Ukraiński	Ukrainskiy
Austrian	Österreichisch	Osztrál	Austriac	Rakouský	Austriacki	Avstriyskiy
Hungarian	Ungarisch	Magyar	Ungar	Uherský, Maďarský	Węgierski	Vengerskiy
Czech	Tschechisch	Cseh	Ceh	Český	Czeski	Cheshskiy
Bohemian	Böhmisch	Bohém	Boehm, de Boehm	Bohémský	Cygański	Bogemskiy
Moravian	Mährisch	Morva		Moravský	Morawski	Moravskiy
Slovakian	Slowakisch	Szlovák		Slovenský	Słowak	Slovatskiy
Carpathian	Karpatisch	Karpatalja	Carpatic, Carpatin			
Ruthenia		Ruszin				
Romanian	Rumänisch	Román	Român, Romanesc	Rumunský		Rumynskiy
Saint	Sankt	Szent	Sfântul, Sfîntu	Svatý	Święty	Svyatoy
(no meaning)					wola, wolka	
(suffix)				á, é, í, ia, ie, ní, ňa, ý, ya, e, i, ie, y	y	a, aya, e, eye, i, iy, iye, yaya, oye, y, yy, yye

Family Names

by Sallyann Amdur Sack

Family names, surnames, or "last names" as they are most commonly called, are the basic building blocks of genealogy. It is with last names that most people begin their research. For many Jews, however—especially Ashkenazic Jews—fixed, hereditary last names as we know them today are a relatively recent phenomenon, adopted only when they were imposed by secular rulers little more than two hundred years ago.

Until modern times, Jews typically called themselves in official Jewish documents by a combination of a Hebrew given name plus his or her father's Hebrew given name, a patronymic. For example, Isaac ben Abraham. In everyday life, they used vernacular names. For Eastern European Jews, these names were Yiddish, sometimes drawn from local names (German, Hungarian, Polish, etc.). For example Zalman ben Isaac. Sephardic Jews, who did not speak Yiddish, tended to use Judeo-Spanish (Judesmo) or Judeo-Arabic names along with the Hebrew ones.

A Jewish male traditionally receives his Hebrew name at the age of eight days at his *brit milah* (ritual circumcision). He uses this *shem hakodesh* (religious name) whenever he is called to the Torah, at his *bar mitzvah*, when he marries, and when he dies. The form of the name is always "[baby's given name] *ben* (son of) [father's *shem hakodesh*]." Jewish females are known as "[baby's given name] *bat* (daughter of) [father's *shem hakodesh*]." Because girls are not called to the Torah in traditional Judaism, they do not need a *shem hakodesh* at birth and often are given only vernacular names. Modern tradition is that their *shem hakodesh* is given at a Sabbath service shortly after their birth. In addition to patronymics and Hebrew and vernacular names, some Jews also carried non-hereditary nicknames that frequently reflected occupations or physical characteristics, (e.g., Isaac the glazier or Jacob the lame).

A handful of families with a tradition of descent from King David carry last names known to date back at least to the Babylonian exile in 580 BCE. Ancient Italian Jewish families adopted fixed last names in the 10th and 11th centuries, and Jews of the Iberian Peninsula began to adopt hereditary family names as early as the 12th and 13th centuries. Many leading Ashkenazi rabbinical families began to do so in about the 14th century as well, but the majority of other Ashkenazim did not acquire last names until centuries later when forced to do so by the civil authorities of the countries in which they lived.

In 1787, Austrian Emperor Joseph II was the first ruler to require that Jews adopt fixed family names. Next was the Russian Czar Alexander I, who made a similar demand in 1804. Napoleon followed suit in 1808; all of the territory under his rule adopted similar rules soon after. Rulers of the several German states issued similar laws during the first third of the 19th century. Turkey did not require family names until the 1930s. In some other parts of the world, Jews did not assume last names until they immigrated to Israel after World War II.

History of Family Name Adoptions
Iberian Peninsula

Jews of Spain and Portugal began to adopt hereditary family names as early as the 12th and 13th centuries, some of which (or their variants) have endured ever since (see INQUISITION). Thus the name Abravanel, Barbanel, Barban and similar variations can be traced back to Don Isaac Abravanel, Chancellor of the Exchequer in pre-Inquisition Spain. At the time of the Spanish edict of expulsion in 1492, Jews were given the choice to convert to Catholicism or to leave the country. Historians estimate that approximately half chose to leave. Those who converted typically adopted new names, often those of their Christian godfathers. For this reason, last name alone does not identify a Spanish family that was originally Jewish.

The situation was different in Portugal. Most of the wealthier Jews who left Spain around the time of the expulsion settled originally in Portugal, where they were forced to convert five years later and were seriously hindered in any attempts to leave the country. Many continued to observe Judaism secretly. These *conversos* are known to have favored certain last names, so Jewish ancestry sometimes may be hypothesized on the basis of name.[1] When they were able to escape from Portugal, Protestant Netherlands was a favored destination. Many merchants managed to make their way there, frequently reverting to open observance of Judaism.

Because many of the secret Jews who escaped to The Netherlands and elsewhere had relatives and business connections back in Portugal or Spain, they often kept their true identities secret. This led to the widespread practice of adopting aliases, much to the dismay of the genealogist.

North Africa, Italy, and the Ottoman Empire were the favored destinations of most Jews who fled the Iberian Peninsula. Although the Ottoman Empire never required Jews to adopt fixed surnames, many Jews did so. Some arrived with names they had assumed earlier in the Iberian Peninsula. Many used last names that reflected earlier geographical origins. Others identified themselves with patronymics and/or occupations. Over time, many last names came to be associated with the Jews of certain localities (e.g., Toledano for Jews from Toledo). Today such names may serve as clues for research. According to Alexander Beider, the most comprehensive list of Sephardic last names from North Africa (although often with incorrect etymological explanations) is found in *Les Juifs de l'Afrique du Nord*, by Maurice Eisenbeth. A thorough discussion of Sephardic surnames may be found in *Sephardic Genealogy*, by Jeffrey Malka. The just-published, massive *Diconario Sefardi de Sobrenomes* (Dictionary of Sephardic surnames) by Ana Rosa Campagnano, Guilherme Faiguenboim and Paulo Valadares, likely outstrips Eisenbeth.

Austrian Empire

As noted above, as part of his modernization program, Emperor Joseph II mandated in 1787 that all Jews of his realm adopt fixed, hereditary family names. Jews of Western Galicia, the area around Kraków acquired by Austria only in 1795, were not required to adopt hereditary surnames until 1805.

By January 1, 1788, Austrian officials ordered all Jews to adopt and use fixed, hereditary German (the official language of the Austrian Empire) surnames and approved German given names. Individuals who previously had used Hebrew names or names of localities were forbidden to continue to use them.

By November 1787, the law required all Jewish heads of households to submit a notification to the local authorities listing both old and new names for each member of their households. The declarant signed the notifications in the presence of the local authorities; the district or chief rabbi countersigned. Local authorities kept the notifications until the next census when they were given to the revision official who registered both the previous and the newly adopted names.

Jurisdictions included in the Austrian Empire at this time were Austria, Bohemia, and Moravia (today the Czech Republic), Bukovina (today part of Ukraine), Galicia (today southeastern Poland and western Ukraine), Hungary, and Slovakia. The fact that a Jewish family name from one of these areas (e.g., Galicia or Hungary) is a classical German name does not mean that the family ever lived in Germany.

Hungarian Jews also had German-sounding last names at first. After the establishment of the Dual Monarchy of Austria and Hungary in the mid-19th century, however, and the subsequent rise of "magyarization" in Hungary, many Jews in that country substituted Hungarian names for their German names.[2]

In Galicia, surnames apparently were assigned by government officials. Folklore holds that Jews who bribed officials received names with pleasant associations—such as Blumberg and Silberstein, while ridiculous, humiliating names such as Kugelmass (mass of pudding) reflected the malevolence of a clerk who perhaps had not been bribed sufficiently.

Under the reign of Maria Theresa (1740–80), mother of Joseph II, only the eldest son of a Jewish family was permitted to marry. One way in which Jews evaded this rule was to have only religious and not civil marriages. Increasingly throughout the 19th century, the authorities sought to force civil marriage, requiring that children of such marriages carry their mothers' family names. Eventually children of such marriages were prohibited to inherit their fathers' property, so there were cases of civil marriages that took place many years after the birth of children, with the result that older children in a single family were registered under the mother's maiden name while later children carried the father's name.

Napoleonic Code

Under the Decree of Bayonne promulgated in 1808, Jewish heads of households residing in lands ruled by Napoleon were required to appear before the mayor of their town and declare for themselves, their wives and minor children, a family name that was written down and required to be used henceforth. Many of these ledgers, from Alsace and Lorraine, from The Netherlands, Belgium and from Italy have survived. The Cercle de Généalogie Juive* (the French Jewish Genealogical Society) especially has located and transcribed ledgers from portions of Alsace and Lorraine that are part of France today. Micheline Guttman of GenAmi, Association de Généalogie Juive Internationale,* has published transcriptions of name adoptions in Brussels and Ghent, Belgium.

Czarist Russia

Alexander Beider's two monumental works, *A Dictionary of Jewish Surnames from the Russian Empire* and *A Dictionary of Jewish Surnames from the Kingdom of Poland*, are indispensable reading for genealogists with ancestral roots in these regions. Especially important are the introductions to both books in which Beider describes in detail the background, process, and types of names chosen.

At the end of the 18th century, most Jews of the Polish kingdom who became Russian subjects as the reins of power changed hands did not have fixed last names. In Christian documents they were known by their vernacular names followed by their patronymic (i.e., their fathers' name with the ending *ovitch* for a man and *ovna* for a woman). On December 9, 1804, Czar Alexander I issued a *ukase* (edict) requiring each Jew in the empire to adopt a hereditary surname to be used without alteration in all registers and transactions. The law was re-issued in 1835, suggesting that not all Jews had complied immediately; late in the 1840s and 1850s, in small communities especially, some Jews still had not adopted last names.

According to Beider, *kahal* (Jewish community) officials were responsible for implementing the process, but no documentation has come to light that describes the exact procedure, and no Russian name adoption registers are known to exist.[3] Analysis of the adopted names suggests that they were chosen by the Jews themselves rather than having been assigned to them, as was the case in Galicia. The most popular category of name was geographical; other names were derived from mother's or father's names, from occupations, or from personal attributes. Some names had no link to any characteristic of the person who first bore them; these names Alexander Beider calls "artificial names."

Spellings of many names did not stabilize for quite a while. Especially in the early 19th century, despite the mandate for consistency in the name-adoption decree, records reveal many variations of the supposedly same name. In addition, the attitudes of most Jews toward these Gentile-mandated names varied between indifference and open avoidance. Registration was the means by which Russian authorities identified young men for the dreaded military conscription. Because the eldest or only son in a family was exempt from the army, many Jewish families sought to have all other sons registered as if they were eldest or only sons. This practice led to a variety of subterfuges in which several brothers would be registered under different, sometimes unrelated, names (see RUSSIAN EMPIRE).

Death record of Abram Blacharz, 1844, Zarki, Poland. It indicates his occupation was that of a blacharz, Polish for "tinker." When Jews acquired hereditary surnames at the beginning of the 19th century, many chose their occupation as their surname.

German States

Early in the 19th century, the sundry German states forced their resident Jews to adopt fixed last names.[4] On the one hand, the purpose of the various mandates was one of liberalization, a step toward emancipation and equality. On the other hand, the laws generally resulted in tighter control by the sovereign. Some laws included a residential quota for Jews; sometimes the law changed and diminished some of the special taxes imposed on Jews. The types of names that could be adopted varied. Women usually were not included in the lists, or else listed as "Sarah, widow of David Rafael."

Newly adopted names typically were recorded in registers maintained by the village priest, mayor, or clerk of the Jewish community. Today, they may be found in regional archives. Before this time, most German Jews were registered with their Hebrew names, their father's given name serving as the "last name." Thus, Isaac son of Jacob would be registered as Isaac Jacob or Jacobs. The son of Isaac Jacob, named in memory of his paternal grandfather, would appear as Jacob Isaac. Lists in which given and "last" name alternate generation after generation commonly are found.

Romania

During the 19th century, the territory that is now contemporary Romania belonged in part to the Austrian (later, Austro-Hungarian) Empire and in part to the Ottoman Empire. Joseph II's decree of 1787 applied to the Austrian portion. For information about Ottoman territories, see "Iberian Peninsula" section above.

Jewish Names in the Twentieth Century
Changes Wrought by Emigration

The massive Jewish emigrations from Eastern European countries of the late 19th and early 20th centuries brought about massive changes in Jewish family names, as the earlier emigration of Jews from German-speaking lands had not. German Jews used the Roman alphabet to spell their names and typically moved to countries that used the same alphabet. Some exceptions occurred among immigrants from Denmark and from the Czech lands, where the alphabets had additional letters, but only a few Jews were part of these groups.

Eastern European Jews were a different matter. Their names were written in the Cyrillic or Hebrew alphabets which typically could not be read by those compiling sailing lists. Clerks unfamiliar with the emigrants' languages sometimes spelled names as they heard them, using the spelling rules of their own language (Dutch, English, French, or German).

United States and Other English-Speaking Countries

Most American Jews today descend from Eastern European immigrants who arrived in the United States between 1880 and the beginning of World War I in 1914. Tales of changes in European names are legend beginning with "The name was changed at Ellis Island," a popular staple of American immigrant mythology. It is just that, a myth. Not only were American immigration officials expressly forbidden to alter the names of immigrants, but these officials simply used the ship manifests prepared in Europe to examine the newcomers. (See IMMIGRATION.)

Names *were* changed in the United States—but generally by the immigrant, not by the government. Most immigrants felt little fidelity to the names imposed by the non-Jewish world and often altered them with little thought. When Abraham Samuels emigrated to Boston from Volhynia, helpful *landsmen* advised him to shed his "greenhorn" name and to adopt a "real American name"—so he became Abraham Grossman! School teachers also had a hand in changing names. Michel Shulkin was told that his given name easily translated into Michael. His Milwaukee schoolteacher had other ideas. As he recalled many years later, she exclaimed, "Michael? That's an Irish name. It's no name for a Jewish boy. You will be Max." Max it became, and Max it remained for the rest of his life.

Name changes occurred in much the same way in Canada, South Africa, Australia, and England.

Although Americans can and sometimes do change their names legally, most immigrants did not bother with the formalities. U.S. courthouses usually do not have records of the changes. A record may exist, however, in the specific case where an immigrant changed the name that was listed on his or her passenger arrival manifest and later sought naturalization. If an immigrant applied for citizenship after September 1906, and the name under which he was applying was different from the name listed on the passenger manifest, the name he used aboard ship may be listed in his naturalization papers. From the beginning of its history, the United States has required that an immigrant live in the country five years before becoming eligible for citizenship. The application process required the immigrant to supply the name he used upon arrival in the United States to permit naturalization clerks to check the manifest to verify that the requisite five years have elapsed (see IMMIGRATION).

The name change may have occurred before your relative ever set foot in his new country. Passenger manifests were created by pursers or ship captains using ticket contracts. Our Eastern European ancestors generally wrote their names using the Hebrew or Cyrillic alphabet. The clerks who wrote the ticket contracts spoke English, Dutch, French, or German—and used the Roman alphabet. As a result, clerks wrote (and spelled) what they heard. Thus, the *sh* sound frequently was rendered *sch* by Hamburg, Germany, shipping agents. Sometimes errors were massive and without obvious logic. A Jewish woman named Laja-Charna who sailed out of French-speaking Antwerp was recorded on the manifest as "Lui" while another woman by the name of "Szeindel H" was listed as "Hen Schneider."

Sometimes, too, the immigrant carried a ticket in a name other than his. On his deathbed, Benny Steinsnider confessed that his real surname had been Dubner. He had been running away from the Russian army and bought papers from someone named Steinsnider. When asked why it had taken him more than 70 years to tell his family, Benny replied, "You never know."

If an immigrant carried a document with his or her name written in Russian, that, too, could be misconstrued. When Abraham Shulkin landed in Cape Town, South Africa, the immigration official there mistook the Cyrillic letter for "the *Sh*" (a Hebrew *shin*) for the letter *W* and wrote the name as Wolkin. The family, seeking a new life in a new country, decided to keep that spelling.

Although research suggests that everyone with the name Shulkin is part of the same family, the following story illustrates the danger of making an automatic assumption about post-emigration Shulkins. Jake Shulkin from Polotsk, Russia, settled in the Saint Lawrence River town of Massena, New York, where he owned a furniture store in partnership with a *landsman* named Slavin. One day Shulkin waited on a non-Jewish Polish immigrant who purchased a houseful of furniture. Writing up the sale, Shulkin asked the customer's name and was startled to hear "Shulkin." Doing a double-take, Jake asked how it was spelled and heard "S-h-u-l-k-i-n." "That's a pretty rare name, isn't it?" Jake commented, to which the immigrant answered, "It isn't really my name, you know. My wife and I are new in town. As we came up over the hill and across the bridge into town, we saw your sign `Slavin and Shulkin Furniture' and I told my wife, `That's what we need; a genuine American name,' so we decided to become Shulkin." Today the only Shulkin living in Massena, New York, is Father Eli Shulkin, a Roman Catholic priest and son of those immigrants.

Many immigrants did not change their name but merely changed the spelling to conform to American pronunciation. Fajnsztajn became Feinstein, Moskowicz became Moskowitz, Tartacki became Tartasky. Anti-immigrant and anti-Semitic attitudes of the existing population caused immigrants to hide their Jewishness by shortening or slightly modifying their European names. Tabashevsky became Tabs, Tartacki became Tarre, Chaikowsky became Shaw.

Immigration to Israel

Not only did many Jews change their names when they emigrated to the United States and other countries, even more did so when they arrived in Palestine/Israel. David Ben Gurion, first prime minister of Israel, actively promoted the idea that Jews should adopt Hebrew names—and many did. Fortunately for the genealogist, many name changes were recorded in Israel and published in the official *Palestine Gazette*. Some years ago, Avotaynu collected all of the published name changes and produced a microfiche listing names alphabetically, both by original and by new name.[5] A copy is available in the Microfilm Reading Room at the Jewish National and University Library in Jerusalem.[*]

Name Changes in Argentina

Argentina was another popular destination for Eastern European Jewish immigrants at the turn of the 20th century. The vicissitudes of last names in this country were rigidly controlled by law. Laws in Argentina forbid name changes. To change either a given name or a surname is difficult, expensive, and generally permitted only in rare cases, such as if a marriage results in a combination of names that might be humiliating or offensive. For example, the surname Barriga means "belly." The woman's name Dolores means "pains." If a woman named Dolores married a man named Barriga, she would become Dolores de Barriga or "pains in the belly." In another case, when a family emigrated from Uruguay, a clerical error resulted in the father and one brother having a name spelled Armoni; the second brother's name was spelled Armony. Armony hired a lawyer, spent considerable money and, after two years, obtained a legal statement that says "Armoni and Armony are the same person."

By law until a few years ago, personal names had to be selected from an official (Catholic) list of names; no other names were permitted. In this way, Jews with the names Moses or Jacob became Martin or Jacinto. The same was true of feminine names.

Name Changes in South Africa and in England

[*Saul Issroff is the source of the information in this section.*] Jews generally felt minimal pressure to change their names in South Africa and few did. Jews were a solid part of the economically active community from its inception and seldom felt the pressures to blend that existed in England. For example, after his World War I army experiences, one Jewish grandfather in the United Kingdom changed his name from Levi to Leigh!

In South Africa various government gazettes were used to publicize name changes. A sample extract from one of the early South African Jewish yearbooks shows the following name changes: Girs (Hersh) changed to Hersman, Kuper to Cooper, Kantorovich to Kentridge, Kollokowski to Colley, Markovitz to Marcow, Margolis to Margo, Lomiasky to Lomey, Lazerowitz to Lazar, Laschinsky to Lasch, Smietsky to Sorel, and Marks Tabakin became Marks (via Manchester, England).

The procedures were identical to those in England. At one time nothing much was required; later legal methods were instituted. To quote from the Public Records Office (PRO) (see UNITED KINGDOM) book:

> Until the 19th century many people used an alias without going through a legal formality. From the late 19th century deed poll changes of names were sometimes (but by no means always) enrolled, and these enrollments may be seen at the PRO. From 1914 all enrolled deeds were published in the *London Gazette* (available at Kew) but for changes of name in the last three years apply to Room 18, Royal Courts of Justice, London. For those deed polls not enrolled look in local and national press, and if all else fails ask your family solicitor. A deed poll change of name has no legal validity, and anyone doing so may continue to use a previous (or indeed another) name.

Irrelevance of Spelling

Just as a careful researcher never assumes that everyone with a given last name is related, the casual way most immigrant names were handled also dictates that no decisions should be made on the basis of spelling. Whether or not a name is spelled with a single or double consonant is irrelevant, as is whether one vowel is used instead of another. When dealing with names that have undergone the process of emigration, only the sound of the name is important. In the Yad Vashem database of Pages of Testimony (see HOLOCAUST) the name Yakubovitz currently is spelled 274 different ways! That is the reason why the "Daitch-Mokotoff Soundex" was developed.

Addresses

Cercle de Généalogie Juive, 14 rue Saint-Lazare, 75009 Paris, France; telephone and fax: 33-1-4023-0490; e-mail: CGIGENEFR@AOL.COM; website: WWW.GENEAOLJ.ORG.

GenAmi, Association de Généalogie Juive Internationale, 76 rue de Passy, 75016 Paris, France; telephone: 33-1-4524-3540; fax: 33-1-4524-2559; e-mail: MICHELINEGUTTMAN@FREE.FR; website: WWW.ASSO.GENAMI.FREE.FR.

Jewish National and University Library, Hebrew University, Givat Ram Campus, mailing address: P.O. Box 34165, Jerusalem, 91341 Israel; fax: 972-2-658-6315; website: WWW.JNUL.HUJI.AC.IL.

Bibliography

Beider, Alexander. *A Dictionary of Jewish Surnames from the Kingdom of Poland*. Teaneck, NJ: Avotaynu, 1996.

———. *A Dictionary of Jewish Surnames from the Russian Empire*. Teaneck, NJ: Avotaynu, 1993.

Eisenbeth, Maurice. *Les Juifs de l'Afrique du Nord* (The Jews of North Africa). [French] Algiers, 1936.

Faiguenboim, Guilherme, Paulo Valadares and Ana Rosa Campagnano, *Diconario Sefardi de Sobrenomes*, 2004. Order from WWW.SEFER.COM.BR.

Malka, Jeffrey S. *Sephardic Genealogy*. Bergenfield, NJ: Avotaynu, 2002.

Notes

1. Mausenbaum, Rufina. "A Painful Portuguese Odyssey," *AVOTAYNU* 13, no. 4 (Winter 1997): 13.
2. Panchyk, Richard. "Given Names and Hungarian Names," *AVOTAYNU* 11, no. 2 (Summer 1995): 24.
3. Beider, Alexander. *A Dictionary of Jewish Surnames from the Russian Empire*. Teaneck, NJ: Avotaynu, 1993: 9–15.
4. Arnstein, George. "Mandated Family Names in Central Europe." *AVOTAYNU* 12, no. 2 (Summer 1996): 34.
5. Sack, Sallyann Amdur. "The Jewish National and University Library Another Israeli Resource," *AVOTAYNU* 9, no. 3 (Fall 1993): 19.

Jewish Given Names
by Warren Blatt

The subject of Jewish given names is a vast topic, enough to fill volumes. This article touches upon only a few aspects: differences between secular and religious names, Ashkenazic naming traditions, the various relationships between pairs of given names, diminutive names and how to interpret names in documents. The Americanization of Eastern European names is used for illustration.

A personal example illustrates the importance of understanding Jewish given names. The author's grandfather had a first cousin who was listed by various names in different sources:

- His 1881 civil marriage registration from Nowogród, Ńomǧa *guberniya,* Poland, lists him (in Cyrillic letters) as Leibka Gershkevich. This means Leib, son of Hersh.
- His tombstone, New York 1926, is inscribed in Hebrew with the name Mordechai Yehudah ben Reb Tzvi, meaning Mordechai Yehudah, son of Tzvi
- His English name engraved on the tombstone is Max.

This article presents the explanations necessary to assume reasonably from the evidence—not from what we know to be true—that this is one and the same man.

Most Jewish men have two names—a religious name, the *shem hakodesh,* and a secular name, called *kinnui* in Hebrew. Many American Jews today have a religious Hebrew name and a secular English name. Among the Jews of Eastern Europe of the past several centuries, Yiddish was the everyday or secular language, so they had a religious Hebrew name and a secular Yiddish name, the *kinnui*. After immigration to a new country—typically around the turn of the 20th century—a new secular name often was chosen, in the language of the new country. For most research, genealogists need to know an ancestor's secular name, the name (or some variant thereof) that appears in civil documents. The *shem hakodesh,* the Hebrew name, generally appears only in connection with Jewish religious observances, for example, a record of a *bris* (circumcision), in a *ketubah* (marriage contract) or *get* (writ of divorce), and on a *matzevah* (tombstone).

Naming Babies After Relatives

A strong tradition among Ashkenazic Jews of Eastern Europe mandated that a baby be named after a deceased relative. (See Sephardic tradition below.) It is important to understand that this was and is tradition, not Jewish law. No evidence of such a practice appears in the Bible, in which most names are unique. The custom seems to have started in the first and second centuries and to have become entrenched by the 12th century. By the 12th century in Europe, we find given names repeating every other generation within families, as a baby was named for a grandfather or grandmother. Generally the child was named for the closest deceased relative for whom no one else in that immediate family was already named. Highest priority was awarded the name of the child's mother, if she had died in childbirth, or the father, if he had died before the baby was born.

If any of the four grandparents were deceased, a baby would be named after one of them; otherwise the newborn would be named for the great-grandparents or, perhaps, a sibling of one of the parents. During the 19th century in Eastern Europe, a girl was typically named after a female relative a boy after a male relative. Usually, a baby was not given the same name as a sibling who had previously died, although some cases of this practice have been seen.

Ashkenazim typically do not name babies after living relatives. Sephardic Jews, on the other hand, name their children in honor of grandparents whether living or dead and usually in a fixed order. The first son is named for the father's father, the first daughter for the father's mother. The next son is named in honor of his mother's father and the second girl for her maternal grandmother. Any subsequent children are named in honor of aunts and uncles.

The tradition to name babies after deceased relatives often enables a researcher to estimate an ancestor's date of death. If, for example, we know that several first cousins born in 1900 were all given their grandfather's name, but that no cousins born prior to that date carried the name, it is safe to assume that the grandfather probably died shortly before 1900.

Other Sources of Given Names

Not all children were named after relatives. A few generations ago, couples typically had many children, and since infant mortality was high, they often ran out of deceased relatives to memorialize. Therefore, sometimes other sources of inspiration were used. A child born on Purim might have been called Esther or Mordechai; a baby born during Passover could have been called Pesach; or Shabbatai, if born on the Sabbath; or Nison, if born during the Hebrew month of Nison. Chanukah apparently was a popular name among some Sephardim. One should not try to draw too many conclusions from such holiday-oriented names. The birth that resulted in a holiday name may have occurred many generations earlier. For example, a baby named Pesach in the late 19th century may have been named in memory of a grandfather named Pesach who had been born during Passover two generations earlier.

Amuletic names are names given for good luck. Examples are Chaim and Chaya, which mean "life." Other examples are Alter and Alta (meaning "old one"), or Bubbe and Zayde (grandmother and grandfather). Often these names were given as a new name when a child became very sick. A Jewish superstition that began during medieval times, and was current up to recent times, imagined the Angel of Death as a bureaucratic fellow with a list of names. It was thought that if the Angel of Death came looking for a sick child with a specific name, and if he could not find a child with that name, then the Angel of Death would spare the sick child. Although amuletic names were sometimes bestowed as second names when children were older, this was not always the case; some children were given these names at birth, with the hope that they would live to fulfill the meaning of their names. A study of birth registrations of children named Alter or Alte in Checiny, Poland, found that in each case the child had been born after the deaths of other siblings in infancy or childhood.[1] Again, make no assumptions; in some cases a baby was named Chaim (or Alter, Zayde or Bubbe) in memory of a deceased relative with that name.

Multiple Names

Today one tends to think that an individual has one name, his or her real name, and it remains that person's name for life. That certainly was not the case for our Jewish ancestors. They frequently answered to many names and nicknames, often in different languages. Genealogists must learn (or know where to research) the commonly related names. Sometimes, when an ancestor cannot be found under one name, he or she may be located under a different name. These names might be unrelated to each other. Unrelated double names are two names that have nothing to do with each other (e.g., Sura Rivka, David Hirsh). The two names might reflect memorialization of two different deceased relatives (for example, a Sholem Wulf named after his two grandfathers). Any given document might show one name, the other name, or both names, in either order. The principle to remember is that the pattern of recording names was completely inconsistent.

Jewish ancestors also had multiple related names—given names that were related to each other in a variety of ways: Biblical associations, other historical associations, calques, variants, diminutives and nicknames, language versions and immigrant adaptations. Each type is explained below.

Biblical associations. A major category of related names is biblical associations, which derive from the blessings that Jacob gave his sons and grandsons (Genesis 48, 49), in which Jacob compared them to various animals. Binyomin was equated with a wolf; the Yiddish name Wulf often is associated with Binyomin. Naftali was compared to a deer, a running stag; the Yiddish word Hirsh means deer. Efraim is associated with fish, the name Fishel in Yiddish. Yissakhar is associated with a donkey or ass to reflect the meaning "hard-working," but considering the donkey's less positive connotation in modern European culture, it has been replaced by the bear, Ber in Yiddish. Yehudah (Judah) is seen as a lion; Leib means lion in Yiddish; the Hebrew name of a man named Leib is likely to be Yehuda. The names Yehudah and Leib are related due to the Biblical association. Hence, in the example at the top of the chapter, Leib appears on a Polish marriage record (Yiddish secular name), and Yehudah appears on the same person's tombstone (Hebrew religious name).

Calques and paired names. Another category of relationships is calques, or loan translations. When the underlying meaning of a name is translated from one language to another,

the result is termed a calque. Names themselves cannot be translated, but many names have underlying meanings, and it is possible to translate the meanings from one language to another. Some typical Hebrew-to-Yiddish calques are Aryeh (lion in Hebrew) and Leib (lion in Yiddish); thus, Aryeh Leib is a common name pair. Ze'ev Wulf is another common pair, the names mean wolf in both Hebrew and Yiddish; Dov and Ber both mean bear; Tzvi and Hirsh mean deer or stag; Tzipporah and Feige mean bird; Asher and Zelig mean happy or joyful; Uri and Shraga mean light or candle.

The lion is the symbol of Yehudah (Judah), so Yehuda, Aryeh and Leib all may occur together or in various combinations (e.g., Aryeh Leib or Yehuda Leib). The following illustrates:

Table 1
Biblical Associations and Calques

Hebrew Name	Biblical Symbol	Hebrew Kinnui	Yiddish Calque	
Yehudah	lion	Aryeh	Leib	
Naftali	deer	Tzvi		Hersh
Beniamin	wolf	Ze'ev	Vulf	
Yissakhar	bear	Dov	Ber	
Efraim	fish	—	Fishel	

Variations between languages. Usually, when a Hebrew name is rendered in Yiddish, its pronunciation changes slightly. Consonants can be elided together or simplified. For example, Yehuda becomes Yuda, Yitzchak becomes Itzik and Mordechai becomes Mordka. Generally the transformations are obvious. Pronunciation is all that changes with most feminine names; the Hebrew consonants remain the same, e.g., Rahel to Rochel.

Diminutives and nicknames. Most English-speakers are familiar with the ways in which nicknames and diminutives are formed in English. Typically the last syllable is omitted and sometimes the long *e* sound is appended to make it diminutive. For example, Joseph is truncated to Joe, and the long *e* sound is added to form "Joey." Anglo-Saxon diminutive names often have changed first letters. Robert becomes Rob becomes Bob becomes Bobby; William becomes Will becomes Bill becomes Billy; Richard becomes Rich becomes Rick becomes Dick. English speakers know Dick usually is short for Richard, but that convention is not at all obvious to the non-English speaker.

The same is true of Yiddish names. Yiddish nicknames are obvious to the Yiddish speaker, but not to someone unfamiliar with the language. To create a Yiddish nickname, often the first part of a Hebrew name is dropped. Examples include Efroyim becomes Froim, Elchanan becomes Chanan, Yeshaya becomes Shaya, Yisrael becomes Srul, Alexander becomes Sender, Eliezer becomes Leizer, Yechezkel becomes Haskel, Yekutiel becomes Kushel, Betzalel becomes Tzalel, Avigdor becomes Vigdor, Yissakhar becomes Socher.

A diminutive name also may be constructed by adding a suffix. Just as Joey means little Joe, so can Moshe become Moshek, Ber become Berel or Berko, Leib become Leibish or Leibke, Hirsh become Hirshel or Hirska. Depending on the region, diminutive suffixes may be formed with *-l*, *-k* or another letter(s). The suffix *-ish* was popular in Galicia, Hungary and Romania. Popular diminutive endings for feminine names were *-el* or *-dl*, such as when Raisa became Raisel and Sheina became Sheindl. Chapter 3 of Alexander Beider's *A Dictionary of Ashkenazic Given Names* describes common suffixes in various regions.

Some Yiddish nicknames are ambiguous, as is true of English names. For example, in English, Al can be a nickname for Alan, Albert, Alfred, Alvin or Alexander. In Yiddish, Nissl might be a nickname for either Nisan or Natan, Chanan for Elchanan or Yochanan, Etta and Ita for Esther or Yehudit.

Some unrelated Yiddish nicknames sound similar to each other, and may easily be confused. Heshel is a diminutive of Yehoshua (Joshua), Hirshel for Hirsh. Shiya is another diminutive of Yehoshua, but Shaya is a diminutive of Yeshaya (Isaiah). Depending on region, pronunciation and/or the way a name was written, it might easily refer to either Hebrew name, e.g., Shaya might be either Yehoshua or Yeshaya.

Yiddish and Hebrew Names: References

The definitive work on Ashkenazic given names is Alexander Beider's *A Dictionary of Ashkenazic Given Names*. Also useful are Beider's *A Dictionary of Jewish Surnames from the Kingdom of Poland* and *A Dictionary of Jewish Surnames from the Russian Empire*. Although these last two books focus on surnames, many Jewish surnames were based upon given names. Beider lists many name variants, and his introductions provide extensive historical background.

In *Jewish Personal Names: Their Origin, Derivation and Diminutive Forms*, Rabbi Shmuel Gorr groups names by their root name, listing all related names and their variants. Gorr died before this book was finished; it was prepared for publication by his literary executor, Chaim Freedman. The book does not indicate when or where particular variants were used, and some common names are missing.

Other sources include a 1998 book by Boris Feldblyum, *Russian-Jewish Given Names*, which is primarily a translation of a 1911 Russian-language book written by Iser Kulisher. Kulisher, a government official, tried to clarify for the Russian bureaucracy the bewildering variants of Jewish given names found in official documents. In the process, he reported every known form he could find. The most valuable part of this book is the introduction, which discusses the history of Jewish names (mostly a translation of Leopold Zunz's 1837 German-language *Namen der Juden* [Jewish names]). Feldblyum's book suffers from an atypical method of transliteration; it does not explain why particular names are related and does not reflect the relative popularity of any given name.

Alfred Kolatch's *The New Name Dictionary: Modern English and Hebrew Names* includes brief etymologies. An interesting appendix organizes the names by their meaning. The book is useful for Hebrew names, but not Yiddish names. A good source for Yiddish given names is Harkavy's 1928 *Yiddish-English-Hebrew Dictionary*. Harkavy lists Yiddish

names with their Hebrew roots and variants and suggested English equivalents on pages 525–30.

Name Popularity Statistics

The following table shows the most popular names used in Eastern Europe.[2]

Table 2
Most Popular Names in Eastern Europe

	Male		Female	
1	Abram	7.4%	Sora	7.2%
2	Mosha	6.9%	Chaya	6.2%
3	Itzik	6.8%	Ryfka	6.2%
4	Lejb	6.4%	Rochel	5.5%
5	Yankiel	6.1%	Leia	5.5%
6	Hersh	5.5%	Chana	4.0%
7	Chaim	4.6%	Feiga	3.7%
8	Meyer	3.7%	Sheina	3.1%
9	David	3.4%	Ester	3.0%
10	Ber	3.3%	Marym	2.4%
11	Shmul	3.0%	Dvora	2.1%
12	Volf	3.0%	Malka	1.9%
13	Yosek	2.9%	Gitel	1.9%
14	Izrael	2.8%	Beila	1.8%
15	Leizor	2.7%	Etka	1.6%
16	Mortek	2.7%	Liba	1.5%
17	Shloma	2.5%	Reiza	1.5%
18	Aron	2.3%	Freida	1.3%
19	Eliash	1.8%	Chava	1.2%
20	Zelman	1.4%	Hinda	1.2%
21	Boruch	1.3%	Tauba	1.1%
22	Mendel	1.3%	Mindel	1.0%
23	Beniamin	1.2%	Rashka	1.0%
24	Zelik	1.1%	Pesha	1.0%
25	Judah	1.0%	Basha	0.9%

Table 3 shows the most popular given names used by Eastern European Jewish immigrants in the U.S., circa 1910.[3]

Table 3
Most Popular Given Names for Jewish Immigrants in U.S.

	Male	Female
1	Louis	Sarah
2	Samuel	Annie
3	Morris	Fannie
4	Joseph	Rose
5	Harry	Ida
6	Jacob	Lena
7	Max	Esther
8	Abraham	Bessie
9	Sam	Mary
10	David	Rebecca
11	Nathan	Jennie
12	Benjamin	Anna
13	Hyman	Rosie
14	Isadore	Celia
15	Isaac	Dora

Case Study

A man who was born in Russian Poland as "Mordechai Leib ben Tzvi Hirsh Dembor" has his name appear in many fashions on various documents and tombstones.

1887 Marriage Record. His name appears in Russian as Lejbka Gerszkievich Dembor, which means "Lejb, son of Gersh, surname Dembor." "Lejbka" is a diminutive (nickname) for "Lejb." In Eastern Europe, Jewish men were familiarly known by their Yiddish names, which is the name used on this civil document. In Russian Poland, he was known to his family and friends (and the government) as Lejb, and his father was known as Hersz. His father's name is spelled as Gersz in this Russian-language document because there is no letter for the 'H' sound in the Russian alphabet, so it is replaced by the 'G' sound.

1905 Report Card. He signs his name "Maks Goldman." In the U.S., Mordechai Leib Americanized his given name to Max, a popular American name at that time. Max starts with the same letter as one of his religious names, Mordechai. "Maks" represents a phonetic spelling of his new given name. (He also Americanized his surname from Dembor to Goldman).

1927 Tombstone. His tombstone in New York identifies him as "Mordechai Yehuda ben Tzvi," in Hebrew. The Hebrew *shem hakodesh*—the religious name—is used on the tombstone. Yehudah has a biblical association with the name Leib. In the Bible, Jacob's son Yehudah was given the sign of the lion, and Leib means "lion" in Yiddish. For his father's name, the Hebrew name Tzvi was used as a calque for his Yiddish name Hersh: Tzvi is the Hebrew word for "deer," Hersz is the Yiddish word for "deer." The English name on the tombstone is "Max Goldman."

1934 Grandson's Birth. The first male grandson born

The Many Names of Max Goldman

1881 Marriage:	"Лейбка Гершкевич Дембор" "Lejbka Gerszkievich Dembor"
1905 Report Card:	"Maks Goldman"
1927 Tombstone:	"מרדכי יהודה ב'ר צבי" "Mordechai Yehuda ben Tzvi" "Max Goldman"
1934 Grandson:	"מרדכי לייב" = "Mordechai Leib" "Morton Leon"
1957 Son's Tombstone:	"... ב'ר מרדכי אריה" "... ben Mordechai Areyeh"

---

after Max's death was given the religious name Mordechai Leib in honor of his grandfather, and was given the secular American names "Morton Leon" – given names fashionable in America in 1934 – which have the same initial letters as the religious name.

1957 Son Harry's Tombstone. His son's name is written in Hebrew as "Tzvi Hirsh ben Mordechai Aryeh." He was named after Max's father Tzvi Hirsh. Harry is a common Americanization of Hirsh, because they both start with the same letter. Aryeh is the Hebrew calque of the Yiddish name Lejb: Aryeh is the Hebrew word for "lion," Leib is the Yiddish word for "lion."

Slavic Languages

Names written in Slavic languages such as Czech, Polish or Russian require other considerations. In civil records in Eastern Europe, names typically are not spelled as the genealogist might expect. Before the 19th century, most Jews did not have hereditary family surnames (see Surnames). Patronymics (father's given names) were used instead, and they typically appeared with the Russian suffix *-vich* (Polish *-wicz*) for a male, or *-ovna* (Polish *-owna*) for a female.

Another consideration is the absence of the *h* sound in the Russian language; no letter represents this sound in the Cyrillic (Russian) alphabet. Foreign words (such as Jewish names) containing the *h* sound were spelled using either the *g* sound (represented by the Cyrillic letter Г) or the guttural *kh* sound (Cyrillic letter X) instead. Thus, Yiddish names such as Hirsh and Hinda in Russian became Girsh and Ginda or Chersh and Chinda. In some Lithuanian and Ukrainian regions, the initial *h* sound tended to be dropped entirely, so Hirsh became Irsh, and Hinda appeared as Inda.

The Polish and Russian languages use declensions; endings of nouns and adjectives change depending where and how they are used in a sentence. This rule includes proper nouns (e.g., names). For example, the name Josek Wolf might appear as Joskiem Wolfem on a civil marriage document in Russian Poland. Researchers need not memorize Polish rules of grammar; it is generally sufficient just to drop or slightly transform the endings of the names to make sense of a name.[4]

Example Explained

Returning to the example at the beginning of this chapter, it now is possible to see why it is reasonable to assume that Lejbka Gerszkiewicz (Russian transliterated into Polish) and Mordechai Yehudah ben Tzvi (Hebrew) are names of the same person. This typifies some of the challenges in Jewish genealogical research, which reveals names written in multiple languages and alphabets. The following features are illustrated in this example:

- Unrelated double names: Mordechai and Yehudah.

Both names appear to be used on the tombstone; in other sources only one name, Yehudah, appeared.

- Related names, biblical association: Yehudah and Leib. The Hebrew name, Yehudah, appeared on the tombstone; its Yiddish *kinnui* Leib appeared in the civil record.
- Related names, Hebrew/Yiddish calque: the father's name appeared in Hebrew on the tombstone, Tzvi; its Yiddish calque, Hersh appeared in the civil record.
- Patronymics, in Russian and Hebrew. Gerszkiewicz = son of Gershka; ben Tzvi = son of Tzvi.
- Russian letter *g*: Yiddish *h* in "Hersh" becomes *g* in Russian.
- Diminutives: The Slavic suffix *-ka* makes Leib into Leibka and Gersh into Gershka.

The English given name used in America, Max, was based upon the initial letter of Mordechai, one of his Hebrew given names.

How to Interpret Names in Documents

Take care not to interpret too literally or definitively any information written in any single document, especially if that information was given orally by the informant to an official who wrote what he or she heard. The clerk recorded what he or she heard through the "ear" of his own particular language and dialect. Genealogists cannot hear a document; they can only see it. Therefore, interpretation is necessary, trying to put oneself into the mind of the individual who wrote the information—not the mind of the informant. Examples from the 1900 U.S. census for Chelsea, Massachusetts, a suburb of Boston, illustrate this point. In the census, a Jewish family has a daughter named Bloomer. If one writes with a Boston accent, in which the name pronounced "Pee-tuh" is written as "Peter," then the name pronounced "Bloo-muh" must be written as "Bloomer"! Another daughter was listed as Solit and a census record from St. Louis, Missouri, listed a man as Iman. These two individuals were actually Charlotte and Hyman. Always try to understand a document through the ears of the individual who recorded it.

The same holds true of documents from Russia or Poland, for example. Christian civil clerks in the "Old Country" did not speak Yiddish, and they wrote what they heard. Sometimes Gimpel might appear as Kimpel or Feivel as Wajwel.

Language Orthography

Another tip is to consider how a certain sound may have been represented in the language of the person writing the document. In English, the letters *sh* represent a certain sound; in German, that same sound is represented as *sch*. That same sound is represented in several ways in Polish (*sz*, *Č*or *s*), Lithuanian and Czech (*Ž*), Hungarian (*s*) and French and Portuguese (*ch*). A ship clerk on a German ship probably wrote the name of a Lithuanian Jewish immigrant named Sheina as Scheine, while a clerk on a Polish ship might write it as Szejna.

Handwriting Was Transferred

If the information was transferred from one written document to an individual who wrote another record, then the added problem surfaces of handwriting interpretation—keeping in mind the principal language of the person writing the second document. For example, in a letter from the Polish State Archives, the name Fishel was transcribed as Fimel. The letter that forms the *sh* sound in the Cyrillic alphabet (ш), resembles the handwritten Cyrillic letter m). Facts can become confused when they pass through layers of interpretation; it helps, wherever possible, to consult original source documents.

Immigrant ship manifests are extremely valuable sources for most North American Jewish genealogists. It is important to remember that these lists were compiled before the ship landed. Thus, these lists contain the European, pre-Americanized names. No Jewish Jennys or Harrys were listed among the immigrants; these are American names.

Note also that Jewish immigrants often Anglicized the names of their parents on civil marriage and death certificates, even if their parents never immigrated. For example, an immigrant whose father's name was Nochum might have told an American government clerk that his father's name was Nathan—even though he was never known by that name.

Spelling

Spelling does not matter in genealogical research. Beginners frequently look for exact spellings, but when they do, they usually do not find what they are seeking. Certain letters often are used interchangeably (e.g., *b* and *p*, *d* and *t*). Thus, Shepsel may have been recorded as Shebsel, and Mordka becomes Mortka. Gorr's "Phonetically Interchangeable Consonants" chart[5] or the Daitch-Mokotoff Soundex System chart (see Daitch-Mokotoff Soundex System) illustrate these types of substitutions. Vowels are particularly interchangeable in various languages and transliteration systems. The Yiddish name for Yitzchak (Isaac) might be written on a ship manifest in a potentially bewildering number of ways—as Icek, Itzig, Hayzjk, Ayzig, Izyk, Eisik, Iccok, Yitzik, Jczek or Idzk.

The Name Was Changed at Ellis Island

No, it was not, despite the popular myth. Many, if not most, Jewish immigrants to the United States (and Israel, Latin America and elsewhere) eventually changed both their given names and surnames, but this change came later, as part of the assimilation process. Often, it wasn't even the immigrant who invented their new name; it might have been a co-worker or perhaps an Irish schoolteacher. Moreover—it cannot be repeated too often—no fixed English equivalents exist for immigrant Hebrew or Yiddish names. The novelist Mary Antin, a Russian Jewish immigrant to Boston, recalls that soon after her arrival:

> With our despised immigrant clothing we shed also our impossible Hebrew names. A committee of our friends, several years ahead of us in American experience, put their heads together and concocted American names for us all. Those of our real names that had no pleasing American equivalents they

ruthlessly discarded, content if they retained the initials.[6]

Patterns existed, but not all immigrants followed them. Rivke might just as easily have become Ruth as Rebecca. Binyomin may have most often become Ben in America, but Moshe became Max, Morris, Maurice, etc. The author's grandfather, born with the Hebrew name Yitzchak, was known at various times and places and in different documents as Icek (in Polish), Itzhak, Itzig, Isidore, Izzy and Jack. Which given name to enter on your family tree may not be an easy decision!

Name Americanization—Statistical Analysis

The author has conducted a statistical analysis of given names from more than 6,000 tombstones in several early 20th-century landsmanshaftn cemeteries in New York and Boston, to discern patterns in the names immigrant Jews adopted when they came to America. Tombstones are a particularly useful source, because they generally include both English and Hebrew given names. Some basic patterns emerged, but there are no hard and fast rules; immigrants chose whatever name sounded fashionable to them.

The new American given names fall into four categories:

Language Versions. Most Biblical names have equivalents in every Western language, because Western Christian nations share some of their cultural roots with Jews. Biblical names came into Western languages from Hebrew via Greek and Latin. If the English equivalent name was considered fashionable at that time, that name was most often the one adopted. In the name study, 77 percent of men with the Hebrew name אברהם (Avraham) adopted the English name Abe or Abraham; 94 percent of men named בנימן (Binyamin) became Ben or Benjamin; and 94 percent of דוד (David) became David. But the English-equivalent name was not always the name chosen. For example, despite the fact that the English-language version of the Hebrew name משה (Moshe) is Moses, only 4 percent of men named Moshe became Moses; 78 percent became Morris. No men named יהזקאל (Yechezkel) became Ezekiel; none of the men named שמשון (Shimshon) became Samson—because these were not popular American names at the time.

No equivalent European-language versions exist for most post-Biblical Jewish names. There is no English version of Nachman or Fruma, and the same is true in reverse. No Hebrew or Yiddish versions exist for the names George or Herman, which have Greek and German roots; there is no Biblical Hebrew root for these two names (and others) to go back to.

Calque (loan translation). This category includes transformations based upon the underlying meaning of a name. For example, 11 percent of Blumas became Flora; both names mean flower. Perl sometimes became Margaret—both mean pearl—but loan translation transformations were extremely rare.

Phonetic Similarity. Names in this category constitute the vast majority: new and old names sound similar. Often, however, no more than the first sound or letters of the name

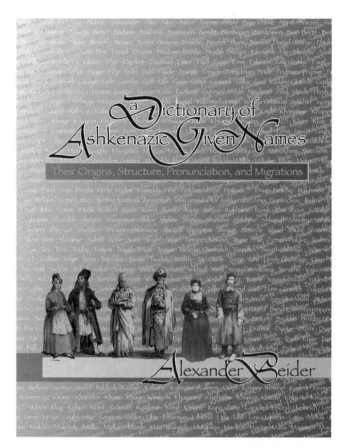

A Dictionary of Ashkenazic Given Names *identifies and describes more than 15,000 Jewish given names from Central and Eastern Europe.*

coincide. For example, of those with the American name Bertha, 26 percent had the Hebrew name Breina, 26 percent had been Beila, 17 percent Bracha and 9 percent Bluma. Of men named Samuel, 40 percent had been Shmuel (the language-equivalent name), but 10 percent were Shimon, 9 percent Yehoshua, 7 percent Simcha, 6 percent Sholem, 6 percent Shlomo, 5 percent Yisrael, 3 percent Yishaya, and smaller numbers of Shimshon, Shabtai, Shaul, Sender, Sinai and Tzadik. In some of the above cases, the Yiddish diminutive name (such as Shaya for Yishaya or Srul for Yisrael) has the common letter *S* with the American name.

Another phonetic factor was assonance, or vowel patterns. 56 percent of women named Chaya, became Ida; 82 percent of Chanas became Anna or Annie; and most Sheinas became Jennie.

It is important to remember that the new American name could have been based on any of the immigrant's Hebrew or Yiddish names. For example, 97 percent of men with the Hebrew name Ze'ev became William, because the Yiddish calque of Ze'ev is Wulf, and Wulf has a phonetic similarity to William. Of men named Aryeh, 70 percent became Louis, because the Yiddish calque of Aryeh is Leib; Leib and Louis both start with the letter *L*. Men named Betzalel often became Charles; a diminutive of Betzalel, Tzali, is phonetically similar to a diminutive of Charles, Charlie.

No Connection. In a small number of cases, immigrants

chose new names that had nothing to do with their Hebrew or Yiddish names. For example, Yitzchak Shlomo became Fred, and Ryfka Leah became Augusta.

Studies of Jewish given name transformations in Argentina, Israel and the Soviet Union (into Spanish, Hebrew and Russian, respectively) show that the same patterns are true elsewhere as well. In each case, a set of given names popular among Jews can be identified and their transformations from Yiddish to the language of the new country seem to follow the same principles as those identified for the United States.

Determining Your Ancestor's Yiddish Name

Since Eastern European civil records reflect the secular (that is, the Yiddish) given name, this Yiddish name is the one a genealogist must know to find official records of previous generations. U.S. passenger arrival manifests are the best source of the Yiddish name of immigrants to America. If one has no idea of a pre-Americanized name, but does know where an immigrant ancestor is buried, look at the tombstone inscription to find the Hebrew name. Use the Hebrew name to form hypotheses about the possible Yiddish name, using the guidance above.

Bibliography

Aleichem, Sholom. "Back from the Draft." *AVOTAYNU* Vol. XIII, no. 2 (Summer 1997): 12–16. A humorous view of the Russian bureaucracy's confusion surrounding Jewish given names.

Antin, Mary. *The Promised Land.* Boston: Houghton-Mifflin, 1912.

Beider, Alexander. *A Dictionary of Ashkenazic Given Names.* Bergenfield, N.J.: Avotaynu, 2001. Comprehensive analysis of the origin and evolution of Ashkenazic given names.

———. *A Dictionary of Jewish Surnames from the Kingdom of Poland.* Teaneck, N.J.: Avotaynu, 1996. The most comprehensive scholarly study of Jewish surnames in Russian Poland.

———. *A Dictionary of Jewish Surnames from the Russian Empire.* Teaneck, N.J.: Avotaynu, 1993. The most comprehensive scholarly studies of Jewish surnames in the Pale of Settlement. For given names, useful because of surnames derived from given names.

———. "Jewish Given Names in the Grand Duchy of Lithuania." *AVOTAYNU* Vol. XIII, no. 2 (Summer 1997): 20–25. A scholarly view of the usage and etymology of Jewish given names in Lithuania from the 14th to 19th centuries.

———. "Jewish Patronymic and Metronymic Surnames in Russia." *AVOTAYNU* Vol. VII, no. 4 (Winter 1991): 3–15. Surnames derived from given names. Includes an excellent table of given names in the Russian Empire.

Davis, Lauren B. Eisenberg. *Autumn Leaves.* Reisterstown, Maryland: self-published, 1997.

Feldblyum, Boris. *Russian-Jewish Given Names.* Teaneck, N.J.: Avotaynu, 1998. Based on Iser Kulisher's 1911 work on Jewish given names used in czarist Russia. Lists more than 6,000 names with variants and combinations.

Gorr, Shmuel. *Jewish Personal Names: Their Origin, Derivation, and Diminutive Forms.* ed. by Chaim Freedman. Teaneck, N.J.: Avotaynu, Inc., 1992. Good coverage of Hebrew and Yiddish names, grouped by root, but no historical context.

Harkavy, Alexander. *Yiddish-English-Hebrew Dictionary*, 2d ed. New York: YIVO/Schocken, 1988.

Hoffman, William F. and George W. Helon. *First Names of the Polish Commonwealth: Origins and Meanings.* Chicago: Polish Genealogical Society of America, 1998. Thorough coverage of first names used in Poland, of all ethnicities.

Kaganoff, Benzion C. *A Dictionary of Jewish Names and Their History.* New York: Schocken, 1977. Mostly covers surnames. Anecdotal, highly readable layman's view, but error prone and no references given.

Kolatch, Alfred J. *The New Name Dictionary: Modern English and Hebrew Names.* New York: Jonathan David, 1989. A revision of the author's earlier works *These Are the Names* (1948), *The Name Dictionary* (1967), and *The Complete Dictionary of English and Hebrew First Names* (1984). Covers Biblical and modern Israeli Hebrew names, and English names.

Lawson, Edwin D. *Personal Names and Naming: An Annotated Bibliography.* New York: Greenwood, 1987, and *More Names and Naming: An Annotated Bibliography.* New York: Greenwood, 1996. Continues Elsdon Smith's bibliography.

Panchyk, Richard. "Given Names and Hungarian Jews." *AVOTAYNU* Vol. XI, no. 2 (Summer 1995): 24–28; "Variations and Changes in Hungarian-Jewish Names." *AVOTAYNU* Vol. XIV, no. 2 (Summer 1998): 41–42. Also his Master's thesis: "Magyarization: A Study of Given Names Among Jews in Buda, 1820–95." (Amherst: University of Massachusetts, Spring 1994).

Rhode, Harold. "Thoughts on Jewish Given Names from Analysis of Czarist Records." *AVOTAYNU* Vol. XI, no. 3 (Summer 1995): 19–21; "Using Litvak Naming Patterns to Derive Names of Unknown Ancestors." *AVOTAYNU* Vol. XI, no. 3 (Fall 1995): 22–23.

Singerman, Robert. *Jewish Given Names and Family Names: A New Bibliography,* David Gold, ed. Leiden and Boston: Brill, 2001. A subject-organized list of more than 3,000 books and articles on Jewish given names and family names throughout history.

Smith, Elsdon C. *Personal Names: A Bibliography.* New York: New York Public Library, 1952. More than 3,400 annotated bibliographic citations on all aspects of names and naming.

van Straten, Jits and Harmen Snel. *Joodse voornamen in Amsterdam: Een inventarisatie van Asjkenazische en bijbehorende burgerlijke voornamen tussen 1669 en 1850* (Jewish First Names in Amsterdam: An inventory of Ashkenazic and matching civil first names). Bennekom, Holland, 1996. Comparisons of civil names associated with Hebrew/Yiddish names, based on civil and Jewish records.

Wilhelm, Y. Z. Ziv HaShemos. *What's in a Name?: Laws and Customs Regarding the Naming of Children and Related Topics.* Brooklyn: S.I.E. Publications, 1998. Orthodox responsa on naming practices.

Wynne, Suzan. *Finding Your Jewish Roots in Galicia.* Teaneck: Avotaynu, 1998.

Zunz, Leopold. *Namen der Juden. Eine geschichtliche Untersuchung.* Leipzig: L. Fort, 1837. The classic work on Jewish given names.

Notes

1. Davis, Lauren B. Eisenberg. *Autumn Leaves.* See Appendix J, "Use of the Name Alter": 382–383.

2. Source: Analysis of all 13,271 Jewish births recorded in the city of Ńomǧa, Poland, 1827–86, as extracted from the Ńomǧa civil records by Michael Tobias. The names have been transliterated from Polish and Russian. Spelling variants have been grouped. Double names (e.g. "Sura Ryfka") have been counted twice.

3. Source: 1910 U.S. Federal Census, a 1-in-250 nationally representative sample. Statistics are for those with a place of birth outside the United States and a native tongue of "Yiddish." See Susan Cotts Watkins and Andrew S. London, "Personal Names and Cultural Change: A Study of the Naming Patterns of Italians

and Jews in the United States in 1910," in *Social Science History* 18, no. 2 (Summer 1994).

4. See any book on Polish grammar; or Fay Vogel Bussgang, "How to Pronounce Your Polish Town and Family Names and Recognize Their Most Common Grammatical Transformations," in *Mass-Pocha* (JGS of Greater Boston) 5, no. 3 (Fall 1996): 7–10; or *Kielce-Radom SIG Journal* 1, no. 3 (Summer 1997): 3–6; or in Suzan Wynne's *Finding Your Jewish Roots in Galicia: A Resource Guide* (Avotaynu, 1998).

5. Gorr, Shmuel. *Jewish Personal Names: Their Origin, Derivation, and Diminutive Forms,* p. xi.

6. Antin, Mary. *The Promised Land*: 187–188.

Jewish Religion, Culture and History

by Harold Rhode

After years of genealogical research, it has become abundantly clear that it is not possible to do effective genealogical research without understanding the cultural context and the local history which so transformed our ancestors' lives. People did not and do not exist in a vacuum. Until the late 18th century, most Jews throughout the world were deeply religious. They lived in different lands, the cultures and rulers of which also influenced their lives and habits.

Jewish religious law—the *Halahkha*—was the one major influence that permeated the lives of all of our ancestors, irrespective of where they lived. Serious genealogists, therefore, must acquire, at a minimum, a basic knowledge of Jewish familial law and religious practices. They must also learn about the local Jewish customs, government regulations and local cultures. Only then can they hope to uncover the secrets behind some of the apparently faulty documentary evidence left behind by our ancestors.

By the end of the 19th century, the majority of world Jewry lived in the Russian Empire. Ancestors of approximately 80 percent of American Jewry, for example, emigrated from that empire. The basic documentary evidence for genealogists from that land are the vital records (i.e., birth, marriage, divorce and death records), and the revisions lists (quasi-census records) that are the basic sources of information about the people of the czarist empire from the late 18th century until the communist revolution in 1917.

The more we study these vital records and revision lists, the more perplexing they become. All too often, we ask questions that make sense in the terms of today's culture. These are very often the wrong questions; they lead us down the wrong trails, give us misleading answers and very often lead to dead ends. Why does the information we find in czarist documents often conflict with what our ancestors told us?

Boris Feldblyum and Yakov Shadevich first posed some of these questions in the Fall 1993 issue of *AVOTAYNU* ("Some Problems in Researching Eastern European Records"). Since then, we have learned that the only way to answer these questions is to understand the cultural milieu, the history of our ancestors and Jewish religious practices. Only by doing so can we ever hope to formulate the right genealogical questions those that will enable us to find the information we want.

Why, for example, are two sons listed as one person? Why do two marriages in the same family take place within a few days of each other or in places that neither seem to have parents? Why aren't children we know survived late into adulthood listed anywhere or listed as having died? Why are ancestors listed as being registered in towns that no family member ever mentioned? We must strive to answer these and other similar questions so that we can gain insight into how our ancestors lived, how they dealt with the authorities and

why what we know from family folk lore very often has little to do with what we find in the myriad of documents to which we now have access in the archives of the successor states of the Soviet Union.

In the West, we usually assume that what is on government vital records documents is true. From time to time, however, exceptions exist that leave us puzzled. Too often rationalizations are created for these discrepancies, but it usually does not enter into our minds that people were trying to fool the government. This is because we usually take for granted that our government is relatively benign and does not threaten us.

Interestingly, our assumptions about government—which are based on our experience with our own governments—very often serve as stumbling blocks that prevent us from asking the correct questions about our ancestors.

Registration with the authorities in Eastern Europe invariably meant trouble. People, therefore, developed methods to evade taxes and military service. Our ancestors' experience in czarist Russia—and for that matter in many other states—taught them that government usually meant trouble. One way to understand this is to remember what Tevya, the main character in "Fiddler on the Roof," asked the shtetl rabbi: "Is there a blessing for the czar?" The rabbi answers: "A blessing for the czar? Of course. May G-d keep the czar far, far away from us!" This short interchange sums up how our ancestors viewed government.

What did the government and its representatives want from its Jews? Money, usually in form of taxes, but even more often in the form of bribes, and male bodies as cannon fodder for its military. Moreover, especially from the late 1820s through the mid-1850s, the czarist government saw the draft as an opportunity to convert young Jewish boys by drafting them at a young age, taking them away from their families, and making them serve in a Christian army for 25 years. In the army, the Jewish boys did not get kosher food, nor observe Shabbat and other Jewish holidays, and—the Russian government hoped—would eventually convert to Christianity. The czarist authorities knew that the traditional Jewish proverb "The more Jews keep the Shabbat, the more the Shabbat enabled the Jews to remain Jews." was absolutely on the mark.

We see evidence of how the Jews dealt with their young boys being taken from them in the revision lists of that time period. Many more young girls are listed than young boys. Living in today's world, we would naturally assume that was obvious because the boys were away in the army. This assumption is incorrect because some boys are listed as having been drafted. By Russian law, boys still had to be listed even if they had been drafted.

Modern biological research demonstrates that a huge preponderance of females could not have been born. So these registers do not reflect a true picture of population makeup of that time. This is because our ancestors developed strategies for averting and circumventing the government decrees that had such enormous potential for destroying and wrecking havoc on our ancestors families.

To the best of our knowledge, our ancestors used the following four strategies and might have also had others which we have not yet discovered:

Males were simply hidden i.e., sent away when the Jews realized that the authorities were coming to record their names. The authorities seem to have had with them copies of previous revision lists, and would ask the whereabouts of people listed in previous registers who were not now present. We know this because of the multitude of notes listed besides males' names indicating that the said male had disappeared without further notice. We have never yet encountered such a note about females. But since the family was the basic building block of Jewish life at that time, it is highly unlikely that such large numbers of males would have vanished into thin air with-out leaving any trace of their whereabouts. As of now, we can only speculate about how the boys were hidden. Yiddish literature from that time period provides some insight in the ways that was done.

Jews sought ways to make their sons appear to be the sole son of parents. According to Russian law, the first male (i.e., the only son of a couple) was exempt from military service. This was because he would later become responsible for taking care of his parents when they became old. There was no Social Security equivalent in czarist Russia and society demanded that children be responsible for the care of their elderly parents. So Jews founds ways to make their sons appear to be the sole sons.

It seems that one of the most common ways this was done is that when the sole son of a couple died, their dead son was buried under the name of someone else's non-only son. Thereafter, at least for governmental purposes, this additional son of the first couple took on the name and identity of the dead boy. For legal purposes, he then appeared to be an only son, and thus exempt from military service. This is one of the main reasons why we find brothers with different family names during that time period.

Register two boys as one person. We have found many instances where two sons were listed as one. One example is my great-grandfather Yitzchak/Itzik Rode and his older brother Moshe Rode, children of Leiba and Hinda Rode. We have never found entries in the revision lists for either boy separately, but twice, in two separate revision lists, we found a listing for Moshe Itzik Rode. Moshe was born around 1838, and Itzik about 1848, but somehow, the family managed to have them registered as one person, neither of whom, to the best of our knowledge, served in the Russian military, probably because for registration purposes, the two were listed an only son. We did find later revision lists and census records for Itzik Rode, but none for Moshe Rode. How then did Moshe Rode survive? We know that he married—the sister of his brother Itzik's wife Asna. Moshe and his wife Etta had at least ten children, so they must have dealt with the authorities somehow. But as of now, we have no idea how.

There are many other instances in today's northern and central Lithuania where two sons are registered as an only son. All of these two son/one son registrations seemed to have occurred during the period when Jewish males were drafted for 25 years. That this had something to do with the draft is probable, because we have not yet come across a situation where two daughters were registered as one person.

No written sources have yet been found which indicate the exact reason for doing so, but it stands to reason that if the government believed that only one son was listed, no son would have had to deal with the military authorities.

Have a son declared dead. There are as number of cases where family lists show sons were listed as having died—but other sources demonstrate that these men were alive and living in other places—in one instance, in Philadelphia. Families were fined if their sons did not appear at the draft inspection board when called up to be examined for potential military service—even if the reason was emigration from Russia. Again, it stands to reason that parents would have done their best to convince the authorities that the boy they were looking for was dead. In this way, the parents would avoid both the fine and their son having to join the czarist military.

Not From One Shtetl

Our ancestors did not come from one particular shtetl. They came from many shtetls, often some distance from each other. Jews were a tremendously mobile people. This is largely because of the nature of the czarist Empire, and for that matter, other empires such as Austria-Hungary as well.

In the medieval world (and the Russian Empire, and its successor state the Soviet Union, functioned largely as medieval states), ethnic and religious groups had roles. Jews were mostly small-time artisans, traders, innkeepers and peddlers. They were responsible for providing the services the farming communities needed, as well as urban services needed by the government. This meant that most of our ancestors had to live in small towns or cities that provided these services. Jews rarely lived on farms because farming was not their role. If they did live on farms, it was almost always to provide the same services listed above, not to farm.

Since Jews were responsible for trade, they needed to have contacts in different towns where they plied their wares on their trading journeys in order to find kosher food and pray with a *minyan* (religious quorum). It is, therefore, not surprising that since a day's journey was between 12 and 20 miles—depending on the terrain—towns sprang up approximately 12 to 20 miles from each other.

Whom could the Jews trust in their trading relationships? Since family relations were the basis of Jewish society, people usually trusted their family members (i.e., brothers, brothers-in-law, and other relatives). Because Jews often married cousins, or uncles married nieces, these relations continued to build up over time.

Since Jews constantly traveled for their livelihood, they often settled in nearby towns, where they set up businesses. Marriages were almost always arranged by parents, so tight familial relations developed between people in whole areas. One sibling might live in the town where he was born; another might live in a nearby town, while still another might live in a town two or three days' journey away.

We, therefore, learn that Jewish families were constantly on the move. Though a family member might have said that he was from a particular town, it is highly likely that his parents were not originally from that town and that his aunts, uncles and grandparents lived in other towns in the vicinity as well. To make matters more complicated, Jewish women often returned to the town where their mothers lived in order to give birth.

So which particular *shtetl* were we from? We now realize that this question can easily lead down a blind alley to nowhere, because families came from large geographic areas, not from one town.

As the following example illustrates, our 19th-century ancestors were so mobile that, at most, we can say they were Litvaks (i.e., roughly from the part of the former Polish-Lithuanian confederation that had been under Lithuanian rule prior to the 16th century).

As a result of researching the Neviazhsky family from Kovno (today Kaunas) guberniya, I knew for many years that my great-great-grandfather, Hirsh Aaron Neviazhsky, had a brother named Shepsel. From the 1816 Kovno City Revision List in the Kovno archives, it appears that before 1811 this family lived in Rassein, Rassein *uyezd* (district), and thereafter, most seemed to have left for either Kelme (also in Rassein *uyezd)* or Kovno city.

As a result of a family gathering in Israel in 1998, I located descendants of Shepsel who told me that he had married Brayna nee Acharkan, and that a young man in Moscow had done a large family tree of the Acharkan family. It showed Brayna's brothers and sisters as Falke, Israel Isaac, Maria (died young), Matla, Feiga and Hatzkel. Their father was Nachman "der Yurburger," indicating that he had come from the town of Yurburg (today Jurbarkas, Lithuania). This Nachman was listed as married to Channa Zeldovich.

By coincidence, not long thereafter, the records for the 1858 Revision List for Vilkomir *uyezd* arrived. Both Vilkomir and Rassein *uyezds* were then in Kovno *guberniya* (province), but they were far from each other. We examined the Vilkomir *uyezd* records, looking for family members from the Vilkomir area. It never crossed our minds to look for the family name Acharkan, because they had come from *shtetlach* (villages) in a completely distant area, far from Vilkomir.

Imagine our surprise when we came across the family name Acharkan as residents of the town of Vilkomir. Even more interesting was the fact that the family listed was obviously the same family listed on the chart sent to me from Moscow.

1858 Vilkomir Jewish Community Revision List Name Entry # 174 (10th Revision List)

	Age in 1850	Age in 1858
Nachman son of Khatzkel	41	48
Nachman's wife: Khana		49
Nachman's 1st son: Khatzkel	18	25
Khatzkel's wife: Shora Mera		20
Nachman's 2nd son: Itzyk Falk	Not yet born	8
Nachman's 1st daughter: Matla		17
Nachman's 2nd daughter: Feiga		13

Clearly, these are almost exactly the same names that appear on the Moscow chart. Even more poignant is the note that appears beside the entry for Nachman:

> Registered until 1851 in the Jewish Community of Shilel (i.e., a shtetl not far from Yurburg), (Kovno *guberniya*). On August 25, 1851, by order of the Kovno Fiscal Office, his registration (and that of his family) was transferred to Vilkomir, (Kovno *guberniya*).

To complicate matters even further, it seems that by the 1890s most of the Acharkan family had moved to Moscow and Warsaw, where they established large businesses involving gold and silver work in Moscow.[1] According to family lore, another branch established an apparel factory in Warsaw that was taken from them during World War I. Extremely few Jews were allowed to live in Moscow in the 1890s. Those who did had to have special skills needed by the government.

Acharkan family lore makes this story even more interesting, because members of different branches heard from their parents and grandparents that the family is descended from a young man who was ritually martyred in 1659 in the town of Rozhani. It is from this person that most of the Sacks, Sack, and Sackheim family is descended; George Sackheim has written about him in his two-volume (unpublished) work, *Scattered Seeds.*

What were the origins of the Acharkan family? Were they from Rozhani, Yurburg, Shilel, Vilkomir, Moscow or Warsaw? Tradition gives us the names of some of these places. The documents tell us about other places. Where was this family from? The best we can say now is that they were Litvaks already in the 1650s and remained so until the early 20th century. Today, descendants of this family live in Moscow, the United States, Israel and possibly other places as well. They have intermarried with Jews from all over, and what remains of their "Litvakness" are subtle cultural aspects passed down from generation to generation, that now appear as family traits more than anything else.

Where to Seek Documents?

Given the above, looking for czarist government documents can be a nightmare. Where should we look? What town or towns should we research? How then can we find documents for our ancestors? How, from a czarist government perspective, could the authorities handle this problem which, from the documents, was a major preoccupation for the bureaucrats?

Clearly, it was difficult for the government to keep abreast of all of these movements of people from place to place, and it needed to do so in order to collect taxes and draft men into the military. It, therefore, developed a system whereby a family was registered as belonging to a particular town, irrespective of where the family actually lived. In fact, a person might never have lived in the town where he was registered.

The government periodically commissioned censuses called revision lists in which officials listed who was registered in/belonged to each town, not who lived there. These revision lists are absolutely critical in order to build our family trees back into the early 19th and even to the 18th centuries. This is because they include references that show us how each family member was related to the head of each household (i.e., brother, nephew, grandparent, uncle, son, relative, etc.) The registers do not usually include information about where the family members actually lived.

Vital records (i.e., birth, marriage, divorce and death records), however, were usually listed in the registers of the towns where these events took place, not by town of registration. From an exhaustive analysis of the vital records of the 19th-century Russian Empire, we learn that approximately 80 to 85 percent of the people were born, married, divorced or died in towns other than those where they or their parents were registered. We know this because in each registration entry, the government official listed the town where the individual or his father was registered. If a researcher insists on getting documents only from the *shtetl* where his ancestors said they lived, he can have at best a 15 to 20 percent chance of finding documents for his family. Flexibility is essential.

The following example illustrates how we might tackle the problem of finding out where our family was from, who our ancestors were, where they actually lived and how to find documents about the family. Even more, it calls into question whether we Jews or our ancestors were correct in labeling ourselves Litvaks, Polish, Russian, Galicianer and so forth.

My paternal grandmother's maiden name was Sarah Hillman. In the mid-1970s, we were told she was named for her paternal grandmother Sara, that the family was from the town of Panemonuk in Kovno *guberniya*, that we were descended from five brothers, and that we were related to Rebbetzin Sara Herzog (nee Hillman), mother of the late President of Israel Chaim Herzog and the U.S. labor leader Sidney Hillman. Two relatives independently confirmed this information.

About a year later, we met Rebbetzin Herzog in Israel. She said that she had met my relatives in Baltimore in the 1940s, knew they thought they were related, but had no further information. She did know, however, that Sidney Hillman was her cousin. We later talked with members of Sidney Hillman's family who knew nothing of us. Since we had no documentary information, we were skeptical about our being related to these people, thinking the story might be a *bubbe myseh* (old wive's tales) invented by people wanting to fabricate *yichus* (pedigree) with well-known people.

We later found citizenship documents for our family confirming the town name Panemonuk and also listing the city Bauska (today in southern Latvia) as place of origin. Nowhere did I find the town named Shadova from which Rebbetzin Herzog's father, Shmuel Yitzhak Hillman, came, nor Zagare, the town where Sidney Hillman was born. To be sure, these towns are in the same general area, but are not the ones from which my family hailed.

With time, we expanded our Hillman family research and learned that my grandmother Sarah's paternal grandfather, Israel, had three brothers. One named Yerucham Fishel died in Kovno *guberniya*. Another—Chaim—used the family name Friedman and immigrated with his family to Baltimore. Still another, the oldest, Avraham Noah, came to Baltimore with his wife and some of his children while some of his sons went to

South Africa. Avraham Noah, Israel and Chaim's gravestones indicate that their father was Yehuda Leib. Thereafter, I received a chart from the South African Hillmans which showed that Avraham Noah's wife, Devorah, was from a town called Krozh (Kraziai). This chart listed Avraham Noah's children as well, one of whom was Lena, who I later found in the 1920 Baltimore census. For town of origin, Lena listed the town of Kelmie (i.e., Kelme in Kovno *guberniya*), a town nor far from Krozh.

When the Lithuanian historical archives in Vilna was opened to foreign researchers in the early 1990s, I obtained a copy of a birth record of this Lena Hillman from the 1869 Kelme Jewish Community Birth Records, where she is listed as Fruma Leah. (The Hebrew name Leah was usually rendered as Lena in English.) Her father, Avraham Noah son of Leib, is listed as having been registered in/belonging to the town of Linkova (in northern Kovno *guberniya*), a town I had never heard mentioned in the family, nor had I ever seen mentioned in any document. I checked with Hillmans from all branches of the family; no one had ever heard of this town.

In 1997, while visiting the Kovno archives, I asked to see the revision lists for the town of Linkova, figuring that since Avraham Noah was listed as belonging to/being registered in that town, I might find more information about the family. Vitalija Gircyte, the archivist, brought me the 1858 revision list and 1883 family lists (roughly the same as revision lists) for Linkova. I quickly realized I had found much more than the gold mine I had hoped for.

Not only did I find records for Avraham Noah, his children and some of his grandchildren, but I also found information for all of the above-mentioned branches of the family. All of the *bubbe mysehs* were confirmed, along with additional details of other previously unknown branches of the family.

We were indeed one big family. Avraham Noah was listed as the first entry. Beside each additional entry, the official noted how the others were related to him. Avraham Noah's three known brothers were listed, along with an additional one whose name we had never heard. This made five brothers, exactly as I had heard from an elderly relative in Baltimore many years ago.

My grandmother's paternal grandmother Sarah, for whom she was named, was listed. I also found information about the ancestors of Sidney Hillman and Rebbetzin Herzog. Beside Sidney Hillman's grandfather's name—Nachum Mordkhel son of Shimkhel Hillman—the scribe wrote the abbreviation *rod* which is short for the Russian word *rodstevnnik* meaning "relative."

Rebbetzin Herzog's grandfather, Avraham Chaim, was listed as Nachum Mordkhel's brother, so we now knew that Sidney Hillman and Rebbetzin Herzog were second cousins. The *bubbe myseh* I had originally heard were 100 percent correct!

Elated, I still did know exactly how we were related to Rebbetzin Herzog and Sidney Hillman, but I strongly suspect that Shimkhel and Leib Hillman were brothers, making their children first cousins. This is because the naming patterns in each family are very similar, pointing to their common grandparents, and because the government scribes very often used the word *rod* to describe cousins.

What seems to have happened is that the Hillmans were first registered in Linkova and then had spread out all along the roads, all the way eastward to Panemonuk (today's Panemunelis) and southward to Kelme and beyond. This conforms perfectly to the typical pattern of Jewish life in that part of the world.

So where was the Hillman family from in Kovno *guberniya*? From all over Kovno and Kurland *guberniyas*. This odyssey might even explain why so many of our ancestors rarely mentioned the exact names of the towns they came from and more often just said Kovno, Vilna or whatever *guberniya*—not the town name—where they lived.

A few more details make this story even more interesting. One source— *Oholei Shem*, a biography of rabbis from all over the world published in Pinsk in 1913—contains an entry for the late President Chaim Herzog's maternal grandfather, Shmuel Yitzchak Hillman, who at that time was a rabbi in Glasgow, Scotland. Rabbi Hillman explains in this entry that he is descended from the Chief Rabbi of Metz (France), Shmuel Hillman, who died in 1763. This Rabbi Shmuel Hillman was born in Krotoszyn, in today's western Poland. His maternal grandfather was Rabbi Natan Nateh Shapiro, the author of one of the greatest kabbalistic books, *Megaleh Amuquot* (He who found the deep secrets of the Torah). Rabbi Shapiro, who died in Krakow in 1633, was descended from the Luria family and through them back to Rashi, who lived in eastern France and western Germany. Tradition has it that Rashi was descended from King David who lived in Eretz Yisrael in Biblical times.

This same Rabbi Shapiro was also descended from Rabbi Yitzchak Abarbanel, the great financier and advisor to the infamous Isabella and Ferdinand of Spain before the Spanish inquisition. Abarbanel also was a great rabbi who ended up in Padova/Padua, Italy, about 20 miles southwest of Venice, where he died and was buried.

So are these Hillman really Litvaks? Their descendants certainly think they are. But their ancestors clearly were not. Some time after 1763, the above-mentioned Rabbi Shmuel Hillman's descendants moved to today's northern Lithuania and southern Latvia. They then obviously became "Litvakized."

Though not all of our ancestors were rabbis, they clearly were extremely mobile. Before the 10th century C.E., almost no Jews lived in what later became the Polish kingdom. The Polish kings invited the Jews to settle in their cities, because they knew the Jews had the trade and commercial skills the Polish nobles needed to make their estates and kingdom prosper. That is how many of our ancestors came to Poland. It was "Go East young man in order to find your fortune." That is how our ancestors eventually became Litvaks, Galicianers, Polish and Russian Jews.

In my case, though I claim to be a "pure Litvak" because all of my eight great-grandparents were Litvaks, some of my more distant ancestors came from other places and underwent a process of "Litvakization" after they settled in "Litvakland," having come there from today's western Poland, France, northern Italy and even Spain.

In the end, all these distinctions among Jews are like the different sections of an orchestra. All are needed and belong; each contributes its part. Together, they form one unit. In terms of the 4,000 to 5,000 years of Jewish history, terms like Litvaks, Galicianers, or for that matter, even Ashkenazim and Sephardim, are of relatively recent origin. We Jews wandered constantly and were influenced by the societies where we settled, and thereby picked up different customs along the way. What matters is that we are all members of the united Jewish people.

Marriage Customs

Often, two or more weddings of members of the same family occurred within days of each other in the same town. From examining Litvak marriage registers, we soon realized that more than one marriage took place in the same family within days of each other. Why was this so? The answer lies in understanding the nature of the Jewish marriage ceremony. Today weddings usually are only one-day affairs. Prior to the turn of the 20th century, Litvak weddings usually lasted a whole week. After the *chupah* (marriage canopy) ceremony is completed, we offer seven blessings for the newly married couple. But traditionally we also say these blessings after each meal during the following six days (except Shabbat). [2] That meant that traditional wedding festivities lasted for seven days.

In addition, it was the usual practice that the groom's relatives moved to the bride's town for the entire seven days. The whole process involved enormous expense and travel. In order to lessen both, families arranged for multiple marriages to take place in the same town within a few days of each other.

The groom's town of registration and that of his father-in-law are usually listed in the marriage register. Since the ceremonies usually took place in the bride's town, the marriage record helps us trace the parents of those getting married even further.

Sometimes, we learn that neither the bride nor groom was from the town where the marriage took place. Given that most weddings were multiple, it is most likely that one of the families of the people getting married also had other relatives living in that same town who were getting married at the same time. (See the example listed after the following point, which illustrates both this point, and the following one.)

It was common practice for first cousins to marry, and for uncles to marry nieces, but not for aunts to marry nephews. In today's world, we have been taught to believe that marriage between close relatives is genetically risky. In fact, what such unions do is to increase the likelihood that recessive traits will appear. These traits might be positive or negative.

From a Jewish point of view, however, different criteria mattered. Examining the marriage registers of Kovno and Vilna *guberniyas*, it seems that a very large portion of Jewish marriages occurred between cousins, or between uncles and nieces. Marriages between aunts and nephews were prohibited by the *Halahkah*.

Keeping this in mind helps us develop research strategies and ask better questions. If you see what appears to be an aunt-nephew marriage, remember that neither the community nor the rabbinate would have sanctioned it. The religious authorities performed marriages, so such marriages could have not taken place. (No secular institutions dealt with personal status.) We must, therefore, think of other possibilities (i.e., maybe the aunt's name was the same as a niece you never heard of before, or that this marriage was not from your family).

The following example illustrates these points. We were looking through the 1878 Ponevezh, Kovno *guberniya* marriage records for the marriage record of Hirsh Aharon, son of Avraham Yitzhak Neviazhsky, to his late wife's sister, Sheitel, daughter of Avraham Tsemakhovich. To the best of our knowledge, he was the only one of his siblings who lived in that town. The others lived either in Rassein, Telzh or in the city of Kovno. We did not find that record, but we did find the record of his brother Yosel's marriage to their niece Fruma Feiga, daughter of Barukh Broida, on March 18. Neither Yosel nor his bride's family lived in Ponevezh. Both, according to Kovno city Jewish Benevolent Society registers lived in Kovno city.

Seeing the family name Broida, we instantly remembered that we had just seen a marriage record on the previous page on March 15 for Shalom Tuvia son of Barukh Broida registered in/belonging to Kelme, to Ayde Rakhel daughter of Yehuda Meizel registered in/belonging to Ponevezh.

What a find! We would never have looked for records for Yosel Neviazhsky in Ponevezh because he never lived there. His only connection—to the best of our knowledge—was that his brother lived there. Yosel married his sister Leah Broida's daughter, again a common practice in Judaism, but why were these two people, who lived in Kovno, being married in Ponevezh? The answer comes from the second record, the one for the marriage of Leah's son, Shalom Tuvia Broida, to a bride whose father was from Ponevezh. Everyone congregated in Ponevezh for the first marriage on March 15, probably because the bride's family lived there. They took advantage of the opportunity of the extended family being there anyway to have a second marriage, that of the groom's sister and their uncle.

Religious Status

Though one's status as a Jew passes from mother to child, one's religious status (Kohen, Levite or Israelite), passes through the father. From time to time, we find people bearing the same surnames from the same towns, but one knows he is a Levite, while the other, bearing the same family name, knows he is an Israelite. Moreover, people were not so committed to their family names as we are today, and often changed them, albeit usually illegally. So if two people have the same family name but do not share the same Jewish religious status, they cannot both be descended from the same male ancestor.

On the other hand, an ancestor might have assumed the family name of his father-in-law, and thus, he might be descended from a female whose father carried that name. If this was not the case, then these two people could not have been related because they could not change their religious status, which, given that Jews knew each other or knew people who knew each other in the area where they lived, could not have been easily fabricated.

The only reason someone might try to fabricate a change in religious status is if a kohen wanted to marry a divorcee or convert which is forbidden in Jewish law. Actually, the problem could only have arisen in the case of a divorcee wanting to marry a kohen, because the number of people who converted to Judaism in the 19th century was almost zero. Also, almost all Jewish marriages were arranged, and families knew each other. This too would have been next to impossible to fabricate.

Therefore, if a researcher finds a marriage record where he/she believes the groom to be a kohen and the bride is listed as a divorcee, he can rest assured that this particular groom could not have been a kohen and that the researcher has found the wrong marriage. No religious official would have performed such a marriage.

Jewish Naming Patterns

Jewish law does not prescribe either what type of names we should give our children or how we should choose these names. Two distinct patterns have developed during the past thousand years. Among Ashkenazic/European Jews, children are usually named after deceased relatives. Ashkenazic tradition—not law—proscribes naming newborns after living relatives.

Sephardic tradition works differently. Children are named after ancestors, whether living or deceased. Usually, the first male child is named after his paternal grandfather, the second male after his maternal grandfather, the first female after her father's mother, and the second female after her mother's mother.

Tradition is not law, but according to Jewish law, if traditions exist for a long time, they acquire the force of law. Many times we see in the Talmud references the sentence, "Beware, the custom of your ancestors is in your hands" (i.e., you must keep that tradition alive, because it helps keep the community together). So even though naming patterns do not stem from Jewish law, they are sacrosanct. Understanding them is, therefore, essential to postulate the correct questions in researching family history.

We can use these traditions to develop research strategies that can help us determine, with a high degree of accuracy, the names of unknown ancestors. Some examples follow:

Ashkenazi subgroups seem to have different traditions governing after which ancestor the first newborns are named. Some Hasidic groups in Jerusalem, for example, give that honor to the mother; the first newborn is usually named for someone in the mother's family.

Litvaks from Kovno and Vilna *guberniya* seem to have different traditions. From careful analysis of more than 15,000 names, the following customs seem evident. Even so, these customs should be looked upon as guides, not ironclad rules, because exceptions do exist.

1. If either parent (usually the father) died before the child was born, the newborn was given the name of his/her deceased parent.

Marriage ceremony in Galicia

2. Male children were usually named for male ancestors; female children for female ancestors.

3. If a newborn's parents' brother or sister was named for his/her grandparent, none of that deceased's grandchildren usually carry that grandparent's name. For example, Avraham and Sheina Tsemakhovich had a son in 1860 whom they named Binyamin, after Avraham's father. None of Avraham and Sheina's 11 children named any of their numerous children Binyamin. Avraham's mother, Hinda, on the other hand, died after Avraham and Sheina stopped having children, so none of their children were named after her. Consequently, each of their children named a daughter after Avraham's mother.

4. If both parents are alive, newborns are named for their grandparents and then their great-grandparents. For example, when Simon Rubin married Lena Menucha Goldberg (changed from Chaitkin) in 1894, both of Lena's parents had already died. Both of Simon's parents were still alive. Their first born was named Avraham, after Lena's father. Their second born, a boy, was not named after Lena's mother probably because of rules #1 and #2. He was named after Lena's maternal deceased grandfather Zvi Hirsh. To the best of our knowledge, Lena's paternal grandfather, Aharon, may still have been alive at that time. Simon's paternal grandparents and maternal grandfather were still alive. Their third child—my grandmother—was the first girl born. She, therefore, received Lena's mother's mother name, Golda. Finally, the fourth child, a girl, was named for Simon's maternal grandmother (according to rules 1 and 2).

5. When a newborn's grandparents are deceased, the newborn, especially a first born, is given a double name, the first being from his father's side, the second being from his mother's side. The following examples illustrate this point.

- The first son of Leiba Mendel and Keila (nee Pazol) Pazernov was born in 1841 in Vilkomir. The parents named him Shlomo Aharon. Shlomo was the name of Leiba Mendel's paternal grandfather. From analysis of the various branches of the Pazol family, it became clear that Aharon seems to have been the paternal grandfather of Keila, although we do not know for sure.

- The above-mentioned Shlomo Aharon and his wife Esther (nee Matuk) had their first born son in approximately 1875. They named him Moshe Elia. Moshe was the name of Shlomo Aharon's paternal grandfather. Elia was his wife Esther's paternal grandfather.

- Sarah Gitel Hillman, my paternal grandmother, was born in 1895 in Baltimore. She was the first child of Morris Hillman and Yetta (nee Naviasky). Both Morris and Yetta's mothers had died earlier. Sarah was her father's mother. Gitel was her mother's mother.

- The above-mentioned Sarah Gitel married Julius Rhode in 1915. By the time their first child—Harold—was born a year later, both of her grandfathers had died. Sarah and Julius named their new son Yisrael Zvi, Yisrael being Sarah's father's father, and Zvi, Sarah's mother's father. They did not name their son after Julius' paternal grandfather probably because of rule #3. (Julius' older brother, Leiba Velvel, was named after Julius and Leiba's paternal grandfather.)

These naming patterns also enable us to predict with a high degree of accuracy the names of the parents and grandparents of our most ancient Litvak ancestors, thereby adding one or two additional generations to our trees. Moreover, putting all this information together helps us connect trees for which we do not yet have any documentary evidence that they are in fact related.

Conclusions

What does the above teach us? It is absolutely necessary to know and understand history of the country and the Jews who lived there. Jews lived under regimes that made the laws with which Jews had to contend. Our ancestors, as do we, developed strategies to deal with governmental restrictions and regulations. Sometimes these regulations worked to our advantage; most often they did not.

Moreover, the technological limitations of the era we are researching determined many aspects of our lives. Clearly, travel was a major undertaking in 19th-century Russia. Nevertheless, Jews by necessity traveled considerably, and thus had contacts all over the area. So the technological and time limitations on travel had less of a bearing on marriage possibilities and familial relations than we otherwise might have expected.

Besides history, it is essential to know as much as possible about our Jewish culture and religion, in order to develop better research strategies for obtaining the documents we need to build our family trees.

We were not from a particular town, but from many towns, which were not necessarily located even in the same district, or even province. It is, therefore, important for us to cast as wide a net as possible in order to find the family records for which we are looking. We found some of the most interesting and useful family records among those of towns where we never imagined we would find any. The best research strategy is to join a group of people researching a particular area, for example a whole *uyezd* (district), and pool everyone's money to order the records for that whole area. These records should be entered into a searchable database which every member of the group can access. That would increase the chance researchers will find the records for their families. It also allows them to discover additional towns where their ancestors lived and to add additional, yet unknown, relatives to their trees.

Finally, understanding naming patterns is crucial to figuring out the names of unknown ancestors.

In short, history, culture and Judaism are the keys to understanding the lives of our ancestors and to obtaining the documents we need.

Notes

1. Source: *Vsia Moskva*—various editions from the 1890s and 1900s.
2. For more information on how this was done, see *Encyclopedia Judaica*, vol. VII,"The Marriage Bene-dictions": 1038.)

Avotaynu

by Gary Mokotoff

Avotaynu, Inc. was founded in 1985 by Gary Mokotoff and Sallyann Amdur Sack. The initial purpose of the company was to publish a journal of Jewish genealogy which the founders named "AVOTAYNU: The International Review of Jewish Genealogy." (*avotaynu* means "our fathers" in Hebrew, but a more modern definition is "our ancestors.") In 1991, Avotaynu added book publishing to its mission and in 1999 started a biweekly e-zine called *Nu? What's New?*

AVOTAYNU:
The International Review of Jewish Genealogy

AVOTAYNU is the largest subscription publication devoted exclusively to Jewish genealogy and family history. The quarterly reviews major events in the Jewish genealogical world, highlights important genealogical resources and features book reviews, letters to the editor and a regular "Ask the Experts" column. Members of its international Board of Contributing Editors regularly report on resources and happenings of Jewish genealogical interest in their countries and abstract publications of all Jewish genealogical societies and special interest groups. The directors of numerous archives and other repositories throughout the world have regularly contributed articles to the journal. Each issue consists of at least 68 pages; issues have been as large as 96 pages. Primary focus is on U.S., Canadian, and Central and Eastern Europe research, but virtually every country in the world has been covered in the more than 70 issues published to date. As an example of the type of articles that appear in the journal, Avotaynu has placed on the Internet (WWW.AVOTAYNU.COM/INDEXSUM.HTM) an index to the articles that have appeared in the first 18 years (1985–2002) of the publication.

Back issues of AVOTAYNU are available on CD-ROM. The most current CD includes all articles published from 1985–2002. The CD is updated typically every three years. A full-word search engine permits the user to search for all occurrences of the name of a particular town, surname, or other topic of interest.

Books

Between 1991 and 2003, Avotaynu published 26 books focusing on the needs of Jewish genealogical research. Three of the books have won the prestigious "Best Reference Book" award of the Association of Jewish Libraries. Descriptions of the available books are located at www.AVOTAYNU.COM/ALLBOOKS.HTM

Books published by Avotaynu are:

1991   *Where Once We Walked.* Gazetteer of 22,000 towns in Central and Eastern Europe where Jews lived before the Holocaust. Winner of "Outstanding Reference Book of the Year" award given by the Association of Jewish Libraries.

AVOTAYNU, The International Review of Jewish Genealogy, is a quarterly that has been publishing articles of use to Jewish genealogical researchers since 1985.

1992   *A Biographical Dictionary of Canadian Jewry: 1909–1914.* Births, bar mitzvahs, marriages and deaths as reported in the *Canadian Jewish News.*

1992   *Jewish Personal Names: Their Origin, Derivation and Diminutive Forms.* 1,200 Jewish given names described.

1993   *A Dictionary of Jewish Surnames from the Russian Empire.* Landmark work on 50,000 Jewish surnames from the Russian Empire showing etymology, districts of the Empire where they appeared and variations of the names.

1994   *Following the Paper Trail.* Helps translate vital records (and other documents) for 13 European languages.

1995   *A Guide to Jewish Genealogical Resources in Israel: Revised Edition.* Collections of Jewish presence throughout the world in Israeli libraries and archives.

1995   *How to Document Victims and Locate Survivors of the Holocaust.* How-to book of Holocaust research.

1995   *Ancient Ashkenazic Surnames: Jewish Surnames from Prague.* Origins of some of the earliest Ashkenazic surnames.

1995 *WOWW Companion*. Given the location of a specific town, permits you to locate other towns in the vicinity. Out of print. Replaced by *Where Once We Walked: Revised Edition*.

1996 *A Dictionary of Jewish Surnames from the Kingdom of Poland*. More than 32,000 Jewish surnames from the Kingdom of Poland showing etymology, districts of the Kingdom where they appeared and variations of the names. Winner of "Outstanding Reference Book of the Year" award given by the Association of Jewish Libraries.

1996 *Documents of Our Ancestors*. Actual forms needed to request documents from various archives and organizations and record the results.

1996 *FAQ: Frequently Asked Questions About Jewish Genealogy*. Out of print. Replaced by *Getting Started in Jewish Genealogy*.

1996 *Jewish Vital Records, Revision Lists and Other Jewish Holdings in the Lithuanian Archives*. Index to the collection of the Lithuanian archives.

1996 *Sourcebook for Jewish Genealogies and Family Histories*. Jewish genealogies and family histories, both published and unpublished, for more than 10,000 family names.

1996 *The German Minority Census of 1939*. Index to the microfilm collection of this census at the LDS (Mormon) Family History Library.

1997 *Eliyahu's Branches: The Descendants of the Vilna Gaon and His Family*. 20,000 descendants of this great scholar.

1997 *Some Archival Sources for Ukrainian-Jewish Genealogy (16th–20th Centuries)*. Index to archival holdings. Out of print.

1998 *Finding Your Jewish Roots in Galicia: A Resource Guide*. Definitive work on Galician-Jewish research.

1998 *Library Resources for German-Jewish Genealogy*

1998 *Russian-Jewish Given Names: Their Origins and Variants*. More than 6,000 variants of Russian-Jewish given names of the 19th and early 20th centuries.

2000 *Getting Started in Jewish Genealogy*. Primer for Jewish genealogy.

2000 *History of the Jews In Russia and Poland*. One of the great histories of the Jews of that area.

2001 *A Dictionary of Ashkenazic Given Names*. The definitive work on the origin and evolution of Ashkenazic given names.

2002 *Between Galicia and Hungary: The Jews of Stropkov*. Yizkor book for this Slovakian town.

2002 *Where Once We Walked: Revised Edition*. Update to this landmark gazetteer. Contains 23,500 towns, 17,500 synonyms. Includes a nearby-town index and soundex index.

2003 *Sephardic Genealogy*. Definitive work on Sephardic genealogy. Winner of the "Outstanding Reference Book of the Year" award given by the Association of Jewish Libraries.

Nu? What's New?

In February 1999, Avotaynu started a biweekly e-mail magazine, *Nu? What's New?* Its purpose is to provide news on a timely basis of recent developments of interest to Jewish genealogists. Each subject is discussed in abbreviated form with links to Internet sites providing detailed information. Subscriptions to the e-zine are free. A link to the subscription page can be found at Avotaynu's home page WWW.AVOTAYNU.COM.

Other Activities

Consolidated Jewish Surname Index. A major database for Jewish genealogy, the Consolidated Jewish Surname Index (CJSI), is located at the Avotaynu Internet site at WWW.AVOTAYNU. COM/CSI/CSI-HOME.HTML. The Consolidated Jewish Surname Index (CJSI) is a gateway to information for more than 500,000 different surnames, mostly Jewish, that appear in 34 different databases. These databases, combined, include more than 2 million entries. By accessing CJSI, you can immediately determine which databases have Jewish names of interest and eliminate the need to waste time referencing each database only to find the surnames of interest to you are not there. CJSI is organized in soundex order using the Daitch-Mokotoff Soundex System rather than pure alphabetical sequence; therefore, the spelling variants of the name you are searching will be grouped together.

Other books, microfiche, maps, CD-ROMs. Avotaynu also sells a large number of books and other resource materials for the Jewish genealogist, all of them listed on its website at WWW.AVOTAYNU.COM/CATALOG.HTM as well as in its printed catalog. Rather than make available every book of potential interest to Jewish genealogists, only those considered the best in their area are sold. Thus, Avotaynu offers for sale only one book on publishing a family history or holding a family reunion.

JewishGen

by Warren Blatt and Gary Mokotoff

The major Jewish genealogical presence on the Internet can be reduced to one word: JewishGen. JewishGen is the brainchild of Susan E. King of Texas and the product of hundreds of volunteers who moderate discussion groups, create databases and web pages, establish educational programs, and maintain the other activities of this vast website at WWW.JEWISHGEN.ORG.

JewishGen started in the late 1980s as a dial-up bulletin board. The JewishGen website started in 1995, with the first online databases accessible in 1996. In January 2003, JewishGen became a division of the Museum of Jewish Heritage in New York (WWW.MJHNYC.ORG). Most major Jewish genealogical organizations that are independent of JewishGen are hosted by JewishGen servers.

The JewishGen homepage provides an overview of the activities of this organization and the independent organizations it hosts. Readers familiar with RootsWeb (WWW.ROOTSWEB.COM) will see that JewishGen's services parallel many of the services RootsWeb provides for American genealogy, although it differs in two significant ways. First, because most Jews worldwide do not live in the countries where their ancestors resided 150 years ago, Jewish genealogical research has an international flavor. Linking up with researchers who share a common ancestor or common ancestral too frequently involves communicating with a person who lives in such diverse areas as France, Argentina, Australia, or Israel.

Second, soundexing is a necessary aspect of Jewish genealogical research. Surnames may be spelled in a variety of ways; Lipshitz, for example, has more than 140 variations. As political borders changed in Central and Eastern Europe over the past 200-plus years, ancestral town names were spelled according to the custom of the conquering power. (Lemberg, Lwów, Lvov, and L'viv, for example, are all names of the same city that has been in four different countries in the past 85 years: Austria, Poland, USSR, and Ukraine.) All databases on JewishGen have a soundexing search option that uses the Daitch-Mokotoff Soundex System (see Appendix C).

Databases

Note: All web addresses described below start with www. JEWISHGEN.ORG. For brevity, this is replaced with ellipses (...).

JewishGen Family Finder (.../JGFF/). The oldest and most frequently used of the JewishGen databases is the JewishGen

Family Finder (JGFF). The JGFF identifies surnames and towns being researched by more than 70,000 Jewish genealogists worldwide. It has more than 300,000 entries, with 90,000 different surnames and 20,000 ancestral towns. The JGFF is designed to bring together genealogists with similar research interests and to allow people researching the same surnames and towns to communicate and share information with one another. A researcher enters a surname and/or town name; displayed are the name(s) and contact information of the researcher(s) with similar research interests. The researcher can then send an e-mail or postal mail message to the submitter, to begin sharing information.

Family Tree of the Jewish People (.../GEDCOM/). The Family Tree of the Jewish People (FTJP) is a lineage-linked database that (as of early 2004) lists more than 2.5 million people on family trees contributed by 2,000-plus Jewish genealogists. For each individual the FTJP displays the date and place of birth, date and place of marriage(s), and date and place of death. Linkages to each individual's parents, spouse(s), and children and also are displayed. Data is submitted to the FTJP in standard GEDCOM (see HOW TO BECOME A GENEALOGIST) format.

The JGFF and FTJP are both interactive databases (i.e., the data is contributed by Jewish genealogists). Both databases have been growing rapidly—more than 3,000 new entries are added to the JGFF every month.

JewishGen's other databases are based on documents abstracted from original historical sources. Most focus on specific geographical areas. Examples include:

- *Vsia Rossiia* (All Russia) Database. More than 34,000 entries from Russian Empire business directories, 1895–1911
- Krakow Ghetto Database. Names of 19,000 Jews in the Kraków, Poland, ghetto in 1940
- Grodno Guberniya 1912 Voters List. Names of 26,000 men of Grodno guberniya (today, western Belarus and northeastern Poland) who were eligible to vote in the Russian parliamentary elections in 1912
- Riga Tax Administration. References to 23,000 individuals living and working in Riga (Latvia), from the Riga Tax records of 1858–1917
- *Aufbau* Survivors Lists. Names of 33,000 Holocaust survivors published in the German-language newspaper *Aufbau*, New York, 1944–46
- The Boston *Jewish Advocate* Obituary Database: Index to more than 23,000 obituary notices from this Massachusetts newspaper, 1905–2002.

In the aggregate JewishGen's databases contain more than eight million records. A complete list of all JewishGen databases can be found at .../DATABASES/.

"All Country" and "All Topic" Databases. JewishGen has begun to combine its databases into multidatabase search engines, so many related databases can be searched at once. The "All Country" databases include The All Belarus Database (.../DATABASES/BELARUS), the All Lithuania Database (.../LITVAK/ALL.HTM), the All Latvia Database (.../DATABASES/LATVIA), the All Hungary Database (.../DATABASES/HUNGARY), and the All Poland Database (.../DATABASES/POLAND). Some of these databases are sponsored by Special Interest Groups (SIGs). These groups index documents such as vital records, voter registration lists, tax and census lists, directories, cemetery lists, and even lists of draft dodgers. "All Topic" databases include the JewishGen Holocaust Database (.../DATABASES/HOLOCAUST) containing 500,000 entries pertaining to Holocaust victims and survivors from many sources, and the JewishGen Online Worldwide Burial Registry (see JOWBR, below) (.../DATABASES/CEMETERY) containing Jewish cemetery and burial records worldwide.

Some other important JewishGen databases include:

- JewishGen ShtetlSeeker (.../SHTETLSEEKER/). A database of 500,000 towns in Central and Eastern Europe, based on data from the U.S. Board on Geographic Names. A search illuminates latitude and longitude for each location, the distance/direction from the country's capital city, and a link to a map. The ShtetlSeeker also can list all of the towns within a certain distance of a given latitude/longitude.
- JewishGen Discussion Group Message Archives (.../DATABASES/ARCHIVES.HTM). An archive of all 100,000-plus messages posted to the JewishGen Discussion Group since 1993, a full-text searchable database of more than 10 million words

Discussion Groups

JewishGen hosts 30 discussion groups—bulletin boards on which subscribers can post messages that are viewed by all persons who are members of the group. The main JewishGen Discussion Group (.../JEWISHGEN/DISCUSSIONGROUP.HTM) has an estimated 5,000 subscribers. Previous postings are accessible via the Discussion Group Message Archives (see above). If you are getting started in Jewish ancestral research, visiting the Discussion Group Message Archives might uncover postings from the past 10 years involving your area of interest.

Most other discussion groups (.../LISTSERV/SIGS.HTM) are oriented toward geographical area of ancestry, which is the essence of Jewish genealogical research. Examples are Belarus, Bohemia/Moravia, Galicia, German, Hungarian, Latin America, Latvia, Litvak (Lithuania), Romania, Sephardic, Scandinavia, South Africa, Ukraine, and United Kingdom. A few discussion groups focus on specific topics, such as rabbinic ancestry or genetics.

InfoFiles

Jewish genealogists throughout the world have contributed files of information (.../INFOFILES/) on a variety of subjects. They are categorized at the JewishGen site by both topic and country. Topics include Basics, Books & Periodicals, Cemeteries, Genealogical Techniques, Genealogists, Genetics,

Holocaust, Immigration/Emigration, Internet Sources, JewishGen Sources, Libraries & Archives, Military, Miscellaneous, LDS (Mormon) Resources, Names, Postal Matters, Preservation, Seminars, Sephardim, Social Security, Special Interest Groups, Translation/Transliteration, Travel, Vital Records. To date more than 200 InfoFiles are posted on JewishGen. Examples of InfoFiles are:

- How to Read a Hebrew Tombstone
- Locating Burial Records in Israel
- Jewish Genealogical Research in Eastern Europe
- Combining Genealogical and Family Trait Genetic Research
- Captured German Records—Microfilms at NARA & USHMM
- Manifest Markings—A Guide to Interpreting U.S. Passenger List Annotations
- Holland-America Line (HAL) Passenger Lists, 1900–1940
- Alternate Surnames in Russian Poland

Projects

A host of projects under the JewishGen umbrella may be useful in your research and the list is growing.

Yizkor Book Project. *Yizkor* (memorial) books are some of the best sources for learning about Jewish communities in Eastern and Central Europe. Groups of Holocaust survivors, former residents, or *landsmanshaftn*, have published these books as tributes to their former hometowns and the people who were murdered during the Holocaust. Yizkor books typically contain descriptions and histories of the shtetl, biographies of prominent people, lists of people who perished, discussions of political, social and religious movements, etc. They often are embellished with photographs, maps, and other memorabilia. Most yizkor books are written in Hebrew or Yiddish, languages that many contemporary genealogists cannot read. The JewishGen Yizkor Book Project (.../YIZKOR/) was organized to facilitate access to information in these books by providing guides and translations. The project features translations, a bibliographic database, a necrology index, InfoFiles, and a discussion group.

- Bibliographic Database (.../YIZKOR/DATABASE.HTML): The Yizkor Book Bibliographic Database lists all known yizkor books (more than 1,200) and their call numbers in more than 50 libraries worldwide. Researchers can search for a particular location to determine if a book exists for an ancestral town. Some communities, especially in Lithuania and Latvia, do not have individual yizkor books, but are described in regional books.
- Translations (.../YIZKOR/TRANSLATIONS.HTML). The core of the Yizkor Book Project is the online English translations of all or part of more than 350 books. Thousands of pages have been translated in this ongoing volunteer project, including chapters about 100 towns from the multivolume *Pinkas HaKehillot*.
- Necrology Database (.../DATABASES/YIZKOR/). The Necrology Database indexes the lists of Holocaust martyrs published in the books appearing in the online translations. Because most of these names were transliterated from Hebrew and

Yiddish, the spellings of the surnames may be different from those used in Roman alphabet sources, so surnames should be searched via soundex. The Necrology Database currently includes information about 250,000 individuals listed in 150 yizkor books.

- InfoFiles (.../YIZKOR/INFOFILES.HTML). Information on libraries that have large collections of yizkor books, retail establishments that sell yizkor books, and professional translators of yizkor books are given here.
- Discussion Group (.../YIZKOR/LIST.HTML). E-mail forum to discuss yizkor books and their translations.

ShtetLinks. JewishGen ShtetLinks (.../SHTETLINKS/) are webpages devoted to individual Jewish communities. The project's purpose is to provide a site at which anyone can commemorate a place where Jews have lived. This is accomplished by creating webpages for that place that include historical information, pictures, memoirs, data, and links to sites that provide additional information. ShtetLinks sites are for those who want to place their own family history in a wider context, to go beyond lists of names and dates. The goal is to develop a grassroots atlas of Jewish life—a way to share the stories and histories of the cities, towns, and villages where our ancestors lived.

JewishGen currently has ShtetLinks sites for more than 200 Jewish communities, primarily in Belarus, Lithuania, Poland, and Ukraine, although there are sites for localities all over the world. Some ShtetLinks sites are very small, while others (such as those for Krakow and Lodz) contain hundreds of pages of information.

Other Features

- *JewishGen Online Worldwide Burial Registry* (JOWBR) (.../DATABASES/CEMETERY/). Information about Jewish cemeteries and burials throughout the world. JewishGen actively collects additional information.
- *Genealogy by Genetics* (.../DNA/). Partnership with a DNA testing laboratory to establish familial relationships through DNA testing.
- *Holocaust Global Registry* (.../REGISTRY/). Lists names of Holocaust survivors, survivors searching for family members, and child survivors searching for clues to their identity.
- *ShtetlSchleppers* (.../SHTETLSCHLEPPERS). Information on planned trips to ancestral towns in Europe.
- *ViewMate* (.../VIEWMATE/). Site on which researchers can place scanned images of photographs or documents, and ask other researchers to help them identify, translate, or analyze their content.

Tools

JewishGen has tools that will:

- Convert a Hebrew date to the secular calendar and vice versa (.../JOS/JOSDATES.HTM)
- Display the dates of all Jewish holidays for any year (.../JOS/JOSFEST.HTM)

- Compute the distance between two coordinates on the earth, in either miles or kilometers (.../JOS/JOSDIST.HTM)
- Supply the Daitch-Mokotoff Soundex code and American Soundex code for any word—typically a surname or town name (.../JOS/JOSSOUND.HTM)

Special Interest Groups

Special Interest Groups (SIGs), whose interests are historical geographical regions of origin, maintain webpages and discussion groups on JewishGen. The webpages contain "how to" information, data on archival resources and specific historical data. Current JewishGen SIGs include: Belarus, Bohemia-Moravia, Courland, Early American, French, Galicia, German, Hungary, Latvia, Litvak, Romania, Scandinavia, Sefard, Southern Africa, Ukraine, the United Kingdom, and a SIG for those with rabbinic ancestry. Links to SIG websites may be found on the JewishGen home page.

Hosted Organizations

JewishGen provides web-hosting services to several independent Jewish genealogical organizations, including Jewish Records Indexing-Poland (JRI-Poland), the International Association of Jewish Genealogical Societies (IAJGS), and several local Jewish genealogical societies (JGSs) (see ORGANIZED GENEALOGY).

Jewish Records Indexing-Poland. JRI-Poland (.../JRI-PL) is an independent non-profit organization whose website and database are hosted by JewishGen. Its stated goal is to index all available Jewish vital records of current and former territories of Poland that are more than 100 years old and is the first place to check for researchers interested in Jewish records from Poland. Where such records are available, JRI-Poland may include towns that are now part of Lithuania, Ukraine and Belarus but once were part of Poland. Operating on the philosophy "if you want your ancestral town's records indexed, volunteer to get it done," JRI-Poland has benefitted from the efforts of hundreds of genealogists; more than two million records were indexed by the beginning of 2004.

The project began by indexing microfilmed records from the LDS Family History Library (see LDS) and expanded when the group signed an agreement with the Polish State Archives, which now provides copies of indexes to later years not available in microfilm at the Family History Library. Data entry is carried out by professionals in Warsaw working directly for JRI-Poland. This work is funded through donations from researchers with an interest in specific towns.

Where no indexes exist, especially for towns in the former Austrian province of Galicia (including towns formerly in Poland, now in western Ukraine), archivists hired by JRI-Poland create indexes from the original records.

At the JRI-Poland site, search for a particular surname (soundexed or exact match) in the complete database or in specific guberniyas or towns. To locate possible relatives who may have moved from the town you know, it usually is best to search by name.

Jewish Genealogical Societies and Special Interest Groups

by Sallyann Amdur Sack

Organized Jewish genealogy as we know it today can be said to have come into existence with the publication of the first "how-to" Jewish genealogy book, *Finding Our Fathers*, by Dan Rottenberg, in 1977, followed in 1980 by *From Generation to Generation*, by Arthur Kurzweil. Readers of these books discovered that—contrary to what many had believed—it is possible to trace Jewish roots and they soon realized the need to form some organizations that would support and facilitate their quests.

Jewish Genealogical Societies (JGSs)

There are more than 70 Jewish Genealogical Societies in 15 different countries. The first was the Jewish Genealogical Society, Inc. located in New York City which incorporated in 1977.[1] Several other U.S. societies formed soon after in other major Jewish population centers of the United States including Boston, Chicago, Los Angeles, Philadelphia, and Washington. The first societies to form outside the U.S. were Israel in 1983 and France in 1984.

These geographically based organizations engage in a variety of activities. The typical JGS holds monthly meetings with programs and speakers of genealogical interest. Many tape record their lectures and lend tapes to members and others. Most produce periodic newsletters and other publications. Some organize workshops, sponsor research, index local records and create computerized databases. Several have hosted annual Jewish genealogical conferences.

Membership typically is open to all interested parties at nominal cost and is an excellent way to exchange information, obtain help with brick walls and blind alleys and share the excitement of new "finds" with people who appreciate them. (Relatives are not always as fascinated as you are.)

Most maintain websites and all are listed on the International Association of Jewish Genealogical Societies (see IAJGS below) webpage at the JewishGen site (www.JEWISHGEN.ORG) (see JEWISHGEN). On the JewishGen homepage scroll down to "Hosted societies." Click onto the link "Jewish Genealogical Societies" and scroll down until you see the JGS closest to where you live. No JGS in your area? Consider forming a society or study group. (Many flourishing JGS began as a study group with a handful of participants.) Contact Avotaynu (see AVOTAYNU) for a list of known Jewish genealogy buffs near you.

Jewish Genealogy Conferences

Every year since 1981, Jewish genealogists have gathered in major cities to conduct facilitated research, listen to speakers, attend workshops, exchange tips and network with fellow enthusiasts from all over the world. The major Jewish genealogical event of each year (initially called "seminars"), the conferences are hosted by local genealogical societies under the sponsorship of the International Association of Jewish Genealogical Societies (IAJGS). Attracting a thousand or more participants in recent years, the gatherings of people with shared interests have spawned numerous projects and Special Interest Groups (SIGs) (see below). Many Jewish genealogists feel that dollar-for-dollar attendance at an annual conference is their most economical genealogical expenditure.

Almost all talks have been taped recorded, most by Repeat Performance.* The proceedings of the 1997 Paris conference were published in a bilingual (French and English) edition,

available from the host society, the Cercle de Généalogie Juive. Tapes of the 2001 London conference are available directly from the Jewish Genealogical Society of Great Britain. For a list of available tapes from all other previous conferences, write Repeat Performances* for a catalogue of offerings from Jewish genealogical conferences. Scan the list of tape recordings from previous conferences and purchase those that seem relevant to your research.

The conference syllabus, often available for subsequent purchase, typically includes (among other items) biographical information about speakers, synopses of each talk and—in most cases—three or four pages of additional information for each talk, frequently including names and addresses of resources.

Other Conferences

Jewish genealogical conferences focus specifically on the needs and interests of those researching Jewish families, but much can be learned at not-specifically Jewish conferences as well.[2,3] In the U.S. consider conferences organized by the Federation of Genealogical Societies (FGS), National Genealogical Society (NGS) and the Federation of Eastern

European Family History Societies (FEEFHS). Jews with roots in North Africa may find material of value in the activities and publication of GAMT*, a French genealogical association for those with roots in Algeria, Morocco and Tunisia.

International Association of Jewish Genealogical Societies (IAJGS)

By the late 1980s, Jewish genealogists in the United States realized the need for an umbrella organization to coordinate conference venues and to speak for the emerging Jewish genealogical community. In 1987 Rabbi Malcolm H. Stern, often called the "father of modern Jewish genealogy" organized a provisional society called the Association of Jewish Genealogical Societies (AJGS). The first officers were elected at the 1988 conference in Washington, D.C. with Gary Mokotoff as president.

To reflect the composition of its membership more accurately, the group changed its name to the International Association of Jewish Genealogical Societies (IAJGS) in 1998. Its annual general meeting, open to all, is held during each yearly conference. Most recently, it has issued a Code of Ethics for Jewish genealogists and has established a committee to monitor archival access issues.

Since 1998, IAJGS has issued annually the *Jewish Genealogy Yearbook*, a compendium of information about and reports on the activities of more than 100 organizations involved in Jewish genealogy. The *Yearbook* typically is provided to registrants at the annual Jewish genealogy conference as a section of the syllabus issued by the conference. An updated electronic version is available at the IAJGS website, WWW.IAJGS.ORG.

The IAJGS website is hosted by JewishGen and accessible also from its homepage at WWW.JEWISHGEN.ORG. Look for the section titled "Hosted Organizations." Consult the IAJGS webpage for a listing of its other activities.

Special Interest Groups

After about a decade of organized Jewish genealogical activity, some researchers realized the benefits of joining with others tracing Jewish families from the same ancestral geographical area. In 1990, Marlene Silverman founded *Landsman*, a publication for those researching Jewish roots in the former Russian provinces of Suwalk and Lomza.[4] This is thought of as the start of Jewish genealogical special interest groups (SIGs). *Landsmen* articles focus on resources and vital statistics abstracts from specific communities in the Suwalk-Lomza area. Similar publications are *the Galitzianer* (Galicia), *Kielce-Radom Journal, Stammbaum* (German) and *Etsi* (Sephardic).

The formation of special interest groups (SIGs) has flourished under the aegis of JewishGen which hosts most of them. *Etsi, Landsman* and *Stammbaum* are independent of JewishGen and maintain separate websites (listed below). To locate a special interest group, look under the SIG heading on the JewishGen homepage.

Unlike the JGSs, SIG membership draws from the entire world. Many actively develop indexing and computerization projects, publish online journals and have active discussion group. Membership is free in those hosted by JewishGen. The vibrant culture of sharing information and knowledge and trading resources makes SIG membership indispensable for most Jewish genealogists. Register for any SIG discussion group via the JewishGen home page. If none exists for an area of interest, consider forming one. Many have grown out of "birds-of-a-feather" gatherings at annual genealogy conferences. Periodically check the JewishGen site to look for newly formed groups.

An exception to the SIGs based on place of ancestry is a relative newcomer, RAVSIG, a special interest group for genealogists researching rabbinical roots, accessed from the JewishGen website.

Addresses

Etsi, c/o L. et. P. Abensur, 77 bd Richard-Lenoir, 75011 Paris, France; website: WWW.GEOCITIES.COM/ENCHANTEDFOREST/1321.

GAMT (Généalogie Algerie, Maroc, Tunisie), Maison Marechal A. Juin 29, avenue de Tübingen, 13090 Aix-en-Provence, France; telephone: 4-42-951-949; website: GAMT.FREE.FR.

Gesher Galicia, c/o Leon Gold, P.O. Box 31093, Santa Barbara, California 93130; website: WWW.JEWISHGEN.ORG/GALICIA.

Kielce-Radom special interest group, c/o Debra Braverman, Gracie Station, P.O. Box 127, New York, New York 10028; website: WWW.JEWISHGEN.ORG/KRSIG.

Stammbaum, publication of the Leo Baeck Institute, Center for Jewish History, 15 West 16 Street, New York, New York 10011; e-mail: KFRANKLIN@LBI.CJH.ORG.

Repeat Performances, 2911 Crabapple Lane, Hobart, Indiana 46342; website: WWW.AUDIOTAPES.COM.

Suwalk-Lomza Interest Group, Box 228, 3701 Connecticut Avenue NW, Washington, DC 20008; website: WWW.JEWISHGEN.ORG/SUWALKLOMZA.

Bibliography

Etsi, Revue de Généalogie et d'Histoire Séfarades (Sephardi Genealogical and Historical Review).

The Galitzianer, publication of Gesher Galicia. Available to members only.

Kielce-Radom Journal, publication of Kielce-Radom special interest group.

Landsmen, publication of the Suwalk-Lomza special interest group.

Stammbaum, publication of the Leo Baeck Institute.

Notes

1. Sack, Sallyann Amdur. "Organized Jewish Genealogy: The Early Years." *AVOTAYNU* 13, no. 1 (Spring 1997): 3–5. See also back cover photograph on pg. 68.
2. Blamont, Claudie. "Non-Jewish Genealogical Associations and Seminars in France: Why the Cercle de Généalogie Juive Participates in Their Activities," *AVOTAYNU* 15, no. 3 (Fall 1999): 14–15.
3. Paulin, Gladys Friedman. "Annual Conferences and the Jewish Genealogist." *AVOTAYNU* 15, no. 3 (Fall 1999): 11–13.
4. Silverman, Marlene. "Landslayt Groups as a Complement to Jewish Genealogical Societies." *AVOTAYNU* 6, no. 4 (Winter 1990): 14–15.

Part II

Topical Section

Holocaust Research

by Gary Mokotoff

Every Jewish family with roots in Continental Europe has family members who were murdered in the Holocaust. Those whose family left that part of the world many years ago and who maintain that their ancestors were safe elsewhere have not yet completed their family trees. As researchers go back in time and discover ancestors, they also come forward in time to document the brothers and sisters of these ancestors and their descendants. Only then can they learn how their families were affected by the Holocaust.

Most family members murdered in the Holocaust died without a tombstone or gravesite to mark their passing. In some cases, the fact that they ever existed was eradicated by acts of war or the deliberate acts of the Germans and their collaborators. Placing them on a family tree documents that they once lived; it is a permanent memorial to them. As author Arthur Kurzweil notes in the Preface of this book:

> When the Nazis rounded us up, they took away our names and they gave us numbers. What we (genealogists) are involved with is taking away the numbers and giving them back their names.

The Holocaust has been described as the most documented event in history. Tens of thousands of books depict the circumstances of this great tragedy. Most books present general histories of the events that transpired during this period. Typically these books and documents are of little or no interest to persons researching individuals; few references identify specific persons. The few books and documents that include lists of individuals nevertheless represent a large collection of information about the millions of people affected by the Holocaust.

Documentation during the Holocaust

Germans have earned a centuries-old reputation for meticulous record keeping. The period of the Holocaust is no exception. Three categories of events took place:

- Events with documented information about individuals
- Events that were documented without recording specific names of individuals
- Events for which there was no documentation

Events That Document Individuals. Two types of camps existed: extermination and concentration/labor. With rare exceptions, persons deported to extermination camps were killed immediately. The Germans made no attempt to document these individuals. Examples of extermination camps are Treblinka and Belzec. No records provide the names of the Jews who were deported from the Warsaw Ghetto to Treblinka or from Lwów to Belzec. Persons deported to a concentration camp who were killed immediately upon arrival also were not recorded at the camp.

The exception is prisoners transported from one camp to another. In this case records would exist at time of departure from the concentration camp. For example, records exist of Jews deported from Theresienstadt (a concentration camp) to Treblinka (an extermination camp).

If a person arrived at a concentration camp and survived the selection, records were kept; some records survive. They include the individual's name, place of birth, birth date and identification number. Often they include the names of parents, name of spouse, occupation and street address before deportation. At times when death from disease, starvation and/or abuse did not occur on a massive basis, these deaths were recorded. Sometimes, as in Dachau, executions in the camp were recorded.

Although many documents were destroyed by the Germans in the late days of the war to hide their atrocities, some documents were captured by United States and British liberation forces. These surviving records have been available to the public for many years—in the United States through the National Archives. Examples include registers from Buchenwald, Mauthausen and Dachau concentration camps. Documents captured by the Soviets have been made available only since the collapse of the Soviet Union.

Documents That Record Events, with No Specific Names. This category includes the records of the *Einsatzgruppen* (mobile killing squads) actions, which provide the dates of death for more than one million Jews. After Germany invaded the Soviet Union in 1942 (today's Belarus, Lithuania and Ukraine), these mobile killing squads of the German SS had the responsibility of killing every Jew, gypsy and political dissident in the towns captured by the regular German army. Consequently, their reports provide the death dates for almost all the Jews of the towns. No German records of these events exist that list individuals. Occasionally individuals escaped the mass killings in their native towns and survived additional days until they were caught or died as part of the partisan resistance, but they were a small minority.

Events for Which No Documentation Was Created. No records were created for the following groups:

- Jews sent to extermination camps (as opposed to concentration camps) unless deported from a concentration camp, in which case, deportation lists may exist
- Jews who did not survive the selection at concentration camps because they were considered unsuitable for slave labor—generally, children under 14, adults over age 50 and mothers with children under age 14. These individuals were gassed immediately; however, they may appear on deportation lists.
- Jews who hid and were discovered. Invariably they were shot immediately and no records were kept of their deaths.

The Hall of Names at Yad Vashem in Jerusalem is the repository of Pages of Testimony that identify more than three million victims of the Holocaust.

Deportation Lists

Deportation lists may provide documentation about individuals sent either to extermination or concentration camps. When Jews were sent from one facility to another, the Germans prepared detailed lists of individuals being transferred. The best-known lists are those of Jews deported from France, primarily to Auschwitz. The lists were published under the title *Memorial to the Jews Deported from France*. More than 70,000 individuals are listed with names, nationalities, places of birth and birth dates. The book is organized by the dates the trains left France, making it possible to determine arrival dates at Auschwitz and, consequently, the death dates of individuals who were gassed immediately. Similar memorial books exist for Belgium and Netherlands. Some books list people chronologically by date of deportation. Where that occurs there may be a finding aid to assist in locating a specific individual. For example, an index to *Memorial to the Jews Deported from France* shows which surnames appear on which deportation lists. A partial index to this list is located at the U.S. Holocaust Memorial Museum site at WWW.USHMM.ORG/UIA-CGI/UIA_FORM/FRDEPORT. A complete index is available on microfiche from Avotaynu at WWW.AVOTAYNU.COM/MICROF.HTM.

Documentation after the Holocaust

After World War II, with hundreds of thousands of Jews scattered throughout Europe and millions having been murdered, attempts were made to identify both the living and the dead, so survivors could locate relatives and friends or know the fate of those who perished. Several important types of resources have been developed to help identify the victims and survivors.

Lists of Displaced Persons. Lists of displaced persons were developed as early as 1943, but the burden of collecting information about both survivors and victims was embraced by the International Tracing Service (ITS) of the International Committee of the Red Cross.* This organization still receives thousands of inquiries each year. The ITS holds 47 million index cards with information about specific individuals.

***Yizkor* Books.** After World War II, the remnant of European Jewry published *yizkor* (memorial) books to document and remember the towns and townspeople destroyed in the Holocaust. More than 1,200 have been published, each for an individual town or region. They include articles written by survivors and often provide a great deal of information about specific individuals from the town. A detailed description appears later in this chapter.

Pages of Testimony. In 1955, Yad Vashem* located in Jerusalem, the primary repository of Holocaust documentation, launched an international effort to document each individual murdered in the Holocaust. It asked people with knowledge of these victims to provide Pages of Testimony vouching that the named person was a Holocaust victim. Approximately three million Pages of Testimony are on file at the Hall of Names; half of the six million victims have been documented individually through this manuscript collection. The Hall of Names is their cemetery, and the Pages of Testimony are their tombstones. A detailed description of Pages of Testimony appears later in this chapter.

Lists of Victims. Lists of victims by country, region or camp have been compiled since the war. Best known is the *Gedenkbuch*, a list of information about 128,000 German Jews murdered in the Holocaust, compiled in the 1990s by the then

West German government from records that survived the war. A comparable book exists for Dutch Jews. Some compiled lists are for regions (for example, Hajdu County, Hungary), cities (for example, Frankfurt am Main) and camps (for example, Theresienstadt).

Locating Survivors Today

Historically, Jews have banded together for mutual benefit and protection. International and national Jewish social service organizations, such as the Joint Distribution Committee and the Hebrew Immigrant Aid Society (HIAS), helped Holocaust survivors relocate in countries that accepted refugees after World War II. Most of these organizations kept records of the individuals they helped, and some records are accessible to the public.

When Jews emigrated from Europe around the turn of the century, they formed *landsmanshaftn* societies in their new lands whose membership typically came from specific regions or towns of origin. When Holocaust survivors left Europe, many joined existing societies or created their own new societies. Some of these groups still exist today. Even if they no longer function, many of their records have survived and may provide clues to help locate survivors.

How to Locate Records

To determine the fate of family members who were caught up in the Holocaust, consider the following strategy:

- If you are unfamiliar with the circumstances surrounding the fate of the Jews of the town where the survivors and/ or victims lived before the Holocaust, read a book on the history of the Holocaust that describes events by town. Two useful books are *Ghetto Anthology* and *Encyclopedia of the Holocaust*.
- Determine whether a *yizkor* book exists for the town in which the people of interest lived. Consult the book to see if there is mention of the individuals or family names you are researching. A database that lists all known *yizkor* books can be seen at WWW.JEWISHGEN.ORG/YIZKOR/ DATABASE.HTML.
- If the fate of a Holocaust victim is not known, write to the Hall of Names at Yad Vashem to determine if a Page of Testimony has been submitted for that individual.
- Check the records of the International Tracing Service* for information about survivors and victims, either by writing to ITS using the Foreign Inquiry Location Service of the Red Cross in your country* or by consulting the microfilm copy at Yad Vashem in person (or by hiring someone to do it).
- If searching for a survivor, write a letter to the organizations in various countries that maintain lists of survivors or that assisted survivors in relocating after World War II. A list of such organizations is posted at WWW.AVOTAYNU. COM/HOLOCAUST/.
- Contact a local Holocaust resource center for information about the latest resources found for Holocaust research. If the local facility does not have a book or record known

to be available elsewhere, ask the staff to obtain a copy of the information for the facility's permanent collection or as a loan copy. New acquisitions are constantly being made, and resource sites regularly share information. A list of many Holocaust resource centers is posted at WWW.AHOINFO.ORG/LINKS.HTML#HOLOCCTRS..

- Consider asking for help from a Jewish genealogical society, whose members are researching their families' histories. Because the Holocaust has had such a profound effect on contemporary Jewish families, many members have developed expertise in Holocaust research. (See JEWISH GENEALOGICAL SOCIETIES AND SPECIAL INTEREST GROUPS.)
- If the options are available of either going to or writing to a major resource center, visit in person. Many research sites are conscientious about processing mail inquiries, but the recipient of your request can devote only a limited amount of time to your inquiry. Individuals who go to the facility can spend the hours necessary to peruse secondary sources of information. Browse through the catalogue of the holdings of the facility. Look for information about any of the towns of interest.

Some references may include details about specific individuals that are not obvious in the catalogue description of the work. Cataloguing is an imperfect process that, to a certain extent, relies on the judgment of the cataloguer. An example is Record Group RG-15.019M at the U.S. Holocaust Memorial Museum. Its description of one collection is "Court inquiries about executions and graves in districts, provinces, camps, and ghettos"—19 microfilm reels. The purpose of the court inquiries was to document Nazi atrocities in Poland. The names of victims are given in many cases.

When writing to a research facility about a specific individual or family, provide as much information as possible—but be concise. Limit the letter to facts about the individual, including exact name, date of birth (even if year only or approximate year), place of birth, names of immediate family members and last known residential address. Any information that can uniquely identify the individual from the thousands, if not millions, of pieces of information at the research site is important. Inadequate information will prompt a rejection of your request, which will only delay the research. Picture yourself at the facility trying to do the research. Could you find the information requested given the information you supply?

Yizkor Books

After World War II, many survivors of the Holocaust published books that memorialized the destroyed Jewish communities of Europe. Called *yizkor* books (*yizkor* means "memorial" or "remembrance" in Hebrew), they commemorate the victims as well as the Jewish communities.

To date, more than 1,200 towns have been commemorated in this manner. *Yizkor* books are particularly associated (in descending order of frequency) with the towns of Poland, Germany, Ukraine, Belarus, Hungary, Lithuania, Netherlands, Romania, Slovakia, Austria, Croatia, Czech Republic, France, Greece, Italy, Latvia, Moldova and Serbia. Determine

לעווין יצחק, אסתר גולדע, שיינדל, נחמן, שרגא יהונה.
לאַנדאַ יחיאל ומשפחתו.
לוסטיג לייזער ואשתו, משה, חנה (שלאַנג), אהרן, שרה.
לאַקסמאַן שמואל, רחל לאה, אלכסנדר, אברהם שלום, אלכסנדר, איטא, ישראל מענדל, רבקה רייזעל.
ליפינסקי אליעזר, גיטל, אברהם, פייגע, טויבע.
לעמפער יאסקע.

מ

מאָדאַנעם בצלאל, מענדל ומשפחותיהם.
מאַנדעלאַייל לייבא, ומשפחתו.
מאַרגאלים אבריש ואשתו.
מאַקמאָב יחיאל-טוביה, רחל, דן, משה ומשפחתו, לייבא אשר.
מיינסטער ישראל הערש ועלוול.
מיינסטער הערש-דוד.
מינץ משה יוסף, חנה אטא, דוד, פייגע, ישראל, וועלוול, אליהו, יעקב, אהרן, שרה (קורנבוים), מאַטעלע, פייגעלע, אהרן, ישראל יצחק (לערמאן).
מנחם מאניע ומשפחתו, אסקה פולה.
מענדזולבסקי נתן דוד, חנה ובניהם.
מעפינג יעקב-הערש ומשפחתו, אליעזר.

ו

זואַרדקע אברהם, חנה, יודל, הערש, רבקה, אהרן, יוסף, דינה.
זאַמסאן אברהם, יהושע, יוסף, ישראל, מענדל, רבקה, מרים פערל, אסתר רחל לאה, שיינדל, צפורה, מענדל, יוסף אברהם, אליעזר.
זואַסערמאן יעקב ומשפחתו, יחיאל ומשפחתו.
זואָסערניר מענדל ומשפחתו.
זואָסעריצוג יעקב, צירל, בריך, ומשפחתו, אהרן יונה ומשפחתו.
זואַרשאווסקי שלמה יעקב.
זואַרשאבסקי אריה ומשפחתו.
זואַרשאוער גרשון, שלמה, יעקב, שלמה, יעקב ומשפחותיהם.
זולמאַן אליעזר ומשפחתו.
זולף אהרן ומשפחתו, מאיר.
זואלפאביץ יוסף, צביה.
זוויינבלום הערש דוד, מיכל, אטמקע, משה, שרה, רפאל, משה, שרה, אבא, אסתר, רבקה, פראדל, פייגע, ישראל, לייבא הערש, ומשפחותיהם.
זוויסבאַרד לוי ומשפחתו.
זוישנוע וואלף ומשפחתו.
זויניצקי ישעיהו ומשפחתו, הענער ומשפחתו.

ז

Portion of the necrology in the yizkor book for Garwolin, Poland, lists Jewish town residents murdered in the Holocaust.

whether your town has such a book by searching on the Internet at WWW.JEWISHGEN.ORG/YIZKOR/DATABASE.HTML.

Although each *yizkor* book was written independently, they share a basic common structure. The first section describes the history of the Jewish community of the town from its inception—sometimes hundreds of years of history—to the events of the Holocaust. This history invariably describes the destruction of all Jewish religious property (synagogues, cemeteries, etc.) and the murder or deportation to concentration or extermination camps of the Jewish population. A map shows the Jewish section of the town, identifying where the synagogue(s), religious school(s) and other Jewish landmarks once stood. For the researcher, this overview provides valuable material about the Jewish communal life of the town. For researchers who want to identify relatives who once lived in the town, pictures of religious, social and welfare organizations may offer clues. The articles and captions associated with the pictures often identify individuals.

The next section consists of personal remembrances of survivors about their individual families. They offer a wealth of information about family members, including names, relationships, ages and sometimes birth dates. Where survivors knew the fate of family members, this may also be included.

The next section often describes families with no survivors. These accounts were contributed by neighbors or friends who had known the family. The articles are brief—one- or two-paragraph descriptions headed by the names of the father and mother, as well as the names of the children. Next may come a necrology—a list of all the victims from the town. The final section includes names and addresses of survivors from the town, usually organized by country of relocation.

Most *yizkor* books are written in Hebrew and Yiddish, although a number have sections in English. *Yizkor* books are a potential link to the present—the articles were written by persons who may still be alive. If not, their children may be alive and able to provide information about their family. If a list of survivors is printed in the book or an address of the society that published the book is given, consider writing to them. First note the copyright year of the publication. If it was pub-

lished decades ago, there is less likelihood that the person is alive or lives currently at the address given.

Telephone books of other countries often are available at major local libraries and foreign consulates. They are also available on the Internet at WWW.INFOBEL.COM/TELDIR. Another alternative is to contact the nearest consulate or embassy for the country of interest. Consulates and embassies have on hand telephone books of the major cities in their country.

The largest collections of *yizkor* books are held at Yad Vashem* in Jerusalem, YIVO Institute for Jewish Research* in New York, the Library of Congress* in Washington, D.C., UCLA Library in Los Angeles and the Jewish Public Library* in Montreal. Substantial collections exist in large public and university libraries throughout the world, as well as in Holocaust research centers.

It is extremely difficult to purchase *yizkor* books. All but the most recently published are out of print, and it is unusual for one to come on the market. When it does, usually a Holocaust survivor has died and the family has given the books to a book wholesaler. Check with dealers in used Jewish books. The National Yiddish Book Center has announced plans to reprint most *yizkor* books. Watch their Internet site at www. YUUDISHBOOKCENTER.ORG. Two companies have developed a reputation as sellers of *yizkor* books; both are located in Israel—both publish catalogues: J. Robinson & Co. Booksellers; 26 Nachlat Benjamin Street; Tel Aviv. Also, Chaim Dzialowski; P.O. Box 6413; 91063 Jerusalem.

JewishGen *Yizkor* Book Project. JewishGen has a project devoted to extracting information from *yizkor* books and making the information available on the Internet. The project is located at WWW.JEWISHGEN.ORG/YIZKOR. There are many subprojects associated with the group. They can all be linked from the home site.

- Translations. Most *yizkor* books are written in Hebrew and Yiddish. The project has translated portions of or complete books. A list is made available.
- Necrology index. More than 150,000 names have been extracted from *yizkor* books and can be searched.

- Database of towns. All known *yizkor* books and the towns/ locales they reference are identified in a searchable database.
- Infofiles exist about libraries that hold large collections of *yizkor* books, retail establishments that see these books and persons who will help in translations.
- The group has its own Discussion Group to which messages can be posted.

Pages of Testimony

The major archives and documentation center for the Holocaust is Yad Vashem in Jerusalem, Israel. Since 1955, Yad Vashem has been attempting to document every one of the six million Jews murdered in the Holocaust in a manuscript collection called Pages of Testimony. To date, more than three million victims have been documented. Persons have been requested to come forward and submit, on a preprinted form, information about the victim, including name; place and year of birth; place, date and circumstances of death; occupation; names of mother, father and spouse; and, in some cases, names and ages of children. Each submitter is required to sign this Page of Testimony and to show his or her name, address and relationship to deceased. By submitting this form, the person testifies that he or she knew of the victim and the circumstances surrounding his or her death. The majority of the submitters are relatives of the deceased. Most Pages of Testimony were submitted in the 1950s when the project started. Most have been submitted by Israelis and, therefore, are written in Hebrew. In recent years, there has been an effort to increase the size of the collection significantly. Holocaust survivors are encouraged to contribute Pages now; otherwise, information that only they can provide will be lost to future generations. The emigration of a large number of Jews from the former Soviet Union has also provided an opportunity to add significantly to the collection.

Pages of Testimony serve two valuable functions: They provide detailed information about the Holocaust victim, and they may offer a link to the present—to a person who either knew the victim or was familiar with the victim's fate. This link becomes weaker as the years pass, because many of the Pages of Testimony were completed in the late 1950s, and many of submitters no longer are living. It may be necessary to locate descendants of the submitters, who may be more difficult to track down and whose knowledge of the victims may be less detailed.

The Pages of Testimony currently are available only at the Hall of Names at Yad Vashem, although there are plans to place them on the Internet. Plans call for making them on the Internet in 2004. They can be accessed in person or by mail inquiry. In response to a mail inquiry, Yad Vashem will send the documents and an invoice; there is no need to prepay. In a departure from the norm, it is usually better to order copies by mail rather than in person. Write to Hall of Names, Yad Vashem, P.O. Box 3477, 91034 Jerusalem, Israel, or e-mail requests to NAMES.RESEARCH@YADVASHEM.ORG.IL. The Hall of Names accepts generic searches, such as "all persons named Mokotow" or "all persons named Mokotow from Garwolin,"

Index card at the International Tracing Service documents the death of Berek (Bernard) Mokotow of Frankfurt am Main, who was born in Warsaw and died at Dachau.

but only for surnames for which they have fewer than 300 documents. The cost averages less than $2.00 per document, but rates may change based on economic conditions, and rules for quality of service may change as demand rises. If you elect to do research in person, check hours of operation before you go.

International Tracing Service

Immediately after World War II, when refugees were scattered throughout Europe, collection points of information about both survivors and victims evolved into what became the International Tracing Service (ITS) of the International Committee of the Red Cross. The ITS endeavored to identify, in an orderly manner, the fate of the millions of persons, both Jewish and non-Jewish, who were displaced or killed during World War II. To this day, data is still being discovered and accumulated by ITS.

The ITS maintains a master index of information. It was compiled in the following manner. For each document they received that contained the names of individuals, they catalogued the document and created an index card for every individual named on the document. If it was a list of persons who died in Dachau during a certain time period and there were 317 persons names, 317 index cards were created extracting the information on the document about each individual (Such as date of birth, place of residence and date of death) and a source citation showing where the information came from. By 1955, ITS had created more than 45 million index cards relating to more than 14 million individuals.

If the person was a survivor, an index card may exist from the time when the individual was in a refugee camp. The card would show his name, age, place of birth, and possibly names of parents and where the person was at the time the information was recorded. When a refugee was relocated, another card would indicate the destination. From information acquired from death lists in cities and concentration camps, the index card would list the name of the individual, date of birth, place of birth, place of death and circumstances of death.

Part of the collection of records about Buchenwald concentration camp in the archives of the International Tracing Service in Arolsen, Germany.

There are also index cards created from inquiries by persons trying to determine the fate of friends or family.

This information can be accessed three ways, each with its own advantages and disadvantages: Write to the ITS directly; use the Foreign Location Inquiry Service of the Red Cross in your country; use copies of ITS records located in the archives of Yad Vashem.

Write Directly to ITS. Address your inquiry to International Tracing Service, Grosse Allee 5–9, 34444 Arolsen, Germany. The ITS will search only for specific individuals. Provide as much information as possible about the person. You must give the name of the individual, either the place of birth or town before the war, and an approximate age. If the name is reasonably unique, this should be sufficient for the ITS to perform the search. If the name is common, provide additional information to identify the individual definitively. One major disadvantage of accessing ITS records by writing to them directly is that it may take years before they reply.

Write to the Red Cross in Your Country. A faster way of dealing with the ITS is through the Red Cross in your country. In the United States and many other countries, the local Red Cross office should be familiar with the procedure to make inquiries to the International Tracing Service.

In 1990, the United States American Red Cross (ARC) made special arrangements with ITS to act as an intermediary. The advantages of working through ARC is that it will process

forms immediately and reject them if insufficient information is provided about the person sought. It may take as long as six months to get a comparable rejection letter for a request sent directly to ITS. The response time from ITS to ARC is faster because ARC constantly monitors its open inquiries. Another advantage is that ARC is part of an international network of Red Cross organizations and will contact its counterpart in another country if evidence indicates a survivor went to that country. For general information about this service, contact the local Red Cross chapter in your area. If the local chapter claims they cannot process the inquiry, contact the national office for advice. Holocaust and War Victims Tracing Center; 4700 Mount Hope Drive, Baltimore, MD 21215-3231; telephone: (410) 764-5311; fax: (410) 764-4638; website: www. REDCROSS.ORG/ SERVICES/INTL/HOLOTRACE/.

Yad Vashem Archives. A third way to access the information is by using the duplicate copy of much of the ITS information located in the Yad Vashem archives in Jerusalem. The facility is open to the public. If a personal visit is not feasible, hire a professional researcher. The major advantage of using the Yad Vashem archives is time; the records can be searched within weeks, if not days. A second important advantage is that it is possible to search for all individuals with a given last name, something that cannot be done via either of the other two methods. The major disadvantage is that the records constitute the ITS collection as of the mid-1950s. With access to records held by formerly communist countries now easing, the ITS has acquired additional Holocaust records. Some of this new information is available at Yad Vashem, but it is not collated with the earlier ITS records. A list of Israelis who conduct this type of research is available at the Association of Professional Genealogists at WWW.APGEN.ORG .

Recommendation: Check the ITS records at Yad Vashem first. If they do not provide sufficient information, then take the more time-consuming approach of using the American Red Cross to check the complete records of ITS .

Internet Sites

American Red Cross Holocaust and War Crimes Tracing and Information Center. WWW.REDCROSS.ORG/SERVICES/INTL/HOLOTRACE/. Expedites record searches at the International Tracing Service in Arolsen, Germany.

Cybrary of the Holocaust HTTP://REMEMBER.ORG. Includes many links to Holocaust-related sites.

List of Holocaust Resource Centers. HTTP://TASKFORCE.USHMM.ORG. Click on link "Directory of Organizations."

JewishGen Infiles about the Holocaust. WWW.JEWISHGEN.ORG/INFOFILES/#HOLOCAUST.

JewishGen *Yizkor* Book Project. WWW.JEWISHGEN.ORG/YIZKOR.

Nizkor Project. WWW.NIZKOR.ORG/. Background information about the Holocaust.

U.S. Holocaust Memorial Museum. WWW.USHMM.ORG/. Includes a search engine to locate record groups or books with their library and archives collection. ·

Yad Vashem. WWW.YAD-VASHEM.ORG.IL/. Currently has no information on the Internet about individuals but it is planned. A good starting point to do research at the Internet site is WWW.YADVASHEM.ORG.IL/ RESEARCH_PUBLICATIONS/INDEX_PUBLICATION.HTML. It provides links to research and publications at Yad Vashem.

Bibliography

Mokotoff, Gary. *How to Document Victims and Locate Survivors of the Holocaust.* Teaneck, N.J.: Avotaynu, 1995. Offers a step-by-step strategy for locating records of victims and survivors. Key portions of the book are available on the Internet at WWW. AVOTAYNU.COM/HOLOCAUST.

Bibliographies of the Holocaust

Edelheit, Abraham J., and Hershel Edelheit. *Bibliography on Holocaust Literature*, 2 vols. Boulder, Colorado: Westview Press, 1986.

Gar, Joseph. *Bibliography of Articles on the Catastrophe and Heroism in Yiddish Periodicals*, 3 vols. New York: Yad Vashem/YIVO, 1969.

Robinson, Jacob, and Philip Friedman. *Guide to Jewish History Under Nazi Impact.* New York: Martin Press, 1960.

Szonyi, David. *The Holocaust: An Annotated Bibliography and Resource Guide.* New York: Ktav, 1985.

Books About the Holocaust

Listed below are books about the Holocaust that contain no information about individuals, but may provide useful background material about the circumstances involving individuals.

Pinkassim HaKehillot (Encyclopedia of towns). [Hebrew] Jerusalem: Yad Vashem. Multi-volume history of the Jewish communities of Central and Eastern Europe. Not all areas are covered, although additional volumes are planned.

Guide to Unpublished Materials of the Holocaust Period. Jerusalem: Hebrew University of Jerusalem and Yad Vashem, 1975–81. Describes the archival collection of Yad Vashem on a town-by-town, camp-by-camp basis.

Arad, Yizhak. *Einsatzgruppen Reports.* Jerusalem: Yad Vashem. Details, day by day, town by town, the actions of the German killing squads throughout Belarus, Lithuania and Ukraine.

Czech, Danuta. *Auschwitz Chronicle 1939–1945.* New York: Henry Holt, 1990. Documents day-by-day events at Auschwitz, identifying incoming and outgoing transports, individual deaths and escapes.

Friedlander, Henry, and Sybil Milton. *Archives of the Holocaust.* New York: Garland. Lists archives holding Holocaust-related material.

Gutman, Israel. *Encyclopedia of the Holocaust*, 4 vols. New York: MacMillan, 1990. Describes events, noted individuals and towns.

Hilberg, Raoul. *Destruction of European Jewry.* New York: Holmes & Meier, 1985. Considered one of the best books on the history of the Holocaust.

Mogilanski, Roman. *Ghetto Anthology.* Los Angeles: American Congress of Jews from Poland and Survivors of Concentration Camps, 1985. Describes events at more than 600 ghettos and concentration camps.

Books Containing Lists of Jews Murdered in the Holocaust

Gedenkbuch. Frankfurt/Main: Johannes Weisbecker, 1986. Lists 128,000 German Jews murdered in the Holocaust. Includes date of birth, place of deportation and, in some cases, date and place of death.

Debski, Jerzy. *Sterbebuecher von Auschwitz (Death books from Auschwitz).* [German] Munich: K.G. Saur, 1995. Identifies about 100,000 persons listed in Auschwitz death books.

Klarsfeld, Serge. *Memorial to the Jews Deported from France: 1942–1944.* New York: Beate Klarsfeld Foundation, 1983. Lists some 70,000 Jews transported by train from France, primarily to Auschwitz. Names grouped by convoy (day of deportation). Often shows date and place of birth.

Steinberg, Maxine, and Serge Klarsfeld. *Memorial de la Deportation des Juifs de Belgique (Memorial to the Jews deported from Belgium).* New York: Beate Klarsfeld Foundation, 1982.

Lijst van Nederlandee jooden die gestorven zijn gedurende de tweede wereld oorlog (List of Dutch Jews, prisoners and missing persons who died in concentration camps during World War II).

Steinhauser, Mary. *Totenbuch Theresienstadt.* [German] Vienna: Vertriebsgesellschaft, 1987. Alphabetical list of persons who died in the Theresienstadt concentration camp.

Books on How to Locate People

Ferraro, Eugene. *You Can Find Anyone!* Santa Ana, Calif.: Marathon Press, 1986.

Hoyer, Frederick Charles, Jr., and John D. McCann. *Find Them Fast, Find Them Now! The Handbook for Finding Missing Persons.* Secaucus, N.J.: Citadel Press, 1988.

Internet

by Gary Mokotoff

The information in this chapter is not intended to describe the thousands of resources available on the Internet for Jewish genealogy. Each chapter of this book contains material regarding the specific Internet resources available for the topic covered. Here, the intention is to present an overview of the Internet for those who are not familiar with its capability.

In recent years, the Internet has impacted enormously our society—and genealogical research. Before the Internet, communication between researchers and their relatives or other genealogists, repositories containing records, and other resources was accomplished in days, weeks or months. Now the Internet has accelerated responses to days, hours and even minutes.

How Does the Internet Work?

In its simplest sense, the Internet allows a computer to access data located on any other computer in the world that grants it access. Why do institutions and/or corporations permit the public to access their computers? Corporations have something to sell or inform. Institutions have information to share.

To access other computers, the researcher's computer must be attached to a telephone or cable television line. This is the method for connecting to the Internet. A modem serves to interface between the computer and the Internet. Special software and hardware, far more expensive than an individual can afford, are necessary to connect to the Internet. A company called an Internet Service Provider (ISP) will, for a fee, serve as an intermediary between the computer and the Internet. The best-known ISP is America Online (AOL). In summary, the computer is connected to a modem, which is connected to the telephone or cable company, which connects to the ISP, which connects to the Internet.

A researcher can connect to a computer anywhere in the world by specifying its Universal Resource Locator (URL) address. Most URLS have the structure WWW.DOMAINNAME.COM. A URL is analogous to a telephone number. Just as telephoning 201-387-7200 connects the caller to Avotaynu's offices, specifying WWW.AVOTAYNU.COM on the Internet connects a person to Avotaynu's Internet site.

Search Engines

The Internet is the world's greatest encyclopedia. Virtually every topic of interest is covered on some web page located somewhere in the world. The only requirement for access is that a researcher know where to find the information.

That is the function of search engines. Search engines are databases that scour the billions of web pages on the Internet and index them, that is, determine their content. A researcher uses a search engine by specifying the "key-words" that identify the information sought. For example, if someone wants a recipe for tuna fish salad, using the keywords "tuna fish salad recipe" will cause the search engine to look into its database and identify all web sites that have the words "tuna" and "fish" and "salad" and "recipe." Tens of thousands of Internet sites may include these words. It is the skill of a search engine to locate those web sites that most likely contain the exact information you want.

Google, at WWW.GOOGLE.COM, is one of the most popular search engines because of its seemingly uncanny ability to locate the exact web sites that satisfy researcher's requests. Here is a genealogical example of how to locate Internet sites that contain useful information.

To research the ancestral town of Lublin, Poland, go to WWW.GOOGLE.COM to find information valuable for genealogical research on the Internet. In the box provided, type the keyword "Lublin," and press the "Google Search" button. Google now searches its database for all web sites relevant to "Lublin" and displays the first several sites that match the keyword. It also states (toward the right of the screen) that 282,000 sites on the Internet have information relevant to "Lublin."

Examination of the results shows that many sites selected by Google are in the Polish language. Sites in English can be requested by clicking the message "Would you prefer to search for English results only?" Click the message; now only sites written in English are displayed. The results demonstrate that there are sites that describe weather conditions in Lublin, hotel accommodations, and even information about people whose surnames are Lublin.

To limit the search further, use the keywords "Lublin Poland genealogy." Now the results come closer to identifying Internet sites of interest to genealogical research. Many sites still appear to be of little value; therefore, add another keyword: "Jewish." Using "Lublin Poland genealogy Jewish" limits the search to Internet sites that are likely to be of greatest value to your research.

Advanced Google Features

Google is a popular search engine because a number of advanced features assist in improving even more the likelihood of finding Internet sites of value to a search. These include Advanced Search, Graphics Search and others.

Advanced Search. Return to WWW.GOOGLE.COM. Click the link to the right of the screen that states "Advanced Search." This feature opens a variety of advanced options to limit the keywords used. One useful function is the "Domain" feature which can include/exclude Internet sites from a specific country. In the example above, in which the keyword "Lublin" identified many sites in Polish, all emanating from Poland, these sites can be excluded by using the Domain line of the Advanced Search. Change the drop-down box from "Only" to

Using the Google search engine to search for web sites that have information about "Lublin Poland genealogy Jewish" locates 735 sites that might have information of value.

"Don't"; in the box on the same line, type the characters ".pl" (every country is assigned a two-character code; Poland's is "pl"). This will exclude in the search any Internet site that has ".pl" as part of its URL.

There are other Advanced Search options noted on the page. Read them and try those that may be of use.

Graphics. Google can select graphics (pictures) appropriate to the keywords selected. Return to WWW.GOGGLE.COM. Above the box for the keywords is the word "Graphics." Click the word "Graphics", type in keywords (for example, "Lublin"), and then click "Google Search." Instead of identifying Internet sites that have information about Lublin, Google identifies and displays graphics associated with web sites about Lublin. Double click any of the graphics, and Google displays the web site that includes the graphic. Right click on the graphic at the web site, and the image can be saved in the researcher's computer. This feature can be very useful, for example, to find maps. Use the keywords "Warsaw maps," and the search engine identifies sites that have maps of Warsaw.

Services and Tools. Go back to www.GOOGLE.COM. Click the link to "Services and Tools." A variety of other Google features may be of value. One link, Google Labs, describes experimental improvements to the Google system. For example, one feature limits searches to glossaries on the Internet. This feature is not that valuable because my personal experience

has been that including the word "glossary" as a keyword invariably identifies sites that provide definitions of terms. For example, to determine the meaning of the Hebrew word *yichus*, use the main Google search engine with the keywords "yichus glossary."

Databases

The term "database" describes a collection of information about a specific subject. A telephone book is a database of names, addresses and telephone numbers of residences and/ or businesses in a specific geographical area. When a family plans a wedding or bar mitzvah celebration, they develop a database of persons who will be invited to attend the event. Placing a database in a computer and making the information accessible on the Internet means that any person in the world can use the information that you want to share.

Ideally, the information in a database can be accessed in a variety of ways in contrast with a printed telephone book which can be accessed only in one way: alphabetical order. It would be valuable if the entries in a telephone book also were accessible by address. For example, if the correct spelling of a person's name is not known, but the street address is, the telephone number can be retrieved.

Clearly, many sequences in a printed telephone book are impractical. If the phone book data existed in a computer, the ability to retrieve the information in all the manners de-

Searching for Surname SPIEGELMAN

Number of hits: 36				
Surname	Town	Country	Last Updated	Researcher (JGFF Code)
Spiegelman	Belgorod Dnestrovskiy	Ukraine	Before 1997	
Spiegelman	Ovidiopol	Ukraine	Before 1997	
Spiegelman	Tashkent	Uzbekistan	4 Dec 1998	
Spiegelman	Lodz	Poland	Before 1997	
Spiegelman	Lodz	Poland	Before 1997	
Spiegelman	Mordy	Poland	Before 1997	
Spiegelman	Warszawa	Poland	Before 1997	
Spiegelman	Siedlce	Poland	Before 1997	
Spiegelman	Ternopol	Ukraine	Before 1997	

The JewishGen Family Finder is a database of more than 300,000 records containing the ancestral surnames and towns being researched by more than 65,000 researchers worldwide. This illustration shows a search for persons researching the surname "Spiegelman." The identifying information about the researcher has been blanked out for privacy reasons.

scribed above becomes very practical. Consequently, it is not uncommon for a computerized database on the Internet to have the capability of retrieving information in a variety of sequences.

An example is the JewishGen Family Finder (JGFF) located at WWW.JEWISHGEN.ORG/JGFF. JGFF is a database of ancestral surnames and towns researched by tens of thousands of Jewish genealogists throughout the world. The content of each entry in the database is the surname, town name, country, name/address of the submitter and submitter identification number. Information can be retrieved from JGFF in a variety of sequences. A list can be requested of all persons researching a specific town or of a specific surname. Because there are many spelling variants of many surnames, the information can be retrieved by a phonetic match (called soundexing). Since submitters may wish to update their contribution to JGFF, a special section of the system makes it possible to retrieve information by submitter control number. Because only the submitter should be able to edit his/her own data, a password is required to gain access to the information.

The ability to access databases from a home computer is one of the most significant benefits the Internet has made to genealogy. Prior to the advent of the Internet, the index to the passengers arriving at Ellis Island from 1892 to 1924 was accessible only on microfilm at selected facilities within the United States. Now it is accessible worldwide at WWW.ELLISISLAND.ORG. Prior to the Internet, the JGFF was distributed two or three times a year as a computer printout to the (then) 50 Jewish genealogical societies throughout the world. To use the database, it was necessary to attend a monthly meeting of a society.

E-mail

This Internet feature has become so commonplace in the past ten years that it requires little description. Electronic mail—that is, e-mail—is the ability to send a message from one computer to another through the Internet. Its principal advantage over postal mail is that delivery of the message is accomplished in seconds. A second advantage is cost. A fixed monthly charge for use of the Internet includes unlimited e-mail.

Discussion Groups/News Groups/ Mailing Lists/Bulletin Boards

E-mail enables an individual to send a message to one recipient or, by adding many addresses, to multiple recipients. Discussion groups, news groups, mailing lists and bulletin boards are terms for the same concept, a variant of e-mail in which a single e-mail message is sent to many recipients. One of the important features of e-mail for genealogical research is the ability to communicate research needs and/or announce a new discovery to many genealogists. A mechanism on the

Internet allows e-mail to be sent to one location and the message then to be broadcast automatically to many people. This mechanism is called discussion groups or one of the other names used above.

The most popular mailing list for Jewish genealogists is the JewishGen Discussion Group. A message sent to the e-mail address JEWISHGEN@LYRIS.JEWISHGEN.ORG is re-sent to more than 5,000 individuals throughout the world, usually within 24 hours. Who receives these messages? Those persons who have indicated an interest and have subscribed to the JewishGen mailing list. Find information on how to subscribe to the JewishGen Discussion Group at WWW.JEWISHGEN.ORG/JEWISHGEN/DISCUSSIONGROUP.HTM

Discussion groups can be subscribed to in one of two modes: digest or mail. Digest mode accumulates the messages sent to the discussion group, and all messages are sent as in a single e-mail once a day. Mail mode sends messages received by the Discussion Group to the subscriber immediately. Always request digest mode. It is not unusual for discussion groups to receive dozens of messages per day. In mail mode, the receiver's e-mail in box can be flooded with e-mail.

Discussion groups may serve purposes that interest only a limited number of people. Many Jewish genealogical Special Interest Groups (SIGs) have their own discussion groups. Information on how to subscribe to these groups can be found at WWW.JEWISHGEN.ORG/LISTSERV/SIGS.HTM.

E-zines

E-mail magazines or e-zines are a variant of discussion groups. You can subscribe to the group but only the creator of the e-zine can post information. Avotaynu publishes the Jewish genealogy e-zine called *Nu? What's New?* In early 2004 there were 6,500 subscribers. To subscribe, go to the Avotaynu home page at WWW.AVOTAYNU.COM.

Ancestry.com's e-zine is called *Ancestry Daily News* with more than 1.5 million subscribers. Subscribe at WWW.ANCESTRY.COM/LEARN.

Instant Messaging and Chat Rooms

The transmission of e-mail is almost instantaneous. It is so fast, it is possible to have a dialogue with the recipient. E-mail can be sent to a person, and that person can respond in less than a minute. The process can continue back and forth. There is a method of carrying on this discussion in a more practical manner. It is called Instant Messaging (IM). Of what value is this feature to genealogical research? Sometimes a discussion between two researchers requires a dialogue where a message begs an immediate response and the response suggests a return message. That is, there should be a dialogue between the individuals.

The IM feature comes free with every new computer, or it can be downloaded at WWW.AIM.COM. A person assigns himself or herself a unique nickname; unique to any of the millions of nicknames created by people already using Instant Messenger. To communicate with someone, that individual's nickname must be determined, and, at a prearranged time, both parties

sign on to Instant Messenger. By typing a message to the individual (by nickname), the message is sent and received instantly. That individual responds immediately, and what ensues is a "chat session."

The IM system permits maintaining "buddy lists," lists of nicknames of people who subscribe to the IM system. When a person signs on to Instant Messenger, the system informs the person whether anyone on the buddy list is online.

Instant Messaging also enables multiple individuals to communicate with one another simultaneously in "chat rooms." IM providers have "rooms" in which any number of individuals can "enter" and chat together. The rooms are dedicated to specific topics (such as genealogy). Alternately, a group of individuals can start a new chat room and limit entry only to people who have a predetermined password.

This method of communicating has become so popular that a new word has entered the language, "IMing," which means "sending an Instant Message."

Fee-for-Service Sites

Access to databases is not necessarily free. Commercial ventures have invested millions of dollars in developing Internet databases, and they recover their costs and generate profits by charging for access to their sites. The best-known genealogy company that offers fee-for-service databases is Ancestry.com, located at WWW.ANCESTRY.COM. Ancestry.com claims that their index contains more than two billion entries. Almost all its records are American plus some English databases. The database include U.S. censuses (including 1920 and 1930), Social Security Death Index, numerous vital records indexes, telephone directories, Civil War and World War I records, various immigration lists (but not Ellis Island), and newspaper and biographical indexes.

Ancestry.com is a fee-for-service site containing more than two billion records. Pictured above is a search for information about any person named "Spiegelman."

Another fee-for-service offering, made by a company called ProQuest, offers online services only to libraries and other institutions, not to individuals. Databases of interest to genealogists include the 1900 and 1910 censuses and an index and copies of all issues of *The New York Times*. Contact your local library to determine if they use ProQuest's services. If so, request that they subscribe to the company's genealogy databases.

Some government agencies charge to use their online databases to defray the cost of developing and maintaining the systems. The Hamburg (Germany) State Archives has indexed names of emigrants from the Port of Hamburg for most of the period 1890B1910. Access to the index is free, but a fee is charged for abstracts of the information contained on the ships manifests. The index is located at www.hamburg.de/fhh/behoerden/staatsarchiv/link_to_your_roots/english/index.htm. Great Britain's Public Records office placed an index to the 1901 census of England and Wales on the Internet at www.pro.gov.uk. To search the name index of more than 32 million individuals is free, but to receive an image download, a fee is imposed. The fee schedule is explained at the site. An account can be established with a credit or debit card.

Jewish Genealogy Link Sites

Some Internet sites' sole function is to provide links to other Internet sites by category. The most famous genealogy (Jewish and non-Jewish) link site is Cyndi's List at www.cyndislist.com. In early 2004, it contained more than 200,000 links to sites of interest to genealogists worldwide. Because Cyndi's List is so comprehensive, it is organized by categories and subcategories. Jewish genealogical links can be found at www.cyndislist.com/jewish.htm. That web page further breaks down Jewish genealogy links into General Resource Sites; History & Culture; The Holocaust; Language & Names; Libraries; Archives & Museums; Locality Specific; Mailing Lists, Newsgroups & Chat; Military; Newspapers; People & Families; Professional Researchers, Volunteers & Other Research Services; Publications, Software & Supplies; Queries, Message Boards & Surname Lists; Records: Census, Cemeteries, Land, Obituaries, Personal, Taxes and Vital; and Societies & Groups

Other sites that offer links to sites of interest to Jewish genealogists include:

- Louis Kessler's site. http://www.lkessler.com
- Jewish Web Index. http://www.jewishwebindex.com
- Jewish Genealogy Links. http://jewish.genealogy.org
- Jewish Roots Ring. http://pw1.netcom.com/~barrison/jewgenwebring.html

Family Histories on the Internet

Many genealogists have published their family trees on the Internet. The trees can be found easily using the Google search engine with "<family name> genealogy tree" as keywords. Some of these sites merely are family trees; others contain complete family histories, including biographies.

Bibliography

Arons, Ron. "Using CD-ROM Databases and the Internet to Research England from Afar" *AVOTAYNU* 16, no. 1 (Spring 2000)

Howells, Cyndi. *Cyndi's List: A Comprehensive List of 70,000 Genealogy Sites on the Internet*. Baltimore: Genealogical Publishing, 2001.

———. *Netting Your Ancestors: Genealogical Research on the Internet*. Baltimore: Genealogical Publishing, 2001.

Kent, Peter. *The Complete Idiot's Guide to the Internet: Seventh Edition*. Alpha Books, 2001.

Luft, Edward David. "Internet Subscription Databases for Genealogical Research." *AVOTAYNU* 18, no. 3 (Fall 2002).

Mokotoff, Gary. "Internet for Greenhorns." *AVOTAYNU* 12, no. 3 (Fall 1996).

———. "Searching for the Descendants of Zelig Ackermann." *AVOTAYNU* 18, no. 1 (Spring 2002).

Savada, Elias. "Only a Mouse Click Away: Using the Internet to Build Your Family Tree." *AVOTAYNU* 16, no. 4 (Winter 2000).

Modern Jewish Migrations

by Sallyann Amdur Sack and Professor Aubrey Newman

Knowledge of the world in which our ancestors lived is essential to any successful genealogical search. It helps us know what information may exist that can tell us about our families; what records were created; why, when, where, and by whom they were created—and where they should be sought today. We look at the world of our forebears both from the viewpoint of the external forces impinging on them—the social, political, cultural, and religious events—and from the perspective of actions our ancestors initiated themselves.

In the category of actions initiated by our ancestors, migration stands out among the most important. Most Jews today do not live where their families lived 150 years ago. Nor for that matter did our 19th-century ancestors live where their ancestors had lived a century earlier. Since the great upheavals of the 17th century caused by the Chmielniki massacres of 1648–49 and the Thirty Years War, Jews have moved continuously. Knowledge of the major migratory patterns helps us know where to look for our ancestors and for the records of them along their travels. At the same time, it must be emphasized that in the great majority of cases the decision to migrate was an individual one; tens of thousands of individuals may have been on the move at any time, but these represented tens of thousands of individual decisions.

Ashkenazi Jewry

Until the mid-17th century, the overall migratory pattern of European Jewry had been from west to east, as the majority of Jews had moved first from southern and western Europe into German-speaking lands and then onward into the Polish-Lithuanian Commonwealth. The trend began to reverse somewhat after the upheavals already mentioned, but well into the 20th century, most of European Jewry lived in Central and (especially) Eastern Europe.

18th-Century Migration within Europe. By the 18th century, most European Jews lived in Eastern Europe where the largest country was the commonwealth of Poland and the Grand Duchy of Lithuania. Because of the Chmielniki massacres and the Great Northern War between Sweden and her Baltic neighbors (which did not end until 1721), the Jewish populations of Poland and Ukraine were unsettled and on the move as the 18th century began. Many settled in northwestern Lithuania, and by the beginning of the 18th century, the Jews were concentrated primarily in the cities of Brisk (today Brest Litovsk), Grodno, Pinsk, and Vilna. When they arrived, they encountered large settlements of German artisans who had organized themselves into trade guilds closed to Jews who practiced the same trades.

Augustus II Sigismund, the duke of Saxony, had been elected to the throne of the Polish-Lithuanian Commonwealth in 1697. His son August III (1733–64) confirmed the ancient Charter of Privileges granted the Jews by the Grand Duke of Lithuania in 1388, but he showed little interest in his Polish-Lithuanian kingdom and this indifference brought about the destabilization of the realm.

Toward the end of the reign of Augustus III, the Lithuanian magnates (those nobles who controlled huge areas of land and private towns dispersed over the entire Polish Commonwealth, representing the bulk of the territory of the state), began thinking about Lithuanian independence and secession from the Polish Commonwealth. The magnates, realizing the economic value of the Jews, invited them to settle on their estates and to serve as equals in the private militias of the nobles. In some instances, the landowners established villages and helped to create cottage industries for the Jews. Most influential was Antoni Tyzenhauz who became treasurer of the court and administrator of the royal estates (1765–80). The movement of Jews onto the large estates was particularly due to his initiative. Tyzenhauz especially encouraged the distilling industry which was almost exclusively in the hands of the Jews. The *kretchmers* served as wayside inns for the Jewish carriers of agricultural produce who plied the export/import trade between Russia and Germany at this time. Kretchmers were also the main centers of liquor distillation and the manufacturers were assisted by the carriers in exporting the liquor manufactured in the distilleries. The profitability of the distilleries was so great that kretchmers—operated by Jews—began to spring up on all of the magnate estates, encouraged by the landowners. For this reason, many Eastern European Jews lived in outlying rural areas during the 18th century.

19th-Century Migration Within Europe. Concomitant with the Industrial Revolution, people throughout Europe—including Jews—moved from the country to the city. Since Jews—with rare exceptions, such as eastern Hungary—were not farmers, the usual Jewish movement was from small market towns to larger cities.

In Russia the Jews generally were not permitted to move out of the Pale of Settlement (that area of the Russian Empire to which Jews had been restricted by Catherine the Great). The Russian Revolution of 1918 abolished the Pale of Settlement [see RUSSIAN EMPIRE], after which Jews flocked to the major cities of the former empire, Moscow, Odessa and Saint Petersburg. Lithuanian Jews moved to Kovno, Vilna, Riga and Dvinsk in the provinces of the previously forbidden territory that became Latvia.

In the Austro-Hungarian Empire, Jews, especially those from Galicia, formerly southeastern Poland, moved steadily toward Budapest and Vienna, often with an intermediate stop along the way. By the turn of the 20th century, so many Jews had settled in Budapest that in some circles it came to be called "Juda-pest." Vienna, in the late 19th century, was to Ashkenazi Jewry what New York became in the 20th century. Great numbers of Jews moved to Berlin, the majority from the former northwestern Polish province of Poznan since Jews from outside Prussian ruled territory faced great difficulties securing residence rights.[1] The British Isles was another area whose Jewish population swelled by the end of the 19th century—from about 60,000 in 1870 to more than 280,000 by 1914. English and Scottish Jewry grew as many Eastern European migrants interrupted their journey to the United States either temporarily or permanently. Lithuanian Jews especially, came to Scotland, with a small number going to Sweden.

19th-Century Migration from Europe. In the mid-19th century, numerous Jews (and others) began to migrate from German-speaking areas to the United States. Some Hungarians emigrated as well. This German migration was the second influx of Jews to the United States, the first—largely Sephardi—having come during colonial times.

The next, and far larger, major migratory wave covered the years 1880 to World War I, when fully half of Eastern European Jewry migrated westward from the Russian and Austro-Hungarian Empires, Romania, and, to a lesser degree, from the Ottoman Empire. Most of the emigrants went to the United States, with the largest number arriving in the first decade of the 20th century. The Russo-Japanese War of 1904 was perhaps the single most important factor causing the largest number to come in that year. Other migrants went to Argentina, Australia, Canada, South Africa, and Western Europe. About one in ten moved to Palestine. Most of the Jews who migrated to South Africa were Litvaks, the majority former residents of Kovno and Vilna guberniyas.

Migratory Routes and Their Records. One of the key factors in such moves, of Jews and non-Jews alike, was the need of the great shipping companies to fill their boats. The development during the second half of the 19th century of the great transatlantic liners meant that the companies competed with each other to attract as many passengers as they could; sometimes they competed by cutting fares, while at other times they attempted to establish a fare cartel and to even out their shipping revenues by controlling the number of passengers each line could carry during a single year.

Emigrants left Europe from a wide variety of ports. Train routes within such countries as Austria, Romania, and Russia, frequently determined the routes taken. So also did the presence of ticket sellers from one or another shipping line.[2] In the late 19th century, Brody, just over the Russian border into the Austro-Hungarian Empire, became a major gathering point for Jewish emigrants, the more so since it was there that the standard Central European railway gauge met the broad gauge Russian lines and passengers were forced to change trains.

Germany. During the 19th and early 20th centuries, most Jews left Europe via German ports, primarily from Bremen initially, but later increasingly from Hamburg. With a minor exception, no records of emigration from Bremen survive today. Happily, Hamburg is a different story. Extensive records exist of immigrants who passed through the Port of Hamburg, and an ongoing project is computerizing the data and posting it on the Internet at WWW.HAMBURG.DE/FHH/BEHOERDEN/STAATSARCHIV/ LINKTOYOURROOTS/ENGLISH/INDEX.HTM. (For more details,

see IMMIGRATION.) Emigrants sailing from Hamburg could have elected the faster, more costly "direct" passage or the less expensive "indirect" route via Southampton, England, LeHavre, France, or other ports where passengers disembarked and reboarded different ships.[3]

Russian emigrants who crossed the German border after the cholera outbreak in Hamburg in December 1894 had to pass through one of several German government border control stations along the eastern frontier with Russia. Control was strict. The German government wanted to prevent the importation of the disease while the Hamburg and Bremen shipping companies, HAPAG and Norddeutscher Lloyd, wanted to maximize the numbers traveling on their ships. Would-be emigrants who did not possess pre-paid tickets often were forced to buy tickets either from HAPAG or from the Lloyd. Emigrants with pre-paid tickets that had been sent to them in advance (generally through one of the immigrant banks in the United States) usually were allowed to pass through Germany to non-German ports. The situation changed after World War I, of course, when Germany no longer had a border with Russia, for Poland had been reconstituted as an independent state. Before 1895, no such restrictions existed. An unknown number of Russian emigrants crossed the border illegally between the control stations and went either westward or southward to reach another, possibly less expensive, European emigration port.

Libau. The path of the Russian-Jewish emigrants was influenced primarily by the pricing policy of the competing European shipping companies, or by which shipping agents had the most persuasive salesmen. Increasingly substantial numbers of Jews from northeastern Lithuania and contemporary Belarus made their way to Libau (today Liepava, Latvia) on the Baltic and from there by boat across the North Sea to Scotland or to London, Hull or Grimsby on the east coast of England. Those who then wished to continue onward took a train across England to Liverpool or Southampton where they boarded ships to the United States and elsewhere. Some crossed Scotland and went from one of the ports on the River Clyde. To date no records of emigrants from the Port of Libau have emerged, and the Latvian archives reports that none are known to exist. No lists exist for immigration into Great Britain for this period, but manifests exist for ships that sailed from the United Kingdom ports for the period after 1890. These lists are held in that country's Public Records Office*, but are not indexed. They are archived by port and the quarter of the year of sailing, and can only be accessed if the port, name of ship and the quarter of the year in which the ship sailed is known.

Other European Ports. Emigrants from the Austro-Hungarian Empire usually could pass freely through the German Empire. They might sail from Bremen or Hamburg or they could make their way to Holland and pass through the United Kingdom. Other emigrants from any part of Europe left from Antwerp, Copenhagen, Le Havre, or Rotterdam. An index to passenger records of the Holland-America Line (1900–40) has been micro-filmed by the Mormons. A few emigrants (usually Hungarian, some from the Ottoman Empire) sailed via the Adriatic port of

Members of the German Central Committee for Jews greet East European emigrants at the port of Hamburg. Courtesy of Hamburg State Archives.

Fiume. Which port was chosen depended on several factors. Sometimes it was cost; sometimes it was restrictions at the desired port of entry. For some it depended on what happened after they crossed into Germany from Russia. In the 1950s, Jews from Romania sailed from Constanza to Israel.

The Jewish Immigrant Aid Committee was formed in New York City in 1870 for the purpose of helping Jews navigate the various steps of the journey from Russia to the United States. Over time this was replaced first by the Hebrew Emigration Aid Society and eventually by the Hebrew Immigration Aid Society (HIAS). In addition, in 1891 Baron Maurice de Hirsch established the Jewish Colonization Association (ICA). Its aim was to assist urban Jews to retrain as agriculturists and to resettle on the land. Eventually it became closely linked with colonizing activities in Palestine, U.S. mid-Western states and, above all, in South America. ICA worked with various aid societies and groups in Europe along the "migration trail", especially the Ezra Society of Antwerp and the Montefiore Vereiningung of Rotterdam. HIAS worked closely with a Canadian steamship company, the Allan Line, since at one point this was the least expensive way to reach the Western Hemisphere.

Cost was not the only reason some Eastern European immigrants entered Canada. Many Jewish immigrants at the turn of the 20th century suffered from the eye disease trachoma, a condition that barred them from entering the United States. Examinations at the Port of New York were more rigorous than those at the crossings between the United States and Canada. Many Eastern European Jews entered Canada destined to the United States and upon entry were transferred immediately to Canadian Pacific trains that entered the U.S. at either Buffalo, New York, or Sault (pronounced "Soo") Sainte Marie, Michigan.

In the United States, the Minneapolis, St. Paul and Sault Line, wanting to compete with eastern American railroads for the lucrative immigrant trade, had entered into a partnership with the Canadian Pacific Railroad around 1885, and in 1887 built an international railroad bridge between Sault Sainte Marie, Ontario, Canada, and Sault Sainte Marie, Michigan. The Canadian Pacific worked closely with the Allan Line and so many Jews passed this way that for many years, HIAS maintained a branch in Sault Sainte Marie, Canada.

In the early 20th century, some long-settled American Jewish leaders established the Industrial Removal Organization to help settle new immigrants across the United States and outside of the crowded eastern seaboard cities. The archives of the Industrial Removal Organization, with its detailed records of the many immigrants helped, are held today by the American Jewish Historical Society* (SEE AJHS).

By the end of the 19th century, all ships carrying immigrants to the United States were required to maintain detailed passenger manifests that were presented to immigration officials upon landing in the United States. Many of these manifests have survived and are among the most prized documents available to Jewish genealogists (see IMMIGRATION). Ships carrying immigrants to other countries carried similar manifests. For further details, consult the chapter on the countries to which your ancestors migrated.

What about migration records in the countries that our ancestors left? For the most part, these are not known to exist, either because they have been lost or because they never were created in the first place. For example, in order to leave Russia legally, men needed to prove that they had fulfilled their military obligation, had paid all taxes, and were not being sought by the police. Since many men fled to avoid service in the Russian army, the majority left clandestinely, along the so-called "Jewish underground," carrying no records, or records that were false and/or forged.

Two series of books listing migrants to the United States may be useful. Created from ship manifests, they are *Germans to America* and *Russians to America*. Unfortunately, they are highly flawed works with many errors and omissions. If one finds an ancestor listed, the specific data should be verified from other sources. Failure to find a relative does not mean that he or she did not immigrate. In the *Russians to America* series, entire ships (and not merely individuals) were not indexed. Another book of interest is *Hamburg Passengers from the Kingdom of Poland and the Russian Empire*, by Marlene Silverman.

Sephardi Migrations

At the beginning of the 20th century, most Sephardic Jews lived in the Ottoman Empire, which included the Middle East, the Balkans, Greece, and Turkey. Large numbers of Sephardim also lived in North Africa—Morocco, Algeria, Tunisia, Libya, Egypt and Sudan. With the exception of some movement from North Africa to the Ottoman Empire, especially the Middle East, this region did not see large-scale Jewish migration during the 19th century. The situation changed, however, early in the 20th century.

Greece. Large waves of emigration began in 1909 in Greece, but especially as a result of the Turkish-Greek population transfer in 1922, many Jews from Salonika especially left for the United States, Europe and Latin America, going to Belgium, France, Italy, Spain, Italy, Argentina, Cuba, and Mexico. An especially large number of Jews from Salonika went to Palestine where they formed the basis of the port workers in Haifa and Jaffa. About 20,000 to 25,000 eastern Sephardim lived in Paris in 1939, at first in the 9th and 11th *arrondisements*. Marseille and Lyons also had substantial Judeo-Spanish populations. Between 1899 and 1924, the number of Ottoman Jews who emigrated to the United States was more than 20,000—most from Thrace and the Aegean regions.

Turkey. From 1900 onward, Sephardim from Rhodes settled in the United States in New York; the southern United States; Seattle, Washington; Belgian Congo; Rhodesia and later, South Africa. After the Young Turk Revolution (1908–09) and subsequent introduction of compulsory military service for non-Muslims, large numbers of Jews from Turkey emigrated to the United States, France, Italy, Morocco and Spain.

Many thousands left Turkey during 1940s for Palestine with a massive emigration in 1949. Between World War II and the mid-1950s, 40 percent of Turkish Jewry moved to Israel. Ten percent returned, but most did not stay.

Balkans. The Jewish populations of Bulgaria and Yugoslavia were stable during the first half of the 20th century, although some moved from Bulgaria to Turkey especially after Balkan Wars of 1912–13.

Ingathering of the Exiles

Jews have come to settle in Palestine/Israel from virtually every country in the world. During the huge migratory waves to the West at the turn of the 20th century, a small percentage of Eastern European Jews elected to go to Palestine. At the end of World War II, most survivors of the Shoah initially settled in Palestine/Israel, many of them entering illegally. A certain percentage of the survivors, especially those with relatives elsewhere, re-migrated to other countries, often the United States, Canada and Australia.

With the establishment of the State of Israel in 1948, most of the Jews of Muslim lands (except for Turkey) made *aliyah* in a massive population transfer. This includes the majority of Jews from Iraq, Lebanon, Syria, Yemen, Egypt, Libya, Morocco and Tunisia. Large numbers of Algerian Jews went to France with another sizeable group going to Israel. A total of about 600,000 Jews came from Muslim lands.

Addresses

American Jewish Historical Society, Center for Jewish History, 15 West 16th Street, New York, New York; website: www.ajhs.org.
Public Records Office, 4 Ruskin Avenue, Kew, Richmond, Surrey TW9 4DU; website: www.pro.gov.uk.

Bibliography

Encyclopedia Lithuania. Boston: J. Kopocius, 1970–1978.
Green Book of Zhagare. (Lithuanian). Vilnius: Versm, 1998.
Hoffman, David B. and Sonia R. Hoffman. "Researching 18th-Century Census and Tax Lists from the Grand Duchy of Lithuania." *AVOTAYNU* 17, no. 3 (Fall 2001): 7.
Hrtckiewicz, Anatol. "The Militias of Magnate's Towns in Belorussia and Lithuania in the 16th to 18th Centuries." [Polish]. *Kwartalnik Historyczny* 77, no. 1. (Minsk, 1970): 47–61.
Klausner, Israel. "Historical Introduction." *Yahadut Lite* [Hebrew]. Tel Aviv, 1968.
Lazuta, Stanislovas and Edwardas Gudavichius. *Privilege to Jews Granted by Vytautas the Great* (Russian and English). Moscow: Jewish University of Moscow, 1993.
Luft, Edward. "How to Determine from Where and When an Ancestor Moved to Berlin." *AVOTAYNU* 17, no. 4 (Winter 2000): 20.
Luft, Edward. Book Review. "Hamburg Passenger from the Kingdom of Poland and the Russian Empire." *AVOTAYNU* 13, no. 2 (Summer, 1997): 65.
Lukowski, Jerry Tadeusz. *Liberty's Folly: The Polish-Lithuanian Commonwealth in the 18th Century, 1697–1935.* Cambridge: Cambridge University Press, 1951.
Moser, Geraldine and Marlene Silverman. *Hamburg Passengers from the Kingdom of Poland and the Russian Empire: Indirect Passage to New York, 1865–June 1873.* Washington: Landsmen, 1996.
Newman, Aubrey. "Lithuania on the Veldt: Jewish Migration to South Africa." *AVOTAYNU* 13, no. 3 (Fall, 1997): 19.
Rossman, M.J. *The Lord's Jews: Magnate-Jewish Relationship in the Polish-Lithuanian Commonwealth During the 18th Century.* Cambridge, Mass: Harvard University Press, 1992.
Sack, Sallyann Amdur. "Can Jewish Genealogists Successfully Research 18th-Century Poland." *AVOTAYNU* 16, no. 3 (Fall 2000): 16. 16.
Yodaiken, Len. "Tackling the Lack of Surnames in 18th-Century Russian Records." *AVOTAYNU* 15, no. 3 (Fall 1999): 17.

Notes

1. Luft, How to Determine: 20.
2. Newman: 19.
3. Luft, Book Review: 65.

Rabbinical Genealogy

by Chaim Freedman

Stymied by the lack of records and/or hereditary surnames, most Jewish genealogists cannot trace their families back more than two or perhaps three centuries. Finding a rabbi in the family, however, can extend a family tree five hundred or more years into the past. The results are a bit like the popular American children's board game called *Chutes and Ladders*, in which landing on the right spot propels a player instantly forward, bypassing several intervening stops. Chances are good that many—if not most—Jewish genealogists who assiduously trace all collateral lines will ultimately find one or more ancestors who was a rabbi. Here is why.

World Jewry was small in number a few hundred years ago—an estimated 2.5 million at the start of the 19th century, roughly divided into 1.5 million Ashkenazim and 1.0 million Sephardim. Improved hygiene and health sparked a population explosion, with the result that most Jews living today are highly interrelated. In an article written some years ago, an Israeli demographer demonstrated statistically how all Ashkenazic Jews alive today probably descend from Rashi, the great 10th-century French rabbi and Torah commentator.[1] In reality, most Jews cannot trace their exact lineage to Rashi.

Finding a rabbi in the family likely will trigger the "Chutes and Ladders" phenomenon. This is because records *do* exist for rabbis who lived hundreds of years ago—most of whom carried hereditary surnames. These rabbis knew and preserved their genealogies; they wrote and published, and their genealogies frequently appeared in the publications. Many of these writings still exist. The rabbinical literature represents an important resource and exists for tracing rabbinical lines into the remote past.[2] This chapter describes how to participate in rabbinical Chutes and Ladders.

The recording of family lineage and pride in *yichus* (eminent lineage or pedigree) has always been an integral part of Judaism.[3] The biblical narrative describes the sequence of generations, from the patriarchs through division of the children of Israel into the 12 tribes, exodus from Egypt, pioneers in the establishment of the Jewish nation in *Eretz Yisrael*, prophets, royal house of David until the destruction of Jerusalem, to exile into the Diaspora.

Until the time of destruction of the first temple in Jerusalem and the exile to Babylonia (586 B.C.), Jews preserved records of their genealogical connection to the nation.[4] To a great extent, however, this continuity has been lost as a result of the Babylonian exile and the creation of the Diaspora.

Jewish tradition has always held that the exilarchs—the leaders of the Jewish community in Babylonia—were descendants of the royal House of David. One such family was the scholarly Kalonymides, who left Babylonia in about the 8th century C.E. They settled first in Italy and then moved to the Rhineland and to France in the ninth and tenth centuries. From this family came the great Biblical and Talmudic commentator Rashi (1040–1105).

Rashi Descent

Traditions of descent from famous rabbis, especially from Rashi, have long intrigued genealogists. The subject was discussed at length in a series of articles in *AVOTAYNU, the International Review of Jewish Genealogy*.[5] Rashi's family and disciples intermarried among themselves, established centers of Jewish learning and laid the foundations of the communities that became hubs of Jewish life in many Western European towns of the early Middle Ages.

Later, in the 14th century, the descendants of Rashi and his disciples moved eastward, creating a vast, interrelated dynasty of rabbinical families that spread throughout Europe. In doing so, they incidentally created a framework for genealogical research. It is from this core group (called the "Jewish intellectual class" by Rapaport) that most Ashkenazic rabbinical families descend.[6] Since the core of medieval rabbinical families all descended from Rashi, the number of rabbinical families whose genealogies must be studied in order to establish specific descent today is extremely large. Some families known to be descendants of Rashi are Epstein, Gunzburg, Heilprin, Heller, Horowitz, Isserles, Jaffe, Katz, Katzenellenbogen, Klausner, Landau, Lipschitz, Luria, Margolis, Rapaport, Shapira, Shorr, Teumin, Treves and Weil. These families compose the root from which most other European rabbinical families stemmed.

The late Paul Jacobi (1911–97) spent 50 years researching the 420 major Ashkenazi European rabbinical families, including the families listed above, as he used to say "from the time that they emerged from obscurity in the 13th or 14th centuries until the French Revolution."[7] His valuable archive, in hard-to-read handwriting, is deposited at the Jewish National and University Library* in Jerusalem. Some duplicate portions are held by the Central Zionist Archives* and the Douglas E. Goldman Genealogy Center at Beth Hatefutsoth* in Jerusalem. Beth Hatefutsoth has computerized some of Jacobi's trees.

Many of the core group of European rabbinical families used hereditary surnames centuries before local governments mandated their adoption. Descendants of the core group of European rabbinical families who migrated eastward from France and Germany to Poland and the Russian Empire took their surnames with them. These names appear in Eastern European Jewish communal records long before the late 18th and early 19th century, when hereditary family names became obligatory.

Like Jewish families generally, rabbinical families are found in both Ashkenazic and Sephardic communities. Spanish and Portuguese families used hereditary surnames prior to their 15th-century expulsions from the Iberian Peninsula, and some of those names subsequently spread throughout Europe after the expulsions. Examples include the Benveniste family, whose male descendants later split into two branches and took the names Epstein and Horowitz. The male line of the Epstein and Horowitz families stems from the male line of the Benveniste family. On the other hand, the Epstein and the Horowitz families also descend from Rashi because of inter-marriages with other families descended from Rashi's daughters. (Rashi had no sons.)

When the Ibn Yechia (later Don Yechia) family left Portugal in 1497, branches settled in many parts of the Mediterranean Basin before spreading to Germany and then into northeastern Russia. The family established a dynasty of rabbis in what is now Belarus and Latvia. The dynasty was composed of various interrelated families such as Don Yechia (sometimes Russified to Donchin), Levin, Tzioni, Zeligman and many others connected by multiple intermarriages between them. A related family with a similar history is the Charlap family, which retains its original surname to this day.[8] Another prominent Sephardic rabbinical line that migrated to Eastern Europe was Abarbanel.

Is There a Rabbi in My Family?

Jews traditionally have cared about their lineage, especially about descent from prominent rabbis, and many families preserved charts and manuscripts detailing their *yichus.* Unfortunately, in the tragedies that mark Jewish history—the expulsions, pogroms and especially the Holocaust—many, if not most, of these records were lost. All that is left for some families is an oral tradition of descent from King David, Rashi, the Vilna Gaon or another rabbinical luminary.

In many cases, not even this much is known today. The Vilna Gaon, for example, embraced the principle of spending as much time as possible in the study of religious texts. One result is that his descendants, and followers generally, often did not emphasize or even impart to their children knowledge of illustrious forebears. The situation tended to be different among the Hasidim whose rabbinical dynasties are revered by adherents and whose sons typically inherit their fathers' courts.[9]

Many contemporary researchers of Jewish genealogy with no known tradition of rabbinical descent—often those whose families have not been strictly observant—discover unsuspected 19th-century rabbis in their families. Others have uncovered charts and manuscripts attesting to an eminent, previously unknown rabbinical line—but without the direct connections explicated. In both cases, whether a family has a tradition of an eminent rabbi, or one simply finds a rabbi in the family in tracing back the family history, further research follows similar steps.

I Found a Rabbi; What Do I Do Now?

Remember that all genealogical research follows the basic principle of tracing back in time, generation by generation. The task is to use the rich existing rabbinical records to move back in time, one person at a time. Be aware that no one can do with this for descent from Rashi (or King David) with all generations named. Jewish tradition is strong that Rashi descended from King David. Similarly, some families have a strong tradition of descent from King David from whom it is believed that the Messiah will come. The most that can be

done, however, is to trace descent from one of the lines believed to have descended from these men, those whom Jacobi said "emerged from obscurity in the 13th or 14th century."

Keep in mind the difference between the two situations. In one case a family has a tradition of descent from a famous rabbi, but the specific generation by generation connections are unknown. In such a situation, pursue research in two directions. Continue to seek records of known ancestors, moving back one generation at a time, remembering to expand knowledge of as many collateral relatives as possible. At the same time, look for other descendants of the rabbinical ancestor.

In the second case, ordinary genealogical research has uncovered a not necessarily famous rabbi who lived within the last few centuries. Because rabbis tended to marry the daughters of other rabbis, chances are good that one rabbi in the family will lead to many, and (for an Ashkenazic family), eventually to one of the 420 families researched by Jacobi. (Unfortunately, the tradition does not necessarily hold for non-traditional 20th-century rabbis.)

What Are the Resources?

The basic resource for tracing rabbis is the vast body of rabbinic literature, much of which is cited below. (see "Sources of Rabbinical Genealogies") As with all Jewish genealogy, English-speaking researchers must deal with resources written in other languages—in this case, almost all the resources are in Hebrew. For convenience it is a good idea to begin with English-language resources; most are 20th-century compilations from earlier Hebrew language works. A list of these resources appears later in this chapter in the section ENGLISH-LANGUAGE SOURCES. After consulting the material written in English, try to tackle the items identified as MOST PROMISING PLACES TO START. The nature of these books requires little more than the ability to identify names in printed Hebrew.

Living people are the other major resource—and infinitely easier for most beginners. Only a scant handful of contemporary Jewish genealogists specialize in broad-based rabbinical research, but many others specialize in research on one particular family. The best way to publicize interest in a particular rabbi or rabbinical line and to make contact with related others or with those who can offer research advice is to log onto JewishGen's rabbinical special interest group, RAVSIG, at WWW.JEWISHGEN.ORG/RABBINICAL/ . This may also be a good place to find experts to translate some of the more difficult Hebrew-language texts.

Ask relatives if they possess any religious books that might have belonged to these ancestors; if so, look for family inscriptions, because they frequently note the names of ancestors. Check Judaica library catalogues to see if relatives wrote any religious books; their introductions may include family details. Many sources depend on who the rabbi was and whether or not he wrote books. If a rabbi was well known and wrote a great deal, chances of learning about his ancestry is greater than it is for a rabbi who was not well known and who did not write.

English-Language Sources

Following are some places to begin.

American Jewish Yearbook. Philadelphia: Jewish Publication Society, 1903, 1904. This source includes lists and short biographies of American rabbis.

Buber, Martin. *Tales of the Hasidim*. New York: Horizon, 1956; reprint Humanities Press, 1988. Stories are compiled about Hasidic masters. A useful source for learning details about the lives of individual ancestors.

Encyclopaedia Judaica. Jerusalem: Encyclopaedia Judaica, 1972, 1987. This major reference work includes many rabbinical biographies, as well as a chart of Hasidic dynasties.

Feuchtwanger, O. *Righteous Lives*. New York: Bloch, 1965. Biographies of prominent rabbis are presented.

Freedman, Chaim. *Eliyahu's Branches: The Descendants of the Vilna Gaon and his Family*. Teaneck, NJ: Avotaynu, 1997. This genealogy of the descendants of the Vilna Gaon and his siblings includes about 20,000 people, with many families updated to the date of publication. Extensive sources and bibliography are presented, along with biographical details (where available), often including personalities previously unknown to English readers. A detailed explanation of research methodology is included.

Frenkel, Rabbi Isser. *Men of Distinction*. Tel Aviv: Sinai, 1967. Biographies of prominent rabbis.

Greenbaum, Masha. *The Jews of Lithuania*. Jerusalem: Gefen, 1995. This history of Lithuanian Jewry mentions rabbinic personalities.

Jewish Encyclopedia. New York: Funk and Wagnalls, 1904. Online at WWW.JEWISHENCYCLOPEDIA.COM, this major reference work includes many rabbinical biographies as well as a chart of Hasidic dynasties. Has more detailed genealogical information than is published in *Encyclopaedia Judaica*.

Jung, Leo. *Jewish Leaders*. Jerusalem: 1964. Biographies of prominent rabbis.

Menton, Arthur F. *The Book of Destiny: Toledot Charlap*. Cold Spring Harbor, NY: King David Press, 1996. Details are presented of research on ancient rabbinical families of Sephardic origin, their settlement in Europe and recent descendants. The book includes scholarly explanations of many versions of the family's descent.

Oshry, Rabbi Ephraim. *The Annihilation of Lithuanian Jewry*. New York: Judaica Press, 1995. This book describes the destruction of Lithuanian communities in the Holocaust and mentions rabbinical personalities.

Rabinowicz, Rabbi Harry M. *The World of Hasidism*. London: Vallentine, Mitchell, 1970. An authoritative, yet concise, introduction to the Hasidic movement and its major rabbinical dynasties.

Rabinowitsch, Wolf Zeev. *Lithuanian Hasidism*. New York: Schocken, 1971. A history is given of Lithuanian and Byelorussian Hasidism with some genealogical charts.

Rosenstein, Emanuel, and Neil Rosenstein. *Latter Day Leaders, Sages, and Scholars*. Elizabeth, NJ: Computer Center for Jewish Genealogy, 1983. Presents lists of rabbis cited in ten Hebrew sources, classified by country, town, surname and personal name. Included are father's name and dates, where known. This is a valuable guide for more detailed research in the sources quoted.

Rosenstein, Neil. *The Unbroken Chain*. New York: Shengold, 1976, 1990. Detailed genealogies of prominent rabbinical families descended from the Katzenellenbogen family are presented. Many families have been updated to current generations. This

The ReMa, Rabbi Moses ben Israel Isserles (1525–1572), Polish rabbi, code annotator, and philosopher

book is one of the most valuable sources available in English. References to Hebrew sources facilitates more detailed research.

———. *The Lurie Legacy*, Bergenfield, NJ: Avotaynu, 2004. History of the Lurie/Luria family with numerous illustrations of documents and family trees.

Sackheim, George I. *Scattered Seeds*. 2 vols. Skokie, IL: R. Sackheim, 1986. This genealogy of 10,000 descendants of the famous martyr Rabbi Israel of Ruzhany, who perished in 1659, includes genealogical tables and biographical details of prominent rabbinical families, many updated to current generations. This book is a useful English accompaniment to *Daat Kedoshim*.

Who's Who. New Providence, NJ: Marquis, many editions for various countries include rabbis.

Most Promising Places to Start

Eizenstadt, Y.T. *Daat Kedoshim*. דעת קדושים. St. Petersburg, 1898. This book continues lines recorded in earlier works, updating them to the end of the 19th century. A major authoritative source of classical rabbinical genealogy, it is often cited in later genealogical works. The work was written as a memorial to two famous martyrs, Yisrael Zak and Tuviah Bachrach, who were burned at the stake in Ruzhany, Belarus, in 1659. They were the ancestors of the Zak and Bachrach families, although the book covers several other major families. It is divided into the following major sections: **Bachrach**, including Altshuler and Jaffe; **Eizenstadt**, including *Shach*; **Gunzburg**, including Landau, Levi and Mirkes; **Heilprin**, including Hochgelerenter, Horowitz, Margolis and Parness; **Mires**, including Ashkenazy, Berlin, Brauda, Frenkel and Neumark; **Posnan**; **Rapaport**, including Ashkenazy, Berlin, Epstein, Ettinger, Halberstadt, Luria, Meizels, Sirkin, Volozhiner and Zusman; **Rokeach**; **Yosef Yoska of Dubno**, including Auerbach, Babad, Berliner, Eskeles, Heilprin, Heshil of Krakow, Kara, Landau, Lipshutz, Meizels, Ornstein, Shorr and Teumim; **Zak**, includes Brauda, Grayever, Katzenellenbogen, Meizel, Polak and Rabbinovitch. Each section is arranged by generation number to facilitate cross-references. Entries include dates, places and biographical material. Daughters are included by name (where known), not just to link rabbinical sons-in-law. Fathers-in-law are noted, as are rabbinical positions held and books written.

Friedman, Natan Tsvi. *Otsar Harabbanim*. (Treasury of rabbis). אוצר הרבנים. Bnei Brak: Israel, 1975. The author presents information on approximately 20,000 individuals covering the years 970–1970. Despite the considerable number of rabbis and scholars described, the names of some known rabbis are omitted. The omissions have no discernible pattern. The entry is coded for each rabbi, his father, father-in-law, sons and sons-in-law. Cross references permit the construction of family trees. *Otsar Harabbanim* is a good first reference work. Although it can provide a direction for further research, it is flawed. Some rabbis are omitted; it is notorious for confusing people bearing the same name; and, because of some circular pathways, one can trace an ancestry line back through its reference numbers and end up at the starting place. The index is not strictly alphabetical; one must scan the entire index to ensure that a person sought has not been missed.

Gottlieb, S. *Ohalei Shem*. אוהלי שם. Pinsk, 1912. This unique book is a compilation of biographies (including family trees) of 1,500 rabbis who held rabbinical positions at the time the book was written. Arranged by country and city, each entry includes genealogical and source material for further research. Most of the data was supplied to the author by the rabbis themselves in reply to the author's request. As a result, the volume and quality of the material varies considerably. This is an essential source in rabbinical genealogical research.

Other Useful Sources

Some additional categories and sources of rabbinical information are listed below. A good working knowledge of Hebrew is necessary to use most of them.

Encyclopedias. Gellis, Y. *Encyclopedia Lekhakhmei Eretz Yisrael* (Encyclopedia of the scholars of Eretz Yisrael) אנציקלופדיה לחכמי ארץ ישראל.

Tidhar, David. *Encyclopedia Lekhalutsei Hayishuv Ubonav* (Encyclopedia of the pioneers of the *Yishuv* and its builders) אנציקלופדיה לחלוצי הישוב ובוניו, Tel Aviv: 1947. Nineteen volumes present detailed biographies with genealogical information for about 50,000 people involved in the development and settlement of Israel. The work includes references to rabbinical ancestry of many of the subjects described.

Prenumerantn and Other Lists. *Prenumerantn*, a Yiddish term meaning "prior numbers," refers to people who ordered copies of a book before its publication and were listed in the book. The lists are a particularly valuable Ashkenazic genealogical source, especially for rabbinical research. The late Beryl Kagan's *Sefer Haprenumerantn*, known in English as *Hebrew Subscription Lists* (1975), is an index by town of about 800 such books covering 8,000 towns. Two additional lists were prepared by Shlomo Katzav (Petah Tikvah, Israel, 1986, 1992). Katzav, formerly associated with Bar-Ilan University in Israel, had the lists printed as pamphlets, some of which may be found in major Israeli libraries. The Central Archives for the History of the Jewish People in Jerusalem[*] holds a manuscript version of a list Katzav prepared from *Hamelitz* (see below under Hebrew and Yiddish Newspaper Lists).

Most of these books, published in Europe in the late 18th century through the early 1940s, were religious in nature. Lists exist for most European towns that had a Jewish community. Names of subscribers from small villages often are listed under the name of the nearest larger community. Some lists include subscribers from communities outside Europe. Genealogists seeking *prenumerantn* lists will find them primarily in old religious Hebrew books. To locate the books themselves, consult libraries with major Judaica collections. Also check special interest groups (SIGS) online;

Rabbi Shlomo ben Yitzhak (Rashi)
(1040–1105) was the outstanding Biblical
commentator of the Middle Ages

some have indexed items related to their geographical areas of interest (SEE SPECIAL INTEREST GROUPS).

Prenumerantn lists are especially valuable for rabbinical genealogical research because the rabbis of particular communities often occupied a prominent position on the lists. Since the lists appear in rabbinical works, the introductions and title pages usually include genealogical information about the author's family, some members of which may be included among the prenumerantn.

Hebrew and Yiddish Newspaper Lists

Another valuable genealogical source, particularly for Eastern European families, are the three major Hebrew newspapers published in the Russian Empire starting in the mid-19th century. Most useful in genealogical research were *Hamelitz* (1860–1904), *Hamaggid* (1856–1903) and *Hatsefirah* (1862–1931). These sources often report details of the lives of local rabbis. As such, these publications offer a treasury of material for the genealogist.

During the period of the "Old Yishuv" in Eretz Yisrael a number of newspapers published in Jerusalem provide rabbinical information. Especially useful is *Halevanon* הלבנון, for which Yad Ben Tsvi[*] has prepared an index. For the period of the new settlement of Israel, useful newspapers are *Hator, Hahed, Hayesod, Hatsofeh, Shearim, Hamodiah* and *Yeted Neeman*. Important Galician newspapers were *Makhzikei Hadaat* (1879–1912) and *Hamitzpeh* (1894–1921). Copies of these publications are available at the Jewish National and University Library in Jerusalem,[*] as well as in some major libraries around the world.

Newspaper research is a painstaking task. Material generally is not indexed by name. Some bound collections may include occasional indexes by town or major personalities. Otherwise one must peruse every page in hope of finding material relative to one's research. Several newspapers ran regular series of articles that carried reports from particular communities. Obituaries of scholars and rabbis frequently provide genealogical information. Some Internet-based Special Interest Groups have created name indexes from newspapers (see SPECIAL INTEREST GROUPS)

Extensive lists of charitable donations were a feature of most Hebrew and Yiddish newspapers. Usually the donor lists were grouped by town, although the lists were rarely alphabetical. (see "donor lists" in the chapter on Israel.) In many cases, rabbis were listed at the beginning of the lists. From time to time special articles included rabbinical biographies and genealogies of prominent families.

Pinkas Hakehillot פנקס הקהילות. This multi-volume series of books about destroyed Jewish communities is a project of Yad Vashem.* Although particular emphasis is given to the Holocaust period, the historical background and development of each of the communities covered in the series are summarized. For many towns, this material constitutes the only extant source of information (see HOLOCAUST for more details). Although *Pinkas Hakehillot* does not present rabbinical genealogies in a formal genealogical structure, this work has considerable value in rabbinical genealogical research. Each town entry includes a list of the rabbis who occupied the rabbinical seat over the period of Jewish settlement in the town. If there was an element of familial succession to this post, then the familial detail supplied is a source for research. Where Hasidic dynasties held court in a town, the familial succession to the title of *Admor* or *Rebbe* is given considerable coverage.

Yizkor Books. Although a full description of the more than 1,200 extant *yizkor* books is beyond the scope of this article, most yizkor books devote a chapter to the rabbis and scholars of the community (see HOLOCAUST.) The amount of genealogical information varies from a simple list of rabbis to books that include detailed biographies and dynastic relationships. JewishGen sponsors a project to locate and translate specific yizkor books at WWW.JEWISHGEN.ORG/YIZKOR/.

Yahadut Latvia יהדות לטביה. (Latvian Jewry) by B. Elav et al. Tel Aviv: Organization of Former Latvians and Estonians, 1953. This volume was the first post-Holocaust attempt to preserve the history of Latvian Jewry. The section on rabbis includes family details.

Yahadut Lita, יהדות ליטה by Garfinkel, N. and L. Goren et al. eds. (Lithuanian Jewry) vol. 1 Tel Aviv: Am Hasefer, 1959, vol. 2, 1972, vol. 3, D. Ripec and R. Hasman et al. eds., 1967, vol. 4. Garfinkel, Lieb and by M. Sudarsky. (Lithuania). New York, 1951. These comprehensive multi-volume histories of Lithuanian communities include historical, socio-economic and biographical material. Considerable rabbinical material is included, but it is not exhaustive. The lists of community histories and tombstone inscriptions that follow the references to rabbinical writings are important references. Litvak SIG has indexed some of the individuals cited.

Research Difficulties

Having a rabbi on one's family tree greatly enhances the possibility of tracing back hundreds of years, but such research is not easy. Several factors contribute difficulties, especially in Eastern Europe.[10]

Identical but Unrelated Surnames. Although Eastern European families bearing classical rabbinical names[11]

Tombstone of Rabbi Judah Loew,
the MaHaRaL of Prague
(1525–1609)

may be able to trace descent from the older Western European root of these families, researchers must remember that these same names also could have been adopted by totally unrelated families. Some families, unrelated to the old lines of known rabbinical families, adopted the same names randomly—or with some view to *yichus* by association—when legislation required Jews to adopt hereditary surnames.

Gaon. The term *gaon* was used sparingly during the lifetime of Elijah ben Shlomo Zalman, the Gaon of Vilna (1720–97). Since then, however, *gaon* has come to be liberally ascribed to rabbinical scholars as a term of honor. As a result, one may have been told that he was descended from "the gaon"—but the term may have referred in fact to another rabbi who was known by that title.

Genealogical Omissions. Genealogies of rabbinical families often omitted sons or sons-in-law who were not scholars. Similarly, daughters were often not recorded in such families.

Lack of Published Information. Certain families, known to be descended from rabbis, simply refuse to publish their family trees for various personal reasons.

Multiple Surnames in One Family. Siblings born to the same father often used surnames different from one another and from that borne by their parents. This practice was prevalent in the Imperial Czarist Empire—a ploy used to confuse the military authorities. The notoriously anti-Semitic practices of the czarist army caused many 19th-century male Jews to use a surname change as a means of evading conscription. Variation of surnames within a single family leads to confusion in genealogical research.

Translation Errors. Some historians and genealogists who are not fluent in Hebrew have used, as the basis of their research, sources translated from Hebrew to English. These secondhand sources are prone to errors. Similarly, some members of families that claim rabbinical descent have been assisted in their research by incompetent translators not familiar with the genealogical nuances of sources.

Some families who have believed that they were descended from prominent rabbis discover, after investigation, that they actually descend either from the siblings of the rabbi or from one of his students. Terminology used to refer to relationships is misleading. "Of the family of the Gaon of Vilna" may mean actual descent, but more often the term refers to the descendants of the Gaon's siblings; sometimes it refers to more distant connections by marriage that lack an actual blood relationship.

Tribal Affiliation: Kohens and Levites

Since certain rabbinical families were Kohens (*kohanim*—descendants of Aaron), and others were Levites (*leviim*—descendants of the tribe of Levi other than Aaron) It is important and helpful to determine the "tribal" descent of alleged descendants. In the technical *halachic* (Jewish law) sense, no person can be a *kohen* unless his father was a *kohen*; the same is true of those with Levite descent. Members of the ancient Rapaport family are known to have been *kohenim*. The Epstein, Horowitz and Landau rabbinical families are known to have been *leviim*. Presumably someone with the name Rapaport who is not a *kohen* (or an Epstein, Horowitz or Landau who is not a Levite) could not be descended from the rabbinical families of that name.

In some cases, however, the situation may be more complicated. An actual relationship may have existed between *kohanic* and *non-kohanic* families that arose in cases when a son-in-law adopted his wife's family name. In Russia especially, this circumstance may have occurred for several reasons, most frequently to avoid military service in the Russian army. Even if the sons-in-law were not *kohanim* or *leviim*, in this particular situation their subsequent descendants are in fact descended from the old rabbinic families—through a female line. This situation is documented in a number of rabbinical families such as the Epsteins, Horowitzes, Landaus and Rapaports.

In the past tribal affiliation was recorded on tombstones. Indeed, the absence or presence of *kohen* or *levi* designation on a tombstone often helped genealogists to clarify relationships. Kohens are commonly depicted with hands held in the traditional rabbinic blessing; a pitcher pouring water is often used for Levites. Some families today, however, have forgotten this aspect of their ancient descent and fail to record it on their tombstones.

Abbreviations and Titles

Many renowned rabbis are known by the acrostics derived from their names; other prominent rabbis are known by the title of their books—usually their most important or famous one. In pursuing rabbinic genealogy, it is essential to know the true name of these individuals. One example is the Maharsha, a name created from the first letters of the name *Moreinu harav Reb Shmuel Edels* (Our great teacher, the rabbi Reb Shmuel Edels). Edels (1555–1631), a prominent rabbinical commentator, is referred to as the Maharsha in most rabbinical texts, whose authors assumed that their readers knew that he was Rabbi Shmuel Yehudah Edels. Perhaps the best known example is Rashi רש"י, the first letters of the name of the famous biblical and Talmudic commentator Rabbi Shlomo ben Yitzhak (1040–1105).

An example of a prominent rabbi known by the title of his most famous book, and not by his name, Rabbi Mordekhai

Jaffe (circa 1530–1612) is known as the *Levush*, the title of his rabbinical commentaries. In some cases, the rabbinical work is known by an abbreviation of the title of the book and the rabbi/author has come to be known by this abbreviation. For example, Rabbi Yoel Sirkes (1561–1640) is known as the *Bakh*, an acrostic composed of the Hebrew letters ב"ח, representing the title of Sirkes's book *Beit Khadash*. Sometimes a combination of these two rabbinical naming techniques applies: The first leader of the Ger Hasidim was Rabbi Yitzkhak Meir Alter. His book is called *Khidushei Harim*. "Harim (הרי"מ) is an acrostic of the author's given name: the Hebrew letters *Resh* [R] for *Reb*, *Yud* [I] for Yitzkhak and *Mem* [M] for Meir. Isaiah Horowitz (1555–1630) is known as the *Sheloh* a name taken from the first initials of each word for his book, *Shene Luhot Ha-Berit*.

A number of honorific titles traditionally have been accorded to rabbis. These include *gaon*, גאון (genius) and *admor*, אדמו"ר (a Hasidic title representing *Adoneinu Moreinu Verabbeinu*, our lord, our teacher and our rabbi). Less famous rabbis may be accorded the title (in written texts) *M'HRR* מ'הרר for *Moreinu Harva Reb* (our teacher, the rabbi so-and-so).

Reb (רב) does not mean rabbi; "*harav*" (הרב) or "*moreinu harav*" (מורנו הרב) are terms for rabbi. The abbreviation *mem hei*, מ"ה, is another common title of honor or respect that does not necessarily signify rabbinic status. *Chevra kadisha* records commonly use this term. For example, the *pinkas* (register) of the *chevra kadisha* (burial society) of Slutsk, Belarus, refers to nearly every male by an honorific title. Obviously not every male in the town over a 300-year period was a rabbi.

Critiques of Published Lineages

Rabbinical genealogical research must also consider critical analyses of some published genealogies that have been conducted by various scholars. Some critical analysis was done close to the time that the early, classical rabbinic genealogical references were written and often are printed as appendixes to those works. Others are modern critical analyses of the classical genealogies.

Particularly important is the work of Rabbi Shlomo Englard of Bnei Brak, Israel. Himself a descendant of prominent rabbinical families, Rabbi Englard has devoted his scholarly research to the task of verifying traditionally accepted lines of descent of the famous rabbinical families. He has re-analyzed the sources quoted by the authors of rabbinical genealogies as the basis for the lines of descent they present. Englard has checked these claims by independent research of additional sources. Painstaking comparison and analysis of rare texts, rabbinical publications and recorded tombstone inscriptions has led Englard to conclude that the some classical authorities erred by confusing the identities of rabbis of the same name, used invalid dates of birth and death that are incompatible with calculated time spans, and presented material that conflicts with facts presented in other verifiable sources.

Englard has published the results of his research in a number of articles in the Hebrew-language journal *Tsfu-*

Encyclopedia Lekhakhmei Galicia (Encyclopedia of Galician Sages), *written by Rabbi Meir Wunder is five volumes of extensively detailed genealogies of Galician rabbinical famalies*

not.[12] Several genealogists have referred to England's work in *AVOTAYNU*. England has studied the methodology and reliability of the classical genealogical scholars and their works: Yisrael Moshe Biderman, Yosef Cohen-Zedek, Avraham Ettinger, Chaim Dov Gross, Tsvi Horowitz, Yosef Levinstein, Tsvi Yekhezkel Michelsohn, Aharon Walden and Mordekhai Weitz.

Families studied by England include Babad, Cohen-Zedek and Luria (and related families such as Shapira, Katzenellenbogen and Margolis) and Rapaport. In addition, England has studied the genealogies of Rabbi Arye Leib *Hagavoah*, Rabbi Arye Leib of Krakow, Rabbi Elimelekh of Lyzhensk, Rabbi Heshil of Krakow, Judah Loew, the *Maharal* of Prague, Rabbi Moshe Isserles *Remo*, Rabbi Tsvi Hersh Ashkenazy *Khakham Tsvi*, Rabbi Yehoshua *Meginei Shlomo*, Rabbi Yehudah Leib and Rabbi Yitskhak Halevy Horowitz of Hamburg. Although a full examination of England's valuable Hebrew-language studies is beyond the scope of this article, his studies must be consulted in any serious research of rabbinical families.

Sources of Rabbinical Genealogies

Numerous sources cited below were written towards the end of the 19th century when access was available to European resources, such as cemeteries and communal registers (*pinkassim*), that later suffered the ravages of wars. The authors of these books lived in a time when the concept of *yichus* was valued and the continuity of oral tradition was maintained. These books and manuscripts constitute the classical (and often rare) resource for genealogical research. The selection presented here is not exhaustive. All the sources cited below are written in Hebrew, unless otherwise

noted, but have been personally consulted by the author and found useful. All books listed are held by the Jewish National and University Library in Jerusalem. Many can be found in other major Judaica collections around the world.

Rabbinical Anthologies

A number of anthologies contain genealogical information about many rabbis. Several of the books, written towards the end of the 19th century, present the only known information about some individuals. Because the inclusion and exclusion of particular rabbis in these anthologies follows no discernible pattern, all the books must be consulted to ensure the fullest possible research. Most books are unindexed and are arranged by first name in the traditional Hebrew style. As a result, it is necessary to review each book in its entirety to determine if a particular rabbi is included.

Azulai, Kh. Y.D. (the *Khidah*). *Shem Hagedolim Hekhadash* שם הגדולים החדש. Warsaw, 1852. Republished Warsaw: A. Walden, 1879, and many other editions. This work provides brief biographical information on 1,500 rabbis who lived over a wide period of time, with no apparent criteria for inclusion. Brief genealogical information includes alphabetically arranged biographies and lists of the books authored by the rabbis. The book list is useful to identify rabbis referred to in other sources by the name of their publication alone.

Beilinsohn, Moshe Eliezer. *Megilat Yukhsin, Shlomei Emunei Yisreal.* מגילת יוחסין, שלומי אמוני ישראל. Odessa, 1863, 1890s. This series of booklets provides detailed genealogical material for mainly Byelorussian rabbinical families. The work is arranged as coded lists or as box charts. The author had included all known members of a family—a valuable source not only for rabbis, but also for their non-rabbinic descendants. This is a rare source. Principal families include Alexandrov; Beilinson; Brauda; Dubnov; Ettinger; Freides; Frumkin; Gunzburg; Heilprin; Katz; Kazarnovsky; Kisin; Judah Lowe, the *Maharal* of Prague; Luria; Margolis; Mirkin; Raskin; Reichenstein; Rozenberg; Simchovitch; Sirkin; Tumarkin; Vilda and Zeitlin.

Braverman, David. *Anshei Shem* אנשי שם. Warsaw, 1892. Biographies of approximately 1,000 rabbis are arranged alphabetically by Hebrew first name up to and including the letter *lamed*.

Efrati, David. *Toldot Anshei Shem.* תולדות אנשי שם. Warsaw, 1875. Detailed notes offer biographical information and sources. This is a precise, usually accurate source. One of the earliest 19th-century rabbinical genealogies, this book traces the descendants of many prominent rabbis and provides copious notes with interconnecting genealogical material. Unindexed, it nevertheless merits lengthy and careful study.

The book is arranged as a main text, entitled *Arzei Banim* (Cedars of the sons), with extensive footnotes (in Rashi script) entitled *Ateret Zekeinim* (Crown of the elders). The author focuses on five primogenitors of his major ancestral lines: Yehuda *Yesod* of Vilna, Yom Tov Heller *Tosfot Yom Tov,* Yehudah Leib *Maharal* of Prague, Moshe *Kremer* of Vilna and Shaul Wahl-Katzenellenbogen.

Each of these five lines is expanded in the footnotes that list all descendants traced by the author. The notes provide considerable details, clearly listing all sons and sons-in-law with their subsequent descendants, including places of residence. Few dates are listed.

Since Efrati's work was written comparatively early, it was available as a source for later works, such as *Daat Kedoshim,* which contributed further information about these families. The major families include Ashkenazi; Berlin; Efrati; Eizenstadt; Eliasberg; Eliash; Epstein; Elijah ben Solomon Zalman, Gaon of Vilna; Gunzburg; Heller; Horowitz; Katz; Katzenellenbogen; Klausner; Landau; Levin; Lipshutz; Judah Lowe, Maharal of Prague; Luria; Mirels; Rapaport; Ratner; Rivlin; Shapira; Shick; Shneurson; Simchovitch; Teumim; Vitkind and Zukerman, with connections to many other families, particularly individuals that lived in Eastern Europe.

Additional notes by Efrati include sources located after publication that expand especially the Katzenellenbogen family. Some brief biographical material is unique. This is a highly recommended source that requires painstaking study of the many footnotes.

Efrati, Eliezer. *Dor Vedorshav* דור ודורשיו. Vilna, 1889. Selected biographies of 66 rabbis whose first names begin with the letter *alef*.

Eizenstadt, B. *Dorot Akharonim, Dor Rabanav Vesofrav, Khahkmei Yisrael Beamerica.*

דורות אחרונים, דור רבניו וסופריו, חכמי ישראל באאמריקה

A series of books of biographies of rabbis who lived mainly in Europe and the United States.

Hakohen, Naftali Yaakov. *Otsar Hagedolim Alufei Yaakov* אוצר הגדולים אלופי יעקב

Heilprin, Refael. *Atlas Etz Khaim.* אטלס עץ חיים. Tel Aviv. This multi-volume work, which discusses rabbis from Biblical times to the present, is the best place to start if you know that you have a rabbinical ancestor. Rabbis are organized by country and/or region and affiliation. Information is presented in several ways such as lists with short biographies and graphic charts showing each rabbi in relation to his major teacher and familial connections. Included are lists of the books authored by the rabbis, which can help readers to identify rabbis referred to in other sources only by the title of their publication. Each volume has separate genealogical charts for selected families, although the charts can be difficult to follow.

Heilprin, Yekhiel. *Seder Hadorot* סדר הדורות. Warsaw, 1862; Jerusalem, 1956. This extensive compilation of rabbis and scholars from biblical times includes genealogical information, but rarely beyond two to three generations.

Kahana, Shmuel Zanvil. *Anaf Etz Avot* ענף עץ אבות. Krakow, 1903. This book is well organized and exact. When facts are unknown to the author, he leaves blank spaces or marks the link with a question mark.

Lewin, Y. *Eleh Ezkerah* אלה אזכרה. New York, 1956. This sevenvolume anthology includes biographies of 368 rabbis who perished in the Holocaust. Genealogical information and photographs are included.

Lipshitz, Arye Yehuda Leib. *Avot Ateret Lebanim* אבות עטרת לבנים. Warsaw, 1927. Although the primary purpose of the book is to present the descendants of the Katzenellenbogen family, many interrelated families are included with coded cross-references. This work is a chronological extension of *Daat Kedoshim*; the book concentrates on the descendants of Shaul Wahl (Katzenellenbogen). Written in the late 1920s, the book is not restricted to rabbinical personalities, although these abound. Changes that occurred in the Jewish social structure in the early 20th century produced later generations whose activities were not limited to the rabbinical sphere. This book is a valuable source for those families whose immediate ancestors may not have been famous rabbis, but who have a tradition of descent from a specific rabbi. The major families covered, in addition to the main Katzenellenbogen lines and their branches, include Alter, Bloch, Finkelstein, Folman, Heilprin, Levin, Lipshutz, Morgenstern, Pines, Rotenberg, Shershevsky, Tsuker and Zabludowsky. A separate section is devoted to the Polish Berliner family who descended from Rabbi Tsvi Hersh of Berlin and

settled principally in Piotrykow, with links to the families Baharier, Gliksman, Michelson, Morgenstern, Posner and Schwerdscharf. Included is a list of people who held a tradition of descent from Shaul Wahl, but whose exact descent the author was unable to determine.

Markovitch, Moshe. *Shem Hagedolim Hashelishi* שם הגדולים השלישי Vilnius, 1910. Biographies are presented of 277 mainly Lithuanian and Byelorussian rabbis whose names begin with *alef*. Updated information is offered on current (as of 1910) generations. Many sources are quoted for each family, and an extensive bibliography is appended

Shapira, Yaakov Leib. *Mishpakhot Atikot Beyisrael* משפחות עתיקות בישראל (Ancient families in Israel). Tel Aviv, 1981. The author traces the ancestry and principal descendants of the classical rabbinical families beginning with Rashi. Summary charts are followed by detailed biographical information and marital connections for each successive generation. In addition, the book includes excellent concise rabbinical biographies.

Shechter-Cohen, Elazar. *Kenet Sofrim* קנת סופרים., Lemberg (Lviv) 1892.

Stern, Avraham. *Melitsei Esh* מליצי אש 1974. Three volumes include information about 2,000 rabbis arranged by date of *yahrzeit* (Hebrew date of death) with an alphabetical index. Includes useful biographical and genealogical information.

Wunder, Meir. *Encyclopedia Lekhakhmei Galicia* אנציקלופדיה לחכמי גליציה (Encyclopedia of Galician Sages). Jerusalem: Institute for Commemoration of Galician Jewry, 1978–97. Five volumes of extensively detailed genealogies of Galician rabbinical families are arranged alphabetically by surname. Most family sections include a genealogical chart. For prominent rabbis of each family, biographical material is included, in particular rabbinical publications, *responsa*, correspondence and photographs. Updated information is given for current generations. Many sources are quoted for each family, and an extensive bibliography is included. An impressive and scholarly work this work is considered to be among the most extensive and reliable sources of rabbinical genealogy written in the 20th century.

Yevnin, Levi. *Nakhalat Avot.* נחלת אבות. Vilna, 1894. Capsule biographies are presented of 83 rabbis with useful genealogical information. The entries are arranged alphabetically by Hebrew first name. With no apparent rationale for selection, the book covers several centuries.

Zarski, S.Z. *Anshei Shem, Toldot Anshei Shem* אנשי שם, תולדות אנשי שם Tel Aviv, 1940; New York, 1950.

Books about Rabbinical Families

Alfasi, Yitskhak. *Sefer Hayakhs Lebeit Eliash* ספר היחס לבית עליאש Jerusalem, 1975. Information is presented on the descendants and ancestors of the Eliash family of Vilna (related to the Gaon of Vilna).

Ehrlich, S. *Ateret Yehoshua* עטרת יהושע. New York, 1982. This is a photocopied version of a pre-Holocaust publication. Presented are a biography and description of descendants of Rabbi Yaakov Yehoshua of Lemberg, Frankfurt am Main, Berlin and elsewhere. Included is considerable genealogical material.

Eisenstadt "Daat Kedoshim (see above)

Epstein, A. *Mishpakhat Luria* משפחת לוריא. Vienna, 1901. This book traces the ancestry of the Luria family and gives details of principal descendants. The work has been criticized for inaccuracies and unsubstantiated claims.

Friedberg, B. *Bnei Landau Lemishpekhotam* בני לנדא למשפחותם. Frankfurt am Main, 1905. Biographical and genealogical material is presented on the early generations of the Landau family.

Friedberg, B. *Toldot Mishpakhat Horowitz* תולדות משפחת הורוויץ Frankfurt am Main, 1911. The author presents detailed material on the early generations of the Horowitz family.

Friedberg, Chaim Dov Berish. *Toldot Mishpakhat Shor* תלדות משפחת שור Frankfurt am Main, 1901. Genealogical material is given for the major personalities in the early generations of the famous Shor rabbinic family, from the time of Rashi through the 17th century.

Heilprin, Y. *Shalshelet Hayikhus* שלשלת היחוס, 1740. This is a manuscript genealogy of the Heilprin family.

Horowitz, Tsvi. *Toldot Mishpakhat Horowitz* תולדות משפחת הורוביץ. Krakow, 1932

Karlinsky, Chaim. *Harishon Leshoshelet Brisk* הראשון לשושלת בריסק. Jerusalem, 1984. This biography of the first rabbi of the Brisk dynasty, Rabbi Yosef DovBer Halevy Soloveitchik, includes material about his family and other prominent personalities in the world of the Lithuanian and Belarussian yeshivas.

Katzenellenbogen, Pinkhas. *Yesh Mankhilin* יש מנחילין Jerusalem, 1986. Based on a manuscript by a member of the Katzenellenbogen family in the mid-18th century, this book is essentially a personal memoir. The author mentions many rabbis and their families. The editor has prepared indexes of individuals mentioned. This is a fascinating and valuable first-hand source of rabbinical genealogy.

Kohen-Tzedek, Yosef. *Dor Yesharim* דור ישרים. Berdichev, 1898. Material is presented on the classical medieval rabbinical families descended from Rashi, through the Treves and Luria families. The author was a renowned 19th-century genealogist. (A number of his claims have been disputed by the modern genealogy critic, Shlomo England).

Levin, N. *Megilat Yukhsin* מגילת יוחסין. Warsaw, 1889. Details are given on selected descendants of the *Maharal* of Prague.

Lipschitz, C.U., and N. Rosenstein. *The Feast and the Fast.* New York: Maznaim, 1984. This biography of Rabbi Yom Tov Lipman Heller (the *Tosfot Yomtov*) includes genealogical charts of many of his descendants.

Maggid, David. *Sefer Toldot Mishpakhat Ginzburg* ספר תולדות משפחת גינצבורג. St. Petersburg, 1899. The author traces various branches of the Ginzburg family and includes biographical material and genealogical charts. The work tends to be disorganized and often fails to show clear linkage between branches. Critical comments by other genealogists appear in appendixes.

Margolis, Efraim Zalmen. *Maalot Hayukhsin* מעלות היוחסין. Lemberg, 1900. A detailed genealogy of the Margolis and Ettinger families is presented.

Michelsohn, Tsvi Yekhezkel. *Tsvi Letsadik* צבי לצדיק. Pietrkov, Poland, 1904. One of a series of books by this renowned classical genealogist, the volume includes detailed information on the descendants of Rabbi Tsvi Hersh Berlin (1721–1800).

Rapaport-Hortschtein, M.E. *Shalashelet Hazahav* שלשלת הזהב. Mukachevo, Ukraine, 1931. The descendants of Rabbi Naftali Katz, the author of *Smikhat Khakhamim,* are detailed.

Rivlin, Eliezer. *Sefer Hayakhas Lemishpakhat Rivlin Vehagaon Mivilna* ספר היחס למשפחת ריבלין והגר"א מווילנא. Jerusalem, 1935. Presents genealogical lists of many Litvak, Byelorussian and Eretz Yisrael families related to or descended from the Vilna Gaon. Descriptions include about 3,000 people traced by the author.

Rozenkrantz, Aharon. *Sefer Yukhsin* ספר יוחסין. Warsaw, 1885. Detailed (and often rare) material about a number of interrelated Eastern European rabbinical families. Included are Berenstein, Deiches, Eiger, Frenkel, Friefberg, Gaon of Vilna, Ginzburg, Gordon, Hamburger, Horowitz, Iserlin, Isserlis, Katz, Katzenellenbogen, Kosman, Levin, Lipshitz, Lopatin, Luria, Meizels, Minkowsky, Morgenstern, Nakhes, Padva, Polka, Rabinowicz, Rachlin. Rapoport, Ratner, Reizes, Rokach, Rozenberg, Rozenk-

rantz, Schwartz, Shik, Simchowicz, Shmeringer, Stern, Tulchinsky, Tumarkin, Yanover and Yevnin.

Schwerdscharf, M.J. *Hadrat Tsvi* הדרת צבי. Sighet, Romania, 1909. This genealogy of a portion of the Schwerdscharf family offers considerable material on ancestral rabbinical lines.

Stern, Y. *Zekher Leyehosef* זכר ליהוסף. Warsaw, 1898. Detailed material on the descendants of several Eastern European rabbinical families, including Broda, Eidels, Epstein, Gaon of Vilna, Heilprin, Horowitz, Isserles, Joffe, Katz, Levin, Luria, Meizels, Shapira, Slutsker, Stern, Temtzes and Yanover.

Wunder, Rabbi Meir. *Elef Margaliot* אלף מרגליות. Jerusalem, 1993. This book traces the ancestry of one of the rabbis of the Margolis family. Extensive biographical information, sources and genealogical charts present a summary of many ancient rabbinical families.

Zeligman, Y. *Megilat Yukhsin* מגילת יוחסין (pre-Holocaust). The book covers a number of interrelated rabbinical and scholarly families who lived in the Latgale region of Latvia and several towns of adjacent Vitebsk guberniya. Families include Altshul, Brauda, Donchin/Don Yechia, Druyan, Eizenstadt, Kissin, Levin, Margolis, Reizes, Rovinson, Shoyer, Sternim, Tzioni and Zeligman. Represents only 49 pages of the original manuscript; the rest disappeared in the Holocaust. The main text was written by Zeligman under the title *Megilat Yukhsin*; extensive footnotes written by Zeligman's relative, Rabbi Benzion Don-Yechia, under the title *Yakhas Avot* reveal keen insight into the historical events involving family members.

Ziv, Asher. *Rabbenu Moshe Isserles* (רמ"א) רבנו משה איסרליש. New York, 1972. The book traces selected descendants of Rabbi Moshe Isserles (the *Rema*).

Hasidic Rabbis

Alfasi, Yitzkhak. *Hakhassidut.* החסידות. Tel Aviv, 1974. This pictorial anthology of major Hasidic dynasties, although incomplete it is a useful reference book; the index lists more than 100 dynasties. A new edition, *Hakhassidut Midor Ledor*, is in publication.

Brandwein, Aharon Yaakov. *Tiferet Banim Avot* תפרת בנים אבות Jerusalem, 1978. Genealogical information is presented on selected Hasidic dynasties. Includes most of the major ones, such as Belz, Chernobil, Ger, Lubavitch, Lublin, Lyzhensk, Przyszucha, Ruzhin-Sadagora and Zanz.

Grossman, Levi. *Shem Veshe'erit.* שם ושארית Jerusalem, 1949. Detailed genealogical material on 79 Hasidic dynasties is presented. A second portion of this study appeared under the title *Kuntrus She'erit Leshe'erit.*

Heilprin, Shmuel Eliezer. *Sefer Hatze'etzaim* ספר הצאצאים Jerusalem, 1980. Descendants of the founder of Chabad (Lubavitch) Hasidism, Rabbi Shneour Zalman of Liadi, are given. Each generation is presented along with biographical material. The book is updated to current generations.

Lewin, Yehudah Leib. *Beit Kotsk* בית קוצק Jerusalem, 1990. This biography of the Hasidic master, Rabbi Menakhem Mendel Morgenstern of Kotsk, includes details of many of rabbis who were his students and followers.

Sephardi and Mizrachi Rabbinic Sources

Ben Naim, Yosef. *Malkei Rabbanan* מלכי רבנן. Jerusalem, 1931. This biographical dictionary of Sephardic rabbis in Morocco is arranged alphabetically by personal name. This highly recommended book of 127 pages covers the period 1275–1929.

In 1995 Yad Ben Tsvi* in Jerusalem published an experimental version of indexes prepared by Mathilde Tagger of Jerusalem. The indexes are arranged by surname, publications written by the rabbis, place of residence and date (both secular and Hebrew). Available at Yad Ben Tsvi or from Tagger.

Cohen, Benyamin Rafael. *Les Rabbins de Tunisie*. (Rabbis of Tunisia). [French and Hebrew]. Jerusalem, 1985. This compilation of biographies of Tunisian rabbis is organized by families (arranged by surname), often with genealogical elements. Although it covers 2,000 years, experts say that only the period 1690–1980 has historical value. Mathilde Tagger created three indexes for the period 1690–1980. Published (in small numbers) by Yad Ben Tsvi* in 1994, they are arranged by surname, publication and place of residence. Indexes are available at Yad Ben Tsvi or from Tagger.

Gaon, M.D. *Yehudei Hamizrakh Be'eretiz Yisrael* (Eastern Jews in the Land of Israel). . 2 vols. Jerusalem, 1936. Volume 2 is a history of Sephardic (and about 10 percent Mizrahi) rabbis and prominent scholars, writers and communal leaders who worked towards the realization of the concept of *shivat Tzion*, (return to Zion) and the rebuilding of the land. Essentially a biographical dictionary, this extensive work includes information about rabbis from Bulgaria, Syria, Turkey and the Balkan communities. It is arranged alphabetically by surname. Mathilde Tagger prepared an alphabetical index of surnames in Roman script with columns for birth date and place and death date and place. The index is available on the Internet at WWW.SEPHARDICSTUDIES.ORG/GAOM.HTML.

Gedolei Salonica. גדולי סלוניקה. Compilation of rabbis from Tripoli, Egypt, Syria and Tripoli.

Laniado, D. *Lakedoshim Asher Baretz*. לקדושים אשר בארץ. Jerusalem, 1980. This is a source about Syrian families.

Laredo, Avraham. *Las Noms des Juifs du Maroc sa essai d'Onomastique Judeo-Marocaine*. (Essay on the Onomastics of Moroccan-Jewish names). [French]. Madrid: Instituto d'Arias Montano, 1978. This is an onomastic analysis of the surnames of the Jews of Morocco that includes biographical material on rabbinical families.

Rozanes, S. *Divrei Yemei Yisrael Betorgama* דברי ימי ישראל בתורגמה. Tel Aviv, 1930. This book details the origins of families in the Turkish Empire, including the Baltic countries.

Tanugi, Y. *Toldot Khakhmei Tunis* תולדות חכמי טונים. Bnei Brak, Israel, 1988.

Toledano, Joseph. *Une Histoire de Familles. Les Noms de Famille Juifs d'Afrique de Nord des Origines a Nos Jours* (A history of families: The names of Jews of North Africa from their beginnings to today). [French]. Jerusalem: Ramtol, 1999. Lists names of families from North Africa and Egypt and their origins.

Books Written by Rabbis

Many books written by rabbis include genealogical information in the introductions or title pages. Following are extracts from some examples:

Rabbi Moshe Isserles, *Av Bet Din* (ABD) (head of rabbinical court) Krakow; his son-in-law Rabbi Moshe Halevy; his son Rabbi Natan Nata; his son Rabbi Moshe Yosef (his father-in-law was Rabbi Leib Khassid ABD Lemberg). Moshe Yosef's son Rabbi Yekutiel Zalmen, ABD Drabitz, (his father-in-law was Rabbi Mordekhai Ashkenazi of Brisk). Rabbi Yekutiel Zalmen had seven sons: Rabbi Yaakov, ABD Polange; Rabbi Yitskhak, ABD Shishburg; Rabbi Simkha, ABD Slonim; Rabbi Mordekhai, ABD Kotsk; Rabbi Natan, ABD Alesk; Rabbi Arye Leib .... (Shmuel Shapiro. *Me'il Shmuel*, Vilnius, 1896)

Rabbi Dovberish Ashkenazi, who sat on the seat of the rabbinate in the Holy Community of Slonim and Lublin,

where he is buried, a descendant of the Gaon Khakham Tsvi. (B. Ashkenzy. *Noda Beshearim*. Warsaw, 1864.)

Avraham Zakheim son of Moshe Natan, son of Rabbi Bentzion, son of Rabbi Yisrael, son of Rabbi Meshulum Zalmen ABD Pokroi, son of Rabbi Khaim ABD Birz, son of Rabbi Sholem ABD Birz, son of the martyr Yisrael who was killed for the sanctification of the Holy Name in the year 5420 [1659] in the city Rozinoi (now Ruzhany) (Avraham Zakheim, *Nitei Eitan*. Warsaw, 1901.)

I am the young Yisrael Moshe son of Rabbi Arye Leib, son-in-law of Uziel RABD Lissa. He was of great *yichus*. On his father's side he was a descendant of Rabbi Yitzhak Khayus, author of *Zerah Yitzhak* in which appears his family tree, and on his mother's side .....(Yisrael Moshe ben Arye Leib. *Rishmei She'elah*. Warsaw, 1836.)

Community Histories

Important sources of genealogical information for Eastern European rabbinical families are community histories published towards the end of the 19th and early 20th centuries. Most of the following books were written at a time when genealogical information was considered worth recording, in contrast to post-Holocaust *yizkor* books, in which precise personal details are rarely published. The older community histories record prominent and not-so-prominent members of the community, often deriving the material from gravestones, most recording selected inscriptions. Most of the books listed below are available in editions reprinted in Israel.

Alter, Avraham Mordekhai. *Bedarkei Polin Aveilot* בדרכי פולין אבלות. Jerusalem, 1987. Descriptions are given of current Jewish monuments and institutions that survived the Holocaust in Polish communities. The book includes details of many rabbis and tombstones in the Warsaw cemetery.

Balaban, Majer. *Dzieje Zydow w Krakowie I na Kazimierzu* [Polish]. Krakow, 1912. A detailed history of the Krakow community is given, with many genealogical charts of famous medieval rabbinical families.

Biber, M. *Mazkeret Gedolei Ostroah*. מזכרת גדולי אוסטרהא. Berdichev, Ukraine, 1907; Jerusalem, 1968. Biographical and genealogical material is presented about rabbis and other prominent people in Ostroah (also known as Ostov or Ostrova), Belarus.

Buber, S. *Anshei Shem* אנשי שם. Krakow, 1895. Biographical and genealogical material is given about rabbis and prominent people in Lwow.

Buber, S. *Kiryah Nisgava* קריה נשגבה. Krakow, 1903. Jerusalem, 1968. Biographical and genealogical material is included about rabbis and other prominent people in Zolkiew, Poland.

Cohen, Y.Y. *Khakhmei Hungaria* חכמי הונגריה. Tel Aviv, 1983. Hungarian community and biographical information.

Cohen, Y.Y. *Khakhmei Transylvania* חכמי טרנסילוואניה Tel Aviv, 1983. Community and biographical information from Transylvania.

Cohen, Y.Y. *Sefer Maramures* ספר מאראמארוש. Tel Aviv: Beit Maramaros, 1983. Community and biographical information about prominent individuals in Maramaros County, formerly Hungary, today Romania and Ukraine.

Dembitzer, Chaim Nathan. *Klilat Yofi* כלילת יופי Krakow, 1888. Biographical and genealogical material is presented about rabbis and other prominent people in Lwow.

Dukas. *Eva Lemoshav* או"ה למושב. The author presents a history of the communities Altona, Wandsbeck and Hamburg, Germany.

Eizenstadt, B. *Rabbanei Minsk VeKhakhameiha* רבני מינסק וחכמיה. Vilnius, 1899; Jerusalem, 1969. This book includes biographical and genealogical material about rabbis and prominent people in Minsk.

Feinstein, Arye Leib, *Ir Tehillah* עיר תהילה - העיר בריסק וגדוליה Warsaw, 1885; Jerusalem, 1968. This community history of Brest Litovsk lists notables divided by century, rabbinical publications and legislation pertaining to the Jews. Correspondence between the author and other prominent authorities about specific biographical and genealogical details is included.

Finn, Shmuel Yosef. *Kiriah Neemanah* קריה נאמנה. Vilna, 1860, 1915; reprinted in Israel in 1968. This historical background of the Jewish community in Vilna (Vilnius) includes quotes from communal records; civil documents; correspondence; legislative enactment pertaining to Jews under successive Polish, Lithuanian and Russian regimes. This is a summary of the earliest Eastern European rabbis, with emphasis on scholastic endeavors and their role in founding prominent *yeshivot*. Biographies of rabbis who held office in Vilna, *maggidim*, members of *beit din*, (rabbinical court) scribes, and other communal functionaries, as well as scholars who held no official position are introduced. Detailed footnotes and additional notes, plus commentaries by scholars and tombstone inscriptions are included. This valuable source of Lithuanian rabbinical genealogy, includes some errors, corrected in additional notes. (Note: Sequential numbers of sections differ among the various editions, resulting in confusion in locating of references quoted in other sources.)

Friedberg, B. *Lukhot Zikaron* לוחות זכרון. Frankfurt am Main, 1904. Biographical and genealogical material is presented about rabbis and other prominent people in Krakow.

Friedenstein, S.E. *Ir Gibborim* עיר גבורים. Vilnius, 1880; Jerusalem, 1969. Biographical and genealogical material is presented about rabbis and prominent people in Grodno.

Frumkin, A. *Toldot Khakhmei Yerushalayim* תולדות חכמי ירושלים. Jerusalem, 1872. This history includes biographies of scholars and rabbis who settled in Eretz Yisrael, particularly in Jerusalem, from the period of the Spanish Expulsion (1492) until the mid-19th century. The Sephardic and Ashkenazic communities are presented separately.

Gliksman, P.Z. *Ir Lask Vekhakhameiha* עיר לסק וחכמיה. Lodz, 1926; Jerusalem, 1968. Biographical and genealogical material is presented about rabbis and other prominent people in Lask.

Grunwald, Y.Y. *Kehilot Yisrael: BeSlovakia, Transylvania VeYugoslavia* קהילות ישראל בסלובקיה, טרנסילבניה ויוגוסלביה 1934, Jerusalem, 1968. Biographical and genealogical material is presented about rabbis and other prominent people in Slovakian, Transylvanian and Yugoslavian communities.

Horowitz, H. *Letoldot Hakehilot Bepolin* לתולדות הקהילות בפולין 1978. Biographical and genealogical information is given for rabbis in about 100 communities in Poland.

Horowitz, Mordekhai. *Rabbanei Frankfurt* רבני פרנקפורט. Jerusalem, 1972. Biographies of selected rabbis of Frankfurt am Main, selected tombstone inscriptions and quotes from the *Gedenkbuch* (memorial book to German Jews who perished in the Holocaust) and other community records are presented.

Kagan, Berel. *Yidishe Shtetl, Shtetlekh, un Dorfishe Yishuvim in Lite.* (Jewish towns, villages and small communities in Lithuania). [Yiddish]. New York, 1991.

A valuable source for Lithuanian genealogy, this book offers a treasure trove of information about many towns. The author has collected references from printed community books, biographies, archival material and the Jewish press in Eastern Europe. Each community is presented with its rabbis, people of notable *yichus,* writers and others worthy of note. For most towns, extensive donor and *prenumerantn* (lists of people who either pre-ordered or donated to be a book prior to its publication) lists are transcribed. Lists of sources make this book an excellent starting point for Lithuanian research.

Klausner, Y. *Toldot Hakehillah Haivrit Bevilna* תולדות הקהילה היהודית בוילנא. Vilnius, 1935, Jerusalem, 1969. Biographical and genealogical material is given about rabbis and other prominent people in Vilna (Vilnius).

Kohen-Zedek, Josef. *Shem Yeshe'erit.* שם ושארית. Krakow, Jerusalem, 1968. Biographical and genealogical material about rabbis and other prominent people in Przemysl, Poland is presented. Recent research has shown some assertions to be false.

Kupernik, A. *Lekorot Bnei Yisrael Bekiev* לקורות בני ישראל בקיוב. Berdichev, Ukraine, 1891; Jerusalem, 1969. Includes biographical and genealogical material about rabbis and other prominent people in Kiev.

Lipman, D.M. *Toldot Hayehudim BeKovno veSlobodka* תולדות היהודים בקובנא וסלבודקא Keidan, Lithuania, 1931. Jerusalem, 1968. Contains biographical and genealogical material about rabbis and other prominent people in Kovno (Kaunas), Lithuania.

Margolis, Kh.Z. *Dubno Rabbati* דובנא רבתי. Warsaw, 1910; Jerusalem, 1968. Biographical and genealogical material is included about rabbis and other prominent people in Dubno, Poland.

Markowitz, Moshe, *Lekorot Ir Rassein Urabbaneihah* לקורות עיר ראסיין ורבניה Warsaw, 1913. Gives the community history of Rassein and was published along with two additional community histories, those of Keidan and Novardok. Detailed biographies are given of the rabbis, scholars and influential people who either functioned in these towns or were born there and functioned as rabbis in other towns. The volume includes considerable genealogical material. This is a rare and almost exclusive source for these communities.

Nissenbaum, S.B. *Lekorot Hayehudim BeLublin* קורות היהודים בלובלין. Lublin, 1900; Jerusalem, 1968. Includes biographical and genealogical material about rabbis and other prominent people in Lublin.

Ovchinsky, L. *Di Geshikhte fun di Iden in Letland.* די געשיכטע פון די אידן אין לעטלאנד (History of the Jews in Letland). [Hebrew, Yiddish] Riga, 1908, 1918. This book offers detailed information on 25 communities located in the former Latvian provinces of Courland and Latgale. A list of the towns rabbis and prominent citizens includes genealogical information.

Schwartz, Pinkhas Zelig. *Shem Hegedolim Hashalem Legedolei Hungaria* שם הגדולים השלם לגדולי הונגריה. New York, 1958. This book provides detailed information on 1,700 rabbis of Hungary, including their communities and publications.

Steinshneider, Hillel Noakh. *Ir Vilna* עיר ווילנא Vilnius, 1900; Jerusalem, 1969. Chapters in this book on Vilna (now Vilnius) arranged by communal function: chief rabbis, *maggidim* (preachers), *dayanim* (judges), *rashei yeshivot* (heads of the *yeshiva*), lay leaders and prominent members of the community. Numerous detailed footnotes expand genealogical connections through in-law relationships. Each entry includes a list of the successive ancestral generations with footnotes pertaining to wives' families. The text for each person includes biography, scholarly publications, children and tombstone inscription. The book quotes communal records now unavailable. This volume is one of the most important sources for Eastern European genealogy.

Teumim, Kh. Z. *Zikaron Larishonim.* זכרון לראשונים. Kolomea, Ukraine, 1914; Jerusalem, 1969. Biographical and genealogical material is presented about rabbis and other prominent people in Kolomea.

Wachstein, B. *Mafteakh Hahespedim* מפתח ההספדים (Index to eulogies), 1924. This useful guide helps the reader locate books that include eulogies about rabbis.

Zinowitz, M. *Mir-Toldot Yeshivat Mir* תולדות ישיבת מיר (The history of the Mir *yeshiva*). Tel Aviv, 1981. This history of the development of the famous Byelorussian *yeshiva* of Mir includes considerable biographical material about the scholars who ran the *yeshiva* and many who attended.

Zunz, Y.M. *Ir Hatzedek* עיר הצדק. Krakow, 1874; Jerusalem, 1970. Biographical and genealogical material is presented about rabbis and other prominent people in Krakow.

Books of Tombstone Inscriptions

Following are some books of tombstone inscriptions, genealogically important because they typically supply such genealogical data as date of death, name of father of the deceased, tribal affiliation (e.g., kohen, levite, yisrael) and perhaps occupation or birthplace.

Berman, S. *Mishpakhot K"K Shklov.* משפחות ק"ק שקלאב Shklov, 1936. Tombstones in Shklov, Byelorussia, are listed by surname with some additional notes about the families.

Brisk, Asher Leib. Khelkat Mekhokek" חלקת מחוקק Brisk is a published work which contains about 3000 inscriptions of tombstones of those who are classified Ashenazim-Perushim, and who were buried in the 'Old Section' on the Mount of Olives in Jerusalem until about 1914. One large Sefardi Block is recorded. For other cemeteries in Israel a series of pamphlets was compiled in the mid-1930's by Pinkhas Grayevsky, giving tombstone lists for Jaffa, Rishon-Letzion, Nes Tziona, Petah Tikvah, Zikhron Yaakov, Ekron, and the Chabad section of the Mount of Olives. The old cemetery of Tel Aviv is listed in a published book *"Lekorot Beit Ha'almin Hayashan BeTel Aviv",* לקורות בית העלמין הישן בתל אביב covering the period until the mid 30's.

Friedman, Philip and Pincus Zelig Gliksman. *Stary Cmentarz Zydowski w Lodzi* (The old Jewish cemetery in Lodz). [Polish with one Hebrew section]. Lodz, 1938. This book records Jews buried in the old cemetery in Lodz from 1826 to 1893. Although written in Polish, genealogical data is easy to understand. Following is a typical sample of the genealogical data provided:

> No. 1286 (page 232) Jacob Saul Berlinski, son of Lejbusza Berliner from Piotrykow, who was known by the name "reb Lejbusz reb Tejweles." Tejwele was a son of Rabbi Hirsz Lewin from Berlin. Tejwele settled in Piotrykow since he married the daughter of a person from Piotrykow. Jacov Saul married the daughter of the Rabbi of Lutermirsk, Nuty Baharjer, and had three sons: Tewel in Lodz, Manele in Piotrykow and Naftali Hirsz, who was a merchant in Dabie. A son of Naftali Hirsz, Lajb Berliner, married a daughter of the Rabbi of Kalisz, Chaim Eliezer Waks. A daughter of Lajb Berliner married a son of the Tsadik of Gory Kalvariji, Majer.

Hock, *Mishpakhot K"K Prague.* משפחות ק"ק פראג. Prague, 1892. Epitaphs in the old Jewish cemetery in Prague are listed by surname of the deceased.

Klausner, Y. *Lekorot Beit Ha'almin Hayashan BeVilna* לקורות בית העלמין הישן בווילנה. Vilnius, 1935. This book lists tombstones located in the ancient cemetery of Vilna (Vilnius), now destroyed. It includes genealogical information.

Moneles, O. *Ketovot Mibeit Ha'almin Hayehudi Ha'atic Beprag* כתובות מבית העלמין היהודי העתיק בפראג (Inscriptions from the ancient Jewish cemetery in Prague). [Earlier editions in Czech and German]. Jerusalem, 1988. Selected tombstone inscriptions from Prague are published, including considerable genealogical information.

Weltsman, Shmuel Tzvi. *Avnei Zikaron.* אבני זכרון (Stones of Remembrance). This manuscript lists tombstone inscriptions in many Polish towns, including (author's Hebrew spelling): Bialystok, Blaszki, Breslau, Dobrin, Dombie, Fabianicz, Golin, Gombin, Grodziensk, Jaroczyn, Kalisz, Kempen, Koblin, Kolo, Konin, Kozmin, Krotoszyn, Kutno, Laki, Lask, Lida, Lipna, Lissa, Lowicz, Lunszyz, Nowy Dwor, Osmenya, Ostroah, Plotsk, Plonsk, Pozen, Praszki, Ripin, Rogozin, Schneidermuhl, Smorgon, Sochachow, Stawiszyn, Szeps, Szwerzentz, Szyraz. Thorn, Turke, Vilon, Wiszegrod, Wreszen, Zagrovi, Zakroczyn, Zdunska Wola and Zloczew.

Yevnin, Shmuel. *Nakhalat Olamin.* Warsaw, 1882. Tombstones from the 19th century in the Warsaw cemetery; genealogical notes are included.

Addresses

Ben Zvi Institute, location: Rehov Abarbanel 12, mailing address: P.O. Box 7660, Jerusalem; telephone: 972-2-539-8888; fax: 972-2-563-8310; e-mail: YADBZ@H2.HUM.HUJI.AC.IL; website: WWW.YBZ.ORG.IL.

Beth Hatefutsoth, Tel Aviv University, Ramat Aviv, Israel; e-mail: BHINFO@POST.TAU.AC.IL; website: WWW.BH.ORG.IL.

Central Archives for the History of the Jewish People, location: Rehov Jabotinsky 46, mailing address: P.O. Box 1149, Jerusalem 91010; telephone: 972-2-563-5716; fax: 972-2-566-7681; e-mail: ARCHIVES@VMS.HUJI.AC.IL; website: SITES.HUJI.AC.IL/ ARCHIVES.

Central Zionist Archives, location 4 Zalman Shazar Blvd., mailing address: P.O. Box 92, Jerusalem; telephone: 972-2-620-4800; fax:. 972-2-620-4837; e-mail: CZA@JAZO.ORG.IL; website: WWW.WZO. ORG.IL/CZA

Jewish National and University Library, location: Givat Ram Campus of Hebrew University, mailing address: P.O. Box 503, Jerusalem 91004; website: WWW.JNUL.HUJI.AC.IL.

Yad Vashem, location: Har Hazikaron, mailing address: P.O. Box 377, Jerusalem 91034; telephone: 972-2-675-1611; fax: 972-2-643-3511; e-mail: general.information@yadvashem.org.il; website: WWW.YADVASHEM.ORG.IL.

Bibliography

Adler, Frank. "The Descendancy of Rashi." *AVOTAYNU* 4, no. 1, (Spring 1988): 9.

Agmon, Chava. "Split Tree—Fragmented Branches: The Kara/Caro Family." *Sharsheret Hadorot* 7, no. 1, January 1993.

Bauer, Yehuda. *The History of the Holocaust.* New York: F. Watts, 1982.

Beller, Eliyahu. "Are All Ashkenazim Descended from Rashi?." *AVOTAYNU* 6, no. 1 (Spring 1990): 28.

Einseidler, David. "Can We Prove Descent from King David." *AVOTAYNU* 8, no. 3 (Fall 1992): 29.

Englard, Shlomo. "Common Errors in Deeds of Family Lineage." *Tsfunot* 3, no. 4, 1991/92.

———. "Common Errors in Deeds of Family Lineage." *Tsfunot* 4, no. 1, 1992.

———. "Common Errors in Genealogical Tables." *Tsfunot* 3, no. 3. 1991.

———. "On Jewish Genealogy." *Tsfunot* 3, no. 2, 1991.

Freedman, Chaim "Prenumerantn As a Source for the Jewish Genealogist." *AVOTAYNU* 10, no. 2 (Summer 1994): 41–45.

———. "Torah and Genealogy," in *Eliyahu's Branches, the Descendants of the Vilna Gaon and His Family.* Teaneck, N.J.: Avotaynu, 1997.

Freedman, Chaim "Beit Rabbanan, Sources of Rabbinical Genealogy", Petah Tikvah 2001.

Honey, Michael. "A Method for Depicting Interconnected Rabbinical Families Simultaneously: The Jewish Historical Clock." *AVOTAYNU* 17, no. 3 (Fall 2001): 10–15.

Hildesheimer, Esriel. "Missing Treves Genealogy." *AVOTAYNU* 5, no. 3 (Fall 1989): 39.

———. "The Treves Families." *AVOTAYNU* 5, no. 1 (Spring 1989): S17–S22.

Jacobi, Paul. "Genesis of the Rapapport Family." *Shersharet Hadorot* 8, no. 2 (March 1994).

———. "The Comradeship Between Historiography and Genealogy." *Studies and Stories in Family History*. nos. 3–4. Jerusalem: Israel Genealogical Society and Hamakor, 5/1990.

———. "The Historicity of the Raschi Descent." *AVOTAYNU* 6, no. 1 (Spring 1990): 17.

———. "Which Rapaports are Also SCHaCH Descendants?" *AVOTAYNU* 11, no. 3 (Fall 1995): 70.

Lamdan, Neville. "A Critique of Richter and Rosenstein." *AVOTAYNU* 5, no. 2 (Summer 1989): S22–S24.

Letter to the Editor. "Comments on Rosenstein's Luria Lineage." *AVOTAYNU* 7, no. 3 (Fall 1991): 47.

Letter to the Editor. "Expands on Chabad Article." *AVOTAYNU* 8, no. 4 (Winter, 1992): 66.

Letter to the Editor. "Questions Luria Documentation." *AVOTAYNU* 7, no. 3 (Fall 1991): 28.

"List of Family Genealogies Developed by Dr. Paul Jacobi Deposited at Beth Hatefutsoth." *AVOTAYNU* 10, no. 2 (Summer 1994): 19.

Menton, Arthur F. *The Book of Destiny, Toldot Charlap*. Cold Spring Harbor, NY: King David Press, 1996.

Richter, John David. "About Some Problems with Rabbinic Genealogies." *AVOTAYNU* 5, no. 1 (Spring 1989): 36.

———. "The Descent from Rashi: A Review." *AVOTAYNU* 6, no. 2 (Summer 1990): 35.

Ronn, Michoel. "Chabad-Lubavitch Literature as a Genealogical Source." *AVOTAYNU* 8, no. 3 (Fall 1992): 40.

Rosenstein, Neil. "A Response to Jacobi's Rashi Article." *AVOTAYNU* 6, no. 2 (Summer 1990): 36.

———. "Ashkenazic Rabbinic Families." *AVOTAYNU* 3, no. 1 (Summer 1987): 7.

———."Englard's Articles on Questions in Rabbinic Genealogy," *AVOTAYNU* 12, no. 1 (Spring 1996): 36–38.

———. "Rosenstein's Rebuttal to Richter." *AVOTAYNU* 5, no. 1 (Spring 1989): 12–13.

———. "A 17th-Century Luria Manuscript Based on an Earlier Manuscript." *AVOTAYNU* 7, no. 2 (Summer 1991): 19–22.

———."Rashi's Descent from King David." *AVOTAYNU* 8, no. 3 (Fall 1992): 31.

———. "Sherwood `Forest' Through the Genealogical Trees." *AVOTAYNU* 14, no. 4 (Winter 1998): 21–22.

———. "Will the Correct Pinchas Horowitz Please Stand Up?" *AVOTAYNU* 15, no. 2 (Summer 1999): 18–20.

———. "Spira and Luria Families Revisited." *AVOTAYNU* 10, no. 4 (Winter 1994): 17.

Rosenstein, Neil and Dov Weber. "Rapaport Family: A Response to Paul Jacobi." *AVOTAYNU* 12, no. 3 (Fall 1996): 46.

———. "The Edelman Hoax and the Origins of Anglo-Jewish Aristocracy." *AVOTAYNU* 14, no. 2 (Summer 1998): 25.

Tauber, Laurence S. "From the Seed of Rashi." *AVOTAYNU* 8, no. 3 (Fall 1992): 32.

Tedeschi, Mark. "Baal Shem Tov Project." *AVOTAYNU* 2, no. 2 (May 1986): 3.

Wunder, Meir. *Me'orei Galicia: entsiklopedia lehokhmei Galicia*. Jerusalem: Institute for Commemoration of Galician Jewry, 1978–2001.

———. "The Reliability of Genealogical Research in Modern Rabbinic Literature." *AVOTAYNU* 11, no. 4 (Winter 1995), 31–36.

———. "The Kollel Galicia Archive." *AVOTAYNU* 7, no. 3 (Fall 1991): 23.

Notes

1. Bauer, Yehuda. *The History of the Holocaust.*
2. Beller, Elyahu, "Are All Ashkenazim Descended from Rashi?" *AVOTAYNU* 6, no. 1 (Spring 1990): 28.
3. *Responsa* are an exchange of letters in the form of a question and an answer in which one party consults the other [a rabbi] on a matter of religion. This literature dates from the Sheirira Gaon (906–1006) and spans every country and continent in which Jews have lived. Essentially commentaries on the Talmud, they typically include the author's genealogy in the preface.
4. Freedman, Chaim. "Torah and Genealogy" in *Eliyahu's Branches, The Descendants of the Vilna Gaon and His Family.*
5. See the writings of Josephus.
6. Articles by Neil Rosenstein and Paul Jacobi in *AVOTAYNU* Spring 1989, Spring 1990, Winter 1994.
7. Rapaport, Chanan. "Development of the Jewish Intellectual Class." *AVOTAYNU* 11, no. 2 (Summer 1995): 32–34.
8. Menton, Arthur F. *The Book of Destiny, Toledot Charlap.*
9. The original students and followers of the Baal Shem Tov regarded the Maggid of Mezerich as his successor for the leadership of the entire group. However, a number of the principal students of the Baal Shem Tov were so highly regarded by their followers that break away groups arose. These were centered in particular towns which gave their name to that sub-group of hasidim. The leaders, known as *admor* or *tzaddik* or *rebbe*, were treated similar to royalty and their homes were regarded like palaces even though many were poor and had modest dwellings. Hence, the term "court" came to describe the rebbe's entourage, his home and his followers. When the followers of a particular court moved away from the rebbe's town, they maintained their identity with the home base and were known as hasidim of Belz, Sadagora, Zunz and so forth. They established their own synagogues and *batei midrash* (houses of study) which were referred to as affiliated with the particular court.

   Some hasidic rebbes behaved like royalty; Ruzhin hasidim and its subdivisions—Chortkov, Sadagora and others—claimed descent from King David and lived in great opulence, dressing in expensive clothing, receiving visitors while seated on a throne and traveling in a coach. The leadership of each court, like the inheritance of a royal crown, usually passed from father to son. Disputes about succession resulted in splinter groups that founded new courts, known by the name of another town.
10. Wunder, Meir. "The Reliability of Genealogical Research in Modern Rabbinical Literature." *AVOTAYNU* 11, no. 4 (Winter 1995): 31–32.
11. The use of the word "classical" as in "classical rabbinical lines" is a matter of consensus and not exact definition. No fixed list exist of classical rabbinical lines. As used here, the term classical refers to any rabbinical families that can be traced back before the 18th century. Likewise, genealogical sources written before the 20th century are a classical fixed list though a general consensus. The terms "ancient" and "medieval" are used interchangeably with "classical."
12. "On Jewish Genealogy." *Tsfunot*. Bnai Brak: 1991, 3, 2; "Common Errors in Genealogical Tables." *Tsfunot*. B'nai Brak, 1991, 3, 3; "Common Errors in Deeds of Family Lineage." *Tsfunot*. B'nei Brak, 1991/92, 3, 2.

Cemetery Research
by Arline Sachs and Warren Blatt

Jewish cemeteries are major resources for genealogists. Tombstones, their placement, the organization of cemeteries and records kept about burials all may yield valuable data. Jewish tradition mandates that cemeteries be kept in perpetuity, a fact that increases the likelihood of finding an ancestor's final resting place. Jewish cemeteries have existed for 800 years in Prague, Czech Republic, and in Frankfurt am Main, Germany. In Israel, archaeologists have found 2,000-year-old burials.

Jews may be buried in exclusively Jewish cemeteries, Jewish sections of Christian cemeteries, or military, municipal and/or nonsectarian cemeteries. The Jewish religion permits burials to be made over previous burials, but only if no other place to bury exists. Thus the ancient Prague cemetery has seven layers of bodies. Jewish law forbids cremation, but some European cemeteries have sections for ashes and tombstones that are memorials to family lost in the Holocaust.

Cemetery organization varies from place to place and over time. In some, burials are placed in sequence according to date of death. Some have separate sections for men, women, children and rabbis, while still others have family plots. The existence of family plots offers the possibility of discovering the graves of related, often unknown, family members. In cemeteries with family plots, entire genealogies sometimes may be constructed merely by observing who is buried next to whom.

Given the difficulty of transporting bodies long distances, plus the Jewish law that burial must occur (usually) within 24 hours of death, it is not surprising that the acquisition of land for a cemetery often was one of the first actions of a newly organized Jewish community. In some cases, however, a central cemetery was used for several neighboring communities that may have been located only a few miles from one another.

Cemeteries generally are closed when all space for burials has been used; then land is bought elsewhere for a new cemetery. Old, no longer used cemeteries often remain in existence and can be fertile ground for genealogical research. Such is the case of a Frankfurt am Main cemetery closed in 1824; many old broken stones are piled in the middle of the cemetery, some of which date from 1200 and still are legible.

Sometimes the existence of old Jewish tombstones is the only known proof of Jewish settlement in a specific time and place. During the 19th century, Jewish tombstones dating from the 13th century were found supporting the Main River bank near Mainz, Germany. Although no one knew exactly where the cemetery had once stood, the stones proved that Jews had been in that area for centuries.

Genealogical Information on Tombstones

Inscriptions on tombstones take many forms. Some are written in both Hebrew and the local secular language, but until very recent times, all would have the name of the deceased written in the traditional Hebrew form (e.g., "here lies *name of the deceased* son (or daughter) of *name of the father of the deceased*"). At a minimum, therefore, a researcher will learn a date of death and the name of the father of the deceased. Occassionally even more information is provided adding the name of the father's father. (e.g., "Batya bat (daughter) of Avraham bar (son of) Isaac")

Sometimes considerable additional information is found. Many tombstones in old cemeteries in the southern United States indicate the deceased's town and country of origin. These cemeteries generally served the wave of immigration from German-speaking lands, so it is not surprising that the most commonly listed places of origin are Alsace, Germany, Hesse and Prussia—along with the exact town in that area.

In general, older tombstones included more data than stones carved today. Many have unfamiliar abbreviations. Often a married woman's stone supplies the name of her husband and her husband's father, in addition to the name of her father. Family names, however, are rare on Ashkenazic tombstones in Western Europe before 1800, and were rarely used on Eastern European tomnbstones before the mid-19th century. Sephardic Jews adopted family names much earlier.

Not everything engraved in stone is necessarily accurate. Mistakes are made. Information for a tombstone often is supplied when the family is grieving and may provide inaccurate data. The person who died may be given a higher age, as a revered elder. A grandparent or even a parent's name may be remembered only by the nickname by which they were known. Sometimes mistakes are made by those who engrave the tombstones.[1,2,3] Records held by the cemetery or the funeral home also may contain errors. In one case, for example, a wife was listed as a daughter—leading to considerable confusion for an unsuspecting genealogist.

If You Cannot Read Hebrew

Here are a few helpful pointers if you cannot read Hebrew. At the top of most Jewish tombstones is the abbreviation פ״נ, which stands for פה נקבר, meaning "here is buried." At the end of many Hebrew tombstone inscriptions is the abbreviation תנצב״ה, which is the abbreviation of a verse from I Samuel 25:29, "May his soul be bound up in the bond of eternal life."

If Hebrew characters are written on a tombstone, they are most likely to be the person's Hebrew name. A Hebrew name always includes a patronymic (e.g., the Hebrew word בן, ben, means "son of," as in "Yaacov ben Yitzhak"; בת, bat means "daughter of." On tombstones these words often appear as

Hebrew Alphabet			Days	
1	א	aleph	א	1
2	ב	bet	ב	2
3	ג	gimel	ג	3
4	ד	dalet	ד	4
5	ה	hay	ה	5
6	ו	vav	ו	6
7	ז	zayin	ז	7
8	ח	khet	ח	8
9	ט	tet	ט	9
10	י	yud	י	10
20	כ	kaf	יא	11
30	ל	lamed	יב	12
40	מ	mem	יג	13
50	נ	nun	יד	14
60	ס	samech	טו	15
70	ע	ayin	טז	16
80	פ	pay	יז	17
90	צ	tzade	יח	18
100	ק	kuf	יט	19
200	ר	resh	כ	20
300	ש	shin	כא	21
400	ת	tav	כב	22
			כג	23
			כד	24
			כה	25
			כו	26
			כז	27
			כח	28
			כט	29
			ל	30

ב׳ר, an abbreviation for ben reb, meaning "son (or daughter) of the worthy," followed by the father's given name. The word reb is a simple honorific, a title of respect; it does not mean rabbi.

Dates are written in Hebrew according to the Jewish calendar. Year 1 of this calendar starts with the creation of the world and probably was designed by the patriarch Hillel II in the fourth century. Hillel calculated the age of the world by computing the literal ages of biblical characters and other events in the Bible, and constructed a calendar that begins 3,760 years before the Christian calendar.

The letters of the Hebrew alphabet each have a numerical value (see above). To calculate a date written in Hebrew letters, add up the numerical values of each letter. This is the date according to the Jewish calendar, not the calendar we use in everyday life, known as the Gregorian calendar (also referred to as the Common Era, civil or Christian calendar). In January 2002, for example, the Jewish year was 5762. Given a Hebrew date, you need to do only a little bit of math to change the Hebrew year into a secular year.

On tombstones, a Hebrew date omits the millennium. For example, the Hebrew year 5680 will be written as 680 rather than 5680. To compute the civil (Gregorian) year, simply add the number 1240 to the shortened Hebrew year.

Here is an example: If the year is written as תרפג, the letter ת is 400, the letter ר is 200, פ is 80, and ג is 3. 400 + 200 + 80 + 3 = 683. The 5000 is usually left off, so the actual year would be 5683. By using this formula, 683 plus 1240 is 1923. That is the civil year.

The Hebrew year begins on Rosh Hashanah, which occurs on the Gregorian calendar in September or October. Therefore, the dates listed for the first months of the Hebrew calendar—Tishri, Heshvan, Kislev and sometimes Tevet—must be read as applying to the preceding year of the civil calendar because they occur after the Jewish New Year but before the Gregorian change of year.

The complete transposition of a Hebrew date to a Gregorian date uses a very complex formula. It is easier simply to refer to one of the published or online reference works such as JewishGen's JOS calculator (WWW.JEWISHGEN.ORG/JOS) or *The Comprehensive Hebrew Calendar, 5703–5860* by Arthur Spier or the *150 Year Calendar* by Rabbi Moses Greenfield. Most synagogues and Jewish libraries possess one of these works. Another alternative is to use one of several computer programs such as CALCONV, JCAL, LUACH. These programs can convert Hebrew to Gregorian dates and vice versa, as well as display calendars and *yahrzeit* (date of death) dates for any year. Use an Internet search engine to locate one of these programs.

Symbols on Tombstones

In addition to the inscription, symbols on the tombstone can be clues. Two hands, with four fingers each divided into two sets of two fingers, is the symbol of a priestly blessing. This signifies a Kohen, a descendant of Aaron. A pitcher signifies a Levite—the Levites were responsible for cleaning the hands of the Temple priests in ancient days. A candelabra often is used on the tombstone of a woman and the six-pointed Star of David on that of a man. A tombstone with the motif of a broken branch or tree stump often signifies someone who died young. There are many other symbols.

Finding the Cemeteries

In the United States and Canada, a person's death certificate, issued by the State or Provincial government, will contain the name of cemetery in which that person was buried.

The best single resource for data about Jewish cemeteries worldwide is the Cemetery Project of the International Association of Jewish Genealogical Societies. Begun in 1992, the project has identified more than 22,000 Jewish cemeteries worldwide, including where known books written about the cemeteries. More than 550,000 names of burials in 1,000 cemeteries were collected; 350,000 names were listed on the preliminary CD-ROM sold by IAJGS in 1998. Most of the information about the cemeteries is available via the Internet at WWW.JEWISHGEN.ORG/CEMETERY. Information supplied by the United States Commission for the Preservation of America's

Heritage Abroad*, which surveyed approximately 4,000 cemeteries, is included in the IAJGS project.

Landsmanshaftn (societies of immigrants from the same European town) in the United States and Canada at the beginning of the 20th century commonly purchased sections of larger cemeteries for the use of members. In cities with large Jewish populations, a single cemetery may be divided into hundreds of sections used by different landsmanshaftn. Some landsmanshaftn had sections in more than one cemetery, and the societies usually kept their own records. The records of many defunct societies now are at YIVO* (see Chapter on YIVO). In other cases, records were passed down within families and may be extremely difficult to locate. Synagogues also purchased sections of cemeteries as did some occupational associations. Ask in cemetery offices for the name of the person who is responsible for the care of the gravesite. This may lead to a living relative you did not know existed.

Finding records may be difficult for cemeteries that are no longer in use. When this is the case, look for Jewish undertakers in the area; they may have the records or know what has become of them. Sometimes one company is bought by another and the existing undertaker will have the older records of the defunct company.

Finding Information About Burials

Not all Jewish cemeteries can be accessed directly. Genealogists seeking material from European and/or Arab communities are often frustrated either by the ravaging effects of war, particularly after the Holocaust, or by access restrictions in certain countries. Especially in those situations, *chevra kadisha* (holy burial society) records are valuable alternate sources of information. The journal in which chevra kadisha records are kept is called a *pinkas* (minute book). In countries and at periods of time when the Jewish community was largely composed of immigrants, the pinkas may record the town of origin of the deceased.

Some of these records have found their way into libraries and archives. Such material includes original manuscripts of *chevra kadisha pinkassim* (or printed versions of them) and published books that record a survey of tombstone inscriptions. Many cemeteries in Europe, the United States and elsewhere have been surveyed and books written about them. A number of books are devoted specifically to recording tombstone inscriptions. Usually, the recording was made before either the cemetery or the records were destroyed. Three of the most valuable books of inscriptions are:

- Berman, S. *Mishpakhot K"K Shklov* (Shklov, 1936) which cites tombstones in Shklov, Belarus, listed by surname with some additional notes about the families.
- Brisk, Asher Leib. *Khelkhat Mekhokek.* This includes approximately 3,000 inscriptions of tombstones of individuals classified as Ashenazim-Perushim buried in the "Old Section" on the Mount of Olives in Jerusalem until about 1914. One large Sephardic block is recorded.
- The Leo Baeck Institute has a series of photocopies of 10,000 deaths (and presumable burials) covering the years

Hebrew Months:

תשרי	Tishri	Sep/Oct
חשון	Heshvan	Oct/Nov
כסלו	Kislev	Nov/Dec
טבת	Tevet	Dec/Jan
שבט	Shevat	Jan/Feb
אדר	Adar	Feb/Mar
אדר ב'	Adar II	Mar
ניסן	Nisan	Mar/Apr
אייר	Iyar	Apr/May
סיון	Sivan	May/Jun
תמוז	Tamuz	Jun/Jul
אב	Av	Jul/Aug
אלול	Elul	Aug/Sep

1200–1828 in Frankfurt am Main compiled by Ettlinger in the early 1900s. Besides the names of the person buried much family information is included such as ancestors, spouse(s) and children is included. Copies are available in Frankfurt at the Jewish museum and at the University of Jerusalem.

Community histories written during the 19th century often also include lists of tombstones and genealogies of prominent personalities (SEE CHAPTER ON RABBINIC GENEALOGY). Such manuscripts do not abound. In Israel several *pinkassim* are held in the Manuscripts Department of the Jewish National and University Library* (JNUL) at Hebrew University in Jerusalem (WWW.HUJI.AC.IL). Others may be found in the JNUL microfilm reading room. Additional *pinkassim* are held in the Central Archives for The History of the Jewish People* also in Jerusalem.

Use of *chevra kadisha* material requires experience in deciphering Hebrew handwriting and a familiarity with relevant terminology and abbreviations. Usually the material is arranged chronologically and has no alphabetical index. Research must be carried out by a painstaking survey of all the material (unless approximate dates are known). Fortunately, this search often can be rewarding, since additional information about the deceased's occupation and family may be included. Individuals may be discovered whose identity as relatives was previously unknown; through marital ties, indicated by the discovery of parent's-in-law, entirely new family lines may be uncovered.

By perusal of *chevra kadisha* records, one may discover unknown siblings who died young, as well as solve the eternal problem of tracing female lines. Researchers of Jewish genealogy frequently are plagued by a dearth of information about their female ancestry. Often the only sources of their names and those of their fathers are in *chevra kadisha* and cemetery records. In these documents, the name of the husband may be recorded with that of the wife. Use of *chevra kadisha* records requires recognition of the arrangement of the entries; in certain cases, separate lists have been kept for males, females, children, and prominent members of the community.

The Diaspora Research Institute* at Tel Aviv University has surveyed all Jewish cemeteries in Turkey. Results of this project are not yet posted on the Internet, although project director Professor Minna Rozen (www.tau.ac.il/humanities/vip/Rozen-Minna.html) promised that they will be eventually. In the meantime, is may be possible to obtain individual listings for a fee. Write directly to the Diaspora Research Institute to inquire.

For those who have relatives buried in Israel, the functioning *chevra kadisha* of each city is the primary resource. Although most use an unindexed chronological system, efforts are being made in several cities to computerize the information. The large Ashkenazi *chevra kadisha* in Jerusalem is completely computerized (see chapter on Israel).

A series of pamphlets was compiled in the mid-1930s by Pinkhas Grayevsky with tombstone lists for Jaffa, Rishon-L'Zion, Nes Tziona, Petah Tikvah, Zikhron, Yaakov, Ekron, and the Chabad section of the Mount of Olives. Burials in the old cemetery of Tel Aviv are listed in *Lekorot Beit Ha'almin Hayashan BeTel Aviv* through the mid-1930s.

Many books have been written about cemeteries; some are general, some deal with specific topics such as engravings, inscriptions or preservation, and some are about a single cemetery. Most of these books are listed on the IAJGS cemetery project webpages. To begin research on the IAJGS cemetery website look at www.jewishgen.org/cemetery. Many of the countries have a general page in addition to listing cemeteries by city. Always look at the general page for the country first. Here are listed books that describe several locations within the country or other important cemetery information about the country. The general page also lists organizations within that country that may be working on restoration of Jewish sites or that may be contacted for additional help. Next look at the general pages for the city of interest; look for a specific cemetery within that city. Many books were written about several cemeteries for a single city, while others describe only one cemetery. The latter are listed with the information about that cemetery.

The JewishGen Online Worldwide Burial Registry ("JOWBR"), is a new online database of Jewish burials worldwide. JOWBR is a volunteer project to catalogue extant names and other identifying information from cemeteries and burial records, from the earliest records to the present. The JOWBR database contains photographs of each tombstone, where available. The initial release of JOWBR, launched in 2003, contains hundreds of thousands of Jewish burial records. The JOWBR database can be accessed at www.jewishgen.org/databases/cemetery.

Addresses

Association for Gravestone Studies, 278 Main Street, Suite 207, Greenfield, Massachusetts 01301; telephone: 3-772-0836; website: www.gravestonestudies.org. The association produces a quarterly newsletter, has scholarships and a lending library for members. (Not exclusively Jewish.)

Central Archives for The History of the Jewish People. Rehov Jabotinsky 46, mailing address P.O. Box 1149, Jerusalem, Israel 91010.

Manuscripts Department, Jewish National and University Library, location: Givat Ram campus, Hebrew University; mailing address: P.O. Box 503, Jerusalem, Israel 91004.

United States Commission for the Preservation of America's Heritage Abroad, 888 17th Street NW, Suite 1160, Washington, D.C. 20006; telephone: 202-254-3824. fax: 202-254-3934. e-mail: uscommission@heritageabroad.gov; website: www.heritageabroad.gov.

YIVO, Center for Jewish History, 15 W. 16th Street, New York, New York.

Bibliography

A few additional references not found on the JewishGen cemetery site are:

"Getting the Most Out of Your Cemetery Visit" *DOROT, the Journal of the Jewish Genealogical Society* (New York) 11, no.2 (Winter 1989–90): 2–3 and

"Tools of the Trade." *DOROT* 11, no.4 (Summer 1990): 16; and 12, no. 1 (Autumn 1990): 8

Berman, S. *Mishpakhot K"K Shklov* (Shklov, 1936). Tombstones in Shklov, Belarus, listed by surname with some additional notes about the families.

Rath, Gideon. "Hebrew Tombstone Inscriptions and Dates," *Chronicles* (Newsletter of the Jewish Genealogical Society of Philadelphia) 5, no. 1 (Spring 1986): 1–4.

Strangstad, Lynne. *A Graveyard Preservation Primer.* Brooklyn, NY: Center for Thanatology Research, 391 Atlantic Ave.

Weltsman, Shmuel Tzvi. *Avnei Zikaron.* Manuscript of tombstone inscriptions in many Polish towns.

Yevnin, Shmuel. *Nakhalat Olamin.* Warsaw, 1882. Tombstones in the main Warsaw Jewish cemetery with valuable genealogical notes.

Notes

1. Bar Zev, Asher. "Epitaphs and Grave Markers: Can You Believe Everything You See?" *AVOTAYNU* 18, no.4 (Winter 2002).
2. Bronstein, Shalom. "Common Hebrew Abbreviations on Tombstones." *AVOTAYNU* 16, no.1 (Spring 2000)
3. Stone, Darla. "Not Everything Carved in Stone is Correct," *AVOTAYNU* 16, no.2 (Summer 2000)

Communal and Synagogue Histories

by Peggy K. Pearlstein

Y ou can begin to research the history of a community, its synagogues, and other institutions by consulting published bibliographies. More recent titles will appear in library catalogues and in journals. Archives possess primary documents such as organizational minutes that are invaluable for anyone engaged in research on communal and congregational histories. Through the Internet it is now possible to search many repository's online catalogues and manuscript collections for records and histories of Jewish communities.

Published Works

American Synagogue History: A Bibliography and State-of-the-Field Survey (Markus Wiener Pub: New York, 1988; Library of Congress call number: Z6373.U5 K67 1988) compiled by Alexandra Shecket Korros and Jonathan D. Sarna lists more than 1200 monographs, pamphlets, and articles published prior to 1988 that give histories of synagogues and Jewish communities in the United States.

Pioneer American Synagogues: A State By State Guide (J.H. Preisler: Wilmington, Delaware, 1995, rev. ed.; Library of Congress call number: BM205.P74 1995) by Julian Preisler lists the oldest existing Jewish congregation in each of the fifty states and the District of Columbia. Founders, charter members, incorporators, and/or early Jewish residents and cemeteries used by each synagogue follow each listing.

The American Synagogue: A Historical Dictionary and Sourcebook (Greenwood Press: Westport, CT, 1996; Library of Congress call number: BM205. O45 1996) edited by Kerry M. Olitzky and Marc Lee Raphael includes representative histories of more than 240 synagogues in North America affiliated with the four major movements in Judaism: Orthodox, Conservative, Reconstructionist and Reform. Concise state-by-state entries give a brief history of the synagogue, its building locations and its rabbinic leaders. References that follow each entry list printed histories and documents and the library and manuscript collections which contain the individual synagogue's archives. Names of individuals can be found in the index.

"Bibliography of North American Jewish Community Books," appears as Section 4 of *Jewish Genealogy Yearbook 2000*, presented by the International Association of Jewish Genealogical Societies (Atlanta, GA: The Association; Library of Congress call number: CS31.J52). Listings appear under individual state for the United States, under the province for Canada, and under the headings Mexico, Caribbean and Central America. Titles also include memoirs, cemetery indexes and some journal articles.

Southern New Jersey Synagogues; A Social History Highlighted by Stories of Jewish Life from the 1880s–1980s (Staples: Marlton, N.J., 1991; Library of Congress call number: BM223.N5 M49 1991) by Allen Meyers is an example of a regional work based on oral histories.

Journals

Judaica Americana: An Annotated Bibliography of Publications from 1960 to 1990 (Carlson Publishing: Brooklyn, N.Y., 1995, 2 volumes; Library of Congress call number: Z6373.U5 K34 1995) ccumulates the bibliographies published until 1990 by the late Dr. Nathan M. Kaganoff in the American Jewish Historical Society's (AJHS) journal, *American Jewish Historical Quarterly* (Library of Congress call number: E184. J5A5; previously titled *Publications of the American Jewish Historical Society* and now *American Jewish History*). The annotated bibliographies list monographic and periodical literature acquired by the library of the AJHS from the United States, Canada and Latin America. There are sections on synagogue histories, local histories and articles contained in selected Jewish journals. A subject index facilitates searching by topic and the names of individual synagogues.

The American Jewish Archives Journal (Library of Congress call number: E184.J5 A37) lists recent acquisitions at the American Jewish Archives in Cincinnati, Ohio. Newsletters and journals of other repositories also contain newly acquired materials. These include records of synagogues, organizations and individuals. The *YIVO News* of the YIVO Institute for Jewish Research at the Center for Jewish History in New York City (Library of Congress call number: DS101. N43) is one example of an archival institution which lists new accessions, including communal records and photographs.

Online Catalogues and Databases

The Library of Congress online catalogue (www.loc.gov) is available to researchers twenty-four hours a day. The most effective way to search the catalogue is by consulting the multivolume *Library of Congress Subject Headings* (LCSH) (Washington: Library of Congress, annual; Z695.Z8 L524a), known familiarly as the "Red Books" and found in most reading rooms of the Library. The highly structured, very specific headings utilize a controlled vocabulary. Many other libraries and research institutions in the United States also use the same subject headings. Most of the Israeli academic libraries use the LCSH too. These institutions often make their own catalogues available on the Internet.

Headings such as Synagogues or Jews can be followed by subdivisions and strung together in a fixed order to limit your search. This is especially helpful if you do not know the exact title or author of a work, or if you want to know what has been published under a certain subject.

The book, *Jubilee: Our First Fifty Years: Kew Gardens Synagogue Adath Yeshurun*, edited by Saul Bernstein (Kew Gardens, NY: Kew Garden Synagogue Kahal Adath Yeshurun, 1990; Library of Congress call number: MLCM 93/04862 (B)) can be found under the subject heading, Synagogues–New York (State)–New York–History. *Roots in a Moving Stream; the Centennial History of Congregation B'nai Jehudah of*

Kansas City, 1879–1970, by Frank Adler (Kansas City, Mo., The Temple, Congregation B'nai Jehudah, 1972; Library of Congress call number: BM225.K35 A64) can be found by searching under two subject headings: Congregation B'nai Jehudah, or Jews–Missouri–Kansas City.

Sometimes there are several subject headings for one title giving different search avenues to other areas you might not have thought about. One example is *The Levin Years, a Golden Era–1929–1951, Dallas, Texas: Hebrew School of Dallas and Its Extended Activities*, conceived, written, and compiled by Ginger Chesnick Jacobs ([Dallas, Texas]: G.C. Jacobs in cooperation with the Dallas Jewish Historical Society, [1989]; Library of Congress call number: BM110. D35 J33 1989). The book appears under the following subject headings: Levin, Jacob, 1905–1983; Hebrew School of Dallas–History; Jewish religious schools–Texas–Dallas–History; and Jews–Texas–Dallas–History.

An example of a book listed under six different subject headings is *Yoyvl-bukh: fertsik yor Sokolover in Shikago: aroysgegebn le-koved dem draysik-yorikn yubileum fun dem Amerikan Sokolover independent fereyn*, edited by Mosheh Mandlboym (Chicago: American Sokolover independent fereyn, 1941; Library of Congress call number: F548. 9. J5 Y69 1941 Hebr). The subject headings for this title are: Amerikan Sokolover independent feryn (Chicago, Ill.); Jews, Polish–Illinois–Chicago–Societies, etc.; Jews–Illinois–Chicago–Societies, etc.; Jews–Poland–Sokolow Podlaski; Chicago (Ill.)–Ethnic relations; and Sokolow Podlaski (Poland)–Ethnic relations.

Some searchable databases of interest to genealogy researchers appear on CDs, often available for individual purchase. One example is "Jewish Records in the Family History Library Catalogue," compiled by Nancy Goodstein-Hilton, a volunteer in the Family History Department of the Church of Jesus Christ of Latter-day Saints (Mormons). Searching state-by-state on this CD will yield small publications about lesser-known communities.

Internet

Researchers of synagogue and communal or organizational histories can benefit from using the websites of archival repositories. The Center for Jewish History in New York City (www.cjh.org) houses the libraries and archives of five major repositories: the American Jewish Historical Society, the American Sephardi Federation, the Leo Baeck Institute, Yeshiva University Museum, and YIVO Institute for Jewish Research. In

Beth Sholom Congregation, Elkins Park, Pennsylvania, was designed by Frank Lloyd Wright.

addition to the printed catalogues, paper inventories and card catalogues onsite, selected electronic finding aids of the five partners are available online. The Jacob Rader Marcus Center of the American Jewish Archives (www.huc.edu/aja) is another example. Its synagogue and local organizations manuscript collections are arranged alphabetically by city. Selected full-text inventories (finding aids) describe contents down to the folder level. The Joseph and Miriam Ratner Center for the Study of Conservative Judaism at The Jewish Theological Seminary of America in New York City (www.jtsa.edu/research/ratner) houses the records of more than one hundred Conservative synagogues and rabbis from throughout the United States.

Don't overlook regional and local repositories which also maintain websites. One example is the Jewish Historical Society of South Carolina (www.cofc.edu/~jhc) which is located at the College of Charleston. The Society's field work files in the Jewish Heritage Collection include organizational and synagogue histories organized first by town and then by family or institution name.

The American Jewish Archives, the Center for Jewish History, (see above) and the Myer and Rosaline Feinstein Center for American Jewish History at Temple University in Philadelphia, Pennsylvania, (www.temple.edu/feinsteinctr) are just three sites that provide links to additional major Jewish historical societies, centers, libraries, archives and organizations.

Other databases, such as "Jewish Records in the Family History Library Catalog" described above, can be accessed with the instructional information on the JewishGen website (www.jewishgen.org).

Compiled Family Histories
and Genealogies

by Peggy K. Pearlstein

Since the early 1970s, there has been a remarkable interest and growth in genealogical research in this country as individuals sought to connect their past with their present. A parallel growth has occurred in the Jewish community too, as individuals began to search for their roots and their missing or unknown relatives. A product of this ongoing research has been the compilation of numerous family histories and genealogies. By and large, the histories are self-published in limited editions. They are distributed primarily to family members and then to select libraries and archives.

Published Works

Sourcebook for Jewish Genealogies and Family Histories, by David S. Zubatsky and Irwin M. Berent (Teaneck, N.J.: Avotaynu, Inc., 1996; Library of Congress call number: Z6374.B5 Z83 1996) contains "published and unpublished Jewish genealogies, family histories and individual family names," available in archival repositories and libraries in the United States. The authors also have added collections of Jewish family papers that are in selected foreign repositories, including Israel. Surnames are listed alphabetically. The book's index to the surnames, using the Daitch-Mokotoff Soundex System, aids the researcher in locating name variants. Some books describe several family genealogies and histories and are listed in this book under General Works.

Finding Our Fathers; A Guidebook to Jewish Genealogy, by Dan Rottenberg (New York, N.Y.: Random House, 1977; Library of Congress call number: CS21. R58) is one of the first books that appeared to help Jewish researchers trace their family roots. The section, "A Source Guide to Jewish Family Genealogies," contains Rottenberg's compilation of 8,000 Jewish family names. Each entry summarizes information that appears on family names in the *Jewish Encyclopedia* (see below on internet access), the *Universal Jewish Encyclopedia* and the *Encyclopedia Judaica* (see below for CD) as well as references in published and unpublished books of Jewish family histories and the genealogy holdings of selected major Jewish archives in the United States and Israel. Due to space constraints, Rottenberg limited references to family relationships "prior to 1900 and outside of the United States."

The Bibliography section of the book contains a short list of multiple-family histories and genealogies and a list of more than 300 individual-family histories and genealogies. Since many are printed in limited quantities and difficult to find, Rottenberg also provided at least one repository location for each title.

Bibliographia Genealogica Judaica, by Hermann M.Z. Meyer (Jerusalem, 1942: Library of Congress call number: Z6374.B5 M4), a 21-page manuscript lists about a thousand Jewish family histories, genealogies and community histories that the author compiled by 1942. Since only 22 copies of the bibliography were published, its availability is limited.

First American Jewish Families: 600 Genealogies—1654–1988, compiled by the late Rabbi Malcolm Stern (Baltimore, MD: Ottenheimer Publishers, 1991, 3rd rev. ed.; Library of Congress call number: CS59. S76 1991) traces the genealogies of Jewish families, many of them Sephardic, from their presence in the United States and Canada prior to 1840, to the present.

The Unbroken Chain: Biographical Sketches and Genealogy of Illustrious Jewish Families from the 15th–20th Century, by Neil Rosenstein (New York, N.Y.: CIS Publishers, 1990, 2nd rev. ed.; Library of Congress call number: CS31 R67 1990) is one example of a work devoted to the descendants of a particular family. The author has traced more than 25,000 descendants of Rabbi Meir Katzenellenbogen of Padua to the present day.

Journals

Avotaynu: The International Review of Jewish Genealogy (Teaneck, N.J.: Avotaynu, Inc., 1985–; Library of Congress call number: DS101. A87) annually publishes a section, "Family Books in Print," in the last issue of the quarterly journal. The annotated list of family histories contains the major names researched, the institutions in which the book is deposited and how to order a copy.

Judaica Americana: An Annotated Bibliography of Publications from 1960 to 1990 (Brooklyn, N.Y.: Carlson Publishing, 1995, 2 volumes; Library of Congress call number: Z6373.U5 K34 1995) ccumulates up to 1990 the late Dr. Nathan Kaganoff's bibliographies which appeared in the American Jewish Historical Society's (AJHS) journal, *American Jewish Historical Quarterly* (Library of Congress call number: E184.J5A5, previously *Publications of the American Jewish Historical Society* and now *American Jewish History*). The annotated bibliographies list monographic and periodical literature from the United States, Canada and Latin America received in the library of the AJHS. A section on genealogy contains individual titles as well as relevant articles from selected Jewish journals. A subject index facilitates searching by name.

The American Jewish Archives Journal (Library of Congress call number: E184.J5A37), published by the American Jewish Archives in Cincinnati, Ohio, and newsletters and journals of other repositories list recent acquisitions to their collections which regularly include family histories and genealogies.

Databases and Online Catalogues

The Library of Congress online catalogue (www.loc.gov) is available to researchers everywhere twenty-four hours a day. A very effective way to search the catalogue is through the use of subject headings, using a highly structured and controlled vocabulary. You can consult the multivolume *Library of Congress Subject Headings* (LCSH) (Washington, D.C.: Library of Congress, annual; Library of Congress call number: Z695.Z8 L524a), known familiarly as the "Red Books," and found in most reading rooms. The identical subject headings are often applied to the holdings of many other libraries and research centers. These institutions usually make their own catalogues available on the internet also (see below, Balch Institute for Ethnic Studies).

A subject heading can be followed by subdivisions and strung together in a prearranged order. The following Library of Congress headings are useful in locating family histories and genealogies.

The subject heading Jews–Genealogy lists everything from archival resources to handbooks to periodicals. More specific subject searches would be Jewish families–[State], Jews–[State]–Genealogy, Jews, [Ethnic Group]–United States–Genealogy, and Family Name.

The Old Country and the New: A Wasserstrom Family History, 1780–1930, by Randy Wasserstrom (Baltimore, MD: Gateway Press; Columbus, OH: Wasserstrom Co. [distribution], 1997; Library of Congress call number: CS71.W3196 1997), is searchable by all of the following subject headings: Wasserstrom family, Jewish Families–Ohio, Jews–Ohio–Genealogy, and Ohio–Genealogy.

When a family name has changed, you can still search by the name that you know. A "see" reference in the Library of Congress catalogue will refer you to the heading used by the Library for a particular family. For example, these subject headings: Oreck family, Jews, Russian–United States–Genealogy, and Russia–Genealogy will all retrieve the title, *The Oreckovsky Family—Orekhovskaia sem'ia: From Russia to America* [compiled and edited by Len Traubman] ([California]: Oreck Foundation, 1994; Library of Congress call number: CS71.O668 1994), a history of the well-known vacuum cleaner manufacturers.

Databases in the form of CDs facilitate research for the genealogist. *AVOTAYNU on CD-ROM* provides quick searching for information about family histories and genealogies. It indexes articles that appeared in the journal from 1985–2002 and is updated every three years. The *Encyclopaedia Judaica* (Shaker Heights, OH: Judaica Multimedia, 1997; Library of Congress call number: DS 102.8 [1998 00002] appeared in a CD in 1997. The 26 volumes of the original text have been updated and hyperlinks have been added.

Internet

The websites of archival repositories are useful for researchers of family histories and genealogies. A prime example of a national repository is The Jacob Rader Marcus Center of the American Jewish Archives in Cincinnati, Ohio (WWW.HUC.EDU/AJA). The personal and family papers in the Center are arranged alphabetically by name. In some cases, full-text inventories (finding aids) describe contents down to the folder level.

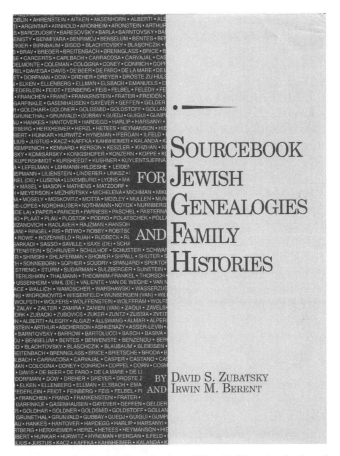

Sourcebook for Jewish Genealogies and Family Histories, *by David Zubatsky and Irwin Berent, (Avotaynu, 1996) is an index to published and unpublished family histories for more than 10,000 different surnames.*

Another major research institution with a website for those interested in family history research is the American Jewish Historical Society (WWW.AJHS.ORG). It is a partner of the Center for Jewish History (WWW.CJH.ORG) in New York City along with the Leo Baeck Institute, the YIVO Institute for Jewish Research, the American Sephardi Federation and Yeshiva University Museum.

Many regional repositories and local historical societies maintain websites that facilitate access to their collections. For example, the Balch Institute for Ethnic Studies of the Historical Society of Pennsylvania houses and administers the manuscript collection owned and funded by the Jewish Federation of Philadelphia. The collection includes some family histories and genealogies. In addition, the Library's catalogue is available online to researchers. Among the titles that appear using the subject heading, Jews–Genealogy is *The Beckwith-Berkowitz Family History: Tales of Life From 1886 to 1996 As Told By Ourselves*, collected and edited by Lolo Beckwith Pike (Kiawah Island, SC: [s.n.], 1996).

The *Jewish Encyclopedia*, originally published in 12 volumes between 1901–1906 is now in the public domain and available on the Internet. More than 15,000 articles and illustrations are searchable by keyword (WWW. JEWISHENCYCLOPEDIA.COM).

Directories

by Alex E. Friedlander

This section will discuss four categories of directories whose contents can be useful for genealogical research: city directories, telephone directories, biographical directories and professional directories. All of these valuable reference sources can be found in the United States and internationally.

Business Directories

Before the telephone was invented—and for many years afterwards—the residents and businesses of most cities and towns in the U.S. were listed in annual directories. These books, generally referred to as city directories, were published by private companies and often included much information now of interest to genealogists. The directories typically date back to the mid-19th century for larger cities, but by the end of the 19th century, even relatively small towns had them. Most city directories continued to be published until the 1930s or 1940s.

A typical city directory includes an alphabetical listing by surname of residents—sometimes only heads of households, but often separate listings for each adult member of the household who had an occupation or was a student. In smaller towns, and even in larger cities for later years, the first name of the spouse often was listed with the head of household. Each listing specifies at least one address, and some directories list both residential and business addresses together. A separate section of the directory usually includes lists by occupation or profession.

Many directories also include a street list. This may be simply a list of each street with the cross streets it bisects, perhaps with house numbers at each cross street, or it may list the residents or businesses for every building, by house or building number, on each block. Usually a section of advertisements is included, and in some cases, maps of the towns are printed with wards denoted. (The ward can be useful in finding census listings.) Additions or changes received after the closing date for inclusion in the main body of the directory typically were printed in a small section near the front.

Genealogical researchers can put these directories to many productive uses. Most obviously, one can track the existence and location of family members and their occupations. For years corresponding to a state or federal census, the directory provides an address to seek in the census. This is one of the most important uses of city directories, since most state censuses are not indexed; the 1910 federal census is not indexed in all states; the 1880 census indexes only heads of households with children younger than 10 years old. Spelling or coding idiosyncrasies or errors may permit an individual being sought to elude detection in soundex or online indexes.

Several cautions must be observed when using city directories as finding aids for censuses. Most important is the need to correlate the closing date of the directory with the

Business directories, the predecessors to the Yellow Pages of telephone books, existed in many countries. Shown here is a section of a 1929 Polish business directory identifying shops in the town of Karczew. Many of the shopkeepers are Jewish. Included is a pharmacy operated by L. Lowensztejn and fabric stores (Blawaty) run by Ch(aim) Goldberg, Sz(lama) Pirowicz, A. Skwara and Sz(lama) Szulman.

date of the census. For example, a 1900 directory may be the wrong directory to use to locate people in the 1900 census—the directory may have closed for publication in the fall of 1899 (or earlier); the 1900 census was conducted in June 1900. In this case, the 1901 directory would be more likely to produce a match. It is important to know the exact date of each census and to look in the first pages of the directory to find its closing date, when given.

A related problem is the fact that new immigrants moved often, sometimes more than once a year, particularly in large cities. This difficulty is compounded by the fact that a given person may not have appeared every year in a directory, and the spelling of the surname may have varied from year to year. A diligent researcher must check several consecutive years and all conceivable spelling variations when looking for an individual.

Always check street listings, both to see if any possible relatives lived in the same building or nearby and to acquire a sense of whether the resident may have owned the building, a possibility if they and their family are the sole occupants. Ownership of a home or business could serve as a pointer to further information in real estate records or corporate records. If a business name is given in the main listing, look for a corresponding entry under the business name (which also may be in the main body of listings), particularly if a title such as "treasurer" or "president" is specified. The business listing may reveal the names of other family members involved in the enterprise. Identification of cross streets in the street directory and of ward boundaries if a map is included, may make it easier to find the person in census documents. Some census indexes and reference tools, including online images, refer to wards rather than enumeration districts. In addition, knowing the ward can narrow the possible range of enumeration districts to seek.

If one is especially lucky, the directory will list surviving spouses as "widow of" and provide the name of the deceased. In some directories, the actual date of death is given in the first directory published after the individual's death.

Most city directories for major cities have been microfilmed and may be found in many libraries. State or local libraries often have at least some years in original bound copies, sometimes on open shelves. Directories for small towns may be available only in the county library or the state library. Sometimes a local history or genealogy association may have copies of directories for small towns that cannot be found anywhere else. In some cases, an individual town may not have published a directory, but its residents may be included in a county directory or a directory for a large adjoining town. The U.S. Library of Congress has an extremely large collection of directories on microfilm.

Some city directories have been abstracted, indexed and put online, particularly for the years surrounding 1890 as a substitute for the destroyed 1890 census. The best source for these listings is ANCESTRY.COM.

City Directories Outside the United States

Outside of the United States, the most easily accessible directories probably are those for the United Kingdom. Similar in many respects to city directories published in the U.S., British directories were often published in parallel with yearly "post office directories," which were for all practical purposes another form of city directories.

Typically the directories have separate sections for different classes of persons, with and without professions, and a street listing. The directories for London and other large cities are available at major libraries, including the LDS (Mormon) Family History Library which has microfilmed series of these volumes. These books may be particularly useful as an alternative to the 1891 census index and 1901 fee-based census index. The same caveats apply as described for U.S. directories.

Business and general directories from the late 19th and early 20th centuries from Lithuania, Poland, Russia and Ukraine are described in the countries chapters elsewhere in this book.

Telephone, Reverse and Electronic Directories

The printed telephone directory replaced most city directories in the United States by the mid-20th century. As telephone directories developed, new formats provided new tools for genealogical research. One important type of directory is variously known as the reverse directory, "criss-cross" directory or Haines Directory. This resource is somewhat akin to the street listings in the old city directories. It contains alphabetical lists of streets and for each street lists subscriber names and telephone numbers for each address. Many directories also include a separate list ordered by telephone numbers that cross-reference the street list. Typically, the street listing shows how long the current occupant has lived there, although this information is not always accurate. Locating people who lived in the same place for a long time can be useful, as they may have known a relative who has since died or moved away. Neighbors may know where the former resident or neighbor moved and may remember information about the next of kin or surviving spouse. Reverse directories often list apartment numbers in multifamily buildings.

Electronic telephone directories are available both on CD-ROM and on the Internet. The former, often generically called "phone disc," are sold in most major computer stores or directly from the publisher (with provisions for periodic updates). The search engines on the more expensive versions of these directories allow searches alphabetically by name, by street address or by telephone number with cross-referencing between these items. For example, one could look up a possible relative in the alphabetical listing, then switch to the specified street address to see if a known spouse or children are shown to verify that the right person has been found.

Some published phone discs have become multi-disk products, requiring that one use different discs for each region of the U.S.; the cost of keeping them updated can exceed $100 yearly. Many libraries now have one or more computers equipped with phone discs in their business, general reference or local history and genealogy divisions.

In the past few years, the development of comprehensive Internet telephone directories has made the purchase of CD-ROM directories unnecessary for most genealogical research. Several web addresses provide the same search capabilities and allow searches for both e-mail and street addresses. Three good sites that offer frequently updated country-wide online directories are SUPERPAGES.COM, SWITCHBOARD.COM and Ancestry's white pages (INFOSPACE.COM). There are subtle differences in format and search screens between these, but the databases appear to be similar. Links are available to international telephone directories.

Biographical and "Who's Who" Directories

Numerous directories around the world publish capsule biographies of people who have achieved prominence in some area of endeavor. Information for each individual typically includes place and date of birth, name (and maiden name) of spouse, and occasionally date of marriage, names of children, education, accomplishments, memberships and residence. Because of the wide variety of specialties in these directories, anyone researching a family tree of reasonable size is likely to find one or more relatives in one of these publications.

Titles range from the well-known and prestigious *Who's Who in America*, published annually by Marquils Who's Who since 1899, to various specialized series that have appeared within the last several decades, also by Marquis, such as *Who's Who in American Law, Who's Who in Finance and Industry*, regional Who's Who editions, and gender- or religion-focused directories. There are also directories for various entertainment and arts fields, including the multi-volume *Contemporary Authors* series found in most libraries. Directories exist for well-known deceased individuals, including several *Who Was Who* series and the *Biography Index*, which contains obituary "who's who" articles.

Because directories are updated either annually or every few years, people who may have been considered worth including in one edition may disappear from the next. The *Biography and Genealogy Master Index (BGMI)* is a comprehensive index to many of these volumes. Gale Publishing offers a multiple-volume series and also a version on two CD-ROMs. The 1980 edition of the BGMI held more than three million biographical listings in eight volumes, referencing more than 350 different biographical dictionaries. Supplements were published for 1981–85, 1986–90 and annually since then, but the easiest way to use the BGMI is through the online and CD-ROM edition, available at many libraries.

The BGMI electronic database lists all published references for each individual, although retrieving past editions of the various volumes referenced can be problematical, depending on the libraries' policy on retaining such books. A two-disk *Consolidated Marquis Who's Who* database, including all the text from 19 of the most popular directories since 1985, is widely available in libraries. The online *BGMI* also is available to some library members through their home computers. For example, the Brooklyn (New York) Public Library provides this service to its card holders.

Many countries have similar biographical directories. Many can be found in major U.S. libraries. Some include only one or a few volumes; others are extensive. Some international directories are current, while others are historical and may cover multiple countries, such as the 45-volume *Biographie Universelle* published in Austria in 1966.

There are also Jewish biographical directories including *Who's Who in American Jewry*, an occasional publication that first published in 1926–28 and 1938, or *The South African Jewish Year Book* published in 1929. An important Israeli bio-graphical encyclopedia, commonly known by its author's name, Tidhar, was published in 19 volumes from 1947 to 1971 (see the bibliographic citation below).

Medical, Legal and Business Directories

The medical and legal professions are notable for their comprehensive directories, which can be found in many libraries. Officials, executives and key managers of major corporations and businesses also publish specialized directories. The information provided for each person in these directories is not as genealogically comprehensive as that given in the various *Who's Who* series, but it usually includes dates and places of birth, education and degrees, current address and other professional details. Major libraries hold previous editions of these directories.

For the legal profession, the most comprehensive directory is the *Martindale Hubbel Law Directory*, an annually updated series of some 20 volumes organized by state and locality. The index volume shows the state and city for each attorney, along with the page number in the appropriate volume. The front section of each book lists all attorneys with brief, coded information on undergraduate and graduate schools. Attorneys affiliated with law firms have their affiliation cited in this section; the attorneys may be listed also in the remainder of the book under their respective firms, listed alphabetically by locality. More detailed information is given for attorneys listed in the latter section. The *Martindale Hubbel* directory is also published as two CD-ROM disks, and the company has a "lawyer locator" on the web at WWW.MARTINDALE.COM/LOCATOR/HOME/HTML.

The equivalent series for the medical profession is the *ABMS Directory of Board Certified Medical Specialists*. This is a series of four large volumes organized by medical specialty. An index volume lists all doctors alphabetically, showing their specialty code plus their index number under that specialty. Information such as the year and place of medical degree, board certification and location of practice also is available for physicians under the "doctor search" option on the American Medical Association (AMA) website, WWW.AMA-ASSN.ORG.

American Medical Association files on deceased physicians, which date back to 1878, have incomplete data through 1905 and more comprehensive data on physicians who died between 1906 and 1969 when the AMA converted to a computerized system. Information includes the date and place of birth and death, medical school, affiliations, place of practice and, sometimes, an obituary. This information through 1929 can be found in the two-volume publication *Directory of Deceased American Physicians* published by the AMA. Covering the years 1804 to 1929, it is available in most major U.S. libraries. The AMA files through 1969 are now in the possession of the National Genealogical Society* (NGS), which will search the files for a research fee of $15 per name, prepaid.

The business world has two major directories. The *Dun and Bradstreet Reference Book of Corporate Managements*, issued since 1968, includes a cross-reference volume that must be consulted first for the name of the individual and the appropriate main volume and business entity under which he or she can be found. Typically, "principal officers" and directors are listed. *Standard and Poor's Register of Corporations, Directors and Executives*, which dates back to 1928, includes similar information. Unlike the medical and legal directories, these annual publications are referenced in the *Biography and Genealogy Master Index*.

Address

National Genealogical Society, Attention: Deceased Physician File, 4527 17th Street North, Arlington, VA 22207-2399; website: WWW.NGSGENEALOGY.ORG.

Bibliography

American Medical Association Directory of Physicians in the United States. Published by AMA Press, annual, 37th edition published 2001. First volume is alphabetical; volumes 2–4 are geographical.

Bibliography and Genealogy Master Index to Biographical Material in Books and Magazines. Published by H.H. Wilson Co. Listings start in 1946. August 2001 edition has 26 volumes. New York Public Library electronic database includes listings through July 1984.

Biographie universelle ancienne et moderne [par] J. Fr. Michaud. (Nouvelle ed.) (Unveränderter photomechanischer Nachdruck der 1854 [i.e. 1843–1865] in Paris erschienenen Ausg.) Graz, Akademische Druk-u. Verlagsanstalt, 1966–70.

Contemporary Authors: A Bio-Bibliographical Guide to Current Writers in Fiction, General Non Fiction, Poetry, Journalism, Drama, Motion Pictures, Television and Other Fields. Published by the Gale Group in multiple volumes each year with more than 100,000 writers listed. A separate cumulative index is published twice a year. Also available through GaleNet's online subscription service.

Current Biography Yearbook. Current ed. Clifford Thompson. Published by H.W. Wilson Co. Annually since 1940. Cumulative index 1940–2000; also a cumulative index for 1991–2000 in the 2000 yearbook.

Entsiklopedyah la-halutse ha-yishuv u-vonav: demuyot u-temunot. David Tidhar. Tel Aviv: Sifriyat Rishonim, 1947–71.

Martindale-Hubbel Law Directory. Published by Martindale-Hubbell, a member of the Lexis-Nexis Group. Annual. 2002 edition has 17 volumes.

The Official ABMS Directory of Board Certified Medical Specialists. Published by Elsevier Science. Four volumes, organized by specialty; volume 4 has master index.

Who Was Who in America. Published by Marquis Who's Who, 55 editions from 1899 to 2002. Currently published annually in two volumes.

Who's Who in American Jewry. John Simons, ed. New York: National News Association, 1926, 1928, 1938–39.

Who's Who in South African Jewry—The South African Jewish Yearbook. South African Jewish Historical Society, 1929.

Newspapers

by Alex E. Friedlander

Genealogists certainly are aware of the published death notices and obituary articles that appear in most newspapers, but those are not the only gems to seek out. If one looks at *The New York Times*, it may be easy to conclude that other social events that appear in print tend to reflect the "monetarily advantaged," but many other newspapers, including those in smaller cities and towns, and/or with a specific ethnic or religious readership—contain numerous other types of information in addition to death notices. These newsworthy items include engagement and marriage announcements, wedding anniversaries, *in memoriam* or unveiling notices, births and even *brit milah* notices. In small-town newspapers, a wedding may merit a feature article that describes at some length all of the guests and their hometowns, the gifts they bestowed on the lucky couple, the outfits they wore and the menu—and perhaps some relationships of guests to the bridal pair.

A family member may also have been involved in some local news event of interest, a business matter, a store opening or expansion—all of which might have occasioned a news article. Personal or social columns may describe the peregrinations of relatives. Many Jews in smaller towns were owners of key retail businesses, and their advertisements often appear in the local newspaper. "Black sheep" may be featured in crime reports.

Obituaries and Death Notices

As noted above, the item most likely to be of genealogical value, of course, is the death notice provided by the family to the newspaper. It is a mistake to think that having a death certificate in hand makes it unnecessary to look for a death notice or obituary. Death notices, which typically appear a day or two after the death (but which may be published for several days in a row, or even show up a week later), may be placed not only by the immediate family but also by other relatives, businesses or fraternal organizations with which the deceased was associated, the synagogue or other religious organizations. In addition to providing genealogical data about the deceased, such notices often reveal the funeral home used, cemetery, and names of previously unknown relatives, as well as names of the spouse, children and even grandchildren. Sometimes surviving siblings were named—and even the place(s) where siblings or children were living. Some newspapers published photographs of the deceased.

Most newspaper indexes (see below) list obituary articles, but it is rare to find death notices included. Many newspapers have an index to the death notices on the page on which they appear, but the greater challenge often is to find the page, the placement of which may vary from day to day. Many newspapers indicate the deaths' page on their front page or overall index page. To locate a death notice, the researcher may need a finding aid, such as (in the U.S.) the

Death notices in newspapers can be valuable because they give the married names of daughters and changes of surname for sons of immigrants.

Social Security Death Index entry that shows at least the month and year of death (see SOCIAL SECURITY DEATH INDEX), a reliable date from a family member, a death certificate or tombstone inscription.

Another problem in locating newspaper death notices is that many cities and towns have, or had in the past, more than one paper. A local history and/or genealogy librarian may be able to offer advice on which resources are more likely to yield results, but it may be necessary to determine by trial and error which were more likely to carry the larger number of death notices and which were more likely to be the paper of choice for Jewish families.

Newspaper and Obituary Indexes

Major newspapers in a number of U.S. and other cities have published indexes. Some newspapers have made their indexes available online. Best known, and widely available in hard cover in libraries, is the index to *The New York Times*, published annually since the middle of the 18th century. Similar indexes are available starting variously between 1972 and 1980 for the *Atlanta Constitution/Journal, Boston Globe, Chicago Tribune, Detroit News, Houston Post/Chronicle, Los Angeles Times, New Orleans Times-Picayune, San Francisco Chronicle* and the *Washington Post*, all published either by the Bell and Howell company in Wooster, Ohio, or University Microfilms in Ann Arbor, Michigan. The indexes for these other papers are not as widely available; when a library does carry them, it may have only the most recent years and the volumes may not be on open shelves.

The New York Times has published two other types of valuable indexes that are less well known. One is *The New York Times Obituaries Index*, a two-volume, separate index to obituary articles: a larger book covering 1856 to 1968 and a smaller volume for the years 1969–1978. A multi-volume *Personal Name Index* (PNI) contains alphabetical listings for every name in an article that has appeared in the paper, including obituary articles. To use the PNI one must have access to the annual index volumes, because the PNI references the pages in these annual volumes, not the actual date and page of the article itself. Although the double lookup process is somewhat awkward, it is far more efficient than looking through every annual volume. The PNI is published in three series that each covers a wide range of years: 1851–1974 (22 volumes), 1975–93 (6 volumes) and 1975–96 (partial series).

A *New York Times Biographical Service* (or *Edition*) published annually since 1970 consists of reproductions of both news articles and obituaries from that year's papers. Each of these volumes is indexed separately.

In England, newspaper indexes exist for *The London Times* and *The Manchester Guardian*. The latter has a microfilm or microfiche index covering the years 1842 to 1945. A three-volume series of obituaries from *The London Times* covering the years 1951 to 1975 may be found in some major libraries. Libraries in various countries are, of course, likely to have more extensive collections of indexes to newspapers in those locations. For example, the Manchester [England] Jewish Museum* has an index of Jewish names from the *Manchester City News* for the years 1875 to 1923.

Some newspapers or indexing services now publish online indexes. These are generally available on a fee basis or through subscriptions to libraries. Most notable is the recently completed index and complete digitization by Proquest of all text and photographs in *The New York Times* from 1850 to the present. The index and images are available on in-library computers at selected libraries and to New York Genealogical and Biographical Society members for home reference. ANCESTRY.COM has a separate and growing index and images service to various newspapers for selected years. This service requires an annual fee or can be accessed at libraries that provide access to ANCESTRY.COM. Indexes to obituary articles in selected newspapers have been developed online by sources other than newspaper publishers. JewishGen, for example, has a small but growing file of obituary indexes ranging from 9,000 obituaries in the *Chicago Tribune* between 1994 and 1998 to more than 21,000 obituaries each in the Boston *Jewish Advocate* and *The Cleveland Jewish News* (see below).

Another important source of indexes to obituaries is the local history and genealogy division in libraries in most cities, as well as local history and genealogy societies. Often these divisions or organizations have card indexes, folder collections or other systems of alphabetical indexes to obituaries assembled from local newspapers. These indexes often include copies of the actual obituaries.

Jewish Newspapers

Many cities around the world had or have Jewish newspapers, often dating back a century or more. The *London Jewish Chronicle* is perhaps one of the best known, but a bibliographical check reveals a wealth of such papers, often changing name and format over time, and with more than one paper for large cities. Many were published in English. Some papers tended to concentrate on Zionist news; these are less likely to have printed genealogically useful information—unless, of course, a family member was active in a Zionist organization. Most have focused more on the local Jewish community and publish(ed) obituaries or death notices for many local citizens.

Newspaper accounts of family events may provide more detail than the version passed down from generation to generation. Courtesy of Melody Amsel-Arieli.

Few of these papers have published indexes, but recent efforts to put some of this data online are creating new finding aids for this resource. JewishGen, for example, makes available searchable indexes to some 23,000 obituaries from the *Boston Jewish Advocate* from 1905 to 2003, and 25,000 obituaries from *The Cleveland Jewish News* (1964 to 2003) at WWW.JEWISHGEN.ORG/DATABASES. Unpublished indexes exist for some years of the *London Jewish Chronicle*, including a card file at the offices of the newspaper and a privately created index to birth, marriage and death notices, 1880–95 at www. JEFFREYMAYNARD.COM. Members of the Jewish Genealogical Society of Great Britain have access to a database of death announcements from the *Chronicle* from 1995 to 2001, but that is not available to the general public.

A number of Hebrew and Yiddish language papers were published in the 19th century in Eastern Europe. These include *HaMagid, HaLevanon* and *HaMelitz*. They were published weekly as early as the 1850s and continued past the turn of the 20th century. Although they sometimes included obituaries, the more interesting contents of these papers included lists of contributors to charities from various towns, notices or articles seeking missing persons, correspondence from various towns, occasional notices of weddings and advertisements for businesses or services. Researchers with any facility in at least visualizing Hebrew characters should make use of these papers.

A comprehensive list of Hebrew language newspapers may be found in the first (index) volume of *Encyclopaedia Judaica* under "Hebrew Newspapers and Periodicals;" unfortunately, the list is alphabetical by title of the newspaper rather than the place of publication. For a shorter list of major European Jewish periodicals, those that existed for at least 20 years, published in Hebrew, Yiddish or the language of the country in which it was published, see the article "Periodicals and Press" in volume 8 of *The Universal Jewish Encyclopedia*. This same article has several other short, but useful, lists of Jewish newspapers published both in the U.S. and abroad. A list of such papers may be found also in volume 9 of the *Jewish Encyclopedia*.

Several online indexes are available for portions of the material in these three publications. JewishGen hosts a list of 5,000 donors from Lithuanian towns published in *HaMagid* in 1871–72, and a list of 20,000 donors from Latvia and Lithuania published in *HaMelitz* from 1893 to 1903. Some 1,500 obituaries, wills and death notices from the entire run (1856–1903) of *HaMagid* were indexed, abstracted and reproduced in a CD ROM entitled *Latter Day Leaders, Sages and Scholars,* volume 2, compiled by Neil Rosenstein.

Addresses

Manchester Jewish Museum, 190 Cheetham Hill Road, Manchester, M8 8LW, England.

Bibliography

Byron A. Falk, Jr. and Valerie R. Falk, eds. *Personal Name Index to the New York Times Index.* Roxbury Data Interface. 1851–1974, 22 vols.; 1975–89, 5 vols. Follow-up series through 1996.

Rosenstein, Neil. *Latter Day Leaders, Sages and Scholars.* Elizabeth, N.J.: Computer Center for Jewish Genealogy, 1997.

The New York Times Index—Death Notices. Four volumes with reproductions of the relevant pages from the full annual indexes, covers the years 1940–64.

The New York Times Obituaries Index 1858–1968. New York: New York Times, 1970. Follow-up volume covers 1969–78.

Part III

U.S. Research

Ship Manifests and
Other Immigration Records

by Nancy Levin Arbeiter, CGRS

U.S. immigration records can provide a wealth of valuable information. Depending on the year, genealogists can learn whom an immigrant ancestor followed to America and whom they left behind, with whom they traveled, where they had last resided, and where they may have been born.

Upon learning the name of your ancestor's steamship and his or her dates and ports of embarkation and arrival, you can then peruse the many historical books and articles written by or about people who followed the same or similar routes to America and whose experiences may have paralleled your ancestors. The result will be a fascinating awareness of what your immigrant ancestors may have encountered on the trip to their new home.

The following are some of the many resources that can help you learn more about your ancestors' immigration experiences:

Reports of the Immigration Commission, vol. 37, *Steerage Conditions, Importation and Harboring of Women for Immoral Purposes, Immigrant Homes and Aid Societies, Immigrant Banks* (1911; reprint, New York: Arno & The New York Times 1970).

Reports of the Immigration Commission, vol. 4, *Emigration Conditions in Europe* (1911; reprint, New York: Arno & The New York Times, 1970).

Anuta, Michael J. *Ships of Our Ancestors* (Baltimore, Maryland: Genealogical Publishing Co., 2002).

Benton, Barbara. *Ellis Island: A Pictorial History* (New York: Facts on File Publications, 1985).

Brownstone, David M. and Irene M. Franck, Douglass Brownstone, *Island of Hope, Island of Tears* (New York: Barnes & Noble Books, 2000).

Coan, Peter Morton. *Ellis Island Interviews: In Their Own Words* (New York: Facts on File, Inc., 1997).

Kapp, Friedrich. *Immigration and the Commissioners of Emigration* (1870; reprint, New York: Arno Press and The New York Times).

Pitkin, Thomas P. *Keepers of the Gate: A History of Ellis Island* (New York: New York University Press, 1975).

Smith, Eugene W. *Passenger Ships of the World Past and Present*, 2nd ed. (Boston, Mass.: George H. Dean Company, 1978).

Steiner, Edward A. *On the Trail of the Immigrant* (New York: Fleming H. Revell Company, 1906).

U.S. Customs Lists

Mandated in 1819 to help deter overcrowding on ships, U.S. passenger lists, also known as manifests, are written records of individuals embarking from foreign ports and arriving at U.S. ports of entry. The federally maintained manifests that date from circa 1820 through 1891 are today commonly called "customs lists," possibly because they were the responsibility of the customs collector at the Customs House in each port.[1]

A federal law of March 2, 1819, required the master of a ship, upon arrival at a U.S. port, to submit a list of passengers to the customs collector of the district in which the ship arrived. Until 1874, customs collectors were then required to submit quarterly abstracts or copies of these lists to the Secretary of State, who, in turn, reported the information to Congress. The U.S. State Department also made its own transcripts of some early lists. The original lists were maintained by the customs collectors, and the abstracts, copies and transcripts were maintained by the State Department. After 1874, customs collectors were not required to send abstracts and copies to the State Department, but instead were required to send statistical reports on the lists to the Secretary of the Treasury.

The original passenger lists, abstracts, copies and transcripts circa 1820 through 1891 make up the "customs lists." They are now the responsibility of the U.S. National Archives and are considered "Records of the U.S. Customs Service, Record Group 36. Note that some of these original lists, abstracts, copies, and transcripts were lost or destroyed. Some states and cities, however, kept their own parallel sets of passenger lists which were required by state or city laws. For research purposes, these state and city lists have been used by the National Archives in place of missing customs lists.

The federal, state, and city lists have been microfilmed and published and are available for research at the National Archives in Washington, DC, and at the various regional branches of the National Archives. This microfilm is also available through the LDS (Mormon) Family History Library (hereafter Family History Library).

The personal information listed on customs lists is minimal, and the amount and kind of data gathered from the passengers remained basically the same from 1820 through 1882. In 1882, some additional information was obtained from the passengers and noted on the customs lists, but personal details remained very superficial. Abstracts contain almost the same information as the originals or copies, but some of the information may have been abbreviated (e.g., a passenger's given name on the original list may have been abbreviated to an initial on the abstract).

Customs lists created between 1820 and 1891 could include the following information:

* Steamship name
* U.S. Customs district and port

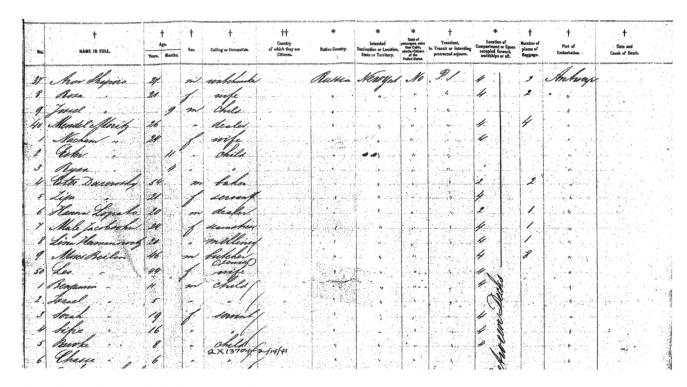

Early ship manifests provided little information about the arriving immigrant. It shows the passenger's name, age, sex, occupation, country of residence and intended destination. This list from 1892 shows the arrival of the Beilin family of Russia on The Rhynland *from Antwerp on September 14, 1893. Their five-year-old son, Israel, became the noted song writer Irving Berlin.*

- Port of embarkation
- Date of the ship's arrival
- Estimate of ship's tonnage
- Passenger data:
- Name
- Age
- Sex
- Occupation
- Country to which they belong
- Country in which they intend to become inhabitants
- Circumstances of death or remarks
- Part of vessel occupied by passenger during voyage
- Country of which they are citizens
- Native country
- Intended destination
- Pieces of baggage

Although of historical and personal interest, customs records are not very genealogically helpful. As they don't provide important personal details, a researcher may even have trouble determining whether he or she has located the correct individual. For example, three unmarried men named Avram Lewin, aged 32–35, all born Russia, immigrated through the port of Boston between 1886–87. All listed the United States as their destination. None was traveling with individuals whose names sounded familiar. Without additional information, how would a researcher identify which of these individuals was the "correct" Avram Lewin? (The researcher *might* obtain additional clues leading to the "correct" Avram

Lewin from his petition for naturalization had Avram later become a naturalized U.S. citizen.)

U.S. Immigration Passenger Arrival Lists

In 1875, undesirable elements were for the first time not allowed entry into the United States by federal law. (State law governed entry prior to this.) This included criminals and prostitutes and charged the customs collectors of ports with enforcement of the law. In 1882, the first federal law regulating immigration was passed, and general supervision of immigration was centralized through the Secretary of the Treasury. At the same time, there were increased restrictions on the kinds of aliens who would be admitted into the United States. "Persons likely to become a public charge" were no longer admissible by federal law.[2] The first law for complete national control of immigration was passed in 1891. Under this law, the Bureau of Immigration in the Treasury Department was established to administer immigration laws. Restrictions on the admissible types of aliens also increased. Along with "persons likely to become a public charge," inadmissible aliens now included "persons suffering from certain contagious diseases, felons, persons convicted of other crimes or misdemeanors, polygamists, and aliens assisted by others by payment of passage."[3]

In 1893 another immigration law was passed. Special boards of inquiry were established to determine an alien's admissibility into the United States, and alien immigrants requesting admission into the United States were required to provide additional information about him or herself before they'd be allowed to enter. This new additional information included the alien's occupation, marital status, ability to read and write, amount of money in their possession, and the name and address of the person the alien was planning to join in the United States.[4] This was all reported on newly created blank manifest forms. It was the first major change to the passenger manifest forms since they were created in 1819 and is the marked beginning of "genealogically helpful" passenger arrival lists.

The Bureau of Immigration became part of the Commerce and Labor Department in 1903. In 1906, its responsibilities broadened, and its name was changed to the Bureau of Immigration and Naturalization. In 1933, it became part of the Immigration and Naturalization Service (INS) and in 2002, services provided by the INS transitioned into the U.S. Citizenship & Immigration Services (USCIS) under the Department of Homeland Security (DHS). Within this chapter, however, this organization will continue to be referred to as the "INS.".[5]

Passenger lists created after about 1891 are commonly called "immigration passenger arrival lists" probably because they were the responsibility of the U.S. Immigration Service. Today these records are in the custody of the National Archives, part of the Records of the Immigration and Naturalization Service, Record Group 85. All of these records have been microfilmed by the INS, but only those that have been published can be researched. The microfilm of all major ports and many smaller ports are available for research at the National Archives branches and the Family History Library.[6] Immigration passenger arrival lists pertaining to the port of New York, 1892–1924, can also be researched on the Internet through the Ellis Island website at www.ELLISISLAND.ORG.

Immigration passenger arrival lists, also called "manifests," provide more personal data on the passengers than the earlier customs lists. As noted earlier, immigration became increasingly restrictive after 1893, and additional questions were asked of aliens requesting admission to the United States. The information was reported on newly created blank manifest forms that were obtained by the steamship lines from the government or printing companies who made the forms according to government specifications.[7] Genealogically important additions were made to the manifests in 1903 (when aliens were asked about their race and "Hebrew" immigrants were thus identified on manifests); in 1906 (when the alien was asked to provide his or her place of birth); and in 1907 (when the alien was asked to provide the name and address of the nearest relative or friend in the "old country").

Immigration passenger arrival lists created between 1891 and early 1893 provide basically the same information as the earlier customs lists. Those created in 1893 and later could—depending on the year—include the following information:

- Name of steamship
- Date of embarkation
- Port of embarkation
- Date of arrival
- Port of arrival

- Passenger data:
- Name
- Age
- Sex
- Marital status
- Occupation
- Ability to read and write
- Nationality
- Last residence
- Final destination
- Who paid for passenger's passage to the U.S.
- Money in passenger's possession
- Ever before in U.S.; if so, when and where
- Whether going to join a friend or relative; if so, who and where
- Condition of health
- Race or people
- Personal description
- Marks of identification
- Place of birth, city and country
- Name and address of friend or nearest relative in country whence alien came
- For naturalized U.S. citizens, date and place of citizenship
- Visa number, place of issue, and date

All individuals on each ship were listed on the ship's manifests, aliens as well as U.S. citizens. Separate manifests recorded those who traveled in first-class cabins, second-class cabins and steerage (sometimes called third-class). Steerage, the least expensive ticket, was the mode of travel for many, if not most, poor Jewish immigrants.

Immigration manifests were not filled out by U.S. immigration officials on American soil. They were completed by the shipping companies at the ports of embarkation. The 1893 U.S. immigration law required that shipping companies obtain basic information about each immigrant before sailing, and this information was to be passed on to the American immigration officials. The result was that at the ports of embarkation or earlier, shipping company officers asked immigrants for their name, origin, destination and other information, and then recorded their answers on the manifests.[8] At the ports of arrival, the completed manifests were given to U.S. immigration officials who subsequently reviewed the information with each passenger. After the 1924 quota law was passed, United States health examiners and immigration inspectors were stationed at American consulates throughout the world. Immigrants applying for visas to America were inspected before arrival in the United States.[9]

Most aliens passed the inspections and were admitted into the United States. Others were detained at the port of entry for a short period of time or held for special inquiry. Detention could occur for medical reasons, lack of money or the absence of anyone at the port to meet the newly arrived alien. The majority affected by lack of money or the absence of a person to meet them were women and children. Once money arrived or someone came to call for them, the individuals would be released. Note, however, that if "no money came

Ship manifest showing the arrival of Albert Einstein and his wife at the Port of New York (Ellis Island) in 1921. The information provided was identical to what every other immigrant to the United States was required to provide. It included occupation, nationality, race, last permanent residence and name and complete address of nearest relative or friend in country whence alien came.

and no one called for them within five days, it was general practice to turn (the immigrants) over to a missionary society or deport them, at their own choice."[10]

Aliens held for special inquiry might have been individuals wanted for criminal actions in other countries, contract laborers, runaway husbands, prostitutes, paupers, or persons "likely to become a public charge." (Some manifests include the abbreviation "L.P.C.". This means "likely to become a public charge.")

Telegraph offices existed at the various ports of arrival. To notify friends and relatives that people were being held at the port and that they needed funding or to be met, the INS sent a telegram to the friend's or relative's residence or work. If the alien or circumstances appeared "suspicious," and the INS had an office located in the appropriate town, the INS might instead send an official to the friend's or relative's residence or work to "check things out."[11]

Many genealogists will not find all relatives who immigrated to the U.S. between 1893 and 1903 listed on the "expanded" 1893 law-based manifests. Depending on the port, some may be listed on the less informative customs, state, or city lists. The reasons vary. Not all ports began using the 1893 law-based manifests immediately. And some ports may have used them but lost them when they were destroyed by a disaster. For example, a fire that broke out shortly after midnight on June 15, 1897, at Ellis Island destroyed the Island's vaults and their contents, including immigration records from both the Barge Office (discussed below) and Ellis Island.[12] The National Archives uses various microfilmed customs and state department lists to cover missing records from the Port of New York. (For other ports they might use state and local records.)[13]

Customs lists and immigration passenger arrival manifests are the best sources for an individual's immigration data. They will tell you the name of vessel, the date of arrival, and the place of embarkation. Depending on the year, genealogists can use the manifest to identify relatives and people who traveled together and to determine whom a relative might have followed to America, why they settled in a specific city, and whom they left behind.

Until visas were required in 1924 there is no way of knowing if an immigrant carried travel documents that could prove any of the personal information supplied to the steamship authorities when he or she boarded a ship. For this reason, the personal information on manifests should be considered secondary evidence and used as clues towards additional research avenues. Remember, also, that passenger manifests are rife with misspellings: last names, places of birth and last residences all may be spelled incorrectly.

Manifest Notations

Once the steamship reached the port of arrival, U.S. immigration officials reviewed each immigrant's manifest listing and sometimes made check marks or other notations on the manifest itself. Among the common notations found on manifests that are based on the 1893 and later immigration laws are the following:

•*X* to the left of the passenger's name indicates that the passenger was detained. (For port of New York passenger lists, a list of detained passengers is provided at the end of the entire ship's microfilmed manifest. The detained passengers list provides the date that the alien was released and admitted into the United States; how many breakfasts, dinners and lunches the alien was provided before he or she

The second page of the manifest included the name and address of the person to whom the immigrant was going, and the final two columns identify his/her place of birth (country and city or town).

was released; and the name and address of the person to whom the passenger was released. The list of detainees is not included on microfilm of port of Boston manifests; it may be on the microfilms of other port manifests.)

•*SI* to the left of the passenger's name indicates that the individual was held for special inquiry. (For port of New York passenger lists, a list of passengers held for special inquiry is provided at the end of the entire ship's microfilmed manifest. This list may include an abbreviation that indicates the reason the immigrant was held, such as the abbreviation "L.P.C.," meaning likely to become a public charge. The special inquiry list is not available on microfilm of port of Boston manifests; it may or may not be on the microfilms of other port manifests.)

Other notations on the manifest could have been written much later, possibly during the naturalization process. These notations tell us that for some reason, the immigrant's legal entry into the United States was checked. For more information on the handwritten notations provided on passenger arrival manifests, see Marian Smith's article "A Guide to Interpreting Passenger Lists Annotations" in JewishGen's info file database: WWW.JEWISHGEN.ORG/INFOFILES/MANIFESTS/.

Family Names Were *Not* Changed at Ellis Island

It is a myth that names were changed at Ellis Island. A U.S. immigration official may have made notations on immigration passenger arrival lists, but that is all. As noted earlier, these documents were not generated in the United States, but by steamship officials at the ports of embarkation or earlier. Although some surnames are misspelled on the manifests, these were probably inadvertent errors. If traditions hold that your family surname was changed, it is most likely that the name

change occurred during the immigrant's process of assimilation. Shortly after arriving—possibly within weeks or a few months—the immigrant may have found that an Eastern European surname with 10 letters, most of which were not pronounced, was a burden and subsequently changed it to something "more American." They may or may not have changed it legally.[14]

Records for U.S. Ports of Arrival

New York was a major port of entry into the United States for Jewish immigrants. Other major ports of entry used by many Jewish immigrants were the ports of Baltimore, Boston, Philadelphia, Galveston (Texas), Philadelphia and the Canada-United States border.

Records for these ports have been microfilmed and published and are available at the National Archives in Washington, DC and at the various National Archives branches. Each branch does not have microfilms for all ports of entry. Most of these microfilms are also available from the Family History Library. (In the Family History Library, the correct microfilm will be found under STATE, COUNTY, CITY, Emigration and Immigration.)

Records for the port of New York, 1892–1924, can also be researched and viewed on the Ellis Island Internet website (WWW.ELLISISLAND.ORG). Copies can be purchased directly from the Ellis Island Foundation; ordering instructions are provided on the website. An excellent set of search tools created for use with the Ellis Island database can be found on the JewishGen Internet website (WWW.JEWISHGEN.ORG/DATABASES/EIDB). Called the "Ellis Island One Step Search Tools," these search engines were originally created by Dr. Stephen Morse. They are sometimes referred to as the "Morse" search tools.

Copies of customs and immigration passenger arrival lists may be ordered directly from the National Archives by submitting a copy of NATF Form 81, *Order for Copies of Passenger Ship Arrival Records*. Obtain a copy of this form from one of the National Archives branches or write to:

General Reference Branch
National Archives
7th and Pennsylvania Avenue, NW
Washington, DC 20408

The form can also be ordered through the Internet at: www.archives.gov/global_pages/inquire_form.html. The search is free. If the desired passenger list is found and you wish to have a copy, the National Archives and Records Administration (hereinafter NARA) will send a bill for $17.25. It is best, however, for each researcher to do his or her own research whenever possible, especially when the exact steamship and date and port of arrival are not known.

The Port of New York

Immigrants who arrived at the port of New York between August 1, 1855, and April 18, 1890, were received at Castle Garden, a circular building originally built as a fort and located at the tip of Manhattan's Battery Park.[15] Castle Garden was administered solely by the State of New York until the early 1880s when control of immigration was given to the U.S. Secretary of the Treasury. The federal government subsequently made a contract with the New York State Commissioners of Emigration to fulfill their immigration responsibilities at the port of New York. The mixed federal–state administering of the facility did not work well and problems abounded. The need for an immigrant receiving station that was completely federally run was identified. Plans for Ellis Island began and the contract with the State of New York Commissioners of Emigration ended on April 18, 1890. The New York State Commissioners of Emigration refused to let the federal government use Castle Garden as a receiving station while Ellis Island was under construction and on April 18, 1890, Castle Garden was closed.[16]

Between April 19, 1890, and December 31, 1891, a building called the Barge Office, located in Battery Park near Castle Garden, was used for immigration purposes. Built in 1879 for the use of the Customs Bureau, the Barge Office was cramped and not considered satisfactory.[17]

Ellis Island opened officially on January 1, 1892, and was used as an immigrant receiving station until June 14, 1897, when a fire that occurred shortly after midnight on June 15, 1897, caused operations to cease. Built entirely of pine, the buildings were destroyed along with immigration records stored for safekeeping in some of the old vaults.[18] The Barge Office was reactivated and used as a receiving station until Ellis Island opened again on December 17, 1900.[19] On March 4, 1955, Ellis Island was closed and declared surplus property.[20]

Contrary to popular thought, not all alien passengers who immigrated through the port of New York were inspected at or even set foot on Ellis Island. After the steamship passed through Quarantine, it would enter New York Harbor and then proceed to its pier. Steamships belonging to the Holland-America Line, North German Lloyd Line, and Hamburg-America Line would go to their piers in Hoboken, New Jersey.[21] The steamships of other transatlantic steamship lines would go to their piers at the lower end of Manhattan Island. First- and second-class passengers would have cursory inspections on board ship. Upon passing inspections, these individuals and U.S. citizens were released onto the steamship's pier and immediately admitted into the United States. All alien steerage passengers and only those first and second-class passengers who were detained were then ferried from the piers in Manhattan and Hoboken to Ellis Island. (Note that the passenger manifests for steamships that docked in Hoboken are part of the port of New York manifest series. There is *not* a separate series of Hoboken manifests.)

Canadian Border Crossing Records

Many Jews and individuals of other ethnicities immigrated first to Canada and then made their way to the United States. Some crossed the border immediately after arriving at a Canadian port of arrival, while others settled in Canada for a long time and became Canadian citizens before moving to the United States. Then others, because the 1921–24 U.S. quota laws did not limit the number of immigrants to the United States from Canada, settled in Canada for the minimal requisite time to establish residency and then moved permanently to the United States.[22]

Individuals who made their way across the U.S.-Canada border during the mid-to-late 19th century did not leave behind border crossing papers. Those, however, who crossed the border after 1894 did indeed leave a document trail behind, and these records are available for research.

As the result of an agreement between the United States and Canada, beginning in 1894 immigrants traveling by steamship to the United States via Canada were listed on U.S. immigration passenger arrival manifests. In order to be listed on these manifests, individuals must have been heading immediately to a specific destination in the United States. Those individuals who planned to go first to a specific destination in Canada and then immigrated later to the United States were not listed on U.S. manifests. They were listed on Canadian manifests which are available for research at the National Archives of Canada.[23]

U.S. immigration inspectors, stationed at the Canadian ports of arrival, inspected immigrants destined for the United States and collected the manifests that they later sent to their district headquarters in Montreal, a headquarters that subsequently moved to St. Albans, Vermont. Until 1929, the district covered the entire Canada-United States border, from the Atlantic Ocean to the Pacific Ocean. In 1929, the district was split, and western arrivals were reported in the Western district records.[24]

Between 1895 and circa 1906, land-border inspection stations were established along the United States-Canada border. Marian Smith's article, "By Way of Canada: U.S. Records of Immigration Across the U.S.-Canadian Border, 1895–1954

(St. Albans Lists)", published in *Prologue* in 2000 and in *Avotaynu: The International Review of Jewish Genealogy* in 1999, provides details about what occurred at the border.[25] In summary, immigrants who passed inspection at Canadian seaports seaports and were traveling immediately to the U.S. were issued a "Certificate of Admission" that they surrendered to U.S. immigration inspectors at the land-border inspection stations. These land-border inspection stations also generated manifests for individuals who had immigrated and settled in Canada for a period of time before crossing later into the United States.[26] These contiguous territory border-crossing lists include the same information as the U.S. ship lists, plus the name of the steamship and the date and port of the individual's original arrival in Canada. Returning U.S. citizens needed to supply their date and place of birth, and naturalized U.S. citizens, their date and place of citizenship.[27]

Like the U.S. immigration inspectors stationed at Canadian seaports, the U.S. land border inspectors sent the manifests that they generated to the district headquarters in Montreal. These U.S. land border and seaport manifests were all bound into volumes and make up what is commonly known in the National Archives as the "St. Albans records." Index cards of these manifests were created and soundexed in the late 1930s. The information on these manifest cards was extracted directly from the manifests.[28] The indexes generally have the same information as the manifests themselves, although they sometimes include additional handwritten details and notations such as "deported" or "debarred" (not allowed to enter).

The St. Albans records and the accompanying soundex index cards, 1895–circa 1952, have been microfilmed and published and are available for research at the National Archives in Washington, DC, and at the various regional National Archives as well as the Family History Library.

(Note that there are immigrants who are listed in the St. Albans index but not in the St. Albans manifests and there are immigrants who are listed in the St. Albans manifests but not in the index. If you can't find your immigrant in the St. Albans records or indices, be sure to check the individual and smaller ports records that are gradually being published and made available for research.[29])

How to Find a Manifest

Millions of people have immigrated to the United States and it can be difficult to locate and identify a specific passenger arrival manifest. To maximize chances of success, before you begin your search try to learn as much as possible of the following information:

- Immigrant's approximate date of arrival in the United States
- Possible port of arrival (not everyone arrived at Ellis Island)
- Surname the immigrant likely used at the time of arrival
- Some idea how the surname might have been spelled on the manifest. Keep in mind Eastern European spelling and sounds. Goldstein, for example, is an Anglicized spelling; in Eastern Europe, and, therefore, on the manifest, it may have been Goldsztejn. Differences in spellings may change the way a surname is indexed

- Immigrant's Yiddish or Hebrew name. Your immigrant ancestor was not listed on the ship's manifest under his or her Anglicized given name. They would have been listed under their Yiddish name, Hebrew name, or secular Eastern European name. An immigrant whose American given name was Phillip may have arrived in the United States under the name "Feiwel"
- Immigrant's approximate age at the time of immigration
- Names of other individuals who might have been traveling with the immigrant

The following resources might provide you with clues about dates and places of immigration:

Census Records. The 1900, 1910, 1920, and 1930 U.S. federal censuses are supposed to provide the year of arrival in the United States for each non-United States-born household member. Some state censuses, such as New York's 1905, 1915 and 1925 censuses, asked for the number of years that each household member had been in the United States. Although these dates often are inaccurate, they are clues to the approximate year of arrival.

Naturalization Records. (1) Certificates of Arrival. Generated by the INS during the naturalization process, certificates of arrival were used to prove that the immigrant had arrived legally in the United States. The certificates list the name of the ship on which the immigrant traveled to the United States; the exact date and port of arrival, and the name that the immigrant used on the ship. This information should not be taken as fact, however, but instead should be used to help locate the actual passenger arrival manifest. Sometimes the wrong certificate of arrival is attached to an individual's set of naturalization papers. For information about the accuracy of information in certificates of arrival see Marian L. Smith, "Certificates of Arrival and the Accuracy of Arrival Information Found in U.S. Naturalization Records."[30]

Certificates of arrival, filed with an individual's petition for naturalization and declaration of intention, usually are not found for individuals who arrived in the United States before June 30, 1906. Given the five-year U.S. residency requirement for naturalization of males arriving in the United States at age 21 and older, the certificates of arrival most commonly are found with petitions for naturalization submitted after June 29, 1911.[31]

Naturalization Records. (2) Declarations of Intent and Petitions for Naturalization. Often referred to as an individual's first and final papers respectively, declarations of intent and petitions for naturalization were generated during the naturalization process. The amount of immigration information on them and the accuracy of the information depend on the year that each document was generated. Documents generated before September 27, 1906, may have extremely limited information, possibly just an approximate date of arrival, sometimes a port, sometimes simply the name of the city at which the immigrant arrived. Even when an exact date is provided, it may be off by days, months, or years. Many declarants and petitioners did not remember the facts and simply fabricated a date.

Declarations and petitions generated after September 26, 1906, usually include port of embarkation, approximate date of embarkation, approximate date of arrival, name of steamship and, possibly, the name that the immigrant sailed under. This information may be inaccurate, but it was checked by the INS before the immigrant was allowed to become a citizen; therefore, it may be your best source of immigration data.[32] It can lead you to the manifest.

Records of the Hebrew Immigrant Aid Society (HIAS). Commonly called HIAS, the Hebrew Immigrant Aid Society, founded in 1880, is the oldest international migration and refugee resettlement agency in the United States. HIAS personnel were at United States ports of entry assisting many (but not all) Jewish immigrants with their entry into the United States. Microfilmed copies of HIAS arrival index cards, 1909–1949, and master index cards, 1950–1979, are available at YIVO in New York City.[33] These early arrival cards may include the name of the immigrant and other people in the traveling party, ship on which the immigrant sailed, date of arrival and where the immigrant intended to go upon arrival. For a fee, HIAS will complete locator searches through arrival cards dating from 1909 (WWW.HIAS.ORG/FIND_FAMILY/OVERVIEW.HTML).

Port of Boston HIAS arrival index cards and case files are held by the American Jewish Historical Society at their new library on the Hebrew College campus in Newton, Massachusetts. Warren Blatt's *Resources for Jewish Genealogy in the Boston Area* provides a fairly in-depth review of their HIAS holdings.[34] Microfilmed copies of the port of Boston HIAS records are available from the Family History Library. Film numbers will be found in the Family History Library catalog under Massachusetts—Emigration and Immigration. A searchable database is now also available on JewishGen (WWW.JEWISHGEN.ORG/DATABASES/USA/BOSTONHIAS.HTM).

Microfilmed copies of the port of Philadelphia HIAS records for various years are available from the Family History Library. Some records from the port of New York are mixed in with the port of Philadelphia records. The HIAS records will be found under: Pennsylvania, Philadelphia, Philadelphia — Jewish records.

The Philadelphia Jewish Archives, located in Center City in Philadelphia, also has HIAS records for the port of Philadelphia, circa 1884–1921 (WWW.JEWISHARCHIVES.NET/GENEALOGY/GENEALOGY.HTML). Their collections are open by appointment only, but they will search the HIAS records for a fee.

U.S. Passport Applications. Among other useful information, passport applications can provide an individual's date and port of arrival in the United States. Not all individuals traveling outside the United States had a passport or filed an application for one. Passports were generally not required until June 1941. The few exceptions were during the Civil War, from August 19, 1861, to March 17, 1862, and from May 22, 1918, until the formal end of World War I in 1921.[35]

Except for certain time periods, aliens were not eligible to obtain passports. The exception most relevant to Jewish genealogists was the time between March 2, 1907 and June 4, 1920, when an alien who declared his intent to become a naturalized citizen could obtain a passport.[36]

The National Archives has microfilm copies of passport applications from October 1795 to March 1925 and indexes to these records. Copies are also available through the Family History Library. Passports applications that date from April 1925 to the present are at the United States State Department. For more information about United States passport applications, see the National Archives passport webpage (WWW.ARCHIVES.GOV/RESEARCH_ROOM/GENEALOGY/RESEARCH_TOPICS/PASSPORT_APPLICATIONS.HTML).

City Directory Listings. Privately printed and published from the late 1700s to the mid-1900s, city directories are secondary and derivative resources designed to provide information about specific cities and their residents. The information was assembled by paid canvassers who went door-to-door collecting names and other data about household members. The directories were sold primarily as marketing tools. Among numerous items, city directories usually include an alphabetical list of the adult male residents and female heads of family in a city, their occupations, and work and residential addresses. New residents in a city often first appear within a year or two of arriving at that location. If you know where the immigrant settled after arriving in the United States, search the relevant city directory for his or her very first listing. This first listing will at least indicate that they had to have arrived in the United States before that date. Be sure to check a few years before the apparent first listing, just to make sure that their first listing was located. Also, check variant surname spellings. It is possible that they lived in that location earlier, but were listed under a slightly different surname. Anglicized names and surnames often evolved over time.

Indexes

Some ship passenger indexes have been published and will help in the search for arrival records. Some are ethnic indexes published in books or on CD-ROMs. Examples are Robert Swierenga's *Dutch Immigrants in U.S. Ship Passenger Manifest, 1820–1880* and *Migrations from the Russian Empire*, a series edited by Ira Glazier, director of the Temple-Balch Center for Immigration Research. The hardcover series of *Migrations from the Russian Empire* is currently six volumes and covers January 1975–June 1891. It is now available on CD-ROM for the years 1850–1896.

Another series of possible interest to Jewish genealogists is Ira Glazier and P. William Filby's *Germans to America*. This 60-volume series covers January 1850–May 1891.

Virginia Steele Wood's online publication, *Immigrant Arrivals: A Guide to Published Sources*, provides a detailed list of many other indexes and immigration resources and is available on the Internet through the U.S. Library of Congress website (WWW.LOC.GOV/RR/GENEALOGY/BIB_GUID/IMMIGRANT/).

Microfilmed passenger indexes are available at the National Archives. With the exception of the individual card manifests that compose the soundex index to the St. Albans records (the Canadian border crossings) and the steamship lines' book indexes, these indexes were completed by the Works Progress Administration in the 1930s. Book indexes are also available: these are alphabetical lists of passengers which were completed by the shipping lines. They often include a printed list of first-class passengers, but the list of steerage passengers usually appears to be incomplete. Unfortunately, because of small print and blurry, scratched images, all of these microfilm indexes are difficult to use.

Information about other federally generated indexes and manifest lists can be found in *A Guide to Federal Records in the National Archives of the United States*, Record Groups 85.3.1 and 85.3.2. This guide is available on the Internet at www.archives.gov/research_room/federal_records_guide/. Microfilm reel numbers can be found in *Immigrant and Passenger Arrivals: A Select Catalog of National Archives Microfilm Publications*, available for use or purchase at the various National Archives branches. Information about the lists and microfilm reels also may be obtained online at the National Archives' web page www.archives.gov/publications/microfilm_catalogs/immigrant/immigrant_passenger_arrivals.html.

For individuals who are researching immigrants who might have come through the port of New York, 1892–1924, there is an excellent online search engine that ties into the Ellis Island database. This is known as the Ellis Island Database One Step Search Tools and can be found on JewishGen's database page (www.jewishgen.org/databases/eidb/). This search engine was originally created by Dr. Stephen Morse and is sometimes referred to as the "Morse" search engine.

Some microfilmed and hard-copy indexes are alphabetical. Other microfilmed indexes are "soundex indexes" (i.e., based on the way the surname "sounds"). This "soundex index" is the same system that is used for the federal census schedules. It is important to remember that surnames are alphabetized and soundexed *using the spelling listed on the manifest*. If the surname was not spelled on the manifest the way you spell it, then it will not be alphabetized or soundexed the way you expect.

When searching indexes, remember that Eastern Europeans did not pronounce all their letters the same way as one does in English; Eastern European alphabets do not contain all the same letters as the English alphabet; most immigrants did not speak English; and many did not know how to write their name in Latin letters. They had no way of knowing if the ship's officer wrote their name "correctly" on the manifest. (Exactly what was *the* correct spelling? The Anglicized version? The transliterated version?) All these factors may have affected the way a surname was listed first on the manifest and later in the index. For example, in Eastern Europe, the letter *w* is pronounced as English speakers pronounce the letter *v*. When searching manifests for individuals from Eastern Europe whose surnames began with the letter *w*, be sure to also check surnames beginning with the letter *v*. The letter *j* was pronounced the way English speakers pronounce a *y* so if you are researching a person whose surname started with *j* be sure to also check *y* or even *i*. A surname that ends in *ovitz* in the United States may have been spelled *ovitz, owitz, ovicz* or *ovic* on a manifest. All lead to different soundex codes.

Note, also, that the Cyrillic alphabet does not have the let-

ters *c* or *h*; the Latin letters *k* and *g* are used instead. Therefore, the Anglicized name Cohen may have been written as Kogan on the manifest—or Kagan, Kan, or other variations; the first name Hirsh could have been listed as Girsh; and the surname Halpern could have been listed as Galpern.

Also remember that a passenger emigrating from Eastern Europe was not listed on the manifest under an Anglicized given name. He or she might be listed on the manifest under their Yiddish name, Hebrew name, secular Eastern European name or some variation that could have been misspelled by the shipping line's authorities. An individual's given name might or might not have been spelled the way that *you* spell it. Shmuel may be Szmuel on the manifest, or the name Feivish listed instead as Fivel, or Zvi listed as Girsh because the names Zvi Hirsh are often used together. Remember also that no Eastern European Jew arrived with the name Harry; look instead for Chaim, Hirsh or some other possibility.

An "info file" on given names is on the JewishGen website. This file, succinctly titled "Given Names," is based on a presentation given by Warren Blatt at past Jewish genealogical conferences. It can be found at: www.jewishgen.org/infofiles/givennames/. In addition, on JewishGen there is also a relatively new database called the "The Given Names Database." It is located at: www.jewishgen.org/databases/givennames/.

Using Immigration List Index Cards to Locate A Manifest

Arrivals between 1893 and 1909. Depending on the port, index cards for people who arrived between circa 1893 and 1897 could be arranged alphabetically or by soundex. They provide the immigrant's previous residence (possibly just the name of the country), age, destination, steamship and date of arrival. There might be a separate card for all individuals traveling together; alternatively, there might be an index card for the head of the family with a notation that he or she was traveling with a specific number of family members. Once you have learned the name of the steamship and date of arrival, you can easily locate the manifest itself.

Arrivals after 1909. Index cards for immigrants who arrived after 1909 may provide the passenger's name, age, and then a code that leads to the manifest. One example is the following index listing for the port of New York: Chaie Goldman 18f 6 39 2959. This tells you that Chaie Goldman, age 18, female, is the sixth passenger listed on page 39 of the ship's manifest in volume 2959. To determine if she is the individual sought, look at the actual manifest for additional information. *Immigrant and Passenger Arrivals: A Select Catalog of National Archives Microfilm Publications* will help identify the volumes and microfilm reels associated with passenger manifests within a specific time frame.[37] According to this catalog, microfilm reel 1343 in the National Archives publication series T715 covers volumes 2958–2959 and includes immigration lists for steamships that arrived at the port of New York between September 26, 1909, and September 27, 1909.[38]

Occasionally, an index listing does not give a page, line or volume number, but instead a "CR#." CR# means certificate of registry number, which *cannot* help you locate the passenger manifest. The number signifies that the INS opened a certificate of registry file on this individual because, for naturalization purposes, INS searched for but could not find this person listed on a manifest. Registry files were opened primarily on people who immigrated to the United States between 1906 and 1924.[39]

(Upon finding a Certificate of Registry number, you can request a search for the pertinent registry records from the INS using the Freedom of Information Act [FOIA]. Note, however, that your request should *NOT* include the CR# that you might have found on the index card. This number will only lead FOIA personnel to the wrong file, and you will receive a negative response.

Your FOIA request *should* include the name of the individual, his date, and his approximate place of birth. Ask for any records available on that person and state that it *might* be a registry file.[40])

Research Aids for Unindexed Years

If a researcher knows the name of the steamship, the port of embarkation and approximate years of arrival in a time period in which there are no indexes, three aids may be useful: *The Morton Allan Steamship Directory*; the National Archives' microfilm publication *A Register of Vessels Arriving at the Port of New York from Foreign Ports, 1789–1919;* and the Hamburg embarkation lists.

The *Morton Allan Steamship Directory* lists dates of arrival and names of steamships that arrived at the port of New York between 1890 and 1930 and at the ports of Philadelphia, Boston and Baltimore between 1904 and 1926. The directory is arranged by year, then by steamship line. The places of embarkation and arrival are listed.

The *Register of Vessels Arriving at the Port of New York from Foreign Ports, 1789–1919*, can also help you identify the ships that arrived at the port of New York in this period and their dates of arrival. This microfilm publication is the National Archives microfilm series M1066 and covers 27 microfilm reels of film. More information can be found at: WWW.ARCHIVES.GOV/PUBLICATIONS/MICROFILM_CATALOGS/IMMIGRANT/CUSTOMS_RECORDS_1820_1891.HTML, Neither this publication nor the *Morton Allan Directory* supplies names of passengers.

The Hamburg, Germany, embarkation indexes and lists, which date from 1850 to 1934, can be extremely useful if you know or suspect that an immigrant emigrated through Hamburg, Germany. The next section describes these records.

Hamburg Emigration Lists

Hamburg, Germany, was a major port of exit for Jews who left Europe for the United States, South Africa, Argentina and a host of other countries.

Emigrants who embarked from Hamburg could either go directly to their destined port of arrival or take the less expensive indirect route, stopping in various European ports of call along the way before reaching their destination.

Embarkation lists for the port of Hamburg, 1850–1934, except 1915–19, and indexes of these lists have survived and are available on microfilm through the Family History Library. Online searches can also be made through the Hamburg State

Archives—Link to Your Roots website FHH1.HAMBURG.DE/FHH/BEHOERDEN/STAATSARCHIV/LINK_TO_YOUR_ROOTS/ENGLISH/. This database currently includes 1890–1905. The preliminary indexing search is free; a fee is charged if the researcher wants more details about the passengers.

The Hamburg lists can supply the name of each emigrant, his or her age, occupation, birthplace or last residence, date of embarkation, name of ship and the ship's destination. The records are in German.

With the exception of a 15-year index to the direct lists of passengers who sailed between 1856 and 1871, most of the microfilmed indexes cover just a couple of years or even just a few months at a time. In order to use these records most effectively, therefore, it is best to have some idea of when an immigrant left Europe. The indexes are arranged alphabetically by the first letter of the surname. The first names of the individuals are usually written in German script. The Family History Library has research aids for reading German script readily available for use onsite. Handwriting aids are also available for purchase from numerous genealogical publishing companies. Several companies are listed in Warren Blatt's FAQ (Frequently Asked Questions) available on JewishGen (WWW.JEWISHGEN.ORG/INFOFILES/FAQ.HTML).

Information from an immigrant's Hamburg embarkation listing can lead you to the correct U.S. passenger arrival record. Much has been written about the Hamburg embarkation lists. For a review of these records and how to use them, see the research outline published by the Family History Library: *The Hamburg Passenger Lists 1850–1934* (Salt Lake City: Church of Jesus Christ of Latter-day Saints, 1992). This guide is also available on the Internet through the Family History Library website: WWW.FAMILYSEARCH.ORG/ENG/SEARCH/RG/FRAMESET_RHELPS.ASP. Additional information on Hamburg embarkation lists can also be found on the German Genealogy webpage at WWW.GENEALOGIENETZ.DE/MISC/EMIG/HAM_PASS.HTML and in Daniel Schlyter's "Hamburg Passenger Lists" in *The Encyclopedia of Jewish Genealogy*.[41] Jürgen Sielemann's chapter on "Eastern European Jewish Emigration Via the Port of Hamburg: 1880–1914" in *The Encyclopedia of Jewish Genealogy* provides background data on the port of Hamburg,[42] and his article on "Lesser Known Records of Emigrants in the Hamburg State Archives" published in Avotaynu 7, no. 3 (Fall 1991) gives added details about the embarkation lists, as well as other key resources available in the Hamburg Archives.

Bremen Emigration Lists

Bremen, Germany, was also a major port of exit for Jewish immigrants going to the United States and other countries. While most of the embarkation lists for this port were destroyed, records from 1920–1939 have been located. The Die Maus Genealogical Society in Bremen, Germany, in conjunction with the Bremen Chamber of Commerce is extracting information from these lists and putting this information into a searchable database. This database currently includes all of 1920–1926 and portions of later years. It provides the names of the immigrants, their ages, their previous residences, their intended destinations, and their occupations. A recent "test" search of

№	Die zu einer Familie gehörenden Personen sind unter einander zu schreiben und durch eine Klammer als zusammengehörig zu bezeichnen.		Geschlecht		Alter (in Jahren)	(Bei deutsch. Männern v. 17 bis 25 Jahren.) Ist die Entlassungs-urkunde oder das Zeugnis (§ 23 des Auswges.) vorgelegt?	Familienstand (ledig u. s. w.)	Bisheriger Wohnort	Staats-angehörigkeit	Bezeich-nung des bisherigen Berufs	Stellung im bisherigen Berufe	Ziel der Auswanderung (Ort und Staat)	Davon sind:	
	Zuname	Vornamen	männ-lich	weib-lich									Erwach-sene und Kinder über 10 Jahre	Kinder unter 16 Jahr / unter 1 Jahr
1	2	3	4	5	6	7	8	9	10	11	12	13		

Emigration lists from European ports can provide useful information that is not present on U.S. immigration lists. For example, Hamburg emigration lists include past residence (Bisheriger Wohnort).

this database listed individuals with the surnames Goldstein, Goldschmidt, Goldfarb, Kagan, Berman and other typically Jewish-sounding surnames. In addition to searching by sur-name, the database allows you to search by "home towns." The English version of the search page can be found at: DB.GENEALOGY.NET/MAUS/GATE/SHIPLISTS.CGI?LANG=EN.

Immigrant Visas

Beginning on July 1, 1924, all alien immigrants arriving in the United States had to present a visa.[43] The type of visa issued depended on the native country of the applicant as well as his or her reason for entering the United States. Immigrants who wanted to come to this country, planned to settle here permanently, *and* who were from a country that was subject to the U.S. immigration quota—such as Poland— would ap-ply for a "quota immigrant visa." Immigrants who wanted to come to this country, planned to settle here permanently, *and* who were from a country that was *not* subject to the U.S. immigration quota—such as Canada—would apply for a "non-quota" immigrant visa.[44] Quota and non-quota immi-grant visa applications can be full of valuable data, including the date and place of birth and places of prior residence. They can be obtained through the Freedom of Information Act (FOIA) from the INS in Washington, DC. For information about FOIA requests, see the FOIA webpage at USCIS.GOV/GRAPHICS/ ABOUTUS/FOIA/INDEX.HTM. More information about visa files can be found in the article "Visa Files, 1924–1944," published on the INS History, Genealogy, and Education online webpages (USCIS.GOV/GRAPHICS/ABOUTUS/HISTORY/IMMRECS/VISA.HTM).

National Archives of Canada

The National Archives of Canada has microfilm copies of manifests for steamships arriving at Canadian ports between 1865 and 1935 and copies of border crossing records for indi-viduals traveling to the United States from Canada between April 1908 and December 31, 1935. The Canadian National Archives' website at WWW.ARCHIVES.CA provides a detailed overview of its immigration holdings. Within this website, immigration information is located at WWW.ARCHIVES.CA/08/ 08_E.HTML and border entry information is located at www. ARCHIVES.CA/02/020202/0202020403_E.HTML.

Holland America Line Microfiche

Holland America Line passenger lists provide information on individuals who departed from Rotterdam on Holland America Line steamships between 1900 and 1940 and landed in New York. This set of lists is on microfiche and is written in Dutch. There is a microfiche index to the lists; surnames beginning with the same first letter are grouped together. An info file written by Donald Campbell Lockhart is on JewishGen's website. It provides details about using the index and pas-senger lists and can be found at WWW.JEWISHGEN.ORG/INFOFILES/ HOLLAM3.TXT. The info file also provides background informa-tion on the Holland America Line (HAL).

According to this Lockard's info file, among numerous items, the lists include the name of the ship; its destination; the date the steamship left port; and the amounts paid for first, second and third class ocean passages and train fares. The name of the person who purchased the passage is provided along with the number of individuals traveling with him or her. If the traveler purchased a "package deal" which included overland service from a main city to Rotterdam or overland service from New York to another town in the United States, the place where the service began and ended may be listed.

Notes

1. Marian L. Smith, Historian, Historian for U.S. Citizenship and Immigration Services (formerly the Immigration and Naturalization Service) (hereinafter M. Smith), e-mail message to N. Arbeiter, October 9, 1998.
2. "Immigration and Naturalization Legislation from the Statistical Yearbook", Bureau of Citizenship and Immigration Services Webpage (hereinafter Statistical Yearbook) U.S. Citizenship and Immigration Services webpage (hereinafter USCIS webpage), accessed by N. Arbeiter, 7 May 2003 (at USCIS.GOV/GRAPHICS/ABOUTUS/STATISTICS/LEGISHIST); M. Smith, conversation with N. Arbeiter, 8 May 2003.
3. Statistical Yearbook.
4. *Ibid.*
5. Marian L. Smith, "Overview of INS History", USCIS webpage, accessed by N. Arbeiter, 7 May 2003 (at USCIS.GOV/GRAPHICS/ABOUTUS/HISTORY/ARTICLES/OVIEW.HTM.
6. M. Smith, conversation, 8 May 2003.
7. *Ibid.*
8. David M. Brownstone, Irene M. Franck, and Douglass L. Brownstone, *Island of Hope, Island of Tears* (New York: Barnes and Noble Books, 2002), , 107–8.
9. Thomas M. Pitkin, *Keepers of the Gate: A History of Ellis Island* (New York: New York University Press, 1975), 156.
10. *Ibid.* 71, 73.
11. M. Smith, conversation with N. Arbeiter, August 1999.
12. Pitkin, 26.
13. Smith, conversation, 8 May 2003.
14. M. Smith, INS Historian, "American Names/Declaring Independence," USCIS webpage, accessed by N. Arbeiter, 7 May 2003 (at USCIS.GOV/GRAPHICS/ABOUTUS/HISTORY/ARTICLES/NAMEESSAY.HTML)
15. Ann Novotny, *Strangers at the Door: Ellis Island, Castle Garden and the Great Immigration to America* (Riverside, Conn. Chatham Press, 1971), 44, 47, 53.
16. Pitkin, 9–16.
17. George Svejda, *Castle Garden As An Immigrant Depot, 1855–1890* (Washington, DC: National Park Service, mimeo, 1968), 105; Pitkin, 14.
18. Pitkin, 26.
19. "Leaving the Barge Office", in *The New York Times,* 16 Dec 1900, p. 14, column 1.
20. Pitkin, 177.
21. "The Abridged History of Hoboken", Hoboken Historical Museum Website, accessed by N. Arbeiter, 8 May 2003 (at WWW.HOBOKENMUSEUM.ORG/ABRIDGED_HISTORY.HTM.
22. Statistical Yearbook.
23. Marian L. Smith, "By Way of Canada: U.S. Records of Immigration Across the U.S.-Canadian Border, 1895–1854 (St. Albans Lists)", *Prologue,* 2000, vol. 32, no. 3; online at the USCIS website (at WWW.ARCHIVES.GOV/PUBLICATIONS/PROLOGUE/FALL_2000_US_CANADA_IMMIGRATION_RECORDS_1.HTML); Marian L. Smith, "By Way of Canada: U.S. Records of Immigration Across the U.S.-Canadian Border, 1895–1854 (St. Albans Lists)", *Avotaynu: The International Review of Jewish Genealogy,* fall 1999, vol. XV, no. 3, pp 4–9.
24. William Schoeffler, "Crossing the Canadian Border: The St. Albans U.S. Passenger Arrival Lists", lecture, 15th Annual Summer Seminar on Jewish Genealogy in Boston, Massachusetts (Hobart, Indiana: Repeat Performance, 1996).
25. Smith, "By Way of Canada
26. *Ibid.*
27. Schoeffler. "Crossing the Canadian Border."
28. M. Smith, conversation, 8 May 2003.
29. *Ibid.*
30. Marian L. Smith, "Certificates of Arrival and the Accuracy of Arrival Information Found in U.S. Naturalization Records," *Avotaynu: The International Review of Jewish Genealogy,* Summer 1998, vol. XIV, no. 2, pp 18–23.
31. M. Smith, conversation with N. Arbeiter, 8 Oct 1998.
32. Marian L. Smith, "Immigration & Naturalization Service Records for Genealogical Research" lecture, 19th Annual Conference on Jewish Genealogy in New York, New York (Hobart Indiana: Repeat Performance, 1999).
33. Estelle M. Guzik, ed., *Genealogical Resources in the New York Metropolitan Area* (New York: Jewish Genealogical Society, 1989), 130.
34. Warren Blatt, ed., *Resources for Jewish Genealogy in the Boston Area* (Newton, Mass.: Jewish Genealogical Society of Greater Boston, 1996), 40.
35. "Passport Applications", NARA Genealogy webpage, accessed by N. Arbeiter, 7 May 2003 (at WWW.ARCHIVES.GOV/RESEARCH_ROOM/GENEALOGY/RESEARCH_TOPICS/PASSPORT_APPLICATIONS.HTML.)
36. *Ibid.* The law that permitted this was repealed on June 4, 1920.
37. *Immigrant & Passenger Arrivals: A Select Catalog of National Archives Microfilm Publications* (Washington, DC: National Archives Trust Fund Board, 1983).
38. *Ibid.* 65.
39. Smith, "Immigration & Naturalization Service Records for Genealogical Research."
40. M. Smith, conversation, 8 May 2003.
41. Arthur Kurzweil and Miriam Weiner, eds., *The Encyclopedia of Jewish Genealogy: Sources in the United States and Canada* (Northvale, N.J.: Jason Aronson, 1991), 9–12.
42. *Ibid.* 7–9.
43. "Visa Files, 1924–1944", USCIS webpage, accessed by N. Arbeiter, 7 May 2003 (at USCIS.GOV/GRAPHICS/ABOUTUS/HISTORY/IMMRECS/VISA.HTM).
44. *Ibid.*

References

Anuta, Michael J. *Ships of Our Ancestors.* Baltimore: Genealogical Publishing Co., 2002.

Bearss, Edwin C. *The Ferryboat "Ellis Island," Transport to Hope.* Washington, DC: National Park Service, 1969.

Blatt, Warren. *FAQ: Frequently Asked Questions About Jewish Genealogy.* Teaneck, N.J.: Avotaynu, 1996.

Brownstone, David, Irene M. Franck, and Douglass L. Brownstone. *Island of Hope, Island of Tears.* New York: Barnes & Noble, 2000.

Chermayeff, Ivan, Fred Wasserman, and Mary J. Shapiro. *Ellis Island: An Illustrated History of the Immigrant Experience.* New York: Macmillan, 1991.

Coan, Peter Morton. *Ellis Island Interviews: In Their Own Words.* New York: Facts On File, 1997.

Colletta, John P. *They Came in Ships: A Guide to Finding Your Immigrant Ancestor's Arrival Record,* 2d. rev. ed. Salt Lake City: Ancestry, 1993.

Eales, Anne Bruner, and Robert M. Kvasnicka, eds. *Genealogical Research in the National Archives of the United States.* 3rd ed.

Washington, DC: National Archives and Records Administration, 2000.

Glazier, Ira A., ed. *Migration from the Russian Empire: Lists of Passengers Arriving at U.S. Ports.* 6 vols. Baltimore: Genealogical Publishing, 1995–97. (Volumes published to date cover January 1875–June 1891)

Glazier, Ira A., and P. William Filby. *Germans to America: Lists of Passengers Arriving at U.S. Ports, 1850 to 1887.* Multiple volumes. Wilmington, Del.: Scholarly Resources, 1988.

Guide to Federal Records in the National Archives of the United States. 3 vols. Washington, D.C.: National Archives and Records Administration, 1995. Internet address: www.archives.gov/research_room/federal_records_guide/.

Kapp, Friedrich. *Immigration and the Commissioners of Emigration of the State of New York.* 1870. Reprint, New York: Arno Press and The New York Times, 1969.

Kraut, Alan M. *Silent Travelers: Germs, Genes, and "the Immigrant Menace".* Baltimore, Maryland: The Johns Hopkins University Press, 1994.

Lainhart, Ann S. *State Census Records.* Baltimore: Genealogical Publishing, 1992.

Kurzweil, Arthur, and Miriam Weiner, eds. *The Encyclopedia of Jewish Genealogy*, vol. 1. Northvale, N.J.: Jason Aronson, 1991.

Morton Allan Directory of European Passenger Steamship Arrivals for the Years 1890 to 1926 at the Ports of New York, Philadelphia, Boston and Baltimore. Baltimore: Genealogical Publishing, 1987.

Moser, Geraldine, and Marlene Silverman. *Hamburg Passengers from the Kingdom of Poland and the Russian Empire: Indirect Passage to New York: 1855–June 1873.* Washington, D.C.: Landsmen Press, 1996.

National Archives Trust Fund Board. *Immigrant and Passenger Arrivals: A Select Catalog of National Archives Microfilm Publications.* Washington, D.C.: National Archives Trust Fund Board, 1991.

Novotny, Ann. *Strangers at the Door: Ellis Island, Castle Garden, and the Great Migration to America.* Riverside, Ct.: Chatham Press, 1971.

Pitkin, Thomas M. *Keepers of the Gate: A History of Ellis Island.* New York: New York University Press, 1975.

Register of Vessels Arriving at the Port of New York from Foreign Ports, 1789–1919. National Archives microfilm publication M1066. 27 reels. Washington, D.C.: National Archives.

Schoeffler, William. "Crossing the Canadian Border: The St. Albans U.S. Passenger Arrival Lists", lecture, 15th Annual Summer Seminar on Jewish Genealogy in Boston, Massachusetts. Hobart, Indiana: Repeat Performance, 1996.

Sielemann, Jürgen. "Lesser Known Records of Emigrants in the Hamburg State Archives." *Avotaynu* 7, no. 3 (Fall 1991).

Smith, Eugene Waldo. *Passenger Ships of the World, Past and Present*, 2d. ed. Boston: G.H. Dean, 1978.

Smith, Marian L. "By Way of Canada: U.S. Records of Immigration across the U.S.-Canadian Border, 1895–1954 (St. Albans Lists)." *Avotaynu* 15, no. 3 (Fall 1999).

———. "Certificates of Arrival and the Accuracy of Arrival Information Found in U.S. Naturalization Records." *Avotaynu* 14, no. 2 (Summer 1998).

———. "Immigration and Naturalization Service Records for Genealogical Research." Lecture, 19th Annual Conference on Jewish Genealogy, New York, August 1999. Audiocassette recording available as 19th Annual Conference on Jewish Genealogy, tape #99-24. Hobart, Ind.: Repeat Performance, 1999.

———. "Interpreting U.S. Immigration Manifest Annotations." *Avotaynu* 12, no. 1 (Spring 1996).

Steiner, Edward A. *On the Trail of the Immigrant.* New York: Arno Press and The New York Times, 1969.

Stolarik, Mark, ed. *Forgotten Doors: The Other Ports of Entry to the United States.* Philadelphia: Balch Institute, 1988.

Svejda, George J. *Castle Garden as an Immigrant Depot, 1855–1890.* Washington, DC: National Park Service, mimeo, 1968.

Swierenga, Robert P., comp. *Dutch Immigrants in U.S. Ship Passenger Manifests, 1820–1880.* Wilmington, Del.: Scholarly Resources, 1983.

Szucs, Loretto Dennis, and Sandra Hargreaves Luebking, eds. *The Source: A Guidebook of American Genealogy*, rev. ed. Salt Lake City: Ancestry, 1997.

Tepper, Michael. *American Passenger Arrival Records: A Guide to the Records of Immigrants Arriving at American Ports by Sail and Steam.* Baltimore: Genealogical Publishing, 1993.

Wood, Virginia Steele, comp. *Immigrants Arrivals: A Guide to Published Sources.* Washington, D.C.: Library of Congress, Local History and Genealogy Reading Room, n.d.

Naturalization Records

by Nancy Levin Arbeiter, CGRS

A large number of foreign-born people who immigrated to the United States became United States citizens. Not all—but many of them. Some became citizens so they could buy land, vote, and take advantage of other benefits brought by citizenship. Others became citizens so they could feel part of this grand country they were adopting as their own. And then some became citizens out of fear that if they didn't, they could be sent back to their old country during war time.

Becoming a citizen was much more involved than simply walking into a courthouse and taking an oath of allegiance. The person applying for citizenship needed to file various documents within specific time periods, locate two (and sometimes more) witnesses who were already citizens (either native-born or through naturalization) who could vouch for the petitioner's moral character and prior residence, and more.

The documents generated in the process of becoming naturalized are often called "naturalization papers," a catch-all phrase referring to one or all pieces of the paperwork. These documents can be extremely valuable for genealogical purposes. Depending on when an individual immigrated and when he or she became naturalized, they may reveal an original surname, a place of birth, an exact or approximate date of arrival, ports of arrival and embarkation, the name of the steamship that brought the immigrant to America, the names of relatives or acquaintances who were already naturalized, and other key data.

Naturalization papers can include:

- The declaration of intention (sometimes called "first papers;" filed with the court)
- The petition for naturalization (sometimes called the "final papers;" filed with the court)
- The order of the court granting or denying citizenship (not a separate piece of paper; usually listed in the court records and noted on the petition for naturalization)
- The certificate of naturalization (given to the citizen after they became naturalized)

Petitioners who arrived legally in the United States after June 29, 1906, should also have a "certificate of arrival" filed with their petition for naturalization. The certificate of arrival was generated by the Immigration and Naturalization Service (INS) and confirms that the alien filing for citizenship legally entered the United States. (In 2002, services provided by the INS transitioned into the U.S. Citizenship & Immigration Services (USCIS) under the Department of Homeland Security (DHS). Within this chapter this organization will continue to be referred to as the "INS.")

Certificates of Arrival provide the name of the steamship or other vessel which brought the alien to the United States border,[1] the alien's port of entry into the United States, the alien's exact date of arrival at the United States port of entry, and the alien's name as listed on the manifest itself. (As noted in the chapter on immigration records, however, this information isn't always accurate and should not be taken as fact. For information about the accuracy of information in certificates of arrival, please see Marian L. Smith, "Certificates of Arrival and the Accuracy of Arrival Information Found in U.S. Naturalization Records.")

Given the five-year U.S. residency requirement for naturalization of males arriving in the U.S. at age 21 and older, certificates of arrival will most commonly be found with petitions for naturalization dated after June 29, 1911.[2]

What Kind of Information Is Included?

The amount and kind of information on the declaration of intention and petition for naturalization depends on when and where the documents were generated. Naturalization documents created before September 27, 1906, were not standardized and could have minimal information on them. It depends on the practices of the court issuing the documents. Alternatively, after September 26, 1906, federal law regulated the process of becoming a U.S. citizen. Preprinted naturalization forms—blank declarations of intention and petitions for naturalization with standardized and specific questions—were issued to the courts for use during the naturalization process. These preprinted forms were periodically changed and the information supplied therein also changed.

- A pre-September 27, 1906, declaration of intention might provide the name of the court, the date of the filing, and the declarant's Anglicized name and country of birth.
- A pre-September 27, 1906, petition for naturalization might provide the name of the court; the date of the filing; the petitioner's Anglicized name and address, occupation, country of allegiance, approximate date of birth, approximate date and port of entry; and witnesses' names, addresses, and signatures. It might also provide much less information.
- Depending on the year, a post-September 26, 1906, declaration of intention provides the name of the court, the date that the declaration was filed, and varying amounts of data about the declarant: Anglicized name, occupation, approximate age, approximate date and place of birth (could be town, district, nearest large town, or *guberniya* [province]), approximate date and port of arrival, embarkation data, vessel name, physical description, name of spouse, spousal birth data, marriage date and place, children's birth data, and a photograph.
- Depending on the year, a post-September 26, 1906, petition for naturalization will provide all of the information present on the declaration of intention plus the name of the court in which the petition was filed, the date of the

filing, witnesses' names and addresses, dates the petitioner was away from the United States, dates and ports of arrival (which for people who arrived after June 29, 1906, will have been verified by the government), and the naturalization certificate number. For those petitions filed July 1, 1929, and later, the petition will also provide spousal naturalization data, including the date and place of the spouse's naturalization and naturalization certificate number.

- If the petitioner legally changed their name at the time of naturalization, a post-September 26, 1906, petition for naturalization should provide information about the old and new name.

Note that the petitioner may have informally started using a changed name before naturalization. If, however, the petitioner arrived after June 29, 1906, and had no court order showing a changed name, they had to naturalize under the name shown on their passenger manifest entry. The index to petitions for naturalization will list the petitioner under the new name with mention of the old name.[3]

Not all of the information on these documents is accurate, especially that of immigrants who arrived prior to June 29, 1906. As with all original records, some of the information included in the petitions and declarations will be primary, and some will be secondary and based on hearsay. Information provided by the court itself (name of court, date of filing, date of admission, naturalization certificate number, etc.) should be considered factual. In general, however, personal information provided by the declarant or petitioner should be considered secondary evidence and used as clues toward further genealogical research.

- The date and port of arrival data can be used to locate the petitioner's actual passenger arrival manifest.
- The certificate of arrival information can be used to locate the actual passenger arrival manifest. Don't assume that the certificate of arrival is always accurate. Sometimes the wrong certificate of arrival could be attached to an individual's set of naturalization papers.
- The petitioner's birth data can be used to locate the petitioner's actual birth place. *Where Once We Walked* can help identify the birth place listed on the petition for naturalization or declaration of intention. While a researcher can not be sure that the town is the petitioner's exact place of birth until he or she finds the petitioner's actual birth record, the name of the town will at least provide the researcher with a geographic area in which to begin the overseas research.
- Naturalization data can be used to locate the spouse's naturalization papers.
- The children's birth data can be used to locate the children's actual birth records or determine where the petitioner was living at a specific point in time.
- The names of the witnesses can be used to identify relatives of the petitioner and lead to locating the relatives' naturalization papers. These, in turn, might provide additional background information on the petitioner himself or herself.

And so forth.

As with all research, be prepared for spelling errors.

Who Filed for Naturalization And What Did They File?

Not everyone was required to file both the declaration of intention and petition for naturalization in order to become a citizen. As a result of derivative citizenship laws, not everyone was even required to file his own set of papers in order to become a citizen. For example, women could have been naturalized through their husbands, and minor children through their parents. In general, it all depended on the naturalization laws in place at the time of each individual's application for naturalization. The laws applied different rules to adult males, women, children, and those in the military, and these laws and rules changed through the years.

Some key naturalization laws that can impact genealogical research strategies are listed below:[4]

- (14 April 1802–present) The petitioner has to have resided for five years in the United States and one year in the relevant state. As a result of the Nationality Act of 1940, the state residency requirement is reduced to six months in October 1940.[5]
- (14 April 1802–present) The petitioner has to prove his residence in the United States through the oaths of witnesses who are already United States citizens.
- (26 March 1790–present) Alien children who are under 21 years of age become citizens through the naturalization of a parent.
  - (10 February 1855–21 September 1922) An alien adult woman's citizenship status depends on her husband's status.
  - If an alien woman marries an alien man between 10 February 1855–21 September 1922 and he becomes a U.S. citizen on or before 21 September 1922, she automatically becomes a citizen at the same time. It does not matter if the woman has not yet immigrated to the United States when her husband becomes a United States citizen.
  - If an alien woman marries a U.S. citizen between 10 February 1855–21 September 1922, then she becomes a citizen at the time of marriage. It does not matter if the marriage occurred outside the United States.
- (1866–1 March 1907) No native-born American woman loses her U.S. citizenship by marriage to an alien.
- (2 March 1907–21 September 1922) A native-born American woman who marries an alien in this time period loses her United States citizenship. If her husband becomes a citizen later in this time period, then she becomes a citizen through him.
- (22 September 1922–present) Wives were no longer naturalized through their husbands. They have to file on their own.
- (22 September 1922–24 June 1936) A native-born American woman who has previously lost her citizenship because of marriage to an alien needs to file her own set of naturalization papers in order to be repatriated, i.e., regain

her citizenship. A declaration of intention and certificate of arrival are not required.

- (25 June 1936–1 July 1940) A native-born American woman who has previously lost her citizenship because of marriage to an alien *and whose marriage shall be or has been terminated* simply needs to apply for and take an oath of allegiance in order to be repatriated
- (2 July 1940–present) A native-born American woman who has previously lost her citizenship because of marriage to an alien *and who has resided continuously in the United States since that marriage* simply needs to apply for and take an oath of allegiance in order to be repatriated. (Marital status is a non-issue.)
- (26 May 1824–26 September 1906) An alien who has resided in the United States for three years before reaching the age of 21 and who has been in the United States continuously for at least five years does not need to file a declaration of intention before applying for citizenship. (This was known as "minor naturalization" because it was the naturalization of immigrants who arrived as minors, not because they were minors when they naturalized.[6])
- (9 May 1918–present) An alien serving in the military can file a petition for naturalization without making a declaration of intention and without proof of the five years residency in the United States. They could also be naturalized at a court near their military base (which was not necessarily located near their personal residence).

For more information about specific naturalization laws, John J. Newman's *American Naturalization Policies and Procedures* provides chronological lists of the laws pertaining to men, women, children, military, and host of other types of individuals. Marian Smith's article, "Any Woman Who Is Now or May Hereafter Be Married: Women and Naturalization, ca. 1802–1940," published in the National Archives publication *Prologue*, provides information about women and naturalization.[7] This article is also available online at www. ARCHIVES.GOV/PUBLICATIONS/PROLOGUE/SUMMER_1998_WOMEN_ AND_NATURALIZATION_1.HTML.

Additional information about naturalization laws can also be found in the new National Archives and Records Administration microfilm series M2033: *Laws Relating to Immigration and Nationality, 1798–1962, and Directories of Courts Having Naturalization Jurisdiction, 1908–1963*. This 2-roll series was published in 2001 and can be found in The National Archives Record Group 287, Publications of the U.S. Government. It may be purchased for private use and can also be viewed at some of the National Archives branches. (For a list of branches which have this microfilm series, search the online National Archives microfilm catalog at WWW.ARCHIVES.GOV/RESEARCH_ROOM/ALIC/RESEARCH_TOOLS/ SEARCH_MICROFILM_CATALOG.HTML. Use microfilm ID "M2033" as the search key and after the brief record is retrieved, request the "full record." The "full record" provides a listing of the National Archives branches with this microfilm series.)

Information Needed to Begin the Search

Before searching for an individual's naturalization papers, some information is needed about the person. This information should include:

- Approximately when your ancestor might have become naturalized. Was it before September 1906? After September 1906? After September 1922?
- The state and county in which your ancestor might have been living when he or she was naturalized.
- The name your ancestor might have been using when he or she was naturalized.
- The courthouses that might have been functioning in the geographic area in which your ancestor may have become naturalized.
- If your ancestor has a common name and was probably naturalized after September 1906, you might also wish to know the name of his or her spouse or children. This can help you determine if you have located the "correct" set of naturalization papers.
- Where copies of naturalization records from that time period might be kept and how you can obtain your own copy.

Sources for Learning the Approximate Date And Place of Naturalization.

Federal census records. The 1870, 1900, 1910, 1920, and 1930 U.S. population censuses each included at least one question about naturalization. The 1870 census asked if the individual was "a male citizen of the U.S., age 21 or older." Alternatively, the 1900, 1910, 1920, and 1930 censuses provide information about each individual's naturalization status. If naturalized, the 1920 census should also provide the individual's approximate year of naturalization as well.

In the 1900, 1910, 1920, and 1930 censuses, if a non-U.S.-born person in the household was not a citizen, the census taker wrote "Al" in the citizenship column. "Al" means "alien." If a non-U.S.-born person in the household had filed his "first papers" for citizenship by the time of the census, the census taker wrote "Pa" in the citizenship column. "Pa" means "filed first papers." Finally, if an individual had completed the naturalization process and had become a U.S. citizen by the time of the census, then the census taker wrote "Na" in the appropriate column. "Na" means "naturalized." The absence of such notations does not necessarily mean that none of the above had actually occurred; the presence of the notations, however, is good evidence that events had transpired.

Census records can also help you determine the geographic area in which you may want to focus your search. If data in census records suggests that an individual was naturalized between 1900–1910 and that the individual was living in one state during this entire period of time, then you will know that the individual was *probably* naturalized in a courthouse in that one state. Alternatively, if data in census records suggests that an individual was living in two different states in this ten-year period (perhaps identified through two birthplaces of two children), then you may have to search for the individual's naturalization papers in two states.

Note that an individual did not necessarily file his declaration of intention in the same courthouse in which he filed his petition for naturalization. An individual may have filed his declaration of intention in a courthouse near his port of arrival or the area in which he lived for an extremely short period of time immediately after arriving in the United States and before he settled "permanently" in any specific location. (Remember, also, that military naturalizations could occur in any court. There was no requirement that the court have jurisdiction over the soldier's residence.)[8]

Microfilmed copies of the federal census records through 1930 can be found and reviewed at the National Archives in Washington, DC, and at the various National Archives branches. Each branch has microfilmed copies of the census records for the entire United States. The LDS (Mormon) Family History Library. also has microfilm copies of the federal census records. Finally, there are some for-profit genealogical companies that have scanned many of the U.S. census returns and have made them available for viewing over the Internet to paid subscribers. (Copies of census returns obtained through these for-profit companies should be saved and reproduced judiciously as the software used by these companies to clean-up and view these scanned images has been copyrighted.)

State census records. Some state censuses provide the naturalization status of household members. Ann Lainhart's *State Census Records* provides details about various state censuses and the information included in them. State census records are generally available at state and city archives and libraries. The Family History Library also has microfilm copies of many of them.

Note that New York 1925 state census provides the naturalization status of each household member and also provides the name of the court in which each individual was naturalized. This census is available at New York City repositories and through the FHL.

Voter registration records. Voter registration records can provide the date and court of a registered voter's naturalization. Many Board of Election offices have retained the voter registration cards of deceased residents of their town. They may let you access them. Some cities require you to have a street address before they will complete the search for you. Some Board of Election offices send old voter registration cards to city or state archives for safe keeping while some routinely destroy them.

The best way to determine whether old voter registration cards exist for a town is to call the Board of Elections department of that town. They may be able to access them immediately, ask you to write, or tell you the disposition of them (sent to an archive or destroyed). If you don't have any success with the Board of Elections, contact the state or city archives for the relevant town. It is possible that the archivists will know where the records are located.

United States passport applications. In general, passports could only be issued to U.S. citizens. Among other useful information, passport applications may provide an individual's date and court of naturalization.

Not every U.S. citizen traveling outside the United States had a passport or filed an application for one. Passports were generally not required for U.S. citizens until 1941. The few exceptions were during the Civil War, from 19 August 1861 to 17 March 1862 and from 22 May 1918 until the formal end of World War I in 1921 when passports were required.[9]

Except for certain time periods, aliens were not eligible to obtain passports. The exception most relevant to Jewish genealogists was the time period between 2 March 1907 and 3 June 1920. During this time period, aliens who declared their intent to become a naturalized citizen could obtain a passport. The act permitting this was repealed on 4 June 1920.[10]

The National Archives has microfilm copies of passport applications from October 1795 to March 1925 and indexes to these records. Copies are also available through the Family History Library. Passports applications dated from April 1925 to the present are at the U. S State Department. Write to:

Department of State
Passport Services
Research & Liaison Section
Room 500
1111 19th Street NW, Suite 200
Washington, DC 20524-1705.

Note that obtaining copies of passport applications that belong to you or your minor children would be done through the U.S. Privacy Act. Requesting an application that belongs to someone other than yourself or your minor children would be a "third party" request. There is currently a $45.00 search fee for each third party application desired. You may also need to provide a copy of a death certificate or another kind of authorization allowing you access to the third party record. For more information about obtaining copies of the applications, see the State Department website at TRAVEL. STATE.GOV/ PASSPORT_RECORDS.HTML.

World War I Draft Registration Cards. One of the questions asked of draft registrants was their naturalization status. While this information won't give you a date and a court, it will give you an individual's naturalization status as of the draft registration time period.

Note that the September 1918 draft asked each registrant if they had filed their declaration, had been admitted as a U.S. citizen on their own, or had been admitted through their father's papers. This will help you determine if you should be looking for the registrant's naturalization papers or his father's.

These documents are available on microfilm at the various National Archives branches and state archives. The Family History Library also has microfilm of them. The original draft registration cards are at the National Archives, Southeast Region in East Point, Georgia. They will complete a search for you upon receipt of a search form. They do require street addresses for some cities. Contact:

National Archives and Records Administration
Southeast Region
1557 St. Joseph Avenue

A petition for naturalization may provide a wealth of information about an immigrant family. In this illustration, the petition includes the birthdates of the immigrant, his wife and all his children; date of marriage; immigrant's town of birth; and the immigrant's date of arrival in the U.S. including name of ship and port of entry.

East Point, Georgia 30344-2593
Phone: 1-404-763-7477
Fax: 1-404-763-7059
E-mail: ATLANTA.CENTER@.NARA.GOV

For more information about World War I draft registration cards, please see the Military InfoFile on JewishGen's web site at WWW.JEWISHGEN.ORG/INFOFILES/WWIDRAFTLEASE. Also see John J. Newman's *Uncle, We Are Ready! Registering America's Men 1917–1918.*

Where Do You Find Naturalization Records? Naturalizations Occurring Before 27 September 1906

Prior to 27 September 1906, an alien could become naturalized at any "court of record" with jurisdiction over his residence.[11] That is, any court that had a seal and a clerk. This would include federal, state, county, city, police, and civil courts. There is no single country-wide centralized index to naturalizations filed in this time period. Each court may have an index to its own naturalization holdings.

There is also no centralized storage facility holding all the records from this early time period or copies of them. Records from the various non-federal courts could still be folded up and sitting in dusty boxes on court shelves. Other non-federal courts may have bound their records and sent their holdings to state, city, or federal archives for safekeeping.

James C. Neagles's *Locating Your Immigrant Ancestor: A Guide to Naturalization Records* can give you clues on a state-by-state basis as to what types of non-federal records are available and where they might be located. Elizabeth Bentley's *County Courthouse Book* provides basic information about the naturalization holdings of county courthouses across the

United States. Many early naturalization records have been microfilmed by the Family History Library. Christina Schaefer's *Guide to Naturalization Records of the United States* provides details on some of these records as well as the FHL microfilm numbers.

The U.S. National Archives branches should have indexes to and copies of the federal naturalizations papers that were generated in their branch jurisdictions in this early time period; some also have copies of naturalization papers generated in the non-federal courts. Via postal mail or e-mail you can request a search of the records and photocopies if any are found. Details about the federal holdings of the various National Archives branches can be found in the *Guide to Federal Records in the National Archives of the United States.* This guide is available on the Internet at WWW.ARCHIVES.GOV/RESEARCH_ROOM/FEDERAL_RECORDS_GUIDE/. There is also information about National Archives naturalization holdings in the National Archives Trust Fund Board's *Guide to Genealogical Research in the National Archives* and in Loretto Dennis Szucs' *They Became Americans: Finding Naturalization Records and Ethnic Origins.*

While there is no centralized location or index for all naturalization records generated in this early time period, in the 1930s there was a project undertaken by the INS to centralize, photocopy, and index original naturalization records which were located at courts within a specific region. To complete this project the INS used labor available through the Work Projects Administration.[12] The project ended before all the work was completed, but there are three major indexes for geographic regions that were finished and are quite useful. These indexes are considered part of the Immigration and Naturalization Service, Record Group 85:

National Archives, Northeast Region, Waltham, Massachusetts. This location has a centralized card index of all individuals who were naturalized in any court in Massachusetts, Maine, New Hampshire, and Vermont from 1791 to 26 September 1906.[13] This is a soundex index published as NARA microfilm series M1299: *Index to New England Naturalization Petitions, 1791–1906.* The Family History Library has this microfilm series.

They have original hard copies and photostatic negatives (dexigraphs) of the declarations and petitions which were generated in the federal courts within their region. They have dexigraphs only of the naturalization records generated in the non-federal courts within their region. (The original copies are at the non-federal courthouses or at various archives.)

This regional archives also has separate state-wide indexes for individuals who were naturalized in this early time period in courts in Connecticut and Rhode Island but these states are not included in the centralized "New England" states index.

For more information about the holdings of the National Archives in Waltham, Massachusetts, please read Warren Blatt's *Resources for Jewish Genealogy in the Boston Area.*

National Archives, Northeast Region, New York, New York. This location has a microfilmed soundex index to petitions for naturalizations that were filed in federal, state, and local courts in New York City, 1792–1906. It is microfilm series M1674: *Soundex Index to Petitions for Naturalizations Filed in Federal, State, and Local Courts in New York City, 1792–1906.* The Family History Library has a copy of the microfilm. The National Archives also has copies of the related petitions and declarations.

For more information about the holdings of this archives, see Estelle Guzik's *Genealogical Resources in New York.*

National Archives, Great Lakes Region, Chicago, Illinois. This location has a soundex index to naturalizations that occurred in federal and non-federal courts in northern Illinois, southern and eastern Wisconsin, eastern Iowa, and northwest Indiana. Chicago and Cook County are included in this index although, as a result of the fire of 1871, references to these records do not begin until 1871.[14] This index has been published as NARA microfilm series M1285: *Soundex Index to Naturalization Petitions for the United States District and Circuit Courts, Northern District of Illinois and Immigration and Naturalization Service District 9, 1840–1950.* The Archives has copies of the related naturalization papers from the federal courts; it does not have copies of the papers from the non-federal courts.

For more information about this index and the specific holdings, please see the *Guide to Federal Records in the National Archives of the United States*, Record Group 85.5.5, at WWW.ARCHIVES.GOV/RESEARCH_ROOM/FEDERAL_RECORDS_GUIDE. Also see the relevant page on the website of the National Archives in Illinois: WWW.ARCHIVES.GOV/FACILITIES/IL/CHICAGO/NATURALIZATION_RECORDS.HTML.

Naturalizations Occurring On and After 27 September 1906

On and after September 27, 1906, an alien could become naturalized at any "court of record" that had a seal, clerk, and jurisdiction over actions in law and equity in which amounts in controversy were unlimited. This would include federal courts and those courts that didn't have financial limitations. This change only eliminated a few courts and the federal, state, county, and some city courts continued to operate. Most police and other small courts were eliminated.[15]

During the naturalization process in this later time period, three copies of the declaration of intention and petition for naturalization were generated. When an individual declared his or her intention to become a citizen of the United States, one copy of the declaration of intention was given to the declarant, one copy was retained by the court, and one copy was sent to the INS in Washington, DC. When an individual subsequently filed his or her petition for naturalization, three copies were again generated: one copy was given to the petitioner; one copy was retained by the court; and one copy of each was sent to the INS in Washington, DC. Upon being admitted as a U.S. citizen, two copies of the certificate of naturalization were created. One was given to the newly admitted citizen and one copy was sent to the INS in Washington, DC.

The copies of the declaration of intention, petition for naturalization, and certificate for naturalization generated between 27 September 1906 and 1956 at any court in the United States and sent to the INS in Washington, DC, were deposited into a centralized INS filing system called the "C-Files" (Certificate Files).[16] The INS has one comprehensive name index to these files. Neither the index nor the files themselves are open to the public, but you can write to the INS to obtain a copy of the naturalization records if you wish.

(Note that there is a large set of naturalization-related correspondence files created by the Bureau of Naturalization between circa 1906–1944. The files are in the National Archives in Washington, DC, Record Group 85, Entry 26 (over 1,700 boxes). While the records' arrangement into topical series makes subject research somewhat simple, finding individual immigrants is impractical without a name index. The name index was recently transferred to NARA and hopefully it will be published soon.[17])

Copies of naturalization records dating after March 1, 1956, were filed by the INS all over the country, and you would need to write to the INS Office in the appropriate state in order to obtain copies.

To write for copies of naturalization at the INS in Washington, DC, you should first obtain a copy of the Freedom of Information Act (FOIA) Form G639, "Freedom of Information/Privacy Act Request." While Form G-639 is not required to make a request, it will expedite handling. You can request a copy of Form G-639 via the telephone, mail, by downloading a copy of it from the INS website, or by ordering the form through the INS website. The INS web address is: USCIS.GOV/GRAPHICS/FORMSFEE/FORMS/.

When writing to the INS for records, you must be prepared for an extended waiting period before receiving them. While you should receive an acknowledgement from the INS that they received your request within ten business days or so, it may be many months before you actually receive any photocopies. Note, also, that the photocopies of the INS records may be difficult to read (possibly because this microfilm was created in the 1950s).[18]

Copies of the petitions for naturalization and declarations of intention that were filed in federal courts in the post-September 26, 1906, time period should be on file in original or microfilm form at the regional branches of the National Archives. . It is faster and easier to search for and obtain photocopies of these records from the regional branches than it is to obtain copies from the INS in Washington, DC. The photocopies will also probably be better. Each regional branch will have their own separate indexes to their specific holdings. Some of these indexes have been microfilmed and are available at through the Family History Library. Copies of naturalizations that occurred in non-federal courts in this later time period could also be located in state archives and or through the Family History Library.

If you are able to obtain your post-September 26, 1906, petitions for naturalization and declarations of intention from the National Archives branches or other non-federal court, do not neglect to write also to the INS for each petitioner's C-File. While you may get some duplicate paperwork, you might get other kinds of additional documentation relevant to your petitioner that was filed by the INS.

There is a directory that was published and updated by the Department of Justice that provides the names of courts that could naturalize people after September 26, 1906. This is the *Directory of Courts Having Jurisdiction in Naturalization Proceedings*. The October 15, 1963, version of the directory provides you with the names of the courts, their court numbers, and whether they were still naturalizing of 1963 and if not, the disposition of their files. Note that the directory does *not* provide you with the date that the court stopped naturalizing.[19] The 1963 book is available at some large libraries and through the Family History Library under microfilm #1730286.

In 2001, NARA published this book along with an important compilation of U.S. immigration and nationality laws in microfilm series M2033: *Laws Relating to Immigration and Nationality, 1798–1962, and Directories of Courts Having Naturalization Jurisdiction, 1908–1963*. An earlier section in this chapter provides more information about this resource.

Locating U.S. Naturalization Records

Once you pinpoint a time period and a geographic location where the naturalization may have taken place, you are ready to begin your search for the actual records.

Using the information found on census records, passport records, voter registration records, or other resources, you can identify an approximate time period in which a person was naturalized and in which to focus your search. If a person was listed in the 1900 federal census as naturalized, then you will know to focus your search on pre-June 1900 naturaliza-tion records and that a duplicate copy of this individual's naturalization papers was not sent to the INS in Washington, DC. If the person was listed in the 1900 census as an alien, but in the 1910 census as naturalized, then you will know that the filing of the declaration and the petition probably occurred between June 1900 and April–May 1910. You won't know, however, if the person had become naturalized after 26 September 1906 and whether or not a duplicate copy of the naturalization papers was filed with the INS in Washington, DC. If the person was listed in the 1920 census as naturalized in 1911, then you'll know that if you can't find a copy of the original papers elsewhere, and if this date is somewhat accurate, then a duplicate copy of this individual's naturalization papers was filed in the INS in Washington, DC.

World War I Military Naturalizations

There is an index that can help you find that elusive set of naturalization papers that might have been generated after the 1918 law was passed which facilitated the naturalization of members of the U.S. Armed Forces. In hard copy only, it is called the "Index to Naturalizations of World War I Soldiers, 1918." It is on file at the Civil Reference Branch of the National Archives in Washington, DC and is Record Group 85, Entry 29, 17W3, 01/35/06-01/36/01.[20]

The index listing will refer you to a certificate and court number. You can match the court numbers with the court numbers listed in the aforementioned *Directory of Courts Having Jurisdiction in Naturalization Proceedings* and use this information to track down a copy of the individual's naturalization papers.[21]

Other Finding Aids

In addition to printed and microfilmed findings aids, there is an online index of naturalizations that occurred in New York's Kings County (Brooklyn) between 1907–1924. This index was completed by members of the Jewish Genealogical Society in New York, the Italian Genealogical Group, and the German Genealogy Group and can be extremely helpful in locating naturalizations that might have occurred in Kings County. The index can be accessed through the website of the Jewish Genealogical Society in New York City: WWW.JGSNY.ORG.

Notes

1. Some immigrants made the journey to the U.S. more than once. They may have come in an early time period and then returned home multiple times in order to escort family members. In her e-mailed comments to me dated 16 February 2003, Marian Smith, Historian for the Citizenship and Immigration Services (formerly the Immigration and Naturalization Service) (hereinafter M. Smith), noted that the certificate of arrival attached to the naturalization papers will not necessarily refer to the petitioner's first arrival in the U.S. It will refer to the arrival used to support the petition.
2. M. Smith, telephone call with N. Arbeiter, 8 Oct 1998.
3. M. Smith, e-mail comments to N. Arbeiter, 16 Feb 2003.
4. John J. Newman, *American Naturalization Processes and Procedures 1790–1985* (Indiana: Indiana Historical Society, 1985), 19–25; Marian Smith, "'*Any woman who is now or may here-*

after be married' Women and Naturalization, ca. 1802–1940," *Prologue: Quarterly of the National Archives and Records Administration,* 1998, vol. 30, no. 2; Carl B. Hyatt, compiler, *Laws Applicable to Immigration and Nationality: Embracing Statutes of a Permanent Character, and Treaties, Proclamations, Executive Orders, and Reorganization Plans Affecting The Immigration and Naturalization Service* (Washington, DC: Immigration and Naturalization Service, United States Department of Justice, 1953).

5. Newman, 20.
6. M. Smith, e-mail comments.
7. M. Smith, "Any woman who is now or may hereafter be married."
8. M. Smith, e-mail.
9. "The Genealogy Page: Passport Applications," National Archives and Records Administration, web site, WWW.ARCHIVES.GOV/ RESEARCH_ROOM/GENEALOGY/RESEARCH_TOPICS/PASSPORT_ APPLICATIONS.HTML.
10. *Ibid.*
11. M. Smith, e-mail. Residency jurisdiction waived for soldiers.
12. *Ibid.*
13. National Archives, Northeast Region, technician, telephone call from N. Arbeiter, 18 Oct 1999.
14. National Archives Trust Fund Board, *Guide to Genealogical Research in the National Archives* (Washington, DC: National Archives Trust Fund Board, 1985), 70.
15. M. Smith, telephone call.
16. M. Smith, e-mail.
17. M. Smith, e-mail.
18. M. Smith, e-mail.
19. M. Smith, telephone call.
20. See also USCIS.GOV/GRAPHICS/ABOUTUS/HISTORY/NATZREC/NATREC.HTM.
21. M. Smith, telephone call; M. Smith, e-mail.

Bibliography

Bentley, Elizabeth Petty. *County Courthouse Book*, 2nd ed. Baltimore, Maryland: Genealogical Publishing Co., Inc., 1995.

Guzik, Estelle, ed. *Genealogical Resources in New York*. New York: Jewish Genealogical Society, 2003.

Lainhart, Ann S. *State Census Records*. Baltimore, Maryland: Genealogical Publishing Co., Inc., 1993.

Mokotoff, Gary and Sallyann Amdur Sack with Alexander Sharon. *Where Once We Walked: Revised Edition*. Bergenfield, N.J.: Avotaynu, 2002.

National Archives Trust Fund Board. *Guide to Genealogical Research in the National Archives: Third Edition*. Washington, DC: National Archives Trust Fund Board, 2001.

Neagles, James C. and Lila Lee Neagles. *Locating Your Immigrant Ancestor: A Guide to Naturalization Records*. Logan, Utah: Everton Publishers, 1986.

Newman, John J. *American Naturalization Processes and Procedures, 1790–1985*. Indianapolis, Indiana: Indiana Historical Society, 1985.

Newman, John J. *Uncle, We Are Ready! Registering American's Men 1917–1918: A Guide to Researching World War I Draft Registration Cards*, North Salt Lake, Utah: Heritage Quest, 2001.

Schaefer, Christina K. *Guide to Naturalization Records of the United States*. Baltimore, Maryland: Genealogical Publishing Co., 1998.

Szucs, Loretto Dennis. *They Became Americans: Finding Naturalization Records and Ethnic Origins*. Salt Lake City, Utah: Ancestry, Inc., 1998.

Smith, Marian L. "*Any woman who is now or may hereafter be married... Women and Naturalization, ca. 1802–1940*". *Prologue: Quarterly of the National Archives and Records Administration*, vol. 30, no. 2 (summer 1998). Also available at: WWW. ARCHIVES.GOV/ PUBLICATIONS/PROLOGUE/SUMMER_1998_WOMEN_AND_NATURALIZATION_1. HTML.

Smith Marian L. "Lesser-Known INS Records Since 1906" Audiocassette, 19th Annual Conference on Jewish Genealogy, New York, Aug 1999. Hobart, Indiana: Repeat Performance, 1999.

Vital Records

by Jordan Auslander

Vital records are the cut gems for those who mine genealogy. Although legally hearsay, they are the admissible records of an event and usually chart two to three generations for an individual while putting them at an address with a date.

Birth, death, marriage and divorce transcripts are also the raw data of family history. Called "vital records" in the United States, these records are termed civil or metrical records in many other countries. In this context, the word vital carries much the same connotation as "vital signs" in medicine, that is, meaning signs of life or essential for life. Vital records may be regarded in much the same way as records that document a person's existence—when and where and with whom they lived. The search for vital records is a primary focus for both novice and experienced genealogists.

Vital records are a snapshot in time that genealogists combine with other information about an individual to provide a time line showing addresses and occupational history (i.e., from peddler to proprietor), all of which must be integrated into the composite picture of a life. From these records, researchers usually can glean clues to additional sources of information. In general, data supplied in vital records varies depending on local requirements and when the event was recorded.

History of Jewish Vital Records

Officially recorded vital records appeared only in recent centuries. Until the 18th or 19th century, most European governments allowed Jewish communities considerable self-government, usually interfering only to levy taxes or to draft men for an army. In an effort to restrict the Jewish population of her realm, the 18th-century Austrian Empress Maria Theresa mandated that only one Jewish man per family might marry, but hers was an exception to the more general *laissez-faire* approach to such matters (see AUSTRO-HUNGARIAN EMPIRE).

Jewish law, which governed European Jewish life, did not need birth and death records, so Jewish communities did not create them. Marriage contracts (*ketubot*), designed to protect the rights of a wife in case of divorce (an action only permitted the husband), were an integral part of Jewish law. They were required and preserved—but within each individual family, not within the community.

The birth date of Jewish men was easy to calculate. All Jewish baby boys had a *brit milah* (ritual circumcision) at the age of eight days. Because the boy would become *bar mitzvah* at the age of 13, the *mohel* (ritual circumciser) kept a record of the event. These record books, however, were the property of the *mohel*, not community property. Jewish women did not know their exact birth dates because Jewish law did not require that they be marked. It is not unusual for Jewish genealogists to be told, for example, that a Russian-born grandmother

never knew her birthday. Perhaps knew only that she was born "around Pesach" (or Chanukah or Yom Kippur). Many simply approximated when required to produce a date, and one finds (on naturalizations) spikes in births on the first, fifteenth and end of months. Death dates were known and necessary so that sons could observe *kaddish* (memorial prayers) for the required length of time. Again, however, these records were maintained by the *chevra kadisha*, the holy society charged with preparing the body for burial. Because the *pinkassim* (registers) of the *chevrot kadisha* were maintained by a community organization and were not in the hands of a single individual, they are found more often than *ketubot* or *mohel* registers.

Civil Registration in Europe

After its 1789 revolution, France became the first European country to institute civil registration of vital events. Napoleon brought the system to the countries he conquered with the Napoleonic Code of 1803. The Russian and Austrian Empires followed suit in the early 19th century, as did most of the German principalities. Knowing the Catholic parish for a Jew's town of origin can lead to pre-civil records.

European Christian churches typically had maintained birth, baptism, marriage and death records even before required to do so by the secular governments. For many years after the creation of civil registration, various governments charged the churches with the registration responsibility. Usually one set of records was kept in the church while a duplicate set was given to the government. For several years in the early 19th century, Jewish birth records were recorded in Christian churches. In Russian Poland, for example, before 1826, Jewish births, marriages and deaths were recorded in local Catholic Church registers. Genealogists who use LDS (Mormon) microfilms for early 19th-century Germany or Poland, for example, should look in church records if no Jewish vital records can be found for that location.

Muslim Countries

Muslim countries established civil registration of vital events even later than their Christian European counterparts. Some, such as Iran, still did not require it even at the time of mass Jewish emigration from their country at the end of the 20th century.

United States Vital Records

The requirement of vital registration in the United States is even more recent than that of many European countries. The laws regarding vital record registration are defined by each state; consequently, the start dates varied by state and even type of record. Some records were recorded at the town level, others at the county or state level. Some states, such as Massachusetts, required the recording of births, marriages and deaths by the mid-19th century; others did not mandate registration until the early 20th century. Chicago did not require the registration of marriages until 1930. Data required on documents also evolved separately by location. The names of parents is a maddening omission on early 20th-century Philadelphia marriage licenses.

U.S. vital records may include birth registrations and certificates, delayed birth registrations or certificates, marriage license affidavits and applications, marriage licenses, registrations and certificates, supplemental marriage papers, marriage banns, death registrations and certificates, amended birth, marriage and death certificates, divorce records, burial records, coroner records (if the individual died in an accident or under suspicious circumstances), Jewish circumcision records, marriage contracts (*ketubot*) or divorce records (*get*). Details vary by location although many of the basic features are common to all.

Birth Certificates

Birth certificates commonly include the official birth name (not the name a person subsequently might have been known by), birth date and place (home or hospital), parents' names, ages, occupations and nationality, number of prior live births, number still living and home address. Home addresses are useful in accessing state and other censuses that are not indexed by name. Sometimes adopted individuals can learn the names of their biological mothers from the name of the hospital in which the birth occurred.

Applications for Marriage Licenses

Marriage applications usually include the age and birth place of bridge and groom, given name of groom, given name and maiden name of bride, names of parents, home addresses, occupations, information about previous marriages, if any, divorce references, names, congregation and address of the rabbi (or sometimes cantor) and witnesses.

Because these records have been created by the individuals involved in the events, they are the most likely to have accurate, and often most detailed, information. The maiden name of a woman married more than once may be retrieved from information in these records. Home addresses listed in applications are useful in providing starting points for city directory and census research. Witnesses often are previously unknown relatives. Note that marriage licenses (held by a couple) have far less information than the applications that led to the issuance of the license. Typically, the genealogically important document is the application for a license, and the congregation of the rabbi who solemnized the ceremony may yield clues to geographical origin—as a burial society does with death records.

Death Certificates

Death certificates may supply given name (and maiden name of women), age, birth date and birth place, parents' names, home addresses, place and cause of death, marital status, name of spouse, name of undertaker and cemetery of burial.

Because the information on these certificates is provided at a time of stress and not by the individual recorded, they are the most likely to be incomplete and/or inaccurate. Even so, undertaker and cemetery information often proves invaluable in leading to individuals who maintain the grave if perpetual care has been provided, or in supplying the names of those who paid for the funeral—perhaps the married names of daughters. A trip to the cemetery or to the cemetery office may reveal the names of other relatives buried nearby or in the same family plot. Date of death may lead to a newspaper obituary or a media story, especially in the case of accidental or tragic death.

Divorce Proceedings

Divorce records supply the date and place of the marriage; addresses; names of the husband, wife and children; property information and allegations.

Where to Search for Documents

Throughout the United States, most (although not all) applications for marriage licenses and certificates of birth and death are filed with a state department of health. Some are filed only with a county clerk or local department of health. No national directory of births, marriages, divorces or deaths exists, but each of the states, commonwealths and territories of

In addition to information about the bride and groom, marriage records usually include the names of parents. In this particular example, also included are the maiden names of the mothers.

the United States maintains indexes of death records. Scope and public access varies. California, for example, publishes alphabetical indexes for each decade. New York State and New York City create annual indexes, but the state indexes are not open to public inspection until 50 years after the death. For U.S. citizens who died after the early 1960s, the Social Security Death Index (see SOCIAL SECURITY DEATH INDEX) is a good place to start. If a desired name is found, the record will yield a date of birth, month and (usually) place of death and/or residence. Where birth and marriage indexes exist, most tend to be for no more than one year—sometimes less, although some cover five years or even a decade. In a few states, the indexes are not made public.

The ease and speed of locating vital records depends primarily on two factors, the jurisdiction of the recording and the accuracy of the information guiding the genealogist. Consider, for example, a relative identified in the 1900 census known to have been born in New York. Was that New York City or New York State? Answer: the relative *may* have been born in New York City, but the census asked for *state* of birth. For births in New York City after 1898, it is helpful to know in which of the five boroughs (Manhattan, Bronx, Brooklyn, Queens or Staten Island) the event occurred. Annual borough indexes were not combined until 1937. If the birth occurred much earlier than 1900, then the month of birth shown on the census—if accurate—will be helpful with some of the contemporary (to the event) indexes. If cumulative, alphabetical county probate indexes exist they can be a helpful start. For example, since the 1900 census provides a birth month, it helps focus a search in places where the indexes are month by month, (and borough by borough in the case of New York City) borough by borough. Note that probate records are filed in county of residence while death records are filed where the event occurred.

State-by-state information often is obtainable on various Internet sites (see INTERNET).

Limitations of Vital Records

Even though vital records may be "official" government documents, do not assume that everything written in them is true. Things are almost never that simple. Vital (and other) records include omissions and (deliberate or inadvertent) misinformation, all of which must be reconciled when assembling the composite picture of a life. In evaluating the data, researchers should ask themselves why a document was generated, who supplied the information and when, who recorded the information and did the informant have any vested interest in concealing or distorting the information supplied.

Often vital records are found to contain information that contradicts other records. Age on a marriage record may not correspond with age on a birth record or death record. Many immigrants approximated dates and years of birth, either out of ignorance or because of difficulties with the Hebrew, Julian and Gregorian calendars used in Russia and in the United States. Names may be misspelled for a variety of reasons or anglicized from the original forms. It is highly unlikely that the Jewish immigrant father of an early 20th-century bride was originally named Harry or Morris or Philip. Much more likely, their the names given at their *brit* were Chaim, Moshe or Pesach. (See "Names"). Some immigrants who traveled alone as young teenagers deliberately told immigrant officials that they were older, tried to lower their ages when they later applied for life insurance and once more raised their ages when applying for social security.

Vital records may answer many questions while generating others. Parents' addresses and occupations may be traced through the birth certificates of their children. Discoveries of children who did not survive to adulthood may be made through comparison of numbers of live births against those still living—which can, in turn, lead to a previously unknown cemetery plot. Spelling variations of maiden names may occur on children's death certificates. Death certificates may help pinpoint an individual's birth—or throw one completely off track.

The reliability of an informant must always be evaluated. Ages and birth dates tend to have the widest variation on marriage license, especially in second marriages for brides in their 30s and 40s!

Access Restrictions

In many ways, the United States is like 50 independent countries that gave up a small number of rights to a federal government. Nowhere is this more evident than in the case of privacy issues. Each state creates its own laws stating when vital records can become publicly available. Most use a 100-year rule for births; restrictions on accessibility to marriage and death records vary. Among the most liberal is Massachusetts, where a birth record can be obtained immediately; strictest is Arizona where one cannot obtain the death record of even a parent without documentation that demonstrates kinship to the deceased.

To help prevent passport fraud, the U.S. Department of State currently is asking states to restrict access to all birth records to only the individual named on the record, immediate family, legal guardians or their authorized representatives. No cutoff date is mentioned in this request. Currently cause of death is restricted on modern death certificates including Florida, Maine and some others. Since 9/11/01, many U.S. jurisdictions have been clamping down on access, among them New Jersey.

Census Records

by Jordan Auslander

At a minimum, census returns allow genealogists to establish exactly where an individual or family lived at a given moment in time. Depending on the years taken, censuses usually provide considerably more information. Indeed, they are among the most valuable of genealogical resources and should be thoroughly investigated at the start of every family history quest.

Microfilmed copies of U.S. federal (national) censuses, taken every ten years since 1790, are open to public access after 72 years. As we go to press, the most recent available census is the one taken in 1930. The sole exception is the 1890 census, most of which burned and was never filmed. The federal censuses exclude armed forces personnel stationed outside the United States.

Census returns are held by the U.S. National Archives* which makes microfilm copies available at all of its regional branches (see U.S. NATIONAL ARCHIVES AND RECORDS ADMINISTRATION).[1] Copies also may be borrowed from LDS (Mormon) Family History Centers, and regional copies often are found in local museums and libraries. Individual reels may be purchased from the National Archives· as well. In recent years, Ancestry.com, HeritageQuest and other Internet-based genealogy companies have created CDs and/or online indexes of a number of U.S. censuses.

Different questions were asked on different censuses. In addition to including the names and ages of all residents at a given address, one or another return may reveal relationships to the head of household, country of birth (and in 1920, province of birth), year(s) of immigration, citizenship status, year(s) of naturalization, occupations, number of years married, number of children born to a female and number of living children. Immigrant households frequently included boarders who were relatives or *landsmen* (persons from the same community in the old country); they, too, are included. Information on a census return often leads one to many additional resources, including vital records, immigrant passenger manifests and naturalization records. Sometimes the name of a boarder reveals a previously unknown maiden name of the wife and an entirely new branch of the family.

Because each census included different questions, and because of the many—often unanticipated—clues provided, experienced genealogists usually try to locate every possible census record of all family members. One may find the names of great-grandparents whom no one knew had visited or emigrated to the United States, or, contrary to oral tradition, it may be that the family lived for a short while in New York City before settling in a small town in the Deep South.

What Censuses to Search

If the year of a family's emigration to the United States is known, begin with the first census following that date. In the many cases when year is not known, it is helpful to recall some facts about Jewish migration to the United States. Most of the Jewish families that lived in the U.S. prior to 1840 can be found in Malcolm Stern's *First American Jewish Families*. Many of the Jews from German-speaking lands who emigrated after the 1848 European revolutions will be found in the 1850 census, the first to list all household members by name. Unfortunately, few additional details are given.

The third and largest wave of Jewish immigrants was composed of Eastern European Jews who came primarily between 1881 and the beginning of World War I in 1914. For them, census research will focus primarily on the 1880, 1900 and 1920 censuses—the surviving, completely indexed years that follow the preponderance of the Jewish migration to the United States. The 1910 census is also valuable, but not completely indexed. This census is discussed further below. The 1930 census also is only partially indexed and offers little genealogically important information not included in 1920 (except the address of residence ten years later). For most Jewish genealogists, the best place to begin is the 1920 census.

For help using the 1930 census, start with Stephen P. Morse's article, "Subtleties in Using the One-Step 1930 Website Address," and his website STEVEMORSE.ORG/CENSUS.[2] Morse also has developed a program for searching names across all censuses, available only to subscribers to GENEALOGY.COM. See also the National Archives website about the 1930 census at 1930CENSUS.GOV.

How the Census Was Taken

Population censuses were compiled by census takers (enumerators) who were hired especially for the task. The area covered by a single census taker was called an enumeration district. To take the census, enumerators went door-to-door, asked individuals in each household a list of required questions and handwrote the answers on a printed form. In immigrant neighborhoods especially, the person who answered the census taker may have spoken English with a heavy accent or might not have spoken English at all. If no adult in the home answered the first time the census taker called, the census taker had the choice of returning another time or simply asking a neighbor or a child for the information. Census takers were not specifically educated or trained for their job, and they were not required to record who supplied the information. As experienced researchers know all too well, householders were not asked to provide proof of their answers.

Because of the way in which the census was taken, most information provided must be viewed as heresay and regarded as clues that need further substantiation. Census returns include many errors. For example, the person who answered the questions may not have known the year of immigration of the head of household or may have forgotten it. Similarly, errors may have arisen because a census taker, unfamiliar with the native (foreign) language of the respondent, misheard a name and recorded it incorrectly. Other errors have arisen because the subsequent indexer misread a handwritten entry.

How to Begin

Census returns are organized by state. First determine which state to research, then decide which year to search and finally learn whether or not an index exists for that state and that census. If the state where an immigrant settled is unknown, it may be necessary to search more than one state. Knowledge about where other family members or *landsmen* settled may suggest logical starting points.

The system used to index U.S. censuses is called "soundex." This is a method of coding names according to how they sound rather than how they are spelled, very important when dealing with immigrant names especially. The entire 1880, 1900 and 1920 censuses have been indexed. To determine which states have been indexed for other years, go to the National Archives website (www.NARA.GOV) and follow the prompts to "research room," "genealogy" and "using census catalogs." Copy the soundex coding rules at the same site.

If the state to be searched has an index, the next step is to code the surnames. Many genealogists find it useful to keep a handy personal research list of all family soundex codes. Surnames that sound different, but that have the same initial letter and similar sounding consonants, may have the same code. If so, names will be intermingled in the index. For example, Goldberg, Goldfinger and Goldfarb all have soundex code G431.

To use the soundex, a researcher must know (or "guesstimate") the first name the head of household used at the time—or else go through the entire soundex code to find the specific family. Immigrants often changed their first names after arrival in the U.S. Someone who arrived with the name Moshe may have become Moe, Morry, Morris and ultimately Maurice. When not certain, the best strategy may be to look at everyone with a name that begins with the letter *M*.

Be aware also that the specific soundex system used for the U.S. census does not work well with Eastern European names. It works much better for English names. An example is the letter *W*. In the census soundex, the letter *W* is silent (e.g., dropped) except when it is the first letter of the name. In indexing the English name Snow, it makes sense to drop the *W*. Not so with Eastern European names where the letter *W* typically takes the sound of a *V*. This means that when searching for individuals from Eastern (or Central Europe whose surnames include the letter *W*), be sure also to code the name as if it might include the letter *V*. The most common problem are names that end with *–witz*. It may be spelled *–vitz*. For example, the name Slomowitz has the soundex code S453, yet the name Slomovitz is coded S451.

Sometimes a researcher cannot locate a soundex listing for a family that he or she knows should be listed. Most of the time the problem arises because the indexer misread an enumerator's handwriting. One researcher named Yentes knew that his parents had lived at a certain address in New York City in 1920, but could not find them until he tried to imagine how the handwritten name could have been misread. He then looked for Yeutes and found them immediately. The names Daniel and David are examples of frequently misread handwriting. Remember also that an immigrant with the name Weinstein would have pro-nounced it Vinestein—and likely was recorded that way (under *V* instead of *W*). Try to summon as much imagination as possible in checking alternate spellings.

Using the Soundex Microfilm

The next step is to locate the roll of microfilm that includes the soundex code for the state and year being searched. A set of directories published by the National Archives provides this information. These are microfilms of individual soundex cards. On each reel of microfilm with a set of soundexes, all the different surnames with the same soundex code are grouped together. Then all of the cards with the same soundex code are arranged alphabetically by first name. In the case of more than one individual with the same first name within a single soundex code, the names are arranged alphabetically by place of birth of the head of household—first those born in the U.S. by state and then those born outside the U.S. by country.

Scroll to the soundex code for the surname being searched. At the beginning of the index cards for that soundex code, go forward to the cards for the desired given name. Remember that many first names can be spelled in a variety of ways (e.g., Joseph, Josef or Yosef).

Information on each card can help determine if it describes the family being sought. In addition to the name of the head of the household, the soundex card includes the names of wife and children if any, and other relatives or individuals living with the family. The data provided for each individual usually is limited to name, gender, age, place of birth, relationship to head of household and citizenship.

Don't stop with the soundex card. Once this has been located, use the information on the card to find the exact page on which the relative's census return is entered. Enumeration district, page and line number are needed, as are county and town. Be certain to note all of this information in your research log.

When the Census Is Not Indexed

Researchers must use a different method for the years and states that are not indexed. It has been estimated that 20 percent of the census is soundexed incorrectly. The same method may be necessary if you do not find a family in the soundex index.

Without a soundex index card, the genealogist must know the address—or town or county name if the individual lived in a small town or rural area. For a small town, a rural area, or even a small city, it sometimes is possible simply to scroll through and visually scan the census returns for that area until the family is found.

Another method is to find an enumeration district map of the area published by the Census Bureau. Major research libraries in large cities, and the National Archives regional

1930 census record that includes the family of Franklin Delano Roosevelt, then governor of New York State. Two years later he became president of the United States. For immigrant ancestors, this census included in columns 22 and 23 the year the person immigrated to the U.S. and whether they were naturalized.

branch for a given area, have such maps as does the LDS (Mormon) Family History Library (see LDS). Consult the map to find the neighborhood and then the enumeration district where a family lived. Often it is useful to know the names of the specific streets surrounding the address and whether the domicile was on the north, south, east or west side of a street because an enumeration district may cover only one side of a block on a given street. Such information frequently is given on contemporary maps or in the city directories (see DIRECTORIES) for the time period of interest. An exact description of the boundaries of an enumeration district is given on the microfilm reel that includes the census returns for that district.

1910 Census

The 1910 census is important for most researchers of Jewish genealogy because the preceding decade was the period of heaviest Jewish emigration to the United States. Unfortunately, the 1910 census was only partially soundexed (actually the system used—similar to soundex— is called Miracode). Consult the National Archives website WWW.NARA.ORG to find the list of 21 states with Miracode. Most major Jewish population centers are not indexed, but finding aids exist for some cities that had large Jewish populations, including New York and Boston. These finding aids, such as U.S. National Archives microfiche publication M1283 and M1860, usually are based upon street addresses.

To use the finding aids a researcher must know the family's address at the time the census was taken. Locate street addresses by using city directories, a family birth, marriage or death record for 1909–11; a naturalization record; or other documents that might supply an address. Because turn-of-the-20th-century Jewish immigrants moved often, try to compile addresses for 1909, 1910 and 1911 before starting to use the finding aids.

State and Municipal Censuses

Several states and even some cities have taken censuses in years between federal censuses. Especially useful for Jewish families are the 1905, 1915 and 1925 New York state census and the 1890 Manhattan police census. The 1925 New York State census is supposed to include the name of the court in which an individual was naturalized, although this is not included in every case. For more information about New York State censuses, see *Genealogical Resources in the New York Metropolitan Area*. A complete list of all state and city censuses can be found in *The Source*. Also check with local historical societies and town halls for possible municipal enumerations.

Mining the Data Further

If immigrant ancestors lived in urban areas, look at census returns for other families living in the same building, in the buildings next door and across the street. In some cases, this will mean looking at other adjacent enumeration districts; often it just means looking through an entire enumeration district to see who else might be there. Early in the 20th century, family members and *landsmen* tended to live close to one another—if not in the same apartment building, then often on the same or nearby street. A neighbor may have become a future spouse.

On the Lower East Side of New York, at this time, Jewish immigrants tended to cluster according to Old Country place of residence (i.e., those from Romania on certain streets; those from Galicia or Lithuania on other streets). Also look at the last few pages of each enumeration district; families that were not home the first time the census taker called often are listed here.

Addresses

National Archives and Records Administration, 700 Pennsylvania Avenue NW, Washington, D.C. 20408; website: WWW.NARA.GOV.

Bibliography

Arbeiter, Nancy Levin. "A Beginner's Primer in U.S. Jewish Genealogical Research" *Avotaynu* 14, No. 3 (Fall 1998).

Guzik, Estelle, ed. *Genealogical Resources in the New York Metropolitan Area,* rev. ed. New York: Jewish Genealogical Society, Inc., 2003.

Lainhart, Ann S. *State Census Records.* Baltimore: Genealogical Publishing, 1993.

Morse, Stephen P. "Subtleties in Using the One-Step 1930 Census Website." *AVOTAYNU* 18, no. 3 (Fall 2002): 3—6.

National Archives Trust Fund Board. *Guide to Genealogical Research in the National Archives.* Washington, D.C.: National Archives Trust Fund Board, 1985.

Stern, Malcolm, H. *First American Jewish Families.* Cincinnati: American Jewish Archives, 1978.

Szucs, Loretto Dennis, and Sandra Hargreaves Luebking, eds. *The Source: A Guidebook of American Genealogy*, rev. ed. Salt Lake City: Ancestry, 1997.

Notes

1. The National Archives in Washington, D.C., holds copies of original census returns for the years 1800 to 1870. In the rare cases where microfilm copies are too difficult to read, a researcher may be granted access to the original paper copy at the National Archives headquarters in Washington, D.C. Original returns for the 1880 census are with each state; no original returns exist after 1880.
2. Morse, Stephen P. *AVOTAYNU*: 3–6.

American Jewish Archives

by Christine Crandall

The Jacob Rader Marcus Center of the American Jewish Archives (AJA) is committed to preserving a documentary heritage of the religious, organizational, economic, cultural, personal, social, and family life of American Jewry. The AJA was founded in 1947 in the aftermath of World War II and the Holocaust. Created at a time when the Jews of America—now the largest and best-educated Jewish community in history—faced the responsibility of preserving the continuity of Jewish life and learning, the AJA has been preserving American Jewish history and imparting it to the next generation for more than half a century,

Located on the Cincinnati campus of the Hebrew Union College-Jewish Institute of Religion,* the AJA houses more than ten million pages of documentation—personal papers of rabbis, secular leaders, and families; congregational records; and organizational records for local, national, and international Jewish groups. The AJA also holds large collections of non-print holdings, including microfilm, audio and video tape recordings, movies, and a large photograph collection. The collections of the AJA are strong in records describing colonial and early American Jewry, records of synagogues and local organizations, documents describing the history of many communities in America, and genealogies and family histories. The AJA is committed to furthering knowledge and awareness of Jewish genealogy and to assisting those who are tracing their Jewish roots.

The AJA welcomes genealogy inquiries and is open to all researchers. All inquiries should be submitted in writing by fax, e-mail or postal mail. Each inquiry receives a personal response. E-mail requests should be made using the research request forms on our website, WWW.AMERICANJEWISHARCHIVES.ORG. Visitors are always welcome to visit the AJA, where the staff will personally assist them in researching their family histories.

The AJA does not perform extensive genealogy searches. Our goal is to assist all who come to us by providing information or guidance that will be of help in a family search. If we locate requested or needed materials in our files, the AJA will—for a fee—provide photocopies or other duplication of requested items in compliance with copyright and restrictions.

The AJA online catalogue (accessible at the AJA website) includes bibliographic records from our collections of manuscripts, microfilm, video and audio materials, nearprint, genealogy files and photographs. The system allows the user to search the catalogue by entering a keyword, personal name, Library of Congress subject heading (see LIBRARY OF CONGRESS) or geographic location. Helpful information is provided for more advanced and boolean search strategies. The AJA online catalogue does not yet, however, contain records for all of the materials available at the AJA. It includes all accessions since 1997, and we are currently working on retro-cataloguing our entire collection. If you do not find what you are looking for or have any questions, please use the reference request form on the website, or contact our reference staff at AJA@HUC.EDU.

Selected Important Collections

Genealogy Files. Of prime interest to genealogy researchers are the genealogy collections. More than 1,500 family histories, ancestor/descendant charts, or other research materials directly related to the genealogy of specific families have been donated to the AJA, usually by the family members who compiled them. The materials are catalogued by the family surname or an individual's name (a family member or the compiler/author of the work in the file). The files may contain family tree charts; lists of family members; vital statistics (birth, death, and marriage dates); places of birth, death, and residence; photocopies or originals of photographs, news articles, obituaries, citizenship records, and other pertinent documents; maps of areas in which the family lived; essays describing the family history or background history of Jews in the areas in which the family lived; and family correspondence. Genealogy collections held by the AJA range in size from one to several thousand pages. The larger collections generally contain data on multiple families and were compiled by collectors. Some genealogies consist of no more than photocopies of materials found in the hands of a family member or in the holdings of another repository. Other family histories have been printed (and may be copyrighted).

Miscellaneous Records. Many, more obscure collections containing materials of interest to genealogists are not cross-referenced to "Genealogies" in the main catalogue. These include congregational records with lists of vital records (birth, death, marriage and divorce), wills, Inquisition records, travel documents, diaries, memoirs, indentures, family correspondence, oral histories, business records, photographs, marriage certificates (*ketubot*), graduation certificates and naturalization records. They usually are filed by the name of the individual or family to whom the document pertains.

Synagogue Collections. Arranged by city, these records usually contain the minutes of governing boards and sometimes also membership lists; birth, marriage, and death records; cemetery plot information; and records of affiliated organizations, such as sisterhoods and brotherhoods. Important among these are the vital records for the synagogues in Barbados and Jamaica. Many of these documents were written in Dutch and Portuguese. The AJA possesses synagogue collections from most major cities in the United States. Due to limitations of time, many materials later than 1850 were not filmed.

Personal and Family Papers. The papers of individuals may contain genealogy-related materials such as obituaries, curriculum vitae, biographical sketches, newspaper articles by or about the person, memoirs, diaries, wills, citizenship papers (including passports and naturalization records), descendant/

ancestor charts, family histories, family correspondence, photographs and vital statistics. Many family papers that contain genealogical information also include histories of families not listed in the collection's title. For example, the Minis Papers include information on the Nunes and Lopez families as well. Specific collections that contain useful genealogical information are the Malcolm H. Stern Papers, Bertram W. Korn Papers, and the Nathan Kraus Family Papers, among many others.

Organizational Papers. Records of organizations to which one's ancestors might have belonged can be enlightening. Among these are some Hadassah, B'nai B'rith, Women of Reform Judaism, or Jewish community boards and group records. Other records to consider are orphanage records—listed under the city in which the person resided. An example of one of the most important resources for individuals researching Cincinnati Jews are the records for the United Jewish Cemeteries, which contain plot listings. Another collection with records of genealogical interest is Cincinnati's Jewish Family Services Records. They consist of correspondence (and biographical data) between Jews in Nazi Germany and Eastern European countries and between rescue agencies in Cincinnati and elsewhere in the U.S. during the period 1936–52. Of worldwide interest are the records of the World Jewish Congress.

Series D holds immigration records, and Series J has photographs with names listed—primarily children survivors of World War II. Consult the inventory and staff members for details on other possible genealogical records.

Rabbis' Papers. Some rabbis saved copies of *ketubot* with their papers, or sometimes kept notes regarding marriages performed, births and deaths in their congregations, and other life-cycle events.

Nearprint. Arranged by city, name or topic, these files contain large ephemeral materials—newspaper and magazine clippings, leaflets, brochures, pamphlets and organizational news releases. This material often is not found elsewhere and can be a great resource for researchers.

Address

The Jacob Rader Marcus Center of the American Jewish Archives; 3101 Clifton Avenue, Cincinnati, Ohio 45220; telephone: (513) 221-1875; fax: (513) 221-7812; e-mail: CCRANDALL@HUC.EDU; website: WWW.AMERICANJEWISHARCHIVES.ORG

American Jewish Historical Society

by Michael Feldberg

The mission of the American Jewish Historical Society (AJHS) is to foster awareness and appreciation of the American Jewish experience and to serve as a scholarly national resource for research through the collection, preservation and dissemination of materials relating to American Jewish history. Founded in 1892 as a membership organization, research library, archives and museum, the AJHS is the oldest ethnic historical organization in the United States.

Genealogical Resources at AJHS

Both the AJHS library and archives can be useful for genealogical research. The AJHS archives holds many records of institutions and individuals. Collections of the personal papers of individuals (mainly well-known individuals and rabbis) are filed in the AJHS card catalogue alphabetically by surname. Institutional records also are filed in the card catalogue alphabetically by name of the institution. The card catalogue may be searched by subject (such as a town name) to locate relevant books or archival collections. Institutional records with great value as resources for family history research include orphanage records, military records, immigration assistance records and New York court records, described below with Record Group (RG) numbers.

Orphanage Records. Each of the orphanages listed here has a different institutional history, but they all eventually merged with the Jewish Child Care Association of New York. AJHS holdings include the following:

- **Brooklyn Hebrew Orphan Asylum**. Holdings include unindexed admission and discharge records, 1879–1953, RG I-230.
- **Hebrew Guardian Sheltering Society of New York.** Holdings include unindexed admission and discharge records, 1907–42, RG I-43.
- **Hebrew Infant Asylum of the City of New York**. Holdings include indexed admission and discharge records, 1895–1908, RG I-166.
- **Home for Hebrew Infants**. Holdings include unindexed admission and discharge records, 1922–53, RG I-232.
- **Hebrew Orphan Asylum**. Holdings include partially indexed admission applications, 1862–79 and 1901–24, and unindexed discharge records, 1899–1940, RG I-42.

Military Records. Military records at the AJHS relate to Jewish soldiers in the American military. They include the following two collections:

- **American Jewish Committee Office of War Records.** Holdings include questionnaires sent to Jewish servicemen after World War I, with data on more than 4,000 Jewish soldiers organized by branch of service, rank, originating city or status (wounded, etc.). To research this material, it is helpful to know a soldier's rank, branch of service (Army, Navy, etc.), and status after the war, RG I-9.

- **National Jewish Welfare Board, Bureau of War Records**. Holdings include data cards on individuals in the service, 1940–69, ordered alphabetically, RG I-52.

Immigration Assistance Records

Immigration assistance records include a large collection of records of various departments of the Baron de Hirsch Fund, the philanthropy of the great Jewish banker and philanthropist Baron Maurice de Hirsch. In addition, the AJHS possesses records of the Jewish Immigrant Information Bureau in Galveston, Texas, relating to the Galveston Immigration Plan, a joint project of several organizations to bring Jewish immigrants into the United States through Texas. One of those organizations was the Industrial Removal Office, devoted to encouraging Jews to settle in the interior of the U.S. Finally, AJHS holdings include records of the Hebrew Immigrant Aid Society (HIAS) in Boston. The HIAS records have been microfilmed by the LDS (Mormon) Family History Library and may be accessed through its Family History Centers (see LDS).

Picture of Jewish farm family about 1910 is part of the photographic collection of the American Jewish Historical Society.

Baron de Hirsch Fund. This collection includes administrative records, deeds and property transfer records, files of student aid recipients, and a list of Jewish farmers. Also in this collection are records of the Jewish Agricultural Society (with loan applications by Jewish farmers), the Woodbine Colony in New Jersey, the Woodbine Agricultural School and the Baron de Hirsch Trade School, RG I-80.

Industrial Removal Office. Included in this record group are approximately 44,000 records of immigrants relocated from big cities to the interior of the U.S. and correspondence from relocated immigrants. The collection is unindexed and arranged by state, RG I-91.

Jewish Immigrant Information Bureau (JIIB), (Galveston, Texas). These records include internal correspondence of JIIB staff, correspondence between JIIB and other organizations, and ship passenger lists of immigrants who came through Galveston from Germany. A grant from the Jewish Genealogical Society of New York permitted the creation of a name index to this collection, RG I-90.

HIAS Boston. These are alphabetically arranged arrival records of immigrants who entered the U.S. through Boston or Providence, Rhode Island, 1882–1929, and an incomplete chronological list of ship arrivals and ships' passenger lists, 1904–1953, RG I-96.

New York County Court Records

These are duplicates of records in the Hall of Records at 31 Chambers Street in New York City, in which the litigants had Jewish-sounding names. They include Mayor's Court Briefs, 1674 to 1860, indexed by last name of the litigant (RG I-151); approximately 500 Declarations of Intent to Become a Citizen and related naturalization documents, 1816–45, indexed by last name of the declarant (RG I-152); Insolvent Debtors Cases, 1787–1861, indexed by last name of debtor (RG I-153); and incorporation papers, 1848–1920, of approximately 10,000 organizations, indexed by name and type of the organization and related European town (RG I-154). The index to the incorporation papers is filed in a card catalogue next to the main card catalogue.

Addresses

American Jewish Historical Society, 160 Herrick Road, Newton Centre, MA 02459; telephone: (617) 559-8880; fax: (617) 559-8881; e-mail: AJHS@AJHS.ORG; website: WWW.AJHS.ORG

Center for Jewish History, 15 West 16th Street, New York, New York 10011; telephone: (212) 294-6160; fax: (212) 294-6161

Bibliography

Arbeiter, Nancy. "New York Orphan Asylum Holdings at the American Jewish Historical Society." *AVOTAYNU* XI, no. 1 (Spring 1995).

Botwinik, Milton. "HIAS-Philadelphia." *AVOTAYNU* II, no. 3 (October 1986).

Bussgang, Fay Vogel. "A Treasure at the American Jewish Historical Society." *AVOTAYNU* XI, no. 4 (Winter 1995).

Cohler, Edward and Linda Levine. "HIAS-Boston." *AVOTAYNU* II, no. 3 (October 1986).

Davis, Fred and Warren Blatt. "Genealogical Resources at the American Jewish Historical Society." *AVOTAYNU* XI, no. 3 (Fall 1995).

Dennis, Marsha Saron. "HIAS-New York." *AVOTAYNU* II, no. 3 (October 1986).

Gerstl, Cynthia. "HIAS-Baltimore." *AVOTAYNU* II, no. 3 (October 1986).

Kaganoff, Nathan M. "American Jewish Historical Society Acquires Early Printed American Judaica." *AVOTAYNU* X, no.4 (Winter 1989).

LDS (Mormon)
Family History Library System

by Gary Mokotoff

Some call the Mormon Family History Library (FHL) in Salt Lake City, Utah, the "candy store" because of all the genealogical goodies it holds, but most genealogists call it simply "The Library." The Family History Library of the Church of Jesus Christ of Latter-day Saints (LDS) is the largest genealogical library in the world. Its five stories house more than 2.5 million rolls of microfilm, 700,000 micro-fiche and more than 280,000 books—all chosen to help genealogists find documentation of their ancestors. The microfilm portion of the collection is available to researchers at both the Library in Salt Lake City and at local institutions called Family History Centers. More than 2,000 Centers are located throughout the world.

Why Are Mormons Interested in Genealogy?

Why do Mormons do family history research? Mormons believe that life does not end at death, but instead our eternal spirits go to a spirit world where they live with our ancestors. Members of the Church believe that their deceased ancestors can receive the same blessings as living members of the Church. For this purpose, they make covenants in temples in behalf of their ancestors, the best known being posthumous baptizing.

In order to identify these ancestors, members of the Church need records. Consequently, the Church, through its records acquisition arm, the Genealogical Society of Utah, goes throughout the world copying records—primarily on microfilm—that will assist its members in identifying their ancestors. These records are available to the public, not just members of the Church.

What is controversial in this practice is that any deceased person can receive these blessings—not just ancestors of Mormons—therefore, the Church has an active program to extract names from the records.

What Kinds of Records Are in the Family History Library Collection?

For decades, the Genealogical Society of Utah, the record acquisition arm of the Mormon Church, has traversed the world to identify records of genealogical value and negotiate the right to microfilm those records. The records, placed in the Library system when acquired and catalogued, include vital records (birth, marriage, death and divorce), censuses, ship passenger manifests and the like. Given the size of its microfilm collection, it is not unreasonable to estimate that the Library has microfilmed more than one billion pages of information about billions of people.

Popular records of interest to Jewish genealogists are:

- Vital records (birth, marriage, death) of many countries in Central and Eastern Europe, especially Austria, Belarus, Hungary, Lithuania and Poland

- Census records for many countries of Central and Eastern Europe
- Census records of the United States, Canada and Great Britain
- Vital record indexes for New York City and many other major U.S. cities. Most of the actual New York City vital records that are available to the public (usually more than 100 years old)
- U.S. naturalization indexes and records for many courts
- Passenger arrival records for all U.S. ports including Ellis Island
- Emigration lists from the port of Hamburg, Germany

Using the Family History Library Catalog

To determine if the Library has records of interest, researchers must use the catalog available at the Library in Salt Lake City and on the Internet at WWW.FAMILYSEARCH.ORG. Alternately, researchers may visit a local Family History Center, where the catalog is available on CD-ROM, computer or microfiche. Volunteers at the Center can offer help in searching the catalog; using it effectively is a bit more complicated than using a standard library catalog.

Because a version of the FHL catalog is on the Internet, genealogists can determine from the comfort of their homes whether the Library has records of interest. To conduct a rigorous search of the catalog, however, is not an easy task. To determine if records exist for a specific town, one cannot merely type in the town name. Researchers who do that may receive a reply that no records are in the collection and may erroneously abandon the FHL as a resource. Another problem may arise when a researcher finds a town of interest in the catalog, but decides without further investigation that the topics listed are irrelevant.

Records in the FHL catalog are defined at three levels: town, province or county, and country. You must search each of the three levels separately. For example, a book on Jewish cemeteries of Poland may include information about the cemetery in your ancestral town. It will not appear in the catalog under the name of a specific ancestral town; rather, it will appear in the catalog under the country name. Records may not be held at the town/city level but at repositories of the province/county/state and, therefore, will be cataloged at that level.

How to Search the Family History Catalog

Use the following procedure for a rigorous search. To illustrate, the following procedure describes a search for the library holdings of the Jews of Warsaw, Poland, using the online version of the catalog. The procedures for using the CD-ROM or microfiche versions found in Family History Centers are similar.

Entrance to the LDS (Mormon) Family History Library in Salt Lake City

Go to the Internet version of the catalog on the web at WWW.FAMILYSEARCH.ORG. At the home page, under the section marked "Family History Library System," click the sentence that states "Search the Family History Library Catalog for Records and Resources." On the next page, click the button to do a PLACE SEARCH. You are now at the page from which you can initiate searches by town.

Type in the name of the town of interest—Warsaw for now—and click the SEARCH button. If the catalog lists more than one town with the name being sought, all possible search results are displayed. In the case of Warsaw, the catalog notes that it has records for many towns in the United States named Warsaw, as well as "Poland, Warszawa, Warsaw."

This display provides important information for the additional searches you must perform; it identifies the province/county and state/country of the town(s) found. Since the goal is to find records for Warsaw, the capital of Poland, note that the city is in Warszawa province and the country of Poland. Province and country are the two other additional categories we must search. The provincial records (Warszawa) may contain information about many towns in the province including Warsaw. The country records (Poland) may contain information about many cities in Poland including Warsaw.

Click the entry for "Poland, Warszawa, Warsaw." The REFERENCE DETAIL page is displayed; this page normally has only one entry. Again, click the entry for Warsaw. This brings up the PLACE DETAILS page. The PLACE DETAILS page describes all the topics for which the library has catalogued records for the city of Warsaw. Note that one of the topics is "Jewish Records." Click the Jewish records entry to see all FHL holdings for Jewish records, Warsaw, Warszawa, Poland.

The computer now presents a list of the FHL record collection for the topic. Do not be concerned if the records description is in an unfamiliar language, in this case Polish. By going to one more level of detail for each collection, a more complete description of the entry is provided in both Polish and English. It shows that the FHL has:

- A book on the Jewish cemetery in Warsaw
- Records of the Evangelical Reform Church in Warsaw
- Metrical (vital) records for the Jewish congregation

In the case of the metrical records for the Jewish congregation, going to still one more level at the Internet site finally produces details of the microfilm collection showing the actual microfilm numbers and descriptions. Why are Evangelical Reform church records catalogued under Jewish records?

The description explains that the records include parish registers of baptisms of Jewish converts.

Searching by Province

We are not finished! The next step is to investigate holdings for the province of Warszawa. Go back to the page where you started the initial search. This time search for Warszawa, the name of the province in which the city of Warsaw is located. Many options are offered:

- Poland, Warszawa
- Poland, Warszawa, Warszawa
- Other entries

The first entry refers to the library's holdings for the province of Warszawa; the second refers to the holdings for the city of Warszawa in Warszawa province. The other entries are for subdivisions of the city. Click the first link and go through the same process for the province of Warszawa as was done for the city of Warszawa. A list of topics for the province appears. Select the topics of interest to determine if there is information of use to you. For example, if you follow the path defined as "Poland, Warszawa-Directories," you will learn that the library has a 1992 Warsaw province telephone directory.

Searching by Country

When you complete the province/county search, go back to the beginning and type the country name: Poland. Again a list of possible locations appears—from the town of Poland in Clay County, Indiana, to the country of Poland. Click the first link and view the list of more than 100 topics the library has for the country of Poland. Browse through all the subjects to educate yourself on how the library catalogs its holdings by topic and to see what records and types of records are available. Note that for the country of Poland, six topics are specifically Jewish:

- Jewish history
- Jewish history-Bibliography
- Jewish history-Periodicals
- Jewish records
- Jewish records-Handbooks, manuals, etc.
- Jewish records-Inventories, registers, catalogs

Browse all pertinent sections.

How to Use a Family History Center

Genealogists use the FHL microfilm resources without ever going to Salt Lake City. Almost every country in the world—with the notable exception of Israel—has local Family History Centers. A Family History Center, typically one or two rooms in the facilities of a Mormon church, has microfilm and microfiche readers, computers, microfilm printers and a small collection of books usually donated by patrons of the Center. They also have finding aids and permanent loan collections of microfilms patrons have requested remain permanently at the Center. Larger cities, such as New York and Los Angeles, have a complete facility dedicated to a Family History Center.

Find the location of the closest Family History Center on the Internet at WWW.FAMILYSEARCH.ORG or call a local Mormon church. The Internet site has a link on its home page to a listing of all Family History Centers. They are listed in (English-language) telephone directories under Church of Jesus Christ of Latter-day Saints. At a center, volunteers who operate the facility can help in your research. They are knowledgable in the operation of the equipment and in the operation of Family Search.

Family History Center volunteers are unlikely to be knowledgable about Jewish research. Do not ask them to help you find records of your ancestors. They will instinctively search two databases that have little Jewish information: Ancestral File, a database of family trees submitted mostly by Mormons, and the International Genealogical Index, a list of 250 million people posthumously baptized by Mormons into their faith. Too often Jewish researchers come to these facilities, have Ancestral File and IGI searched unsuccessfully, and leave thinking the Family History Library has no information about their ancestry.

Instead, search the Locality Catalog for records groups that might have information about your ancestors, as described above. If you find microfilms of interest to you, fill out an order form provided by the volunteer who will order a copy sent from Utah to your local facility; typically, it arrives in two to three weeks. A nominal charge covers the costs of shipping and postage. When the film arrives at your Center, use one of the microfilm readers to locate records and the microfilm printer to make duplicate copies for your research files.

Visiting the Family History Library In Salt Lake City

The ultimate experience is to visit the Family History Library in Salt Lake City. It is a five-story building totally oriented toward genealogical research. Here you have access to their microfilm, microfiche and book collection in an open-stacks environment. You just help yourself to the film, fiche or book of interest. There are more than 600 microfilm work stations; 50 computer terminals all with Internet access; work tables; microfilm, fiche and book copying equipment; help desks manned by professionals; and volunteers at strategic locations to answer simple questions. Because of space limitations, only about one million of the 2.5 million microfilm rolls are within the Library. The remainder, usually available within 24 hours, must be ordered from a storage facility. The permanent microfilm collection includes all U.S. and Canadian holdings plus all European Jewish films.

The floors of the Library are organized by geographical region. Most of the activity occurs on three floors—on the second floor (U.S./Canada), Basement 1 (International) and Basement 2 (British Isles/Ireland). On each of these three floors, hundreds of thousands of microfilm reels are available in open stacks. Visitors remove a film of interest from its drawer, take it to one of the hundreds of microfilm readers on the floor, locate the items of interest on the reel, take the microfilm to a film copier, make a copy of the record(s) you have had the good fortune to find, and then return the film to the drawer where it was found.

Each of the three research floors has a copying room where researchers can make paper copies of film, fiche, or pages from a book in the book collection. Each microfilm reader has its own work station that includes:

- subdued lighting for better viewing
- lighted work space for personal papers next to each reader
- an electrical outlet to plug in a laptop computer (Be sure to bring a lock to secure your computer when you retrieve microfilms, etc.)

Each floor has a Help Desk manned by professionals and trained volunteers who can answer questions and help visitors with problems. For example, on the European floor, personnel can help translate documents in German, Polish, Russian and other European languages.

Each floor has books of finding aids to shortcut the process of identifying the microfilm number for a specific record group. For example, the U.S./Canada floor has a finding aid book that identifies the microfilm number for the collections of passenger arrival records to all U.S. ports. Another aid identifies the city directories in the collection, while a third lists vital records for New York City and Chicago. On the European floor there is a finding aid for the Hamburg Emigration Lists. In 2000, a finding aid for Jewish records, created by a Library volunteer, identifies all records in the collection identified specifically as Jewish. This information is provided in loose-leaf binders on each floor; the spine of the binder is labeled "Jewish."

The main floor includes an information desk to greet new visitors, many computer work stations and work desks and the U.S./Canadian book collection.

The third floor contains the Library offices and is closed to the public.

Master copies of the microfilms are kept in a nuclear bomb-proof vault dug into Granite Mountain near Salt Lake City. Duplicates of the films are available at the Family History Library and for loan to Family History Centers. Because of space limitations, not every film resides at the Library. Rarely used films must be ordered from the vault. If a film must be ordered and a copy is already part of its circulating library system, it can be brought to the Library within hours. If a duplicate must be made from the vault—and this is very rare—it may take a day or two.

Library hours are 8:00 a.m. to 9:00 p.m., Tuesday through Saturday, and 8:00 a.m. to 5:00 p.m. on Monday. The Library is closed on Sunday. It is also closed on the following holidays: New Years' Day, Independence Day (July 4), Thanksgiving Day (fourth Thursday in November), Christmas Day and the day after Christmas. It closes at 5:00 p.m. on Pioneer Day (July 24), Halloween (October 31), Thanksgiving Day Eve, Christmas Eve and New Year's Eve.

Address

Family History Library
35 North West Temple Street
Salt Lake City, Utah 84150-3400

Bibliography

Warren, Paula Stuart and Jim W. Warren. *Your Guide to the Family History Library*. Betterway, 2001.

Leo Baeck Institute

by Karen S. Franklin

L eo Baeck Institute (LBI), located at the Center for Jewish History,* was founded in 1955 to document the history and culture of German-speaking Jewry, a remarkable legacy that the Nazis sought to destroy. Its archives and library offer the most comprehensive collection of documents, memoirs, photographs and books dealing with the life and history of Jews in German-speaking lands, including Alsace Lorraine, Austria and Germany, from earliest times until the present. The materials are mostly in German, with some in Hebrew and many in English.

Genealogical Resources at LBI

The LBI collections are bountiful sources of material for German-Jewish genealogical research. Archival holdings include family collections, plus large genealogical collections compiled by historians. Almost all include family trees, vital records, community histories, and other materials relevant to family and community research. The library collections include biographical dictionaries, biographies and surveys of archives in Germany.

All of these sources may be identified by using the computerized LBI master catalogue, online at WWW.LBI.ORG. The computerized LBI master catalogue also can be accessed on the computers in the public area outside the Center Reading Room. The "simple search" option is sufficient for most genealogical research. Begin the research by typing the family surname and/or the town name into the keyword search and click "submit query."

Following is a list of selected library and archival holdings most relevant for genealogical research. This list includes a few of the many books and archival collections of family and community histories, vital records and biographies that can be identified through surname and town searches of the master catalogue. For more extensive lists, see Estelle Guzik, *Genealogical Resources in New York* (New York: Jewish Genealogical Society, Inc., 2003) and Gary Mokotoff, *How to Document Victims and Locate Survivors of the Holocaust* (Teaneck, N.J.: Avotaynu, 1995).

General Sources

Berthold Rosenthal Collection (1875–1957). Manuscripts and correspondence on the history and genealogies of the Jews in Baden and *Memorbuecher* (memorial books) of many other communities. Includes family trees, surname adoptions and lists of residents. Call number AR 637.

Dokumentation zur juedischen Kultur in Deutschland 1840–1940: die Zeitungsausschnittsammlung Steininger (Documents of Jewish Culture in Germany from 1840 to 1940: The Collection of newspaper clippings by Steininger). Muenchen. Archiv Bibliographia Judaica, K.G. Sauer Verlag. Call number X Mfiche 1.

Ellmann-Krueger, Angelika G. *Auswahlbibliographie zur juedischen Familienforschung vom Anfang des 19. Jahr-* *hunderts bis zur Gegenwart* (Selected Bibliography for Jewish Family Research from the Beginning of the 19th Century to the Present). Call number Ref Z 6374 B5 E4.

Jacob Jacobson Collection (1888–1968). The Jacobson estate includes substantial sections of the *Gesamtarchiv der deutschen Juden* (Archives of German Jewry) established in Berlin in 1905 as the central repository for the records of German-Jewish communities and organizations. Call numbers AR 7002; AR 246; MF134 (2); MF 447, reels 1–37.

John H. Richter Collection (1919–1994). Various family histories and genealogies. John Henry Richter was born in Vienna, Austria, in 1919 and emigrated to the United States in 1941. A librarian at the University of Michigan, his avocation was family research. Call number AR 1683 or MF 534, reels 1–73.

Juedische Familien-Forschung, edited by Arthur Czellitzer, nos. 1–50. Berlin, 1924–1938. The journal of Jewish genealogy published in pre-war Berlin. Call number P-B 184.

Stammbaum: Journal of German-Jewish Genealogy, 1993–present. Published entirely by volunteers until 1995, LBI now oversees publication with strong volunteer support. Call number Gen C121.

Wininger, Salomon, *Grosse juedische National Biographie, mit mehr als 8000 Lebenschreibungen namhafter juedischer Maenner und Frauen aller Zeiten und Laender* (Jewish National Biography with more than 8,000 Life Stories of well-known Jewish Men and Women of all Times and Countries). Call number Ref DS 115 W5.

Holocaust Victims, Survivors, and Refugees

Gedenkbuch: Opfer der Verfolgung der Juden, 1933–1945 (Memorial Volume: Victims of the Jewish persecution, 1933–1945). Koblenz: Bundesarchiv, 1985. 2 vols. (With cooperation from Yad Vashem, Jerusalem), this book lists Jews of Germany who perished, with place of birth and death and cause of death, if known. Call number Ref. DS 135 G33 G38.

1938 German Census. The 1938 census, an official census of all "non-German" minorities living in German territory in 1939, included the region of Sudetenland that had been annexed from Czechoslovakia. Call number MF 466.

Spalek, John M, with Adrienne Ash and Sandra H. Hawrylchak. *Verzeichnis der Quellen und Materialen der deutschsprachigen Emigration in den USA seit 1933* (Guide to the Archival Materials of the German-Speaking Emigration to the United States after 1933). Charlottesville: University Press of Virginia, 1978. Call number Ref E 184 G3 S68.

Geographical Regions

Bavaria, Schwierz, Israel. *Steinerne Zeugnisse juedischen Lebens in Bayern: eine Dokumentation.* (Witnesses in Stone of Jewish Life in Bavaria: A Documentation). 1992. Call number DS 135 G36 S395

Berlin, northern Germany. The Rudolf Jakob Simonis Collection (1749–1965) contains several hundred family trees, family histories and related correspondence for Berlin, northern Germany and Sweden. Call number AR 7019.

Bohemia. Gold, Hugo. *Die Juden und Judengemeinden Boehmens in Vergangenheit und Gegenwart* (Jews and Jewish Communities of Bohemia's Past and Present). Prague: Bruenn, 1934. Call number q DS 135 C954 G63.

Former East Germany. Jersch-Wenzel, Stefi, et. al. *Quellen zur Geschichte der Juden in den Archiven der neuen Bundeslaender* (Sources for the history of the Jews in the archives of the lands of the new Germany), 1996, 1999. Call number Ref. CD 1222. Q8

Frankfurt. *Ele Toldot*. A 32-volume collection of transcriptions of genealogical records of the Jewish community of Frankfurt am Main covering the years 1241 to 1824, compiled by Shlomo Ettlinger from originals located in the Stadtarchiv Frankfurt am Main. Call number AR 5241; MF 452; MF 458.

Hesse. Arnsberg, Paul. *Die Juedischen Gemeinden in Hessen* (Jewish Communities in Hessen). Frankfurt am Main, 1971. Call number Ref DS 135 G4 H48 A75; Heinemann, Hartmut. *Quellen zur Geschichte der Juden im Hessischen Hauptstaatsarchiv Wiesbaden, 1806–1866* (Sources for the history of the Jews in the major archives of the State of Hessen in Wiesbaden, 1806–1866). Wiesbaden: Kommission fuer die Geschichte der Juden in Hessen, 1997. Call number Ref DS 135 G4 H43 Q445 1997

Palatinate. *Dokumentation zur Geschichte der juedischen Bevoelkerung in Rheinland-Pfalz und im Saarland von 1800 bis 1945* (Documentation of the History of the Jewish Population in the regions of the Rhein, Pfalz, and Saarland from 1800 to 1945). Koblenz: hrsg. von der Landesarchivverwaltung Rheinland-Pfalz in Verbindung mit dem Landesarchiv Saarbruecken, 1982. Call number DS 135 G4 P35 P3

Posen. Heppner, Aron, and Isaac Herzberg. *Aus Vergangenheit und Gegenwart der Juden und der jued. Gemeinden in den Posener Landen* (From the Past and Present of the Jews and the Jewish Communities in Posen). Koschmin, 1909. Call number Ref DS 135 G4 P69 H41.

Schwaben. Doris Pfister, ed. *Dokumentation zur Geschichte und Kultur der Juden in Schwaben* (Documentation of the history and culture of the Jews of Schwaben). 1993. Call number q DS 135 G37 D6. John H. Bergmann Collection includes a history of the Jews of Laupheim (Schwaben), with family trees for most families and information and files on surrounding communities in Schwaben, including Augsburg, Buttenhausen, Huerben and Isschenheim. Call number AR 4861.

Shanghai: The LBI holds significant archival holdings on the community of Jews living in Shanghai during World

Reading room of the Center for Jewish History, home of the Leo Baeck Institute

War II. Collections include clippings, interviews, posters, correspondence, videos, municipal records, address books and a list of refugees who died in Shanghai.

For Further Information

Contact LBI's family research department by postal mail or e-mail. First complete the family research form available at WWW.LBI.ORG/FAMILY.HTML, or include your name, mailing address, specific family names, and, if possible, specific locations (regions, towns, villages) where your family lived. The more specific the search criteria, the better.

Address

Leo Baeck Institute, Center for Jewish History, 15 West 16th Street, New York, NY 10011; telephone: (212) 744-6400; fax: (212) 988-1305; e-mail: LBIGENEALOGY@LBI.CJH.ORG; website: WWW.LBI.ORG

Library of Congress

by Sharlene Kranz

The U.S. Library of Congress is located in three massive buildings in Washington, D.C. Although its primary function is to serve members of Congress, the library also is open to the public, free of charge. Materials do not circulate. The stacks are closed, but copying machines are readily available. Use the library's website to search its catalogue and to obtain information about the reading rooms and collections. Not all holdings are stored onsite. Researchers who plan to visit the library should write in advance to consult with reference librarians and to order desired materials.

The library is composed of three buildings connected by an underground tunnel—the Thomas Jefferson Building, John Adams Building and James Madison Building. Holdings of greatest interest to genealogists are described below.

Thomas Jefferson Building

Main Reading Room

Telephone reference: (202) 707-4773; website: LCWEB/LOC/GOV/ RR/MAIN.

A biographical reference collection holds current *Who's Who*, biographical dictionaries, alumni directories and other materials. A subject guide to the Main Reading Room at the reference desk lists the other biographical materials available here. Current U.S. and foreign telephone directories, city directories and reverse telephone directories are arranged alphabetically by state and then by country. A card catalogue lists the city directory for every locality. A good strategy when searching the computer catalogue is to use keywords, for example, Jews [specific geographic location].

The *American Jewish Year Book* (call number E184.J5 A6), published annually since 1900 by the American Jewish Committee, is an excellent source of general information. Each year book includes advertising and essays on current Jewish-American affairs and on Jewish international interests. Included is a directory of national and local organizations that list all officers, staff and trustees. The section on New York City, for example, lists congregations, Jewish hospitals, social welfare institutions (such as the Clara de Hirsch Home for Working Girls), the Educational Alliance, Hebrew Aid Societies, *landsmanshaftn* (townsmen societies), statistics and demographics and necrology. Volume 42 (1940) includes an index to Volumes 1–41.

Microform Reading Room

Telephone reference: (202) 707-5471. Microform is a term that includes microfilm and microfiche.

A large self-service collection of U.S. city directories (see below) on microfilm and microfiche is held in this room. More than 150 cities are represented in this collection whose years of coverage span colonial times to 1935. Also held here are 19th- and early 20th-century Russian and Berlin city directories, including:

- *Vsia Rossia* (All Russia) for 1895, 1899, 1903, 1911–12, and 1923 (microfilm #24185). These directories include most of the small towns of the Pale of Settlement, where most Russian Jews of that era were required to live. The directories include lists of people who owned businesses, from large factories to small grocery stores. A large proportion of names are Jewish.
- *Petersburg/Petrograd/Leningrad* (All St. Petersburg/ Petrograd/Leningrad) for 1894–1934, with the exception of 1918–21. These extremely detailed city directories sometimes include telephone numbers (microfilm #04676).
- *Vsia Moskva* (All Moscow) for 1896–1936 (microfilm #30585)
- *Berlin 1891–1941* (microfilm #32901 and microfiche 85/161)
- *Russian Imperial Government Serials on Microfilm in the Library of Congress* (microfilm #83/5231). This list of uncatalogued works from the Russian Empire includes many city directories for localities throughout the empire. One of the most interesting items is #335, *Heshbod Va'ad Ha-Hevra,* a list of contributors in the Russian Empire to agricultural settlements in Syria and present-day Israel for the years 1890–1901.
- U.S. telephone directories (1976–91) on Phonefiche, a microfiche listing. This self-service collection consists of yellow (commercial) and white pages (residential) telephone directories for most U.S. cities and towns. For most years, there is a published guide to the collection entitled *Community Cross-reference Index*. Non-current U.S. telephone directories (white and yellow pages) for years not included in the set of Phonefiche are available.
- Various Jewish newspapers on microfilm are available here, including the *London Jewish Chronicle* (1841–June 1960, indexed for the first 50 years), *The Jewish Messenger* (1857–1902, an English-language weekly focused on Anglo-Jewry in North America, published in New York City), *Carolina Israelite* (Charlotte, North Carolina, 1944–68), *American Israelite* (Cincinnati, 1854–1947) and *The Jewish Exponent* (Philadelphia 1887–present, weekly).

Local History and Genealogy Reading Room

Telephone reference: (202) 707-5537; website: LCWEB/LOC/GOV/ RR/GENEALOGY.

This reading room houses a large collection intended primarily to facilitate research in U.S. local history and genealogy. Card catalogues include a family name index, surname index, coats-of- arms index, U.S. biographical index and a U.S. local history shelf list. General genealogical and local history guides are stored on the reference shelves. Organized by state, volumes include published lists of vital records, census indexes, gazetteers, manuals on research for various ethnic groups, indexes to genealogical periodicals, books on immigration, directories of addresses of historical and genealogical societies and guides to vital records for U.S. states and counties and for many foreign countries. Lists of places of worship compiled in the 1930s are here. To identify books catalogued after 1980, it is necessary to use the *Online Computer Catalogue*, CATALOG.LOC.GOV.

Hard copy U.S. city directories may be requested in this room. More than 1,000 city directories, most published before 1935, are available on microfilm in the Microform Room. City directories in the library cover about 250 American cities and towns before 1861, and more than 1,000 cities from 1861 to 1935. The Library of Congress holds the largest collection of city directories in the U.S. Also available are U.S. telephone directories and reverse telephone directories (often called street address or criss-cross directories).

Business directories list the names and addresses of businesses for major cities. *Family Search on CD-ROM*, the LDS automated system of family history information, is available here (see LDS). The CD-ROM includes the Social Security Death Index (SSDI) (see U.S. SOCIAL SECURITY DEATH INDEX). *Family Search* also includes a military index that lists nearly 100,000 U.S. servicemen who died in the Korean and Vietnam conflicts, including date of birth and death, residence, place of death, and rank and service number.

Non-current editions of foreign telephone and city directories, shelved in closed stacks, may be requested here. Holdings are uneven. Computer terminals for access to the library's automated files are available here, as are computers to consult online data bases including ANCESTRY.COM, HERITAGEQUEST and PROQUEST.

European Reading Room

Telephone reference: (202) 707-4515; website: LCWEB/LOC.GOV/RR/EUROPEAN.

The European Reading Room's reference collection contains materials on Europe (excluding the British Isles, the Iberian Peninsula and Turkey) and the republics of the former Soviet Union. Of special interest is the collection of approximately 800 uncatalogued telephone directories from the former Soviet Union. Most date from the 1950s to the present, with some earlier items. *Directories from the Countries of the Former Soviet Union* (February 1995) is a finding aid to the collection. Most directories are printed in Russian, but some are in the language of the particular country (primarily the more recent directories of the independent states). The Library of Congress does not have recent residential directories for many of the largest cities of the former Soviet Union, typically because they have not been published. Books are listed under seven headings: Baltic States, Belarus, Caucasus, Central Asia, Moldova, Russia, Soviet Union, and Ukraine. Additional directories, mostly older ones, have been catalogued and are accessible through the card and computer catalogues.

The pre-revolutionary, 41-volume Russian encyclopedia *Entsiklopedicheskii slovar'*, published between 1890 and 1907, is valuable for its treatment of historical and geographical subjects and Russian literary and cultural figures. A second edition, *Novyi entsiklopedicheskii slovar'* (1911–16), has only 29 volumes and stops at the letter O. The three editions

of the *Bol'shaia Sovetskaia Entsiklopediia* (1926–47, 1950–56, and 1970–78) and the English translation of the third edition, *Great Soviet Encyclopedia 1973–1983,* also are useful for geographical, biographical, and historical information.

Polish city directories in the library's collection include *1916 Directory of Lwow* (call no. WMLC91/1014); *1930 Telephone Directory for Poland: Upper Silesia and Cracow* (95/2971 Microform Reading Room); *Address Book City of Cracow 1926* (cat. #SF86-92379); Address Book Pomeranian Region 1929 (West Prussia) and Poznan Region 1926, call no. 4HD1481; 1TF91-2448; *Address Book Cracow region*, LCN60, call no. #DK403.K75; *Commercial Directory, Gdansk*. HF3636.83; *Directory Warsaw 1870* (DK4614.D95 1987 reprint) and *Directory Warsaw 1869* (DK4614.D952 1983 reprint). *Lists of Jews of West Prussia and Bromberg 1806* (DS135.P62P687); and *Lists of Jews of West Prussia and Bromberg 1810* (DS135.P62P684). For other Polish directories, check the computer catalogue under Directories–Poland.

Hebraic Section

Telephone reference: (202) 707-5422; website: LCWEB.LOC.GOV/RR/AMED/HEBRAIC.HTML.

One of the most valuable repositories for Jewish genealogy is the Library of Congress's Hebraic Section, long recognized as a major center for the study of Hebrew and Yiddish materials. The collection and the staff are duplicated nowhere else. Most of the materials in this section are written in Hebrew and Yiddish, but some are written in Ahmharic, Coptic, English, Judeo-Arabic, Judeo-Persian, Ladino and Syriac. Highlights of the collection for genealogists include:

- A broad selection of Hebrew periodicals, current and retrospective, and a variety of Yiddish and Hebrew newspapers
- *Yizkor* books for Jewish communities destroyed in the Holocaust
- Books on rabbinic genealogy
- Local histories and some histories of cemeteries for some towns in Eastern Europe that include lists of graves
- Israeli telephone books on CD-ROM

Jewish researchers may find their family surnames in the Author/Subject National Union Catalogs of Hebraica and Yiddica if a family member has written materials in these languages. Other reference works located here are the *Encyclopaedia Judaica, Jewish Encyclopedia, Evreiskaia Entsiklopediia*, directories, yearbooks, and standard indexes to the periodical and scholarly literature.

John Adams Building
Science and Technology Reading Room
And Business Reference Services

Telephone reference: (202) 707-6401; website: LCWEB.LOC.GOV/RR/SCITECH.

The value of this specialized collection to the genealogist lies in its holdings of biographical material, from a vast assortment of *Who's Who* in various fields to book-length biographies and alumni directories. Bound editions of some Jewish newspapers are held here as well.

Thomas Jefferson Building of the Library of Congress houses many departments including the Hebraic section. Photo by Lisa Whittle for the Library of Congress.

James Madison Building

Geography and Map Reading Room

Telephone reference: (202) 707-6277; website: LCWEB.LOC.GOV/RR/GEOMAP.

This largest map collection in the world holds almost 5 million maps, 53,000 atlases, and 8,000 reference works. It includes cartographical and geographical information for all parts of the world. There is no comprehensive catalogue of map holdings; researchers must work with one of the specialists on duty. Of particular interest to genealogists and local historians are the following materials:

- A large collection of U.S. county maps and atlases that show land ownership published in the 19th and early 20th centuries
- Fire insurance maps and atlases published by the Sanborn Map Company, beginning in 1867. The collection includes detailed plans of 12,000 American cities and towns. Houses, synagogues, and businesses are detailed.
- Detailed topographical maps by the German government (1890s–1930s), the Austrian-Hungarian government (1870s–1914) and the Polish government (1920s and 1930s) that show very small towns, as well as other series covering Eastern Europe
- Current and historical gazetteers and atlases
- Ward maps of American cities that help locate a family's city ward in an unindexed census
- Town plans of USSR cities indicating major street grids and points of interest, such as cemeteries and synagogues, made by the German military, 1930–44

Newspaper and Current Periodical Room

Telephone reference: (202) 707-5690 and 5691; website: LCWEB.LOC.GOV/RR/NEWS/NCP.HTML.

Issues of U.S. and Roman-alphabet foreign-language newspapers owned by the library are available in hard copy or microform in this reading room. (Current and old non-Roman alphabet foreign language newspapers are available in the Area Studies reading rooms appropriate to the language.) Collections include:

- Current periodicals. Approximately 70,000 titles are retained for up to 24 months. (Older materials are bound or microfilmed and stored in the Adams and Jefferson Buildings.)
- Newspapers. Approximately 350 domestic and 1,000 foreign titles are retained on a permanent basis. The collection includes loose papers, microfilm, microprint and bound volumes. Most newspapers in non-Roman alphabets are available in specialized reading rooms (for example, Hebrew and Yiddish papers are held by the Hebraic Section). Finding aids include:
- Newspapers received currently in the Library of Congress
- *Chronological List of American Newspapers in the Library of Congress, 1801–1967*
- *Checklist of Foreign Newspapers in the Library of Congress, 1801–1950s*
- Complete microfilm sets of seven newspapers are available by self-service: *London Times, London Sunday Times, Los Angeles Times, New York Times, Wall Street Journal, Washington Evening Star* and *Washington Post.* (A few

newspapers have indexes; for example, *The New York Times* is indexed from 1851; *The London Times* is indexed from 1868; *The Washington Post* and *Los Angeles Times* are indexed from 1972). Some Jewish newspapers held in this reading room include:

- *The American Israelite* (Cincinnati 1946–88; the Microform Reading Room holds editions 1854–1947 and 1989–92 on 46 reels, microfilm #02649)
- *The Jerusalem Post*, 1950–
- The Jewish Daily Forward
- *Aufbau,* an American Jewish weekly in German. The library holds bound copies for 1940–2001 (DS101.A75) in the Main Reading Room, and 2002–03 issues in the Newspaper and Current Periodical Room.

Consult the reference librarian for the most useful indexes. *The New York Times Obituary Index* is an index often useful to genealogists. The *Personal Name Index to the New York Times Index* (PNI) (Z5301.F28) cross-references all names indexed in the annual *Times* indexes. PNI comes in two series: 22 volumes covering 1851 to 1974, and 5 volumes covering 1975 to 1989. PNI includes all names from society notices, including marriage listings.

Manuscript Reading Room

Telephone reference: (202) 707-5387; website: LCWEB.LOC.GOV/ RR/MSS.

The Manuscript Reading Room makes available for inspection and study more than 35 million manuscripts and documents relating to United States history. The collection includes the personal papers of 23 U.S. presidents and the papers of other great Americans. Also included are papers of government officials and records of organizations that have significantly affected American life. Consult *The Jewish Experience: A Guide to Manuscript Sources in the Library of Congress*, by Gary J. Kohn, The American Jewish Archives, 1986) (Z6373.U5K64) which indexes collections of papers and holdings on Jewish individuals, institutions, organizations and publications. The personal papers of hundreds of noted Jewish Americans are held here.

Biographical and historical manuscripts donated by organizations and individuals are kept here. Individuals researching a person or group of any note should check the catalogue for this room. Use the index to the *Dictionary Catalogue of Collections for the Manuscript Division.*

Performing Arts Reading Room

Telephone reference: (202) 707-5507; website: LCWEB.LOC.GOV/ RR/PERFORM

This collection includes biographies and obituaries, autographed manuscripts, letters and correspondence, copyright deposits, books and scores, periodicals and special materials.

Motion Picture and Television Reading Room

Telephone reference: (202) 707-8572; website: LCWEB.LOC.GOV/ RR/MOPIC

This collection includes biographies and obituaries from the entertainment industry, as well as histories, movie reviews, magazines and newspapers, including a complete run of the publication *Variety*.

Prints and Photographs Division

Telephone voice mail: (202) 707-8867; telephone reference: (202) 707-5836; website: LCWEB.LOC/GOV/RR/PRINT/P_ABOUT.HTML

This division provides assistance and delivery of materials for pictorial items not in book format. Included are photographs, prints, drawings, posters and architectural records. Numerous images relate to Jewish history, both in the U.S. and abroad.

Law Reading Room

Telephone reference: (202) 707-5080; website: LCWEB.LOC.GOV/ GLIN/LL-ABOUT.HTML

Copies of the Martindale-Hubbell directory of American lawyers from 1900 to present may be obtained here. Here also is the complete set of Nuremberg trial documents.

Address

Library of Congress, Washington, DC 20540 (at Independence Avenue and 2nd Street, SE); telephone: (202) 707-5000; website: LCWEB.LOC.GOV

Bibliography

Luft, Edward. "Internet Subscription Databases for Genealogical Research." *AVOTAYNU* 18, no. 3 (Fall 2002).

Savada, Eli. "Using *The New York Times* Online Backfile." *AVOTAYNU* 18, no. 2 (Summer 2002).

National Archives and Records Administration

by Sharlene Kranz

The U.S. National Archives and Records Administration is the governmental repository for non-current federal records. It does not have state records (birth, marriage, death) or local records. Records are arranged by federal agency and come in many forms—loose papers, bound volumes, motion picture films, videotapes, sound recordings, still photographs, maps, microfilm, microfiche and electronic records.

The key to using records held by the National Archives is to determine "How did my ancestor interact with the federal government?"

Records held by the Archives are housed in two locations in the Washington, D.C. metropolitan area:

- Archives I*, the main building, which occupies a full city block between 7th and 9th Streets at Pennsylvania Avenue, N.W.
- Archives II* in College Park, Maryland

A publication sales office in Room 404 at Archives I offers free pamphlets and finding aids in addition to books for sale.

Archives I

Major genealogical records held at Archives I are: U.S. census 1790–1930; passenger ship arrival records; military records up to, but not including, World War I; naturalization records and records of various federal agencies. Most genealogists will use records in Room 400, the Microfilm Research Room, telephone: 202-501-5400; genealogical reference: 301-837-2000.

Federal Censuses. Federal censuses, taken every ten years, are opened for public inspection after 72 years (see NATURALIZATION). The 1930 census and all previous years are now open. The 1890 census was almost totally destroyed by fire. To access the census you must know the state in which your subject lived. It is helpful to know the county, city, and street address. Depending on the year, census records provide such information as name of household members, age, occupation, state or country of birth, year of marriage, year of immigration, citizenship status and more.

Use clues from the census to lead you to immigration and naturalization records. Soundex, a phonetic index, is used for all 1880 households with children age 10 or younger and for all 1900, 1920 and 1930 (11 southern states only) data. For 1910 Soundex and Miracode, a variation, applies to 21 states; a street index (Microfilm M1283) is available for 39 cities. To use the Soundex effectively, search for the name under every possible spelling; census takers may not have understood clearly your immigrant ancestor's foreign accent and/or language.

Commercial publishing firms have created name indexes to census records through 1860 and have completed indexes

to the 1870 census for most states. During the 1930s, the federal government created an index to the 1880 census, but it includes only households with children under age 10; the 1910 census was indexed for some states, but the project ran out of funds before indexing New York and New Jersey, among other states. Censuses taken before 1880 do not include street addresses; they are tied to the ward structure of the city. Some census and ward maps are in the library in Room 402.

Each National Archives microfilm has a name and a number (such as M1066 or T1288). Location registers at the front and back of the Microfilm Reading Room list the exact location (cabinet and drawer) of each microfilm publication.

Ship Arrival Records. Ship Arrival Records (1820–1957) provide information about immigrants to the United States (see IMMIGRATION). Some records are customs lists; others are immigration lists. For genealogical purposes, they are essentially the same; only the amount of information provided varies. More recent manifests provide more information. Lists normally include the following information for each passenger: name, age, sex, occupation, country of embarkation, country of destination. Most Jews came to the United States through the Port of New York, but other important entry points included Philadelphia, Boston, Galveston and Baltimore.[1] After 1895, many Jewish immigrants came across the Canadian border. Indexes to ship passenger lists exist for some ports, but the time period covered varies:

Port	Lists	Indexes
Atlantic & Gulf Coast ports	1829–73	1829–73
Baltimore	1820–1909	1820–1952
Boston	1820–1943	1848–1940
Canadian border[2]	1929–54	1895–1952
Detroit	1906–57	1906–54
Galveston, Tx.[3]	1896–1951	all
Gloucester, Mass.	1918–43	none
Key West, Fl.	1898–1945	none
Misc. Great Lakes Ports	1820–73	none
Misc. Southern Ports	none	1890–1954
New Bedford, Mass.	1902–43	1902–54
New York	1820–1957	1820–46; 1897–1948
New Orleans	1820–1945	1853–1952
Philadelphia[4]	1800–1945	1800–1948
Port Townsend/Tacoma, Wash.	1894–1909	none
Portland, Maine	1893–1943	1893–1954
Providence, R.I.	1911–43	1911–54
San Francisco	1882–1957	1893–1934
Savannah, Ga.	1906–45	none
Seattle/Port Townsend, Wash.	1882–1957	none

The National Archives publishes *Immigrant and Passenger Arrivals*, which lists the microfilm records for ship's arrivals.[5] A copy of the *Morton Allan Directory of European Passenger Steamship Arrivals* is located in Room 400; it lists immigrant ship arrivals by date (1890–1930), port and steamship company.

To find a given person in the ship records, you must know the date of arrival, port of entry and name of ship. Look up the name in the microfilmed index, and then find the list, filed by port, the name of the ship and that date. Check with staff for research tips if the records are not where you expect them to be based on published guides. Weather or other variables may have resulted in a ship arrival that did not conform with the listed date.

Naturalization Records. Naturalization records held in Washington include an eclectic mixture of *federal* naturalization indexes and records on microfilm. Before 1906 a person could become naturalized in any court of record—city, county, state, or federal. Most naturalizations took place in the county court where the person resided. From September 1906 onward, with rare exceptions, all naturalizations were conducted in federal courts. For soldiers naturalized during World War I, see the section on military records below.

Federal naturalization records are held by the regional archives serving the state in which the federal court is located. Archives I, Room 400, however, has microfilm copies of some naturalization indexes and some federal records for some federal courts. These microfilm rolls include declarations of intention, naturalization petitions, citizenship records, and soundex indexes for some states, local and federal courts.[6]

Additional films on a number of states are currently available only at certain regional archives. LDS (Mormons) Family History Centers have copies of all films held by the National Archives (see LDS).

Subject Index to Correspondence and Case Files of the Immigration and Naturalization Service, 1903–52 (T458). This collection consists of 31 reels of microfilm of index cards organized alphabetically by subject. Reel 16 includes topics related to "Hebrew;" Reel 18 includes "Jewish" and "Judaism;" Reel 17 lists "Israel" and Reel 19 has "Palestine."

Military Records. Military records held at Archives I include service records and pension files for the military services from the American revolution up to, but not including, World War I. More recent military records are generally held in St. Louis, Missouri. Military Reference telephone: (202) 501-5385. Among the items held at Archives I are:

- Revolutionary War. Alphabetical index
- War of 1812, Indian Wars, Mexican War, Patriots War (fought 1837–40 on the Niagara frontier)
- Civil War. Union service records (consult state indexes); Union pensions (consult alphabetical *General Pension Index*); Confederate service records (look up name in *Consolidated Index)*
- War with Spain Philippine Insurrection. Consult indexes
- Veterans Administration Payment Pension Card. Alphabetical index 1907–33

Retrieval of service records is requested in Room 400 with a wait of up to two hours. Records are brought to Room 203 for

use. Three requests per hour are pulled for each researcher; the last pull is at 3:30 p.m. Monday through Friday. Records are not pulled on Saturday. Records are held in Room 203 for three working days. To check if records have been pulled, the telephone number in Room 203 is (202) 501-5405.

A name index to file cards of soldiers who were naturalized at the beginning of World War I (RG85 of the Immigration and Naturalization Service, entry 29) may be consulted in Room 11E. The cards provide the soldier's name, date of naturalization, court and certificate number. For information on this index, call (202) 501-5395.

World War I Draft Registrations. World War I draft registration cards for all states are on microfilm M1509 (see WORLD WAR I DRAFT REGISTRATION). NARA regional archives have films for the states in their area, (e.g., the regional archives in Massachusetts have the cards for Connecticut, Maine, Massachusetts and New Hampshire; the Pacific Northwest regional archive in Seattle has registrations for Alaska, Idaho and Oregon). Check with other regional archives for availability.

Passport Records. Passport records include regular and emergency passport applications, 1725–1925. Overseas travel by 19th-century American citizens was fairly common, but passports were not required in the U.S. until passage of the 1924 Immigration Act. Many early 20th-century immigrants went back to Europe for a visit in the 1920s and 1930s. These passports are especially valuable if you have been unable to find European birthplaces. The applications usually give the exact town of birth and date of immigration to the U.S., and sometimes even the name of the ship. Microfilms of passport applications are:

- M1371, indexes for passport applications, 1810–1906
- M1372, passport applications, 1795–1906
- M1848, index to passport applications, 1850–52, 1860–80, 1881, 1906–23[7]
- M1490, passport applications, 1906–25
- M1834, emergency passport applications (passports issued abroad) 1877–1907

The Jewish Genealogy Society of Greater Washington (JGSGW) has indexed Jewish names on emergency passports (1914–25), issued by U.S. consular officials to wives and children of naturalized citizens living overseas; the microfiche index is available in Room 400.

Archives II, College Park, Maryland

The holdings at the National Archives at College Park[*] include the cartographic collection; the Nixon Presidential Materials; electronic records; motion picture, sound, and video records; the JFK Assassination Records collection; still pictures; the Berlin Documents Center microfilm; and records of many federal agencies, including the U.S. Department of State.

Records cannot be retrieved from stack areas during evening hours or on Saturday; requests should be made early in the day. Last pull time Monday through Friday is 3:30 p.m.

Archives II can be reached by automobile; by Metro (Prince Georges Plaza Metro, then the R3 Metrobus; on Saturdays a free shuttle travels from the Metro to Archives II);

Main building of the U.S. National Archives and Records Administration

or by free shuttle bus from Archives I (on the hour between 8 a.m. and 5 p.m. Monday through Friday; this is a staff bus, and researchers can board only when space is available).

Researchers must first speak with a consultant archivist in Room 1000 off the main lobby. Security is strict; bags must be checked, but laptop computers are allowed. Paper-to-paper copies cost 15 cents per page; microfilm-to-paper copies are 30 cents per page.

Listed below are some Archives II materials of special interest to genealogists.

U.S. Department of State (RG59) 1789–1963 (except microfilmed passport applications [1795–1925] and indexes [1810–1923], which remain at Archives I downtown). These records include the Central Decimal Files of the Department of State, 1789–1963. Records of genealogical value include birth, marriage, and death of U.S. citizens abroad; settlement of the foreign estates of U.S. citizens who died abroad; claims by U.S. citizens against foreign governments; lists of U.S. citizens temporarily or permanently residing abroad; and correspondence regarding U.S. citizens residing abroad.

JGSGW has issued a three-microfiche set of *Indexes to Department of State Records Found in the U.S. National Ar-*

chives, which is available in the Microfilm Reading Room 4050, cabinet 48, first drawer. Users can search for names in this index on Avotaynu's Consolidated Jewish Surname Index at WWW.AVOTAYNU.COM/CSI/CSI-HOME.HTML. Records can be pulled prior to your arrival by calling a civilian records archivist at (301) 837-3480.

Microfiche I includes:

- Index of Jewish applicants for emergency U.S. passports (1915–24)
- Index to registration of U.S. citizens, Jerusalem (1914–18)
- Index to Jewish names in "Protection of Interests of U.S. Citizens 1910–29 in Germany, Lithuania, Poland and Romania"[8]
- Index to Jewish names in "Protection of Interests of U.S. Citizens 1910–29 in Russia"
- Index to Jewish names in "Protection of Interests of U.S. Citizens in Austria-Hungary"

Microfiche II includes (1910–29) an index to Jewish names for the countries of Austria, Balkan States, Baltic Provinces, Bessarabia, Bulgaria, Czechoslovakia, Free City of Danzig, Estonia, Hungary, Latvia, Lithuania, Turkey, Ukraine and the Kingdom of Yugoslavia. Microfiche III covers Palestine (1910–29).

Federal Bureau of Investigation (FBI RG65). These field agent investigative case files, 1908–22 (M1085), 955 rolls, consist primarily of records of people suspected of being German agents or sympathizers. Many Jews are included.

Captured German Records (RG242) on microfilm, in German, include:

- Name Index of Jews Whose German Nationality was Annulled by the Nazi Regime (Berlin Documents Center) (T355)
- Documents Concerning Jews in the Berlin Documents Center (T457)
- Death books of camps liberated by American forces: Matthausen Death Books (1939–1945, T990); Dachau list of inmates; Flossenberg and Buchenwald
- Prussian Mobilization Records (1866–1918, M962)
- Arolsen (Red Cross Tracing Service) films (also available at U.S. Holocaust Memorial Museum): Bergen-Belsen, Buchenwald, Constanz (Feldkirch), Dachau, Gestapo transport lists, Gross Rosen (Breslau), Jewish Agency for Palestine, Matthausen, Middlebau (Songerhausen), Natzweiler and Sandbostel (Bremerforde)

Other captured records pertain to Belarus, Hungary, Italy, Latvia, Lithuania and Poland. The collection also includes lists prepared by Allied personnel of people in the camps at the time of liberation.

Records of the All-Union (Russian) Communist Party (Smolensk Archives), 1917–41, T87, RG242. For details see *Guide to the Records of the Smolensk Oblast of the All-Union Communist Party of the Soviet Union 1917–1941,* Archives document, indexed by subject and document number.

Russian Consular Records, 1862–1922 (RG261) (M1486), indexed by the JGSGW are files of correspondence, passports, proof of citizenship, and much more, from various Russian consular offices. The files include correspondence between early 20th-century immigrants from Russia, often Jewish, and official representatives of the czarist government. They often include considerable personal information such as date and place of birth; parents' names; data on education, marriage, arrival in the United States; addresses lived in the United States; births of children, etc. To access these records, first consult *Index and Catalog to the Russian Consular Records*, by Sallyann Sack and Suzan Wynne, microfilm M1710.[9] Records of Imperial Russian Consulates in Canada, 1898–1922, are found in (M1742).

Records of foreign service posts of the Department of State (RG84) include records of genealogical value such as births, marriages, and deaths of American citizens; records of passports or visas issued; records about the disposal of property, the settlement of estates and the protection of American citizens; court records of certain posts where ministers and consuls exercised judicial authority over American citizens; records of services performed for American ships and seamen; lists of seamen shipped, discharged or deceased; and records of claims made by American citizens against foreign governments. Records of diplomatic

posts cover the period 1788–1945; consular posts cover 1790–1949. The collection includes records of the U.S. consulate in Jerusalem (1857–1934). For information call textual reference at (301) 837-3480.

Cartographic Branch. This branch owns more than two million World War II-era, highly detailed German aerial reconnaissance maps of Europe (RG373) and 1:50,000-scale maps of Europe and elsewhere for the 1950s and later (Army Map Service, RG77). Inexpensive photocopies or very high-quality, high-gloss photographs can be made. Also available are maps of regions that were included in Foreign Service inspection reports (1906–39); most are base maps on which additional information has been annotated, such as significant buildings, harbor facilities and business districts. The telephone number for cartographic reference is (301) 837-0868.

Still Pictures Branch, This branch owns *New York Times* Paris Bureau photographs prior to World War II. Still Pictures telephone reference number is (301) 837-1956.

Motion Picture, Sound, and Video Branch. The index held here includes such topics as Holocaust, Israel, and the Jews. The films were made by the U.S. armed forces, civilians, and commercial companies. The telephone reference number is (301) 837-1956.

Addresses

Archives I, Pennsylvania Avenue at 8th Street, N.W., Washington, DC 20408; telephone: 202-501-5400; e-mail: INQUIRE@ARCH1.NARA.GOV; website: WWW.NARA.GOV/GENEALOGY

Archives II at College Park, 8601 Adelphi Road, College Park, MD 20740; telephone: 301-837-2000; e-mail: INQUIRE@ARCH2.NARA.GOV

Addresses of Regional Archives

Alaska, Anchorage. Pacific Alaska Region; 654 West Third Avenue, Anchorage, AK 99501-2145; telephone: (907) 271-2441; fax: (907) 271-2442; e-mail: ARCHIVES@ALASKA.NARA.GOV

California, Laguna Niguel. Pacific Southwest Region; 24000 Avila Road, 1st Floor, East Entrance, Laguna Niguel, CA 92677-3497; e-mail: CENTER@LAGUNA.NARA.GOV

California, San Francisco. Pacific Sierra Region, San Bruno; 1000 Commodore Drive; San Bruno, CA 94066-2350; e-mail: CENTER@SANBRUNO.NARA.GOV

Colorado, Denver. Rocky Mountain Region; Bldg. 48, Denver Federal Center, West 6th Avenue and Kipling Street, Denver, CO 80225-0307; mailing address: P.O. Box 25307, Denver, CO 80225-0307; e-mail: CENTER@DENVER.NARA.GOV

Georgia, Atlanta. Southeast Region; 1557 St. Joseph Avenue, East Point, GA 30344–2593; e-mail: ARCHIVES@ATLANTA.NARA.GOV

Illinois: Chicago. Great Lakes Region; 7358 South Pulaski Road; Chicago, IL 60629-5898; e-mail: ARCHIVES@CHICAGO.NARA.GOV

Massachusetts, Boston. New England Region, Waltham, MA; Frederick C. Murphy Federal Center, 380 Trapelo Road, Waltham, MA 02452-6399; e-mail: ARCHIVES@WALTHAM.NARA.GOV

Massachusetts, Pittsfield. NorthEast Region; 10 Conte Drive, Pittsfield, MA 01201-8230; e-mail: ARCHIVES@PITTSFIELD.NARA.GOV

Missouri, Kansas City. Central Plains Region; 2312 East Bannister Road; Kansas City, MO 64131-3011; e-mail: ARCHIVES@KANSASCITY.NARA.GOV

New York, New York. Northeast Region; 201 Varick Street, New York, NY 10014-4811; telephone: (212) 401-1620; fax: (212) 401-1638; e-mail: ARCHIVES@NEWYORK.NARA.GOV

Pennsylvania: Philadelphia. Mid-Atlantic Region; 900 Market Street, Philadelphia, PA 19107-4292; telephone: (215) 597-3000; fax: (215) 597-2303; e-mail: ARCHIVES@PHILARCH.NARA.GOV

Texas, Fort Worth. Southwest Region; 501 West Felix Street, Building 1, Fort Worth, TX 76115-3405; mailing address: P.O. 6216, Fort Worth, TX 76115-0216; e-mail: ARCHIVES@FTWORTH.NARA.GOV

Washington, Seattle. Pacific Northwest Region; 25 Sand Point Way NE; Seattle, WA 98115-7999; e-mail: ARCHIVES@SEATTLE.NARA.GOV

Notes

1. What to do if your relative came in a period for which there is no existing index? The best source of a date of arrival is a naturalization record, although dates are not always correct. The 1900 and 1910 censuses provide the year of immigration, and the 1920 census provides the year of naturalization, but these dates, too, are often incorrect.

2. *Indexes to Canadian Border Entries* include:

    M1461 Soundex index to Canadian boarder entries through the St. Albans, VT district 1895–1924. 400 rolls.

    M1462 Alphabetical index to Canadian Border entries through small ports in Vermont 1895-1924. 6 rolls (includes Norton & Island Point, Beecher Falls, Highgate Springs, Swanton, Alburg & Richford, St. Albans & Canaan).

    M1463 Soundex index to entries into St. Albans from Canadian Pacific and Atlantic ports, 1924–52. 98 rolls.

    M1464 Manifests of passengers arriving at St. Albans, Vermont through Canadian Pacific and Atlantic ports 1895–1954. 640 rolls.

    M1465 Manifest of passengers arriving at St. Albans, VT through Canadian Pacific ports 1929-49. 25 rolls.

    M1478 Card manifests (alphabetical) of individuals entering through the Port of Detroit, MI 1906–54. 117 rolls.

    M1479 Passenger and alien crew lists of vessels arriving at the Port of Detroit 1946–57. 23 rolls.

3. *Indexes for Galveston, TX* include:

    M1357 Index to passenger lists of vessels arriving at Galveston, TX 1896–1906. 3 rolls.

    M1358 Index to passenger lists of vessels arriving at Galveston and the subports of Houston and Brownsville 1906–51. 7 rolls.

M1359 Passenger lists of vessels arriving at Galveston 1896–1951. 36 rolls.

4. *Philadelphia records* include:

    M1500 Records of the Special Board of Inquiry, Dist. 4 (Philadelphia), Immigration and Naturalization Service 1893–1909. 18 rolls.

5. "Immigrant and Passenger Arrivals: A Select Catalog of National Archives Microfilm Publications" may be consulted online at WWW.JEWISHGEN.ORG/INFOFILES/FAQ.HTML#NA, click on Passenger Lists, click on the port of interest to you.

6. For example, M1674 Index (Soundex) to Naturalization Petitions Filed in Federal, State and Local Courts in New York, Including New York, Kings, Queens, and Richmond Counties, 1792–1906.

7. M1848 contents: Index, 1850-52, rolls 1–28, created by NARA staff many years ago, which duplicates the information in M1371, rolls 2-4; Index, 1860–80, rolls 28–29, created by NARA staff many years ago, partially duplicates the information in M1371, rolls 3–4, and researchers should use M1371, rolls 3–4, instead of this; Index, 1881, roll 29, created by NARA staff many years ago, which duplicates the information on M1371, roll l5; Index, 1906–23, rolls 30–52; and Index to Passport Extensions, 1917–20, rolls 53–57.

8. The series "Protection of Interests of U.S. Citizens" consists of correspondence from American citizens or their representatives who appealed to the U.S. Department of State for help in tracing relatives or sending food, money and other assistance to family members in Europe.

9. The Philadelphia branch of the Archives has created two finding aides for the records of the Philadelphia Russian Consulate, rolls 3–36 of M1486: a two-page "instructions to use Russian Consular Records," and an 11-page detailed roll listing. Anyone using the *Index* will get a reference to a Consulate—Box Number—Folder/Volume Number—and page number. He must then use the conversion charts to find the correct roll, then wind through that roll to find the correct box number, folder number and page number. The problem is that unless you know ahead of time how many boxes are on each roll, and how many folders are in each box, it is difficult to know where you are on the film. With the 11-page list prepared in Philadelphia, the search is much easier. No lists exist for the other rolls.

U.S. Holocaust Memorial Museum

by Sharlene Kranz

The Holocaust Memorial Museum, opened in 1993, is America's national institution for the documentation, study and interpretation of Holocaust history and serves as this country's memorial to the millions of people murdered during the Holocaust. In addition to the permanent and temporary exhibits, the Museum has seven departments of interest to genealogists: Library, Archives, Registry of Jewish Holocaust Survivors, Photo Archives, Oral History Department, Film and Video Department, and Center for Advanced Holocaust Studies.

Entrance to the Museum is from either the 14th Street or 15th Street side; to reach the library take the elevator inside the 14th Street door to the fifth floor. No admission ticket is required to use the library or archives. When you reach the fifth floor you will be required to check in at the guard's desk and to leave briefcases, purses, etc. in nearby lockers. Bring a quarter for the locker.

The Museum is a no-smoking building. Do not bring children to the library/archives; facilities are crowded and a research atmosphere prevails. A kosher cafe is open 9 a.m.– 4:30 p.m.; it is located on the 15th Street entrance plaza in an Annex building.

Please remember that, while institute staff will attempt to help you, their primary responsibilities do not relate to genealogy. Also, do not expect research materials that predate or postdate the Holocaust.

Library

The Library is accumulating one of the world's most important collections of printed and other material on the Holocaust. At present, the collection numbers more than 44,000 books, films and video materials, as well as an extensive collection of periodicals. Its focus is on the years 1933–45. It is an open-shelf library and is organized according to the Library of Congress system. Using this system, which also can be accessed online on the muse-um's website, visitors may browse among the collection's holdings. It is not a lending library. A copy machine is available for public use.

The computerized reference system, which combines the holdings of the Library, Archives, and Oral History Department, is far more detailed and cross-indexed than those of most other institutions. For example, under the heading "Dachau" there are 15 subheadings (compared to six in the Library of Congress) and 119 holdings are listed. For the genealogist looking for information relating to specific persons, the key notation to be used is "name lists." Thus, the material under Dachau can be keyed in under Dachau-Name Lists, eliminating all the general material on Dachau and focusing on lists of people. The institute follows the Library of Congress' approach to geographical locations, i.e., current name and nationality apply. Thus, 1939 material on Breslau, Ger-

many, is located under Wroc»aw, Poland, even though the material predated the change in borders and names; material relating to Galicia might be listed under Ukraine.

While many valuable sources of information are located in the library stacks, the most important reference books containing lists of Holocaust victims and survivors are located in one section of the reading room. It is impossible to list all the books located there, but a few books, which contain extensive name lists, are mentioned here. There are also over 600 *yizkor* (remembrance) books.

Anthology of Armed Jewish Resistance. 4 volumes with index of names and places.

Auschwitz Chronicle. Day by day account of events. Useful in conjunction with transport lists.

Belzec, Sobibor, Treblinka. Few names but useful to identify transports.

Counted Remnants. 1946 list of 74,000 Budapest survivors.

Cracow Ghetto Registration Forms. 38 volumes containing individual forms.

Gedenkbuch. List of 128,000 West German and Berlin Jews who perished in the Holocaust. There are also memorial books for many individual German cities and towns.

Il Libro della Memoria. List of Jews deported from Italy.

In Memoriam. List of Jews deported from the Netherlands.

Jewish Community of Salonika. Community list in 1943.

La Memorial de la Deportation des Juifs de France. List of Jews deported from France.

Lithuanian Jewish Communities. Includes about 6,000 names.

Lodz Names. 10-volume list of Jews held in Lodz ghetto 1940–44.

Memorial de la Deportation des Juifs de Belgique. List of Jews deported from Belgium.

Names of the Deported Jews from Hajdu County. List of Hungarian Jews.

Sharit ha-Platah. List of 55,000 survivors from all over Europe, mostly located in displaced persons camps.

Sterbebhcher von Auschwitz. List of 80,000 persons who died in Auschwitz.

Terezinska Pametni Kniha. List of Bohemia/Moravia Jews sent to Theresienstadt.

Totenbuch Theresienstadt. List of Austrian Jews deported to Theresienstadt.

Vilnius Ghetto. List of Jews in Vilna ghetto.

Archives

The Library and Archives share a computerized catalog system. There are, however, some fundamental differences, the most obvious of which is the open stack library system and

the need to request material from the Archives. Persons using the archives must obtain a researcher's card. This is quite easy and only requires presenting a photo ID and familiarizing oneself with archive rules. The archives are closed on weekends and holidays, but material from the archives will be held in the library on such days if it has been requested on the previous Friday or other open day.

The archives contain primary documents, largely on film, on all aspects of the Holocaust. Film reading machines are available. The bulk of archive holdings relate to Eastern Europe and the former Soviet Union as well as extensive records from concentration camps. Although a major effort has been made to break down and identify the contents of these collections, and much of the material relates to individuals, it is not indexed in that way. For example, from the hundreds of filmed collections, take "Captured German Records" collection (1996 A0342), 189 reels of film with about 189,000 pages of material, which contains information on millions of individuals in concentration camps such as Dachau, Buchenwald and Mauthausen. The finding aid for this collection only identifies the nature of the documents appearing on each reel and does not list the names which appear in these documents. Similarly, the 34-reel collection of material from the Lwow archives (RG 1995 A1086) lists documents and not names. This is also true of the 305-reel collection of Stutthof material (RG 04.058M) and the even larger collection of material acquired from the Moscow Osobyi archives (RG 11.001M).

In some cases, the filmed material in itself consists of name lists, e.g. an alphabetical list of over 200,000 Polish survivors prepared by the Polish Jewish community (RG 15.057M), and this material is easy to search. However, in most cases the researcher must be patient and examine large amounts of material in an effort to locate individual names. Requests for copies of material may be made during visits or by mail; however, requestors should be aware that the archivists do not have the time to undertake extensive searches of filmed material.

USHMM staff is constantly filming new material for the archives, and there is often a backlog in cataloging this material. Accordingly, while a web-based search of holdings is a useful first step, visitors to the USHMM should always consult with an archivist to determine whether additional material is also available. For example, a major collection of Hungarian files from 1944 and a collection of Warsaw ghetto material are currently in the process of being catalogued.

Registry of Jewish Holocaust Survivors

The Registry of Jewish Holocaust Survivors was developed by the American Gathering of Jewish Holocaust Survivors located in New York City and relocated to the Museum in 1993. The Registry continues to register survivors and currently has the names of about 160,000 survivors and their families in its computerized database. While this database is not available on the web, a published form of this information is issued every few years, and this is available at research institutes and libraries around the world. A list of the institutions where this is available is carried on USHMM's website. By now, however, its name is somewhat of a misnomer, since its principal focus has become the collection of information on and computerization of names of Holocaust victims. It, therefore, differs from the library and archives since its concentration is on the fate of individuals.

While some of the Registry's administration functions are carried out on the museum's fifth floor, its public access facilities are located on the second floor, immediately to the right when one goes up the long stairs from the lobby. This public area is staffed at all times when the museum is open.

Far more important than its listing of survivors, moreover, is the project to include in a single database all the names of Holocaust victims and survivors. This massive effort differs from Yad Vashem's Hall of Names, which is based on voluntary personal submissions, in that the name lists are all drawn from Holocaust records. While this project is still in its beginning stages, and is not publicly available outside the USHMM, it has grown to over one million names and this number steadily increases. Much of these name lists come from other institutions, such as concentration camp memorials/museums and survivor groups, and there is continuing cooperation with institutions around the world. In a parallel effort, the Registry has developed a "list of lists", i.e. a list of sources of information, organized by locality, where names of Holocaust victims and survivors can be found. This permits the Registry to locate names in response to the thousands of requests for information received every year (see below).

Particular interest at present is focused on material acquired from Moscow, the files of the Extraordinary State Commission. This unique Russian-language collection consists of material identifying about one million persons, Jews and non-Jews, who were Holocaust victims in all areas of the former Soviet Union occupied by Germany. Up to now, Russian reading volunteers have screened this material in answering inquiries, but this is time consuming and, since the material is organized by town, impossible unless one knows where a person resided in 1941–44. Recently, the Registry has begun to computerize all the names which appear in this massive collection and to transcribe the names from Cyrillic into Latin letters. This project will take several years to complete, but should open an entire new area of information to genealogists.

Since very little of the USHMM's holdings are available

on the web, and it is difficult for many interested persons to make a personal visit there, the museum, on its web site, has constructed an information request form on which you can request that a search be made. Go to WWW.USHMM.ORG, then Research, the Survivors Registry and then Research Request Form. Limit such requests to Holocaust related events, e.g. deportations, concentration camps, survivors, and provide as much information as you can, e.g. do not ask for all Polish Goldbergs, but rather Jakob Goldberg born in 1915 in Warsaw.

Photo Archive

The Photo Archive is a repository for still, historical photographs that have been collected and copied from individuals and archives around the world. It is organized by topic and covers the period from the end of World War I to the close of the displaced persons camps. Interwar Jewish life is a major focus of the collection, as well as the events of the Nazi period and its aftermath. The genealogist seeking to understand pre-war Jewish community life, the Jewish refugee experience, life under Nazi domination, and the immediate post-war experience, will find a wealth of visual material.

While the chances of finding photos of one's immediate family are slight overall, certain sections of the collection have lent themselves to many such matches. This is especially true of the portions of the collection dealing with pre-war Jewish life in Bedzin, Poland; the SS St. Louis refugee ship; the Kovno ghetto; Jewish children's homes in France; and DP camps in Germany. Donated family collections are generally documented with extensive biographical summaries, and all

notable figures are key-worded for easy retrieval. Over 5,000 copyright free images from the Photo Archives are available online at WWW.USHMM.ORG/RESEARCH/COLLECTIONS. The Photo Archive is not open on weekends or holidays.

Oral History Department

The Oral History Department collects and distributes video and audio taped testimonies relating to the Holocaust. At present, it has 3,000 interviews in various languages, some of them produced by the USHMM and others obtained from different Holocaust centers. An alphabetical list of the persons who were interviewed can be consulted in the Archives. While the chances of finding a recording relating to one's own family are small, the material is useful to understand the environment in which Jewish families lived and died.

Film and Video Department

This office collects material in audiovisual form relating to the Holocaust and World War II. Categories include prewar Jewish and shtetl life, the rise of Nazism, ghettos, concentration camps, etc. This Department is located in the USHMM annex adjacent to the main building and is only open weekdays.

Center for Advanced Holocaust Studies

While it is far larger than the Departments described above, the Center primarily focuses on academic work relating to the Holocaust. It supports and assists researchers preparing books, monographs and articles on specific subjects, and is unlikely to be of direct interest to genealogists unless, by chance, a resident researcher is working on a subject of direct interest to you. This Department also publishes a journal, Holocaust and Genocide Studies and sponsors lectures and other public events.

Address

United States Holocaust Memorial Museum
100 Raoul Wallenberg Place, SW
Washington, DC 20024
Hours: 10 a.m.–5 p.m. seven days a week except Yom Kippur and Christmas
Telephone: (202) 488-0400 Museum
(202) 479-9717 Library
(202) 488-6113 Archives
(202) 488-6130 Survivors Registry
Museum: WWW.USHMM.GOV
Library: WWW.USHMM.GOV/RESEARCH/LIBRARY/

YIVO Institute for Jewish Research

by Fruma Mohrer

The YIVO Institute for Jewish Research in New York is one of the world's most important research centers for genealogists of East European descent. The collections of the YIVO library and of the YIVO archives provide a wealth of information that both the novice and the experienced genealogist will find significant. YIVO's primary value for genealogists resides in its holdings in the following categories:

- Geographical and historical source materials on Jewish life in Europe, with emphasis on Eastern Europe
- Biographical materials on Jews around the world
- Materials on the Holocaust, including information on victims and survivors of the Holocaust
- Source materials on American Jewish life, with emphasis on the period of major immigration
- Family histories, family papers and genealogy collections

Because of the vast scope of the YIVO library and archives which hold 350,000 volumes and approximately 22 million documents, photographs, films, art works and sound recordings, only selected collections are mentioned below. For additional information refer to the YIVO Library Online Catalog at WWW.YIVO.ORG. The Center for Jewish History Online Public Access Catalog, which will include YIVO holdings, will be posted on the Web by summer of 2003 and will be available at WWW.CJH.ORG. The reader is also referred to the *Guide to the YIVO Archives;* to the *Guide to YIVO's Landsmanshaftn Archive* (1986); and "People of a Thousand Towns," YIVO's online photo collection of Eastern Europe.

Geographical and Historical Source Materials On Jewish Life in Europe

YIVO Library. The YIVO library's publications on the geographical background of Eastern European Jews, include rare foreign-language almanacs, gazetteers, atlases, maps, lexicons and encyclopedias. These include, to mention a few examples, the *Yevrayskaya Entsiklopedia* (Russian-Jewish encyclopedia), the *Słownik Geograficzny Krókestwa* (Geographical dictionary of the Kingdom of Poland) and the *Skorowiez Miejscowości Rzeczpospolitej Polskiej* (List of localities of the Republic of Poland). Published in Warsaw in 1938, *Skorowiez* includes Polish administrative divisions, the seat of the courts, railroad stations and other items. YIVO also holds more than 600 *yizkor* (Memorial) books, written primarily in Hebrew and in Yiddish published by survivors from towns and cities throughout Poland, Ukraine, Belarus and other East European countries, as well as countries in Central and Western Europe. The *yizkor* books provide important historical information about these localities. These published geographical resources in Hebrew, Polish, Russian, Yiddish, Lithuanian and German provide authoritative and historically accurate data on villages, hamlets, towns and cities.

Genealogists beginning their research path will discover that determining the names of their ancestral towns, which may appear to be a straightforward process to a lay person, is often a complicated matter. Numerous visitors to YIVO arrive with the name of their ancestral town as "Guberniya," a name quoted affectionately and reminiscently by many genealogists' favorite great aunt. "Guberniya," as Jewish genealogists soon learn, simply means "province," a term used in the czarist period that by no means refers to any specific cartographic coordinates.

Other visitors to YIVO believe they have their ancestral town well identified, but do not realize that the same town name is found in dozens of places on Polish and Russian maps. Just as the American map has many towns by the name of Maple Grove or Smithtown, so too the territories of Belarus, Poland, Russia, and Ukraine are full of hamlets, villages and towns that bear similar names. A well-known example is Dı browa. Sixteen different Dı browas are listed in *Where Once We Walked* by Gary Mokotoff and Sallyann Amdur Sack. How to figure out in which Dı browa one's ancestors resided is a challenge of no small proportions.

YIVO's rich resources on the cartography and history of these thousands of places provide the tools necessary for genealogists to determine the actual identity of their towns, as they move back and forth among family anecdotes, family interviews and official gazetteers.

Once towns and cities are identified, the visitor to YIVO is equipped with one of the essential clues for successful family research. Without this information the researcher cannot continue his or her search for the appropriate *landsmanshaftn* records, *yizkor* books, photograph collections or Holocaust-related records.

YIVO Archives. Doing genealogical research in the YIVO archives reveals that certain geographical areas are more richly reflected in the collections than others. The scope of this discussion does not permit a complete listing of these areas. Instead, the general characteristics of the YIVO archives collections are described with examples.

While the more than 600 *yizkor* books in the YIVO library span the entire range of central and Galician Poland and include eastern Poland and Lithuania, the YIVO archives collections significant for genealogical research are limited to certain cities and certain geographical ranges. The largest group of genealogically rich materials pertains to the Vilna region and to the territory of pre-war independent Lithuania. The Records of the Vilna Kehilla and the Records of Lithuanian Jewish Communities, in which more than 120 communities are reflected, are two of this collection type. The pogrom files

Family members celebrate the wedding of Jean Yudenfreund to Hymen (Max) Schure, New York City, circa 1930. Courtesy of the YIVO Institute for Jewish Research photo archives. Donor: Aviva Weintraub.

in the Tcherikower Archives, gathered by YIVO founder and historian Elias Tcherikower, include hundreds of lists of victims compiled on the spot at the initiative of Jewish relief organizations. These files constitute the world's most comprehensive original documentation on the pogroms of 1918–20. The Records of the Vaad Hayeshivot (1924–36), an organization founded in Vilna that functioned as a central office for all the famous *yeshivot* of higher learning in eastern Poland, contain lists of Jewish residents of more than 450 communities in the five eastern provinces (Bialystok, Nowogrodek, Polesie, Vilna and Volhynia) of interwar Poland.

Other geographical areas represented in the YIVO archives include, for example, the Records of the Minsk Jewish Community Council; and fragmentary 16th- through 19th-century records of a number of Jewish communities contained in the Papers of Simon Dubnow, the first modern Jewish historian to issue an appeal for the preservation of Russian-Jewish historical documents. Two collections on Germany (Record Groups 31 and 116) contain a rich range of 17th- through 20th-century German-Jewish communal records. The Records of Krotoszyn, Ostrowo and Briesen are three collections of Jewish communities that first belonged to the

Prussian or German Empire and later became part of Poland.

The YIVO Archives Photo Collection, entitled "People of a Thousand Towns," searchable by name of town, is available on the Internet at WWW.YIVO.ORG. Poland, Lithuania, Latvia, Russia, Czechoslovakia and Romania are the primary countries reflected in this photo collection, frequently used by genealogists.

Biographical Sources on Jews Around the World

YIVO Library. The YIVO library holds multilingual biographical sources on Jewish communal and political leaders, rabbinical figures, and cultural and literary personalities. Most valuable for those genealogists whose families distinguished themselves in the ancestral Jewish community or in the rabbinical or cultural world, readers will not be surprised to learn that many researchers have relatives who were active in at least one of these fields.

Biographical sources include the *Polski Słownik Biograficzny*, which contains information on Jews in Poland; the *Yevrayskaya Entsiklopedia* (mentioned above), which has information on Russian Jews in the czarist period; the *Lexi-*

con of *Modern Yiddish Literature*; Zilbercweig's *Lexicon of the Yiddish Theater*, which has hundreds of biographies of theater personalities unavailable anywhere else; biographies of rabbis, such as *Meorei Galicia*, by Meir Wunder; lexicons and encyclopedias on the history of Zionism; the Hebrew-language encyclopedia of early Jewish settlers in Palestine, edited by David Tidhar; *Who's Who in American Biography*; and *Who's Who in Canadian Biography;* and the *Magyar Zsido Lexikon*, the Hungarian-Jewish lexicon that contains entries about well-known Hungarian Jews.

YIVO Archives. The YIVO archives holds several collections that include information about Jewish personalities active in the cultural, artistic, political, spiritual and literary fields of endeavor. A few will be mentioned here. The records of the Jewish Actors Union in Warsaw, an interwar professional association, contains files of actors, playwrights, producers and directors, most of whom perished in the Holocaust. Genealogists whose relatives were active in the Yiddish theater may find references and information even on little-known Polish-Jewish actors.

The Bund Archives, a vast collection of more than 700 linear feet representing the archives of the Jewish Labor Bund, which was transferred to YIVO in 1992, contains biographical files, both European and American, of political figures of the early to mid-20th century who were affiliated with the socialist, anarchist and other political movements. The YIVO Photo and Film Archive holds photographs of Jewish personalities. The Collection of Art and Artifacts has a Biographical Series with information about Jewish artists. The records of the *Vaad Hayeshivot* (mentioned above) contain correspondence of well-known *roshei yeshivah* (heads of yeshivas) in Eastern Poland; the Papers of Samuel Tiktin contain biographical files, collected in the mid-1940s, of rabbinical figures worldwide. The records of Ezras Torah, an American institution devoted to assisting Jewish communities in Europe, contain original correspondence, primarily from the 1920s, from rabbis in Jewish communities throughout Eastern Europe. Finally, several hundred collections in the YIVO archives are papers of Yiddish writers. Their correspondence files cover the entire Yiddish literary community.

Holocaust Sources

YIVO library. The library's genealogical sources on the Holocaust include a large part of the English, Yiddish, Hebrew, Polish and French language published historiography on this subject. The several hundred *yizkor* books mentioned earlier in this article, are a significant source on the history of the destruction of the Jewish communities of Europe. Written and edited by the survivors themselves, these works include lists of victims as well as information on daily life in the ghettos, roundups, deportations, executions, and resistance activities. In addition to the *yizkor* books, the multivolume *Pinkas Hakehillot* in the original Hebrew, whose newest volumes are acquired regularly by YIVO, is the most noteworthy. Yad Vashem's more recent *Encyclopedia of Jewish Life* provides a much needed research tool for English language readers but the full text of the original Hebrew language *Pinkas Hakehillot* continues to be the single most useful lexical work on the

Jewish communities eradicated in the Holocaust. Also of interest to genealogists are the newspapers of the Jewish Displaced Persons Camps, available on microfilm, printed for the most part in romanized Yiddish. Serge Klarsfeld's *Le Mémorial de la Déportation des Juifs de France* contains lists of transports of Jews to concentration camps. Zosa Szajkowski's *Analytical Franco-Jewish Gazetteer, 1939–1945*, a lengthy and detailed gazetteer of place names, concentration camps and detention camps in France, is organized by name of *département*. The *Gazetteer* informs the reader of all archival collections throughout the world that hold original documents on the Holocaust in France. The Register of Jewish Survivors in Poland, published in 1945, contains numerous lists of survivors liberated in concentration camps. Similar lists exist for Latvia, Yugoslavia, Italy and other countries. These survivors lists are used regularly by genealogists searching for family members who might have survived the Holocaust.

YIVO Archives. The YIVO archives genealogical sources of the Holocaust period are not as geographically wide ranging as those of the YIVO library. In general, the Holocaust collections in the archives are of historical rather than genealogical significance. Many documents, however, contain names of individuals, although no cumulative index of names exists at this time. Included in this category is the Zonabend Collection, which contains records of the Lodz ghetto *Judenrat* (Jewish governing body appointed by Nazis), and which has, among other things, an original album of about 15,000 signatures of school children in the Lodz ghetto, who sent their new year's wishes to Rumkowski, the Eldest of the Ghetto; eyewitness accounts of several thousand survivors; the Sutzkever-Kaczerginski Collection, which contains records of the Vilna Ghetto Administration and includes original ghetto diaries—files on daily health, educational, cultural, sports and other activities; fragments of the Emanuel Ringleblum Oneg Shabbat Archive known at YIVO as the Hersh Wasser Collection and which has original eyewitness accounts collected by the Underground Archive. The Bund Archives holds two original documents from Auschwitz with lists of names: a logbook dated 1944 with handwritten lists of prisoners, many of them non-Jewish, a few of them Greek Jews; and a small group of Auschwitz prisoner registration sheets of Greek Jews. The Records of the Salonika Jewish Community (RG 207) include communal metrical books for Greek Jews of the 1930s, most of whom were murdered in the Holocaust. The HIAS Paris and Lisbon office records, as well as the AJDC Lisbon records, contain numerous case files of French and other European Jewish refugees as well as passenger lists of refugees traveling from Europe to countries offering safe haven during the war. The HIAS Holocaust microfilms provide information on more than 45,000 survivors of the Holocaust who were processed by HIAS.

Related collections, such as the National Refugee Service Records and the German Jewish Children's Aid Collection, are among the many immigration collections in the YIVO Archives with extensive case files of, and information about, German and Austrian and other refugees from Nazi persecution. The records of the *Union Générale des Israélites de France* in

Paris contain original copies of the Census of Jews of 1941 decreed in conjunction with a one billion franc indemnity levied upon the Jewish population. The same collection also contains lists of deportees and names of children living in Jewish children's shelters in Paris. None of these names are indexed. The Shanghai Ghetto Collection, gathered by YIVO in the late 1940s as preparation for an exhibition, contains original documents from Shanghai and includes fragmentary lists of names. The Collections of Displaced Persons Camps in Austria, Germany and Italy contain fragmentary lists of survivors.

Jewish Life in the United States With Focus on Immigration

YIVO Library. The YIVO library's genealogical materials on the immigration period include a book listing Jewish *landsmanshaftn* active in 1938, published with the assistance of the WPA, titled *Jewish Landsmanshaftn of New York*. *Landsmanshaftn* are mutual aid societies founded by American Jewish immigrants from the same hometown in Europe. A second book, called *Yidishe famliyes un familye krayzn* (Jewish families and family circles) lists family circles. In addition, the library has a variety of anniversary journals published by *landsmanshaftn*. The YIVO Bibliography of *American and Canadian Jewish Memoirs and Autobiographies* edited by Ezekiel Lifschutz is a resource on memoirs by Jewish immigrants.

YIVO Archives. The YIVO archives is noted for its rich and wide ranging collection of *landsmanshaftn* records. More than 1,000 *landsmanshaftn* are represented in the YIVO archives, either as separate collections or as part of the miscellaneous Landsmanshaftn Collection (RG 123). The HIAS archive at YIVO, a vast collection numbering hundreds of linear feet, includes the HIAS arrival records as well as records of HIAS branches worldwide. Of these, the Ellis Island records, 1905–23, contain hardship and deportation cases of those prospective immigrants whose health or other status prevented them from entering the United States.

Family Histories, Family Papers and Genealogy Collections

YIVO Library. In addition, genealogical sources in the YIVO library can be accessed via keyword searches such as "genealogy," "family history," "tombstones," "Jewish history, Poland," "Hasidism," etc. For example, doing a keyword search for the subject heading "tombstones" yields *Bibliography of Jewish Cemeteries,* by Kaufman Kohler, 1916; *Some References to Early Jewish Cemeteries in New York City; Der alte Judenfriedhof in Prag; The Old Cemetery in Charleston; Old and New Cemeteries in Odessa, 1888; Matsevot kvarot harabanim v'anshei shem,* by M. Piner. Similarly, the subject heading "Family History" yields a number of family histories that otherwise might be overlooked. These include *Zur Geschichte der Familie Yomtob Bondi (1921)* and *Stammbaum Bletter der Familie Grafenberg (1916),* as well many other family histories

YIVO Archives. The YIVO archives holds some collections of family papers. The several collections of family papers are most easily accessible by consulting the subject heading FAMILY SOCIETIES in the Index to the *Guide to the YIVO Archives* and also by searching for the name of the family in the Index to the *Guide to YIVO's Landsmanshaftn Archive*. In addition, the YIVO archives holds the Collection on Genealogy and Family History (RG 126), which has dozens of small family collections, accessible by name of family and consisting of passports, family trees, photographs and other items. A much smaller collection entitled Collection of Genealogy and Family History (Vilna Archives) (RG 44) was collected in Europe before World War II. The Papers of William McCagg contain extensive files and index cards pertaining to this historian's research on the genealogy of ennobled Hungarian and Hapsburg Jews. The Records of the *Personenstandarchiv Koblenz* (RG 242) consist of photostatic copies of original documents made in 1950–51 by a YIVO representative in Germany. Included are copies of birth, marriage, death and cemetery records and community registers from a wide range of communities in Germany and places formerly in Poland.

Online Electronic Resources at YIVO

In addition to information about YIVO holdings available on the YIVO website at WWW.YIVO.ORG, the Center for Jewish History (CJH) Online Public Access Catalog (OPAC) will reside on the CJH website at WWW.CJH.ORG. The OPAC, to be posted on the Internet by summer of 2003, will provide access to information about the collections of all Center partners, including the YIVO library and archives collections

YIVO Public Service Information

Address: YIVO Institute for Jewish Research, Center for Jewish History, 15 West 16th Street, New York, NY 10011; website: WWW.YIVO.ORG. The YIVO website contains public services telephones and e-mail addresses of librarians and archivists.

Reproduction Services: The YIVO library and archives provide reproduction services on the premises of the Center for Jewish History. Permission to produce photocopies is granted on a case-by-case basis, depending on the condition or legal status of the original publications or documents. A price list is published on the YIVO website.

Availability. YIVO library and archival collections are available in the Center for Jewish History Reading Room, Monday-Thursday, 9:30 am–5:00 pm, with the exception of Jewish and civil holidays. The library is open to the public without appointment. The archives is open to qualified researchers by appointment with an archivist. This is to ensure that the collection to be consulted is not at the Preservation Départment or being used by another researcher. Photo and film collections are available for consultation in the YIVO Photo and Film Archives. An appointment should be made with the Photo and Film Archivist.

Jewish Museums and Historical Societies

by Dianne Weiner Feldman

Many Jewish historical societies and museums hold materials of great value for family research. These materials may include *mohel* (ritual circumciser) books, midwife records, *yizkor* (memorial) books, cemetery records, genealogies, ethnic newspapers, passenger lists and photographs. Records of marriages, confirmations, synagogues and *landsmanshaftn* (societies of immigrants from the same locality) sometimes are housed in a Jewish historical society. Some Jewish museums, in addition to storing and displaying objects, also may function as historical societies, collecting and preserving archival material useful for genealogical research.

Materials held in the collections of historical societies include original and secondary sources on life in America, as well as information on life abroad. Immigrant ancestors may have lived on more than one continent; when they immigrated to America (or elsewhere), they brought items from abroad with them. For example, the Jewish Museum of Maryland* has items in its collections from many parts of the world, because Jewish residents of Maryland came from many parts of the globe. You might find a foreign birth certificate, a passport, or a *ketubah* (marriage contract) brought to America from abroad and subsequently deposited in an American Jewish museum or local historical society.

The names and addresses of Jewish historical societies and museums can be obtained in a number of ways. The American Jewish Historical Society* compiles and maintains a list of community level and national Jewish historical societies in the U.S. and abroad. The list is available on the web at WWW.AJHS.ORG/ACADEMIC/OTHER.CFM.

The National Foundation for Jewish Culture* has a directory of Jewish museums, WWW.JEWISHCULTURE.ORG/MUSEUMS that includes American Jewish museums and links to Jewish museums worldwide.

The Myer and Rosaline Feinstein Center for American Jewish History of Temple University has a directory of American Jewish historical repositories that can be reached at WWW.TEMPLE.EDU/FEINSTEINCTR.

Published guides to historical societies and museums are available for sale and can be found in the reference section of libraries. One such guide is *The Official Museum Directory*. Addresses for historical societies can also be found in published guides to genealogy.

Non-Jewish Sources

Jewish ancestors were citizens of the larger community in which they lived, and information about them need not be confined to an agency that specializes in Jewish history. State archives, state historical societies, city archives, county and town historical societies and libraries with local history collections should be searched for information of genealogical value.

State archives and historical societies typically have information on land records, wills, city directories, census records, local newspapers, reference books, laws, vital records, corporate charters, ships passenger records, photographs, personal papers of prominent individuals and organizations.

Historical societies may be national, regional, state, county, local or municipal. Several books list and describe the names and locations of historical societies; many can be located via the Internet. The *Directory of Historical Agencies in North America* may be found in the reference section in libraries along with other directories of historical societies. The *National Union Catalog of Manuscript Collections* is a cataloging program operated by the U.S. LIBRARY OF CONGRESS with links to the resources of archives and manuscript repositories other than the Library of Congress. State and municipal governments can refer researchers to their respective archives; public historical societies may know of private collections and museums, and large historical societies can tell you of small societies. Telephone directories under headings such as "historical places," "societies," or "museums" are another source of names and addresses of repositories.

Recommendation for All Types of Repositories

Some records are unique to one historical society, but there may also be some duplication. Information available from Jewish and non-Jewish organizations and between statewide and local historical organizations may overlap. Institutions often can supply a description of their collections that assist in directing your research.

The collections of an institution are not static; they are usually growing larger and evolving. In addition to acquiring new material that might be useful, institutions also develop better finding aids for existing material; more foreign-language documents are translated. After a lapse of time, re-check a repository to see if new items of interest have been acquired or become available for use.

A wide range of policies and of days and hours of operation exist among organizations. Some organizations may have a research service; others do not. Some locales charge a fee for use of the facility. Hours of operation and holiday closures of museums and historical societies vary greatly. In addition to national and local government holidays, Jewish institutions may be closed on Jewish holidays. Always check directly with the institution to determine when the building is open to the public for research and whether an appointment is needed.

Addresses

American Association of Museums, 1575 Eye Street, NW, Suite 400, Washington DC 20005-4002

American Association for State and Local History, 1717 Church Street, Nashville, TN 37203-2991; website: WWW.AASLH.ORG

American Jewish Historical Society, 15 West 16th Street, New York, NY 10011 and 160 Herrick Road, Newton Centre, MA 02459

Museum of Jewish Heritage, New York

Jewish Museum of Maryland, 15 Lloyd St., Baltimore, MD 21202; website: WWW.JHSM.ORG

Myer and Rosaline Feinstein Center for American Jewish History of Temple University, 1515 Market St., Suite 215, Philadelphia, PA 19102

National Foundation for Jewish Culture, 330 Seventh Avenue, 21st floor, New York, NY 10001

National Union Catalog of Manuscript Collections (NUCMC), WWW.LOC.GOV/COLL/NUCMC/

Bibliography

Directory of Historical Agencies in North America. Nashville, Tenn.: American Association for State and Local History.

Official Museum Directory. Washington: National Register Publishing and American Association of Museums.

New York City Research

by Eileen Polakoff

Why does the *Guide* have a separate chapter for New York City? The answer is that so many Jews settled there between the 1850s and the early 20th century that today New York has the world's largest Jewish population. Almost every Jewish genealogist has or did have relatives who lived in New York within the past 150 years.

New York City, as we know it today, was incorporated in 1898. Before that, New York City meant Manhattan and part of the Bronx. Brooklyn, Queens, Staten Island and the remainder of the Bronx were all separate entities until they joined Manhattan and part of the Bronx to become a larger New York City. These are the five boroughs of New York City. The equivalent counties (and their significance) are discussed in the section below on Jurisdiction of Records.

It is important to know this history, because the creation of records often is based upon jurisdictions. Thus, death records exist for Manhattan from 1866 to the present; for the other boroughs, death records from 1866 onward are variable. Some additional vital records also exist for various sections of what is today New York City from about 1812, but they are incomplete.

This chapter focuses primarily on records created since the beginning of the large wave of immigration to New York in the 1880s.

Immigration to New York City

Since 1829, New York has been the largest city in the United States, home of the port where the majority of immigrants to America disembarked between 1880 and 1925. Experts variously estimate that between 62 and 80 percent of all immigrants to the United States in those years entered via the Port of New York. Most genealogists know about Ellis Island; fewer are aware that before Ellis Island opened on January 1, 1892, immigrants landed on the lower part of Manhattan at a place called Castle Garden.[1] Two million immigrants arrived at Castle Garden in the decade between 1880 and 1890. Sixteen million immigrants came to Ellis Island between 1892 and 1923; an additional number of would-be immigrants, probably fewer than 500,000, were returned to Europe. Approximately two-thirds of the immigrants who landed in New York migrated to other places, which means that more than five million immigrants remained in New York City.

Beyond the basic sources of city directories, censuses, vital records, naturalization and court records, it is important to understand the jurisdictional aspects of research in New York City and to know the migratory patterns within the city.

Migration Patterns Within New York

At the beginning of the 20th century, the Lower East Side of Manhattan was the place where thousands of new immigrants first settled, usually in tenement buildings. The term *tenement* referred to any multiple dwelling, but on the Lower East Side, the typical tenement building had six floors. The first and second floors usually housed businesses with tiny living spaces in the back; the remaining four floors each had four tiny three-room apartments. Census records show that immigrants tended to cluster with other immigrants from the same country (e.g., Romanian Jews on one block; Russian Jews on another).

Wherever they lived, as the immigrants prospered they sought to move out of their crowded neighborhoods. Among the patterns of migration within the City of New York are the following:

- When the Williamsburg Bridge was completed in 1903 connecting the Lower East Side section of Manhattan to the Williamsburg section of Brooklyn, many residents of the Lower East Side moved to Brooklyn.
- As larger apartment houses were built in upper Manhattan in the second and third decades of the 20th century, immigrants took the subway north to Harlem or the Bronx. As more immigrants moved to such neighborhoods as Harlem, some families that now considered themselves Americanized moved across town to the Upper West Side.
- From about 1910 to 1930, immigrants who had moved to Williamsburg in Brooklyn moved on to better neighborhoods in Brooklyn. Later they moved to newly developing neighborhoods in Queens, or, if they had really made money, they moved back into fashionable areas of Manhattan.
- After World War II, many Jewish families moved to the suburbs—to various areas in New Jersey, Long Island beyond Brooklyn and Queens (Nassau County), or north of the city to Westchester County.

From the turn of the 20th century to post-World War II, it was not uncommon for a single family to move from Lower Manhattan to Jersey City, New Jersey, then to Brooklyn, to Queens, and finally to the suburbs in Nassau County. This often happened within a single generation. The challenge to the genealogist is to track his or her families' movements using the wealth of tools available.

No Home Ownership: Vertical, Not Horizontal

When conducting research on an urban population, it is important to remember that people primarily live vertically rather than horizontally. Not all of New York City—or any other city—is composed of huge skyscrapers, but most cities have many multiple-dwelling buildings. In New York City this can mean a two-family house; a brownstone, a four- or five-story building that could house just one family or residents of 4 to 10 apartments; or an apartment building of any number of floors—usually from 4 to 25, though many are 40–50 stories high.

Jurisdictions of Records

The five boroughs are geographically coterminous with the five counties that comprise New York City, but some boroughs and counties may have different names. Manhattan is short for Manhattan Island, which is the borough of Manhattan and the county of New York. This is the section of New York City that most people think of when they think of New York.

Brooklyn is a borough, but the county name is Kings County. Queens is both a borough and a county. The Bronx is also a borough and a county. Staten Island is a borough; its county name is Richmond. New Yorkers tend to ignore county designations and simply refer to the borough name.

New York City's Equivalent Boroughs and Counties Today

Boroughs	Counties
Manhattan	New York
Brooklyn	Kings
Bronx	Bronx
Queens	Queens
Staten Island	Richmond

Not all New York City records are centralized. In many cases, a researcher must know the borough or county in which a person lived in order to find records about that individual. A simple way to look at jurisdictional aspects of records is to remember that records related to the State of New York are maintained by the county. Records related to the City of New York are maintained by the borough. For example, vital records were created by the Department of Health and, therefore, are maintained by the City of New York. In the state of New York, vital records are created by local towns and cities for the state, and duplicate copies are filed with the New York State Department of Health. Exceptions to this rule exist for large cities within the state, such as Albany, Buffalo, New York City and Yonkers. Court records, such as name changes, are created by state supreme courts and are maintained by the counties throughout the state.

In addition, one must remember that the areas surrounding New York City may also be important for genealogical research. New Jersey is only a river (the Hudson) away, and four counties in that state—Bergen, Essex, Hudson, and Union—are places where New Yorkers may have lived. North of New York is Westchester County; to the east, on Long Island, are Nassau and Suffolk Counties. All of these places may be important to the genealogist with roots in New York City.

Genealogical Research Facilities In New York City

Not only has New York City been the largest city in the United States since 1829, it also has more genealogical research facilities than any other American city. One resource book, *Genealogical Resources in New York*, lists more than 100 facilities in the metropolitan area. The book should be read from cover to cover with a notebook next to it to make notes about resources to explore more thoroughly. In addition to describing the location of specific record groups, the book supplies clues to sources not previously considered by the average researcher. The list of record groups at YIVO* is

a good example (see YIVO). Although YIVO focuses primarily on records from Eastern Europe, a perusal of its record groups shows that it also holds records of the Holocaust era French *Judenrat* (Jewish council that worked with the Nazis).

In addition to these facilities, one could argue that each religious building—church, temple, synagogue or meeting house—and every cemetery (New York has more than 75), fraternal or social or labor organization also should be considered a resource.

The New York Public Library* is world renowned and second only in size to the Library of Congress* in holdings. The governmental office most used by genealogists is the New York City Municipal Archives;* many of its indexes and records have been filmed by the LDS (Mormon) Family History Library* (see LDS). The Municipal Reference Library* is primarily a place where information about government operations is deposited, including information about employees of the City of New York. In addition, it has considerable information about the city of New York itself, such as files of clippings about New York neighborhoods.

Vital Records

Marriage records often are the best source of information. Unlike death records, for which a person supplies data about another individual, marriage records are based upon interviews with the persons to be married. The format and number of questions for a license have changed over the years. Some early records are especially good because they provide towns of birth for bride and groom.

Although they provide a wealth of material, marriage records also present a challenge to the researcher. The New York City Department of Health was responsible for issuing marriage certificates from 1866 to 1937. In 1908, the City Clerk of New York City began to keep a set of records that consists of the application filed by the couple before the wedding, a summary of the application and the marriage license filed after the wedding by the person officiating. From 1908 until May 1943, applications had to be filed in the borough where the bride lived. After May 1943, they were filed in the borough where the couple obtained their license. From 1908 to 1937, therefore, two sets of marriage records were maintained in New York City, one by the Department of Health,* the other by the City Clerk. One may find the marriage record of a couple in one set, both sets or neither set of records. The Municipal Archives* has all New York City Department of Health* marriage certificates for all boroughs and any existing indexes (1855–1937).

City Clerk records after 1929 are not open to the public at this time, but for a fee, it is possible (with some restrictions) to obtain information from the City Clerk. The Municipal Archives* has City Clerk Bride and Groom indexes for all boroughs (counties) for the period 1908–52 (the Bronx index begins in 1914, when it became a county). After obtaining information from the indexes, one can order the actual records from the City Clerk or the Municipal Archives.* The record consists of an affidavit (sworn application), summary, license and parental approval page. If either party had been divorced,

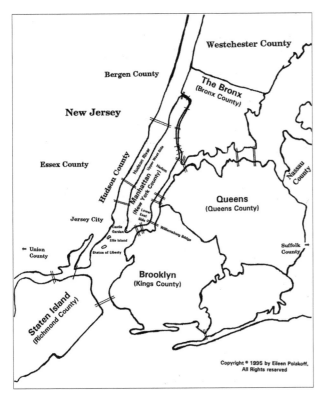

Greater New York City area showing the five boroughs of the city (Manhattan, Brooklyn, Bronx, Queens and Staten Island) with their county names (New York, Kings, Bronx, Queens and Richmond).

the date and place of divorce are provided, as well as a statement as to whether the previous spouse were still living.

In 1937 the Department of Health* stopped marrying people, so the only agency responsible for marriages in New York City was the City Clerk. The Department of Health* marriage records (1866–1937) have been microfilmed and are available at the New York Municipal Archives* and from the LDS (Mormon) Family History Library (see LDS). Microfilming has begun on the City Clerk marriage records. To date, the indexes for both bride and groom (1908–51) have been filmed and are available at the Municipal Archives.* The indexes are arranged by borough for each year with four volumes per year (Jan-Mar, April-June, July-Sept and Oct-Dec) with separate books for brides and grooms. After the date and marriage license number is found in the indexes, the actual City Clerk marriage record may be obtained for a fee of $10 per record. The City Clerk will accept only money orders while the Municipal Archives will take personal checks (drawn on U.S. banks) or money orders. In New York State, marriage records are private for 50 years.

The New York City Department of Health* is responsible for birth and death records. The agency has published annual indexes to births and deaths (1888–1985). Access to the records varies according to time period and privacy laws. Birth records to 1909 and death records to 1949 are available at the Municipal Archives.* The indexes and records have been microfilmed, and copies of most may be ordered from the LDS (Mormon) Family History Library. Post-1949 death records are available to family members from the Department

of Health.* At this time, birth records after 1909 are not available to the public.

Additional earlier birth and death indexes and records are available for many areas that now constitute New York City. The consolidation of the city in 1898 joined the areas of Manhattan and Brooklyn, as well as small towns in Brooklyn, Bronx, Queens and Staten Island, into the large metropolis of New York City. See *Genealogical Resources in New York* for details.

A microfilm copy of indexes to vital records filed with the New York State Health Department* is available at the U.S. National Archives Northeast Branch*. Indexes cover births (1888–1921), deaths (1881–1946) and marriages (1881–1946). Exceptions are birth and death indexes for Albany, Buffalo and Yonkers prior to 1914 and marriages for the same cities before 1908.

Divorce records for all jurisdictions in New York State are maintained by the county Supreme Court and are sealed for 100 years. Indexes to these records are available at the courts, but the files themselves are not open to the public.

City Directories

City directories for the years before most families had telephones are very useful for genealogical research. In New York City, they are critical. The 1910 U.S. census has a wealth of information, but State of New York returns are not indexed. To find a family in that census, one must have an address. The city directories may supply the address. For New York (and other large urban areas) research, always do a year-by-year search of city directories, because city dwellers moved often and each directory may provide new clues about a family. Remember also to look at all variant spellings of the surname. In New York City, check all boroughs. The Bronx always was included with Manhattan except in the early years when eastern and northern portions of what is now The Bronx were part of Westchester County.

The first city directory for New York City was published in 1786; they continued to appear until approximately 1914. For Manhattan, the directories continue until 1925. In 1931, a residents-only directory (no business listings) was published for Manhattan. The next directory available for all boroughs of New York City is 1933/34, but it is also the last one available. This directory includes all adults in a household—including adult children; the wife is listed in parentheses, and often an apartment number is given.

Naturalization

Citizenship records are extremely important to immigrant research. Often they are the only source that names an ancestor's town of birth. A number of different sets of citizenship records exist for New York City. The strategy to locate these records depends on when the relative arrived in the United States.

If the arrival was prior to 1900, it is possible that the name may be found in the pre-1906 Soundex Index to records that cover all New York courts. These are known as the "Old Law" records and names are arranged according to the Soundex system used by the National Archives. The records are made up of an index card containing a summary of the information on the actual record and a dexograph (early version of photocopying) copy of the petition. The index card supposedly contains all the information but, it is always important to get a copy of any original record. One rarely finds information that was not on the card, but it is possible. One item not on the card is the signature of the applicant. Original dexograph copies are maintained by the National Archives regional branch in New York City.*

The LDS (Mormon) Family History Library* has microfilmed copies of the pre-1906 naturalization index cards. It also has microfilmed copies of the federal court indexes and the New York State Supreme Court indexes. Many—but not all—of the actual records also have been filmed by the Family History Library.

After 1906, a person in New York City could be naturalized in any of seven different courts: two federal courts—the U.S. District Court for the Southern District (Manhattan, the Bronx, Westchester, Putnam, Rockland, Orange, Dutchess, and Sullivan counties) or the U.S. District Court for the Eastern District (Kings, Queens, Richmond, Nassau, and Suffolk counties)—or one of the five county supreme courts: Bronx, Kings, New York, Queens, or Richmond. (see NATURALIZATION).

Begin with the federal courts and always check both Southern and Eastern districts. Indexes (available from the Family History Library) exist for each of the districts. Then check the supreme court for the county where the person lived. If records do not surface, check the court in the area where the person worked.

One exception to remember when seeking naturalization papers for someone who became a citizen while serving in the military is that military naturalizations have less information than the standard variety. They do not include the so-called "first papers" (Declaration of Intent to Become a Citizen) or a Certificate of Arrival (see NATURALIZATION).

Pre-1906 naturalization records have little information of value to genealogists. Post-1906 records include (at a minimum) the Declaration of Intent to Become a Citizen, Petition for Naturalization and Certificate of Arrival. Ship arrival data is asked as part of the naturalization process (see NATURALIZATION).

Court Records

Name changes. Today, we are much more aware of formal name changes and their implications than were our ancestors. Since many Jewish immigrants arrived in the United States with names that here were considered unpronounceable, the immigrants easily Anglicized them and didn't think to do it formally. In some cases, however, individuals did undergo a legal process to change their names. Such records are filed in the county supreme courts in New York.

Probate and administration files. Probate of wills and letters of administration, in cases where an individual died without a will, are filed in the surrogate's court where an individual had lived, not where he or she died. Each of the five New York City counties has a surrogate's court (see PROBATE).

New York.	80,565	820,000
Albany (1661)	2,000	4,000
Amsterdam (1865)	......	250
("Ararat" on Grand Island, Niagara Falls [1825], near Buffalo).		
Arverne.		
Bensonhurst.		
Binghamton	......	250
Brooklyn (1850)	13,000	100,000
Buffalo (1825)	775	7,000
Coney Island.		
Elmira (1801)	300	1,500
Flushing	......	25
Glens Falls.	27	
Ithaca (1891)	55	100
Kingston (1853)	68	600
Newburgh (1865)	158	500
New York (1654)	60,000	672,000
Port Chester	......	300
Poughkeepsie.	......	75
Rochester (1840)	1,175	5,000
Schenectady (1856)	......	550
Sharon Springs.		
Staten Island	......	750
Syracuse (1839)	......	5,000
Tannersville.		
Troy	500	3,000
Utica.		
(Wowarsing [Sholom] Agr. Col., Ulster County, 1837).		
Yonkers (1882).		

Comparison of the 1877 and 1900 Jewish populations of New York State showing the enormous influx of Jews to New York City, Brooklyn and Buffalo during that period.

Voting Records

New York City has maintained voter records since 1872 for Manhattan. Brooklyn has records from 1890 and Queens and Staten Island from 1897 or 1898. Not all records for all years have survived. As with many types of records, questions asked of a person registering to vote changed over the years. In the 19th century, prospective registrants were asked such questions as number of years they had lived in the county or state, age and physical description. In the 20th century, questions included name of head of household, occupation of voter, where voter employed and years employed. Women were allowed to vote in New York in 1918 (not 1920, when the amendment giving suffrage to women was passed by Congress). Most important, if the voter was an immigrant, it includes the name of the court where the voter was naturalized.

It is possible to learn if an ancestor was registered to vote. Voter registration information may be obtained in several places: at the New York Public Library,* the various boards of elections and the Municipal Archives.* The microform division of the New York Public Library* has the *List of Registered Voters*, arranged by Assembly District, Election District and then specific address. A researcher who is not certain of an address for an individual being sought, but does know the neighborhood of residence, should use the *List of Enrolled Voters*, an alphabetical list of voters by borough, arranged by Assembly District, Election District and then by initial of surname. Pick years that are critical to the search. For example, if trying to find someone in a census but lack an address, search the years just prior to the census or pick a presidential election year. People are more likely to vote in a presidential election year than in "off" election years.

Deeds and Property Records

Most immigrants to New York City did not own real estate initially, but they may have bought some after living in the city for a while. Deed and property records include names of sellers and buyers. To find information in deeds, look up the block and lot number in the ledger books which are arranged by address and kept at the City Registrar's office in each borough. All transactions are in chronological order. Scan the block information for family names. Note the *liber* (book or volume) and page numbers, then look at the microfiche files of the original deeds. Also look at the Name Indexes for Grantor/Grantees (seller/buyer) for a specific block and lot number, (i.e., the address).

World War I Draft Registration Cards

One of the great sources for research on immigrants is the World War I draft registration cards. In some cases, the information on these cards is the only source for learning the birth place of men who never became citizens or who became citizens before 1906 via their fathers' naturalizations. In addition to looking at the cards, if your relative served in the war, check the state records of men who served. The New York State Archives* in Albany has a summary of military records for all men who served in World War I from New York.

All men ages 18–45, whether native or foreign born, were required to register in one of three draft registrations conducted in 1917 and 1918. Only those who were already in military service, volunteers, and diplomats were exempt. More than 24 million men registered (see WORLD WAR I DRAFT REGISTRATION).

Researchers need a specific address to search these records. Because of the size of the population in 1917 and 1918—estimated at 5.5 million—New York City had 189 local draft boards, each representing 5,000 men, for a total of nearly one million individuals. Without an address, a search would be impossible. Fortunately, a finding aid exists to help the researcher. On September 11, 1918, *The Evening Mail* newspaper published a map outlining and describing 170 draft boards in Brooklyn, Bronx and Manhattan. After finding a relative's address on a present-day map, find the appropriate draft board on the *Mail's* map. Copies of the map are available at the U.S. National Archives Northeast Branch* in New York City and at the LDS (Mormon) Family History Library. Some indexing has been done for New York City draft registrations, but most is still unindexed (see WORLD WAR I DRAFT REGISTRATIONS).

Censuses

New York is unique in having had two federal censuses conducted, six months apart, in 1870. The city claimed an undercount, hence the second enumeration. This second enumeration was the first time addresses were supplied. The first enumeration had to be accessed by map and ward (political division of the city). The second census had addresses along the side of the page. This can assist the researcher to find the first census and, thus, compare information.

Almost the entire 1890 federal census was destroyed in a fire, including all for New York City. Fortunately, a separate census, called the Police Census, was taken in Manhattan in 1890. Although it does not include as much data as the federal census of that year, it does cover Manhattan and the western Bronx for that year.

New York State conducted "off-year" censuses—from 1825 to 1925 in ten-year intervals. Not all records have survived for all counties. When doing research on immigrants, the most important state census is the one from 1925, which asks for court of naturalization. An address is needed to search any of the state censuses, but finding aids exist that can help. The extant censuses and finding aids have been microfilmed by the LDS (Mormon) Family History Library.*

The New York Times Index

A commercial firm, ProQuest, has scanned all issues of *The New York Times* from its founding in 1848 to 1998 as part of its Historical Newspapers project.[2] Researchers may search for any name, place or event in articles advertisements, birth, marriage and death notices. Searches can be limited by date. Results, viewed as an entire page or as just an article, can be saved to disk. Many genealogists have been surprised to find cites of ancestors in these pages.

Conclusion

Research in New York City can be complex and time-consuming, but it often is rewarding. If ancestors lived in New York City at almost any time since the Civil War, research likely will reveal at least one reference to them. Among the keys to research in New York City are: never give up, systematically review all possible record sources, do neighborhood searches for family members and research collateral lines. Then review once more all the information gathered and begin again.

Addresses

New York City Department of Health, Bureau of Vital Records, 125 Worth Street, Room 133, New York, New York 10013; telephone: (212) 788-4520

New York Municipal Archives, 31 Chambers Street, Room 103, New York, New York 10007; telephone: (212) 788-8580

New York Municipal Reference Library, 31 Chambers Street, Room 112, New York, New York 10007

New York City Public Library, 476 Fifth Avenue, New York, New York 10018; telephone: (212) 930-0561; website: WWW.NYPL.ORG

New York State Archives, Cultural Education Center, 11th floor, Empire State Plaza, Albany, New York, website: WWW.SARA.NYSED.GOV

U.S. National Archives, Northeast Branch, 201 Varick Street, 12th floor, New York, New York 10014; telephone: (212) 337-1301; e-mail: ARCHIVES@NEWYORK.NARA.GOV.

Bibliography

Guzik, Estelle, ed. *Genealogical Resources in New York*. New York: Jewish Genealogical Society, 2003.

Notes

1. Castle Garden opened again for two and a half years following the fire at Ellis Island on June 14, 1897.
2. Savada, Elias. "Using *The New York Times* Online Backfile," *AVOTAYNU* 18, no. 2 (Summer 2002): 22–25.

Wills and Probate Records
in the United States

by Charles B. Bernstein

A check of the local probate court should be a manda-tory step in every genealogical search—even though the deceased was not wealthy and the researcher already knows all about the individual or that branch of a family. Frequently, information is uncovered that can be found no-where else.

A probate court is a special court whose jurisdiction originally was the proving of wills of deceased persons. To probate a will is to prove to the satisfaction of the probate court that the will is the authentic and valid will of the decedent, signed in accordance with the local law applicable for the signing of wills. The jurisdiction of the probate court grew to include the administration of the estates of persons who left wills—testate estates—and also the administration of estates of persons who did not leave wills—intestate estates. Finally, the jurisdiction of probate courts expanded to include supervision of the administration of minors' and incompetents' estates.

In most states, the probate court is part of the county court system and is located in the county seat. The specific names given to a probate court vary from state to state. In Illinois, for example, it is called the Circuit Court of [county name] County Probate Division. In California, it is the Superior Court for the State of California, in and for the County of [county name]. In New York it is called the Surro-gate's Court, County of [county name], an independent court with countywide jurisdiction. In Pennsylvania it is called the [county name] County Orphan's Court. In some states such as Connecticut and Indiana the probate court is part of the town governmental system.

Probate courts are part of the county judicial system in many metropolitan U.S. areas with large Jewish populations, a fortunate situation for researchers since the Jewish popula-tion of the United States has lived primarily in suburban metropolitan areas since the mid-20th century. This is true — for example in Cook County — the county in which Chicago is located, as well as Los Angeles, Philadelphia, Nassau and Suffolk Counties on Long Island (New York) or northern New Jersey, where there are many suburbs and the Jewish popu-lation is widely distributed. If probate courts were organized by municipality in these metropolitan areas, probate research would be impractical and onerous.

A will should be probated in the county of the person's legal residence (domicile) at the time of death. Some elderly Americans divide their time between winter homes in warm climates and their legal domicile in a more northern state. That could lead to some difficulty finding a will. For example, if a decedent had a New York City driver's license and voted in New York, then the legal residence probably was New York. On the other hand, if a person moved all household furnishings to Florida and died in Florida, but was buried in New York City because that was where a spouse or other family members had been buried, the legal residence of that person was Florida. Traditionally, the law provided that an individual can only have one domicile at a time, but that rule seems to have become blurred in recent years.

Probate court estates are contained in court files. A researcher must determine the case number from an index in the office of the clerk of the court and then order the file. If the case was filed many years ago, the file might be in an offsite warehouse. Plan ahead when visiting an out-of-town probate court. Contact the clerk's office by telephone or mail; order the file and establish when it will be there. For offsite files, different jurisdictions take differing amounts of time (from three days to three weeks) to bring a file into the clerk's office. Some jurisdictions charge a fee to bring a file from storage.

Difficulties sometimes arise when contacting an out-of-town probate court to ascertain that an estate exists and to obtain the case number. New York State, for example, charges $40 to search the index to determine if an estate exists; requests must be submitted in writing with an enclosed check. San Francisco charges a search fee of $5 per year with a lengthy waiting period for a reply. I once wrote to the probate court in Los Angeles to inquire if an estate had been probated for a certain person. Six months later, my letter was returned along with a printed slip of paper saying that the clerk requires a $2 fee and self-addressed stamped envelope in order to respond.

Most probate courts in less densely populated areas will supply a case number over the telephone, and may even pull the file and offer some basic information. Iowa is a notable exception. In Iowa, a clerk will not provide any information even in response to a written request. Researchers must hire a local lawyer or genealogist to do in-person research.

Once a file is in hand, researchers usually can make photocopies of salient documents. Sometimes they can be made on a public machine available for use in the office of the probate court clerk. More frequently, copies can be made only by the clerk—usually more expensively.

Probate estates come in three varieties: minors' estates, incompetents' estates and decedents' estates. Since the original purpose of probate estates was to prove wills, and since the majority of probate estates are decedents' estates, the term "probate estate" has acquired the secondary meaning of "decedent's estate."

Minors' and incompetents' estates, however, offer many genealogical facts and should not be overlooked. A routine review of the index to minors' and incompetents' estates, as well as decedents' estates, should be made for every person on a family tree.

Minors' Estates

A minor's estate is usually opened for one of two reasons: The child received a settlement from a personal injury action, or the child received an inheritance or is the beneficiary of an insurance policy. Since a minor (a child under the age of 18 or 21, depending upon the particular jurisdiction) is not a legal entity and cannot hold title to property—much like a woman prior to the latter part of the 19th century—a minor's estate must be established. A guardian of the child is appointed to receive the minor's property and to administer it until the child comes of age. Minors' estates are valuable genealogically because they supply, at a minimum, the child's birth date. Also, by the time the child comes of age, the family may have moved and the estate file may offer a clue to the family's current whereabouts. The estate probably will include names of the parents and possibly names, addresses and ages of siblings of the minor. Finally, names of people mentioned in the estate and the name of the lawyer may offer sources for personal interviews, if not too much time has elapsed since the event and if these persons are still alive. These names could provide sources for interviews with their descendants or persons who were associated with them.

Two examples of the usefulness of a minor's estate and the surprises that it might provide follow. I had completed practically the entire family tree of the descendants of an immigrant to the United States, but was having trouble making a connection across the seas. I did not know the name of the German town from which the family had originated. I routinely checked for a minor's estate not expecting to find anything useful—and was amply rewarded for the effort. In 1880, a minor's estate was opened in Chicago for four siblings because a great-aunt in Germany had bequeathed them a total of $100. The dollar amount was meaningless, but now I had the name of the town in Germany from which the family had come to America and the name and approximate date of death of the great-aunt. This information enabled me to access the birth, marriage and death records of the German town and find an additional two earlier generations on this family tree.

Another example resulting in a surprising information bonanza involved a minor's estate opened because a 17-year-old boy wanted to enlist in the U.S. Navy during World War I. He was an orphan and needed to have a guardian appointed who could sign for him to enlist. He had an unusual surname, and I suspected that he was a member of a certain family that had had six siblings born between 1862 and 1884—his parent's generation. I could not, however, figure out whose child he was. Research revealed that his mother was the eldest of the six siblings. She and her husband had both died young; their son had gone to live with maternal grandparents. The boy had taken his mother's maiden name (the name of the grandfather with whom he was living). Since his mother had died so young, those who told me about the family had forgotten about her. The family also had forgotten about the young

man because he settled in another part of the country after the war.

Incompetents' Estates

The second category of probate estates is incompetents' estates. In some jurisdictions, incompetents' estates are referred to as disabled person's estates, mentally ill estates or similar appellations. Estates with property probably constitute the majority of incompetents' estates. Such estates can be subdivided into two categories. The first subcategory involves people who are physically or mentally unable to administer their property. In addition, the family might need a court order to commit an individual to a mental or physical health care facility when the person is mentally or physically unable to give his or her consent. The second subcategory involves situations in which a family needs a court order to commit an individual to a mental hospital. In both cases, the estate file includes the incompetent person's date of birth, address and the names and addresses of his or her next of kin and—in modern times—probably his or her Social Security number. The file usually also contains a physician's report on the physical and mental condition of the patient. An incompetent's estate is closed when the person dies, so if a file was filed several years before you research it, the chances are that the incompetent person will have died and the file will provide the date of death.

Decedent's Estates

Decedents' estates also fall into two subcategories, testate and intestate. Testate estates are opened for persons who died with a will. Intestate estates are estates of individuals who died with property to be distributed but who left no will. Not all wills, however, result in the opening of an estate.

Wills also can come in two categories. One is the unprobated will, which is less common. More common is the probated will, meaning a will which is proved (probated) to have been signed by the testator (the person who made the will) and witnessed in accordance with the statute of the state pertaining to wills and is then declared by the court to be the official will of the decedent.

Even if a person is penniless, he or she can write a will and that will may include much information about the person, his or her family, thinking and perhaps even fantasies. In some states, even if a person has no assets in his or her own name, (i.e., subject to probate), but the person leaves a will, the law requires that after the person has died, the person in possession of the will must file it in the probate court. One state requires that one who has possession of a will must file it with the clerk of the probate court within 30 days after the date of death. Then the will simply sits in a file—forever. No further action need be taken, but whatever information is in the will is available to a researcher. The will may contain previously unknown information, such as names of next of kin, whether immediate or distant, friends, witnesses to the will and the lawyer who prepared the will. These individuals can be contacted if the will is not too old and the people are still alive; such persons may be able to reveal further information.

I, JULIUS ROSENWALD, residing and domiciled in the City of Chicago, County of Cook, and State of Illinois, being of sound and disposing mind and memory, do hereby make, ordain, publish and declare this to be my Last Will and Testament, and I do hereby revoke and annul any and all other wills, testaments or codicils heretofore made by me.

First: I direct my Executors to pay all my debts as soon after my death as conveniently may be.

Second: I give, devise and bequeath, and direct my said Executors, as soon as convenient after my death, and in any event within the period of two (2) years after the date of my death, to set over and deliver unto the ROSENWALD FAMILY ASSOCIATION, a corporation with philanthropic, educational, scientific, and charitable purposes as its corporate purposes, now in the process of organization as a corporation not for pecuniary profit under the laws of the State of Illinois, assets which in the unqualified judgment of my Executors shall, together with the value of such gifts as I may make to said corporation prior to the date of my death, have an aggregate value of Eleven Million Dollars ($11,000,000.00). I direct my Executors, in transferring said assets to said corporation, and as a condition precedent thereto, to receive satisfactory assurances from the corporation that it will use such portion of such assets as my Executors in their unqualified discretion shall determine, for the use and benefit of the MUSEUM OF SCIENCE AND INDUSTRY FOUNDED BY JULIUS ROSENWALD, situated in Chicago, Illinois.

Third: All the rest, residue and remainder of my estate, of every kind, nature and sort whatsoever, remaining after carrying out the foregoing provisions of this, my Last Will and Testament, I give, devise and bequeath absolutely, in equal shares, share and share alike among my children, LESSING J. ROSENWALD, EDITH R. STERN, ADELE R. LEVY, MARION R. STERN, and WILLIAM ROSENWALD.

Fourth: I hereby appoint as Executors of this, my Last Will and Testament, my son LESSING J. ROSENWALD and my daughter MARION R. STERN and the survivor of them and I direct that neither of them be required to give bond. Each of said Executors shall have full power to bind my estate.

IN WITNESS WHEREOF, I have hereunto set my hand and seal this 12th day of December A. D. 1931.

Julius Rosenwald (SEAL)

Initial page of the Last Will and Testament of Julius Rosenwald. He is the man attributed to making Sears, Roebuck & Company a successful retail chain.

NAMES	RELATIONSHIP	RESIDENCE
ADELAIDE R. ROSENWALD	Widow	Drake Towers, Chicago, Ill.
LESSING J. ROSENWALD	Son	Drake Hotel, Chicago, Ill.
WILLIAM ROSENWALD	Son	Washington Lane Elkins Park, Pennsylvania.
EDITH R. STERN	Daughter	Metairie Lane, New Orleans, Louisiana.
ADELE R. LEVY	Daughter	950 Park Avenue, New York, New York.
MARION R. STERN	Daughter	1701 South Sheridan Road, Highland Park, Illinois.

Petitions for Probate include the names of the heirs, a source of the married names of daughters.

Many states do not require unprobated wills to be filed. Therefore, when checking with the clerk of a probate court to see if a probate estate is on file for someone, if told that there is no probate estate on file, always ask—as a separate question—if an unprobated will is on file. Sometimes, unprobated wills are kept in an index separate from the index used for probate estates.

Both intestate and testate estates have almost the same contents, except that the intestate estate does not have a will and the money goes to the decedents heirs—next of kin—in the proportions dictated by the law of the state. An intestate estate may be more useful genealogically. For example, a petition, or initial paper filed in an estate in both an intestate estate and a testate estate, lists the names and addresses of heirs, those who by the law of the state are entitled to inherit the decedent's property. In a testate estate, however, only the persons named in the will and not necessarily all of the heirs receive the proceeds of the estate. Therefore, when the estate is closed, the paperwork will contain no further information about the heirs who did not receive any property pursuant to the will. In an intestate estate on the other hand, the closing papers will provide up to date information about the heirs. If they have moved, the closing papers will include their current addresses. An occasional bonanza occurs if a daughter of the decedent has married

since the death of the decedent, because then the married name and name of the husband of the daughter will be revealed by the closing papers.

Most probate estates contain several key documents.

Petition for Probate

The first document filed to commence probate proceedings is the Petition for Admission of a Will to Probate for testate estates or the Petition for Letters of Administration for intestate estates. A petition in a testate estate has two purposes. The first is to ask the court to admit the will to probate, i.e., to declare that the will was signed under circumstances that fulfills the statutory requirements of the state and to be the officially recognized will of the decedent that will control how the decedent's assets are to be distributed. The second purpose is to ask the court to appoint the person the decedent named in the will to administer the affairs of the estate. That person, where there is a will, is called the executor or, if a woman, sometimes an executrix, although usually just a generic "executor" is used for both sexes. In an intestate estate, the petition will ask for an administrator to be appointed to administer the affairs of the estate.

The petition will probably contain much of the following important genealogical information: the name of the decedent, his or her address, place and date of death, names and addresses of heirs (next of kin even if they receive nothing under the will) and legatees and devisees (those who receive property under the will; legatees receive personal property; devisees receive real estate). Usually the heirs and legatees/devisees are the same persons, but not always, particularly if the decedent did not have a spouse or child. The list of heirs and legatees/devisees also indicates whether these persons are minors or incompetents and what their genealogical connection is to the decedent, particularly if they are heirs.

Affidavit of Heirship

Most states make provision for an affidavit (or declaration) of heirship, i.e., a statement showing the next of kin of the decedent and how they are related to the decedent. This document of course is extremely valuable for the genealogist. In some states, the affidavit of heirship is an important component of the file because the heirs—next of kin who

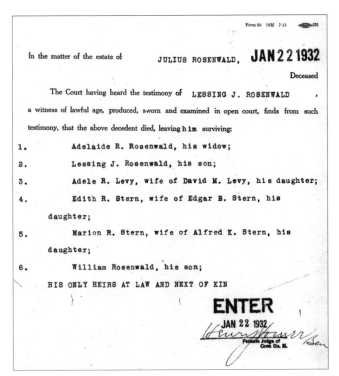

In the matter of the estate of   JULIUS ROSENWALD,   **JAN 22 1932**

Deceased

The Court having heard the testimony of   LESSING J. ROSENWALD   ,

a witness of lawful age, produced, sworn and examined in open court, finds from such

testimony, that the above decedent died, leaving h im surviving:

1.   Adelaide R. Rosenwald, his widow;

2.   Lessing J. Rosenwald, his son;

3.   Adele R. Levy, wife of David M. Levy, his daughter;

4.   Edith R. Stern, wife of Edgar B. Stern, his
         daughter;

5.   Marion R. Stern, wife of Alfred K. Stern, his
         daughter;

6.   William Rosenwald, his son;

HIS ONLY HEIRS AT LAW AND NEXT OF KIN

ENTER

JAN 22 1932

Probate Judge of
Cook Co. Ill.

*The transcript of the Proof of Heirship procedure can include
additional information about the family.*

would be entitled to receive the estate if there were no will—
are entitled to notice of the will being presented for probate
so that they can file a will contest, an objection to the will
being admitted to probate and thus obtain a share of the
estate. In some states, if there is a will, the provision to provide
notice to the heirs seems to be somewhat lax, if existent at all.
Therefore, if an estate is intestate, the likelihood is usually
greater that a more serious effort will be put into the preparation
of the affidavit of heirship and that it will be thorough.

Depending on the court and the era, affidavits of heirship
take different forms and are of varying degrees of thorough-
ness. They may include names of the spouses of the heirs,
mentions of adoptions and divorces, copies of the adoption
and divorce decrees, ages of the heirs and statements that
they are adults and mentally competent. In one state, the custom was to have a relative testify in court as to the heirship,
with the judge asking the questions. The testimony went according to a specific format. At a certain point, the judge was
required to ask whether each heir was an adult and mentally
competent, because if the heir were not, the court would appoint a guardian *ad litem* to represent his or her interests in
the hearing on whether the will should be admitted to probate.
The judge would ask the witness to the heirship: "Are you
over eighteen years of age?" "Are you mentally competent?"
This often resulted in an embarrassing or amusing scene. One
stately, middle-aged woman who was testifying to the heirship
of her mother was perfunctorily asked: "Are you over the age
of eighteen?" She replied, "A little." Then the judge had to ask,
"Are you mentally competent?" The woman's glibness left her.
She gave a trace of a smile and simply shrugged.

Heirship also can reveal any illegitimate children and,
depending upon the state, children given up for adoption. In
Illinois until recent years, children given up for adoption
theoretically remained heirs of their biological relatives as
well as of their adoptive relatives. If an adopted child knew
who his or her biological relatives were, he or she could
exercise the right to an inheritance from a biological relative
who had died intestate. This is not the case in New York,
however, where, once adopted, an individual no longer is an
heir of his or her biological family.

Different courts use different formats for putting the
heirship of the decedent in the record, and this can result in
different types of information being required. For example, in
some states, heirs are the decedent's next of kin no matter
how distant. If the decedent was an only child of an only
child, his or her next of kin would be third cousins, the descendants of the siblings of his or her great-grandparents. On the
other hand, in New York no relative more distant than a first
cousin can be an heir. Even a first cousin once removed does
not qualify as an heir, and in the case of an intestate estate,
the estate would be forfeited to the State of New York, which
would get the money. If there was a will leaving property to
parties who were not heirs of the decedent, the judge would
not make an effort to get the information on the heirship into
the public records, since third cousins would have no right to
contest the will anyway.

As a practical matter, judges and lawyers frequently do not
make as strong an effort as genealogists would like to present
as thorough an affidavit of heirship as possible. Just as in
death certificates where an informant who is the child of the
deceased answers the question for names of parents of the
decedent, or particularly maiden name of the mother of the
decedent as "unknown" because he or she does not want to
bother to think about it or to check it out, so do those involved
with assembling affidavits of heirship usually put little effort
into it.

An estate of a decedent who has no spouse or children is
more valuable to a genealogist than an estate of a person with
a spouse and children, because the heirship extends to collateral heirs. In one state, until about 1960, the law of heirship said
that if a person died with a spouse but no children, the spouse
was entitled to all of the decedent's personal estate, but the
decedent's other heirs were entitled to half of the real estate. Because of this statute, the decedent's collateral heirs had to be
included in the affidavit of heirship. Unfortunately, the law was
changed to eliminate the collateral heirs. As a result, when the
first spouse died, his or her entire heirship beyond the spouse
is lost to the public records, and only the name of the spouse
is included in the estate. When a person who is the last survivor of many siblings and who has many nieces and nephews
and maybe even grandnieces and nephews as heirs dies before
his or her spouse, this rule wipes out the potential preservation
in the public record of the heirship for that entire family.

The Will

The next document in the file is the will. It may contain
personal information not otherwise available, and estates

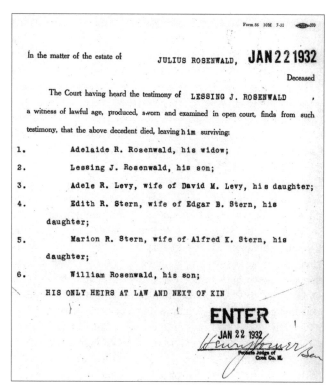

Form 86   10M   7-31   ⊂▦▭▶370

In the matter of the estate of   JULIUS ROSENWALD,   **JAN 22 1932**

Deceased

The Court having heard the testimony of   LESSING J. ROSENWALD   ,

a witness of lawful age, produced, sworn and examined in open court, finds from such

testimony, that the above decedent died, leaving h im surviving:

1.   Adelaide R. Rosenwald, his widow;

2.   Lessing J. Rosenwald, his son;

3.   Adele R. Levy, wife of David M. Levy, his daughter;

4.   Edith R. Stern, wife of Edgar B. Stern, his
          daughter;

5.   Marion R. Stern, wife of Alfred K. Stern, his
          daughter;

6.   William Rosenwald, his son;

HIS ONLY HEIRS AT LAW AND NEXT OF KIN

ENTER

JAN 22 1932

Probate Judge of
Cook Co. Ill.

Testimony at a Proof of Heirship hearing can provide genealogically relevant information.

may have been opened for odd reasons even though they are small in monetary amount. Thorough genealogists should always check for a decedent's estate and will even if they think they already know all about the person and his or her descendants. For example, once I was operating on the hypothesis that two men—both with an unusual last name—were brothers, but I could not find proof of the relationship. One was rich and prominent and had a large number of children; the other was a poor ne'er-do-well, also with many children. In the will, the rich man left $100 to his poor brother. It was a token amount—but the information was sufficient to document that these two men were brothers.

Bond of Personal Representative (Executor or Administrator)

The next document to seek in the probate file is the bond. If a will exists, the bond usually will be just a personal bond of the executor, equal to a certain percentage of the value of the personal property (as opposed to real estate) of the estate. The requirement of a bond and the calculation is based on the theory that the executor or administrator cannot just walk off with the real estate. An administrator must be bonded by an insurance company. In the event that the estate owns real estate, an additional bond must be posted only if the real estate is sold during the administration of the estate to assure the court that the executor or administrator will not abscond with the proceeds of the sale.

Occasionally, an executor or administrator will have two persons be sureties on his or her bond instead of getting a bond from an insurance company. The entry of a private

bondsman — the person who agrees to act personally as the surety — into the scenario can sometimes generate genealogical information, since they are usually relatives of the executor or administrator. Sometimes the bondsman is required to file a financial statement with the court. If the bondsman owns real estate, that can be helpful, because frequently real estate stays in the family and passes to heirs. After the bondsman's real estate has been sold eventually, a title search may enable a genealogist to extend the family tree to the bondsman's heirs.

Frequently, estate papers are prepared in such a way that the value of assets of the estate either are not given or are given in vague terms. A bond, therefore, is sometimes the only decipherable clue to the value of the estate. Although a bond does not include any specifically genealogical information, except in the rare case of a personal bondsman, discussion of the bond is included to provide a comprehensive understanding of the probate process.

Inventory

Another important document in the court file is the inventory. This document lists all of the property in the decedent's name. It does not include joint tenancy property which passes to the surviving joint tenant at the decedent's death or assets that pass to a named beneficiary, such as the proceeds of an insurance policy or an Individual Retirement Account (IRA). The inventory may, however, provide a good idea of the value of the estate.

If the decedent owns real estate or an interest in real estate, the legal description of it should be copied from the inventory. With this, one can easily research the chain of title to the real estate in the office of the county recorder of deeds. Sometimes a family holds real estate, especially commercial real estate, for a long time. On a few occasions, I found that families kept a parcel of real estate that was in a prominent location in the business center of a city for 100 years after the estate was probated. As a result, I was able to trace the great- and great-great-grandchildren of the original owner when they eventually sold the property. By this time, family members had proliferated all over the country, but when someone signs a deed, the signature usually is notarized in the place where it is signed, thus enabling a researcher to determine the locations of heirs three or four generations after the death of their ancestor.

Claims of Creditors

In the course of the probate proceedings, creditors of the decedent may file claims for debts that were owed at the time of the decedent's death. These claims may provide insight into the person's life. Sometimes, although not often in modern times, such claims involve disputes by business partners that can reveal more information about the inner workings and value of the decedent's business.

Frequently claims are filed by funeral homes. This can be a helpful means of determining where a person is buried. Sometimes the decedent did not have a funeral notice published in a newspaper, or the funeral notice—especially in New York—does not state the cemetery of burial. If the person died long ago, the funeral home may no longer exist, or perhaps it does not have the record, or it charges for the record, or it will not give the record to a stranger. Sometimes a non-immediate relative is not eligible to purchase a copy of the death certificate, or at any rate, the death certificate costs several dollars. By determining the place of burial from a claim filed by the funeral home in probate proceedings, the information is obtained at no cost. For an active genealogist dealing with thousands of names and tens of thousands of dollars of potential costs, it is helpful to obtain this information for free. Some probate courts require that a copy of the death certificate be included in the probate court file.

In older estates, claims by funeral homes can shed light on the religious practices of the family. For example, a charge may appear on the bill for *tachrichim* (burial shrouds), $3.00; or for *shomrim* (around-the-clock body watchers), $2.00; or *chevra kadisha* (burial society for washing and preparing the body), $4.00. In the case of Reform Jews of German, Hungarian or Bohemian background, a charge for an organist might appear. The bill may include funds advanced by the funeral home to newspapers for funeral notices.

Listings of newspaper(s) in which the funeral notices appeared might be helpful. Before the 1940s, immigrant Russian Jews who were poor generally did not place funeral notices in the newspaper of record of the city in which the person died (such as the *New York Times* or the *Chicago Tribune*). They may have placed notices in newspapers with a more working-class readership, however, such as the *New York Post* or *Chicago Herald-American*, or in Yiddish newspapers such as the *Forward, Morgan Journal* or *Chicago Yiddishe Courier*. The funeral bill may provide a clue that leads to a funeral notice in one of the second-tier newspapers in which one might not ordinarily look or in which one might not want to take the time to look unless certain that the funeral notice was published there.

Federal Estate Tax Return

The Federal Estate Tax Return provides detailed information about the value of each asset of the estate and distribution of the assets and payment of debts of the decedent. Sometimes this information would not be in the other probate court documents because many of the decedent's assets are not subject to probate, for example, joint tenancy property, insurance policies and IRAs payable to a named beneficiary. Yet these assets are included in a Federal Estate Tax Return. Federal Estate Tax Returns usually are not part of the probate court file, but they are in some states, most importantly New York.

Final Account and Receipts on Distribution

The last important document usually included in a probate file is the Final Account. This document itemizes the receipts and disbursements of the estate and sets forth the distribution to the persons entitled to the estate. The receipts are the assets of the decedent when he or she died, (i.e., a recapitulation of the inventory) plus all income for the estate earned by the administrator or the executor during the course of the probate process. Disbursements include funeral expenses,

administration expenses such as attorney's fees and court costs, and other expenses involved in the business of administering the assets of the estate. There may be a disbursement for funeral expenses or for the purchase of a grave or for perpetual care, which will lead to the location of the grave.

Sometimes the honorarium given to the rabbi for conducting the funeral will reveal who conducted the funeral services, which in turn will identify for the researcher the name of the synagogue to which the decedent or his children belonged— or in the case of a lay person or clergy of another faith officiating, the falling away from the Jewish fold of that branch of the family.

Also the funeral home patronized may be an indication of the socio-economic class and the European origins of the family. For example, certain funeral homes were patronized by upper-class German Jews, others by Workman's Circle members and still others by Orthodox Jews from Lithuania. If the rabbi of Temple Emanuel in New York City officiated at a funeral in 1915, a researcher might reasonably assume that the decedent came from a well-to-do family with origins in Germany. If a funeral was conducted by a rabbi of the Congregation Anshe Tarnopol on the Lower East Side of New York, one might conclude that the decedent or his or her family came from the area of Tarnopol.

A sometimes important part of the Final Account are the Receipts on Distribution. These are documents signed by those who are entitled to the proceeds of the estate indicating that they approve of the Final Account and have received the correct amounts of their inheritances, whether an heir who receives his or her share which is determined by the law of intestacy, or a legatee or devisee who is entitled to a distribution by virtue of a will. The Receipt on Distribution usually will supply a current address of an heir, legatee or devisee. Since most estates are in probate for a year or two, individuals may move during this period. It is always helpful to obtain an updated address. In addition, widows and female heirs sometimes marry during the course of the probate proceedings; the Receipt on Distribution will reveal the new, married name.

Anti-Genealogical Factors

The future does not bode well for preserving all the information set forth in this article in future probate estate files. Three factors work against the genealogist. The first is what in one state is called Independent Administration. This means that once a petition, will and heirship are presented to the court and the administrator or executor is appointed, the inventory and final account and, in some cases, claims, do not need to be filed with the court unless the persons monetarily interested in the estate demand it—probably because they do not trust the executor or administrator. This reduces the amount of information available to the researcher, especially the details in the inventory and final account. New York recently reduced the requirements for documents that must be filed with the court.

The second factor, which is akin to Independent Administration, is the small estate affidavit. By statute, some states have provided that an estate worth less than a certain amount need not be opened in probate court. The assets can be transferred with an affidavit by someone seeking the transfer who swears as to who the heirs, legatees and devisees are if a will exists and that all debts of the decedent have been paid. In Illinois, the small estate affidavit concept applies to estates with assets less than $50,000.

The third major deleterious factor is the book *How to Avoid Probate*, by Norman Dacey—and its progeny and kindred. This book publicized and encouraged the availability of living trusts. In a living trust situation, a person transfers all of his or her assets into a living trust during his or her lifetime. At the death of the maker of the trust, the assets of the trust are either distributed directly to the beneficiaries named in the trust or are kept in the trust with the beneficiaries receiving the income for the rest of their lives before the principal is distributed. Upon the death of the maker of the trust, the successor trustee need not file anything with the probate court in order to transfer the assets to the persons entitled to receive them. However otherwise useful, this procedure eliminates from the public record all of the information now obtainable from a probate estate file.

One other value of a probate record is that it provides an easy method to determine a date of death without researching death records that in some jurisdictions are not available to the public and in others require a search fee. Moreover, in most jurisdictions, searches of death records are conducted by clerks, so a genealogist can never be sure if a completely thorough search took place. To the extent that living trusts have reduced the number of estates, genealogists have been deprived of one method of obtaining this information easily.

Conclusion

The importance of conducting a routine search for a probate file for every person on a family tree cannot be overemphasized. One never knows what information will be in a probate file. Once I was researching a family of four brothers and two sisters. The four brothers had estates probated. The estate of one brother showed that he had two children. Because the attorney handling the estate was inexperienced, he thought that he needed to include in the petition for probate the names of the decedent's brothers and sisters and also the children of deceased brothers and sisters of the decedent. The petition, therefore, included a third sister who had remained in Europe and had died leaving five children. The names of the third sister and her children, unexpectedly and unnecessarily named in the petition for probate, had been unknown to present-day members of the family.

World War I Draft Records

by Eileen Polakoff

Twenty-four million American men registered for the draft during World War I, nearly one quarter of the entire population of the United States. Many of the men were immigrants, born as early as 1872, who may not have become naturalized citizens. Chances are excellent that some members of every immigrant family are represented in these records. All of the records may be viewed on microfilm either at the U.S. National Archives* in Washington, D.C. or at any LDS (Mormon) Family History Center. Branch archives have collections based on their locations; cards for Minnesota are at the regional archive center in Chicago.

On May 18, 1917, passage of the Selective Service Act authorized the president of the United States to increase the American armed forces during wartime. Local draft boards established throughout the nation created draft registration cards for the eligible males in their district. All residents— aliens as well as citizens—had to register. Not all served, of course, and those who volunteered to serve did not register for the draft. Some who later volunteered, however, had actually registered for the draft and may be found in these records.

On June 5, 1917, all men between the ages of 21 and 31 were required to register (i.e., men born as early as June 6, 1886). One year later, on June 5, 1918, those who had attained the age of 21 since the first registration were now required to register. A supplemental registration was held on August 24, 1918, for those who had become 21 years of age after June 5, 1918. The final registration was on September 12, 1918, for all men ages 18 through 45 (i.e., men born between September 13, 1872, and September 12, 1900). This expanded the ages to men not yet 46 years old and the thousands of young men under the age of 21. Table 1 summarizes the information provided on each registration.

All the registrations have been microfilmed by the Mormons (see LDS) and are available at the Family History Library (FHL) or through loan to a Family History Center. To locate the 4,383 microfilms in the FHL catalogue, look under

- United States. Selective Service System
- Draft-United States
- United States-Military Records-World War I, 1914–1918
- (state name)-World War I Selective Service System

The original cards are stored at the National Archives Southeast Region branch near Atlanta, Georgia, a full set of microfilms is available at the National Archives in Washington, D.C., and the 13 regional archives have microfilms for the states and territories within their region.

Each registration district covered up to 30,000 men. Each draft board arranged its own registration cards alphabetically (except Connecticut, Massachusetts and Rhode Island) within the district. Small towns and some counties had only one draft

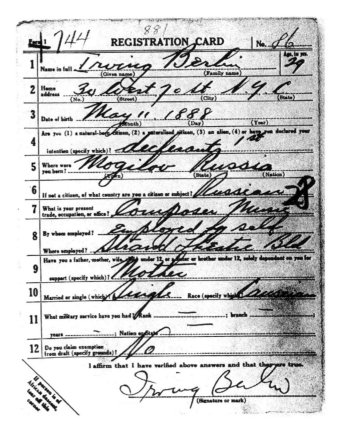

World War I draft record of the noted composer, Irving Berlin. Courtesy of the U.S. National Archives and Records Administration.

board; for them the cards are in one group and easy to search. This is not the case for large cities, of course, and most Jews lived in large cities with many draft boards. To locate the correct draft board and its records, researchers need the address (or series of addresses) where family members lived in 1917 and 1918. Look for addresses in city directories, vital records or the 1920 census (see CENSUS). In some cases, it may be less time consuming to look at all draft boards within a city. For example, Pittsburgh had 21 draft boards. Searching 21 draft boards for one or two surnames should take only a few minutes per board. For larger cities, such as New York with its 189 draft boards, determine if a finding aid, such as a map, has been made. Family History Library microfilm number 1,498,803 is composed of a series of maps of draft boards that can help with the larger cities.

The information listed on each registration differs somewhat but the general information recorded included full name, home address, date and place of birth, age, race, citizenship, if not a U.S. citizen, country of citizenship, occupation, employer, personal description (color of hair and eyes, height, missing arm/leg or other disability) and signature. Additional information could include address of nearest relative, depen-

Information Asked on World War I Draft Registration Cards

There were three separate registrations for the World War I draft: June 5, 1917; June and August 1918; and September 12, 1918. For each regis-tration, a different form was used and different information was re-quested. Information asked on all draft registration cards: name, home address, date of birth, age in years, by whom and where employed, citizenship, race, color of eyes/hair, height/build, date of registration and signature of applicant.

Information asked:	June 5, 1917	June & Aug. 1918	Sept 12, 1918
Age of men registered	21–31	21 since June 5, 1917	18–21 and 31–45
Time period of birth	6 June 1886–5 June 1896	6 June 1896–24 August 1897	13 Sept 1872–12 Sept 1900
Birthplace	–	–	no
Present trade	–	no	–
Dependents	–	no	no
Nearest relative & address	no	–	–
If bald	–	no	no
Married or single	–	no	no
Previous military service	–	no	no
If exemption claimed	–	no	no
Father's Birthplace	no	–	no

dent relative, father's birth place, marital status, bald or not, or previous exemption from service.

If a name is not found in the draft board alphabetically, look at the end of that board's registration for "strays." In smaller cities and towns, look in nearby counties. As always, be creative with the spelling of names, and watch for others with the same surname.

It is possible that the most important bit of information on the first and second registration cards is the exact place of birth for those between the ages of 21 and 31.

The most genealogically valuable registration is the second (June and August 1918), which asks for both father's name and birth place. Unfortunately, only the country name usually is given for birth place—but not always. In about 10 percent of the records, one is fortunate enough to find the elusive overseas town of birth.

The Selective Service System was responsible for all aspects of the military process up to the time the soldier reported for duty. This means that in addition to registration the System classified them; considered needs of families, industry and agriculture; handled appeals, medical fitness and order in which registrants would be called; calling for the appearance of registrants and handled the transportation to a center for training.

As we go to press, there are two online data bases to the World War I draft registration cards. The first was started by Ray Banks in 1995 and is now available at WWW.ANCESTRY.COM. This data base includes five percent of the men who registered, or just over one million names. Six states (Alaska, Delaware, Florida, Idaho, Mississippi and Nevada) are complete. The second data base was created by Carol Glick Feinberg and includes all of two draft boards plus part of a third for New York City. The area covered is on the Upper East Side of Manhattan from 96th to 106th Streets and includes 13,000 names. This data base is available at WWW.JGSNY.ORG, the website of the New York-based Jewish Genealogical Society, Inc. Ancestry.com is in the process of scanning all of the draft registration cards to create an online resource.

Internet

WWW.JEWISHGEN.ORG/INFOFILES/WWIDRAFT.HTM.

Address

U.S. National Archives, Pennsylvania Avenue, Washington, D.C.

Bibliography

Newman, John J. *Uncle, We Are Ready! Registering America's Men, 1917–1918*. North Salt Lake City: Heritage Quest, 2001.
Polakoff, Eileen. "World War I Draft Registrations." *Ancestry Magazine*, Vol. 20, No. 5, Sep/Oct 2002.

Part IV

Researching Country of Ancestry

Austro-Hungarian Empire

by Suzan F. Wynne

The Austro-Hungarian Dual Monarchy ceased to exist after World War I. At its greatest extent, the Habsburg Austrian monarchy (after 1867, the Dual Monarchy) in the center of Europe had included portions of what is now Austria, Bosnia, Croatia, the Czech Republic, Germany, Herzegovina, Hungary, Italy, Poland, Romania, Slovakia, Slovenia, Switzerland, Ukraine and Yugoslavia. The Habsburgs called territories that came into their Empire "Crownlands."

Catholic Austria had little tolerance for those who practiced other religions and never invited Jews to settle in its lands. Its Jewish population was small until the partitions of Poland late in the 18th century. In 1772, 1775 and 1795 the rulers of Austria, Prussia and Russia partitioned the territory of Poland among themselves. Austria absorbed the poor and mostly rural southeastern portion of Poland and renamed it the Kingdom of Lodmeria and GaliciaCusually known only as Galicia. Galicia had a Jewish population second only to that of Russian Poland.

In 1867, the Austrian Empire entered into a political compromise with the Hungarians and created a new entity henceforth known as the Austro-Hungarian Kingdom or the Dual Monarchy.

Crownlands were administered by governors appointed by the ruling monarch. In a general sense, laws were generated by the emperor and passed by the legislature based in Vienna, but the laws did not always apply to all parts of the Empire, nor did they necessarily go into effect at the same time in all parts of the Empire. Specific legislation might address a particular perceived problem in one or more of the Crownlands and then be administered by the local governor in ways that often were influenced by local political bodies.

A weak central government and a chronic lack of money determined that legislative bodies of the Crownlands (known as Diets) continued to play an important role in all of the Empire's territories throughout much of its history. Policies toward the Jews on taxes, military service, restrictions and other matters tended to be similar, but minor differences appeared when the laws were applied in the various Crownlands.

As the Empire expanded, Jews living in the newly acquired territories came under generally strict Austrian laws that sought to control population expansion by birth or immigration restrictions and to ensure that no Jews from outside the Empire would be attracted to relocate within its borders. Heavy taxes were placed on Jews, along with severe restrictions on movement, occupation, trade and worship. Jews needed permission to marry, to build a synagogue, or to move elsewhere with the Empire. Jews were forbidden to appear on the streets at certain times, periodically required to adopt distinctive dress, and prohibited to engage in many occupations or to serve non-Jews in other occupations. Virtually every aspect of daily life was circumscribed by government regula-

tions until Emperor Franz Josef began to abolish these laws in 1848.

Until the mid-18th century, the Jews of Poland, including what became Galicia, governed themselves with the *kehillah*, an elected body of representatives comprised of elders and wealthy men. In her 1772 *Galizische Judenordnung,* an edict that established how Jews were to be taxed and treated under Austrian rule, Maria Theresa, wanting as little as possible to do with governing Jews, reinstituted the *kehillah* in Bukowina and Galicia. In 1789, Joseph II, believing that the *kehillah* was incompatible with his desire to encourage a greater level of Jewish integration, abolished the *kehillah* although his successor reestablished it 10 years later.

Under the *kehillah* system, each Crownland within the Empire had a chief rabbi who oversaw the affairs of the Jewish community, especially its legal matters. The *kehillah* was charged with collecting taxes owed to the throne and other matters as assigned. The leader of the *kehillah* mediated between the Jewish community, the nobility and the government.[1] (McCagg, p. 14). Later, the *kehillah* was an elected body with many duties and responsibilities to both the Jewish community and the Austrian government. The *kehillah* became the body through which Jews could work to moderate or stave off restrictive policies or alter new requirements.

Jews of the Austrian Empire were always vulnerable and subject to the whims of a ruler who at times submitted to pressures from the clergy and othersCsuch as local diets, which sometimes objected to Jews having the right to live in their towns.

The first effort to reform the relationship between the state and the Jewish community came under Joseph II (1780–90) who concluded that the solution to the "Jewish problem" was to reform laws to open Austrian economic, political and social life to Jewish participation. Joseph issued a Patent of Toleration that elaborated a radically different relationship between Austria and its Jews. The Patent was followed by numerous laws that specifically altered established policies.

The entire Jewish community did not wholly support the reforms, since Joseph abolished the *kehillah* and established a system to regulate marriage under civil law. The Jews of Galicia especially actively resisted government interference with this important religious function. Joseph's reforms were largely moribund by the end of his brief reign, and most of the rest were overturned by his brother and successor, Leopold II (1790–92) and, subsequently, Leopold's son Franz II (1792–1835). Conditions for the Jews did not improve measurably until well after Franz Joseph assumed power in 1848.

Prior to Franz Joseph's emancipation of the Jews in 1868, government regulation of Jewish rights and internal movement generally was harsh and arbitrary, but the way the Jews chose to manage this problem differed dramatically and resulted in substantial differences in Jewish economic, educational and social conditions in various parts of the Empire. Many Jews in Bohemia and Moravia, for example, embraced the government's universal education requirement. When emancipation came, they were well educated secularly and ready and eager to participate in the economy and social institutions of those Crownlands. In Bukovina and Galicia, however, most Jews strongly resisted governmental efforts toward assimilation; as a result, they were less interested in or capable of engaging in social and economic integration at the time of emancipation.

Governance of the Jewish Community

The Jewish community was granted rights of self-governance for most of the years of the Empire. Each Crownland had a central *kehillah* except for post-1868 Hungary which had two. In each Crownland, the central *kehillah* had a similar structure with a central governing body. Almost all matters concerning the Jewish community were overseen by this body. The central *kehillah* oversaw legally established *kehillot* in some Crownlands, while smaller countries, such as Moravia, had just the central body. Whether central or regional, the *kehillot* were headed by elders and elected representatives. Their duties were established by laws that specified the geographical territory each covered.

The *kehillot* were designed to collect taxes and to perform a variety of functions to maintain Jewish institutions and life. In addition, the *kehillah* was mandated to tax members for support of its own administration, officially recognized synagogues, *mikvot* (ritual baths) educational organizations, courts, and social welfare institutions within its jurisdiction. Some taxes were collected by Jewish schools. Taxing powers were enforced by the state because the *kehillah* was perceived as an arm of the Austrian government, even though *kehillot* leaders generally had no role in imposing most of the taxes. Everyone born and/or recognized as a Jew was required to register with the *kehillah* that covered his or her official place of residence.

Rabbis were selected by the district-level *kehillah* as the official rabbi for the district and was paid by the *kehillah*. When a Crownland had only one district, that rabbi served in the only officially recognized synagogue. This tended to keep the Jewish population living near the synagogue and close to each other. Official rabbis were responsible for representing the Jewish community; conducting religious services in officially sanctioned synagogues; conducting officially approved marriages; collecting birth, marriage and death information as prescribed by civil law; and overseeing Jewish laws and institutions. Civil and religious matters were addressed by *bet din* (religious courts). Criminal matters were heard by local civil courts. Some *bet din* records have been found in major national archives of countries that were part of the Empire, but most probably disappeared in the Holocaust.

Religious and secular politics played an important role in determining who would be the official district rabbi. Over time, more stringent qualifications crept into Austrian law. By the time of the emancipation in 1868, every sector of the empire had laws requiring official rabbis to show evidence of having had a certain amount of education and having passed secular philosophy courses as part of that education.

Even after emancipation, the Jewish communities of the empire continued to govern themselves. The structure of the governance and the number of districts in each Crownland changed several times during the reign of Franz Joseph, but the concept remained intact. A law of March 21, 1890, confirmed that every Jew must belong to the one congregation designated for the district that was his official place of residence. The congregation was held responsible for maintaining a register of members. Taxes were compulsory and the Dual Monarchy enforced the right of congregations to tax their members.

Residence Laws Affecting the Jewish Community

Prior to emancipation, Jewish residence in some major cities of the Empire, including Lemberg (today L'viv), Prague and Vienna, was subject to restrictive laws. Jews able to obtain permission to live in these cities were restricted to designated areas. Permission was granted on the basis of income and other requirements. Non-residents could secure limited permission to visit and conduct trade in these cities, but their official addresses remained with the *kehillah* where they were registered for tax and voting purposes.

Marriage and Family Laws: Their Impact on Civil Registration Of Vital Events

On September 23, 1726, Charles VI decreed that only one member of a Jewish family be allowed to marry and be recognized as a legitimate household. Recognition as a legitimate household, a *familiant*, initially required registration and payment of a substantial tax. In practical terms, however, because of quotas that existed in many places in the Empire at that time, permission to marry was granted only if and when a death or movement of official registration to another jurisdiction created a vacancy in a locality. No interruption of religious marriage occurred, but members of these unofficial unions were at a disadvantage when they applied for business licenses, permission to engage in certain occupations or to move their households to major cities, or to conduct a host of other activities covered by the family laws.

Marriages, births and deaths were registered by the Catholic parish where the family lived. A law of May 14, 1734, established the minimum marriageable age for Jewish males and females at 18 and 15, respectively. The law required that the parties document their ages on the basis of birth or circumcision registers. If no registers existed, a local nobleman could attest to the ages.

Unlike earlier *Judenpatents* (laws regulating Jews), the *Judenpatent* for Galicia issued in 1789 included no restriction on the number of marriages permitted. Jews living in the Lemberg district, however, fell under special constraints that included a quota for the number of families that could live there. With some variations, these limitations generally remained in place until 1868. Reforms in 1848 abolished the *familianten* restrictions in Bohemia and Moravia, but it was not until 1868 that all vestiges of these harsh marriage laws finally disappeared.

Surname Adoption

Most Jews who lived in the Austrian Empire did not carry fixed, inherited family names prior to January 1, 1788, when Emperor Joseph II ordered their adoption, recognizing that surname adoption was essential to regulate and track Jews for many official governmental purposes, such as conscription and taxation. West Galicia, the portion of Poland annexed by Austria in the 1795 partition, was ruled as a separate administrative entity until 1803 and did not require permanent surnames until February 21, 1805.[2]

No registers of Austrian name adoptions are known to survive, although Alexander Beider has described a German-language description of the process written approximately one hundred years later.[3] If such registers were made (and even this is not certain), they likely were maintained by the governors of the individual countries within the Empire. No English-language references exist that describe the actual procedures involved, but some reference materials reveal that the surname adoption law required Jews to adopt German-language surnames, although some names were forbidden to Jews. Jew who already had a fixed surname based on some other language of the land were not required to alter their names.

The 1787 law gave heads of households until January 1, 1788, to register. Logically, name adoption should have been the responsibility of the local *kehillah*, but because some surnamesCespecially from GaliciaCwere unflattering and even cruel, most assume that the process was handled by government bureaucrats assigned by the governors of the Crownland. Because the process resulted in a wide variation of names from appealing to insulting, many assume that money helped secure a pleasant name. Whether the fee was official or unofficial is not known.

Military Service

Jews were required to serve in the military after 1788, but this requirement was riddled with exceptions. After Joseph II's death in 1790, Jews generally paid fines in order to avoid military service. The Austrian military leadership was no more eager to have Jews serve than most Jews were eager to serve. An agreement with the government placed most Jews in commissary service, where most Jews served after 1868. Jews who could afford to do so, paid a special tax to avoid service entirely. Because military service was considered a lifelong occupation rather than a brief period of required service, Jewish men who wanted access to the larger society were more open to serving in the military (McCagg, p. 66). Empire-wide military records are held today in the Kriegsarchiv* (military archives) in Vienna.

Travel

All residents of the Empire carried identification papers, and movement from one's place of residence required that the individual or head of household register with the local authorities. Jews, like other citizens, needed passports when they wanted to leave the Empire. Internal travel between Crownlands also necessitated travel documents. Jews conducted considerable trade between Crownlands, so many of them must have been able to pay the fees required to obtain the required authorization. For example, Jews in northern Hungary grew wine grapes for kosher wine imported for use in Galicia and elsewhere in the Empire. Within the various Crownlands, the Diets regulated internal movements of their populations.

Following emancipation, when Jews were freer to engage in higher education and the professions, many were attracted to cities such as Vienna and those in Bohemia, Hungary and Moravia. They sought to improve their economic standing and gravitated toward law, literature, medicine, music and other performing arts. Banking, wholesale businesses in textiles, oil and petroleum products, tobacco, diamonds, silver and gold, were occupations that led to gentility for a small number of Jewish men.

Land Ownership and Residence Laws

Until the era of Franz Joseph, Jews could not own agricultural land. Some Jews did own real property, however, in the form of houses where they lived in cities and towns. Much of the Empire was still dominated by feudalism, and major tracts of land were held by members of the nobility; Jewish ownership of land was rare. Small numbers of Jews owned land and property in pre-1772 Poland, and it appears that when Poland was partitioned, ownership was not disrupted despite the imposition of Austrian law.

In 1840, the Hungarian Diet voted to void existing restrictions on Jewish residency, and Jews responded by emigrating to Hungary in large numbers. After 1848, at the beginning of the long reign of Franz Joseph and in response to Hungary's growing restiveness and influence in the Empire, efforts were made to reform Austrian land-ownership laws. Even after emancipation lifted all residence and land-ownership laws based on religion, local Diets sometimes instituted restrictions of their own. Land ownership maps may be found in archives of individual countries.

Education

In an effort to encourage assimilation of the Jews into mainstream society, Joseph II developed a universal education requirement. Although short-lived, it mandated the creation of German-Jewish schools and required Jews to acquire a knowledge of German before achieving the right to marry. Bohemian Jews responded eagerly to the opportunity and established a system of schools for Jewish children, although some children attended Christian schools. Elsewhere in the Empire, notably in Galicia, education was viewed with deep suspicion and fear that it would lead to the assimilation that Joseph II was promoting.

In 1849, Franz Joseph spearheaded legislation to require universal education for Jewish children ages 7–14, but in 1855, the Austrian Parliament banned Jews from attending public schools and barred Jewish teachers from employment

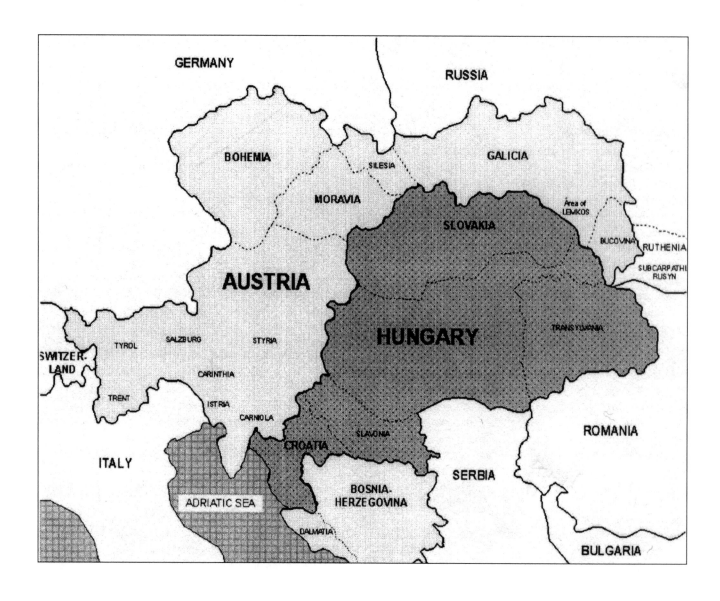

in public schools. This ban persisted until full Emancipation in 1868.

Post-emancipation educational records were maintained by local governments, and those that have survived are in local repositories and archives.

Language Issues

Ethnic groups throughout the Empire had their own languages, and Austria's imposition of the German language was often a contentious issue. Jews used Hebrew in a religious context and Yiddish in their daily lives. At various times, the Austrian Parliament ordered the Jews to cease publishing in Yiddish and Hebrew and to discontinue its use in communal and official documents. This stricture had significant effects in various parts of the Empire. Some Jews concluded that it was best to align themselves with the German-speaking population. German was considered an international language among the educated. Associating oneself with German as a primary language spoke to the desire of some Jews to melt into the larger society. This was especially true in Bohemia and Moravia.

On the other hand, some Jews were drawn to the various nationalist movements that developed in the middle of the 19th century. They identified with those who desired more autonomy from Austria if not downright independence. Galicia's Polish and Ruthenian nationalist movements competed for the same territory around Lemberg, a complication that confounded the situation. Jews attracted to nationalist movements tended to be those who were less attached to the Jewish community religiously. While they hoped for a warm welcome from the nationalists, they frequently were disappointed. Use of a language and declarations of nationalist aspirations were insufficient to overcome deeply ingrained anti-Jewish feelings. The Ruthenians (Ukrainians) perhaps were most accepting of Jewish overtures, but this alliance afforded opposing Polish forces an excuse for pogroms against Jews after World War I. In Hungary, significant numbers of Jews joined the movement to have Magyar recognized as the official language. When the Dual Monarchy was created, Magyar was made the official language of Hungary. In general, Yiddish receded in importance as a instrument for daily communication by Jews the more the Jews found acceptance by the larger society.

Genealogical Resources

Property Tax Maps. Josephine Metrics were maps created in 1800 for the taxation purpose of showing who lived in properties in a town. The maps were revised in 1815 and called Franciscan Metrics. Properties were numbered, and the numbers were used as the house numbers seen in vital, tax and voting records. The maps included the names of the owners of the property and land. The maps were used locally and today are held in the archives of each country. Since the spelling of surnames tended to be fluid in the early 19th century, the maps can be especially useful when used in conjunction with vital and other records.

Notary Records. Prior to the invention of mechanical copiers, notary publics served as officially licensed producers of copies of documents. People needing copies of vital records and military, school and other similar documents turned to notaries for this service. For a small fee, the notary made a copy and certified it as an exact duplicate of the original. Notaries were supposed to retain a copy for their own files and periodically to bind the files into books. At some point, the books became government property. Some are housed today in the archives of the contemporary countries that once composed the Austrian Empire.

In Poland, these documents come under the jurisdiction of the Ministry of Justice and, therefore, are governed by restrictive privacy laws. Only direct descendants may have access to ancestors' records and the ancestry must be proven. In addition, a death certificate is required to prove that the individual is deceased. Some leeway has been granted to Jews who have noted that death certificates were not issued for victims of the Holocaust.

Vital Records. Until the system was dismantled after the Empire ended, Jewish vital records were collected and maintained by the official rabbi appointed to each administrative district under the *kehillot* in each Crownland. A single district included many towns, and events were recorded in the order of their occurrence. In some parts of the Empire, wars caused the destruction of these records. Today the surviving records are in bound books in various archives. Some Jewish records have been filmed and are available from the LDS (Mormon) Family History Library (see LDS). See also individual chapters for details of specific countries.

Addresses

Kriegsarchiv, A-1030 Vienna, Nollendorfergasse 2; telephone: 01-0043-179540-504; website: www.oesta.gv.at/engdiv/adresses.htm

Bibliography

Kaganoff, Benzion C. *A Dictionary of Jewish Names and Their History*. New York: Schocken, 1977.

Luft, Edward D. "Map Resources for the Genealogist at the U.S. Library of Congress." *AVOTAYNU* 7, no. 4 (Winter 1991): 43–46.

Austro-Hungarian Empire

Beider, Alexander. *A Dictionary of Jewish Surnames from the Kingdom of Poland*. Teaneck, N.J.: Avotaynu, 1996.

Brook-Shepherd, Gordon. *The Austrians: A Thousand Year Odyssey*. New York: Carroll and Graf, 1996.

Deutsch, Gotthard. "Austria." *Jewish Encyclopedia*, vol. 2. New York: Funk and Wagnalls, 1902.

Duker, Abraham G. "Galicia." *Universal Jewish Encyclopedia*. New York: Universal Jewish Encyclopedia.

McCagg, William O., Jr. *A History of Habsburg Jews, 1670–1918*. Bloomington: Indiana University Press, 1992.

Panchyk, Richard. "Genealogy and Migration: Jewish Movement in 19th-Century Austro-Hungary." *AVOTAYNU* 12, no. 1 (Spring 1996): 25–28.

Pauley, Bruce F. *From Prejudice to Persecution: A History of Austrian Anti-Semitism*. Chapel Hill: University of North Carolina Press, 1992.

Rosanes, Salomon A. *Divre Yemei Yisrael be-Togermah* History of the Jews in Turkey and the Levant). [Hebrew] Tel Aviv, 1930.

Stein, Wilhelm. "Austria." *Universal Jewish Encyclopedia*. New York: Universal Jewish Encyclopedia, 1939.

Czech Republic and Slovak Republic (formerly Bohemia and Moravia)

Arnstein, George. "History of Jewish Record Keeping in Bohemia." *AVOTAYNU* 7, no. 3, (Fall 1991): 22.

Brilling, Bernhard. "History of Personal Records of Jews in Germany." *AVOTAYNU* 7, no. 2, (Summer 1991): 9–10.

Bruell, Claire. "Connections to the Czech Republic." *AVOTAYNU* 12, no. 2 (Summer 1996): 21–26.

Gladstone, Bill. "The Jews of Bohemia and Moravia: A Historical Reader." *AVOTAYNU* 10, no. 1 (Spring 1994): 60–61.

Gruber, Ruth E. "Recommends Source for Genealogical Inquiries in Czech Republic." *AVOTAYNU* 9, no. 4, (Winter 1993): 70.

Kestenberg-Gladstein, Ruth. "The Jews Between Czechs and Germans in the Historic Lands, 1848–1918." *The Jews of Czechoslovakia*, vol. 1. Philadelphia: Jewish Publication Society of America; New York: Society for the History of Czechoslovakia, 1968.

Kisch, Guido. "Jewish Historiography in Bohemia, Moravia and Silesia." *The Jews of Czechoslovakia*, vol. 1. Philadelphia: Jewish Publication Society of America; New York: Society for the History of Czechoslovakia, 1968.

Kohn, Hans. "Before 1918 in the Historic Lands." *The Jews of Czechoslovakia*, vol. 1, Philadelphia: Jewish Publication Society of America; New York: Society for the History of Czechoslovakia, 1968.

Luft, Edward D. "The Complete Catalogue of Records for the Jewish Communities of Bohemia and Moravia, Excluding that of Prague." *AVOTAYNU* 7, no. 3 (Fall 1991): 20–21.

CCCC. "Guide Book: Jewish Sights of Bohemia and Moravia," *AVOTAYNU* 9, no. 1 (Spring 1993): 63.

CCCC. "Parish Registers in Slovakia." *AVOTAYNU* 9, no. 4 (Winter 1993): 67.

Rakov, Lipman. "Gives Hints on Slovak Research." *AVOTAYNU* 10, no. 3 (Fall 1994): 65.

Rothkirchen, Livia. "Slovakia: I, 1848–1918." *The Jews of Czechoslovakia*, vol. 1. Philadelphia: Jewish Publication Society of America; New York: Society for the History of Czechoslovakia, 1968.

Sack, Sallyann Amdur. "More Resources in Israel." *AVOTAYNU* 7, no. 2 (Summer 1991): 7–8.

Hungary (including portions of territory now in Romania)

Bercuvitz, Rick. "Revisiting Our Romanian Roots." *AVOTAYNU* 9, no. 4 (Winter 1993): 302.

Clapsaddle, Carol. "Beit Maramaros." *AVOTAYNU* 7, no. 2 (Summer 1991): 7–8.

Etvos, George. "Resources for Jewish Genealogical Research in Hungary." *AVOTAYNU* 13, no. 4 (Winter 1997): 17–19.

Goldstein, Irene Saunders. "Romanian Records at the Holocaust Memorial Museum; Research Strategies for Records Still Held in Romania." *AVOTAYNU* 9, no. 4 (Winter 1993): 18–19.

Gyemant, Ladislau. "Sources of Research for Jewish Genealogy in Transylvania." *AVOTAYNU* 11, no. 2 (Summer 1995): 29–30.

Gyemant, Ladislau. "Genealogy and History: Sources of Jewish Genealogical Research in Romania (18th–20th Centuries)." *AVOTAYNU* 13, no. 3 (Fall 1997): 42–48.

Luft, Edward D. "Jewish Records in Sopron, Hungary." *AVOTAYNU* 14, no. 2 (Summer 1998): 51.

Landeszman, Gyorgy. "Jewish Records in Hungarian Archives." *AVOTAYNU* 3, no. 2 (Spring 1987): 13–15.

Landeszman, Gyorgy. "Some Problems of Genealogical Research in Hungary." *AVOTAYNU* 7 no. 3 (Fall 1991): 17–19.

"New Records of Hungary and Russia Available at the LDS Library." *AVOTAYNU* 13, no. 1 (Spring 1997): 51.

Panchyk, Richard. "Given Names and Hungarian Jews," *AVOTAYNU* 11, no. 2 (Summer 1995): 24–28.

Panchyk, Richard. "What Hungarian Censuses Can Tell Us." *AVOTAYNU* 13, no. 3 (Fall 1997): 34–36.

Perlman, Robert. "Books on Hungary." *AVOTAYNU* 9, no. 4 (Winter 1993): 69.

Regenstreif, Dan. "Origins of the Jews of Romania and Their History Up to the Basic Rules of 1831–32." *AVOTAYNU* 8, no. 2 (Summer 1992): 19–24.

Skowronek, Jerzy, "Jewish Genealogical Research in Polish Archives," *AVOTAYNU* 10, no. 2 (Summer 1994): 5–8.

Teitelbaum, Stephen U., "Is My Name Teitelbaum, Farkas, Wolf or What?" *AVOTAYNU* 9, no. 3 (Winter 1993): 45–46.

Poland (formerly Galicia)

Berglass, Itzhok and Shlomo Yahalomi-Diamand, ed. *The Book of Strzyzow and Vicinity.* Israel: Natives of Strzyzow Societies in Israel and the Diaspora, 1969. Trans. and republished by Harry Langsam, Los Angeles, CA.

Bussgang, Fay Vogel. "Census Records and City Directories in the Krakow Archives." *AVOTAYNU* 12, no. 2 (Summer 1995): 27–28.

Levite, Avraham, ed. *A Memorial to the Brzozow Community.* Israel: Survivors of Brzozow, 1984.

Papakin, Heorgij V. "The Practicalities of Genealogical Research in Ukraine. " *AVOTAYNU* 10, no. 4 (Winter 1994): 3–4.

Solomowitz, Benjamin H. "Some Discoveries in Galician Records." *AVOTAYNU* 13, no. 4, (Winter 1997): 45.

Wynne, Suzan F. *Finding Your Jewish Roots in Galicia: A Resource Guide.* Teaneck, N.J.: Avotaynu, 1998.

Trieste

Dubin, Lois C. *The Port Jews of Trieste: Absolutist Politics and Enlightenment Culture.* Palo Alto: Stanford University Press, 1999.

Ukraine (now includes territory once part of Hungary and then Czechoslovakia as well as part of Galicia)

Lozytsky, Volodymyr. "Sources for Jewish Genealogy in the Ukrainian Archives." *AVOTAYNU* 10, no. 2 (Summer 1994): 9–14.

Subtelny, Orest. *Ukraine: A History.* Toronto: University of Toronto Press, Canadian Institute of Ukrainian Studies, 1988.

Wynne, Suzan F. *Finding Your Jewish Roots in Galicia: A Resource Guide.* Teaneck, N.J.: Avotaynu, 1998.

Yugoslavia

Freidenreich, Harriet Pass. *The Jews of Yugoslavia: A Quest for Community.* Philadelphia: Jewish Publication Society of America, 1979.

"Research Projects at the Diaspora Research Institute." *AVOTAYNU* 10, no. 3 (Winter 1994): 54–55.

Notes

1. McCagg: 14
2. Beider: 9
3. Beider: 8–9

Ottoman Empire

by Sallyann Amdur Sack

For many centuries, large numbers of Jews lived in the Ottoman Empire where governmental actions created records valuable for genealogical research. This chapter addresses issues and records that were common to the entire empire. Individual countries created after the dissolution of the empire are discussed in their own chapters. The countries formed after the dissolution of the empire include Bulgaria, Egypt, Greece, Israel, Iraq, Jordan, Syria, Tunisia and the former Yugoslavia; each are discussed separately elsewhere in this book.

History

After the establishment of the Spanish and Portuguese Inquisitions more than five centuries ago, many of the Jews who left the Iberian Peninsula went to live in the Ottoman Empire, where Sultan Beyazid II welcomed them for the help they could provide in developing commerce. The Ottoman Empire had been founded in 1289. Its early capitals were Bursa in Anatolia and Edirne (Adrianople), where the contemporary borders of Bulgaria, Greece and Turkey meet. Constantinople (today Istanbul and the current capital of Turkey) remained in Byzantine hands until the Ottomans captured it in 1453. In the 16th century, the Ottoman Empire, a strong rival to Christian Europe, saw the Jews as desirable allies in this competition.

Constantly varying in size at different periods of time, at its peak, the Ottoman Empire covered all of the Arab world from Yemen to North Africa and all of the land bordering the Black Sea, the Caucasus, southern Ukraine, Persia and portions of Yugoslavia. It occupied parts of Hungary and from the 1500s to about 1720 surrounded Vienna twice, once in the 16th century and again in the 17th century, and controlled most of Romania until the late 19th century. The Empire lasted until the end of World War I (technically November 17, 1922, when Sultan Mohammed VI fled from Turkey); in its heyday the Ottoman Empire was the superpower of its time.

When the Jews from the Iberian Peninsula first came to the Ottoman Empire, they encountered already existing Jewish communities in such places as Salonika (today Thessaloniki, Greece), Smyrna (today Izmir, Turkey) and Constantinople. These Jews were known as Romaniote Jews. The term Romaniote comes from the word Rome and refers to those Greek-speaking Jews who inhabited the Byzantine Empire, that is, the true Roman Empire. (The Byzantines believed themselves to be the true heirs to early Roman Christianity and referred to themselves as such. They despised the heretical Roman Catholic establishment that presided over western Christendom from Rome.)

The Spanish and Portuguese Jews settled Constantinople, Salonika and Smyrna in great numbers. Salonika quickly became more than 50 percent Jewish and the working language of the city became Judeo-Spanish, the language of the Sephardim—medieval Spanish with Hebrew, Arabic, and later, some southern European Slavic, Greek and Turkish words. At first the Sephardim and Romaniotes lived in different sections of the cities and maintained their separate languages and rituals.

By the mid-16th century, Sephardic Jews outnumbered their Romaniote brethren and Romaniotes began to assimilate into Sephardic culture. The process was given added impetus, especially in Istanbul, because of a large number of serious fires in Romaniote quarters. The survivors moved into Sephardic quarters, were absorbed into the larger group and became Sephardim.

Many Jews from Central and Eastern Europe and (later) Russia also settled into the Ottoman Empire. They, too, eventually assimilated into the predominant Sephardic culture. Their descendants have family names such as Eskenazi, Franco and Ruso, which mean Ashkenazi, "Franks" (westerners) and Russian, respectively—even though they swear today that they are Sephardim.

Status of the Jews in the Islamic World

Jews living in North Africa, Spain and the Middle East had come to live under Islamic rule as a result of the Arab conquests of the 8th century even before the Ottoman Empire conquered North Africa and the Middle East in the 16th century.

Because they are also "People of the Book" (i.e., descendants of the Prophet Abraham), the Islamic religion accords Jews and Christians the status of *dhimma*, a protected and tolerated—yet inferior—minority, permitted to live under Islamic rule but subject to specific restrictions and taxes. With some exceptions, especially in Persia and portions of North Africa, Jews were not subject to forced conversions. Conditions varied from country to country, but on the whole, Jews of the Ottoman Empire did not endure the brutal massacres and pogroms that occurred in Christian Europe.

Generally, in exchange for the safeguarding of life and property and the right to worship their own religion, Jews lived under a variety of restrictions, many of them humiliating, fit for a subjected population. At various times and places, they were forbidden ever to strike a Muslim even in self-defense, could not carry arms, ride horses or use normal saddles on their mounts, could not pray too loudly, proselytize, build new houses, worship or dress like Muslims. In some places, specifically Iran, they were required to wear special badges on their clothing or specially dyed outer garments. They were forbidden to make fermented beverages and were not permitted to work in any government service. Most of all, they were to pay the *jizya*, the tax on all non-Muslims.

Ottoman Census Registers

The Ottomans were good tax collectors. One of the first things they did was to make registers listing all male heads of households. They went from town to town, village to village so that everyone they could find was listed. The registers were created for the purpose of collecting taxes. Since the non-Muslims paid a head tax, they also had to be listed. At times, the Jews made deals with the Ottoman authorities, agreeing to pay a specific amount that was almost always less than what they would have paid had the Ottomans registered each and every Jewish head of household. For this reason, the Ottoman registers do not include the names of every head of household.

At least two copies of the registers were made. One was kept locally; the other was sent to the authorities in Istanbul.

The registers, called *mafassal defters*, are written in Turkish using Arabo-Persian script. In addition, the scribes used their own special version of this script, called *siyaqat* which only they could read. Even today, these documents are extremely difficult to decipher. A few have been transliterated and published in Roman script. Harold Rhode has transliterated the register that includes the Jews of Safed in the 16th century.[1] It includes almost no family surnames; men are listed in the traditional Jewish way as "X" son of "Y." Some additional clues may be found, such as "the carpenter" or "from such and such a place." Some registers have been published for Buda (now part of Budapest, Hungary) and for Tiflis (i.e., Tblisi, the capital of Georgia).[2] Often different groups of people lived in different quarters of the city, according to their places of origin.

Turkish Archives

Given the history of the Ottoman Empire, it is obvious that *Bas Bakanlik Arsiui*[*] the Ottoman Archives in Istanbul are a vast treasure of material. Jewish culture flourished in the 16th century, and, for this period especially, many valuable documents are held in the archives.[3] The Turkish authorities allow access to the records, but a researcher must first prove that he or she can read the Ottoman script. For practical purposes, therefore, this source still is inaccessible to genealogists.

Millet System

From the 16th century onwards, the Jews of the Ottoman Empire generally lived in their own independent communities that were subdivided according to ethnic group, for example, Arabic-speaking Jews, the *Musta'rabim* (Arab culturally), Sephardim, North Africans, Italians and sometimes, Ashkenazim.

The Ottoman Empire generally allowed its minorities to govern themselves. In addition, the extent of Ottoman control over the functionaries who administered the far-flung empire varied from place to place and time to time. The situation of the Jews in any specific place at any given time varied accordingly. In the early 19th century the central government in Constantinople attempted to liberalize the situation of the *dhimmis,* but these reforms were not always put into operation, especially in North Africa and Palestine.

On February 18, 1856, the sultan issued a new reform decree under which the insulting term *dhimma* was to be eliminated from official documents. Non-Muslims were given the right to repair their houses of worship and (indirectly) even to build new ones. The *jizye* was abolished—but replaced by a new "military substitution tax" (*bedel-i askeri*). For the first time, non-Muslims also were subject to military conscription.

The new edict also reorganized religious communities into recognized, autonomous bodies, called *millets. Millets* were constitutionally recognized groups with lay and religious governing bodies and leaders. Jews often had a chief rabbi, the *hakham-bashi*, first in Constantinople and eventually in other cities as well.

Capitulation Treaties

The Ottoman Empire established rules to deal with two non-Islamic groups. One group was the *dhimmas*; the other consisted of foreigners, usually European merchants and/or diplomats who, officially at least, resided only temporarily in the Ottoman lands. The rules for dealing with the second group are called *capitulation treaties*; the first treaty was signed with France in 1536. Treaties with other European countries and with the United States followed thereafter.

According to the capitulation treaties, individuals living within the Ottoman Empire who were citizens of other nations were entitled to be protected and, if need be, judged by the embassies and consular officers of their own countries. Over time, especially in the 19th and early 20th centuries, as the Ottoman Empire progressively weakened, increasing numbers of Jews and others successfully sought this form of protection. Especially attractive for Jews was the fact that they were thereby exempt from Ottoman military service. Typically individuals employed by foreign consulates automatically received protection; merchants and other wealthy persons were the most likely to be protected. Both foreign and locally born men could be included. In the Ottoman Empire the foreign-born protected Jews were called *francos*; the few who were locally born were *beraths* (i.e., possessors of a special patent called *berat*). In 19th-century Romania, both foreign and native-born protected Jews were called *sudits*.

Some Jews gained foreign nationality; others merely obtained protected status. Records of both types may be found in the archives of the various European countries; some are in consular records, others in national archives. France and Italy were popular protectors for the Jews of Greece, North Africa, Istanbul and western Anatolia. Spain sometimes also was a protector of North Africans. Especially noteworthy are the many Jews who emigrated to Palestine in the late 19th and early 20th century and were given British protection by its consulate in Jerusalem. The United States protected a sizeable number as well. For more details see especially the references to Abensur-Hazzan and Kark listed below.

Contemporary Special Interest Groups

Two Jewish genealogical societies with a large Sephardic membership, the (French) Cercle de Généalogie Juive[*] and the Israel Genealogical Society[*] both have Ottoman Empire

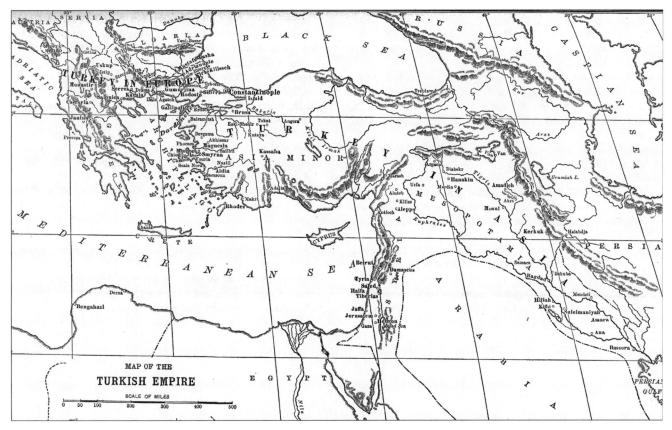

Ottoman Empire at the beginning of the 20th century showing towns where Jews lived

Special Interest Groups. Contact them for the best current information on Empire-wide resources.

Jewish Records in Muslim Lands Today

At the end of World War II, nearly 40 percent of world Jewry (the Sephardim) lived in Muslim lands in North Africa, Turkey, Iran and the Middle East. With the establishment of the State of Israel in 1948 and the rise of virulent anti-Semitism, the majority of Jews fled these countries. Most went to Israel where they comprise 50 percent of the population. The initial exceptions were Iran and Turkey. After the flight of the shah, when Iran joined the ranks of the stridently anti-Israel, this ancient Jewish population left its homeland *en masse*.

One thing characterizes the genealogical research efforts of Jews who ancestors came from Arab lands, the fact that it is next to impossible to obtain records from any of their governments. Iran is not Arab, but it falls within the same category—a place where many Jews once lived, from which it is impossible to obtain any records. Egypt which has signed a peace treaty with Israel in 1979 is theoretically an exception, but at this writing, the peace is a cold one, and we have not heard of any records being sent by that government. Secular Turkey has remained an ally of Israel from the start. Although many of its Jews have made *aliyah*, this has not taken the form of a mass exodus in response to organized persecution. Nevertheless, genealogists have not yet gained access to government-held records, apparently because of limitations of its system.

In this respect, Jewish genealogists with roots in Arab countries are today in much the same state that Ashkenazic genealogists were before the dissolution of the Soviet Union and the collapse of communism in Eastern and Central Europe. Lacking access to governmental archives and record repositories, genealogists must pursue intensely all other possible avenues of information, however scanty. This orientation characterizes virtually all of the Arab (and Iran) countries described here.

Addresses

Basbakanlik Devlet Arsivleri, Genel Mudurlugu, ivedik Caddesi, no. 59, 016180 Yenimahalle Ankara; telephone: 0312-344-5909; fax: 0312-315-1000; e-mail: DAGM@DEVLETARSIVLERI.GOV.TR.

Cercle de Généalogie Juive, 14, rue Staint-Lazare, 75009 Paris, France; telephone/fax: 33-1-4023-0490; e-mail: CGJGENEFR@AOL.COM; website: WWW.GENEALOJ.ORG.

Israel Genealogical Society, P.O. Box 4270, 01041 Jerusalem, Israel; telephone: 972-8-688-0884; e-mail: IGS@ISRAGEN.ORG.IL; website: WWW.ISRAGEN.ORG.IL

Bibliography

Abensur-Hazzan, Laurence. "The Current State of Sephardic Jewish Genealogy." *AVOTAYNU* 14, no. 1 (Spring 1999): 37–38.

Benbassa, Esther, and Aron Rodriques. *Juifs des Balkans: Espaces judeo-iberiques, XIVth–XX siecles.* (Judeo-Balkan Jews from the 14th to the 20th centuries). [French]. Paris: Ed. La Decouverte, 1993.

Blumberg, Arnold. *A View from Jerusalem, 1849–1858: The Consular Diary of James and Elizabeth Anne Finn.* Cranbury, N.J.: Associated University Press, 1980.

Bornstein-Makovetsky, Leah. "Jewish Names in Istanbul in the 18th and 19th Century." *AVOTAYNU* 14, no. 3 (Fall, 1998): 63–65. Includes reference to empire-wide list of Jewish names used in *gets* (Jewish divorces).

Contributing Editor (France). *AVOTAYNU* 8, no. 3 (Fall 1992): 51.

———. *AVOTAYNU* 14, no. 3 (Fall 1998): 70–71.

Contributing Editor (Israel). *AVOTAYNU* 8, no. 4 (Winter 1992): 56.

Contributing Editor (Turkey) *AVOTAYNU* 9, no. 1 (Spring 1993): 43.

Daitch, Randy. "Ottoman Empire Resources" *AVOTAYNU* 8, no. 1 (Spring 1992): 18–19.

Friedman, Isaiah. "The System of Capitulations and its Effects on Turco-Jewish Relations in Palestine, 1856–1897." In David Kushner, David, ed. *Palestine in the Late Ottoman Period: Political, Social and Economic Transformation*. Jerusalem: Yad Izhak Ben Zvi and Leiden: E.J. Brill, 1986.

Getz, Mike, and Sallyann Amdur Sack. "American Consulate, Jerusalem, 1857–1924." *AVOTAYNU* 10, no. 4 (Winter 1994): 13–16.

Gocek, Fatma Muge. "Archival Information on Ottoman Jews: Inheritance Register of the Chief Rabbi, 1769 C.E." In Avigdor Levy, ed. *The Jews in the Ottoman Empire*. Princeton, NJ: Darwin, Washington, D.C.: Institute of Turkish Studies, 1994.

Kark, Ruth. *American Consuls in the Holy Land*. Detroit: Wayne State University, 1994.

Kerem, Yitzchak. "Greek Jewry: Sources for Genealogical Research." *AVOTAYNU* 10, no. 4 (Winter 1994): 11–12.

Rhode, Harold. "The Ottoman Empire and Jewish Genealogy." *AVOTAYNU* 8, no. 1 (Spring 1992): 17.

Sack, Sallyann Amdur. "Israel Revisited: A genealogical trip." *AVOTAYNU* 3, no. 2 (Summer 1987):14–16.

Shaw, Stanford. *The Jews of the Ottoman Empire and the Turkish Republic. New York: New York University Press, 1991.*

"Three Important Archives in Israel." AVOTAYNU 9, no. 4 (Winter 1993): 11–13.

Notes

1. Rhode, Harold. M.A. Thesis, Columbia University, Department of History, 1973.
2. See articles on southeastern Europe in *Bulletin* by Tibo Halasi-Kun, Studia Turcica and Archivum Ottomanicum.
3. See various articles by Professor Bernard Lewis.

Russian Empire

by Vladislav Soshnikov

Note to reader: Do not overlook important information about the Eastern European database of Jewish archival records described at the end of this chapter—Ed.

The Imperial Russian Empire occupied a vast territory in both Europe and Asia. This chapter provides an explanation of basic historical and genealogical information about Jews who lived in the European part of the Russian Empire (excluding the Kingdom of Poland) and a general description of the archival system and genealogical resources preserved in the archives of the former Soviet Union.

The European portion of the Empire traditionally was composed of territories initially acquired more than 1,000 years ago from the medieval principalities of Kievan Rus, a state of the Eastern Slavs that included nearly all of contemporary Belarus, Ukraine and portions of northwestern Russia. In the 18th century, Russia acquired much of Poland and territories along the Baltic Sea at the same time that it expanded southward into lands conquered from Ottoman Turkey. In the 19th century, the Russian Empire added Finland and many territories in Asia, becoming the largest country in the world. In the 20th century, the Soviet Union included most of the territories of the former Russian Empire with the exception of Finland and Poland.

National boundaries have changed dramatically over the past two centuries; so have administrative districts within countries. The Russian Empire was divided into *guberniyas* (provinces), *uyezds* (districts) and *volosts* (subdivisions of uyezds). After the demise of the empire, the former capital cities of most guberniyas became centers of *oblasts* (regions) in the successor Soviet Union. Many exceptions exist, however, and many *oblasts* are different in size and name from the former *guberniyas*. Pre-revolutionary *uyezds* are comparable to *raions*, a subdivision of the *oblast* in contemporary Russia, Belarus and Ukraine. See also separate chapters on Belarus, Estonia, Latvia, Lithuania, Moldova, Poland, Russia and Ukraine.

Jewish History

Jews first appeared on European Russian territory more than one thousand years ago, but they did not inhabit Russia in great numbers until after the partitions of Poland in the years 1772–95. The three partitions brought almost one million unwelcome Yiddish-speaking, Ashkenazic Jews into the Empire, where they faced hostility from the Christian clergy and commonly experienced anti-Semitism from the majority of Russian citizens.

In 1791, Russian Empress Catherine the Great established the Pale of Settlement, an area along Russia's western border, and decreed that all Jewish inhabitants of her realm (with minor exceptions) live within its borders. The Pale had four major regions: 10 Polish *guberniyas* (see the chapter on Russia

Poland); six in northwestern Russia (Grodno, Kovno, Minsk, Mogilev, Vilno and Vitebsk); five in southwestern Russia (Chernigov, Kiev, Podolia, Poltava and Volhynia) and four in southern Russia (Bessarabia, Ekaterinoslav, Kherson and Taurida). With some adjustments, this residency restriction remained in force until 1917. At the time of the first All-Empire Census in 1897, 94 percent of the Empire's Jews still lived in the Pale, and only 208,000 of the 5.2 million Jews lived in the interior of Russia or in Finland.

The major areas where Jews lived, Belarus, Estonia, Latvia, Lithuania, Moldova (formerly Bessarabia) and Ukraine (with the exception of Bukovina and Galicia), were part of the Russian Empire from the late 18th century until the czar was overthrown during the 1917 Russian Revolution.

Social Status of Jews in the Russian Empire

Imperial Russia created a variety of laws that generated records about its Jewish subjects, many of which survive in archives and are valuable sources of genealogical information today. In order to understand the types of records created and to know where to seek them, the researcher needs to be familiar with the class structure formulated by medieval Russian law. The Russian Empire was a Christian state ruled by an autocratic czar with the help of an extensive bureaucracy. Every inhabitant was seen as belonging to one or another class, each of which served a specific function within the society and had different, specific duties and obligations toward the crown. These classes were nobility, clergy, military, peasants, town dwellers and artisans. Jews were officially classified as *inorodtsy*, non-Christian strangers of foreign origin, required to be good citizens and to take an oath of loyalty to the czar.

Initially, when the Jews of the western provinces became subjects of the Russian crown in 1772, they were allowed to keep the long-standing community organizations and privileges that they had enjoyed in the Polish-Lithuanian state. The situation changed in the 1790s, however, when the Pale of Settlement was established along with special laws and regulations that limited the Jews' social status and established particular obligations and duties. Jewish merchants, for example, were forced to pay taxes twice as high as those paid by non-Jews. Although the *kahillas* (Jewish communities) were allowed to exist for the first 50 years after creation of the Pale, they were forced to carry out the discriminatory policies of the State.

An urban population, Jews engaged primarily in banking, industry and trade, operating small shops and businesses. They resided in small Jewish market towns (*shtetls*) (*evreiskie obschestva mestechka*) and in separate communities within larger towns (*gorodskie meschanskie evreiskie obschestva*) and were registered separately in revisions of government tax census records (*reviskie skazki*) conducted in the corresponding districts (*uyezd*). The Crown Treasury Chambers (*Kazennaya Palata*) in each guberniya compiled lists of taxpayers during periodic revisions in 1795–1858. Some professionals, artisans, merchants and farmers were exempted from these revision lists.[1] In addition, Jews paid a number of special taxes, including the *korobochny sbor*, the main community tax used to support community institutions and mutual aid, and *svechnoi sbor*, a tax on Sabbath candles used to support Jewish schools.

Among others, additional individual taxes were levied on inheritances, the lease of buildings, distillery and liquor trade, industry, ownership of cattle and the right to wear Jewish clothing. The taxes were established by local governments and approved by the czar's interior and financial ministries. All the specific Jewish community taxes were paid and registered at the corresponding city governmental bodies. From 1836 to 1875, this was the *Duma, Ratusha, Magistrat*; after 1875, it was *Gorodskaia Uprava*.

Significant changes occurred in the organization of Jewish life during the 19th century. The *kahals* were abolished in 1844, and Jews of the Pale came under the governance of the general police administrations in the districts. City governments were responsible for economic and tax matters. Government-appointed rabbis were added to the list of Jewish community officials who, by that time, already had diminished control over business practices. Jewish courts continued in existence. *Chevrot* (brotherhoods of the Jewish community) increased in importance and number, many assuming the role of trade union, while synagogues became meeting places for various new political parties.

For taxation and military conscription purposes, the Russian government devised a special system of registration to track Jewish movement within the country. No one was permitted to move from his place of residence without special written consent issued from a specific governmental office. Despite the law, however, Jews moved frequently both within the Pale and even to the interior of the country, citing such reasons as travel for business, attendance at one or another educational institution, to visit relatives or even to resettle in newly allowed areas. Much migration was done without official approval, especially when the need arose to evade military service.

In the early 1800s, Czar Alexander I devised a plan to resettle some Jews from the Pale of Settlement to agricultural colonies in Novorossia (New Russia), the vast southern territories seized from the Ottoman Empire. Although thousands of Jews moved to agricultural colonies in the southern guberniyas of Bessarabia, Ekaterinoslav, Kherson and Taurida throughout the 19th century, few succeeded as farmers, despite certain privileges granted to colonists. At the same time, however, many Jews settled in south Russian towns and established prominent communities in Ekaterinoslav (today, Dnepeprotovsk), Elisavetgrad (today, Kirovograd) and Odessa. Nonetheless, Jewish agricultural colonies formally existed until the beginning of the 20th century.

Military Duty

In 1827, Czar Nicholas I decreed that Jews, who heretofore had been exempt from military service, were now liable for up to 25 years of army service as common soldiers—and the *kahals* were made responsible for delivering the required number of recruits. Jews employed many methods to avoid induction, including the use of false documents and officially permitted ransom. Many young men simply ran away from their communities when their draft date approached. In every community, however, some men fulfilled the military obligations and had the rank of reserve soldiers. In every *guberniya* and district, draft offices (*rekrutskie prisutstviya* before 1874 and *po voinskoi povinnosti prisutstvie* in 1874–1917) kept registers of all males eligible for conscription; in addition, family lists showing all males and their dates of birth were compiled periodically.

Vital Record Registration

As noted above, all Jews were registered in or assigned to a specific geographical location even if they actually resided elsewhere. Beginning in 1826, Jews were required to register all births, marriages, divorces and deaths in the synagogue in the locality to which they were assigned. In 1835, new regulations ordered the rabbis to keep registers (*metricheskie knigi*) of all Jewish vital events; after 1857, these registers were kept by government-appointed "crown rabbis," who usually were not the spiritual leaders of the respective communities.

For the years 1835–1917, Jewish vital records were collected annually by municipal institutions—initially by *Gorodskaia Duma* or *Ratusha/Magistrate*, and after 1870 by *Gorodskaia Uprava*. Beginning in 1844, these institutions compiled family lists of all resident Jewish families every two years; periodically, they also created alphabetical lists of the heads of local Jewish families. In addition, many other documents about Jews were created: registers of conscription dates, local tax records, copies of revision lists, registers of specific taxes for Jewish communities, registers of community members and registers of permission to leave.

According to the class structure of the 19th-century Russian Empire, different administrative institutions were responsible for different classes in each city. For the years 1870–1917, the *Meschanskaia Uprava* was responsible for town dwellers; *Remeslennaya Uprava* handled matters for craftsmen; and *Kupecheskaia Uprava* dealt with the merchants. These institutions were responsible for collecting taxes and administering military recruitment for their class of the population; their records are each kept separately in archives today. Jewish shtetls were administered by the local government of the *volost*, a smaller administrative subdivision of the *uyezd*.

Police Records

For administrative control purposes, district and city police kept their own files on Jews. Among their records after 1844 were lists of residents, petitions to establish a business, registers of internal travel passports and other miscellaneous documents. During the late 19th and early 20th centuries, when liberal and revolutionary political parties appeared (e.g., Bund, Social-Democratic and Zionist parties), Jewish activists became a special focus of attention for the police departments of each guberniya. An alphabetical card catalogue of names was created at the headquarters of the czar's police department in Moscow. Today this unique catalogue, which lists alphabetically hundreds of thousands of individuals, is in the custody of the Russian State Archives* in Moscow.

Temporary Amelioration of Burdens Under Czar Alexander II

During the reign of Czar Alexander II (1855–81), life improved somewhat for Russia's Jews. After 1859, Jewish merchants of the First Guild (i.e., the richest) and foreign Jews "noted for their social position" could reside permanently in St. Petersburg and Moscow. After 1861, Jews who had academic degrees and worked for the government could reside anywhere in the Empire, and, after 1879, any Jew with an academic degree, regardless of his employment, might do likewise. Merchants of the first and second guild were allowed to live in Kiev, and after 1865, Jewish artisans, mechanics and distillers could reside outside the Pale.

Even before the end of Alexander II's reign, however, the trend had begun to reverse, and it deteriorated even further under the last two Romanovs, Alexander III (1881–94) and Nicholas II (1894–1917). In 1887, the government introduced strict limits on Jewish educational access and began to enforce residency requirements more rigidly. In 1891, 20,000 of the 30,000 Jews who lived in Moscow were expelled to the Pale, many of them in chains. The list of restrictions on Jews grew longer and longer. The Pahlen Commission, created in 1883 to study "the Jewish question," reported that no fewer than 650 restrictive laws directed against the Jews may be enumerated in the Russian code, and the discriminations and disabilities implied in these laws are such that they have naturally resulted in making, until now, the life of an enormous majority of the Jews in Russia exceedingly onerous.

Local judicial and municipal reform had permitted Jews equal representation, but a law of 1879 restricted Jewish representation on local governmental bodies to no more than one-third—even in areas where Jews were a much larger percentage of the population.

Emigration, Assimilation and the Tragedy of Russian Jewry

Jewish life in the Pale did not see much social change before the Russian Revolution. Poverty was widespread, and the separation of the Jews existed until the fall of the Czarist Empire in 1917. Approximately 1.5 million Jews from the Russian Empire (excluding Russian Poland) emigrated to the United States between 1880 and 1914, at the same time that half a million went to Canada, South Africa, South America, Western Europe and Palestine.

Emigration was not legally regulated in Russia until 1892, but everyone who wished to travel abroad was required to obtain permission from his hometown government and a travel passport from the local governor's office. Jews, most leaving illegally, migrated from the western provinces of the Russian Empire chiefly by railway to the German seaports of Bremen and Hamburg to board ships for America. Beginning in 1888, the Baltic port of Libau (today Liepava) also offered service.

Emigration ceased during the Russian Revolution (1917) and subsequent civil war (1918–21) and almost no one emigrated from the successor Soviet Union. In the great social changes after the Revolution, Jewish religious communities and the traditional way of life were assimilated and dispersed in the growing industrial country. Many Jews left their *shtetls* for cities such as Moscow and Leningrad. During Stalin's Great Terror in the 1930s, millions of Soviet citizens, including many Jews, died in prisons and labor camps. Only in the western parts of Belarus, Lithuania and Ukraine, which were under Polish rule during the years 1921–39, was traditional Jewish life preserved longer.

The USSR annexed the western Belorussian, Lithuanian and Ukrainian regions in 1939, as well as Bessarabia in 1940, and brought dreadful political repression and a socialist economy on these territories. Nazi Germany's invasion during World War II completed the destruction of the remaining Jewish communities, and millions died in the Holocaust. After World War II, the Jews who remained alive in the USSR lived under the strict totalitarian regime of the Cold War until the 1970s, when the Soviet regime yielded to political pressure from the West and allowed limited Jewish emigration. A total of 700,000 Soviet Jews had emigrated by the end of the 1980s, some to Israel, the majority to the United States.

After the collapse of the Soviet Union in 1991, Jewish religious, community and cultural life could once more be re-established under the democratic laws of the newly independent states. Today, more than one million Jews still live in Russia, Ukraine, Belarus and other republics, but Jewish emigration continues.

Adoption of Jewish Surnames

With the exception of some rabbinic and other notable lines, most Polish Jews who came under Russian sovereignty at the end of the 18th century did not have true surnames, but identified themselves for religious purposes by their traditional Hebrew names (e.g., So and so, the son of So and so) (see JEWISH CUSTOMS). In December 1809, the Russian government ordered all Jews to adopt fixed, hereditary family names so that they might be more easily identified for taxation and conscription.

No name adoption registers are known to have survived, but each individual Jewish community apparently was responsible for administering the process.[2] Given the increasingly harsh laws under which Russian Jews were forced to live, it is not surprising that many evaded the law in a variety of ways and to the best of their abilities. As late as the middle of the 19th century, government officials complained about the frequent change of family names among Russian Jews who lived in different communities under different names. The Jews of 19th-century Russia were extremely mobile; they moved often in search of a better life and to avoid military conscription and extremely harsh taxes. Often they lived in different communities under different surnames, frequently adopting the name of their previous community as a surname. Thus, even close relatives might have different last names, and every Jew probably lived in (and created a paper trail in) many *shtetls,* not just the single one cited by an immigrant ancestor. Until the Russian Revolution, Jews had been forbidden to change the names by which they were recorded in their official birth register. For many reasons, this was a law more honored in the breach than in the observance.

Resources for Genealogical Research

Archival Sources

As is true in most places, archival collections are the major source of Jewish genealogical information, but the complete holdings of Jewish genealogical records are still being uncovered after years of official indifference, neglect and secrecy. In general, archival sources document Jews in Russian controlled territory since the 1790s, but in many cases, only limited information is available for a given historical period. Wars, revolution and divisions between neighboring countries caused the destruction of many archival records from the Imperial Czarist Empire. Provenance determines where records are to be kept. That is, records are held in the archives where they were created, despite changes in sovereignty. In the case of the Russian Empire, however, not only did boundaries between countries change, but so also did administrative divisions within the Empire. Especially after World War II, archival holdings were exchanged and moved between neighboring regions and/or countries. In order to know which archives to search for possible records of interest, genealogists need to study comprehensively the administrative divisions within the 19th-and early 20th-century Pale of Settlement.

Central historical archives hold the bulk of the most ancient and historically important records of the country. For example, the central historical archives of Russia in Moscow and in St. Petersburg hold the archival collections of the central government of the Russian Empire. In addition, regional archives exist in each oblast center today in Moldova, Russia and Ukraine. They usually hold both pre-revolutionary and Soviet records, including most of the genealogically relevant documents for the corresponding *guberniyas* and *uyezds.* The situation is different in Belarus and the Baltic States (Estonia, Latvia and Lithuania), where nearly all genealogically useful records have been concentrated in central state historical archives. In these countries, regional archives usually hold no pre-World War II records.

Fond, obis and K (delo) are archival designations of the record storage system that enables an archivist in the former Soviet Union to retrieve records, much as a librarian relies upon a cataloguing system. A fond corresponds to a record group, an obis to an inventory of a subject or records within a specific fond; a K is a file within an obis. As a result of Russian archival descriptive practice, each item in an archive is defined by three numbers: fond, obis and K.

The records in a fond are the records of a single specific organization or individual. The organization might be a unit of a government institution; in the case of the Russian Empire,

the individual was usually a rich landlord, merchant, prominent artist, scientist, cultural activist or industrial capitalist. Archivists and researchers can find an archival record by the institution or individual that created it. Therefore, when seeking genealogical information for a certain town resident, one must locate record groups (fonds) of the corresponding *guberniya,* district and town administrative institutions and religious and pubic organizations, and then look through inventories and indexes in search of interesting items. An individual file (K) usually is a bound volume of old papers that varies in size from a single sheet to a thousand pages. The handwriting is in Old Russian script and requires specific language expertise in order to understand the contents.

Basic reference aids in the archives are archival guides (*putevoditeli*) and traditional archival inventories (*opisi fondov*). Officially published archival guides in Russian, Ukrainian or other national languages have been published in almost every archive of the former Soviet Union and include general summaries of the records in each fond and collection. They may be found in many libraries as well. Archival inventories (*opisi fondov*) show the ordinal numbers and brief titles of every item (K) within the record group (fond). Each fond may have several *opisi.* The archival guides generally have been compiled in the 20th century and are typewritten in Russian, Ukrainian or other national languages. Indexes (*ukazateli*) and card catalogues (*katalogi*) sometimes are created for particular record groups. The aids may be a geographical index to a collection of vital records or a subject index listing names of government and public institutions mentioned in a collection of governor's office records. If these reference aids exist, they are generally fragmentary and not genealogically oriented; genealogy was not a priority in Soviet archives.

In recent years, some central historical archives in Russia and in Belarus started compilations of computerized databases of genealogical archival sources; unfortunately, these files are for the internal use of archivists only and are not available to outside researchers. On the other hand, the most advanced archives have started to build websites and to provide information about their holdings and services on the Internet. A comprehensive list of Russian archival addresses and a standardized description of their holdings and conditions for researchers compiled by Patricia Kennedy Grimsted is available online at www.LISG.NL/~ABB..

Types of Records

The primary sources for genealogical research during the time of the Russian Empire are:

- Revision lists (*reviski skazki*) for the years 1794–1808, 1811–12, 1815–25, 1833–35, 1850–52, and 1857–59
- Supplemental revision lists from 1860 to the end of the 19th century
- Local censuses of householders for the years 1862 to 1916
- Surviving portions of the All-Empire 1897 universal census
- Family and local residential lists (*posemeinye spiski* and *obyvatel'skie knigi*)

- Class lists for merchants (*spiski kuptsov*) and members of town communities (*spiski meschan* and *spiski evreiskih obschestv*)
- Lists of voters eligible to vote for the city council
- Jewish vital records (*metricheskie knigi*) for the years from 1835 to 1918
- Military conscription records (*posemeinye spiski* and *svidetelstva o voinskoi povinnosti*)
- Land and property records in corresponding town administrations
- Records of educational and cultural institutions

Because Jews were active in the economic life of the areas in which they lived, such documents as commercial contracts, documents about debts, protests, lending contracts, purchase orders—all stored in the collections of city governments—may be valuable to the family historian.

Another group of valuable documents are books of residents (*domovye knigi*), which may be found in some archives today. In the beginning of the 19th century, inhabitants of municipal, institutional and privately rented homes were registered in special lists that were updated yearly—and are still maintained today. Information collected includes surname, given name and patronymic, age of the inhabitant, locality from which the inhabitant came with the precise name of former place of residence, religion, date of entry into the quarters and upon leaving, the date and place to which the occupier moved. The source of the data is the internal passport issued to each resident of Russia upon reaching the age of 16. The St. Petersburg municipal archives* holds 547 files of residency books for the period 1843–1922. Similar books for Moscow are scattered among various archives. For more details see article by Vladimir Paley.[4]

After 1905, when Russian law allowed elections of the people's representatives to the Duma (parliament), lists of voters—men over the age of 25—were published in the official government regional newspapers (the *Gubernskie Vedomosti*) in 1906, 1907 and 1912.

After the Russian Revolution in 1917, the old governmental institutions ceased to function, and new state structures were created in the Soviet Union. In 1918, religious institutions were separated from the state, and the registration of Jewish births, marriages, divorces and deaths was transferred to civil institutions. In the 1920s, a system of local registry offices (ZAGS) of the Ministry of Justice was established. The ZAGS offices continue to function in Russia, Belarus, Moldova and Ukraine, and keep registers for the last 75 years.

Records created prior to 1920–25 normally have been transferred to the state archives of the appropriate oblast center. ZAGS archives do not provide services for genealogists and issue legal copies of vital records only to relatives of the person for whom information is required. Requests with notarized copies of proof of relationship should be sent through one's embassy or directly to the Ministry of Justice of the country involved.

Nonarchival Resources

Business, Provincial and City Directories. Business directories, such as the all-Russia *Vsia Rossia*, regional directories (*Ves Severo-Zapad*) and city directories, such as *Ves Kiev*, were published in Russia during the 1890s and the first decade of the 20th century. Listed in them are the names of many people who engaged in crafts, trade and small business—including many Jews.

Provincial directories (*gubernskie pamyatnye knishki*), published periodically in each guberniya from 1850 to 1916, cover all public institutions and offices, including Jewish institutions. Included are rabbis, other religious functionaries, doctors, hospital staff members, pharmacists and teachers; many of the latter were Jewish.

Many directories are held in major libraries around the world, including the U.S. Library of Congress* and the library of Columbia University* in New York.

Vsia Rossia 1895 Database. Jewish names from Ukrainian regions Jews names from an 1895 *Vsia Rossia* (business directory) for the Ukrainian guberniyas of Chernigov, Kiev and Poltava may be found on JewishGen (see JewishGen) under the title "Vsia Rossia 1895 Database." Another database on the same site, entitled "Jewish Religious Personnel in Russia, 1853–54" lists more than 4,000 synagogue employees from 900 towns throughout the Pale of Settlement.

Yiddish and Russian-Language Newspapers. Prior to World War I, many Yiddish and Russian-language Jewish newspapers existed in the Russian Empire. They often included marriage and death notices as well as articles of interest to family historians. Large collections of such newspapers may be found at the U.S. Library of Congress,* the YIVO Institute for Jewish Research,* the New York Public Library*—Jewish Division, and the Jewish National and University Library* in Jerusalem.

Museums and Cemeteries. Regional museums and Jewish cemeteries are potential sources of additional information, but both suffered considerable loss and damage during World War II. Researchers should always attempt to investigate these sources. Letters [in Russian] may be addressed "Administration" and the name of town of interest. Ask about the status of a Jewish cemetery in the community; also request that the letter be forwarded to the director of any local museum.

Languages Used in Records

Throughout this article, country and town names are rendered in transliterated Russian spelling. Russian was the official language of the Czarist Empire and most archival documents, inventories and reference aids created in that period are written in Russian. Some records in Belarus and western Ukraine are in Polish for the period when portions of these countries were under Polish administration; in the western part of Ukraine that belonged to Hungary until World War I and to Czechoslovakia in the interwar years, records are in those languages. Yiddish (written in Hebrew script) records usually are written parallel to Russian text in Jewish vital statistics registers. The Ukrainian and Belarussian languages appear in some records after 1918; the Lithuanian, Latvian and Estonian languages became official in those countries after 1918.

Calendar Considerations

Prior to 1918, Russia used the Julian calendar. In 1918, the Soviet government adopted the Gregorian calendar used in the

West. This means that dates in records from the 19th-century Russian Empire are 12 days earlier than the corresponding date on the Gregorian calendar. In addition, the Jewish calendar—months and days—appear in Jewish registry books that are written in Russian and Yiddish alongside the Christian calendar dates. A lack of correspondence between dates may occur also because the Jewish day begins at sundown.

Archival Conditions for Researchers

During the Soviet period, archives traditionally were not open to the public. Since 1991, in the newly independent countries, archives have been officially open to domestic or foreign researchers, including genealogists. Some countries, specifically the Baltic States, have established procedures helpful to researchers. Unfortunately, in Belarus, Russia and Ukraine a difference still exists between official national policy and local practices with the result that the archives in these countries are still not as helpful to genealogists as they might be.

Genealogists who wish to do their own on-site research should apply in writing to the archival director for formal approval of the proposed research; even if granted, the researcher's work in the reading room may be supervised by archivists. In many archives, because of a poor economic situation and slack bureaucratic discipline, procedures remain complicated and unfavorable to individual genealogists. Many genealogists report difficulty gaining access to records and favoritism by the directors of various archives. As a result, genealogists often must depend upon good luck and the mercy of one or another archivist. Frustrating limits on the delivery of archival files to the reading room and problems obtaining photocopies often are encountered. Although most archives have obtained photocopy machines in recent years, the number of copies a researcher may make is sometimes limited. Users are not allowed to make copies themselves, but must fill out a special application for copying permission that then must be considered by the archives director. Every photocopy made must be checked by an authorized archivist and imprinted with an archival copyright stamp. Photocopying an entire file is not permitted. Charges for copies vary; the range is US$1 to US$10 per page of European letter-size paper. Sometimes archivists mask part of the document, allowing users to obtain only the record pertaining to the approved subject of research.

Genealogical Services

In recent years, many archives, especially central historical archives in major cities, have begun to offer genealogical services for a fee. Unfortunately, most archives have received more inquiries than they can handle and lack adequate resources for speedy service. In addition, mail correspondence and money transfers tend to be very complicated in Belarus, Russia and Ukraine? It typically takes many months—even years—for a foreigner to obtain an answer, and even then the results often are unreasonably expensive and incomplete, primarily because of inexperience and lack of finding aids.

Anyone who requests research by mail initially will be charged from $50 to $80 simply for the archives to accept the request. Basic fees for genealogical research vary from $4 to $10 per hour of searching. Every photocopied page of a document costs from $1 to $10—and even higher. Photocopies are sent from the archives only after receipt of the full payment. An average search costs approximately $300. A final archival report, typewritten in the language of the particular county, usually consists of a list of all archival records inspected during the search and a line-by-line translation of records found that are relevant to the search. Photocopies of original records usually must be ordered separately.

A competent local genealogist or professional genealogical service usually can provide better and quicker service. Lists of professional genealogists who specialize in a particular country are available in genealogical reference books and magazines and on the Internet.

Microfilmed Genealogical Records

The LDS (Mormon) Family History Library in Salt Lake City, Utah, is now acquiring genealogical records from the republics of Armenia, Belarus, Estonia, Georgia, Lithuania, Moldova, Russia and Ukraine. A substantial number of Jewish vital records and revision lists, particularly from Belarus, became available in recent years. For the latest detailed information, always consult the latest edition of the Family History Library Catalog, Locality section, available on microfiche or CD-ROM at your local LDS Family History Center or on the WorldWideWeb.

United States Holocaust Memorial Museum (USHMM)*

The USHMM holds microfilm copies of Holocaust-era records from archives in Kiev, Minsk, Kishinev, Minsk, Moscow, Riga and other cities. Among others, these include ghetto records, death books from concentration camps, reports of the Soviet Extraordinary Commission to Investigate and Establish War Crimes of the German-Fascist Invaders.

Online Database of Archival Holdings for Jewish Genealogy

The Routes to Roots Foundation (RTRF) website (www. RTRFOUNDATION.ORG) features a town-by-town inventory of archive documents in a consolidated database from archives in Belarus, Lithuania, Moldova, Poland and Ukraine—all of the territory that once was part of the Pale of Settlement. The Consolidated Eastern European Archival Database is updated on an continual basis as new material is received from the archives. Postings of new archive data can be found on the "News Alert" feature of the website home page. The website also includes articles by archivists and historians, maps, related websites and other pertinent material for researching Jewish family history.

Bibliography

Altskan, Vadim. "Jewish Genealogical Material in the Archives of the Former USSR." *AVOTAYNU* 9, no. 1 (Spring 1993): 9–10.
Baker, Zachary. Bibliography of Eastern European Memorial (Yizkor) *Books.* New York: Jewish Genealogical Society, 1992.
Beider, Alexander. *A Dictionary of Jewish Surnames from the Russian Empire.* Teaneck, NJ: Avotaynu, 1993.

Bolotenko, George. "Beyond the Metricals: Records from the Russian Department of Police." *AVOTAYNU* 11, no. 4 (Winter 1995): 3–12.

Boonin, Harry. "Russian Business Directories." *AVOTAYNU* 6, no. 4 (Winter 1990): 23–32.

———. "Vital Statistics in Czarist Russia." *AVOTAYNU* 5, no. 3 (Fall 1989): 6–12.

Deych, Genrich M. *A Research Guide to Materials on the History of Russian Jewry (19th and Early 20th Centuries) in Selected Archives of the Former Soviet Union.* Moscow: Blagovest, 1994.

Dubnow, S.M. *History of the Jews in Russia and Poland.* Trans. by I. Friedlander. Philadelphia: Jewish Publication Society of America, 1916. Reprinted Teaneck, NJ: Avotaynu, 2000.

Encyclopedia Judaica: 17 vols. and index. Jerusalem: Keter, 1972–82.

Everett, Joseph. "`Soul' Searching in the Russian Census of the 18th and 19th Centuries." *FEEFHS Newsletter* 5:3–4 (August 1998): 34–42.

Evreiskaia Entsiklopedia (Jewish Encyclopedia). [Russian] 16 vols. St. Petersburg, 1915.

Feigmanis, Aleksandrs. "Gubernskie Vedomosti: A Genealogical Resource." *AVOTAYNU* 12, no.4 (Winter 1996): 27–28.

Feldblyum, Boris. "Russian Revision Lists: A History." *AVOTAYNU* 14, no. 3 (Fall 1998): 59–61.

Feldblyum, Boris and Yakov Shadevich. "Some Problems in Researching Eastern European Records." *AVOTAYNU* 11, no. 3 (Fall 1993): 12–13.

Freedman, Chaim. "Pseudo-Adopted Sons in Russian Revision Lists." *AVOTAYNU* 14, no. 3 (Fall 1998): 62.

Freeze, ChaeRan. "To Register or Not to Register: The Administrative Dimension of the Jewish Question in Czarist Russia." *AVOTAYNU* 13, no. 1 (Summer 1997): 6–11.

Gessen, Valery. "Some Glimpses of Studying Jewish Genealogy in Russia." *AVOTAYNU* 8, no. 4 (Winter 1992): 31–34.

Gilbert, Martin. *The Jews of Russia: Their History in Maps and Photographs.* Jerusalem: National Council for Soviet Jewry for the United Kingdom and Ireland, 1979.

Glazier, Ira, ed. *Migration from the Russian Empire. Lists of Passengers Arriving at U.S. Ports.* Vol 1–4. Baltimore: Genealogical Publishing, 1995–1998.

Grimsted, Patricia Kennedy. *Archives and Manuscript Repositories in the USSR.* Princeton, NJ: Princeton University Press, 1981.

Greenberg, Louis. *The Jews in Russia*, 2 vols., New Haven, Conn.: Yale University Press, 1944, 1951.

Jewish Encyclopedia. 12 vols., 1901–12.

Kronik, Alexander and Sallyann Amdur Sack. *Some Archives Sources for Ukrainian-Jewish Genealogy.* Teaneck, NJ: Avotaynu, 1997.

Levitas, Isaac. *The Jewish Community in Russia.* Jerusalem: Posner and Sons, 1981.

Luckert, Yelena. *Soviet Jewish History, 1917–1991: An Annotated Bibliography.* New York: Garland, 1992.

Mehr, Kahlile. "Russian Archival and Historical Terminology." *AVOTAYNU* 12, no. 3 (Fall 1996): 35–37.

———. "Russian Research Sources. *FEEFHS Newsletter* 5:3–4 (August 1998): 50–51.

Olson, James S., ed. *An Ethnohistorical Dictionary of the Russian and Soviet Empires.* Westport, CT: Greenwood Press, Inc., 1994.

Paley, Vladimir. "Russian Books of Residents as a Genealogical Resource." *AVOTAYNU* 12: no. 1 (Spring 1996): 23.

Rhode, Harold. "What May be Learned from 19th-Century Czarist Jewish Birth Records and Revision Lists." *AVOTAYNU* 10, no. 3 (Fall 1994): 3–5.

Room, Adrian. *Place Names of Russia and the Former Soviet Union: Origins and Meaning of the Names for Over 2,000 Natural Features, Towns, Regions and Countries.* Jefferson, NC: McFarland, 1996.

Russisches Geographisches Namenbuch (Russian Geographical place Names.) [German] Wiesbaden: Otto Harrassowitz, 1964.

Sack, Sallyann Amdur. "How to Do Research in the Former USSR." *AVOTAYNU* 9, no. 3 (Fall 1993): 39–43.

Sallis, Dorit and Marek Web, eds. *Jewish Documentary Sources in Russia, Ukraine and Belarus: A Preliminary List.* New York: Jewish Theological Seminary of America, 1996.

Shadevich, Yakov. "More Russian Genealogical Resources Found at the U.S. Library of Congress." *AVOTAYNU* 8, no. 1 (Spring 1992): 7–8.

Shea, Jonathan D. and William F. Hoffman. *Following the Paper Trail: A Multilingual Translation Guide.* Teaneck, NJ: Avotaynu, 1994.

Sistematicheskii Ukazatel Literatury o Evreyah na Russkom Iazyke s 1708 goda po Dekabr 1889 (Systematic guide to publications on the Jews in the Russian language from 1708 to 1899.) [Russian] St. Petersburg: Landau, 1892.

Soshnikov, Vladislav. "About the Russian Archivist's Soul." *AVOTAYNU* 14, no. 3 (Fall 1998): 66–67.

———. "Jewish Agricultural Colonies in New Russia." *AVOTAYNU* 12, no. 3 (Fall 1996): 33–34.

———. "Procedures for Genealogical Requests According to Official Regulations in Russian, Ukrainian and Belarussian Archives. *East European Genealogist* 6:3 (Spring 1998): 21–22.

———. "Russian Genealogy: Research in Russian, Ukrainian and Belarussian Archives." *Family Chronicle* (May/June 1998): 13–16.

———. "Russia's Economic Crisis and Its Effect on the Archives and Genealogists." *RAGAS Newsletter* 5:3 (Fall 1999): 5–7.

———."Libau: A Gateway for Emigration from the Russian Empire." *AVOTAYNU* 15, no. 1 (Spring 1999): 20.

———. "Sources for Genealogy in the Archives of the Former Soviet Union." *RAGAS Report.* 1:1 (April 1995): 2–5.

———. "The Current State of Archival Research in the CIS." *AVOTAYNU* 12, no. 1 (Spring 1996): 6–9.

Spiski Nasellenykh Mest Rossiiskoi Imperii (Lists of populated places of the Russian Empire). 62 vols. St. Petersburg: Tsentralnyi Statisticheskii komitet ministerstvo vnutrennikh del, 1861–85.

Thaden, Edward C. *Russia's Western Borderland, 1710–1870.* Princeton, NJ: Princeton University Press, 1980.

Universal Jewish Encyclopedia: 10 vols., 1939–43.

Valdin, Anton. "Little Known Sources of Russian-Jewish Data." *AVOTAYNU* 9, no. 1 (Spring 1993): 6–8.

Weiner, Miriam. *Jewish Roots in Ukraine and Moldova: Pages from the Past and Archival Inventories.* Secaucus, NJ: Miriam Weiner Routes to Routes Foundation; New York, NY: YIVO Institute for Jewish Research, 1999.

Yodaiken, Len. "More on Revision Lists." *AVOTAYNU* 13, no. 4 (Winter 1997): 46–48.

Notes

1. Hoffman, David B. "Constructing a Mid-19th-Century Census of Jews in Lithuania." Presentation at August 1999 Jewish genealogical conference, New York City.

2. Beider, Alexander. *A Dictionary of Jewish Surnames From the Russian Empire*: 9–15.

3. Grimsted, Patricia. *Archives and Manuscript Repositories in the USSR.*

4. Paley, Vladimir. "Russian Books of Residents as a Genealogical Resource: 23.

Pale of Settlement Including the Kingdom of Poland

After the first partition of Poland (in 1772), Russia annexed the eastern Polish territories, which were home to numerous Jewish families...In 1793 and then again in 1795, Russia annexed more Polish territory...As a result of these territorial changes, a massive Jewish population abruptly became subjects of the Russian czar...Migration of the new Jewish subjects into other areas of the empire was vigorously restricted. On June 23, 1794, for the first time, the Pale of Settlement—the only area in which Jewish settlement was permitted—was defined. [From *A Dictionary of Jewish Surnames from the Russian Empire*, by Alexander Beider, published by Avotaynu, Inc.]

After Napoleon's defeat in 1815, the Congress of Vienna divided the Duchy of Warsaw into three parts: the Grand Duchy of Posen (Poznań), which was returned to Prussia; the Kraków area, which became the independent Free City of Kraków (which, after 1846, belonged to Austria); and the largest portion, which was ceded to Russia and received the official name of Kingdom of Poland (*Tsarstvo Pol'skoe* in Russian). Other names used in literature for the same geographical area are Congress Poland, the Congress Kingdom and Russian Poland. [From *A Dictionary of Jewish Surnames from the Kingdom of Poland*, by Alexander Beider, published by Avotaynu, Inc.]

Inquisition Records

by Jeffrey S. Malka

Until recently, Jews had not lived openly as Jews in Spain or Portugal for 500 years. The order of expulsion from Spain in 1492 and the subsequent establishment of the infamous Spanish Inquisition effectively ended centuries of Jewish life in that country. In 1497, Portuguese Jews—most of them recent refugees from the Spanish Expulsion—were forcibly converted to Catholicism. Portugal's inquisition was instituted not long after and remained in effect until the early 19th century. A very small organized Jewish community has emerged in Spain and Portugal in the past few decades, but they are too recent to be genealogically relevant in terms of Jewish history.

The Iberian Peninsula has long been known as Sepharad, the word from which is derived the term *Sephardim*—Jews descended from ancestors who lived in the Iberian Peninsula or culturally and religiously associated with them (in contrast to *Ashkenazim*, European Jewry designated by a derivation from the word Ashkenaz, a Hebrew term for Germany). Following the Moors' conquest of Spain in 711 C.E., Iberian Jewry became part of the larger Jewish world that lived under Islam. Opposed and decimated by the preceding vicious Visgoth rule, Iberian Jews welcomed the Moorish conquest and were able to regain Jewish knowledge they had lost when under oppression. Iberian Jews became part of the large cultural and historical Jewish world that centered on Baghdad (Babylon) and the Babylonian Jewish centers of learning. Because of shared cultural and religious values as well as several back and forth population migrations, the term *Sephardim* today covers a much wider spectrum than just the 1492 exiles. (For a further discussion of this complex topic, see Malka, Jeffrey, *Sephardic Genealogy*.)

As interest in genealogy has burgeoned, individuals with Sephardic roots are beginning to learn that a surprising wealth of Inquisition and other earlier, pre-Inquisition Portuguese and Spanish records may permit them to trace their families back to when they resided on the Iberian Peninsula. In addition to records of the Inquisition in Portugal and Spain, the Canary Islands, Mexico and Peru, church and notarial records going back many centuries offer possibilities for genealogical research. (For discussion of European notarial records see AUSTRO-HUNGARIAN EMPIRE.)

The 1492 Spanish order of expulsion offered Jews two choices: They could convert to Catholicism and continue to live in Spain, or they could remain Jews and leave. In reality, a century of anti-Jewish riots and massacres had preceded the order of expulsion, resulting in a number of conversions and massive Jewish flight from Christian Spain toward Moslem-controlled regions and North Africa, so by 1942 the number of Jews remaining in Spain was markedly reduced. Once populous Jewish communities, such as that of Barcelona were reduced to 20 or so families by 1492 and other Spanish Jewish communities had already disappeared.[1]

Individuals who can trace their Jewish roots back to Spain or Portugal, both prior to and at the time of the expulsion, fall into two major categories. One group consists of descendants of people who had always remained Jewish and left Spain voluntarily, primarily for Portugal, North Africa or the Ottoman Empire, with some going to Italy and southern France. The other major group are descendants of Jews who had at one time converted to Catholicism, either sincerely, or insincerely. Among the group who converted (*conversos* or New Christians) some continued Jewish practices in secret (crypto-Jews) and some of these later returned to Judaism. Also among descendants of conversos today are growing numbers of non-Jews whose ancestors had not returned to Judaism and only recently have learned (or suspect) that they are descended from Jews and want to determine if this is true. The Jews who never converted have usually retained Hebrew or Arabic names such as Shaltiel, ibn Ezra, Cohen or Malka, while the *converso* group carry Spanish names such as Perera, Nunes or de Sola—names they often acquired at the time of conversion. Names such as Toledano arising from Spanish towns do not denote prior *converso* ancestry.

Numbers are hard to determine, but historians estimate that after 1391 about one third of the Jews of Spain left Iberia, one third converted and one third fled to Spain (see *Sephardic Genealogy* for more details). Descendants of Spanish Jews who converted frequently remained Christian and already were or became fully integrated and assimilated; only a few are aware of a Jewish past. The secret Jews, called crypto-Jews or the preferred term today, *anusim* (forced ones, in Hebrew) generally descend from the group forced to convert—many were Jews who originally fled Spain for Portugal.[2]

In 1492, when Spanish Jews who refused baptism were expelled from Spain, the largest group fled to neighboring Portugal, which already had a Jewish population of approximately 75,000.[3] The exact number of newcomers from Spain is unknown, but it is estimated at about 120,000 although these numbers vary widely. But Portugal (which charged a fee for entry) was a safe haven for only five years.

Don Manuel, who ascended to the throne of Portugal in 1495, wished to marry Princess Isabella of Castile. In return he had to agree that his country would be rid of its Jewish residents. When the marriage contract was concluded in December 1496, a decree of expulsion of the Jews from Portugal was announced at the same time. Although the Jews were given 10 months in which to leave the country, King Manuel did not want to lose his useful subjects. Portugal was entering a period of economic expansion, and he knew that the Jews, who then constituted one third of his subjects, would be helpful commercially.

A second law was published in March 1497 ordering baptism of all Jewish children in Portugal between the ages of 4 and 14 years of age (see *Sephardic Genealogy*). Even so, the Jews continued their preparations to leave Portugal. When they arrived in Lisbon, however, the only port of embarkation open to them, no ships were available and with the expiration of the allowed 10 months, all were given only two choices: to be declared slaves of the king or to accept baptism. Thus most of the Jews of Portugal accepted Catholicism by force, and, not surprisingly, a substantial number of the so-called New Christians continued to observe Jewish customs and religion in secret (crypto-Jews).

Soon after this event, yet another decree was promulgated. It ordained that the Portuguese government would make no inquiries for 20 years, to allow these forced converts to learn their new faith. The result was that Jews continued to live in Portugal (from which they were generally forbidden to leave) and appeared in church, but many continued to observe Jewish customs at home. This decree was renewed until 1526 when King Joao began to negotiate and finally obtained Papal consent to install an Inquisition in Portugal (in 1536). This began centuries-long persecutions of New Christians, ostensibly aimed at those accused of still following Jewish customs but involving many others as well, at times for ulterior motives of revenge or financial gain. Therefore, when they could, many secret Jews attempted to flee the country; Protestant Netherlands was a favorite destination, as was Dutch Brazil and other places in Latin America and the Caribbean.

As far as Spanish records are concerned, three groups of Jews may be distinguished:

- Those Jews investigated by an Inquisition tribunal and about whom trial records were kept
- Those who remained in Spanish or Portuguese lands but were not accused of judaizing (secretly observing Jewish laws and rituals)
- Those who fled Iberia

Records of the Inquisition apply only to the first group—those who were suspected of judaizing (although not all so accused were necessarily guilty of the accusation). Spanish notarial records created before the order of expulsion includes data on all three groups. Catholic church records include, in theory, data on all inhabitants, including Jews prior to the expulsion, as well as post-conversion data on the lives of those Jews who converted and either became sincere Christians or never were caught practicing Judaism.

Spanish Notarial Records

Voluminous notary public records in Spain that document sales of land, loans of money and other commercial transactions are among the most useful resources available to the genealogist researching Jewish or non-Jewish roots in pre-Inquisition Spain. They commonly date back to the 12th century or earlier and may consist of as many as 3,000 or more unindexed, difficult-to-read handwritten pages of data per year, even for small towns. The search can be rewarding, however, because these records almost always identify the religion and profession of the individuals recorded as well as their relationships.

For instance, Alfonso Gonzalez, silversmith, sold to Jacob Abensamerro, Jew of Toledo, an estate (inheritance) in Gaudaxaras, known as the Batida (field) of don Simuel el Levi that borders on the estate (inheritance) of Mose el Maleque and with old road that goes to Guadamur.[4,5]

Because these records are unindexed, reading them can be enormously frustrating unless one knows exact details about the event or person sought. Research only can be done onsite, so one should allow plenty of time to do it in a relaxed fashion. It is necessary to be able to read the cryptic handwriting of the period. Spanish has changed little since the Middle Ages, but the penmanship can look very strange to someone unfamiliar with the script. As preparation for a research trip, the researcher should study examples in books of 11th-century Spanish.[6]

Notarial records are harder to decipher than most records because scribes tended purposely to make them difficult to read; they earned their living by being able to read what no one else could decipher.

Notarial records help locate families in medieval Spain, where they lived, the properties they owned and taxes they paid. They can also document alternate names used by the same individuals or families and variants of names that permit further research. One of numerous examples is a case in which documents concerned a property sale in which the same person was referred to in one document as Lesar Maleque and in another as Lesar Abenrey. In another document, a different Yucaf Abenrey was called Yucaf Maleque. Maleque means king in Arabic, while Abenrey means son of king (ben Maleque).[7] Both are known variants of the Sephardic family name Malka, which means king in Aramaic.

Notarial records are kept in the local provincial historical archives or sometimes, for very small towns, in the mayor's office. The immense genealogical value of the notarial records can be realized by consulting the few books in which researchers have published summaries of selected documents that mention Jews.[8,9] Because these records go back centuries, the notarial records are important for the pre-expulsion period of Jews in Spain.

Spanish Inquisition Records

Records of the Spanish Inquisition still exist. They were kept meticulously and, therefore, are an invaluable resource for genealogists tracing Jewish roots in Spain and Portugal, sometimes including entire family trees. The Inquisition focused not on Jews who remained Jewish (they had been expelled), but rather on Jews who had converted to Christianity, the so-called New Christians, whom Inquisition officials suspected of secretly continuing Jewish practices.[10] The records are especially valuable to descendants of those converts, some of whom returned to Judaism.

La Inquisicion Espanola (Spanish Inquisition) was the official, government-run organization; The *Santo Oficio de la Inquisicion* (Holy Office of the Inquisition) operated its central headquarters in Madrid and held tribunals in various localities in Spain and later in the Americas.

Although the edict of expulsion and the events leading to the establishment of the Spanish Inquisition occurred more than five centuries ago, the Inquisition was not officially

Auto-da-fe in the Plaza Mayor of Madrid in 1680

abolished until relatively recently. Its last known execution was that of a woman burned at the stake in 1821; she was accused of having had sex with the Devil and having produced eggs that foretold the future.

Spanish Repositories That Hold Inquisition Documents

Archivo Historico Nacional. With 5,344 manuscript bundles and 1,463 manuscript books on the Inquisition, Madrid's Archivo Historicao Nacional's* holdings are a great, largely unmined source of Jewish genealogical information. Records include papers of the Supreme Council of the Inquisition; correspondence of the Supreme Council with other tribunals in Spain, the Americas and Italy; and records of tribunals in Spain that were brought to Madrid before or after dissolution of the Inquisition. These records include court cases from the tribunals of Cordoba, Corte, Granada, Llerena, Logrono, Murcia, Santiago, Seville, Toledo, Valencia, Vallodolid and Zaragoza. Each tribunal was responsible for a large area that included many communities. Published catalogues exist for the documents from the tribunals of Murcia and Toledo, but the catalogues are incomplete.[11]

Archivo Diocesano de Cuenca* (records of the diocese of the town of Cuenca) are an important source for this town. A guide is in preparation and will be obtainable from the Archivo.

Archivo General de Simancas (Valladolid)* holds government records, not of the Inquisition itself, but of governmental actions that resulted from it. In order to maintain the myth that the church did not actually harm anyone, victims of the Inquisition tribunals were "relaxed" (transferred) after their torture and trials to the government authorities who then administered the recommended punishments. In this manner the Inquisition could avoid having blood on the hands of its holy clerics. A useful guide exists for this archive, but familiarity with Spanish documentation is necessary in order to use it.[12]

Archivo de La Real Audiencia de Zaragoza* holds documents from the Kingdom of Aragon, many of which involve Jews. **Archivo de Museo Canario*** in Las Palmas holds Inquisition records for the Canary Islands, while the **Archivo de Real Corona de Aragon*** holds records of Jews living in Barcelona and Catalonia.[13]

Numerous provincial historical archives have forwarded a wealth of records useful to Jewish genealogists to the major archives cited above.

Repositories in the Americas

During the first century of the Spanish colonies, the colonial bishops administered the Inquisition in the New World. Their files, therefore, would originally have been sent to the episcopal archives in their territories and probably still are in some of those repositories. The early Inquisition records deal primarily with Indians and clerical malfeasance. The Spanish Inquisition headquartered in Madrid and aimed squarely at judaizing New Christians did not officially come to the Americas until close to the end of the 16th century. It established three tribunals in the Americas, in Cartagena, Columbia; Lima, Peru; and Mexico City. The Mexico City tribunal served the North American mainland and extended south to Panama and west to the Philippines. Lima, Peru's tribunal served most of South America, while Cartagena (then called Nueva Granada or the Audiencia de Santa Fe), attended to the northern coast of South America and the Caribbean Islands.

The archives from Lima and from Mexico City have survived. Those from Cartagena disappeared many years ago. Correspondence between the three New World tribunals and the Supreme headquarters in Madrid is kept at the Archivo Historico Nacional in Madrid. They consist of only 175 manuscript bundles and 78 manuscript books. Among them are the few remaining references to cases tried in Cartagena.

Records of the Mexico City tribunal are in the Archivo General de la Nacion (AGN)* in Mexico City. They consist of 1,555 bound volumes dating from 1522 to 1819 and include the Inquisition records of the bishops as well as records of the official tribunal of the Holy Office of the Inquisition (*Santo Oficio de la Inquisicion*) established in Mexico in 1569. Many of the bishops' Inquisition records concerns trials of Indians; arrival of the Inquisition from Spain intensified the search for secret Jews.

Colonial records at the AGN, including those of the Inquisition, are detailed and well organized. Every bound volume of Inquisition records includes a brief abstract of each of the files in the volume, which permits rapid searching. A comprehensive guide to the records will soon be available on CD-ROM at the AGN.

Church Records

Extant church records consist of baptismal, matrimonial and *defunciones* (deaths) for an entire community; they usually date back centuries and are easy to use. Permission of a local bishop to use these records generally is required, but this is usually granted on request. They can only be researched onsite at the hundreds of churches in Spain.

Ministerio de Cultura Identification

For personal, onsite research in Spain, one should obtain a Ministerio de Cultura ID, which generally provides access to all government archives. To obtain one, bring a passport, a letter of recommendation from a university or an embassy and two passport photographs to any of the major governmental archives, such as *Archivo General de Indias** in Seville or AHN in Madrid.

About Surnames and Aliases

Hereditary surnames existed in Christian Spain since the 12th century; Jews in Moslem Spain used surnames even earlier than this, as did Moslems. The use of aliases by Jews is a phenomenon that occurred primarily with the 16th-century marranos' exodus mostly from Portugal. After the 1492 and 1497 expulsions from Spain and Portugal, "New Christians" were viewed with suspicion and were not allowed to travel out of the country. A century later an exodus of *conversos* occurred, mainly from Portugal and toward the Netherlands, England and the New World. Others went to Italy (Livorno) and the Ottoman Empire. The *conversos* who formed this later exodus were often merchants and highly assimilated Portuguese and Spaniards. They moved to Amsterdam because of the trading opportunities it provided. From there, they could trade with England and other countries hostile to Spain and

Portugal. The also used their language skills and connections to trade with Portugal or Portuguese and Spanish possession in the New World. Those who had returned openly to Judaism could not use their converso names to visit and trade with their connections in Spanish and Portuguese lands because this would put their relatives who remained behind in jeopardy. They, therefore, used aliases to protect their families in Spain and Portugal.

In contracts and other documents drawn in the Netherlands, England and elsewhere, both the alias and the original name often were listed, allowing the researcher to determine which aliases correspond to which converso names.[14]

Addresses

Archivo Diocesano de Cuenca, C/Obispo Valero 2, Palacio Episcopal. 16001 Cuenca; telephone: 96-621-2461

Archivo General de la Nacion (AGN), Eduardo Molina y Albaniles s/n, Col. Penitenciaria Ampliacion, Deleg. Venustiano Carranza, 15350, Mexico, D.F.; website: WWW.AGN.GOB.MX/INDICE.HTML

Archivo de La Real Audiencia de Zaragoza, Archivo Histórico Provincial, Villalpando, 7, 49071, Zaragoza, Spain; telephone: 976-397-566.

Archivo de Museo Canario in Las Palmas, Plaza de Santa Ana, 4, 35071 Las Palmas, Spain; telephone: 928-323-020; fax: 928-322-134; website: WWW.MCU.ES/LAB/ARCHIVOS/ARP12A.HTML#6A.

Archivo de Real Corona de Aragon, Calle Condes de Barcelona 2, Barcelona, Spain; telephone: 93-315-0211; website: WWW.MCU.ES/LAB/ARCHIVOS/ACA.HTML.

Archivo General de Simancas (Valladolid), Carretera de Salamanca-Simancas Valladolid, Spain; website: WWW.MCU.ES/LAB/ARCHIVOS/AGS.HTML.

Archivo Historico Nacional (AHN), Concepcion Contel Calle Serrano 115, 28006 Madrid, Spain; telephone: 91-563-5923; website: WWW.MCU.ES/LAB/ARCHIVOS/AHN.HTML.

Bibliography

Abecassis, Jose Maria. "Contributing Editor Portugal). *AVOTAYNU* 8, no. 3 (Fall 1992).

Abecassis, Jose Maria. *Genealogia Hebraica: Portugal e Gibraltar, Secs. XVII a XX* (Jewish genealogy: Portugal and Gibraltar, 17th to 20th centuries). Lisbon: Author, 1990. Five volumes of documented family trees.

Ashton, Eliyahu. *The Jews of Moslem Spain.* Philadelphia: Jewish Publication Society, 1993.

Assis, Y.T. *The Jews of Santa Coloma de Queralt: An Economic and Demographic Case Study of a Community at the End of the Thirteenth Century.* Jerusalem: Magnes, 1988.

———. *Jews in the Crown of Aragon, 1213–1327.* Jerusalem: Central Archives for the History of the Jewish People, 1995. Thorough study of Jews in northeast Spain.

———. *Jewish Economy in the Medieval Crown of Aragon, 1213–1327.* Leiden, The Netherlands: E.J. Brill, 1997. Companion volume providing the Jewish economic information on the Jews of Aragon.

Baer, Yitzhak. *History of the Jews in Christian Spain.* Philadelphia: Jewish Publication Society, 1993. A classic.

Beinart, Haim. "The Great Conversion and the Converso Problem." Haim Beinart, ed. *The Sephardi Legacy.* Jerusalem: Magnes, 1992.

———. *The Expulsion of the Jews from Spain.* English translation of *Gerush Sefarad.* Portland, Ore.: Littman, 2002.

———. *Conversos on Trial: The Inquisition in Ciudad Real.* Jerusalem: Magnes, 1981.

———. "The Jews in Castile." *The Sephardi Legacy.* Haim Beinart, ed. Jerusalem: Magnes, 1992.

Benbassa, Esther and Aron Rodrigue. *Sephardi Jewry: A History of the Judeo-Spanish Community, 14–20th Centuries.* Berkeley: University of California, 2000.

Blazquez Miguel, Juan. *La Inquisición* (The Inquisition). [Spanish]. Madrid: Ediciones Penthalon, 1988.

———. *Ciudad Real y la Inquisición, 1483–1820* (Ciudad Real and the Inquisition). [Spanish]. Ciudad Real: Comision Municipal de Cultura, 1987.

———. *Toledot: Historia del Toledo judio* (Generations: History of Jewish Toledo). [Spanish]. Toledo, Spain: Editorial Arcano 1989.

———. *La Inquisición en Cataluòa: el tribunal del Santo Oficio de Barcelona, 1487–1820* (Inquisition in Catalonia: Holy Office Tribunal of Barcelona, 1487–1820). [Spanish] Toledo, Spain: Editorial Arcano, 1990.

———. *Madrid-judios, herejes y brujas: El Tribunal de Corte (1650–1820)* (Jews of Madrid, heretics, and witches: The Royal Tribunal (1650–1820)). [Spanish]. Toledo, Spain: Editorial Arcano, 1990.

———. *La Inquisición en Castilla-La Mancha* (Inquisition in Castile-La Mancha). [Spanish]. Cordoba, Spain: Universidad de Cordoba, 1986.

Bonnín, Pere. *Sangre judia: Espanoles de ascendencia hebrea y antisemitismo cristiano.* (Jewish blood: Spaniards of Jewish ancestry and Christian anti-Semitism). 2d ed. [Spanish]. Barcelona: Flor del Viento Ediciones, 1998.

Cortes i Cortes, Gabriel. *Historia de los Judios Mallorquines y sus descendientes cristianos* (History of the Majorcan Jews and their Christian descendants). [Spanish]. Palma de Mallorca: Imagen, 1985. Posthumous two-volume book by a right-wing (Falangist) Catholic author descendant. Name lists and some family trees.

Donate Sebastia, J. and J.R. Magdalena Nom de Deu. *Jewish Communities in Valencia.* Jerusalem: Magnes, 1990.

———. *Three Jewish Communities in Medieval Valencia: Castellon de la Plana, Burriana, Villareal.* Jerusalem: Magnes, 1990. Extensive study that includes multiple documents referring to Jews from the archives.

Elnecave, Nissim. *Los Hijos de Ibero-Franconia* (Sons of Iberia-Franconia). [Spanish]. Buenos Aires: Ediciones La Luz, 1981.

Epstein, Isidore. *The Responsa of Rabbi Solomon ben Adret of Barcelona (1235-1310) As a Source of the History of Spain.* London: Ktav, 1968.

Gerber, Jane. *The Jews of Spain: A History of the Sephardic Experience.* New York: Free Press Macmillan, 1992.

Greenleaf, Richard. *The Mexican Inquisition of the Sixteenth Century.* Albuquerque: University of New Mexico Press, 1969.

Hinojosa Montalvo, Jose. *The Jews of the Kingdom of Valencia: From Persecution to Expulsion, 1391–1492.* Jerusalem: Magnes, 1993. The most complete study of the Jews of Valencia (present-day provinces of Castellon, Valencia, and Alicante). Includes translations of archival documents, extensive name lists, and related bibliography.

Hordes, Stanley. *The Crypto-Jewish Community of New Spain, 1620–1649: A Collective Biography.* PhD diss. Tulane University, 1980.

Isaacs, Abraham Lionel. *The Jews of Majorca.* London: Methuen, 1936.

Laredo, Abraham. *Les Noms des Juifs du Maroc* (Names of the Jews of Morocco). [Spanish]. Madrid: Institut Montano, 1978.

Leon Tello, Pilar. *Judios de Toledo* (Jews of Toledo).[Spanish]. Madrid: Institut Arias Montano, 1979. Lists Jews who lived in Toledo and court documents about them.

Leroy, Beatrice. *The Jews of Navarre in the Late Middle Ages.* Jerusalem: Magnes Press, Hebrew University, 1985.

Liebman, Seymour B. *The Inquisitors and the Jews in the New World: Summaries of Procecesos, 1500–1810, and Bibliographical Guide.* Miami: University of Miami Press, 1975. Following a brief introduction, lists Inquisition Records in the New World.

Malka, Jeffrey S. *Sephardic Genealogy: Discovering Your Sephardic Ancestors and Their World.* Bergenfield, N.J.: AVOTAYNU, 2002.

de Molina, Rafael, Conde y Delgado. *La Expulsion de Los Judios de la Corona de Aragon* (The expulsion of the Jews of the Aragon Crown). [Spanish]. Zaragoza, Spain: Institucion Fernando el Catolico, 1991.

Mausenbaum, Rufina Bernardetti Silvo. "A Painful Portuguese Odyssey." AVOTAYNU 13, no. 4 (Winter 1997): 13–14.

Netanyahu, B. *The Origins of the Inquisition in XIV Century Spain.* New York: Random House, 1995.

O'Callaghan, Joseph F. *A History of Medieval Spain.* Ithaca, N.Y.: Cornell University Press, 1975.

Ortiz, Dominguez. *Judeoconversos en la espana y America* (Jewish *conversos* in Spain and America). [Spanish]. Madrid: Ediciones Istmo, 1971.

Ortiz, Dominguez. *Judeoconversos en la espana moderna* (Jewish *conversos* in modern Spain). [Spanish]. Madrid: Editorial Mapfre Paseo de Recoletos, 1992.

Pflaum, H. "Une ancienne satire espagnole contre les marranes." (An ancient Spanish satire against the marranos). [Spanish] *Revue des Etudes Juives* 86 (1928): 131–50.

Raphael, David. *The Expulsion 1492 Chronicles.* North Hollywood, Calif.: Carmi House; New York: Sephardic House. Translations of contemporary writings about Sephardim and the expulsion, 1992.

Regne, Jean. *History of Jews in Aragon: Collection of Regesta and Court Documents 1213–1327.* Jerusalem: Magnes, 1978.

Rodriguez Fernandez, Justiniano. *La Juderia de la Ciudad de Leon* (Jewish quarter of the city of Leon). [Spanish] Leon, Spain: Centro de estudios e investigacion "San Isidro," Archivo Historico Diocesano, 1969. Lists Jews and 11th– and 12th-century Jewish tombstones.

Roth, Cecil. *A History of the Marranos.* 4th ed. New York: Hermon, 1974.

———. *The Spanish Inquisition.* New York: W.W. Norton, 1996.

Roth, Norman. *Conversos, Inquisition, and the Expulsion of the Jews from Spain.* Madison: University of Wisconsin Press, 1995. Information about *converso* families; lists *converso* names.

Sachar, H.M. *Farewell Espana: The World of the Sephardim Remembered.* New York: Vintage, 1995.

Sack, Sallyann Amdur. "Jewish Life in Portugal Today." AVOTAYNU 13, no. 4 (Winter 1997): 15–15.

Sealtiel-Olsen, Vibeke. "Aliases in Amsterdam." *Etsi* 4, no. 12 (March 2001): 3–7.

Singerman, Robert. *The Jews in Spain and Portugal.* New York: Garland, 1975.

Valadares, Paulo. "Converted and Reconverted: History of the Jews Who Stayed in Portugal (1497–1997)." AVOTAYNU 13, no. 4 (Winter 1997): 9–12.

Zafrani, Haim. *Juifs d'Andalousie et du Maghreb* (Jews of Andalusia and the Maghreb). Paris: Maisonneuve & Larose, 1996.

Notes

1. Benbassa, Esther and Aron Rodrigue. *Sephardi Jewry.*
2. Jews who converted to Catholicism under pressure in Spain and, later, in Portugal, have been called by a number of names other than New Christian. *Anusim,* the forced ones, has come to be

popular among some as preferable to the better known term *marrano*, which means pig and, therefore, is considered pejorative and insulting. Another commonly used term is *converso*.

3. Modern authors feel the number of Jews left in Spain by 1492 did not exceed 50,000, because so many had already fled Spain in prior centuries. See Benbassa, Esther and Aron Rodrique, *Sephardi Jewry.*

4. Madrid, Archivo Historico National, clero, papeles, leg 7041. *Clero, papeles* and *leg* are Spanish archival terms used to locate documents.

5. Another example from February 20, 1477, reads:
"Don Culeman (Suleman) Abensabad obtained permission from the San Clemente convent, in the name of his daughter, Clara, wife of Rabbi Mose Maleque, surgeon, to sell some houses that the said Mose possesses in the parish of San Tome, adjoining the castillo of the juderia, (castle of the Jewish quarter) next to Santa Maria la Blanca. Sale of these houses to Salamon Abenhumayd, Jew, and to dona Cadbona, his wife, for 25,000 marevides."

6. Examples of old Spanish script may be seen on the Internet at WWW.ORTHOHELP.COM/GENEAL/INQUIS.HTM.

7. Tello, Pilar Leon. *Judios de Toledo.* 2 vols. (Madrid: Instituto B. Arias Montano, 1979).

8. Asis, Yom Tov. *The Jews in the Crown of Aragon: Regesta of the Cartas Reales in the Archivo de la Corona de Aragon, 1828–1493.* (Jerusalem: Central Archives for the History of the Jewish People, 1995). See discussion of notarial records.

9. The Spanish Inquisition concerned itself not only with New Christians accused of judaizing but also with detecting and stopping crypto-Moslems, fornicating clergy, and those who engaged in blasphemy and witchcraft.

10. Feldman, *Anglo-Americans.*

11. Angle de la Plaza Bores. *Guia del Investigador, Archivo General de Simancas.* (Madrid: Ministerio de Cultura, 1992).

12. Asis, *Jews in the Crown.*

13. Blazquez, Miguel, Juan. *La Inquisicion en Castilla-La Mancha.* (Inquisition in Castile-La Mancha). [Spanish] (Cordoba, Spain: Universidad de Cordoba, 1986).

14. Sealtiel-Olsen, Vibeke, "Aliases in Amsterdam."

Algeria

by Philip Abensur

Historians believe that some Jews, together with Phoenicians, may have founded warehouses in Algeria as early as the 11th century BCE. The oldest Jewish inscriptions, however, date from the Roman period, after 40 CE, in Constantine and in a few other small cities. The first known synagogue was in Setif in the 3rd century CE.

The Arabs conquered North Africa in 688. Few Jews lived in Algeria until the end of the 14th century, but immigration of Jews from Spain between 1391 and 1492 greatly increased the number and the organization of Algerian Jewry. During this time, Algeria became the Jewish spiritual center of North Africa. It was a time of relative calm and security, during which close ties were maintained with the Jews of Tunisia.

Algeria came under Ottoman rule from the 16th to the 18th centuries and was conquered by the French in 1830. In 1870, a decree of French minister Adolphe Crémieux conferred French citizenship on the majority of Algerian Jews. The Jewish population of Algeria increased from 20,000 in 1830 to 150,000 in 1960. Though they suffered restrictions in some occupations, no Jews were deported from Algeria during the Shoah. Most Jews had left by the time of Algerian independence in 1962. The majority went to France, others to Israel. A tiny community remains in Algiers with a synagogue, but no rabbi.

Resources for Genealogists

Genealogical research is extremely difficult for Jews with Algerian roots. The political situation had made it almost impossible to obtain records from Algeria, although many archives remain in that country. A portion of them, however, is now in France and can supply valuable information from the beginning of the French period (1830). A few resources can be classified as Jewish, but most are secular (much more important; mainly French civil status records).

Jewish Records

Cemeteries. According to a survey of Algerian Jewish cemeteries made in 1993 by the Algeria Cemeteries Preservation Society, most Jewish cemeteries in Algeria have been almost completely destroyed, although those in the main cities of Algiers, Constantine and Oran seemed to be well preserved.

Since then, a French Jewish journalist, Elisabeth Schemla, has published a book about her stay in her native country between November 1999 and January 2000.[1] Looking for her brother's tombstone in the Algiers cemetery located in Saint-Eugene, she found broken tombstones and bones lying on the ground. Some names could be read: Achouche, Akoun, Bakouche, Enot, Farro, Garrus, Gharbi, Kespi, Lachkar, Loufrani, Maklouf, Mesguish, Nebot, Saffar, Seror, Solal, Sonigo and Tabet.

In the village of Khenchela where her father was born and her grandfather buried, Ms. Schemla again found broken stones in the Jewish cemetery bearing the names Elbaz, Guedj, Touitou. Another informant who lives in Miliana reports that the Jewish cemetery still exists but is in a precarious state because of landslides caused by bad weather.

Except for a partial record published in 1888[2], however, no list of burials is available, and onsite research in Algeria appears to be extremely difficult. For further details, see "Jewish Cemeteries in Algeria," *Etsi*, no. 3, Winter 1998.

Jewish Registers. Jewish registers of any sort from Algeria are very rare. A marriage register of Algier is kept by the synagogue Berit Shalom* in Paris.

Jewish Marriage Contracts (*Ketubot*). *Ketubot* from Algeria are extremely rare and supply little genealogical information, usually just the given names of the fathers of the newlyweds and sometimes the given names of their paternal grandfathers.

Alliance Israélite Universelle Records. The Alliance Israélite Universelle opened schools in Algeria at the end of the 19th century as a result of growing anti-Semitism in the country. Information about local committees, member lists and pupil lists, can be found at the Alliance archives* in Paris.

Other Jewish Repositories. The Central Archives for the History of the Jewish People* holds the community archives of Constantine for the years 1795–1960. The YIVO Institute for Jewish Research* holds records of the arrival of Jews in Algeria.

Secular Records

Civil Status Records. Civil status records represent the most complete source for genealogy in Algeria. About two-thirds of the French civil status records in Algeria from 1830 to 1962 have been microfilmed by the French government. The original registers have remained in Algeria.

Microfilms of records more than 100 years old are kept at the Centre des Archives d'Outre-Mer in Aix-en-Provence, France.* The microfilms may be freely consulted and photocopied, but the Centre does not do research or send photocopies. However, an index to all the records is available on the Internet at HTTP://SDX. ARCHIVESDEFRANCE.CULTURE.GOUV.FR/ECFA/ REPORT.XSP. The Centre also holds additional documents from Algeria that may provide genealogical information, such as censuses, electoral and military lists, and files of individual who applied for a colonization plot.

Microfilms of civil records less than 100 years are held at the Direction des Français de l'étranger, Sous-direction de l'état civil*, in Nantes, France. These microfilms are not freely available, except for deaths registers if the exact date of death is known.

In the births registers, one can find the names of the newborn and of the parents and, in the margins, mention of the marriage (if any) and of death. Marriage registers supply place and date of birth of the newlyweds, as well as names of their parents. Death registers give the names of the parents of the deceased. In each register, the names of the witnesses may prove valuable because they sometimes are family members.

National Archives Documents. Documents about the Jews of Algeria between 1842 and 1906 can be found at the Archives

Nationales (French National Archives)* (series F19/11143 to 11157), among them lists of consistory members, individual files, donors names and similar items. (The Consistoire is the official Jewish representative in France.)

French Naturalizations. Few Jews were naturalized before 1865, when Emperor Napoleon III passed a *senatus-consulte* (law) that offered the possibility for Jews and Muslims to become French citizens. Only about 300 Jews used this method to become French citizens, but a few years later, in 1870, French minister Adolphe Crémieux announced a decree that accorded French citizenship to about 40,000 *indigenous* (individuals born in Algeria of Algerian-born parents) Jews.

Every French naturalization file more than 60 years old is open to the public. There are, however, no naturalization files for the Jews naturalized as a result of Crémieux's decree. Apparently, naturalization was automatic, with no need to file applications. Some files provide considerable information, such as birth date, emigration, profession, names of parents and children, and even a copy of a Jewish marriage contract. Other are less informative and provide only date and place of birth and occupation. Naturalization files from before 1931 can be accessed at the Archives Nationales* in Paris. Naturalization files from 1931 to 1954 are kept at the Centre des Archives Contemporaines* in Fontainebleau. Photocopies are not permitted, but microfilms can be ordered. Files to be consulted must be ordered in at least 15 days in advance.

Newspapers. Daily or weekly French newspapers were published beginning in the second half of the 19th century. Announcements of births, deaths or marriages can be found in them, as well as extracts of civil status records—for example, a list of all births registered in the city during a period of days.

Addresses

Alliance Israélite Universelle, 45 rue La Bruyère, 75009 Paris, France; e-mail: biblio@aiu.org; website: WWW.AIU.ORG.

Archives Nationales (CARAN), 11 rue des Quatre Fils, 75003 Paris, France; website: WWW.ARCHIVESNATIONALES.CULTURE.GOUV.FR/CHAN.

Association Consistoriale Israélite d'Alger, 6 rue Hassena Ahmed, Algiers.

Association Consistoriale Israélite de Blida, 29 rue des Martyrs, Blida, Algiers.

Berit Shalom synagogue-Comité algérois, 18 rue Saint-Lazare, 75009 Paris, France.

Central Archives for the History of the Jewish People, P.O. Box 1149, Sprinzak Building, Givat Ram Campus-Hebrew University, 91010 Jerusalem, Israel.

Centre des Archives Contemporaines, 2 rue des Archives, 77300 Fontainebleau, France; telephone: (01) 6431-7300; website: WWW.ARCHIVESNATIONALES.CULTURE.GOUV.FR/CAC/FR.

Centre des Archives d'Outre-Mer (CAOM), 29 chemin du Moulin de Testas, 13090 Aix-en-Provence, France; telephone: (04) 4293-3850; fax: (04) 4293-3889; website: WWW.ARCHIVESNATIONALES. CULTURE.GOUV.FR/CAOM/FR and HTTP://SDX.ARCHIVESDEFRANCE.CULTURE. GOUV.FR/ECFA/REPORT.XSP .

Consistoire Central, 19 rue Saint-Georges, 75009 Paris, France.

Direction des Français de l'étranger, Sous direction de l'état civil, 11 rue de la Maison Blanche, 44941 Nantes cedex 9, France; telephone: (02) 5177-3030; fax: (02) 5177-3699; website: WWW. DIPLOMATIE.FR/ARCHIVES.

Etsi, Sephardi Genealogical and Historical Society, 77 bd Richard-Lenoir, 75011 Paris, France (mailing address only); website: www. GEOCITIES.COM/ETSI-SEFARAD.

Bibliography

"Archival Publications as Sources of Data." *AVOTAYNU* 1, no. 1 (January 1985). See entry for Jewish Theological Seminary.

Attal, Robert. *Les Juif d'Afrique du Nord: Bibliographie* (Bibliography: Jews of North Africa). [French and Hebrew] Jerusalem: Ben Zvi Institute, 1993.

Ayoun, Richard and Cohen, Bernard. *Les Juifs d'Algérie: Deux mille ans d'histoire* (The Jews of Algeria: Two thousands years of history). [French] Paris: Lattes, 1982.

Bennett, Ralph. "About the Jews of Morocco, Algeria and Libya." *AVOTAYNU* 10, no. 3 (Fall 1994).

Bloch, Isaac. *Inscriptions tumulaires des anciens cimetières israélites d'Alger.* (Inscriptions of old Jewish cemeteries of Algiers). [French]. Paris, 1888. Index by Philip Abensur in *Etsi*, no. 3, Winter 1998.

Chouraqui, André. *Histoire des Juifs en Afrique du nord.* (History of the Jews in Northern Africa) 2 vols. [French]. Paris: Rocher, 1998.

Contributing Editors (France). *AVOTAYNU* 2, no. 2 (October 1986).

———. *AVOTAYNU* 3, no. 1 (Spring 1987).

———. *AVOTAYNU* 4, no. 4 (Winter 1988).

———. *AVOTAYNU* 7, no. 4 (Winter 1991).

———. *AVOTAYNU* 8, no. 1 (Spring 1992).

———. *AVOTAYNU* 8, no. 2 (Summer 1992).

———. *AVOTAYNU* 8, no. 3 (Fall 1992).

———. *AVOTAYNU* 9, no. 2 (Summer 1993).

———. *AVOTAYNU* 11, no. 1 (Spring 1995).

———. *AVOTAYNU* 12, no. 1 (Spring 1996).

———. *AVOTAYNU* 12, no. 2 (Summer 1996).

———. *AVOTAYNU* 14, no. 1 (Spring 1998).

Eisenbeth, Maurice. *Les Juifs de l'Afrique du Nord: Démographie et onomastique.* (Jews of Northern Africa: demography and onomastics). [French]. Algier: Imprimerie du lycée, 1936; Paris: Cercle de Généalogie Juive and Gordes: La Lettre Sépharade, 2000.

Faraggi-Rychner, Anne-Marie. "Etat des cimetières juifs en Algérie (suite)." (Jewish Cemeteries in Algeria, following)," *Etsi*, no. 11, December 2000.

Haddey, J. M. *Le livre d'or des Israélites algériens* (Golden book of the Algerian Jews). [French] Algier, 1871.

Hirschberg, Haim-Zeev. *A History of the Jews in North Africa.* 2 vols. Leiden: Brill, 1974, 1981.

"Index." *AVOTAYNU* 15, no. 1 (Spring 1999).

"Jews of Livorno, Italy in 1841." *AVOTAYNU* 12, no. 4 (Winter 1996).

Latapie, Roger. "Etat actuel des cimetières juifs d'Algérie." (Present state of Jewish cemeteries in Algeria). [French] *Etsi*, no. 3, Winter, 1998.

Les Juifs d'Algérie, Images et textes. (The Jews of Algeria, pictures and texts). [French] Paris: Editions du Scribe, 1987.

Schemla, Elisabeth. *Mon journal d'Algérie, Novembre 1999–Janvier 2000.* [French] Paris: Flammarion, 2000.

"Sephardic Reference Sources." *AVOTAYNU* 12, no. 3 (Fall 1996).

Notes

1. Schemla, *Mon journal d'Algérie*. Ms. Schemla reports that civil state archives still exist in Algeria and appear well preserved. In Khenchela, she found the birth registrations of her father and all of his siblings, dating from 1896 to 1915, offering the hope that some day these records may be available to Jewish genealogists.

2. Bloch, *Inscriptions tumulaires*.

Argentina

by Paul Armony

Jews were not permitted to live openly in Argentina until the adoption of its 1853 constitution. Before the Spanish Inquisition was abolished in 1813, no Jews were allowed to live in any territory that belonged to Spain, including the "Provincias Unidas del Rio de La Plata," as Argentina originally was called. Exceptions existed, of course; all of the Spanish colonies had individuals of Jewish heritage. Some were arrested and burned at the stake for judaizing, and the word "Portuguese" was understood to mean Jew, just as "Russian" assumed that connotation in the 20th century. In the years before 1853, individual Jews were buried in Protestant cemeteries which had been opened after a treaty with England in 1825.

Historians can document only six Jews living in Argentina before 1855. Starting in that year, some Jews trickled into the country as military and commercial agents of French and English firms, as jewelers, adventurers and as dealers in "white slavery" (Jewish prostitution).

Jewish History of Argentina

Jewish Community from 1860 to 1889

The first official Jewish wedding in Argentina took place in November 11, 1860; before then, the Jewish ceremony had been forbidden. By 1862, a group of several dozen Ashkenazi Jews had founded the first Jewish society in the country, one that within six years became the Israeli Community of the República Argentina (CIRA). The society has existed continuously since then. Its synagogue, *Templo Libertad,** was built in 1897 and replaced in 1932 by the current building.

The Argentinean government opened the country to European immigration in 1854, offering special inducements to both immigrants and to those who sold them land. Most original immigrants were Italians and Spanish, augmented by some Swiss, Welsh and Volga Germans. Individual Sephardic Jews began to arrive in the 1880s, primarily from Morocco, Syria and Turkey. With no central organization and well able to speak Spanish (because of their knowledge of *Ladino* [Judeo-Spanish]), most assimilated easily and dispersed around the country as traveling salesmen and then tradesmen. In January 1889, José Elías Maman requested permission to establish a Sephardic synagogue, and the first Judeo-Sephardi organization was founded in 1891.

Great Jewish Immigration of 1889

By 1889, Argentina had 1,572 Jewish residents. In August of that year, the first contingent of 819 Jews from Kamenets-Podolsk arrived in Buenos Aires aboard the ship *Weser*. In Paris, they had purchased from an Argentinean agent some land around La Plata, about 50 kilometers from Buenos Aires. When the emigrés arrived, however, they were forced to accept instead new land near the recently inaugurated train station Palacios, in the province of Santa Fe, 650 kilometers from Buenos Aires. After many painful incidents, including an epidemic that claimed the lives of 62 children, the new immigrants established the first Jewish city in Argentina, which they called Moisesville.

Their misfortunes were reported to the Alliance Israelite Universelle by a Jewish scientist, W. Lowenthal, who visited Argentina at the end of 1889. The Alliance had helped the group by partially paying its passage, and they felt responsible for its bad luck. The Lowenthal report stimulated Baron Maurice de Hirsch to found the famous Jewish Colonization Association (JCA), which bought land in Argentina, Brazil, Canada, the United States and elsewhere, to colonize Russian Jews as farmers and agricultural workers. Baron de Hirsch wanted to prove that Jews could adapt to productive occupations, not only those of usury and trade.

Jewish Colonization Association

JCA wanted to settle 3,000 colonists yearly in Argentina, but its goal was frustrated by ignorance of the country and ill-chosen, uneducated administrators who sometimes were venal as well. Baron de Hirsch's untimely death in 1896 and the resultant elaborate bureaucracy based on the colonial English model all prevented the program from reaching the goals foreseen by its founder. During the 80 years of JCA existence in Argentina, only about 35,000 individuals were settled on the land. Most soon abandoned the program (3,393 families remained with about 20,000 individuals), primarily because of major disagreements with the rigid and inflexible administration. JCA was able to bring only a few German Jews (430 families) to Argentina at the end of the 1930s.

Although they never settled in one of the Baron de Hirsch colonies, the existence of the program itself determined the destinations of many Polish and Russian Jews. Because of JCA, they knew of the existence of Argentina, and many immigrated to Argentina and other South American countries on their own. Some had relatives there and knew that one could live freely and make a living. Thus were formed the Jewish communities of Brazil, Uruguay and other Latin American countries. Many did not want to be farmers, but JCA offered no other alternative.

Jewish Immigration to Argentina

Approximately 238,000 Jewish immigrants came to Argentina, out of a total of three million during the period of open immigration from Asia and Africa, Asia and Europe between 1880 and 1914. Argentina was one of the major destinations for Ashkenazic Jews from Russia and Poland, but also of the Sephardim from such places as Syria, Turkey and the Greek island of Rhodes. A smaller number of Moroccan Jews arrived beginning in 1956, the last of the Jewish immigrants to Argentina.

At its peak size, during the decade of 1950s, between 400,000 and 500,000 inhabitants of Jewish origin lived in Argentina. At that time, Argentina's Jewish community was one of the six or seven largest Jewish populations in the world and the second largest in the Western Hemisphere. After that time, Jews began to emigrate from Argentina, primarily to Israel—the destination for more than 70,000—but to many other countries as well. Today approximately 220,000 Jews live in Argentina. Canada has a larger Jewish population, and soon Brazil will as well.

How many Jews lived in Argentina during the past 110 years cannot be known with accuracy. After 1960, the census no longer asked religion, and for a number of reasons (assimilation, cremation, leftist politics), many Argentinean-born Jews were not buried in Jewish cemeteries.

Genealogical Research in Argentina

Any genealogical investigation in Argentina must begin with the answers to two basic questions: Where did the ancestor live? Where did that person die and when? The first question divides into two further questions: in Buenos Aires or in the interior of the country? If in the interior, then one has 30 or more places to investigate. Did the individual live on a Baron de Hirsch colony? At least 16 were founded by JCA.

If some possible ancestor was originally a colonist but subsequently left the colony, then he or she may have resided in one of the 16 largest cities in Argentina: Bahía Blanca, Catamarca, Córdoba, Corrientes, La Plata, Mendoza, Neuquén, Paraná, Posadas, Resistencia, Rosario, Salta, San Juan, Santa Fe, Santiago del Estero and Tucumán.

In addition, there are dozens of small towns in the 22 Argentinean provinces where there were, and still are, small Jewish communities. To obtain the addresses for these Jewish communities, consult the *Israeli Directory* published in 1946/47/50; the only remaining copies are available in the library of AMIA* (Asociacion Mutual Israelita Argentina); the main Jewish association in Buenos Aires. Its building was destroyed by a terrorist attack in July 18, 1994, but it has been rebuilt and, since September 23, 1999, is located once again at its old address.

Knowing when a person arrived in Argentina often helps determine where he or she lived. Certain records were started or existed only during certain years. Unfortunately, during the 110 years of Jewish communal existence in Argentina, many institutions were established that no longer exist; often their records and registrations also are missing. This is especially true of the first immigrants and in the interior of the country where some Jewish communities have disappeared. For this reason alone, any indication of where to look is extremely valuable.

At the end of 2000, 31,200 Jews lived in the interior of Argentina, while 190,000 lived in the Greater Buenos Aires area. Demographics dictate that the easiest and often fastest

Portraits of some of the early Jewish colonists of Entre Rios appear in a museum in the town of Dominguez.

way to search is to begin with Buenos Aires, where 80 to 85 percent of Argentinean Jews live and have lived.

Today, approximately 13 million individuals live in Greater Buenos Aires (the city of Buenos Aires and the towns within a 50-kilometer radius), more than one third of the total national population of 36 million. Also 85 percent of the Jews reside there. Despite the fact that the first immigrants settled initially in Baron de Hirsch colonies, the majority moved to the cities after a few years.

Once the place of residence is known, the second question is whether the ancestors were Ashkenazi or Sephardi; for in Buenos Aires and in some of the other big cities, the cultures remain divided. In other localities, their communities have united to create communal cemeteries. There is no fixed rule, of course, but in most cases, the two groups have lived separately. When they intermarried, the husband's origin almost always prevailed, unless the wife was not Jewish.

Research in Buenos Aires

Books and pamphlets on where to obtain birth, marriage and death certificates, immigrant arrival records, names of parents and other data do not exist in Argentina, especially in Buenos Aires. For that reason, the **Asociación de Genealogía Judía de Argentina** (AGJA),* the Jewish Genealogical Society of Argentina, makes particular efforts to guide new genealogists. The AGJA has no physical office and, thus, is unable to handle requests in person, unless arranged by prior appointment.

Records divide into three major groups: those of official government origin, those of private Jewish origin and those that are private and non-Jewish.

Government Records

Below are listed the possible records that can be obtained.

- Vital records from the *Registro Civil* (civil register). By law since 1886, all births, marriages and deaths are registered here. To obtain any of these certificates, it is necessary to go to any Registro Civil office.
- Ship arrival records (immigrants)
- Records of all Argentinean citizens.

- Probate records, including all the various steps involved in claiming inheritances
- Files of the Argentina federal police. These and other political registrations are very difficult to access and legal action may be necessary to obtain them.
- Voter lists are now available on CD-ROM. Similar lists for earlier years may exist but, at present, they have not been located.
- Telephone directories. The current directories are available on CD-ROM and online via the Internet at HTTP://WWW.PAGINASAMARILLAS.COM.AR/HOME_GUIA.ASP?IDIOMA=EN; HTTP://WWW.PAGINAS-DORADAS.COM.AR/PDPORTAL/GT. Earlier directories are available in telephone company offices, libraries and other institutions. There is no centralized national directory or bureau of telephone listings.
- School records for university students, professional centers and so forth exists, but are difficult to access officially. Sometimes access is possible through personal friendships.
- The Museum of Immigrants, owned by the Immigrants Bureau, is very small and new, but has some historical information, such as maps and pictures.
- *Archivo General of the Nation.** Located here are copies of the national census, old pictures and considerable historical information. Unfortunately, it holds only the records of immigrants who arrived before 1880 (the big Jewish immigration began in 1889).

Records of Jewish Origin

Materials useful to genealogists may be found in many of the following institutions. Because of the two attacks against the Jewish community—the bombing of the Israeli Embassy in 1992 and the AMIA building in 1994—stringent security measures now impede formerly free access to these places.

- Jewish Museum Dr. Salvador Kibrick; Libertad 769, Buenos Aires
- YIVO Institute, "IWO of Argentina," Pasteur 633, Buenos Aires
- Mark Turkow Center of Jewish Documentation, Pasteur 633, Buenos Aires
- AMIA, Pasteur 633, Buenos Aires, holds the list of individuals buried in Ashkenazi cemeteries (see cemetery information below for more details).
- Organizations of immigrants from Europe and other places. Few organizations still exist today: those formerly from Poland, from Galicia and from Germany. Addresses may be obtained from AMIA.
- Lists of marriages, burials and other life events held by the various Jewish communities
- Lists held in temples and synagogues of marriages, bar mitzvahs and other events. Only a few synagogues have records of the marriages; information about these synagogues may be obtained from the Bureau of the Chief Rabbi of Buenos Aires, Pasteur 633.
- Lists held by various Jewish institutions, such as homes for the aged and orphans, hospitals and beneficent associations

- Directories of Jewish people in Argentina. These directories were issued from 1946 till 1971 or latter, the copies of years 1946/1947/1950 are in the AMIA library the AGJA has copies of them and originals of years 1954, 1960 and 1971. The 1960 directory was computarized by AGJA and the 1954 is in process.
- *Yizkor* books published in Argentina and other books written in memory of the deceased. Some copies are in the library of the Latin American Jewish Seminar.*
- Jewish newspapers and publications: *Idishe Zeitung, Di Presse* and others—none still published. The complete collections were in the AMIA library destroyed in the bombing; some copies are in other Jewish libraries and private collections such as the Library of the IWO (YIVO)* and the New York Public Library.*
- Lists of students at Jewish schools exist, but security rules make it difficult to obtain this information. The same is true of membership lists for Jewish clubs and sport associations.
- Association of Jewish Genealogy of Argentina (AJGA) does not have permanent physical headquarters. It is an organization of hobbyists and cannot undertake to do research for others, but its members are willing to help with advice. The society meets the first Tuesday of each month at 6:30 p.m. To confirm a meeting, telephone 54-11-4701-0730 or send an e-mail to GENARG@INFOVIA.COM.AR.

Many in the Argentinean Jewish community are not affiliated with temples or synagogues, making it difficult to reach the group as a whole.

Non-Jewish Private Institutions

- The Center for Latin American Immigration (CEMLA)* has the records of approximately three million immigrants who arrived in Argentina between 1880 and 1930 (see below under arrival records).
- Newspapers such as *La Nacion* and *Clarin* publish death notices.
- At the main National Library, researchers can use telephone directories and other books. At the Congress Library, the public can see the old newspapers; *La Nacion* and *Clarin* do not have public libraries.

How to Obtain Genealogical Information in Buenos Aires

Civil Vital Records

The central office of vital registration for Buenos Aires is located at Uruguay 753, but 14 other neighborhood centers are located throughout the city. Generally, the offices are open to the public weekdays from 7:30 a.m. to 3 p.m., but variations in the schedule occur throughout the year.

Two personal visits are necessary in order obtain a copy of a birth, marriage or death record. Records can be obtained for any year from 1890 onward. One must first make the request and then return between 15 and 20 days later to obtain the copy. If one does not know the exact number of the document, book and folio, then it is necessary to pay a nonrefundable research fee of approximately 20 pesos charged whether or not the record can be found. You must indicate the approximate date (year); only three to five years before and after the year indicated are searched. If the record is not found and a researcher wants additional years searched, the fee must be paid again. The research fee is in addition to the approximately 15 pesos charged per certificate. Sometimes it is possible to obtain a specific date from AMIA and avoid the research charge. If express service is needed (i.e., less than the usual five days), an additional fee is levied. These offices do not respond to mail requests; several private agencies will do this, but they charge substantial fees.

The certificates include considerable information: name, nationality, profession, home, age of the individual(s) involved, parents, spouses and children. Sometimes the names of witnesses are included and/or causes of the death and other miscellaneous data. A researcher who knows only a last name and no other information should hire a registered lawyer who can request the information in writing (with a requisite fee). This fee is in addition to the fee charged per certificate. Usually responses come within one month.

Arrival Records

The following organizations hold records of immigrants to Argentina.

CEMLA, a private Catholic organization located at Independence 20, corner at Av. L.M. Huergo, originally held registrations of three million immigrants who came to Argentina between 1882 and 1926. (CEMLA continues to process later arrivals, but had reached till 1930 as of this writing.) Many records were lost especially from the first decade of this century, due to fire. CEMLA is open to the public Tuesday and Thursday from 10 a.m. to 2 p.m. A search fee per person is charged whether or not a record is found; an additional fee is charged for each certificate. Telephone: 54-11-4342-6749/54-11-4334-7717; fax: 54-11-4331-0832; e-mail: CEMLA@CIUDAD.COM.AR. Mail or e-mail inquiries are accepted, but payment must be sent in advance. CEMLA has placed an index to these arrivals on the web at http://www.CEMLA.COM/PAGINAS/C_BUSQUEDA.HTM. After locating entries of interest, you can contact them and get copies of the originals for a fee.

The **Electoral National Court**, 25 de Mayo, 245 1002 Buenos Aires, has alphabetical registers of all Argentinean citizens, alive or dead. The office is open daily from 8:30 a.m. to 1:30 p.m. but is closed all of January. Information is available only to a direct relative of the individual sought—with proof of relationship required. In other cases, an attorney must make the request. After sending a completed form and payment of 10 pesos, a response comes within 30 days. Included are the names of the parents and all addresses of the person.

The *Archivo General de la Nación*, at Av. Leandro N. Alem 246, has records of immigrants who arrived before 1882; the major Jewish immigration did not begin until 1889, the holdings are of use to few Jewish genealogists. In addition, the archives has a publication office as well as files of photo-

Old section of the Moisesville cemetery which was created in 1891

graphs and other graphic documents. The archives are closed during January.

Temples and Religious Congregations

Records are held by temples, synagogues and Jewish associations, but details can be obtained only by consulting each individual organization. The *Community Chalom*, which holds records of the Ladino-speaking Jews of the Balkans, Greece, Rhodes and Turkey, has computerized information about all of marriages performed in their temple; AGJA has a copy.

The Libertad Temple also has files of all of its marriages and, for a fee, will send a copy of the marriage certificate. Other important temples, such as the Temple in Paso Street, have records, but they are not computerized.

Jewish Genealogy Society of Argentina (AGJA)

AGJA has numerous valuable genealogical lists such as:

- lists of immigrants from the holdings of the Jewish Museum
- lists of passengers who arrived on the *Weser*, the *Tokyo*, the *Lisbon*, the *Pampa* and other ships
- list of JCA colonists; records of students in schools in Moisesville
- children of JCA colonists
- records of cemeteries
- and other databases

The database, which includes more than 200,000 records, is the most important Jewish database in Argentina. The information is not free; for more information, please contact AGJA by e-mail at GENARG@INFOVIA.COM.AR or request an appointment by telephone at 54-11-4701-0730.

AGJA is a nonprofit organization that receives no subsidies from any outside group. It has neither funds nor personnel to carry out genealogical investigations for third parties, but is willing to help other Jewish genealogists in a spirit of mutual cooperation. Some of its members will undertake private investigations for moderate fees, but AGJA cannot assume responsibility for their work. AGJA publishes the magazine *Toldot* three times per year in Spanish; subscriptions are available to all.

Cemeteries in Greater Buenos Aires

Eleven Jewish cemeteries are located in Greater Buenos Aires, all outside the city limits. They are Liniers, Ciudadela (Ashkenazi), Tablada and Berazategui, of the AMIA Ashkenazi; Lomas de Zamora Ashkenazi, of the Community of Lomas de Zamora; Avellaneda (Moroccans); Ciudadela of the Alepinos; Ciudadela and Bancalari of the Ladino-speaking Jews from Greece and Turkey; Lomas de Zamora of the Sephardim from Damascus and Beirut; and Tablada Sefaradí for Jews of Turkish origin.

In addition, there is one abandoned cemetery where dealers in prostitution and some of their ladies are buried. This cemetery, which belonged to the Jewish Zwi Migdal prostitution organization, is close to the Moroccan cemetery and is maintained by it. No records or any information exist about the people buried there.

The following Jewish communities administer the 11 existing cemeteries in Buenos Aires:

AMIA administers Liniers (opened in 1910), Ciudadela (opened in 1929), Tablada (opened in 1930) and Berazategui (opened in 1957). Only Tablada and Berazategui with more than 110,000 records are computerized; the information is in the AMIA system. Because of the destruction of its building in the terrorist attack of 1994, AMIA lost most of its 150,000 original registrations; these records are being recreated from the books that were kept in the cemeteries. Records of Liniers (with 23,000 registrations) and Ciudadela (with more than 6,000 registrations) have been computerized by the AGJA.

Association Community Israeli Latin of Buenos Aires (ACILBA), an organization of Jews of Moroccan origin, has its cemetery in Avellaneda (Provincia de Buenos Aires). The list of those buried in this cemetery—more than 2,200 names—was computerized by the AGJA. Established in 1900, ACILBA's cemetery was the first Jewish cemetery in the Greater Buenos Aires area.

In reality, the first Jewish cemetery in Buenos Aires was the cemetery for the dealers in Jewish prostitution. In 1898, when the newly founded Ashkenazi *chevra kadisha* (burial society) needed money to buy a cemetery, the very rich *T'mein* (dealers in Jewish white slaves), offered to be its partner, providing the needed money in exchange for the right to be buried in the cemetery. When the *chevra kadisha* rejected the offer, the slave dealers bought their own land for a cemetery, which they continued to use until approximately 1945; although the organization that owned it was dissolved in 1934. The registration book of the individuals buried in this cemetery is missing. Most of the tombs were vandalized by grave robbers to see if they contained jewels.

Bene Emeth is used by Jews from Damascus and Beirut. This cemetery was opened in 1913 in Lomas de Zamora, Provincia de Buenos Aires. More than 6,000 Jews are buried here; AGJA has a copy of its computerized list.

Association Israeli Community Sefaradí (ACIS) buries Jews from the Balkans, Greece, the island of Rhodes and Turkey (all those who spoke Ladino). They began with the cemetery of Ciudadela and then acquired that of Bancalari, also located in the Province of Buenos Aires. AGJA has just computerized the names of individuals interred in both cemeteries, Ciudadela with 2,500 registrations and Bancalari with 3,700 registrations.

The Israeli Association Sefaradí Argentina (AISA), composed of Syrian Jews from Aleppo, have their cemetery in Ciudadela, Province of Buenos Aires. Opened in 1929, this cemetery also has a section that belongs to the AMIA Ashkenazi and another to the Ladino-speaking Jews from Turkey (ACIS). The section that belongs to AISA has more than 4,400 computerized registrations, a copy is held by AGJA.

The Hebrew Association of Mutual Aid (AHSC) buries Jews of Turkish origin in the Tablada cemetery opened in 1930. AGJA is computerizing their roughly 1,000 registrations.

The South Ashkenazi Jewish Community of Buenos Aires has its own cemetery located in Lomas de Zamora, Province of Buenos Aires, where 2,200 Jews are buried. The information from this cemetery has been computerized by the AGJA.

For administrative reasons, all the cemeteries listed above, except for the community of Lomas de Zamora, use death certificates issued by the City of Buenos Aires even if the person died in the Province of Buenos Aires. This is fortunate for genealogists, who can request a death certificate in the City of Buenos Aires instead of having go to La Plata, the capital of the province of Buenos Aires, which is 60 kilometers from Buenos Aires.

Jews are buried also in Colinas del Tiempo, a nonsectarian, private garden cemetery. Incorporation of this cemetery into the AMIA failed because Orthodox Jews objected that some "non-Jews" (children of mothers who had been converted by a Reform community) are buried here. The cemetery has existed for approximately five years; AGJA does not have records of its burials.

Some Jews are buried in other nonsectarian cemeteries, such as the municipal cemeteries of Chacarita and Flores. Records of burials in municipal cemeteries are held by the municipality of Buenos Aires. Also nonsectarian are private garden cemeteries such as Jardin de Paz and Memorial Park, where one may buy a tomb and be buried without religious specification. AGJA has no records of Jews buried in nonsectarian cemeteries.

No specifically Jewish private cemetery exists inside Buenos Aires proper, the result of a special prohibition that, in 1898 and 1926, canceled authorization for the opening of the Ashkenazi Jewish cemetery in the city. Consequently, between approximately 1860 and 1892, Jews were buried in the Second Cemetery of Dissidents in Buenos Aires, today First of May Park; later, between 1892 and 1900, in Chacarita-sector city cemetery for dissidents; and from 1900 until 1910, in the Municipal Cemetery of Flores (170 of the approximately 800 graves were moved to Liniers Cemetery at various times). Information about the 800 individuals buried here has been computerized by AGJA from old cemetery records. AGJA also has the records of the people buried in the First of May Park and in Chacarita-sector city cemetery for dissidents. In 1910, Liniers Cemetery was opened in the Province of Buenos Aires, across Avenida Gral. Paz, just outside the city limits from the neighborhood of that name.

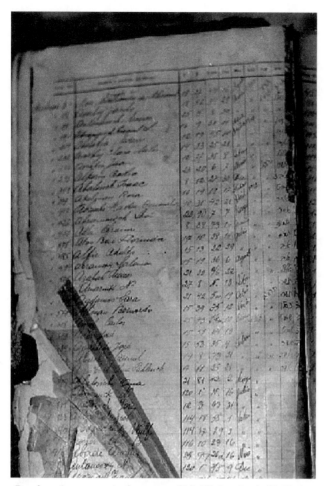

Death registers contain the names of 23,400 Jews buried in Liniers.

How to Search for Cemetery Information

If the person being sought was Ashkenazi, begin with AMIA. AMIA has computerized the names of people buried in the cemeteries of Tablada and Berazategui. The database of 110,000 names may be accessed via the last name or the year of death. Resulting information includes the specific date of death and location of the grave. Consultation can be made either in person at the AMIA central headquarters or at the cemetery, where one is given a computer-printed map showing the location of the grave and the way to reach it. (The cemetery is very large.) The computer report shows the date of death. AGJA has a copy of this database. Telephone to learn when the cemeteries may be visited: Tabled, 4652-8288; Berazategui, 4255-1494; Liniers, 4653-1883; and Ciudadela, 4653-2351.

Most Sephardi burials have been computerized. This includes Avellaneda (Moroccans) with 2,200 records, Ciudadela (from Aleppo) with 4,400 burials, Bancalari (Ladino-speakers) with 3,700 graves, Ciudadela (Ladino-speakers) with 2,500 deceased, Tablada Sephardim with 1,000 records, and Lomás of Zamora Sephardim with 6,500 deceased. Remember that AGJA has all the above information. AMIA provides the information without cost; AGJA charges a fee, but a search through AGJA may be done by e-mail and saves re-

searchers the necessity of visiting distant cemeteries in person.

Genealogical Research Outside of Buenos Aires

Genealogical research outside of Buenos Aires is difficult because much information is not centralized. At one time, Jews were dispersed throughout the entire country, constituting large communities in Córdoba and Rosario, smaller ones in Neuquén and San Juan. Some Jews lived in small towns where they maintained stores and warehouses. One can request the addresses of all existing Argentinean Jewish communities from AMIA.

An important guide to locating Jews outside Buenos Aires is the Israelite Guide published form 1946,till 1972, copies of years 1946/47/50 are found in the AMIA library and 1954, 1960 and 1972 in the AGJA library.

The *Guía Telefónica* (telephone directory) is the best source to find individuals. Each city has one, so there are many to check. Today they also are available on CD-ROM and on the Internet for the entire country. In a single, integrated directory one can search by surname, address or telephone number. These CDs may be purchased either at telephone company offices or at newsstands. Some old directories are available in the National Library, but a great problem exists. Because of the politics of the state telephone company that existed during the period 1945–92, one could not obtain telephones without paying large sums of money. The results were a black market in the sale of telephones, and telephones that were not charged to the real user's name. Even today, people who rent a property do not have the telephone in their name, but rather in the name of the owner of the property. This situation enormously hinders locating people. In addition, many people do not update their listings, with the result that many telephones are listed in the directories at addresses where the holders have not lived for more than ten years.

Until the 1950s a directory called the *Green Guides* was published in Argentina. People registered their home and business addresses here, whether or not they had a telephone. Some libraries have copies of the *Green Guide*, but they are difficult to locate.

Electoral Censuses

Another source of information is the electoral censuses, in which women appear with both maiden and married surnames. Because these documents provide legal home addresses, it is possible to check them against the telephone CD-ROM guide and discover the telephone number, even when the phone is registered in a different name.

Civil Registrations

All counties in Argentina are divided into departments; each has a civil registration office where one must go to seek death certificates. The offices do not answer requests by mail; most employees do not understand English. For these reasons, it is extremely difficult to obtain a death certificate without local help. The other possibility is to hire one specialized agency.

Jewish Institutions

The interior of Argentina once had many Jewish institutions, but as the Jewish population has declined, some institutions have disappeared and others are greatly reduced. Places such as Basavilbaso, Carlos Casares, Domínguez and Moisesville, which once had a Jewish majority, also had many cultural and other societies. All that remains today is their memory; in some places there is not a single halachically Jewish family. Many books and commemorative magazines of these communities with their many lists of names still exist; they can be consulted in the AMIA library. Considerable information is available to help one look for family, but time is required and one must travel and know Spanish well enough to be able to read the documents.

List of Colonists

If a family being traced arrived in Argentina as part of the Baron de Hirsch program, one can search lists of colonists who owned land and lists of former colonists who abandoned and sold their farms. AGJA has some lists, but they are incomplete. The JCA (Baron de Hirsch Fund) created at least 16 colonies and many subcolonies. In addition, other Jewish immigrants and former Baron de Hirsch colonists established four independent colonies.

The table below indicates the names of the colonies, corresponding subcolonies and the name of the nearest train station and/or Argentinean town. Often, a colony is identified by its Argentinean name, not by the JCA name.

Cemeteries in Argentina

More than 70 jewish cemeteries are currently in use in Argentina. Records of the 56 cemeteries included larger ones — Catamarca, Cordoba, La Plata, Mar de Plata, Mendoza, Rosario, Paraná, Moisesville, Rivera, Santa Fe, Santiago del Estero, Tucuman, etc. — are already computarized by the AGJA. Other important cities, such as La Plata, Mar del Plata, Mendoza and Rosario, likely have registrations of their cemeteries, but these have not yet been integrated into the files of the AGJA.

Numerous cemeteries in the province of Entre Rïos, the center of Jewish colonization, seemingly have no records of burials. For these, the only possibility is to record the cemetery *in situ*. Such a project is possible, but it requires considerable work, time and money.

In sum, genealogical research in Argentina is possible, but one must either do the research personally or hire local researchers. Jewish institutions in Argentina are not economically able to do free searches; most lack computers and are managed with few employees and a corps of volunteers. Genealogical investigation is not a major priority.

Although it possesses neither the economic means nor volunteers to carry out such searches, AGJA wishes to help genealogists all over the world. In the six years since it was founded, AGJA has created a cemetery database of more than 280,000 entries, 210,000 dead persons and 70,000 maiden surnames of married women (as of June 2003). Beside the other databases have around 100,000 more entries. AGJA accepts consultations with payment of a fee or contribution. Recently, may 2003, AGJA issued a booklet "La Investigación Genealogica en Argentina" (Spanish). This booklet will be translated to English as "The Jewish Genealogical Research in Argentina" to be presented in the Seminar in Washington in July 2003 and to be included in the Jewishgen files.

Addresses

AGJA. Juana Azurduy 2223, piso 8 (1429) Buenos Aires; e-mail: genarg@infovia.com.ar; telephone: 54-11-4701-0730.

AMIA (Asociacion Mutual Israelit Argentina, Pasteur 633, Buenos Aires.

Archivo General of the Nation, Av. Leandro Alem 246, Buenos Aires.

CEMLA Independencia 20, Buenos Aires.

Latin American Jewish Seminar, Jose Hernandez 1750, Buenos Aires.

Library of the IWO (YIVO), Pasteur 633, Buenos Aires.

New York Public Library, Fifth Avenue at 34th Street, New York.

Templo Libertad, Libertad 785, Buenos Aires.

Bibliography

AMIA. *Comunidad Judia de Buenos Aires 1894–1994.* (The Jewish community of Buenos Aires, 1894–1994). [Spanish]. Buenos Aires: Mila, 1994.

Avni, Haim. *Argentina y la Historia de la Inmigracion Judia, 1810–1950.* (Argentina and the history of Jewish immigration). [Spanish] Buenos Aires: Magnes, 1983.

Avni, Haim. *Argentina and the Jews: A History of Jewish Immigration* Tuscaloosa, AL: University of Alabama Press, 1991.

Carioli, Susana B. Sigwald. *Colonia Mauricio* (Mauricio Colony). [Spanish] Carlos Casares: Del Archivo, 1991.

Cociovitch, Noe. *Genesis de Moises Ville* (The birth of Moises Ville). [Spanish]. Buenos Aires: Mila, 1987.

Cymbler, Jeffrey. "Argentina, the Other Golden Land," *AVOTAYNU* 5, No. 1, (Summer 1989).

Elnecave, Nissim. *Los Hijos de Ibero Franconia.* (The children of Ibero Franconia). [Spanish] Buenos Aires: La Luz, 1981.

Feierstein, Ricardo. *Historia de los Judiios Argentinos* (History of the Jews of Argentina). [Spanish] Buenos Aires: Planeta, 1992.

Gerchunoff, Alberto *The Jewish Gauchos of the Pampas* (originally published in 1940 as *Los Gauchos Judios de las Pampas*). Albuquerque: University of New Mexico Press, 1953.

"HIAS in Argentina," Letter to the Editor, *AVOTAYNU* 5, no. 1, (Spring 1989).

Lewin, Boleslao. *Como fue la Inmigracion Judea en la Argentina* (What Jewish immigration to Argentina was like). [Spanish] Buenos Aires: Plus Ultra, 1983

Mirelman, Victor A., ed. *En Busqueda de una identidad* (Looking for an identity). [Spanish] Buenos Aires: Mila, 1988.

Mirelman, Victor A. *Jewish Buenos Aires, 1890–1930: In Search of an Identity.* Detroit: Wayne State University Press, 1990.

Pardo, Oscar. *AVOTAYNU*, Contributing Editor columns 2, no. 3, (October 1986); 3, no. 2, (Summer 1987).

Presencia Sefaradi en la Argentina. (Sephardic presence in Argentina) [Spanish] Buenos Aires: C.E.S., 1992.

Wolf, Martha, et al. eds. *Los Inmigrantes Judios* (The Jewish immigrants) [Spanish] Buenos Aires: Manrique Zago, 1989.

Notes

1. *History of the Argentinean Jews*, by Ricardo Feierstein.
2. *Toldot* 9, May 1999.

Australia

by Sophie Caplan

Jews have lived in Australia since the first day of European settlement, January 26, 1788, when the First Fleet from England arrived in what later became Port Jackson, the harbor of Sydney. The first colony was named New South Wales; its original European population consisted of convicted felons plus a regiment of marines to guard them and to run the colony for a few years.

The major stimuli for bringing convicts to the southern continent were the discovery and mapping of the Australian east coast by Captain Cook and his crew in 1770 and the American Declaration of Independence in July 1776, which closed the former American colonies of the British Crown to further transportation of British convicts there.

Between 1788 and 1852, when transportation of convicts to the Australian east coast ceased, approximately 145,000 convicts were brought to New South Wales, about 1,000 of whom are believed to have been Jews. From 1816 onwards, an ever-growing number of Jews also came as free settlers, some of them relatives of the convicts. (The convicts subsequently were called emancipists). In 1828, the person first accredited to perform Jewish marriages, Phillip Joseph Cohen, had arrived, and the Jews of New South Wales came under the *hechsher* (jurisdiction) of the Chief Rabbi of England. This ensured a continuing link with British Jewry and its Orthodox religious modalities as the main strand of Jewish religious expression in Australia. For many years, the London *Beth Din* (religious court) was the only court of religious appeal.

A burial society was organized in Sydney in 1817 and several *minyans* with unofficial religious leaders existed during the 1820s. The first formal congregation in Australia was founded in Sydney in 1831; the first synagogue opened in 1844. Religious status differences between the emancipists and the free settlers for several decades in the 19th century led to schisms in the community.[1] Eventually unity prevailed, and the present Great Synagogue of Sydney, the mother congregation of Australia, opened in 1878.

Gold was discovered in 1823, but the news was suppressed for nearly three decades for fear of social disruption. The discoveries were finally made public in 1851 in New South Wales and in Victoria. This led to a gold rush and to an appreciable rise in immigration—including that of young, single Jewish men. Most came from England, but many also from Germany and some from Eastern Europe. Often they came after a sojourn in England or the California gold fields. Jews usually did not remain miners, but returned to their trades as butchers, bakers and shopkeepers, supplying the needs of the miners. A few became gold buyers and later founded banks.

The towns of Ballarat, Bendigo and Geelong in Victoria; Hill End in New South Wales; and Kalgoorlie in Western Australia all developed small Jewish communities as a result of the gold rush. All have died out now except for a vestigial community in Ballarat with a synagogue which is a museum.

Small Jewish communities developed in such district market towns as Maitland, Port Macquarie and Tamworth, or in mining towns such as Broken Hill and Newcastle—all in New South Wales. In these places Jews often ran the general store, the inn and the pubs. These communities have since disappeared except for Newcastle; the Jewish families either moved to the state capitals so that their children might find Jewish marriage partners, or they intermarried and became part of the general community. Hence the assertion that between 25 and 33 percent of pre-1948 Australians have some Jewish ancestry.

The promulgation of the May Laws of Czar Alexander II in 1881 brought some Russian Jewish immigrants directly to Australia, primarily to Sydney. Other Russian Jews who had emigrated in the 1880s to England, Scotland or Ireland came to Australia as immigrants after a sojourn of one or two generations in the United Kingdom. These early Russian Jews brought some intensification of Jewish religious and cultural life.

In the 1920s, some Russian Jews who had gone on *aliyah* (immigration) to Eretz Yisrael resettled in Australia, primarily in Perth, after economic conditions became bad in Palestine. From 1910 onward, other Russian Jews who had gone to Manchuria via Siberia came to Australia through China or Japan. They settled initially in Brisbane. These included Jews from Harbin, Shanghai and Tientsin.

The last two decades of the 19th century saw the arrival of Jews from the dismembered parts of Poland, including Galicia. This immigration increased in the early 1920s until, in 1926, Australia passed a law that specifically excluded immigrants from Greece, Italy and Poland.

A trickle of Jewish immigrants from Germany started to arrive in 1936, rising in 1938 despite the fact that Jewish immigration was severely restricted with stringent requirements, including so-called "landing money."[2] After *Kristallnacht*, the Australian government initially offered to allow immigration of 15,000 Jews over the next three years. The offer was amended to 15,000 over five years after the intervention of the then Anglo-conformist Jewish leadership, which feared that the arrival of European Jews would place their own acceptance in jeopardy.[3]

At the outbreak of World War II in September 1939, fewer than 2,000 Jews actually had arrived, some from Czechoslovakia. Those from Austria and Germany included Jews who had emigrated to these countries from Poland a generation earlier. A number of converted Hungarian Jews also came at this time; some of their grandchildren returned to Judaism 40 or 50 years later. Many surnames were Magyarized, e.g., Schlesinger to Sirmai.

The oldest place of Jewish worship in Australia

Designed by convict architect James Thomson 1843

Sketch of the Hobart Synagogue in Tasmania, the oldest existing synagogue in Australia

Hobart Synagogue as it exists today

In July 1940, the British government deported to Sydney a large boatload of men of Austrian and German origin. This was the notorious *Dunera,* which landed on September 6, 1940. Included were both Nazis and Jews who had come to England as refugees, had originally been interned in England and then sent to Australia to be interned by proxy.[4] After some time in internment, the Jewish men gradually were released. Some joined the Australian army "employment company."[5] Others went back to fight in the British army, or to settle in Israel.

After World War II, Australia felt the need to increase its population in order to discourage future invaders. Australian Jews were allowed to nominate as immigrants 2,000 close relatives who had survived the Holocaust in Europe.[6] Eventually a total of about 17,000 survivors are estimated to have arrived in Australia between 1946 and 1952. In addition, approximately 1,500 to 2,500 Jewish immigrants came from Shanghai—despite discriminatory policies against Jewish immigrants. Survivors included those of Czech, French, German, Hungarian and Polish origin, and a few Dutch. British ex-servicemen had the right to be demobilized anywhere in the British Commonwealth; a number of Jews and their families availed themselves of this provision.

In 1957, about 1,000 Hungarian Jews who had fled during the 1956 Hungarian Revolution, arrived in Australia. At the same time, Egyptian Jews who had fled or been expelled when Nasser took over came—primarily to Adelaide. Polish Jews without Australian relatives were sponsored by *landsmanshaftn* (town societies) in Melbourne. To this day,

Melbourne is perceived as a Polish Jewish *shtetl,* with Sydney seen as a place that attracted Austrians, Germans and Hungarians. In truth, immigrants of all origins are scattered among every Jewish population center.

From the late 1950s onwards, many Jews who earlier had made *aliyah* to Israel re-emigrated to Australia, often joining relatives. Other Israelis have continued to settle in Australia, some coming as spouses of young Australian visitors to Israel or as families. Polish anti-Semitism in 1968 brought additional small groups of Polish Jews directly from Poland, while renewed Russian emigration started in the 1980s and continued until the mid-1990s.

The most distinctive group of new Jewish immigrants to Australia have been South Africans and a few from Zimbabwe. Starting as a trickle in the mid-1960s, their immigration became a flood in the 1980s and continues to the present. English-speaking, affluent and well educated, they have been very successful immigrants, many filling gaps as highly trained professionals, innovative businessmen, dedicated rabbis and educators. Coming from a community that is structured similarly to the Australian Jewish community, the South Africans have easily joined boards and committees and taken positions of leadership in many communal areas.

The successive waves of Jewish immigrants have served to vary the Jewish religious spectrum. While some German Jews joined Orthodox congregations as congregants, rabbis and cantors, others recreated the Reform temples of Central Europe. Some of the Hungarian and Slovak Jews created the extreme Orthodox Adas Israel communities in Melbourne and Sydney. British ex-servicemen were active in establishing new congregations in outlying suburbs; Sephardic Jews established congregations that use the Sephardic rites. Even Russians now have their Russian-speaking congregation in Sydney with an Australian-educated, Russian-speaking rabbi whose family had been divorced from Jewish practices for three generations.

Australia has become a country where a large percentage of current Jewish school children attend Jewish day schools, 70 percent in Melbourne and 60 percent in Sydney. Day schools exist also in Adelaide, Brisbane, Perth and Surfers

Paradise. No Conservative brand of Judaism as such exists in Australia, but the branch known variously as Reform/Progressive/Liberal Judaism is probably closer to Conservative Judaism than to U.S.-style Reform. There is now a Conservative congregation as part of the first Sydney Liberal congregation, the Neuweg shul.

In 1851, the southern colony of Victoria, with Melbourne as its capital, separated from New South Wales, and gold discoveries brought an immediate growth of population. Today and for many years, Melbourne has been the most important Jewish population center in Australia. It is known as "the *shtetl* on the Yarra," the Yarra being the river that flows through Melbourne.

Queensland separated from New South Wales in 1859, and Jews have lived in its state capital, Brisbane, since at least 1865. They live as well in a number of smaller towns such as Boonah, Cooktown, Nambour, Toowoomba and Townsville, and now also along the so-called Gold Coast, with its main town of Surfers' Paradise to which many Australian Jews retire.

Tasmania has two small Jewish communities. One is in Hobart in the south of the island, from which vessels sail to Antarctica and which has the oldest extant synagogue building in Australia, built in 1845. The second town is Launceston, also with a 19th-century synagogue. This community survives because of the Hasidic organization Chabad. On Australia's west coast, Jews played a leading role in the 1829 foundation of the Swan River colony, later Perth, but the first religious congregation was not organized until 1887.

The Australian Jewish Historical Society (AJHS) was founded in Sydney in 1938, its Melbourne branch in 1953. Branches now exist also in Perth and in Canberra. The society journal, *Australian Jewish Historical Society Journal*, has been published continuously since 1939. Now published twice yearly, each volume has both a name and a subject index. The AJHS has published special issues on Canberra and Perth Jewries, as well as numerous articles on Melbourne, Sydney and other towns.

Genealogical Resources

The single most useful book for any genealogist researching family in Australia is Nick Vine Hall's *Tracing Your Family History in Australia, a National Guide to Sources*, now in its fifth edition. Because Australia is organized into six states and two territories, Vine Hall divides his book into chapters for each state or territory, listing the registries, archives and other sources for each. Each chapter, following Hall's plan, lists birth, marriage and death registries in each state and territory; it also describes the holdings of the National Archives and all Jewish archival repositories.

Jewish Archives and Libraries: Genealogical and Historical

Few Australian Jewish organizations, libraries or archives can afford to employ a paid archivist/researcher to answer genealogical or historical inquiries. Most individuals who respond to queries are part-time volunteers, and mail generally is not answered as quickly as in the commercial world. Occasionally an organization will charge a fee for responding.

Sydney, New South Wales

The **Australian Jewish Historical Society*** holds books, journals, photographs, clippings and other material on Australian Jewish history and shares a website with the Australian Jewish Genealogical Society in Sydney. The society responds to some genealogical inquiries if they do not require hours of research. Fees for inquiries are US$30 per inquiry; photocopies and faxes of documents are charged separately.

The **Australian Jewish Genealogical Society*** holds books on worldwide Jewish genealogical research, CD-ROMs and microfiche, as well as some family trees. Monthly workshops are held on Sunday mornings at the Reverend Katz Library. Fees are charged for responses to time-consuming inquiries.

The Archive of Australian Judaica* is a special collection at the Fisher Library of the University of Sydney. Established in 1983, it has become the most important Jewish archive in Australia, but for the personal researcher of history, rather than for genealogy *per se*. It holds books, theses, personal archives of several Australian Jewish personalities both alive and dead, minute books, ephemera, photographs and most Jewish journals published in Australia. The archives does not respond to genealogical inquiries.

Jewish Care.* Formerly **Jewish Community Services*** (and before that, the Australian Jewish Welfare Society), Jewish Care has a computerized database of everyone who has received assistance since 1936. In genuine family reunion cases, the Services will search its database, advertise in the *Australian Jewish News* and coordinate with other Jewish Care offices throughout Australia. Ask for Bella Sharp-Collins. It is not able to undertake genealogical research.

Sydney Jewish Museum* Focusing on the Holocaust and Australian Jewish history, the museum's library specializes in books on the Holocaust, including memorial books that list victims. Holdings may be consulted when the library is open, but neither the museum nor the library engages in genealogical correspondence. All such letters are referred to the Australian Jewish Genealogical Society.

Melbourne, Victoria

Makor Jewish Community Library and Research Centre,* the leading Jewish library in Australia, answers in person and by mail, fax and telephone, simple queries which can be answered by consulting (for ten minutes or less) a book named by the inquirer that is present in the library. More complex research questions are referred to appropriate experts. Interlibrary loans or direct loans may be negotiated throughout Australia but not to overseas borrowers. The Australian Jewish Genealogical Society (Victoria) keeps its holdings for members in the library.

Jewish Museum of Australia* The museum holds important exhibitions on Jewish subjects. The archives soon will go to the State Library of Victoria on permanent loan. The museum focuses on the Australian Jewish experience. Its collection of some 10,000 items includes personal and community memorabilia, documents and photographs, among other items. The museum also holds the most significant archive of *Dunera* material in Australia, including an indexed list of all passengers, Jewish and non-Jewish. The index gives first name, family name and internment number. Researchers estimate that 80 percent of the passengers were Jewish. The collection and archives are accessible for research purposes by prior arrangement.

Jewish Holocaust Museum and Research Centre[*] is an organization run by volunteers, most of whom are Holocaust survivors. The library specializes in holdings about the Shoah and includes a number of *yizkor* (memorial) books. Ursula Flicker will do research free of charge for people seeking to learn the fate of family members; incidental expenses incurred in the research, such as mailing and photocopying costs, must be paid by the inquirer.

Australian Jewish Genealogical Society (Victoria).[*] The society holds lectures and workshops and maintains a collection of books for its members to use in researching Jewish genealogy worldwide. Details of meetings and membership are available at WWW.AJGS.ORG.AU. The archives of the Australian Jewish Historical Society (Victoria) are now on permanent loan at the Latrobe Library, the State Library of Victoria.

Adelaide, South Australia

The honorary archivist of the **Adelaide Hebrew Congregation**[*] was the former honorary secretary of the South Australia branch of the Australian Jewish Genealogical Society and willingly continues to provide information on the following holdings. Material held includes original records of the only Orthodox Jewish congregation in South Australia since 1848, including some birth, marriage, death and cemetery records. This material is being indexed gradually. Because the records are confidential, no access is given to the public directly, but must be by written inquiry. Contact Dr. Klee Benveniste.[*]

Basic inquiries about dates of Jewish births, deaths and marriages in South Australia are researched without charge, but a small donation to the congregation's charitable fund is encouraged. The records are incomplete.

Copies of family history material compiled by the previous honorary archivist have been deposited in the State Library of South Australia,[*] the South Australian Genealogy and Heraldry Society[*] and the Australian Jewish Historical Society (Victoria).[*] No catalogues of holdings exist.

Perth, Western Australia

Perth Hebrew Congregation[*] founded in 1887, has a library and archives run by a part-time honorary archivist, Louise Hoffman. Inquiries should be addressed to her in care of the congregation.

Australian Jewish Genealogical and Historical Society of Western Australia[*]. This group is small but welcomes new members. The chairman Michelle Urban[*] responds to inquiries by fax or by e-mail.

Brisbane, Queensland

The **Brisbane Jewish Congregation**[*] was founded in 1865, but no Jewish community archive exists in Brisbane or elsewhere in Queensland. Morris Ochert,[*] the Brisbane correspondent of both the Australian Jewish Historical Society and the Australian Jewish Genealogical Society has a vast knowledge of Brisbane cemeteries and of the Jewish community. He will attempt to answer inquiries if possible; a small donation to buy books for the genealogical society in Brisbane would be appreciated.

Canberra, Australian Capital Territory

The Canberra Jewish community developed only in the 1950s. Its history is told by Rabbi Dr. Israel Porush in a special issue of the *Australian Jewish Historical Society Journal* (vol. 9, no. 3). No archives are readily available. Members of the Australian Jewish Genealogical Society Canberra Group are unable to do research for others, but inquiries sent by mail to ACT Jewish Community[*] are printed without charge in *Hamerkaz*, the monthly community newsletter.

Darwin, Northern Territory

Darwin has never had a Jewish community, only isolated families or individuals. The Australian Jewish Genealogical Society has two members in Darwin. Lily Segall (BUBBLES@ OCTA4.NET.AU) is willing to answer some questions.

State Genealogical Societies

Every Australian state or territory has a major general genealogical society in the state capital and sometimes also in major towns. While their libraries generally do not hold much material of specific interest to Jewish family history researchers, some of the general material held may be useful. This includes old street maps and especially town directories which index residents alphabetically by surname, address and occupation. In Sydney, these are known as *Sands Directories* and were issued yearly until telephone directories made them redundant.

National Archives of Australia

The National Archives of Australia[*] are user friendly and have recently published sets of *FactSheets* available from its Publications Manager detailing their services and *modus operandi*. Research inquiries may be submitted by post, telephone, fax or e-mail. The archives does not undertake extensive research, but if that is required, they send a list of private researchers. Reading room services include up to 20 pages of photocopies free of charge, 10 per person per day. Overseas inquirers may receive up to 50 pages free of charge. Holdings of interest to Jewish genealogists include immigration records, internment records from Hay and Taiura camps during World War II and guides to the collections. Dr. Malcolm Turnbull, former editor of the Melbourne edition of the *Australian Jewish Historical Society Journal*, has written a guide to records of Jewish interest in the National Archives of Australia.[*] Entitled *Safe Haven: Records of the Jewish Experiences in Australia*, it is available from the Archives for AU$10 plus packing and postage.

National Archives in Western Australia[*] Because Perth is located so far from Canberra where the main national archives is located, a separate branch exists in Perth. Holdings from 1901 include immigration records, naturalization applications, alien registrations and shipping lists. In the past, naturalization could be applied for after five years of continual residence in Australia, with a preliminary application possible after three years. Currently, only two years of continuous residence is required. Alien registration was instituted during wartime when alien residents were required to report regularly to their local police stations.

The **Battye Library of Western Australian History*** holds many references to Jews in Western Australia—photographs, local Jewish newspapers and communal newspapers, books and short histories in journals. The current Jewish newspaper is *The Maccabean*; an earlier Jewish newspaper was entitled *The Western Judean*. A major book on the history of the Jews in Western Australia is *Hebrew, Israelite, Jew: The History of the Jews of Western Australia* which has an index and excellent bibliography on the Jews of Western Australia. Also potentially useful is the **Library and Information Service of Western Australia*** and the Western Australia Records Office; telephone: 61-8-9427-3360.

Registries of Births, Marriages and Deaths

Each Australian state or territory has its own registry. Addresses, telephone and fax numbers, e-mail addresses, websites, prices, rules and methods of delivering information all differ. Policies on access also vary. The genealogical section of the State Library in the capital city of each state and territory holds some microfiche, CD-ROMs, indexes and books published by the registries.

New South Wales Registry of Births, Marriages and Deaths,* the oldest registry in Australia, holds valuable historical records dating from the beginnings of European settlement on the continent. (Aborigines had only oral records, which they transmitted by song.) Until now, old certificates were produced as black and white photographs. Soon a conversion method will produce certificates up to 1952 digitally. Delivery time will be faster and on paper that will not fade or discolor.

Prices for certificates vary according to the number of years for which registry books must be searched to yield a record. If the inquirer knows the date of birth, marriage or death within a 10-year period, the certificate costs AU$26. If the period is two decades, the cost is AU$51. The price increases by AU$25 for every 10-year period or part thereof after the initial 10-year period. For a search of an entire century, the cost is AU$251.

Victorian Registry of Births, Marriages and Deaths.* Registry records in Victoria began in 1836 and the Registry has issued a number of microfiche and CD-ROMs available for purchase. These include the Victorian Pioneer Index (1836–88) of consolidated births, deaths and marriages at AU$220; Federation (1889–1901) at AU$189; Edwardian Index (1902–13) at AU$189; Great War Index (1914–20) at AU$209; and a Death Index (1921–85) at AU$250. The cost for microfiche and CD-ROM versions is the same. Overseas postage is an additional AU$10.

Certificates cost AU$17 each. Death records are available to anyone, but the policy on access to certificates defines individuals eligible to obtain birth and marriage records. Eligibility requirements have changed recently; researchers must make inquiry to determine access.

Australian Capital Territory Registry of Births, Deaths and Marriages.* The Territory restricts access to birth, death and marriage certificates to next of kin, guardians or legal representatives. An applicant must prove his or her identity with two personal identity documents. No provision has been made for family history researchers. Applications may be made in person or by mail. Applications by telephone, fax or through the Internet are not accepted. Current cost is AU$30 per certificate.

Queensland Registry of Births, Deaths, and Marriages.* Certificates cost AU$23 each; additional postage for overseas mailings. Priority certificates by fax. Payment in advance in Australian currency.

Northern Territory Registry of Births, Deaths and Marriages.* Each certificate costs AU$25.

South Australia Registry of Births, Death and Marriages.* Each certificate costs AU$29, postage included. This registry requires an application on the letterhead of the Australian Jewish Genealogical Society* before supplying the information above.

Tasmanian Registry of Births, Deaths and Marriages.* This registry charges AU$25 for any certificate for any search period not exceeding five years. An additional AU$10 is added for each additional five-year search period.

Western Australia Registry of Births, Deaths and Marriages.* All birth, death and marriage certificates from before 1942 where the registration number can be cited cost AU$20 each. If the registration number and district of birth are not known, the cost is AU$30. Later death certificates also are AU$30 each.

Addresses

The country code for telephone calls to Australia is 61. If calling within Australia, insert a zero in front of the city code; if calling from overseas, use only the city code without a zero in front of it.

ACT Jewish Community, P.O. Box 3105, Manuka, Canberra, ACT 2603.

Adelaide Hebrew Congregation, P.O. Box 320, Glenside, South Australia, 5065.

Australian Capital Territory Births, Deaths and Marriages, Registrar General's Office (B1) Allara House, Corner Allara Street and Constitution Avenue, Canberra, A.C.T. 2601; mailing address P.O. Box 225, Civic Square, ACT 2608; telephone: 61-2-6207-6444; fax: 61-2-6207-0895; website: WWW.RGO.ACT. GOV.AU.

Australian Jewish Genealogical Society, Beth Weizmann, 306 Hawthorn Road, Caulfield South, Melbourne, 3162; telephone: (Les Oberman) 61-3-9571-8251 or (Lionel Sharpe) 61-3-9523-6738; e-mail: OBERMAN@TRNXMELB.MHS.OZ.AU or SHARP@PA.AUSOM. NET.AU.

Australian Jewish Genealogical Society, P.O. Box 42, Lane Cove, Sydney, NSW 1595; fax: 61-2-9427-7530; e-mail: SOCIETY@ AJGS. ORG.AU; website: WWW.AJGS.ORG.AU.

Australian Jewish Genealogical Society of Western Australia, c/o Michelle Urban; fax: 61-8-9375-3574; e-mail: URBAN@WANTREE. COM.AU.

Australian Jewish Historical Society, Mandelbaum House, 385 Abercrombie Street, Darlington, Sydney 2008, NSW, telephone/fax: 61-2-9518-7596; e-mail: AJHS@OZEMAIL.COM.AU; website: WWW.ZETA.ORG.AU/~FERALTEK/HISTORY/AJHS.

Battye Library of Western Australia History, telephone: 61-8-9427-3291.

Carol Stirk, P.O. Box 7192, East Brisbane, 4169 Queensland; e-mail: STIRK@UG.NET.AU.

Jewish Care, Fischl House, 4a Nelson Street, Woollahra, Sydney, 2025, NSW, telephone: 61-2-1300-133-660; fax: 61-2-9302-8001; e-mail: INFO@JEWISHCARE.COM.AU; website: WWW.JEWISHCARE.COM.AU.

Jewish Holocaust Museum and Research Centre, 13 Selwyn Street, Elsternwick, Victoria, 3185; telephone: 61-3-9528-1985; fax: 61-3-9528-3758; e-mail: HC@SPRINT.COM.AU; website: WWW.ARTS.MONASH.EDU.AU/AFFILIATES/HLC.

Jewish Museum of Australia, director, Dr. Helen Light, 26 Alma Road, St. Kilda, Melbourne 3182; telephone: 61-3-9534-0083; fax: 91-3-9534-0844; e-mail: INFO@JEWISHMUSEUM.COM.AU; website: WWWJEWISHMUSEUM.COM.AU.

Klee Benveniste, P.O. Box 195, Melrose Park, Adelaide, 5039, S.A.

Library and Information Service of Western Australia; fax: 61-8-9426-3256; website WWW.LISWA.WA.GOV.AU.

Makor Jewish Community Library and Research Centre, 306 Hawthorn Road, Caulfield South, 3162, Melbourne, Victoria; telephone: 61-3-9272-5611; fax: 61-3-9272-5629; e-mail: JLIBRARY@VICNET.NET.AU; website: WWW.VICNET.NET.AU/~JLIBRARY.

Morris Ochert, 3/23 Lucinda Street, Taringa, Brisbane, 4068, Queensland.

National Archives of Australia, P.O. box 7425, Canberra Mail Centre, A.C.T. 2610, Australia; e-mail: REF@NAA.GOV.AU; website: WWW.NAA.GOV.AU.

National Archives of Australia in Western Australia, 384 Borwick East, Victoria Park, Peth, W.A. 6101, Australia; telephone: 61-8-9470-7500; e-mail: REFWA@NAA.GOV.AU.

New South Wales Registry of Births, Marriages and Deaths, 191 Thomas Street, Haymarket, Sydney 2000; mailing address: Box 30, G.P.O. Sydney, 2001, NSW; telephone: 1-300-655-236; e-mail: PIANNUCO@NSW.GOV.AU or RFEENY@AGD.NSW.GOV.AU or BDM.MAIL@AGD.NSW.GOV.AU; website: WWW.LAWLINK.NSW.GOV.AU/BDM.

Northern Territory Births, Deaths and Marriages, mailing address: G.P.O. Box 3021, Darwin, N.T. 0801; telephone: 61-8-8999-6119; fax: 61-8-8999-6324.

Queensland Registry of Births, Deaths and Marriages, mailing address: P.O. Box 188, Albert Street, Brisbane, Queensland 4002; telephone: 61-7-3247-5795; fax: 61-7-3247-5818; website: WWW.JUSTICE.QLD.GOV.AU.

Perth Hebrew Congregation, Freedman Road, Menora, Perth, Western Australia 6050, fax: 61-8-8271-9455.

South Australia Births, Deaths and Marriages, mailing address: G.P.O. Box 1351; Adelaide, S.A. 5001; telephone: 61-8-8204-9599; fax: 61-8-8204-9605; website: WWW.OCBA.SA.GOV.AU.

Southern Australian Genealogy and Heraldry Society, GPO Box 592, Adelaide, South Australia 5001; telephone: 61-8-8272-4222; fax: 61-8-8272-4910; e-mail: SAGHS@CHARIOT.NET.AU; website: USERS.CHARIOT.NET.AU/~SAGHS.

State Library of South Australia, North Terrace Adelaide, South Australia 5000; telephone: 61-8-8207-7200; fax: 61-8-8207-7249; website: WWW.SLSA.SA.GOV.AU.

Sydney Jewish Museum, 148 Darlinghurst Road, Darlinghurst, Sydney 2010, NSW; telephone: 61-2-9360-7999; fax: 61-2-9331-4245; e-mail: ADMIN@SJM.COM.AU; website: WWW.SYDNEYJEWISHMUSEUM.COM.AU.

Tasmanian Registry of Births, Deaths and Marriages, Registry of Births, Deaths and Marriages, Department of Justice and Industrial Relations, Level 3, 15 Murray Street, Hobart, 7000; mailing address: G.P.O. Box 198, Hobart, Tasmania 7001; telephone: 61-3-6233-3793.

The Archive of Australian Judaica, Fisher Library of the University of Sydney, NSW; telephone: 61-2-9351-4162; fax: 61-2-9351-2890; e-mail: MDACY@LIBRARY.USYD.EDU.AU; website: WWW.LIBRARY.USYD.EDU.AU/JUDAICA.

Victorian Registry of Births, Marriages and Deaths, Department of Justice, Registry of Births, Deaths and Marriages Victoria, 589 Collins Street, Melbourne 3000; mailing address: G.P.O. Box 4332, Melbourne, Victoria 3001; telephone: 61-3-9693-5815; fax: 61-3-9603-5858; website: WWW.MAXI.COM.AU.

Western Australia Registry of Births, Deaths and Marriages, mailing address: P.O. Box 7720; Cloisters Square, Perth, W.A. 6850; telephone: 61-8-9264-1555; fax: 61-8-9264-1599; e-mail: RGOPERTH@JUSTICE.MOJ.WA.GOV.AU; website: WWW.JUSTICE.WA.GOV.AU.

Bibliography

Genealogy

Hall, Nick Vine. *Tracing Your Family History in Australia, a National Guide to Sources.* 2 vols., reprinted 2002; website WWW.VINEHALL.COM.US lists distributors worldwide.

General Works

Apple, Raymond. "The Jews." *Making Australian Society.* Melbourne: Thomas Nelson, 1989.

Levi, John S. and George F.J. Bergman. *Australian Genesis, Jewish Convicts and Settlers 1788–1850.* Adelaide: Rigby, 1974, 2nd. ed. 2002, Carlton South: Melbourne University Press.

Rubinstein, Hilary L. *The Jews in Australia: A Thematic History,* Vol. 1, 1788–1945. Melbourne: William Heinemann, 1991.

Rubinstein, William D. *The Jews in Australia: A Thematic History* Vol. 2, 1945–91. Melbourne: William Heinemann, 1991.

Rubinstein, W. D. *Judaism in Australia.* Melbourne: Bureau of Immigration, Multicultural and Population Research, no date given.

Rutland, Suzanne D., *Edge of the Diaspora, Two Centuries of Jewish Settlement in Australia.* Sydney: Collins Australia, 1997.

Rutland, Suzanne D. and Sophie Caplan. *With One Voice: The History of the New South Wales Jewish Board of Deputies 1945–1995.* Sydney: Australian Jewish Historical Society, 1998.

Particular Groups or States

Aaron, Aaron. *The Sephardim of Australia and New Zealand.* Sydney: self-published, 1979.

Norst, Marlene J. and Johanna McBride. *Austrians and Australia* Sydney: Athena, 1988.

Adelaide, South Australia

Munz, Hirsch. *Jews in South Australia, 1836–1936.* Adelaide: Adelaide Hebrew Congregation, 1936.

Hyams, Bernard. *Surviving: A History of the Institutions and Organisations of the Adelaide Jewish Community.* Adelaide: The Jewish Community Council of South Australia, 1998.

The Adelaide Hebrew Congregation and Massada College commemorate the opening of the Nathan and Miriam Solomon Centre, Adelaide, July 1990. Gives a brief account of the Jewish community in Adelaide.

Brisbane, Queensland

Fabian, Rabbi D. Alfred has written about the community of Surfers Paradise in the *Australian Jewish Historical Society Journal.*

Ochert, Morris. "History of the Brisbane Hebrew Congregation." *Australian Jewish History Society Journal*, vol. 9, part 7. This author has written several other articles about Brisbane and smaller Jewish communities in such places as Boonah, Cooktown, Nambour and Toowoomba, all of them published in the historical society journal.

Trone, John, "The Jewish Enclave in Brisbane," in Rod Fisher and Barry Shaw, eds. *Brisbane: The Ethnic Presences Since the 1950s.* Brisbane History Group, Papers, no. 12. Brisbane: Kelvin Grove, 1993.

Early Jewish History

Several books document the early decades of Jews in Australia. Rabbi John Simon Levi and Dr. George F. J. Bergman wrote the epochal *Australian Genesis: Jewish Convicts and Settlers, 1788–1850*, which relates the personal histories of many Jews and became a rare book within one year of publication. A revised edition entitled *Australian Genesis: Jewish Convicts and Settlers, 1788–1860* (i.e., ten more years) was published by Melbourne University Press in March 2002. Rabbi Levi also wrote *The Forefathers: A Dictionary of Biography of the Jews of Australia, 1788–1830*, which included biographical details about almost every Jew in Australia at that time. This book, now out of print, is being updated to 1850 and will list a larger number of Jewish men, women and children. The new edition is likely to be printed under the title *Dictionary of Australian Colonial Jewry, 1788–1850*, also by Melbourne University Press in 2004.

Rabbi Levi found 530 Jewish children born between 1830 and 1850, in the then much larger colony of New South Wales. Because of the relative scarcity of Jewish marriage partners available to Jewish men in the 19th century, however, many intermarried. As a result, today there are no Jewish descendants of the Jewish convicts of the First Fleet.

The history of Sydney, cradle of Australian Jewry, is detailed in the general history books listed in the bibliography such as *Australian Genesis,* Suzanne Rutland's *Edge of the Diaspora* and Hilary and W.D. Rubinstein's two volumes, *The Jews, a Thematic History.* Also important is *Jewish Sydney: the First Hundred Years, 1788–1888,* by Helen Bersten, long-time honorary archivist of the Australian Jewish Historical Society. Most of the history and biography books listed have name indexes.

Rabbi Lazarus M. Goldman's *The Jews in Victoria in the 19th Century* describes these developments, while Hilary Rubinstein's *The Jews in Victoria, 1835–1985,* continues that history into the 20th century. A number of histories of congregations in Victoria also help the Jewish genealogist with names of congregants and burial lists, such as Newman

Rosenthal's *Formula for Survival: The Saga of the Ballarat Hebrew Congregation,* which describes the life of a congregation in a gold mining town.

So far no one has written a complete book about Jews in Queensland or in Brisbane, but a number of articles written by Morris Ochert and by Rabbi Alfred Fabian on Queensland Jewry have been published over the years in the journal of the Australian Jewish Historical Society.

Hedi Fixel, a long-time resident of Hobart and pre-war refugee from Vienna, has written the history of *Hobart Jewry: 150 Years of Survival Against All Odds.*

Bibliography—Tasmania

Elias, Peter and An [eds.]. *A Few from Afar: Jewish Lives in Tasmania from 1804.* Hobart: Hobart Hebrew Congregation, 2003. [She adds the following. I don't know that we should: ISBN 42207 3, Aus. $30, plus postage and packing, Aus.$9 within Australia; Aus. $17 elsewhere..]

Notes

1. As there were many more Jewish male convicts than Jewish female convicts, the Jewish emancipists often married women from Ireland who agreed that the children would be brought up as Jews, without the mother or children having been formally converted. The free settlers often came with Jewish wives.

   The schism occurred when a religious official omitted a prayer at the *brit milah* (ritual circumcision) of the grandson of an emancipist whose wife had not been Jewish. Since that particular emancipist was by then a wealthy man and a leader of the community, he led a departure from the York Street Synagogue and established the Macquarie Street Synagogue.

2. "Landing money" was a sum of £50 sterling per person required to show that the immigrant could afford to support himself until he found work. Often the British Jewish emigration societies lent this money until arrival in Australia when it was collected by the local Jewish Welfare Society for return to Britain.

3. "Anglo-conformist" refers to a desire to assimilate to Anglo-Celtic names, mores, outlook and way of life.

4. "Interned by proxy" refers to the fact that these men were interned in Australian internment camps instead of camps in Britain where they originally were held. The prisoners were still considered internees of the British government.

5. "Employment companies" did not carry weapons or fight the enemy. Instead, they did military labor such as loading and unloading cargo, digging trenches and laying roads.

6. No files are known to exist, but newfound immigration files from the Australian Jewish Welfare Society (now Jewish Care) currently are being researched by the Australian Jewish Genealogical Society. The National Archives in Canberra have files on pre-war applications for Australian landing permits indexed by surname of sponsors and would-be immigrants. These files are available to researchers.

Austria

by Henry Wellisch

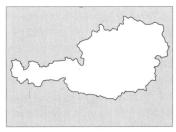

Austria, a largely German-speaking Alpine country, approximately the size of the U.S. state of Maine and with seven and a half million inhabitants, is located in the heart of Europe. Until 1918, the German-speaking provinces were at the center of the great Austro-Hungarian Empire, which included all of (the former) Czechoslovakia and Hungary and also large parts of Italy, Poland, Romania and Yugoslavia.

The Hapsburgs became rulers of this land in the 13th century and, by shrewd political moves, added country after country to their holdings, culminating in the 19th century with the formation of the Austro-Hungarian Empire. Vienna, capital of today's Austria, was also the glittering capital of this empire that covered most of Central Europe. Vienna and its Jewish community were renowned the world over, and, since the vast majority of Jews in the current territory of Austria lived in Vienna, this article focuses mainly on that city and its Jews.

Jewish History in Austria

Jews are first recorded on Austrian territory in the year 903 CE, when the *Raffelstatten* customs ordinance referred to Jewish merchants. Around that time, the first Jewish settlements sprang up in various places in the provinces of Lower Austria and Styria; today the names of towns such as Judenburg, Judendorf and Judenau testify to the presence of Jews.

It is in Vienna, however, that the first Jewish resident known by name (Scholom) is recorded in 1203. Scholom was employed by the reigning duke as master of the mint and, as such, negotiated with the English for the ransom of their King Richard the Lionhearted, who had been kidnapped returning home from a crusade. Scholom and 15 other Jews later were killed by a band of Crusaders during a quarrel; the culprits were all executed, however, by order of the duke. This is one of the few early incidents of attacks on Jews recorded by both Jewish and Christian sources.

The first organized Jewish community in Vienna dates back to the beginning of the 13th century, when in 1238 the rulers granted the first charter giving some autonomy to that community. Jews lived in their own quarter near the center of the city; they owned 70 to 80 houses, a synagogue, *mikvah* (ritual bath), school and cemetery. The walls surrounding the quarter had five gates; at its center was a square called the *Schulhof* (synagogue court). Today, it is known as *Judenplatz* (Jewish Square).[1]

Many Jews engaged in money lending and numerous records from this period have survived. Although the records give the names of both the borrower and lender, they are not particularly useful for genealogical research. The date of the record is given in parentheses, for example, Pendit (1249); Isserl son of Aron (1370); Jakob the Hungarian, son of Mosche (1398); Peltlin the Jewess (1373).

By the end of the 14th century, Jewish Vienna had grown to approximately 1,000 souls and was considered one of the leading Jewish communities in the Germanic lands. At this time, the situation of Vienna's Jews began to deteriorate. Christian Viennese merchants became hostile; Jews were accused of supporting the anti-Catholic sect of Hussites; and Jews were held responsible for a series of fires. The accusations culminated in the expulsion edict of Duke Albert in the year 1421, recorded in Jewish history as the *Wiener Geserah* (Viennese edict). By order of the duke, poor Jews were expelled, while the well-to-do were asked to convert. When they refused, more than 200 Jews were burned alive. After this event, Vienna was known in Jewish circles as the *Ir Hadamim* (city of blood).

At about the same time, Jews were expelled from other places in Austrian territory. They and the survivors of the Vienna massacre were able to find refuge in the Hungarian cities of Oedenburg (Sopron), Ofen (Budapest), Pressburg (Bratislava) and Wiener Neustadt in Lower Austria. Just a few decades later, however, Jews were again present in Vienna. Some Jewish doctors practiced in the city during the middle of the 15th century; 12 Jewish families were recorded in 1512; and in 1582, a Jewish cemetery existed.

The number of Jews grew, and in 1624 Emperor Ferdinand II permitted the establishment of a Jewish ghetto outside the walled city, across the arm of the Danube.[2] A large and relatively prosperous settlement was established, which grew to more than 3,000 inhabitants over the next few decades. By 1670, approximately 500 families lived in 136 houses; the community maintained two synagogues, two hospitals and various other institutions.

Starting in 1635, Jews were allowed to own shops and to trade during daylight hours in the inner city. Others worked as exporters and importers, artisans, petty traders, bakers and butchers. Detailed lists of owners of houses from this period have survived and may be found in *Das Wiener Ghetto*, by I. Schwarz. Yom Tov Lipman Heller and Sheftel Horowitz were among the well-known rabbis serving in Vienna.

Among the documents that have been preserved from this period are lists of the owners of houses in the ghetto and death records for the years 1634–66. Unfortunately, for the genealogist, geographical rather than hereditary family names were used by most.[3] Following are the owners of the houses on the right side of the third street; in italics are the geographically derived names: 35, Jodl Herlinger; 36, Joseph *Welscher*; 37, Gerstl *Khalstatt* and Josef his son-in-law; 38, Mayr *Pruckh*; 39, Victor Gerstl.

Conditions for Viennese Jewry again deteriorated during the second half of the 17th century. Christian merchants complained about competition, and the Catholic bishop and the empress pressured the emperor to take measures against the Jews. Finally in 1670, the Emperor Leopold I ordered Jews expelled from Vienna and other parts of the Austrian territory. Several prominent individuals intervened unsuccessfully, among them Queen Christina of Sweden and Pope Clemens IX. The second Jewish community of Vienna ended with its dispersion to the smaller towns of Moravia and Bohemia; 50 wealthy families were allowed to settle in Berlin. For the period of the two ghettos and the expulsion in 1670, see the books by Kaufmann and Schwartz noted in the bibliography. Both books include extensive lists of Viennese Jews, but few have family names.

Some Viennese Jewish families who had found refuge in Moravia, together with a number of Moravian and Bohemian Jews, were allowed to settle on the estates of the Esterhazy princes in Burgenland, which, at that time, belonged to Hungary but was part of the Austrian Empire. The following communities were established on the Esterhazy land around the beginning of the 18th century: Deutschkreutz, Eisenstadt, Frauenkirchen, Kittsee, Kobersdorf, Lackenbach and Mattersdorf. On the Burgenland estates of Count Battyany, Jews were permitted to settle in Rechnitz and Güssing. Unusual in Western Europe, these communities remained traditional and Orthodox throughout the succeeding centuries, and dissolved only in 1938 when the Nazis forced most Jews to move to Vienna.

At this time, the Austrians were involved in a war with the Ottoman Empire, which had occupied most of Hungary. In 1683, a large Turkish army reached Vienna, and after a two-month siege, the city was relieved by a combined European army under the command of Polish King John Sobiesky. To assist the Austrian state with its finances, Emperor Leopold I invited a number of Jewish financiers to act as suppliers for the army and the court. The most famous of these court Jews (*Hofjuden*) was Samuel Wertheimer. It is said by some that the Austrians could not have won the war against the Turks without his help. He was succeeded by his nephew Samson Wertheimer, who, since he was a learned man, eventually received the honorary title of chief rabbi of Moravia and Hungary from the emperor. Both men intervened with the authorities when the Jewish communities in the Burgenland and in Moravia needed assistance.[4] These privileged Jewish families and several others received permission to settle in Vienna, but were not allowed to form a community or construct a synagogue or school. They were exempted, however, from wearing traditional Jewish dress and a few were even raised to nobility. During the reign of Empress Maria Theresa (1740–80), an additional number of Jewish bankers and industrialists were allowed to reside in Vienna under the status of "tolerated Jews." Permission usually had to be renewed every three years, and the tax for the privilege was quite high. Maria Theresa limited the number and type of Jewish economic activities, prohibited direct ownership of real estate and imposed other limitations.

Maria Theresa's son, Emperor Joseph II (1780–90), introduced far-reaching changes in the situation of Austrian Jews. Feeling that the Jews should be made more useful to the state, the emperor wanted the Jews to enter schools and universities and to speak the German language. Jews were no longer made to wear special dress, and various other restrictions were removed. The general ban on Jewish residence in Vienna was retained, however, as was the tolerance tax for those few privileged families who had a special residence permit. Under the new law, Jews also had to serve in the army for the first time. Some progress was made, but Jews were still second-class citizens.

In 1787 Emperor Joseph II proposed a law on Jewish names—the first in Europe—a measure that has had considerable significance for genealogists. All Jewish heads of families, their wives and children, and single Jews were obliged to adopt a permanent family name by January 1, 1788. Unmarried females had to take the name of their father. All persons were required to select a German given name that could not be altered during their lifetime. Jewish names related to a locality were prohibited. Starting January 1, 1788, all circumcision, marriage and death registers had to be written in German with all persons identified by both their family and first names. The Jewish community of Prague, as the largest in the empire, conducted negotiations with the court chancellery on the subject of first names and eventually reached a compromise list of 120 masculine and 37 feminine first names. It is not clear how strictly the law was enforced, but as late as 1835, a Jew from Prague was refused permission to name his son Ferdinand, and in 1847, a Bohemian Jew was not permitted to change the names of his children from Wolf and Julie to Wilhelm and Juliane.

Starting in 1836, Jews could choose almost any German first name, as long as the name was not that of a Christian saint. Even then, however, changes to existing first names were usually rejected by the authorities. All restrictions ended on December 21, 1867, with the passage of the general emancipation law.[5]

With the sudden death of Emperor Joseph II in 1790, the era of limited rights for Jews came to an end. Some former restrictions on Jews were even reintroduced during subsequent decades.

By the end of the 18th century, approximately 100 "tolerated" families lived in Vienna, consisting of about 400 persons including Jewish servants. Most were well-to-do bankers, industrialists, importers, exporters and merchants. No permission existed for an organized community, synagogue or school. Prayer services were conducted and students were taught at private homes by imported preachers and teachers with temporary residence permits. A list dated December 31, 1804, shows 119 tolerated Jewish families.[6] The Orthodox communities in the Burgenland, then in Hungarian territory, continued their steady growth.

In 1823, the authorities finally approved construction of a complex of buildings in Vienna consisting of a synagogue together with administrative offices, *mikvah* (ritual bath) and a kosher butcher shop. The synagogue was consecrated in 1826 with a ceremony of splendor and dignity; Isaac Noah Mannheimer was brought to Vienna from Copenhagen to lead the congregation. In the same year, the congregation began to register births, marriages and deaths. Because of restrictions still in force at this time, the synagogue was referred to as a house of prayer (*Bethaus*), and Rabbi Mannheimer's official title was teacher of religion (*Religionslehrer*). The formal establishment of the community occurred in 1852.[7]

When Emperor Franz Joseph I ascended to the throne in 1848, revolutions erupted in many European countries; Austria was no exception. The Vienna uprising was brutally suppressed, but the march of emancipation could not be stopped. In 1867, with the founding of the Austro-Hungarian monarchy, discrimination based on religion was abolished. Residence restrictions for Vienna were progressively relaxed, and a great wave of immigrants including many Jews descended on Vienna. The modern Jewish community of Vienna dates from this time. After 1848, the restrictions on the movement of people (Jews and non-Jews) to Vienna were abolished. As a result, large numbers of people began to move to Vienna and its population grew rapidly. [see public records at the FHL]

Table 1 shows growth of numbers of Jewish residents in Vienna and percentage of the total population. Marsha L. Rosenblit, *The Jews of Vienna 1867–1914*

Plan of the Old "Judenstadt" in Vienna

Table 1. Growth in Population of Viennese Jewry

Year	No. of Jews	Pct. of Pop.
1830	200	
1847	4000	
1857	6200	1.3
1869	40,200	6.6
1880	73,200	10.1
1890	118,000	8.7
1900	147,000	8.8
1910	175,300	8.6
1923	201,500	
1936	176,000	8.0

Figures for 1830 and 1847 are approximate, and the latter may include illegal residents. Before 1848, only "tolerated" Jews were allowed to reside in Vienna, but it is assumed that a large number without permits also lived there. The rest are based on official censuses, but the figure for 1857 includes legal residents only.

The first wave of Jewish immigrants came primarily from Moravia and Bohemia. They were followed by Jews from western Hungary and Slovakia, and in the 1890s and the early years of the 20th century, Jews from Galicia, the so-called *Galitzianers*. Because members of the first two groups primarily spoke German, they had little difficulty integrating into the local society and quickly became assimilated. The Galitzianers, on the other hand, usually spoke Yiddish, were poorer and less educated, and had more difficulty assimilating.[8]

During the second half of the 19th century, Jews established a firm foothold in Vienna. They started retail and wholesale businesses, department stores, factories, banks, newspapers and many other enterprises, but since they were still prevented from entering government service, many entered the professions. By the turn of the 20th century, Vienna had a large and prosperous Jewish middle class, which greatly influenced the life of the city. Most significantly, they made

a determined effort to provide higher education for their children. At this time, more than half of all medical doctors and lawyers in Vienna were Jewish, as were most of the editors of the leading newspapers.[9]

In literature, music, the arts and sciences, Vienna's Jews made historic contributions that greatly influenced the modern world. Sigmund Freud, Gustav Mahler and Theodor Herzl all lived in Vienna and considered themselves to be Viennese, although none had been born in the city. To become conductor of the Vienna Symphony Orchestra and director of the Vienna Opera, Mahler had to be baptized, but he never denied his Jewish origins.

With the rapid rise of the Jewish community of Vienna in the second half of the 19th century came a rise in anti-Semitism. It accelerated after the stock market crash of 1873, and the subsequent recession was blamed on Jewish stockbrokers who were accused of manipulating the market, contributing to its collapse and driving thousands into bankruptcy. The liberal parties declined, and the largely lower-middle-class Christian-Socialist party, under the leadership of a populist anti-Semitic lawyer named Karl Lueger, gained in popularity. In 1897, Lueger was elected mayor of Vienna. Once in office, he toned down his rhetoric, but is known for the notorious statement: "I decide who is a Jew."

The other emerging political movements were the Marxist Social Democratic Party, founded by Victor Adler, an assimilated Moravian-born Jew, and the Pan-German anti-Semitic nationalists. From this time onward, Austrian Jews, if they wanted to vote or participate in Austrian politics, were restricted to the Social Democratic Party. This situation continued until the end of the first republic in 1938.[10]

With the outbreak of World War I, the golden period of Viennese Jewry ended. Occupation of Galicia by the Russians triggered a mass exodus of Jews from that region. Many thousands fled to Vienna, where they were cared for by the community and the government. After the recapture of Galicia by the Austrians, most Jews returned, but more than 20,000 remained in Vienna.

The lost war and the collapse of the empire transformed Austria from a major power into a small country with fewer than seven million inhabitants. There the Socialists, with the participation of many Jewish intellectuals, formed a left-wing and progressive city administration that, in the 1920s, was the envy of many other European cities. But the misfortunes following the war created a sharp rise in anti-Semitism in provincial Austria as well as in Vienna.

After some recovery in the late 1920s, the 1929 depression dealt the Austrian economy a death blow, radical political parties increased in popularity, and parliamentary democracy came to an end in the early 1930s. In February 1934, after an unsuccessful uprising by the Socialists, their party was outlawed. This event was followed in July 1934 by an unsuccessful *coup d'etat* and murder of the chancellor by the illegal Nazi party.

The interwar years were difficult for all Austrians, Jews and non-Jews. As a result of the demise of the empire, Jews suffered economically with the rest of the population, but life continued more or less normally. All normal life came to a sudden and disastrous end, however, in March 1938, with the occupation of the country by Nazi Germany, which was welcomed by huge and enthusiastic crowds. In Vienna as well as in the provinces, anti-Semitic outrages occurred as had not been seen in Western Europe since the Middle Ages. Hundreds of Jews committed suicide; within a few months many lost their businesses and jobs, and thousands were reduced to poverty. Practically all Jews living in the provinces were evicted and had to move to Vienna.

There followed an immediate surge to find places of refuge. Although most countries closed their doors, nearly 130,000 Jews (out of almost 200,000) were able to escape. About 16,000 were caught later in European countries such as France and Belgium. On *Kristallnacht*, November 10, 1938, all Austrian synagogues were destroyed and thousands of Jews were sent to concentration camps.

Some deportations to the East (Nisko in Poland) started as early as the fall of 1939, but they were discontinued. In February and March 1941, about 5,000 Jews were deported to several ghettos in the Kielce, Poland, area and in October, another 5,000 were sent to Lodz, Poland. Large-scale deportations to the East started in the fall of 1941 to Auschwitz, Izbica, Kovno, Minsk, Riga, Sobibor and other places. More than 16,000 Viennese Jews were deported to the "model ghetto" of Theresienstadt. The last transport left Vienna for Theresienstadt a few days before the capture of the city by the Russians. Approximately 50,900 Austrian Jews perished, and 2,000 deportees survived. Together with the 16,000 emigrants to other European countries, the total was about 65,000 victims.

According to the Council of Elders of Viennese Jews, 5,992 Jews lived in Vienna in December 1944. Of these, 4,839

Interior of the synagogue known as the "Leopoldstädter Tempel", in the Tempelgasse of Vienna, at the beginning of the 20th century

lived in mixed marriages, 804 were Jewish according to the racial laws, 195 were full Jews, 70 had Aryan relatives and 13 were foreign citizens. Lower Austria was home to 118 Jews at this time.[11]

With the end of hostilities, thousands of Jews from the East poured into Western occupation zones. In 1946, more than 35,000 Jewish displaced persons lived in the American zone of Austria. Following the establishment of the State of Israel in 1948, this number dropped rapidly. Very few former Austrian Jews who had escaped chose to return to their former home country. In 1950, 13,396 individuals were registered with the Jewish community, but by 1965 this number had dropped to 9,537, of whom 8,930 lived in Vienna. In 1956, as a result of the Hungarian revolution, about 20,000 Jewish refugees crossed the border, but most continued on to various destinations overseas and only a few hundred remained.

The Jewish community was reconstituted in 1945, and the Central Synagogue, which had not been completely destroyed during *Kristallnacht*, was reopened. Other Jewish institutions such as the old peoples' home, and a number of charitable institutions, also were reconstituted. In Vienna, Eisenstadt and Hohenems near the Swiss border, Jewish museums have reopened and the huge Central Cemetery is looked after with the voluntary assistance of Walter Pagler, a non-Jew.

Exterior of the synagogue, known as the "Polnische Schule", in the Leopoldsgasse in Vienna at the beginning of the 20th century

At the end of the war, the Austrians declared that they were its first victims and that the Austrian state could not be held responsible for the persecution of its Jewish citizens. Only in recent years has the Austrian government been more forthcoming about Austria's role during the war.

Genealogical Resources

As a practical matter, Jewish genealogical research in Vienna can begin only at the start of the 18th century. Pribram's book provides extensive lists of the "tolerated" Jewish inhabitants and their marriages for the 18th century through 1848. Wachstein also includes considerable genealogical information on Jews of Vienna. For later centuries, an excellent overview of genealogical research in Vienna is found in the English-language guidelines published on the Internet by the City of Vienna archives. In general, researchers may write in English to the various archives and institutions in Austria. Replies will be in either English or German.

If your ancestors lived in Vienna, begin your research first by reading the pamphlet prepared by the Vienna City Archives. Then go to the catalog for the LDS (Mormon) Family History Library. The Mormons have done extensive microfilming in Austria, and most of the records you will want to research are available this way.

In 1782, the Austrian government first mandated that Jewish communities maintain birth, marriage and death registers. For Vienna and the Burgenland communities, these are the most important source of genealogical information. The registers of both areas have been microfilmed by the Mormons and are available from LDS Family History Centers. Jewish vital records for Vienna are available also at the Vienna Jewish Community offices* and the Vienna City Archives.* Civil registration of births and marriages did not begin in Austria until 1938; prior to that time, religious authorities were responsible for registration. Records created after 1938 are in local city archives.* The original Burgenland records are in the regional archives in Sopron, Hungary.

Only a few thousand Jews lived outside of Vienna and Burgenland. For those locations, contact local municipal authorities to inquire about civil records. Graz,* Innsbruck,* Linz* and Salzburg* currently have small Jewish communities.

In Austria, even today all inhabitants are required to register their addresses with the local police; some of these records have been microfilmed by the Mormons.[12] The Vienna City Archives* has addresses prior to 1948; the *Zentralmeldeamt* holds addresses after that date. Wills and other probate records after 1850 are kept in the Vienna City Archives; wills for Vienna earlier than 1850 have been microfilmed by the Mormons.

Two other categories of records filmed by the Mormons are useful for genealogical research; these are Austro-Hungarian Empire military records and passport registers. Vienna has a huge military archive that holds records for the entire Austro-Hungarian Empire. All male Jews in the empire were required to register for the draft at age 18, whether they ultimately served or not. Many Jews served as Austrian soldiers in the War of 1870 and in World War I. Indexed draft records, called "muster rolls" are filed under Vienna.

Cemetery research, a staple of Jewish genealogical research, is easily handled, thanks to the efforts of Walter Pagler.* Pagler compiled a huge database of Jewish cemeteries in Vienna and the provinces and will respond to English-language letters. He does not charge for his services, but gratefully accepts donations. The International Association of Jewish Genealogical Societies cemetery project is another source of information.

A list of approximately 61,000 Jewish Holocaust victims is now available in a searchable database on the website of the Dokumentationsarchiv des osterreichischen Widerssstandes (Documentary archives of the Austrian Resistance) at WWW. DOEW.AT. Click on PROJECT: NAMENTLICHE ERFASSUNG, then on VORNAME (given name), and on NACHNAME (family name), SUCHE (search), NEUE SUCHE (new search). The result will display given name, family name, date of birth and—if known—place of deportation and date of death. The website includes considerable additional information on the Holocaust in Austria, all in German. This organization also may be contacted in English via e-mail at ERFASSUNG@DOEW.AT. Deportees to Theresienstadt are listed in the *Totenbuch Theresienstadt*, while names of approximately 2,000 survivors of the deportations may be found in Gertrud Schneider's book.

The archives of the Viennese Jewish community—other than vital statistics records—were transferred to the Central Archives for the History of the Jewish People in Jerusalem* where they comprise the largest single collection in that repository. These records include statutes, correspondence, minutes, financial records, personnel files, material on eduction, synagogues, welfare and other Jewish institutions. Although this material is not directly genealogical in nature, it may provide additional other clues, especially for the advanced genealogist.

Some Comments on Viennese Birth, Marriage and Death Records

Here are some abbreviations and words that often are used in Viennese German-language birth, marriage and death records.

Konfessionslos: non-denominational
Mos=Mosaisch: Jewish (by religion)
Zust.=Zustandig: This designation refers to the home-town (domicile) of the person in question

Birth registers sometimes show the following in a column marked *Anmerkung* (remarks): *Trg*: 20/3/1892. Wien. *Trg.* is the abbreviation for *Trauung* (wedding of the parents of the newborn) followed by the date and the place of the wedding of the parents of the newborn child.

In 1939, the German government decreed that all Jews had to take on the additional first names of Israel or Sara. Jews were ordered to present personal documents (birth, marriage certificates, etc.) at the *Bezirkshauptmannschaft* [B.H.] (government district office) where a stamp similar to the one shown in Figure 1 below was affixed. It is clear that wherever such a stamp appears in the Vienna birth, marriage and death registers, that person was in Vienna on the date shown on the stamp. However, if no stamp shown, it does not necessarily mean that the person was not in Vienna in 1939.

> Annahme des Zusatznamens ISRAEL/SARA angezeigt
> (Acceptance of the additional name ISRAEL/SARA noted)
> B.H. IV.   2/8/1939

Figure 1.

Jewish Records at the LDS (Mormon) Family History Library

Vienna. Birth, marriage and death registers of the *Israelitische Kultusgemeinde—Wien* (Jewish religious community-Vienna), 1826–1938

Burgenland and Niederoesterreich (Austrian Provinces). Birth, marriage and death records for the following Burgenland communities: Eisenstadt, Deutschkreuz, Frauenkirchen, Gattendorf, Guessing, Kittsee, Kobersdorf, Lackenbach, Mattersdorf, Rechnitz and Stadt Schleining, 1833–95. Birth, marriage and death records for St. Poelten, 1874–1938. 1848 Jewish census for Frauenkirchen.

Public Records Microfilmed by the Mormons (for Vienna, unless otherwise noted)

Civil Registration

Death register, 1648–1920, partially indexed
Birth register of males, 1858–1901
Daily account of deaths in Vienna hospitals, 1848–1942
Birth, marriage and death records for Burgenland communities, 1895–1920

Population Records

Meldezettel der Stadt Wien (Domicile registration of Viennese inhabitants). Includes names of husband, wife, children, place and date of birth, occupation, religion, former and new place of residence. 1850–1920, grouped alphabetically.

Probate Records

Magistrates court, 1548–1850, indexed

Military Records

Mustersheets of Viennese soldiers arranged alphabetically, 1760–1900

Emigration and Immigration

Passport registers, 1792–1918, partially indexed

Occupations

Register of workbooks, 1860–1919, indexed

Directories

City directories, 1870, 1902, 1906, 1908 and 1925
Telephone directory, approximately 1920

Cemeteries

Central Cemetery register, 1875–1904 (Christian and Jewish)
    See the Family History Library catalogue for birth, marriage, death, and other records from other cities in Austria.

Jewish Community Organizations

Graz: Israelitische Kultusgemeinde Graz; Synagogenplatz 1
Innsbruck: Israelitische Kultusgemeinde Innsbruck, Sillgasse 15
Linz: Israelitische Kultusgemeinde Linz, Behlehemstrasse 26
Salzburg: Israelitische Kultusgemeinde Salzburg, Lasser-strasse 8

Internet Sites

German Genealogy: Austria:
WWW.GENEALOGIENETZ.DE/REG/AUT/AUSTRIA-EN.HTML
Institute for Historical Family Research:
WWW.IHFF.AT
Jewish community of Vienna:
WWW.IKG-WIEN.AT
City of Vienna Archives:
WWW.MAGWIEN.GV.AT/ENGLISH/ANCESTORS
Vienna GenWeb
WWW.ROOTSWEB.COM/~AUTWIE/

Addresses

Allgemeines Verwaltungsarchiv; (General administrative archive); Wallnerstrasse 6, A-1010 Wien; (Records of the first republic 1918–38)
Bundespolizeidirektion Wien (Federal Police Directorate, Vienna), Zentralmeldeamt (Central Registry Office) Rossauerlande 5, 1092 Wien; (Population records on Vienna [Meldezettel]—after 1948)
Dokumentationsarchiv des Oesterreichischen Widerstndes (Austrian resistance archives); Wipplingerstrasse 8, A-1010 Vienna; telephone 01 534 36; Archive and library of the Nazi period
Haus-, Hof- und Staatsarchiv; (State and court archive); Minoritenplatz 1, A-1010 Wien; Records of aristocratic titles, distinctions and diplomatic service 1848–1919
Israelitische Kultusgemeinde Wien; (Jewish Community of Vienna); Seitenstettengasse 4, A-1010 Wien; telephone 01 531 040; Holds birth, marriage and death records 1826–1938
Jewish Welcome Service; (Jewish tourist information service); Stephansplatz 10, A-1010 Wien

Juedisches Museum Wien; (Vienna Jewish Museum); Dorotheergasse 11, A-1010 Wien; e-mail: INFO@JMW.AT; has excellent book store.

Library of the Vienna Jewish Museum; Seitenstettengasse 4; A-1010, Wien; e-mail: BIBLIOTHEK@JMW.AT

Oesterreichisches Staats und Kriegsarchiv; (State and war archive, Austro-Hungarian armed forces); Nottendorfplatz 2, A-1030 Wien; telephone 01 795 400

SCHALOM, *Verein zur Wiederherstellung und Erhaltung der jud. Friedhofe in Wien*; (Society for the restoration of Jewish cemeteries in Vienna); telephone and fax: 01 76 15 07

Walter Pagler; Zentralfriedhof Tor 1, A-1110 Wien

Wiener Stadt und Landesarchiv; (Vienna county and city archives at city hall); Magistratsabteilung 8 (MA 8), Rathaus, A-1010 Wien; telephone: 01 4000 8408; fax: 01 4000 7261; e-mail: POST@M08.MAGWIEN.GV.AT

Wiener Stadt und Landesarchiv, Zentralevidenzstelle; (Central Documentary Office); Magistratsabteilung 61 (MA61), Rathaus, A-1082 Wien Recruitment lists, testamentary provisions, proof of domicile, proof of death certificates

Wiener Stadtbibliothek; (Vienna Municipal Library at City Hall); Rathaus A-1010 Vienna; telephone: 01 4000 84808; City directories [Lehmann] 1859–1942

Bibliography

Berkeley, George E. *Vienna and Its Jews: The Tragedy of Success, 1880s–1980s.* Cambridge Mass.: Abt Books, 1987.

Bussgang, Fay, "Archives of the Jewish Historical Institute in Warsaw," AVOTAYNU 10, no. 1 (Spring 1994). Has Jewish Community of Vienna registers 1880–1937, 45 items.

Die Juedische Wochenschrift, a weekly newspaper that began in 1885 as *Die Wahrheit*. The nearest thing to a national weekly for the Jews of the Austro-Hungarian Empire, it was published from 1885 to 1938. For the last ten years, it was the official organ of the Jewish community. Available on microfilm in large university libraries, especially those that have Jewish Studies programs.

Fraenkel, Josef, ed. *The Jews of Austria: Essays on Their Life, History and Destruction.* London: Vallentine-Mitchell, 1970.

Freidenreich, Harriet Pass. *Jewish Politics in Vienna, 1918–1938.* Bloomington: Indiana University Press, 1991.

Geadelte Juedische Familien (Titled Jewish families). Salzburg: Kyffhauser, 1891.

Grunwald, Max. *Vienna.* Philadelphia: Jewish Publication Society of America, 1936.

Kaufmann, David. *Die Letzte Vertreibung der Juden aus Wien und Niederoesterreich* (Last expulsion of Jews from Vienna and Lower Austria). Vienna: Carl Konegen, 1889.

Lowe, Peter. "LDS Films of Viennese Registration Forms (*Melezettel*) As a Genealogical Resource." AVOTAYNU 16, no. 3 (Fall 2000).

Pribram, A.F. *Urkunden und Akten zur Geschichte der Juden in Wien.* (Documents and registers for the history of the Jews in Vienna). Vienna: Braumuller, 1918.

Rozenblit, Marsha L. *The Jews of Vienna, 1867–1914: Assimilaton and Identity.* Albany: State University of New York Press, 1983.

Sack, Sallyann Amdur. "Report on a Return Trip to Israel," AVOTAYNU 11, no. 4 (Winter 1995). Resources at Central Archives for the History of the Jewish People.

Schmidl, Erwin A. *Jews in the Hapsburg Armed Forces, 1788–1918.* Eisenstadt: Osterreichisches judisches Museum, 1989. Covers Jews in and outside of Vienna.

Schneider, Gertrud. *Exile and Destruction: The Fate of Austrian Jews, 1938–1945.* Westport, Conn.: Praeger, 1995.

Schwartz, Ignaz. *Das Wiener Ghetto* (Viennese ghetto). Vienna: Braumuller, 1909.

Steinhauer, Mary. *Totenbuch Theresienstadt* (Theresienstadt death book). Vienna: Junius, 1987.

Tranicek, Peter. AVOTAYNU 12, no. 4 (Winter 1996). Lists of foreigners, and census of 1938/39—unfilmed.

Wachstein, Bernhard. *Die Inschriften des alten Judenfriedhofes in Wien* (Inscriptions of the old Jewish cemetery in Vienna). Vienna: Braumuller, 1917.

Wistrich, Robert S. *The Jews of Vienna in the Age of Franz Joseph.* Oxford: Oxford University Press, 1989.

Notes

1. The Austrian government has decided, with the cooperation of the Jewish community of Vienna, to erect a Holocaust memorial on this square for the 65,000 Jewish victims from Austria. A list of the victims will be displayed in a building nearby.

2. This area, between an arm of the Danube and the Danube River, forms an island now known as Leopoldstadt. During the 19th and 20th centuries, a large part of Vienna's Jews lived there, and in pre-World War II days the district was nicknamed Mazzesinsel (Matzos Island).

3. Although it is known that famous rabbinical families had hereditary surnames, it is not clear if the names of persons on this list were permanent. Some of these records are at the Oesterreichische Staats und Kriegsarchiv and at the Wiener Stadt und Landesarchiv.

4. Samuel Oppenheimer and Samson Wertheimer both used their influence at court to intervene repeatedly to assist Jewish communities in various ways. Several hundred Jews from Buda who, after its capture were held captive by the Austrian forces, were released after Samuel Wertheimer intervened.

5. Wenzel Zacek, "Eine Studie zur Entwicklung der jüdischen Personennamen in neuerer Zeit" (Study on the development of Jewish personal names in modern times), *Jahrbuch der Gesellschaft für Geschichte der Juden in der Czechoslovakischen Republik* (Yearbook of the Society for the History of the Jews of Czechoslovakia), vol. 7. For an English summary see the newsletter of the JGS of Canada (Toronto) *Shem Tov* 7, no. 2, (June 1991).

6. For the 18th century and the 19th century up to 1848 see (in German): Pribram, A.F. *Urkunden und Akten zur Geschichte der Juden in Wien.* This book includes extensive lists of "tolerated" Jewish inhabitants of Vienna and their marriages.

7. See Max Grunwald, Vienna.

8. See G.E. Berkeley, *Vienna and Its Jews* and R.S. Wistrich, *The Jews of Vienna in the Age of Franz Joseph*

9. Same as note 6.

10. R.S. Wistrich, *The Jews of Vienna in the Age of Franz Joseph* and H.P. Freidenreich, *Jewish Politics in Vienna 1918–1938*

11. Jonny Moser, *Demographie der judischen Bevolkerung Osterreichs 1938–1945; Schriftenreihe des Dokumentationsarchives des osterreichischen Widerstandes*, Vienna 1999

12. Lowe, Peter. "LDS Films of Viennese Registration Forms (*Meldezettel*) as a Genealogical Resource."

Belarus

by Vladislav Soshnikov

Read the chapter entitled RUSSIAN EMPIRE *before reading this section. Also consult the section on* JRI-Poland *and the Eastern European Database in the introduction to* POLAND. *Considerable information and many terms are discussed there that apply to Belarus but are not repeated below—Ed.*

This chapter is a guide to sources of genealogical information about Jews who lived in Grodno, Minsk, Mogilev and Vitebsk guberniya and parts of other historical districts whose territories today are included in the Republic of Belarus. Town names are rendered in transliterated Russian because records, inventories and reference aides in Belarussian archives are written almost exclusively in Russian.

History

Jews have lived in the territory of contemporary Belarus since the late 1380s when the medieval territories of White Rus and Black Rus became part of the Grand Duchy of Lithuania, Rus and Samogitia. Historically, Belarus is part of *Litve* (Lithuania) and its Jews were considered "Litvaks." They were Ashkenazic, spoke Yiddish, and Hebrew knowledge was widespread. Many of the celebrated Lithuanian *yeshivot* actually were in Belarus, those of Mir and Volozhin among others.

Jews from Poland and Germany settled in Brest and Grodno in the late 1380s. With the development of trade between Poland, Russia and the Lithuanian lands, additional Jewish communities developed in Minsk, Mogilev, Orsha, Polotsk and Vitebsk. In 1692, the Slutsk community achieved the status of a principal community, that is, it became a city (*gorod*) instead of a town (*selo*) and was no longer subject to a district center, but rather to the guberniya directly. Smaller communities sprouted under the protection of landowners who rented their inns, towns and villages to Jewish lease-holders (*arendars*). Jews enjoyed certain privileges in the Grand Duchy of Lithuania. According to a Polish census, 62,800 taxpaying Jews lived in Belarus in 1766, 40 percent of Lithuanian Jewry. The largest communities were Minsk with 1,396 Jewish inhabitants and Pinsk with a Jewish population of 1,350.

The Grand Duchy of Lithuania formally existed until the fall of the United Kingdom of Poland and Lithuania in 1792. Partitions of Poland in 1772–95 brought more than one million Jews into the newly acquired western provinces of the Russian Empire. From 1791 until 1917, the Belarussian territories were included in the Pale of Settlement established for the Jews restricting them from moving into the interior of Russia (see RUSSIAN EMPIRE).

Despite Russian discrimination, Jews grew in number. By 1847, 225,725 Jews lived in the three guberniyas that today are Belarus (Grodno, Minsk and Mohilev); the number grew to 724,548 at the time of the 1897 all-Empire census, 13.6 percent of the total population. Jews were the majority in the

principal cities of the regions— 47,561 in Minsk (52.3 percent of the total population), 32,369 in Dvinsk (46.6 percent), 21,536 in Mogilev (50 percent), 21,000 in Pinsk (72.4 percent), 20,759 in Bobruisk (60.5 percent) and 20,385 in Gomel (54.8 percent). In 1914, 1,250,000 Jews, about 12 percent of the total population, lived on Belarussian territories.

Emigration

During the 19th and early 20th centuries, extreme poverty led large numbers of Jews to emigrate from Belarus to the Ukraine, southern Russia and, beginning in the 1880s, to the United States. Emigration ceased with the outbreak of World War I in 1914, the Russian Revolution in 1917 and the ensuing Russian civil war (1919–21). Only a few Jews managed to emigrate after 1921 from western Belarus, ruled by Poland in the decades of the 1920s and 1930s.

After World War II, even after all of the Jewish communities had been destroyed during the Holocaust, a large number of Jews still lived in Belarussian territories, most having returned from wartime evacuation to the interior of the Soviet Union. With changes in the political regime, many were able to emigrate to Israel and the United States in the 1970s and especially in the late 1980s and early 1990s. By the mid-1990s, an estimated 40,000 Jews remained in Belarus, primarily in Bobruisk, Gomel, Minsk, Mogilev and Vitebsk. Jewish religious and cultural life has been re-established under the democratic laws of the independent Republic of Belarus, but emigration continues, primarily to Israel.

Boundaries and Historical Geography

Belarus as a country name was not used officially until 1918; in 1991, it asserted its independence from the former Soviet Union. The territory of contemporary Belarus includes, with adjustments, the former 19th- century guberniyas of Grodno, Minsk, Mogilev, Vitebsk and portions of Vilna guberniya, all of which were part of the Pale of Settlement. Geographically, this land is bounded by Lithuanian and Belorussian forest lands, the Pripet Marshes and the eastern plains and forests on the border of Smolensk province.

After the third partition of Poland in 1795, Belarus became part of the northwestern provinces of the Russian Empire. Belarus' national boundaries have changed dramatically over the last two centuries, as have administrative districts within the country. The administrative division of the Belarussian provinces of the Russian Empire was established in the late 1790s and early 1800s, and had minor changes in the 19th century. After the 1917 Russian Revolution, boundaries changed in the period between 1920 and 1939 when Belarus was divided between Poland and the Soviet Belarussian

Republic of the USSR, and in the years 1940–45 during World War II and the expansion of the Soviet Union.

A researcher who seeks 19th-century records from towns in contemporary Belarus must check both town records and corresponding *uyezd* (district) and guberniya records. A comprehensive history of administrative division of Belarussian lands may be found in the bibliography in the end of this chapter.

Guberniya Districts during the Second Half of the 19th Century

During the 19th century and until the Russian Revolution in 1917, Belarus consisted primarily of four guberniyas—Grodno, Minsk, Mogilev and Vitebsk. These in turn were divided into districts called *uyezds*. Following are the names of these districts along with information about the recent sovereignty of the guberniyas; the 19th- century Russian name is first, followed by the modern Belarussian, Lithuanian or Polish name and the name of the country to which it now belongs.

Grodno, annexed from Poland in 1795, belonged to Poland during the years 1920–39 and from 1939 until 1991 was part of the USSR. The traditional Russian and Belarussian name of this ancient city is Grodno (Hrodna); Grodno is the Polish version, but this variant was accepted in the USSR. Districts of Grodno guberniya were:

Belsk/Bielsk, Poland
Belostok/Bialystok, Poland
Brest/Brest, Belarus
Grodno/Hrodna, Belarus
Kobrin/Kobryn, Belarus
Pruzhany/Pruzany, Belarus
Slonim/Slonim, Belarus
Sokolka/Sokolka, Poland
Volkovysk/Vavkavysk, Belarus

Minsk, annexed from Poland in 1793, has been the capital of the Republic of Belarus since 1918. From 1922 until 1991, it was part of the Soviet Union. Its western districts belonged to Poland during the years 1920–39. Districts of Minsk guberniya were:

Bobruisk/Babruisk, Belarus
Borisov/Barsav, Belarus
Igumen/Cherven, Belarus
Minsk/Minsk, Belarus
Mozyr/Mazyr, Belarus
Novogrudok/Navagrudak, Belarus
Pinsk/Pinsk, Belarus
Rechitsa/Rechitsa, Belarus
Slutsk/Slutsk, Belarus

Mogilev, annexed from Poland in 1772, was included in the Gomel region of the Russian Federation between 1919 and 1924. From 1926 until 1991, it was part of the Soviet Socialist Republic of Belarus. Districts of Mogilev guberniya were:

Chausy/Chavusy, Belarus
Cherikov/Cherykav, Belarus
Gomel/Homel, Belarus

Gorki/Gorki, Belarus
Klimovichi/Klimavichy, Belarus
Mogilev/Magilev, Belarus
Mstislavl/Mstislav, Belarus
Orsha/Orsha, Belarus
Rogachev/Ragachov, Belarus
Senno/Syanno, Belarus
Stari Bykhov/Bykhav, Belarus

Vitebsk was annexed from Poland in 1772. It was part of the Russian Federation between 1919 and 1938, although its two western districts belonged to Poland in the years 1920–39. Dvinsk (Daugavpils), Rezhitsa (Rezekne) and Lyutsin (Ludza) were acquired by Latvia before World War II; Nevel, Sebezh and Velizh districts became part of Pskov oblast of the Russian Federation in the 1920s. The remaining districts, Drissa, Gorodok, Lepel, Polotsk and Vitebsk, became part of Belarus after World War II. Districts of Vitebsk guberniya were:

Drissa/ Drissna, Poland; Verhnyadzvinsk, Belarus
Dvinsk/Dinaburg; Daugavpils, Latvia
Gorodok/Haradok, Belarus
Lepel/Lepel, Belarus
Lyutsin/Ludza, Latvia
Nevel/Nevel, Russia
Polotsk/Polotsk, Belarus
Rezhitsa/Rezekne, Latvia
Sebezh/Sebezh, Russia
Velizh/Velizh, Russia
Vitebsk/Vitebsk, Russia

Four southern districts of Lithuania became part of Belarus at the start of World War II. Vilna guberniya, annexed from Poland in 1795, was part of the Lithuanian Federation during the years 1796–1801, after which a separate Vilna guberniya was formed. In 1920, Vilna guberniya was captured by Poland; in 1939–40, the western portion of Vilna guberniya was included in the Republic of Lithuania while the eastern part was incorporated into the Republic of Belarus. The entire region was part of the USSR until 1991. The four districts acquired by Belarus are:

Disna/Dzisna, Belarus
Lida/Lida, Belarus
Oshmiany/Ashmyany, Belarus
Wileika/Vileika, Belarus

Although these southern districts are part of Belarus today, the revision lists from the 19th century, taken when the region was part of Vilna guberniya, remain in the Lithuanian State Historical Archives* in Vilnius.

From the late 19th to the early 20th century, the following towns belonged to different districts.

• Braslav was part of the Novo-Aleksandrovsk district of Kovno guberniya, but today belongs to the Vitebsk region of Belarus.

• Druskieniki was part of Grodno district; after World War II, it became Druskeninkai in Lithuania

Street scene in Brest, Belarus, at the beginning of the 20th century showing Jewish shops. Courtesy of Tomasz Wisniewski.

- Sapotskin belonged to Augustow district in Suwalki guberniya, Kingdom of Poland; since World War II is has belonged to Belarus.

Archival Sources

Archival collections are the primary source of Jewish genealogical information. Provenance determines where records are to be kept. Wars and boundary changes, however, frequently affect the location of records. In the Soviet Union, especially after World War II, archival holdings were exchanged and moved between neighboring regions and/or countries.

In the case of Belarus, some exceptions exist from the international archival standard which mandates that records be held in the archive of the country that today governs the land where they were created. For example, some archival holdings in Grodno, cover Polish territory in Bialystok region because it was part of records created by the Grodno guberniya administration. On the other hand, records pertaining to contemporary Belarussian territories (Lida, Oshmiany and Vileika districts of the former Vilna guberniya, and Braslav area of the former Novo-Aleksandrovsk district of Kovna guberniya) are in the Lithuanian historical archives in Vilnius and Kaunas. The Grodno archive has some vital records from Vilna guberniya separated from the holdings of the Lithuanian historical archives in Vilnius. Latvian archives hold some records of the former Dvinsk and Rezhitsa districts of Vitebsk guberniya.

The most important genealogical records in Belarus are held in the national historical archives in Minsk* and the central historical archives in Grodno*. Some records of genealogical value for the 20th century are stored in regional (oblast) state archives in Brest, Gomel, Grodno, Minsk, Molodechno (a branch archives of Minsk archive), Mogilev and Vitebsk.

National Historical Archive of Belarus in Minsk

The LDS (Mormon) Family History Library has microfilmed extensively in the National Historical Archives in Minsk. As of fall 1999, about three-quarters of the Jewish vital records held in this repository had been filmed. Microfilms are available at the Family History Library in Salt Lake City and the Family History Centers worldwide.

Jewish Vital Records (registry books of births, marriages, divorce and deaths)

Abbreviations:
    B=Birth, M=Marriage, D=Death, V=Divorce
    Hyphen (-) indicates most years included
    Slash (/) indicates several years missing
    "Members" and "Tax" mean community records but not vital records.

Jewish Records from the Historical Archive in Minsk

Inventory of the first Jewish records that have been filmed is given below. Additional filming is currently underway; the Family History Library catalogue should be consulted for towns not listed here. Each entry below shows the town, record type, years and microfilm number.

    David-Gorodok B 1893/1898 1,794,311
    David-Gorodok B 1899–1910 1,920,791
    David-Gorodok BMD 1874/1892 1,794,310
    David-Gorodok BMD 1874/1892 1,794,311
    Gorodok D 1860–1863 1,920,792
    Gorodok M 1913 1,920,795
    Ivenets D 1857 1,920,794
    Kamen B 1866 1,920,794
    Kamen B 1891/1911 1,920,795
    Kamen D 1860 1,920,792
    Kamen V 1908 1,920,795
    Karolin B 1860–1872 1,794,309
    Kojdanov B 1896 1,920,795
    Kojdanov D 1867 1,920,794
    Lakhva M 1879/1915 1,920,792
    Lepel Members 1841 1,920,795
    Minsk B 1840, 1847 1,920,793
    Minsk B 1852/1869 1,920,794
    Minsk B 1882, 1895 1,920,795
    Minsk B Doc 1899–1907 1,920,793
    Minsk BMD 1836/1839 1,920,792
    Minsk D 1840, 1846 1,920,793
    Minsk D 1861 1,920,793
    Minsk D 1861 1,920,794
    Minsk M 1857 1,920,794
    Minsk School 1906–1916 1,920,793
    Minsk V 1840 1,920,793
    Mogilev B 1837–1838 1,920,796
    Mogilev B 1854/1883 1,920,796
    Mogilev B 1864/1893 1,920,800
    Mogilev B 1870/1875 1,920,797
    Mogilev B 1872–1875 1,920,798
    Mogilev B 1876–1880 1,920,798
    Mogilev B 1879–1880 1,920,799
    Mogilev B 1881–1882 1,920,799
    Mogilev B 1883–1886 1,920,800
    Mogilev B 1887–1889 1,920,800
    Mogilev B 1887–1889 1,920,801
    Mogilev D 1853/1857 1,920,796
    Mogilev D 1870–1874 1,920,797
    Mogilev D 1875–1878 1,920,798
    Mogilev D 1879–1882 1,920,799

Mogilev D 1883–1886 1,920,799
Mogilev D 1883–1886 1,920,800
Mogilev D 1887–1890 1,920,802
Mogilev D 1891–1894 1,920,802
Mogilev M 1857/1879 1,920,796
Mogilev M 1880–1892 1,920,801
Mogilev M 1880–1892 1,920,802
Mogilev V 1877/1890 1,920,796
Ostroshitskij G. B 1905 1,920,795
Ostroshitskij G. D 1872–1917 1,794,308
Ostroshitskij G. D 1872–1917 1,794,309
Pinsk B 1882, 1922–1929 1,794,309
Pinsk B 1924–1926 1,794,310
Pinsk D 1930–1939 1,794,310
Rakov B 1869 1,920,794
Rakov B 1877/1889 1,920,793
Rakov B 1897/1917 1,920,795
Rakov D 1860/1864 1,920,792
Rakov D 1903 1,920,795
Rakov M 1908 1,920,795
Rubezhevichi B 1904/1912 1,920,795
Rubezhevichi D 1861, 1864 1,920,792
Rubezhevichi M 1860 1,920,792
Rubezhevichi Taxes 1839 1,920,793
Samokhvalovichi B 1865 1,920,792
Samokhvalovichi D 1859 1,920,794
Samokhvalovichi D 1860, 1864–1865 1,920,792
Senno B 1861–1864 1,920,795
Stolin B 1911 1,794,309
Stolptsy B 1860 1,920,792
Stolptsy D 1860–1864 1,920,792
Zaslavl' D 1856–1857 1,920,794
Zembin M 1905 1,794,309

It may appear that dates on different films overlap, but this is misleading. The description of each film's contents has been simplified for this list. Most of the films include records for scattered years; the births, marriages and deaths for similar ranges of years may appear on different films. For example, film 1 may have births from 1860, marriages 1870–80, and deaths from 1865 to 1890. film 2 may have births from 1865 to 1880, marriages from 1881–90 and deaths from 1860. Each film is given the simplified description of BMD 1860/1890 even though the records are different. This leads to some of the descriptions of consecutive films seeming to contain duplicate records when they do not. For full details about the contents of a film, see its entry in the Family History Library catalogue, locality section under the heading "Belarus, (Town)—Jewish Records."

The following Jewish vital records for communities of Mogilev guberniya have not been microfilmed but are found in archival fond 2003 of the Mogilev provincial government (gubernskoe pravlenie) and collections of Jewish Religious Communities of Mogilev and Vitebsk guberniyas (Fond 3410) and Zhlobin Religious Community (Fond 2457):

Gomel, 1882–1906
Goretsk, 1894–1917

Dashkovka, 1857–1916
Klimovichi M, 1912
Knyazhitsy, 1871–1916
Lyady, 1893–1917
Mogilev, 1890–1917
Mstislavl B, 1916
Mstislavl D, 1872
Mstislavl district communities B, 1883–94
Rogachev, 1885–1896
Romanovo, 1897–1917
Seletsk, 1871–1917
Tishovsk, 1871–1917
Vorotinsk-Zaverezhsk, 1872–1917
Zembin M, 1905 (only this file appears to be microfilmed)
Zhlobin, 1867–1906

Revision Lists of Minsk Guberniya

In addition to vital records, the Mormons have filmed some Jewish revision lists for the years 1795, 1811, 1816, 1842 at the Minsk archives. Shown below is the town, year and microfilm number.

Bobriusk 1795 1,925,366–378
Bobriusk 1806 2,008,324–326
Bobriusk 1816 2,008,268–270; 2,010,469
Borisov 1795 1,925,378–379
Borisov 1811 2,008,326–329; 2,010,468–469; 2,010,473
Borisov 1816 2,008,263–268
Davidgorod 1795 1,925,405–407;1,925,409–413;
1,925,399–401;2,008,319–320
Dokshitsy 1795 1,925,366 and 1,925,367
Igumen 1795 1,925,380–396; 2,008,317–319
Igumen 1811 2,008,329–330; 2,010,467–468
Igumen 1816 1,925,180–181; 2,008,262–264
Igumen 1842 2,008,280–281
Koidanova 1811 2,008,322–324 1,921,924–930; 1,922,324–325;
Minsk 1795 1,922,327; 1,923,577–579; 2,008305;
2,008,316–317
Minsk 1811 2,008,322–324
Minsk 1816 2,008,270–278
Minsk 1842 2,008,278–280 1,925,403–405; 1,925,409;
Mozyr 1795 1,925,396–399; 1,925,401; 2,008,306–308; 2,008,320
Mozyr 1811 1,925,413–415
Mozyr 1816 1,925,415–416
Nesvizh 1795 2,008,282–283
Novogrudok 1795 2,008,281–282
Novogrudok 1806 2,008,321
Novogrudok 1811 2,008,472–473
Novogrudok 1816 2,010,469–470; 2,008,471
Pinsk 1795 1,922,326
Pinsk 1811 2,008,471–473
Pinsk 1816 1,925,416 and 1,925,180
Postavy 1795 2,008,303–304
Rechitsa 1816 2,010,469
Slutsk 1795 2,008,2–303; 2,008,306–308; 2,008,320–321
Slutsk 1811 2,010,468–469
Slutsk 1816 2,008,471
Velejka 1795 1,923,579; 2,008,308; 2,008,315–316

These records are from Fond 333, opis 9. More than half of the microfilms are for the revision of 1795, the period before Jews had family names. Revision lists in the fond of the Minsk Treasury (*Kazennaya Palata*) have not been filmed yet. Records created after 1860 are "supplemental revision lists." The recorded individuals are not registered in the main revision lists (up to 1858) because they were absent when these lists were made. Supplementary revisions continued until the end of the 19th century. Jews are listed separately in the revision lists, but to locate Jewish records it is necessary to search every file, page by page.

Revision Lists for Mogilev Guberniya

Among the records in Fond 2151 of the Mogilev Treasury (*Kazennaia Palata*) are revision lists and alphabetical lists of Jewish town dwellers and farmers for a number of districts, towns and shtetls; (the first number is the *delo* (file) number. The following files are in opis (series) 1:

68.   Jewish town dwellers of Mogilev guberniya, 1868–1869
69.   Jewish farmers of Mogilev guberniya, 1873–1874
70.   Jewish farmers of Mogilev guberniya, 1873–1875
71.   Mogilev guberniya, 1878–1879
82.   Bykhov, 1861
86.   Gomel district, 1858
90.   Rossasny, Goretzky district, 1867–1874
98.   Dubrovny, Goretzky district, 1874–1876
99.   Liadny, Goretzky district, 1874–1877
100. Rossasny, Goretzky district, 1874–1877
104. Kopys, 1874
105. Kopys, 1874–1876
108. Klimovitchi and neighboring townships, 1816
111. Klimovitchi and neighboring townships, 1834
127. Mogilev City, 1858
131. Mogilev district, 1874
132. Mogilev district, 1881
134. Shklov, Mogilev district, 1874
145. Dubrovka, Orsha district, 1852
150. Jewish farmers of Goretsk and Savsk communities, Orsha district, 1858
152. Goretsk community, Orsha district, 1858
153. Dubrovensky Community, Orsha district, 1858
154. Liadny Community, Orsha district, 1858
155. Bayevsky and Rossasinsky Communities, Orsha district, 1858
159. Rogachev district, 1818
160. Rogachev district, 1831
167. Cherikov, Krichev and Molostovitchi, Cherikov district, 1816
200. Jewish farmers of Cherikov district, 1864–1874
207. Cherikov community, 1874
209. Jewish farmers and retired soldiers of Cherikov district, 1881–1886

Revision Lists for Vitebsk Guberniya

In Fond 1640 of the Vitebsk Treasury (*Kazennaia Palata*) are 455 files for the years 1778–1887, but it is not clear if the

original revision lists exist. These files probably are minutes, correspondence and other important documents. Archivists in Minsk say that they hold no revision lists for Vitebsk.

Other Types of Archival Records

Vital records (called "rabbinate records") are either fragmentary or not available for many communities. In addition, it is often impossible to find information for a particular family in revision lists. In such cases, genealogists may find data in other sources that are rarely used but are available for research in the Minsk archives.

The following Jewish records from Minsk, Mogilev and Vitebsk guberniyas have not been filmed. Note that "Jewish community records," "rabbinate records" and "religious congregation records" are just small collections of clerical records of administrative bodies (*kahals* and rabbis) and are not the vital registry books.

Belitsy: Jewish Community Records, 1856–1862
Borisov: Rabbinate Records, 1905
Cherikov District: Jewish School Commission Records, 1853
Cherikov: Jewish State School Records, 1880
Dashkovka: Jewish Community Records, 1857–1914
Dobromysl: Jewish Community Records, 1854
Dubrova: Jewish Civic Association Records, 1862
Es'mony: Jewish Community Records, 1914
Gomel: Jewish Community Records, 1853–1876
Gorsk: Jewish Community Records, 1911
Gorodok: Rabbinate Records, 1872–1917
Karpilov: Jewish Community Records, 1890–1906
Kazimir-Sloboda: Jewish Community Records, 1862
Khotimsk: Jewish Community Records, 1880
Klimovichi: Jewish Community Records,1854–1915
Lepel': Jewish Community Records, 1833–1844
Liady: Jewish Community Records, 1899
Minsk: Jewish Burial Association Records, 1909–1918
Mstislavl': Jewish Elementary School Records, 1862–1864
Nosovichi: Jewish Community Records, 1855–1917
Novogrudok: Jewish Community Records, 1800–1850
Orsha: Jewish Community Records, 1840–1915
Polotsk: Jewish Community Records, 1826–1840
Rogachev: Jewish Elementary School Records, 1857–1875
Staryi-Tolochin: Jewish Community Records, 1861
Streshin: Jewish Community Records, 1861–1877
Surazh: Jewish State School Records, 1855–1877
Uvarovich: Jewish Community Records, 1883
Zabychansk-Neginsk: Jewish Community Records, 1858–1903
Zakharino: Jewish Community Records, 1875
Zhuravichi: Jewish Community Records, 1860–1875

Records of Government Institutions

In the years 1835–1917, Jewish vital statistic records were collected annually by the offices of city administrations (initially by Gorodskaia Duma and after 1875 by Gorodskoe Pravlenie). Among the documents created by these institutions were family lists of all resident families, alphabetical lists of local Jewish heads of families, registers listing dates of military induction, local tax records, copies of revision lists, registers of specific Jewish community taxes, records about admission or dismissal of community members by class (town dwellers, merchants) and registers of permissions to leave. Many records about Jews have been collected by guberniya-level administrative bodies of the governor's office (*kantseliaria Gubernatora*) and provincial government (*Gubernskoe Pravlenie*). While many records did not survive, existing archival collections of these institutions may be useful for genealogical research.

The fond of the Minsk city government (*Gorodskaia Uprava*) consists of 9,391 files for the years 1870–1918. Among the records of its Jewish department, a section responsible for Jewish matters, are the revision lists of citizens for the years 1858; family lists of Jews in the town of Minsk for 1894; lists of Jews who suffered damages during the pogrom in Minsk in 1905; voter lists for the Constituent Assembly for the year 1917; lists of newborns; lists of residents; applications for membership in the town community; lists of town dwellers; annual lists of merchants; applications for membership in the merchants' class; lists of other specially licensed groups of people such as craftsmen and cabmen (*izvozchiki*); permissions to trade (including small trade); permissions to erect buildings; lists of real estate owners; tax and property records and many individual files about Jewish town dwellers.

Also, among the records of the Jewish Department are "Lists of Male Jews" (1874) for the following settlements of Minsk guberniya: David-Gorodok, Elskin, Karobin, Igumen, Khalui, Konatkevichi, Lahvy, Lapichi, Lemchitzy, Lyachovichi (file in bad condition), Lyanina, Lyna (Igumen district), Makavno Mozyr and Mozyr district, Petrikov (Mozyr district), Pogostnya, Pogosty (Igumen district), Puhovichi, Romanovo, Shatzk, Sinyavka, Skrygalov, Slutsk, Smilovichi, Starobin, Timokovichi, Turov and Uzmyany.

The fond of the Minsk Town Dweller Administration (*Meschanskaya Uprava*) consists of 2,028 files for the years 1876–1918. Included are family lists from the late 1800s to the early 1900s and alphabetical lists of taxpayers from the early 1900s. Some files of particular interest are:

- File 2002 which includes a family list of Jewish town dwellers of Minsk in 1894 (884 families). These names were translated from Russian into English and appeared in *RAGAS Report*.[1]

The following are in other files:

- Case about the exclusion of town dwellers from Minsk because of high school graduation or baptism, because they received the title of dentist or became merchants or because they transferred to another community, 1916.
- Copies of registry books (births, marriages and deaths) of Jews from Novogrudsky district in 1849. This includes the communities of Delyatichi, Eremichi, Gorodische, Korelichi, Kroshin, Lyubcha, Mir, Negnevichi, Novaya Mysh, Polonka, Snov, Stvolovichi, Turen, Tzyrin and Vselub.

Police records are in the fonds of town and district police administrations (*gorodskie/uyezdnye politseiskie upravlenia*). Local police kept their own lists and files on Jews for admin-

Wooden synagogue in Grodno, Belarus. It was burned to the ground by the Germans during the Holocaust. Courtesy of Tomasz Wisniewski.

istrative control purposes. Among the records are petitions for the opening of a business, information about members of the Zionist Party, registers of passports and other similar documents.

Records of the political police are in the fonds of the provincial gendarmerie. (Political police might be considered analogous to the Federal Bureau of Investigation in the United States, as opposed to local police.) For example, in the fond of the Vitebsk provincial gendarmerie, among records for the years 1899–1917, inventories one, two and three have items related to Jewish topics.

Military draft lists for the years 1812–74 are in the fond for the Minsk provincial recruitment office (*gubernskoe rekrutskoe prisutstvie*); draft lists from 1874 to 1917 are in the fonds of the district draft offices (*uyezdnye po voisnkoi povinnosti prisutstviya*). It is hard to work with these lists because they are arranged chronologically by district, and the inventories supply no indication of the class of the draftee.

Other individual lists of Jews are found in several archival collections. For example, lists of Jews living in Vitebsk guberniya, 1910–10, and a list of Jews who owned real estate in Slutsk in 1908. In the fond of the Minsk provincial committee for urban resettlement of rural Jews are ten items for the years 1798–1835. In fond 2003 for the Mogilev provincial government (*gubernskoe pravlenie*) are lists of Jewish employees of pharmacies of Mogilev guberniya, 1914–18.

Information for Vitebsk Guberniya

The National Historical Archives in Minsk[*] has neither Jewish metrical books (vital statistics) nor revision lists for this area. What they do have is a series of family and merchant lists beginning in 1874, with entries through 1919. Often the books include data from the 1858 revision list as well. Each year, new entries were added for births, marriages, deaths and military inductions.

Fond 2496, records of the Vitebsk town government (*gorodskoe pravlenie*) has 88 books pertaining to the city of Vitebsk. They have not been microfilmed by the Mormons, and because the books are unusually large, photocopies are not permitted. All citizens are recorded together with no separation by religion. No indexes exist; each book must be searched, page by page. Records include:

- Family lists, 1874–1919 (files 2529–2550)
- Supplemental revision lists, 1882–3 (files 2608, 2617)
- Voter registrations, 1892–97; 1906 (opis 1, file 1821)
- Property records, 1910–11 (opis 1, files 5133–5134)
- An extract from the metrical records of Jews born in 1894 in the town of Lutzin and in Lutzin district (opis 1, file 2164)
- Draft registration, 1892–96
- A general list of male Jews in the city of Vitebsk, 1874 (fond 1416, opis 1, file 2680)

Separate fonds of Jewish organizations from Vitebsk guberniya that have not been microfilmed include the following. All appear to be guberniya (and not city) level records.

- Vitebsk Jewish community (*kahal*) records, 1827–95, primarily administrative.
- Orphanage records, 1911–1918
- State Jewish school records, 1849–1867
- Vitebsk provincial committee to study the census of the Jews, 1875
- Vitebsk Jewish association of agricultural colonies and children's orphanages, 1911–1918.

National Historical Archive of Belarus in Grodno

This historical archive holds records of Grodno guberniya, including the district of Belostok (today, Bialystok, Poland) and some records for Disna, Lida, Oshmiany and Vileika districts of the former Vilna Guberniya. The Mormons have filmed the Jewish vital records in the archive.

Jewish Vital Records

The archive has no rabbinate books of births, marriages, divorces or deaths for the Jewish communities of Grodno guberniya; records did not survive World War II. On the

other hand, the archives does have a collection of Jewish vital records for Lida district:

Belitsy synagogue (m. 1887–1900; v. 1898; d: 1897–99)
Orlya (m. 1889–1900, v: 1887–1900; d: 1897–1900)
Osmiany (m., v. and d. 1897–1900)
Ostryno (marriage, divorce and death: 1897–1900)
Radun (m. 1900, v and d: 1897–1900)
Rozhanka (m. 1897–98, v: 1897–1900, d: 1897–1900)
Schuchin (v: 1897–99)
Vasilishki (v: 1897–99, d: 1897–99)
Voronovo (marriage, divorce, death: 1897–1900)
Zheludok (marriage, divorce, death: 1897–1900)

Records of Jewish Organizations

Separate fonds exist for some Jewish organizations. Note, however, that those listed as "Jewish community records," "Rabbinate records," and "Religious congregation records" are simply small collections of clerical records of administrative bodies (*kahals* and rabbis). They are not vital registry books.

Belostok: Jewish hospital records, 1832–1913
Belostok: Jewish religious congregation records (undated)
Bel'sk: Jewish religious congregation records (1835–1846)
Brest: Jewish hospital records, 1913
Brest: Jewish community records, 1874–1897
Brest: Jewish religious congregations records (synagogue), 1852–1910
Disna district: rabbinate record, 1893–1901
Grodno: Jewish community records (municipal), 1838–1912
Grodno: Jewish hospital records, 1889
Kobrin: Jewish community records, 1838–1912
Olita (Vilna guberniya): Jewish religious community records, 1836–1846
Orlya (Lida district): Jewish religious community records, 1836–1846
Ostrolenka: Jewish community records, 1838–1867
Prensk (Suwalki guberniya): Jewish religious community records, 1895–1902
Pruzhany: Jewish religious community records, 1856–1869
Shaki (Suwalki guberniya): Jewish religious community records, 1842–1911
Suwalki: Jewish hospital records, 1863–1869
Volkowysk: Jewish religious community records, 1865

Revision Lists

Numerous revision lists for the years 1795 to 1900 (records after 1858 are "supplemental lists") are in fond 24 of the Grodno treasury (*kazennaya palata*). Revision lists are for the districts of Bel'sk, Belostok, Brest, Grodno, Kobrin, Pruzhany, Slonim, Sokolka and Volkovisk.

Among other records are alphabetical lists of Jews for the years 1853 for Brest, Pruzhany, Slonim and Sokolka districts. Revision lists of Lida district for the years 1834 and 1863–1884 are in the fond of the Lida district treasury (*kazennaya palata*).

Records of the 1897 All-Empire Census

Most of the 1897 census schedules (i.e., returns that list individuals) were destroyed by the government soon after

Interior of a wooden synagogue in Grodno, Belarus. It was destroyed during the Holocaust. Courtesy of Tomasz Wisniewski.

the census. However, some of the original records with personal information survive in fond 100 of the Grodno Guberniya Census Commission. Among 397 files of this collection, information about Jewish residents appear in records for Belostok, Belsk, Brest-Litovsk, Dyatlovo, Grodno, Ivanovo, Kamenets-Litovsk, Lyskovo, Narevka, Peski, Ross, Svisloch, Volkovisk, Yalovka, Zelva and Zditova. Records for the cities of Grodno and Belostok only partly survived and cover less than half of the population.

Records of Government Institutions

The largest institutional collection is that of the fonds of the Grodno governor's office (*kantseliaria gubernatora*) which includes 58,451 items for the years 1802–1917 and the Grodno provincial administration (*gubernskoe pravlenie*) which includes 79,980 items for the years 1802–1916. These state administrative institutions supervised all others and, thus, have documents about various cases that reflect the everyday life of the guberniya, including information about Jews—for example, individual applications for passports and permission to travel abroad.

In fond 1021 of the Grodno Guberniya Commission for the Jewish Censuses, the following files are of particular interest:

- Registration records of Jewish town dwellers and name lists of Jews, 1875
- Name lists of those Jews who purchased certificates for release from military service, 1871–74.
- Family lists of the Bereza Jewish community, 1874
- Petitions of Jews to issue birth certificates, 1875

Many documents concerning military conscription are in the fonds of the Guberniya Recruitment Office (*rekrutskoe prisutsvie*); this includes records for the years 1808–74. The guberniya military draft office (*gubernskoe po voinskoi povinnosti prisutstvie*) includes records for the years 1874–1917 as well as fonds of the corresponding district institutions (*uyezdnye po voinskoi povinnosti prisutstviya*). Records include family lists and lists of males arranged chronologically by induction date and by district.

Information about town dwellers is concentrated in the fonds of the town governments (*gorodskie upravy*) for the cities of Brest, Grodno, Lida and Slonim. Among various records for the years 1895–1916 are lists of residents and taxpayers, individual petitions of community members; family lists of town dwellers; lists of merchants and proprietors; lists of reserve soldiers, property and tax records.

Members of the class of town dwellers are recorded in records of the administration for town dwellers (*meschanskie upravy*). Fonds for 12 towns include documents for the years 1879–1917. The biggest collections are for the towns of Brest, Schuchin, Selets and Volkovysk. For example, in fond 116 for the Brest administration are records concerning the issues of passports, 1895–1915; registers of the candle tax, 1913–14 and information about the election of deputies to the town council, 1913.

Miscellaneous data about residents of Jewish communities in small towns are held in the record groups of *volost* governments, the smallest administrative division in the Russian Empire. There are 115 record groups for the years 1861–1917 for the districts of Grodno guberniya and the districts of Disna, Lida and Oshmyany of Vilna guberniya. For example, an alphabetical list of the Jewish community of Yalovka (155 pages for the year 1907 alone) appears in the record group of the Shimkov *volost* government.

In the fonds of the police administration (*politseiskie upravlenia*) for Brest district (fond 674, 457 items, 1886–1915) and Grodno district (fond 117, 59 items, 1905–1917) are many records of particular interest. For example, information about members of the Zionist Party, registers of fines for those who failed to report for induction into the army, petitions to open businesses and for certificates of loyalty and registers of travel passports.

In fond 508 of the Senior Notary of Grodno district court (30,000 files for the years 1883–1914) appear many records of genealogical value. Among them is information about commercial and property transactions, rental agreements, loan certificates and copies of notarized documents. The archival inventory lists thousands of names, but there is no index and a specific name can only be found through a page-by-page search.

Among the records of the fonds of the district tax collectors (*uyezdny podatnoi inspektor*) are payment books and lists of real estate property by district for the years 1908–15. In the fond of the Lida district treasury the following files are of particular interest:

- Lists of creditors to the state treasury (1904–1915)
- Lists of depositors to he savings bank (1914–1916)
- Lists of payers of the Lida town resident's tax, 1915

Similar accounts may be found in other archival collections as well.

Jewish Vital Statistics Records for Bialystok District

The following microfilms pertaining to Jewish communities of the former Grodno guberniya apparently were made by the LDS (Mormon) Family History Library in the Bialystok, Poland, regional archives. Records are in Russian and Polish. Jewish vital statistics records include:

Bialystok BMD 1835/1939
Bielsk-Podlaski BMD 1835
Choroszcz V 1883/1913
Ciechanowiec BMD 1839/1935
Orla BMD 1836–1866
Suraz BMD 1870/1914
Trzcianne BV 1871–1919
Wasilkow BMD 1818/1933

Records for Belarus in the Lithuanian Archives

The following list of holdings in the Lithuanian historical archives in Kaunas and Vilnius related to Belarussian territories was taken from *Jewish Vital Records, Revision Lists and Other Jewish Holdings in the Lithuanian Archives*, by Harold Rhode and Sallyann Amdur Sack.

Asmena (Oshmyany, Lida district). Revision lists, 1795–1831

Kaunas archive, Fond 515, Op. 15, File 1032

Novy Dvor (Lida district). Vital records BMD: 1896–1914, Fond 728, Op. 4, File 319–320

Orlya/Orly (Orlowa, Lida district). Vital records B,M: 1896–1914. Fond 728, Op. 1, File 962, 965, 969, 976, 984, 993, 1017, 1026, 1042–44, 1053–54, 1061, 1069, 1078, 1084, 1088, 1095

Radun (Lida district). Vital records B,M: 1896–1914; Fond 728, Op. 1, File 955–1094

Shchuchin (Lida district). Vital records BMD: 1896–1914, Fond 728, Op. 1, File 956–1096

Sokolka, Poland (Sokolka, Grodno guberniya); Vital stat. rec. B,M,D: 1835, Fond 1108, Op. 1, File 15

Vidzy (Novo-Alexandrovsk district); revision lists: 1816–827, 1871–94; Kaunas archive, Fond 208, Records of Novo-Aleksandrovsk (Zarasai) county

Vileika (Vileika district); revision lists, 1795–1831; Kaunas archive, Fond 515, Op. 15, File 1032

Zaskevichi (Oshmyany district); Vital records BMVD: 1855–72. Fond 728, Op. 1, File 1103–1122.

State Archives of Minsk Oblast

The state archives of Minsk oblast keeps records of Soviet organizations for the period 1918–90. Among others, the following records may be useful for Jewish genealogical research:

- Jewish Club of the Poale-Zion Organization of Chita records, 1919–23
- Poale-Zion Party of Belorussia, Central Committee records, 30 items, 1917–921
- Yugend Bund, Gomel' Branch records, 1918–19
- General Jewish Workers' Bund, Mozyr Committee records, 1920s
- Records of the Jewish Public Committee to Aid Victims of Pogroms in the Borisov district records, 1920–23

Branch Archive of Minsk Oblast in Molodechno

This branch archive of Minsk oblast keeps records of the Polish state for 1919–39 and records of Soviet organizations for the period 1939–90. Among others the following records may be useful to Jewish genealogists: Jewish elementary school of Rabbi M. Shatsker, 18 items, 1929–34.

State Archive of Grodno Oblast

The state archive of Grodno oblast keeps records of the Polish state for the years 1919–39, and records of Soviet organizations for the period from 1939 to 1990. Among others, the following records may be useful for Jewish genealogical research:

Grodno: Jewish religious community records, 164 items, 1899–1939

Grodno: Jewish religious community records, 158 items, 1929–36

Grodno: Tarbut Jewish Teachers' Seminary records, 72 items, 1926–36

Szczuczyn: Jewish religious community records, 2 items, 1915–39

Lida: Moses Dvorzecki Jewish High School records, 1918–39

Volkowysk: Herzliya Coeducational High School records, 121 items, 1921–39

State Archive of Brest Oblast

The state archive of Brest oblast keeps records of the Polish state for the years 1919–39 and records of Soviet organizations for the period 1939 to 1990. Among others, the following records may be useful to Jewish genealogists:

Bereza Kartuska: Jewish religious community administration records, 3 items, 1936–1937

Brest: Jewish religious community administration records, 17 items, 1928–1937

Brest: Jewish People's Bank records, 1 item, 1938–1939

Drohiczyn district: Society of Jewish craftsmen records, 1938–1939

Domachev: Jewish religious community administration records, 2 items, 1928–1937

Kobrzyn (Kobrin): Jewish religious community administration records, 4 items, 1936–1938

Mamorita: Jewish Cooperative Bank records, 1 item, 1928

Pinsk: Jewish religious community administration records, 15 items, 1934–1939

Pinsk: Yudel Piekacz Jewish Vocation School records, 238 items, 1921–1939

Pinsk: Jewish Municipal Hospital records, 2 items, 1919–1939

Pinsk: District Aid Committee for Jewish victims of war, 7 items, 1920–1925

Pinsk: Guardianship Society for Jewish orphans, 46 items, 1921–1939

Pinsk: Guardianship Society for Jews, 86 items, 1921–1939

Pinsk: Jewish Cooperative Agricultural Society, 1 item, 1933–1938

Pinsk: Jewish Society for Labor Organizations, 3 items, 1934–1938

Telechany: Jewish Credit Bank records, 1 item, 1932–1936

Wysokie Litewskie: Jewish religious community administration records, 1 item, 1928

State Archive of Gomel Oblast

The state archive of Gomel oblast keeps records of Soviet organizations of the period 1917–90. Among others, the following records may be useful for Jewish genealogical research:

Gomel: Jewish National Chamber of the People's Court records, 1926–30

Gomel: National Jewish Court records, 1931–34

Rechitsa district: Plenipotentiary of the Jewish Public Committee to Aid Victims of Pogroms, 1923

Sources Beyond the Archives

Organizations

The most important non-archival source is the Belarus Special Interest Group (SIG) sponsored by JewishGen and accessible at WWW.JEWISHGEN.ORG/BELARUS. Sign on to receive the SIG's digest and to access its All-Belarus database. Be sure to access and read carefully the JewishGen discussion group message archives (1993-present) as well as relevant Infofiles (see JEWISHGEN).

Information about a long list of Belarus Jewish cemeteries may be found at WWW.JEWISHGEN.ORG/CEMETERY/INDEXOLD.HTM. Narrative information exists for the following Jewish cemeteries in Belarus: Baranovichi, Bobruysk, Borisov, Brest, Butin, Craisk, Derezhin, Dyatlowo, Gomel, Grodno, Ivenets, Karpilokov, Kletsk, Kobylnik (today, Naroc), Luban, Lyakhovichi, Mikhanovichi, Mir, Mogilev, Molchadz, Mysh, Neshvizh, Novogrudock, Novy Sverzhen, Ostrovy, Pinsk, Polotsk, Rogachev, Ruzhany, Samohkvalovichi, Seliba, Shklov, Slonim, Smilovichi, Sopotkin, Svir, Timkovichi, Vasilishki, Vidzy, Vitebsk, Volozhin, Vorotinschina, Yehzona, Zaslavi, Zaverezh'ye, Zhetel, Zhlobin.

The Index to Religious Personnel in Russia 1853–54 has data for Minsk, Mogilev and Vitebsk. This database may be found on the website of the Jewish Genealogical Society of Rochester, New York (see ORGANIZED GENEALOGY).

Addresses
Genealogical Societies

East European Jewish Heritage Project, Jewish Revival Charitable Mission, 13b Dauman Street, Minsk 220002 Belarus; telephone/fax: +375-172-34; e-mail: EEJHP@USER.UNIBEL.BY

Belarussian Genealogical Society, Kollektornaia ulitsa 10, Room 208, Minsk 220084 Belarus

Minsk Historical Genealogy Group, Zhukovskogo 9-2-190, Minsk 220007 Belarus; e-mail: MINSKHIST@YAHOO.COM

Archives

National Historical Archive of Belarus, Kropotkina ulitsa 55, Minsk 22002 Belarus; website: WWW.PRESIDENT.GOV/BY/GOSARCHIVES.

National Historical Archive of Belarus in Grodno, Tesingausa ploschad 2, Grodno 230023 Belarus

State Archive of Brest Oblast, Sovietskih Pogranichnikov ulitsa 34, Brest 224000 Belarus

State Archive of Gomel Oblast, 8th pereulok Ilyitcha 26a, Gomel 246042 Belarus

State Archive of Grodno Oblast, Akademicheskaia ulitsa 7a, Grodno 230023 Belarus

State Archive of Minsk Oblast, Kozlova ulitsa 26, Minsk 220039 Belarus; Branch Archive of Minsk Oblast in Molodechno, Revolutsionnaia ulitsa 69, Molodechno, Minsk oblast, 222310 Belarus

State Archive of Mogilev Oblast, Chelyuskintsev ulitsa 172a, Mogilev 212014 Belarus

State Archive of Vitebsk Oblast, Kalinina ulitsa 22, Vitebsk 210015 Belarus

Main Archival Administration of Belarus, Kollektornaia ulitsa 10, Minsk 220084 Belarus

Lithuanian State Historical Archives in Vilnius, Gerosios Vilties 10, Vilnius 2009, Lithuania

Bibliography

Administrativno-territorialnoye ustroistvo BSSR Administrative territorial division of the Belarussian Soviet Socialistic Republic for the years 1917–85. [Russian] vols. 1–2. Minsk, 1985.

Boonin, Harry. "Belarussian Archival Holdings." *AVOTAYNU* 6, no. 3 (Fall 1990): 10–15.
———. "What We Know about Genealogical Records in Belarus." *AVOTAYNU* 9, no. 4 (Winter 1993): 6–8.

Feigmanis, Aleksandrs, "Genealogical Resources in Minsk for Jews of Vitebsk Guberniya." *AVOTAYNU* 14, no. 3 (Fall 1998).

Krutalevich, V. A. *Administrativno-territorialnoye ustrostvo BSSR* (Administrative territorial division of the Belarussian Soviet Socialistic Republic). [Russian] Minsk, 1966.

Rapanovich, Y.N. *Slounik nazvau nasellenych punktau Brestzkoi oblasti* (Dictionary of place names of the Brest region). [Belorussian] Minsk, 1980.

Rapanovich, Y.N. *Slounik nazvau naellenych punktau Minskoi oblasti* (Dictionary of place names of Minsk region). [Belorussian] Minsk, 1981.

Rhode, Harold and Sallyann Amdur Sack. *Jewish Vital Records, Revision Lists and Other Jewish Holdings in the Lithuanian Archives.* Teaneck, N.J.: Avotaynu, 1996.

Sallis, Dorit and Marek Web [eds.]. *Jewish Documentary Sources in Russia, Ukraine and Belarus: a preliminary list.* New York: Jewish Theological Seminary of America, 1996.

Shiriayev, E.E. *Rus Belaya, Rus Chyornaya i Litva v kartakh* (Maps of White Russia, Black Russia and Lithuania). [Russian] Minsk, 1991.

Soshnikov, Vladislav "Belarussian Archives Revisited." *AVOTAYNU* 10, no. 3 (Fall 1994).
———."Belarus Revisited." in *RAGAS Report* 5, No. 2 (Summer 1999): 1–4.
———."RAGAS Provides Mogilev Guberniya Inventory." *AVOTAYNU* 13, No. 3 (Winter 1997): 31–32.
———. "Sources for Jewish Genealogy in Belarussian Archives." *AVOTAYNU* 11, no. 3 (Fall 1995).

Spisok volostei, obschestsv i selenyi Minskoi guberniyi (List of smaller administrative districts, communities and settlements of Minsk province). [Russian] Minsk, 1870.

Spisok volostei i vazheishikh selenyi Evropeiskoi Rossii: Guberniye LItovskoi i Belorusskoi oblastei (List of smaller administrative districts and main settlements of European Russia: provinces of Lithuanian and Belorussian regions). [Russian] St. Petersburg, 1886.

Spisok naselennykh meste Minskoi guberniyi (List of settlements of Minsk province). [Russian] Minsk, 1909.

Spisok naselennykh mest Minskoi guberniyi (List of settlements of Minsk province). [Russian] Minsk, 1912.

Ukazatel naselennykh mest Grodnenskoi guberniyi (Index of settlements of Grodno province). [Russian] Grodno, 1905.

Zaprudnik, Jan. *Historical Dictionary of Belarus.* Lanham, MD: Scarecrow Press, Inc., 1998.

Zhivopisnaya Rossia: Litovskote i Byelorusskoye Polesye (Pictorial Russia: Lithuanian and Belorussian Forest Lands). [Russian] Minsk: *Belarusskaya Encyclopaedia*, reprint of a 1882 publication, 1993.

Zhuchkevitch, V. A. *Kratky toponimichesky slovar* Belorussii (Brief dictionary of Belarusssian place names). [Russian] Minsk, 1974

Note

1. Reprinted in "About the Russian Archivist's Soul," *AVOTAYNU* 14, no. 3 (Fall 1998): 66.

Belgium

by Marcel Apsel, Daniel Dratwa and Bob Drilsma

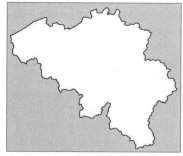

Jews immigrated to the territory of Belgium in three major time periods. Between the 12th and 14th centuries, Jews, primarily from Rhenish German areas, scattered throughout various duchies and counties of Brabant (with its capital in Brussels), Hainaut (with its capital in Mons) and other places. They formed tiny communities, and during the Black Death (1348–49) were accused by the Catholic Church of having profaned the host (holy bread). As a result, in 1370, the Jews who had survived were burned at the stake in Brussels, and the community almost entirely disappeared. The oldest remaining material presence of Jews is a tombstone of a Jewish woman of Tienen/Tirlemont from 1255; in addition, the university library of Hamburg, Germany, has a 1310 Hebrew manuscript written by a Brussels scribe.

The second major period of immigration began with the expulsion of the Jews from Spain in 1492 and from Portugal in 1497. Educated and sometimes quite wealthy Jews, disguised as *marranos* (also called crypto-Jews), dispersed over Europe coming also into the 17 provinces under Spanish rule—today, the Low Countries of the Netherlands and Belgium. Geographically, the former Southern Provinces correspond to contemporary Belgium, the Northern Provinces to The Netherlands. The *marranos* who settled in Antwerp at the end of the 15th century and the beginning of the 16th century played an important economic and financial role in the city. Because of pressure from the Spanish, however, most *marranos* left Antwerp during the years 1540–50, ending both the second period of Jewish presence in Belgium and the economic prosperity of 16th-century Antwerp.

Although some *marranos* returned to Antwerp in the 17th century, they were unable to assume the same economic and financial position they had occupied a century before. A secret synagogue existed in Antwerp during the years 1650–94, and a number of *marrano* poets lived in Brussels. During the 18th century, the Jewish presence in the southern provinces, then under Austrian administration, was very small; about 100 Jews lived in Brussels in 1756.

With the French conquests, the Southern Provinces were incorporated into the French Republic in 1795. Decrees about equality of all citizens, including Jews, also were applied to the Jews of the Southern Provinces. On March 17, 1808, Napoleon legally recognized Judaism as a religion organized by synagogues and administered by consistories. (A consistory is an officially recognized organization whose primary purpose is to organize Jewish religious worship and related religious activities such as circumcisions, marriages, burials, education, and religious slaughtering.) The small Belgian Jewish community was incorporated into the consistories of Krefeld and Trier (Treves), France. After Napoleon lost his last battle and his crown at Waterloo near Brussels, Belgium was incorporated into the Kingdom of The Netherlands.

Following a revolution in 1830, Belgium gained its independence and became the Kingdom of Belgium.

Religion and state were legally separated in the Belgian constitution of 1831. The Jewish religion received official recognition and freedom, and Jewish life was legally organized by the national authorities (Department of Justice). Today, the Central Israelite Consistory of Belgium is charged with all practical matters concerning Jewish life, such as nominating rabbis, cantors, sextons, ritual slaughterers and religious teachers, and the maintenance of synagogues and Jewish schools.

During the 19th century the Jewish population grew slowly by immigration mostly from Alsace and Lorraine to the southern part of Belgium, from Germany to Brussels, and from Holland to Antwerp. The structure of Jewish religious organization followed the French consistory system instituted by Napoleon. From 1880 onwards, a new influx of immigration came from Eastern Europe, the result of pogroms after the assassination of the Russian czar in 1881. For many, Belgium, and especially Antwerp, was a stop on the way to the United States. Sephardic Jews came from the Ottoman Empire during the Greek-Turkish War just before the turn of the 20th century.

In the middle of the 19th century, Antwerp developed one of the largest harbors in Europe and, therefore, enjoyed regular shipping connections to the United States. Some refugees originally bound for the United States preferred, however, to stay in Antwerp, Brussels, Liege and other places. After the United States restricted immigration in 1921, most in-transit Russian-Jewish emigrants had no choice but to remain in Belgium, where many worked in the flourishing diamond industry.

More than economic reasons motivated Jews to settle in Antwerp during the interbellum period. By then, Antwerp had developed a strong religious community that became well known to the Polish emigrants of the 1920s and 1930s. Many of the more religious Jews saw it as a safe environment in which to settle. With the arrival of German refugees in the 1930s, Belgian Jewry reached its peak in 1939 with a population estimated at approximately 65,000, located primarily in Antwerp (25,000), Brussels (30,000), Liege (5,000) and Charleroi (3,000). Others Jews settled in Ghent, Ostende, Namur and Arlon.

Approximately 30,000 Jews from Belgium were killed in the Holocaust—roughly 25,000 were deported from Mechelen, Belgium, and approximately 5,000 from Drancy, France. The Register of the Jews in Belgium of 1940 lists 56,000 Jews living in Belgium.[1] Apparently, 10,000 Jews who had been living in Belgium just before World War II managed to flee (or hide) by 1940.

Rebuilding the Jewish communities was the first and primary goal of those who survived the war. The Belgian

Memorial to Belgian Jews murdered in the Holocaust is located in Brussels.

Jewish communities today consist of those who succeeded in hiding, plus the 1,207 who returned from the camps (and their descendants). Some other survivors of concentration camps and displaced people who had never lived in Belgium before the war joined them. The latter were largely Eastern European Jews (Czech, Hungarian, Polish, and, in the mid-1950s, Romanian Jews). Some had family ties, friends or *landsleit* (members of the same former town) in Belgium. The flourishing diamond business in Antwerp also attracted many Jews; other business possibilities prompted some refugees to try their luck in Brussels. Minor Jewish communities developed again in Arlon, Charleroi, Gent, Liège and Ostende.

Some Jews settled temporarily in Belgium after the war because of the impossibility of emigrating legally to Palestine under the British Mandate. Other survivors were obliged to remain in Europe because of immigration quotas imposed by the United States. In the 1960s, the worldwide economic boom allowed Belgian Jewish organizations to develop strongly. Today most of the structure of Jewish organized Jewish life in Belgium dates from the 1960s.

Generally speaking, however, Jewish genealogical research in Belgium should be focused on the years 1870–1940, when Belgium was a stopping place for many Eastern European Jews headed for the United States.

Genealogical Resources in Belgium

Because church and state are legally separate in Belgium, Jewish birth, death and marriage records are intermingled with those of the rest of the population. To a great extent, Jewish genealogical research in Belgium since 1830 is no different from research for the rest of the population—except for some additional Jewish resources. An English-language website, ARCH.ARCH.BE, provides good basic information on how the archival system in Belgium works.

Belgium has four basic civil resources for genealogical research: the national state archives, provincial archives, city archives and civil town records. Birth, marriage and death records from 1811 until 1900 may be found on microfilm in the National State Archives, the Rijksarchieven/Archives de l'Etat. Each of the nine Belgian provinces has a public records office in its respective provincial archives. They generally are open weekdays from 8:30 a.m. to noon and from 1 p.m. to 4:30 p.m. These records have been microfilmed by the Mormons (see LDS) and may be ordered through their Family History Centers worldwide. Original records are kept in the municipalities where access to them is determined on a case-by-case basis depending usually on the physical condition of the records. In some cases the originals have been microfilmed and the films are available—but in other cases, they are not.

Records less than 100 years old are kept at the Dienst Burgerlijke Stand en Bevolking/Service de l'Etat Civil et de la Population, the registrar's offices. These town offices keep birth, civil wedding and death records of every resident in Belgium, whether Belgian citizen or foreigner. Even in cases where an Orthodox Belgian Jew is buried in a cemetery in The Netherlands, a death certificate will be filed in his town of residence. All deaths must be certified by a physician who attests to the cause of death. Death certificates do not record where the deceased will be buried or cremated. If the deceased had died someplace other than his or her normal place of residence, the death record will be transferred to the town of residence. To determine where a Jewish person has been buried, it is necessary to check with the Jewish community or the "Frechie Burial Foundation" a private burial society that primarily buries Dutch Jews who live in Antwerp.

A federal privacy law forbids research into records about individuals that are less than 100 years old—with two exceptions. A person may always have access to his or her own records. In addition, if records are needed in order to prove descent (or some other legal reason), one may seek permission to view the records from the local court in each city (*Rechtbank van Eerste Aanleg/Tribunal de première instance*), with costs paid by the individual making the inquiry.

Addresses

The following is a list of state, provincial and city archives that may be useful to Jewish genealogical researchers.

Brussels

Algemeen Rijksarchief/Archives Générales du Royaume (National Archives of Belgium—main branch) Ruysbroeckstraat 2, 2 rue Ruysbroeck, 1000 Brussels; telephone: 02-513-7680; e-mail: MERCKAERT@ARCH.BE. This repository holds the archives of the central governmental institutions of the government, records for all of Belgium and also the archives and records of the province of Brabant. All records are on microfilm. The annual cost for research in all Belgian archives is 15 Euro.

Antwerp

Rijksarchief Antwerpen: (National Archives—Antwerp branch) Door Verstraeteplaats 5, 2018 Antwerpen; telephone: 03-236-7300; e-mail: RIJKSARCHIEF.ANTWERPEN@ARCH.BE. Open Tuesday through Saturday, 8:30 a.m. to noon and 1 p.m. to 4:30 p.m.; Saturday until 4 p.m., but Saturday closed July and August. The civil records of the registrar's office of the city of Antwerp until 1900 are found here (on microfilm).

Stadsarchief Antwerpen (City Archives of Antwerpen): Venusstraat 11, 2000 Antwerpen; telephone: 03-206-9411; fax: 03-206-9410; e-mail: STADSARCHIEF@STAD.ANTWERPEN.BE; website WWW.STADSARCHIEF.ANTWERPEN.BE/STADSARCH. Open Monday through Friday, 8:30 a.m. to 4:30 p.m. The most important records found here are records of the Foreign Police. These consist of individual folders with various information about each foreigner living in Belgium (in this case, in Antwerp). Most other cities in Belgium have in their archives also their records of the Foreign Police. The Algemeen Rijksarchief/Archives Générales du Royaume has similar records for the entire country. Personal access to records in the city archives is possible only to direct descendants and then only after an official request to the City Archives. In turn, the City Archives must obtain permission from the City Council. After permission is granted, the folder may be consulted only on the premises of the archives.

For copies of Antwerp records after 1900, write to *Dienst voor Burgerlijke Stand van de stad Antwerpen*: Lange Gasthuisstraat 21, 2000 Antwerpen; telephone: 03-201-3511; e-mail: DISTRICT.ANTWERPEN@STAD.ANTWERPEN.BE. For the borough of Berchem: F. Van Hombeekplein 29, 2600 Berchem; telephone:

03/230.99.40. For the borough of Borgerhout: Moorkensplein 19, 2200 Borgerhout; telephone: 03/270.17.11. To obtain permission for research on records created after 1900, write to de *Voorzitter van de Rechtbank van Eerste Aanleg*, Britselei 55, 2000 Antwerpen if permission to view such records was not obtained at the registrar's office. Records more than 100 years old are readily obtainable. If one is not a close relative, the ability to obtain records less than one hundred years old depends on the willingness of the town registrar. Permission may never be refused to a direct descendant, but access to records of aunts, uncles and first cousins depends on the good will of the registrar. Access to the records of more distantly related relatives or those of non-relatives is more difficult to achieve without a proper reason. The Civil Court may grant such permission, but the chance of success is much like a lottery.

Mechelen

Stadsarchief Mechelen (City Archives of Mechelen): Hof van Habsburg, Goswin de Stassartstraat 145, 2800 Mechelen; telephone: 015-20.43.46 and 015-20.39.43; fax 015-21.64.48; e-mail: STADSARCHIEF@MECHELEN.BE; website : HTTP://WWW.MECHELEN.BE/ARCHIEF. Open Monday through Friday, 8:30 a.m. to 12.30 p.m. and 3.30 p.m. to 5 p.m. Because a death record must always be made in the place where a person died, this archive holds records of the Jews who died in the Dossin Barracks in the town of Mechelen (Malines). In some cases, if the deceased used to live in Antwerp, Brussels or elsewhere, a copy of the death record will be sent to the town of the deceased's official residence.

Brabant

Stadsarchief Brussel/Archives de la Ville de Bruxelles (City Archives of Brussels): 65 Huidevetterstraat/Rue des Tanneurs 65, 1000 Brussels; telephone: 02/523.62.80. Open Monday through Friday, 8 a.m. to 1 p.m. and 2 p.m. to 4:30 p.m. Civil records of the registrar's office from the 18th century onwards are held here. For copies of Brussels records after 1900 write to Dienst voor Burgerlijke Stand van de stad Brussel/Echevin de l'Etat Civil de Bruxelles: 6 Boulevard Anspach, 1000 Bruxelles.

Hainaut

Archives de l'Etat Mons (National Archives – Hainaut Branch): 23 Place du Parc, 7000 Mons; telephone: 065-35-4506; e-mail: ARCHIVES.MONS@ARCH.BE. Open Monday through Friday, 9 a.m. to noon and 1 p.m. to 4:30 p.m. Civil records of the registrar's office from the 18th century onwards are held here.

Limburg

Rijksarchief Hasselt: (National Archives—Limburg branch) (province of Limburg): Bampslaan 4, 3500 Hasselt; telephone: 011-22-1766; e-mail: RIJKSARCHIEF.HASSELT@ARCH.BE. Open Monday through Friday, 9 a.m. to noon and 1 p.m. to 4:30 p.m.

Liege

Archives de l'Etat à Liege (National Archives—Liege branch) (province of Liege): rue du Chera 79, 4000 Liege; telephone: 04-252-0393; e-mail: ARCHIVES.LIEGE@ARCH.BE. Open Monday

Naam : APSEL

Voornamen : Moses, Pinkas

Geboren te Doliniany, Pol. den 11 November 1909

Beroep : Handelsreiziger   Nationaliteit : Poolsche   Godsdienst : Joodsche

Burgerstand : ong.

OUDERS

geboren te _____, den _____

zoon (dochter) van Markus

geboren te Olchowiec, den 1880

en van Pepa Apsel

geboren te Doliniany, den 1878

GROOTOUDERS

Vaderszijde

klein zoon van Salomon, Apsel

geboren te Doliniany, den _____

en van _____

geboren te _____, den _____

Moederszijde

van _____

geboren te _____, den _____

en van _____

geboren te _____, den _____

(zie keerzijde)

Registration form used during the Holocaust by the Belgian Judenrat. It shows the person's name (Mozes Pinkas Apsel), date and place of birth (Doliniany, 11 November 1909), occupation (salesman), nationality (Polish), information about father (Markus, born in Olchowiec in 1880), mother (Pepa Apsel, born Doliniany in 1878), father's father (Salomon Apsel). Provision is made for information about the other grandparents but it is left blank.

through Friday, 8:30 a.m. to noon and 1 p.m. to 5 p.m. City Archives of Liege: rue Velbruck 9-11, 4000 Liege.

Luxembourg

Archives de l'Etat à Luxembourg (National Archives—Luxembourg branch) (province of Luxembourg): Parc des Expositions, 6700 Arlon; telephone: 063-22-0613; e-mail: ARCHIVES.ARLON@ARCH.BE. Open Monday through Friday, 9 a.m. to noon and 1 p.m. to 4:30 p.m.

Namur

Archives de l'Etat à Namur (National Archives—Namur branch) (province of Namur): rue d'Arquet 45, 5000 Namur; telephone: 081-22-3498; e-mail: ARCHIVES.NAMUR@ARCH.BE. Open Monday through Friday, 9 a.m. to noon and 1 p.m. to 4:30 p.m.

Oost-Vlaanderen

Rijksarchief Beveren (National Archives—partly Oost-Vlaanderen branch) (province of Oost-Vlaanderen), Kruibekesteenweg 39, 9120 Beveren; telephone: 03-775-3839; e-mail: RIJKSARCHIEF.BEVEREN@ARCH.BE. Open Monday through Friday, 8:30 a.m. to noon and 1 p.m. to 4:30 p.m. In addition to information from the province of Oost-Vlaanderen, this archive also holds data on all of Flanders that other, local branches of the National Archives do not have.

Rijksarchivef Gent (National Archives—Oost-Vlaanderen branch) (province of Oost-Vlaanderen): Geerard de Duivelstraat 1, 9000 Gent; telephone: 09-225-1338; e-mail: RIJKSARCHIEF.GENT@ARCH.BE. Open Monday through Friday, 8:30 a.m. to noon and 1 p.m. to 4:30 p.m.

West-Vlaanderen

Rijksarchief Brugge (National Archives—West Vlaanderen branch) (province of West Vlaanderen) Academiestraat 14, 8000 Brugge; telephone: 050-33-7288; e-mail: RIJKSARCHIEF.BRUGGE@ARCH.BE. Open Monday through Friday, 8:30 a.m. to noon and 1 p.m. to 4:30 p.m.

Jewish Genealogical Sources

Because the Belgian constitution enforces complete separation of state and religion, the religion of Belgian residents is mentioned only twice in official population registers: twice in the censuses of 1835 and 1842 and again during World War II. This is one reason why the Germans could not learn easily who was Jewish during World War II. Some individuals never mentioned their religion and were not known publicly as being Jewish; as a result, these Jews were never identified as such during the war.

The first place to look to determine who was Jewish are lists of Jewish cemeteries, but these present a serious problem. In Belgium, cemeteries can be obliged to dig up graves after 15 years, but old burial books still exist. For records of Antwerp, one may consult the burial books of the Schoonselhof cemetery. This primarily affects records of Jews buried in mixed Jewish and Gentile cemeteries because long ago, the Jewish community of Antwerp and the Orthodox Jewish community of Brussels purchased a plot in the Netherlands, near the Belgian border, in order to bury their dead, for in the Netherlands cemeteries can remain undisturbed forever—and thus they observed the Jewish prohibition against disturbing graves.

Putte has three Jewish cemeteries, the cemetery of the Shomre Hadas of Antwerp, the cemetery of the Machzike Hadas of Antwerp and Brussels and the cemetery of the Frechie Burial Foundation.* A cultural gap exists between Dutch Jews and Eastern European Jews. The Frechie Burial Society* primarily serves Dutch Jews who did not belong to the Jewish communities of Antwerp because of this cultural gap.

Thus, there is no difficulty proving the Jewishness of those buried in Jewish cemeteries in the Netherlands. Most Jewish communities have lists of members buried in their cemeteries, but it can be difficult to find lists of Jews buried in mixed cemeteries. A researcher should begin at the offices of the local Jewish community. These offices generally have lists of death records of individuals who were members of the Jewish community and buried through the burial society of that Jewish community. If the deceased wished to be buried in a non-Jewish cemetery, this could occur.

A second place to find data about Jews is the so-called wedding books. In most cases, every Jewish community that performs a marriage lists these weddings in special books. Under Belgian law, however, the burgomaster or an alderman of a local community must perform a civil wedding before a religious wedding can take place. A non-observant Jewish couple may legally choose to have only a civil wedding. On the other hand, it also may happen that a religious couple has only a Jewish ceremony, disregarding Belgian law. No officially appointed rabbi will perform such weddings but Jewish law requires only that a *minyan* (quorum) be present to perform a wedding ceremony. Under Belgian law, however, such marriages are not legally recognized. Religious only marriages may occur between elderly widows and widowers with pensions from the Belgian or German authorities (a *Wiedergutmachung*) who might lose the pensions if they remarry. A third possibility are lists of Jewish social, religious, sport,

cultural and other organizations, insofar they have kept records of their members and if their archives have survived war and/or neglect.

Much information has been lost—because of the Holocaust, lack of interest of keeping archives, lack of space, neglect, inability to maintain repositories and carelessness. The following sections list first Jewish institutions and organizations that keep data of genealogical value and then, national, provincial and local institutions levels where civil birth, wedding, divorce and death records may be found. Notary or court records are areas for more specialized and specific research.

Jewish Archives

Various Jewish institutions keep records of their members and activities. Below are some organizations that may have records of genealogical value.

Antwerp

Centrale (Welfare Institution and Home for the Aged): Jacob Jacobstraat 2, 2018 Antwerp; telephone: 03-232-3890; e-mail: INFO@CENTRALE.BE; website: WWW.CENTRALE.BE. This institution keeps lists of residents of their home for the aged.

Brussels

Consistoire Central Israélite de Belgique: 2 rue Joseph Dupont, 1000 Brussels; telephone: 02-512-2190; e-mail: CONSIS@ONLINE.BE; website: WWW.JEWISHCOM.BE.

Cercle de Généalogie Juive de Belgique–Kring voor Joodse Genealogie in Belgie (Jewish Genealogical Society of Belgium). See *Musee Juif de Belgique* below.

Centrale d'Oeuvres Sociales Juives (Welfare Institution); 91 Avenue Henri Jaspar; 1060 Brussels; telephone: 02-538-8036; e-mail: LACENTRALE@SWING.BE.

L'Enfant Caché – Het Ondergedoken Kind (Hidden Children); 68 Avenue Ducpétiaux, 1060 Bruxelles; telephone 02/538.75.97; e-mail: ENFANTCACHÉ@SKYNET.BE.

Institut d'Etudes du Judaisme (Institute of Jewish Studies); 17 Avenue Franklin Roosevelt, 1050 Brussels; telephone: 02-650.3348 or 3460; e-mail: IEJ@ULB.AC.BE; website: WWW.ULB.AC.BE/PHILO/JUDAISM.

Institut Sépharade Européen: 52 Rue Hotel de Monnaies, 1060 Brussels; telephone: 02-534-9812; e-mail: MOISE.RAHMANI@SEFARAD.ORG; website: WWW.SEFARAD.ORG.

Musée Juif de Belgique-Joods Museum van Belgie (Jewish Museum of Belgium); 21 Rue des Minimes, 1000 Bruxelles; telephone: 02/5121963; fax: 02/5134859; e-mail: D.DRATWA@MJB-JMB.ORG; website: WWW.MJB-JMB.ORG. The Jewish Genealogical Society (JGS) of Belgium is a non-profit organization independent of the museum, but incorporated as a separate unit within the museum. Thus, the address of both is the same. Officially, all of the holding of the JGS are incorporated into the museum holdings as well.

The museum holds a list of more than 56,000 Jews registered in Belgium in 1940, including names, birth dates and birth places of parents, grandparents and children. In addition the following records may be found at the museum:

- Register of the Jews of Brussels in the censuses of 1756, 1803, 1815, 1829, 1835 and 1842. After 1842, religion ceased to be recorded in the census.
- Register of Jewish refugees. In 1947 the authorities allowed 5,000 Jewish refugees to settle in Belgium. Most came from Poland and from Displaced Persons camps.
- The database of the address book of the Jews of Antwerp of 1902 can be found on the website of the museum: choose language, genealogy and search for the address book of the Jews of Antwerp.
- Jewish cemeteries of Belgium
- Records of youth organizations
- Records of people registered for alyah between 1945–1947

Useful Jewish Organizations
Brussels
Administration des Victimes de Guerre (Administration of War Victims), 31 Square de l'Aviation, 1070 Brussels; telephone: 02-522-7860; e-mail: SQUARE.31@SKYNET.BE.

Union des Déportés Juifs de Belgique: 68 Avenue Ducpétiaux, 1060 Brussels; telephone: 02-538-9666.

Mechelen
Joods Museum van Deportatie en Verzet-Musee Juif de la Deportation et de la Resistance (Jewish Museum of Deportation and Resistance): Goswin de Stassartstraat 153, 2800 Mechelen; telephone: 015-29-0660; e-mail: INFOS@CICB.BE; website: WWW.CICB.BE.

This museum is situated in the former Dossin Barracks, where the Germans gathered most of the Jews of Belgium to be sent to Auschwitz. Between August 4, 1942, and July 31, 1944, 28 convoys deported 25,257 Jews from Mechelen (Malines) to Auschwitz. More than two-thirds were gassed upon arrival; of those deported, only 1,207 survived.

Jewish Communities
It is always good to check with the Jewish community offices to see what information they may be able to offer.

Antwerp
Israelitische Gemeente van Antwerpen Shomre Hadas (Jewish Congregation of Antwerp), Terliststraat 35, 2018 Antwerpen; telephone: 03/232.01.87. E-mail: INFO@SHOMRE-HADAS.BE; website: HTTP://WWW.SHOMRE-HADAS.BE.

Israelitische Orthodoxe Gemeente van Antwerpen Machzike Hadas (Jewish Orthodox Congregation); Jacob Jacobsstraat 22, 2018 Antwerpen; telephone: 03/233.55.67.

Israelitische Sefardische Gemeente van Antwerpen (Jewish Sephardi Congregation of Antwerp); Hoveniersstraat 31, 2018 Antwerpen; telephone: 03/232.53.39.

Arlon
Communaute Israelite d'Arlon: Rue des Martyrs 11, boite 16, 6700 Arlon; telephone: 063/21.79.85. E-mail: JEANCLAUDE.JACOB1@SKYNET.BE; website: HTTP://SITE.VOILA.FR/SYNAGOGARLON

Brussels
Communauté Israélite de Bruxelles: 2 rue Joseph Dupont, 1000 Bruxelles; telephone: 02-512-4334.

Communauté Israélite Orthodoxe Machzike Hadas (Jewish Orthodox Congregation), 67a rue de la Clinique, 1070 Bruxelles; telephone: 02-521-1289.

Communauté Israélite Liberale: 96 Avenue Kersbeek, 1190 Bruxelles; telephone: 02-332-2528; fax: 02-376-7219; e-mail CILB@SKYNET.BE.

Communauté Israélite Orthodoxe de Schaerbeek: 126 rue Rogier, 1030 Bruxelles; telephone: 02-241-1664.

Communaute Israelite de St-Gilles: 73 Rue de Thy, 1060 Bruxelles.

Communauté Israélite Sépharade de Bruxelles: 47 rue de Pavillon, 1030 Bruxelles; telephone: 02-215-0525.

Communauté Israélite d'Uccle-Forest (Maale): 11 Avenue Messidor, 1180 Bruxelles; telephone: 02-344-6094; e-mail: INFO@MAALE.ORG; website: HTTP://WWW.MAALE.ORG.

Charleroi
Communaute Israelite de Charleroi: 56 Rue Pige-au-Croly; 6000 Charleroi; telephone: 071-32.80.49.

Ghent
Joodse Gemeenschap van Gent: Veldstraat 60, 9000 Gent; telephone: 09-225-7085.

Heide
Heide has no organized Jewish community, but information about Jewish life in Heide before World War II may be obtained from the Jewish Genealogical Society of Belgium. (See *Musee Juif* above.)

Knokke
Israelitische Gemeente van Knokke Adat Yisrael: Van Bunnenlaan 30, 8300 Knokke; telephone: 050-61-0372.

Liege
Communaute Israelite de Liege: 19 rue Leon Fredericq; 4020 Liege; telephone: 043-43-6106. E-mail: COMMULIEGE@HOTMAIL.COM.

Oostende
Israelitische Gemeente van Oostende: Filip Van Maestrichtplein 3, 8400 Oostende; telephone: 059-80.24.05.

Waterloo
Communaute Israelite de Waterloo et du Brabant Sud: 140 Avenue Belle-Vue, 1410 Waterloo; telephone:02-354-6833.

Jewish Cemeteries
Local Jewish communities are generally the best sources of cemetery information, but some additional information is noted below.

In Antwerp, the former Kiel cemetery was closed in 1935. Information may be found at the Schoonselhof cemetery. Schoonselhof information, including the book of the old

Jewish cemetery of Kiel, may be found at the Schoonselhof cemetery administration office: Krijgsbaan 1, 2710 Hoboken (Antwerp); telephone: 03-830-5417; fax 03-830-5417.

Dratwa, Daniel, *Répertoire des périodiques juifs parus en Belgique de 1841 à 1986*, (Repertory of Jewish Journals published in Belgium between 1841 and 1986), Brussels :Pro Museo Judaico-Centre D'Etudes du Judaisme Contemporain, 1987. In each newspaper you can find obituaries and informations on birth and wedding of people.

Frechiestichting, the two Antwerp Jewish communities have also their cemeteries in Putte, Holland. Information may be obtained at the administrative office at Cuperusstraat 26, 2018 Antwerp, Belgium; telephone: 03-239-2105; e-mail: B.DRILSMA@ VILLAGE.UUNET.BE. For burials in the town of Eijsden, contact the Jewish community of Liege; for information about burials in Luxembourg, contact the Jewish community of Arlon.

Jewish Newspaper

Belgisch Israelitisch Weekblad, a Dutch-language Jewish weekly that has published births, wedding and death notices for Jews living in Antwerp and surroundings since 1954. Available in Jewish bookstores and by subscription. E-mail: BIW@PLANETINTERNET.BE.

Bibliography

Apsel, Marcel. *AVOTAYNU* Contributing Editor—Belgium. See the following issues: 1, no. 1 (January 1985); 1, no. 2 (July 1985); 3, no. 1 (Spring 1987); 3, no. 2 (Summer 1987); 4, no. 1 (Spring 1988); 6, no. 2 (Summer 1990); 6, no. 3 (Fall 1990); 7, no. 2 (Summer 1991); 8, no. 2 (Summer 1992); 10, no. 1 (Spring 1994); 11, no. 1 (Spring 1995); 11, no. 3 (Fall 1995); 12, no. 1 (Spring 1996); 12, no. 4, (Winter 1996); 13, no. 3 (Fall 1997); 14, no. 1 (Spring 1998); 15, no. 1 (Spring 1999); 17, no. 1 (Spring 2001); 17, no. 4 (Winter 2001); 18, no. 4 (Winter 2002) Teaneck: Avotaynu, 1999-present.

Brachfeld, Sylvain. *Brabosh: beelden uit het Antwerps Joods Verleden/ Images Anversoises d'Antan* (Short stories about Jewish life in the past). [Dutch] Published by the author in 1986; stories from Jews living in Antwerp and surrounding areas, mostly before World War II. e-mail of publisher: BRASYLV@NETVISION.NET.IL

———. *Uit vervlogen tijden: Wetenswaardigheden uit het Antwerps Joods Historisch Archief* (Information from the Antwerp Jewish historical archives). [Dutch] Antwerp, Belgium; Herzlia, Israel, 1987; e-mail: BRASYLV@NETVISION.NET.IL. Stories about people and institutions of Antwerp.

———. *Ils n'ont pas eu les gosses* (They did not get the children). [French] Belgium/Israel: Sylvain Brachfeld, 1989. The stories, filed with the Gestapo, of the more than 500 Jewish children staying in orphanages of the *Association de Juifs de Belgique/ Joodenvereniging van België* (Organization of Jews of Belgium) during World War II.

———. *Ze hebben het overleefd* (They survived). [Dutch] Brussels: Vubpress, 1997. Story of how half the Jewish population of Belgium was hidden and rescued by non-Jewish civilians during the German occupation of World War II, and the story of how 500 Jewish children known to the Gestapo survived the war.

Caplan, Sophie. *AVOTAYNU*, Contributing Editor—Australia, 3, No. 4, (Winter 1987) and 4, No. 2, (Summer 1988).

Catalogue: Consistoire Central Israelite de Belgique, 1980. [Dutch and French] Exhibition of 150 years of Jewish life in Belgium with a short bibliography of publications about the Jews of Belgium.

Communaute Israelite de Bruxelles: La Grande Synagogue de Bruxelles, Contribution a l'histoire des Juifs de Bruxelles, 1878–1978. (Jewish community of Brussels; contribution to the history of the great synagogue of Brussels, 1878–1978). [French] Brussels, 1978.

Genami (WWW.CHEZ.COM/GENAMI), a member society of the International Association of Jewish Genealogical Societies, has lists of names of Belgian Jews and a partial name list of Jews in Antwerp for 1913.

Gutmann, Micheline and Ronald D. Courtney, *AVOTAYNU* 14, no. 4 (Winter 1998).

Klarsfeld, Serge, and Maxime Steinberg. *Memorial de la Deportation des Juifs de Belgique—Memoriaal van de Deportatie der Joden uit Belgie* (Memorial to the deportation of the Jews of Belgium) [French] New York: Organization of the Jewish Deportees of Belgium, Children of the Deportation and the Beate Klarsfeld Foundation: New York, 1982. 2d., enl. ed. [French and Dutch], 1995.

Michman, Dan. *Belgium and Holocaust: Belgians, Jews, Germans*. Jerusalem: Yad Vashem, 1999.

Pierret, Philippe. *Ces pierres qui nous parlent* (Stones that are speaking). [French] Brussels: Olivier Devillez, 1999. The story of the Jewish cemetery of Dieweg (Brussels) with information about those buried there.

Saerens, Lieven: *Vreemdelingen in een wereldstad: een geschiedenis van Antwerpen en zijn joodse bevolking (1880–1944)* (Foreigners in a cosmopolitan town: a history of Antwerp and its Jewish population 1880–1944). [Dutch] Tielt: Lannoo, 2000; website: WWW.LANNOO.COM.

Schmidt, Ephraim. *Geschiedenis van de Joden in Antwerpen* (History of the Jews of Antwerp). [Dutch] Antwerp: Ontwikkeling 1963. French ed. Antwerp: Excelsior, 1969; 2d. Dutch ed. Antwerp: Devries-Brouwers, 1994.

Schreiber, Jean-Phillippe. *Dictionnaire Biographique des Juifs de Belgique* (Biographical dictionary of the Jews of Belgium). [French] Brussels: De Boeck, 2002. Includes more than 600 biographies of Belgian Jews.

———. *Politique et Religion, Le Consistoire Central-Israelite de Belgique au 19ieme siecle* (Politics and religion; the Jewish consistory of Belgium in the 19th century).[French] Brussels: Presse Universitaire de Bruxelles, 1995.

———. *L'Immigration Juive en Belgique du Moyen Age a la premiere guerre mondiale* (Jewish immigration to Belgium from the Middle Ages until World War I) [French] Brussels: Presse Universitaire de Bruxelles, 1996.

Steinberg, Maxime. *Extermination et Resistance des Juifs en Belgique*. (Extermination and resistence of the Jews in Belgium) [French and Dutch] Brussels: Comite d'Hommage des Juifs de Belgique a leurs heros et Sauveurs, 1979.

——— *L'etoile et le fusil: La traque des Juifs, 1942–1944*. (The star and the rifle: the hunting of the Jews, 1942–1944) [French] 2 vol. Brussels: Vie Ouvriere, 1986.

Note

1. The German occupying forces installed the *Association de Juifs de Belgique/Joodenvereniging van België (AJB)* (Organization of Jews of Belgium), better known under its German name *Judenrat*. Its purpose was to organize Jewish life during the Nazi occupation and to pass all German orders to the Jewish population. In fall 1940, the Germans ordered the AJB to register all Belgian Jews. This handwritten database survived the war and is—except for Charleroi and Liege—almost complete. Public access is not permitted, but complete information from a file may be supplied upon written request from a direct descendant of the listed individual (if the list exists). Consult *musée juif de Belgique—Joods Museum van België* in the listing of Jewish archives.

Brazil

by Egon and Frieda Wolff

Brazil became a Portuguese colony in 1500 and was ruled by Portugal uninterruptedly, except during the Dutch occupation from 1630 to 1654, the so-called colonial period. In 1822, Brazil declared its independence from Portugal and established a monarchy that existed until the country became a republic on November 15, 1889.

Although not always easy to document, Jews have lived in Brazil for all of its 500-year history, first as *conversos* from Portugal and later as Sephardim from Holland (during the Dutch years). During this time, however, no organized Jewish communities or synagogues were permitted to exist. The only exception was during the Dutch occupation of the State of Pernambuco and other part of northeastern Brazil. At that time, some of the secret Jews returned to open observance of Judaism. Other European Jews came during these years and established the first synagogue in the Western Hemisphere. The reconquest of Pernambuco forced these Jews to flee. Brazil officially opened to the immigration of individuals other than Portuguese Catholics (the so-called "Opening of the Ports") only in 1808, and small numbers of Jews migrated to this country throughout the 19th century.

The first imperial constitution of 1824 declared total liberty of religion—with some restrictions, the most important that places of worship other than Catholic ones had to be in private buildings with no outside appearance of a church or synagogue. After that, Jews from North Africa—especially Morocco—established their first centers and synagogues in Belem, in the State of Para, in 1826 and 1828.

Large-scale Jewish immigration began in 1848, when restrictions on personal liberties by European governments caused some Jews to come to the Western Hemisphere. After the Franco-Prussian War of 1870–71, when French Jews suffered the cession to Prussia of their homelands, Alsace and Lorraine, many decided to go to Brazil, where relatives from the 1848 immigration had already settled. Three 19th-century congregations are known to have existed, one in Rio de Janeiro and two in Belém, but none has left even a single document recording the birth, marriage or death of a congregant.

Despite the lack of official documents, our research has yielded the names of approximately 3,000 Jewish immigrants during the 19th century. Baron Maurice de Hirsh's Jewish Colonization Association (ICA) devised the first plans for Jewish agricultural colonies in southern Brazil at the end of the 19th century, although they were not realized (in the State of Rio Grande do Sul) until the beginning of the 20th century.

From the end of the 19th century to World War I in 1914, many Polish and Russian Jews went to Brazil. Afterwards, Russians who did not agree with the Bolshevik regime and Germans driven by the 1923 inflation also came to Brazil. Ten years later, refugees came from Hitler's Germany and Mussolini's Italy. The last wave of immigrants were Egyptians after the Suez crisis and Hungarian Jews in 1957 after the ill-fated revolt against the communist system in Hungary.

Today, Brazil is home to approximately 100,000 Jews, most in São Paulo (45,000) and Rio de Janeiro (25,000). Smaller communities exist in Bahia and Recife with a scattering elsewhere. Ninety percent are Ashkenazim.

Like other countries in the Western Hemisphere, most Brazilian Jews descend from European immigrants who began to arrive at the start of the 20th century, but especially after World War I, during the 1930s and after World War II. A notable group was the Sephardim from Morocco, Syria and other Arab countries, who opened up the hinterland of the Amazon and the State of Para. Attracted by economic opportunities offered secondary to rubber production in the interior of the Amazon Basin, unmarried men began to arrive in the middle of the 19th century, settling in Belém at the mouth of the Amazon and in Manaus, capital of Brazil's largest state, Amazonas. Many worked as traders along the river and married native women. Married Moroccan men began to arrive only in the second half of the 19th century.

Sources for Genealogical Research

Colonial and Imperial Period

Knowledge of the Spanish and Portuguese Inquisitions is needed to understand early Jewish settlement in Brazil. In 1492, Jews who did not consent to be baptized were expelled from Spain. An estimated 120,000 moved to neighboring Portugal, which already had a Jewish population of about 75,000. When King Manuel of Portugal sought to marry Spanish Princess Isabella, a condition of the agreement was that he make his country free of Jews. Accordingly, in December 1496, a decree of expulsion was announced, giving the Jews 10 months in which to leave. The king did not really want to lose these useful subjects, however, so a second law was announced in March 1497 ordaining the baptism of all Jewish children between the ages of 4 and 14. Most Jews continued preparations to leave Portugal, but when they arrived in Lisbon, the only port of embarkation open to them, no ships were available. With the expiration of the allowed 10 months, the Jews were given a choice of slavery to the king or forced baptism. Thus, the Jews of Portugal accepted the Catholic faith only under force, and a large number of so-called "New Christians" continued to observe Jewish customs and religion in secret.

A new decree that promised no inquiries into lingering Jewish practices if these people observed their new religion during the next 20 years had the desired effect. The New Christians continued to live in Portugal, appearing in church, but continuing their Jewish practices as home. In 1536, the Portuguese king obtained papal consent to install the Inquisition in Portugal, thus beginning centuries of persecution of New Christians accused of continuing to follow Jewish customs. As a result, many secret Jews made strenuous efforts to flee Portugal, often to Brazil, sometimes with a sojourn in Holland first.

No court of Inquisition existed in Brazil. Accusations against secret Jews (also called Crypto-Jews or judaizers) were first accepted and judged by the bishops until the arrival of the first Inquisition official (*visitador*) in Bahia and later one in Recife. The *processes* of the First Visitation (records of the Inquisition) have not been published in Brazil, but the second was made public knowledge by Eduardo D'Oliveira Franca and Sonia A. Siqueira in their book *Segunda Visitacao de Santo Oficio as Partes do Brazil*. New Christians found guilty of judaizing by the bishops or *Visitadores* were sent to be judged in Portugal. Records (called *processes*) of these trials are available at the Nation Archives, the Torre do Tombo, in Lisbon.* This is one of the best sources for researchers interested in the origins of Catholics believed to be descendants of Portuguese or Spanish Jews.

Genealogies of some families, almost none of them still Jewish, have been published in Brazil, mostly by their descendants. A book about this phenomenon is *Os Heredeiros do Poder*, by Francisco Antonia Dória; one about the Dutch period in Brazil is *Gente da Nacao,* by José Antonio Gonsalves de Mello.

Descendant of Jews who came from Holland during the Dutch occupation of northeastern Brazil during the years 1630–54 have vast documentation at their disposal in the Amsterdam Municipal Archives* and the Dutch National Archives* in The Hague. In these repositories, one may find not just commercial and religious archives, but also such genealogically valuable data as birth, marriage and burial certificates. For those with such roots, it is not impossible to trace all the way to the present time.

We have written and published two books that might be useful in this context. The first is *Judeus ëm Amsterdã— Seu relacionamento com o Brasil 1600–1620* (Jews in Amsterdam—their relations with Brazil 1600–1620); the other is *Quantos Judeau estiveram no Brasil Holandës? e outros ensaios* (How many Jews lived in Dutch Brazil? and essays). *Dictionario Biográfico I: Judeus e Judaizantes no Brasil, 1500–1808* (Biographical dictionary: Jews and Judaizers in Brazil, 1500–1808) consists of entries about Crypto-Jews and Jews, starting with the discovery of Brazil in 1500 and going to the Opening of the Ports in 1808. Information in the books comes from two sources. One is the registers of Visitations of the Holy Office (the Inquisition) in Brazil during the 16th and early 17th centuries. The other is the Inquisition trials in Lisbon of judaizers born in, or residents of, Brazil. Records of these trials are kept in the National Archives* in Lisbon. In *Dicionario Biográfico II* researchers will find genealogies of some Jews who came to Brazil during the 19th century—especially Americans, English and French. Also helpful is Rabbi Malcolm Stern's *First American Jewish Families*.

For a few years during the colonial period, at the time of the Dutch occupation of the northeast from 1630 to 1654,

Jews could openly practice their religion. Some people from this region and time are included in the book; hence, the word "Jews" in the title. Information about them was researched in the archives of Amsterdam and The Hague.

The first book which we authored, *Judeus no Brasil*, (Jewish in Imperial Brazil) included the beginnings of some family trees. A later book, *Dicionário Biográfico: Genealogias Judaicas* (A biographical dictionary: Jewish genealogies), includes genealogies of a number of families; several arrived in Brazil during colonial times. Another source for some families is Jose Maria Abecassis' *Genealogia Hebraica: Portugal and Gibraltar, Seventeenth to Twentieth Centuries*, which includes references to several Brazilian branches.

18th and 19th Centuries

A researcher who descends from Jews who came to Brazil during the late 18th and 19th centuries must depend largely on oral history, unless the family has managed to keep such documents as passports, birth and religious marriage certificates from the county of origin and, possibly, naturalization papers from Brazil.

Brazil started civil registration of births and marriages only after becoming a republic on November 15, 1889. Only one Jewish congregation existed in Rio de Janeiro at that time, but its archives do not hold even a single birth, marriage or death documents of a congregant.

Municipal (non-denominational) cemeteries were established only in the 1840s. In 1810, while Brazil was still a colony of Portugal, a treaty of "friendship and peace" was signed by Portugal with its old ally England. Included in the treaty was a paragraph allowing freedom of religion to members of all friendly nations. Intended to refer especially to Anglicans, the provision also covered English Jews who soon began to settle and work in Brazil. Thus, when a Protestant section was reserved in the Sao Francis Xavier Cemetery in Rio, Jews also were allowed to be buried in it. The second Brazilian-Jewish cemetery opened in 1921; the first had been present in Recife during the Dutch occupation of that city from 1630 to 1654. The Recife cemetery disappeared, although there has been talk of excavating in the area where it is supposed to have been located.

Births, marriages and deaths were registered only in parish churches. This excluded those Jews who came to Brazil shortly after the colony was opened to non-Portuguese people (in 1808). Foreigners sometimes married in their consulates, however, and it has been possible to obtain copies of such records from London, for example by accessing the records of the British consuls to Brazil. Such records are held in the Public Records Office in London.* In addition, notices sometimes were placed in newspapers, especially English and French journals. A few families have managed to save annotated family bibles, another source of marriage information. Until the 1970s, divorce was illegal in Brazil; legal separation was permitted, but partners could not remarry in Brazil. According to Brazilian law, death certificates may not state the religion of the deceased.

```
                    - 63 -

S.P.  419              SAHDA BOHABOT
H.              nacida en Iquitos (Perú)
               el 11 de Setbre de 1901
            fallecida el 19 de Enero de 1928
               Recuerdo eterno de tu
                 inconsolable Esposa
               Hijos y demas Familia


                      *  *  *


S.P.  689             SALOMÃO BONOMO
M.D.  H.        Eternas Saudades de seus
               Filhos, Genro,Nora e Netos
                    F. 21-4-1947


                      *  *  *


N.  610              À minha querida
H.              e inesquecida, Esposa
                  ROSA BUTLER BORGES
                  nascida a 7-9-1891
                   em Lodz - Polonia
                 fallecida a 10-3-1945
                  Com eterna Saudade
              e como Preito de Gratidão
           do teu querido e inesquecido
               Esposo Alberto Borges


                      *  *  *


N.  1017             REGINA BORNSTEIN
M.D.                   Nasc. Kunz
                19-1-1874  31-12-1942


                      *  *  *
```

Page from Sepulturas de Israelitas, S. Francisco Xavier, Rio de Janeiro *(Jewish graves in S. Francisco Xavier [cemetery] in Rio de Janeiro) shows inscriptions on tombstones*

Cemetery Data

For genealogists researching Jewish roots in Brazil, cemetery data may be among the best available sources. Until the middle of the 19th century, Brazilians were buried in and around churches. The first public cemeteries were established in 1851; in 1855, a part of Sao Francisco Xavier Cemetery was reserved for Protestants who were almost all non-Brazilians— as were the more than one thousand Jews who also were buried in that section.

An error on a death certificate issued in the 1880s, aroused our curiosity and caused us to check a tomb in a cemetery where we subsequently discovered one thousand Jewish burials. We copied the tombstone inscriptions from these graves and published the results in 1976 in *Sepulturas de Israelitas.* Encouraged by what we had found, we researched other non-Jewish cemeteries and eventually checked more than 100,000 Brazilian Jewish graves and published several more books of tombstone inscriptions.

Naturalization Records

Naturalization documents, kept in Brazil's National Archives,[*] are another important source of genealogical data. Applicants

were required to list parents, spouse and children (if married), and their ages. Witnesses usually were Jews, another factor that may be helpful in genealogical research.

Dictionario Biografico IV: Processos de Naturalizacao de Israelitas Seculo XIX (Biographical dictionary IV: 19th-century Jewish naturalization records) lists information on 456 Jews who obtained Brazilian citizenship during the 19th century, records of whom are on file at the Brazilian National Archives.[*] The list represents only a fraction of the Jews who lived in Brazil at the time. Most were relatively poor Moroccan immigrants; many others who applied for citizenship were not accepted. European Jewish immigrants, usually from England, France, Germany or Hungary, generally more prosperous than the Moroccans, tended to retain their original citizenship, becoming naturalized only when necessary for their professions.

Wills and Testaments

Wills and heirs have proven valuable in completing Brazilian Jewish family trees. Wills must be researched in local *cartorios* (notary offices). Commercial contracts of businesses with Jewish partners, death announcements mentioning children and other relatives, newspaper clippings,[1] memoirs of parents, grandparents and other relatives, also can be good sources of information. Whenever possible, however, memoirs must be checked against documentary evidence since memories sometimes are imprecise or inaccurate. See also *Dicionário Biográfico III—Testamentos e Inventários* (Testaments and inventories), which also includes many documents kept in the Brazilian National Archives.[*]

Ship Records

Other sources for a search of forefathers during the 19th century are registers of arrivals of boats and foreigners (up to 1842), which are kept at the National Archives. After that date, records are available only for 20th-century arrivals. If, however, the immigrant sailed from the Port of Hamburg, Germany, it may be possible to find him or her on the Hamburg Emigration Lists (WWW.HAMBURG.DE/FHH/BEHOERDEN/ STAATSARCHIV/LINK_TO_YOUR_ROOTS/ENGLISH/INDEX.HTM), which include place of destination. Archives of the British Church in Rio, in Salvador da Bahia and in Recife sometimes yield unexpected Jewish information. For example, Isaac Amzalak was buried in the Salvador British Cemetery in 1872.

Some published genealogies of Jewish immigrants to Brazil go back to the end of the 18th and the 19th centuries.

For 20th–century information, write to the Jewish Genealogy Society of Brazil[*] and to the Jewish community offices in the city of interest. Use the *Jewish Traveler's Guide* to find addresses of Jewish community offices.

Addresses

Algemeen Rijksarchief (Dutch National Archives), Prinswillem-Alexanderhof 20; P.O. Box 90520, 2509 LM The Hague, The Netherlands.

Arquivo Nacional, Rua Azeredo Coutinho 77, Centro, 22230-170 Rio de Janeiro, Brazil.

Biblioteca Mario de Andrade, Rua de Consolacão, 94, São Paulo, Brazil.

Biblioteca Nacional, Rio Branco 219-39, Rio de Janeiro 20040-008, Brazil.

Gemeentearchief (Amsterdam Municipal Archives), Amsteldijk 67, 1074 HZ, Amsterdam, P.O. Box 51140, 1007 EC, Amsterdam, The Netherlands; website: WWW.GEMEENTEARCHIEF.AMSTERDAM.NL; e-mail: SECRETARIAT@GAAWEB.NL.

Instituto dos Arquivos Nacionais/Torre do Tombo (National Archives of Portugal), Amameda da Universidade, 1649-010 Lisbon, Portugal; tel.: +351-21-781-1500; website: WWW.IANTT.PT; e-mail: DC@IANTT.PT.

Jewish Genealogical Society of Brazil, P.O. Box 1025, CEP 13001-970 Campinas, S.P. Brazil.

Public Records Office, 4 Ruskin Avenue, Kew, Richmond, Surrey TW9 4DU; website: WWW.PRO.GOV.UK.

Bibliography

Abecassis, José Maria. *Genealogia Hebraica Portugal e Gibraltar Sécs. XVII a XX.* Lisbon: Livraria Ferin, Lda. Rua Noa do Almada 72-1200 Lisboa, 1990.

Azevedo, J.L. "Notas sobre Judaisme e Inquisicao no Brasil." *Revista de Instituto Hist. e. Georg. Brasileiro.* (Notes on Judaism and the Inquisition in Brazil). [Portuguese]. Rio de Janeiro: 1907.

Bigazzi, Anna Rosa Campagnano. "History of the Jews of Italy: Migration to Brazil during the Holocaust Period," *AVOTAYNU* 15, No. 3 (Fall 1999).

Calmen, Pedro. *Historica de Brasil, 1500–1600* (History of Brazil). [Portuguese] Rio de Janeiro: Editera Nacional, 1939.

Contributing Editor (Brazil) "History of the Jews of Brazil." *AVOTAYNU* 4, no. 3, (Fall 1988): 19.

———. "Books on Jewish Tombstone Inscriptions in Brazilian Cemeteries." *AVOTAYNU* 4, no. 3 (Fall 1988): 19.

———. *Dicionario Biografico: 1500–1800. AVOTAYNU* 5, no. 3 (Fall 1989): 23.

———. "Crypto Jews in the State of Pará." *AVOTAYNU* 6, no. 1 (Spring 1990): 29.

———. "Sources of Genealogical Records." *AVOTAYNU* 6, no. 3 (Fall 1990): 20.

———. "Famous Jewish Brazilian Families. *AVOTAYNU* 6, no. 4 (Winter 1990): 50.

———. "Jews, Judaizers and Their Slaves." *AVOTAYNU* 7, no. 1 (Winter 1991): 20.

———. "Additional Books by Egon and Frieda Wolff." *AVOTAYNU* 7, no. 3 (Fall 1991): 28.

———. *Dicionario Biografico—Volume 4. AVOTAYNU* 7, no. 4 (Winter 1991): 58.

———. "Memorial to Two Jews Buried in Vassouras." *AVOTAYNU* 8, no. 4 (Winter 1992): 53.

———. "Jews in the Amazonian Rain Forest." *AVOTAYNU* 9, no. 1 (Spring 1993): 35.

———. "Books Available on Brazilian Jewish History." *AVOTAYNU* 9, no. 3 (Fall 1993): 47.

———. "Jews and Marranos in Northern Brazil." *AVOTAYNU* 9, no. 4 (Winter 1993): 48.

———. "'Jewish Priest'" of Caico." *AVOTAYNU* 9, no. 4 (Winter 1993): 49.

———. "The Amzalak Family History." *AVOTAYNU* 10, no. 1 (Spring 1994): 43.

———. "Jewish Migration Pattern." *AVOTAYNU* 10, no. 4 (Winter 1994): 62.

———. "Using Inquisition Records." *AVOTAYNU* 10, no. 4 (Winter 1994): 62.

———. "Jews in the Amazon." *AVOTAYNU* 11, no. 2 (Summer 1995): 47.

———. "Bentes Family of Brazil." *AVOTAYNU* 11, no. 2 (Summer 1995): 47.

———. "Jewish Memorial Opens in Vassouras, Brazil." *AVOTAYNU* 11, no. 3 (Fall 1995): 63.

———. "Early Jewish Presence in Brazil." *AVOTAYNU* 13, no. 3 (Fall 1995): 49.

Dória, Franciso Antonia. *Os Heredeiros do Poder* (The power brokers). [Portuguese]. Rio de Janeiro: Revan, 1995.

Franca, Eduardo D'Oliveira and Sonia A. Siqueira. *Segunda Visitacao do Santo Oficio as Partes do Brasil* (Second visit of the Holy Office to the territory of Brazil). [Portuguese]

Gonsalves de Mello, José Antonio. *Gente da Nacao* (Our people's nation). [Portuguese] Recife: Massangana, 1990.

Jewish Travelers Guide. London: *Jewish Chronicle*, 2002.

Malcolm Stern's *First American Jewish Families.* Cincinnati: American Jewish Archives, 1978.

Novinsky, Anita. *Cristaos Novos na Bahia* (New Christians in Bahia). [Portguese] São Paulo: Universidade de São Paulo and Editora Perspectiva, 1970; 2nd. ed., 1992.

Rheingantz, Carlos G. *Primeiras Familias de Rio de Janeiro (Secuilos XVI e XVII)* (First families of Rio de Janeiro). [Portuguese] Rio de Janeiro: Livraria Brasileira Ediera, 1965.

Salvador, J.G. *Cristaos-novos, Jesuitas e Inquisicao* (New Christians, Jesuits and the Inquistion). [Portuguese] São Paulo: Livraria Pioneira Editora, 1969.

Southey, Robert. *History of Brazil.* New York: Burt Franklin, 1971.

Wolff, Egon, and Frieda Wolff. *Dicionário Biográfico: Genealogias Judaicas* (Biographical dictionary: Jewish genealogies). [Portuguese] Rio de Janeiro: Instituto Historico e Geográfico Brasileiro, 1990.

———. *Dicionário Biográfico I: Judaizantes e Judeau no Brasil 1500–1808* (Biographical Dictionary I: Jews and Judaizers in Brazil). [Portuguese] Rio de Janeiro: Instituto Histórico e Geográfico Brasileiro, 1986.

———. *Dicionário Biográfico: Processos de Naturalizacao de Israelitas: Século XIX* (Biographical Dictionary: 19th century Jewish naturalization records). [Portuguese] Rio de Janeiro: Instituto Histórico e Geografico Brasileiro, 1987.

———. *Documentos V* (Documents V). [Portuguese] Rio de Janeiro: Instituto Histórico e Geografico Brasileiro, 1993/1994.

———. *Sepulturas de Israelitas* (Jewish tombstones). [Portuguese] São Paulo: Centro de Estudos Judaicos, 1976.

———. *Sepulturas Israelitas II* (Jewish tombstones II). [Portuguese] Rio de Janeiro: Cemitério Comunal Israelita do Rio de Janeiro, 1983.

———. *Sepulturas Israelitas III: As Mishpakhot de Belem* (Jewish tombstones III: Families of Belem). [Portuguese] Rio de Janeiro: Instituto Histórico e Geográfico Brasileiro, 1987.

———. *Genealogia Carioca* (Rio de Janeiro genealogy). [Portuguese] Rio de Janeiro: Colégio Brasileiro de Genealogia, 1990.

———. *Guia Histórica-Sentimental Judaico Carioca* (Historical/ Sentimental Guide to the Jews of Rio de Janeiro). [English and Portuguese] Rio de Janeiro: Instituto Histórico e Geografico Brasileiro, 1987.

Note

1. The *Jornal do Brasil* and *O Globo* from Rio de Janeiro and *Folha de São Paulo* and *O Estado* probably can be found in such large libraries as the U.S. Library of Congress. Usually, however, they only print death notices. See also *Jornal do Commercio* in the National Library in Rio and the *Rio News*.

Bulgaria

by Mathilde A. Tagger

Jews have lived in Bulgaria since the second century of the Common Era as shown by graves from that time excavated from Bulgarian archeological sites. Most were Romaniote Jews, observers of the Byzantine rite who read the Torah in its original Hebrew and translated it into Greek. They were joined by Bavarian and Hungarian Jews during the 14th century; both groups were totally absorbed into the masses of newcomers from Spain following the Expulsion Edict of 1492. From then on, Judeo-Spanish was the language of all Bulgarian Jews.

Bulgaria was incorporated into the Ottoman Empire in 1396 and gained independence in 1878, after which equal rights were given to all minorities, including the Jews. Many Russian and Romanian Ashkenazi Jews emigrated to Bulgaria at the turn of the 20th century. They joined the Jewish community and lived in perfect harmony within it.

After the publication of Herzl's *The Jewish State* in 1896, the Zionist movement in Bulgaria developed quickly and assumed a major place in Jewish life there. Bulgaria became unique among Jewish communities. Instead of extremist religious belief, as experienced in many other parts of the Diaspora, Bulgarian Jews preserved a Jewish national feeling, reflected in all the branches of the community's public activities. All the Jewish institutions were headed by democratically elected Zionists.

Bulgaria allied itself with Nazi Germany in 1941, as a result of which some anti-Semitic laws were passed by the Parliament. In April 1943, Bulgaria acquired Thrace and Macedonia. Nearly 12,000 Jews from these provinces were immediately deported to their death in Auschwitz. Many members of Parliament and Orthodox Church leaders protested the deportation of the Jews and managed to stop it, but as a compromise, the 25,000 Jews of Sofia were expelled from their homes and sent to live in small localities.

King Boris III died suddenly in August 1943. Italy had been occupied by the Allied Forces, and Soviet troops were on their way to the Bulgarian frontiers. As a result of this political situation, the government softened its attitude towards the Jews. Bulgaria was occupied by the Russian army on September 9, 1944, and a communist regime was installed immediately. Nevertheless, in September-October 1948 the government allowed the Jews of Bulgaria the opportunity to leave the country and settle in Israel on two conditions: loss of Bulgarian nationality and forfeiture of all their property. Approximately 45,000 Jews left Bulgaria between October 1948 and May 1949. The 6,000 who remained were primarily from Sofia. Most were intermarried families, families with a very ill member and/or fervent communists.

The arrival in Israel of all social classes of this community, intellectuals as well as small merchants, is one of the major reasons that the process of their integration into their new homeland was fast and complete.

Genealogical Resources in Israel

The Central Archives for the History of the Jewish People in Jerusalem* holds microfilmed group passports of the immigrants who arrived in Israel from all Jewish-Bulgarian communities between October 1948 and May 1949. Unfortunately, the lists are not arranged alphabetically and some pages are illegible.

Each group passport lists 300 to 500 people. For each individual one can find the surname name, given name, birth place and date. A photograph and the signature of the head of the family often can be found as well. The archives also has lists of immigrant surnames by ship. The ship lists of vessels that carried the immigrants from the ports of Varna and Burgas to Israel include the number of passengers for each ship, the number of group passports and the number of persons on each group passport.

In addition to the records that document nearly 45,000 immigrants from all over the country, the Central Archives has records from a number of communities as shown in Figure 1.

The Diaspora Research Institute at Tel Aviv University* holds the results of a 1990–94 project that collected photographs and documentation on Bulgarian Jewish archives, cemeteries, institutions, religious objects, neighborhoods, private and public libraries and synagogues. Project personnel made a systematic photographic record of the archives of Jewish communities kept in the State Archives in Sofia. The collection includes the archives of all the Jewish communities from the 16th century until 1960, except those of Ruse and Vidin, two provincial towns. Additional material was photographed in provincial archives and in the archives of the Jewish communities of Macedonia.

Some Holocaust-era material held by the State Archives in Sofia and filmed by the U.S. Holocaust Memorial Museum* and at the U.S. National Archives, Archives II* facility, has been described by Yitzhak Kerem.

Bulgarian Newspaper

A Bulgarian-language daily newspaper, *Izraelski Far*, or just *Far*, as it was best known, began publishing in 1949. In 1955, it changed its name to *Tribuna Izraelski Far*. The publication became a weekly in April 1982, but ceased publication in January 1998. One may find many obituaries, often with photographs. The newspaper may be found in the library of the Ben Zvi Institute* and in the Jewish National and University Library,* both in Jerusalem.

Benjamin Arditti has written or edited several major books about Bulgarian Jews. One, *Vidni evrei v Bulgaria* (Well-known Jews in Bulgaria), includes 124 biographies for 89 different persons (some women) who played a role in the Jewish communities. Covers approximately 1850–1970. Mainly Sephardic Jews, but some Ashkenazi. Some photo-

Town	Period	Description	Rec. Group
Kiustendil	1912–18	952 Jewish victims of war	HM2/7893
Pazardjik	1897–1922	Birth of males	HM2/8230
Pazardjik	1921–40	Birth and marriage	HM2/8223-27
Pazardjik	1942–45	Jews deported to Chepelare from Pazardjik	HM2/8234.6
Pazardjik	1943	Family cards	HM2/8231-32
Pazardjik	1943–44	List of Sofia Jews deported to Pazardjik	HM2/8229
Pazardjik	1945–42	Marriage certificates	HM2/8234.2
Pleven	1944	Family cards of the community; some deported from Sofia	HM2/7869.3
Plovdiv	1949	Immigrants from Plovdiv to Israel	HM2/7852.5
Ruse	1829–1952	Death register	HM2/7875.1
Ruse	1912–13	Birth certificates	HM2/7870.2
Ruse	1912–13	Jewish soldiers and marriages	HM2/7870.4
Ruse	1914–46	List of graves	HM2/7880.6
Sofia	1949	Jews remaining in Sofia after last departure in 1949	HM2/7845.14
Varna	1885	Jews killed in Bulgarian wars	HM2/7859.4
Varna	1912–18	Jews killed in Bulgarian wars	HM2/7859.4
Varna	1932–44	Poor Jews	HM2/7858.5
Varna	1935–39	Teachers' biographies	HM2/7867.14

Figure 1. Bulgarian records at the Central Archives for the History of the Jewish People

graphs. The biographies were written by different persons including the editor. Articles are classified in alphabetic order renewed in each volume. Some include onomastic analysis.

All of Arditti's articles end with bibliographical notes. This compilation is a very good genealogical source especially when one is aware of the fact that Bulgarian Jews, like Russian Jews, use patronymics; that is, their father's name follows the given name. Surnames included are: Adroke, Aftaliyon, Aladjem, Alfasa, Alkalay, Almosnino, Alshekh, Arditti, Arie, Arueti, Asseo, Asher, Assa, Azaria, Aziel, Bakish, Bali, Barukh, Bassan, Bashmutski, Behar, Belkovsky, Ben Shushan, Benmayor, Bentsion, Benun, Benyamin, Berakha, Bidjirano, Daniel, Dankovits, Davidov, Erenprays, Eshkenazi, Farkhi, Gabe, Geron, Graciani, Haimov, Hananel, Herbst, Isakov, Israel, Kalev, Kalmi, Kamerman, Kaneti, Katalan, Khezkiya, Koen, Kordoba, Koso, Krispin, Levi, Menahemov, Meshulam, Mevorakh, Mezan, Miko, Mushonov, Navon, Nitsani, Ovadia, Pardo, Pasken, Perets, Pipo, Piti, Rabiner, Rimalovski, Romano, Rozanes, Ruetel, Semo, Shats, Shekerdjiyski, Shishedji, Sidi, Surudjon, Tadjer, Tsadikov, Ventura, Yasharov, Yosef, Yosifof and Zilbershtain.

Arditti's book, *Yehudei Bularia-Kehilat Shumla* (Jews of the Bulgaria-Shumen community), has four chapters that deal with the history of the community from the beginning of the 18th century till 1948, when the massive *aliyah* to Israel began. The last chapter consists of alphabetically arranged biographies of individuals well known in the community. Includes list of family names current in Shumen, with their origins and meanings; 60 Sephardic names and five Ashkenazi; a list of 54 teachers at the local Jewish school; biographies of the nine Shumen Jews who earned a diploma from the Ecole Normale Orientale de Paris of Alliance Israélite Universelle; chronological list of 28 Jewish soldiers from Shumen killed

during the Bulgarian wars (1912–18) and soldiers killed during the Israel War of Independence in 1948.

Records Access

Most of the archival material of the Sofia Jewish community was burned by the community itself before Jews were deported from the capital during World War II. Death registers for Sofia, however, are held both in the synagogue and in the Jewish Plot Office of the Municipal Cemetery. The records cover a period of at least 100 years; the first registration date is unknown.

In the municipal government administration, vital records exist from 1878, the year Bulgaria became independent. For Sofia, which included half of the Jewish population in 1948, these records are kept in *Rayonen Obshtinski Savet* (municipal district councils). It is not possible to obtain copies of birth, marriage or death certificates by mail. One must go in person to request the record, but an attorney or a notary holding a proxy in proper form can be delegated this task. Some Israeli attorneys who were born in Bulgaria and can read and write the language handle such matters. Small fees are required for each certificate. Since the only language spoken in these offices is Bulgarian, someone who does not speak the language must bring a translator.

The Shalom Organization of the Jews of Bulgaria has published its *Annual* (formerly: *Godishnik*) since 1966. The annual includes many biographies. The full collection of the *Annual* is held at both the Ben Zvi Library* and the Jewish National and University Library.*

LDS (Mormon) Microfilms

The Mormons have microfilms of civil registration for the districts of Sofia and Pazardzhik that begin in 1893.

Internet

For links to Internet sites for Bulgarina genealogical research, go to MAXPAGES.COM/POLAND/BALKAN_RESEARCH. There is a Bulgarian genealogical discussion group at GENFORUM. GENEALOGY.COM/BULGARIA.

Addresses

Ben Zvi Institute, P.O. Box 7600/7504, Rehavia, Jerusalem, Israel 91076

Central Archives for the History of the Jewish People, P.O. Box 1149, 91010 Jerusalem, Israel

Diaspora Research Institute, Humanities Faculty, Tel Aviv University, Ramat Aviv, Israel; telephone: 972-3-640-9462; 640-9799; fax: 972-3-640-7287; e-mail: DIASPORA@POST.TAU.AC.IL

Jewish National and University Library, P.O. Box 503, Givat Ram Campus Hebrew University, Jerusalem, Israel 91004

Bibliography

Arditti, Benjamin. *Yehudei Bulgaria bishnot ha-mishtar ha-natsi: 1940–1944* (Bulgarian Jews under the Nazi regime 1940–1944). [Hebrew] Tel Aviv: 1962. First historical and well-documented analysis of the miraculous salvation of the Bulgarian Jews during World War II. Large bibliography and detailed index.

Arditti, Benjamin, ed. *Vidni evrei v Bulgaria* (Well-known Jews in Bulgaria). [Bulgarian] Tel Aviv: 1969–72. 4 vols.

Arditti, Benjamin. *Yehudei Bulgaria—Kehilat Shumla.* (Jews of the Bulgaria—Shumen community). [Hebrew] Tel Aviv: 1969.

"Bulgaria." *Encyclopedia Judaica.* Jerusalem: Keter, 1972. Lists rabbis and scholars.

Chary, Frederick B. *The Bulgarian Jews and the Final Solution, 1940–1944.* Pittsburgh: University of Pittsburgh Press, 1972.

Gruenwald, Mordechai. *Algo di la istoriya di la comunidad israelita di Vidin* (History of the Jewish community of Vidin). [Judéo-Spanish, Rashi letters] Sofia: 1894. Includes chronological list of chief rabbis of the community and alphabetical list (by first name, father's first name and family name) of the 442 Jewish males inhabitants in 1894.

Ilel, Joseph, "The Participation of the Bulgarian Jews in the Wars of 1885, 1912–1913 and 1915–1918," In *Social, Cultural and Educational Association of the Jews in the People's Republic of Bulgaria Annual*, Vol.XXII, 1987: 121–176. This article contains the list of the 954 Bulgarian Jews who perished in the wars of 1912–1913 and 1915–1918. For each individual it includes the year of birth, the military unit and the date of death.

Kasheles, Haim. *Korot Yehudei Bulgaria* (History of the Jews of Bulgaria). [Hebrew] Tel Aviv: Dvir, 1971. 5 vols. In vol. 5: List of the Jewish periodicals in Bulgaria.

Kerem, Yitzchak. "Documentation on Sephardic and Balkan Jewry at the U.S. Holocaust Memorial Museum and the U.S. National Archives." *AVOTAYNU* 15, no. 4 (Winter 1999): 20–22.

Moskona, Isak M. "Za proizkhoda na familinite imena na belgarskite evrei." *Obshtestvena kulturno prosvetna organizatsiya na evreite v narodna republika Bulgariya* (On the origin of the family names of the Bulgarian Jews in Educational and Cultural Organization of the Jews in the Popular Republic of Bulgaria). [Bulgarian] Annual 1 (1967), 111–37. Onomastic analysis, including the towns where specific names were current.

Pinkas Kehilot (Encyclopedia of Jewish Communities) Vol. 10: Bulgaria. [Hebrew] Jerusalem: Yad Vashem, 1967. Includes many names and photographs, an index and detailed bibliography.

"Project for Research of Turkish and Balkan Jewry." *Report for 2000/2001, Diaspora Research Institute.* Ramat Aviv: Tel Avi University, 2002.

Rosanes, Salomon A. *Istoriya di la komunidad yisraelita di Rushtchuk.* (History of the Jewish community of Roustchouk). [Judeo-Spanish, Rashi letters] Rustchuk: 1914. History begins in 968. No index. The text includes many biographies, alphabetical lists of families residing in the town 1800–10 and 214 Jewish male inhabitants in 1852/53.

Tadjer, Abram. *Notas istoricas sovri los djudios di Bulgaria* (Historical notes on the Jews of Bulgaria). [Judeo-Spanish, Rashi letters] Sofia: 1932. Includes many biographies of leaders in various Jewish communities.

Tagger, Mathilde. "Les Juifs bulgares pendant la seconde guerre mondiale" (Jews of Bulgaria during World War II). [French] *Revue du Cercle de Généalogie Juive*, 13: 51 (1997). Family names borne by the 163 Bulgarian Jews who were deported from France, based on Serge Klarsfeld's *Mémorial de la Déportation de Juifs de France*. Includes birth places of these Jews.

Tamir, Vicki. *Bulgaria and Her Jews: The History of a Dubious Symbiosis.* New York: Sepher-Hermon Press for Yeshiva University Press, 1979. The most comprehensive and scientific study on the subject. The index has hundreds of names. Large bibliography.

Canada

by Lawrence Tapper

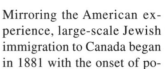

On July 1, 1867, under the terms of the British North American Act, the four British North American colonies of Prince Edward Island, Nova Scotia, New Brunswick and the Province of Canada (divided into two new provinces of Ontario and Quebec) entered into confederation to become the Dominion of Canada. Until the Canadian legislature passed the Citizenship Act of 1947 which created a separate Canadian nationality, Canadians were still British subjects, and, prior to 1947, immigrants were naturalized as British subjects.

Canada's ten provinces, three northern territories and the year in which they joined the Confederation are as follows. The Atlantic provinces are Newfoundland (1949), Nova Scotia (1867), Prince Edward Island (1867) and New Brunswick (1867); Ontario (1867) and Quebec (1867) comprise central Canada. The Prairie provinces are Manitoba (1870), Saskatchewan (1905), and Alberta (1905). British Columbia (1871) is the westernmost province. The territories are Nunavut (1999), Yukon (1898), and Northwest Territories (1870). Canada is the world's second largest country and has a population of 31 million. The three levels of government are federal, provincial or territorial, and municipal.

Jews have lived openly in Canada since the days of the British conquest of New France in 1759. From its founding in 1605, Jews, Catholics and other Nonconformists were not officially permitted to live in New France although evidence reveals that several individuals did so illegally. Those Jews who were discovered either were deported or forced to convert to Roman Catholicism. For a history of Jewish presence in New France, see *Les Juifs et la Nouvelle-France*, by Denis Vaugeois. By the mid-18th century, North America had become a battleground between the French and the English. The loss of New France was confirmed in the Treaty of Paris in 1763. Jews, however, moved in before the treaty was signed and ratified.

The David, Franks, Hart, Jacobs and Joseph families were among the first Jews to settle in Canada. Some like Aaron Hart came with the British forces as traders and suppliers and, as non-Catholics, were treated by the British colonial administration as loyal English settlers. They became landholders, married, raised families, engaged in business, served as minor office holders, and were active in the French-Canadian communities where they lived. By 1768, Montreal had sufficient Jews to form the Congregation of Spanish and Portuguese Jews, *Shearith Israel*. The community flourished and, by 1832, Jews achieved full civil and political emancipation. A second Ashkenazi congregation, *Shaar Hashomayim*, formed in 1846.

By 1881, Canada had a well-established, viable Jewish community of 2,443 persons living mostly in Ontario and Quebec. The community remained small, static and cohesive until the great wave of Eastern European immigration began.

Mirroring the American experience, large-scale Jewish immigration to Canada began in 1881 with the onset of pogroms and state-sponsored anti-Semitic discrimination in countries such as czarist Russia and Romania.

By 1896, colonization of the Canadian northwest with agricultural immigrants from the United States, Britain and Continental Europe had became an instrument of national policy. Although most Jewish immigrants did not come to Canada to farm, they, too, benefitted from this relatively open-door policy. A substantial number of Jewish immigrants did farm in the provinces of Alberta, Manitoba and Saskatchewan from the 1880s until the 1930s, when most lost their farms to the Great Depression and the drought of the 1930s.

Between 1900 and 1921, Jewish immigration was largely unrestricted. Except for a brief hiatus during World War I, Jewish migration from Eastern Europe continued unabated until the early 1920s, when the Canadian government enacted legislation limiting Jewish immigration; in the 1930s, the doors closed.

According to Louis Rosenberg in his pioneering 1939 demographic study, *Canada's Jews: A Social and Economic Study of the Jews in Canada*, the net increase in Jewish population by immigration between 1900 and 1931 was approximately 116,000. The Jewish population had climbed to more than 157,000 according to the 1931 census. The tragic history of Canada's treatment of Jewish refugees is described in *None is Too Many: Canada and the Jews of Europe 1933–1948*, by Irving Abella and Harold Troper. Not until 1947, when immigration controls were relaxed, were Jewish refugees admitted to Canada to work in the needle trades in meaningful numbers.

To this day, Canada continues to be a preferred destination for Jewish immigrants. Canada's Jewish population has grown steadily over the decades and, by some estimates, now stands at almost 400,000. To learn more about Canadian immigration policy, consult *The Making of the Mosaic: A History of Canadian Immigration Policy*, by Ninette Kelly and Michael Trebilcock. Researchers should also see the Pier 21 website www.PIER21.CA. Located in Halifax, Pier 21 was a major immigration port of entry through which more than one million immigrants passed between 1928 and 1971.

Sources of Genealogical Information

Six major sources of genealogical material and information exist in Canada. These are: documentation in the National Archives of Canada* and the National Library of Canada;* records held in various federal government departments; information in provincial archives; vital statistics records; data in various Jewish archives, synagogues and organizations; and the Jewish genealogical societies in Canada.

Record keeping and management of archival resources in Canada are similar to those processes in the United States. At the federal level, the National Archives of Canada* exists to serve the government of Canada and to acquire and preserve nationally significant records from the private sector. Provincial archives exist in every province and territory and are listed below. Municipal archives exist in all urban centers. Universities and other institutions have numerous specialized archives. For a detailed list of all Canadian repositories that hold archival records, visit *Canadian Archival Resources* on the Internet at WWW.USASK.CA/ARCHIVES/MENU.HTML.

Accessibility to material and quality of service provided to researchers by Canadian archival repositories varies widely and is largely dependent on the size and resources of each institution. Most have well-developed websites. Some facilities provide detailed reference service by telephone, e-mail and regular mail. Some of the smaller archives, however, managed by volunteers, cannot provide the same high level of service. Visitors are welcome, but it is important to check hours of operation beforehand.

Library and Archives of Canada
(formerly the National Archives of Canada and the National Library of Canada)

In October 2002, the federal government announced its intention to merge the administration and operations of the National Archives of Canada* (NA) and the National Library of Canada* (NL), both located in Ottawa, to create the new Library and Archives of Canada. Both institutions have significant collections of interest to genealogists who will benefit by getting help from one centralized reference service center.

National Archives. The National Archives of Canada,* WWW.ARCHIVES.CA, preserves passenger lists (1865–1935), border entry records (1908–35), federal census records from 1851, federal voters lists since 1935, military personnel records, the Russian consular records (1898–1922) and a rich collection of Jewish community records. These records are fully described on the Genealogy Research page at the National Archives* and in its publication, *Tracing Your Ancestors in Canada.* Another publication, *Archival Sources for the Study of Canadian Jewry,* lists 150 Jewish collections found at the National Archives.* Both are available from them free of charge. The latter publication contains outdated information on the National Archives* archival holdings, but has a useful bibliography of historical works on Jewish life in Canada, as well as a select list of history theses up to 1987.

National Library. The National Library of Canada,* WWW.NLC-BNC.CA, preserves published material about Canada. It has the most complete collection of reference resources, telephone and city directories, community or local histories, government publications and many current Jewish and Canadian daily newspapers. Many are available on microfilm and circulate on interlibrary loan. The library has the most complete collection of city directories published in Canada.

The earliest directory is a microfilm copy of the 1790 directory for Quebec City. The collection is housed in the National Library Reference Room; its original directories do not circulate on interlibrary loan. The Canadian Institute for Historical Microreproductions* (CIHM) has made microfiche copies of many pre-1900 city, county and provincial directories. They are available in many libraries and also may be purchased directly from CIHM.

The National Library* has 20,000 published local and community histories that may be borrowed on interlibrary loan. Its government publications include the *Canada Gazette* and the Canadian Parliamentary *Sessional Papers.* The NL has a complete set of Canadian telephone directories on microfiche. To locate the address and telephone number of a person living in Canada, go to CANADA411@SYMPATICO.CA.

Two separate databases compiled by *La Societé de Généalogie de Quebec* may be used only in the reference room. The first consists of Quebec marriages 1926–96; the second contains deaths 1926–96. The search page is written in French, but librarians will assist researchers.

The Canadian Genealogy Centre (WWW.CGCCCG.ARCHIVES.CA) is an initiative of the National Archives,* the National Library,* the federal government's Department of Canadian Heritage,* and partners in the genealogical community. Its goal is to provide Canadian genealogical resources on the Internet at one central site. It expects to go online in 2003.

Records Held in Governmental Departments

The second source for genealogical information consists of record groups still kept by various federal government departments that have not transferred them yet to the custody of National Archives.* These departments include Citizenship and Immigration Canada,* which controls the records of immigrants arriving at Canadian ports since January 1, 1936, as well as records of naturalization and citizenship dating back to 1854, and Statistics Canada,* which retains control of the 1940 National Registration census.

Provincial Archival Repositories

Canada's ten provincial archival repositories are responsible for acquiring and preserving provincial government records, including education, health, labor, the judicial system, vital records usually more than 100 years old, as well as some private collections of Jewish organizations, synagogues and individuals. In most provinces, the same types of records are found in different repositories. For example, in some provinces, judicial records such as court, land titles and estate records are kept by the provincial court system and the provincial archival repository. Most provincial archives and libraries also have valuable collections of city directories, newspapers, periodicals, and regional and local histories for their provinces.

Vital Statistics Records

The most important source for personal information is vital records. Birth, marriage and death records less than 90 years old are kept by provincial ministries of health. Older records are usually transferred to provincial archival repositories and often are incomplete. The civil registration of vital data is collected and administered solely by the provinces, except for Quebec where religious institutions collected the information and submitted it to the province. Record keeping in the provinces began in the late 1800s. Jewish immigrants commonly did not register events with civil authorities. For details about obtaining civil registration records from provincial and territorial ministries see *Tracing Your Ancestors in Canada* and visit WWW.ARCHIVES.CA or WWW.GENEALOGY.COM.

Material in Jewish Organizations

A large body of material is found in Jewish community-sponsored archives, historical societies and synagogues. Here one finds records of *landsmanshaftn*, free loan and sick benefit societies, synagogues, personal papers of individuals, as well as oral histories and photographs. The largest repositories with valuable genealogical holdings are the Canadian Jewish Congress National Archives and Reference Centre* in Montreal (WWW.CJC.CA); the Ontario Jewish Archives* in Toronto (WWW.FEDUJA.ORG/PUZZLED/INFOHIGH/ARCHIVES.STM; the Winnipeg-based Jewish Heritage Centre of Western Canada* (WWW.JHCWC.MB.CA) and the Jewish Public Library of Montreal* (WWW.JEWISHPUBLICLIBRARY.ORG).

The Canadian Jewish Congress National Archives holdings in Montreal include the United Jewish Relief Agencies of Canada case files, United Restitution Organization claim files, Jewish Colonization Association, Jewish Immigrant Aid Services of Canada case files, CJC War Efforts Committee military personnel case files, Harry Hershman War Orphan files of 1921, Hebrew Sick Benefit Association membership and burial plot information files 1892–1989 and the Montreal Baron de Hirsch burial register.

The Ontario Jewish Archives (OJA) in Toronto has oral histories, Jewish directories, synagogue and cemetery records, marriage registers and photographs from Toronto and other Ontario Jewish communities. The OJA also has JIAS Canada Central Region case files from the 1930s to the 1980s. The Jewish Heritage Centre of Western Canada holds the records of the Winnipeg Jewish Community Council, and the Jewish Public Library in Montreal has the most comprehensive collection of books, periodicals and other published materials about Jews in Canada as well as a large collection of *yizkor* (memorial) books.

Jewish Genealogical Societies

The six Jewish genealogical societies in Canada are a major source of genealogical information and support. Societies exist in Calgary, Montreal, Ottawa, Toronto, Vancouver and Winnipeg. Most have created excellent genealogical reference libraries and websites, hold research meetings and host guest speakers. Many have undertaken research projects and created information databases. The Jewish Genealogy Society of Montreal* (JGSM) has indexed the Rabbi Colton *mohel* (ritual circumcision) diaries and all of the Jewish vital records of Quebec (1847–1942) in the Drouin microfilm collection held at the main branch of the Montreal Municipal Library. The surname list is available online at the JGSM website (WWW.GTRDATA. COM/JGS-MONTREAL).

The Jewish Genealogical Society of Ottawa (WWW.JGSO.ORG) conceived and fund a project to digitize Canadian naturalization records for the years 1915–32 from the Canadian Sessional Papers. Working with the JGSM which scanned and provided indices for the naturalization database, the two societies agreed to have the database hosted by the Canadian Genealogy Centre's* website. JGSO has digitally scanned and indexed approximately 55,000 headstones in several Jewish cemeteries in Ukraine including the main Jewish cemetery in Chernivtsi, Ukraine. The society has funded the *Keneder Odler* obituary index created by the Canadian Jewish Congress National Archives.*

The Jewish Genealogical Society of Canada (Toronto)* has created a database of all 14,000 headstones at Roselawn Cemetery.* It publishes the newsletter *Shem Tov* and has hosted two IAJGS annual conferences on Jewish genealogy. The Jewish Genealogical Society of Southern Alberta* has its Calgary Cemetery Project Database and publishes a biannual newsletter *Shorashim*.

For a current list of all Canadian Jewish genealogy societies' addresses and telephone numbers, visit WWW. JEWISHGEN.ORG/IAJGS/AJGS-JGSS.HTML.

Overall, the best sources of information for genealogists are found in the following categories of records: records of entry to Canada and border crossing records, military records, civil and legal status records, Jewish community records, cemeteries, funeral homes and *chevrot kadisha* (burial societies), federal censuses at the National Archives,* orphanage records, domicile records and published sources.

Records of Entry to Canada

One of the most popular sources for genealogists at the National Archives of Canada* is the passenger arrival record group. These records consist of microfilmed copies of passenger manifests and border entry lists from 1865 to 1935. The archives has records for every Canadian port of entry. The resources most often consulted by Jewish genealogists are the arrival lists for the port of Quebec City from 1865 to 1935; Halifax, Nova Scotia, from 1881 to 1935; Saint John, New Brunswick, from 1900 to 1935; and Vancouver, British Columbia, from 1905 to 1935. For a detailed description of these records, visit the Immigration Records page found under "Genealogy" at the National Archives* website WWW. ARCHIVES.CA.

Immigration has always been a federal government responsibility in Canada. It has been controlled by various federal departments since Confederation. The Department of Citizenship and Immigration was created in 1950. Prior to 1908, persons were able to move freely across the international boundary between Canada and the United States, and the Canadian government did not document immigrant arrivals over the U.S. border before that time. Beginning in 1908, border ports were established along the international boundary,* and records of crossings were made. The National Archives* has border entry records from 1908 to 1935, but those from 1908 to 1918 are not indexed; indexes exist to records created between 1918 and 1935. The Montreal Municipal Library*

Jewish immigrant family from Russia in 1911. Courtesy of National Archives of Canada.

holds a microfilm copy of the St. Alban's border crossing (to the U.S.) records.

Microfilmed individual immigration forms (Form 30A) for immigrant arrivals were used by the Department of Immigration and Colonization between 1919 and 1924. They are arranged in quasi-alphabetical order. Passenger lists of ships arriving via New York from 1906 to 1931 and other eastern American ports from 1905 to 1928 are in the archives as well. The U.S. lists identify the names of only those passengers who stated their intention to proceed directly to Canada, but no nominal record of emigrants from Canada to the United States was kept.

Approximately 187,000 Jews entered Canada between 1900 and 1931 via ocean ports or across the American border; more than 68,000 passed through Canada en route to the United States during the same period. Most Jewish immigrants landed at Quebec City or Halifax or came via U.S. ports. The original manifests held by the National Archives* were destroyed long ago; only the microfilm copy is available for consultation. The manifests include the name, age, occupation and intended destination of passengers. No index to the lists from 1870 to May 1921 exists, so unless a researcher knows a passenger's name at time of arrival, the exact date and port of arrival and the ship's name, this research could be similar to seeking the proverbial needle in a haystack and is best deferred until more information has been obtained.

The microfilm is difficult to read. Names of persons entered on the manifests by ships' pursers sometimes are illegible or so faint that they can barely be read. To speed up research, visually scan the column designated for racial origin on each page frame for the words "Jewish" or "Jews" and ignore the rest of the names. Generally, Jews are grouped together under steerage or third class because that is how almost all of them traveled to Canada.

For further information about accessing ship manifests, researchers should write to the Canadian Genealogy Centre of the National Archives and National Library,* supplying as much information as possible. Staff will not do individual research but will provide an appropriate microfilm reel number

and will recommend that it be borrowed on international interlibrary loan. The National Archives* imposes no charge for interlibrary loan or reference service. Those without Internet access can request a copy of *Tracing Your Ancestors in Canada.*

For arrivals after January 1, 1936, Canadian citizens or residents must submit an *Access to Information Request Form* together with a CAN$5.00 fee to the Department of Citizenship and Immigration Canada.* Proof must be supplied that the person whose data is sought is dead. Under Canadian privacy laws, only a Canadian citizen or resident may apply for an arrival record. Foreigners must ask a Canadian to apply on their behalf; the JGS in Toronto* and other cities are prepared to help.

The Canadian Jewish Congress National Archives* (www. CJC.CA./ARCHIVES) also has some arrival information for the years 1921–81 in the form of case files from the Jewish Immigrant Aid Services of Canada* (JIAS) collection. JIAS (WWW.JIAS.ORG) has assisted Jewish settlement in Canada since the organization's founding in 1922. It also holds colonist case files and records of the Jewish Colonization Association of Canada (JCA) and case files of refugees, war orphans and German-Jewish internees helped by the United Jewish Relief Agencies of Canada (UJRAC). Inventories describing these collections and alphabetical indexes are available on the Canadian Jewish Congress website. Experienced researchers who find a JIAS record usually compare the information contained in it with the matching official record of entry from the Department of Citizenship and Immigration and the naturalization record for corroborating information and anomalies.

The JIAS collection has two key series for genealogists, those of the migration records series, which holds case files of persons and families JIAS helped to settle in Canada, and the citizenship and naturalization case files series of individuals whom JIAS helped to obtain citizenship. The UJRAC records can be especially valuable to genealogists seeking information about interned Jewish refugees, war orphans, refugee skilled laborers and other Holocaust survivors, who came to Canada before, during and after World War II. For further information about these collections, contact the Canadian Jewish Congress National Archives.*

Case files of JIAS Central Division,* which is based in Toronto, date from 1935 and are arranged alphabetically. Interested researchers should write directly to JIAS* in Toronto. The JIAS-Western Division records form part of the Jewish Heritage Centre of Western Canada's* (JHCWC) archival holdings. They consist of alphabetical lists of immigrant case files for the years 1923 to 1950. The National Archives* has a microfilm copy of these records and a corresponding finding aid (#955). For access, contact the JHCWC.

Two useful collections at the National Archives* complement the JIAS and UJRAC records. The first is the records of the Canadian National Committee on Refugees (call number MG 28, V 43). From 1938 to 1948, the Committee fought for the legal admission of Jews and other refugees who were interned in Canada. Of particular interest are the case files of European refugees who entered Canada. The second collection, Jewish Family Services of the Baron de Hirsch Institute of Montreal (call number MG 28, V 86), has the post-war Refugee Youth Programme case and subject files from 1947 to 1952.

Colonization records assume great importance to those whose ancestors homesteaded in the Canadian prairie provinces of Alberta, Manitoba and Saskatchewan. Valuable information about these pioneers may be found in several collections, including the JCA of Canada records (1884–1978) at the Canadian Jewish Congress Archives* and the JCA London office records on microfilm at the National Archives.*

The JCA was established by railroad magnate Baron Maurice de Hirsch of Paris, in 1891. The JCA's goal was to promote the large-scale emigration of persecuted Eastern European and Russian Jews to North and South America and to resettle them on farm colonies primarily in western Canada and later in southern Ontario and Quebec. The Canadian Committee of the JCA was established in 1906. Before the JCA became involved, some farm colonies already had been founded by the Young Men's Hebrew Benevolent Society of Montreal and its successors. Records exist for the period until the JCA ceased operations in the late 1970s. Some of the more valuable series found in this fond include prepaid travel and arrival lists of Jewish refugees coming to Canada 1906–26 and subject and colonist case files from 1904. For access, apply to the Canadian Jewish Congress Archives.*

The National Archives* has microfilmed records of the JCA's Canadian operations for the period 1891–1919. They were obtained from the JCA's international headquarters in London, England. The National Archives call number for its JCA microfilm is MG 28, V 83, reels A-935 to A-939, and the collection is available on interlibrary loan. The JCA London office records have been transferred to the Central Archives for the History of the Jewish People* in Jerusalem (see ISRAEL). The Canadian JCA microfilm chronicles the cooperation between the JCA and its forerunner agencies, the Young Men's Hebrew Benevolent Society of Montreal and the Baron de Hirsch Institute, in their attempts to promote Jewish colonization.

The National Archives* also preserves on microfilm the personal papers of Louis Rosenberg, Canadian Jewry's leading demographer. Early in his career Rosenberg served as the Western Canadian director of the JCA, based in Winnipeg from 1919 until 1940. The Rosenberg Papers include much valuable data on Jewish farmers plus information about the founding and operation of many Jewish farm colonies in western and eastern Canada. The call number for this collection is MG 30, C 119, and the finding aid number is 966.

Note should be made of the records of the Imperial Russian consulates known as the LI-RA-MA collection (MG 30, E 406), which operated in the Canadian cities of Halifax, Montreal and Vancouver between 1898 and 1922. The consulates dealt with some 11,400 former subjects of the Russian Empire resident in Canada at that time. Most of the case files were created for men of draft age during World War I. Approximately 2,462 names have been identified as Jewish. Priceless genealogical information found in the Passport/Identity Papers series. This series has been microfilmed and is available on interlibrary loan. Most of the contents of the case files are in Cyrillic. A copy of the microfilm is available from the LDS (Mormon) Family History Library (see LDS). The finding aid #1411 is available on microfilm reel M-7591.

Below is the list of the Passport/Identity Papers Series nominal card index found on the genealogy page at the National Archives of Canada* website (WWW.ARCHIVES.CA).

Reel No.	First Entry/Last Entry
H-1971	Aaltonen, Kalle Emil/Glinskii, Egor Nikolaev
H-1972	Glinksy, George/Labluk
H-1973	Labon, Sergei Stepanov/Popofsky, Moses
H-1974	Potsokhoto/Vishniak
H-1975	Vishtak, Avtonom Iakovlevich/Zywic

After consulting the index reel and identifying the relevant file, researchers can obtain that file by searching the shelf list at the LI-RA-MA page on the National Archives* website and then borrowing it through interlibrary loan. The case files are found on reels M-7620 to M-8271.

Military Records

Canada's Jews have served in every military conflict from the Conquest to the Rebellion of 1837–38, the Fenian Raids in 1870, the Riel Rebellion, the South African War, the two Great

Teferis Israel School and Synagogue at the Litpon colony in Saskatchewan. The colony was founded in 1901 by Jews from Romania. Courtesy of National Archives of Canada.

Wars and Korea. The National Archives* has an online index at its website WWW.ARCHIVES.CA of 600,000 Canadians who enlisted in the Canadian Expeditionary Force (CEF) during World War I, including members of the Jewish Reinforcement Draft Company, Montreal, and a Jewish section of the Third Battalion (Queen's Own Rifles of Toronto). More than 5,000 Jews served in the CEF. About 300 transferred to the Jewish Legion when it was established in 1917 to fight under General Sir Edmund Allenby's British army which liberated Palestine from the Ottoman Empire in December of that year. The National Archives also has the personal chaplaincy records of Rabbi Samuel Cass (MG 30, D225). H/Major Cass served with the First Canadian Army and at Canadian Military Headquarters, London 1942–46. He succeeded Rabbi S. Gershon Levi as Senior Jewish Chaplain. See *Breaking New Ground: The Struggle for a Jewish Chaplaincy in Canada*. Rabbi Levi's papers are kept by the Canadian Jewish Congress National Archives.* For biographies of Jewish casualties and decorations in World War II, see *Canada's Jews in World War II*. For information about veterans, contact the Jewish War Veterans of Canada* which maintains posts in cities across the country or the following branches of the Royal Canadian Legion: Brigadier General Frederick Kisch Branch #97 in Montreal, General Wingate Branch #256 in Toronto, Maccabee Branch #343 in Hamilton, Balfour Branch #362 in Windsor, General Monash Branch #115 in Winnipeg and Shalom Branch #178 in Vancouver. The Baron de Hirsch cemetery, de la Savane, Montreal has a memorial to deceased members of the Kisch Branch.

Civil and Legal Status Records

In the category of records of personal status are citizenship, civil registration and vital records, and census returns. Also in this category are the vital records of the Jewish community through its communal institutions, synagogues and clergy.

Canadian citizenship and naturalization records created between 1854 and 1917 were destroyed in the Parliamentary fire in Ottawa in 1917. The Department of Citizenship and Immigration* still controls the card index to these and subsequent records, but these records provide only limited genealogical information. Included for each person are present and former place of residence, former nationality, occupation, date of certification, and name and location of the court responsible for granting the naturalization. More detailed records created after 1917 are also kept by the Department of Citizenship and Immigration.* They include such information as date and place of birth, date of entry into Canada, occupation, place of residence and names of family members. The records are organized alphabetically by surname and date of birth. For an ordinary search, knowledge of the full name and at least approximate (or exact) date of birth is needed. To discover if a person was naturalized, consult the Canadian Naturalization Records Index on the Canadian Genealogy Centre's* website.

Because of restricted access to information and privacy laws, only a Canadian citizen or resident of Canada can apply for and obtain copies of naturalization and citizenship records. Non-Canadians should arrange for a Canadian citizen to apply for a record on their behalf. Canadians must complete an *Access to Information Request Form* and submit it together with a Canadian $5.00 fee to Citizenship and Immigration Canada.* The form can be obtained from most Canadian public libraries and federal government offices and is online at INFOSOURCE.GC.CA under Access to Information and Privacy, Request Forms, ATIP-Access to Information, ATIP-Access to Information, Form Number TBC 350-57.

The date of arrival of a naturalized citizen in Canada may be estimated from the date of the person's naturalization. Before 1917 and after 1977, a three-year residence was required before citizenship could be granted. Between these dates, a five-year residence was required.

As mentioned above, the official recording of vital information is solely a provincial responsibility. Civil registration records of recent vintage are kept by the provincial and territorial offices of vital statistics. Earlier records are usually transferred to provincial archives.

In Nova Scotia, birth and death records before 1908 and marriage records prior to 1907 are held by Nova Scotia Archives and Records Management.* Records created afterwards are held by the Vital Statistics, Department of Business and Consumer Services.* In the case of New Brunswick, births from 1886–1905, and marriage and death records 1888–1950 are held by the Provincial Archives of New Brunswick and thereafter with the Vital Statistics Office, Health and Community Services.* Ontario's vital records (births 1869–1905, marriages 1801 (predominately 1835–1918 and deaths 1869–1930) are at the Archives of Ontario. For subsequent records, contact the Office of the Ontario Registrar General.* On the other hand, Manitoba's vital records have not been transferred to the Provincial Archives of Manitoba. Manitoba's Vital Statistics* retains control of all of its vital records created after 1882 while Saskatchewan's start in 1895. Alberta's records from 1898–1905 are with the Provincial Archives of Alberta. Thereafter, they are with Alberta Registries.* For British Columbia, researchers should visit the British Columbia Archives website WWW.SEARCH.BCARCHIVES. GOV.BC.CA. Indexes are online for birth registrations, 1872–99; death registrations 1872–1979 and marriage registrations 1872–1924. In Quebec, pre-1900 records are kept in the regional offices of the Archives nationales du Quebec. Post-1900 records are with the Ministere de la Justice, Direction de l'Etat Civil (Department of Civil Status).* The best source for information about Quebec's Jewish vital record keeping and practices and the Drouin Genealogical Institute microfilms of Quebec vital records is found in the *AVOTAYNU* article "Indexing the Jewish Vital Records of Quebec, 1841–1942"[1] or at the Jewish Genealogical Society of Montreal's website WWW.GTRDATA.COM/JGS-MONTREAL. See also Stanley Diamond's InfoFile "Jewish Vital Records Research in Montreal (Quebec)" at WWW.JEWISHGEN.ORG/INFOFILES/#CANADA.

Researchers should be aware of several rules and procedures when filing genealogy applications with provincial authorities. For example, none of these agencies conduct speculative searches where the required identifying information is not provided, and searches are done only as time permits. Requesters must state their relationship to the person whose record is to be searched. For privacy reasons, information about a living person is released only to that person or upon that person's authorization. Proof of death is required in the case of deceased persons. A fee is always charged. Applications must indicate clearly that the information requested is for genealogical purposes. Supply as much accurate information about the event in question as possible. In general, searches of up to three consecutive calendar years will be performed, if required, for an additional fee.

Jewish Community Records

Considerable vital information is found in Canada's Jewish communities. This includes many genealogically useful records of Jewish religious events that are not part of the government record, such as *brit milah* (ritual circumcision), the naming of baby girls, *bar* and *bat mitzvahs*, confirmations, conversions, Jewish marriages, divorces, deaths and *yahrzeit* notices, all of which are usually found in synagogues. Jewish death records also are found in funeral chapels in major cities with large Jewish populations. In some cases, Jewish vital records have been deposited with local community archives. No central repository for these records exists, and no systematic effort has been made to acquire them.

In larger Jewish communities, genealogists should contact Jewish historical and genealogical societies or community archives for help, or they can contact the synagogues directly. The quickest way to find a synagogue in Canada is to visit the Canadian Jewish Congress'* synagogue directory list on its website www.cjc.ca or by contacting CJC offices across Canada. Many synagogues perform a limited amount of reference work for individuals using their own records. Many historical and genealogical societies are under-funded and are staffed by volunteers. Donations are always appreciated. Researchers also can contact local Jewish community centers for help; most have websites.

Records in Ottawa, Vancouver and Winnipeg. Here are three examples of what might be found in the medium-sized Jewish communities of Ottawa, Winnipeg and Vancouver. Some synagogues in Ottawa have donated their records to the Ottawa Jewish Historical Society,* while others have not. The Society also preserves records of the Ottawa Talmud Torah that date from 1932 and the local community paper, the *Ottawa Jewish Bulletin*, from 1937. The National Archives* has the private papers of the Reverend Joseph Rabin (MG30-D 198), including his personal circumcision and marriage registers from 1919 to 1968, and the personal papers of Rabbi Reuven Bulka (MG31-F 14), one of Canada's prominent Orthodox rabbis.

In Calgary, the Historical Society of Southern Alberta* maintains a variety of genealogical useful material from the Jewish community of Southern Alberta. Its holdings include a local Jewish press collection, the Harry and Martha Cohen Library, an oral history collection, the JHSSA photograph collection. The Jewish cemeteries file which consists of photographs of every headstone in the five Jewish cemeteries of Southern Alberta, and an obituaries file started in 1994. It

publishes *Discovery* three times a year and has published a history book *Land of Promise: The Jewish Experience in Southern Alberta* Calgary, 1996.

In Vancouver, records are kept by the synagogues themselves. The Jewish Historical Society of British Columbia* has a family histories collection. It also has custody of the records of the Canadian Jewish Congress, Pacific Region, the Canadian Zionist Federation, Canadian Hadassah-WIZO and other communal organizations. The Jewish Genealogical Institute of British Columbia's large genealogical reference collection is located in the Isaac Waldman Jewish Public Library.* To learn more about life in British Columbia's largest Jewish community, visit the Jewish Federation of Greater Vancouver website at www.jfgv.com. A useful history is *Pioneers, Peddlers and Prayer Shawl: The Jewish Communities in British Columbia and the Yukon.*

In Winnipeg, the Jewish Heritage Centre of Western Canada* and its Jewish Genealogical Institute should be contacted first. The Centre has custody of the archival collections of the Jewish Historical Society of Western Canada as well as a large reference library of materials about Jewish life on the Prairies. Its computer database contains more than 18,000 genealogical references extracted from local Jewish newspapers dating back to the early 1900s. Visit its website www.jhcwc.mb.ca for the best guide to doing genealogical research in the Canadian Midwest. Winnipeg's synagogues, including the two largest, *Shaarey Zedek* and *Rosh Pina*, maintain their own vital records. All synagogues answer genealogical inquiries. For a list of Winnipeg synagogues visit the Jewish Federation of Winnipeg website www. jewishwinnipeg.org. In the 1990s, the National Archives* and the Provincial Archives of Manitoba (PAM)* microfilmed *Shaarey Zedek*'s original birth, marriage and death records 1907–73. Microfilm copies are available at the National Archives,* Provincial Archives of Manitoba* and the Canadian Jewish Congress.*

Cemeteries, Funeral Homes and Chevrot Kadisha. For a comprehensive listing of all Jewish cemeteries in Canada, visit The International Association of Jewish Genealogical Societies Cemetery Project at www.jewishgen.org/cemetery/northamerica.

Funeral Homes and *Chevrot Kadisha.*The microfilmed records of Toronto's Steeles-College Memorial Chapel are available at the National Archives* (call number MG28-V 141). The records consist of Statement of Death forms and related invoices for deceased persons for 1949 and for 1951 to 1975. No formal records were kept for this nonprofit, community-run chapel before 1949. The records are arranged alphabetically. Each form lists the name of the deceased; dates and places of birth, death and burial; age, occupation, civil status and last residence; next of kin; names and birthplaces of parents.

Records of Benjamin's Park Memorial Chapel of Toronto (MG28-V 140), Toronto's oldest and largest funeral home, consist of two parts. First is the seven original record books kept by founder Joseph Benjamin from 1930 to 1980 (finding aid number 1450). Each book provides the following information on deceased individuals: date of death, *yahrzeit* date (anniversary of Jewish date of death), cemetery section, name of cemetery. The second part of the collection consists of a file card index of deceased persons arranged alphabetically for the years 1936 to 1945 and 1954 to 1976 (vols. 1–21). Records are arranged chronologically for the years 1946 to 1957 (vols. 21–24). The cards provide additional information about the deceased supplementing that found in the record books. The collection also includes an alphabetical list of synagogues and societies and their affiliated cemeteries. Benjamin's Park Memorial Chapel* has a computerized index of all its clients, beginning in the mid-1980s, and answers telephone inquiries. For records of events prior to the mid-1980s, they prefer that researchers contact the National Archives.*

Ottawa has two Jewish cemeteries, the Jewish Community Cemetery on Bank Street and the new one in Herbert's Corners, Osgoode Township. The Jewish Genealogical Society of Ottawa* is digitally scanning and indexing the headstones in both cemeteries. The Ottawa Chevra Kadisha is located at the Jewish Community Memorial Chapel, 1771 Cuba Ave. Its records are kept by the Ottawa Jewish Archives.*

For information about the five Jewish cemeteries in Winnipeg and elsewhere in the province of Manitoba, researchers should visit the Genealogical Institute of the Jewish Heritage Centre of Western Canada at the Jewish Genealogical Institute's website WWW.JHCWC.MB.CA/GENINST.HTM. The four operational cemeteries are *B'nai Abraham, Beth Israel, Rosh Pina* and *Shaarey Zedek* The oldest, the Children of Israel Cemetery 1883–1933, is closed. The Institute's Cemetery Photography Project contains more than 15,000 photographs of headstones from eight Jewish cemeteries in the province. For access to the collection, contact the Jewish Historical Society of Western Canada.* The National Archives* has a microfilm copy of the *Chesed Shel Emes* Chapel's directory of all Jewish burials in Winnipeg from 1946 to 1969 (MG28-V 153, microfilm reel number M-7752). The Chapel, located at 1023 Main Street, R2W 3P9, phone: (204) 582-5088; was established in 1930. The microfilm provides the names of the deceased, the dates of death and burial, and the cemetery of interment. The entries, written in English and Hebrew, are arranged alphabetically and chronologically.

In Montreal, the largest and oldest Jewish funeral chapel is Paperman and Sons Inc.* (WWW.PAPERMAN.COM). Its burial permits date back to 1913 and are computerized. *Beth Olam Levayah**, which served the francophone Sephardic community from December 1997, closed in 2001. *Chesed Shel Emes**, 935 Beaumont, Montreal H3N 1W3, phone: (514) 273-3211; serves the haredi community. The Canadian Jewish Congress Archives* has membership and death records of Montreal's Hebrew Sick Benefit Association from its founding in 1892. Both the Baron de Hirsch Cemetery, 5015 de la Savane, Montreal H4P 1V1, phone: (514) 735-4696; and the Back River Cemetery records have been digitized. The first burial in the Baron de Hirsch cemetery occurred in 1904. Its burial register is kept at the office and a duplicate is at the Canadian Jewish Congress National Archives.* The Back River Cemetery is Montreal's oldest Jewish cemetery. Its first recorded burial took place in 1889. Now known as the Back River Memorial Gardens Cem-

etery Inc., it is fully being restored by Montreal's community umbrella organization, Federation CJA. For further information, contact Park Maintenance Corporation,* 7700 Route Transcanadienne, Montreal, Quebec, H4T 1A5, phone: (514) 738-5356; Park Maintenance Corporation has burial indexes for Back River Memorial Gardens; Kahal Israel Memorial Park* 4189 Sources Rd., Dollard Des Ormeaux H9B 2A6, phone: (514) 684-3441; and Eternal Gardens* 33 Elm Ave., Beaconsfield H3Y 2P4, phone: (514) 695-1751. The *Shaar Hashomayim* Congregation, phone: (514) 937-9471; the Spanish and Portuguese Congregation-Shearith Israel, (514) 737-3695; and Temple Emanu-El Beth Shalom, (514) 937-3575; all have their cemeteries on Mount Royal. Paperman's and all of Montreal's Jewish cemeteries welcome written and telephone inquiries.

For information about the six cemeteries in British Columbia, five of which are in the greater Vancouver area, contact the Jewish Genealogical Institute of British Columbia.* It has a list of burials in the Temple Emanuel Cemetery (established 1859) in Victoria. See the Institute's publication, *B.C. Jewish Cemeteries: Lower Mainland and Victoria.* Richmond B.C.: B.C. Genealogical Society, 1993.

Censuses at the National Archives

Canada has taken a national census every ten years since the mid-1800s, but because large-scale Jewish immigration to Canada did not begin until 1881, only the 1881, 1891 and 1901 censuses are of interest to most Jewish genealogists. (The 1911 census opens in 2003.) These unindexed census returns list each person individually and include details of age, gender, country or province of birth, religion, racial origin, occupation, marital status, education and physical disabilities, where applicable. The 1881 census has been indexed and may be found at the Family History Library website, WWW.FAMILYSEARCH.ORG (see LDS).

To find a microfilm reel number, consult the current edition of the checklist of Canadian census returns, *Catalogue of Census Returns on Microfilm, 1666–1891* and the *Catalogue of Census Returns on Microfilm, 1901*. They include all major census returns for Canada available on microfilm at the National Archives of Canada.* Published by the National Archives,* it is available at most public libraries and should be online in the near future. A useful strategy to locate the record of a Jewish person living in Canada is first to consult the index "Jewish Residents in Canadian Censuses," produced by Glen Eker and available on microfiche from Avotaynu*. For example, if an individual is found in Eker's list for the 1891 Montreal census, locate the corresponding microfilm reel for Montreal by consulting the *Catalogue of Census Returns on Microfilm*. The census microfilm circulates on interlibrary loan. The 1901 census has been digitized and is online at the National Archives* website but has not been indexed by name.

The 1906 census taken in Manitoba, Saskatchewan and Alberta is available on the National Archives website WWW.ARCHIVES.CA. The 1911 census is currently not unavailable for genealogical research purposes. Only individuals named in his or her record can have access, but only for pension,

Jewish market day on Kensington Avenue in Toronto, 1924. Courtesy of Metropolitan Toronto Reference Library.

citizenship and passport purposes. A legal representative of a deceased person can obtain access, but only to settle the affairs of that person's estate. The record can be obtained from Statistics Canada* under the Access to Information Act.

While many of the post-1911 censuses that are particularly useful for Jewish genealogists are closed, researchers can still access the 1940 National Registration Records maintained by Statistics Canada.* These records contain detailed personal information relating to all persons 16 years of age or older. Excluded from the enumeration were all serving members of the armed forces and children under the age of 16. The information was originally obtained under the authority of government legislation to mobilize the nation's war effort. To gain access for genealogical purposes, the 1940 records may be accessed under the Access to Information Act in those cases where the individual in question has been deceased for more than 20 years and proof of death is provided. An individual enumerated in 1940 may access his or her own record. To obtain a transcript, download an electronic version of the Access to Information Request Form TBC 350-57 from the INFOSOURCE.GC.CA website and forward the completed inquiry with fee to Statistics Canada.*

Orphanage Records

The National Archives* holds Jewish orphanage records from homes that operated in Winnipeg and Montreal. The records and case files of the Montreal Hebrew Orphans Home from 1924 to 1940 are found in the Jewish Family Services of the Baron de Hirsch Institute collection (MG28-V 86). Minutes of the various committees of the Jewish Children's Home and Aid Society of Western Canada from 1937 to 1950 are found in the Harry Walsh Collection (MG 30, E 255).

Growing up in the Winnipeg orphanage is the subject of the personal memoirs of Rabbi Reuben Slonim in his book, *Grand To Be An Orphan.* Considerable research material and correspondence about the orphanage are included in his personal papers (MG31-F 7).

Domicile Records and Published Sources

While they usually provide only minimal information, domicile records can help pinpoint the exact whereabouts of a person. Several useful sources worth consulting are such items as voters lists prepared for federal and provincial elections. The National Archives* has the federal lists for election years since 1935. Municipal government offices or their archives usually preserve assessment rolls, while land titles and homestead patents are usually kept by provincial archives. In order to file a patent to a homestead, it was necessary to show proof of citizenship. Citizenship documents often are included in homestead files. Homestead records are found in provincial land record offices and in the Department of Interior fonds Dominion Lands Branch series and its sub-series at the National Archives of Canada.* The Department of the Interior administered the Dominion Lands Act by which many Jewish immigrant homesteaders obtained patents to 160 acres of free land.

Membership records of Jewish organizations and agencies with which many Jews were affiliated can be useful. For example, in the collections of B'nai Brith Canada, Jewish National Fund and Hadassah-WIZO Organization of Canada at the National Archives* are numerous membership lists that provide names and addresses. The Toronto *landsmanshaftn* records which are preserved in the Ontario Jewish Archives* fall into this category as well.

Published materials, including Canadian-Jewish newspapers and genealogical reference works, should be consulted. They contain valuable sources of genealogical information including birth, confirmation, *bar* and *bat mitzvah*, marriage announcements and death notices and obituaries. Many are unindexed and available on microfilm. They usually are found in both Jewish and public libraries in cities with organized Jewish communities. The National Library of Canada* has an extensive collection. Jewish genealogical societies in Toronto, Montreal, Ottawa, Toronto and Winnipeg maintain specialized reference libraries. The largest and best known Jewish library in Canada is the Jewish Public Library of Montreal* (JPL)* (WWW.JEWISHPUBLICLIBRARY.ORG), with more than 125,000 books in five languages, including the largest collection of Canadian Judaica in Canada. The JPL Special Collections department preserves one of the most significant collections of *yizkor* books in Canada. The JPL's catalogue is online.

For a history of the Jewish press in Canada, researchers should consult Lewis Levendel's *A Century of the Canadian Jewish Press: 1880s–1980s.* The JPL has a complete microfilm run of *Der Keneder Adler* (Canadian Jewish Eagle), published in Montreal 1907–80. The Jewish Genealogical Society of Ottawa* and the Canadian Jewish Congress Archives* has produced an indexed database of obituaries for the early years from this Yiddish-language daily. The project was funded by the Jewish Genealogy Society of Ottawa.* The Jewish Historical Society of Western Canada* has created a computer database of personal information extracted from the pages of *The Jewish Post* and the *Israelite Press* and is preparing an index of the *Western Jewish News.* The National Library of Canada* has runs of many Anglo-Jewish newspapers and periodicals including the *Jewish Times* 1897–1909, the *Canadian Jewish*

Times 1909–14, the *Canadian Jewish Chronicle* 1914–66, and the *Canadian Jewish Review* 1922–66.

Some of the major Jewish biographical works include *The Jew in Canada: A Complete Record of Canadian Jewry from the Days of the French Regime to the Present Time*, by Arthur Daniel Hart; *Canadian Jewry: Prominent Jews of Canada. A History of Canadian Jewry Especially of the Present Time Through Reviews and Biographical Sketches*, by Zvi Cohen; *Who's Who in Canadian Jewry*, by Eli Gottesman, as well as the 1969 and 1976 editions of *Family Who's Who* published by the Hebrew University of Jerusalem. Consult *A Biographical Dictionary of Canadian Jewry 1909 to 1914* (Tapper) and its electronic companion for the years 1897 to 1909 on the Ancestry website (WWW.ANCESTRY.COM) for the earlier period. They are indexes of vital information extracted from the pages of *The Jewish Times* and its successor, *The Canadian Jewish Times*, which was published in Montreal. They chronicle the lives of many of Canada's founding Jewish families.

The two most definitive history books about Jews in Canada were written by Gerald Tulchinsky. They are: *Taking Root: The Origins of the Canadian Jewish Community* and *Branching Out: The Transformation of the Canadian Jewish Community*. The best bibliographical reference work is *Jews and Judaism in Canada: A Bibliography of Works Published Since 1965*, Canadian Jewish Studies, Special Issue, 1999–2000.

Addresses

Alberta Registries, Vital Statistics, Box 2023, Edmonton, Alberta T5J 3W7; website: WWW.GOV.AB.CA/GS/SERVICES/VPE/INDEX.CFM/.

Avotaynu, 155 North Washington Ave, Bergenfield, New Jersey 07621; telephone: (201) 387-7200; website: WWW.AVOTAYNU.COM.

Benjamin's Park Memorial Chapel, 2401 Steeles Avenue West, Toronto, Ontario; telephone: (800) 579-9060; website: WWW.BENJAMINS.CA/DEFAULT.HTM.

Beth Olam Levayah, 8255 Bougainville, Montreal, Quebec, Canada H4P 2T3; telephone: (514) 736-8888.

British Columbia Vital Statistics Agency, P.O. Box 9657, Stn. Prov. Govt., Victoria, British Columbia V8W 9P3; website: WWW.VS.GOV.BC.CA/.

Canadian Genealogy Centre, 395 Wellington Street, Ottawa, Ontario K1A 0N3; WWW.GENEALOGY.GC.CA.

Canadian Heritage, 25 Eddy Street, Hull, Quebec K1A OM5; telephone: (819) 997-0055.

Canadian Jewish Congress, 1590 Avenue Docteur Penfield, Montreal, Quebec, H3G IC5; telephone: (514) 931-7531; website: WWW.CJC.CA.

Central Archives for the History of the Jewish People, P.O. Box 1149, Jerusalem 91010, Israel; telephone: +++ 972-2-563-5716.

Chesed Shel Emes, 935 Beaumont, Montreal, Quebec H3N 1W3.

Department of Citizenship and Immigration Canada, Public Rights Administration, 365 Laurier Street, 15th Floor, Ottawa K1A 1L1, Canada.

Isaac Waldman Jewish Public Library, Jewish Community Centre, 950 West 41st. Street, Vancouver, British Columbia V5E 2N7.

Jewish Community Memorial Chapel, 1771 Cuba Ave., Ottawa K1G 1L7; telephone: (613) 526-9192.

Jewish Genealogical Institute of British Columbia, #206-950 West 41st Avenue, Vancouver, British Columbia V5Z 2N7.

Jewish Genealogical Society of Canada (Toronto), P.O. Box 446 Station A, Willowdale, Ontario M2N 5T1.

Jewish Genealogical Society of Montreal, 5599 Edgemore Avenue, Montreal, Quebec H4W 1V4; WWW.GTRDATA.COM/JGS-MONTRAL/.

Jewish Genealogical Society of Ottawa, c/o Jewish Community Library, Soloway Jewish Community Centre, 21 Nadolny Sachs Private, Ottawa, Ontario K2A 1R9; WWW.JGSO.ORG.

Jewish Genealogical Society of Southern Alberta, 1607–90 Avenue SW, Calgary, Alberta T2V 4V7.

Jewish Heritage Centre of Western Canada, C116-123 Doncaster Street, Winnipeg, R3N 2B2; telephone (204) 477-7465; WWW.JHCWC.ORG/.

Jewish Historical Society of British Columbia, Jewish Community Centre, 950 West 41st Street, Vancouver, British Columbia V5Z 2N7; telephone: (604) 257-5199.

Jewish Historical Society of Western Canada, C116-123 Doncaster Street, Winnipeg, Manitoba R3N 2B2.

Jewish Public Library of Montreal, 1 Carre Cummings Square, Montreal, Quebec, H3W 1M6, telephone: (514) 345-2627; website: WWW.JEWISHPUBLICLIBRARY.ORG.

JIAS Central Division, 4600 Bathurst Street, Suite 325, Toronto, Ontario, M2R 3V3.

Manitoba Office of Vital Statistics, Consumer and Corporate Affairs, 254 Portage Avenue, Winnipeg, Manitoba R3B OB6; telephone: (800) 282-8069, extension 3781; e-mail: WITABLSTATS@GOV.MB.CA.

National Archives of Canada, 395 Wellington Street, Ottawa, Ontario K1A 0N3; telephone: (toll free in Canada and USA) (866) 587-7777; website: WWW.ARCHIVES.CA.

National Library of Canada, 395 Wellington Street, Ottawa, Ontario K1A ON3.

Ontario Jewish Archives, 4600 Bathurst Street, Toronto, Ontario, M2R 3V2; telephone: (416) 635-2883; website: WWW.FEDUJA.ORG/PUZZLED/INFOHIGH/ARCHIVES.STM.

Ottawa Jewish Historical Society, Soloway Jewish Community Centre, 21 Nadolny Sachs Private, Ottawa, Ontario, K2A 1R9; telephone: (613) 798-4696, extension 260.

Paperman and Sons, 3888 Jean Talon Street West, Montreal, Quebec, H3R 2G8, telephone: (514) 733-7101; website: WWW.PAPERMAN.COM.

Roselawn Lambton Cemetery Association, 61 Alness S. @218, Toronto, Ontario M3J 2H2.

Saskatchewan Vital Statistics Unit, Department of Health, 1942 Hamilton Street, Regina, Saskatchewan S4P 3V7.

Statistics Canada, Access to Information and Privacy Office, 25B R.H. Coats Building, Tunney's Pasture, Ottawa, KlA 0T6.

Vital Statistics, Department of Business and Consumer Services, P.O. Box 157, Halifax, Nova Scotia B3J 2M9.

Vital Statistics Office, Health and Community Services, P.O. Box 6000, Fredericton, New Brunswick E3B 5H1.

Provincial Archives Addresses

Provincial Archives of Newfoundland and Labrador; Colonial Building, Military Road, St. John's NF A1C 2C9; telephone: (709) 729-3065; website: WWW.GOV.NF.CA/-PANL.

Nova Scotia Archives and Records Management, 6016 University Avenue, Halifax, NS B3H 1W4; telephone: (902) 424-6060; website: WWW.GOV.NS.CA/NSARM/.

Public Archives and Records Office (Prince Edward Island), P.O. Box 1000, Charlottetown PE C1A 7M4; telephone: 902 368-4290; website: WWW2.GOV.PE.CA/EDUC/ARCHIVES/ARCHIVES_INDEX. ASP.

Provincial Archives of New Brunswick, P.O. Box 6000, Fredericton NB E3B 5H1; telephone: (506) 453-2122; website: WWW.GNB.CA/ARCHIVES.

Archives nationales du Quebec (Western Quebec); Direction des Archives nationales de l'Ouest du Quebec; 535, avenue Viger est; Montreal QC H2L 2P3; telephone: (514) 873-6000.

Archives nationales du Quebec (Eastern Quebec), Direction des Archives nationales de l'Est du Quebec 1210, avenue du Séminaire C.P. 10450, Sainte-Foy QC G1V 4N1; telephone: (418) 643-8904; e-mail: WWW.ANQ.GOUV.GC.CA.

Archives of Ontario, 77 Grenville Street, Unit 300, Toronto ON M5S 1B3; telephone: (416) 327-1600 or (800) 668-9933 (Ontario Only); website: WWW.ARCHIVES.GOV.ON.CA.

Provincial Archives of Manitoba; 200 Vaughan Street; Winnipeg MB R3C 1T5; telephone: (204) 945-3971 or 945-3972; website: WWW.GOV.MB.CA/CHC/ARCHIVES.INDEX.HTML.

Saskatchewan Archives Board, Regina Office: University of Regina, Regina SK S4S 4A2; telephone: 306-787-4068

Saskatoon Office: University of Saskatchewan, Murray Building, 3 Campus Drive, Saskatoon SK S7N 5A4; website: WWW.SASKARCHIVES.COM

Provincial Archives of Alberta, 12845-102 Avenue, Edmonton AB T5N 0M6, telephone: 780-427-1750; website: WWW.CD.GOV.AB.CA/PRESERVING/INDEX.ASP.

British Columbia Archives, 655 Belleville Street, Victoria BC V8V 1X4, telephone: 250-387-1952; website: WWW.BCARCHIVES.GOV.BC.CA

Yukon Archives, P.O. Box 2703, Whitehorse YT Y1A 2C6; telephone: 867-667-5321; website: WWW.GOV.YK.CA/DEPTS/EDUCATION/LIBARCH/YUKARCH.HTML.

Archives of the Northwest Territories, c/o Prince of Wales Northern Heritage Centre; P.O. Box 1320; Yellowknife NT X1A 2L9; telephone: 403-873-7698; website: WWW.PWNHC.LEARNNET.NT.CA/.

Nunavut Archives; P.O. Box 310; Igloolik NU X0A 0H0; telephone: (867) 934-8626; e-mail: EATKINSON@GOV.NU.CA.

Bibliography

Abella, Irving and Harold Troper. *None is Too Many: Canada and the Jews of Europe 1938–1948*. Toronto: Lester and Orpen Dennys, 1982.

Brown, Michael, et al. *Jews and Judaism in Canada: A Bibliography of Works Published Since 1965*. Toronto: Canadian Jewish Studies, 2000.

Canada Gazette. The official newspapers of the government of Canada, published since 1841.

Cohen, Zvi. *Canadian Jewry: Prominent Jews of Canada. A History of Canadian Jewry Especially of the Present Time Through Reviews and Biographical Sketches*. Toronto: Canadian Jewish Historical Publishing Co., 1933.

Diamond, Stanley and Ruth Diamond. "Indexing the Jewish Vital Records of Quebec 1841–1942." *AVOTAYNU* 18, no. 2 (Summer 2002).

Godfrey, Sheldon J. and Judith C. Godfrey. *Search Our the Land: The Jews and Growth of Equality in British Colonial America, 1740–1867*. Montreal and Kingston: McGill-Queen's University Press, 1995.

Gottesman, Eli. *Who's Who in Canadian Jewry*. Ottawa: Canadian Jewish Literary Foundation, 1965.

Hart, Arthur Daniel. *The Jew in Canada: A Complete Record of Canadian Jewry from the Days of the French Regime to the Present Time*. Toronto and Montreal: Jewish Publications Ltd., 1926.

Kelly, Ninette and Michael Trebilcock. *The Making of the Mosaic: A History of Canadian Immigration Policy*. Toronto: University of Toronto Press, 1998.

Leonoff, Cyril. *Pioneers, Peddler and Prayer Shawls: The Jewish communities in British Columbia and the Yukon*. Victoria: Sono Nis, 1978.

Levendel, Lewis. *A Century of the Canadian Jewish Press: 1880s–1980s*. Ottawa: Borealis, 1989.

Rosenberg, Louis. *Canada's Jews: A Social and Economic Study of the Jews in Canada*. Montreal: Canadian Jewish Congress, 1939.

Slonim, Harry. *Grand to be an Orphan*. Toronto and Vancouver: Clarke, Irwin, 1983.

Tapper, Lawrence. *A Biographical Dictionary of Canadian Jewry*. Teaneck, N.J.: Avotaynu, 1992.

Tulchinsky, Gerald. *Branching Out: The Transformation of the Canadian Jewish Community*. Toronto: Lester, 1998.

———.*Taking Root: The Origins of the Canadian Jewish Community*. Toronto: Lester, 1992.

Notes

1. Diamond, Stanley and Ruth Diamond. "Indexing the Jewish Vital Records of Quebec 1841–1942." *AVOTAYNU* 18, no. 2 (Summer 2002).

Caribbean Basin

by Irene Saunders Goldstein

Researchers with roots in Denmark, France, Germany, Great Britain, The Netherlands, Portugal, Spain, Turkey, other European countries, and even North America, may be surprised to find traces of family members whose paths took them to the Caribbean. This chapter presents a patchwork-quilt compilation of historical and genealogical information about the Jewish communities of the Caribbean.

Following a synopsis of Caribbean Jewish history and a list of general genealogical resources available to Caribbean researchers, country-specific discussions are presented in sections on Aruba, the Bahamas, Barbados, Costa Rica, Cuba, Curaçao, Dominican Republic, French Guyana, Guadeloupe, Haiti, Jamaica, Martinique, Nevis, Panama, Puerto Rico, St. Eustatius, Suriname (formerly Surinam), and the U.S. Virgin Islands (St. Croix and St. Thomas).

Difficulties inherent in genealogical research in the Caribbean area include changing jurisdictions (records typically are held separately by the country that ruled a nation or territory for a particular time period, and many localities experienced a succession of rulers); records that are disorganized, restricted or inaccessible, and/or water-logged, destroyed, or missing; and the fact that researchers may not be available onsite.

The lists of repositories and references presented in this chapter, although not encyclopedic, offer the reader a flavor of the rich resources available. Special emphasis has been placed on compiling histories and resources with Jewish content. Addresses of all repositories and institutions mentioned are listed at the end of this chapter.

Caribbean Jewish History

In the 16th and 17th centuries, eager to escape the dangers and persecutions of the Inquisition (see INQUISITION RECORDS), significant numbers of Spanish and Portuguese Jews and conversos followed the burgeoning, lucrative trade routes from Europe to seek refuge and to make a fresh start in the New World. Jews flourished in the Brazilian city of Recife for a quarter century following the 1630 Dutch ouster of the Portuguese until the 1654 Portuguese reconquest of the territory. Most of the 150 Recife Jewish families departed with the Dutch, the majority to Amsterdam. A small group—captured by pirates on their way to Holland, rescued by a French warship and then abandoned in the Caribbean—made its way to North America to become the first Jews in New Amsterdam (later New York). Some of the Recife families settled in the Caribbean, where European Jews had begun to arrive from Europe in the 1620s and 1630s. Jewish communities were established by the 1660s in Suriname (then Dutch Guyana) in South America, Barbados, Curaçao, Jamaica and the Virgin Islands. Jews also settled in Dutch Brazil, Guadeloupe, Haiti, Martinique, Nevis and Tobago.

The early history of the Jews of the Caribbean Basin influenced the early history of the United States. In a review of Malcolm Stern's *First American Jewish Families,* Eli Faber notes:

Jews left Holland, England, and various Caribbean islands to settle in North America during the 18th century prior to the American Revolution. Jewish newcomers to England's New World colonies settled in the seaboard towns in search of success as international merchants who traded in the goods shipped through the Atlantic world. Family genealogies reveal that an appreciable number of these Jewish settlers had relatives scattered in other ports around the Atlantic, thereby verifying that trading ventures during the 18th century depended, to a considerable extent, on conducting commerce with correspondents with whom one had personal ties.

From the mid-18th to the mid-19th centuries in Curaçao, St. Croix, St. Eustatius and St. Thomas, Jews capitalized on their knowledge of the Spanish language and their kinsmen residing in the Spanish colonies in America to develop trade with those colonies. From the mid-19th to the mid-20th centuries, liberation of the Spanish colonies in the New World opened the doors to Jewish settlement in Colombia, Costa Rica, the Dominican Republic, El Salvador and Panama. Panama is the only Jewish community among these former Spanish colonies that remains today.

Overview of Resources

An important step in conducting genealogical research, suggested on the Caribbean Genealogy Research website www. CANDOO.COM/GENRESOURCES, is determining which country owned the island or territory during the period researched. The Caribbean-L discussion list CARIBBEAN-ADMIN@ROOTSWEB. COM offers the ability to contact people with research experience in a particular location.

Stern's *First American Jewish Families* documents the earliest Jewish families in the New World. The book's 600 genealogies include not only Americans, but also their family members who lived on the Caribbean islands of Barbados, Curaçao, Jamaica, St. Eustatius and St. Thomas. Although the book's name index is extensive, no locality index is included to help the reader sort through the approximately 300 pages of descendancy charts. An extensive bibliography leads the reader to the author's sources.

The American Jewish Archives* (AJA) holds extensive Caribbean genealogical and historical resources (see AJA). Among other collections, Rabbi Stern's correspondence and research documents are held by the AJA; its website posts an inventory of these papers. The website, WWW.HUC.EDU/AJA, does not feature a complete index of its holdings, but staff is responsive to researchers' requests for information. Some AJA resources are described in detail below and in the discussions about resources for the Jewish communities in the various Caribbean countries.

Miscellaneous Caribbean Information Sources

The following sources at the AJA are collections for which no specific country is given:

- Cardoze, David, biographical and other information, 1973 (Flat File C5:D10)
- Cordova, Jesua H., biographical information, 1963 (SC-2503)
- Cortissos family, family tree, 1656–1899 (Genealogies File)
- De Mesquita, Joseph B., will, 1708 (SC-2782)
- Fidanque family, genealogical information, 1729–1956 (Genealogies File)
- Ligier, Leon A., "The Odyssey of the Jews of Spain and Portugal: Sephardim in Transition," 1957 (SC-13520)
- Lindo family, biographical information, 1757–1881 (SC-7271)
- Loker, Zvi, "Jewish Presence, Enterprise, and Migration Trends in the Caribbean," 1654–1789 (Small Collections); "Material for a General Index of Post-Exilic Iberian Jews (including Conversions), XXXVI to End of V Century," n.d. (SC-7370)
- Maduro family, 1612–1948 (Genealogies File)
- Maslin, Simeon J., "Toward the Preservation of Caribbean Jewish Monuments," 1969 (Miscellaneous File)
- Mesquita, Benjamin Bueno de, brief biography by Arnold Wiznitzer, 1950s (SC-8065)
- New Amsterdam, paper on provenance of first Jews in New Amsterdam, by Egon and Frieda Wolff, n.d. (SC-8827)
- Philately
- Piza family genealogical information, 1723–1950
- Roseman, Kenneth, maternal family genealogy, 1864-1969
- Sasso, Isaac, 1920, 1978 (Correspondence File)
- "The Search for the Elusive Caribbean Jews," by Franklin B. Krohn, 1992 (SC-13816)
- Stein family, Philadelphia, 1795–1963 (Genealogies File)

The collections of the American Jewish Historical Society* include all of the Americas, including the Caribbean (see AJHS).

The LDS (Mormon) Family History Library (FHL) collection includes microfilms of interest to Jewish genealogists researching a number of islands and territories in the Caribbean Basin. A database of Jewish records prepared by the FHL for the International Association of Jewish Genealogy Societies (IAJGS) is available on the JewishGen website, WWW.JEWISHGEN. ORG/DATABASES/FHLC. The full FHL catalogue may be consulted online at WWW.FAMILYSEARCH.ORG. LDS microfilm indexes are presented below in several of the sections on specific countries. Johni Cerny and Wendy Elliott's *The Library* summarizes FHL holdings and offers brief country histories.

Among the most useful Caribbean resources hosted by JewishGen (see JEWISHGEN) are SefardSIG's Sephardic

Websites for Genealogy in the Caribbean, IAJGS International Jewish Cemetery Project, and Jewish Genealogy Family Finder.

Robert Swierenga discusses Dutch Jewry who entered the Caribbean and North America during the period 1800–80 in his book *The Forerunners: Dutch Jewry in the North American Diaspora.*

Editors Martin A. Cohen and Abraham Peck, in *Sephardim in the Americas,* describe the communities of Barbados, Curaçao, Martinique, New Amsterdam, Recife, St. Eustatius, St. Martin and Suriname.

With specific reference to several Caribbean nations, Jeffrey S. Malka's *Sephardic Genealogy* and Sephardic Jewish Genealogy website present methodologies and describe resources for Sephardic genealogy.

Records for the Netherlands Antilles (the islands of Aruba, Bonaire, Curaçao, St. Eustatius, St. Maarten and Saba), if not held in repositories on the islands themselves, may be found in The Netherlands, particularly in Amsterdam. The Netherlands Society for Jewish Genealogy holds resources on Jews with connections to The Netherlands and the Caribbean. The society hosts a website and publishes the journal *Misjpoge.*

Trouwen in Mokum, 1598–1811 (Marriages in Amsterdam), by Dave Verdooner, provides data on more than 15,000 marriages that may help genealogists trace Dutch-Jewish family members in the Caribbean.

Gail Greenberg writes that the Jewish Historical Society of England's* *Index to Transactions I–XXV* and *Miscellanies I–X* provide information on articles about the large Sephardic community in London linked to communities in Amsterdam and the West Indies. Marriage and other records held by London's Spanish and Portuguese Jews' Congregation,* by New York's Shearith Israel Congregation,* and by Charleston, South Carolina's Kahal Kadosh Beth Elohim* may be useful resources.

Judith Laikin Elkin published an online "Bibliography of Books and Articles in Latin American Jewish Studies, 1991–96."

Civil records for islands under British control, including Barbados and Jamaica, if not held in repositories on the islands themselves, may be found in London repositories (see UNITED KINGDOM).

Websites

American Jewish Archives, WWW.HUC.EDU/AJA
American Jewish Historical Society, WWW.AJHS.ORG
Bibliography of Books and Articles in Latin American Jewish Studies, 1991–96, WWW.H-NET.MSU.EDU/~LATAM/BIBS/BIBJEWISH.HTML
Bibliography of North American Jewish Community Books: Carribbean [sic], WWW.JEWISHGEN.ORG/AJGS/BIBLIOGRAPHY/CARRIBBEAN.HTM
Caribbean-L discussion list, e-mail CARIBBEAN-ADMIN@ROOTSWEB.COM
Caribbean Genealogy Research, WWW.CANDOO.COM/GENRESOURCES
Caribbean GenWeb, WWW.ROOTSWEB.COM/~CARIBGW
Center for Research on Dutch Jewry, DUTCHJEWRY.HUJI.AC.IL
IAJGS International Jewish Cemetery Project, WWW.JEWISHGEN.ORG/CEMETERY
Jewish Communities of the World (abridged), WWW.WJC.ORG.IL/COMMUNITIES/JEWISH_COMMUNITIES_OF_THE_WORLD
JewishGen, WWW.JEWISHGEN.ORG
JewishGen Online Worldwide Burial Registry, WWW.JEWISHGEN.ORG/DATABASES/CEMETERY

Jewish Historical Society of England, WWW.JHSE.ORG

Netherlands Society for Jewish Genealogy, WWW.NLJEWGEN.ORG

Sephardic Jewish Genealogy, WWW.ORTHOHELP.COM/GENEAL/SEFARDIM.HTM

SefardSIG's Sephardic Websites for Genealogy in the Caribbean, WWW.JEWISHGEN.ORG/SEFARDSIG/CARIB_SITES.HTM

Spanish and Portuguese Jews' Congregation (Bevis Marks), WWW. JEWISHGEN.ORG/JCR-UK/COMMUNITY/BEVIS/HISTORY.HTM

Bibliography

Arbell, Mordechai. "Genealogical Research on Portuguese Jews in the Caribbean and the Guineas: Facilities and Difficulties." *Sharsheret Hadorot* 11, no. 1 (February 1977): 4–6.

———. "'La Nacion': Los Judios Hispano-Portugueses del Caribe." *Sephardica* 1, no. 1 (March 1984): 85–94.

———. *The Jewish Nation of the Caribbean: The Spanish-Portuguese Jewish Settlements in the Caribbean and the Guianas.* Jerusalem: Gefen, 2002.

Arbell, Mordechai, comp., et al. *Spanish and Portuguese Jews in the Caribbean and the Guianas: A Bibliography.* New York: John Carter Brown Library, 1999.

Beker, Avi, ed. *Jewish Communities of the World.* Jerusalem: World Jewish Congress & Lerner Publications Company, 1998. Abridged version: WWW.WJC.ORG.IL/COMMUNITIES/JEWISH_COMMUNITIES_OF_THE_WORLD.

Bennett, Ralph. "Book Reviews: Marriages in Amsterdam." *AVOTAYNU* 10, no. 2 (Summer 1994): 60–61.

———. "History of the Jews of the Caribbean." *Los Muestros,* (1993): 11.

———. "The Case of the Preteenage Grooms." *DOROT* (Spring 1994): 10.

Bohm, Gunter. "The First Sephardic Synagogues in South America and in the Caribbean Area." *Studio Rosenthaliana* 22, no. 1 (Spring 1988): 1–14.

Cerny, Johni, and Wendy Elliott. *The Library: A Guide to the LDS Family History Library.* Salt Lake City: Ancestry, 1988.

Cohen, Martin A., and Abraham J. Peck, eds. *Sephardim in the Americas: Studies in Culture and History.* Tuscaloosa: University of Alabama Press/American Jewish Archives, 1992.

Cohen, Robert. "Early Caribbean Jewry: A Demographic Perspective." *Jewish Social Studies* 45, no. 2 (Spring 1983): 112–34.

Faber, Eli. "Book Review: First American Jewish Families." *AVOTAYNU* 8, no. 2 (Summer 1992): 53–54.

———. *A Time for Planting: The First Migration 1965–1820.* Baltimore: Johns Hopkins University Press, 1992.

Fidanque, E. Alvin. "Early Sephardic Settlers in North America and the Caribbean." *Journal of Reform Judaism* (Fall 1978): 77–82.

Fortune, Stephen Alexander. *Merchants and Jews: The Struggle for British West Indian Commerce, 1650–1750.* Gainesville: University Presses of Florida, 1984.

Hebrew University of Jerusalem, Institute of Contemporary Jewry. *Oral History of Contemporary Jewry: An Annotated Catalogue.* New York: Garland, 1990.

Institute for Research on the Sephardi and Oriental Jewish Heritage. *Jews in the Caribbean: Evidence on the History of the Jews in the Caribbean Zone in Colonial Times.* Author, n.d.

Jewish Historical Society of England, *Index to Transactions I–XXV* and *Miscellanies I–X.*

Kaganoff, Nathan M. *Judaica Americana: An Annotated Bibliography of Publications from 1960 to 1990.* 2 vols. Brooklyn, N.Y.: Carlson, 1995.

Krohn, Franklin B. "The Search for the Elusive Caribbean Jews." *American Jewish Archives* 45 (1993): 2, 147.

Liebman, Seymour B. *New World Jewry, 1493–1825: Requiem for the Forgotten.* New York: KTAV, 1982.

Loker, Zvi. "Economic Activities of Jews in the Caribbean in Colonial Times." In *Jews in Economic Life: Collected Essays in Memory of Arkadius Kahan,* 121–32. Jerusalem, 1985.

———. "Conversos and Conversions in the Caribbean Colonies and Socio-Religious Problems of the Jewish Settlers." In *Proceedings of the Ninth World Congress of Jewish Studies,* Division B, vol. 3: The History of the Jewish People, 205–12. Jerusalem, 1986.

Malka, Jeffrey S. *Sephardic Genealogy.* Bergenfield, N.J.: Avotaynu, 2003.

Oliver, V.L. Caribbeana. CARIBBEANA@CANDOO.COM.

Postal, Bernard, and Malcolm Stern. *Tourist Guide to Jewish History in the Caribbean.* New York: American Airlines, 1975.

Smith, Marian L. "Jewish Immigration to the U.S. via Mexico and the Caribbean, 1920–1922." *Generations* (Jewish Genealogical Society of Michigan) 14, no. 2 (Spring 1999): 8–13, 17.

Stern, Malcolm H. "Portuguese Sephardim in the Americas." *American Jewish Archives* 44 (1992): 1, 141.

———. "Sephardic Research." Lecture at 10th Summer Seminar on Jewish Genealogy, Salt Lake City, July 1991 (audio tape).

Stern, Malcolm H., comp. *First American Jewish Families: 600 Genealogies, 1654–1988,* 3d ed., updated and rev. Baltimore: Ottenheimer, 1991.

Swierenga, Robert P. *The Forerunners: Dutch Jewry in the North American Diaspora.* Detroit: Wayne State University Press, 1994.

Tigay, Alan M., ed. *The Jewish Traveler:* Hadassah Magazine's *Guide to the World's Jewish Communities and Sights.* Northvale, N.J.: Jason Aronson, 1994.

Verdooner, Dave. *Trouwen in Mokum, 1598–1811* (Jewish marriages in Amsterdam). 2 vols. The Hague, Netherlands: Warray, 1992.

Aruba

History. Aruba, Bonaire, Curaçao, Saba, St. Eustatius and the Dutch portion of St. Maarten compose the Netherlands Antilles. The first Jews arrived in these islands from Amsterdam in 1651; they were joined later by Jewish refugees from Brazil following the Portuguese recapture of that country in 1654.

In 1946 Jews in Aruba established a social center and began to worship together and to offer Jewish education. The community established a synagogue in 1962. Warren Freedman's *World Guide for the Jewish Traveler* notes that the island's old Jewish cemetery contains gravestones dating from 1563, almost a century before the first Jewish settlement on neighboring Curaçao. Regular use of the cemetery began in 1837. Most Aruban Jews were buried in Curaçao.

Resources. Civil records in The Netherlands may provide information on Jewish families in Aruba (see THE NETHERLANDS). The American Jewish Historical Society* holds microfilmed periodicals from Aruba.

The Family History Library (FHL) collection includes microfilms of interest to Jewish genealogists researching the Netherlands Antilles.

Websites

American Jewish Archives, WWW.HUC.EDU/AJA

American Jewish Historical Society, WWW.AJHS.ORG

Aruba Tourism Office, WWW.ARUBATOURISM.COM

Family History Library, WWW.FAMILYSEARCH.ORG

IAJGS International Jewish Cemetery Project, WWW.JEWISHGEN.ORG/CEMETERY/ATL-CARIBBEAN/ARUBA.HTML

JewishGen, WWW.JEWISHGEN.ORG

Congregation Beth Israel in Aruba

Bibliography

Emmanuel, Isaac S., and Suzanne A. Emmanuel. *History of the Jews in the Netherlands Antilles.* 2 vols. Cincinnati: American Jewish Archives, 1970.

Freedman, Warren. *World Guide for the Jewish Traveler.* New York: E.P. Dutton, 1984.

Malka, Jeffrey S. *Sephardic Genealogy.* Bergenfield, N.J.: Avotaynu, 2003.

Bahamas

History. Relatively few Jews came to the Bahamas when the islands were first settled by the British in 1620, but several Jewish families from Poland, Russia and the United Kingdom settled in Nassau after World War I. Jews came to Freeport on Grand Bahama Island later. England ruled the Bahamas until 1973, when the British Crown ended the islands' 300 years of colonial status.

Resources. Some ancient Jewish gravestones exist in Nassau. The IAJGS International Jewish Cemetery Project notes the presence of Grand Bahama Memorial Park in Freeport. Questions may be addressed to the United Bahamas Hebrew Congregation.*

The Bahamian government has published a guide to Bahamian records (available at the LDS Family History Library). LDS microfilms may be consulted for several Bahamas record groups: vital records, 1850–1960, #222931–223062, and probate records, 1954–60, #223485–223498 (includes wills). Cerny and Elliott's *The Library* lists additional resources, including books and/or microfilms on court records, history, land and property and immigration.

The Bahama Islands GenWeb Project website lists the LDS microfilm catalogue and provides additional information and links to record repositories and libraries, the Bahamas Historical Society, history of the islands, surname index and other genealogically relevant data.

Freeport boasts both a Conservative synagogue and a Reform congregation, joined together in the United Bahamas Hebrew Congregation.*

Websites

Bahama Islands GenWeb Project, WWW.ROOTSWEB.COM/~BHSWGW

Bibliography of Bahamian Genealogy, WWW.GSU.EDU/~LIBPJR/BAHGEN. HTM

Caribbean Genealogy Research, WWW.CANDOO.COM/GENRESOURCES

Family History Library, WWW.FAMILYSEARCH.ORG/GENEALOGY

United Bahamas Hebrew Congregation, WWW.UAHCWEB.ORG/CONGS/OT/ OT031

Bibliography

Cerny, Johni, and Wendy Elliott. *The Library: A Guide to the LDS Family History Library.* Salt Lake City: Ancestry, 1988.

Saunders, D. Gail, and E.A. Carson. *Guide to the Records of the Bahamas* (Nassau: Government Printing Department, Commonwealth of the Bahamas, 1983), cited in Cerny and Elliott, *The Library* (1988): 696.

Barbados

History. A year after Barbados was settled by the British in 1627, Spanish and Portuguese Jews from Dutch Brazil, Cayenne, England, Hamburg, Leghorn (Livorno, Italy) and Suriname came to the island. The Jews of Barbados were granted the right to worship in public before the Jews in London. By the 1660s, the Jewish community, Nidhei Israel, built a synagogue in Bridgetown. Nidhei Israel synagogue was rededicated in 1987, and the old Jewish cemetery was restored for use.

The community grew to more than 300 by 1860 and then to 800 by the mid-1700s. The Jews prospered in the sugar business and also in trading and banking. Some Barbados Jews may have resettled in Newport, Rhode Island.

According to a 1680 census, the Barbados Jewish community consisted mostly of Sephardim. About 170 Jewish families lived on the island in 1710, according to a contemporary observer.

In response to the threat of rising Nazism, 30 Eastern European Jewish families went to Barbados, joined by Jews from Trinidad.

Resources. The Caribbean Genealogy Research website lists contact information for government record repositories, the museum and historical society, resources and the LDS microfilm index.

Shilstone's tombstone translations inform a researcher about the Jewish community's cemetery. The cemetery's burials date from 1654 to 1929 and then again from 1932.

Communal and religious life centers around two organizations, the Caribbean Jewish Congress* and the Jewish Community Council.*

The American Jewish Historical Society* holds the archives of the Barbados Jewish community, 1679–1901.

Barbados census returns of 1715 are published in David Kent's *Barbados and America.* The 1715 returns are also available on Family History Library (FHL) microfilms (#1162149 and #1162150, item 2); the original census records are held by the Barbados Department of Archives.

The FHL collection includes microfilms on Jewish births (1779–1884) and burials (1660–1886) in Barbados (#1159601) plus tombstone inscriptions in Bridgetown and other records. A database of Jewish records prepared by the FHL for IAJGS is available on JewishGen; the full FHL catalogue may be consulted online.

"Barbados Jewish History" includes information on the circa-1830 migration to Philadelphia.

The American Jewish Archives[*] collection includes the following files of Jewish interest (among others):

- Malcolm H. Stern Papers, Barbados research, 1971–84 (box 15, files 18–19)
- Bridgetown synagogue. Newspaper article on consecration, 1835 (flat file, C3:D6)
- Burial records, 1690–1855 (SC-13554)
- Burial records and ledger books of Jewish community, 1696–1887 (microfilm 822)
- Census of inhabitants, 1715 (SC-13554)
- Census of Jews, 1679–80 (SC-13488)
- Gomez, Mordecai, trade authorization, 1718 (SC-4129)
- Jewish Community of Barbados, 1654–1833. M.A. thesis by J. Westphal, 1993 (SC-14016)
- Lopez, Mathias, account book, 1779–89 (microfilm 1687); naturalization record, 1725 (SC-7417; rare documents file)
- Philately, 1987 (SC-13497)
- Plantation and house list of Jews in Jamaica and Barbados, 1692 (SC-12932)
- Stouse, Samuel S., memorandum of visit, 1962 (SC-13490)
- Vital records, n.d. (SC-13555)
- Wills (alphabetized list) (SC-13465)
- Picture Collection, for photograph(s) of Nidhe Israel Cemetery

The 600 genealogies in Stern's *First American Jewish Families* include Jews who lived in Barbados.

Websites

American Jewish Archives, WWW.HUC.EDU/AJA
American Jewish Historical Society, WWW.AJHS.ORG
Barbados Tourism Authority, WWW.BARBADOS.ORG
Caribbean Genealogy Research, WWW.CANDOO.COM/GENRESOURCES
Cemetery: WWW.JEWISHGEN.ORG/JCR-UK/COMMUNITY/BEVIS/HISTORY.HTM
Family History Library, WWW.FAMILYSEARCH.ORG
IAJGS International Jewish Cemetery Project, WWW.JEWISHGEN.ORG/CEMETERY
Jewish Barbados, WWW.HARUTH.COM/JEWSBARBADOS.HTML
JewishGen, WWW.JEWISHGEN.ORG

Bibliography

Barbados Board of Tourism. *A Chronological Account of the Barbados Jewish Community.* (Pamphlet).

"Barbados Jewish History." *Philadelphia Chronicles* 16, no. 2 (Summer 1997): 3.

Cerny, Johni, and Wendy Elliott. *The Library: A Guide to the LDS Family History Library.* Salt Lake City: Ancestry, 1988.

Dunn, Richard S. "The Barbados Census of 1680: Profile of the Richest Colony in English America." 3d ser., *William and Mary Quarterly* 26 (1969): 23.

Faber, Eli. *A Time for Planting: The First Migration 1654–1820.* Baltimore: Johns Hopkins University Press, 1992.

Funke, Phyllis Ellen. "Barbados." In *The Jewish Traveler:* Hadassah Magazine's *Guide to the World's Jewish Communities and Sights,* Alan M. Tigay, ed., 35–39. Northvale, N.J.: Jason Aronson, 1994.

Kent, David L. *Barbados and America.* Arlington, Va.: C.M. Kent, 1980.

Cohen, Martin A., and Abraham J. Peck, eds. *Sephardim in the Americas: Studies in Culture and History.* Tuscaloosa: University of Alabama Press/American Jewish Archives, 1992.

Samuel, Wilfred S. "Review of Jewish Colonists in Barbados, 1680." *Transactions of the Jewish Historical Society of England* 13 (1932–35): 73.

———. *A Review of the Jewish Colonists in Barbados in the Year 1680.* London: Purnell & Sons, 1936.

Shilstone, E.M. *Monumental Inscriptions in the Burial Ground of the Jewish Synagogue at Bridgetown, Barbados.* New York: American Jewish Historical Society, 1956; New York: Macmillan, 1988.

Stern, Malcolm H. "Portuguese Sephardim in the Americas." *American Jewish Archives* 44 (1992): 1, 141.

Costa Rica

History. The Jewish history of Costa Rica is divided into phases. The first group of settlers arrived during the period of exploration in the late 15th century, which coincided with the imposition of the Inquisition in the Americas as well as in Spain. No cases against Jews in Costa Rica were registered in the Archivo de Indias in Spain.

Most early Costa Rican Jewish colonists originated in Castille and Andalusia in Spain, via Panama, bearing such surnames as Castro, Carazo, Carvajal and Naranjo. Jews who came during the 16th and 17th centuries engaged in agriculture, and they maintained the secrecy of their Judaism. A number of unusual practices persist today among their descendants that point to their Jewish heritage.

The second group of immigrants arrived in the 19th century, Sephardic Jews from Curaçao, Jamaica, St. Croix and St. Thomas. The first official recording of a Jewish birth occurred in Aljuela. Most descendants of this group retain their Judaism; among their surnames are de Castro, Lindo, Maduro, Robles, Salas and Sasso.

Ashkenazic Jews began arriving in Costa Rica before the turn of the 20th century. The best-known immigrant among this group was Samuel Zemurray of Bessarabia, the founder of United Fruit Company. Other immigrants came from Austria, Czechoslovakia, Poland and Russia. According to Luis Kleinman, a large number of Polish Jews arrived in the 1930s.

Resources. Several resources are listed on the website of the AOL Hispanic Genealogy Special Interest Group, HTTP://USER.AOL.COM/MROSADO007/CR.HTM#ARCHIVES

Bibliography

Encyclopaedia Judaica, c.f. Costa Rica.

Kleiman, Luis. "History of the Jews of Costa Rica." *AVOTAYNU* 5, no. 4 (Winter 1989): 56.

Cuba

History. Jewish converts numbered among the first European settlers on the island of Cuba in 1492; the *Encyclopaedia Judaica* describes several of these earliest immigrants. During the 17th-century Portuguese reconquest of Brazil from the

Dutch, groups of Jews fled Brazil to settle in Cuba, where they developed an active trade with the Antilles and other islands that eventually expanded to Amsterdam, Hamburg and New York.

The contemporary Cuban-Jewish community is not linked to the settlers of the 15th through 18th centuries. Following the Spanish-American War (1898), American Jews began to establish themselves on the island. By 1904, they had founded the Union Hebrew Congregation, and, in 1906, they purchased a cemetery. Prior to World War I, according to Yitzhak Kerem, immigrants arrived from Turkey and the Near East. In 1920, many more Jews from Istanbul fled to Havana. In 1914, these Sephardic Jews established a community organization called Union Hebrea Shevet Ahim.

In 1920–21, Eastern European Jews began to arrive in Cuba. For the majority, the island was merely a transit point en route to the United States; by 1925, most of the Jews who had arrived in Cuba between 1920 and 1923 had left. But when the U.S. tightened its immigration rules in 1924, thousands of Jews found themselves compelled to remain in Cuba, and even after 1924, thousands of Jews entered the island nation.

American organizations dedicated to Jewish welfare, including HIAS and the American Jewish Joint Distribution Committee, provided assistance to the impoverished immigrant Jews in Havana. In about 1925, the Centro Israelita was founded and served as the principal communal body of Eastern European Jews in Havana.

In the 1930s, a central Jewish committee was created to represent all Cuban Jewry—Americans, Sephardim and Ashkenazim. Ashkenazim had arrived during the build-up to World War II. By 1949, the Ashkenazic community had founded the Patronado de la Casa de la comunidad Hebrea.*

Jews left Cuba for Miami, Florida, in 1960 to seek political asylum in the wake of Fidel Castro's communist takeover. Many of these Jews had come to Cuba in the 1920s and 1930s, when immigration quotas to the United States had been sharply limited.

Resources. The Caribbean Genealogy Research website includes information on libraries and other resources in Cuba. The Cuban Genealogy Society publishes a guide to genealogical research in Cuba.

A chronology of Cuban-Jewish history appears in the appendix of Robert Levine's *Tropical Diaspora*, hosted also on the JewishCuba website.

For information about Jews in Cuba, write to the congregations.* For information about Cuban Jews in the United States, contact Cuban Hebrew Congregation* in Miami Beach and Sephardic Temple Tifereth Israel* in Los Angeles. See also the JewishCuba website; among its many references is a database of Cuban-Jewish burials and book indexes.

In 1808, Napoleon decreed that all Jews were to adopt hereditary surnames. Working with the records of these name adoptions in the archives of Bordeaux, France, genealogist Stephane Toublanc demonstrated that the families listed in those records included members born in Cuba.

The IAJGS International Jewish Cemetery Project presents information and additional references on cemeteries in Camaguay, Cienfegos, Havana, Santa Clara and Santiago de Cuba. The project also lists websites and books on the Jews of Cuba, cemeteries in a number of Cuban cities and references that describe tombstone inscriptions and photographs. Photographs and some tombstone inscriptions of Jewish cemeteries in Havana may be seen online.

The U.S. National Archives* holds a chronological file of registrations of American citizens in Cuba for the period 1871–1935 (Record Group 84). The list includes the registration number, useful in accessing the record in the file "Registration of American Citizens, 24 January 1869–31 December 1935." The records include such information as name, date and place of birth, date and place of residence, purpose of stay, wife's name and place of birth, children, how citizenship was obtained and passport number. The register is also available from the *Caribbean Historical & Genealogical Journal*; an index appears online.

The 1969 *American Jewish Year Book* includes an article by Seymour B. Liebman on the Cuban-Jewish community in South Florida. Betty Heisler-Samuels's 2001 article in *The Miami Herald* brings the reader up to date.

The websites of the Cuban Genealogy Center and the Cuban Genealogical Society may have resources of interest to Jewish genealogists.

Websites

Caribbean Genealogy Research, WWW.CANDOO.COM/GENRESOURCES
Caribbean Historical & Genealogical Journal index, WWW.ROOTSWEB. COM/~CARIBGW/CGW_ARCHIVE/CUBA/HAVANA.HTM
Cuban Genealogy Center, WWW.CUBAGENWEB.ORG
Cuban Genealogy Society, WWW.ROOTSWEB.COM/~UTCUBANGS
IAJGS International Jewish Cemetery Project, WWW.JEWISHGEN.ORG/ CEMETERY/ATL-CARIBBEAN/CUBA.HTML
Jewish Cuba, WWW.HARUTH.COM/JEWSCUBA.HTML
JewishGen, WWW.JEWISHGEN.ORG/CEMETERY
The Jews of Cuba, WWW.JEWISHCUBA.ORG
Photographs and tombstone inscriptions, WWW.SUEGERSTEN.COM/CUBA/ CUBA_JCEM.HTM
World Jewish Congress, WWW.WJC.ORG.IL/COMMUNITIES/JEWISH_COMMUNITIES_ OF_THE_WORLD

Bibliography

Bejarano, Margalit. *La Comunidad Hebrea de Cuba: La memoria y la historia* (Jewish community of Cuba: Memory and history). Jerusalem: Instituto Abraham Harman de Judaismo Contemporaneo Universidad Hebrea de Jerusalem, 1996.

———. "*Los Sefaradies: Pioneros de la Immigracion Judia a Cuba*" (Sephardim: Pioneers of Jewish immigration to Cuba). Jerusalem: *Rumbos* 14 (1985): 107–22.

Beker, Avi, ed. *Jewish Communities of the World*. Jerusalem: World Jewish Congress & Lerner Publications Company, 1998.

Bettinger-Lopez, Caroline. *Cuban-Jewish Journeys: Searching for Identity, Home, and History in Miami*. Knoxville: University of Tennessee Press, 2000. (Index: WWW.JEWISHCUBA.ORG/FAMTIES/ INDEX.HTML)

Center for Latin American Studies. *The Texture of Jewish Immigrant Life in Cuba, 1910–1984*. Gainesville: Granter Galleries, University of Florida, 1987.

Cuban Genealogy Society. *Research Guide for Cuba*. Available from the society, P.O. Box 2650, Salt Lake City, Utah 84110.

Encyclopaedia Judaica, c.f. Cuba.

Heisler-Samuels, Betty. *The Last Minyan in Havana: A Story of Paradise, Hope, and Betrayal*. Aventura, Fla.: Chutzpah Publishing, 2000.

———. "Forced to Leave Homes, Cuban Jews Thrive in Miami." *The Miami Herald*, 17 January 2001. WWW.JEWISHCUBA.ORG/MIAMI.HTML.

Hirsch, Claus W. "Using the *American Jewish Year Book* in Family History Research." *AVOTAYNU* 17, no. 4 (Winter 2001): 17.

Kerem, Yitzchak. "Greek Jewry: Sources for Genealogical Research." *AVOTAYNU* 10, no. 4 (Winter 1994): 11–12.

Levine, Robert M. *Tropical Diaspora: The Jewish Experience in Cuba*. Gainesville: University Press of Florida, 1993.

Liebman, Seymour B. "Cuban Jewish Community in South Florida." *American Jewish Year Book*, vol. 70, edited by Morris Fine and Milton Himmelfarb. New York: American Jewish Committee/Philadelphia: Jewish Publication Society, 1969.

Margolis, Paul. "Tropical Remnants: The Architectural Legacy of Cuba's Jews." *Jewish Heritage Report* 1, nos. 3–4 (Winter 1997–98). WWW.ISJM.ORG/JHR/NOS3-4/CUBARCH.HTM.

———. "Jews of Camaguey, Cienfuegos, Santa Clara, and Santiago, Cuba." WWW.JEWISHCUBA.ORG.

Sapir, Boris. *The Jewish Community of Cuba*. Trans. by Simon Wolin. New York: Jewish Theological Seminary Press, 1948.

Smith, Marian L. "Jewish Immigration to the U.S. via Mexico and the Caribbean, 1920–1922." *Generations* (Jewish Genealogical Society of Michigan) 14, no. 2 (Spring 1999): 8–13, 17.

Wynne, Suzan. "Third International Seminar (1991, Salt Lake City): An Update." *AVOTAYNU* 7, no. 1 (Spring 1991): 7–8.

Curaçao

History. Curaçao, together with Aruba, Saba, St. Eustatius and the Dutch portion of St. Maarten, compose the Netherlands Antilles. The first permanent Jewish settlers, between ten and twelve families who had escaped to The Netherlands from the oppression of the Inquisitions of Spain and Portugal, arrived in Curaçao from Amsterdam in 1651; in that year they founded Congregation Mikve Israel and Beth Haim cemetery. These settlers were joined by Jewish refugees from Brazil following the Portuguese recapture of that country in 1654. The Jewish community was founded and Bet Haim cemetery consecrated in 1659, and in Willemstad, Mikve Israel synagogue was consecrated in 1732.

The Jews engaged in agriculture; on their plantations they grew sugar cane, tobacco, cotton, indigo and citrus fruits. They also played a critical role in the commerce of the area, facilitating imports of supplies from Europe and the export of tropical produce. The Jewish community's family and ethnic connections with Jewish financiers and industrialists in Amsterdam, Bordeaux, Hamburg, Lisbon, London, Madrid and New York enabled them to dominate trade throughout the Caribbean. Jews similarly dominated the shipping and then the insurance businesses.

When the French expelled the Jews from Martinique and Guadeloupe in 1685, many Jews fled to Curaçao. By the end of the 17th century, approximately 125 Jewish families had settled in Curaçao. Their numbers grew to 140 families by 1713 and then to 250 families by the mid-1700s, when the Jews in Curaçao constituted the single largest Jewish community in the New World.

Interior, Congregation Mikve Israel synagogue on Curaçao

The Curaçao Jewish community became the "mother community" of the Americas, in that it assisted other communities in the area, mainly in Suriname and St. Eustatius. The Curaçao community also helped to finance construction of the first synagogues in New York City and Newport, Rhode Island.

In 1808, Napoleon decreed that all Jews were to adopt hereditary surnames. Families listed in records in the archives of Bordeaux, France, show that the families included members born in Curaçao, according to Suzan Wynne.

In 1864, a number of families separated from Mikve Israel to found one of the few Sephardic Reform congregations, Temple Emanuel. A hundred years later, the two congregations merged to form United Congregation Mikve Israel-Emanuel*.

The early 20th century brought Ashkenazic Jews, mainly from Central Europe, to Curaçao, where they founded Shaarei Tzedek Orthodox* congregation. By the middle of the century, the number of Jews began to decline.

Resources. The Jewish community publishes a monthly journal, *Mikve Israel*. A Jewish museum exists in the old Portuguese synagogue in Willemstad. The current Mikve Israel-Emanuel Synagogue, which celebrated its 350th anniversary in 2001, may be of assistance to researchers.

The National Archives in Curaçao* holds some civil records. Documents about Curaçao's Jews also may be found (among other repositories in THE NETHERLANDS) at the Rijksarchief* in The Hague. The Jossy Maduro files about many Sephardic families are held by the Central Bureau of Genealogy also in The Hague (see THE NETHERLANDS). The *Studia Rosenthaliana* journal article "Discovering and Utilizing Sources for the History of the Jews in the Netherlands" describes, in English, genealogical resources in Holland.

The S.A.L. Mongui Maduro Jewish Library* holds an extensive collection of Judaica plus materials of specific genealogical interest. Birth, marriage and death registers; periodicals; local synagogue publications; almanacs; agendas and calendars; and constitutions and bylaws are included in the library's holdings.

Mikve Israel-Emanuel's Jewish Cultural Historical Museum* tells the Jewish history of Curaçao and preserves its most precious religious and cultural artifacts.

Isaac S. Emmanuel and Suzanne A. Emmanuel listed marriage records in their *History of the Jews in the Netherlands Antilles.*

The American Jewish Historical Society* holds microfilmed copies of Curaçao marriage records and microfilmed periodicals.

The Joint Distribution Committee* archives in New York holds lists of people who sailed to Curaçao from Holland during the 1940s (Record Group Ar33-44, files 370–371, 533).

Beth Haim cemetery, consecrated in 1659 and the oldest existing Jewish cemetery in the Western Hemisphere, contains 2,500 graves. Replicas of some of its tombstones are presented at the Jewish Cultural Museum.* The newer cemetery is located near town on Berg Altena. These cemeteries are described in the IAJGS International Jewish Cemetery Project website. The 17th-century Jewish cemetery in Blenheim is one of the oldest in the New World.

In a study on tombstone-decorating traditions, Rochelle Weinstein presents the pedigree of Curaçao's 18th-century Senior family, which reveals connections to family members in Amsterdam, The Hague, Hamburg and London.

The genealogies in Stern's *First American Jewish Families* include Jews who lived on Curaçao.

The American Jewish Archives* collection includes the following files of Jewish interest (among others):

- Malcolm H. Stern Papers, files on Curaçao families and Curaçao marriages (box 17, files 1 and 2, respectively); file on Maduro family (box 21, file 4).
- Birth and circumcision records, 1700–1815 (SC-13495)
- Commercial documents, 1708–90 (SC-13552)
- Congregation Mikve Israel, membership list, 1825–99? (SC-13496); catalogue of materials in congregational archives, n.d. (SC-13506); congregational records, 1672–1817 (SC-13505)
- Congregation Mikve Israel-Emanu-El, essay, "The Other Synagogue," by Charles G. Casseres, to commemorate the 250th anniversary of the synagogue, 1982 (SC-13508)
- Curiel, A., official correspondence, 1856–57 (microfilm 3488)
- Epitaphs from headstones in Jewish cemeteries, trans. by Isaac S. Emmanuel (SC-13609–SC-13613)

- Hart, Naphtali, and Company, legal documents and correspondence re captured Dutch ships, 1763–64 (SC-4650)
- Lindo, Solomon, miscellaneous documents, 1825–99 (SC-13496)
- Lyon, Lewis, trading records, 1813–14, 1829 (SC-7569)
- Marriages performed in Amsterdam, Curaçao and St. Eustatius of couples born in the United States, 1717–96 (SC-7816, microfilm 3002)
- Old Curaçao Archives (List SC-2562)
- Peixotto, Solomon C., miscellaneous documents (SC-13496)
- Portuguese Congregation, birth roll of female Portuguese Jews, 1743–1831 (SC-13503); constitution, 1833 (SC-13502); register of births and deaths, 1722–1831 (SC-13504)
- *Santa Companhia de Dotar Orphas e Doncellas,* historical information, letter from Isaac S. Emmanuel, 1960 (SC-13467)
- Temple Emanu-El, copies of temple bulletins, 1960–62 (SC-13507)
- Maps, Flat file, Cabinet 4, Drawer 4

The Center for Research on Dutch Jewry* of Hebrew University in Jerusalem has compiled a number of genealogically useful databases and other resources.

The Family History Library (FHL) collection includes microfilms of interest to Jewish genealogists researching Curaçao. A database of Jewish records prepared by the FHL for IAJGS is available on the JewishGen website. The full FHL catalogue may be consulted online.

Websites

American Jewish Archives, WWW.HUC.EDU/AJA
American Jewish Historical Society, WWW.AJHS.ORG
Beth Haim cemetery, WWW.JODENSAVANNE.SR.ORG/ARTICLE6.HTML
Center for Research on Dutch Jewry, DUTCHJEWRY.HUJI.AC.IL
Family History Library, WWW.FAMILYSEARCH.ORG
IAJGS International Jewish Cemetery Project, WWW.JEWISHGEN.ORG/CEMETERY
JewishGen, WWW.JEWISHGEN.ORG
Mikve Israel-Emanuel Congregation, WWW.SNOA.COM
Netherlands Society for Jewish Genealogy, WWW.NLJEWGEN.ORG
S.A.L. Mongui Maduro Foundation, WWW.MADUROLIBRARY.ORG

Bibliography

Alvarez Correa, H.M. *The Alvares Correa Families of Curaçao and Brazil: A Genealogical Study.* The Hague: Végron, 1965.

Arbell, Mordechai. *The Jewish Nation of the Caribbean: The Spanish-Portuguese Jewish Settlements in the Caribbean and the Guianas.* Jerusalem: Gefen, 2002.

Arbell, Mordechai, comp. *Spanish and Portuguese Jews in the Caribbean and the Guianas: A Bibliography,* edited by Dennis C. Landis and Ann P. Barry. Providence, R.I.: John Carter Brown Library, 1999.

B'nai B'rith Curaçao 2389. *10th Anniversary, 1962–1972.* [Curaçao, 1972].

Bohm, Gunter. "Edward Edwards, Primer Consul de Hamburgo en Curaçao." *Judaica Iberoamericana,* no. 2. Santiago: Universidad de Chile, 1978.

Cohen, Martin A., and Abraham J. Peck, eds. *Sephardim in the Americas: Studies in Culture and History*. Tuscaloosa: University of Alabama Press/American Jewish Archives, 1992.

Congregation Mikve Israel-Emanuel. *Our "Snoa," 5492–5742*. Curaçao: Author, 1982.

"Discovering and Utilizing Sources for the History of the Jews in The Netherlands," *Studia Rosenthaliana*, 1981: 75–84.

Goslinga, C.C. *Curaçao and Guzman Blanco: A Case Study of Small Power Politics in the Caribbean*. The Hague: Martinus Nijhoff, 1975.

Emmanuel, Isaac S. *Precious Stones of the Jews of Curaçao, 1656–1957*. New York: Bloch, 1957.

Emmanuel, Isaac S., and Suzanne A. Emmanuel. *History of the Jews in the Netherlands Antilles*. 2 vols. Cincinnati: American Jewish Archives, 1970.

Faber, Eli. *A Time for Planting: The First Migration 1654–1820*. Baltimore: Johns Hopkins University Press, 1992.

Funke, Phyllis Ellen. "Curaçao." *The Jewish Traveler:* Hadassah Magazine's *Guide to the World's Jewish Communities and Sights*, edited by Alan M. Tigay, 156–59. Northvale, N.J.: Jason Aronson, 1994.

Karner, Frances P. *The Sephardics of Curaçao: A Study of Sociocultural Patterns in Flux*. Assen, Netherlands: Van Gorcum, 1969.

Katzner, Kenneth. "Dutch Gem in Caribbean." *Washington Jewish Week*, 29 April 1999, 31.

Krafft, A.J.C. *Historie en oude families van de Nederlandse Antillen: het Antilliaanse patriciaat: met een historische unlading, zest uitgewerkte genealogieën, genealogische aantekeningen, fragmenten van genealogieën, ongepubliceerde documenten en een overzicht van bronnen zowel gedrukte als in handschrift/door* (History and old families of the Dutch Antilles [Dutch West Indies]; Antillian patriciate: with a historical introduction, sixty genealogies, genealogical notes, fragments of genealogies, unpublished documents and a survey of sources both printed and in handwriting). The Hague: Nijhoff, 1951.

Likuski, Sita. "The Dutch Connection." *Zichron-Note* (San Francisco Jewish Genealogy Society) 18, no. 4 (November 1998): 13.

Maduro, J.M.L. "*De Joden en hun Rabbijnen*." In *Historie en oude families van de Nederlandse Antillen* (History and old families of the Dutch Antilles [Dutch West Indies]), edited by A.J.C. Krafft, 44–55. The Hague: Nijhoff, 1951.

———. "*De Portugese Joden in Curaçao*" (Portuguese Jews in Curaçao). *Gedenkboek Nederland-Curaçao 1634–1934: Uitgegeven ter gelegenheid der herdenking van de drie-honderdjarige vereeniging van Curaçao met Nederland* (Memorial book Netherlands-Curaçao 1634–1934: Published at the commemoration of 300 years of unification of Curaçao with the Netherlands), edited by A. Euwens et al. Amsterdam: De Bussy, 1934.

———. "Maduro Genealogy." *Historie en oude families van Nederlandse Antillen* (History and old families of the Dutch Antilles [Dutch West Indies]), edited by A.J.C. Krafft, 100–17. The Hague: Nijhoff, 1951.

Maslin, Simeon J. *Guidebook: The Historic Synagogue of the United Netherlands Portuguese Congregation Mikve Israel-Emanuel of Curaçao*. Willemstad, 1964.

———. "The Sephardim of Curaçao: Can These Bones Live?" *CCAR Journal* 11, no. 3 (October 1963): 23–30.

S.A.L. Maduro Foundation. *The S.A.L. (Mongui) Maduro Library, "Lanhuis Rooj Catootje," Curaçao*. Curaçao, 1989.

Stern, Malcolm H. "Portuguese Sephardim in the Americas." *Sephardim in the Americas: Studies in Culture and History*, edited by Martin A. Cohen and Abraham J. Peck, 141–78.

Tuscaloosa: University of Alabama Press/American Jewish Archives, 1992.

Stern, Malcolm H., comp. *First American Jewish Families: 600 Genealogies, 1654–1988*, 3d ed., updated and rev. Baltimore: Ottenheimer, 1991.

Swierenga, Robert P. *The Forerunners: Dutch Jewry in the North American Diaspora*. Detroit: Wayne State University Press, 1994.

Ucko, Enrique. "*Los judios sefardies de Curazao (en Santo Domingo)*" (Sephardim in Curaçao [and Santo Domingo]). In *Presencia judia en Santo Domingo* (Jewish presence in Santo Domingo), edited by Alfonso Lockward. Santo Domingo, D.N.: Taller, 1994.

van Son, Sol. "From Our Contributing Editors—Holland." *AVOTAYNU* 5, no. 1 (Spring 1989): 16–18.

van Wijngaarden, Rene. *Engraved in the Palm of My Hands: Delvalle van Daelen*. Schoorl, Holland: Pirola, 2002.

Vlessing, Odette. "Book Reviews: *Sephardim in America*," *AVOTAYNU* 9, no. 4 (Winter 1993): 65–67.

Weinstein, Rochelle. "Stones of Memory: Revelations from a Cemetery in Curaçao." *Sephardim in the Americas: Studies in Culture and History*, edited by Martin A. Cohen and Abraham J. Peck, 81–140. Tuscaloosa: University of Alabama Press/American Jewish Archives, 1992.

Wynne, Suzan. "Third International Seminar (1991, Salt Lake City): An Update." *AVOTAYNU* 7, no. 1 (Spring 1991): 7–8.

Dominican Republic

History. Christopher Columbus discovered the island of Hispaniola in 1492; the few settlers he left were killed by Indians. Upon his return, Columbus established another colony that initially flourished, but was virtually abandoned by 1550. The French eventually claimed the western portion of the island, which later would become the independent nation of Haiti.

The Spanish ceded the remainder of the island to France in 1795, but the natives soon overthrew colonial rule. The colony reunited with Spain in 1809, and the Dominican Republic declared its independence in 1821. A few weeks later, the Haitians staged a successful coup, setting the stage for the rule of a succession of Haitian and Dominican Republic dictators. During the period 1916–24, the United States controlled the Dominican Republic, following which another series of dictators has ruled the country.

During the 19th century, Jews from Curaçao settled in Hispaniola, but they did not organize a community. Today, most of the approximately 250 Jews in the Dominican Republic, mainly of Central European origin, live in Santo Domingo, while some reside in Sosua.

The Dominican Republic Settlement Association (DORSA) was formed with the assistance of the Joint Distribution Committee and helped settle Jews in Sosua. About 700 European Jews reached the settlement, where they were assigned land and cattle. Other refugees settled in Santo Domingo. In 1943, the number of Jews in the Republic peaked at a thousand. A high percentage of the Jews has intermarried, but many non-Jewish spouses and the children of mixed marriages participate in Jewish communal life.

Resources. Jewish life is organized by the Parroquia Israelita de la Republica Dominicana. Two synagogues serve the Jews of

Santo Domingo and of Sosua. The community publishes the bimonthly magazine *Shalom,* and a small Jewish museum is open to visitors in Sosua.

The Family History Library (FHL) microfilm collection includes a large number of Dominican Republic civil registration records, catalogued by city or town. The Caribbean Genealogy Research website offers an index to the FHL collection, in addition to information on repositories and libraries.

The 1972 edition of the *American Jewish Year Book* features an article by Stanley T. Samuels on the development of the Sosua Jewish community.

The website of *Genealogie et Histoire de la Caraibe* (in French with some English) offers insights to genealogists.

Websites

AmYisrael, WWW.AMYISRAEL.CO.IL/NA/CENTRAL_AMERICA/DOMINC.HTM
Caribbean Genealogy Research, WWW.CANDOO.COM/GENRESOURCES
Family History Library, WWW.FAMILYSEARCH.ORG
Genealogie et Histoire de la Caraibe (Genealogy and History of the Caribbean), MEMBERS.AOL.COM/GHCARAIBE
Netherlands Antilles GenWeb, WWW.ROOTSWEB.COM/~ANTWGW

Bibliography

Deive, Carlos Esteban. *Heterodoxia e Inquisicion en Santo Domingo 1492–1822.* Santo Domingo: Taller, 1983.
Lockward, Alfonso, ed. *Presencia judia en Santo Domingo* (Jewish presence in Santo Domingo). Santo Domingo: Taller, 1994.
Samuels, Stanley T. "Moshav in the Caribbean: Sosua Revisited." In *American Jewish Year Book,* vol. 73, edited by Morris Fine and Milton Himmelfarb. New York: American Jewish Committee/Philadelphia: Jewish Publication Society, 1972.

French Guyana

History. Portuguese Jewish refugees from Brazil settled on the island of Cayenne in a community called Remire. Sephardic Jews from Leghorn (Livorno), Italy, joined this group. Approximately 20 Jewish families from North Africa and Suriname founded a successor community in Cayenne in 1992; the Chabad organization assists this group in maintaining Jewish life.

Resources. The website of *Genealogie et Histoire de la Caraibe* (in French with some English) offers insights to genealogists.

Websites

Caribbean Genealogy Research, WWW.CANDOO.COM/GENRESOURCES
Genealogie et Histoire de la Caraibe (Genealogy and History of the Caribbean), MEMBERS.AOL.COM/GHCARAIBE
Jewish Communities of the World, WWW.WJC.ORG.IL/COMMUNITIES/JEWISH_COMMUNITIES_OF_THE_WORLD

Bibliography

Arbell, Mordechai, comp. *Spanish and Portuguese Jews in the Caribbean and the Guianas: A Bibliography,* edited by Dennis C. Landis and Ann P. Barry. Providence, R.I.: John Carter Brown Library, 1999.
Beker, Avi, ed. *Jewish Communities of the World.* Jerusalem: World Jewish Congress & Lerner Publications Company, 1998.
Loker, Zvi. "Cayenne: A Chapter in the Jewish Settlement of the New World in the Seventeenth Century." *Zion* 48, no. 1 (1983): 107–16.

Guadeloupe

History. In 1654, three shiploads of refugees from Brazil became the first Jewish settlers on this French-owned island. The new residents established sugar cane plantations, and the products of refineries were the island's principal exports. In 1685, Louis IV ordered the expulsion of Jews. In the second half of the 20th century, Jews from North Africa and France came to the island to live. In 1988, Or Sameach synagogue was founded, along with a community center, Talmud Torah, kosher food store and cemetery.

Resources. The Caribbean Genealogy Research website offers information on records repositories, researchers and other information, including an index of LDS microfilms.

Contact the community organization, Communaute Culturelle Israelite*.

The website of *Genealogie et Histoire de la Caraibe* (in French with some English) offers insights to genealogists.

Websites

Caribbean Genealogy Research, WWW.CANDOO.COM/GENRESOURCES
Genealogie et Histoire de la Caraibe (Genealogy and History of the Caribbean), MEMBERS.AOL.COM/GHCARAIBE
Jewish Communities of the World, WWW.WJC.ORG.IL/COMMUNITIES/JEWISH_COMMUNITIES_OF_THE_WORLD

Haiti

History. The first group of Jewish immigrants to Haiti set out from Brazil in the 17th century after the island was conquered by the French. At the beginning of the 20th century, Haiti was the destination for Jews from Egypt, Lebanon and Syria, followed by Jews from Eastern Europe in the 1930s. After steady emigration during the second half of the 20th century, most of the remaining Jews live in Port-au-Prince.

Resources. Although Haitian Jews never have established a community organization, contact with a member of the community* is possible.

The American Jewish Archives* holds a 1976 article on Lopez De Paz (biographies file).

Websites

American Jewish Archives, WWW.HUC.EDU/AJA
Caribbean Genealogy Research, WWW.CANDOO.COM/GENRESOURCES

Bibliography

Beker, Avi, ed. *Jewish Communities of the World.* Jerusalem: World Jewish Congress & Lerner Publications Company, 1998. Abridged version: WWW.WJC.ORG.IL/COMMUNITIES/JEWISH_COMMUNITIES_OF_THE_WORLD.
Cohen, Martin A., and Abraham J. Peck, eds. *Sephardim in the Americas: Studies in Culture and History.* Tuscaloosa: University of Alabama Press/American Jewish Archives, 1992.
Loker, Zvi. *"Un diplome de Montpellier: Lopez de Paz 'Medecin du Roy'" a Saint Domingue [Haiti]; Un document inedit de l'epoque coloniale." Revue d'Histoire de la Medecine Hebraique* 29, no. 4 (December 1976): 53–55.
———. *"Un Cimitiere Juif au Cap-Haitien"* (Jewish cemetery in Cap-Hatien). *Revue des Etudes juives* 136, no. 3–4 (July-December 1977): [425]-27.

Jamaica

History. During Jamaica's Spanish rule from 1494 to 1655, crypto-Jews streamed to the island from Spain and (mainly) Portugal, most via England. When the British took over the island in 1655, Jews could return to the open practice of their religion. In the 17th and 18th centuries, Jews played prominent roles in the economic life of the island, and in the 19th century, they held important positions in political and cultural life. While the Jewish population grew during the 20th century as Jews from Syria and Germany came to the island, the Jewish population has since diminished, due to economic decline, emigration and intermarriage.

Resources. A time line of Jewish Jamaica is available on the Sephard website.

The Jamaican Jewish Genealogical Society* has created a Jewish genealogical database.

The Caribbean Genealogy Research website lists information on Jamaican archives, libraries, the historical society and other resources, including a microfilm index to holdings of the Family History Library.

Jews settled throughout the island of Jamaica; synagogues existed in Kingston, Spanish Town, Port Royal and Montego Bay. Visitors can see the ruins of many synagogues as well as 14 Jewish cemeteries.

The American Jewish Historical Society* holds the archives of the Jewish community of Jamaica, West Indies, 1674–1900.

For selected British holdings, see Sephardim's webpage.

A.P.M. Andrade's *Jews of Jamaica: A Record of the Jews in Jamaica from the English Conquest to the Present Time* is enhanced by a typescript index compiled by Paul F. White held at both the American Jewish Archives* (record SC-13479) and the New York Public Library's Dorot Jewish Division.*

The American Jewish Archives* collection includes the following files of Jewish interest (among others):

- Malcolm H. Stern Papers, including files on the Jews of Jamaica (box 20, file 2); Kingston Jamaica English and German Congregation 1788–1918 (box 20, file 8); vital records for Kingston, 1809–1907 (box 20, file 9); miscellaneous files on the West Indies (box 4)
- "Aspects of the Economic, Religious, and Social History of the 18th-Century Jamaican Jews Derived From Their Wills," term paper by Melvin R. Zager, 1956 (SC-13486)
- Birth, marriage, death, circumcision and other vital records of Jews, 1800–1950 (manuscript collection 465; microfilms 3002–4)
- Carillon, Rabbi Benjamin C., dedication certificate for temporary synagogue in Montego Bay, 1845 (SC-13468)
- Commercial documents, 1708–90 (SC-13552)
- D'Aguilar family, journal of voyage to New York from Port Royal, 1807 (SC-2589)
- Delgado family, genealogical information, 1725–1973 (Genealogies file)
- De Sola family, birth and marriage records, 1798–1821 (SC-2794); receipts for snuff (rare documents file)
- Enriques, Jacob Jeosua Bueno, petition to king of England, 1996 (SC-3232)

- His, Jeossuah, of Cordova, philosophical treatise, n.d. (SC-9725)
- History of Jews of Jamaica (partial), by Jeorge F. Judah, 1901 (SC-13484)
- Kingston, Jamaica, marriage registers at English and German synagogues, 1788–1842; 1853 (SC-6306)
- Kingston, Jamaica, registers of births, deaths and marriages, 1788–1918 (SC-13463, SC-13464, microfilm 3003)
- Lee, John, will, 1831 (SC-6729)
- Lopez, Aaron, correspondence mentioning Abraham Pereira Mendes, 1768 (manuscript collection 231; rare documents file)
- Mendes, Abraham P., sermon in tribute to Rev. Moses N. Nathan, n.d. (SC-8040)
- Moreno, Gabriel, will, 1695 (SC-8450)
- Nieto, David H., and Esther Belasco, *ketubah*, 1873 (SC-9125; flat file C5:D15)
- Petitions and other materials re Jews in Jamaica (and Bermuda), 1698 . . . 1776 (microfilm 578)
- Plantation and house list of Jews in Jamaica and Barbados, plus petition of Jews to queen of England, 1692 (SC-12932)
- Stanton, Miriam, account of escape from Nazi Germany in 1941, 1989 (SC-11893)
- "Study of the Life of the Jews in Jamaica, as Reflected in Their Wills, 1692–1798," term paper by David M. Zielonka, 1963 (SC-13489)
- Synagogue of the amalgamated Israelites, programs 1884, 1885 (SC-13477)
- Touro, Isaac, Papers, Kingston, Jamaica, 1760 (SC-12400)
- Wills, 1692–1798 (microfilm 140); 1768–1800 (SC-13478); alphabetized list filed in AJA (SC-13465)
- Miscellaneous documents and prayer books, 1913– (manuscript collection 339)
- Miscellaneous pages from journals of the assembly, 1760, 1774, 1808, 1809, 1820 (SC-13476)

London's Spanish and Portuguese Jews' Congregation* holds a list of Jewish tombstones in Jamaica.

Daniel Silvera's website on Jamaican-Jewish genealogy includes information on the Silvera family genealogy, studies of 19th-century Jewish families, newspaper clippings and a surname index.

The Family History Library (FHL) collection includes microfilms of Jamaican records of interest to Jewish genealogists. A database of Jewish records prepared by the FHL for IAJGS is available at WWW.JEWISHGEN.ORG; the full FHL catalogue may be consulted at WWW.FAMILYSEARCH.ORG. The FHL also holds microfilms of Jamaican wills; an alphabetical index appears online.

The contemporary Sephardic and Ashkenazic Jewish communities of Jamaica have joined to form the United Congregation of Israelites.*

Websites

American Jewish Archives, WWW.HUC.EDU/AJA
American Jewish Historical Society, WWW.AJHS.ORG
Caribbean Genealogy Research, WWW.CANDOO.COM/GENRESOURCES

Family History Library, WWW.FAMILYSEARCH.ORG
IAJGS International Jewish Cemetery Project, WWW.JEWISHGEN.ORG/
CEMETERY
Jamaican Jewish Genealogy, WWW6.PAIR.COM/SILVERA/JAMGEN
Jamaican wills, WWW.APEX.NET.AU/~TMJ
Jewish Communities of the World, WWW.WJC.ORG.IL/COMMUNITIES/
JEWISH_COMMUNITIES_OF_THE_WORLD
JewishGen, WWW.JEWISHGEN.ORG
New York Public Library, Dorot Jewish Division, WWW.NYPL.ORG/
RESEARCH/CHSS/JWS/JEWISH.HTML
Sephard, WWW.SEPHARDIM.ORG/JAMGEN
Sephardim, WWW.SEPHARDIM.ORG/JAMGEN/JGLDSRESOURCES.HTML
Spanish and Portuguese Jews' Congregation (Bevis Marks),
WWW.JEWISHGEN.ORG/JCR-UK/COMMUNITY/BEVIS/HISTORY.HTM

Bibliography

Andrade, A.P.M. *Jews of Jamaica: A Record of the Jews in Jamaica from the English Conquest to the Present Time.* Kingston: Jamaica Times, 1941. (See Paul White, below, for index information.)

Arbell, Mordechai. *The Portuguese Jews of Jamaica.* Kingston: Canoe Press, 2000.

Barnett, Richard D. "The Correspondence of the Mahamad [Council] of the Spanish and Portuguese Congregation of London during the Seventeenth and Eighteenth Centuries." *Transactions of the Jewish Historical Society of England* 20 (1959–61): 10.

Barnett, Richard D., and Philip Wright. *The Jews of Jamaica: Tombstone Inscriptions 1663–1880,* edited by Oron Yoffe. Jerusalem: Ben Zvi Institute, 1997.

Beker, Avi, ed. *Jewish Communities of the World.* Jerusalem: World Jewish Congress & Lerner Publications Company, 1998. Abridged version: WWW.WJC.ORG.IL/COMMUNITIES/JEWISH_COMMUNITIES_OF_THE_WORLD.

Cohen, Martin A., and Abraham J. Peck, eds. *Sephardim in the Americas: Studies in Culture and History.* Tuscaloosa: University of Alabama Press/American Jewish Archives, 1992.

Collins, Kenneth E. "Jewish Medical Students and Graduates in Scotland, 1739–1862." *Jewish Historical Studies* (Jewish Historical Society of England) 29 (1982–86): 75–96.

"Discovering and Utilizing Sources for the History of the Jews in The Netherlands," *Studia Rosenthaliana* (1981): 75–84.

"The Earliest Extant Minute Books of the Spanish and Portuguese Congregation Shearith Israel in New York, 1728–1786." *Publications of the American Jewish Historical Society* 21 (1913): 77.

Faber, Eli. *Jews, Slaves, and the Slave Trade.* New York: New York University Press, 1998.

Fortune, Stephen Alexander. *Merchants and Jews: The Struggle for British West Indian Commerce, 1650–1750.* Gainesville: University of Florida Presses, 1984.

Holzberg, Carol S. *Minorities and Power in a Black Society: The Jewish Community of Jamaica.* Lanham, Md.: North-South, 1987.

Hurwitz, Samuel J., and Edith Hurwitz. "The New World Sets an Example for the Old: The Jews of Jamaica and Political Rights 1661–1831." *American Jewish Historical Quarterly* 55 (1965–66).

"Jamaica Synagogue Ruins & Jewish Cemetery to Be Protected, Rebuilt." *Jewish Heritage Report* 1, nos. 3–4 (Winter 1997–98); WWW.ISJM.ORG/JHR/NOS3-4/JAMSYN.HTM.

Korn, Bertram W. "The Haham DeCordova of Jamaica." *American Jewish Archives* 18 (1966): 141–54.

Lindo, Donald. *Out of Many, One People.* CD-ROM of Jamaican genealogy (50,000 names). Cited in MacFarlane, *Shem Tov,* and WWW6.PAIR.COM/SILVERA/MAIN.HTML.

MacFarlane, Anthony. "Jamaican Jewish Genealogy." *Shem Tov* 15, no. 4 (December 1999): 1, 3.

Mitchell, Madeleine E. *Jamaican Ancestry: How to Find Out More.* Bowie, Md.: Heritage Books, 1998.

Porter, Stephen D. *Jamaican Records: A Research Manual.* Available from the author, WWW.SEPHARDIM.ORG/JAMGEN/SPORTER.HTML.

Rosenbloom, Joseph R. "Notes on the Jews' Tribute in Jamaica." In Jewish Historical Society of England, *Transactions,* Sessions 1959–61, vol. 20 (1964).

Schlesinger, Benjamin. "The Jews of Jamaica: A Historical View." *Caribbean Quarterly* 13, no. 1 (March 1967): 46–53.

de Souza, Ernest Henriques. *Pictorial: Featuring Some Aspects of Jamaica's Jewry.* Kingston, 1986.

White, Paul F., comp. Table of contents and biographical index (typescript) to Andrade's *A Record of the Jews of Jamaica.* Montego Bay, Jamaica: Author, 1964.

Martinique

History. Early in the 17th century, the first Jews in French Martinique settled in Dutch commercial outposts. The first synagogue was founded in 1667. In 1685, when Louis XIV expelled the Jews from the French islands, most of the 96 remaining Jews departed for Curaçao. Jews from France and North Africa settled in Fort de France, Martinique, in the 1960s and 1970s.

Resources. The Caribbean Genealogy Research website presents information on Martinique's archives and other resources. The website of *Genealogie et Histoire de la Caraibe* (in French with some English) offers insights to genealogists.

Martinique's Jewish community* maintains a synagogue and community center, including a Talmud Torah, youth club and *chevra kadisha.*

Websites

Caribbean Genealogy Research, WWW.CANDOO.COM/GENRESOURCES
Genealogie et Histoire de la Caraibe (Genealogy and history of the Caribbean), MEMBERS.AOL.COM/GHCARAIBE

Bibliography

Cohen, Martin A., and Abraham J. Peck, eds. *Sephardim in the Americas: Studies in Culture and History.* Tuscaloosa: University of Alabama Press/American Jewish Archives, 1992.

Faber, Eli. *A Time for Planting: The First Migration 1654–1820.* Baltimore: Johns Hopkins University Press, 1992.

Liebman, Seymour B. "Anti-Semitism in Martinique in the 17th Century." *Tradition* 10, no. 4 (Fall 1969): 40–47.

Netherlands Antilles
(see Aruba; Curaçao; St. Eustatius)

Nevis

History. The Sephardic community on Nevis was part of the extensive Caribbean Jewish trading network that flourished during the 17th century.

Resources. The Caribbean Genealogy Research website presents information on Nevis's archives and other resources. The St. Kitts-Nevis GenWeb Page offers links to a number of genealogy websites.

Civil records in The Netherlands may provide information on Jewish families in Nevis (see THE NETHERLANDS).

Rabbi Malcolm Stern discovered in 1957 on Nevis the ruins of a 17th-century synagogue and an abandoned cemetery with legible tombstones. His 1971 article cites the inscriptions on the tombstones, translated from the Portuguese.

The American Jewish Archives* collection of Malcolm H. Stern Papers includes files on the Jews of Nevis (box 22, file 7) and vital records for Nevis (box 27, file 12). "Some Notes on the Jews of Nevis," by Malcolm Stern, is held in record SC-13476. Microfilm 2594 includes photographs and transcriptions of old tombstones.

Fifteen of the grave markers at the Nevis Jewish Cemetery are decipherable. The Jewish Community of Nevis Archaeology Project website posts a great deal of information:

> The Jewish Cemetery in Charlestown . . . contains gravestones that are engraved in English, Hebrew and Portuguese, dating from 1679 to 1768. Once constituting 25% of the island's population, the Sephardic Jews of Nevis brought to the island the secret of how to crystallize sugar. . . . A stone-walled path, known as the 'Jews Walk,' leads from the cemetery to the supposed site of the community's synagogue, which is believed to have been built in 1684.

The IAJGS International Jewish Cemetery Project website on JewishGen provides information on Nevis.

The Center for Research on Dutch Jewry* at Hebrew University in Jerusalem has compiled a number of genealogically useful databases and other resources.

The Family History Library (FHL) collection includes microfilms of interest to Jewish genealogists researching Nevis. A database of Jewish records prepared by the FHL for IAJGS is available on the JewishGen website.

Websites

American Jewish Archives, WWW.HUC.EDU/AJA
Caribbean Genealogy Research, WWW.CANDOO.COM/GENRESOURCES/DETAILS.HTM
Center for Research on Dutch Jewry, DUTCHJEWRY.HUJI.AC.IL
Family History Library, WWW.FAMILYSEARCH.ORG
Florida International University Library, WWW.FIU.EDU/~LIBRARY/INTERNET/SUBJECTS/JEWISHSITES.HTML
IAJGS International Jewish Cemetery Project, WWW.JEWISHGEN.ORG/CEMETERY
Jewish Cemetery of Charlestown, WWW.GEOGRAPHIA.COM/STKITTS-NEVIS/KNPNT03.HTM
Jewish Cemetery in Nevis, WWW.TC.UMN.EDU/~TERRE011/CEMETERY.HTML
Jewish Community of Nevis Archaeology Project, WWW.TC.UMN.EDU/~TERRE011/NEVIS.HTML
JewishGen, WWW.JEWISHGEN.ORG
Jewish Latin America and the Caribbean, WWW.FIU.EDU/~LIBRARY/INTERNET/SUBJECTS/JEWISHSITES.HTML
Nevis Genealogical Information, WEBSITE.LINEONE.NET/~STKITTSNEVIS/NEVRECD.HTM
RootsWeb Caribbean-L Archive, ARCHIVER.ROOTSWEB.COM/TH/INDEX/CARIBBEAN/
St. Kitts-Nevis GenWeb Page, WEBSITE.LINEONE.NET/~STKITTSNEVIS/GENEALOG.HTM#ISLAND SPECIFIC

Bibliography

Cohen, Martin A., and Abraham J. Peck, eds. *Sephardim in the Americas: Studies in Culture and History.* Tuscaloosa: University of Alabama Press/American Jewish Archives, 1992.
Faber, Eli. *A Time for Planting: The First Migration 1654–1820.* Baltimore: Johns Hopkins University Press, 1992.
Malka, Jeffrey S. *Sephardic Genealogy.* Bergenfield, N.J.: Avotaynu, 2003.
Stern, Malcolm H. "A Successful Caribbean Restoration: The Nevis Story," *American Jewish Historical Quarterly* 61, no. 1 (1971–72).

Panama

History. In their hundred-year history of Jewish life in Panama, E.A. Fidanque and colleagues note the connection of a number of Panamanian families to Sephardim from Hamburg, Germany. In their discussion of the Sephardim of the Altona Cemetery, Marian and Ramon Sarraga observe that "several epitaphs in Altona and in Hamburg's modern Jewish cemetery (Ohlsdorf) attest to the 19th-century migration of Hamburg Sephardim to the Caribbean."

Resources. The American Jewish Archives* holds a file on the Robles family genealogy and documents (Flat File C5:D7).

The Panama GenWeb website presents information of interest to genealogists researching Panama.

Websites

American Jewish Archives, WWW.HUC.EDU/AJA
Panama GenWeb page, WWW.ROOTSWEB.COM/~PANWGW/PANAMA_HOME.HTM

Bibliography

Fidanque, E.A., et al. *Kol Shearith Israel: A Hundred Years of Jewish Life in Panama.* Panama, 1977.
Sarraga, Marian and Ramon. "The Sephardim of the Altona Cemetery." *AVOTAYNU* 8, no. 1 (Spring 1992): 14-17.

Puerto Rico

History. Christopher Columbus discovered Puerto Rico in 1493. In 1808, Napoleon decreed that all Jews were to adopt hereditary surnames. According to Suzan Wynne, records of these name adoptions in the archives of Bordeaux, France, show that the families listed in those records included members born in Puerto Rico.

In 1898, at the conclusion of the Spanish-American War, virtually no Jews lived on the island. As the Nazis rose to power, European Jewish refugees fled to Puerto Rico. In 1942, they established the Jewish Community Center. In the 1950s and 1960s, Jews from the United States and Cuba swelled the community. Most Jews live in San Juan; a number of families reside in Ponce and Mayaguez.

Resources. The Caribbean Genealogy Research website presents information on Puerto Rico's archives, libraries, census records and other resources. The Puerto Rico GenWeb page also offers a number of links to information of interest to Jewish genealogists.

Communal life is varied in Puerto Rico. In San Juan there are a Reform and a Conservative synagogue.*

The U.S. National Archives, Northeast Region,* holds hardcopy naturalization records for Puerto Rico. Also at this National Archives branch are World War I draft registrations for Puerto Rico. Microfilmed records also are available through the Family History Library (FHL), searchable online.

The U.S. Bureau of the Census issued a 1900 report on an 1899 census of Puerto Rico, available at the FHL. The FHL also holds a number of English-language histories of Puerto Rico, plus a Spanish-language guide to the Historical Archives of Puerto Rico and a Spanish-language catalogue of resident foreigners in Puerto Rico in the 19th century. A Spanish-language work on 19th-century immigration to Puerto Rico is available in Salt Lake City in book form, and at LDS Family History Centers on microfilm (#924457, item 1).

Websites

Caribbean Genealogy Research, WWW.CANDOO.COM/GENRESOURCES
Family History Library, WWW.FAMILYSEARCH.ORG
Jewish Communities of the World, WWW.WJC.ORG.IL/COMMUNITIES/ JEWISH_COMMUNITIES_OF_THE_WORLD
Puerto Rico GenWeb, WWW.ROOTSWEB.COM/~PRWGW/INDEX.HTML

Bibliography

Beker, Avi, ed. *Jewish Communities of the World.* Jerusalem: World Jewish Congress & Lerner Publications Company, 1998. Abridged version: WWW.WJC.ORG.IL/COMMUNITIES/JEWISH_COMMUNITIES_OF_THE_WORLD.

Cifre de Loubriel, Estela. *Catalogo de Extranjeros Residentes en Puerto Rico en el Siglo XIX* (Catalogue of resident foreigners in Puerto Rico in the 19th century). Rio Piedras: Ediciones de la Universidad de Puerto Rico, 1962.

————. *La Immigracion a Puerto Rico durante el Siglo XIX* (Immigration to Puerto Rico during the 19th century). San Juan: Instituto de Cultura Puertoriqueno, 1964.

Gomez-Canedo, Lino. *Los Archivos Historicos de Puerto Rico* (Historical Archives of Puerto Rico). San Juan: Archivo General de Puerto Rico, 1964.

Guzik, Estelle. *Genealogical Resources in the New York Metropolitan Area.* New York: Jewish Genealogical Society, 1989.

United States Bureau of the Census. *Report on the Census of Puerto Rico, 1899.* Washington, D.C.: Government Printing Office, 1900.

Wynne, Suzan. "Third International Seminar (1991, Salt Lake City): An Update." *AVOTAYNU* 7, no. 1 (Spring 1991): 7–8.

St. Eustatius

History. In the 18th century, St. Eustatius was the most prosperous mercantile center in the Caribbean. Many members of its large Jewish population were engaged in trade. From four families on the island in 1722, the number grew large enough to build a synagogue. By 1795, upon occupation by the British and French, most Jews had left St. Eustatius. Only five inhabitants remained there in 1818.

Resources. Inscriptions on the gravestones in the small Jewish cemetery have been copied and published by John Hartog. Names listed indicate that both Ashkenazim and Sephardim lived on St. Eustatius.

The American Jewish Archives* collection includes the following files of Jewish interest (among others):

- Archaeology (SC-13493; SC-13491)
- Commercial documents, 1708–90 (SC-13552)
- "Congregation 'Honen Daliem' of St. Eustatius," by John Hartog, 1976 (SC-13472; microfilm 3002)

- "Debate on Seizure and Confiscation of Private Property in St. Eustatius," *Parliamentary History of England,* 1781 (SC-13484)
- Dutch pamphlet, *Missive,* 1778 (microfilm 60)
- "Genesis and Exodus: Some Aspects of the Early Jewish Community on the Island of St. Eustatius in the Netherlands Antilles," by Samuel S. Strouse, 1962 (SC-13480)
- Hart, Naphtali, Jr., correspondence, 1773 (manuscript collection 231)
- Marriages performed in Amsterdam, Curaçao and St. Eustatius of couples born in the United States, 1717–96 (SC-7816; microfilm 3002)
- Newspaper article, plight of Jewish community, 1781 (SC-5103)
- Resident list in 1781 (SC-13492)
- Tombstones, letter from Rabbi Leo M. Abrami, 1974 (SC-3234; microfilm 2594); inscriptions from St. Eustatius Jewish cemetery, 1700–1825 (SC-13483; microfilm 3004)

In *First American Jewish Families,* Rabbi Malcolm Stern's genealogies include Jews who lived on St. Eustatius.

The Center for Research on Dutch Jewry* has compiled a number of genealogically useful databases and other resources.

The Family History Library (FHL) collection includes microfilms of interest to Jewish genealogists researching St. Eustatius. A database of Jewish records prepared by the FHL for IAJGS is available on the JewishGen website. The full FHL catalogue may be consulted online.

Websites

American Jewish Archives, WWW.HUC.EDU/AJA
Center for Research on Dutch Jewry, DUTCHJEWRY.HUJI.AC.IL
Family History Library, WWW.FAMILYSEARCH.ORG
JewishGen, WWW.JEWISHGEN.ORG
Netherlands Antilles GenWeb, WWW.ROOTSWEB.COM/~ANTWGW

Bibliography

Cohen, Martin A., and Abraham J. Peck, eds. *Sephardim in the Americas: Studies in Culture and History.* Tuscaloosa: University of Alabama Press/American Jewish Archives, 1992.

Emmanuel, Isaac S., and Suzanne A. Emmanuel. *History of the Jews in the Netherlands Antilles.* 2 vols. Cincinnati: American Jewish Archives, 1970.

Faber, Eli. *A Time for Planting: The First Migration 1654–1820.* Baltimore: Johns Hopkins University Press, 1992.

Freedman, Warren. *World Guide for the Jewish Traveler.* New York: E.P. Dutton, 1984.

Hartog, John. "The Honen Dalim Congregation of St. Eustatius." *American Jewish Archives* 19 (1967): 65.

————. *The Jews and St. Eustatius: The Eighteenth-Century Jewish Congregation Honen Dalim and Description of the Old Cemetery.* Aruba: Dewit Scores, 1976.

"St. Eustatius." *AVOTAYNU* 2, no. 2 (May 1986): 31.

Suriname (Dutch Guyana)

History. The Jewish community of Suriname, on the northern coast of South America, probably was founded during the 1660s. Following the Dutch occupation in 1668, Portuguese and Spanish Jews arrived from Amsterdam. By 1694, 92 Sephardic and approximately 12 Ashkenazic families resided

Interior of synagogue in Suriname. Note the sandy floor.

in the community, along with 50 unmarried individuals. By 1685, a Sephardic synagogue had been constructed, and, by the 1730s, at least two synagogues operated, one Sephardic and one Ashkenazic. The Jews there traded actively with fellow Jews throughout the Caribbean area. A group of Italian Jews also established a 17th-century settlement in Dutch Guyana. In the first half of the 18th century, Ashkenazic Jews from Rotterdam followed. Special privileges granted by the British and then by the Dutch permitted the Jews to settle in the "Jodensavanne," the "Jewish savannah," a region in which Jews owned more than 115 plantations specializing in sugar and refining.

Resources. The Central Record Bureau (Burgerlijke Stand) in Suriname holds all birth, marriage and death records after 1816, but political considerations have made these records unavailable to the public. Sea-damaged pre-1816 records are held by the National Archives (Rijksarchief)* in The Hague, Netherlands, but the documents may be unavailable for research pending restoration.

Civil records in The Netherlands may provide information on Suriname Jewish families (see THE NETHERLANDS). Microfilmed Suriname records also are available at the Centraal Bureau Voor Genealogie* in The Netherlands.

American Jewish Archives* holdings include:

- Congregational and community records (microfilms 67–67n, 176–198; SC-6851; 527-527t)
- Philately: Neveh Shalom Synagogue, 1961 (Miscellaneous file); Old Synagogue, 1968 (SC-13473)
- Parimaribo correspondence, ledgers, congregational records (Manuscript Collection No. 505, Box No. X-364, SC-13498 to SC-13501)
- Maps (Flat file, Cabinet 4, Drawer 4)
- Miscellaneous (microfilm 316, Picture Collection, Nearprint Box-Geography)
- Nassy family documents, letters, papers, 1765–1800 (Miscellaneous file and others)
- Genealogies for Bennett families (Genealogies file)

The FHL microfilm collection includes records held by the American Jewish Archives,* including the full records of the Sephardic synagogue, 1754–1920.

Suriname's Jewish communal organization is the Kerkeraad der Nederlands Portugees Israelitische Gemeente in Suriname.* The two 18th-century synagogues in Paramaribo serve the needs of the Jewish community. The community publishes *Sim Shalom,* a Dutch-language newspaper.

The American Jewish Historical Society* holds *mohel* books and other records from the Suriname Jewish community, 1746–1968, and microfilmed periodicals. A list of Jewish planters circa 1700–50 is published in Ralph Bennett's Summer 1992 *AVOTAYNU* article. Bennett also reviews Verdooner's *Trouwen in Mokum, 1598–1811,* which provides data compiled from 119 vital statistics registers on more than 15,000 marriages in Amsterdam.

The Center for Research on Dutch Jewry* of Hebrew University in Jerusalem has compiled a number of genealogically useful databases and other resources.

The Family History Library (FHL) collection includes microfilms of interest to Jewish genealogists. A database of Jewish records prepared by the FHL for IAJGS is available on the JewishGen website; the full FHL catalogue may be consulted online.

The publication *Genealogie et Histoire de la Caraibe* (Genealogy and history of the Caribbean), no. 50, June 1993, reports on documents pertaining to individual Jewish families in Suriname and Amsterdam in the late 18th century.

Websites

American Jewish Archives, WWW.HUC.EDU/AJA
American Jewish Historical Society, WWW.AJHS.ORG
Caribbean Genealogy Research, WWW.CANDOO.COM/GENRESOURCES
Center for Research on Dutch Jewry, DUTCHJEWRY.HUJI.AC.IL
Family History Library, WWW.FAMILYSEARCH.ORG
Genealogie et Histoire de la Caraibe (Genealogy and history of the Caribbean), MEMBERS.AOL.COM/GHCARAIBE
History of Jews in Suriname, WWW.ANGELFIRE.COM/MB2/JODENSAVANNE
Jewish Communities of the World, WWW.WJC.ORG.IL/COMMUNITIES/JEWISH_COMMUNITIES_OF_THE_WORLD
JewishGen, WWW.JEWISHGEN.ORG
Netherlands Society for Jewish Genealogy, WWW.NLJEWGEN.ORG

Bibliography

Abensur, Philip. "From Our Contributing Editor—France." *AVOTAYNU* 9, no. 4 (Winter 1993): 53.

Beker, Avi, ed. *Jewish Communities of the World.* Jerusalem: World Jewish Congress & Lerner Publications Company, 1998. Abridged version: WWW.WJC.ORG.IL/COMMUNITIES/JEWISH_COMMUNITIES_OF_THE_WORLD.

Bennett, Ralph. "Filling in the Blanks in Dutch-Jewish Genealogy." *AVOTAYNU* 9, no. 2 (Summer 1993): 28–31.

———. "The Jews of Exotic Surinam and Their History." *AVOTAYNU* 8, no. 2 (Summer 1992): 16–18.

Caplan, Judith Shulamith Langer. "Another Surnamer Surfaces." *AVOTAYNU* 13, no. 4 (Winter 1997): 51–57.

Cohen, Martin A., and Abraham J. Peck, eds. *Sephardim in the Americas: Studies in Culture and History.* Tuscaloosa: University of Alabama Press/American Jewish Archives, 1992.

Cohen, Robert. "The Misdated Ketubah: A Note on the Beginnings of the Surinam Jewish Community." *American Jewish Archives* 36, no. 1 (April 1984): 12–15.

———. *Jews in Another Environment: Surinam in the Second Half of the Eighteenth Century.* New York: E.J. Brill, 1991.

Seventeenth-century view of the "Joode Savaane," Dutch Guiana (now Suriname)

Cohen, R., ed. *The Jewish Nation in Surinam: Historical Essays.* Amsterdam: S. Emmering, 1982.

Cohen, Simon, trans. *Essai historique sur la colonie de Surinam: English Historical Essay on the Colony of Surinam, 1788,* edited by Jacob R. Marcus and Stanley F. Chyet. Cincinnati: American Jewish Archives, 1974.

Emmanuel, Isaac S., and Suzanne A. Emmanuel. *History of the Jews in the Netherlands Antilles.* 2 vols. Cincinnati: American Jewish Archives, 1970.

Genealogie et Histoire de la Caraibe (Genealogy and history of the Caribbean), no. 50 (June 1993). MEMBERS.AOL.COM/GHCARAIBE.

Hilfman, P.A. "Notes on the History of the Jews in Surinam." *Publications of the American Jewish Historical Society* 18 (1906): 179–207. See also Index to vols. 1–20 for articles on Suriname.

Malka, Jeffrey S. *Sephardic Genealogy.* Bergenfield, N.J.: Avotaynu, 2003.

Oudschans Dentz, Frederik. *American Jewish Historical Society Journal* (1906).

———. *De kolonisatie van de Portugeesch Joodsche natie in Suriname en de geschiedenis van de Joden Savanne.* Amsterdam: M. Hertzberger, 1927(?). [Dutch]

Stern, Malcolm H., comp. *First American Jewish Families: 600 Genealogies 1654–1988,* 3d ed., updated and rev. Baltimore: Ottenheimer, 1991.

Stern, Malcolm H. "Portuguese Sephardim in the Americas." *Sephardim in the Americas: Studies in Culture and History,* edited by Martin A. Cohen and Abraham J. Peck, 141–78. Tuscaloosa: University of Alabama Press/American Jewish Archives, 1992.

Swierenga, Robert P. *The Forerunners: Dutch Jewry in the North American Diaspora.* Detroit: Wayne State University Press, 1994.

Verdooner, Dave. *Trouwen in Mokum, 1598–1811* (Jewish marriages in Amsterdam). 2 vols. The Hague, Netherlands: Warray, 1992.

U.S. Virgin Islands (St. Thomas and St. Croix)

History. The first Jews in the Virgin Islands arrived in 1655—Portuguese and Spanish ship owners, planters of sugar cane and producers of rum and molasses—from Barbados, France, Holland, Recife (Brazil) and Suriname. Gabriel Milan, a Jew, was sent to the islands by Denmark's King Christian in 1684 to serve as governor. When the British attacked the island of St. Eustatius for having assisted in the American Revolution, the Jewish community was destroyed; the Jews moved to the islands of St. Thomas and St. Croix. Denmark ruled St. Thomas and St. Croix until 1917.

When the Panama Canal opened in 1914, most of the islands' Jewish population emigrated to Panama. The Jewish population is currently on the rise, principally from the North American mainland.

In 1796, the synagogue Berakha v'Shalom v'Gmilut Hassadim was founded; the congregation continues to the present, known as the Hebrew Congregation of St. Thomas.* The congregation conducts services in the oldest synagogue building in continuous use under the American flag.

Resources. The Caribbean Genealogy Research website lists information on vital records, libraries and museums in the U.S. Virgin Islands and the holdings of the Northeast Branch of the U.S. National Archives,* government record repositories, the museum and historical society, resources, and the LDS microfilm index.

Two U.S. Virgin Island cemeteries* are located in Charlotte Amalie, St. Thomas. (Some researchers have reported that the cemeteries are in dangerous locations.) Julius Margolinsky indexed 299 epitaphs, compiled from records in the archives of the Jewish Community in Copenhagen. The Scandinavia SIG plans to digitize and post this list on its website. The IAJGS International Jewish Cemetery Project website on JewishGen provides information on cemeteries on St. Croix and St. Thomas.

Records for the period of Danish rule are held by the Danish National Archives.* Danish-language information is available online. Information in English can be found in Erik Gøbel's *A Guide to Sources for the History of the Danish West Indies (U.S. Virgin Islands), 1671–1917.*

The American Jewish Archives* collection includes the following files of Jewish interest (among others):

- Malcolm H. Stern Papers, Piza family of St. Thomas, 1657–1951 (box 24, file 6); records of St. Thomas and the Virgin Islands, 1837–1973 (box 25, file 8); vital records for St. Thomas, St. Croix and Nevis (box 27, file 12).
- List of epitaphs, Christiansted Jewish cemetery, St. Croix, 1957, 1958 (SC-13471)
- Levi, George, and Robles, E.A., document fragments, 1914 (SC-13551)

The following American Jewish Archives resources provide information on St. Thomas:

- Birth records, 1786–1954 (microfilm 125; SC-13730)
- Birth, marriage, death, circumcision and other vital records of Jews (also in Jamaica), 1800–1950 (manuscript collection 465; microfilms 3002–4)
- Danish historical and commercial records
- De Sola, Hannah, confirmation certificate, 1844 (SC-2795)
- Epitaphs from the Jewish cemetery in St. Thomas, 1837–1916 (microfilm 3002; SC-3233)
- "Jews in Nineteenth Century St. Thomas: The Relationship of a Peripheral Jewish Community in the Caribbean with an Established Community of Coreligionists in Europe," thesis by Judah M. Cohen, 1995 (SC-14309)
- Levy, Nathan, American consul on St. Thomas, official U.S. correspondence, 1836–40 (SC-7105)
- Marriage and other life-cycle records, St. Thomas Hebrew Congregation, 1786–1969 (microfilm 3612)
- Milan, Gabriel, biography by Fredrik J. Krarup, Denmark, 1893 (microfilm 523) governor of St. Thomas, records, 1684–1685 (SC-8179)
- St. Thomas Hebrew Congregation documents
- Sasso, Rabbi Moses D., papers, sermons, miscellaneous, 1914–66 (microfilm 1384; SC-13550)
- Savan Jewish Cemetery history, including sampling of tombstone inscriptions, 1978 (SC-13494)

The American Jewish Historical Society* holds microfilms of vital records from the 18th through the 20th centuries and a family tree of Joshua Piza by Dida Lindo Guiterman (1772–1850).

The Family History Library (FHL) collection includes microfilms of interest to Jewish genealogists researching the U.S. Virgin Islands. A database of Jewish records prepared by the FHL for IAJGS is available on the JewishGen website. The full FHL catalogue may be consulted online. Danish civil records for the time period when the Virgin Islands were un- der Danish rule also may be consulted. In addition, naturalization records from U.S. courts may be available.

The Scandinavian SIG's webpages on the Virgin Islands offer information and links on history, census and vital records, maps and an LDS microfilm index. The USVI GenWeb page offers many links to resources and sites of interest.

In *First American Jewish Families,* Rabbi Malcolm Stern's genealogies include Jews who lived in St. Thomas.

Websites

American Jewish Archives, WWW.HUC.EDU/AJA
American Jewish Historical Society, WWW.AJHS.ORG
Caribbean Genealogy Research, WWW.CANDOO.COM/GENRESOURCES
Danish National Archives, WWW.SA.DK/RA/BRUGEARKIVET/RAsamL/FOER1848/VESTIND.HTM (in Danish)
Family History Library, WWW.FAMILYSEARCH.ORG
Hebrew Congregation of St. Thomas, WWW.ONEPAPER.COM/SYNAGOGUE
IAJGS International Jewish Cemetery Project, WWW.JEWISHGEN.ORG/CEMETERY
JewishGen, WWW.JEWISHGEN.ORG
Scandinavia SIG, WWW.JEWISHGEN.ORG/SCANDINAVIA/VIRGINISLANDS.HTM
USVI GenWeb, WWW.ROOTSWEB.COM/~USVI

Bibliography

Cohen, Martin A., and Abraham J. Peck, eds. *Sephardim in the Americas: Studies in Culture and History.* Tuscaloosa: University of Alabama Press/American Jewish Archives, 1992.
Gøbel, Erik. *A Guide to Sources for the History of the Danish West Indies (U.S. Virgin Islands), 1671–1917.* Odense: University Press of Southern Denmark, 2002.
Encyclopaedia Judaica, c.f. Virgin Islands.
Margolinsky, Julius, comp. *299 Epitaphs on the Jewish Cemetery in St. Thomas, W.I. 1837–1916.* Copenhagen, 1957.
———. *Jodiske Dodsfald i Danmark 1693–1976* (Jewish deaths in Denmark 1693–1976). Lyngby, Denmark: Dansk Historisk Handbogsforlag, 1977.
Paiewonsky, Isidor. "Jewish Historical Development in the Virgin Islands, 1665–1959." Charlotte Amalie, 1959.
Relkin, Stanley T., and Monty R. Abrams, eds. *A Short History of the Hebrew Congregation of St. Thomas.* St. Thomas, V.I.: Hebrew Congregation of St. Thomas, 1983.
Swierenga, Robert P. *The Forerunners: Dutch Jewry in the North American Diaspora.* Detroit: Wayne State University Press, 1994.

Addresses

American Jewish Archives, 3101 Clifton Avenue, Cincinnati, OH 45220; telephone: (513) 221-1875; fax: (513) 221-7812; website WWW.HUC.EDU/AJA
American Jewish Historical Society, 15 West 16th Street, New York, NY 10011; telephone: (212) 294-6160; fax: (212) 294-6161. New England branch, 160 Herrick Road, Newton Centre, MA 02459; telephone: (617) 559-8880; fax: (617) 559-8881; web-site: WWW.AJHS.ORG
Association Culturelle Israelite de la Martinique, Maison Grambin, Platean Fofo Voie Principale, 97233 Schoelcher, Martinique; telephone: 596 61 51 31
Bahamas Ministry of Tourism, P.O. Box N-3701, Nassau, B.F.
Barbados Board of Tourism, 800 Second Avenue, New York, NY 10017
Caribbean Historical & Genealogical Journal, TCI Genealogical Resources, P.O. Box 15839, San Luis Obispo, CA 93406; website: WWW.ROOTSWEB.COM/~CARIBGW/CGW_ARCHIVE/CUBA/HAVANA.HTM

Caribbean Jewish Congress, P.O. Box 1331, Bridgetown, Barbados; telephone: 809 436 8163

Center for Research on Dutch Jewry, Hebrew University, Mount Scopus, 91905 Jerusalem, Israel; fax: 972-2-5880242; website: DUTCHJEWRY.HUJI.AC.IL

Centraal Bureau Voor Genealogie, Prins Willem-Alexanderhof 22 NI, 2595 BE The Hague, Netherlands

Centro Israelita de la Republica Dominicana, P.O. Box 2189, Santo Domingo; telephone: 809 535 6042; fax: 809 542 1908

Comision Coordinadora de las Sociedades Religiosas Hebreas de Cuba, Calle 1 Esq. 13, Vedado-Cuidad de la Habana 10400; telephone: 53 7 328 953; fax: 53 7 333 778

Communaute Culturelle Israelite, 1 Bas du Fort, 97190 Gosier, Pointe-a-Pitre, Guadeloupe; telephone: 590 90 99 08

Communidad Hebrea HaTikva Pio Rosado, 268 e/Habana y Trinidad, Santiago de Cuba 90100; telephone: 53 226 51078; website: WWW.JEWISHCUBA.ORG/HATIKVA/HATIKVA.HTML; e-mail: HATIKVA@CHH.CIGES.INF.CU

Congregation Shearith Israel, 8 West 70th Street, New York, NY 10023; telephone: (212) 873-0300; fax: 212.724.6165; website: WWW.SHEARITHISRAEL.ORG; e-mail: OFFICE@SHEARITHISRAEL.ORG

Costa Rica Board of Trade, 108 East 66th Street, New York, NY 10021

Cuban congregations in Cuba and the United States:

Conservative: Patronado de la Casa de la Communidad Hebrea de Cuba, Calle 13 e I, Vedado, Havana, Cuba

Orthodox: Hadath Israel, Calle Picota 52, Havana Vieja, Cuba

Reform: Av. de los Presidentes 502, Havana, Cuba

Sephardic: Centro Hebrea Sephardi de Cuba, 17th Street, #462, at E St., Vedado, Havana, Cuba; telephone: 53 7 326 623

Cuban Hebrew Congregation, Temple Beth Shmuel, 1700 Michigan Avenue, Miami Beach, FL 33139

Greater Miami Jewish Federation, 4200 Biscayne Blvd., Miami, FL 33137

Temple Tifereth Israel, 10500 Wilshire Blvd., Los Angeles, CA 90024

Curaçao Tourist Board, 19495 Biscayne Blvd., #804, Aventura, FL 33180; telephone: (305) 466-1900 or 800-3-CURACAO; fax: (305) 705-1234; e-mail: JOEL@AVENTURA.NPIPB.COM; additional offices: 475 Park Avenue South, #3209, New York, NY 10016; Curaçao Tourism Development Bureau, P.O. Box 3266, Curaçao, Netherlands Antilles; telephone: 011-599-9-461-600; fax: 011-599-9-461-2305

Family History Library, 35 North West Temple Street, Salt Lake City, UT 84150-3400; telephone: (801) 240-2331 or (800) 453-3860 x22331; fax: (801) 240-5551; website: WWW.FAMILYSEARCH.ORG

Haiti Jewish community, P.O. Box 687, Port-au-Prince, Haiti; telephone: 509 1 20 638

Hebrew Congregation of St. Thomas, P.O. Box 266, St. Thomas, VI 00801; telephone: 809-774-7704; website: WWW.ONEPAPER.COM/SYNAGOGUE

Index of Jewish Records at the Family History Center, website: WWW.JEWISHGEN.ORG/AJGS/FHLINDEXCD.HTML; WWW.IAJGS.ORG

Jamaican Jewish Genealogy Society, 58 Paddington Ter., Kingston 6, Jamaica; telephone: 1 876 927-9777; fax: 1 876 927-4369; e-mail: AINSLEY@CWJAMAICA.COM

Jewish Community, Pilo Sav 19, Av d'Estrees, Cayenne 97300, PB 655 Cayenne, Guyane Francaise (French Guyana) CEDEX 97335; telephone: 594 30 39 34; fax: 594 31 78 93

Jewish Community of Aruba, Beth Israel Synagogue, P.O. Box 50, Oranjestad, Aruba; telephone: 297 823 272; fax: 297 836 032

Jewish Community Council, P.O. Box 256, Bridgetown, Barbados; telephone: 809 432 0840

Jewish Cultural Historical Museum, adjacent to Mikve Israel-Emanuel Synagogue, Hanchi di Snoa 29, Punda, Curaçao; telephone: 461-1633; fax: 461-1214; website: WWW.SNOA.COM

Jewish Historical Society of England, 33 Seymour Place, London W1H 5AP England; telephone: 020 7723 5852; website: WWW.JHSE.ORG

Joint Distribution Committee Archives, 711 Third Avenue, New York, NY 10017; fax: 212-370-5467; website: WWW.JDC.ORG/WHO_ARCHIVES.HTML

Kahal Kadosh Beth Elohim, 86 Hasell Street, Charleston SC 29401; telephone: (843) 723-1090; fax: (843) 723-0537; website: WWW.KKBE.ORG

Kerkeraad der Nederlands Portugees Israelitische Gemeente in Suriname, P.O. Box 1834, Paramaribo, Suriname; telephone: 597 471 313; fax: 597 471 154

S.A.L. Mongui Maduro Library, P.O. Box 480, Curaçao, Netherlands Antilles; telephone: 599 9 737 5119; fax: 599 9 737 6875; website: WWW.MADUROLIBRARY.ORG

Nationaal Archief (National Archives) of the Netherlands Antilles, Scharlooweg 77, Willemstad, Curaçao, Nederlandse Antillen; telephone: 599 9 461 4866; fax: 599 9 461 6794; e-mail: NA@NATIONALARCHIVES.AN

New York Public Library, Dorot Jewish Division, Fifth Avenue and 42nd Street, New York, NY 10018-2788; telephone: (212) 930-0601; fax: (212) 642-0141; website: WWW.NYPL.ORG/RESEARCH/CHSS/JWS/JEWISH.HTML

Patronado de la Casa de la Communidad Hebrea de Cuba, Calle 13 e I, Vedado, Havana, Cuba

Rijksarchief (National Archives), Algemeen Rijks-archief, Prins Willem-Alexanderhof, ZO, The Hague, Netherlands

Shaare Zedek Synagogue-Community Center, 903 Ponce de Leon Avenida, Santurce 00907, Puerto Rico; telephone: 809 724 4157

Shaarei Tsedek Orthodox, Lilieweg 1A, Mahaai, Curaçao

Spanish and Portuguese Jews' Congregation (Bevis Marks), 2 Heneage Lane, London, EC3A 5DQ; telephone: +44 0171-6261274; fax: +44 0171-6261274; website: WWW.JEWISHGEN.ORG/JCR-UK/COMMUNITY/BEVIS/HISTORY.HTM; e-mail: BEVISMARKS@FIRST-STEP.DEMON.CO.UK

United Bahamas Hebrew Congregation, P.O. Box F1761, Freeport, Grand Bahama Island; telephone: 242 373 2008; website: WWW.UAHCWEB.ORG/CONGS/OT/OT031

United Congregation of Israelites, Shaare Shalom Synagogue, P.O. Box 540, Kingston 6, Jamaica; telephone: 809 927 7948; fax: 809 978 6240

United Congregation Mikve Israel-Emanuel, Kerk Strat, P.O. Box 322, Willemstad, Curaçao, N.A.; telephone: 599 9 461-1067; fax: 599 9 465-4141; website: WWW.SNOA.COM; e-mail: INFO@SNOA.COM

U.S. National Archives, Northeast Region, 201 Varick Street, 12th Floor, New York, NY 10014; telephone: (212) 337-3000

U.S. Virgin Islands cemeteries: The larger cemetery is located across the street from the general cemetery in downtown Charlotte Amalie. The other is situated on Jews' Street in Charlotte Amalie.

China

by Peter Nash

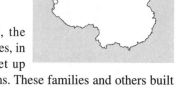

Genealogical research for former residents of China is hampered by a lack of official and vital records. The methodology one must use, therefore, requires ingenuity in order to extract maximum benefit from a variety of indirect resources. Success is also achievable by maximizing networking. Earliest tracing of Jews in China starts in 1850.

History

According to historians,[2] the Jewish presence in China probably goes back two thousand years, but the earliest references to Jews trading in China, made by Arab travelers, date from the eighth century. Jews of Persian and Arabian origins were among the merchants who plied the Old Silk Road from Rome to China dealing in silk, spices and furs. They established trading posts along the caravan routes in Afghanistan, India and China and later on the Chinese coast, including Canton. During a Christian-Arab conflict in the ninth century, Jewish merchants carried the bulk of the trade from Asia to Europe.

The city of Kaifeng in China's central plains had the largest, most enduring and stable Jewish community, which existed for more than eight hundred years. Jewish history in Kaifeng is inscribed on three stone tablets, a traditional Chinese method of transmitting history. Two tablets dating back to 1489 and 1512 are now housed in the Museum of Kaifeng. The third tablet dates back to 1663. Its location is unknown.

China's turbulent history in the 19th and 20th centuries led to the dissolution of the Jewish community of Kaifeng. The Yellow River floods in 1850 destroyed the already dilapidated synagogue in Kaifeng (but Jewish artifacts from Kaifeng can be found in several museums around the world). As the Kaifeng community declined, a new Jewish presence emerged in Shanghai. During the Opium Wars of the 1840s waged first by the British and then by the Americans and the French, parts of China were devastated. Under the Treaty of Nanking in 1842, the Chinese government opened its ports to foreign settlement and trade. The British chose the banks of the wide and navigable Whangpoo River as their international trading port. On this site the cosmopolitan city of Shanghai developed.

Shanghai

Former Baghdadi Sephardic Jews, British subjects who lived and traded in Bombay, saw the potential for trade between both India and China with Great Britain and followed in British footsteps to Shanghai. These Jews included the Sassoon family. Elias David Sassoon, son of David Sassoon, was the first to open a branch of the Sassoon company in Shanghai in 1850, dealing in opium and soon expanding into other imports and exports. As the firm grew, other Baghdadi families joined the Sassoon enterprises as clerks and managers. Two families, the Hardoons and the Kadoories, in time branched out and set up their own independent firms. These families and others built up enormous fortunes and helped to turn the quiet port of Shanghai into a metropolis.

The Sephardic families who made their homes in India distanced themselves from the intense traditional lifestyle of their ancestors in the Arabian subcontinent and attempted to emulate all things British. The wealthiest, such as the Kadoories and the Sassoons, sent their children to English public schools and joined English sporting and social clubs. At home, however, they observed Jewish laws, retained many aspects of their culture and kept most traditions, especially in their cuisine, dress, music and language. Some continued to speak Arabic. The first synagogue and Jewish school in Shanghai, built in 1900, was aided financially by the wealthy Sephardim. By 1920, one thousand Sephardim lived in Shanghai.

After World War I (1914–18), some groups of Ashkenazi Russian and Polish refugees escaping the Russian Revolution made their way to Shanghai. To accommodate the needs of the growing community, the Shanghai Jewish School was built in 1932 next to Ohel Rachel synagogue (built in 1917). Children of both the Sephardic and Ashkenazic communities attended this school. By 1933, an estimated ten thousand Jews lived in Shanghai, but a breakdown by Sephardic and Ashkenazic origins does not exist.

The next major wave of Jews arrived in Shanghai in the years 1938–39. These were Central European refugees—mainly German and Austrian, but also Czechoslovakian—fleeing from the Nazis. Unlike most Western bloc allies—including the United States, Canada, Great Britain, Australia and New Zealand—Shanghai required no entry visa. The Japanese who controlled Shanghai after 1937 kept the city open to Jewish refugees, because they believed that Jews had considerable influence on the international scene. Some, including Polish and Lithuanian Jews, arrived in Shanghai as late as the end of 1941, traveling by rail across Siberia and through Manchuria in the north. Estimates show that approximately eighteen thousand Central European Jews entered Shanghai, but the number may actually have been greater than twenty thousand.

The Shanghai Jewish community was a linguistic, cultural and religious mosaic. There were German-, Russian- and English-speaking Jews. Among the Jews from Poland and Lithuania were several thousand Orthodox and Reform Jews. The Jewish community of Shanghai, old and new alike, was in no sense unified; little social interaction transpired among the various groups.

Daily life was strongly affected, however, by the Japanese occupation of China after its declaration of war on the United

Jews of K'ai-Fung-Foo (Kaifeng) at the end of the 19th century

States at the end of 1941. Soon thereafter, many among the Sephardic community who held British citizenship were interned by the Japanese, who gradually came more directly under Nazi influence, resulting in a reversal of their previously pro-Jewish policy. Most of the European refugees were stateless, unlike the Russian Jews who held Soviet passports, and were forced to live in a ghetto area called Hongkew. Survival was not endangered so much by the activities of war as by poor diet and sanitation and low resistance to tropical diseases.

The end of World War II in August 1945 did not bring peace to China; civil war erupted between the Communists and the Nationalists. The dispersion of the entire Shanghai Jewish community commenced in 1946 and accelerated by the time the Communists took over and the People's Republic of China was established in September 1949. Most Jews went to Israel, at least initially, and many migrated to other countries later. Others traveled directly to the United States, Australia and elsewhere.

Harbin, Manchuria

At the turn of the 20th century, Harbin was an insignificant, muddy outpost on China's northeastern frontier. Russians, including some Jews, migrated to Harbin in the 1890s, following Russia's successful bid to build the Chinese Eastern railway linking the two countries. The earliest group of Jews in Harbin came from Siberia. They were engaged in cattle and dairy production, but were soon joined by Jewish soldiers, many of

whom were deserters seeking new opportunities after the Russo-Japanese War of 1904–05.

By 1908, approximately eight thousand Jews lived in Harbin and had built their first synagogue, Talmud Torah (religious school) and high school. Jews fleeing the Russian Revolution after World War I augmented the numbers, and although Jews settled in other Manchurian cities, including Mukden (now Shenyang), Dairen, and smaller towns, by 1920 Harbin had between 12,000 and 13,000 Jewish residents.

The Japanese occupation of Manchuria in 1931 created many economic and social disruptions, and an atmosphere of intolerance and harassment forced Jewish families to leave. Some went to Palestine, others to the United States, but the majority moved to Shanghai and Tienstin. By 1935, only about five thousand Jews remained in Harbin. For the Jews, the World War II years were difficult, but not catastrophic. The Chinese Communists' victory in 1949 prompted most to leave, although more than three hundred Jews waited until 1956 to emigrate. A small number never left and died in Manchuria.

Tienstin (Now Tianjin)

This city on the North China coast was one of the treaty ports opened to Western trade following the Opium Wars. Some Jews from Russia may have settled there as early as 1870, but it was not until 1904 that a Jewish cemetery was established and a viable community structure formed. Compared to Shanghai and Harbin, Tienstin's community was poorer and smaller, numbering about 2,500 and consisting primarily of Russian Jews, with a small number from Poland and Germany. After the defeat of Japan in 1945 and the subsequent success of the Chinese Communists, the Jews of Tienstin also began to leave China. By 1955, 130 Jews were still in Tienstin, but then the community faded away.

Hong Kong

Jewish community life began in Hong Kong in the mid-1850s. Its origins, like those of Shanghai, stem from the same former Baghdadi families. Hong Kong continued to grow with the Russian-Jewish migration to China following the pogroms of the Russian Revolution in 1917. The migration never reached the numbers of the other Jewish communities in China. About two hundred Jews resided in Hong Kong after the takeover of China by the Communists in 1949. The Jewish Historical Society of Hong Kong* was established in 1984 to collect, preserve and study materials of Jewish relevance.[3] Hong Kong returned to Chinese rule in 1997.

Tracing and Accessing Records
Birth and Marriage Records

The customary method of researching vital records does not apply to Jews in China. Systematically kept, centralized civil records of births and marriages probably existed, but none has come to light, except for records of Sephardic Jews who were British citizens. The Family Records Centre* in London has birth and marriage records for British citizens resident in

Shanghai Ashkenazi Jewish Communal Association

BIRTH CERTIFICATE

No. 307/151

Date of Birth		Child named	Sex	Address where Born	Name of Father	Age	Name and Maiden Surname of Mother	Age	Signature and Address of Informant	Signature of Mohel	Nationality
Hebrew	Civil										
%-th of Kislav 5699	27th November 1938	LEIB /LEO/	male	Country Hospital	David B. Vilensky	35	Haya Hasanoff	26		H. Plotkin	Ex-Russian

Birth record from the Ashkenazic (Russian) Jewish community in Shanghai, 1938

China over a wide range of cities and towns. These records originally were kept in British foreign office registers.

Birth and marriage certificates for the Russian Ashkenazic Jews were issued by the Shanghai Ashkenazi Jewish Communal Association. For the Central European Jews, birth certificates were issued by the Health Department of the Shanghai Municipal Council. Marriage certificates were issued by the Communal Association of Central European Jews. Whether they still exist in China or were taken out of China and archived elsewhere is not known.

Tracing, therefore, is essentially random, and success relies on following the trail of migration to and from China—that is, tracking the country of origin (not necessarily birth), prior to migration to China or the country of resettlement.

Burials and Cemeteries

Jewish cemeteries and sections within larger non-Jewish cemeteries existed where the various communities were established. The International Association of Jewish Genealogical Societies Cemetery Project describes the fate of a number of cemeteries in Harbin and Shanghai under the Communist regime (see "Cemeteries" on JewishGen website). In the case of the four Jewish cemeteries in Shanghai, 1,692 monuments were dismantled and remains exhumed in 1958, and re-interment of very few remains and resetting of monuments (some partial) took place in a new cemetery in 1959. Information on this event, with photographs and names on some monuments, can be found in a book entitled *God and Country.*[4]

In 2002, *Igud Yotzei Sin's Bulletin* reported that tombstones, with inscriptions in Hebrew and English unexpectedly were found outside of Shanghai. At least 55 names, some with dates and origins have been listed.[5] *Igud Yotzei Sin* in Israel is the Association of Former Residents in China.*

In 1958, the 853 graves of the old Jewish cemetery in Harbin were transferred to a new location; an additional 23 burials occurred between 1958 and 1965, the year the Jewish community stopped functioning as reported by Ted Kaufman in the *Bulletin* of Igud Yotzei Sin. Only 515 graves have been identified; the list of names (in Russian Cyrillic) with burial dates was published by Igud Yotzei Sin.[6] Maida Dacher of Los Angeles has supplied the author with a transcript in English letters. A website exists with the names in English.* In

addition, the JewishGen Online Worldwide Burial Registry focusses on a searchable burial database.*

YIVO Institute for Jewish Research in New York,* located at the Center for Jewish History, has a Hebrew Immigrant Aid Society (HIAS) list of 1,433 Jews who died in Shanghai from 1940 to 1945. In 1946, the list appeared in four consecutive issues of the German-language newspaper *Aufbau*, published in New York. The *Aufbau* list included dates of birth and death and place of last residence in Europe. The list is searchable at WWW.JEWISHGEN.ORG. YIVO also holds a list of 74 deaths in Shanghai during 1948.[7]

The Family Records Centre* in London has death records of British citizens, including Jews, who resided in China.

Tracing and Accessing Records: Lists, Registers, and Institutions

Sugihara Visa List. Japanese consul-general Chiune Sugihara was stationed in Kaunas, Lithuania, as the Germans advanced in July 1940. Desperate Jews, mostly Polish but also some Central Europeans (including about four hundred from the Mir Yeshiva in Poland) by then had reached Kaunas. Unable to obtain visas anywhere, they sought help from Sugihara. Acting against orders from Tokyo and aided by his wife, Sugihara issued more than 3,500 Japanese transit visas that enabled the Jews to reach Kobe, Japan.

Through the second half of 1940 and first half of 1941, two thousand Jews with Sugihara visas reached Kobe via Siberia and Vladivostok. About one thousand with family connections migrated onward to such destinations as Australia, South America and the United States. Prior to the Japanese attack on Pearl Harbor in December 1941, the Japanese authorities made a concerted effort to resettle the remaining stateless refugees and allowed them to be sent to Shanghai.[8]

David Egelman of San Diego, California, has created a database of 2,139 Jews on the Sugihara visa searchable on the JewishGen website.* The vast majority of the visa holders (91 percent) are of Polish nationality, with Lithuanians, Germans, Czechs and others making up the remaining numbers.

The Central Archives for the History of the Jewish People. This Jerusalem repository holds a collection of files that belonged to the Far Eastern Jewish Central Information Bureau, established by the Hebrew Immigrant Aid Society (HIAS) in Harbin in 1918. The Bureau later moved to Shanghai

Sephardic (British subject) birth record, 1930

and dissolved about 1948. The files with more than 2,500 typed sheets, include lists of refugees registered with HIAS in Shanghai in the years 1943–45 who sought assistance for onward migration. The final destination up to 1949 can also be found. One list contains approximately 16,000 to 18,000 names with birth and marriage data, occupation, when and how arrived in Shanghai and details of possible sponsors for onward migration.[9] (Also see YIVO below)

Gross-Hongkew List. The Gross-Hongkew 1943–44 list holds nearly 14,800 names and is a census entitled "Foreigners Residing in Dee Jay Police District, Including Foreigners Holding Chinese Naturalization Papers." The district is Hongkew (now Hongkou) where European refugees were forced to reside, thus becoming a ghetto. The area was maintained by the Chinese police, but was under Japanese (occupier) control. The typed list includes "foreigners" from many countries; a minority of names were non-Jews. The list is searchable as an adjunct in CD-ROM form to the book *Exil Shanghai 1938–1947.*[10]

Police Records for Shanghai and Tsingtao. The register of the Municipal Police Records for Shanghai and Tsingtao (a naval port now Qingdao) is available for research at the U.S. National Archives in College Park, Maryland.[11] The records of the Shanghai Municipal Police date from 1894 to 1949 and were handed over in 1949 by the non-communist Nationalist Chinese garrison to American intelligence officers based in Shanghai. They are kept in RG 263, Records of the CIA. Tsingtao also was a haven for refugees, some briefly in transit while others stayed for several years. Many rolls of microfilm covering different time periods have a vast amount of personal information, and although the classifications of "Jew" or "Jewish" are not used routinely, Jewish identification frequently can be made by name.

Aktives Museum, Berlin. The Aktives Museum* has files from political archives of the former *Deutsche Reich's* foreign ministry that pertain to approximately 5,500 German refugees in Shanghai who contacted the German consulate in Shanghai after their arrival in that city in 1938–40. The Shanghai files were sent to the Gestapo and the interior ministry in Germany. They may include names of those left behind.[12]

Consular Records in Shanghai Concerning Jewish Refugees. Jonathan Goldstein visited Polish, Russian, and U.S. consulates in Shanghai in 1992, but only the Polish consulate confirmed the existence of a 200-page register (in Polish) of Polish citizens, including Jews, who passed through Shanghai or Nanjing (formerly Nanking) between January 9, 1934, and October 29, 1941. This register is held at the Hoover Institution Archives* located on the campus of Stanford University in Palo Alto, California.[13] The unindexed register, searchable manually at the Hoover Archives, contains the surname and given name, profession, religion (therefore, if Jewish), place and date of birth, marital status, last known address in Poland, address in China and other registration data. A list of Polish refugees analyzed by place of origin and occupation also is held at the Hoover Archives.

YIVO Institute for Jewish Research. YIVO Institute for Jewish Research in New York has extensive files on the activities of HIAS in Shanghai, including correspondence on emigration from Shanghai. YIVO also holds many donated files relating to activities of communal organizations, synagogues, cemeteries and burial societies as well as books, newspapers, youth organizations and schools. YIVO has acquired microfilms of the HIAS lists of Shanghai refugees held at the Central Archives for the History of the Jewish People.*

Leo Baeck Institute. The Leo Baeck Institute in New York City has collections containing 44 items of correspondence, reports, unpublished manuscripts, diaries and similar material relevant to Shanghai both during and after World War II. Its journal Stammbaum has published articles on German and Austrian refugees in China.

American Jewish Historical Society. This institution has the Boston HIAS collection containing an estimated 12,000 alphabetically arranged individual case files covering the 1920s and 1930s. Each file includes such items as correspondence, requests for immigration, certificates of support by U.S. residents, visa applications, certificates of good moral character, certificates of funds transmitted and other similar papers. Although most case files originated in Europe, many were opened in China and some resulted in admission to the United States. The HIAS collection is not catalogued and can be searched only in Waltham, Massachusetts.[14]

Australian National Archives. The National Archives of Australia* has files spanning the years 1938–58 relating to

	Date & place of birth	Nat.	Profession	Date & place of arrival in Sh'ai	Relatives:
1. ABEE Siegbert (single)	13.2.06 Breslau	Germ.	Musician, Pianist	28.6.39 from Breslau, S/S " Usaramo "	Aunt: Henriette DANIEL, 1703 Colonial Str. Phila.Pa.
2. ABEL Theodor wife: Lilli daughter: Edith Weiss	8.3.83 Hamburg 28.5.86 " 16.5.13 "	Germ. " "	Dealer in watches	16.8.39 from Hamburg, S/S " Suwamaru "	grand children, Eva & Rolf WEISS, c/o Ref.childrens Movemen London WC1,Bloomsbury H.
3. ABELSON Chaim single)	15.9.16 Wisock near Pinsk	Pol.	Rabbi-student (Mir.Yesh.)	22.8.41 from Kaunas S/S " Asama-Maru"	Ezrath Tora: Rabbi KALMANOWICZ, 540 Bedford Ave. Brcklyn New York.
4. ABISCH Adolf married	16.691 Czerno-witz	Franz.	Manufact.of Perfumes	1939 from Vienna,	
5. ABISCH Dr.David wife: Martha nee Lieber	1.1.05 Slobanila (Bukovina) 8.6.13 Berlin,	Germ.	Physician	25.4.39 from Berlin, S/S "Biancamano "	Nephew: Fred RUBIN, 994 Intervale Ave. Brookl.N.Y.
6. ABOLNIK Dr.Salomon	1904 Wilna,	Spain.	Physician	1938 from Barcelona,	
7. ABRAHAM, Albrecht wife: Ida son : Harry	22.12.1900 Altenkirchen	Germ.	Colonist	15.3.39 from Frankfurt a.M. S/S " Jul.Caesare "	Brother: Ernest BRANDON(Abraham) 32 Wadsworth Terrace N.Y.
8. ABRAHAM Arthur wife: Hertha, son : Erwin	9.7.97 Strelno 2.12.00 Wronke	Germ. "	Merchant	15.5.39 from Berlin, S/S " Ciu.Cesare "	cousin:Jennie ADLER, Lombardo hotel 111 East 56th Str.New York
9. ABRAHAM Benno (divorced)	15.5.92 Hohen-salza	Germ.	Merchant	15.5.39 from Berlin	Cousin: I. MENGER, 2760 Sakramento str. S. Freisc.
10. ABRAHAM, Flora nee Traube (widow) son: Fritz	19.3.76 Gleiwitz 8.5.03 Berlin	" "	without Merchant	28.9.40 from Berlin via Siberia	Son: Joachim ABRAHAM, 9,Grandview Grove Armandale,Vict.Austr.

Record of Jews fleeing German anti-Semitism entering Shanghai from Europe in 1939-41. This document is part of the records of HIAS, the Hebrew Immigrant Aid Society.

Jewish refugees. The files cover such matters as the plight of Jewish refugees in Shanghai; evacuation of Polish refugees in Japan, Shanghai, and Russia; and the granting or rejection of landing permits for named applicants from China. They have original ship manifests for sailings from Shanghai and Hong Kong to Australia.[15]

***National Archief Nederland.**[*] The National Archives of The Netherlands has records of the departure of Dutch Jews from Shanghai for the period 1941–42 in Inventory No. 375. The source of these records was the Ministerie van Buitenlandse Zaken* (Ministry of Foreign Affairs).[16]

Publications in China

Directories and Registers. A number of city directories are accessible. Very useful, at least for tracing Central European refugees who landed in Shanghai, is the Emigranten Adressbuch fuer Shanghai (Immigrant address book for Shanghai), published originally in November 1939 and reprinted by the Old China Hand Press* in 1995. This valuable directory lists the full names, local addresses, previous occupations and cities of origin of about 5,000 refugees who had escaped to

Shanghai by mid-1939. It also includes lists by occupations. Only the "head of the house" is included; the directory thus represents about 10,000 refugees. The gap between this estimate and the total number of about 18,000 refugees who came to Shanghai is probably due both to failure to register of some refugees and the arrival of many refugees after the closing date for publication.

Another useful directory for Shanghai is the Adressbuch der Emigranten-Betriebe (Classified directory of immigrant firms, ADEB). Originally published in 1939, it includes names, addresses, and telephone numbers of businesses or proprietors of goods and services, listed alphabetically and by service classification. A facsimile copy of the May 1941 (third) edition is accessible at the Jewish Museum of Australia.*

Two other directories for the wider (not just Jewish) community can be referenced, the Shanghai Directories for the years 1929–48 and the Hong Books for all of China for only 1934 and 1941. The Shanghai Directories list businesses, personal addresses, schools, universities, churches and synagogues. They have a street directory with every Western (British, French, American) concession or district street listed, as well as the names of those who lived on them. The Hong Books for mostly Shanghai, but also Tienstin and Tsingtao, list businesses and names, but not addresses.[17]

Newspapers. Newspapers for the Jewish communities were published in various languages—German, Polish, Russian, and Yiddish as well as English. They printed news of world and local affairs and activity reports on social, cultural, Zionist youth, scouts and sport groups, advertisements, personal announcements and many photographs.

The English-language *Israel's Messenger* was the most enduring regular newspaper, published in Shanghai 1904 to 1941. Published monthly, it contained political commentary, social news, obituaries, sports events and other items. All issues are available on microfilm.[18]

A number of other German-language newspapers were published during the period 1939–49 mostly for relatively short periods and were quickly replaced by others. Among these were *Shanghai Woche, Shanghai Echo, Shanghai Post* and *Gelbe Post.* An exception was *Shanghai Jewish Chronicle*, published continuously from 1939 to 1945. The Council for the Jewish Experience in Shanghai has a database of worldwide collections.[19]

Some newspaper issues are held privately, and others are in public collections such as the Queensborough Community College, New York, which holds a complete collection of the *Shanghai Post* and *Mercury*.[20] The *Gelbe Post* (14 issues), *Acht-Uhr-Abendblatt* (56 issues) and *Tribüne* (13 issues) are searchable on the Internet.[21] Reprints of the first seven 1939 issues of *Gelbe Post* are available.[22]

The *ALMANAC-Shanghai 1946–47*, a post-World War II commemorative issue published by the *Shanghai Echo*, featured many names associated with the life and times of the Shanghai Jewish community across the wide spectrum of communal associations, social, sporting and cultural groups.[23]

Miscellaneous Lists

Aufbau. The German-language newspaper *Aufbau*, published in New York since 1934, has been a valuable link for refugees with German-speaking backgrounds. Indexing of all *Aufbau's* obituaries and family announcements (including those for former China residents) is in progress. Information about the project may be found in the GerSig discussion group on the JewishGen website.*

The story of the approximately 100 members who belonged to the Jewish Company attached to the Shanghai Volunteer Corps in the period 1933–42 has been published published and can be found on the Internet.*

Shipping or Passenger Lists. Some former China residents including Ashkenazim originally from Russia, came by ship to Seattle, Washington, via Yokohama, Japan. Passenger lists on microfilm (for 1890–1957) are held by the Pacific-Alaska Region (Seattle branch) of the U.S. National Archives and Records Administration.[24]

The impending takeover by the Chinese communists after 1948 forced the emigration of all remaining European, Russian and Sephardic Jews from China. By the end of 1951, the numbers of refugees who emigrated to other countries were approximately: United States (7,000), Israel (5,000), Australia (3,000) and other countries combined (3,800).[25] Many left by air, but few arrival lists are available.

Many refugees sailed from Shanghai to the United States during the years 1946–49 on the American President Line whose ships operated under contract to the U.S. Maritime Commission (later the Maritime Administration). The Historic Documents Department of the San Francisco Maritime National Historical Park has confirmed that lists for these sailings do not exist.[26]

YIVO Institute of Jewish Research has microfilm of considerable HIAS correspondence relating to sailings from Shanghai to other countries.[27] It has the names of 892 emigrants who sailed on the International Relief Organization ship, *Wooster Victory*, that left Shanghai on December 24, 1948, for Haifa, Israel.[28]

On December 31, 1948, some 900 refugees sailed from Shanghai on the *Castel Bianco* via Cape Town to Naples, where they transferred to two smaller ships, *Casserta* and *Tetti*, finally arriving in Haifa on February 17, 1949. Passenger lists of these sailings are not known to exist. Accounts of the voyage are given in several issues of the *Igud Yotzei Sin Bulletin.*[29]

The Shanghai International Relief Organization ship *Marine Lynx* sailed from Shanghai on July 25, 1947, with refugees who chose to return to Austria or Germany. It sailed to Naples where 650 refugees disembarked. About 476 traveled on to Germany and 174 to Austria. No passenger manifest has been located, but a list of about three hundred scheduled to return to Berlin is available at the Aktives Museum in Berlin, including notation of their preferred choice of sector, i.e., whether British, French, Russian or U.S.[30]

Refugees sailed to Australia either directly from Shanghai or from Hong Kong. The first disembarkation port usually was Sydney; others disembarked in Melbourne or Brisbane. Many ships with numbers of refugees varying from one to more than three hundred sailed to Australia in the years 1946–49. The author has recorded many such sailing and passenger lists at the National Archives of Australia in Canberra.[31]

Jewish Care Australia (formerly Australian Jewish Welfare Society) compiled lists of Shanghai refugee arrivals for 1946, together with names and addresses of sponsors. On December 28, 1946, 306 refugee Jews sailed on the *Hwa Lien* from Shanghai and arrived in Sydney, Australia, on January 28, 1947. This passenger list is among those compiled by Jewish Care.

*Landesarchiv Berlin.** This repository has an incomplete list of about 1,700 emigrants who traveled from Germany to Shanghai in the late 1930s; dates of birth are often noted. In many instances, the lists also note return to Berlin and, in some instances, onward emigration to, for example, the United States.

*Jewish Care Australia.** Many refugees from China registered with Jewish Care (known then as Australian Jewish Welfare Society) for assistance in migration and sponsorship. The relevant files are still available and search requests may be sent to Jewish Care.

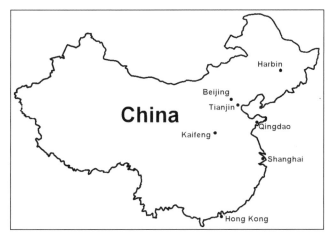

Map of China showing cities where Jews lived

A list of 108 former Shanghai residents who settled in Melbourne was compiled in conjunction with the exhibition *Story of a Haven: The Jews of Shanghai*, held in 1997 at the Jewish Museum of Australia* in Melbourne.

Steve Hochstadt of Bates College in Lewiston, Maine, U.S.A., has conducted an oral history project based on interviews of Holocaust survivors who found refuge in Shanghai. Although still incomplete, more than 110 individuals have been interviewed in Austria, Germany, Shanghai and the United States.[32]

Associations, Groups and Institutes

Many organized Jewish associations and groups functioned during decades of community life in various Chinese cities. These included Scouts and Guides, Betar, Jewish Recreation Club (for various sports), Organization for Educational Resources and Technological Training (ORT), and cultural activities such as theater and music. Today a number of associations and friendship groups exist outside of China. Their primary aims are to maintain a channel of communication for the former Jewish residents of China and also to collect and preserve materials of historical value especially related to 19th- and 20th-century Jewish communities in China. Communication is facilitated by distribution of journals or newsletters to lists of subscribers.

Reunions, including trips to China, of groups of former China residents with a common Jewish community life experience are popular and held all over the world. One benefit for the researcher is the accompanying list of participants. A former resident could be sought by contacting any or all of the groups mentioned below.

*Igud Yotzei Sin.** The Association of Former Residents of China (Igud Yotzei Sin), formed in 1951 in Tel Aviv, provides links for various backgrounds and interests, especially by Chinese city, and is probably the most organized and significant such group worldwide. Since May 1954, the group has published a periodic newsletter, *Bulletin*, in English, Russian and Hebrew. It covers all aspects of the former Jewish communities of China including a wide range of biographical, social and historical matters, as well as current and forthcoming events. Photographs with names of former residents are abundant, and the bi-monthly *Bulletin* frequently announces individual occasions for celebration as well as obituaries. Advertising a search for lost relatives or friends is allowed.

Igud Yotzei Sin published a documentary on various sports entitled *Participation of Chinese Jewry in Sports*. Names and results for a range of sports are covered for the period from the 1920s to the 1940s.[33]

Old China Hands. No overall association of former China residents, so-called Old China Hands (OCH), exists, although an unknown number of groups have formed under this name. Each group has a certain common China interest, but not necessarily a Jewish focus. OCH reunions have been held all over the world attended by both Jewish and non-Jewish OCH. The Old China Hands Archive has been founded in the Special Collections Department of the Library of California State University, Northbridge, California.* It collects various materials of historical interest dealing with the China experience and also reunion attendance lists.

*Sino-Judaic Institute.** This Palo Alto, California, institution is dedicated to facilitating the study of the history of Jews in China. It publishes a periodic newsletter called *Points East* and has given documentary material from former refugees of Shanghai and elsewhere to the Hoover Institution Archives located on the same site.*

*The Council for the Jewish Experience in Shanghai** was created in 1994 to preserve the history of the Central European refuge in Shanghai. The Council also aims to facilitate access to archival materials for researchers without itself holding archival collections. Projects undertaken include the digitization of deaths in Shanghai, 1940–45, now a JewishGen searchable database.

Reunions of Former Central Europeans. So-called "Rickshaw Reunions" have been held in Oakland, California (1980); Catskills, New York (1985); Jerusalem, Israel (1988); Philadelphia, Pennsylvania (1991); Chicago, Illinois (1993); Catskills, New York (1997); Philadelphia, Pennsylvania (1999) and San Francisco, California (2002). Attendance lists with current addresses accompanied each gathering. The Rickshaw Express Internet website is a forum for China life experiences, searches, photo identifications and historical information.

Modern China

Today, about 250 Jews and a rabbi constitute the Jewish community of Shanghai; Beijing has a community of about 100 Jews. Virtually all are there only for business. Since the establishment of diplomatic relations between Israel and China in 1991, however, Chinese intellectuals have shown a burgeoning interest in the 2000-year Jewish presence in China. Conservation and restoration of Jewish heritage sites, including synagogues and burial sites, have been implemented. The study of the traditions and heritage of Judaism and Hebrew literature and comparisons with Chinese cultural traditions and literature are being fostered. Four education centers have been established. The first was the Center for Jewish Studies* at the Shanghai Academy of Social Sciences, with a focus on the past 150 years. The research of director

Dr. Pan Guang has been published in both English and Chinese. Similarly, Professor Xu Xin, director of the Center for Jewish Studies at Nanjing University* has published extensively on the former Jewish communities of China. The new Center of Jewish Studies at the Heilongjiang Academy of Social Sciences in Harbin, headed by Professor Qu Wei, promises to be significant as archives of the former Harbin Jewish community are known to exist.[34] The Institute of Jewish Studies at Henan University in Kaifeng*, under Professor Zhang Qianhong, was established in 2002.

An Israel-China Friendship Society was established in March 1992 by the Igud Yotzei Sin in Israel. A newsletter is published concurrently with the *Bulletin* by the Igud Yotzei Sin.

Restitution Claims Agencies. Upon arrival in Shanghai in 1939, the author's family first resided with his maternal grandmother's cousin Leopold Steinhardt and family, who also had fled Berlin. After emigration from Shanghai, all contact was lost for decades. The author eventually tried to find descendants of his cousin, but various efforts failed, even though his relative had been a prominent member of the Shanghai Jewish community. Finally a suggestion led to contacting the *Landesregierung – Entschädigungsstelle Berlin** (formerly the *Landesverwaltungsamt Berlin*), the German government department that processed applications for restitution claims. It was possible to request the forwarding of a letter to persons who may have made a claim for any reason associated with their forced emigration from Nazi Germany. Soon thereafter, the family was reunited.

Addresses

Aktives Museum, Chausseestr. 8, 10115 Berlin, Germany; e-mail: INFO@AKTIVES-MUSEUM.DE

American Jewish Historical Society, 2 Thornton Road, Waltham, MA 02453; e-mail: AJHS@AJHS.ORG

Australian Jewish Historical Society, 385 Abercrombie Street, Darlington NSW 2008, Sydney, Australia; e-mail: AJHS@OZEMAIL. COM.AU

Bates College, Lewiston, ME 04240; Steve Hochstadt; e-mail: SHOCHSTA@ABACUS.BATES.EDU

Center of Jewish Studies Shanghai, 622-7 Huai Hai Road (M) Suite 352, Shanghai 200020, China; Professor Pan Guang; e-mail: GPAN@SRCAP.STC.SH.CN

Center of Jewish Studies, Heilongjiang Academy of Social Sciences, 501 Youyi Road, Daoli District, Harbin 150018, China; Ms Fu Ming Jing; e-mail: FMJ0451@YAHOO.COM.CN

Center for Jewish Studies, School of Foreign Studies, Nanjing University, Nanjing 210093, China; Professor Xu Xin; e-mail: XUXIN49@JLONLINE.COM

Central Archives for the History of the Jewish People, PO Box 1149, Jerusalem 91010, Israel; e-mail: ARCHIVES@VMS.HUJI.AC.IL

Council for the Jewish Experience in Shanghai, 3500 Race Street, Philadelphia, PA 19104; Ralph B. Hirsch; e-mail: CJES@CJES.ORG

Hoover Institution Archives, Stanford University, Stanford CA 94305; e-mail: ARCHIVES@HOOVER.STANFORD.EDU

Igud Yotzei Sin (Association of Former Residents of China), PO Box 1601, Tel Aviv, 61015 Israel; e-mail: IGUD-SIN@BARAK-ONLINE.NET

Institute of Jewish Studies, College of History and Culture Henan University, Kaifeng City, 475001 China; Professor Zhang Qianhong; e-mail: ZHANGQUANHONG@YAHOO.COM

Jewish Care Australia, 332 Oxford Street, Bondi Junction, NSW 2022, Australia; e-mail: INFO@JEWISHCARE.COM.AU

Jewish Historical Society of Hong Kong, c/o Jewish Community Centre, One Robinson Place, 70 Robinson Road, Mid-Levels, Hong Kong; e-mail: SCRIBE@DANGOOR.COM

Jewish Historical Society of Hong Kong, c/o Jewish Community Centre, One Robinson Place, 70 Robinson Road, Mid-Levels, Hong Kong; e-mail: JCCLIB@HK.SUPER.NET

Jewish Museum of Australia, 26 Alma Road, St. Kilda, Victoria, Australia 3182; e-mail: INFO@JEWISHMUSEUM.COM.AU

Jewish National and University Library, PO Box 34165, Jerusalem 91341 Israel; Benjamin Richler; e-mail: BENJAMINR@SAVION.HUJI.AC.IL

Landesarchiv Berlin, Eichborndamm 115-121, 13403 Reinickendorf, Berlin, Germany; e-mail: INFO@LANDESARCHIV-BERLIN.DE

Landesregierung-Entschädigungsstelle, Ferbelliner Platz 1, 10707, Berlin, Germany (formerly Landesverwaltungsamt Berlin, Entschädigungsbehörde Abt III); e-mail: ENTSCHAEDIGUNG@LVWA. VERWALT-BERLIN.DE

Leo Baeck Institute, 15 West 16th Street, New York NY 10011; e-mail: LBAECK@LBI.CJH.ORG

Nationaal Archief, Nederland, Prins Willem Alexanderhof 20, The Hague, The Netherlands; e-mail: INFO@NATIONAALARCHIEF.NL

National Archives and Records Administration, Pacific Alaska Region, 6125 Sand Point Way NE, Seattle, WA 98115; e-mail: SEATTLE.ARCHIVES@NARA.GOV

National Archives of Australia, PO Box 7425, Canberra Mail Centre, ACT 2610, Australia; e-mail: WW1PRS@NAA.GOV.AU

Old China Hand Press, 91-3-2A Jianguo Xi Lu, Shanghai 200020, China; e-mail: DEKEERHC@ONLINE.SH.CN

Old China Hand Research Service, 1500-2-2B Huai Hai Zhong Lu, Shanghai 200031, China; e-mail: TESS_SH@ONLINE.SH.CN

Old China Hands Archive, California State University, 18111 Nordhoff Street, Northbridge, CA 91330; Professor Robert Gohstand; e-mail: ROBERT.GOHSTAND@CSUN.EDU

Queensborough Community College, 222-05 56th Ave., Bayside NY 11364; e-mail: HRCAHO@QCC.CUNY.EDU

Sino-Judaic Institute, 232 Lexington Drive, Menlo Park, CA 94025; Ms. Rena Krasno; e-mail: LAYT@SEATTLEU.EDU

Verlag Turia & Kant, A-1010 Wien, Schottengasse 3A/5/DG 1, Austria; e-mail: INFO@TURIA.AT

YIVO Institute for Jewish Research, 15 West 16th Street, New York, NY 10011; e-mail: YIVOMAIL@YIVO.CJH.ORG

Internet sites

WWW.JEWISHGEN.ORG/DATABASES. JewishGen Online Worldwide Burial Registry, Aufbau Shanghai Death Lists, Sugihara Visa Lists

WWW.EXIL-SHANGHAI.DE. Details of the book *Exil Shanghai 1938–1947*

WWW.RICKSHAW.ORG. Rickshaw Express: Forum for China life experiences, searches, photo IDs and other material

WWW.LBI.ORG. Leo Baeck Institute, New York

WWW.YIVOINSTITUTE.ORG. YIVO Institute for Jewish Research, New York

WWW.AJHS.ORG. American Jewish Historical Society, New York

WWW.SINO-JUDAIC.ORG. Sino-Judaic Institute, Mountain View, CA

SITES.HUJI.AC.IL/ARCHIVES. HIAS files for Harbin and Shanghai

WWW.PRO.GOV.UK. Public Record Office, Kew, London

WWW.STATISTICS.GOV.UK/REGISTRATION/FAMILY_RECORDS.ASP. Family Records Centre, Myddleton Street, London

SITES.HUJI.AC.IL/JNUL/IMHM. *Israel's Messenger.* Vols. 1–37 (1904–41)

DEPOSIT.DDB.DE. *Deutsches Exilarchiv* (member of Deutsche Bibliothek, Frankfurt aM, Germany). Shanghai Newspapers

WWW.NAA.GOV.AU. National Archives of Australia—for refugee entry
WWW.KU.EDU/~KANSITE/WW_ONE/COMMENT/SVC.HTM. Shanghai Volunteer Corps
WWW.HRBJEWCEMETERY.COM. Jewish Burials in Harbin

Bibliography

Dicker, Herman. *Wanderers and Settlers in the Far East*. New York: Twayne, 1962

Goldstein, Jonathon. ed. *The Jews of China*. Armonk, NY: M.E. Sharpe, 2000. Vol I : Historical and Comparative Perspectives. Vol II: A Sourcebook and Research Guide with comprehensive. Bibliography, by Frank J. Shulman

Kranzler, David. *Japanese, Nazis and Jews — The Jewish Refugee Community of Shanghai 1938-45*. New York: Yeshiva University Press, 1976

Meyer, Maisie J. *From the Rivers of Babylon to the Whangpoo — A Century of Sephardi Jewish Life in Shanghai*. Lanham MD: University Press of America, 2003

Tokayer, Marvin & Swartz, Mary. *The Fugu Plan*. New York: Paddington Press, 1979

Notes

1. Exhibition 1986: *Passage through China — the Jewish Communities of Harbin, Tienstin and Shanghai*. Beth Hatefusoth, The Nahum Goldman Museum of the Jewish Diaspora, Tel Aviv, Israel. Illustrated brochure with history of the Jews in China

2. Exhibition 1997: *The Story of a Haven: the Jews of Shanghai*. Jewish Museum of Australia.* Illustrated brochure with history of the Jews in China and exhibit catalogue

3. Leventhal, Dennis. *Igud Yotzei Sin* Bulletin #347 (September-October 1996): 20–21

4. Johnston, Tess and Erh, Deke. *God and Country*. Hong Kong: Old China Hand Press, 1996: 118–124

5. *Igud Yotzei Sin* Bulletin #372 (June-July 2002): 14; #376 (June-July 2003): 31

6. Kaufman, Ted. *Igud Yotzei Sin* Bulletin #335 (May-June 1994): 46–52

7. YIVO Institute.* Shanghai Collection 1926–1948 RG 243/Folder 28

8. Kranzler, David. *Japanese, Nazis and Jews - The Jewish Refugee Community of Shanghai 1938–45*. New York: Yeshiva University Press, 1976: 309–346

9. Nash, Peter. *AVOTAYNU* 17, no. 4 (Winter 2001): 19

10. Armbrüster, Georg; Kohlstruck, Michael and Mühlberger, Sonja. ed. *Exil Shanghai 1938–1947*. Teetz, Germany: Hentrich and Hentrich, 2000

11. Amdur Sack, Sallyann. *AVOTAYNU* 16 no. 1 (Spring 2000): 33

12. Armbrüster et al. See chapter by Hoss, Christiane; (Aktives Museum, Berlin*): 103–132 (in German)

13. Goldstein, Jonathon. *AVOTAYNU* 10 no. 2 (Summer 1994): 23–24

14. Davis, Fred and Blatt, Warren. *AVOTAYNU* 11 no. 3 (Fall 1995): 33

15. National Archives of Australia.* See website for refugee entry search

16. Heidebrink, Iris. *Misjpoge* 11 no. 4 (1998), 109 (in Dutch); abstracted in *AVOTAYNU* 14 no. 4 (Winter 1998): 73

17. Old China Hand Research Service, Shanghai*

18. Jewish National and University Library*; Call No. Pfi 99 for Israel's Messenger (Vols 1–37) on microfilm

19. Council for the Jewish Experience in Shanghai*

20. Hirsch, Claus. *STAMMBAUM* no. 20 (Winter 2002): 7

21. *Deutsches Exilarchiv* (member of Deutsche Bibliothek, Frankfurt aM, Germany). See website to view Shanghai newspapers

22. Verlag Turia and Kant, Wien, Austria.*

23. Australian Jewish Historical Society, Sydney*

24. Private communication from Eileen Price, Denver Colarado

25. National Archives of Australia.* Statistics from Department of External Affairs for Refugees & Displaced Persons in Shanghai 1948–1953 showing countries of emigration, Series No. A1838/1, Item No. 861/5/7, Annex 1

26. Private communication from Roberto Landazuri, Historic Documents Department, San Francisco Maritime National Historic Park, California

27. Private communication from Claus Hirsch, New York

28. YIVO Institute*: Shanghai Collection 1926–1948 RG 243/Folder 47

29. Maimann, Kurt. *Igud Yotzei Sin* Bulletin #298 (June 1988): 6; Bulletin #305 (May-June 1989): 12; Bulletin #307 (September 1989): 14

30. Private communication from Sonja Mühlberger, Berlin, Germany

31. Author has approximately 1000 names of refugees who arrived in Australia by sea and air

32. Private communication from Steve Hochstadt, Lewiston, Maine

33. Documentary by Eliahu Bar-Josef, Haifa, Israel; published in 1995 by *Igud Yotzei Sin**

34. Zeev, Benjamin. "A Delegation of the Heilongjiang Academy of Social Sciences Visited Israel" *Israel-China Voice of Friendship* no. 37 (August-September 2001) Supplement to *Igud Yotzei Sin* Bulletin #369: 2

Czech Republic

by Nora Freund

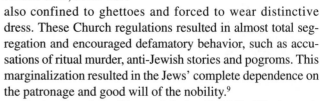

Read the chapter AUSTRIAN EMPIRE *before reading this section—Ed.*

The Czech Republic consists of the area known as the Czech Lands—the provinces of Bohemia, Moravia and a small part of Silesia—and is situated in Central Europe bounded by Germany, Poland, Austria and Slovakia. This area has always had affinity with Western Europe rather than Eastern Europe; it was part of the Holy Roman Empire during the Middle Ages, and then was ruled for 400 years by the Hapsburg Empire of Austria. This territory seldom has had independence from other major powers, and many towns and villages are known by both Czech and German names. Old atlases can help to pinpoint the location sought, as can books such as *Where Once We Walked*[1] and *Jewish Sights of Bohemia and Moravia*.[2]

History

Earliest Jews

The first mention of a Jewish presence in the Czech Lands occurred in the ninth century, when Jewish merchants were mentioned passing through the customs houses.[3] A Jewish settlement was recorded in the area of the Prague market in the middle of the 10th century and another settlement in the second half of the 11th century.[4] This settlement was destroyed during the first Crusade (1096–98), but another, under the Prague castle, was mentioned in the 12th century.[5] By the time of the reign of Wenceslas I (1230–53) and the founding of the Old Town of Prague, the Jewish settlement played an important part in the economy. Eventually it became a separate entity, with a wall and six gates and independent control of its social, political and legal affairs.[6]

Middle Ages

During the Middle Ages, the Jews were guaranteed the same rights and privileges as the Roman and German traders and were granted permission to build homesteads along the trade routes and near the market places. At that time, the Jews of Bohemia traded mainly in cattle, cloth, furs, grain, tin, wax and wool. They imported luxuries, arms, salt, spices and wine. Some Jews were active as physicians and court officials.[7]

During the 12th and 13th centuries, the Jewish community of Prague was a significant cultural center, with the earliest preserved Hebrew manuscript dating from the 12th century. Manuscripts from the time reveal that the scholars used Old Czech, a Slavic language, to explain difficult Hebrew texts, showing that they were fluent in the language of the surrounding population.[8]

Conditions worsened during and after the Crusades, until Jews were no longer permitted to practice crafts, hold land or engage in trade—except restricted money lending, which was forbidden to Christians. At this time, Jews were also confined to ghettoes and forced to wear distinctive dress. These Church regulations resulted in almost total segregation and encouraged defamatory behavior, such as accusations of ritual murder, anti-Jewish stories and pogroms. This marginalization resulted in the Jews' complete dependence on the patronage and good will of the nobility.[9]

During the reign of Premysl Otakar II (1253–78), the position of the Jews was legalized as being under the protection of the king and, therefore, they were treated as royal property. This arrangement was not always enough to protect the Jews, but it resulted in very high taxes paid to the king for his "protection." Whenever the king needed money, the Jews were always good for ransom.

In the 14th century, German anti-Semitism spread to the Crown Lands, and in 1389 the worst pogrom in Prague history caused the death of about 3,000 people. Rabbi Avigdor Kara, who witnessed and survived this pogrom, wrote an elegy, which was recited annually in the Prague Altneushul on Yom Kippur.

The Hussite Wars (Reformation) in 1419–37 resulted in a weakening of the power of the king and Church and a loosening of restrictions against Jews. The Catholic Church considered Hussites a Judaizing sect, and the Jews supported the Hussites. Nevertheless, anti-Jewish feeling resulted in riots, and Jews were expelled from many towns for siding with the Hussites.

Competition from the new burgers, who assumed many of the commercial functions that had belonged to the Jews, led to more expulsions from the towns. During the second half of the 15th century, the Jews who left the towns settled where possible in small countryside towns or on the estates of the nobility where they were able to find protection. Laws confirming the Jews' rights to settlement frequently alternated with expulsions from the towns during the 16th century.

At the time of Ferdinand I (1526–64), the Czech Lands came under the rule of the Habsburgs, rulers of the Austrian Empire. Ferdinand reaffirmed the Jewish privileges, but under pressure from the burgers repeatedly expelled the Jews—and postponed his edicts time and again. Maximillian II (1564–76) reaffirmed the Jewish privileges. Under the rule of his successor, Rudolph II, who transferred his seat to Prague from Vienna, a period of outstanding development began. During that time, the Jewish community regained its autonomy.

This period of the Renaissance resulted in a great flowering of Jewish culture in Prague. Jesaia Halevi Horowitz was one of the first printers. The first Hebrew press north of the Alps was established in Prague in 1512. His son, Aaron Mesullam Horowitz, built the Pinkas Synagogue. Rabbi Eleazar Ashkenazi formed the first burial society in 1564.

Altneuschul (Old New Synagogue) in Prague is the oldest surviving synagogue in Europe. Some claim portions date back to the 11th century. There are two clocks in its tower. The higher one has twelve Roman numerals depicting the hours of the day. The lower clock is marked with the Hebrew equivalent of 1–12 counterclockwise and rotates in that direction.

Marcus Mordecai Maisel (1528–1601) was financier to the emperor Rudolph and responsible for the building of the Jewish Town Hall, High and Maisel synagogues as well as the foundation of the hospital. The most outstanding personality of the time was Judah ben Bezalel (1512–1609), known in Jewish tradition as Rabbi Loew or the Maharal of Prague. He was known as the maker of the *golem*, a mythical figure said to protect the Jews of Prague. He was followed by Rabbi Yom Tov Heller Wallerstein, famous for his *Mishna* commentary.

In return for massive financial support to the emperor, the Jews were given further privileges and extra land in the ghetto. In the defeat of the invading Swedes by the Austrians in the Thirty Years War, the Jews helped to defend the city and as a reward were given permission to build a belfry onto the Jewish town hall and to hang a flag with a depiction of a Swedish cap inside the Star of David. This became the emblem of the Prague Jewish Community and the flag still hangs in the Altneuschul today.

At the conclusion of this campaign, the emperor granted the Jewish community permission to stay wherever they had settled. Jews were allowed to practice all arts and crafts and to set up their own shops and stalls in marketplaces and squares.

Despite the emperor's opposition, Jews were again expelled from several towns between 1650 and 1700. Meanwhile,

Jews from Poland and Ukraine were flooding into the country, escaping from the Chmielnicki pogroms of 1648. The expulsion of Jews from Vienna in 1670 sent refugees into the rural communities. In 1650, the Bohemian Diet curtailed the number of Jews permitted to reside in Bohemia and restricted their residence to places where Jews had been permitted to settle before 1618. The plague of 1680, which claimed 3,500 lives in the Prague ghetto alone, put an end to efforts to control the Jewish population.

In spite of the hardships, the population of Jewish Prague grew until, at the end of the 17th century, it was the largest Jewish population of any city in the world. The rural population also grew until it formed two-thirds of the Jewish population of the Bohemian Crown Lands. This resulted in the formation of an independent Jewish entity for the rural areas, the *Boehmische Landesjudenshchaft* (Bohemian Jewish rural society), which was authorized to manage legal matters and religious questions. From 1659 to 1749, the Czech Lands had *Landesrabbiner*, (Land Rabbis) among whom were Aaron Spira Wedeles, Abraham Broda, Wolf Spiro Wedeles and David Oppenheim.

The small Jewish communities of Moravia formed a council in the 15th century to collect and distribute taxes, represent Jewish interests to the government and deal with legal matters of the community. Among the Land Rabbis of Moravia were some of the most prominent personalities of Bohemia, such as Rabbis Jehuda Lowe ben Bezalel (before he went to Prague), Yom Tom Lippmann Heller and Menachem Krochmal. In general, despite continued difficulties, Jewish life in Czech lands tended to be less precarious than in the surrounding countries.

The Jewish "Family Law"

During the reign of Charles VI (1711–40) renewed efforts were made to limit the number of resident Jews; for this purpose, a census was taken in 1724. After the census, a fixed number of Jewish families was established: 8,541 for Bohemia and 5,106 for Moravia. In order to maintain this number, the so-called "family law" was passed. (See below).

On December 18, 1744, Empress Maria Theresa issued an edict that the presence of Jews would no longer be permitted in the Bohemian Crown Lands. Despite deputations from the Bohemian court and estates and ambassadors of several countries, she refused to rescind her decision and only postponed it temporarily. The economic effect in Prague was so severe that the guilds demanded a change. In the meantime, vandals and neglect had wrecked the ghetto area.

Eventually, in July 1748, Maria Theresa permitted the Jews to return to Prague, but she taxed them so heavily for the privilege that they could not regain their former economic situation. During the time of expulsion, many Jews had settled in Liben, a small town near Prague; others scattered throughout the rural area, settling wherever they could find a haven.

With the reign of Joseph II and the Enlightenment (1780–90), the passage of the Edict of Toleration canceled the obligation of Jews to wear distinctive clothing and began to create conditions that permitted the Jews to engage fully in the economic life of the community.[10] German schools not only were

Jewish cemetery on Josefstrasse in Prague at the beginning of the 20th century contains some of the oldest tombstones in Europe.

open to Jews, but Jews were required to attend. Jews (as well as Czechs) had to adopt German surnames, and to choose given names from a restricted list of 109 male names and 35 female names. Only in 1849 were Jews given equality with other populations.

The abolition of restrictions and the so-called "family law" produced many demographic changes in the Jewish population. Jews left the ghettos and moved to the small villages; the population increased so that by 1890 there were almost 95,000 Jews in Bohemia and 45,000 in Moravia. Then they began to migrate to the cities, and many small communities disappeared. Emancipation led to closer ties with both the Czech and German populations. Jews integrated into both groups, and, by 1900, about half used German and the other half Czech as their main language. The German cultural circle was considered the more intellectual with a large Prague Jewish-German presence including Franz Kafka, Max Brod, Franz Werfel, Oscar Baum and others.

On October 28, 1918, the Czechoslovak Republic was born out of the remnants of the Austro-Hungarian Empire. This new republic included all of Bohemia and Moravia as well as Slovakia and Carpatho-Ruthenia (today, western Ukraine). Out of a population of about 13 million, less than 2 percent were Jews. On September 30, 1938, with the signing of the Munich agreement, Czechoslovakia was forced to cede its border areas to Germany, which declared the Sudetenland, as it was called, to be part of Germany, and thus under Nazi control.[11] About 25,000 Jews, as well as many of the Czechs, fled to what remained of Czechoslovakia. Synagogues were burned and cemeteries vandalized or demolished.

In 1938, approximately 300,000 Jews lived in Czechoslovakia. About 122,000 of these resided in the Czech Lands (i.e., the western part of Czechoslovakia). This figure included refugees from other places. Germany marched into what re-

mained of Czechoslovakia on March 15, 1939, and declared it to be the Protectorate of Bohemia and Moravia. About 89,000 were eventually deported to Terezin (Theresienstadt) and other camps, where most perished.

After World War II, Czechoslovakia was again a complete country, but now without Carpatho-Ruthenia, which was ceded to the Soviet Union and had a very large Jewish population. In 1948, the Communists took over Czechoslovakia, and some of the few remaining Jews fled. The rest, for the most part, hid their Jewish identity. Only in 1989, after the so-called "Velvet Revolution," did Jewish life begin again. In 1993, Czechoslovakia divided forming the two countries of Slovakia and the Czech Republic. The cultural flowering of Czech Jewry lasted only 20 years, the time of the First Republic (1918–39).

Surnames

Not until the time of the Enlightenment, during the reign of Joseph II (1780–90), was the population required to adopt surnames. This applied not only to Jews but to the Czechs as well, all of whom were required to adopt German names from an approved list.

Before that time, only prominent people were likely to have surnames. Many rabbinic families, for example, already had family names. Many typically Czech Jewish names end in *eles*, such as Abeles, Muneles and Pereles.

Surnames were chosen in various ways. Some people already had names denoting where they came from, such as Wiener (from Vienna). Others used their father's names, possibly the source of the "eles" endings. Others came from occupations such as Glaser, Holzer or Lederer. Many are German names, but may be considered typically "Czech" since they were more common in Bohemia and Moravia than they were in Germany. In this category are such names as Berg, Baum and Stein. It was rare to see such names Germany without one

Interior of the Altneuschul (Old New Synagogue) in Prague as it existed in the 19th century. The banner was presented to the Jewish community by Emperor Ferdinand in 1648.

or another prefix attached to it. Other common names are Adler, Freund, Heller and Popper. Czech Jewish names usually were not insulting or ridiculous.

After the Reformation and the defeat of the Hussites in the 15th century, some Protestants preferred to convert to Judaism rather than to return to the Catholic Church. Czech and Moravian Jewish families occasionally maintain that they have Hussite ancestry, and thus Slavic names such as Kotouc or Lipa.

Given names of Czech ancestors often are confusing to genealogists, for one and the same person may have been known by several different names. In the early part of the 19th century, most Czech Jews had both a Hebrew as well as an official given name. Thus, Israel also would be Ignatz. One Jewish great-grandmother was known as Shaindl, but was officially both Suzanna and Charlotte. After 1848, Jewish given names tended to be the same secular common names as the rest of the population. Hebrew names would appear only on Jewish records, such as circumcision, marriage or *b'nai mitzvah*—just as in North America today.

Familianten Law (The "Family Law")

The census of 1724, mentioned above, listed by village and by family all Jews who lived in the Czech Lands. First, the heads of household were listed, followed by spouse and children, without surnames. At that time, 30,000 Jews lived in 168 towns and 672 villages in Bohemia, and 20,000 in Moravia. This did not include the Jews of Prague, where the census was not conducted until 1729. The Prague census showed 2,335 families totaling 10,507 Jews. After the census was complete, the "family law" was promulgated, which limited the number of Jewish families in Bohemia to 8,541 and 5,106 in Moravia. Families were given a "family number" that brought with it "domicile rights" equivalent to citizenship. Only the eldest son in each family was permitted to marry; families with daughters only were destined to die out. Younger sons remained single or emigrated.

Many younger sons moved to Poland or Hungary, where this law did not apply. By 1800, thousands of Moravian Jews had moved to Hungary and Slovakia. Some also went to the United States. For example, Isaac Mayer Wise (1819–1900), the founder of Reform Judaism in America, left from Steingrub (today Lomnicka) for the U.S. because of this law.

In some cases, religious marriages were performed, but not registered officially. This resulted in many so-called illegitimate births on the official birth registers. Registers were kept listing the *familiant*—that is, the head of the family—and his sons in order of birth. Girls were not listed in the *familianten* books, although wives might be. When a father died, the eldest son was permitted to marry. These registers were often not actually compiled in written form until many years after the event and were backdated. Naturally, there were times when false information was given. Upon their marriage, some couples "adopted" the wife's surname, especially if that family had only daughters. Generally, however, the registers are accurate and correspond with the vital statistics records.

In 1789, Emperor Joseph II slightly raised the number of permitted Jews to 8,600 in Bohemia. Moravia remained at 5,106. In addition, Jews engaged in agriculture or in such trades as butcher or glazier were allowed to apply for special permission to start a family. In one case, for example, the aide-de-camp of a high army officer obtained his superior's recommendation for a permit to marry, because the officer was so pleased with his subordinate.

Genealogical Resources

The Austrian Empire lasted for almost 400 years and the Czechs were under its rule for most of that time. They had a strong and efficient record keeping bureaucracy. Although compliance was often slow, especially in the villages, most communities kept good records, most of which have been preserved. In small places, church parishes often included Jewish records. These church records are not part of the Jewish archive.

The vital statistics and the *familianten* records now are held in the state archives in Prague.* This building, which once was the entire national archives, now is dedicated to Jewish records. It also holds many censuses, maps and reference works.

The family law was repealed in 1849, and many unofficial marriages were subsequently registered. In one small village alone, approximately 50 marriages were registered during the years 1849 and 1850, an absurdly high number under normal circumstances.

During the 200 years Jewish families were domiciled and registered, their mobility was limited. Except for those who emigrated, people tended to stay where they were, and immigration was not permitted. Several brothers often married sisters (not their own) or cousins, so families often were related in multiple ways. Researchers should, therefore, gather *all* names in collateral families, not just those in one's direct lines. Often, one finds second and third cousins by chance because of familiarity with a tangential family name. One Bohemian Jew maintains that if you go back far enough, all Bohemian Jews are related—an exaggeration, perhaps, but with a kernel of truth.

Familiantenbucher (family books) are available to researchers. To be sure of finding the correct family, a researcher should know the area, preferably the village or town, where the family lived. Because of the limited number of names that Jews were permitted to take, totally unrelated families often had the same names. The fact that the given names often repeated within a family can cause confusion, as well. Birth, marriage and death records are essential tools for comparison. The vital statistics records, called *Matrices,* also are held in the same archive and are available for research. Although quite extensive, the Matrices are not complete. Some birth, marriage or death records are missing for some towns; sometimes the earliest records exist, but not later ones.

Not only are the *familianten* records written in old Gothic German, but they often are difficult to read. Sometimes the handwriting is poor as if the clerks were quite elderly or not well educated. Some have faded; many are more than 200 years old. On the other hand, the archivists, who speak Czech, German and a little English, are helpful, and researchers can hire translators when necessary. To use the Matrices, a researcher must know the village where the ancestors resided. Indexes held at the archives list even the smallest community. These in turn point one to the town where the records were held. The Archives charges a small fee (about US$1) for accessing each volume, but reference books and the *familianten* records are free. Archivists will perform individual research for a fee and may be reached by mail or e-mail.

The main archive for Moravia is in Brno. Many genealogically useful records are held there. Property and/or court records are held in municipal archives.

The records of the LDS (Mormon) Family History Library are only minimally useful to Czech and Moravian researchers, as the Czech authorities have not permitted their records to be filmed.

Holocaust Records

Records of Czech and Moravian Jewish victims of the Shoah are numerous and informative. The Pinchas Synagogue in Prague has on its walls as a memorial the names and birth dates of more than 77,000 Jewish victims of Nazism. The same information is in the two-volume Terezin memorial books that provide a complete listing of all deportees from Bohemia and Moravia to Terezin and other locations. The books are ar-

ranged chronologically by transport number and include a complete alphabetical index. A separate section for each transport lists survivors. Although written in Czech (with a small companion volume in English), the lists are self-explanatory. The books may be purchased directly from the publisher and are available in many large libraries. Both the Prague Jewish Museum* and Beit Terezin* at Kibbutz Givat Chaim Ichud in Israel have the individual cards for each deportee from which these volumes were compiled.

Many towns have their own lists of former Jewish residents. For example, Plzen has a memorial at the site of the old synagogue with a stone showing the name and birth date of all its Holocaust victims.

Cemeteries

In the Czech Republic, many cemeteries were basically preserved, although they were vandalized during the Nazi era. Some were later demolished by the Communist regime. The most infamous is the old Zizkov cemetery in Prague, located where a large communication tower now stands. In use until 1891, the Zizkov cemetery was closed when the new cemetery at Strasnice was opened. At first the stones were buried, but later they were removed and destroyed when the tower was built.

In many cases, tombstones were stolen for reuse, and, of course, age and neglect have taken their toll. Jiri Fiedler, a Czech researcher who has devoted his life to the subject, has produced an excellent resource of Jewish sites past and present. His guidebook, *Jewish Sights of Bohemia and Moravia*, provides detailed identification of cemeteries, synagogues, prayer rooms and locations where Jews lived, showing their proximity to major centers.

The U.S. Commission for the Preservation of America's Heritage Abroad and the Jewish Heritage Council of the World Monuments Fund identified 412 cemeteries and 212 synagogues. An *AVOTAYNU* article lists the locations surveyed.[12] Some of the cemeteries have lists of the graves; others do not. Information about these cemeteries may be found on the JewishGen website (see JEWISHGEN).[13]

Onsite visits provide much information unavailable from lists. Persons buried nearby, maiden names and much other information may be gleaned. Hebrew names often can provide information on additional generations, especially if the previous generation also was buried there. Families tended to be buried in the same area within a cemetery. Although the oldest gravestones usually were engraved in Hebrew, those of the last hundred years were often in Czech or German as well. In any case, inscriptions can be translated once the researcher has returned home. Be sure to record the exact location of the grave and the complete inscription. Now that some of the stones have been exposed to the elements again, older inscriptions are becoming illegible quickly. Careful photography can provide the researcher with a permanent record. Rubbings can be made of gravestones, which provide the researcher with a full-sized record and do not harm the stones. In any case, since the Velvet Revolution of 1989, a number of towns have undertaken to maintain or restore their Jewish cemeteries. Usually it is easy to find a local resident who can direct one to a site, even when the cemetery no longer exists.

Available Records

Central Archives. The determination of the German Nazis to construct a "Museum of the Extinct Race" in Prague ensured that they preserved and consolidated the Jewish records of the Czech lands. This practice contrasted with the wholesale destruction of Jewish works in other areas. These records are now kept in the main archives in Prague,* where they are available for research. The vital records in this collection often include not only the names of parents, but often the grandparents and even the grandmothers' maiden names.

The records were kept in German Gothic script; sometimes the handwriting is very poor, because the clerks were either old or not well educated. However, the archivists are helpful, and researchers may hire translators to assist them.

In addition to the specifically Jewish records of birth, circumcision, marriage and death, and the *Familianten-bucher*, useful civic records also exist. These can be found in the municipal archives of the relevant towns, as well as in regional archives. The Moravian records are held in Brno. These include land transfer and ownership, military records, court and property records. The Catholic parishes, which kept the Jewish records as noted above, may still have some of these records; they were not included in the Nazi centralization of Jewish records.

Jewish Museum. The Jewish Museum in Prague* holds many records and reference materials pertaining to Czech Jewry, including cemetery and community records. Most of its holdings are stored out-of-town and must be requested.

Other Sources of Information

Nobility Records. In the German areas, Jews sometimes were protected under the patronage of the nobles who viewed them as property. Such a Jew was known as a *Shutzjude* (protected Jew). At times, Czech Jews were also known by this term if they were under the protection of a German who had land in Bohemia. The local nobility also kept records. The records were privately held and may still exist, depending on the whim or fate of the particular noble. Books about the history of individual noble families held in the collections of large research libraries may include information about the Jewish families under the noble's patronage.

Books. The history of the Jewish families of Prague in the 17th century is recorded in Simon Hock's book *Die Familien Prags*. Daniel Schlyter's *Handbook of Czechoslovak Genealogical Research* also includes a survey of early Prague Jewish families. A Czech language history of the Jews of Bohemia and Moravia written by Tomas Pekny presents a detailed history of Jewish life from the 10th century to 1867, the date of Jewish emancipation in the Austro-Hungarian Empire. A more recent survey is Rudolf Wlaschek's German-language book of lectures on the history of 19th- and 20th-century European Jews. An example of books about the social life and customs of the Jews of the Prague ghetto is Milada Vilimkova's work, *La Ghetto de Prague*, in French; Wilma Iggers's *The Jews in*

Bohemia and Moravia is available in both English and German.

A number of researchers have published their family histories. These are too specific to be included here. Although no central index of such stories exists, some may be found in Holocaust libraries, at Yad Vashem, in large general libraries and on the Internet (see also FAMILY HISTORIES).

The town of Boskovice in Moravia once had a large Jewish population. A book, *The Jews of Boskovice*, has been published in Czech with a short summary in English and German.

Internet. The Internet facilitates genealogical research enormously. Of particular interest is the Boh-Mor (Bohemia-Moravia) special interest group website found under JewishGen (see JEWISHGEN). Another valuable site is the immigrant's newspaper *Aufbau* at WWW.AUFAUONLINE.COM. The annual journal, *Judaica Bohemiae*, is held in major research libraries; an index to its articles can be found at WWW.JEWISHMUSEUM.CZ. The journal has been published since 1965 and covers all aspects of Jewish Bohemian life through the centuries. WWW.COLLEGIUM-CAROLINUM.DE/DOKU/LIT/JUEDG/BIBL-JUD-P.HTM is a bibliography compiled by Robert Luft listing books of Jewish interest in the Charles University collection in Prague. The website WWW.ZCHOR.ORG/CZECH.HTM is the forum of the Jewish communities of the former state of Czechoslovakia. This site can help with tracing information about lost communities.

Military Records. Military records may be useful. Jews from the Czech lands served in the Austro-Hungarian army and often attained high rank. The military archive in Prague* holds recruit books for men inducted into military service prior to 1918.

Regional Archives. Regional archives in the Czech Republic are an important source for detailed information about the lives of ancestors. The central archive in Prague holds primarily vital statistics and references, but the regional archives holds lists of former residents, censuses, property and court records and sometimes even such things as seating lists for synagogues.

Other Archival Collections. The Archives of the Capital City of Prague* holds such items as property and legal records plus general vital statistics. The Czech and Slovak Jewish Communities Archives* in New York produced one issue of a journal called *Phoenix* and may hold useful material. The Leo Baeck Institute,* devoted to Jews from German-speaking areas, includes the areas of Czechoslovakia where German was spoken. It holds a number of family trees and research material.

The Czechoslovak Genealogical Society International* is concerned primarily with immigration from the former Czechoslovakia to the United States. It holds conferences, publishes books and has a newsletter that includes searches. Although mostly not relevant for Jewish researchers, some articles and information about early immigration to the United States may be useful.

Addresses

Archives of the Capital City of Prague, Husova 20, 110 01 Praha, Czech Republic

AVOTAYNU 12, no. 3 (Fall 1996) contains a complete listing of the public archives in Bohemia and Moravia. These include regional and city archives with addresses and phone numbers as well as the current directors.

Bet Terezin, Kibbutz Givat Chaim, Israel; e-mail: BTEREZIN@INTER.NET.IL

Czechoslovak Genealogical Society International, P.O.Box 16225, St. Paul, MN 55116-0225

Czech and Slovak Jewish Community Archives, 86-17 139th Street, Jamaica, New York 11435

Jewish Museum of Prague: Zidovske Muzeum v Praze, Jachymova 3, 100 01 Praha 1 Czech Republic

Leo Baeck Institute, Center for Jewish History, 15 West 16th Street, New York, NY; e-mail: WWW.CJH.ORG

Moravsky zemsky archiv v Brne (Regional Archive of Moravia in Brno) Zerotinovo nam.3-5 p.p. 22 656 01 Brno

Prague Jewish Community, Maislova 18, Prague 1, Czech Republic

Prague Jewish Museum, U Stareho hrbitova 3a, 110 01 Prague 1, Czech Republic; telephone: 02-223-17-191

Statni Ustredni Archiv (Czech State Archives), Tr Dr. M Horakove 133, 16621 Praha 6, Czech Republic; e-mail: SUA@MVCR.CZ

Vojensko historicky ustav (Military archive), U Pamatniku 2, Praha 3, Czech Republic

Bibliography

Beider, Alexander. *Jewish Surnames in Prague: 15th to 18th Century.* Teaneck N.J.: Avotaynu, 1994.

Dagan, Avigdor, ed. *Jews of Czechoslovakia: Historical Studies and Surveys.* 3 vols. Philadelphia: Jewish Publication Society, 1968.

Dolista, K. "The Complete Catalogue of Records for the Jewish Communities of Bohemia and Moravia Excluding that of Prague." *Judaica Bohemiae* 7, no. 21, (1971), Reprinted in *AVOTAYNU* 7, no. 3 (Fall 1991).

Epstein, Helen. *Where She Came From.* Boston: Little, Brown (1997).

Fiedler, Jiri. *GuideBook: Jewish Sights of Bohemia and Moravia.* Prague: Sefer (1991).

Gold, Hugo. *Die Juden und Judengemeinden Mahrens in Vergangenheit und Gegenwart-Ein Sammelwerk. Judischer Buch und Kunstverlag* (Jews and Jewish communities of Moravia in past and present). [German] Brno: Jewish Book and Art Publishers, 1929.

Gold, Hugo. *Die Juden und Judengemeinden Boehmen in Vergangenheit und Gegenwart. Judischer Buch und Kunsterlag* (Jews and Jewish communities of Bohemia in past and present). [German] Prague and Brno: Jewish Book and Art Publishers, 1934.

Hock, Simon. *Die Familien Prags nach den epitaphien des alten Judischen Friedhof in Prag* (Jewish families of Prague based on the epitaphs of the old Jewish cemetery in Prague. [German] Pressburg, 1892.

Honey, Michael. "Historical Clock: Rabbinic Dynasties of Bohemia." Jewish Cultural Centre in Prague, 25 Maislova, Prague, Czech Republic.

Iggers, Wilma. *Historical Reader of Jews of Bohemia and Moravia.* [German] Munich: Verlag C.H. Beck, 1986; *The Jews of Bohemia and Moravia: A historical reader.* [English] Detroit: Wayne State University, 1992.

Judaica Bohemiae. [Czech] Prague: Jewish State Museum, 1965.

Mokotoff, Gary and Sallyann Amdur Sack. *Where Once We Walked.* Teaneck, NJ: Avotaynu, 1991.

Pekny, Tomas. *Bistorie Zidi v Cechach a Na Morave* (History of the Jews of Czech and Moravia). [Czech] Prague: Sefer, 1993.

Phoenix, Journal of Czech and Slovak Family and Community History. Czech and Slovak Jewish Community Archives, 1997.

Schlyter, Daniel M. *A Handbook of Czechoslovak Genealogical Research.* Buffalo Grove, IL: Genun, 1985. *Terezinska Pametni Kniha. Terezinska Initiativa* (Terezin memorial books). 2 vols. [Czech] Prague: Melantrich, 1995.

Vilimkova, Milada. *La Ghetto de Prague.* [French] Paris: Aurore d'Art, 1990.

Wlaschek, Rudolf. *Juden in Boehmen: Beitrage zur Geschichte des Euopreanischen Judentum 19 und 20 Jahrhundert.* [German] Munich: Aldenhaurg, 1997.

Notes

1. Mokotoff and Sack. *Where Once We Walked.*
2. Fiedler, Jiri. *Guidebook: Jewish Sights of Bohemia and Moravia.*
3. *Ibid.*
4. *Ibid.*
5. *Ibid.*
6. *Ibid.*
7. *Ibid.*
8. *Ibid.*
9. *Ibid.*
10. Edict of Toleration, October 13, 1781, was the most important change in legal status for the Jews since the 13th century. It permitted the building of prayer houses and conferred most civil rights such as schooling, and choice of occupation.
11. Signed by Neville Chamberlain and Adolf Hitler, the Munich Agreement ceded the Czech border areas known as the Sudetenland to Germany on condition that Hitler make no further territorial claims. This was against existing international agreements and left Czechoslovakia defenseless.
12. *AVOTAYNU* 9, no. 2 (Summer 1993): 22.
13. WWW.JEWISHGEN.ORG/CEMETERY

Denmark

by Elsebeth Paikin

The First Wave—"Old Danish Jews" (1633–1880).[1] Exactly when the first Jews came to Denmark is veiled in the mists of time. Surely some of the many Jewish wanderers who roamed Europe from the Middle Ages onward, driven by need, wars, plagues and persecutions, must have found their way to Denmark. It is also likely that merchants, traders and peddlers tried their luck in Denmark from early on.

Numerous laws and regulations that prohibited the entry of beggars, vagrants, gypsies, Jews and Papists into Denmark indicate that Jews must have existed in Denmark at that time, and numerous reports by the police confirm the existence of poor, wandering Jews in Denmark, where they were as unwanted as in all other countries. Time and again, new laws and regulations were passed as old ones proved ineffective. Some of the Jews that came illegally to Denmark eventually managed to stay, sometimes after having first been fined and expelled more than once.

Usually, the history of the Jews in Denmark is said to begin in 1622, when King Christian IV officially invited Jews of the "Portuguese Nation" (Sephardic Jews) from Amsterdam and Hamburg to settle in Glückstadt, a newly founded town in Holstein on the Elbe River. The Jews were offered "letters of protection," many privileges and freedom of religion. The King hoped that, with the help of enterprising and wealthy Jewish merchants, Glückstadt could become an important competitor to Hamburg. Glückstadt never prospered, however, but together with Altona (which King Christian IV inherited in 1640), it became a haven of refuge for the Jews of Hamburg whenever persecutions threatened them.[2] The Danish kings were not only kings of Denmark, but also hereditary dukes of Schleswig and Holstein (see below).

- 1460–1658: Holstein and Slesvig are twin duchies. All or parts of the duchies are held by the King of Denmark, other parts by brothers and cousins. The dukes strive for independence from the Danish Crown.
- 1658–1721: Half of the Duchies of Holstein and Slesvig ruled by a sovereign duke; the other half ruled by the King of Denmark
- 1721–1773: All of the Duchy of Slesvig and half of Holstein ruled by the King of Denmark
- 1773–1864: All of the Duchy of Slesvig and all of Holstein ruled by the King of Denmark
- 1864–1920: All of the Duchy of Slesvig and all of Holstein incorporated into the German Empire
- 1920: The northernmost part of the Duchy of Slesvig (Sønderjylland) returned to Denmark

At first, the Jews' privileges were valid only for Schleswig and Holstein—not for the kingdom itself.

In the middle of the 17th century, several wars, ensuing epidemics and economic collapse devastated Denmark. In some areas the population was decimated; many farms and towns were derelict and deserted. To revive the country and raise money, the king provided optimum conditions for all who would settle in the deserted towns and start a trade. In the 1660s and 1670s, therefore, the privileges issued to Sephardic Jews in Schleswig and Holstein were extended to the entire kingdom. From that time onward, Jews (mainly Ashkenazim from Hamburg and Altona) began to settle officially in the kingdom of Denmark, in the towns of Aalborg, Aarhus, Assens, Faaborg, Fredericia, Horsens, Køge, Nakskov, Odense, Randers, Slagelse—and in the capital, Copenhagen. The Ashkenazim were not allowed, however, to move from town to town. They had to remain in the town where their family originally had been granted permission to settle.

The privileges only applied to the wealthy. Poor Jews, like other paupers, were not allowed to come to Denmark. Those who did were fined and expelled—some several times, as they kept coming back. Over time the privileges were extended and circumstances for the Jews improved steadily. Contrary to the situation in many other parts of Europe, no special taxes, special garments, restrictions on marriage or areas of the towns in which to live were imposed on Danish Jewry. Denmark was no breeding ground for persecution, forced conversion or the like, and the Danish kings were praised as "mild and just."[3]

King Frederik VI (ruled 1808–39), who was personally very sympathetic to the Jews, was called "King of the Jews." As early as 1684, Jews were granted internal self-rule. In 1809, Jews were permitted to live anywhere they wanted in Denmark, and in 1814 they obtained permission to enter into any trade or occupation of their choice. Finally, the Constitution of 1849 granted them rights equal to those of all other Danish citizens.

Throughout the 18th century, more Jews—particularly from Poland and Germany—settled in Denmark, but immigration started to ebb around 1800. In 1885, the Jewish population was estimated at 3,542. Several of those who came to live in Denmark but did not succeed or thrive did not, as might be expected, move to other Danish towns, but very often returned to their original town or country.[4]

Second Wave—Russians or "New Jews" (1880–1917). Beginning in about 1880, Jewish emigration from Eastern Europe increased steadily, peaking in the years 1900–15. From the western and northern parts of Russia and Poland, emigrants embarked primarily from ports on the Baltic coast (especially Libau, Königsberg and Stettin), where they sailed to Denmark or Sweden and then on to England and the United States. Most wanted to go to America, and many succeeded, but some, who could not pay the fare all the way to America, went to Denmark (or Sweden), where they worked hard trying to save enough money for the next leg of the journey. Although some eventually made it to America, others, by choice or by circumstances, settled in Denmark, which was considered an "America for the poor."

Danish immigration regulations were tightened beginning in 1912 because of the strained international situation; in 1917 the Danish authorities formally stopped further immigration.

Immigrants were not registered upon arrival, so precise statistics do not exist. Data from various sources, however, indicate that approximately 10,000 Jews came to Denmark between 1900 and 1917; 40 to 50 percent of them remained in Denmark.

Throughout the years, increasing numbers of Danish Jews have integrated, assimilated and intermarried into Danish society. At the turn of the 20th century, approximately 50 percent of the marriages were intermarriages. Today, a great part of the Jewish population does not observe Jewish rituals. At the other end of the spectrum is a small congregation of a few hundred ultra-Orthodox Jews who live in Copenhagen. It is, thus, difficult to provide numbers or statistics on Danish Jewry today, because one would first need to define who is a Jew. The narrowest definition would include only those who are paying members of the Jewish congregation. The widest would be the genealogical definition (i.e., all those with Jewish roots).

Immigration Since 1930. The most recent Jewish emigration to Denmark consisted of refugees primarily from Germany before World War II; refugees from the 1956 Hungarian uprising and from Czechoslovakia in 1968; and a significant influx from Poland during the years 1969 to 1972. Because legislation protects individual privacy, however, it is difficult, if not impossible, for researchers to gain access to archival documents and records about these immigrants.

Research in Denmark

Because of the widespread, longstanding assimilation and integration of Danish Jews, genealogical research should not be restricted to Jewish records alone, but researchers should encompass ordinary Danish records as well. On the other

Permit to settle in Copenhagen in 1768 given to Joska Isach Israel as a result of his marriage to Reusche, daughter of Isach Lazarus

hand, until the beginning of the 19th century, most Jews, assimilated or not, lived in relatively few towns; in Copenhagen they lived only in a small part of the city. The few exceptions can be rather difficult to find.

Before delving into records, researchers must learn to read Gothic script and some special Danish alphabet characters. The Danish alphabet has three letters not found in other languages: æ, ø and å. In upper case letters they are rendered Æ, Ø and Å. The letters usually are transcribed as follows: æ = ae, ø = oe and å = aa. (Both "å" and "aa" are used randomly in some Danish names and places, [e.g., Århus and Aarhus; Faaborg and Fåborg].

The Danish word for Jew is "jøde"; for Jewish it is "jødisk", but sometimes the term "mosaisk" is used instead. Thus, *Mosaisk Troessamfund* is the official name for the Jewish community in Denmark.

In addition, until approximately 1900, the typical Danish handwriting was Gothic script.

The Gothic script (or Old German Script) was used until 1875 (see WWW.SA.DK/SA/BRUGEARKIVER/GOTISK/1700SMAA.HTM for the Gothic alphabet used circa 1700, WWW.SA.DK/SA/BRUGEARKIVER/GOTISK/1800HAAND.HTM for the alphabet used circa 1800 and WWW.SA.DK/SA/BRUGEARKIVER/GOTISK/ in Danish only: introduction to Gothic script and examples from various periods.)

The Gothic script and specifically Danish characters mean that a genealogist cannot expect to come to Denmark, walk into an archive, ask for a census from 1845 and be able to read it—even if the genealogist knows Danish! This obstacle can be overcome, but not overnight; learning to read Gothic script takes time. Fortunately, some records have been transcribed and are available electronically (see The Danish Demographic Database, DDD.SA.DK).

Names and Naming Traditions

Patronymics were used in Denmark until after 1850; that is, a son was given a surname consisting of his father's first name plus the suffix *sen* (meaning "son"). A daughter's surname was constructed similarly with the father's name and the suffix *datter* (meaning "daughter"). This pattern also applied to the Jews in Denmark. David's son would be given the surname Davidsen, and a daughter of Joseph would be Josephsdatter. Or, as was very common in the 18th and beginning of the 19th centuries, the surname of a child was the father's given name and surname. For example, Rachel, the daughter of Nathan Cohen, would be known as Rachel Nathan Cohen, and the son Jacob would be known as Jacob Nathan Cohen—Nathan being part of the surname and not a given or middle name.

A further complication arose from the fact that names were often changed or misspelled upon immigration.

Jews in Denmark—as elsewhere—sometimes changed their names for practical reasons, to escape discrimination, to obtain jobs or because they converted to Christianity. For example, in 1813 Jacob Philip and his wife Doba were christened in Aarhus and given the names Christian and Christine Dessau.[5] Dessau and Dessauer are known Jewish names, however, so Jacob Philip's family name might have been Dessau from the beginning; unfortunately, the records do not supply that information.

Another example is the Ashkenazic Jew, Moses Aaron Nathan, who was born and raised in Altona and Glückstadt. In 1711, he was allowed to settle in Nakskov on the island of Lolland, where he married the daughter of a Jew, who had lived in Nakskov for 30 years. Their son, Pinches (Danish version of Pinchas) took the name of the town in which he was born, Nakskov or Nasschou. When Pinches wanted to move to Copenhagen, however, he was prevented from doing so because of the requirement that Ashkenazic Jews remain in the town where their family was first granted permission to settle. Pinches then recalled that his grandmother in Glückstadt had been both born and married to a Henriques, one of the Sephardic families. He changed his name, therefore, to Bendix Henriques, and, as a "Jew and according to the Portuguese Jews' privileges," he easily obtained citizenship in Copenhagen.[6]

The first Jew given a "letter of protection" in 1619 by King Christian IV (1588–1648) and appointed mintmaster in Glückstadt is usually known by the name of Albert Dionis (or Denis), but, as many Portuguese Jews did at that time, he used several other names (i.e., Alvaro Denis, Albrecht de Nyes, Albertus Dionysius, Samuel Hyac and Samuel Jachja)![7]

Scandinavian Mobility and Migration

Inter-Scandinavian mobility and migration—particularly among Jews—has always been significant. Jews who could not find work in Copenhagen often went to Sweden or Norway to work, with or without their families, for a period of time. Most often, they just crossed the narrow sound between Denmark and Sweden, but occasionally they traveled to Stockholm or Oslo. Inter-Scandinavian migration varied over time due to different judicial measures and, of course, the current employment situation. A genealogist with a family history in Denmark who does not find a particular record in Denmark should try repositories in Sweden or Norway. In fact, even if some ancestors lived in Sweden or Norway, they might have emigrated via a Danish harbor, and thus reported that they came from Denmark—or vice versa.

Danish Colonies

From the beginning of the 17th century, Denmark had colonies, possessions, protectorates or extensive commercial relations with other countries. These included the Faroe Islands, Greenland, Iceland, the Danish West Indies: St. Thomas, St. John and St. Croix, which were sold in 1917 to the United States and today are the U.S. Virgin Islands; Guinea on the Gold Coast of Africa (sold in 1850 to England); and Trankebar on the southeastern coast of India (sold in 1845 to England). As a result, some records from these places are kept in the Danish Archives (see CARIBBEAN).

Genealogical Research
Research from Abroad

For genealogists who do not live in Denmark, the easiest way to start the research is via the Internet, CD-ROMs and printed sources.

Emigrants' Records. Records of ancestors who emigrated from or via Denmark after 1868 may be found in official Danish emigration records kept by the Copenhagen police. In the mid-19th century, mass migration had became an increasingly prosperous market for shipping companies and travel agents, and some tried to earn quick money by cheating the emigrants. In order to regulate the activities of the shipping agents and to protect emigrants from fraud, the police kept lists of all tickets purchased from Danish travel agents. Records were kept for both direct and indirect traffic (i.e., via Germany or England); records exist of emigrants from Denmark who bought tickets from a Danish agent. The records include name, occupation, place of birth and/or last residence, age, destination, number of the contract, date of police registration and, in the case of direct transportation from Denmark, name of the ship.

Emigration records (passenger lists) are available for the years 1869 to 1908 (360,000 emigrants) in the online searchable Danish Emigration Data Base (WWW.EMIARCH.DK) or DDD.DDA.DK compiled by the Danish Emigration Archives* and the City Archives of Aalborg.* In addition, 4,109 records of emigrants from Denmark for the years 1879–87 are listed in the Emigration Records from VEJLE (WWW.AALBORG.DK/BORGERPORTAL/APPLIKATIONER/UDVANDRER/SoegpostEngelsk.asp. The emigration records, also available on a CD-ROM, may be purchased from *Det Danske Udvandrerarkiv* (Danish Emigration Archives).*

Immigrants' Records. Before 1776, immigration into Denmark was not controlled much, except for Jews and Catholics. Because of attempts to keep poor Jews out of Denmark, Jews had to apply for a permit or passport and were required to pay a fee. The passport applications can be found in *Danske Kancelli** (Danish Chancellery) *1773–1799* at *Rigsarkivet** (Danish National Archives) in the police archives at *Landsarkivet i København** (the Provincial Archive, Copenhagen*.) After 1914, the State Police issued permits (*opholdsbøger*) to aliens; these registers also are kept at the Provincial Archive, Copenhagen.

The police archives holds many other records of interest, among them a register of Jews in Copenhagen for 1780–1835, a register of Jews born outside Denmark 1844–46 and a register of non-Danes of the Mosaic religion. Consult the JewishGen's Scandinavia SIG website: WWW.JEWISHGEN.ORG/SCANDINAVIA for access details.

Naturalization Records. All naturalizations were granted by issuing a law of naturalization, usually once a year. Until 1850, naturalizations were only necessary for a public or government officer or a civil servant. Information about naturalizations for the period 1776–1850 can be found in *protokoller for naturalisationspatenter* (registers of naturalization papers), from 1850–1960 in the official reports of parliamentary proceedings—or more easily available from 1850 in *Lovtidende*, an official gazette in which the government publishes new laws, rules and regulations. *Lovtidende* is issued annually and may be found in all Danish libraries and some major libraries abroad. *Lovtidende* provides the number of the naturalization law and the date it was issued, together with the *tillaeg* (appendix) number. With that, one can request the petition for naturalization for the individual in question at *Rigsarkivet** (the National Archives).

Without knowledge of the exact year of naturalization, this can be a vexing job. In some cases, applications for naturalization was not made until many years after arrival in Denmark. Someone who came to Denmark in 1905 and lived there since might not have applied for naturalization until the 1940s or even later. Fortunately a short-cut exists. *Rigsarkivet* has a card index of all immigrants who became naturalized citizens. Typed lists of the card index exist for the period 1850–1915 and are accessible at the *Rigsarkivet*. Although the Danish National Archives does not undertake individual research, genealogists may write to inquire about one or two names (with possible spelling variations).

Even better, the Danish Immigrant Museum* currently is making naturalization and other immigration-related records available for online search at WWW.IMMIGRANTMUSEET.DK/IMMIBAS/IMMIBAS.HTM. At present, one can find the items listed below. This is a work in progress and new items will be added periodically. Researchers can find translations and advice at the Scandinavian SIG website at WWW.JEWISHGEN.ORG.

- *Arbejdsophold* (work permits), 1812–1924 for Frederiksborg County, the northern part of Zealand only, 1812–75 (towns 1812–54) based on information from parish registers, and from 1875 onwards from the police records listing *opholdsboger* (work permits).
- *Indfødsretstildeling* (naturalizations) (1776–1960) list all individuals who became naturalized Danish citizens in the years 1776–1960. (50.317 records). For the years 1776–1849 the *Indfødsretstildeling* is based upon a register of naturalizations; for the years 1850–1960, it is based on the comments to the proposals for naturalization laws. After 1898, married women and minor children are not found in the records, because they automatically obtained naturalization together with the husband or father. Widows who applied independently and obtained Danish citizenship usually are listed under their married names.
- *Udviste* are names of individuals expelled from Denmark in the years 1875–1919; this source includes 31,000 records, with some duplicates, as many individuals were expelled several times. Names have been taken from the internal police publication *Politiefterretninger*. Most of the expulsions were based on the *Fremmedloven* (aliens act)

Immigration records may be searched online at the Danish Demographic Database DDD.SA.DK, or directly at DDD.SA.DK/IMMIBAS/HTM/IMMIBASLINK.HTM. Additional information about the material, the database and new or updated databases may be found at WWW.IMMIGRANTMUSEET.DK. The Immigrant Museum* may produce a CD-ROM in the near future; if it does, information about such a CD-ROM could also be found on the website. Currently, the website is written in Danish only.

Census. The censuses might be an easy way to find information about ancestors if a researcher knows where they lived at a specific time. A search is relatively easy because Jews lived in only a few towns, and most immigrants at the beginning of the 20th century initially lived in a small area of Copenhagen.

Noted Danish Jewish pianist and comedian, Victor Borge (1909–2000)

The first Danish census was held in 1787; afterwards they were held in 1801, 1834, 1840, 1845, 1850, 1855, 1860, 1870, 1880, 1890, 1901, 1906, 1911, 1916, 1921, 1925 and then every fifth year until 1970. In 1970 the Central National Register was established, thus eliminating the need for censuses. In 1885 and 1895, censuses were taken of Copenhagen only.

From 1845–1901 (in 1916 only for Copenhagen) the censuses have information about place of birth, and from 1855 onward, information about religious affiliation. Censuses are available from 1803, 1835, 1840, 1845, and 1855 (incomplete) for the former Danish parts of Schlesvig and Holstein. Censuses were taken in the Danish West Indies in 1841, 1846, 1850, 1855, 1857, 1860, 1870, 1880, 1890, 1901 and 1911. The most recent publicly accessible census was taken in 1921, but genealogists can request, and customarily obtain, permission to see later censuses.

Census data generally are reliable, but, of course, the information is based on what the clerks were told. Names are spelled inconsistently, especially in the older censuses; at times persons are found under one name in one census and under another name in the next census. Ages might differ for various reasons; older people might not have remembered their exact age, or an erroneous age might have been given in order to avoid special taxation or conscription. Jews may have had specific reasons to avoid being listed at all—particularly if they were illegal immigrants.

Two published articles claim that the listings of Jews in the censuses are not reliable. In some cases, the persons are listed twice; in other cases, not at all. The articles have information about Jews in some of the towns in question, as well as those missing from the censuses.[8]

In addition to ordinary censuses, special censuses called *mandtal* were conducted frequently. Between the censuses in 1787 and 1801, *mandtal* lists for Copenhagen were done in 1784, 1790, 1791, 1793, 1794, 1795 and 1798 to survey the supplies of corn and other provisions. These *mandtal* also included Jews living in Copenhagen. Other *mandtal* were created for conscription or to collect extra taxes. Joseph Fischer copied all information pertaining to Jews in Copenhagen (see the Jewish Community Archive, miscellaneous, below); he also extracted information on the Jewish population from the regular censuses. They are all found in his archival collection in *Rigsarkivet.**

Census Data on the Internet, CD-ROM and Microfilm. For the Source Entry Project, initiated in 1992, volunteers transcribe records—primarily censuses, but also some parish registers and probate records—and donate them to the Danish Data Archive.* In turn, the Archive makes the data accessible for online Internet search on the Danish Demographic Database and also produces a CD-ROM, updated once or twice yearly. Because the volunteers usually focus on censuses in which they have interest, these enumerations now electronically accessible represent a random choice. Nevertheless, it is a good tool for researchers from abroad, and the number of electronically accessible censuses increases daily.

Currently, searches can be made by name, birth place and occupation, but unfortunately, not by any soundex method. Wildcard searches, however, are possible. It is not possible to search by religion, although the censuses do list this information. Occasionally, in the older censuses *jøde* (Jew) is listed as an occupation.

Microfiche. *Statens Arkivers Filmningscenter** (National Archives' Film Center) sells microfilms of censuses up to 1916 and parish registers to 1891. Also available are microfiche of the Mosaic Community's vital records (births more than 100 years old, marriages and *bar mitzvas* [called confirmation in Denmark] more than 50 years old). If a particular microfiche has information about birth, marriage and death, the limit is 100 years; if the microfiche has only marriage records, the limit is 50 years. For deaths the limit is only 10 years, but the records since 1935 have not been deposited yet with the provincial archive. Information on deaths since 1935 can be obtained by writing to the Mosaic Community.*

Josef Fischer (1871–1949), founder of Jewish genealogy in Denmark

The LDS (Mormon) Family History Centers have microfilms of the publicly available Danish censuses and parish registers.

Onsite Research in Denmark
Taken in the aggregate, the Danish National Archives, the four provincial archives, the Danish National Business Archives and the Danish Data Archives comprise the Danish State Archives.

Archives and Libraries
Two important archives located in Copenhagen are *Rigsarkivet** (The National Archive) and *Landsarkivet* for *Sjælland** (Provincial Archive for Zealand). The Danish State Archives will do a few straightforward searches, but it does not undertake any genealogical research; instead, it makes available a list of professional genealogists.

Erhvervsarkivet (The National Business Archives) may be useful if an ancestor were a businessman or owned or established a firm in Denmark.

Arbejder bevægelsens Bibliotek og Arkiv (Library and Archive for Laborers and the Labor Movement) is the place to look for information about laborers and their living and working conditions.

Det Kongelige Bibliotek (The Royal Library) has an extensive collection of Judaica as well as some biographies and genealogies of Danish Jews.

Frederiksberg Bibliotek (Frederiksberg Municipal Library) has specialized in genealogy for many years. It has an immense collection of published and unpublished family histories, genealogies and pedigrees, so this is a good place to look. Search online at its website WWW.FKB.DK.

If You Know Only the Name, but Little Else
Even if a genealogist knows nothing but the names of some ancestors and the fact that they came from Denmark, it may be easy to find them if they also died in Denmark. Julius Margolinsky, Hans Metzon and most recently Elias Levin have published several books on Jewish burials in Denmark 1693–1998.[9] If a family lived in Denmark for a relatively long period, then it is fairly easy to find a year of death for someone—and that is a good place to start. Even if a family stopped in Denmark for a short time someone may have died here. Remember to try alternate spellings.

City directories exist for some of the larger towns for various periods. For Copenhagen the city directory is *Kraks Vejviser* (Krak's directory) or Copenhagen *Vejviser*. Published since 1770, these directories may be found at the Provincial Archives in Copenhagen and the *Raadhusbiblioteket* (City Hall Library).

Jewish Community Archives
Vital Records
Vital records for the Jewish community, called the Mosaic Community in Denmark are found in the Provincial Archives* in Copenhagen as well as in the National Archives;* some are available on microfiche (see above).

Judaism became a recognized religion by a royal decree of March 29, 1814. Until then non-Lutherans had only been accepted and permitted to on an individual basis, in 1814 the

Jews were given official permission to practice their religion. Vital records since that date are found primarily in the Provincial Archives (on microfiche). Jewish vital records for Copenhagen exist from 1810; copies of the originals are found in the National Archives. Most vital records from 1810 forward have been well preserved, but many earlier documents were lost in the great Copenhagen fire of 1795 and during the bombardment of Copenhagen in 1807 during the Napoleonic wars. All births, marriages and deaths of persons who did not belong to a recognized religion were registered in local Lutheran parish registers. This means that it may be possible to find Jewish births, marriages and deaths from before 1814 in the Lutheran parish registers. In cases of conversions, christened Jews naturally will be found in the parish registers and usually they have acquired a new Christian name also after 1814.

Probate Records

As early as 1736, the Jewish community was granted the right to administer the estates of deceased members of the community. Later in the 18th century these rights were regulated and, to some extent, restricted, but some probate records exist from 1760 until 1814 in the Mosaic Community's archive kept at Rigsarkivet.* Since 1814, Jewish probate records have been kept with all other Danish probate records. (see "General Danish Records" below) Probate records were written primarily in Hebrew or Yiddish until 1805; thereafter they were written in Danish. The community distinguished between the estates of the German (Ashkenazi) and the Portuguese Nation (Sephardi).

Not only do these records name relatives of the deceased, but the total amount of the estate, and often, all the possessions of the deceased are listed in the protocol, along with their value (e.g., furniture, clothing, jewelry, candlesticks, household items).

Registers of the Jewish Community's Poor Relief

Jewish community archives include a variety of registers, among them registers for charity and relief given to poor immigrants at the turn of the 20th century. For various reasons, many poor Jews did not apply for poor relief. One reason is that Jews who had received poor relief were not granted citizenship. Some lists name the ports of emigration, usually Königsberg, Libau or Stettin.

Miscellaneous holdings at *Rigsarkivet** include a membership list (1913–15) for Russian-Polish immigrants; a register (1925–32) concerning Russian-Polish immigrants that includes information on place of birth, year of immigration (1905–20), occupation, political and labor union affiliations; school records; and records about illness and hospitalization.

Most valuable is Joseph Fischer's archive. Joseph Fischer (1871–1949) was a central figure in the Jewish community for many years and a pioneer in Jewish genealogy, having published several genealogies of old Danish Jewish families. In his archive are notes, correspondence, transcripts and extracts of various records related to the history of the Danish Jewry. Even photographs, personal papers, letters and wills are found occasionally. Material is written in Danish, Hebrew or Yiddish.

Specifics of all the Jewish records kept at *Rigsarkivet** may be found in the register of the holdings of the Mosaic

Community's archive, which can be bought from Rigsarkivet. See www.sa.dk/ra/salgservice/bestil.htm for details. It is a great help for anyone undertaking Jewish genealogical research in Denmark.

General Danish Records

Jewish ancestors who assimilated and were integrated into the Christian population must be researched in general Danish records. Although some Lutheran parish registers date back to the 1650s, many have been lost; from about 1750, most parish registers have survived. After 1812–14, parish registers were made in duplicate and never kept under the some roof overnight. From that time, at least one copy of practically all parish registers have survived.

Research in parish registers created since 1812–14 is relatively easy, because the information is entered in specific columns and in separate parts of the register (e.g., all deceased women or all male children born). Before 1812–14, information was entered chronologically and with no specific columns for any data. The vicar just wrote as in a diary—in more or (often) less illegible handwriting.

As mentioned above, some transcribed parish registers have been donated to the Danish Data Archive* for the Source Entry Project, but the registers have not yet been made available online. All parish registers until 1891, however, exist on microfiche, which can be purchased from *Statens Arkivers Filmingscenter.**

Civil marriage was introduced in 1851 for persons who did not belong to any of the recognized religions, or for situations in which the bride and groom belonged to different religions. Later, others, such as communists and social-democrats who shunned any religion, often chose civil marriage. For this reason, the civil marriage records should be researched as well. Provincial archives have indexes of names, and the records are available on microfiche.

Oldest existing Jewish tombstone in Copenhagen, that of the jeweler David Israel, who died 16 September 1693 (15 Elul 5453)

LDS (Mormon) Family History Centers have microfilms of most Danish parish registers and censuses.

Probate Court Records

Probate court records after 1814 are found in provincial archives. Each provincial archive holds the extant records for its judicial area, and the records are generally accessible after 50 years. Lists after 1860 are kept on microfilm and in original at the National Archives.

Photographs

The Royal Library* has a vast collection of photographs—including portraits, historical topographical photos, and photograph albums—as do most local historical archives. Addresses for the local historical archives may be found on the websites WWW.LOKALARKIVER.DK and WWW.LOKALARKIVER.DK/ARKIVVEJVISER2000/ARKIVVEJVISER.HTM or write to the Union of Local Historical Archives.* The Royal Library's collection of photos can be found at WWW.KB.DK/KB/DEPT/NBO/KOB/BILLED/INDEX-EN.HTM where you can make an online search. Many of the photos are online. Several have collections of negatives from old photographers, so that it is possible to have copies made of photographs that have long since disappeared. Searching these collections is not easy, but most rewarding if the genealogist finds a photograph of an ancestor or the house in which he or she lived.

Suggested Reading

Louis Frænkel's *Forgotten Fragments of the History of an Old Jewish Family* is an excellent source on European (including Danish) Jewish history. It embraces Jewish families from many European countries encompassing several centuries and more than 5,000 people.

Because of the high incidence of Jewish assimilation and integration into Danish society, relevant information can be found in many bibliographies, reference books and directories. Among the most useful are the following:

Erichsen, B. and A. Krarup's *Dansk Historisk Bibliografi*. Vol. III: *Personalhistorie* (Danish Historical Bibliography. Vol. III: Personal History). Copenhagen, Gad, 1929.

Steen, Poul and Julin, A. *110 Års Indholdsfortegnelse—Personalhistorisk Tidsskrift 1880–1990*. (Index of Journal of Personal History 1880–1990) Copenhagen: Samfundet for dansk genealogi og Personalhistorie, 1992. Includes author and title indexes. Also available on disk, and online at WWW.GENEALOGI.DK/110.HTM

Steen, Poul and A. Julin. *Tusindvis af navne...Register til Personalhistorisk Tidsskrift 1966–1996*. (Thousands of names .... Index to Personalhistorisk Tidsskrift 1966–1996). Copenhagen, Samfundet for dansk genealogi og Personalhistorie, 1998. Also available on disk. The last two items may be ordered on Samfundet's website: WWW.GENEALOGI.DK—click on "Bogliste og bestilling af bøger".

Addresses

Rigsarkivet (National Archive), Rigsdagsgaarden 9, DK-1218 Copenhagen K Denmark; fax: 45 33 15 32 39; website: WWW.SA.DK/RA/

Landsarkivet for Sjælland m.m. (Provincial Archives for Zealand etc.) Jagtvej 10 DK-2200, Copenhagen N Denmark; fax: 45 35 39 05 35; website: WWW.SA.DK/LAK

Landsarkivet for Fyn (Provincial Archives for Funen), Jernbanegade 36, DK-5000 Odense C. Denmark; fax: 45 66 14 70 71; website: WWW.SA.DK/LAO/DEFAULT.HTM

Landsarkivet for Nørrejylland (Provincial Archives for North Jutland) Lille Sct. Hansgade 5, DK-8800 Viborg Denmark; fax: 45 86 60 10 06; website: WWW.SA.DK/LAV/DEFAULT.HTM

Landsarkivet for de Sønderjyske Landsdele (Provincial Archives for South Jutland), Haderslevvej 45, DK-6200 Aabenraa Denmark; fax: 45 74 62 32 88; website: WWW.SA.DK/LAA

Statens Arkivers Filmningscenter, Landsarkivet for Nørrejylland, Lille Sct. Hans Gade 5, DK-8800 Viborg Denmark; fax: 45 86 60 10 06; e-mail: SAF@SA.DK; website (in Danish only): WWW.SA.DK/SAF/DEFAULT.HTM

Dansk Data Arkiv (Danish Data Archive), Islandsgade 10, DK-5000 Odense C Denmark; fax: 45 66 11 30 60; website: WWW.DDA.DK

Det Danske Udvandrerarkiv (Danish Emigration Archives), Arkivstræde 1, Postbox 1731, DK-9100 Aalborg Denmark; fax: 45 98 10 22 48; website: WWW.EMIARCH.DK; online searchable database: DDD.SA.DK; e-mail address: EMIARCH@EMIARCH.DK

Immigrantmuseet (Immigrant Museum), Farums Arkiver og Museer, Paltholmcentret (E), 3520 Farum Denmark; fax: 45 42 95 28 33; website: WWW.IMMIGRANTMUSEET.DK; e-mail: INFO@IMMIGRANTMUSEET.DK

Erhvervsarkivet (National Business Archives), Vester Allé 12, DK-8000 Aarhus C. Denmark; fax: 45 86 12 85 60; website: WWW.SA.DK/EA/DEFAULT.HTM

Arbejderbevægelsens Bibliotek og Arkiv (Library and Archive for Laborers and the Labor Movement), Nørrebrogade 66 D, DK-2200 Copenhagen N Denmark; fax: 45 35 36 32 22; website: WWW.ABA.DK

Det Kongelige Bibliotek (Royal Library), Christians Brygge 8, DK-1219 Copenhagen K. Denmark; fax: 45 33 93 22 18; website: WWW.KB.DK

Statsbiblioteket (State Library), Universitetsparken, DK-8000 Aarhus C. Denmark; fax: 45 89 46 21 30; website: WWW.SB.AAU.DK/ENGELSK/WELCOME.HTM

Frederiksberg Kommunebiblioteker (Frederiksberg Municipal Libraries), Solbjergvej 21–25, DK-2000 Frederiksberg Denmark; fax: 45 38 33 36 77; website: WWW.FKB.DK

Samfundet for dansk genealogi og Personalhistorie (Society for Danish Genealogy and Biography), President Birgit Flemming Larsen, Klostermarken 13, DK-9000 Aalborg Denmark; e-mail: INFO@GENEALOGI.DK; website: WWW.GENEALOGI.DK/INDEX_US.HTM and a webpage with a thorough survey on "Facts about genealogical research in Denmark": WWW.GENEALOGI.DK—go to the English page and choose FACTS ABOUT GENEALOGY IN DENMARK:

Hvem Forsker Hvad (Danish Genealogical Research Journal), Editor Michael Bach, Rolfsvej 14, 3.tv., DK-2000 Frederiksberg Denmark; e-mail: INFO@HVEMFORSKERHVAD.DK; website: WWW.HVEMFORSKERHVAD.DK

Sammenslutningen af Lokalhistoriske Arkiver (Union of Local History Archives), Enghavevej 2, P.O. Box 235, DK-7100 Vejle, Denmark; fax: 45 75 83 18 01; e-mail: SLA@VEJLE.DK; website: WWW.LOKALARKIVER.DK

Mosaisk Troessamfund (Jewish Community in Denmark), Ny Kongensgade 6, second floor, Postboks 2015, DK-1012 Copenhagen K Denmark; fax: 45 33 12 33 57; website: WWW.MOSAISKE.DK

Selskabet for Dansk-Jødisk Historie (Society for Danish-Jewish History), Kaare Bing, Kulsvierparken 81, DK-2800 Lyngby Denmark; fax: 45 45 88 24 68; e-mail: INFO@RAMBAM.DK; website: WWW.RAMBAM.DK

Bibliography

Arnheim, Arthur: "Samuel Jachja/Albert Dionis liv og Chr. IVs privilegier til jøderne (Samuel Jachja/Albert Dionis's life and King Christian IV's privileges to the Jews)." [Danish] *Rambam* 7, (1998): 18–36.

Blum, Jacques: *Dansk og/eller jøde. en kultursociologisk undersøgelse af den jødiske minoritet i Danmark* (Danish and/or Jewish. A cultural-sociological study of the Jewish minority in Denmark). [Danish] (Chapter 2). Copenhagen: Gyldendal, 1972.

Blüdnikow, Bent. "Dansk/Jødisk historie. En forskningsoversigt." (Danish-Jewish history) *Politihistorisk Aarskrift* (Journal of police history). [Danish] Copenhagen: Politihistorisk Selskab, 1982.

Blüdnikow, Bent, ed. *Fremmede i Danmark—400 års fremmedpolitik* (Aliens in Denmark: 400 years of alien policy) [Danish] Odense, Denmark: Odense University Press, 1987.

Blüdnikow, Bent. *Immigranter. Østeuropæiske jøder i København 1904–1920* (Immigrants: Eastern European Jews in Copenhagen). [Danish] Copenhagen: Borgen, 1986.

Boolsen, Vibeke E.: "En, to mange ... Invandrerstatistik og dansk jødisk historieskrivning. Om Faaborgs Jøder" (One, two, many... immigration statistics and Danish Jewish history: on the Jews of Faaborg). [Danish] *Rambam* 2, (1993): 26–37.

Borchsenius, Poul. *Spredt blandt folkeslagene—Historien om de danske jøder* (Dispersed among the peoples). [Danish] Denmark: Fremad, 1969. (A special Danish volume; Vol. 4, printed as an epilogue to Keller, Werner. *Und würden zerstreut alle Völker.* (Vol. 1–3) München/Zürich: Droemersche Verlagsanstalt, 1966).

Engman, Max. *Norden och flyttningarna under nya tiden* (The Nordic countries and migration in recent times). [Swedish] Copenhagen: Foreningerne Nordens Forbund, Projekt Nordliv, 1997.

Felding, Steen. "De mange og de få. Folketællingerne 1787 og 1801 og det jødiske befolkningstal i Danmark," (The many and the few: the censuses of 1787 and 1801 and the Jewish population in Denmark). [Danish] *Rambam* 5, (1996): 6–37.

Frænkel, Louis. *Forgotten Fragments of the History of an Old Jewish Family* (2 vol. illustrated 1: Text and indexes 2: genealogical tables). Copenhagen, 1975. Newly revised and updated: *Genealogical Tables of Jewish Families 14th–20th Centuries*; *Forgotten fragments of the history of an old Jewish family.* München, Germany: K.G. Saur Verlag GmbH, 1999.

Gøbel, Erik. *A Guide to Sources for the History of the Jewish West Indies (U.S. Virgin Islands), 1671–1917.* University Press of Southern Denmark, 2002.

Hameln, Glückel von: *The Memoirs of Glückel of Hameln.* New York: Schocken, 1977.

Krag, Helen and Margit Warburg: *Der var engang—amol iz geven* (Once upon a time). [Danish]. Copenhagen: Gyldendal, 1986.

Larsen, Birgit Flemming, et al. "On Distant Shores." *Proceedings of the Marcus Lee Hansen Immigration Conference*, Aalborg, Denmark, June 29–July 1, 1992. Aalborg, Denmark: The Danish emigration Archives, 1993.

Levin, Elias. *Den gamle jødiske begravelsesplads i Møllegade 1694–1994* (Old Jewish Cemetery in Møllegade 1694–1994) [Danish] Copenhagen: self-published, 1994. (With photographs of existing tombstones)

Levin, Elias. *Jødiske gravstene...på Mosaisk Vestre begravelsesplads* (Jewish tombstones...in Mosaisk Western Cemetery, Copenhagen, Denmark). [Danish] Copenhagen: self-published, Vol. 1: 1885–1900. (1986); Vol. 2: 1901–1915 (1987); Vol. 3: 1991–1998. Text is in both Danish and English; includes photographs of all existing tombstones.

Margolinsky, Julius. *Jødiske dødsfald i Danmark 1693–1976* (Jewish deaths in Denmark 1693–1976). [Danish] Copenhagen: Dansk Historisk Håndbogsforlag, 1978.

Margolinsky, Julius. *299 Epitaphs on the Jewish cemetery in St. Thomas, W.I. 1837–1916.* Compiled from records in the archives of the Jewish Community in Copenhagen, indexed. Copenhagen, photostatic edition.

Metzon, Hans. *Jødiske begravelser i Danmark 1977–1983.* Copenhagen, 1984.

Metzon, Hans. *Jødiske begravelser i Danmark 1984–1990.* Copenhagen, 1991.

RAMBAM Tidsskrift for jødisk kultur og forskning (Journal for Jewish culture and research). [Danish]. Copenhagen: Society for Danish Jewish History, since 1990. From 1888–1990 published under the name *Tidsskrift for dansk jodisk historie* (Journal for Danish Jewish history).

Salomon, Karen Lisa Goldschmidt, ed. *A Guide to Jewish Denmark.* Copenhagen: C.A. Reitzels, 1994.

Svenstrup, Thyge and Vello Helk. *Det Mosaiske Troessamfund i København med nedlagte troessamfund i provinsen. En Registratur.* (The Jewish community in Copenhagen and previous Jewish communities in the provinces: an archives registry with an English survey). [Danish with a history in English). Copenhagen: Rigsarkivet, 1993.

Tidsskrift for jødisk Historie og Literatur (Journal for Jewish history and literature) 1917–1925.

Welner, Pinches. *Fra Polsk jøde til dansk* (From Polish Jew to Danish). [Danish]. Copenhagen: Steen Hasselbalchs, 1965.

Worsøe, Hans H. *Håndbog i Slægtshistorie* (Guide to genealogy). [Danish]. Copenhagen: Politiken, 1997.

Østergaard, Bent. *Indvandrernes danmarkshistorie* (The immigrants' history of Denmark). [Danish] Copenhagen: Gad, 1983.

Notes

Postal and web addresses may change. Periodically check the Scandinavian SIG website at www.JewishGen.org/scandinavia/denmark.htm for current updates. Also check the website for information about Danish privacy laws which were being revised at the same time this book was being revised.

1. See especially Blum, Blüdnikow, Borchsenius (listed in Bibliography section of this chapter) for more information on Danish and Danish-Jewish history.

2. Hameln, Glückel von, *Die Memoiren der Glückel von Hameln* (Memoirs of Glückel from Hameln). New York: Schocken, 1977, 21ff.

3. *Die Memoiren*, 25 (1996): 6–37.

4. *Rambam*, 5(1996): 6–37.

5. *Rambam* 5 (1996): 17; Parish Register for Vor Frue parish 1749–1813, folio 154a.

6. Poul Borchsenius, *Spredt blandt folkeslagene: Historien om de danske jcder.* Denmark: Fremad, 1969): 43.

7. *Rambam*, 7 (1998): 19.

8. Steen Felding, *Rambam*, 5 (1996), 26–37; Vibeke E. Boolsen, *Rambam*, 2 (1993): 26–37.

9. Levin, Elias. *Den gamle jødiske begravelsesplads i Mølle-gade 1694–1994* (Old Jewish Cemetery in Møllegade 1694–1994) [in Danish]. Copenhagen, 1994.; Levin, Elias. *Jødiske gravsten på Mosaisk Vestre begravelsesplads* (Jewish tombstones in Mosaisk Western Cemetery, Copenhagen, Denmark). [in Danish & English]. Copenhagen, 1994. Vol. 1: 1885–1900. (1986); Vol. 2: 1901–1915 (1987); Vol. 3: 1991–1998 . Text is in both Danish and English text; includes photographs of all existing tombstones.

10. Svenstrup, Thyge, and Vello Helk, eds. *Det Mosaiske Troessamfund i Kobenhavn med nedlagte troessamfund i provinsen—en arkivregistratur* (With a survey in English). Copenhagen: Rigsarkivet, 1993.

Egypt/Sudan

by Jeffrey S. Malka

Egypt

Home to such Jewish notables as Jacob and Joseph, Moses, Philo of Alexandria, Jeremiah the prophet, Moses ben Maimon (Maimonides), the gaon Saadia and others, boasting the oldest known synagogue (Ben Ezra) and the second oldest Jewish cemetery (Bassatine), the historical link between Jews and Egypt is ancient indeed. After the Exodus from Egypt, Jews are known to have returned in 586 BCE[1] and then maintained an uninterrupted presence ever since. Others say that there have been Jews in Egypt since the days of Joseph. Fargeon, editor of the *Annuaire des Juifs* (the yearbook of Jews in Egypt) writes in the 1942 yearbook that when Moses led the Israelites out of Egypt, some Jews remained and settled in Asyut where they formed a warrior tribe thereby maintaining a Jewish presence in Egypt since those early biblical days.[2]

In the early 20th century, the multilingual and cosmopolitan Jews of Egypt maintained 37 synagogues in Cairo alone, several all Jewish orchestras, 3 Jewish theaters (one in Yiddish), nearly a dozen Jewish newspapers in a variety of languages, as well as Jewish hospitals and old age homes while the Jewish aristocracy entertained and hobnobbed with Egyptian and European royalty. Largely European in outlook, the 20th-century Egyptian-Jewish population can be divided into four main groups.

In order of their numbers, these were the Sephardic Jews, the Ashkenazi Jews, the indigenous Egyptian Jews and the ancient Karaites. The first two groups were mainly francophone in language and culture while the latter two, who had inhabited Egypt for more than a millennium, were more likely to speak Egyptian Arabic and to wear Egyptian-style clothing. Even so, as Patai states, nearly all the Jews felt themselves entirely separate and distinct from the surrounding Egyptian Arab culture.[3] As a result of the Israeli-Arab wars and the deteriorating economic and political situation under Nasser, most of the Jews of Egypt either left or were expelled so that the present population is down to about 20–50 elderly Jews in Cairo with an average age greater than 70–80 and an even smaller number of holdouts in Alexandria.

In 1948, 70–80,000 Jews lived in Egypt; about 55,000 in Cairo and most of the rest in Alexandria, with smaller communities in Port Said and smaller towns.[4] Of relevance to genealogists searching for documents, 5,000 to 10,000 held Egyptian citizenship, 40,000 were stateless and 30,000 were foreign nationals (Italian, French, British, etc)—even though most of the latter had also been born in Egypt.[5]

The Sephardim were by far the most numerous group. Arriving in the 12th century (Maimonides came to Egypt in 1165), their numbers were augmented by a large influx of exiles from Iberia in 1492 and the ensuing years.[6] Their ranks were further swelled in the 19th century by Sephardim from other areas of the Ottoman Empire, mainly Aleppo, Baghdad, Izmir, Livornia, Salonika and Tunis.[7]

The next group are the indigenous Jews, possibly 20,000 in number, who were Egyptian in both language and culture. They were mostly goldsmiths and merchants and often lived in Cairo's *harat al Yahud* (Jewish lane or quarter) and Alexandria's port district.

Next in size were the Ashkenazim, almost all of whom came to Egypt in the late nineteenth century fleeing the pogroms and anti-Semitism in Russia, Romania and the like. These were often economically poorer than the local Sephardim, and many lived in the *hart-al-barabra* (quarter of the foreigners). They spoke Yiddish and maintained their own separate synagogues, a Yiddish theater and a Yiddish radio station that existed until 1950.

Relatively less known are the Karaite Jews, who numbered about 5,000 in Egypt in 1947. The Karaites are a Jewish sect that broke away from rabbinic Judaism in the first millennium C.E. Rejecting rabbinic teachings (Talmud, etc.), Karaites base their religion and practices on the written texts of the five books of Moses (*Kara'a* means to read) and they maintain their own separate synagogues.[8] In the twentieth century, the largest remnants of Karaites lived in Egypt (5,000) and Russia (10,000), but unlike the Karaites of Lithuania, Poland and Crimea, who did not consider themselves Jews —a designation with which both the Nazis and fellow rabbinic Jews agreed[9]— in Egypt, both Karaites and the rabbinic Jews considered Karaites a Jewish sect, although both groups banned marriage with each other's members. While many lived elsewhere, the traditional home of the Karaites was in Cairo's *harat al Yahud al Kar'in* (Karaite Jewish lane or quarter), which adjoins the other *harat al yahud*. The Karaites buried their dead in their half of the Jewish Bassatine cemetery of Cairo, separated by a wall from the half used by the rabbinic Jews. Arabic speakers, this community of numerous goldsmiths and jewelers produced several notable poets and playwrights. Their last chief rabbi in Egypt, Tuvia Bakovitch, served from 1934 to 1956. Like the rest of Egyptian Jewry, they too have left and can now be found in the United States, mostly in the San Francisco area.

Jewish Records

Cairo

The Jewish archives are held at the Jewish Community Center (JCC) of Cairo.[9*] Unfortunately, the holdings of the archives are disorganized and they are difficult to read because many are written in either Hebrew or Arabic script. At present, the only way to get information from these voluminous archives is to request it from the Jewish Community Center of Cairo.

Sketch of synagogue in Cairo, Egypt

Even academics have been denied permission, however, to search the archives themselves.[11] Written requests must be accompanied by a donation of $100–150 to the JCC at the time of the request, with a similar amount sent when notified that the information is ready. Because of the records' disarray, information may take years to obtain—if at all. The elderly members of the JCC are interested in hosting volunteers from abroad, who are knowledgeable in Hebrew, to spend time in Cairo helping to organize the records.[12]

The Jamie Lehman Collection at New York's Yeshiva University is a small subset of the Cairo archives that were secreted out of Egypt and housed in the university archives.[13] Catalogued but not indexed, it consists of a mix of rabbinic records and letters, Cairo B'nai B'rith records and accounts of the charity activities of the community. The collection is part of the Yeshiva University Archives, and advance permission is needed to use it.

Alexandria

Requests for record searches should be addressed to the Jewish Community Center of Alexandria[14*] accompanied by a donation. Responses are slow to come. Records are similar in type to those in Cairo, but limited to Alexandria, whereas Cairo holds records from outlying Jewish communities such as Ismailia, Port Said, Tanta and others.

Montefiore Censuses

These censuses conducted at the behest of Sir Moses Montefiore in 1839, 1849, 1855, 1866 and 1875 were taken of the Jewish population of Palestine, but they also include (on reel 3) a census of the Sephardim of Alexandria, Egypt, taken in 1840. The originals are in London; microfilm copies are in Jerusalem (see ISRAEL).[15]

Synagogues

Because of the dwindling Jewish population and lack of funds, only three synagogues remain functioning in Cairo: Shaar Hashamayim, Meir Enaim and Ben Ezra. The Cairo Jewish community struggles to maintain and restore the others with the sporadic assistance of badly needed donations from its diaspora.

Ben Ezra Synagogue* in old Cairo (Fostat-Goshen) is the world's oldest known synagogue.[15] Believed to have been founded by Ezra the Scribe half a millennium before the Common Era, it stands at the site, according to both Jewish and Coptic tradition, where Moses was retrieved from the Nile by Pharaoh's daughter. The waters of the Nile still flood its basement today. The medieval Jewish chronicler Benjamin of Tudela visited the synagogue in his travels in 1169.[16] It was in the forgotten *geniza* (storehouse of discarded holy documents) of the Ben Ezra Synagogue that the treasure trove of ancient documents that have yielded so much information about medieval Jewish history, especially from around the tenth century, were found. Shaar Hashamayim* is the main Cairo synagogue and well worth a visit now that it has been restored. Meir Enaim Synagogue* is under the supervision of the Jewish Community of Cairo* and may be visited upon request.

Cemeteries

The main Jewish cemetery of Cairo is the Bassatine. It is the second oldest Jewish cemetery in the world, second only to the cemetery on the Mount of Olives in Jerusalem. Originally 120 *feddans* in size (a *feddan* is approximately 4,200 square meters), it was divided by a wall into two halves of 60 *feddans* each for the Karaite and the rabbinic Jewish burials. The Karaite half has been sold; only the rabbinic half remains. In the 1960s, marble stones were ransacked from the Bassatine by vandals to be used in the building boom in Cairo, and hoodlums set up homes and even businesses in the deserted mausoleums. To visit the Bassatine, it is necessary to contact the JCC for permission. A substantial donation towards cemetery upkeep is solicited at the time of a request.

Cairo also has a number of smaller private cemeteries belonging to some of its prominent Jewish families such as the Ades, Cattaui, Levy, Mosseri and Sapriel families. Walled and with private watchmen, these cemeteries are better preserved and can be visited again through the JCC of Cairo.

Alexandria has three Jewish cemeteries. Two located in Chatby and one in Mazarita (sometimes called Chatby 1 cemetery). All three Alexandria cemeteries are walled and have largely escaped vandalism. They are overgrown with vegetation at most times of the year, but the gravestones show only the ravages of time and weather. The Alexandria Jewish community has a listing of burials in its archives, although obtaining information or a response is difficult, as noted previously.

According to Morris Bierbrier, an Egpytologist at the British Museum in London, the Alexandria synagogue has death records from 1860 (although not all burials were registered there), marriage records from about 1907 and birth records (not in consecutive order because families often delayed the registration of births).

Libraries

The Library of the Jewish Heritage in Egypt* at the century-old Shaar Hashamayim Synagogue is the largest Jewish studies library in Cairo. The library of Jewish history in the historic Ben Ezra synagogue is smaller but holds some useful material.

Egyptian Diaspora

With the dispersal of Egyptian Jewry, groups of Egyptian Jews have formed around the world, especially in Adelaide and Sydney, Australia; London; Brooklyn, New York; and Geneva, Switzerland. Although members may not be especially interested in genealogy, they can be useful sources of information. Among the associations are:

- Association of Jews From Egypt in Israel, 56 Pinsker Street, Tel Aviv; telephone: 03-528-5534
- International Association of Jews from Egypt, a group headed by Victor Sanua, Ph.D., St. John's University, 2416 Quentin Road, Brooklyn, New York 11229; telephone: (718) 339-0337. Their purpose is to preserve the memories and culture of the expatriates before they are lost. Lectures are given and articles published in *Image Magazine*.*
- Historical Society of Jews from Egypt, P.O. Box 230445, Brooklyn, NY 11223; e-mail: DSAKKAL@HSJE.ORG. According to the group's literature, "the aims of this society are to preserve, maintain and coordinate the implementation, and to convey our rich heritage to our children and grandchildren, using all educational means at our disposal to bring into being the necessary foundations." The society wants to create a museum of Egyptian Jewry in New York with *sepharim* (Torah scrolls) and other objects that illustrate the life of Jewry in Egypt.

Non-Egyptian Sources

Morris Bierbrier reports finding birth, marriage and death records from 1866 onward for Egyptian Jews who held foreign nationalities at the Dutch, French and Italian consulates in Alexandria and Cairo, as well as British consular records in the Public Records Office, Kew, London.*

Civil Records

To request certificates from Egyptian civil authorities, one must know the exact date and the specific district in Cairo or Alexandria that the event occurred. Mail requests are not known ever to get replies, and even onsite requests are not likely to succeed unless one goes in person to the proper place and persuades (monetarily) the official in charge to look. Even then, you will usually be told that nothing can be found. Unfortunately, one must know from family sources where an event occurred; no other means exists to obtain this information.

Internet Resources

Bassatine News at WWW.GEOCITIES.COM/RAINFOREST/VINES/5855 is the website of the Jewish Community Center (JCC) of Cairo. Under the leadership of Carmen Weinstein with the help of Samir Raafat, the JCC of Cairo provides updates of their efforts to restore and preserve Jewish cemeteries and landmarks, as well as news of the community. Requests for information can be made through this website, but responses will take some time and often remain unanswered.

Samir Raafat is an Egyptian writer of books and articles in Egyptian newspapers about Cairo and its history in the 19th and 20th centuries. An alumnus of Cairo's prestigious Victoria College, a boy's school where Egyptian society's upper classes sent their sons, Raafat uses his considerable writing skills and knowledge to write about events and families that were part of life in Cairo. Although not Jewish, Raafat has written excellent histories of some of the notable Egyptian-Jewish families and events. His website at WWW.EGY.COM/JUDAICA/ contains many of his articles, including those dealing with Jewish topics, and is of considerable interest and value in providing a true flavor of Jewish life in Cairo during the 19th and 20th centuries.

Egyptian-Jewish Identities at SHR.STANFORD.EDU/SHREVIEW/5-1/TEST/BEININ.HTML presents an interesting perspective on Egyptian Jewry and their identity conflicts in the 19th and 20th centuries.

Cattaui Family Tree at WWW.GEOCITIES.COM/RAINFOREST/VINES/5855/CATTAUI.HTM.

Jabes Family Tree at WWW.GEOCITIES.COM/RAINFOREST/VINES/5855/JABES1.HTM.

Sephardic Genealogy Sources at WWW.ORTHOHELP/GENEAL/SEFARDIM.HTM is the most comprehensive Internet site for Sephardic genealogy sources. It includes history, maps, internet links, archives and book lists.

Addresses

Ben Ezra Synagogue, 6 Harett il-Sitt Barbara, Mari Girges, Old Cairo; telephone: 2-847-695

Eliahu Hanavi Synagogue, 69 Nebi Daniel Street, Ramla Station, Alexandria; telephone: 3-492-3974; 597-4438

IMAGE Publications, P.O. Box 290642, Brooklyn, New York; telephone: (718) 627-4624; fax: (718) 627-4284; e-mail: IMAGE@IMAGEUSA.COM; website: WWW.IMAGEUSA.COM

Jewish Community Center (JCC) of Alexandria, 69 Rue Nebi Daniel, Ramla Station, Alexandria.

Jewish Community Center (JCC) of Cairo, #13 Sabil El Khazinder Street, Abbassia, Cairo, Egypt; telephone: 20 2 482-4613; fax: 20 2 482 4885

Library of the Jewish Heritage in Egypt, Adli Pasha Street, downtown Cairo. Across the street from Shaar Hashamayim. Ask synagogue guards for key.

Meir Enaim Synagogue, 55 No. 13 Street, Maadi, Cairo. Permission to visit must be obtained from Jewish community.

Public Records Office, Kew, Ruskin Avenue, Richmond Surrey, TW9 4DU, England.

Shaar Hashamayim, 17 Adli Pasha Street, downtown Cairo; telephone: 2-749-025.

Bibliography

History

Adler, Elkan Nathan. *Jewish Travellers in the Middle Ages*. New York: Dover, 1987.

Beinin, Joel. *The Dispersion of Egyptian Jewry: Culture, politics and the formation of a modern diaspora*. Los Angeles: Univ of California Press, 1998. Follows up where Kramer stops.

Bennett, Ralph. "History of the Jews of Egypt" in *AVOTAYNU* 10, no. 1 (Spring 1994).

Fargeon, Maurice ed. *Annuaire des Juifs d'Egypte et du proche orient*. [French] 1942, 1943. Cairo: La Societe des Editions Historiques Juives d'Egypte. Similar to U.S. city directories.

Fargeon, Maurice ed. *Annuaire des Juifs d'Egypte et du proches orient, 5706/1945–6*. [French] Cairo: La Societe des Editions Historiques Juives d'Egypte.

Juifs d'Egypte, Images et Textes. 2nd Ed. [French] Paris: Les Editions du Scribe, 1984. Compendium of photographs and images compiled by Jews from Egypt.

Kramer, Gudrun. *The Jews in Modern Egypt, 1914–1952*. Seattle: Univ of Washington Press, 1989. The most comprehensive study of that period.

Laskier, Michael. *The Jews of Egypt, 1920–1970*. New York: New York University Press, 1992. Excellent review.

Malka, Eli. *Jacob's Children in the Land of the Mahdi. The Jews of the Sudan*. Syracuse, NY: Syracuse University Press, 1998. History of the Jews of the Sudan and the Malka rabbinic family. The appendix includes a listing of all Jewish marriages in the Sudan. Since these Jews were, with rare exceptions, from Egypt, the missing link to many family histories can be found here.

Malka, Jeffrey S. *Sephardic Genealogy: Discovering Your Sephardic Ancestors and Their World*. Bergenfield, NJ: Avotaynu, 2002.

Nemoy, Leon. *Karaite Anthology*. New Haven: Yale Univ. Press, 1952, 1980.

Patai, Raphael. *The Vanished Worlds of Jewry*. New York: Macmillan, 1981.

Rosanes, Salomon A. *Korot Hayehudim Beturkia Vebeartzot Hakedem: Devrei Yemai Yisrael Betogarma Al-Pi Mekorot Rishonomim* (History of the Jews of Turkey and of the Middle East). [Hebrew] 6 vols. vol.1 Tel Aviv, 1930; vols. 2–5 Sofia, Bulgaria: 1934–8; vol. 6 Jerusalem: 1948. Covers the period from 1300 onwards.

Rosenstein, Neil. "The 19th-Century Montefiore Census." *AVOTAYNU* 8, no. 2 (Summer 1992).

Shamir, Shimon. *The Jews of Egypt; A Mediterranean Society in Modern Times*. Boulder, CO: Westview, 1987.

Taragan, B. *Les Comunautes israelites d'Alexandrie; apercu historique depuis les temps des Ptolémées jusqu'a nos jours*. Alexandia, Egypt: Editions juives d''Egypte, 1932.

Family Trees and Research

Aciman, Andre. *Out of Egypt*. New York: Farrar Straus Giroux, 1994, 1995. An Alexandrian Jewish family.

Alhadeff, Gini. *The Sun at Midday*. Tales of a Mediterranean Family. New York: Pantheon, 1997. Family stories of the Alhadeff-Pinto families in Turkey, Rhodes, Egypt, South America and elsewhere.

Alhadeff, Victtorio. *La cita en Buenos Aires. Saga de una gran familia Sefaradi*. Family story of the Alhadeff family of Rhodes.

Malka, Eli. *Jacob's Children in the land of the Mahdi. The Jews of the Sudan*. Marriage lists (see above).

Perera, Victor. *The Cross and the Pear Tree*. New York: Knopf, 1995. The author relates his search for his ancestors, some of whom lived in Alexandria, Egypt.

Sudan

Sudan, the largest country in Africa, lies just south of Egypt and has a long shared history with Egypt. Jewish history starts in the Sudan in the late 19th century when a half dozen Jews from Egypt came to start businesses in what was then the wild and not-fully-charted African interior. These early settlers went through a turbulent time as prisoners of a fundamentalist Muslim leader known as the Mahdi. The Mahdi routed both British and Egyptian armies and ruled the Sudan for 13 years until he was defeated by the British.

Building on these adventuresome beginnings, a flourishing Jewish community developed under the security blanket of British rule and the leadership of Shlomo Malka, a young rabbi recruited from Tiberias, Israel, in 1906. An elaborate synagogue was built and served a united congregation of Sephardim and Ashkenazim in Khartoum. A number of Jewish institutions evolved such as a large Jewish recreation club and the only B'nai B'rith lodge in the African interior. Jewish businesses flourished and many of the largest British and foreign trading companies had Jews in leadership positions.

Similar to Egypt, the Arab-Israeli conflict spelled doom for this small but vigorous Jewish community resulting in a mass exodus to England, Israel, Switzerland and the U.S. No Jews live in the Sudan today. Members of the exiled Sudan community prospered greatly abroad. They donated millions of dollars to Jewish and Israeli causes, revived the World Sephardic Federation, provided huge subsidies and scholarships to universities in Israel, owned and ran deluxe hotel chains and international firms in Israel and throughout the world, and became major contributors to Jewish and Sephardic causes wherever the need arose. The ancient Adli synagogue in Cairo was refurbished with a $700,000 grant from Nessim Gaon, the most prosperous exile of the Sudan community. Funds from other Sudan Jews helped preserve the historic Bassatine cemetery in Cairo (see Egypt).

Archives

The only archival material concerning the Jewish community in the Sudan are the rabbinic records maintained by Rabbi Shlomo Malka. Microfilmed copies of the records can be found at the Jewish National and University Library* in Jerusalem (call number 4 7306/1-2), but are difficult to use because they are written in Sephardic cursive script unfamiliar to those just familiar with Hebrew block lettering or the Ashkenazi cursive used in Israel.[17]

Interior of synagogue in Khartoum, Sudan. When the last Jews left the Sudan, the Khartoum synagogue was torn down 20 years ago by the Sudan government, ostensibly to build another structure. The site has remained empty since.

Several hundred articles written over a period of years by Rabbi Malka in the Cairo Jewish periodical *Shams* (the Sun) cover a large range of religious, political and social topics and give a good picture of the thinking of the time. They do not, however, supply directly genealogical information as do the rabbinical records. Copies of the articles may be found at the Ben Zvi Institute* in Jerusalem.

Cemetery

The Jewish cemetery in Khartoum was vandalized and desecrated after the Jews left in the late 1950s. Many of the gravestones have been overturned or broken. As a result many relatives arranged to transfer the remains of their rabbi and families for reburial in Israel in the Sudan section of Jerusalem's Givat Shaul cemetery. The only listings of burials is in Eli Malka's book.

Addresses

Ben Zvi Institute, P.O. Box 7600/7504, Rehavia Jerusalem 91076, Israel

Jewish National and University Library, P.O. Box 503, Jerusalem 91004, Israel; telephone: +++ 972- 2-660-0351

Bibliography

Malka, Eli. *Jacob's Children in the Land of the Mahdi. The Jews of the Sudan*. Syracuse Univ Press, 1998. The only book in print on the history of the Jews of the Sudan and the Malka rabbinic family. The appendix includes a listing of all Jewish marriages in the Sudan.

Malka, Jeffrey. *Sephardic Genealogy: Discovering Your Sephardic Ancestors and Their World*. Bergenfield, NJ: Avotaynu, 2002.

Notes

1. Bennett, 1994.
2. Fargeon, 1942.
3. Patai, 1981.
4. Beinin, 1998.
5. Patai
6. Patai
7. Patai
8. Nemoy, 1952, 1980.
9. Beinin, 1998
10. Bassatine News at WWW.GEOCITIES.COM/RAINFOREST/VINES/5855
11. Beinin
12. Write to JCC in Cairo: Jewish Community Center of Cairo, Address: #13 Sabil El Khazinder Street, Abbassia, Cairo, Egypt.
13. Jamie Lehman collection. Yeshiva University Archives, 500 West 185th Street, New York, NY 10033.
14. Jewish Community Center of Alexandria, 69 Rue Nebi Daniel, Alexandria, Egypt.
15. The Montefiore censuses are kept at Jews College, Albert Road, London NW$ 2SJ England. A microfilm copy is at the Jewish National and University Library in Jerusalem from whom copies may be purchased for $120.
16. Adler 1987.
17. See Malka, Jeffrey S.. *Sephardic Genealogy* which discusses this script in detail.

England and Wales

by Anthony Joseph

The Anglo-Jewish community has made a significant contribution to the story of the Jewish people worldwide. An important community in its own right, Anglo-Jewry also was one of the most pivotal staging posts for hundreds of thousands of migrant Jews who left Eastern Europe for the United States and elsewhere. With the development of steam-powered ships and the consequent ability to move large numbers of people across the oceans cheaply and relatively comfortably, mass migration of many European folk on an enormous scale became commonplace throughout the 19th and early 20th centuries. An estimated sixty million individuals left Europe for the United States between 1830 and 1914. Probably five million of this total were Jews. Not all passed through the United Kingdom[1] and of those who did, not all left their trace within the English recording system. Nevertheless, significant numbers of the transmigratory population left some record of their temporary presence in England and Wales, enough to make English records among the most valuable in following the genealogical threads of a family dispersion.

History

Before considering details of genealogical research in English, Welsh and Anglo-Jewish sources, it is useful to understand the growth and development of the Jewish community as a whole. We do not know the precise date that Jews first settled in the British Isles. Some speculate that Jews set foot in Britain in Roman times, or even earlier, but 1066, the time that William I of Normandy conquered Britain, is the first documented date of any Jewish presence. Prior to this, the Normandy French-Jewish community was thriving and well established, primarily as bankers and financiers to the Court and the population at large.

This group established a medieval Anglo-Jewish community that flourished for more than two centuries, despite occasional tensions and unspeakable massacres, such as occurred at York in 1189. From time to time, deaths in suspicious circumstances occurred in the English countryside and activated, especially if a child perished, the grotesque ritual murder charge to scapegoat the Jews. It was not until well into the 13th century, however, that increasing hostility to the perceived power of the Jewish financiers led to the Edict of Expulsion by Edward I, implemented on August 1, 1290. At that time, the entire Jewish population was ordered either to leave the realm, be forcibly baptized or be put to death. With this edict, the medieval Anglo-Jewish community came to an abrupt and effective end.

After 1290, for more than three and a half centuries, scarcely any Jews resided in England. Although we have evidence of the occasional Jewish adventurer, such as Sir Edward Brampton (in reality, a Portuguese Jew called Edvardo Brandao), who plays some part in the fabric of English history, no recognizable Anglo-Jewish community existed as such. During the reign of Elizabeth I (1558–1603), small numbers of mostly Portuguese Jews, known as *marranos*, established themselves in London as a fledgling clandestine community. Overtly, they were as Christian as their neighbors, but in secret they maintained their Jewishness. Expansion of this group continued slowly but steadily throughout the first half of the 17th century. Although of Portuguese background, many had lived in Amsterdam and come to Britain as part of the increasing Anglo-Dutch trading development.

In 1656, the Lord Protector, Oliver Cromwell, granted the petition of the Portuguese-Dutch Jew Menassah ben Israel, who pleaded that the Edict of 1290 should be lifted and Jews be allowed to live freely in England. Although there was no formal act of readmission, Cromwell and his advisors had contact with covert Jews who lived in England and found them politically useful. Menassah ben Israel's subsequent report in Amsterdam resulted in significant immigration from the Dutch capital to London over the next few years. At this time, the migration was almost exclusively Sephardic; they established the first Resettlement Anglo-Jewish Congregation, that of Bevis Marks. This is the most senior Anglo-Jewish congregation, and some of its records date back to the late 17th century.

The Edict of 1290 was never formally repealed, either during Cromwell's time or subsequently. That Cromwell indicated it would no longer be used as an instrument of oppression against the Jews did not prevent occasional episodes over the next three centuries during which anti-Semitic agitators attempted to harass Anglo-Jewish citizens in an effort to force Jewish people to leave England. For numerous technical legal reasons, these attempts have never had any chance of success, nor any adverse effect on the modern Anglo-Jewish community.

After the path breaking by the Portuguese-Dutch Sephardic settlers in London, Jews from other, more widespread, European communities began to settle in England. Many more were Ashkenazim, and by about 1680, they established their first congregation, the Great Synagogue in Dukes Place, the second oldest congregation in Britain.

Some studying Anglo-Jewish history have speculated about a possible relationship between the medieval Anglo-Jewish settlements ended in 1290 and the latter day one that began in 1656. It should be noted categorically that there are no connections whatever between these two entirely separate Jewish presences; no one has ever been able to trace any modern living descendants of the medieval community, although it certainly is possible to trace modern-day Jewish families in England back to the mid-17th century.

A Historic Wedding Anniversary

August 5th, 1810, at Godmanchester, Huntingdonshire, at two o'clock p.m., by the Reverend Simon Lepseker, Mr. Jonas Lazarus, Silversmith and Jeweller of Lincoln, to the beautiful and accomplished Miss Rosceia Nathan, daughter of Mr. M.I. Nathan, Silversmith and Jeweller of the former place. The marriage ceremony was performed in Mr. Nathan's garden, in the presence of a numerous company of Jews and Christians (at least two hundred persons) under an elevated canopy supported by four youths. A band of music playing a grand martial air, preceded the bridegroom who was attended by the bride's father and grandfather; some minutes later they were followed by the bride (veiled) attended by her mother and grandmother. Four green wax tapers were burned during the ceremony; the bride was led several times around the bridegroom and the ring was put on the forefinger of her left hand, where it remained until the next day, and was then placed on the usual finger appropriated for that purpose. At the conclusion a glass was handed round to the happy couple and their relations, out of which they all drank; it was then laid under the bridegroom's feet and by him stamped to pieces. After the ceremony a large part of their friends sat down to a handsome dinner provided for the occasion. *The Gentleman's Magazine* (August, 1810).

The biggest of the six precursors of the United Synagogue was the 18th-century Great Synagogue, the one with which the "Chief Rabbi of the German and Polish Jews" became associated. The membership list of this congregation through to 1790 been published in the Miscellanies of the Jewish Historical Society of England, with annotations, comments and details of family interrelationships. Other important sources that have appeared in the *Miscellanies* include the Plymouth Aliens' Register (with many Jewish names) and lists of Jewish stockholders recorded with the Bank of England.

(Jonas and Rosceia Lazarus were Anthony Joseph's great-great-great-grandparents.)

An estimated 3,000 Jews lived in Britain, almost exclusively in London, by the end of the 17th century. The numbers multiplied tenfold during the next century, in part through natural increase but also by ever-expanding immigration from other, less tolerant, European countries. Although the modern Anglo-Jewish community has lived primarily in London, it established several other smaller provincial communities early in the 18th century, in part because of employment difficulties in the capital. The guild system, which controlled many jobs in London, insisted on Saturday work, an impossibility for the Orthodox Jew, who insisted on observing the Sabbath. The guild had less of a strangle hold outside of London, so an exodus from the capital resolved the difficulty for the observant Jews who found it so difficult to earn a living in London. These people became peddlers who worked largely along a swathe of the English southern coast from Ipswich in the east to Penzance in the west. The pattern of these communities was virtually identical. A base was established in one of the port towns, and the community gathered each week at the commencement of the Sabbath to maintain their observances. When the Sabbath concluded on Saturday evening, the hawkers and peddlers would recommence their rounds and roam the countryside. One or another of the community would be released from secular business activities to return to base early enough on Friday to prepare the Sabbath meal and other necessities for the rest of the community. In addition to the exodus from London, some direct migration occurred to the port towns from continental Europe, as a result of the trading activities of the various ports and continental counterparts.

By the early 19th century, with the change of economic habits following the Industrial Revolution, the hawking and peddling communities declined rapidly. In many cases, Jewish contribution to local life disappeared, leaving only a few traces. Today, the occasional building, defunct Jewish cemetery or memorial is the only trace of these vanished communities. In a few other towns, more modern Jewish communities developed independently of the hawking and peddling families, but building on institutions established by their pioneering predecessors. Numerous records of these smaller and earlier communities have survived and are available for use as genealogical sources. All histories and details of articles containing published vital records are listed in the four Anglo-Jewish bibliographies issued since 1937. They are included in the Mordy guide listed in the bibliography.

During the Industrial Revolution, modern-day, larger Jewish communities established themselves in such provincial English cities as Birmingham, Bristol, Leeds, Liverpool and Manchester. All of these towns existed before the Industrial Revolution, but only in the 19th century did their growth and rapid expansion give them the importance they have now in Anglo-Jewish life.

Massive migration from Eastern Europe to the United States and elsewhere was particularly intense between 1881 and 1914; during that period, 250,000 Jews settled permanently in Britain. The arrival of this vast tide of Jewish humanity to the British shores provoked a political backlash that resulted in the Aliens Act of 1905, legislation that considerably restricted, but did not altogether terminate, Jewish migration into England.

The interwar period, 1919–39, saw the rise of the Nazi party and its subsequent domination of Europe, with it the frequent, desperate attempts of Jews to flee the terrors of their native lands. A large number of those who successfully fled Germany and German-controlled territories, came to Britain, although as with previous migrations from the European mainland, many simply passed through the United

Kingdom on their way to the United States, South America or elsewhere.

Since World War II, the Anglo-Jewish community has declined considerably from approximately 450,000 at its height to approximately 300,000 individuals today. Even in its heyday, Jews have never been more than one percent of the British population, but the community has had a marked impact on British society generally.

Vital Records

For genealogical research, it is convenient to divide English and Welsh records into those applicable to all citizens and those that are more specifically Jewish. In 1836, two acts of Parliament established primary vital registration applicable to all to take effect July 1, 1837. For various reasons, in the early years, a significant proportion were never registered—births especially. The Registration of Births and Deaths Act of 1874 considerably tightened registration procedures, initiated penalties for non-compliance and greatly reduced the incidence of evasion although some instances of failure to register persisted throughout the 19th century.

For the purpose of administering the registration acts, England and Wales were divided into local registration districts and sub-districts. All recorded events were combined quarterly and a copy submitted to the Registrar General. Another copy was kept by the superintendent registrar of each local district. At the Office for National Statistics (ONS),* the ONS processes the material sent them from the local Superintendent Registrars. Indexes dating back to the inception of the system in 1837 are available at the Family Records Centre.* There are no restrictions on consulting the indexes, but for births registered since 1951 and the deaths of children under the age of 16 occurring since that year, researchers must satisfy the authorities that their need for a certificate is not for misuse. The indexes of birth, marriage and death are quarterly and in separate volumes up to 1983 and annual thereafter. The latest processed year is 2000.

Access to the centralized national indexes is available at the Family Records Centre, but the volume of certificates themselves are not open to the public. These records also have been copied in numerous forms, most notably by the LDS (Mormon) Family History Library who have made microfiche or microfilms. The quality of many copies is poor; many early indexes were handwritten and may not be clearly readable on microfilm. In addition, the process of integrating the various district returns and then making copies has created considerable scope for errors of transcription. Alphabetization of the information is another source of error. It is important to recognize as well that the references to volume and page number given in these indexes are not the same as those in the finding aids of the local superintendent registrar's offices. A joint reference system has only been introduced within the past decade. Since the spelling of names frequently is fluid and inconsistent, failure to locate an entry may simply result from lack of knowledge of how a particular entry was spelled. For example, a name like Weinstein may be recorded as Winestein or Wienstein, or even Veinstein/Vinestein. One unexpected

variation of this name that caused considerable difficulty researching one family was the spelling Wainstain.

As a result of transcription errors that may occur in the indexes, sometimes a reference found in the "master copy" may not lead to the issuing of a particular certified event. Usually, however, if the reference to an indexed entry is identified, it is possible to obtain a copy of the actual certificate. A fee for such copies is set by the ONS and is subject to periodic increases. It usually is possible to view local registrar indexes for a particular geographical district; simply consult the telephone directory for the address of registration of births, deaths and marriages. Note that these indexes only include events registered within their area of jurisdiction. Only the integrated central indexes provide national coverage, but it can be useful to consult local indexes if the central one appears deficient. Boundaries of specific registration districts have altered periodically in response to population shifts and administrative changes. For example, a birth known to have occurred in or near Birmingham in 1850 may have been registered in the then subdistrict of Aston. To be thorough, researchers must learn the names of all the districts and subdistricts and how they have varied over time. The ONS has produced numerous booklets listing all the changes since 1837; they are available from Her Majesty's Stationery Office. These offices exist in many towns and are listed in local telephone directories.

Contents of Vital Records

The details supplied on English and Welsh vital records often is less informative than that obtained from other countries, even such a closely allied one as Scotland. Over time, however, the ONS has increased the amount of information required. Birth certificates supply the name of the child, place and date of birth, name of father, name and maiden name of mother, occupation of father and of the informant and the signature of the registrar. Sometimes, the mother's occupation is included. Up to 1911, the mother of an illegitimate child could name the father of her child verbally, if the father was agreeable. This led to abuses, so from that time both parties have to sign in the "informant" column.

Marriage certificates give the date and place of the event, names of the bride and groom, their marital status at the time (bachelor/spinster/divorcee/widower, etc.), their addresses at the time of marriage, occupations and the names of the fathers of the bride and the groom, names and signatures of witnesses and of the officiant who performed the marriage. Names of the mothers of the couple usually are not given, but whether or not the fathers are alive at the time is included. The latter information, however, frequently is unreliable. Instances have been found within a single family grouping where the father of one sibling is described as deceased, but apparently is alive a few years later at the marriage of another sibling. Since 1911, marriage indexes cross reference the bride's name to the groom's surname and vice versa.

Death certificates give the name of the deceased; the date and place of death; occupation; usual place of residence; name of the informant and frequently, relationship of infor-

A page from the 1891 census of England and Wales shows a Jewish section of London.

mant to the deceased; and signature of the registrar. Usually the parentage of the deceased is not listed, but it may be recorded when a child has died and a parent is the informant. The end of each quarterly volume of death registrations almost always has a section of unknown persons. These are murder victims, inmates of institutions whose background is totally unknown or someone whose body has been discovered only a considerable time after death making identification impossible. In the latter case, nicknames such as "Old Moses" are used instead. On more than one occasion, this practice has given rise to the unreliable speculation that the deceased may have been Jewish. Since 1969, death registration indexes should list both the date and place of birth of the deceased. For foreign nationals, only the country is given in many instances—usually the name of the current state controlled the place of birth.

Unrecorded Marriages

Numerous problems confront the genealogist using vital statistics records. When a name is so common that it is virtually impossible to identify the correct person from the index alone, the only solution may be to purchase the full certificate to establish if it is, indeed, the individual being sought. No phonetic (soundex) listings exist. Another problem, known as *stille chuppah* (silent canopy) is specific to Jewish family research. The requirement to record in civil fashion all marriages occurring in England and Wales since July 1, 1837, also involved certain expenses associated with giving statutory notice of intention to marry. Under Jewish law, two Jewish people of the opposite sex may stand under any symbolic canopy, and if the man pronounces the appropriate words in the presence of two religiously-fit witnesses, a legal marriage has been contracted under Jewish law. For religious Jews, especially if poor, such a ceremony was perfectly adequate for their consciences, and a couple could then regard themselves as husband and wife henceforth. Of course, this failed to satisfy the requirements of English civil law, since no secular counterpart was recorded and, therefore, no registration of the marriage would have been filed with the authorities.

A serious view of the situation was taken if secular officials discovered any such irregular practice, and especially if a rabbi or other religious leader was known to have connived at it. Under such circumstances, a secretary for marriages who held a license from the Registrar General to solemnize Jewish weddings and record them for secular purposes would lose that license. This threat, however, was not sufficient to prevent the practice happening quite widely. Apart from religious witnesses, who could testify that they had been present at such an occasion; no written record of the event is available. The costs of undergoing such a ceremony were minimal, and no statutory fees were paid to the secular authorities. This, of course, appealed to the impoverished Jews applying the system to themselves. In theory, the officiant should have issued a *ketubah* (religious marriage contract) to the bride, but since these events occurred a century ago, the chances of such a document surviving in personal custody is minimal. The apparent secular non-registration of marriages, that by all rights should have appeared in the vital registers, may well have been occasioned by this practice.

Sometimes, on the secular marriage documentation, the addresses of the bride and groom may appear identical or virtually identical. Do not infer that this means that the couple were already living together as husband and wife. This would have been extremely unlikely in religious Jewish communities. However, the secular costs of giving notice of intent to marry doubled if the parties came from different parishes. If it could appear that they lived in the same parish, this halved the expense. In such circumstances, bride and groom frequently gave an identical address to reduce the impact on their finances. Many addresses were multi-occupation, and owners with any spare space frequently took lodgers who would, therefore, have the same address. The same address does not presuppose cohabitation, although they may all have shared the same stove and lavatory in the back yard.

Census Records

Following recourse to the ONS and/or various local registry offices, the next most useful source is the decennial census. The first countrywide census was taken in 1801 and they have been repeated every ten years since with the exception of 1941. Most returns for 1801–31 have been destroyed, although some scattered returns are held in local hands. Generally, only statistic abstracts of no value for genealogical research exist. Returns from 1841 onwards exist, but may be consulted only after one hundred years. This means that censuses 1841–1901 currently may be consulted by the general public.

The original 1901 census data was supposed to have been completed, in each case, by the head of the household and then gathered by an enumerator who went to each house in the district to personally collect the forms. Often, an enumerator had to assist the head of the household to complete the return, partly because of general illiteracy or, in some cases, because of inability to record the information in English. Errors arose if an enumerator failed to understand the informant correctly. Details such as variations in name spelling or inaccuracies concerning ages and relationships between members of the household may easily now have an official place in the records. In addition, individual returns gathered by enumerators were transcribed in the process into the format in which they have been preserved. All of these steps may have created errors, a fact to remember when consulting the census.

The 1841 census recorded the head of the household and all other occupants listed as living with him or her. Relationships, such as spouse or child, are not specified and can only be inferred. Because many streets were not numbered at that time, or a house number was omitted, it may be necessary to examine a wide section of the census before finding the family sought. The ages of all adults were rounded up to the nearest five years. If the grouping of people living within a household did not fit the standard pattern, it may be that other relatives, such as nephews or cousins, are confused with the children of the head of the household. Occupations of the residents usually are given, but place of birth is non-specific. If the person was born within the same county as they were living in 1841, this is indicated by a "yes." If he or she was born outside the county, this is indicated by "no." Someone born abroad is indicated by "f" for foreign.

Returns for the 1851 and subsequent censuses provide information much superior to that for 1841. The ages of the

inhabitants, relationship to the head of the household, a more accurate place of birth and details of occupation are more standard. In many cases, place of birth is simply listed as the particular country from which a person came, but not infrequently a more specific region or town is given. By the 1891 census, with greatly increased numbers of Jews lived in certain districts, such as the East End of London, enumerator forms printed in Yiddish were issued upon request to enable the head of the household to record the details more accurately.

Many of the censuses have been at least partially transcribed, indexed or otherwise voluntarily recorded by family history societies and enthusiastic individuals in many parts of the country. With the exception of the 1881 census, however, there is no comprehensive listing of all the data available. The 1881 census, however, has been alphabetized and transcribed, county by county, for all of Great Britain. A comprehensive index covers England and Wales by given name, surname and birthplace. Microfilm copies are available in many parts of the world. As with the vital registration records, much of the impetus to disseminate the census data has come from the LDS (Mormon) Family History Library in Salt Lake City which offers the 1881 census on CD.

The key to obtaining maximum benefits from the various censuses is to have a good idea of the address at which the person was living at the time the census was taken. The organization of the census is strictly geographical. An administrative area of a local authority was enumerated street-by-street throughout the area. A large city like London has 20 or more administrative areas. Addresses usually may be obtained from relevant birth, marriage or death certificates, street directories or other classified listings.

Another important item of information that may be available from the censuses is whether or not the head of the household (or other occupant) had become a naturalized British subject. If the delineation is simply "British Subject," the person may or may not have undergone naturalization. If, on the other hand, the description is "naturalized British Subject," then almost invariably that person would have acquired British citizenship—although they may have changed their name upon naturalization and thus not be found in indexes of naturalization. This has implications for research in the Public Record Office that will be examined below.

Wills

Wills are another useful source for investigating pedigrees. Since January 13, 1858, the Family Division of the High Court has operated a central probate system that annually indexes all grants. The Calendars of these grants indicate the town in which administration of the deceased's effects has occurred. For this information to be available, the deceased must have had assets in England or Wales under the jurisdiction of the Court. For such purposes, the place of death is immaterial. If the deceased was a foreign national, he or she must have had English-based assets that would have needed an English-based agent to administer. The essential purpose of the probate system is to allow open access to wills before the assets have necessarily been distributed, in case a challenge must be mounted as to whether the estate is being administered lawfully. Therefore, once a grant of probate has been obtained, the documentation is public. Microfiche copies started in 1982; since 1998 they are computer indexed. Some district registries have placed their sets, along with their older original wills, in the nearest record office.

For the location of pre-1858 probate records, consult the 4th editions of Jeremy Gibson's *Probate Jurisdictions: Where to Look for Wills* (Federation of Family History Societies, 1994). This work touches on post-1858 records in public repositories, but the current situation is fluid. For this reason, plus the fact that older probate grants and letters of administration can only be found in at First Avenue House,* it is best to concentrate on that repository. First Avenue House is the present address of the head Probate Office; it moved from Somerset House a few years ago.

Although the centralized probate system has existed only since 1858, many wills are available from before that time. Discovering their whereabouts, however, may be complicated. Essentially, the administration of these grants is in the hands of local consistory courts, usually loosely based on a county town. There were two much larger courts, however, the Prerogative Court of Canterbury and the Prerogative Court of York, that were used much more frequently than the consistory courts for issuing grants of administration. These courts are, therefore, the logical first place to consult, but it may be necessary to roam much more widely over England and Wales if the grants are not discovered at Canterbury or York. A partial index for the Prerogative Court of Canterbury for all grants from 1750–1800 is available from the Society of Genealogist whose holdings are discussed below. Research has shown that the majority of Jews who left a probate record of any description applied to the Prerogative Court of Canterbury.

Records Housed in the Public Records Office

Many items of considerable genealogical research value are housed at the Public Record Office in Kew, Surrey.* This repository may be formidable in some respects to those unfamiliar with using it. It is sometimes advantageous to obtain the professional services of a guide and researcher who knows the facilities. Various booklets, called PRO publications, give would-be researchers guidance to the nature and extent of various holdings. From the viewpoint of the Jewish genealogical researcher, the most important sources are likely to be those that deal with naturalizations or denizations, war service records and shipping lists. For consular records, consult *Guildhall Library Research Guide 2, The British Overseas, a guide to records of their births, baptisms, marriages, deaths and burials.* Guildhall Library, third revised edition, 1994.

Naturalization Records

It never has been necessary to naturalize in order to live in Britain, but in modern times some careers, especially political ones, have been unavailable to non-British Subjects. Although naturalization was relatively expensive, in some circumstances it was essential. Naturalization papers exist back to the early 19th century; prior to that date, acquiring citizenship was done by denization with an Act of Parliament. This was relatively uncommon because of the cost involved. Naturalization papers vary considerably in the quantity of information the applicant supplied, but the length of time resident in the United Kingdom, place of origin (town and country) and original nationality always are given. The addresses at which the applicant had lived for a considerable period of time prior to undergoing naturalization usually are specified. Of course, this can be useful in supplying addresses to examine in one of the decennial censuses. In many cases, the applicant specified details of parentage although the information may contradict other sources. Spouses of married applicants rarely are named, but the names and dates of birth of children of the marriage usually are listed. Police reports, sponsorship character references and other miscellaneous data sometimes are included. Privacy laws usually prevent access to applications made within the past 75 years, although this is left to the discretion of Public Record Office officials.

Military Records

The Service Records of soldiers, sailors and other military personnel may be very informative, but it is necessary to know details of the regiment to which the person belonged or to have some idea about where he served. The *British Jewry Book of Honour*, issued in 1922, attempted to list all English Jews who had fought in World War I, both those who had died and those who had survived. Inevitably, there are errors of omission and commission, the indexing is less than perfect, and, here too, it is important to know the regiment in which the person served—although not for fatalities. Two volumes of World War II fatalities have been published. For detailed information about servicemen write to the archivist at AJEX Jewish Military Museum.*

Passenger Lists

Shipping registers maintained at the Public Record Office are of variable quality. Nothing exists prior to 1878, and registers are unindexed. Board of Trade registers of passengers exist arranged by date, port and ship. Passenger lists exist for transatlantic and longer voyages for 1878–1960 inward and 1890–1960 outward. No lists of air passengers exist. If the name of the ship on which a passenger sailed is known, as well as the date and port of departure, consulting the registers is a worthwhile exercise. Arrival records are equally unindexed and require exact details to make them researchable. The passenger manifests frequently supply considerable detail about the passengers and their families, ports of destination and places of origin. Relationships within the family of passengers also is frequently supplied. Unless more or less accurate details of the sailing are known, however, it is a Herculean task to go through all the registers on a "just in case" basis.

Other Registers

Local English and Welsh authorities have made available through their own offices many of the records concerning citizenry that lived in their areas. Useful examples are electoral

Wentworth Street, formerly "Petticoat Lane", London, at the beginning of the 20th century

registers and school registers of pupils and staff. Much of this information is not indexed, however, and may require tedious searching to locate useful facts. If, for example, details of a particular school attended by a pupil are known, this might yield an address that can be used effectively to locate a family in one of the censuses. Electoral rolls suffer the same disadvantage as the census in that they are listed in street order and are not indexed. The London Metropolitan Archives is the largest such repository of this nature and one that covers more Jewish families than any other in the kingdom. For details of local record offices, libraries with extensive local history departments containing manuscripts, consult The Royal Commission on Historical Manuscripts.*

Periodicals

Newspapers, magazines, printed periodicals and the like may be a mine of genealogical information—if they can be accessed appropriately. Many local public libraries have all copies of their local newspapers and, in some cases, many of the national and ethnic papers. The most comprehensive holding within the United Kingdom, however, is at the Colindale Newspaper Reference Library, near London.* This repository has virtually a complete set of every regularly published journal that has ever appeared in England or Wales. Of particular relevance for Jewish genealogical research is the Jewish press, especially the London-based *Jewish Chronicle* which has published since 1841. Other more local Jewish publications,

and of a much later period. also are useful sources with their announcements of births, marriages, deaths, bar mitzvahs, engagements, in memoriam and so forth. Although the *Jewish Chronicle* is the oldest such publication, and extremely useful, it suffers from the fact that its indexing has not had the needs of genealogical research in mind. One decade, however, (1870–80) has been indexed and published in a valuable exercise by Doreen Berger called *The Jewish Victorian.* Of the non-Jewish press, other than secular, regularly published newspapers (frequently daily), the *Gentlemen's Magazine* (1731–1868) is the most notable. This has much of enormous Jewish interest and genealogical value within its columns. The National Newspaper Library may be accessed either with a British Library reader's ticket or an annual pass issued on production of proof of identity such as passport or driver's license, plus evidence of permanent address from a legal document such as income tax payment, insurance policy or utility bills.

Societies

The records of professional bodies, trade unions, universities and a few other statutory organizations such as the General Medical Council or General Dental Council, may provide addresses for individuals and sometimes other linking details. In a few cases, such as at Cambridge University, studies have been made of the Jewish contribution to the institution. The information included can be quite useful. No general statements can be made, however, about which records have or have not survived; the only course is to pursue each on an individual basis.

Learned societies to which Jews may have belonged or may have contributed their records should be considered. The London-based Society of Genealogists* whose collections range widely over many aspects of Jewish genealogical activity is the most useful for information and assistance. The Society also houses many specific pedigree books, including those of numerous upper class Jewish families and some Jewish genealogical collections that have been bequeathed to it. The Colyer-Fergusson Papers, the D'Arcy Hart Collection and the Mordy Bequests cover a wide range of Jewish material. Microfilm copies of the Society of Genealogists' Collections may be available and have been disseminated to many other repositories. Details are available from the Society. The Society of Genealogists has sponsored a series of volumes under the general heading of The National Index of Parish Registers. Volume 3 of this series has a chapter by Edgar Samuel devoted to Jewish births, marriages and deaths, including a compendium of various sources such as those already discussed in this account. The Jewish collections within the Archives of the College of Arms (the body that confer coats of arms) is treated in the same National Index of Parish Registers. Apart from the registration of individual pedigrees, the Jewish collections consist of registers of births that cover the years 1707–63; they contain only a handful of entries relating to prominent families. The births have been transcribed also in *Bevis Marks Records*, vol. 5.

The Society of Genealogists has published a series under the general title "My Ancestor Was....: How Can I Find Out More About Him?" Within this series, the late Isobel Mordy supervised "My Ancestor Was Jewish: How Can I Find Out More About Him?" The booklet, periodically updated, is available from the Society of Genealogists and is an essential guide for those researching Anglo-Jewish genealogy.

Church of England Records

Although not a secular source and supposedly applicable only to citizens who belonged to the Church of England, some Jewish representation exists within the English parish register system. This was initiated by Henry VIII in 1538 when the monarch ceased to pay allegiance to the Church of Rome. If an individual, Jewish or otherwise, converted to the Protestant faith, details of their marriages, baptisms, etc. are likely to appear in the parish registers. Quite apart from this function, however, the same registers were sometimes used by Jewish people who felt it preferable that some record should attest a birth, albeit in the somewhat alien milieu of a parish baptismal register. Attention to this phenomenon has been drawn by Edgar Samuel in Volume 3 of the National Index of Parish Registers published by the Society of Genealogists. The International Genealogical Index (IGI) of the LDS (Mormon) Family History Library includes a transcription and indexation of many parish registers since 1538, although many of the earlier years are very fragmentary.

Other Jewish Sources

In addition to the many secular records available to the genealogist, the researcher also has available many much more specific Jewish sources. In many cases, the Jewish sources act in parallel with already analyzed secular data, but they may provide additional information and amplify known details. Sometimes also they are the only source of data for a particular family. The most important of these repositories are those of the older Sephardi and Ashkenazi London congregations.

For the past 60 years, the elders of the Sephardic congregation based at Bevis Marks, have been transcribing and publishing their older vital records. Six volumes are now in the public domain and may be purchased from Bevis Marks. Many are available in public libraries and similar institutions worldwide. (Although no law mandated it, most English Jews adopted fixed, hereditary family names by the early 19th century.[2]) The congregation's birth registers up to 1881, marriage registers to 1901 and death registers to 1918 have been published as well as an especially valuable indexed circumcision register from the 18th century. The latter, maintained between 1715 and 1785 by Isaac de Paiba and his son Abraham de Paiba, covers 1,500 cases attended by them. Although most were London-based Sephardim, a significant minority were Ashkenazi and also lived some distance from London. All of the individuals recorded in birth and burial registers were Sephardim and most, but not all, lived in London. Most, but not all, individuals recorded in the marriage registers lived in London. Some reflect a marriage between a Sephardi and an Ashkenazi, or a Sephardi and a convert.

All births, marriages and deaths that occurred after July 1, 1837, the beginning of national registration, may have a second, parallel listing in that record base. For events that occurred prior to July 1, 1837, however, the religious registers may be the only record. In some cases, translation difficulties (from Portuguese, Ladino and even Hebrew) have led to identification problems. Nevertheless, the general results of the published Bevis Marks records are excellent and cohesive. Occasional annotations, asides and other comments add to their social history value. In 1870, six Ashkenazi synagogues, three dating back to the 18th century, merged into one body called the United Synagogue. Their records are now in the custody of the Archive Department, Office of the Chief Rabbi.* These records constitute most of the data about the early London Ashkenazi community. Some of the early records have been microfilmed by the Mormons. The request will be searched only upon receipt of written inquiries providing a full address and signature. A search fee is charged. This same office holds records belonging to defunct London suburban and provincial congregations. Although a few Sephardi congregations existed outside of London—notably in Manchester—the majority were Ashkenazi, some dating back to the 18th century. Fragmentary records survive. Morris Bierbrier has researched the pedigrees and history of the Manchester Sephardic community, which had its origins in Aleppo, Baghdad, Caofu, Damascus and North Africa.

Details of records held by existing provincial congregations may be learned from the secretaries of these groups. The most important examples include Birmingham, Bristol, Leeds, Liverpool, Manchester, the North East (Newcastle-upon-Tyne and Sunderland) and the South West (Exeter and Plymouth). Many of these communities have been studied by local Anglo-Jewish historians, and a number have published histories. For details, consult the communal sections in Roth's bibliography and later compendia. Several include primary data such as lists of seat holders of the synagogue, details from marriage and burial registers and accounts of numerous communal organizations, including details about the individuals who ran them.

Attempts have been made recently to collate data from several different Jewish cemeteries, both in London and the provinces, but the results are still fragmentary. The burial grounds in Bristol,[4] Cheltenham[5] and Plymouth[6] have been well transcribed as have a few London Jewish cemeteries. Sometimes, specific Jewish cemeteries have been examined, but often it is simply a Jewish enclave within the grounds of a municipal (secular) cemetery. This means that the records of this community may be in the hands of the civil or secular authorities as much as in the hands of the local Jewish community. No full listing of cemeteries has been made. Those serving the London area are described in *Greater London Cemeteries and Crematoria*, revised by Clifford Webb. London: Society of Genealogists (latest edition); the Jewish section by Charles Tucker is revised continuously. Telephone the local Jewish community office to determine where the records are.

An organization of particular relevance for Jewish genealogical research is the Jewish Historical Society of England, founded in 1893. Since then, its publications include a series of *Transactions, Miscellanies* and *Historical Studies*. To date, 37 volumes have appeared at regular intervals; the first 25 are indexed. An index of the next 10 volumes has now appeared (vols. 26–35). Within these published sources are numerous genealogical-style articles and accounts of specific families. The emphasis is toward the smaller old, established, wealthy and acculturated section of the community, not the mass of immigrants who arrived after 1880. Additional references to various Jewish pedigrees are scattered within other occasional publications of the Society. Some examples include Jewish probates up to 1848, the names of Jews naturalized during the years 1609–1799 and an abstract of events of particular Jewish interest that have appeared in the *Gentleman's Magazine*. Colorful Jewish ceremonies frequently figured in its columns, often in a wealth of detail. This is especially true in the obituary notices and the reporting of weddings. Recognizably Jewish entries in the calendars of wills and administrations located in the Act Book of the Prerogative Court of Canterbury through 1848 are found in "Anglo-Jewish Wills and Letters of Administration," by Arthur P. Arnold in *Anglo-Jewish Notabilities. Their Arms and Testamentary Dispositions.* The Jewish Historical Society of England, 1949: 129–225.

The Jewish Genealogical Society of Great Britain,* established in 1992, publishes a quarterly, *Shemot*, that is a worthwhile starting point for learning background information on Anglo-Jewish research.

Various, miscellaneous early sources, not yet fully explored for public use, may prove to have considerable Jewish genealogical research potential. For example, records of Jews who purchased insurance policies during the 18th century are currently being examined; this is likely to prove a very fruitful study. Attempts to absorb the large numbers of poor Jewish immigrants, who arrived in Britain between 1880 and 1905, generated considerable social unease. The well-established and relatively wealthy Anglo-Jewish population had mixed views about the best method of treating them. On one hand was the traditional Jewish charity, represented by the generosity of such families as the Rothschilds and the Montefiores. On the other hand, the arrival of such clearly "foreign" people was not always welcomed openly. Desperate problems of poverty, sickness and accommodation came with the mass of immigrants, and even generous contributions from those who could afford them were not enough.

One of the welfare organizations established to cope with the situation was the Poor Jews' Temporary Shelter (WWW.ITS. UCT.AC.ZA/SHELTER/KAPLAN.HTM) started by Simon Baker in 1889. His accommodation was illegal, grossly overcrowded and insanitary—but it did represent an attempt to cope with the problem. Incomplete Shelter records for the years 1895–1914 chronicle the arrival and departure of several thousand Jewish families. Some were ultimately absorbed into the Anglo-Jewish community, but many others were dispatched to continue their journeys overseas. The surviving records to 1914 have been computerized and are soon to be published. At present, the database is in the custody of the Department of History at the University of Leicester, where Professor Aubrey Newman oversees the project of making the data partially available. The original records have been transferred to the London Metropolitan Archives. Admission and discharge registers are closed for 65 years.

The London and provincial Jewish communities have had much interaction. Cecil Roth's study of the growth and development of provincial Jewish communities between 1740 and 1840 was published in 1950. A series of provincial historical essays, it is a useful source on the existence and fate of earlier Anglo-Jewish communities. If Roth has not mentioned it, it probably did not exist; no additional organized communities have come to light since this work.

Many other studies have been published of individual Jewish families and charismatic Jewish people who have contributed to the development of British society as a whole. Notable is *The Jews of Britain*, by Paul Emden, although, as with so many other similar approaches to the study of Anglo-Jewish history, the emphasis is on the wealthy and industrious people. With the growth of interest in genealogical studies generally, a growing number of desktop family histories appear each year. It is impossible to generate a completely current list, but the *Jewish Chronicle's Jewish Year Book,* published annually since 1896, is a great overview of the Anglo-Jewish community (and covers many aspects of Jewish interest in other countries of the world). It includes a list of existing synagogues and congregations as well as a "Who's Who" section with a list of obituaries of important individuals who died within the previous year.

Addresses

Archive Office of the Chief Rabbi, 735 High Road, Finchley, London N12 0US

Association of Jewish Ex-Servicemen and Women (AJEX) AJEX House, East Bank, Stamford Hill, London N16 5RT

Federation of Synagogues, 65 Watford Way, London NW4 3AQ

General Register Office, 1 Myddleton Street, Islington, London EC1R 10W

Family Records Centre, 1 Myddelton Street, Islington, London, EC1R 10W

Jewish Genealogical Society of Great Britain, P.O. Box 13288, London N3 3WD

Office for National Statistics, P.O. Box 2, South Port, Merseyside PR8 2JD

Probate Office, Principal Registry of the Family Division, First Avenue House, 42–49 High Holborn, London WC1V 6NP

Public Record Office, 4 Ruskin Avenue, Kew, Richmond, Surrey TW9 4DU; website: www.pro.gov.uk

Reform Synagogues of Great Britain and Council of Reform and Liberal Rabbis, the Sternberg Centre for Judaism, 80 East End Road, London N3 2SY

Royal Commission on Historical Manuscripts, Record Repositories in Great Britain (latest edition), PRO Publications

Society of Genealogists, 14 Charterhouse Buildings, Goswell Road, London EC1M 7BA; website: www.sof.org.uk

The Jewish Year Book, Valentine Mitchell, Newbury House, 900 Eastern Avenue, London IG2 7HH

Spanish and Portuguese Jews' Congregation, Bevis Marks, 2 Ashworth Road, London W9 1JY

Bibliography

Arnold, Arthur P. "Anglo-Jewish Wills and Letters of Administration." London: Jewish Historical Society of England.

Berger, Doreen. *The Jewish Victorian*. London: Robert Boyd, 1999.

Bevan, Amanda, ed. *Tracing Your Ancestors in the Public Record Office*. London: Public Record Office, 5th rev, ed., 1999.

Bierbrier, M. "The Manchester Sephardi Community and Its Sources." *Etsi-Sephardi Genealogical and Historical Review* 1, no. 3 (Winter 1998): 10–12.

Emden, Paul H. *Jews of Britain: a series of biographies*. London: Sampson Low, 1943.

Joseph, Anthony P. "Genealogy and Jewish History," Transactions of the Jewish Historical Society of England, vol. 34, London: Jewish Historical Society of England, 1997.

Joseph, Anthony P. "Contributing Editor (England), *AVOTAYNU* 1–19, (Winter 1985 to present).

Joseph, Anthony P. "Guide to British Census Records," *AVOTAYNU* 2, no. 2 (May 1986).

Joseph, Anthony P. "How to Obtain Vital Statistics Records from the United Kingdom," *AVOTAYNU* 2, no. 1 (January 1986).

Joseph, Anthony P. "The Value of Wills to the Genealogist," *AVOTAYNU* 3, no. 1 (Winter 1987). "London Seminar: Highlights and Summary," *AVOTAYNU* 3, no. 2 (Summer 1987).

Miscellanies of the Jewish Historical Society of England, vols. 1–6, Jewish Historical Society of England.

Kershaw, Roger and Mark Pearsall. *Immigrants and Aliens: A guide to sources on U.K. Immigration and Citizenship*. Public Record Office Readers' Guide no. 22. London: Public Record Office, 2000.

Kushner, Tony, ed. *The Jewish Heritage in British History: Englishness and Jewishness*. London: Frank Cass, 1992. "Directory of Jewish Historical and Heritage Resources in the United Kingdom,": 212–229.

Mordy, Isobel. "My Ancestors Were Jewish." London: Society of Genealogists, 2002.

Proceedings of the Second International Jewish Genealogical Seminar (London, 1987), available from International Jewish Genealogical Resources (U.K.). Records of the Bevis Marks Congregation, vols. 1–6, (Bevis Marks, 2 Ashworth Road, London W9).

Raymond, Stuart. *English Genealogy: A Bibliography*. Birmingham: Federation of Family History Societies (latest edition).

Rosenstein, Neil. "Hyamson and Colyer-Fergusson Collection," *AVOTAYNU* 7, no. 2 (Spring 1991). Note that the collections are held by the Society of Genealogists, not at the University of Southampton as claimed.

Roth, Cecil. "The Rise of Provincial Jewry." London: *The Jewish Monthly*, 1950.

Samuel, Edgar R. "Sources for Roman Catholic and Jewish Genealogy and Family History," National Index of Parish Registers, vol. 3. London: Society of Genealogists.

Tucker, Charles. "More on the Colyer-Fergusson Collection," *AVOTAYNU* 3, no. 2 (Summer 1987).

Wenzerul, Rosemary, ed. *Jewish Ancestors? A Beginner's Guide to Jewish Genealogy in Great Britain*. London: Jewish Genealogical Society of Great Britain, 2000.

Wynne, Suzan. "An American Perspective on London Research." *AVOTAYNU* 2, no. 3 (October 1986).

Notes

1. The United Kingdom is composed of Great Britain (England and Wales) and Northern Ireland.

2. In English law, one may possess as many names as one likes provided that all the authorities with whom one deals are informed and there is no intention to deceive or defraud. The only restriction was on aliens between 1914 and 1971, where it was not permitted to change the name by which one was known on August 1, 1914, (or when one entered the country subsequent to that date) unless one was first naturalized. Even so, the military authorities provided Jews of foreign origin who were permitted to go on active duty during World War II with neutral identities, and most encountered few if any problems keeping these names after the war was over.

3. *Etsi* 1, no. 3 (Winter 1998).

4. Available from Sam Silverman.

5. Hand typed copy is out-of-print, but a copy is held by the author.

6. Similarly, out of print, but the author has a copy. The Plymouth Public Library and/or the Plymouth Hebrew Congregation may also possess a copy.

Estonia

by Len Yodaiken

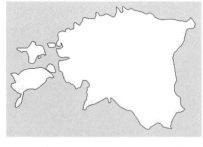

When we speak of Estonia, we think of the present-day state, which first achieved independence in 1918. During the period of the Czarist Empire, however, the *guberniya* (province) of Estonia was a smaller area than the current nation's boundaries. At the time of independence, the province of Livonia was divided, with part going to each of the new states of Estonia and Latvia. This is important to know, because many of the records that relate to the current Latvian portion of Livonia repose in the Historical Archives of Estonia (see LATVIA). Similarly, one must not ignore the possibility that some Estonian records may also be in Latvian archives.

History

Jews first appeared in Estonia as early as the 14th century, probably trading within the framework of that great and unique medieval trading organization, the Hanseatic League. At that time, the city of Reval (today, Tallinn) was the most easterly of the Hanseatic ports, and much of the beautiful medieval city is preserved and in use today both for dwellings and offices as well as a vibrant tourist center.

This was not, however, the starting point of a permanent Jewish settlement. The various powers that occupied Estonia—Lithuania, Poland, Russia and Sweden—prohibited Jewish residence until the latter part of the 19th century. Jewish settlement in Estonia began formally only when Czar Alexander II granted that right to some Jews in 1865. This statute permitted the so-called *Nikolai Soldaten* (Nicholas soldiers),[1] cantonists and their descendants,[2] tradesmen of the first guild, artisans and Jews with higher education to settle in Estonia. Members of these groups founded the first Jewish congregations in Estonia.

Tallinn had a Jewish congregation, the largest in Estonia, as early as 1830, but it was recognized officially only with the promulgation of the 1865 statute. The Tartu congregation was established in 1866 when the first 50 families settled there, and by 1875 a synagogue had been built in Võru. The pre-World War II Jewish community never exceeded 4,500, more than half of whom escaped into Russia before the German invasion. That post-war Jewish community was the only one in Europe to exceed its pre-war numbers. It reached 5,000 as a result of the return of those who had fled, augmented by Russian Jews included in the population sent by the Soviets to russify Estonia. In addition to Tallinn, Tartu and Võru, Jews settled in Narva, Parnu, Rakvere, Valga and Vilandl. A handful of Jewish families were found also in a number of other towns such as Haapsalu, Kuressare, Lihula, Mustvee, Paide and Tapa.

Most of the larger towns have Jewish cemeteries in various stages of repair or disrepair. To this day, a considerable amount of vandalism has been inflicted upon Jewish cemeteries. Tallin has only the modern cemetery, which is well tended. In Tartu there is both a new cemetery and one from before the war, both being meted out their share of vandalism. The old cemetery has some very beautiful and elaborate headstones. In Võru, the local Christian community has encroached upon the Jewish cemetery, and one finds 15 to 20 Jewish headstones standing between graves marked with crosses.

Vital Records

The State Archives of Estonia holds birth, marriage and death records from the czarist era, but the holdings are not complete. Birth records indicate the place of origin of the father and, sometimes, of the mother. Because these families were the first Jewish immigrants in Estonia, the information is invaluable for tracing family to earlier geographical locations. These records have been filmed by the LDS (Mormon) Family History Library and may be obtained from their libraries. As far as can be determined, all Jewish communal records not in the various national archives have vanished. Mormon holdings of Jewish vital records include:

- Tallin (Reval): Births, marriages, divorces and deaths 1872–1940; film numbers 1921300, 1921301 and 1921257
- Tartu (Dorpat): Births, marriages, divorces and deaths, 1897–1926; film numbers 1921257 and 1921258
- Valga (Walk): Births, marriages and deaths, 1919–1925; film number 1921258
- Võru (Werro): Births and deaths, 1883–1925; film number 1921269
  Also at the State Archives of Estonia* (*Eesti Riiklarhiv, Maneezl*) are the following Jewish records:
- Estonian Jewish Autonomous Administration, fond 1107, 228 files, 1928–1941
- Estonian Jewish School Administration, fond 4167, 9 files, 1928–1941
- Tartu Jewish Union Files, fond 2283, 127 files, 1887 and 1917–1940

Estonian Historical Archives

The Estonian Historical Archives* (*Eesti Riiklik Ajaloo Keskarhiv*) has vital statistic records for the years 1918–41, plus:

- Chancellery of Estonia guberniya, fond 29; 21,907 files, 1794–1917

Also held in the Historical Archives are academic records, including those for Jewish students at Tartu University. The *Album Academiucum* (see Bibliography) has a complete list of all the University students, including their patronymics,

Synagogue in Tartu at the beginning of the 20th century

dates of birth and academic achievements. A list of 800 Jewish students has been extracted from the three volumes; a copy is at the Central Archives for the History of the Jewish People* in Jerusalem, file number INV./8174. Gurin's *Statistics of the Jewish Population in Estonia* has a detailed inventory of the 1935 Jewish population of Estonia, town by town, street by street and name by name. Martinson's *Eesti Riklik Kirjastus* lists many of the Jews murdered by the Nazis, including their patronymics and dates of birth. The names of a few cantonists and *Nikolai Soldaten* are dispersed throughout the books by Jokton and Levin. All in all, there is a considerable body of records for this small, relatively unknown community.

Addresses

Archives of the Estonian and Latvian Immigration Society, Kibbuyz Shefayim, Israel

Central Archives for the History of the Jewish People, P.O. Box 1149, Jerusalem, Israel

Estonian Historical Archives *(Eesti Riiklik Ajaloo Keskarhiv)*, Liivi St. 4, Tartu, Estonia

State Archives of Estonia *(Eesti Riikiarhiv)*, Maneezi 4, Tallinn 15019

State Historical Archives *(Ajalooarhiiv)* Juhan Llivi 4, 202400 Tartu, Estonia

Bibliography

Album Academicum Universitatis Tartueniis (Academic album of Tartu University). 1918–44. 3 vols. [Estonian]. Tartu: Pühendatud, 1986.

Amitan-Wilensky, Ella. "Estonian Jewry: A Historical Summary." In M. Bobe, *The Jews in Latvia.* Tel Aviv: Reshafim, 1971.

Dworzecki, M. *Mahanoth HaYehudim beEstoniyah* (Camps of the Jews in Estonia). English summary. Jerusalem, 1971.

Genss, Nosen. *Zur Geschichte fun der Juden in Livonia und Estland 1933–1937* (History of the Jews in Livonia and Estonia 1933–1937), 2 vols. [German]. Tartu, 1933.

———. *Bibliografie fun Yidishe Druk-Oysgabn in Estl* (Bibliography of Yiddish publications in Estonia). [Yiddish] Tallinn, 1937.

Gurin, Samuel. *Juudi Kultuurvaltsuse väljaanne* (Statistics of the Jewish population of Estonia). Tallinn, 1936; second ed. Scarborough, Canada: Kirjastus Maarjamaa, 1988. Includes a set of names and addresses in Latin script.

Gurin-Loov, Eugenia. *Holocaust of Estonian Jews.* Tallinn: Eesti Juudi Kogukond, 1994.

Jokton, K. *Di Geshikhte fun di Yidn in Estland* (History of the Jews in Estonia). [Yiddish] Tartu: R. Salmanovich'I, 1927.

Juudi Vahemusrahvuse Kultuuromavlitsuse Juubell Album (Jubilee album of the Autonomous Cultural Administration of the Jews of Estonia). [Estonian]. Tallinn, 1926.

Levin, Dov. *Pinkas Hakehillot Latvia and Estonia* (History of the communities). Jerusalem: Yad Vashem, 1988. (in Hebrew)

Levin, Dov. "Estonian Jews in the USSR 1941–45: Research Based on Survivors' Testimony." *Yad Vashem Studies.* Jerusalem: Yad Vashem, 1976.

Martinson, E. *Eestl Riklik Kirjastus* (Estonia under the heel of the swastika). [Estonian] Tallin: 1962. There is also a Russian edition.

Nodel, Emanuel. *Life and Death of Estonian Jewry.* Cleveland, Ohio:, 1973.

Sher, Tatiana. "Judaica in the Historical Archives of Estonia." *Avotaynu* 9, no. 4 (Winter 1993).

Yodaiken, Len. *The Judeikin Family History and Tree,* (private ed. 1998.

Yodaiken, Len. "Pre-independence Estonian Birth Documents." *Sharsheret HaDorot* 12, no. 2 (June 1998).

Notes

1. *Nikolai Soldaten* were Jewish soldiers drafted into the Russian army for 25 years during the reign of Nickolas I. The government reasoned that by removing them from their communities for 25 years, they would be completely assimilated when finally released.

2. Cantonists were males between 8 and 11 years of age who were snatched from their families and raised in the Russian Orthodox faith as cadets in military cantons. Many are said to have died of loneliness.

France

by Basile Ginger

History[1]

Jews have lived in France since the start of the Gallic-Roman period during the second century C.E. They lived first in Provence and Aquitaine, and then also to the north of the Loire, almost to the border with Belgium. Just as a locality such as Villejuif (literally, city of Jews or Jewish city) testifies to their presence, so also do the numerous *rues des Juifs* (street of the Jews) and *rue de l'ancienne juiverie* (street of the old Jewish quarter) that one finds scattered throughout the country.

Only from the time of the First Crusade at the end of the 11th century did Jews begin noticeably to lose their rights; for example, the right to own land and the right to work at something other than money lending. They lived in certain quarters of the cities and periodically were accused of ritual crimes. Finally, they were periodically expelled from the realm: by Philippe-Auguste in 1182; by Philippe the Handsome in 1306 (an estimated 100,000 Jews); and then by Charles VI in 1394, the so-called "definitive banishment," as opposed to previous similar orders that generally had been rescinded.

Banished Jews often settled in neighboring countries outside of the realm of the king of France: Alsace, Lorraine, Provence (including the Papal *Comtat Venaissin*), Franche-Comté (between Alsace and Savoy), Savoy, Dauphiné, northern Italy, the Rhine Valley and Switzerland. Expelled eventually from these places as well, many Jews later moved to Poland or to Central Europe. Those banished from Provence in 1501 sought refuge primarily in the Comtat.

From the middle of the 16th century until nearly the middle of the 19th century, the Jews who lived in the present-day territory of France were concentrated in four specific regions: in Alsace, in Metz and Lorraine, in the Papal states of Avignon and the Comtat Venaissin, and along the southwestern coast, especially Bordeaux and Saint-Esprit (suburban Bayonne). The first three regions eventually became part of France through the progressive expansion of the country.

With the provisional exception of Mulhouse and Strasbourg, Alsace became part of France in 1648. Jews go back to the Middle Ages in Alsace. The feudal system allowed them to maintain certain communities, but the hostility of the towns and large cities gave Alsatian Jewry an almost exclusively rural character. On the eve of the French Revolution, Alsatian Jewry was far and away the most important Jewry in France.

In Metz, conquered by French troops in 1552, a new community was not only permitted but positively encouraged, since it provided provisions for the French garrison. At the end of the 17th century, the dukes of Lorraine welcomed Jews to this region.

In the papal realms of Avignon and Comtat Venaissin (in the present *département*[2] of Vaucluse), Jewish presence was uninterrupted from the Middle Ages onward, but the number of communities diminished progressively. By the start of the 17th century, the six communities initially allowed were reduced to only four: Avignon, Carpentras, Cavaillon and l'Isle-sur-la-Sorgue. There Jews lived in ghettos called *carrières*. After this region became part of France in 1791, its Jewish inhabitants dispersed throughout the country.

On the southwestern coast of France, essentially Bordeaux and Saint-Esprit, lived descendants of Spanish Jews who had been forcibly converted to Christianity in Portugal in 1497. They had been admitted to France as "New Christians of the Portuguese Nation." In fact, they were *marranos,* secret Jews, who progressively practiced, more and more openly, the Jewish religion they had never really abandoned in spite of their forced conversion. They formed the Spanish and Portuguese Jewish nations. The French rulers closed their eyes to this situation because Jewish merchants and ship owners brought important returns to the realm and contributed to the prosperity of the region.

Mention also should be made of the community of Nice, a possession of the Dukes of Savoy, and Paris, with several hundred families, most of whom generally originated in the other four areas. Of the nearly 40,000 Jews estimated to live in France on the eve of the French Revolution, 23,000 lived in Alsace, 7,000 in Lorraine, 5,000 in the Southwest, 1,800 in the Comtat Venaissin and about 2,000 elsewhere—especially in Paris, which had 600 Jews.

Jews were emancipated in two stages at the time of the Revolution. On January 28, 1790, the Portuguese and Spanish Jews of the French southwest and those of the Comtat Venaissin were emancipated. The largest group, those from Alsace and Lorraine, were emancipated on September 27, 1791.

In July 1870, France entered a disastrous war against Germany (Prussia, at that time), and on May 10, 1871, under the Treaty of Frankfurt, France lost "Alsace-Lorraine." This term designates specifically those territories annexed by Germany between 1871 and 1918. From Alsace, it encompasses the departments of the Bas-Rhin and the Haut-Rhin, without the territory of Belfort. From Lorraine, it is the part that currently constitutes the department of the Moselle. Alsace-Lorraine must be differentiated from the expression "Alsace and Lorraine," which means, in addition to the departments already cited, departments of the Meurthe-et-Moselle, of the Meuse and of the Vosges.

In the revolutionary activity of 1871, among the casualties were the Paris *Hôtel de Ville* (city hall) and the *Palais de Justice;* the state civil archives were lost to fire.

The Jewish population of France expanded especially after 1881, the date of the first Russian pogroms, following which tens of thousands of immigrants came from Russia,

Poland, Central Europe and Germany. After 1962, Jews came *en masse* from Algeria, joining those who had already come from Egypt, Greece, Lebanon, Morocco, Tunisia and Turkey. Thus, the majority of Jews in France today are of Sephardic origin—using the word in its broadest sense to mean those of the Mediterranean Basin, not the strict meaning of from the old Iberian Peninsula.

Some additional historical detail appears in the sections that follow, one for each of the major former Jewish settlements in France.

Décret de Bayonne

On July 20, 1808, Napoleon enacted a decree, commonly called *Décret de Bayonne*, that required registers to be opened in every French commune (city, town or village) where Jews lived. In these registers, every Jewish inhabitant was required to record the permanent family name and given name that he or she declared to adopt or to keep henceforth. The head of household made a name declaration for his minor children, indicating their dates and places of birth. The decree applied to all of the Napoleonic Empire, including at that time Belgium, Italy, western Germany and the Netherlands. A typical example:

Before the mayor of the community of Weshoffen, canton of Wasselonne, district of Strasbourg, department of Bas-Rhin, comes Abraham Moyse who declares that he is taking the name Blum as his family name and that he will keep Moyse as his given name. Signed before us October 9, 1808.

This Moyse Blum is the ancestor of Léon Blum, a French prime minister whose father was born in Westhoffen in 1831.

These registers, called *prise de nom* (name adoption), number about 46,000 and were created by the mayors in conformity with the decree. Most have survived and are held today in departmental, mayoral or municipal archives. Very often the Jews have maintained the names that they were bearing when the decree was enacted: in general they adopted as family name their hereditary surname if they already had one, or their father's or their own Hebrew name, or a secular transformation of their Hebrew names.

These lists are a valuable source of information for genealogists today. A systematic index has been largely completed, especially for Alsace and Lorraine, by the Cercle de Généalogie Juive (CGJ).[3] The Cercle has published these lists, with regrouping by families—a significant help for the researcher.

Civil Records

Vital Records

Civil records (*état civil*) did not exist in France before 1792; instead, the Roman Catholic Church registered vital events of its parishioners. Some specifically Jewish vital statistics can be found for Bordeaux (after 1738), for Metz (as early as 1717), in the Comtat Venaissin (beginning in 1736), and in Alsace (1784 census) (details below).

A law enacted on September 20, 1792, instituted secular civil registration applicable to everyone in France. Three registers (one each for births, marriages and deaths) were started in the town hall of every town or village in France, in

Actual text of "Decret of Bayonne" issued by Napoleon on July 20, 1808. It required the establishment of registers in which every Jewish inhabitant was required to record the permanent family name and given name that he or she declared to adopt or to keep henceforth.

which all such events were recorded yearly in chronological order. At the end of each year, an alphabetical index was created that specified the date and record number of each event. Before 1910, however, it was not unusual for the index to be arranged only according to the initial letter of a name.

Between the end of 1793 and September 1805, the "Republican calendar" was the only calendar used for the records. Researchers can use the resources of the website at WWW.FOURMILAB.CH and its page WWW.FOURMILAB.CH/documents/calendar (the last words are case-sensitive) to convert dates from the Republican calendar to the current Gregorian calendar. Alternately, if they can read French they can download the RamCal converter at RAMSESGEN.ONLINE.FR.

The creation of an alphabetical 10-year index (*table décennale*) also was mandated. The first such index, which covered the period 1793 to 1802, often is missing in repositories. Subsequent indexes covered 1803 to 1812 and so on. These indexes include the same information as the annual indexes. The 10-year index is the first document to consult if one does not know the exact date of an event.

Until 1808, the date of the *Décret de Bayonne*, the recording of Jewish events was not reliable due to the lack of hereditary surnames. Until 1884, when family record books (*livrets de famille*) became mandatory—and sometimes even until the beginning of the 20th century—the recording clerk usually relied only upon his ears and wrote a surname as he heard it. Even the initial letter of a name might vary from one record to another; for example, the letters P and B occasionally were interchanged. This is especially true in Alsace, because of pronunciation customs there. More generally, genealogists should never take the content of any specific vital record as unquestionable truth.

All events are recorded in two copies. The first is held in the town hall; the second is sent to the court house. The family record book is kept by the parents.

Content of the Records

Listed below is information not usually found in vital records of other countries. Birth records include, for the parents, their residence, occupation and age, or, since 1922 (and occasionally prior to 1922), their date and place of birth. Since 1897, written as margin notes (except for Alsace-Lorraine until 1920, because French laws were not in effect in this area between 1871 and 1920), are the date and place of the marriage, the family and given names of the spouse and, on occasion (since 1886), the date and place of divorce, of remarriage, of a second divorce, etc. The same information is given for the witnesses as for the parents (witnesses were discontinued in 1924), plus any possible relationship to one member of the couple. Since 1945, the date and place of death has been written as a margin note.

Marriage records include the given and family names of the spouses, their date and place of birth, their residence, occupation and the names of their parents (and, should the case arise, mention of their death), mention of a possible marriage contract (since 1850), and, should the case arise, mention of the name of the previous spouse of each one of the couple, with the date and place of the death or of the divorce (since 1886). The same information is given for the witnesses (present even after 1924) as for the parents, plus any possible relationship to one of the couple. Since 1913 (and often before, especially in Paris), the bride's maiden name (and no longer only the groom's family name) appears in the appropriate alphabetical place in both the annual and the 10-year indexes. Nationality is never indicated. The marriage record is usually kept in the locality where the bride lives. Marriage banns were posted at the town hall of both the bride and groom, but publication of banns was not required after 1927. Many registers of banns were destroyed later.

Death records cite the date and place of birth (since 1823, in principle), occupation, names of parents (since 1823) with possible mention of their deaths, as well as information on the informant (i.e., the person who reported the death at the town hall) and, should the occasion arise, the informant's relationship to the deceased, the surname and given names of the spouse or mention of "widow of" or "widower of." Note that almost any information in death records may be inexact or approximate, since the record generally reflects only what is reported by the informant. Experience has shown that the only reliable fact, in addition to the name of the deceased, is

the name of his/her spouse or the mention "widow(er)." The name of the spouse can help one differentiate the decedent from possible namesakes. Since 1910, the maiden name of the wife (no longer only her married name) appears in the appropriate alphabetical place in the annual and 10-year indexes. Since 1924, no witnesses are required. The death record is kept in the locality where the event occurred and also is fully transcribed into the record book of the last place of residence, if the death occurred elsewhere—such as a hospital.

Where the Records and Indexes Are Kept

Vital records are not centralized. Registers less than 100 years old are always kept in the local town hall. If the locality has more than 2,000 inhabitants, records more than 100 years old are kept in the town hall indefinitely, unless they have been deposited at the municipal archives (in the cities) or, after 150 years, in the departmental archives (*Archives Départementales*) located in the capital city of each department. Registers of towns with fewer than 2,000 inhabitants generally are deposited in the departmental archives. The 10-year indexes are kept with the registers.

Special Case of Paris

The departmental archives of Paris and its inner suburbs (the former *département de la Seine*) are called the *Archives de Paris*; a well-done booklet explains in detail the steps to follow to access the records (and many other sources).[4] Since 1903, registers and indexes have been kept in the town hall of the *arrondissement* where they occurred.[5]

A researcher who does not know the *arrondissement* where the event occurred less than 100 years ago should write (enclosing a self-addressed envelope and two international postal coupons, if writing from abroad)

- *Bureau des mairies,* 4 rue Lobau, 75004 Paris. Indicate the date (or a range of a few years for the date) of the event and request an extract of the certificate, without the names of the parents (unless it is a death record). To get a complete copy, with the names of the parents, you have to indicate these names (see below). Expect to wait a few months for a reply (a few weeks for events that have taken place since 1976).

Town hall addresses can be found in the *Proceedings of the 1997 Paris International Seminar,*[6] or in the booklet issued by the Archives, but the letter will arrive if you just put on the envelope "*Mairie du N* ^{e} *arrondissement* (N^e being its number)," *Paris*. If a complete copy is desired, do not omit the names of the parents, unless it is a death record. But it is even simpler and much faster to request a copy or an extract, without knowing the *arrondissement* but with supplying the other information as seen above, on the website (in French) WWW.PARIS.FR. Click on the *vos démarches,* then *vos actes d'état civil*. Do not send any self-addressed envelope; they should send you the paper free of charge.

For events more than 100 years old, two different cases must be distinguished: basically, copies of both registers and indexes created before 1860 were burned by rioters in 1871.

Table 1. Selected Departmental Archives for Jewish Research

Department	Address	Postal code	City	Phone	Fax	Operation hours and periods
ALPES MARITIMES	Centre Administratif, route de Grenoble	06036	Nice Cedex	04 93 18 61 70		M–F 8:45–5:45
Bouches du RHONE	66 bd St Sébastien	13259	Marseille Cdx 6	04 91 04 72 00	04 91 57 17 54	M–F 8:30–12:45 & 1:45–5:00
	23 r Gaston Saporta	13100	Aix–en Provence	04 42 21 09 08	04 42 21 42 65	M–F 8:30–12:00 & 1: 00–6:15
DOUBS	r Jules Gauthier mail address: BP 2059	25000 25050	Besançon Besançon Cedex	03 81 52 97 50	03 81 51 61 63	M–F 9:00–6:00, Sat 9:00–12:00; closed July 1–15
GIRONDE	13 r Aviau	33081	Bordeaux Cedex	05 56 52 14 66	05 56 29 18 16	M–F 8:30–5:00, Sat 8:30–11:45; closed July 1–15
	imp. Poyenne	33000	Bordeaux	05 56 79 19 93	05 56 29 13 32	M–F 9:00–12:00 & 2:00–5:00; closed July 1–15
MEURTHE & MOSELLE	1 rue de la Monnaie, CS 5202	54052	Nancy Cedex	03 83 35 40 52	03 83 37 81 11	M–F 8:30–6:00, Sat 8:30–12:00; closed July 1–15
MEUSE	20 r Monseigneur Aimond	55000	Bar-le-Duc	03 29 79 01 89	03 29 77 20 13	M–F 8:30–5:00, Sat (except Jul–Aug) 9:00–4:45
MOSELLE	1 allée du Château	57070	St Julien les Metz	03 87 76 26 26	03 87 36 96 98	M–F 9–5:45; closed July 16–31
PYRÉNÉES–ATLANTIQUES	bd Tourasse, cité administrative	64000	Pau	05 59 02 67 06		M–F 8:30–12:30 & 1:30–5:30 Sat 8:30–12:00
BAS RHIN	5 rue Fischart	67000	Strasbourg	03 88 45 94 54	03 88 60 44 52	M–F 8:45–11:45 & 2:00–5:45
HAUT RHIN	3 r Fleischauer (cité administrative)	68000	Colmar	03 89 41 36 41	03 89 24 14 42	M–F 8:15–11:45 & 2:15–5:00, Wed 8:15–5:00
RHONE	2 r Montauban (section ancienne et notaires) 57 r Servient (section moderne: 19e–20e s.)	69005 69003	Lyon Lyon	04 78 28 05 73 04 72 61 10 73		M–F 9:00–6:00, Sat 9:00–12:00; closed July 1–15 M–F 9:00–4:00, Sat 9:00–12:00; closed July 1–15
PARIS	18 bd Sérurier Metro Porte des Lilas	75019	Paris	01 53 72 41 23	01 53 72 41 34	M 1:30–5:30, T–F 9:30–5:30
VAUCLUSE	Palais des Papes Minutier notarial	84000 84200	Avignon Carpentras	04 90 86 16 18 04 90 63 56 81	04 90 82 75 95	M–F 8:30–12:30 & 1:30–6:00 M–F 9:00–12:00 & 2:00–5:00; closed Aug.15–Sept.15

About one-third of the data in these registrations has been reconstructed from notarial acts and other sources and may be consulted at the *Archives de Paris*. Paris had only 12 *arrondissements* before 1860, and their boundaries were different from their current boundaries. The procedure is explained in the booklet issued by the Archives de Paris. If one is researching a record before 1860, it is unnecessary to know the *arrondissement*.

Microfilms of registers and indexes for the years 1860–1902 may be consulted directly either at the Archives de Paris or at LDS (Mormon) Family History Centers, but since each of the 20 *arrondissements* has a separate register, it will usually be necessary to search the 10-year indexes for each of them—or at least a good portion of them.

Contrary to the general case, registers that are more than 100 years old may not be consulted in Paris town halls. On the other hand, for localities of inner suburbs of Paris (the present departments 92, 93 and 94), records and indexes of birth, marriage and death for the years 1793 to 1859 usually have survived and are kept in the corresponding town halls, just as those from 1860 to 1902. Some parts of these localities were included in Paris before 1860 (see the booklet by the

Archives de Paris). One can find much additional information (in French) on FBEZIAUD.FREE.FR/parisgenweb and its various headings (note that "parisgenweb" is case-sensitive).

Access to Vital Statistics Information

Access to the records obey "the 100-year law;" that is, records less than 100 years old are not open to the public; but since the most recent accessible 10-year index covers the period 1883–1902, the term "less than 100 years" really means that from 1903 until today, the records cannot be freely consulted (and until the year 2013). Throughout this chapter, therefore, the term "less than 100 years" really means from 1903 until today.

Records Less Than 100 Years Old

Inspection of registers and indexes for events that occurred less than 100 years ago is forbidden to private individuals, even to those directly related (the individual himself, his ancestors, descendants or spouse). Only professional genealogists, notaries and similar individuals are given this privilege (though some municipal clerks, in small localities, may grant it to a private individual). An individual or his descendants cannot inspect registers, but they may obtain a complete copy of the record if they supply the name of the parents.

In principle, however, a professional genealogist will not give out the complete information other than about a deceased individual, except to direct relatives. On the other hand, the town hall is required to release the information described below. If you make the request in writing, attach a self-addressed, stamped envelope (or two international postal reply coupons, if you write from abroad). In principle, the requester should furnish the exact date of the event, but the town halls of villages and small towns (and often of cities as well) are content with approximate dates (a few years). This way it is possible to obtain the following documents:

• Complete copy of all death records
• Complete copy of a birth or marriage record, if you are directly related (sometimes it is sufficient to indicate, in the letter of request, that you are), and if you give the names of the parents of the person whose record is requested.

   This last condition was not required until a decree of September 1997. Currently, it is not enforced everywhere, but is strictly enforced in Paris and the other large cities. There, one must indicate the names of the parents, even to get one's own birth certificate.

• Extract (without the name of the parents) of a birth or marriage record including, in addition to the usual information except the parents' names, the margin notes recording marriage(s), death, etc. This is particularly useful when one is researching cousins. You may learn of an eventual divorce, and, if such should have been the case, even the name of an earlier spouse, if you specifically request it. Requests must always be made at, or sent to, the town hall that holds the records. Many practical details can be found in a guide to genealogy in France authored by Jean-Louis Beaucarnot.[7]

Records More Than 100 Years Old

Here the situation is more complex: access to records is open, but that does not mean that one always has the right to obtain a photocopy, a complete copy or even an extract, because onsite inspection of the records is possible (except when the administration holding the record refuses for a valid reason; for example, in cases where the register is in fragile condition). Town halls of small towns, if the registers are held there and if they have the necessary personnel, often respond to written requests (accompanied by a self-addressed, stamped envelope or several international postal coupons), even if they are given only approximate dates.

   Some town councils tax the cost of "research and copies" quite freely. Some reply that their staff, which often is small, is not obliged either to make copies or extracts by hand (which is true, for records more than 100 years old). They do it sometimes, perhaps more willingly if the request comes from a foreigner. The problem is that, as already mentioned, they are not allowed to make photocopies.

   Always check to see if the Mormons have microfilmed any of these records, which is the case, for instance, for

Transcription on the "Service Central de l'etat civil" of the birth certificate of a Polish Jew who was a naturalized Frenchman. Information also includes marriage and death information.

Alsace, for Lorraine, for Paris after 1860, and for many other departments. If so, then for most foreigners, it is easier to research the records in an LDS Family History Center. Actually, the microfilms that can be consulted in the departmental archives in France were furnished by the Mormons in return for permission to do microfilming.

Practical Details about Departmental Archives

Continental France is divided into 96 departments, numbered from 01 to 95 (Corsica is divided into two departments numbered 2A and 2B, instead of 20), and their archives have different hours of operation. Information is given in Table 1 on the most useful archives for foreigners searching for Jewish ancestors or cousins in France. To get information for any other archives, write: *Archives départementales de* (the name of the department), followed, on the next line, by the postal code and the name of the capital city of the department. Even better, consult the web pages WWW.FRANCEGENWEB.ORG/ archives.htm (note that "archives.htm" is case-sensitive) which supply a list of archives' addresses. Note that for some documents (other than vital records) of interest to genealogists, the Archives of Paris covers not only Paris (number 75), but also three other departments, numbers 92, 93 and 94, called *la Petite Couronne* ("the small crown," because they surround Paris). For the address and hours of operation, see Table 1 or the website cited above.

Records Created Outside Continental France

Records of French people, whether born French or naturalized, created in a foreign country or in a former French colony that since has become independent, are in principle kept in Nantes:

- Records less than 100 years old in the *Service Central de l'état civil.** The accessibility of complete records is restricted in the same manner as it is for records created in France. One can utilize the website WWW.DIPLOMATIE. GOUV.FR/FRANCAIS/ETATCIVIL/DEMANDE_INTERNET.HTML. This may be useful in particular for Jews from Algeria.

- Records more than 100 years old in the *Centre des Archives Diplomatiques.** No mail requests.

Most Jews born in Algeria before 1962 are French citizens, thanks to the *décret Crémieux,* which naturalized their ancestors all at one time in 1870 on the condition that they were born in Algeria and were living there at the time the decree was enacted. These Jews are now considered by the French authorities to be born in a foreign country, and their records less than 100 years old are kept in Nantes in the *Service Central de l'état civil.* The majority (not all) of the microfilms of records more than 100 years of age can be consulted at the *Centre des Archives d'Outre-Mer.** A copy of the microfilms may be borrowed (one at a time) to be read in official archives (in Paris, at CARAN)*. No mail requests.

Research on Jews from Algeria is discussed in another chapter of this book.

Sources Other Than Civil Records[7]

Naturalization Files

Naturalization files are especially useful to Jews whose family emigrated from Eastern Europe. French naturalization documents are centralized, a great advantage to genealogists. They usually include considerable valuable information, specifically the date and place of birth of the individual, the name of his or her relatives, often their date and place of birth, as well as many other biographical details. If one has a rare family name, it is even possible to make a systematic search of all the naturalizations with that name and sometimes to discover information about family members whose residence in France had not even been known.

The procedure to find a file may be quite tedious; the reader is referred to a detailed discussion in *AVOTAYNU.*[8] The current discussion should be considered a summary and update to the *AVOTAYNU* article. The main new points are the finding aids in the CARAN*, the reduced time limit for direct consultation of the files, which is now 60 years instead of the previous 100 years and, last but not least, the availability of a searchable CD-ROM which gives the portion of the *Liste alphabétique* (see below) corresponding to the years 1900 to 1950. This CD-ROM may be ordered from *"Chercheurs d'Ancêtres"** and enables one to easily find the file.

Until 1889, an *admission à domicile* (residence permit), which conferred provisional status between alien and citizen,

was an obligatory preliminary to naturalization. When citizenship was conferred, the two records were combined before they were placed in archival storage, and one can now see that often the thickest file by far is the one created at the time of the request for a residence permit.

Requests made before 1930 were later sent to the National Archives whose research center in Paris is called CARAN. The request, if it was accepted, served as the basis of the decree that was published in the *Bulletin des Lois* or, after 1924, in the *Journal Officiel.* Naturalizations that occurred after 1930 are discussed below.

The three documents that can direct one to a naturalization file are the *Liste alphabétique des personnes ayant acquis la nationalité française par décret* (alphabetical list of those who acquired French citizenship by decree), the *Bulletin des Lois,* and the *Journal Officiel.*

La Liste Alphabétique (Alphabetical List)

This publication, which we shall call simply "the List," is also known as *Preuve de la nationalité* (proof of French citizenship). It is a 10-year table (20 years for the first period) that began in 1900 and was kept until 1979. It consists of 37 volumes. Following each surname, one finds for men, for unmarried women, and for minor children, their given name, date and place of birth, date of naturalization, and reference to the decree. In the case of married women, given names are replaced by their maiden names, and only their married names are given in the alphabetical listing.

A genealogist researching an ancestor or cousin who was naturalized by decree after 1900—but not by marriage or by declaration—can obtain all this data by just consulting the List. Generally, however, researchers can learn a great deal more by consulting the file. A file, here, is a set of about 10 to 30 sheets of paper collected together and put into a folder.

Le Bulletin des Lois (Bulletin of Laws)

For naturalizations and residence permits granted before 1900 or for finding a woman whose married name is unknown, it is necessary to use the *Bulletin des Lois* or an index at the CARAN (see below). For naturalizations granted between 1900 and 1923, the *Bulletin* may also provide some additional data: occupation and place of residence, and, for married women, their given names.

Beginning with 1836, the *Bulletin's* supplementary section provides information on the decrees that interest us. If you do not know the year in which naturalization was granted, use whenever possible (if you search from Paris) the alphabetical indexes in the *Salle des Inventaires* of the CARAN: on microfiche (from 1802 to 1813), on an internal computer network (from 1814 to 1832), and on microfilm (from 1848 to 1883). The period 1833–47 is rarely relevant for Jewish research; the primary time of interest to Jewish genealogists is 1884 to 1899, so it is for this period—or if you do not search from Paris, that you must consult the 10-year tables for the supplements of the *Bulletin des Lois.* Be aware, however, that the notice of a naturalization often was not published until many years after that status had been conferred. More details about the research into the *Bulletin des Lois* may be found in the *AVOTAYNU* article of Winter 1996 cited in note 8.

Le Journal Officiel (The Official Journal)

The decrees of naturalization after 1924 appear only in the *Journal Officiel*. Notices there supply the same information as those in the *Bulletin*.

The List may usually be found in the departmental archives, in the *préfectures* (offices of the departmental administration) and in some administrative libraries (libraries devoted to official administrative matters). In Paris, it can best be consulted at the *Archives de Paris*,* where direct access is permitted (but the first volume, letters A to K for 1900–20, is missing) or at the CARAN on microfiche.

The *Bulletin des Lois* may be found in the departmental archives, in the municipal or administrative libraries of big cities, and in some large libraries. In Paris, it may be consulted at the CARAN[9] (but not at the *Archives de Paris**); here one has the advantage of direct access by the public. On the other hand, the *Bulletin* is slightly incomplete. The collection at the *Bibliothèque Administrative* (City of Paris Administrative Library)[10] is complete; its call number is 2.

In Paris, *le Journal Officiel* may be consulted at the Administrative Library where the call number is 7, or at the CARAN (until 1940). Outside Paris, it may be found in the same places as noted in the discussion of the *Bulletin des Lois*.

Practical Details

After—but only after—you have located the date of the decree of naturalization, you can submit (either on the spot or by mail) a written request for research of the complete file. No proof of relationship is required.

1. If the naturalization was granted no later than 1930, submit the request in the CARAN reading room as a *demande de consultation de dossier de naturalisation* (request to consult a naturalization file). Indicate at least the names and the date citizenship was granted or the reference of the decree. If you prefer, you may also send the request to the CARAN, *Service des Recherches, section Moderne*, but you would have to supply the same information (they will not research it, in spite of their name). Telephone requests are not accepted.

Whether you go to the CARAN or make your request by mail (after you have obtained the necessary information from the CD-ROM or from a friend in Paris), expect to wait about three weeks for a reply, which is typically, "The record has been, or has not been, found." The reply will be by mail if you enclose an SASE or an international reply coupon.

Then, if the file was found, you (or the person who made the request) can inspect it at the CARAN reading room and/or request a photocopy of its contents (but photocopying is not allowed unless it is from a microfilm that you first must order). To begin with, you will receive a quotation. If ordering from abroad, payment should be made by international money order.

2. If the naturalization was enacted after 1930, the record is not kept at the CARAN. Write to one of the following services, providing the same information as for the CARAN.

a. Naturalizations from 1931 through 1975: *Centre des Archives Contemporaines*.* If the file is more than 60 years old, you can inspect it (in Fontainebleau) or directly order a photocopy by mail. If the file is less than 60 years old, you will not be allowed to refer to it, even if you are a direct descendant, and you must first ask for a special permit at the CARAN (although the record is not kept there). Whether or not it will be granted (expect to wait several months for the reply) depends on the content of the file; privacy of medical information is especially protected.

b. Naturalizations after 1975: *Ministère des Affaires Sociales*.* This is also the place to write if you receive a response saying that the file (even before 1930) could not be found.

Notarial Archives (Archives notariales)

In France, a notary drafts and keeps copies of wills, land transfers and important contracts (such as marriage contracts). In principle, but not always in practice, notarial acts more than 100 years old are deposited in the departmental archives.

After 1850, the existence of a marriage contract is indicated in the act of marriage, with the name and address of the notary to whom it was given. If an inventory of the estate has been made after a person's death (*inventaire après décès*), it also gives the reference to the marriage contract. The *déclaration de succession* (declaration for death duties), when it exists, gives information about the heirs, which is very valuable for collateral genealogy, and sometimes about the deceased's way of life.

Starting with the residence of the deceased (indicated in the death record), one can search at the departmental archives for the corresponding *bureau d'enregistrement* (registration bureau), then the registration itself (series Q at the departmental archives), which is drafted six months after death. As with civil vital registers, direct descendants can obtain a copy of a declaration for death duties less than 100 years old, but cannot consult the registers themselves.

Outside Paris, notarial acts are held at the departmental archives in series E, where they are classified by *Etude* (notarial office) and in chronological order for a given *Etude*. For Paris, acts more than 100 years old are at the CARAN, in the *Minutier central* (the name given to the collection of records of the Paris notaries), and are freely available for consultation.

Censuses (Recensements)

In principle, censuses have been taken every five years since 1836 and may be consulted after 30 years, but in the large cities it is necessary, in practice, to know the address of the family being researched (see the section below on voter registration).

In Paris, however, no censuses were taken before 1926, and the only ones that exist (accessible in the Archives de Paris*) are those for 1926, 1931, 1936 and 1946. In the immediate suburbs, the first (incomplete) censuses date from 1891 and can be inspected in the archives of the corresponding departments (92, 93 and 94).

Between 1836 and 1962, the information recorded was last name, given names and age; then (since 1906) year of birth (or, since 1968, date of birth), gender, profession, address (and, since 1962, residence at the time of the preceding census), nationality (in 1851, 1872, 1876, and since 1886), and relation to the head of the household. The place of birth (generally only the country of birth if it was outside of France) appeared in 1872, 1876 and from 1906 to 1936. Religion was recorded only in 1851.

Although the censuses are often unreliable, they can be useful to the researcher, especially for tracing collateral relatives, since they indicate the composition of a household. Sometimes they are useful for retrieving the place of birth when one knows only an individual's subsequent domicile. Census returns may be consulted either in town halls or in departmental archives.

Voter Registration Lists (listes électorales)

Until 1848, voter registration lists included only men of wealth at least 30 years of age; from 1848 to 1974 the age was 21 or older, and in 1974 the age of majority dropped to 18 years. Women do not appear in these records until 1945, when they were first allowed to vote. After 1852, the lists include last name, first name, date and place of birth, domicile and profession. This data enables one to find a birth record of someone with French nationality when all that is known is the locality of residence at a given time. Above all, the voter registration lists are useful for researching collateral genealogy since the indication of domicile allows one to refer to censuses.

The lists are found either in the city hall or in municipal or departmental archives. They are immediately consultable by any French citizen in possession of a voter registration card (on condition that he is not acting with a commercial purpose). Thus, those who are not French must seek assistance from someone who is. Paris voter lists may be consulted in the *Archives de Paris* for 1848 to at least 1976, but there are many gaps before 1900.

Military Records (dossiers militaires)

If possible, first read (in French) a well-done website, PERSO.CLUB-INTERNET.FR/parbelle/serv_hist/shat.htm (note that "parbelle" is case-sensitive).

For the files of an officer, first ask the *Service Historique de l'Armée de Terre* (SHAT).[11] The files of all career military personnel are open to public view only 120 years after the date of birth; the delay is 150 years if any medical information is included. Nevertheless, an exception is generally made for descendants, who are given an abstract of the files including dates and essential events.

For the files of noncommissioned officers and other ranks, it is necessary to know the regiment, even in modern times. For that, and also for other information, one may consult at the Departmental Archives, in series R, recruitment registers (*registres matricules du recrutement)* from 1867 (since 1859 for Paris). They include annual indexes and indicate changes of address, but since these registers also contain medical information, they are made available only to direct descendants. The files of those given military decorations, such as the

Legion of Honor, the *médaille militaire* or the *médaille de Sainte-Hélène,* are also rich sources of genealogical information. In principle, they are found at the CARAN.

The CGJ library has an out-of-print book, *Les Israélites dans l'Armée Française.*[12] Note that at the CARAN, in the microfilm room open to the public, is a copy of the card index of all those who died for France during World War I: soldiers and noncommissioned officers (number 323 Mi and following), officers (number 331 Mi and following). Included are their dates and places of birth and death.

Additional Sources or Methods

Some additional sources are useful especially for collateral genealogy; among these are various collections of notifications (e.g., of marriage or death). The *Bibliothèque Généalogique** (Genealogical Library) has several hundreds of thousands of these notifications, arranged alphabetically.[13] They also can often be found in departmental archives, usually in series J.

When a family name is not too common, the Minitel, the electronic telephone directory, can give the addresses and telephone numbers of possible cousins, although the names of at least 10 percent of the subscribers are unpublished. Minitel may be accessed from overseas at WWW.PAGESBLANCHES.FR (the database of *France-Telecom*, the official French telephone agency): Indicate the last name and the number of a department. It is unnecessary to indicate the locality or even a given name except in the case of a family name that is very common. The search is done by department or *région*. For example, Paris proper is 75; for Paris and its region, type *ile de france* or *idf*. Alsace is 67 and 68; the Moselle is 57; Lyon is 69; Marseille, 13 and Nice is 06.

In fact, one can quickly research all of France by using WWW.INFOBEL.COM/: choose *France, white pages*, enter the last name, keep blank the box *where,* then *find.* The addresses shown are sometimes approximate, but the numbers of the departments are given by the first two digits of the postal code, so you can check the address as indicated above. If there are too many hits, you can choose *Extended search* and enter the first name.

For Paris and even for all of France, it is often useful to consult old telephone directories to determine, for example, the year of death or the year that a household moved. These books have existed since 1883. For Paris, most of them may be consulted at the *Bibliothèque Historique.** For all of France, they may be found at the *Bibliotheque Nationale de France** (BNF). But remember that until at least 1980 they indicate only initials of given names. One can also use the Bottin directory (*annuaire Bottin*), which can be found among others at the Paris Administrative Library,* at the *Archives de Paris** and at the BNF (the most complete collection). Formerly limited to merchants, artisans and industrialists of Paris, this directory progressively included professional people, magistrates, civil servants and others, and later covered all of France. As for the *Bottin Mondain* and other directories that one can find in the same places as the *annuaire Bottin,* they concern only celebrities and notables, but often supply biographical information.

Note an additional feature about the following sources already discussed above: Extracts of birth certificates less than 100 years old, without the names of the parents, are available to anyone. Generally, it is sufficient to indicate in the request the date with a span of a few years, but you may need to wait a few weeks, or even to repeat the request. From 1897 onwards, they can reveal the marriage of a distant cousin whose married name is not known. On a death certificate, one can sometimes read the date and place of death of the spouse.

It is also possible, of course, to engage the services of a professional genealogist, especially for research in Paris. Several may be found on the websites WWW.CGPRO.ORG or WWW.CSGHF.ORG. Click on *Annuaire*, do not choose a name followed by *succ* (inheritance), then search the e-mail address on Google.

Specifically Jewish Sources
Consistories and Their Archives
By a decree of March 15, 1808, Napoleon officially recognized the Jewish religion. Rabbis were not paid salaries by the state at that time (although they were after 1831 and until the official separation of church and state in 1905). The decree provided, under the tutelage of a Central Consistory in Paris, a consistory (an assembly of elected rabbis and laymen) in each department that had at least 2,000 Jews, or a district consistory corresponding to a cluster of at least 2,000 Jews living in several departments. The members of each consistory were elected by 25 leading citizens. Between 1808 and 1831, the expenses of the religion were covered by the Jews within each district; the registers for the apportionment of taxes were set each year by the consistory.

These tax lists have genealogical value; they included for the heads of families—and sometimes for each member of the family—the family name, given name, age and place of birth, occupation and, for the men, their assets. The tax lists that have survived are kept in the various departmental archives in series V of the ministry of religion.

The consistory controls the religious life of the community. In the departments annexed by Germany between 1871 and 1919, the pre-annexation laws applicable to religions in France remained in full force when this region was returned to France, because the law of 1905 that mandated the separation of church and state had been instituted at a time when Alsace-Lorraine (Bas-Rhin, Haut-Rhin and Moselle) were not part of France. Thus, the Jewish structure there was (and still is) supported by the state, which pays the rabbis' salaries and ensures the maintenance of Jewish religious property and records. The Jewish cemeteries are the property of the departmental consistories; the consistory archives are deposited in the departmental archives.

Because of limited space, those who wish to access the archives of the Consistoire of Paris* or of the Central Consistory* must make an appointment with the director or send questions in writing.[14]

Consistory archives offer less information than the civil vital records, but the archives of the Consistory of Paris and the Paris region (in the 19th century, Fontainebleau, Orléans

and Rouen belonged to this consistory), which began in 1809, hold various lists of names (e.g. consistory electors, pupils, teachers, community employees and others).

The registers of religious marriages (series GG) have been kept since 1822. They are arranged by synagogue, with indexes (between 1887 and 1903, and after 1913) arranged alphabetically according to the first letter of the last name of the bride and of the groom. Although the parents, unfortunately, are not recorded, it is possible to discover in these records traces of marriages celebrated in Paris from 1822 to 1860, the civil records of which were lost in the Commune fire of 1871. Until 1872, the records provide only family names, given names (sometimes lacking), usually the addresses, and class of ceremony (i.e., how sumptuous). After 1872, the dates and places of birth are most often indicated. Anne Lifshitz-Krams has compiled an index of the religious marriages celebrated between 1848 and 1872.[15]

From 1877 onwards, several synagogues functioned in Paris. The most prestigious marriages were performed by the chief rabbi of France in the synagogue in rue de la Victoire. The synagogue in rue des Tournelles was mostly used by Eastern European immigrants; thus, the names and places of birth are often imprecise and/or incorrectly spelled.

Religious death registers (series NN) have been preserved since 1880. They indicate last name, maiden and married name for married women (sometimes with the notation " wife of" or "widow of"), given name (but not always), age, address, name of the cemetery, sometimes location of the grave and class of ceremony. For a century, *brit milah* (ritual circumcision) has been a private matter. In principle, the *consistories* do not have knowledge of births.

The *Consistoire de Paris* has records of three censuses: The first, for 1809–10, lists 2,914 Jews in Paris, grouped by family with name, date and place of birth, address, occupation of the head of the family, date of arrival in Paris and remarks. A census taken in 1852 is limited to the heads of families. The best-known census, taken in 1872 after the fire in the city hall set by the revolutionary Commune, lists by *arrondissement* some 23,000 Jews attached to the *Consistoire*. The following information is given for the head of the family: last name, first name, occupation, year of birth (or age) and place of birth; for his wife: given name and, sometimes, number (and gender) of minor children—without given names or ages, except in the 11th *arrondissement*; and address. The lists for each *arrondissement* are alphabetical by first letter of the last name. Unfortunately, experience has shown that the information in these lists is often only approximate—if not false.

Cemeteries
Cemetery research can be very helpful in tracing collateral genealogy, especially in those localities that are small enough not to have too many cemeteries. It is possible, however, to find the right cemetery if one knows the city, the name of the deceased and the date of death by sending this information, plus an SASE to the *Service des cimetières** (cemeteries department). Expect to wait several months, but usually you will receive the name of the cemetery.

For deaths more than 100 years ago, if you know the location but not the date, it is more practical to consult the civil 10-year death indexes. If the ancestral town has a Jewish cemetery (and there are many, especially in Alsace and in Lorraine), however, a visit is in order.

The 10-year indexes cannot be used for deaths less than 100 years ago, and although anybody can obtain a copy of the record, you run the risk of not getting it if you ask the town hall of a city without knowing the exact date of death. The discovery of the tombstone can then prove useful, even if there is no Jewish cemetery.

In Paris, several burial records have been computerized—among others, those of Bagneux and Pantin. The following cemeteries include areas for Jewish burials: Montparnasse, Montmartre, Passy, Père-Lachaise and also some that are outside of Paris proper but are called Parisian cemeteries (*cimetières parisiens*). When you look for one of these (in Bagneux[16], Pantin[17] or Thiais[18]), it is important to specify with this degree of precision so as not to risk being sent to the community cemetery.

No official Jewish divisions have existed for several years, however, and recent Jewish graves are mixed in among the others. This is true even in the old plots when a space becomes free—except in the numerous perpetual allotments which nevertheless are taken back by the municipal government if the grave is no longer properly maintained.

If the registers are computerized, and if one can be sure of the spelling written on the act, one can obtain instantly in person (but not generally by mail) at the cemetery office, the location of the grave, date of burial and the *arrondissement* where the individual died, all of which will facilitate an eventual search for the death certificate.

For inscriptions on old gravestones (those before the middle of the 19th century), it usually is necessary to decipher Hebrew characters and to know some of the formulas and abbreviations generally used.

Memorial to the Jews Deported from France

One can find in this book by Serge Klarsfeld the names, nationalities, and usually dates and places of birth of about 80,000 Jews (approximately one-fourth of the Jewish population of France in that period) who were deported from France between 1942 and 1944.[19] Most were foreigners or naturalized (many Jews had fled to France to escape Nazi tyranny, were later interned as enemy aliens, and still later by the Germans, as Jews). The book contains some errors, which is unavoidable in such a work. A microfiche sold by Avotaynu indicates the numbers of all the convoys where a given surname appears, which then allows a quick search of the book. It is easier, however, to use the CD-ROM, *L'Histoire de la Shoah*, which may be ordered from the *Centre de Documentation Juive Contemporaine* (CDJC). On the CD, just click on *La France et la Shoah*, then *Les déportés*, then type the surname (*nom*), enter, etc. You can also sort the deportees, for instance, by their date or place of birth. The CD-ROM also includes considerable information (in French) about the Shoah.[20] See also the websites www.

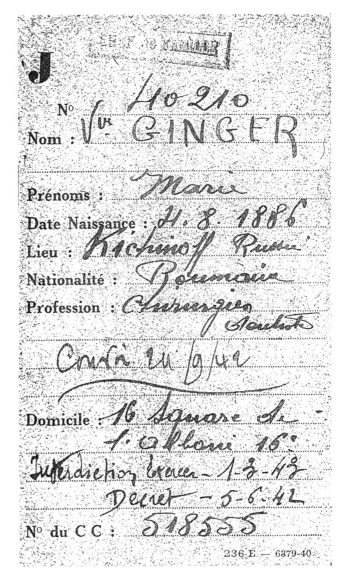

A card created by the French government ordering the arrest of a Jew, Marie Ginger, during World War II on the orders of the German occupation forces. Copies of these documents are on microfilm at CARAN.

JEWISHGEN.ORG/INFOFILES/FR-KLARS.TXT and WWW.MEMORIAL-CDJC.ORG/INDEX_EN.HTM.

Deportations from France during World War II

On the website DANIEL.CAROUGE.DE-FRANCE.ORG one can find a list of persons, Jews and non-Jews who died in the concentration camps. To date it comprises only about 30,000 people out of an estimated total of about 80,000 Jews and some tens of thousands of non-Jews. This alphabetical list has been compiled by Daniel Carouge from the French *Journal Officiel* issues from 1991 to 2001. For Jews, one can see from this list that, more than once, the information found in the *Memorial* was completed and probably corrected, especially for date and place of birth.

Note that French Jews (and even many non-Jews, such as the daily paper *Le Monde*) generally do not use the term "Holocaust" (which literally in ancient Greece meant "entirely

Birth registry of the Jews of Metz for 1728

burned" in a religious sacrifice of an animal); what happened to European Jewry during World War II was not a sacrifice. *Shoah* is the Hebrew word for catastrophe.

Records of Arrested Jews (le Fichier des Juifs arrêtés)

Much discussion has taken place about the true meaning of this record, discovered in 1991 by Serge Klarsfeld among the files of the War Veterans Ministry. Created on cards between 1941 and 1944, it lists the names of tens of thousands of Jews who were arrested, usually by the French police, on the orders of the German occupiers. Most of them (but not all) were later deported and can also be found in Klarsfeld's book or the associated CD-ROM. For them, one may find here some additional data: date of arrest, maiden name, occupation, exact address at the time of their arrest. This file may be consulted on microfilm at the CARAN or a copy pertaining to a given person may be requested for free by mail.

Other Jewish Sources

One must mention the following important sources:

- Jewish genealogical societies in France,
- *Cercle de Généalogie Juive* (CGJ)* WWW.GENEALOJ.ORG, e-mail: OFFICE@GENEALOJ.ORG
- GenAmi* HTTP://ASSO.GENAMI.FREE.FR, e-mail: ASSO.GENAMI@ FREE.FR
- ETSI,* focusing on Sephardi genealogy, WWW.GEOCITIES.COM/ EnchantedForest/1321 (note that "EnchantedForest" is case-sensitive), e-mail: LAURPHIL@WANADOO.FR

In addition, a researcher can fruitfully use three Jewish libraries in Paris; the first two are not specifically oriented toward genealogy:

- Library of the *Alliance Israélite Universelle, 45 rue La Bruyère, 75009 Paris*, telephone: (0)1-533-288-55, website: WWW.AIU.ORG/BIBLIO/PRESENTATION/INDEX.HTML; e-mail: BIBLIO@ AIU.ORG. Jewish periodicals, mostly published in France; and Jewish encyclopedias and books.
- *Medem* library, *18 passage Saint-Pierre Amelot, 75010 Paris*, telephone: (0)1 470-014-00; website: WWW.YIDDISHWEB. COM/medem (note that "medem" is case-sensitive); e-mail: MEDEM@YIDDISHWEB.COM. This library has Europe's largest collection of Yiddish books.
- Library of the *Cercle de Généalogie Juive* (CGJ), housed in the *Bibliothèque Généalogique* (Genealogical Library), but the use of this collection is normally limited to CGJ members; others need specific authorization.

Alsace

The Thirty Years War (1618–48) ravaged Alsatian lands; the province lost almost half of its population and most of its Jewish communities were annihilated. The Treaty of Westphalia put Alsace under French rule, but the feudal structure was maintained, and each local lord decided for himself whether or not to welcome Jews into his realm. About 3,000 Jews were counted in Alsace in 1689; by 1784, the number was greater than 20,000.

This impressive growth came partly from a high birth rate (not limited only to Jews), but family names reveal that the increase can be attributed also to substantial immigration from such German-speaking lands as Bavaria, the Palatinate, the Rhineland and Swabia.

On the eve of the French Revolution, Alsatian Jewry was the largest Jewish community in France: 23,000 persons of a total of approximately 40,000 individuals. Acquisition of French citizenship in 1791 stimulated an evolution: the Jewish communities continued to grow, but the urban ones developed more rapidly than the rural, as citizenship allowed Jews to move to cities if they wished, a choice that had not been freely available before. By the middle of the 19th century, most rural communities had begun to disappear.

In 1871, at the time of German annexation, Alsace had about 34,000 Jews, but almost 10,000 of them chose to live in France, where they reinforced existing communities such as Paris, and also created new ones in Besançon, Dijon, Elbeuf and Lille. In 1910, only about 23,000 Jews remained in Alsace.

DÉNOMBREMENT GÉNÉRAL DES JUIFS,

Qui font tolérés en la Province d'Alface, en exécution des Lettres-Patentes de Sa Majefté, en forme de Règlement, du 10 Juillet 1784.

LIEUX qu'ils habitoient à la fin de l'année 1784. par N.os & ordre alphabétique.	NOMBRE des Familles.	QUALITÉS.	NOMS DES INDIVIDUS.		TOTAUX des Individus.
1. ARTZHEIM. *Etat du 21 Décembre 1784.*	Unique.	Chef, Femme, Mère, Fils, Filles, Valet, Servante,	Abraham. Schönel. Breinel. Abraham. Malgen Johanna Baden Joseph. Jachet.	} Abraham.	9
2. AVENHEIM. *Etat du 15 Novembre 1784.*	Unique.	Chef, Femme, Fils,	Hirtzel Dreyfus. Mümel. Jegel Dreyfus.	}	3
3. BALBRONN. *Etat du 14 Février 1785.*	1.ere	Chef, Femme, Valets, Servantes,	Samuel Levy. Efther Bloch. Sander. Meyer. Rella. Hanna.	}	6
	2.de	Chef, Femme, Fils, Filles, Servantes,	Macholen Levy. Mariani Baruch. Kotfchel Männel Lippmann Schielen Heya Guttel Ella Hanna Heya Coffa.	} Levy.	10
	3.	Chef, Femme,	Jacob Gotfcher. Barrar Levy.	}	2
	4.e	Chef, Femme, Fils, Fille, Précepteur, Servante,	Baruch Levy. Honna Macholen. Salomon Raphael Schielen Leyfer Jacob Barras Löw David. Sara.	} Levy.	10
	5.e	Chef, Femme, Fils, Filles,	Löw Jofeph. Schönel Abraham. Jofeph Abraham Hirfch Simon Wolff Jüttel Zürla	} Jofeph.	7
			A		35

First page of the census of 1784 of the Jews of Alsace

Formerly cattle merchants and peddlers, the Jews were now merchants, industrialists, doctors and lawyers. Judeo-Alsatian, which had been the community's language for six centuries, was slowly being abandoned by the young people.

The dark years of 1940–45 completed the evolution. Today, most of the rural communities are extinct; all that exists are some unused synagogues and cemeteries, and one can be assured of a regular *minyan* only in Colmar, Haguenau, Mulhouse or Strasbourg.

Family and Given Names[21]

Until the beginning of the 19th century, the Jews preserved their ancestral naming habit: a baby received a given name followed by the given name of his or her father, and sometimes a nickname. Gradually, this nickname, or sometimes the father's name, became transferable from father to son, and thus took the appearance of a patronymic. But not until 1808 did the *Decree of Bayonne* impose on the Jews the obligation to adopt fixed, inherited surnames.

In the meantime, however, the 1784 Census of the Jews of Alsace (see below) showed that more than half of the Jews had stable surnames that could be considered as patronymics (but with certain caution). Among these pseudo-patronymics, the Lévys and the Kahns constituted 17 percent of the total families; 13 percent carried the names Bloch, Dreyfus and Weil (with every imaginable orthographic variation). Among the other relatively frequent names were Bernheim, Blum, Brunschwig, Frank, Gougenheim, Moch, Nettter and Schwob in Lower Alsace (the present *département du Bas-Rhin*). Common in Upper Alsace (*Haut-Rhin*) were Geismar, Greilsamer, Grotwohl, Haas, Haguenauer, Kintzburger, Nortemann, Spira, Ulmann and Wormser.

Many of these surnames are toponymical, linking the families to origins more or less distant. One finds German localities such as Braunschweig, Guntzburg, Spire, Ulm and Worms, or a reference to a region or district: Bloch, derived from *Welsh*, is associated with Romance-language countries, Frank with France or with German Franconia, Schwob with Swabia and, by extension, with all of southern Germany.

For the families whose surname was not yet stabilized, the custom was for the son to add his father's given name. Thus, the son of Wolff Isaac (who was Wolf, son of Isaac) carried the name of Moyses Wolff, that is, Moyses, son of Wolff. But since the town hall's clerks did not always know the Jewish naming custom, another son of the same family might be recorded as Jonas Isaac and not as Jonas Wolff.

As a general rule, in most of the families where a surname had been transformed into a pseudo-patronymic, the latter was kept as the family name after the Decree of Bayonne was enforced. An exception to this rule were some of the very common patronymics such as Lévy. Thus, in Hégenheim which had more than 30 Lévy families, some of them adopted the following surnames: Barth, Bluem, Blum, Lauff, Leo, Levaillant, Lewall, Leweil, Leyman, Wolff. These choices, however, were not always final: one often finds in civil registers from the first half of the 19th century a return to the old nickname, or to the given name of the father.

The animals, to which the patriarch Jacob on his death bed compared his sons, were the source of several patronymics: Naphtali, compared to a deer, became Cerf or Hirsch, with all the variations imaginable, Hersch, Hirtz, Hertz, Hirtzel, Herschel and even Zvi and Ziwy (deer in Hebrew). Judah, compared to a lion (Loeb in German and Leib or Leibel in Judeo-Alsatian) became Lehmann, Leo, Léon, Leopold, Lion, Loeb, Loewel or Leype. Benjamin, compared to a wolf, became Wolf, and as a given name, Wolfgang and Louis. The Issachars often became Baer, although Jacob did not compare his son to a bear but to a donkey; in turn, Baer became Ber, Behr, Bermann, Bernhard, Bernard or Berr.

Lastly, it is not necessary to attach much importance to the spelling. This often depended simply on the town hall clerk's knowledge of German and French, as well as on the pronunciation in Judeo-Alsatian. Thus, some Levys became Lefi, Lefy, Levis, Levi, Lewi and Lewies; Kahn became Caen, Cahen, Cohen, Caim, Cain, Kan, or even Kannweiller or Katz, an acronym of Cahen Tzedek (righteous priest).

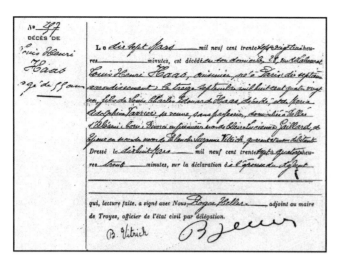

Death certificate includes date of birth, occupation, names of parents, names of first spouse and last spouse and name of informant (spouse).

As for the choice of given names: the imagination of the Alsatian Jews—as well as their fondness for puns and plays on words—was given free rein, resulting in the addition of diminutive suffixes, variations in pronunciation, transcriptions of typical Jewish given names into de-judaized given names, translations and equivalences, sometimes erroneously (for example, the Biblical given name Uri, which evokes the idea of light, became Phoebus, Greek epithet for Apollo, the god of light, or Fabius, and then, in Yiddish, Feisel, Feist, Feit or Veit, in French Felix or Philippe, all this being the consequence of a false etymology).[22] The same was true of female given names where they generally took care to preserve the initials—embroidered as monograms on pieces of their trousseaus.

For all these reasons, a researcher must be very careful about using "lists of correspondence" between old and new given names. A Blümel could have become either Blanche (to conserve the initials) or Fleur or Florette (the French translation of the name), or Rose or Rosette (to preserve the floral image).

Census of 1784

The oldest general source of genealogical information about the Jews of this region comes from the *Dénombrement général des Juifs qui sont tolérés en la Province d'Alsace, du 10 juillet 1784* (Census of the Jews permitted to live in the Province of Alsace, of July 10, 1784), ordered by Louis XVI. It can consulted on the website WWW.NGJ.ENS.FR. Choose *Menu de consultation* then *Dénombrement des Juifs d'Alsace de 1784*. The census has been microfilmed by the LDS (Mormon) Family History Library (see LDS).[23] A reissue of the census was made by the CGJ in 1999.[24] An index has been created by Daniel Leeson and constitutes a separate book.[25]

Since the purpose of the census was to limit the number of Jews in Alsace by a restriction on marriages and control of immigration from Germany, many Jews of irregular status sought to avoid being registered. Very often, individuals inscribed as members of the domestic staff were Jews who did

not have proper authorization to settle in the locality; so the presence of domestic staff is not necessarily an indication of a high social position.

Nevertheless, this is a source of inestimable value that records, locality by locality (184 in all), 3,913 families—2,806 from Lower Alsace (Bas-Rhin, and Landau area in the Palatinate, currently in Germany) and 1,107 from Upper Alsace (Haut Rhin). Recorded for each family are the head of the household (who is not necessarily the father of the children, because of remarriages), his wife (who is not necessarily the mother), children, their maids, male servants and tutors. In all, 19,624 individuals from Alsace are included; about 2,000 more are estimated to have escaped registration.

Generally speaking, Jewish genealogical research in Alsace is strewn with obstacles and snares, as Pierre Katz explains below.[26] Katz came to his conclusions after analyzing several hundred name adoption registers.

Traps for Research in Alsace

The amateur Jewish genealogist has at his or her disposal three major sources for researching in Alsace: the 1784 census; the civil registers starting in 1792, where one theoretically finds records of birth, marriage and death; and the registers of name adoption (or more exactly fixation) of 1808. Anyone who has tried this, however, can testify that it is not always easy to identify the same individual in each of these sources.

For example, in the 1784 census of Haguenau, we find a Koppel, son of Leyser Nephtali. In 1808, he should be listed in the register of declarations under the name Koppel Leyser. Actually, he appears as Jacques Hirsch (which he keeps for his new names), butcher. In between, we find him in the civil registers as Koppel Nephtali, Jacques Leyser-even as Jacob Katsef (Katsef is the Hebrew word for butcher) or Jacob Haguenauer, because the family is originally from Haguenau. Sometimes, it is only the signature on a record that allows us to confirm an individual's identity.

Problems of Language

The records of name declarations, as well as the civil registrations, were often drafted in German, and the clerks wrote in Gothic script. To decipher them requires not only knowledge of Gothic handwriting, but equally some mastery of the German language for, after identifying three or four letters, it becomes necessary to imagine what the word might be. In addition, there is the fact that most of the clerks spoke the Alsatian dialect, which possessed neither fixed grammar nor fixed orthography, and its pronunciation varied from locality to locality.

The problem does not vanish even when the forms were written in French, because many clerks had only scant knowledge of the language and recorded names phonetically (with the Alsatian accent understood) using whimsical separations into words. Other phenomena complicate the situation, especially with given names: These include variations in pronunciation; addition of suffixes; "dejudaizing" the names (after 1791–92, the dates of acquisition of French citizenship by Jews and creation of a secular civil state), by translation or by a choice based on similar sounds; and exploitation of biblical history— as we have already seen.

Thus, reconciling these sources requires some knowledge of languages, including Judeo-Alsatian (with its multiple local variants), as well as familiarity with the mentality of Alsatians and rural Alsatian Jews, notably their love for puns and plays on words.

Geographical Problems

The ability to connect individuals across sources also necessitates precise identification of places, because the names and their administrative structures evolved over time. For example, in 1784, Alsace did not include the canton of Sarre-Union. On the other hand, a part of the Palatinate, with some very important Jewish communities around Landau, shows up in the census. These changes of names and of jurisdiction coincided with the transfers of Alsace between France and Germany, (e.g. the French suffixes *le-Haut* and *le-Bas* correspond to Ober and Nieder in German). Thus, Hagenthal-le-Haut and Hagenthal-le-Bas are respectively Oberhagenthal and Niederhagenthal in 1784 (and between 1871 and 1919).

Credibility of Dates

In most 1808 registers, heads of households made name declarations for their minor children, indicating their dates and places of birth. In principle, then, it should be possible to retrieve records of these births from the civil records, if they occurred after 1792, to learn the name of the mother and in this way reconstitute an entire family. In practice, one often finds that the dates of birth indicated in the 1808 registers do not coincide with the civil records, the town hall clerk having entered this information without verifying it with the civil records. This is especially true when the child was born in a different community.

The same problem arises when one tries to find a birth date from ages listed in a death record or from parents' ages listed upon the birth of a child. In fact, to reconstruct families from the 1808 registers, it may be necessary to look at all of the Jewish civil records for a given community between 1792 and 1808 (sometimes, even beyond that); connections can be made only laboriously and painstakingly.

Evolution of the Concept of Civil Status

Behind all of these problems lies another, more profound issue: the concept of civil status and what it represented to the individuals concerned. For us today, the civil status is an intangible entity, that which is recorded is essential—the names, dates, down to the orthography. A person who is not registered does not exist! This modern concept developed slowly; Thus, our concept of the importance of civil records leads us to assume that the act of adopting a name (in 1808) was important to the Jews involved and that they approached it seriously.

Nothing could be further from the truth. For instance, one can find several cases in which the head of the family chose the exact same name for each of his sons and another, single name for each of his daughters: the five Abrahams and

the four Sarahs continued to be called by their Jewish given names, which were completely different.

We see then that Jewish genealogical research in Alsace is strewn with barriers. This is not said to discourage the amateur. In the final analysis, these problems are the spice that gives taste to the genealogical cuisine!

18th-Century Jewish Marriage Contracts

The book *Mémoire juive en Alsace: Contrats de mariage au 18ᵉ siecle* (Alsatian Jewish Memory: Marriage contracts from the 18th century) includes 6,500 Jewish contracts from both Upper and Lower Alsace between 1702 and 1791, researched by André Aaron Fraenckel and Salomon Picard.[27]

Contracts are grouped in alphabetical order by towns and villages served by a notary and chronologically within each grouping. They record the names of the marriage partners, their parents (and sometimes grandparents), witnesses, guarantors, sometimes the rabbi, as well as place of residence of most of the individuals named. The financial arrangements are indicated and, often, the manner in which the assets were acquired. Often Torah and Talmud scrolls were included in the dowries.

Not only is the history of Jewish Alsatian families of the 18th century illuminated, but equally that of the neighboring provinces when one of the couple came from Lorraine, the Palatinate and so forth. Our ancestors used different notaries from their own village or the place where they married, or even neighboring localities. We find, divided between different notaries, therefore, marriage contracts passed down in a single village; the presence of the names of the father, mother, grandparents, of successive partners—all this usually allows us to recover different familial branches.

The researcher's difficult task has been eased by an index of family names prepared by Daniel and Rosanne Leeson and published by the *Cercle de Généalogie Juive*.[28]

Sources by Departments

Numerous sources with lists of Jews have survived.[29] Below is an index of locations for which at least one such source (in addition to the 1784 census and to the book by Fraenckel) is cited, either in the book by Gildas Bernard or in the catalogue of the library of the *Cercle de Généalogie Juive*.[30] With the exception of those marked with the letter M, K or K' they all were created prior to 1792. The letter code indicates the type of source and location where the reference can be consulted:

- M (middle) applies to sources for the years 1792 to 1815 (the end of the period covered by Bernard). These are in addition to the 1808 name adoption lists.
- K (Katz) designates the work of Pierre Katz: the lists of 1808 with regrouping by families.[31]
- K' (Katz) denotes the work of Pierre Katz that gives (with regrouping by families) the names of the individuals who had indicated in the 1851 census for the Bas-Rhin that their religion was "Jewish."[32]
- D (Departmental) refers to one or more sources found in departmental archives of the given departement.

- C (Communal) refers to one or more sources in communal archives of the indicated locality.
- L (Library) indicates that the library of the *Cercle de Généalogie Juive* has at least one document, in addition to name adoption lists (for these lists, one may order photocopies for specific localities). Some sources of D and L may be identical.

Vital records and ten-year indexes of all the Alsatian *communes* (communities, not only those with Jewish population) have been microfilmed by the Mormons, generally from 1792 to 1882.

In what follows, a given department will be referred to by its 2-digit number.

Bas-Rhin (67)

All of the following localities are found at least in K and K', with the exception of Dangolsheim, Dinsheim, Eschbach, Forstheim, Hoelschbloch, Lalaye, Lobsann, Mattstall, Merkwiller and Niederlauterbach and also with the exception of the names followed by (K'), which means that they are not in (K). Most of the original lists of name adoptions have been microfilmed by the Mormons—but without regrouping by families:[33]

Balbronn, Bassemberg (D), Batzendorf (D), Benfeld (K'), Birkenwald, Bischeim (D), Bischoffsheim, Bischwiller (K'), Bitschhoffen, Boesenbiesen, Bolsenheim, Bouxwiller (D), Brumath, Buswiller, Dambach-la-Ville, Dangolsheim (D), Dauendorf (D), Dehlingen, Dettwiller (D), Diebolsheim, Diemeringen, Dinsheim (D), Dossenheim-sur-Zinsel (D), Drachenbronn, Duppigheim, Duttlenheim (D), Eckwersheim, Epfig, Erstein (K'), Eschbach (D), Ettendorf (D), Fegersheim, Forstheim (D), Fouchy (D), Froeschwiller, Gerstheim, Goetsdorf, Gundershoffen, Gunstett (D), Haegen, Haguenau (D,C), Harskirchen, Hatten, Herrlisheim (D,L), Hochfelden, Hoelschbloch (D), Hoenheim, Illkirch-Graffenstaden (K'), Ingenheim (D), Ingwiller (D), Itterswiller (D), Krautergersheim, Kuttolsheim, Kutzenhausen (D), Lalaye (D), Langensoultzbach, Lauterbourg (D,L), Lembach, Lichtenberg (D), Lingolsheim (D,K', L), Lobsann (D), Mackenheim, Marckolsheim, Marmoutier (D), Mattstall (D), Matzenheim, Merkwiller (D), Mertzwiller, Minversheim, Mittelhausen, Mommenheim, Mulhausen, Muttersholtz, Mutzig (D), Neuwiller-lès-Saverne (D), Niederbronn, Niederlauterbach (D), Niedernai, Niederroedern, Niederseebach, Oberbronn, Oberlauterbach, Obernai(D), Oberschaeffolsheim, Odratzheim, Offendorf (D,L), Offwiller (D), Osthoffen, Osthouse, Ottrott, Pfaffenhoffen (D), Plobsheim (K'), Quatzenheim, Reichshoffen (D), Riedseltz, Ringendorf, Romanswiller, Rosenwiller (L), Rosheim (C,L), Rothbach, Sarre-Union (D,L), Saverne (D), Schaffhouse-sur-Zorn, Scharrachbergheim, Scherwiller, Schirrhoffen, Schleithal (K'), Schweighouse (K'), Schwenheim, Schwindratzheim (D), Seebach (K'), Sélestat, Soultz-sous-Forêts, Stotzheim, Strasbourg (D), Struth (D), Surbourg (D), Tieffenbach, Traenheim (K'), Trimbach, Uhlwiller (D), Uhrwiller, Uttenheim, Valff, Villé (K'), la Walck, Waltenheim, Weinbourg, Weiterswiller, Westhoffen, Westhouse (L), Wingersheim (D), Wintzenheim-Kochersberg (D), Wissembourg (D), Wittersheim (K'), Wolfisheim, Zellwiller, Zinswiller.

In (L), are some documents that refer to several localities, for example "*Etat de tous les Juifs des territoires de la Noblesse Immédiate de Basse-Alsace en 1725.*" (A list of all the Jewish heads of households in the territories of the nobility of Lower Alsace in 1725), 360 families.

Haut-Rhin (68) and the Territory of Belfort (90)

The *Territoire de Belfort* is a small department composed of the portion of the Haut-Rhin that was not annexed (with the rest of Alsace) by the Germans in 1871. Today this department belongs to Franche-Comté and not to Alsace.

Upon request by e-mail, the *Centre Départemental d'Histoire des Familles*[*] (the departmental Family History Center—CDHF) will do simple research in the records of Haut-Rhin for a modest fee. See the details on its website WWW.CDHF.NET/FR. On the French page click *services*. Despite the similarity in names, this center is not connected with the Mormons. Several original lists of name adoptions have been microfilmed by the Mormons—but without regrouping names into families. This approach may be more fruitful than using Mormon microfilms, especially for the years 1883 to 1902 for which the Mormons have not done any filming.

Blotzheim (D,D90), Bollwiller (DA,DM,L), Buschwiller (D90), Cernay (D), Colmar (D), Dornach, Durmenach (D,L), Folgensbourg (DM), Foussemagne (D,D90), Froeningen (D,L), Grussenheim (L), Guebwiller (D67), Habsheim (L), Hagenbach (C), Hagenthal-le-Bas (D90,L), Hagenthal-le-Haut (D90,L), Hartmannswiller, Hattstatt (L), Hegenheim (L), Herrlisheim-près-Colmar (DM), Hirsingue (D), Horbourg (D,L), Ingersheim (L), Issenheim (D,DM), Jungholtz (D,L), Kembs (D), Luemschwiller (D,L), Mulhouse, Murbach (L), Oberdorf (D,L), Pfastatt, Réguisheim (L), Ribeauvillé (D,L,LM), Riedwihr (D,DM), Rimbach (D), Rixheim (D,L), Seppois-le-Bas (D), Sierentz (D), Soultz-Haut-Rhin (L,DM), Soultzmatt, Steinbrunn-le-Haut (D), Thann (D), Turckheim (D,LM), Uffheim (D), Uffholtz (D,D67,L,LM), Voegtlinshoffen (DM), Wattwiller (D,D67), Wettolsheim (D), Wintzenheim, Wittenheim (D), Zimmersheim (D,DM), and Zillisheim (D,LM).

Some documents that concern a number of different communities are found in L. An example is a booklet by Dr. Peter Stein.[34]

Another Source

After the peace treaty of May 10, 1871, those who formerly lived in Alsace-Lorraine (the areas of Alsace and Lorraine ceded to the Germans) and who had left that region, were permitted, until October 1, 1872, to declare to the mayor of their new community of residence that they wanted to remain French citizens. Among the approximately 100,000 who made this declaration (*déclaration d'option*) were an estimated 15,000 Jews.

The great practical value of this source is its centralization: All of these dossiers have been kept at CARAN,[*] the French national archives in Paris. A card index, kept in strict alphabetical order, has been microfilmed and constitutes 87 reels of microfilm (numbered 226 to 312). These reels may be used by the researcher in the *Salle des Inventaires* (Inventory Room).

All of the information which has been published in the *Bulletin des Lois* (Bulletin of Laws) appears on the microfilms, that is, family name (maiden name for married women and widows), given names, married name for widows and married women, date and place of birth, community of residence at the time of this declaration (thus, outside of the ceded territory), date of the declaration of opting for French citizenship. We may also find additional observations such as "widow" or "assisted by the husband."

Before 1922, the dates and, above all, the places of birth of parents were usually not recorded on birth certificates. In such a case, one can often find them on the microfilms of the options. In addition, the names, dates and places of birth of minor children are particularly valuable information for extending one's genealogy to collateral relatives.

Internet Sources

Researchers can put questions, in French or in English, on the CGJ site, www.genealoj.org under the heading *questions and answers*. The answers generally will be written in French. Another website, *Généalogie (juive) alsacienne* (Alsatian Jewish genealogy), provides considerable information about Alsace and can be accessed easily via the CGJ home page. Its heading *Petites annonces* (small announcements) currently is not very active, but one should try it. For the Bas-Rhin, one can find on the website of the *Cercle Généalogique d'Alsace* (Alsatian Genealogical Society, not specifically Jewish), www.alsace-genealogie.com, how to order a copy or a translation of a vital record more than 100 years old. This may be more interesting than utilizing the Mormon microfilms, especially for the years 1883 to 1902.

Some Details About Alsatian Civil Records

This paragraph uses information taken from the *Guide des recherches généalogiques en Alsace* (Guide to Genealogical Research in Alsace), by Christian Wolff, a book out of print; its essential information is given here.[35]

Up to 1810, registers often are written in German, except in cities; those created between 1871 and 1918 are always in German (in Gothic handwriting). Until 1920, they do not have the margin notes, introduced in France in 1897. On the other hand, from 1876 until 1918, these records include religion.

German was the official language between 1879 and 1918, but the use of French was forbidden only between 1914 and 1918 (and, naturally, between June 1940 and November 1944). In Alsace, more systematically than in the rest of the country, notarial archives more than 100 years old (and often less than that) have been deposited in the departmental archives, since German law mandated this.

Lorraine

After a brilliant presence from the Early Middle Ages until the 13th century, when they were expelled from Metz, Jews reappeared in Lorraine in the middle of the 16th century.

After the conquest of the Three Bishoprics of Metz, Toul, and Verdun by French forces in 1552, four Jewish families obtained permission to settle in Metz in 1567. Because Jews furnished necessary provisions for the army garrison, especially the cavalry, this facilitated a steady increase in their numbers; by 1595, 20 Jewish families officially organized themselves into a community.

The Jewish population of Metz numbered an estimated 2,200 in 1789, which made it the second largest Jewish community in France (after that of Bordeaux).

From looking at their surnames (see below), it seems that the majority of families appeared to have come originally from the German Rhineland. The country around Metz furnished an important segment of the new population as well, and some Alsatian family names also appear. The great rabbis of Metz were always called from foreign countries (e.g. Poland and Bohemia), so that no one could impugn the impartiality of their judgments.[36] Their prestige was considerable in the world of Ashkenazi Jewry, but most members of the community were quite poor and encased in a classical range of occupations: dealing in money, grain, horses, cattle and second-hand goods.

The wars of the 17th century favored the settlement of Jews in the countryside around Metz, where they were in the majority in the villages. In fortified areas such as Thionville, Sarrelouis, Sierck, Phalsbourg and Sarrebourg, their numbers were limited to one or two families.

The Duchy of Lorraine was nominally independent, but in fact it was occupied by France from 1633 to 1697 and remained under French influence until the official return of Lorraine to France in 1766. In 1721, recently settled Jews were expelled and only 73 officially tolerated families remained, scattered among 24 localities, most of them in "German" Lorraine.

Family and Given Names[37]

The family names of the Jews of Lorraine often were nicknames. They generally indicated the place where the family had lived in the more or less recent past. These surnames of origin tended to be hereditary, but sometimes they were lost after several generations. Some names referred to a country, such as Polacque or Polacke (meaning from Poland) or Franck which might indicate that the family originally came from Western Europe (France) and had lived several generations in Slavic countries before moving back to Alsace or Lorraine. Some referred to a province such as Swabia, including the names Chouabe, Chevaube, Schwab, Schwaube or Job. Most frequently, the names referred to a locality, including cities in Germany such as Bonn, Coblenz or Frankfurt or localities in Lorraine (essentially in the countryside around Metz), such as Altroff or d'Altroff, Augny, Boulay and Créange. Naturally, we also find religious names such as Cahen or Caen and Lévy.

When the decree of Bayonne mandated the adoption of family names, the Jews of Lorraine generally took their hereditary surname or, by default, the given name of their fathers. Sometimes they transformed into a family name the given name associated with their religious name, as is explained in the section devoted to Alsace, for instance, Cerf (Naphtali) and Lion

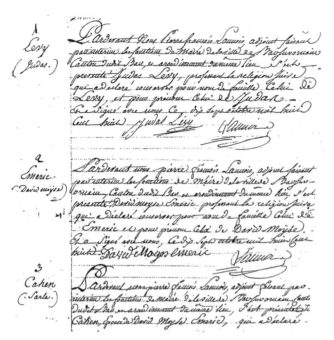

First page of the register of name adoptions in 1808 for the Jews of Bar-sur-Ornain (now Bar-le-Duc) in Lorraine

(Judah) became surnames. Jews adopted these French surnames even in the German-speaking part of Lorraine.

Given names peculiar to Lorraine include: Baroukh which became Boris, or, by translation from the Hebrew, Bénédict, Bendit or Benoît; Gershom became Garçon; Elhanan became Alcan; Mordekhaï (Mardochée) is Marc or Marque (Marx in Alsace); Jonas and Yohanan are Lajeunesse; Menahem is Mendel, Manuel or Michel; Meïr became Mayer or Meyer. Many of these given names were adopted as family names in 1808. In a general way, more in Lorraine than in Alsace, given names (both masculine and feminine) are more or less French.

Old Genealogical Sources: Introduction

Metz[38]

Uneasy about the growth of the Metz Jewish community, the French authorities in 1717 imposed vital statistics registration (in French) on its *syndics* (Jews elected in a large community to be in charge of some administrative tasks). Although the first records date from that year, they were not kept regularly until after 1720. The system remained the same until 1792 when secular registration was instituted. The absence of indexes makes use of these early registers difficult; except in the final years, events are recorded in chronological order, without separation for births, marriages and deaths. It especially is not easy to differentiate between innumerable individuals all named Salomon Cohen or Abraham Lévy. Pierre-André Meyer has done much to fill these omissions. Using a method developed by demographers, Meyer has reconstituted whole families from the registers[39].

Other genealogical sources for Metz include many Hebrew-language manuscript *memorbücher*, books created to remember the deceased. A single book has survived in France. Its trans-

lation into French by Simon Schwarzfuchs was published in Metz in 1971. It includes 865 death notices for the years 1576 to 1724 and is deposited at the municipal archives of Metz. An additional *memorbuch* may be found in the New York Jewish Theological Seminary:[*] 1,217 death notices for the period 1720 to 1849, for which a microfilmed copy has been deposited at the library of the *Alliance Israélite universelle* in Paris.[*] A list of names of individuals covering the entire period 1721–89, prepared by Jean-Claude Bouvat-Martin, has been published by the Cercle de Généalogie Juive.[40]

Memorbücher, however, are not a substitute for vital records. In the book that has been translated into French, for example, many items list an individual only by a given name followed by the name of his or her father. Family names often are not recorded.

Marriage contracts are documents of immense value not only for genealogists but also for social, economic and cultural historians. In general, the Departmental Archives has collections that go back to 1713. One work by Jean Fleury which supplies considerable valuable information for genealogists, was taken from 2,021 marriage contracts created between 1693 and 1792 in the territory that is currently the Department of the Moselle.[41]

Many other lists of names exist, including censuses, assessment books, voter registration lists for the Jewish community—but until 1802 these lists only indicate the heads of the families. Several lists are kept at the New York Jewish Theological Seminary.

Documents created for lawsuits and petitions also have survived. A list of these documents for the years 1595 to 1796 with numerous and diverse names may be found in a work by Zosa Szajkowski.[42]

Countryside Around Metz

In addition to the work on marriage records by Jean Fleury, we should note the 1702 fiscal census of Saint-Contest and other analogous lists, as well as numerous extracts from the assessment lists of the *taxe Brancas*, a special tax for Jews created in 1718. Copies of many of these documents may be found in the library of the Cercle de Généalogie Juive.[*]

Duchy of Lorraine

Among other documents are three lists of families with residency permission, dated 1705, 1721 (73 families in 24 localities), and 1753 (180 families in 52 localities of the former States of Lorraine and Barrois, including Nancy and Lunéville). Copies of these lists are deposited in the CGJ library.

Old Sources by Departments

Numerous lists of specifically Jewish names have survived. The following is an index of localities for which at least one list of names is cited either in *Les famillles juives en France* by Bernard or in the catalog of the library of the CGJ. The departments are listed by number. Thus, the archives of department 57, for example, is designated as (D57).

In the lists that follow, works already indicated in the notes are not repeated. (L) designates the CGJ library, (LE) designates a copy, on deposit in the CGJ library, of the *Etat (liste) général des 180 familles tolérées en Lorraine et Barrois*. Among the relatively recent books that include lists of names are monographs by Françoise Job, Jean-Pierre Bernard, Jean-Louis Calbat and Jean Daltroff.[43] As with Alsace, works designated (K) are the 1808 name adoptions with groupings by families done by Pierre Katz for the Moselle and the Meurthe-et-Moselle.[44]

The civil registers and 10-year indexes have been microfilmed by the Mormons for the civil parishes in Lorraine until the following dates, different for each department: 1875 for department number 54, 1882 for number 55, 1872 and sometimes 1892 for number 57 and number 88.

Meurthe-et-Moselle (54)

All of the following localities are found at least in (K), with the exception of Essey-lès-Nancy, Lay-Saint-Christophe, Longwy, Malzéville and Rosières:

Azerailles, Baccarat, Blâmont, Blénod-lès-Toul, Bulligny, Choloy, Cirey-sur-Vezouze, Domgermain, Einville, Essey-lès-Nancy (LE), Foug (LE, D57), Herbéviller, Lay-Saint-Christophe (LE), Longwy (D75M), Lunéville (LE, D57), Maizières (LE), Malzéville (LE), Moncel, Nancy (C, LE, D57), Parroy, Pont-à-Mousson (D57), Rosières (DM), Thiaucourt, Tomblaine and Toul.

Some name adoption records (not grouped by families) have been microfilmed by the Mormons.[45]

Meuse (55) Only Bar-le-Duc (ex-Bar-sur-Ornain) and Vaucouleurs are in (K). For the following localities there are documents where indicated. Bar-le-Duc (LM), Chalaines (D, DM), Etain (LE, D, DM), Fresnes-en-Woëvre (DM), Gondrecourt (DM), Saint-Mihiel (DM), Sampigny (D), Vaucouleurs (DM), Verdun (DM, LM).

Moselle (57) Not included in (K) are: Achâtel, Anzeling, Barchain, Baudrecourt, Basse-Yutz, Bliesbruck, Bourgaltroff, Domnon, Eberswiller, Edling, Ennery, Les Etangs, Fameck, Forbach, Freistroff, Freyming, La Grange, Grening, Guinglange, Halstroff, Haute-Yutz, Hellering, Helstroff, Jouy-aux-Arches, Kédange, Koenigsmaker, Ladonchamps, Lorry, Loupershouse, Luttange, Marly, Marsal, Metz, Metzervisse, Mey, Moulins-lès-Metz, Nelling, Niedervisse, Petit-Rhorbach, Pontpierre, Rémering, Richemont, Rurange, Sansonnet, Sierck, Thionville, Tragny, Tromborn, Uckange, Vantoux, Vaudréching, Waldweistroff, Waldwisse and Welferding.

All of the following are included in (K) as well as in the indicated documents. Achâtel (D), Anzeling (LE); Augny (D, L), Bacourt (L), Barchain (D), Baudrecourt (D, D54), Basse-Yutz (D), Bionville-sur-Nied (D, L, LM), Bliesbruck (L, LM, LE, D75M), Boulay (D, L, LE), Bourgaltroff (D), Bourscheid (LM), Bouzonville (D, L, LM, LE), Chambrey (D), Château-Salins (D, D75M, L, LM), Courcelles-Chaussy (D, D75M, L, LM), Créhange (D, L), Delme (D), Denting (D), Dieuze (LE), Domnon (LE), Donjeux (D), Donnelay (D), Eberswiller (LE, D75M), Edling (LE), Ennery (D, L, LM), Erstroff (D), Les Etangs (D75M), Fameck (LE); Faulquemont (L), Fénétrange (L, LE, LM), Fèves; Forbach (D, D75M, L, LE, LM), Francaltroff (=Altroff), Frauenberg (D54, D75, C, L, LM), Freistroff (L, LE); Freyming (LE); Gelucourt,

Gorze, Gosselming (L, LM, LE), La Grange (D), Grening (LE), Grosbliederstroff (=Bliderstroff) (L, LE, LM), Guenwiller; Guéblange-lès-Dieuze; Guinglange (D); Halstroff (LE); Haute-Yutz (D); Hellering (D, LE); Hellimer (D, LE); Helstroff (LE); Héming; Imling (D); Insming (L, LM); Jouy-aux-Arches (D); Kédange (D); Koenigsmaker (D, D75M); Ladonchamps (D); Langatte (K, LM, LE); Lhor (LE); Liocourt; Lixheim (D, LE); Longeville-lès-Metz (D); Lorry (D); Loudrefing (LE); Loupershouse (LE); Louvigny (D, L, LM); Luttange (D, D75M); Maizières-lès-Vic; Marly (D, D75M, L, LM); Marsal (LE); Metting (LE); Metz (D, D75M, L, LM); Région de Metz (L); Metzervisse (D, D75M); Mey (D); Mittelbronn (D); Montenach; Morhange (D, LE); département of Moselle (L, LM); Moulins-lès-Metz (D, L); Moyenvic; Nelling (D75M, LE); Niedervisse (D, D75M); Petit-Rhorbach (LE); Phalsbourg (D, L, LM); Pontpierre (D, D75M); Puttelange (LE); Raville; Réchicourt-le-Château; Rémering (LE); Réning; Richemont (D75M); Rouhling; Rurange (D); Saint-Avold; Saint-Jean-Rohrbach; Sansonnet (D); Sarrebourg (LM); Sarreguemines (D54, D, LE, LM); Saulny; Schalbach (LE); Sierck (D); Talange (K); Thionville (D, DM, D75M); Tragny (D, D75M); Tromborn (LE); Uckange (D, D75M); Vallières (D, K); Vantoux (D, D75M); Vaudreching (LE, LM); Vergaville (K); Vic-sur-Seille (K); Volmerange-lès-Boulay (K,LE); Waldweistroff (LE); Waldwisse (D,D75M); Welferding (D); Woippy (D, K).

Vosges (88) Bruyères (D,DM,LM); Bulgnéville (DM); Charmes (DM); Châtel (D); Châtenois (DM); Damblain (DM); Darney (LM); Epinal (DM,LM); Lamarche (DM); Liffol-le-Grand (DM); Luxeuil (LM); Mirecourt (DM); Neufchâteau (D,DM,LM); La Neuveville (DM); Rambervillers (LM); Raon l'Etape (DM); Remiremont (DM,LM); Saint-Dié (D,DM); Vrécourt (D);

A Not-Specifically Jewish Source

Remember the *déclarations d'option* that were described in the section devoted to Alsace. These lists apply as well to the Moselle which also was ceded to the Germans in 1871, and they constitute a valuable genealogical resource.

Some Details
About the Civil Records of the Moselle

As the Moselle was ceded to the Germans with Alsace, all of the remarks concerning language and margin notes made at the end of the section devoted to Alsace apply here as well.

Comtat Venaissin[46]

Papal Jews

The Comtat Venaissin belonged to the *Saint-Siège* (the papal power) beginning in 1274; beginning in 1348 Avignon also belonged to the *Saint-Siège*. The areas were not made part of France until 1791, and in 1793 they constituted the main part of the department of Vaucluse.

Unaffected by the expulsion decrees from France of 1306 and 1394, and from Provence in 1501, these Jewish communities existed without interruption, probably since Roman times. Conditions of life deteriorated after 1525, however, following the introduction of rigorous and vexatious rules: the obligation to wear a yellow hat and for women the *pécihoun* (a piece of material sewn over their linen cloth), the requirement to be confined in overcrowded ghettos called *carrières* (a word that means street in *Provençal* dialect), and narrow streets that were locked each night by a Christian porter whose salary the Jews were forced to pay.

After 1624, Jewish ghettos were permitted in only four towns—called by the Jews the four holy communities (in memory of the four holy communities of Jerusalem, Hebron, Safed and Tiberias)—Avignon, Carpentras, L'Isle-sur-la-Sorgue and Cavaillon (plus Bédarride, until 1694).

Between 1750 and 1789, the four communities lost nearly a quarter of their population because of emigration to France (where, however, they were officially forbidden to live). In 1776, many of the *Avignonnais* (so called, if they came from any of the four communities) tried to profit from the residency rights given by Louis XVI to the *Juifs Portugais* (the so-called Portuguese Jews), those living in Bordeaux or Bayonne. Only 350 to 400 Jewish families lived in the whole of the Comtat on the eve of the Revolution. Emigration increased considerably after the emancipation and union with France in 1791; by 1808, only several dozen Jewish families (631 individuals) remained in the entire department of Vaucluse. Most of the "Papal Jews" went to live in Provence (in Arles, Aix-en-Provence and Marseilles), in Languedoc (especially Montpellier and Nîmes) and, above all, in Paris.

Today, the ancient Jewish families from the Comtat, who assimilated into the general French population, would be difficult to find if not for some characteristic surnames. The majority of Jews who live in the Vaucluse today are Sephardim from North Africa. Some individuals of Judeo-Comtadine origin are Adophe Crémieux, author of the 1870 decree that gave French citizenship to the Jews of Algeria; the composer Darius Milhaud; and René Cassin, winner of the Nobel Peace prize in 1968 and one of the authors of the Universal Declaration of the Rights of Man.[47]

Family and Given Names[48]

In the 18th century, the 2,000 to 2,500 Papal Jews used no more than 45 different family names. A few, such as Crémieux, Millaud, Monteux or Naquet, accounted for the lion's share.

As a general rule, the typical surnames were names of places, the majority outside of the Comtat (and sometimes outside of France) preceded by *de*, a particle dropped after the Revolution: Ascoli (in Italy), Beaucaire, Bédarrides, Carcassone, Cavaillon or Cavailhon, Courthoison (Courthézon), Crémieux (Crémieu), Digne, Largentière, Laroque or La Roque, Lattes, Lisbonne, Lunel, Meyrargues, Milhaud, Monteux, Narbonne, Pampelonne, Perpignan, Puget, Sampal (i.e. Saint-Paul), Valabrègue (Vallabrègues), etc.

There were also some names of Biblical origin: Mossé or Mosset (Moshe), Avidor or Avigdor, Cohen; or Hebrew: Vidal or Vives (translated from Haïm which means life), or Cassin (a Hebrew sobriquet that means rich), Bendic or Bendit (translated

from Baruch, blessed); or of Provençal origin: Astruc or Astruget or Benestruc, which signifies "born under a good star." Equally, some patronymics came originally from the East (Allemand or Lallemand), are Arabic (Alphandéry), or have uncertain etymology: Naquet, Pourfat or Profa, Sasias or Sazias or Sasia.

As for given names, some masculine given names took a Provençal sound (Haïm became Aïn; Joseph, Jass or Jessé; Noé, Noël; Yehuda, Jassuda), some were translated from Hebrew, as can be seen with some of the family names (thus, we find Benestruc for Gad; Ange or Lange for Mordecaï; Salvador for Yehoshua), some were used in a diminutive form (Caï or Cacaï for Mordecaï; Isseron for Israël; Jacoulet for Jacob). Some feminine names are biblical names transformed into regional diminutives: Hana into Nanousse; Lea into Liotte or Hiotte; Miriam into Millian or Mejan. Some diminutives do not have Biblical connections, but are French words, e.g. Belle or Belette, Blanquette, Doucette, Gentille, Précieuse or Roussette (René Moulinas indicates that these given names were written in Hebrew letters by the rabbi in the registers maintained since 1763). Some are translations: Nerto, meaning myrtle, translates the Hebrew Hadassa.

Old Sources

An interesting source are four civil registers begun in 1763 by order of Brother Jean-Baptiste Mabil, Inquisitor of the Holy Office. They cover the years 1763–92 and are deposited in the Departmental Archives of Vaucluse: Avignon (number GG226), Carpentras (number GG47), Cavaillon (number GG29), l'Isle-sur-la-Sorgue (number GG24). These registers have been microfilmed by the departmental archives. As has been shown by René Moulinas, the registers have some major gaps, particularly in the registration of births (see also the website WWW.NGJ.ENS.FR. Choose *Bases de données*, then click on *Menu de consultation* and *Dépouillement de Jean-Claude Cohen*).[49]

Numerous additional sources exist for the four communities, plus one just for Pertuis. A civil register for Carpentras, similar to one mentioned above, with some more details, is at YIVO (Institute for Jewish Research in New York)* and another, covering the years 1738 to 1769, is in Jerusalem at the Central Archives for the History of the Jewish People.* These two registers are written in Hebrew.

Some 1808 name adoption registers have survived: Avignon, Carpentras, Cavaillon, Pertuis and Saint-Saturnin-lès-Avignon. These lists may be consulted on the above-mentioned website. Choose *Menu de consultation* and *Base des déclarations de 1808*, then click on the green region at the extreme southeast of France, the *région PACA,* department of Vancluse. The lists sometimes include professions, date and place of birth, parentage and, of course, date and place of birth of minor children. For Carpentras, the register includes parentage.

The Mormons have done no microfilming in the department of the Vaucluse.

Southwest of France

In 1492, after the expulsion from Spain, many Jews who refused to convert became refugees in Portugal; in 1497, however, they were forcibly baptized and became so-called "New Christians." The Inquisition was established in Portugal in 1536 and hunted down the New Christians who judaized in secret (the Crypto-Jews), as it had already done since 1482 to the New Christians in Spain. In both countries, even after several generations, they and their descendants were always called New Christians or *marranos*, a pejorative that means "pig." In addition to being watched by the Inquisition, New Christians were the focus of popular animosity and were treated at best as second-class citizens.[50]

Portuguese New Christian merchants first arrived on French shores at the end of the 15th century. Slowly they organized and facilitated additional settlement of their compatriots, as well as of numerous New Christian Spaniards with whom they sometimes shared family lines. This immigration lasted until the end of the 18th century. The newcomers spoke Spanish at home as well as inside their communities, which came to be known as the "Spanish and Portuguese Nations."

In spite of *Lettres Patentes* (privileges granted in writing by the king) awarded by Henri II in 1550 and renewed by his successors, this group was continually the target of denunciations and accusations of secretly practicing their original Judaism (which was, most often, true). In 1723, the *lettres patentes* of Louis XV used, for the first time, the expression *Juifs Portugais* (Portuguese Jews); the camouflage was a known sham. Besides, by the end of the 17th century, well entrenched both economically and socially, the rich merchants of Bordeaux especially had begun openly to practice their Judaism in circumcisions, marriages, Jewish cemeteries and Jewish prayer houses. They had a web of family and commercial relationships with the avowed Jews of the Netherlands, especially those of Amsterdam. Often the French Southwest was only a stop on the route to Amsterdam, the metropolis of the Portuguese Jewish Nation.

The *marranos* lived primarily in two regions, Bordeaux and Bayonne. In Bordeaux, they had significant economic weight, thanks to foreign commerce, and in spite of their small numbers, up to the end of the 18th century (260 individuals in 1615, about 100 families in 1718; 327 in 1751).[51] They were concentrated as well in the region of Bayonne, in the suburb of Saint-Esprit (where they numbered 2,500 in 1785), in Bidache, Dax, Labastide-Clairence and Peyrehorade. *Marranos* were not admitted to Bayonne itself until 1790.

Family Names[52]

At the time of their forced baptism at the end of the 15th century, the *marranos* adopted names of Spanish or Portuguese families, often those of their Christian sponsors. They kept these names even after their open return to Judaism several centuries later.

We find among them the names Albouquerque, Alvares, Azevedo, Carvalho, Cardozo or Cardoze, Castro or de Castres, Da Costa or Dacosta, Da Silva, Dias, Fonseca, Foy, Francia or France, Gomès or Gomez or Gommes, Gonsalès, Gradis, Henriques, Julian, Lemeyra, Léon or de Léon, Lopes, Mendès, Molina, Nunes, Peixotto, Pereyra or Pereire, Perpignan, Petit,

Pimentel, Pissaro, Raba, Robles, Rodrigues, Salzedo, Silva, Torres and others.

Old Sources

Gironde (33). All of the sources described here pertain to Bordeaux. Among them, in the Departmental Archives of Gironde is a *Déclaration des juifs* (declarations of the Jews) dated 1751, recording 1,451 individuals, with names, ages of children, occupations and dates of arrival in the city.

In the Communal Archives (*Archives communales*) of Bordeaux, we find 13 lists of names covering the years 1618–1792, as well as a register of name adoptions from 1808. A microfilmed copy of the 1808 declarations is in the CGJ library.

We may also consider as a source the *Dictionnaire du judaïsme bordelais* (Dictionary of Bordeaux Jewry), by Jean Cavignac,[53] in spite of numerous errors. At the end of an analysis of the 1808 declarations of 2,063 Jews, Cavignac reconstituted their families and family lines from the beginning of the 18th century to about 1850. Simplified genealogies are given for the families Astruc, Azevedo, Cardoze, Gradis, Lemeyra, Lopès-Dias, Perpignan, Raba, Rodriguès-Henriques and Roget.

Landes (40). In these departmental archives are some documents about Jews from Dax and Peyrehorade. The Communal Archives of Peyrehorade hold a register of name adoptions for that locality.

Pyrénées-Atlantiques (64). Many sources for Bayonne-Saint-Esprit can be found in the departmental archives, as well as in the communal archives of Bayonne. In addition, registers of name adoptions for Bayonne-Saint-Esprit and Pau are held in the corresponding communal archives.

A copy of a circumcision register for Bayonne (for the years 1725–73), edited by Gérard Nahon, is in the CGJ library.

Other Regions of France

The edict of "permanent banishment" of 1394 prevented all official Jewish settlement in France (with the exception of the *marranos* in the Southwest and the Papal Jews) in any way other than the progressive expansion of the royal domain beyond its 14th-century limits.

Beginning in the early 18th century, however, a small number of Jews were allowed in Paris and in some cities of Languedoc and Provence. Later, a community composed of Jews originally from Alsace was formed in Besançon, starting in 1787.[54] The Mormons have filmed those records up to 1892.

Paris

The first community that was larger than a few families appeared during the reign of Louis XIII (1610–43), but it was only under Louis XV (1715–74) that one saw the formation of three different communities, closely watched by the police but increasingly tolerated, then officially established from the beginning of the reign of Louis XVI (1774–91):[55]

• So-called German Jews, the oldest and largest group, composed primarily of those from Metz and some from Alsace, to which were added, during the 18th century, Jews from Poland and German lands

- *Avignonnais* from the Rhône Valley, sometimes after a sojourn in Bordeaux
- So-called Portuguese Jews from Bordeaux, forming a restrained but influential group

On the eve of the French Revolution (1789), Paris had an estimated (legally authorized) 500 to 600 Jews. This group was augmented by an unknown number of unauthorized foreigners.

A few documents with names from before the Revolution are held in the National Archives and in the *Bibliothèque de l'Arsenal* (Library of the Arsenal);* some are limited to the heads of households, and there are never more than about a few hundred names.

A work by Paul Hildenfinger gives the family name, given name and, sometimes, the name of the father, date and place of death of 171 Jews buried in Paris between 1717 and 1789.[56] The *Revue* of the *Cercle de Généalogie Juive* has published a list of about 140 Jewish volunteers in the National Guard in 1790,[57] but this list, taken from a book by Léon Kahn entitled *Les Juifs de Paris pendant la Révolution*[58] (Jews in Paris during the Revolution), generally just has given name or family name and name of the street on which the person lived.

After their emancipation in 1791, Jews moved to Paris with much eagerness, especially because this residence had been almost forbidden before then. By 1808, the number was somewhat greater than 3,000. The 1808 name adoption register disappeared, along with the rest of the civil records, in the Commune fires of 1871, but the Jewish Theological Seminary in New York has a copy made by the Consistoire in 1809 (see above). An index of Jewish marriages in Paris from 1793 until 1802 has been reconstructed by Claudie Blamont.

The Jewish population was approximately 10,000 in 1830 and more than 25,000 in 1872. At this time, after the 1870–71 war against the Germans, and at least until the end of the 19th century, Jewish life in Paris was dominated by the Alsatian element. It is estimated, however, that in 1885, a third of the Jews living in Paris had been born outside the country, primarily in the Russian Empire (including Poland).

Details of 19th- and 20th-century genealogical research for Paris are described above. The Mormons have microfilmed the civil vital records for Paris and its immediate suburbs for the years 1860 to 1892. On site the films extend to 1902.

County of Nice

A few Jews lived uninterruptedly in Nice from the Middle Ages onwards; they numbered fewer than 300 on the eve of the Revolution and about the same number in 1808. Under Sardinian rule before 1792, they pursued banking, international commerce and medicine. Nice, conquered by the Republic in 1792, was part of France until 1814. From 1814 to 1860, it reverted to Sardinian rule before coming back to France in 1860. From 1792 to 1814, and from 1860 onwards, civil vital records were maintained in the same manner as in the rest of France. The 1808 name-adoption register with 183 declarations corresponding to 256 persons is kept in the communal archives. It can be consulted on the above-mentioned website, WWW.NGJ.

ENS.FR. Click on *menu de* consultation, *base des déclarations de 1808, région PACA* (South-East), and finally *Alpes Maritimes*. Family names were hereditary, however, even before 1808.

Records for the years 1814 to 1860 were held by the Catholic Church, except, after 1837, in places where non-Catholic worship was tolerated. In these localities, a rabbi was made responsible for Jewish vital records; because of negligence, however, many events were not recorded. Italian-language registers for the years 1838–59 are kept in the departmental archives of the Alpes Maritimes, where the collections for Sardinia include lists of Jewish families for 1829 and 1835. The Mormons have microfilmed Jewish civil records from 1800 to 1814 and from 1838 to 1859 (see *Alpes Maritimes* in their catalogue), and secular civil records from 1860 to 1892.

The library of the *Cercle de Généalogie Juive* holds indexes of the Jewish civil records for the years 1792–1815 and for 1838–60 called *baptêmes* (baptisms)—probably births—as well as a partial copy of the 1808 name-adoption register.

Languedoc and Provence

At the end of the 18th century, some Jews lived in Montpellier, Narbonne and Nîmes. This situation came about because some of the Jews of the Comtat, the so-called Avignonnais, had tried to profit, before 1791, from the residency rights accorded to the Portuguese Jews. Thus, the departmental archives of Hérault hold lists of Jewish shopkeepers and dealers in old clothes; the lists cover the years 1731–86, primarily for Montpellier. In the notarial acts, the Jews living in Montpellier, not having the right to live officially in the French kingdom, appear as residents of different localities in the Comtat.

The communal archives of Nîmes has a birth, marriage and death register of 194 individuals for the years 1781–92, a copy of which is in the CGJ library. In addition, Dr. Lucien Simon has created a large index with civil records concerning many Jews from Nîmes that has been published by the CGJ.[60] Technically speaking, this is not an old source, since it covers the 19th and 20th centuries, but it often indicates two or three earlier generations. The published version includes no information about living persons. The departmental archives of Marseille has a document that includes the residency declarations of 13 Jewish merchants who lived in that city in 1782. Several name adoption registers have been preserved, for Aix-en Provence, Arles, Eygalières, Marseille, Nîmes and Tarascon; except for the one for Nîmes, they can be consulted on the above-mentioned website, department of Bouches-du-Rhone. The CGJ library has numerous documents with names for Marseille and the surrounding region in the 18th and 19th centuries, particularly indexes about Jewish cemeteries.

Addresses

To call a French telephone or fax number from abroad, after dialing 33 do not dial 0 before the 9 remaining digits. If you speak in English, you probably will not be well understood most of the time.

Archives de Paris, 18 boulevard Sérurier, 75019 Paris; telephone: (0)1-537-241-23; fax: (0)1-53-72-41-34.

Alliance Israélite Universelle, 45 rue La Bruyère, 75009 Paris; telephone: (0)1-533-288-55; fax: (0)1-487-451-33.

Bibliothèque Administrative de la Ville de Paris, Hôtel de Ville, entry 5 rue Lobau, 75004, 4th floor, staircase W1; telephone: (0)1 427-648-87.

Bibliothèque de l'Arsenal, 1 rue de Sully, 75004 Paris.

Bibliothèque Généalogique, 3 rue de Turbigo, 75001 Paris; telephone: (0)1 42 33 58 21, open on Tuesdays 12 a.m. to 6 p.m.; Wednesdays 2 p.m. to 8 p.m.; Fridays 10 a.m. to 6 p.m.; open in July and August.

Bibliothèque Historique de la Ville de Paris, 24 rue Pavée, 75004 Paris; telephone: (0)1 44 59 29 40.

CARAN, Centre d'Accueil et de Recherche des Archives Nationales, 11 rue des Quatre-Fils, 75003 Paris; telephone: (0)1-402-760-00; fax: (0)1 40 27 66 28; Temporary address (until 2005): 60 rue des Francs-Bourgeois, 75003 Paris.

Central Archives for the History of the Jewish People, POB 1149, 91010 Jerusalem, Israel; telephone: 972-2-563576; fax: 972-2-566766.

Centre des Archives Contemporaines, Service des Communications, 2 rue des Archives, 77309 Fontainebleau cedex; telephone: (0)1 64 31 73 00, e-mail: CAC.FONTAINEBLEAU@CULTURE.GOUV.FR.

Centre des Archives Diplomatiques 17 rue de Casternau, 44036 Nantes cedex; telephone: (0)2 51 77 25 25.

Centre des Archives d'Outre-Mer, 29 chemin du Moulin Detesta, 13090 Aix-en-Provence; telephone: (0)4 42 26 43 21.

Centre de Documentation Juive Contemporaine, 17 rue Geoffroy l'Asnier, 75004 Paris; telephone: (0)1 42 77 44 72, e-mail: CONTACT@MEMORIAL-CDJC.ORG; Temporary address: 37 rue de Turenne, 75003 Paris.

Cercle de Généalogie Juive, 14 rue Saint-Lazare, 75009 Paris; telephone and fax: (0)1 40 23 04 90.

Chercheurs d'Ancêtres, 6 rue de l'Oratoire, 75001 Paris; telephone (0)1 55 35 06 57; e-mail: BOUTIQUE@ANCETRES.COM.

Cimetière parisien de Bagneux, 45 avenue Marx Dormoy, 92220 Bagneux.

Cimetière parisien de Pantin, 164 avenue Jean Jaurès, 93500 Pantin.

Consistoire de Paris, 17 rue Saint-Georges, 75009 Paris; telephone: (0)1 40 82 26 26, fax: (0)1 42 81 92 16. Closed in August.

ETSI, association de généalogie et histoire séfarades, c/o P. et L.Abensur, 77 boulevard Richard-Lenoir, 75011 Paris.

GenAmi, c/o Micheline Gutmann, 76 rue de Passy, 75016 Paris.

Jewish Theological Seminary, 3080 Broadway, New York, New York 10027.

L'Association Culturelle des Juifs du Pape, Musée juif comtadin, rue Hébraïque, 84300 Cavaillon; telephone: (0)4 90 76 00 34.

Ministère des Affaires Sociales, Sous-Direction des Naturalisations, 93 bis rue de la Commune, 44404 Rezé-lès-Nantes.

Service Central de l'état civil, 11 rue de la Maison Blanche, 44941 Nantes cedex 9; telephone (0)2 77 30 30, fax (0)2 51 77 36 99.

Service des cimetieres, (only for Paris) 71 rue des Rondeaux, 75020 Paris.

Service Historique de l'Armée de Terre, Pavillon des Armes, Vieux-Fort, château de Vincennes, 94300 Vincennes; telephone: (0)1 41 93 34 33.

Bibliography

Archives de Paris. *Sur les traces de vos ancêtres à Paris.* Paris, 1997.

Beaucarnot, Jean-Louis. *Généalogie mode d'emploi.* Paris: Guides Marabout, 2002.

Beider, Alexander. "The Evolution of Ashkenazic Given Names: Some General Aspects." *AVOTAYNU* 17, no. 1 (Spring 2001): 18–22.

Bernard, Gildas. *Les familles juives en France, XVIᵉ siècle–1815: Guide des recherches généalogiques et biographiques.* Paris: Archives Nationales, 1990. May be purchased on site at the CARAN for 17.5 euros or by mail (first request information by mailing to *La Documentation française,* e-mail LIBPARIS@LADOCUMENTATIONFRANCAISE.FR.

Bernard, Jean-Pierre. *Relevés des cimetières de Moselle.* Paris: CGJ, 2002.

Blamont, Claudie. *"Mariages juifs à Paris de 1793 à 1892."* Revue du Cercle de Généalogie Juive, No. 57 and 58, 1999.

Bouvat-Martin, Jean-Claude. *Tables du Memorbuch de Metz (1720–1849).* Paris: CGJ, 2001.

Calbat, Jean-Louis. *Les mariages juifs en Moselle.* Paris: CGJ, 2001.

Cavignac, Jean. *Dictionnaire du judaïsme bordelaise aux XVIIIᵉ et XIXᵉ siècles.* Bordeaux: Archives départementales de la Gironde, 1987.

Cercle de Généalogie Juive. *Proceedings of the 5th International Seminar on Jewish Genealogy, Paris, July 13–17, 1997.* Paris, CGJ, 1998. May be ordered from CGJ using Eurocard, MasterCard or Visa.

Cercle de Généalogie Juive. *Revue du Cercle de Généalogie Juive.* Paris: CGJ, from 1985.

Chipaux, Roger. *Recensements de la population israélite de Besançon en 1839 et en 1851.* The documents are held at the CGJ library.

Daltroff, Jean. *Les Juifs de Niedervisse.* Sarreguemines: for the author, 1992.

Fleury, Jean. *Contrats de mariage juifs en Moselle avant 1792.* Paris: CGJ, 1997.

Fraenckel, André Aaron. *Mémoire juive en Alsace: Contrats de mariage au 18ᵉ siècle.* Strasbourg: éditions du Cédrat, 1997.

Ginger, Basile. "Use of French Naturalization Documents." *AVOTAYNU* 12, no. 4 (Winter 1996): 11–14.

Hildenfinger, Paul. *Documents sur les juifs de Paris au XVIIIᵉ siècle; actes d'inhumation et scellés.* Paris: Champion, 1913.

Job, Françoise. *Le cimetière israélite régional de Lunéville, 1759–1998.* Paris: CGJ, 1999.

Job, Françoise. *Les Juifs de Lunéville aux 18ᵉ et 19ᵉ siècles.* Nancy: PU Nancy, 1989.

Job, Françoise. *Les Juifs de Nancy.* Nancy: PU Nancy, 1991.

Kahn, Léon. *Les Juifs de Paris pendant la Révolution.* Paris: Ollendorf, 1898; reprinted New York, B. Franklin, 1968.

Katz, Pierre. "Jewish Genealogical Research in Alsace," *AVOTAYNU* 10, no. 2 (Summer 1994).

Katz, Pierre. *Les communautés juives du Bas-Rhin en 1851.* Paris: CGJ, 2000.

Katz, Pierre. *Les communautés juives du Haut-Rhin en 1851.* Paris: CGJ, 2002.

Katz, Pierre. *Recueil de déclarations de prise de nom patronymique des Juifs en 1808 pour la Moselle et la Meurthe-et-Moselle.* Paris: CGJ, 1998.

Katz, Pierre. *Recueil des déclarations de prise de nom patronymique des Juifs en 1808 pour le Bas-Rhin.* Paris: CGJ, 1999.

Katz, Pierre. *Recueil des déclarations de prise de nom patronymique des Juifs en 1808 pour le Haut-Rhin.* Paris: CGJ, 1997.

Klarsfeld, Serge. *Le Mémorial de la déportation des Juifs de France.* Paris: Fils et Filles des Déportés Juifs de France, 1978; English ed: *Memorial to the Jews Deported from France 1942–1944.* New York: Beate Klarsfeld Foundation, 1983.

Kleitz, Jean-Pierre. *"La recherche en généalogie juive en Alsace avant la création de l'état civil"* Actes du Vᵉ congrès de généalogie juive. Paris: CGJ, 1998.

Leeson, Daniel. *Index du Dénombrement de 1784*. Paris: CGJ, 1999.

Leeson, Rosanne and Daniel Leeson. *Index to Mémoire juive en Alsace*. Paris: CGJ, 1999.

Les Israélites dans l'Armée Française, 1914–1918. Angers: Gaultier, 1921.

Mendel, Pierre. *"Note sur les noms des Juifs français modernes," Revue des Etudes Juives*. Paris, 1950.

Meyer, Pierre-Andre. *"La communauté juive de Metz au 18ᵉ siècle*. Nancy: Serpenoise, 1993.

Meyer, Pierre-Andre. *"Les immenses ressources de la généalogie judéo-messine," Proceedings of the 5th International Seminar on Jewish Genealogy Paris, July 13–17, 1997*. Paris: CGJ, 1997.

Meyer, Pierre-Andre. *Tables du registre d'état civil de la communauté juive de Metz (1717–1792)*. 2nd. ed. Paris: CGJ, 1999.

Moulinas, René. *Les Juifs du Pape en France*. Paris: Privat, 1981.

Nahon, Gérard. *"Communautés espagnoles et portugaises de France"* in *Les juifs d'Espagne, histoire d'une diaspora, 1492–1992*. Paris: Liana Lévi, 1992.

Netter, Nathan. *Vingt siècles d'histoire d'une communauté juive: Metz et son grand passé*, 2d. ed. Marseille: Jeanne Laffitte, 1995.

Proceedings of the 5th International Seminar on Jewish Genealogy, Paris, 1997; see "Cercle de Généalogie Juive."

Revue du Cercle de Généalogie Juive, no. 19. Paris: CGJ, 1989.

Simon, Lucien. *Etat civil de Nîmes et de Pont-Saint-Esprit*. Paris: CGJ, 2000.

Stein, Peter. *Verzeichnis der Juden des südlichen Elsass und der benachbarten Gebiete*. Basel: for the author, 1997.

Szajkowski, Zosa. *Franco-Judaïca: An Analytical Bibliography, 1500–1788*. New York: American Academy for Jewish Research, 1962. Available at the *Bibliothèque Nationale de France* (French National Library), Paris.

Wolff, Christian. *Guide des recherches généalogiques en Alsace*. Strasbourg: Oberlin, 1975.

Notes

1. Gildas Bernard. *Les familles juives en France, XVIᵉ siècle-1815: Guide des recherches généalogiques et biographiques* (Jewish families in France, 16th century to 1815: a guide to genealogical and biographical research). [French] Paris: Archives Nationales, 1990. After a large historical introduction, indicates nearly all the sources, department by department, that the various French Archives have to offer to Jewish genealogists. This book is also available in the New York Public Library.

2. The *département* is an administrative subdivision of the country. Continental France has 96 departments created in 1789. The former *provinces* (replaced with several changes by the *régions*) are usually composed of two to eight departments.

3. *Cercle de Généalogie Juive* (or CGJ), 14 rue Saint-Lazare, 75009 Paris; telephone: (0)1 402-304-90, e-mail: OFFICE@GENEALOJ.ORG; website: WWW.GENEALOJ.ORG.

4. Archives de Paris. *Sur les traces de vos ancêtres à Paris* (On the track of your ancestors). [French] Paris: 1997.

5. The *arrondissement* is an administrative subdivision of a large city, specifically Paris, Marseille and Lyon. Currently, Paris has 20 *arrondissements*. The town halls of the *arrondissements* are annexes of the central city hall.

6. *Proceedings of the 5th International Seminar on Jewish Genealogy, Paris, July 13–17, 1997*. Paris: Cercle de Généalogie Juive, 1998.

7. Jean-Louis Beaucarnot. *Généalogie, mode d'emploi* (Genealogy, directions for use). [French] Paris: Marabout, 2002. The best current book on genealogical research in France, not specifically Jewish, but not for beginners only.

8. Basile Ginger. "Use of French Naturalization Documents." *AVOTAYNU* 12, no. 4 (Winter 1996): 11–14.

9. Fees in 2002: yearly card 20 *euros*, temporary card (15 days) 5 *euros*, free pass one day per year.

10. Free entrance with identification.

11. No mail requests. Monday 1 p.m. to 5 p.m.; Tuesday to Friday, 9 a.m. to 5 p.m., closed in August.

12. *Les Israélites dans l'Armée Française, 1914–1918* (Jews in the French Army, 1914–1918). [French] Angers: Gaultier, 1921. Officers and soldiers, either dead while fighting for France or mentioned in dispatches.

13. Genealogists can order from the *Bibliothèque Généalogique* a search in the Archives de Paris for a record created before 1903. See details on its website, WWW.BIBGEN.ORG/mail-usa.html (note that "mail-usa.html" is case-sensitive).

14. Closed in August.

15. Anne Lifshitz-Krams. *Les mariages juifs à Paris, 1848–1872* (Jewish marriages in Paris, 1848–1872). [French] Paris: CGJ, 1996.

16. Created in 1886, includes 27 Jewish areas with many graves of Jews from Poland and Lithuania.

17. Also created in 1886, it has 33 Jewish areas.

18. *Cimetière parisien de Thiais* was created in 1929.

19. Serge Klarsfeld. *Le Mémorial de la déportation des Juifs de France*. Paris: *Fils et Filles des déportés juifs de France*, 1978. English ed: *Memorial to the Jews Deported from France, 1942–1944*. New York: Beate Klarsfeld Foundation, 1983. A new edition in French, with corrections and additional information, should be published soon in Paris.

20. CDJC has original lists of the deportation convoys and might sometimes give hints for research on a given deportee.

21. Pierre Mendel. "Note sur les noms des Juifs français modernes" (A note on the modern names of French Jews). *Revue des Etudes Juives*. Paris: 1950: 15–65. "Modern names" must be understood here as opposed to those used during the Middle Ages; André Aaron Fraenckel *Mémoire juive en Alsace: Contrats de mariage au 18ᵉ siècle* (Alsatian Jewish Memory: marriage contracts from the 18th century). [French] Strasbourg, éditions du Cédrat, 1997.

22. Alexander Beider. "The Evolution of Ashkenazic Given Names: Some General Aspects." *AVOTAYNU* 17, no. 1 (Spring 2001): 18–22.

23. Microfilms #1069535, item 3, or #1071438, item 1.

24. *Dénombrement de 1784 des Juifs d'Alsace*. Paris: CGJ, 1999.

25. Daniel Leeson. *Index du Dénombrement de 1784*. Paris: CGJ, 2000.

26. Pierre Katz "Jewish Genealogical Research in Alsace." *AVOTAYNU* 10, no. 2 (Summer 1994): 31–32.

27. André Aaron Fraenckel. *Mémoire juive en Alsace*.

28. Rosanne and Daniel Leeson. *Index to Mémoire juive en Alsace*. Paris : CGJ, 1999.

29. Jean-Pierre Kleitz. "La recherche en généalogie juive en Alsace avant la création de l'état civil" (Jewish genealogical research in Alsace before the introduction of civil records). [French] *Actes du 5ᵉ congrès de généalogie juive* (Proceedings of the 5th Seminar on Jewish Genealogy. [French] Paris: CGJ, 1998: 341–46.

30. Gildas Bernard *Les familles juives en France, 16ᵉ siècle-1815*. The catalogue of the library may be consulted on the CGJ website, WWW.GENEALOJ.ORG.

31. Pierre Katz *Recueil des déclarations de prise de nom patronymique des Juifs en 1808 pour le Bas-Rhin*. Paris: CGJ, 1999; Pierre Katz *Recueil des déclarations de prise de nom patronymique des Juifs en 1808 pour le Haut-Rhin*. Paris: CGJ, 1997.

32. Pierre Katz *Les communautés juives du Bas-Rhin en 1851* (The Jewish communities of the Bas-Rhin in 1851). [French] Paris: CGJ, 2000; Pierre Katz, *Les communautés juives du Haut-Rhin en 1851* (The Jewish communities of the Haut-Rhin in 1851). [French] Paris: CGJ, 2002.

33. Microfilms #1070259 to 0263, and 1070123.

34. Peter Stein. *Verzeichnis der Juden des südlichen Elsass und der benachbarten Gebiete* (Tables concerning Jews of Upper Alsace and neighboring areas, 13th-18th centuries). Basel, 1997.

35. Christian Wolff. *Guide des recherches généalogique en Alsace* (Guide to genealogical research in Alsace). [French] Strasbourg: Oberlin, 1975.

36. Pierre-Andre Meyer. *La communauté juive de Metz au 18th siècle* (The Jewish community of Metz in the 18th century). [French] Metz: Serpenoise, 1993: 67.

37. Pierre Mendel. *Note sur les noms des Juifs français modernes*; Pierre-André Meyer *La communauté juive de Metz au 18ᵉ siècle*.

38. Pierre-André Meyer. "Les immenses ressources de la généalogie judéo-messine." *Proceedings of the 5th International Seminar on Jewish Genealogy*. Paris, CGJ, 1998: 33–45.

39. Pierre-André Meyer. *Tables du registre d'état civil de la communauté juive de Metz (1717–1792)* (Indexes of the civil registers of the Jewish community of Metz [1717–1792]). [French] Paris: CGJ, 1999); 2d ed.; Pierre-André Meyer, *La communauté juive de Metz au 18ᵉ siècle*; Nathan Netter *Vingt siècles d'histoire d'une communauté juive: Metz et son grand passér* (Twenty centuries of history of a Jewish community: Metz and its great past). [French] Marseille: Jeanne Laffitte, 1995.

40. Jean-Claude Bouvat-Martin. *Tables du Memorbuch de Metz (1720–1849)* (Indexes to Metz memorbooks [1720–1849]). [French] Paris: CGJ, 2001.

41. Jean Fleury *Contrats de mariage juifs en Moselle avant 1792* (Marriage contracts of the Jews in Moselle before 1792). [French] Paris: CGJ, 1997.

42. Zosa Szajkowski *Franco-Judaïca: An Analytical Bibliography, 1500–1788* (New York: American Academy for Jewish Research, 1962). Available at the *Bibliothèque Nationale de France* (French National Library, Paris).

43. Françoise Job. *Les Juifs de Lunéville aux 18ᵉ et 19ᵉ siècles* (The Jews of Luneville in the 18th and 19th centuries). [French] Nancy, PU Nancy, 1989; Françoise Job. *Le cimetière israélite régional de Lunéville, 1759–1998* (The regional Jewish cemetery of Luneville, 1759–1998). [French] Paris: CGJ, 1999; Françoise Job. *Les Juifs de Nancy* (The Jews of Nancy). [French] Nancy, PU Nancy, 1991; Jean Daltroff. *Les Juifs de Niedervisse* (The Jews of Niedervisse). [French] Sarreguemines: by the author, 1992; Jean-Pierre Bernard. *Relevés des cimetières de Moselle* (Indexes to the graves of the Moselle). [French] Paris, CGJ,

2002; Jean-Louis Calbat. *Les mariages juifs en Moselle* (Jewish marriages in Moselle). [French] Paris: CGJ, 2001.

44. Pierre Katz. *Recueil des déclarations de prise de nom patronymique des Juifs en 1808 pour la Moselle et la Meurthe-et-Moselle.* Paris: CGJ, 1998.

45. #107022, item 3 and #1114842, item 1.

46. Gildas Bernard. *Les familles juives en France, XVIe siècle-1815*; René Moulinas. *Les Juifs du Pape en France* (The Papal Jews in France). [French] Paris: Privat, 1981.

47. The museum often publishes articles about individuals from the Comtat in its review.

48. René Moulinas. *Les Juifs du Pape en France*.

49. *Ibid.*

50. Gildas Bernard. *Les familles juives en France, XVIe siècle-1815*; Gérard Nahon. "Communautés espagnoles et portugaises de France" (Spanish and Portuguese communities in France). [French] *Les Juifs d'Espagne, histoire d'une diaspora, 1492–1992* (The Jews of Spain: history of a diaspora, 1492–1992). [French] Paris: Liana Lévi, 1992.

51. Gilda Bernard. *Les familles juives en France, XVIe siècle-1815*: 41.

52. Pierre Mendel. *Note sur les noms des Juifs français modernes*; Jean Cavignac *Dictionnaire du judaïsme bordelais aux XVIIIe et XIXe siècles* (Dictionary of the Jews of Bordeaux in the 18th and 19th centuries). [French] Bordeaux, 1987.

53. Jean Cavignac. *Dictionnaire du judaïsme bordelais aux XVIIIe et XIXe siècles*.

54. Pierre Katz. *Prise de nom de 1808 à Besançon, avec regroupement par familles* (Name adoptions of 1808 with regrouping by families). [French]; Roger Chipaux. *Recensements de la population israélite de Besançon en 1839 et en 1851* (Censuses of the Jewish population of Besancon in 1839 and 1851). [French] These documents are held in the CGJ library.

55. Gilda Bernard. *Les familles juives en France, XVIe siècle-1815*.

56. Paul Hildenfinger. *Documents sur les juifs à Paris au XVIIIe siècle; actes d'inhumation et scellés* (Documents on the Jews of Paris in the 18th century; burials and seals). [French] Paris: Champion, 1913.

57. *Revue du CGJ* 19 (1989): 697–99.

58. Léon Kahn. *Les Juifs de Paris pendant la Révolution* (The Jews of Paris during the Revolution). [French] Paris: Ollendorf, 1898; reprinted New York: B. Franklin, 1968.

59. Claudie Blamont. "Mariages juifs à Paris de 1793 à 1802." (Jewish marriages in Paris from 1793 to 1802). *Revue du Cercle de Généalogie Juive.* no. 57 and 58. [French] Paris: CGJ, 1999.

60. Lucien Simon. *Etat civil des Juifs de Nîmes et de Pont-Saint-Esprit* (Civil records of the Jews of Nîmes and of Pont-Saint-Esprit). [French] Paris: CGJ, 2000.

Germany

by Peter Lande

In seeking information on one's German-Jewish roots, the genealogist has the advantage that this was probably the best documented of all European Jewish communities, both in book form and in civil and community records. While access to some of this information requires a trip to Germany, much is available in major libraries around the world. In addition, most community records and a few civil records may be accessed at LDS (Mormon) Family History Centers (see LDS). For the purpose of this article, Germany is defined according to its present borders, although occasional references are made to sources of information relating to larger areas, such as former German or Prussian localities.

History

Germany was united only in 1874, but Jews have lived in the area for nearly two thousand years, probably coming to western Germany with the Romans. They were primarily traders and craftsmen who settled in the river valleys where commerce took place, first along the Rhine and later along the Elbe and Danube. Written records of Jewish presence date back to the fourth century in Cologne. By the 10th and 11th centuries, Jews were accorded special status, and the communities were large enough to have founded *yeshivas* (religious schools).

The oldest Jewish cemetery in Germany, located in Worms, dates back to 1076; the Worms synagogue was built in 1034. In some cases, Jews obtained charters of rights, were allowed to manage their own civil affairs, and often were excused from compulsory military service. By the 11th century, several thousand Jews lived along the Rhine, in the Palatinate and along the Danube in Bavaria.

Like Jews in other parts of the world, German Jews suffered from periodic persecution. Large-scale massacres occurred in the 11th century at the time of the First Crusade. In the 13th century, Jews were driven from much of southern, southwestern and central Germany, but such actions often were followed by invitations to return to the same towns a few years later. In the 14th century, the Jews were blamed for the plague, or Black Death, and were largely expelled, although they never completely left Germany. Most went east and settled in what later became Czechoslovakia and Poland, where local rulers welcomed them.

Yiddish, although it has older linguistic roots in Aramaic and Hebrew, developed in Germany between the 9th and 12th centuries and has major Germanic components. It moved with the Jews who fled eastward and flourished there, while largely ceasing to be used in Germany itself.

The return of significant numbers of Jews to Germany occurred over several centuries and included the arrival of some Sephardic Jews in northwest Germany during the 16th century. Gradually, Jews from Eastern Europe moved back to Germany, where they sought and found greater economic and, later, political and social opportunity. At the end of the 19th and start of the 20th centuries, an even larger number of Eastern European Jews left from German ports on their way to the United States and elsewhere.

By the 17th and 18th centuries, many Jews had attained considerable social and economic success, some as *Hof Juden* (court Jews), who handled the financial affairs of local rulers. Most Jews remained poor, however, with precarious or nonexistent legal status, until the early 19th century, when many were given equal rights. Some of these rights were later rescinded, and it was not until much later in the century that at least formal equality was granted. Even then, widespread anti-Semitism restricted Jewish access to universities and the civil and military services. Economic change and the search for greater opportunities led to movement from smaller towns and villages to cities such as Berlin, Breslau, Cologne, Frankfurt, Hamburg and Leipzig. By the beginning of the 20th century, approximately one-third of all German Jews lived in Berlin.

The number of German Jews peaked in 1910 with 610,000 residents, but, even then, they constituted less than one percent of the total population. These numbers gradually declined, and, in 1933, when Hitler assumed power, the census recorded 503,000 individuals who considered themselves Jews. Undoubtedly, many more had converted or simply did not choose to record themselves as Jews. Between 1933 and 1939, about 300,000 Jews fled Germany for the United States, Palestine, United Kingdom, South America and anywhere else that would admit them. Some only reached neighboring countries such as Belgium, France or Poland and later were swept up in the Holocaust.

Jewish presence in post-World War II Germany is small, but increasing, reaching close to 100,000 residents, the majority from the former Soviet Union and Poland.

Sources for Genealogical Research

Civil Records

Germany does not maintain national civil (birth, marriage and death) records, and most census records, with one exception noted below, are not useful for genealogists. Standardized German civil records have existed only since 1876, after Germany was unified. For centuries before, what became Germany had consisted of a large number of states of varying size, all of which spoke German but had their own laws and citizenship practices. Since the 1870s, records have been held in *Standesämter* (civil registry offices) located throughout Germany. Large cities such as Berlin have several such offices, while a single office may serve several small villages. No single list exists of German *Standesämter*, but this does not hinder research.

Given the decentralization of records, a researcher must establish when and where an ancestor was born, married or died. Each event may have occurred in a different locality; if so, the relevant records will be held by different offices. To complicate matters further, some town names exist in many localities. For example, more than 75 localities with the name Neustadt are listed in an 1870 finding aid for Austria, Germany and Prussia. After World War II, 38 localities in West Germany carried that name. Nevertheless, most localities can be located using the References at the end of this chapter.

It is not necessary to know the exact address of the relevant *Standesamt*. Simply write to the mayor of the town of interest and request that your inquiry be passed to the relevant office. In the case of larger cities that are likely to have more than one such office, include the street address where the ancestor resided at the time the birth, marriage or death occurred. Suggestions for determining addresses are given below. A more serious problem arises if the date of an event is unknown. In theory, a *Standesamt* will look for information without a date, but in practice, given small staff and other priorities, such a search may take years. Accordingly, when a date is unknown, look first in Jewish community records (see below) before turning to civil inquiries.

German civil records are generally fairly complete, although some have been lost to fire or wars. No distinction is made between Jewish and non-Jewish civil records, but during Nazi times, the personal names "Israel" and "Sarah" were added to many individual Jewish records. In some places, these designations still have not been removed. Personal inspection of files is not allowed, so there is little point in visiting a *Standesamt*, although officials in small towns sometimes ignore these restrictions for foreigners. A printed form exists for use in requesting information, but seems not to be required when one writes from outside Germany. In theory, the form must be notarized, but again, this requirement does not seem to apply to foreign researchers.

A small fee is charged, but many offices will do the research first and send a bill subsequently. Given the problems of nonresidents in making payment in Euros, and the problems for German offices in cashing foreign checks, many offices simply do not bill foreign researchers. In every case, however, one should include a self-addressed envelope and one or two international postal coupons with the letter of inquiry.

Stringent restrictions, based on *Datenschutz* (privacy laws), govern the information that is made public. A researcher may obtain copies of birth, marriage and death records only for himself and direct ancestors (e.g., parents, grandparents, great-grandparents and their spouses). One may not obtain records for other relatives such as uncles and aunts. Some exceptions to the direct descendant rule are made in legal matters such as inheritance, but these rarely apply to genealogists. Do not expect speedy replies to inquiries. *Standesamt* officials are busy, and genealogical inquiries are not their priority task.

One exception exists to the rule that one must approach the *Standesamt* in the place where an event occurred. This is the case of records for areas that once were, but no longer are, part of Germany; in most cases, these are towns now in Poland. To the extent that such records are held in Germany, they are maintained at *Standesamt I.** The holdings of this office are listed in *Standesregister und Personenstandsbücher des Ostgebiete im Standesamt I in Berlin* (Civil registries held in Standesämt I in Berlin). This source should be consulted when researching areas that were once part of Germany. The same procedures and restrictions described above apply to this *Standesamt*.

Local Registration of Births, Marriages and Deaths
Births, marriages and deaths were registered in Germany locally or regionally long before 1876, first by Jewish and other religious communities and later directly by various German states and localities. These records, therefore, are just as likely to turn up in archival as in community collections (see community records, below). Later civil records almost always are found in local, regional or state archives. There is no known complete list of such records but, as the following list of the most important collections shows, some began as early as the end of the 18th century. The maintenance of almost all such local records was terminated in the 1870s, although exceptions have been found. Such sources of information often are available at LDS (Mormon) family history centers and may fill some of the gaps in information when community records are not available.

Following are the dates that local registration began in various German states and localities.

Baden	1810–70	Registration by Christian communities as agents for the state, with copies to courts
Bavaria (Bayern)	1813–69	Vital records kept by local authorities
Frankfurt	1850–	Public registration
Hannover	1809	Local registration with copies to state
Hesse	1808–76	Local registration with copies to state
Lübeck	1809	Civil registration
Oldenburg	1811	Civil registration
Palatinate (Pfalz)	1795	
Prussia	1809	From 1711 onward, Jewish congregations required to keep birth and marriage records; after 1750, these had to be reported to state. Police registered all births 1816–47; after 1847, congregations were required to keep birth, marriage and death records.
Rhineland (Rheinland)	1798	Civil registration
Saxony (Sachsen)		Urban birth registration beginning in 1802, marriage and death registration beginning in 1813
Westphalia (Westfalen)	1804	Civil registration

Wedding ceremony during 18th century in Germany. From Boden-schatz, Kirchliche Verfassung, *1748.*

Researchers should seek civil records other than births, marriages and deaths. For example, one problem in researching German-Jewish family history is that most Jews did not adopt fixed family names until the late 18th or early 19th centuries. The requirement to take family names was imposed at different times in different states in Germany, beginning in the 1780s; the last state action was in 1852. It is difficult to conduct research before that time, except where a rabbinical or other prominent family had adopted fixed surnames earlier. Fortunately, a number of name adoption lists have been preserved, some as published books, others in official registers that may be consulted. Known sources are listed in References. In most cases, however, one must search archival sources for towns and areas where the ancestors lived. In a few cases, registers of name adoptions and naturalizations (see below) were collected in the *Gesamtarchiv** or *Zentralstelle für Genealogie** and have been microfilmed by the Mormons. Major cities where name adoption lists exist include Bonn, Karlsruhe, Koblenz, Mainz, Trier and Zweibrücken. Such lists frequently include information on a person's prior name, as well as information on a man's spouse and children.

Prior to 1874, many German states required foreigners to register, and these people often applied for citizenship. For example, in the case of Hamburg, from 1834 to 1929, the *Einwohnermeldeamt* (residents' registration office, discussed below) maintained records on residents who were not citizens, while separate registers of non-citizen workers (from 1834 through 1890) also were kept. Other Hamburg records

exist for individuals who applied for citizenship. This information is particularly important for families with roots in that city, since applicants often chose new, more German-sounding names that often are impossible to link to their previous names unless the records are examined. A few naturalization lists for other localities have been filmed by the LDS (Mormon) Family History Library. Over the past 200 years, the boundaries of Germany and its predecessor states have varied widely. Many localities that once were German are now Danish, French, Polish and even Russian. Most libraries, including the Mormon Family History Library, categorize records under the country in which a locality is currently located. A researcher should look there first. Also consider the possibility that civil records for periods when a locality outside Germany was under German jurisdiction might be held in a German archive, as in the case of records in *Standesamt I*. A good example is cited by Edward D. Luft who describes how he found in an East German archive, 18th-century records for a town that has been part of Poland since 1945.[1] In addition, a large collection of German records is held at the Jewish Historical Institute in Warsaw, but it has not been fully catalogued or filmed yet. In other cases, German civil records are held in the original town or regional center. Access to such records will follow the policies of that country (for example, see POLAND).

Emigration Lists

While not technically a civil record, never overlook ship departure records. Beginning on a large scale in the mid-19th century, more than one million persons, many of them Jews, departed from Hamburg for the United States and elsewhere.[2] Similar records for Bremen, the other major German port of embarkation, have been lost except for a partial list covering the years 1847 to 1871.[3] Most Jewish emigrants came from Eastern Europe, but many came from various parts of Germany. Hamburg records have been microfilmed by the LDS (Mormon) Family History Library.[4] Emigration records also are available for Baden and a number of individual cities, such as Aachen, for example (see References and LDS holdings).

Jewish Community Records

Existing Jewish community records date to the late 17th century. Most common are *mohel* (ritual circumciser) records, held by the individual *mohels* as their private, rather than communal, property, although they often ended up in community collections. Unlike vital statistics records, which were removed from community collections by Nazi authorities and filmed, *mohel* records generally remained with the bulk of community records and probably are the most useful part of the *Gesamtarchiv* collection discussed below.[5] Some lists have been published in *Jüdische Familienforschung* and some in *Maajan*. Most were written in Hebrew, with a few in German. Many histories of prominent German-Jewish families have been published, mostly as articles but some as books. Like the mohel records, no comprehensive bibliography of sources yet exists, and the sources that do exist are difficult to locate.

Many communities kept records of marriages, because it was customary to give a portion of the dowry to the community. Such records were maintained in Hamburg as early as 1686 and in Prussia beginning in 1914. Death records date back even further, at least to the mid-17th century. These records usually were kept by *chevrot kadisha* (burial societies), but sometimes the communities maintained death records themselves, with a few, such as Frankfurt am Main, going back to 1600.

Unfortunately, no centralized source or collection of all Jewish community birth, marriage and death records has ever existed, much less of other community records. Historically, the records have been held on a local level by synagogues or city and provincial associations. In the 1920s and early 1930s, the *Gesamtarchiv der deutschen Juden* (Collected Archives of German Jews) in Berlin attempted to collect all German-Jewish community records. The *Gesamtarchiv* was a great success, since many communities had found it difficult to maintain old records. This was especially true in small, rural towns whose Jewish communities had shrunk as Jews left for larger cities and other countries. On the other hand, many major Jewish communities continued to keep and maintain their records, while many southern German communities were not interested in sending records to Berlin.

The *Gesamtarchiv* collection of thousands of documents included not only vital statistics data, but also various types of administrative records, such as land purchase, building receipts and elections of rabbis. When the Nazis assumed power, the vital statistics data was transferred to the *Reichsippenamt* (racial ancestry office) and used to determine who was a Jew under Nazi racial laws. The originals of this part of the collection were destroyed during the war, but photocopies had been made. Most are available through the LDS (Mormon) Family History Library.*

The largest collection of *Gesamtarchiv* records other than birth, marriage and death is held at the Stiftung Neue Synagoge Berlin—Centrum Judaicum.* These holdings are listed in volumes 5 and 6 of *Quellen zur Geschichte der Juden in den Archiven der neuen Bundeslaender*. There is another large part at the Central Archives* in Jerusalem; a small portion is held at the Leo Baeck Institute* in New York. In some cases, the only copies of such records are held in German local, regional or state archives (see archives below). The Hamburg collection is particularly extensive. Branch and state archives in Augsburg, Ludwigsburg and Nuremberg, as well as the principal state archives in Munich and Stuttgart, reportedly have major Jewish collections. Thorough researchers must explore each possibility.

A combined list of all known birth, marriage and death recrds is provided at the end of this chapter titled "The Complete Archives of the German Jews." A single asterisk by the name of the town indicates the LDS (Mormon) Family History Library has the records. In many cases both the Family History Library and the Central Archives for the History of the Jewish People have the same material, while in other cases, they both may have material but for different years. For records other than birth, marriage and death, localities are marked by *B* for Berlin (Centrum Judaicum-Neue Synagoge,* a memorial site

for one of Berlin's major synagogues that also hold a useful library and archives pertaining to Berlin Jews); *J* for Jerusalem (Central Archives*) and *N* for New York (Leo Baeck Institute*). All of the collections are publicly available, but none of the institutions that holds them will research names or cities in response to mail inquiries; a personal visit is required. The Centrum Judaicum material has been filmed, but is difficult to read. Little of this material beyond the *mohel* records is directly useful to genealogists, except for rabbinical or other prominent community figures.

After the war, the newly created German Democratic Republic (East Germany) created a *Zentralstelle für Genealogie* (central office for genealogy) in Leipzig. This office had immense files on all aspects of genealogy, including a large collection of birth, marriage and death records of German Jews, mostly taken from the *Reichsippenamt*. Some of this material had come originally from the *Gesamtarchiv*, but other portions seem to have been obtained from different sources. Without comparing lists, however, it is impossible to know if the Leipzig material is the same as the material from other sources.

Fortunately for the genealogist, the LDS (Mormon) Family History Library filmed the entire *Zentralstelle* collection when the communist East German government collapsed. Provenance of information may vary. For example, the records on the town of Gandersheim from 1853 through 1896 may have come from the *Gesamtarchiv* via the *Bundesarchiv*, while records on Gemmingen from 1811 to 1879 may have been acquired in Leipzig. As a result, the Mormons hold records for most German-Jewish communities for the period of the 19th century before civil registration was established. No index to family names exists, but a guide to the massive collection of mostly non-Jewish family records has been published by the Family History Library (see LDS).*

Separate from these community records, the *Zentralstelle* holds extensive family records in the Ahneneliste collection, and these were filmed for the Family History Library.* Although these are mostly non-Jewish records, they are worth checking. A guide to this massive collection has been published by Thomas Edlund for the Family History Library (see references).

When looking for any of the above-cited material, always begin at an LDS (Mormon) Family History Center. An excellent discussion of the advantages and problems involved in using the Mormon catalogue is included in Ralph Baer's ar-

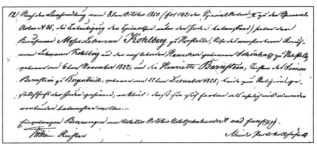

Marriage record of Moses Lehmann Kohlberg of Herstelle, a businessman, son of Lehmann Kohlberg and Hannchen Schoenholz of Herstelle and Henriette Bernstein, daughter of Simon Bernstein of Borgentreich. The record says that Henriette was born on 22 December 1825.

Synagogue on Oranienburgerstrasse, Berlin. It was severely damaged by Allied bombing during World War II but rebuilt after the war.

ticle, "German-Jewish Records in the Mormon Library."[6] For example, some microfilms hold both Catholic and Jewish records, but are catalogued only under the Catholic heading. Some town names were omitted when the filmed material was collected by a regional court or other administrative unit. Particularly for small towns and villages, always search for nearby towns, county (*Kreis*) or even provincial records when you cannot find a desired record.

Records of Jewish Organizations

German Jews maintained a multitude of educational, religious and social organizations. During the 20th century, many of the organizations came under the umbrella of the *Reichvereinigung der Deutschen Juden* (Association of German Jews). When Hitler came to power, he would not accept the notion of "German" Jews, so he forced the organization to be renamed *Reichsvereinigung der Juden in Deutschland* (Association of Jews in Germany). This organization functioned under Nazi supervision almost until the end of the World War II.

The *Reichsereinigung* records were not destroyed and can be consulted on microfiche at the Bundesarchiv branch

in Berlin[*] and at the United States Holocaust Memorial Museum[*] in Washington. This huge collection has been well catalogued by subject matter (e.g., hospital, school, personal file) for persons who emigrated, died or were deported. A list of hundreds of individuals on whom files were opened is available on JewishGen.

Censuses

National and local censuses, traditionally major sources of information for genealogists, have little relevance in Germany. Although censuses were conducted in Germany every 5 or 10 years since 1871, only aggregate information is available to researchers (i.e., the number of persons in various categories for a city or a region). Older censuses were held in various cities and states, but generally these do not yield information on individuals. The one exception is the May 1939 Nazi census designed to identify all Jews and persons with Jewish ancestry. This is discussed below under Holocaust Records.

Holocaust Records

The *Gedenkbuch*, a German government publication, lists approximately 128,000 German-Jewish victims of the Holocaust. It lists first and last name, maiden name where applicable, date of birth, last place of residence and what is known about the individual's fate. In many cases, there is simply the word *verschollen*, which means vanished and assumed dead, or *für tot erklärt*—declared dead by a court proceeding. The book was published in 1986 before the reunification of Germany and, therefore, only covers what was West Germany and West Berlin. A new edition in preparation will cover all of Germany within its 1937 borders and is expected to include approximately 50,000 additional names.

Well before publication of the *Gedenkbuch*, and continuing to the present, many German cities and individuals prepared *yizkor* (memorial) books or articles for individual localities and regions. In addition to information about the history of the Jewish community, these books often provide additional information about the victims and, in some cases, about survivors. Such books exist for almost all major cities where German Jews lived, such as Berlin (55,000 names), Hamburg (nearly 9,000 names), Cologne (7,000 names), Leipzig, Stuttgart and dozens of other smaller communities. The library at Yad Vashem[*] in Jerusalem has the largest collection of *yizkor* books but extensive collections exist also at the United States Holocaust Memorial Museum (USHMM) and various other libraries (see HOLOCAUST). Many sources for information on specific German towns are cited in an appendix to volume 2 of the *Gedenkbuch*.

Prior to large-scale deportations of Jews from Germany (to concentration camps in Eastern Europe) in 1941–42, many German Jews fled to neighboring countries, in most cases only to be arrested and deported from there. A number of books list Jews deported from Belgium, Czech Republic, France and Holland (see References). Although the lists are not arranged by nationality, place of birth often is cited, and, thus, German Jews can be identified. Unfortunately, such identification is difficult for persons born in third countries, such as someone born in Poland, who might have lived all of his life in Germany. Deportation lists exist (at Yad Vashem[*] and the USHMM[*]) for most major German cities, but they rarely need to be consulted because the same information is usually given in memorial books for the relevant community.

Another (incomplete) source of information on German Jews who fled the Nazis is *Die Ausbürgerung deutscher Staatsangehörigkeit 1933–45* (see References). This lists the names of those stripped of their German citizenship, usually after they fled from Germany. It does not indicate where they fled or whether they were caught later, but it does at least provide a researcher a reason to search records in other countries.

An unusual and valuable source of information is the May 1939 census of Jews—sometimes called the 1938 census, the year in which it was planned. This census, organized by city and town and then alphabetically, includes individual returns on 233,000 Jews then living in Germany or the Sudetenland, a portion of Czechoslovakia seized by the Germans in 1938. The census forms for the province of Thuringia and a few cities in the northern Rhineland have been lost, but otherwise the collection is complete. Data on the missing locations may be obtained from city and/or provincial memorial books. Although the census was taken in Austria as well, those forms have disappeared.

The census records are available from any LDS (Mormon) Family History Center[*] and include name, maiden name, date and place of birth and residence, and whether any of that person's four grandparents were Jewish. The material is relatively easy to use for large towns, which are identified in a finding aid for the collection (see References). It is more difficult to use in the case of small towns and villages; several localities often were merged together under one heading, e.g., Pfalz Land (Palatinate countryside).

The extent of information from the concentration camps themselves varies widely. Extensive name lists exist for Buchenwald, Dachau and Flossenburg with limited lists from Bergen Belsen (see HOLOCAUST.)

Just as no complete record of all German-Jewish victims exists, the same is true of a complete list of German- Jewish survivors. Some memorial books list survivors. The *Emigranten Adressbuch* for Shanghai lists heads of families for the 17,000 Jews, most of them Germans, who reached that city in the late 1930s and early 1940s, more than 90 percent of whom are known to have survived (see CHINA).[5] An unpublished list of Jews, mostly German, who were granted refuge in Switzerland is available at the U.S. Holocaust Memorial Museum (USHMM).[*] A list of more than 30,000 survivors, many German, culled from lists that appeared in the New York German-language newspaper *Aufbau* is available on JewishGen.[*] More general sources of information are discussed in the chapter HOLOCAUST. In 2001, the USHMM Survivors Registry published its most recent edition of persons registered as survivors and their families (see References). These lists are arranged according to wartime and prewar places of residence.

Archives

Small villages are unlikely to have their own archives, but most towns and regions, and all states, have archives to which public access is permitted. Even in the case of small villages, one should check with the town hall, mayor's office or other local authority to see what records are available or where a Jewish cemetery might still be located. An alphabetical list by town of the principal public and private archives in Germany is included in *Taschenbuch für Familiengeschichtsforschung* (Pocketbook for family genealogical research), the basic reference on genealogical research in Germany. Recent editions include a chapter on German-Jewish research. An English-language book by Brandt, *Germanic Genealogy*, also has a chapter on German-Jewish records, but it is much less detailed. Onsite access to archival material is far less restricted than in a *Standesamt*, although much of the same material is available in both places.

Virtually every German town has an *Einwohnermeldeamt* (residence registration office), which maintains records on all residents. Although these offices tend to be extremely busy and highly protective of their records, one can usually gain access to the records indirectly. This is true because such records are ultimately transferred to the local archives where access is easier. The legal basis for making records available varies state by state, but in Hamburg, for example, records are restricted for a term of 50 years, beginning 5 years after a registrant's death or departure from Hamburg. Since most genealogists research records created before the end of World War II, when the Jewish presence in Germany all but ceased to exist, virtually all records of interest may be consulted. Many records were lost or destroyed during World War II, of course, but they should always be sought anyway.

More generally, a genealogist should examine archive catalogues to find material related to Jews, which often is catalogued separately. Do not expect every archive to have the same types of material. The Hamburg state archives, for example, has a list of Jews who converted to the Lutheran church that dates back to the 17th century; the Nazis ordered the Lutheran church to compile the list during the Holocaust era, but the work proceeded so slowly that the task was never completed. The Nazis demanded such lists of all religious communities, but the Catholic Church refused to prepare them. Lutheran officials were more cooperative in Berlin, but these extensive lists are held by a Lutheran organization—not by the Berlin state archives. Access to the records is permitted at Evangelisches Zentralarchiv[*] in Berlin. The Leipzig *Zentralstelle*[*] also has a list of Jews in Berlin who converted to the Lutheran church. The list has been microfilmed by the Mormons, but it is not known whether or not these records are identical with the material held in Berlin. Similar lists may exist in other states, but they are difficult to locate.

Archives are often a useful place to seek Jewish community records. The Institut fuer Stadtgeschichte[*] (Frankfurt am Main city archives) holds Jewish community records that date back several hundred years; in other places, the same records are held by the local Jewish community. In archives and libraries, check also for old *Bürgerbücher* or *Adressbücher*. *Bürgerbücher* date back several hundred years and list those inhabitants of a city who held citizenship—rare for Jews before the 19th century. *Adressbücher*, similar to city

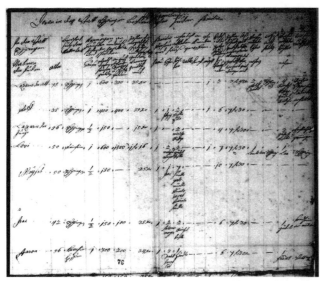

1736 census document listing Jews of Eppingen.
Courtesy of Werner Frank.

directories that existed throughout Europe and North American until the 1930s, often go back 200 years and are a useful way to search for a family's presence and address in a given locality. A partial list of *Bürgerbücher* and *Adressbücher* is available in *Familiengeschichtsforschung.*

As a rule, a researcher must visit an archive to know what it holds; an exception pertains to the former Deutsche Demokratische Republik (former East Germany). A 1996 book, *Quellen zur Geschichte der Juden in den Archiven der neuen Bundesländer*, lists, archive by archive, all material relating to Jews. Considerable material dating back several hundred years is available. Where no material exists, this fact is noted, thereby saving a researcher a visit. In addition, the state of Rheinland-Pfalz has published a multi-volume guide to its archival holdings from Jewish communities in that state and the Saar; this is indexed by town and major personal names (see References).

The Jewish Museum* in Frankfurt am Main has an extremely useful collection of genealogical material from various areas of Germany. It also holds the largest formerly private genealogical collection of German Jewish data, the Brilling collection.[7] This collection, which has never been fully catalogued, is particularly rich in material from Silesia. The small staff cannot respond to mail inquiries; a personal visit is required.

Libraries

The search for books and printed material is both more difficult and easier than an archival search. It is more difficult because thousands of books, monographs and articles have been written about the Jewish presence in Germany, many including extensive information on individuals and their families. It is easier because of Ellmann-Krüger's *Library Resources for German-Jewish Genealogy*, which identifies 18 major German libraries open to the public that have significant collections of Judaica. In each case, the book supplies such pertinent information as address, hours open to the public and nature of the collection(s). It also tells the researcher how to search holdings, either through printed

catalogues or through online public access catalogues. This allows a researcher who does not live in Germany to identify items of interest and, perhaps, to locate the same item in a local library or to order via international interlibrary loan.

As might be expected, no one catalogue lists all publications related to Jews in Germany. *Library Resources* discusses categories of printed material, such as genealogies, regional and local histories, cemeteries, memorbooks, encyclopedias, biographical and other directories of interest, and offers examples under each category. The book identifies a number of specialized bibliographies listing literature pertaining to Jews in major areas and cities of Germany, such as Bavaria, Frankfurt, Hamburg, Hesse, the Palatinate and Silesia. Ellmann-Krüger's earlier *Auswahlbibliographie zur jüdischen Familienforschung vom Anfang des 19, Jahrhunderts bis zur Gegenwart* lists more than 2,500 publications of possible interest to Jewish genealogists. This book is unusually well indexed by family name and locality. (It is expected to be replaced soon by a new and expanded version.) Consult also *Arbeitsinformationen*; published every three years, it lists ongoing research projects and supplies the names and addresses of authors, thus allowing the genealogist to contact persons whose works may never get published.

The best single collection of German Jewish literature, including genealogy, is held by the Leo Baeck Institute* in New York. Its annual yearbook includes a list of materials relating to German Jews published the preceding year, providing a useful means to keep up to date on new material. Another sizeable collection is at the Wiener Library* in London.

Jüdische Familien-Forschung (Jewish genealogical research) was published quarterly by the *Gesellschaft für*

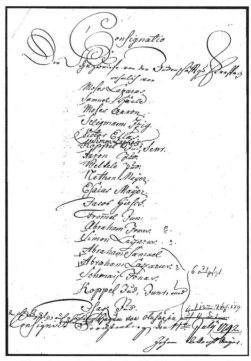

List of Jews in Ernsbach with Schutz (protected)
status, 1792. Courtesy of Werner Frank.

jüdische Familien-Forschung from 1924 until the mid-1930s. The publication includes information on individual families, community records available then—that may still exist—and even a *Suchblatt*, similar to the "Ask the Experts" column of *AVOTAYNU*. Copies are available at the U.S. Library of Congress (see LIBRARY OF CONGRESS) and in the LDS (Mormon) Family History Library (see LDS) in Salt Lake City. Other publications of interest are *Maajan/Die Quelle* and *Stammbaum*.

Cemeteries

Nazi authorities never made the same effort to destroy Jewish cemeteries in Germany as they did in Eastern Europe. Despite neglect and the passage of time, an estimated 2,000 Jewish cemeteries with 600,000 tombstones still exist. This does not include the many cemeteries and gravestones no longer extant that have been recorded in printed material. See CEMETERIES for information about the International Association of Jewish Genealogical Societies Cemetery Project.

Major efforts are underway in Germany to photograph all existing gravestones.[7] Most work thus far has been done in the states of Baden-Württemberg, Hamburg, Hesse and Lower Saxony. The Weissensee Cemetery* in Berlin, Germany's largest, has complete records of burials and has computerized them. The list may be consulted on site; mail inquiries are accepted.

Onsite cemetery visits often are easy; one simply walks into them. Do not assume, however, that any given city has only one Jewish cemetery. Five still exist in Hamburg, for example. Some cemeteries are enclosed by a wall with a locked gate and no indication of where to turn for access. In Frankfurt, a nearby florist has the key; sometimes it may be necessary to scale the wall and search through tombstones overgrown by vegetation.

Jewish Communities in Germany Today

Almost 100,000 Jews live in Germany today, but most are relatively recent immigrants, especially from Eastern Europe. The community is headed by a *Zentralrat der Juden in Deutschland** with headquarters in Berlin and offices in approximately 50 other German cities. To locate them, look in a local telephone directory under *Jüdisches*. Most do not hold extensive historical documentation themselves, but will know where such material is held. They also typically know the location of cemeteries.

Addresses

Bundesarchiv Berlin, Herbert-Baum Strasse 45, 12205 Berlin, Germany; website: WWW.BUNDESARCHIV.DE/ STANDORTE/BERLIN

Central Archives for the History of the Jewish People, 46 Jabotinsky Street, Jerusalem 91010, Israel

Deutsche Zentralstelle fuer Genealogie, Tucholskystr. 9, 04329 Leipzig, Germany

Evangelisches Zentalarchiv, Bethaniendamm 29, Berlin, Germany

Institut fuer Stadtgeschichte Frankfurt am Main, Muenzgasse 9, D-60311 Frankfurt am Main; website: WWW.STADTGESCHICHTE-FFM.DE

Juedischer Friedhof Berlin Weissensee, Herbert-Baum-Strasse 45, 13088 Berlin, Germany; telephone and fax: 30 9-250-833.

Juedisches Museum, Untermainkai 14/15, 100 60311 Frankfurt/M., Germany; e-mail: INFO@JUEDISCHESMUSEUM.DE

Family History Library, 35 North West Temple Street, Salt Lake City, Utah 84150

Leo Baeck Institute, Center for Jewish History, 15 West 16th Street, New York City, N.Y. 10011; website: WWW.LBI.ORG

Standesämt I, Rückerstrasse 9, 10119 Berlin, Germany

Stiftung Neue Synagoge Centrum Judaicum, Oranienburgerstr. 28/30, D 10117 Berlin, Germany; e-mail: CJUDAICUM@SNAFU.DE

United States Holocaust Memorial Museum, Raoul Wallenberg Place, Washington, D.C. 20024; website: WWW.UHSMM.ORG

Wiener Library, 4 Devonshire Street, London W1W 5—14, England; website: WWW.WIENERLIBRARY.CO.UK

Yad Vashem, P.O. Box 3477, Jerusalem 91034, Israel

Zentralrat der Juden in Deutschland, Schongauerstrasse 1, 10117 Berlin, Germany; website: WWW.ZENTRALRATJUDEN.DE

Bibliography

Hundreds of books and articles that document Jewish history in Germany generally, as well as in specific towns, regions and states may be useful to genealogists. The following list is intended to be more indicative than exhaustive:

Historical Setting

Fogel, Rolf. *Ein Stueck von uns. Deutsche Juden in deutschen Armeen 1813–1876. Ein Dokumentation* (A piece of us. German Jews in German Armies 1813–1876, a documentation). [German] Mainz: Hase & Koehler, 1977.

Friedländer, Saul. *Nazi Germany and the Jews. The Years of Persecution, 1933–1939.* vol.1. New York: Harper Collins, 1997.

Gidal, Nachum Tim. Jews in Germany from Roman Times to the Weimar Republic. Köln: Könemann, 1998.

Kampmann, Wanda. *Deutsche und Juden, Die Geschichte der Juden in Deutschland wom Mittelalter bis zum Beginn des ersten Weltrkieges* (The history of Jews in Germany from the Middle Ages to the beginning of the first World War). [German] Frankfurt am Main: Fischer, 1994.

Leo Baeck Institute. *Year Book.* London: Secker & Warburg, 44 annual issues.

Meyer, Michael and Michael Brenner ed. *Deutsche-jüdische Geschichte in der Neuzeit* (German-Jewish history in recent times). [German] München: Beck, 1996–97.

Trepp, Leo. *Geschichte der deutschen Juden.* (History of German Jews). [German]. Stuttgart: Kohlhammer, 1996.

Civil and Community Records

Brandt, Edward et al. *Germanic Genealogy: A Guide to Worldwide Sources and Migration Patterns.* St. Paul: Germanic Genealogy Society, 1995.

Edlund, Thomas. *Register to the Ahnenstammkartei des deutschen Volkes.* St. Paul, MN.: Germanic Genealogy Society, 1995.

Glazier, Ira and P. William Filby. *Germans to America: Lists of Passengers Arriving at U.S. Ports 1850–1897.* Wilmington: Scholarly Resources, 1988–95.

Jüdische Familien-Forschung (Jewish family research). [German] Berlin:Gesellschaft für jüdische Familien-Forschung, 1924–38.

Maajan/Die Quelle. (The source). [German]. Zurich: Schweizerische Vereinigung für jüdische Genealogie, quarterly 1986–2000.

Ribbe, Wolfgang and Eckhardt Henning ed. *Taschenbuch für Familiengeschichtsforschung* (Reference book for genealogical research). [German] Neustadt an der Aisch: Degener, 1995.

Schrader-Muggenthaler, Cornelia. *The Baden Emigration Book.* Apollo, PA: Closson Press, 1992.

Stammbaum. New York: Leo Baeck Institute, quarterly 1992–2000

Standesregister und Personenstandsbücher der Ostgebiete in Standesämt I in Berline (Civil registries and personnel books held in Standesämt I in Berlin). [German] Frankfurt am Main & Berlin: Verlag für Standesämtwesen, 1992.

United States Board of Geographic Names. *West Germany.* Washington, D.C., 1960.

United States Defense Mapping Agency. *Gazetteer of the German Democratic Republic and Berlin.* Washington, 1983

Zimmermann, Gary and Marion Wolfert. *German Immigrants: Lists of Passengers Bound from Bremen to New York, with Places of Origin, 1847–71.* Baltimore: Genealogical Publishing Co., 1985–1993.

Holocaust

Boberach, Heinz et al., ed. *Quellen zur deutschen politischen Emigration 1933–1945* (Sources of information on German political emigration). [German] Munich: Saur, 1994.

Edlund, Thomas. *The German Minority Census of 1939.* Teaneck: Avotaynu, 1996.

Freie Universität Berlin. *Gedenkbuch Berlins der jüdischen Opfer des Nationalsozialismus* (Berlin memorial book for the Jewish victims of National Socialism). [German] Berlin: Hentrich, 1995.

Gedenkbuch Opfer der Verfolgung der Juden unter der nationalsozialistischer Gewaltherrschaft in Deutschland, 1933–1945 (Memorial book for the victims of persecution under the National Socialist 1933–1945). [German] Koblenz: Bundesarchiv, 1986.

Hepp, Michael ed. *Die Ausbürgerung deutscher Staatsangehörigkeit 1933–1945* (The striping of German citizenship 1933–1945). [German] Munich: G. Saur, 1996.

Institut Theresienstädter Initiative Academia Prag. *Die Opfer der Judentransporte aus Deutschland nach Theresienstadt 1942–1945* (The victims of the Jewish transports from Germany to Theresienstadt 1942–1945). [German] Prague: Institut Theresienstaedter Initiative, 2000.

Klarsfeld, Serge. *Memorial to the Jews Deported from France.* New York: Beate Klarsfeld Foundation, 1983.

Klarsfeld, Serge and Maxime Steinberg. *Memorial de la Deportation des Juifs de Belgique* (Memorial to the Jews deported from Belgium). [French] Brussels Beate Klarsfeld Foundation, 1982.

Mokotoff, Gary. *How to Document Victims and Locate Survivors of the Holocaust.* Teaneck: Avotaynu, 1995.

Reichsbund Juedischer Frontsoldaten. *Die juedischen Gefallenen des deutschen Marine und der deutschen Schutztruppen 1914–1918: Ein Gedenkbuch* (Jewish naval and army casualties in World War I). [German] Berlin: Der Schild, 1932.

United States Holocaust Memorial Museum. *Registry of Jewish Holocaust Survivors.* Washington: U.S. Holocaust Memorial Museum, 2001.

Libraries and Archives

Arbeitsinformationen über Studienprojekte auf dem Gebiet der Geschichte des deutschen Judentums und des Antisemitismus (Information about current research projects concerning German Jewry and anti-Semitism). 17 eds. [German] Cologne: Germania Judaica, 1963–1998.

Ellmann-Krüger, Angelika, with Edward Luft. *Library Resources for German-Jewish Genealogy.* Teaneck, N.J.: Avotaynu, 1998.

Ellmann-Krüger, Angelika. *Auswahlbibliographie zur jüdischen Familienforschung vom Anfang des 19. Jahrhunderts bis zur Gegenwart* (Selected bibliography regarding Jewish genealogical research from the beginning of the 19th century to the present). [German] Wiesbaden: Otto Harrassowitz, 1992.

Heinemann, Hartmut ed. *Quellen zur Geschichte der Juden im Hessischen Hauptstaatsarchiv Wiesbaden* (Sources in the main state archives of Hesse on the history of the Jews). [German] Wiesbaden: Kommission f.d. Geschichte d. Juden in Hessen, 1997.

Jersch, Wenzel and Reinhard Rürup ed. *Quellen zur Geschichte der Juden in den Archiven der neuen Bundesländer* (Sources of information on the history of Jews located in the archives of the new federal states). 5 vols. [German] Munich: Saur, 1996–99.

Verzeichnis der im Schleswig-Holsteinischen Landesarchiv befindlichen Quellen zur Geschichte des Judentums (Sources in the Schleswig Holstein archives relating to he history of Jews). 3 vols. [German] Schleswig: 1963–66.

Zimmer, Theresia ed..*Inventar des Quellen zur Geschichte der jüdischen Bevölkerung in Rheinland-Pfalz und im Saarland von 1800/1815–1945* (Inventory of sources of information relating to Jews in Rhineland-Palatinate and Saarland from 1800 to 1945). 6 vols. [German] Koblenz: Landesarchivverwaltung Rheinland-Pfalz, 1982.

Cemeteries

Arnstein, George. "German Cemeteries, Overview and Notes." *Stammbaum,* no. 6–7 (December 1995): 14–32.

Arnstein, George. "More on Jewish Cemeteries in Present-Day Germany, Austria and Switzerland." *Stammbaum,* no. 8–9 (July 1996): 13–24.

Brocke, Michael. "Erbe und Aufgabe. Jüdische Friedhöfen in der Bundesrepublik Deutschland." (Jewish cemeteries in Germany). [German] *Tribune:* Frankfurt am Main: 1984, 23, no. 92: 67–76.

Brocke, Michael and Christiane Mueller. *Haus des Lebens: Juedische Friedhöfe in Deutschland* (House of life: Jewish cemeteries in Germany). [German] Leipzig: Reclam, 2001.

Brocke, Michael, Eckehart Ruthenberg and Kai Uwe Schulenberg. *Stein und Name: Die juedischen Friedhoefen in Ostdeutschland* (Stone and name: Jewish cemeteries in East Germany). [German] Berlin: Institut Kirche und Judentum, 1994.

Diamant, Adolf. *Jüdische Friedhöfe in der Bundesrepublik. Eine Bestandsaufnahme* (Jewish cemeteries in Germany). [German] Frankfurt am Main: Selbstverlag, 1982.

Honigmann, Peter. *"Dokumentation jüdischer Grabinschriften in der BRD. Ein kurzer Überblick anhand der Erfahrungen in Baden-Württemberg"* (Documentation regarding Jewish tombstone inscriptions in Germany). [German] *Aschkenas* 3, 267–73, 1993.

Peters, Dieter. *Land zwischen Rhein und Maas Genealogische Daten von jüdischen Friedhöfen in der ehemaligen Rheinprovinz und in den niederländischen Provinz Limburg* (Territory between the Rhine and Maas genealogical data from Jewish cemeteries in the former Rhine Province and the Dutch Province of Limburg). [German] Kleve: Mosaik Familienkundliche Vereinigung für das Klever Land, 1993.

Weissleder, Wolfgang. *Der gute Ort: Juedische Friedhöfe im Land Brandenburg* (The good place: Jewish cemeteries in the state of Brandenburg). [German] Verein zur Foederung Antimilitarischer Traditionen in der Stadt Potsdam e.V. 2002.

Notes

1. Luft, Edward. "Records for West Prussia Found in East German Archives." *AVOTAYNU* 15, no. 1 (Spring 1999).
2. Sielemann, Jürgen. "Emigration from the Port of Hamburg, Germany, *AVOTAYNU* 14, no. 4 (Winter 1998):19–20.
3. Sielemann, Jürgen. "Bremen Emigration Lists Found." *AVOTAYNU* 13, no. 3 (Fall 1997):11
4. Sielemann, Jürgen. "Hamburg Emigration Lists Are Being Computerized." *AVOTAYNU* 15, no. 2 (Summer 1999): 3.
5. Lande, Peter. "The Complete Archives of the German Jews." *AVOTAYNU* 9, no. 1 (Spring 1993)
6. Baer, Ralph. *AVOTAYNU* 6, no. 3 (Fall 1990): 4.
7. "Shanghai Jewish Refugee Book Now Available." *AVOTAYNU* 12, no. 1 (Spring 1996): 66
9. Luft, Edward. "Brilling Archives in Frankfurt Museum." *AVOTAYNU* 11, no. 1 (Spring 1995): 11
13. Polevoy, Nancy. "German-Jewish Gravestones on the Internet." *AVOTAYNU* 15, no. 1 (Spring 1999): 66

The Complete Archives
of the German Jews

Gesamtarchiv der Deutschen Juden (The Complete Archives of the German Jews), collected by Jacob Jacobson in the 1920s and early 1930s, is undoubtedly the best single source of genealogical information on German Jews. As a result of World War II, the collection today is housed in three different locations: Potsdam, Germany; the Leo Baeck Institute in New York City: and the Central Archives for the History of the Jewish People in Jerusalem. Many of the vital records that once formed part of the collection have been microfilmed by the LDS (Mormon) Family History Library..

The columns represent (1) locality or province; (2) # of documents in collection; (3) inclusive years; (4) location of documents. J=Central Archives for the History of the Jewish People, Jerusalem; P=Potsdam/ Coswig Archives; N=Leo Baeck Institute in New York City. Note that the compilation does not explain the nature of the documents. An asterisk (*) after the locale indicates that birth/death/marriage material is available through the LDS (Mormon) Family History Library. This list originally appeared in the Spring 1993 issue of *AVOTAYNU*.

Locality	#	Years	Loc
Aachen	3	1896–1912	J
Abterode*	1	1853–1854	J
Abterode*	9	1827–1920	P
Adelebsen	2	1857–1889	J
Ahlem	2	1893–1917	J
Ahrensdorf	1	1827–1833	J
Allenstein*	7	1854–1910	J
Allenstein*	80	1854–1913	P
Allersheim*	1	1779–1903	N
Alt–Landsberg*	8	1860–1922	P
Altona	1	1870–1914	J
Altona, Hamburg, Wansbek	46	1647–1938	N
Altstrelitz	1	1740–1923	N
Alzey	1	1913	J
Andernach	6	1827–1906	P
Ansbach*	19	1748–1916	J
Apolda*	1	1899–1905	P
Arnswalde (Brandenburg)	62	1829–1897	P
Arnswalde	1	1780–	N
Aschaffenburg	1	1837–1839	J
Aschenhausen (Thuringia)*	13	1740–1913	J
Aschenhausen (Brandenburg)*	34	1802–1914	P
Aschersleben*	2	1849–1891	P
Aschersleben*	1	1805	N
Auerbach	8	1836–1901	P
Auerbach	12	1848–1899	J
Augsburg	1	1809	J
Aurich (Hannover)*	5	1811–1861	J
Aurich (Hannover)*	4	1811–1898	P
Bad Kissingen	1	1908–1912	J
Bad Segeberg	1	1934	J
Beczk	1	1689	N
Beeskow	5	1817–1925	J
Belgard (Persante)*	2	1823–1914	P
Bergen (Hanau)*	1	1829–1881	P
Berlin*	177	1671–1946	J
Berlin*	340	1804–1924	P
Berlin*	90	1675–1925	N
Bernburg*	6	1831–1871	J
Bernkastel	1	1856–1863	J
Bernkastel	11	1848–1936	P
Beuthen*	114	1818–1897	P
Beuthen*	34	1810–1895	J
Beverungen	12	1709–1901	J
Beverungen	49	1708–1906	P
Bielefeld*	61	1791–1912	P
Bielefeld*	9	1809–1862	J
Billerbeck	1	1821	J
Bingen	1	1800–1872	J
Bingen	1	Middle Ages	N
Birstein*	1	1890–1920	P
Birstein*	1	18th century	N
Bleicherode	4	1847–1927	J
Bleicherode	1	1805	N
Bleicherode	9	1760–1932	P
Bocholt*	3	1909–1912	P
Bochum*	30	1833–1912	P
Bochum*	8	1851–1900	J
Bodenfelde	2	1807–1870	P
Boizenburg*	9	1794–1858	J
Boizenburg*	11	1799–1862	P
Bomst*	3	1891–1915	P
Bomst*	3	1868–1897	J
Bonn*	3	1738–1796	J
Bonn*	2	19th century	P
Borek*	181	1825–1907	P
Borek*	23	1834–1905	J
Borghorst*	2	1871–1904	P
Braetz*	5	1877–1927	P
Brakel	1	1764	J
Brandenburg*	5	1821–1912	P
Brandenburg*	1	1876–1929	J
Braunsberg	40	1854–1938	P
Braunschweig*	5	1880–1910	P
Breisach	29	1803–1937	P
Breisach	18	1801–1920	J
Bremen	3	1906–1928	P
Bremke	1	1899–1900	J
Breslau*	12	1748–1866	J
Breslau*	5	18/19 cen	N
Breslau*	137	1817–1936	P
Brest Kujawsk (Warsaw)	30	1826–1928	P
Brieg*	— —		P
Brieg*	1	1841	J
Bromberg*	17	1809–1884	J
Bromberg*	138	1815–1900	P
Bruchsal	6	1840–1895	J
Bruttig	1	1831–1838	J
Bublitz*	11	1813–1880	J
Bublitz*	9	1820–1935	P
Buergel	80	1726–1882	P
Buergel	23	1748–1829	J
Bunzlau*	1	1867–1887	N
Burg	1	1873	J
Burg	13	1872–1933	P
Burgbernheim	1	1825	J
Burgsteinfurt	18	1763–1904	J
Burgsteinfurt	44	1759–1837	P
Buttenhausen	1	1835–1850	J
Butzbach*	2	1838–1870	J
Christburg	15	1858–1934	P
Cleve	2	1799–1923	J
Coepenick	1	1830–1832	J
Coethen*	1	1856	J
Cologne see Koeln			
Corbach*	1	1876	N
Cosel (Saxony)	8	1823–1875	J
Cosel (Silesia)	2	1868–1908	P
Crailsheim	3	1810–1920	P
Crailsheim	6	1779–1911	J
Culmsee	13	1843–1910	P
Czempin*	5	1838–1862	J
Czempin*	55	1795–1899	P
Danzig*	9	1850–1935	P
Danzig*	2	1793	N
Darmstadt*	29	18th century	P
Darmstadt*	98	1663–1918	J
Deggingen (Wuerttemberg)	8	1825–1870	J
Deggingen (Bavaria)	10	1805–1859	P
Delitzsch	2	1911–1928	P
Delmenhorst	2	1830–1911	P
Derenburg	1	1805	N
Dessau	2	1902–1907	P
Dessau	2	1764–1772	J
Detmold*	2	1810	N
Dettelbach	1	1790	J
Dettelbach	4	1871–1899	P
Dettensee*	19	1855–1930	J
Dettensee*	138	1811–1923	P
Deutsch–Eylau	1	1869	J
Deutsch–Krone*	15	1623–1871	J
Deutsch–Krone*	12	1780–1917	P
Diespeck	7	1723–1825	J
Diespeck	27	1801–1902	P
Diez a.d.Lahn*	1	1863	J
Diez*	14	1860–1935	P
Dinslaken	6	1801–1888	J
Dinslaken	3	1839,1922–31	P
Dirschau*	1	1850	J
Dobrzyca	3	1841–1873	J

Place	Count	Years	Code
Dobrzyca	24	1834–1892	P
Donauworth	1	1383	J
Dortmund	6	1899–1912	P
Dramburg*	2	1856–1889	J
Dresden*	5	1788–1919	J
Dresden*	2	1786–1840	N
Dresden*	43	1835–1932	P
Driesen	58	1791–1924	P
Driesen	1	1864	N
Driesen*	6	1818–1861	J
Drossen*	8	1811–1887	J
Drossen*	14	1836–1888	P
Duesseldorf	3	1822–1933	J
Duesseldorf	1	1714	N
Dyhrenfurt	1	1782–1807	N
Dziekanka	1	1909	N
East Prussia	1	1800	N
Ederheim	15	1791–1874	J
Eichstetten*	2	1831–1885	J
Eichtersheim	1	1774	J
Eiterfeld*	1	1891–1928	J
Elberfeld	3	1899, 1913	P
Elbing (Danzig)*	90	1817–1936	P
Elbing (Posen)*	28	1811–1913	J
Ellar	13	1841–1887	P
Ellar	1	1846	J
Ellrich*	1	1816–1858	J
Ellrich*	1	1805	N
Ellrich*	3	1790–1907	P
Elmshorn	25	1828–1932	P
Emden*	1	1855–1895	J
Emmendingen*	3	1816–1923	P
Emmendingen*	5	1796–1928	J
Emmerich	4	1825–1911	P
Erfurt*	111	1817–1917	P
Erfurt*	30	1823–1923	J
Ermershausen	1	1769–1922	J
Ermershausen	5	1778–1909	P
Ermetzhofen*	6	1837–1922	P
Eschau	2	1830–1918	P
Eschwege*	3	1825–1930	P
Esens*	1	1854–1855	J
Esens*	21	1845–1891	P
Ettenheim*	1	1860–1874	J
Euerbach	1	1703	J
Feuchtwangen*	27	1822–1902	P
Feuchtwangen*	7	1830–1846	J
Filehne	23	1829–1921	P
Filehne	4	1835–1846	J
Flatow*	30	1787–1907	P
Flatow*	1	1828–1874	N
Flatow*	4	1790–1897	J
Floss*	55	1700–1892	P
Floss*	128	1682–1889	J
Fordon*	1	—	J
Fordon*	1	—	P
Forth*	3	1719–1914	J
Frankenau*	1	1823–1853	P
Frankenberg*	3	1822–1899	J
Frankenberg*	12	1802–1906	P
Frankershausen*	11	1825–1923	P
Frankfurt a.M.*	19	1820–1913	P
Frankfurt a.M.*	13	1614–1938	J
Frankfurt a.M.*	2	1805–1808	N
Frankfurt a.O.*	74	1736–1926	J
Frankfurt a.O.*	114	1751–1929	P
Frankfurt a.O.*	5	1759–1847	N
Fraustadt*	69	1818–1928	P
Fraustadt*	22	1802–1866	J
Freiburg*	2	1897–1922	P
Freiburg*	1	1895	J
Freienwalde*	32	1857–1932	P
Freienwalde*	5	1857–1914	J
Freystadt*	1	1857	P
Friedeberg*	22	1834–1913	P
Friedeberg*	14	1814–1910	J
Friedrichstadt*	22	1825–1917	P
Friedrichstadt*	11	1802–1910	J
Fuerth*	3	1913	P
Fuerth*	3	1773–1872	J
Fuerth*	1	1761–1806	N
Fulda	85	1731–1898	J
Gadebusch*	1	1801–1843	P
Gadebusch*	1	1783–1786	J
Gandersheim*	3	1856–1927	P
Gandersheim*	1	1844	J
Gedern*	26	1832–1936	P
Gedern*	15	1867–1933	J
Gehaus*	1	1822–1909	J
Geinsheim	1	1783–1786	J
Geisa*	1	1872–1891	J
Geisa*	31	1811–1929	P
Geldersheim	1	1842–1860	J
Gemuenden	2	1821–1857	P
Genthin	1	1855–1905	P
Georgenberg	4	1854–1874	P
Georgensmuend	1	1844	J
Georgensmuend	1	1836–1898	P
Gerolzhofen	1	1807–1904	P
Gersfeld	2	1837–1934	J
Gersfeld	1	1827	P
Geseke*	1	1858–1934	J
Giebelstadt	1	1730	J
Giebelstadt	2	1861–1919	P
Gladenbach	1	1788–1849	P
Gleiwitz*	3	1889–1917	P
Gleiwitz*	1	1890–1896	J
Glogau*	1	1864	N
Glogau*	20	1718–1845	J
Glogau*	28	1744–1922	P
Gnesen*	1	1858	P
Gnesen*	1	1840–1852	J
Gnesen*	8	1783–1909	N
Goch	1		N
Gochsheim*	4	1823–1886	J
Gochsheim*	3	1845–1887	P
Goettingen	3	1894–1906	P
Goettingen	1	1348	J
Gollnow*	1	1867	J
Goslar	3	1845–1888	P
Gostyn	6	1862–1891	P
Grabow*	7	1823–1901	P
Graetz*	139	1754–1900	P
Graetz*	45	1749–1901	J
Grajewo	4	1874–1877	P
Graudenz	3	1851–1936	P
Gravenhage (The Hague)	1	1760–1915	N
Greifenhagen	1	—	N
Greifenhagen	29	1821–1906	P
Greifenhagen	2	1888–1891	J
Greifswald	2	1863–1902	J
Greifswald	17	1851–1913	P
Grevesmuehlen	1	1844	J
Gross–Bieberau*	19	1802–1929	J
Gross–Bieberau*	11	1848–1930	P
Gross–Steinheim	10	1845–1912	P
Gross–Steinheim	1	1822	J
Gross–Zimmern	1	1756	J
Gruenberg	7	1847–1940	P
Gruenberg	1	1855–1899	J
Guestrow*	33	1719–1922	P
Guestrow*	30	1794–1831	J
Gundersheim	1	1844	J
Gunzenhausen*	1	—	J
Guttstadt*	3	1846–1902	J
Guttstadt*	31	1834–1904	P
Hadamar	1	1854–1869	J
Hagen	61	1832–1938	P
Hagen	51	1854–1910	J
Haigerloch	2	—	N
Halberstadt*	3	1731–1803	N
Halberstadt*	106	1661–1913	P
Halberstadt*	64	1700–1903	J
Halle*	3	1700–1770	N
Halle*	22	1800–1897	P
Halle*	21	1767–1903	J
Haltern	9	1843–1925	P
Haltern	2	1856	J
Hamburg*	13	1857–1917	P
Hamburg*	2	1890–1903	J
Hameln*	7	1710–1924	P
Hameln*	14	1723–1872	J
Hamm	8	1813–1926	P
Hamm	39	1732–1835	J
Hammerstein	6	1812–1869	P
Hanau*	2	1813–1899	J
Hannover	6	1790–1914	P
Hannover	1	—	N
Hannover	4	1848–1911	J
Harburg	74	1750–1934	P
Harburg	39	1754–1902	J
Harburg	1	—	N
Havixbeck	1	1831–1871	P
Hechingen	25	1751–1906	J
Hechingen	2	1635–	N
Hechingen	45	1637–1930	P
Heidelberg*	5	1714–1869	J
Heidelberg*	1	1900–1914	P
Heidingsfeld	8	1764–1853	J
Heidingsfeld	9	1816–1879	P
Heilsberg	3	1852–1912	P
Helmstedt*	1	1750–1754	N
Herborn	7	1860–1928	P
Herford	4	1849–1899	J
Herford	31	1827–1912	P
Herxheim	1	1864	J
Hessdorf	1	1822–1833	J
Hesse see Kurhessen			

Place	No.	Years	Code
Hesse	2	1826	N
Hessen–Darmstadt	10	1524–1930	J
Heubach*	1	1764	J
Hildburghausen*	2	1774–1824	J
Hildesheim	2	1711–1830	J
Hirschhorn*	4	1808–1872	J
Hirschhorn*	7	1789–1935	P
Hoechberg	13	1763–1881	P
Hoechberg	12	1720–1888	J
Hoeringshausen	12	1824–1914	P
Hoeringshausen	24	1828–1910	J
Hoerstein	1	1844–1868	N
Hoexter	1	1882–1890	J
Hoexter	5	1887–1912	P
Hohenlimburg	8	1869–1921	P
Holzminden*	1	1845	J
Holzminden*	1	1838	P
Homberg/Hesse*	17	1774–1913	P
Homberg*	12	1827–1898	J
Huerben	1	1800–1837	N
Huettenheim	8	1769–1933	P
Inowroclaw	1	1846	J
Insterburg*	32	1858–1917	P
Insterburg*	7	1858–1927	J
Ittlingen*	2	1837–1917	P
Jarotschin*	17	1834–1914	P
Jaratschewo	6	1740–1848	P
Jastrow*	3	1814–1879	J
Jastrow*	1	1810–1816	N
Jastrow*	11	1852–1907	P
Jesberg	1	—	J
Jesberg	2	1838–1857	P
Johannisburg	1	1836	J
Jugenheim	2	1833–1880	P
Jutroschin	6	1854–1899	P
Kallies/Kalisch*	3	1858–1938	P
Kallies/Kalisch*	1	1836	J
Karbach	9	1804–1869	P
Karbach	5	1809–1842	J
Karge	1	1832–1834	N
Karlsruhe*	55	1809–1940	J
Karlsruhe*	16	1770–1839	P
Kassel	2	1871–1912	J
Kassel	2	18th cent	N
Kattowitz*	17	1865–1911	J
Kattowitz*	71	1861–1920	P
Kiel*	1	1859–1861	J
Kippenheim	4	1793–1903	J
Kirchhain*	1	1850–1900	P
Kissingen	1	1907–1911	J
Kleinbardorf	1		P
Kleineibstadt	1	1871–1926	J
Kleineibstadt	1	1864–1918	P
Kobylin	2	1778–1856	P
Koeln*	6	1887–1930	J
Koeln*	1	1830	N
Koeln*	7	1847–1914	P
Koenigsberg*	8	1812–1931	J
Koenigsberg*	6	1798–1847	N
Koenigsberg*	3	1871–1912	P
Koenigshuette*	1	1876–1886	J
Koenigshuette*	64	1855–1921	P
Koeslin*	14	1817–1906	P
Koeslin*	1		N
Kolberg	1	1876	J
Kolberg	2	1854–1919	P
Kolmar	4	1813–1891	J
Kolmar	21	1818–1865	P
Konstanz*	1	1864–1910	J
Koschmin*	13	1808–1905	J
Koschmin*	118	1800–1912	P
Kosten	67	1834–1895	P
Kosten	11	1838–1876	J
Kostschin	5	1849–1903	P
Kowal	16	1837–1939	P
Krakow*	21	1820–1905	P
Krefeld	1	1816	J
Kreuzberg/Silesia*	56	1823–1918	P
Kreuzberg/Silesia*	7	1863–	J
Kroeben	4	1835–1883	P
Krotoschin*	3	1785–1831	N
Krotoschin*	51	1825–1901	P
Kurhessen	2	1648–1841	N
Kurmark	5	1743–1812	N
Kurnik*	22	1809–1866	P
Ladenburg*	1	1872	J
Landau*	1	1860–1886	P
Landau*	1	1711	J
Landeck*	2	1869–1885	P
Landsberg*	52	1733–1898	P
Landsberg*	73	1717–1912	J
Landsberg*	2	1765	N
Landshut	1	1705	J
Langendernbach*	1	1882	J
Langendorf*	9	1758–1922	P
Langendorf*	2	1783–1824	J
Lauenburg*	1	1936–1938	J
Laupheim	19	1741–1902	J
Lautenburg	1	1898–1912	J
Leipzig	23	1834–1931	P
Leipzig	18	1814–1912	J
Leipzig	1	1675–1764	N
Lengfeld	3	1834–1938	J
Lenzen	2	1769–1877	J
Leschnitz*	1	1857–1912	P
Levern	1	1872–1900	P
Lichenroth	3	1825–1923	P
Liebenwalde*	1	1831	N
Lieberose	1	1841	J
Liebstadt	1		J
Liegnitz*	1	1822	P
Liegnitz*	5	1815–1910	J
Limburg	9	1846–1901	P
Lippe–Detmold	1	1810	N
Lippehne	11	1773–1903	P
Lissa	1	1839	N
Lissa	3	1905–1917	P
Loetzen	54	1870–1923	P
Lomscha	6	1877–1920	P
Lorsch	1	1900	J
Lubacz–Sieszewa	1	1806	N
Luebbecke	1	1595–1701	J
Luebeck	6	1880–1913	J
Lubien	12	1837–1894	P
Lublinitz*	1	1855–1865	P
Lubraniec	19	1826–1930	P
Ludwigsburg	2	1812–1911	J
Lyck	17	1804–1919	P
Märkisch-Friedland*	111	1700–1912	P
Märkisch-Friedland*	3	1784–1815	N
Märkisch-Friedland*	107	1706–1880	J
Magdeburg*	2	1874–1912	P
Magdeburg*	4	1702–1927	J
Mainz*	10	1758–1920	P
Mainz*	5	1729–1929	J
Malchin*	2	1814–1852	P
Mannheim*	1	1830–1880	J
Marienburg*	18	1841–1921	P
Marienburg*	2	1857–1902	J
Marienwerder*	1	1830–1880	J
Marienwerder*	22	1785–1938	P
Marisfeld*	2	1846–1857	J
Markoldendorf–Luethorst	1	1836–1903	P
Marksteft	1	1812–1853	J
Marlow*	4	1801–1877	J
Marlow*	12	1818–1914	P
Maroldsweisach	1	1868–1882	J
Massbach	18	1750–1909	J
Massbach	3	1837–1909	P
Meiningen (Thuringia)*	5	1837–1911	J
Meiningen*	2	19th cent.	N
Meiningen (Saxony)*	4	1864–1885	P
Mellrichstadt	1		J
Melsungen*	10	1825–1899	J
Memel	4	1882–1912	P
Memel	1	1881–1897	J
Memelsdorf	2	1808–1825	J
Meseritz*	4	1815–1898	J
Meseritz*	42	1796–1929	P
Meseritz*	2	1805	N
Mewe	1	1869	J
Michelfeld*	1	1846–1854	P
Militsch	44	1828–1917	J
Militsch	27	1823–1917	P
Miloslaw	1	1839–1909	P
Mirow	2	1803–1853	J
Moenchengladbach	1	1873–1878	N
Moenchsroth	4	1766–1937	J
Moenchsroth	2	1839–1893	P
Moerfelden	1	1829	J
Mohrungen	2	1885–1917	P
Mosbach	1	1900–1923	P
Muehlhausen*	3	1761–1888	J
Muehlhausen*	6	1850–1940	P
Muenster*	42	1827–1912	P
Muenster*	6	1846–1914	J
Muensterberg	6	1842–1900	J
Muensterberg	25	1821–1903	P
Muenzenberg	1	1823–1876	J
Murowana–Goslin	23	1827–1873	P
Myslowitz	37	1854–1913	P
Nakel*	1	1835	N
Nakel*	2	1843–1897	P
Namslau*	19	1836–1899	P
Naumburg*	1	1793–1795	J
Neckarkreis	1	1812–1863	J
Neisse*	3	1857–1912	P

Place	Number	Dates	Code
Neuenkirchen	18	1767–1889	J
Neuenkirchen	44	1768–1927	P
Neumark	6	1722–1813	N
Neustadt (Silesia)*	18	1825–1920	P
Neustadt (Silesia)*	4	1849–1918	J
Neustadt/Pinne	28	1829–1904	P
Neustadt/Warthe	23	1821–1900	P
Neustadt, see Nove Meste			N
Neustadt–Eberswalde	2	1856–1918	J
Neustettin*	5	1856–1889	J
Neustettin*	25	1865–1913	P
Neustrelitz	1	1835–1838	N
Neutershausen	5	1865–1930	P
Neutomischel	2	1861–1925	P
Niederaula	5	1823–1929	P
Niederbreisig	1	1878	P
Niederklein	1	1899–1901	P
Niedermarsberg	6	1898–1923	P
Niederwerrn	22	1785–1873	J
Nienburg	1	1833–1838	J
Nordeck*	1	1862–1881	P
Nordhausen*	23	1827–1925	P
Nordhausen*	7	1820–1874	J
Nove Meste	1	1689	N
Obbach	1	1842–1872	P
Oberaula*	1	1835–1876	P
Oberdorf	8	1747–1913	J
Oberdorf	6	1804–1933	P
Obereuerheim	1	1845–1868	P
Obereuerheim	1	1871	J
Oberlangenstadt	1		N
Oberlauringen	9	1815–1891	P
Obernik/Posen*	23	1834–1899	P
Oberseemen	1	1799–1850	N
Oberseemen	9	1812–1937	P
Oels	1	1860–1878	P
Oettingen	2	1819–1866	P
Offenbach	1	1823	N
Offenbach	118	1614–1932	J
Offenbach	115	1710–1938	P
Ohlau*	8	1816–1881	P
Oppeln*	28	1829–1839	P
Oppeln*	2	1858–1936	J
Oranienburg	5	1813–1882	J
Oranienburg	18	1838–1924	P
Orb	1	1823–1880	P
Orth	1	1825	J
Osnabrueck*	1	1309–1321	J
Osterholz–Scharmbeck	40	1839–1938	P
Ostrowo*	1	—	N
Ostrowo*	24	1814–1912	P
Ottensoos	9	1619–1890	J
Ottensoos	13	1828–1920	P
Paderborn*	3	1855–1935	J
Paderborn*	8	1819–1935	P
Partenheim	1	1842–1877	P
Pasewalk*	9	1816–1937	J
Pasewalk*	97	1816–1937	P
Pattensen	1	1870–1890	P
Pattensen	2	19th cent.	J
Penzlin*	3	1749–1846	J
Perleberg*	11	1861–1923	P
Pfalz (Palatinate)	1	1782–1823	N
Pfungstadt*	3	1704–1754	J
Pleschen*	176	1827–1906	P
Pless*	5	1797–1890	P
Pollnow	5	1859–1932	P
Polzin*	3	1838–1906	P
Pommern (Pomerania)	4	18th cent.	N
Posen*	3	19th cent.	N
Posen*	5	1841–1939	P
Potsdam*	2	1491–1836	N
Potsdam*	2	1801–1888	J
Potsdam*	9	1743–1912	P
Prague	1	1782–1823	N
Prenzlau*	6	1754–1865	J
Prenzlau*	36	1790–1912	P
Prenzlau*	2	1751–1841	N
Preussen (Prussia)	1	18th cent.	N
Preussen	17	1777–1932	J
Preussisch–Friedland	10	1864–1903	P
Preussisch–Oldendorf	6	1846–1902	P
Preussisch–Oldendorf	2	1798–1889	J
Preussisch–Stargardt*	15	1851–1895	P
Priegnitz, see Neumark			N
Przedecz (Warsaw)	8	1835–1877	P
Pudewitz	17	1868–1902	P
Pyritz*	111	1841–1906	P
Pyritz*	73	1772–1912	J
Raboldshausen	7	1876–1913	P
Randegg*	1	1827–1851	P
Rastatt	1	1871–1880	J
Rastenburg*	26	1844–1915	P
Ratibor*	28	1786–1918	J
Ratibor*	98	1821–1918	P
Rauschenberg*	1	1893–1901	P
Ravensburg	1	1796–1802	N
Rawitsch	91	1701–1909	P
Reckendorf	2	1828–1867	J
Reckendorf	2	1834–1892	P
Reetz	2	1829–1896	P
Regensburg	1	1912	J
Reichenbach*	16	1832–1939	P
Reichensachsen	1	17–20 cent.	N
Reichensachsen	1	1674–1837	J
Rehna	11	1845–1849	J
Rehna	12	1859–1882	P
Rendsburg	18	1695–1930	J
Rendsburg	1	1795–1844	N
Rendsburg	56	1824–1938	P
Rheda	2	1822–1859	J
Rheda	17	1798–1906	P
Rheinberg	8	1773–1829	J
Rheinberg	1	1704–1877	P
Rhina*	3	1833–1927	P
Rhina*	2	1829–1883	J
Riesenberg*	2	1843–1920	P
Rietberg*	1	1767	J
Rimpar	3	1832–1926	J
Rimpar	6	1815–1922	P
Rimpar	1	1795–1804	N
Roedelsee	2	1798–1825	J
Roessel	6	1884–1937	P
Rogasen*	13	1834–1914	P
Rogasen*	1		N
Rohrbach*	3	1806–1884	P
Romrod	2	1836–1901	J
Romrod	12	1827–1934	P
Romsthal–Eckardroth	2	1799–1925	P
Rosenberg (Oberschlesien)*	2	1859–1888	J
Rosenberg (West Prussia)*	11	1849–1910	P
Rosenberg (West Prussia)*	1	1899–1929	J
Rosenthal*	2	1821–1851	P
Rotenburg*	2	1735	J
Roth*	2	1780–1877	J
Roth*	22	1825–1903	P
Rottenberg	2	1653–1747	J
Ruegenwalde*	3	1835–1859	J
Ruegenwalde*	11	1833–1894	P
Rybnik	44	1834–1916	P
Saalfeld	2	1860–1896	P
Sachsen (Saxony)	1	1840	J
Sachsen–Meiningen	2	19th cent.	N
Sachsen–Weimar–Eisenach	1	1901	J
Salmuenster*	6	1865–1921	P
Salzkotten	1	1801	J
Samotschin	17	1831–1926	P
Sandersleben*	1	1867	J
Sandersleben*	4	1848–1938	P
Sandersleben*	1	1795–1835	N
Santomischel*	72	1820–1898	P
Sarne	73	1829–1892	P
Scharmbeck	4	1878–1915	J
Schermeisel	2	1798–1805	N
Schermeisel	11	1816–1905	P
Schildberg*	1	1876–1882	P
Schildberg*	1	1833–1876	N
Schlawe	3	1846–1902	J
Schlawe	7	1876–1907	P
Schlesien (Silesia)	2	1751–1845	J
Schleswig–Holstein	1	1866	J
Schleswig–Holstein	1	1775–1817	N
Schlettstadt	1	1910–1911	P
Schlichtingsheim	2	1834–1856	P
Schlochau	4	1850–1908	P
Schloppe*	4	1807–1906	J
Schloppe*	2	1885–1904	P
Schnaittach	25	1874–1906	P
Schnaittach	19	1671–1858	J
Schneidemuehl	9	1773–1881	J
Schneidemuehl	10	1778–1921	P
Schoenfliess	8	1866–1920	P
Schoenfliess	1	1776	J
Schoeningen*	1	1900	P
Schoenlanke*	23	1790–1897	P
Schoenlanke*	6	1779–1853	J
Schokken	1	1834–1865	P
Schopfloch	6	1754–1891	J
Schopfloch	16	1767–1938	P
Schottland	1	18–19 cent.	N
Schriebens	2	1896–1908	J
Schrimm*	47	1830–1916	P
Schroda	53	1819–1922	P
Schwabach			

Place	No.	Dates	Type
(Brandenburg)*	7	1760–1880	J
Schwabach (Bavaria)*	24	1722–1934	P
Schwandorf	1	1927	J
Schwebheim	1	1859–1861	P
Schwedt*	7	1814–1897	J
Schwedt*	82	1819–1912	P
Schweinsberg*	1	1896–1900	P
Schweinsfurt	12	1731–1920	J
Schweinshaupten	3	1816–1882	P
Schwerin*	8	1774–1904	J
Schwerin*	11	1736–1935	P
Schwerin/Warthe*	5	1711–1865	J
Schwerin/Warthe*	1	19th cent.	N
Schwerin/Warthe*	7	1834–187	P
Schwersenz	185	1735–1897	P
Schwiebus	20	1890–1921	P
Seelow*	33	1757–1906	P
Seesen	32	1808–1911	P
Seesen	23	1820–1867	J
Segeberg	24	1793–1936	P
Sickenhofen	3	1842–1917	P
Sievershausen	3	1847–1912	J
Soegel*	7	1867–1919	P
Soest	76	1819–1906	P
Soest	15	1829–1855	J
Sohrau*	15	1821–1893	P
Soldin*	1	1847	J
Solms–Braunfels	1	1736–1816	N
Sommerhausen	14	1827–1889	J
Sommerhausen	11	1827–1890	P
Spangenberg*	1	1836	N
Stadtlengsfeld*	8	1798–1939	J
Stargard*	53	1709–1918	J
Stargard*	142	1769–1925	P
Stavenhagen*	1	1776–1813	P
Stavenhagen*	3	1762–1848	J
Steele	1	1744–1827	J
Steinbach (Wuerttemberg)	2	1811–1860	J
Steinbach (Hesse)*	1	1808–1850	P
Sternberg*	14	1825–1897	P
Sternberg*	5	1838–1878	J
Stettin*	34	1816–1897	J
Stettin*	171	1820–1916	P
Stolp*	8	1852–1901	P
Stolp*	6	1840–1892	J
Storkow*	1	1842–1869	J
Stralsund	77	1854–1924	P
Stralsund	19	1774–1924	J
Straussberg	3	1835–1878	J
Straussberg	5	1827–1920	P
Strelitz*	316	1704–1931	P
Strelitz*	143	1755–1911	J
Strelitz*	1	1825–1846	N
Stuhm*	2	1873–1920	J
Stuhm*	28	1857–1936	P
Stuttgart	1	1911	P
Stuttgart	2	1838–1939	J
Suechteln	1	1902–1905	P
Suedpreussen	1	1806	J
Sulzbach/Oberpfalz	85	1811–1927	P
Sulzbach/Oberpfalz	103	1682–1924	J
Sulzbach	1	—	N
Sulzbuerg	2	1813–1926	J
Sulzbuerg	4	1838–1925	P
Tangermuende*	4	1768–1905	P
Tangermuende*	3	1856–1908	J
Tempelburg*	10	1839–1906	P
Tessin*	25	1821–1886	J
Thalheim	5	1842–1970	P
Thalmaessig	3	1804–1849	J
Tilsit	1	1818–1914	P
Tirschtiegel*	2	1748–1888	J
Tost*	6	1820–1898	P
Tost*	1	1831–1877	J
Trappstadt	1	1811–1923	P
Trebbin*	13	1780–1874	P
Trebbin*	1	1692–1812	N
Trebur	20	1836–1933	P
Trebur	2	1846–1862	J
Tremessen*	1	1886–1887	P
Treuenbrietzen	4	1816–1902	J
Trier*	1	—	J
Tuetz	1	1891	N
Tuetz	8	1835–1901	P
Tuetz	1	1837	J
Ulm	2	1865–1875	J
Unruhstadt*	1	1817–1874	N
Unruhstadt*	3	1836–1878	P
Untereisenheim	1	1860–1922	P
Unterriedenberg	1	1843	P
Vlotho	1	1796	J
Voehl	3	1829–1920	J
Voehl	27	1835–1924	P
Voelkershausen*	13	1817–1903	P
Voelkershausen*	3	1830–1864	J
Voelkersleier	4	1840–1902	J
Waag–Neustadt, see Nove Meste			N
Wachenheim	6	1834–1916	P
Wallau	1	1742	P
Walldorf a.d.Werra*	23	1779–1885	J
Walldorf a.d.Werra*	74	1797–1902	P
Wallerstein	31	1700–1850	J
Wallerstein	1	—	N
Wallerstein	23	1789–1870	P
Wandsbeck	6	1745–1893	J
Wandsbeck	2	1888–1908	P
Wanfried*	1	1764–1830	P
Wanfried*	1	1659–1778	J
Warburg*	14	1706–1914	J
Warburg*	15	1758–1912	P
Waren*	1	1830	J
Wassertruedingen	4	1832–1872	P
Wassertruedingen	7	1809–1910	J
Weener*	3	1843–1870	J
Weener*	5	1849–1856	P
Weilburg	12	1874–1931	P
Weilburg	26	1818–1930	J
Weiler*	1	1912	J
Weimar*	1	1840	J
Welbhausen	1	1839–1879	J
Werl	1	1826	J
Werneck	2	1857–1902	J
Wertheim	1	1818–1840	J
Wesel	5	1739–1855	P
Westerburg	1	1851–1886	J
Westfalen	1	1737	N
Westheim*	14	1780–1920	P
Westpreussen	4	1800–1845	N
Westpreussen	3	1773–1812	J
Wetzlar	13	1725–1860	J
Wiesbaden	2	1841–1880	J
Wiesbaden	21	1825–1915	P
Wiesenbronn	1	1815	J
Wiesenfeld	4	1861–1865	J
Wilhermsdorf	3	1753–1870	J
Windsbach	1	1794	J
Wittstock*	1	1875–1908	J
Witzenhausen	4	1892–1928	P
Wolbeck*	1	1822	J
Woldenberg*	26	1845–1897	P
Wolfenbuettel*	58	1755–1925	P
Wolfenbuettel*	37	1809–1922	J
Wolfenbuettel*	3	18/19 cent	N
Wollmirstedt	2	1809–1863	J
Wongrowitz	38	1744–1898	P
Worfelden	6	1893–1925	P
Worms*	54	1831–1936	P
Worms*	2	1877	J
Worms*	2	1782–1823	N
Wriezen*	2	1808–1847	J
Wriezen*	14	1800–1889	P
Wronke*	73	1817–1895	P
Wuerttemberg	1	1828	J
Wuerzburg	3	1814–1880	J
Wuerzburg	3	1862–1913	P
Wuerzburg	1	—	N
Xions	4	1862–1904	P
Zeckendorf	2	1817–1913	J
Zeilitzheim	1	1889–1926	J
Zeitlofs*	2	1831–1932	J
Zossen	9	1753–1765	J
Zuellichau	1	—	N
Zuelz*	135	1627–1913	J
Zuelz*	68	1698–1922	P
Zwesten	1	1832–1863	N
Zwingenberg*	1	1826–1936	J

Greece
by Yitzchak Kerem

*T*o understand the Ottoman Empire laws that applied in this region, read the chapter entitled OTTOMAN EMPIRE before starting this section—Ed.

History

Until the 19th century, the country we know today as Greece was part of the Ottoman Empire. Greece became independent in stages: Attica, Evia and the Peleponnesia in 1821, Thessaly in 1881. Jews mostly lived in Macedonia and Epirus which became part of Greece in 1912. (Peleponnese is the large peninsula south of Athens.)

Greek Jewry dates back as early as antiquity when Aristotle had a debate with a Jew under a tree. In 142 B.C.E. Thessaloniki had two reported synagogues, Etz Hachaim and Etz Hadaat. According to oral tradition, a Jewish community existed in Paramithia in the late classical period. After the fall of Jerusalem in 70 C.E., Jews arrived on the Greek mainland as Roman slaves. The remains of a synagogue on the island of Delos date back to antiquity. By the Middle Ages Greek Jewry had developed a culture that remained distinct until it was destroyed in the Holocaust.

During the Muslim invasion of the Near East and North Africa during the seventh and eighth centuries, all that remained of the Roman Empire was located in the southern Balkans and part of Anatolia. The area that is contemporary Greece was called Romania, and the Jews of the Greek peninsula (and Italy) were correspondingly called Romaniote Jews.[1] By this time, its population center Salonika (today Thessaloniki) had a relatively large Jewish population that later was augmented by German Jews fleeing the Black Death persecution in the 14th century and by Sephardic Jews fleeing the Spanish Inquisition and Iberian expulsions at the end of the 15th century and into the 16th century. With the exception of the Ionian islands, where the Jews had an Italian-Jewish background, most of Greek Jewry was under Ottoman rule from the Middle Ages onward; this larger area (except for modern-day Turkey) is discussed here.

Greek was the native language of the Romaniote Jews. Prayers and Torah readings were translated into Greek. Religious poetry was written in Hebrew script, but in a dialect of Epirotic Greek that had an admixture of Hebrew words and grammar. This Jewish dialect became known as Judeo-Greek. The five *megillot* of the Bible (Book of Esther, Book of Ruth, Song of Songs, Book of Ecclesiastes, and Book of Lamentations) were recited in Greek but written in Hebrew letters. Influences from the Palestinian Talmud, late Hellenistic culture and the Byzantine Empire contributed to the evolution of the *minhag* Romaniote (the Greek prayer rite), little traces of which remain today. Much of the Romaniote prayers were handwritten religious poems passed from generation to generation, (or written in modern times by *hahamim*, wise, older religious leaders who often were rabbis) recited on special occasions like Succot. When the Sephardic exiles arrived in the region after 1492, much of their prayer and ritual dominated the Romaniote customs. Romaniote liturgy and traditions from Ioannina were preserved there until the Holocaust and in the New York City area until recent decades.[2]

No laws fixed Jewish family names in this part of the world. Romaniote custom was for first and last names to be inverted generation after generation, e.g., Moses son of Abraham was Moses Abraham; his son may have been Abraham son of Moses, or Abraham Moses. Sephardim adopted last names after the Spanish Expulsion.

As they did in other parts of the Ottoman Empire, Jews from Spain and Portugal who settled in Greece organized their local Jewish communities according to the original town or region in which they had lived on the Iberian Peninsula. Before 1900, the stronghold of Greek Jewry was Salonika in Thrace, where the majority of the population was Jewish, and Judeo-Spanish was the language of commerce. In 1912, the Jewish population numbered between 70,000 and 80,000. In the first decade of the 20th century, Ioannina had a Jewish population of 7,000; Corfu, 5,000; Rhodes, 4,000; and Larissa, about 2,000. In the last quarter of the 19th century, the Jewish population of Hania, Crete, was about 2,000.

Greece conquered Salonika in 1912 during its struggle for independence from Turkey. After that, Jews began to leave Salonika as Greeks came to settle. Several years before Turkey ceded Salonika to Greece in 1912, in 1906 a door-to-door cenus was taken. Salonika to Greece in 1912, a door-to-door census was taken. Written in Turkish, it is held by Greece's Macedonian State Archives.[*] By 1922, Salonika had a Greek majority. The Jewish population in Greece, which stood at 100,000 after the annexation of Thrace following the Balkan War of 1912–13, dropped to 77,000 on the eve of World War II.

Most Greek Jewry were destroyed following the German occupation of World War II. In less than a year, between March 1943 and February 1944, more than 46,000 Jews from Salonika were deported to Auschwitz and Bergen Belsen, 95 percent of whom perished. A similar fate befell the Jews of East Thracia and central and eastern Macedonia. By the end of World War II, only 10,000 Jews remained in Greece; today this number has dwindled to little more than 5,000. The main Jewish communities today are located in Athens, Larissa, Salonika and Volos. The Central Board of Greek Jewish Communities[*] is the legal guardian of settlements with fewer than 20 Jews.

Resources for Genealogical Research

For practical purposes, Greek-Jewish genealogical research is possible only from the middle of the 19th century, when the

Paris-based Alliance Israelite Universelle* began to establish schools in the area. Records prior to that time have been lost, mostly in fires and other disasters. These were primarily Jewish communal records of circumcisions, marriages and deaths plus religious exegeses with genealogical details about the author on the introductory pages. In addition to information generated by Alliance activities, publications and some extant cemetery data, the primary source of data is individuals in the so-called "Sephardic diaspora" scattered all over the world. In the absence of community or civil archival records, genealogists must turn to a variety of other sources, at the same time developing a strategy that focuses on family names and the locations where individuals with these names lived. Often if one knows a family name and where they lived, it is possible to find someone who can help.[3]

Alliance Reports

Alliance schools generated numerous reports, including lists of principals and (sometimes) students, political reports about local communities, and Ottoman Empire-wide events. The records, written in French, sometimes included supplementary information in local languages such as Greek, Italian and Judeo-Spanish. For example, if disasters such as major fires occurred in a community, reports exist of the committees formed to deal with them. Some Alliance records may be seen at its archives in Paris* (see FRANCE); others are held in Jerusalem at the Central Archives for the History of the Jewish People* (see ISRAEL).

Publications

Among the best sources of information are 19th- and 20th-century serial publications from this area and from major Jewish communities in western Europe. Included are those of the Alliance Universelle Israelite* (in French), the French Jewish weeklies L'Univers Israelite and Archives Israelites, The [London] Jewish Chronicle and a periodical written in Italian called Mose, published on Corfu. A vast Judeo-Spanish press from Salonika, including daily or periodic newspapers, existed from 1876 until the Holocaust. The main Judeo-Spanish newspapers were La Epoca, La Verdad, El Jidyo, La Renaissancia Judia and La Axion. In French there were Le Progres, l'Independant, Pro-Israel and l'Opinion. Because of the large number of names mentioned, particularly valuable sources for genealogy are the Zionist Israel from Salonika and Foni in Athens. Articles about Ottoman Empire Jewry, including Greece, may be found in the Proceedings of the Jewish Historical Society of England, Studia Rosenthalia from Amsterdam, Revue des Etudes Juives (Paris), Pe'amim (Ben-Zvi Institute, Jerusalem) and even Archivum Ottmanicum and Neve Romania from Germany. In addition to the Alliance schools, British (Anglo-Jewish Association) and German Ezra (Hilfsverein) schools in Salonika also generated reports and publications.

The Jewish National and University Library* (see ISRAEL) in Jerusalem has complete sets of many publications, and Bar-Ilan University* also has some. The best collection of publications is at the Ben Zvi Institute* in Jerusalem, where newspapers published in Salonika, Istanbul, Vienna, Cairo, and even New York may be found. The archives of the Alliance Israelite Universelle* in Paris has the most complete collection of its publications. Publications and other information also may be found at the Italian Museum* in Jerusalem.

Since the mid-1980s, the scholarly publication of the faculty of Oriental Studies at Cambridge University,* Bulletin of Judaeo-Greek Studies has appeared twice yearly. The leading Sephardic cultural and communal publications around the world include Los Muestros (Brussels),* La Lettre Sefarade (France),* Aki Yerushalayim (Jerusalem),* Sephardic House Newsletter (New York),* La Erensia Sefardi (New York),* Association of American Jews from Turkey (AAJFT) Newsletter (New York),* Shalom (Istanbul),* Tiryaki (Istanbul),* Chronika (Athens),* Magen Escudo (Caracas),* Sefardica (Buenos Aires),* Shajar (Montevideo)* and El Vocero (Chile).* All of the publications occasionally have published information about Greek Jewry. In recent years, the publication of the Jewish Museum in Athens included an article about Greek-Jewish names.

Yizkor Books

Several yizkor books on Greek Jewry have been published by survivor groups in Greece and Israel. They include:

- Michael Mohlo, ed. In Memorium: Hommage aux Victimes Juives des Nazis en Grece (In memory of to the Jewish victims of the Nazis in Greece). [French] Thessalonika: Communauté d'Israelite de Thessalonique, 1973.
- Saloniki ir va-em be-yisrael (Salonika, mother city in Israel). [French, Hebrew, Yiddish] Jerusalem-Tel Aviv: Centre de recherches sur le Judaisme de Salonique, Union des Juifs de Grece, 1967.
- David A. Rencanti, ed. Zikhron Saloniki: Gedulata ve-hurbana shel Yerushalyim de-Balkan (A memorial of Saloniki: the grandeur and destruction of Jerusalem of the Balkans). [Hebrew, Judezmo] Tel Aviv: Committee for the Publication of the Salonikan Memorial Book, 1971/72.

Salonika Records

Communal records of the Athens and Salonika Jewish community, 1870–1941, confiscated by the Nazis during World War II, were recaptured by the Soviet army and today are held in the Osobyi Archives* in Moscow. Still unknown are the nature and breadth of these records, but it is possible that they may include such valuable genealogical material as birth, marriage and death records since the 1860s. The collection includes 400 files from the Salonikan Jewish community and three files from the Athenian Jewish community. Also at the Osobyi are records of the Stock Company Saloniki-Palestine and of the Great Lodges of the Jewish Order B'nai B'rith in Yugoslavia and Greece.

Professor Minna Rozen, former director of the Diaspora Research Institute at Tel Aviv University,* has made a digitized video record of these documents and is in the process of computerizing the data for public use. The files also are accessible on microfilm at the archives of the U.S. Holocaust Memorial Museum* (see HOLOCAUST).

New York's YIVO Institute for Jewish Research (see YIVO) has a collection of Jewish vital records of Salonika from the 1920s and the Central Archives for the History of the Jewish People* has Jewish community records for the years 1913–46.

Circumcision Registers

Books kept by individual *mohels* (ritual circumcisers) are prime genealogical records, but they were the private property of the mohel and they, like other Jewish community records, today are scattered all over the world. The Central Archives for the History of the Jewish People* in Jerusalem has a late 19th-century mohel book from Izmir, Turkey, while others are in private hands. If one knows the history of individual communities, especially where the residents went when they emigrated, then it is sometimes possible to find sources. For example, the circumcision registers from the communities of Castoria and Ioannina at the end of the 19th and beginning of the 20th centuries are in the hands of descendants of the *mohelim* who created them. Sol Matsil of Great Neck, New York, has the circumcision book of his father who was from Ioannina. Information about the circumcision books of Jews from Castoria may be obtained from Rabbi Marantz, The Sephardic Temple, Cedarhurst, New York.*

Existing Jewish Cemeteries

Jewish cemeteries still exist and can be visited in the following cities and towns: Athens, Corfu, Didymotiko (Demotica), Drama, Ioannina, Kavalla, Larissa, Patras (current state of this cemetery is unknown), Rhodes, Thessaloniki (Salonica), Trikala, Veria (currently neglected and pillaged), Volos and Zakynthos. For information on visiting them, contact the Athens Jewish community.*

Judeo-Greek Diaspora

Beginning in the 19th century, Jews of the Ottoman Empire, including those from today's Greece, migrated all over the world, usually to communities where they had *landsmen* (relatives or people from the same localities). It is essential to know where most of the Jews of an ancestral Greek town emigrated; they usually maintained separate synagogues,

Interior of the Italian synagogue in Thessaloniki at the beginning of the 20th century. Courtesy of Tomasz Wisniewski.

burial societies, Talmud Torah schools, cemeteries and communities because they generally were not accepted by the local Ashkenazic community. It is a wandering diaspora, and one needs to read history and literature to trace much of it. More than 40 communities of former Greek Jews exist throughout the world today in North and South America, Africa and Europe. To find traces of this diaspora, consult literature about the Greek Jewish diaspora annotated by this author in *Greece in Modern Times*.[4] Toward the end of the 19th century, some Jews moved from Russia to Turkey and Greece. At the same time, other Greek-Jewish communities existed in Bohemia and Hungary.

The area of Greece known as the Peleponnesia had nine active Jewish communities (Argos, Corinth, Hydra, Kalamata, Mistra, Nauflion, Patras, Sparta and Tripoli) that were destroyed in a war between the Greeks and Turks early in the 19th century. In the Attica region, Jewish communities were destroyed in the cities of Agrineon, Naufpaktos and Thebes. The communities were comprised of Romaniote and Italian Jews originally from Venice. Survivors, taken as slaves, were redeemed by the Jewish community of Smyrna (today Izmir, Turkey). Others went to Corfu and to Eretz Yisrael.

The diaspora from the Greek island of Rhodes was one of the largest among Ottoman Jewry. From 1895 to 1940, Jews from Rhodes migrated primarily to what was then the Belgian Congo (Zaire [1971–97], today Democratic Republic of Congo) and to Seattle, Washington, in the United States. Many of the first emigrés, at the end of the 19th century, just traveled wherever a boat went, often as stowaways. Thus, some Jews from Rhodes landed in Elizabethville in the Belgian Congo and ended up establishing commerce for the conquering Belgian army. Their descendants may be found today in a remote valley in Zaire, in Burundi and in Rwanda. Along with Romanian Jews, they were among the first Jews in Rhodesia (now Zimbabwe), where they became merchants. After Mobuto assumed power in the Congo (in 1965) and fully enacted nationalization in 1973, a large group went to Cape Town, South Africa; another group went to Brussels; smaller numbers settled in Atlanta, Georgia; Buenos Aires; Montgomery, Alabama; Rio de Janeiro and Sao Paulo in Brazil; and in Venezuela.

Salonikan Jewry has a huge diaspora in Paris. Many left Greece after anti-Semitic riots in Salonika in the 1930s. Because of the influence of the Alliance schools, the more educated bourgeoisie tended to travel toward Paris, while the laborers emigrated mostly to Palestine. Today, between 15,000 and 18,000 former Salonikan Jews live in the South Tel Aviv/Jaffa area. They are also easy to find in Paris, where they tend to gather in certain neighborhoods and in certain industries. They largely control the fashion industry in the 16th *arrondissement* (district) and in the 9th arrondissement are clustered in an area colloquially called "Salonika City," where they have their own restaurants and clubs. The poorer worker population from Salonika and other parts of Turkey lived in the 11th arrondissement of Paris.

Another large group of former Salonikan Jews once lived in Alexandria, Egypt, but after 1956, they moved to Rome and

London. Other Greek Jews in Alexandria came from Corfu and Ioannina. The whereabouts of their archives is unknown.

A large number of Jews from the Ionian island of Corfu went to Manchester, England, in the 1840s because they were cotton merchants and wanted to go into the lucrative fabric trade at the beginning of the Industrial Revolution in that city. Some emigrated in the late 19th century and early 20th centuries to Alexandria, Egypt; others went to Trieste. A blood libel in Corfu in 1891 caused many more Jews to leave.

Little intermarriage between Greek Jews and Christians has taken place, although some occurred in colonial America. Most Greek Jews (primarily from Ioannina and Salonika) came to the United States in the first two decades of the 20th century. Because Greek Jews did not speak Yiddish, there was little mixing with Ashkenazic Jewry at first. Among those who emigrated overseas, the distinctions of separate synagogue affiliation, marriage with descendants of fellow townspeople and parochial Sephardic and Judeo-Greek identity had largely disappeared by the third generation, except perhaps among the Jews from Rhodes who settled in Seattle, Washington. Although not religiously observant, Rhodes Jews typically have not assimilated and tend to marry among themselves. Even in the third generation, it is common to find them marrying fellow "islanders."

Geographical Name Changes

One of the major difficulties in tracing the Sephardic diaspora is the fact that communities often had many different names at different times, some reflecting first Turkish and then Greek hegemony. Within a country, differing communities may have similar-sounding names, like the Greek island of Zante (from the Venetian period or when referred to in Italian) and the mainland town of Xanthi. In Greek, the Ionian island and town Zante are called Zakynthos. This community should not be confused with Xanthi in the Thrace region in northeastern Greece. It should not be further confused with the German town Xantin. Consult historical atlases to be certain of the location of a town.

Useful Institutions in Greece Today

The following institutions hold archival and historical material, newspapers, journals and other publications relevant to the history of Greek Jewry. KIS's monthly historical magazine *Chronika* has great value as do the Jewish newspapers held at the Jewish National and University Library. The Greek National Archives holds material on Greek Jews from the Greek revolution (1821–33) to World War II.

In Athens, information may be found at the following institutions: the Greek Foreign Ministry, Benaki Archives, Benaki Library, National Archives, National Library, Parliament Library, Jewish Museum, Central Board of Jewish Communities (KIS), Souliote History Center, and the E.L.I.A. Archive.

In Thessaloniki, useful addresses include: Albert Nar, Thessaloniki Jewish Community,* 24 Tsimiski Street, Thessaloniki; Salonikan Jewish History Study Center and Salonikan Jewish Museum;* YMCA Library, Ottoman Macedonian Archives;* Macedonian Studies Library;* Aristotle University,

Sketch of the Monastirlis Synagogue in Thessaloniki. Copyright by Elias V. Messinas, AssocAIA Architect.

main library,* Thessaloniki Municipality* (houses the former City of Thessaloniki Study Center) and Institute of Balkan Studies*. Other potentially helpful institutions in Greece include the Corfu Reading Room,* Historical Archives and Library in Chios,* Ottoman Archive (Iraklion*), Municipal Library (Chania),* Jewish Synagogue and Museum (Chania),* and in Larissa, the office of the lawyer Moisi Esdras and Rabbi Shabetai Azaria at the offices of the local Jewish community.

Resources Outside of Greece

Salonikan and other Greek Jewish records can be found in numerous institutions in Israel including the Central Zionist Archives,* Ben-Zvi Institute Library and Yad Ben-Zvi Archive,* the Israel State Archives,* the Labor Archives,* Haganah Archives,* Jabotinsky Archives,* Hebrew University and National Library Archive,* the Institute for Microfilmed Manuscripts (National Library),* Jerusalem Municipal Archives,* Yad Vashem,* Lochamei Getaot Holocaust Museum,* Salonikan Jewry Research Institute (Tel Aviv),* and the Ladino Literature Unit at Bar Ilan University.* The largest collection for Salonika is at the Central Archives.*

In the United States, the following institutions hold some useful information: U.S. National Archives,* U.S. Holocaust Memorial Museum,* Library of Congress,* YIVO,* the Joint Distribution Committee,* and the Jewish Heritage Museum (New York City).*

Internet and E-mail Resources

Following are some valuable Internet sources for researching Judeo-Greek genealogy:

- *Sefarad, the Sephardic Newsletter,* a monthly publication edited by Yitzchak Kerem. Among other features, it includes a Sephardic genealogical database, bibliography, developing archives and Sephardic researcher directory (SPIDER.HUJI.AC.IL/~MSSEA).

- Sephardic genealogy sources coordinated by Dr. Jeff Malka, ORTHOHELP.COM/GENEAL/SEFARDIM.HTM..
- Jewish Museum of Rhodes. WWW.RHODESJEWISHMUSEUM.ORG.
- Rhodesli Sephardic Family Trees Database—Jewish names from Rhodes compiled by Petro Michailidis, WWW.GEOCITIES.COM/HEARTLANDVALLEY/2177.
- *Etsi*, the online version of a quarterly publication about Sephardic Jewry with considerable Ottoman content. WWW.GEOCITIES.COM/ENCHANTEDFOREST/1321.
- Ottoman Sephardic Page compiled by Scott Marks, WWW.GEOCITIES.COM/THETROPICS/CABAN/5947.
- *Ha-Kehillah*, a publication on Greek synagogues edited by Elias Messinas, WWW.SEFARAD.ORG/HOSTED/ENGLISH/KHK/.
- Sephardic last names, a database of more than 2,300 names compiled by Harry Stein, WWW.SEPHARDIM.COM.
- Sephardic last names, WWW.ONELIST.COM/SUBSCRIBE.CGI/APELLIDOS-SEFARDITAS.
- Sefard SIG, a Sephardic discussion group, SEFARD@MAIL.JEWISHGEN.ORG or SEFARD2@JEWISHGEN.ORG.

Addresses

Aki Yerushalayim, P.O. Box 8175, Jerusalem 91080, Israel; e-mail: JUDEOSPA@TRENDLINE.CO.IL

Alliance Israelite Universelle, 45 rue de la Bruyè, Paris 95009, France

Aristotle University, Thessaloniki, Greece; website: WWW.AUTH.GR

Association of American Jews from Turkey Newsletter, New York; e-mail: AAJFT@AOL.COM; website: MEMBERS.AOL.COM/AAJFT/FRIEND

Central Archives for the History of the Jewish People, 46 Jabotinsky Street, Jerusalem 91010; telephone: 972-2-566-7686; e-mail: ARCHIVES@VMS.HUJI.AC.IL; website: SITES.HUJI.AC.IL/ARCHIVES

Central Board of Greek Jewish Communities, 36 Voulis Street, Athens, Greece 10559

Chronika, Central Board of Jewish Communities, 36 Voulis Street, Athens, Greece 10559

El Vocero, Comunidad Israelite Sefardi, Av. Ricardo Lyon 812, Santiago, Chile

Faculty of Oriental Studies, Sidgwith Avenue, Cambridge CB3 9DA, United Kingdom

Institute of Balkan Studies, 45 Moskovska Street, 1000 Sofia, Bulgaria; telephone/fax: 359-2-980-6297; e-mail: BALKANI@CL.BAS.BG; website: WWW.CL.BAS.BG/BALKAN_STUDIES

Jewish Museum of Greece, 39 Nikis Street, Athens, Greece 10557.

La Erensia Sefardi, 46 Benson Place, Fairfield, Connecticut 06430; website: MEMBERS.AOL.COM/ERENSIA/ERENSIASEFARDI.INDEX.HTML.

La Lettre Sefarade, Jean Carasso, 84220 Gordes, France; fax: 33-4-9072-3839; e-mail: SEPHARADE@WANADOO.FR; English edition: Rosine Nussenblatt, P.O.Box 2450, Kensington, Maryland 20891; e-mail: LETTRESEPHARADE@EARTHLINK.NET

Larissa Jewish Community, 29, Kendavron Street, Platteis Evraion Martyron Katchis, Larissa 412 22, Greece; telephone/fax: 041-532-965, 041-534-410; website: WWW.ATLANTIS.GR/KIS/LARISAHISTORY_EN.HTML.

Los Muestros, 25, rue Dodonée, 1180 Brussels, Belgium

Macedonia State Archives, Kambounion 9, Thessaloniki, Greece

Magen Escudo, Av. Principal de Mariperez, Los Caobos, Caracas 1050, Venezuela

Salonikan Jewry Research Institute, 68 Levinsky Street, Tel Aviv, Israel

Sefardica. Paraguay 1535, 1061 Buenos Aires, Argentina; telephone: 812-4995; fax: 814-0890

Sephardic House Newsletter, Center for Jewish History, 15 West 16th Street, New York, New York 10011

Shajar, Comunidad Israelita Séfaradi Uruguay, Calle Buenos Aires 234, Montevideo, Uruguay

Shalom Atiye Sok. Polar Apt. No. 12/6 Tesvikiye, Istanbul, Turkey

The Sephardic Temple, Branch Blvd. at Halevy Drive, P.O. Box 392, Cedarhurst, NY 11516; telephone: 516-295-4644

Tiryaki Gazete Idare Merkezi, Tunel, Kumbaraci Yokusu 131, Beyoglu, Istanbul, Turkey; Attention: Mose Grosman; telephone: 245-2479, 245-5946; fax: 245-2479

Bibliography

Listings followed by an asterisk (*) have high genealogical value.

Salonika (Thessaloniki)

Benveniste, David. *MiSaloniki LeYerushalayim* (From Salonica to Jerusalem, my life). [Hebrew] 2 vols. Jerusalem: Vaad Eidat HaSephardim Veidot Hamamizrah with the Saloniki Jewry Research Center and Hamerkaz Leshiluv Hamoreshet Shel Yahadut Sefarad Vehamizrah, 1981 and 1982.

Emmanuel, Isaac S. *Matzevot Saloniki* (Precious stones of the Jews of Salonica). [Hebrew] vols. 1 and 2. Jerusalem: Ben-Zvi Institute, Hebrew University and Kiriyat Hasefer, 1963 and 1968.*

———. *Histoire de Israelites de Salonique T.I. 140 av.J-C a 1640* (History of the Jews of Salonika, 140 B.C.E.–1640). [French] Paris: Thonon, 1936.

Goodblatt, Morris S. *Jewish Life in Turkey in the XVIth Century as Reflected in the Legal Writings of Samuel de Medina*. New York: Jewish Theological Seminary of America, 1952.

Kerem, Yitzchak. "Crypto-Jews Around The World. Part III: The Deunme," *Sharsheret Hadorot* 12, no. 3 (December 1988): VII-IX.*

Matkovski, Alexander. *A History of the Jews in Macedonia*. Skopje, Yugoslavia: Macedonian Review Editions, 1982.

Molho, Isaac Raphael. *Matzevot Saloniki* (Tombstones of the Jewish cemetery of Salonica). [Hebrew] Tel Aviv: Saloniki Jewry Research Center, 1974.*

———. "The Jewish Community of Salonica in the 19th Century and Before." [Hebrew] *Otsar Yehudei Sefarad* 8 (1965).*

Nehama, Joseph. *La ville convoitee, Salonique* (The coveted city, Salonica). [French] Paris 1914.

———. *Histoire des Israelites de Salonique* (History of the Jews of Salonica). 7 vols. [French] Thessaloniki: Communaute Israelite de Thessalonique, 1979. Reprint, published originally 1935-1959.

Recanati, David ed. *Zichron Saloniki, Gedulata Vehurvata Shel Yerushalayim Debalkan* (Saloniki memorial, the grandeur and destruction of Jerusalem of the Balkans). [Hebrew] 2 vols. Tel Aviv: Havaad Lehotsaat Sefer Kehilat Saloniki, 1972 and 1986.*

Saloniki, Ir Ve'em Beyisrael (Saloniki, A Jewish metropolis). [Hebrew] Tel Aviv: Saloniki Jewry Research Center, 1967.*

Other Greek Jewish Communities

Argenti, Philip Panteles. *The Religious Minorities of Chios: Jews and Roman Catholics*. Cambridge: Cambridge University Press, 1970.

Dalven, Rae. *The Jews of Ioannina*. Philadelphia: Cadmus Press, 1990.*

Kerem, Yitzchak. "The Jews of Ioannina between Ottoman Loyalty and Greek Insurrection, 1900-1913." [Hebrew] *The New East* 39 (1997-98): 47-54.

Molho, Michael. *Histoire des Israelites de Castoria* (History of the Jews of Castoria). [French] Thessaloniki, 1938.

Preschel, Pearl L. "The Jews of Corfu" (doctoral dissertation). Department of Near and Eastern Languages of the Graduate of Arts and Sciences of New York University, February 1984.*

Sack, Sallyann Amdur. "Report on a Return Trip to Israel." *AVOTAYNU* 11, no. 4 (Winter 1995): 21–24.

Rhodes

Angel, Marc D. *The Jews of Rhodes: The History of a Sephardic Community*. New York: Sepher-Hermon Press and Union of Sephardic Congregations, 1980.*

Galante, Abraham. *Histoire des Juifs de Rhodes, Chi, Cos, Etc.* (History of the Jews of Rhodes, Chios, Cos, etc.) [French] Istanbul: l'Imprimerie Babok, 1935.

Levy, Isaac Jack. *Jewish Rhodes: A Lost Culture*. Berkeley: Judah L. Magnes Museum, 1989.

Levy, Rebecca Amato. *I Remember Rhodes*. New York: Sepher-Hermon Press, 1987.*

Holocaust

Ben, Yosef. *Yehudi Yavan Beshoa VeBihitnagdut 1941–1944* (Greek Jewry in the Holocaust in the Resistance, 1941–1944). [Hebrew] Tel Aviv: Saloniki Jewry Research Center, 1985.*

Bowman, Steve B. "Jews in Wartime Greece" *Jewish Social Studies*, 48, no. 1 (Winter 1986): 46-62.

Franco, Hezkia. *Les martyrs juifs de Rhodes et de Cos* (The Jewish martyrs of Rhodes and of Cos). [French] Elizabethville: author, 1952. (Reprinted in English as Hizkia M. Franco, *The Jewish Martyrs of Rhodes and Cos* Harare). Zimbabwe: Harper Collins, 1994.*

Kerem, Yitzchak. "Rescue Attempts of Jews in Greece in the Second World War." [Hebrew] *Pe'amim* 27 (1986), 77-109.

———. "The Survival of the Jews of Zakynthos in the Holocaust," *Tenth World Congress of Jewish Studies*. Division B, II: 387–94, vol. 2. Jerusalem: World Union of Jewish Studies, 1990.

Matsas, Michael. *The Illusion of Safety: The Story of the Greek Jews During the Second World War.* New York: Pella, 1997.

Menashe, Albert. *Birkenau (Auschwitz II)*. New York: Isaac Saltiel, 1947.

Refael, Shmuel. *Sh'ol, Yehudei Yavan Beshoah, Pirkei Eidut* (Routes of Hell: Greek Jewry in the Holocaust). [Hebrew] Tel Aviv: Saloniki Jewry Research Institute and Irgun Nitsulei Machanot HaHashmada Yotsei Yavan Beyisrael, 1988.*

Vivlio Mnimis. (Memorial book). [Greek] Athens: Board of Greek Jewish Communities, 1979.*

Greek Jewish Diaspora

Dassa, David R. *Sefarad VeYerushalayim* (Spain and Jerusalem). [Hebrew] Jerusalem, 1992.*

Emmanuel, Yitzhak-Moshe. *Eretz Yisrael, Kur Hachituch* (Eretz-Yisrael melting pot: family heritage). [Hebrew] Holon: Ami's, 1988.*

Kerem, Yitzchak. "Corfiote Triestians: A Jewish Diasporic Community from Greece." *Eleventh World Congress of Jewish Studies*, Division B, vol. 3: Jerusalem: World Union of Jewish Studies, 1994.

———. "The Migration of Rhodian Jews to Africa and the Americas, 1900-1914: The Beginning of New Sephardic Communities." Aubrey Newman and Stephen Massil, eds., *Patterns of Migration, 1850–1914, Proceedings of the International Academic Conference of the Jewish Historical Society of England and the Institute of Jewish Studies, University College, London*. London: The Jewish Historical Society of England and the Institute of Jewish Studies, University College, London, 1996: 321–334.

———. "The Settlement of Rhodian and Other Sephardic Jews in Montgomery and Atlanta in the Twentieth Century." *American Jewish History* 85, no. 4 (December 1997): 373-391.

———. "The Vivante Family History and the Holocaust," *Sharsheret Hadorot*, 13, no. 1 (Spring 1999), XVII–XXII.*

Overview of Greek Jewry

Attal, Robert. *Les Juifs de Grece de L'Expulsion a nos Jours* (The Jews of Greece from the Expulsion to our days). [French, English, Greek, and Hebrew] Jerusalem: Yad Izhak Ben-Zvi and the Hebrew University of Jerusalem, 1984.

Benveniste, David. *Kehilot Hayehudim Beyavan, Richmai Masa* (Jewish communities of Greece, notes and impressions). [Hebrew] Jerusalem: Vaad Eidat HaSephardim BeYerushalayim with the Department of Sephardic Communities of the World Zionist Organization, 1979.

Bowman, Steve B. *The Jews of Byzantium, 1204–1453*. Tuscaloosa: University of Alabama Press, 1985.

Franco, M. *Essai sur l'histoire des Israelites de l'Empire Ottoman depuis l'origine jusqu'a nos jours* (Essay on the history of the Jews of the Ottoman Empire from its origin until today). [French] Paris: Durlacher, 1897.

Kerem, Yitzchak. "Genealogical Research on Greek Jewry." *Sharasheret Hadorot* 6, no. 3 (October 1992): 2-3.

Rivlin, Bracha; Yitzchak Kerem and Lea Bornstein-Makovetsky *Pinkas Hakehillot Yavan* (Encyclopedia of Jewish communities from their foundation until after the Holocaust in Greece). [Hebrew] Jerusalem: Yad Vashem, 1998.

Rozanes, Shlomo Avraham. *Korot Hayehudim Beturkia Vebeartzot Hakedem. Divrei Yemai Yisrael Betogarma Al-Pi Mekorot Rishonim* (A history of the Jews in Turkey and in ancient lands). [Hebrew] vols.1-5: Tel Aviv: Dvir, 1930-38. Jerusalem: Mosad Harav Kook, 1945.

Sevillias, Errikos. *Athens-Auschwitz*. Athens: Lycabettus Press, 1983.

Stavrolakis, Nikos. *The Jews of Greece, an Essay*. Athens: Talos Press, 1990.

Notes

1. The term "Romaniote" comes from the word Rome and refers to those Greek-speaking Jews who inhabited the Byzantine Empire; that is, the "true" Roman Empire. The Byzantines believed themselves to be the true heirs to early Roman Christianity. See Harold Rhode,"The Ottoman Empire and Jewish Genealogy," *AVOTAYNU* 8, no. 1 (Spring 1992).

2. The Jews of Ioannina had specific customs for the dowry, life cycle and Jewish holidays that differed from Sephardic customs in the region. In Ioannina and Chalkis, the Romaniote Jews celebrated the holiday of Irtaman two weeks before Purim, to welcome the joy of the Jewish month of Adar. On Rosh Hashanah in Ioannina, the prayer, *I Demiourghía tov Kósmou* (The creation of the world) was recited, a unique custom found nowhere else. No traces of Romaniote liturgy were ever recorded in the smaller Romaniote community of Chalkis.

3. Numerous researchers today specialize in the Jewish populations of one or another Ottoman Empire Jewish community. For the most current list, see George K. Zucker, ed., *International Directory for Sephardic and Oriental Jewish Studies* (Cedar Falls, Iowa: University of Northern Iowa, 1993). For European experts in Sephardic studies, consult Annette Winkelmann, ed., *Directory of Jewish Studies in Europe* (Oxford: European Association for Jewish Studies, 1998).

4. Yitzchak Kerem, "Diaspora Studies: Greek Jewish Diaspora," in *Greece in Modern Times*, Stratos E. Constantinidis, ed. Lanham, Maryland: Scarecrow Press, 2000.

Hungary

by Louis Schonfeld

The territory of Hungary has not been easy to define in modern times. During the 19th century, the Magyars, the dominant ethnic group since the start of the second millennium, barely constituted a majority in the country they once called the Kingdom of Hungary, or Greater Hungary.[1] Until 1867, this territory, often called "historical Hungary," was the largest geographic entity in the Austrian Empire. But in 1867, as an outgrowth of Hungarian nationalist pressures, the Austrian Empire officially became the Austro-Hungarian Empire, and its monarch Franz Joseph became Emperor of Austria and King of Hungary in a new political entity called the Dual Monarchy.

Of all the 19th-century European countries with a sizable Jewish population, Hungary was the most diverse. The earliest Jewish census, dated 1725, was recorded in Latin even though German was the official language of government discourse from the beginning of the 17th century until the middle of the 19th century. With the institution of the dual monarchy in 1867, Hungarian became the language of record throughout the country.

Hungary became an independent nation only after World War I, but as a member of the losing Central Powers, it was punished by the forfeiture of two-thirds of its territory. Among the major geographical divisions that had been part of Greater Hungary but were lost as a result of the 1920 Treaty of Trianon are the Banat, Burgenland, Croatia, Maramaros, parts of Serbia, Slovakia, Slovenia, Subcarpathian Ruthenia and Transylvania. Burgenland was ceded to Austria; Croatia, parts of Serbia and Slovenia were ceded to form part of Yugoslavia; Romania acquired the Banat, Transylvania and half of Maramaros. To the newly created Czechoslovakia went Slovakia and Subcarpathian Ruthenia, also known as the "tail" of Czechoslovakia.

Archeological evidence from the third century C.E. has shown that Jews resided in this territory even before the arrival of the Magyars, a tribe that some historians say emerged from the steppes of Central Asia and settled in the Carpathian Basin several decades prior to the year 1000 B.C.E. Historians believe that Jews came to this region along with the Romans, who referred to these lands as Pannonia and Dacia.

The Jewish population in this region ebbed and flowed. At the beginning of the 18th century, few Jews were left, except for remnants of the Spanish expulsion who, after finding haven in Turkey, participated in the occupation of Hungary during the Ottomans' 150-year rule which lasted until the end of the 17th century. The remainder of the Jewish population in Hungary lived in Burgenland, an area along Hungary's western border with Austria. Here were the *siben gemeindes*, (seven communities) of Deutschkreutz (Német-Keresztur), Eisenstadt (Kismarton), Frauenkirchen (Boldogasszony), Kittsee (Köpscény), Kobersdorf (Kábold), Lakenbach (Lakompak) and Mattersdorf (Nagymarton), the only independent Jewish communities officially permitted in Hungary during the reign of Empress Maria Theresa (1740–80). (Names in parentheses are the former Hungarian names.)

At that time, the Hungarian lands belonged to noblemen, many of whose estates were large enough for them to be considered "magnates," that is, those with immense landholdings. The magnates needed Jews to run their estates and collect taxes. Despite Maria Theresa's official position of not tolerating Jews in this area, on almost every Hungarian noble's estate, several Jewish families worked as managers, tradesman or other functionaries. These *schutzjuden* (protected Jews) either had migrated or were recruited from the German-speaking lands of Austria, Bohemia, Germany and Moravia to the western and central parts of Hungary and from the Galician areas and towns of Brody, Lemberg and possibly Krakow to the border areas of eastern Hungary, especially Slovakia and Subcarpathian Ruthenia. This development began in the early 18th century and continued for nearly 150 years.

By 1780, an estimated 100,000 Jews lived in Hungary; several factors soon caused the number to swell. Maria Theresa died. Joseph II, her relatively progressive son, assumed the throne and instituted measures that made it easier for Jews to enter the country. In 1772, as a result of the first partition of Poland, (see HABSBURG EMPIRE) the Austro-Hungarian Empire had acquired the southeastern portion of Poland which it renamed Galicia. Joseph II's liberal laws, combined with the more tolerant Gentile population found in multi-ethnic Hungary, fueled the movement of Galician Jews into the Hungarian border areas. These Galician Jews quickly adapted to the ethos of Hungarian society, and as they and future generations became more comfortable in the milieu of Slovakia and Subcarpathian Ruthenia, they moved further inland looking for additional opportunities.

The Golden Age of Hungarian Jewry coincided with the duration of the Dual Monarchy. For nearly 50 years, ending with the onset of World War I, Jewish community life flourished, its members prospered and communities grew in size and influence. In the 1910 national census, Hungarian Jewry reached its numerical zenith of 910,000. When Jews who had converted to Christianity are included, the number exceeds one million. The 1910 census also shows the remarkable penetration of Hungarian Jewry into the economic life of the country at that time: no fewer than 30 percent of all merchants, 40 percent of doctors, 45 percent of journalists and a remarkable 49 percent of all lawyers and jurists were either Jews or of Jewish origin.

Nineteenth-century Hungarian Jews were zealous in their identification with Magyar culture, language and national as-

Map of the Kingdom of Hungary showing towns with significant Jewish populations

pirations. This was especially true among the members of two polar factions of the Jewish community, the assimilationists and the Hasidim. The Hasidim were loyal to the Magyar cause because of the freedoms they enjoyed in comparison with other Jews of Central and Eastern Europe. In Hungary, the Hasidim largely were free to manage their institutions with only minor infringements imposed from time to time.

Assimilationists, lured by the sensuality of Hungarian secular life, found acceptance among the intelligentsia and cosmopolitan citizens of Budapest and other large cities. The Magyar plurality was able to claim the majority ethnic position in the kingdom only by including the more-than-willing, Hungarian-speaking Jewish population. Many Jews purchased titles of nobility; others converted to Christianity to advance their careers or to ingratiate themselves with the aristocracy and intelligentsia. Nearly 100,000 Jews in Budapest converted to Christianity during the Golden Age. Conversions were documented by the government and those records, for Budapest at least, are extant and may be published in the future.[2]

In the first decade of the 20th century, Budapest's Jewish society was a Magyar version of Jewish life in Vienna, from the perspective of the Jewish community's cultural, economic and religious appearance. Coincidentally the Jewish population of both cities in the years preceding World War I peaked at about 200,000. It was not uncommon to hear anti-Semites of the day refer to Budapest as "Yudapest." During World War I, the Jewish population suffered along with the rest of the country, but the war's end did not bring relief to the Jews. Perhaps as an omen of impending disaster, the Jews were the disproportionate targets of a socialist revolution and a counter-revolution that plagued Hungary in the years immediately following World War I.

After World War I, Hungary became the first country in Europe to institute a new anti-Semitic law: the *numerus clauses*. It restricted the number of Jews who could enter the universities and was designed to limit the number of Jews in the professions to no more than their proportional numbers in the general population.

Religious Life. Religion played a significant role in Hungarian-Jewish life. Many Jews who emigrated from Hungary beginning in the late 19th century did so because they could not or would not adhere to the strictures of local religious life. A strong correlation exists between areas of heavy Jewish emigration and areas of strict adherence to Orthodoxy—especially Hasidism.[3]

Orthodoxy and Neology (Reform) separated themselves into distinct groups at the 1868/69 Congress. In 1895, when Judaism was given status equal to those of other religions, it only exacerbated the tension between the religious factions. As a result, the government decided that both would be recognized as distinct Hungarian-Jewish communities. The most strident elements acquired leadership of the Orthodox group, and the more worldly members of the community found that they had no voice. The latter petitioned the government to form their own distinct body, one that came to be called the Status Quo Ante. They held a centrist position, and they wanted to return to the situation that existed before the Congress. In the years preceding World War I, a fourth group emerged that wanted to isolate itself even further from external secular influences, but did not want to join any of the three other groups. This group comprised nearly all Hasidic groups including the Satmar and the Munkatcher Hasidim. They took the appellation "Sephardim" because this was an effective means to exclude themselves from any Hungarian-Jewish organizational intrusion.

Hungarian Hasidism is an almost exclusively Galician phenomenon. Not only did those Jews who entered Hungary after Joseph II's Edict of Toleration come from the Hasidic shtetls of Galicia, but nearly all the popular Hasidic dynasties that flourished throughout Hungary were Galician in origin. Satmar originated in Drohobycs (lead by Rabbi Moses Teitelbaum), Klausenberg (led by Rabbi Chaim Halberstam) originated in Nowy Sancz, Munkacs (led by Rabbi Zvi Elimelech Spira) originated in Dynow, and Belz originated in Belz (led by Rabbi Aharon Rokeach). Other popular groups such as Spinka and Vishnitz also could trace their origins to Galicia. The only indigenous Hungarian Hasidic community was started by Rabbi Eizik Taub (1795–1840) of Nagy Kallo in Szabolcs county.

Because few Hasidic rebbes lived in Hungary in the earliest years of emigration from Galicia, most Jews settled first in

villages near the Galician border, where they were close to the Hasidic centers and could easily seek their rebbe's advice and celebrate with him on holidays. Ironically this settlement pattern also facilitated their annihilation during the Holocaust. Not only did the Hasidim live in areas close to the extermination camps, the most notorious of which were in Poland, but Himmler and Eichmann harbored a zealous hatred for these foreign-looking *ostjuden* (Eastern Jews). In fact, when Eichmann and his coterie entered Budapest to take personal charge of the deportation of Hungarian Jews, the Hasidic Jews of Maramaros and the sub-Carpathian region comprised the first transports sent to Auschwitz.

Locating Your Ancestral Town

Determining the towns and villages where an ancestor lived is essential to genealogical research. This can be especially difficult for those with Hungarian ancestry, many of whose ancestor's emigrated from pre-World War I Greater Hungary, from places that today belong to neighboring countries and have different names. A most formidable gazetteer, which includes all place names that were once and are currently in Hungary, is *Magyar Helysegnev-Azonosito Szotar*. Edited by Gyorgy Lelkes and published in 1998 by Talma Konyvkiado, this 1,000 page gazetteer includes all the location names, their county and district affiliations, population by nationality and references to the full-color county maps in the book. The localities are listed in the language of today's jurisdiction along with their Hungarian translations. The gazetteer lists all 64 historical counties with district breakdowns and is referenced to 64 excellent color maps of these counties. The book's introduction is in Hungarian and German. The format for the town listings is similar to that of *Where Once We Walked*. This is the book for someone who must have the best.

Due to the multi-ethnic nature of the Austro-Hungarian Empire and the political vicissitudes of East Central Europe, an additional important reference tool is a geographical dictionary for the area. The ancestral names and the names of the towns and villages where those ancestors lived are the fundamental pieces of information upon which all future research is built. To find the contemporary name of the Hungarian town your ancestor may have called Ratsferd in Yiddish, additional sources specifically tailored to the Jewish researchers' needs may be consulted. The most useful guide is Yitzchak Cohen's, *Chachmei Ungaria*. The book is primarily a reference on Hungarian rabbis, but an introductory chapter has a gazetteer that helps locate the contemporary town name whose Jewish name may be the only information a researcher knows. For many years, the mid-sized town of Ujfeherto in the center of Szabolcs county had a large, almost exclusively Orthodox Jewish population. Jews throughout Europe knew the town name as Ratsferd, and that town name may have been the only one passed down to the descendants of a Jewish emigrant.

Knowing the Jewish names of towns is also important when using *prenumerantn* (Jewish subscription lists), a Jewish source for discovering information about ancestors.

Synagogue in Kecskemet at the beginning of the 20th century. Courtesy of Tomasz Wisniewski.

These lists can help the researcher locate a person in a specific time and town. Hungary was a major center of Jewish printing and many *seforim* (religious books) were published in Munkacs, Nagyvarad, Vranov, Pecs and other locations.

An example of the value and use of *prenumerantn* is presented by the author in a file on the Hungarian JewishSIG website www.JEWISHGEN.ORG/HUNGARY. A list appears of 525 names sorted alphabetically by name and also a list by town order as shown in *Sefer Schne Apharim*, written by Shimon Broida in 1825 and published in Prague. Hundreds of *seforim* published in Hungary from the end of the 18th century until 1944 include lists of subscribers. Although the lists are usually called *prenumerantn*, they may also be found with titles such as *Mitnadvim* (donors) or *Michabdim* honorees).

Resources And Finding Aids

The quality and quantity of finding aides that can assist researchers locate information are impressive. Following are the most important of the guides that focus on sources related to Hungarian-Jewish communities. In 1993, Gyorgy Haraszti prepared a two-volume work entitled *Magyar Zsido Leveltari Repertorium* (Directory of archival holdings relating to the history of Jews in Hungary) under the auspices of the Center of Jewish Studies at the Hungarian Academy of Sciences in Budapest, the Central Archives for the History of the Jewish People in Jerusalem and the Rosenfeld Project on the History of Hungarian and Habsburg Jewry at the Dinur Center at The Hebrew University in Jerusalem. At the end of volume B, an English-language summary describes the purpose, methodology and difficulties encountered in bringing to light all the necessary archival sources. Even though the title states that the focus is historical, considerable information is included that could be helpful to the family researcher. Not the least of these benefits are the inclusion of many Hungarian-Jewish personalities, organizations and place names listed in the index. Except for the summary, the entire two books are in Hungarian. An experienced researcher could easily learn the methodology, however, and thereby gain information about access to these archival resources.

Published in the same year as the books by Haraszti and by the same three sponsoring organizations was a volume titled *Magyar Zsido Hirlapok es Folyoiratok Bibligorafiaja 1847–1992*, (Bibliography of Hungarian Jewish newspapers and journals). It was edited and annotated by the most distinguished postwar scholar of Hungarian Jewry, Dr. Sandor Scheiber. While there is no English summary for this book, it is a relatively simple resource to use by experienced researchers. For the most comprehensive study of Jewish life in Hungary since its inception until just a few years ago, there is *The Jews of Hungary: History, Culture, Psychology*, by Raphael Patai. In this landmark work, one learns the history of the Jews in Hungary. The author also discusses the Hungarian national character and Jewish attitudes in this regard, which helps explain the synergy that contributed to the development of Hungarian science, culture and social behavior. Since Patai's focus is on the major players and issues of the times, the book is less helpful in giving the reader an appreciation of the more prosaic activities and lifestyle of our ancestors.

In order for the English reader to learn of the daily activities of our Hungarian ancestors, one should also read *Journey to Vaja*, by Ellen Kalman Neves, and *Thorns and Apples in Tokaj Valley*, the Jewish history of Abauj-Szanto, by Zehava Szass Stessel. A popular, yet comprehensive, biographical and geographical dictionary [in Hungarian] focusing on the Jewish community is *Zsido* (Jewish) *Lexicon*, by Peter Ujvari. It was first published in 1929 and reprinted in 1987.

Obituary Notices

Unique genealogical documents may be found in the Hungarian National Library* in Budapest. In the Special Collections room, researchers can see the obituary notices that were commonly issued from early in the 19th century until the end of World War I. More than 800,000 of these notices, which contain the name of the deceased, surviving relatives, dates and indicators of religion have been alphabetized by Jozsef Kiss, a prominent Hungarian genealogist who specializes in rabbinic genealogy.

Yizkor Books and Memoirs

Yad Vashem has the largest collection of Hungarian *yizkor* books; approximately 110 are for towns and regions of the former Kingdom of Hungary, few of them in English. (For more about *yizkor* books see HOLOCAUST). Hungarian survivors have written a number of books in a variety of languages throughout the past 50 years describing life in pre-war Hungary and the Hungarian Holocaust.

Onsite Research

The main Hungarian National Archive* facility where one goes to do hands-on research is in Obuda, about six miles from the center of Budapest. Look for the sign *informacio*; feel free to ask for someone who speaks English. Call in advance to verify dates and times when the archives are open to the public. You will be working with microfilmed records, the accommodations here are modern and comfortable. If you prefer working with the original documents, as opposed to microfilm, you will be more successful in the regional archives. The previous research location on Becsikapu ter is still the central office of the Hungarian National Archives,* but it no longer serves as a research location for genealogists. The excellent website has a special section for genealogists. One can write in English directly to the archives to purchase copies of the microfilms. Write: Attention head of copying department. The archives has a number of useful publications. Janos Lakos edited a comprehensive guide, history and overview holdings entitled *A Magyar Orszagos Leveltar* (The Hungarian National Archives). The book was published in 1996 in Hungarian with a thoughtful English summary on pages 265–292. A four-volume index of archival holdings is called *A Magyar Orszagos Leveltar Fondjainak es Allagainak*

Jegyzeke. The index and inventory of the Hungarian National Archives was published in 1996. Finally, a pamphlet entitled *Magyarorszag Leveltarainkas Cimes Nevjegyzeke* (Hungarian National Archives address and employee listing) published in 1994 is especially useful for travelers to the regional and district archives in Hungary.

This booklet lists the names and positions of employees throughout the archive system and the addresses and telephone numbers of the archive locations. A schedule for each location shows dates and times of operation. Keep in mind that the information is some years old; it is wise to confirm the information in advance of a trip. All three of these publications are available for purchase at the Becsikapu ter administrative office. Personal data on individuals is made available 90 years from the date of birth, 30 years from the date of death or, if these dates are unknown, 60 years from the date the document was created. Documents concerning personal data are accessible with no restrictions for individuals concerned or their relatives who can prove legal relationship to them.

Vital Records. On October 1, 1895, Hungary established a secular governmental agency responsible for keeping all vital records in the country. From that time onward, Jewish births, marriages and deaths were incorporated together with the other religious groups into a single civil administration. Prior to this date, documentation was the responsibility of the religious authorities. For the Jews, a designated rabbi recorded all these events and submitted the requisite information to the proper authorities. Up to 1895, birth, marriage and deaths of each religious community were kept in separate volumes. Some Jewish registrations in Hungary (e.g., Trencsen County) began at the end of the 18th century, but in most cases records were kept regularly only after 1851, birth records especially. Most of these can be found in the Hungarian National Archives* and in the county archives.

Areas with a Jewish population too small to support its own rabbi reported vital events to the rabbi in the nearest organized congregation. The 1877 gazetteer *Magyarorszag helysegnevtar ket kotetben* (Hungarian place names) lists every settled area within greater Hungary and notes the Jewish population and the closest established synagogue; this is where the vital records were kept. Therefore, a researcher not able to locate vital record information for a small village should refer to this two-volume gazetteer for guidance. The gazetteer is a crucial reference tool because records are indexed by these record-keeping centers. A copy is available from the LDS (Mormon) Family History Library, (see LDS) microfiche #6000840. In addition, Avotaynu will soon publish a CD of the gazetteer, compiled by Jordan Auslander. The index appears in volume I; volume II contains listings of localities arranged by counties (*megye*) and then districts (*jaras*). The three numbers after a place name in the index represent the county, the district and the locality in Volume II. Researchers should note the following significant features:

- If "IZR" is written in bold capital letters, the synagogue was located in that town.

- If not, look in the town name immediately after the number indicating how many Jews lived there. The associated synagogue may be in that adjacent town.
- If neither of the above is shown, look for a town with "IZR" in bold capital letters near the town that concerns you. The location of the synagogue tells you the town in which the records for the smaller surrounding communities were kept.

The Mormons have microfilmed most Jewish birth, death and marriage records up to 1910 for the area that is Hungary today, and copies may be ordered at LDS Family History Centers throughout the world. A set of the microfilms is also available to researchers in Budapest at the *Magyar Orszagos Leveltar,* the National Archives of Hungary*. Bound paper copies are kept in the various regional archives throughout the country. One may purchase copies of any microfilms made by the Mormons at an approximate cost of US$20 per roll. They may be ordered (in English) directly from the National Archives.* Send request to the attention of Laszlo Kalniczky, head of copying department.

Censuses. The first official census of Hungarian Jews, in a series initiated by Emperor Charles IV, was in 1725. An even earlier census, believed to have been taken in 1712, and only for the city of Pest, shows 1,100 Jews living there. These early lists taken during various times between 1725 and 1775 are classified under the generic Latin term *Conscriptio Judaeorum*. Their value to genealogists is limited because few Jews had family names at that time; therefore, it would be an exceptional entry that listed a family name. Information shown includes the name of the head of household, sometimes a wife's and children's names, at other times just the number of family members, the number of servants and their religion, the name of landlord on whose land they lived, possessions and taxes assessed. The census lists are arranged in alphabetical order by county name written in Latin, which in most cases is different from the Hungarian spelling. The LDS Family History Library has microfilmed this census with the assigned numbers 1529693 through 1529699.

19th-Century Censuses. Tax censuses taken in the 19th century are similar to the earlier enumerations, but sometimes it is possible to find surnames listed among the entries. The censuses of 1827–28 and the Jewish censuses of 1848 and 1869 have been at least partially microfilmed by the Mormons. The 1827–28 census includes both Jews and non-Jews and may prove helpful to some in locating an ancestor in a specific time and place. Only a small portion of the Jewish population is included, however, because this census was limited to property owners, and few Jews owned property at that time.

Many similar local and county tax records and lists were made during the first half of the 19th century. Most of these documents have remained at the regional archives and have not been microfilmed by the Mormons. In 1965, the Mormons filmed Jewish records at the Hungarian National Archives* in Budapest. Some counties where the 1848 Jewish census records have survived were not in the possession of the National

Archives* at that time and, therefore, were not filmed. Among the unfilmed, but extant, records is the entire 1848 census records for Szatmar County, which at that time was held at the regional archives for Szabolcs-Szatmar County in Nyiregyhaza. Professor Gyorgy Haraszti, a former archivist of the Central Jewish Authority,* reports that the complete 1848 census is located in the archives of that organization. The original documents were photographed, page by page, during the years 1942–44 by the Jewish employees working there, fearing that the original books might be destroyed if the building became a target of the Fascist regime. Only the photographed pages remain today. The Jewish Archives* is not open to the public and restricts visits to unpublished hours.

In an issue of Avotaynu, (Winter 2003) the former archivist of the Hungarian Jewish Archives, Kinga Frojimovics, states in "Documents of the Hungarian Jewish Archives" that there are "363 registers of births, marriages and deaths of various Jewish communities of the provinces. There are also a few *mohel* (circumcision) books in the collection. The majority of registers are from the period from 1886 until 1945." A catalogue of items in this vital yet still shrouded archive has been in preparation for several years and will hopefully be published soon. She concludes: "We expect the published catalogue to be an important reference book for conducting research in the archives of Hungary." It remains to be seen if the publication of this guide will encourage the protectors of this archive to allow reasonable public access to it. Excluding certain functionaries of the Central Jewish Authority or approved academicians, no one has ever been allowed to view its contents. We understand the sensitivity of the community defenders, however, we must continue to insist that those of us who wish to learn about our ancestors be given the opportunity to do so.

Jewish Census of 1848. Concurrent with the unanticipated uprising of 1848, the first modern census of Hungarian Jews was taking place. This is the well-known Jewish census of 1848. Approximately 25 percent of the census has survived and has been microfilmed by the Mormons (the portion found at the Hungarian National Archives at the time of filming). Included are the counties of Baranya, Bekes, Bihar, Csanad, Esztergom, Fejer, Gyor, Hajdu, Komarom, Kosep-Szolnok, Krasso, Kraszna, Maramoros, Moson, Szabolcs, Tolna, Trencsen, Turocz, Ung, Vas, Veszprem and Zala. In addition the 1848 census records for the following cities have also been filmed: Eperjes (Presov), Gyongos, Gyor, Miscolz, Modor (Modra), Nagyszombat (Trnava), Pecs, Sopron, Szakolcza, Ujvidek, Temesvar, Trenscen and Zombor. According to Professor Haraszti, about 300,000 Jews lived in Hungary at the time of the 1848 census. The Hungarian SIG currently is computerizing the 1848 Jewish census (estimated date of completion in 2005).

Another census that was regional in scope was the 1857 census. Only some areas of Saros and Zemplen County census records survive and have been located in the county archives. The first modern national census was the 1869 census, which is also widely available. Other important censuses were the 1890 and 1910 national census, the last census taken before

the Treaty of Trianon drastically reduced the size of Hungary. The 1920 Czechoslovakian census is known to be complete, but is only available in the archives in Prague.

Jewish Census of 1869. The Jewish census of 1869 is especially helpful to genealogists because it lists all residents of a household and identifies father, mother (including maiden name where known), children and other residents, such as servants. Age, occupation and gender are listed for each person.

The censuses of 1725, 1848 and 1869 have been microfilmed by the Mormons; like all Hungarian microfilms made by the Mormons, copies may be purchased directly from the Hungarian National Archives* at a reasonable price.

Other records not yet microfilmed by the Mormons can be viewed at various regional archives in Hungary. This includes the Jewish census of 1808/9; the census of 1857; tax lists of Judaeorum and Ignoblium for the years 1838, 1840 and probably others as well; the census of 1880; notary records; school records and emigration papers. Genealogically valuable records come to light regularly as increasing numbers of genealogists mine the regional archives. This writer recently discovered a listing of Jewish heads of households in 1843 for the city and district of Mukachevo at the State Archives in Berehovo.*

Military Records. Until the end of World War I, the Hungarian army was under the command of the Austrian military. The 1877 *Gazetteer of Hungarian Church Parishes* identifies the army units associated with various areas, thereby supplying the information needed to access the Austrian military records (see HABSBURG MONARCHY). In addition to the number of inhabitants for each town, their religious affiliation and the location of the nearest official church and synagogue, the gazetteer also notes, county by county, the character and name of the auxiliary and national army division affiliated with that location and tells in which of the nearby towns the unit was stationed.

Cemeteries. Most Hungarian-Jewish cemeteries remained intact during the years of the Holocaust and after. Although some isolated cases of vandalism and desecration took place, most damage to tombstones has come from weather erosion and lack of proper maintenance in subsequent years. In the more traditional Jewish areas of Hungary, especially in the northeastern quadrant, tombstones tend to be written entirely in Hebrew, some with engraved family names; others have only the traditional Hebrew names of the deceased followed by the father's name. As Reform Judaism became more influential throughout the 19th century in Hungary, inscriptions were introduced using both Hebrew and German or Hebrew and Hungarian.

20th-Century and Holocaust-related Records. New materials are being discovered or being made available as interest in these matters has increased. A two-volume work that deals with the Holocaust era is *Magyorszagi Zsido Hitkozsegek—1944 Aprilis* (Data from a census organized by the Central Council of Hungarian Jews on the order of the German authorities). Included is an English summary. These books report the information compiled by the Jewish

Holocaust memorial in Nyregyhaza lists Jews from the town who were murdered. Courtesy of Roberta Solit.

communities of Hungary (740 communities, towns and villages). Of this number, 165 communities/congregations belonged to the Neolog, 38 were Status Quo Ante communities, and the remainder of about 550 were Orthodox. Among the items of information that were included for each location are as follows:

- Affiliation and administrative status of the community
- Name and profession of the president of the community
- Name(s) of the rabbi(s) of the community
- Number of taxpaying members
- Schools
- Total number of paid functionaries and officials of the community
- Foundations, their assets and property

The publication is well documented and indexed. Of the eight indexes, the two most useful to the genealogical researcher are the general index of personal names and the index of rabbis serving in communities.

Not to be confused with the April 1944 census of Jewish communities is another type of census prepared under the jurisdiction of the Gendarmerie, the Hungarian national police, at the insistence of the Germans. The area under Hungarian administration at that time was divided into national police districts. These districts were Budapest, Debrecen, Kassa, Kolozsvar, Marosvasarhely, Miskolc, Pecs, Szekesfehervar and Szombathely. The order called for local authorities to prepare a list of all the Jews in four copies, one for the local police; the second one to the gendarmerie, the national police force who had authority over the local police; the third copy was sent to the Ministry of Interior in Budapest; and the fourth stayed with the local Jewish *Judenrat* (prominent Jews in the community who liasoned with the government authorities). It appears that every Hungarian Jew except those living in Budapest completed one of these forms

in March and April 1944. The lists were used to register Jews entering the ghetto and to ration their food, inventory property and determine the communities wealth, and finally this information was used as the basis for preparing the deportation lists.

During the past 15 years these registration documents have been located in various repositories throughout Hungary. Yad Vashem has published several books using these materials. Four volumes in the series entitled, *Names, Nevek, Shemoth*, by Yad Vashem, have been published in the past ten years:

- Victims of deportations from Hajdu county
- Two volumes on Jewish men in forced labor battalions
- Hungarian Jewish women in Stuthoff concentration camp
- Victims of deportations from Zala county

In the Hajdu volume, Professor Gabrial bar Shaked writes that the lists are being computerized so that eventually it will be possible to find those registered, not only according to the names, but also according to place of birth, occupation as well as other variables. Bar Shaked believed that such information might help to establish family connections and construct family trees. Reportedly Bar Shaked, who no longer works at Yad Vashem, has a similar list from other sources of Jews in the Budapest area.

Many more deportation lists, as yet not catalogued repose within the Yad Vashem archives in Jerusalem. As a result of an agreement between Hungary and Israel, Yad Vashem received an additional 150,000 microfilmed pages of documentation from the Hungarian archives in October 2002. Included is information pertaining to the roundup of the Jews, "aryanization" of Jewish property and deportation. In total, more than one million pages of documentation are slated to come to Yad Vashem from Hungary over the next few years.

In less than one year, beginning in April 1944, when the

Nazi defeat was predicable, two-thirds of Hungarian Jewry, nearly 600,000 men, women and children were annihilated in a paroxysm of violent murderous activity; thus initiating the last chapter of this remarkable Jewish community.

To learn more about the tragic events of this period please refer to the writings of Professor Randolph L. Braham, the leading scholar of this subject.

Hungarian Rabbinic Ancestry

Additional sources are available to genealogists with ancestors who were rabbis. Because the information is so rich in materials the researcher should explore these sources even if he or she has no tradition of rabbis in the family. Books specific to rabbis in Hungary include *Toldot Geonei Ungaria* (Sages of Hungary), by Pinchas Zelig Schwartz, published in 1912 in Paks and *Chachmei Ungaria* and *Chachmei Transylvania*, written by Yitzchak Cohen and published by Moreshet in 1995 and 1997, respectively. Hasidism was especially strong in subcarpathian Ruthenian, Maramaros especially.

Pre-World War II Transylvania had strong "Oberlander" and Status Quo communities. The designation Oberlander and Unterlander was specific to Hungarian Jewry. The former were rigidly Orthodox in their beliefs and followed the customs of Orthodox German Jewry as taught by the renowned Rabbi Moses Schreiber, known throughout the Jewish world as the Chatam Sofer. His *yeshiva* in Pressburg (today Bratislava, Slovakia) was the preeminent institution of Jewish scholarship in the 19th century, and his students traveled throughout the Hungarian kingdom to spread their message of Torah and decorum. Initially, the term "Oberlander" had a geographical designation, (northerner) and referred to the German origins of the Chatam Sofer who was born in Frankfurt, Germany. Later the geographical designation became secondary as the disciples and students of the Chatam Sofer settled throughout the entire area of Hungary. Then the designation Oberlander became more of a socio-religious term. In addition to the famous Sofer-Schreiber family, other well-known Oberlander families are the Reichmanns of Toronto and the Gestetner family of London.

Unterlanders were Hasidim, and the entire eastern region of Hungary may be considered to be inhabited by Unterlanders, many of whom were descendants of Hasidic families, but who may have abandoned the strict lifestyle of their origins and joined the Status Quo Ante or the Neolog movements.

Addresses

Central Board of the Federation of Jewish Communities in Hungary, VII, Sip utca 12, Budapest; telephone: 361-342-1355; fax: 361-342-1790; e-mail: BZSH@MAIL.MATAV.HU.

Hungarian National Archives, Central Building, I. ket. Bécsi kapu tér 4, postal address: 1250 Budapest, P.O. Box 3; telephone: 36-1-156-5811; fax (Obuda research center and the repository of the microfilms): 36-1-436-0729; e-mail: INFO@NATARCH.HU; website: WWW.NATARCH.HU.

Hungary Szechenyi Library, H-1827 Budapest, Buda Royal Palace, Wing F; telephone: 361-224-3700; fax: 361-2-2-0804; website: WWW.OSZK.HU/ENG/KOSZONTE.HTML.

Jewish Museum and Archives, Dohany u. 2, 1077 Budapest; telephone: 361-342-8949; fax: 361-342-1790; e-mail: BPJEWMUS@c3.HU; website: WWW.C3HU/~BPJEWMUS. Archivist: Zsuzsanna Toronyi

State Archives in Berehovo – see UKRAINE. Current information is that the Jewish material in the Berehovo Statny Archiv is to be (has been?) transferred to Uzhgorod, which is the central archival administration for Zakarpatskaya Oblast (Subcarpathian Ruthenia).

Bibliography

Bar Shaked, Gabriel. "Books on Hungarian Jews Planned." *AVOTAYNU* 8, no. 2 (Summer 1992): 15.

Bar Shaked, Gabriel. *Names of Jewish Victims of Hungarian Labor Battalions*, 2 vols. Jerusalem: Yad Vashem, 1992.

Beller, Steven. *Vienna and the Jews 1867–1938*. Cambridge, 1989.

Benedik, S. *Andras Karpatalja Tortenete es Klturtortenete Beremenyi*, 1994.

Benoschofsky, Ilona. *History of Jewry in Hungary*. New York: American Joint Distribution Committee, 1988.

Berend, I.T. & Ranki Berend. *Hungary: A Century of Economic Development*. New York: Barnes & Noble, 1974.

Beth Hatefutsoth. *Story of the Jews in Hungary*, 1984.

Bindman, Yirmeyahu. *On Two Fronts* (CIS, 1990).

Bodolai, Zoltan. *Timeless Nation*. Sydney, Australia: Hungaria, 1978).

Body, Paul. *Joseph Eotvos and Modernization of Hungary 1840–70*. New York: Columbia University, 1985.

Borsody, Stephen. *Hungarians—A Divided Nation*. New Haven: Yale, 1988.

Braham, Randolph L. *The Nazi's Last Victims: The Holocaust in Hungary*. Detroit: Wayne State, 1998.

Braham, Randolph L. *The Politics of Genocide: The Holocaust in Hungary*. Detroit: Wayne State, 2000.

Brandt, Edward Reimer. *Content and Addresses of Hungarian Archives*. 2nd. ed. Baltimore: Genealogical Publishing, 1993.

Chater, Melville. *Danube, the Highway of Races*. Washington: National Geographic, 1929.

Clapsaddle, Carol. "Group to Document All Hungarian Holocaust Victims." *AVOTAYNU* 8, no. 1 (Spring 1992): 37.

Cohen, Yitzchak Yosef. *Chachmei Transylvania*. Jerusalem: Machon Yerushalayim, 1989.

Dalmat, Dan. *Bibliographica Hungarica-Judaica*. Budapest: Geniusz, 1991.

Deak, Istvan. *Lawful Revolution*. New York: Columbia University, 1979.

Denes, Dr. Friedman *Az Ujpesti*. Dr. Venetianer Lajos, Israelita., Ujpest, 1937.

Dernoi-Kocsis, Laszlo. *Politikusok es Kalandorok*. Kossuth, 1973.

Dolinay, Gyula. *Magyar Kiralyok ezs Hosok Arczkepcsarnoka*. Szerzo Sajat, 1886.

Doman, Istvan. *Gyori Izraelita Hitkozseg Tortenete 1930–47*. Orszagas Kepviseletenek, 1979.

Don, Yehuda and Victor Karady, eds. *Social and Economic History of Central Europe*. New Brunswick, N.J.: Transaction Press, 1990.

Dotam, Yehudis. *B'Brit Yachad* (Agency, 1985)

Eotvos, George. "Resources for Jewish Genealogical Research in Hungary." *AVOTAYNU* 13, no. 4 (Winter 1997): 17.

Eotvos, Jozsef. *Szidok Emancipatioja, A Nepszeru Zsido Konyvta*.

Eppstein, John, ed. *Hungary*. Cambridge U. Press, 1986.

Epstein, Benjamin R. *T.G. Masaryk and the Jews—A Collection of Essays*. New York: B. Pollak, 1941.

Frankel, Jonathan. *Assimilation and Community*. Cambridge, 1992.

Freidenreich, Harriet. *Jewish Politics in Vienna 1918–1938*. Bloomington: Indiana University Press, 1991.

Frojimovics, Kinga. *Magyarorszagi Zsido Hitkozsegek 1944*. Registered Hungarian Jewish Communities. [Hungarian] Budapest: MTA Judaisztikai, 1994.

Frojimovics, Komorocz. *Zsido Budapest*, Vols. 1 & 2. Budapest: MTA Judaisztikai, 1995.

Fuchs, Abraham. *Yeshivot Hungaria*, 2 vols. Abraham Fuchs, 1987.

Fugedi, Erik. *Elefanthy*. Budapest: Central Europe University Press, 1998.

Funder, Friedrich. *From Empire to Republic*. New York: Albert Unger, 1963.

Gates-Coon, Rebecca. *Landed Estates of the Esterhazy Princes*. Baltimore: Johns Hopkins, 1994.

Gedye, G.E.R. *Betrayal in Central Europe*. New York: Harpers, 1939.

Gero, Andras and Janos Poor. *Budapest, a History from Its Beginnings to 1938*. New York: Columbia University, 1997.

Glatz, Ferenc. *Viragkor es Pusztulas*. Budapest: MTA Tortenet-tudomany, 1996.

Glicenstein, Ze'ev. "Hungary's Secret Jewish Collection." *AVOTAYNU* 12, no. 2 (Summer 1996): 36.

Goldfarb, Jeffrey. *After the Fall*. New York: Basic Books, 1992.

Gonda, Laszlo. *Zsidosag Magyar-Orszagon, 1526–1945* Szazadveg, 1992.

Gracza, Rezsoe. *Hungarians in America*. Minneapolis: Lerner, 1969.

Gruber, Ruth Ellen. *Upon the Doorposts of Thy House*. New York: John Wiley, 1994.

Gruenwald, Yehuda. *Toysent Yor Yidish Leyben Iyn Ungarn*, 1976.

Gruenwald, Yekutiel. *Hayehudim B'Ungaria R'Moshe Kahn in Vatz*, 1913.

Gruenwald, Yekutiel. *L'Flagot Yisroael B'Hungaria*. 1968.

Grunvald, Fulop. *Magyar-Zsido Okleveltar*. (Hungarian Jewish documents). [Hungarian] 1960

Gyertyan, Ervin. *Szemuveg A Porban Magveto* 1975

HaCohen, Pinchas *Hadafus Halvri B'Hungaria*. Kiryat Sefer, 1956.

Hajdu, Janos. *Ujbol es Mindorokke Omike*. 1996.

Hanak, Peter ed. *One Thousand Years (Hungary)*. Budapest: Corvina, 1988.

Handler, Andrew. *Blood Libel at Tiszzaeszlar*. New York: Columbia University, 1980.

Haraszti, Gyorgy. *Magyar Zsido Leveltari Reportorium* (Directory of archival holdings relating to the history of Jews in Hungary). [Hungarian] 2 vols. Budapest: Center of Jewish Studies, Hungarian Academy of Sciences, 1993.

Hartog, Jan de. *Isten Utan Az Elso*. Alapkiadas, 1989.

Herczeg, Ferenc. *Het Svab, A Singer es Wolfner*. 1936.

Hoffman, Charles. *Gray Dawn: The Jews of Eastern Europe in the Post-Communist Era*. New York: Harper & Collins, 1992.

Hoffman, Eva. *Exit into History*. New York: Viking, 1993.

Horecky, Paul L. ed. *East Central Europe*. Chicago: U. of Chicago Press, 1969.

Horvath, Pal ed. *Het Evtized A Hazai Zsidosag Eleteben*, vol. 1 & 2. MTA, 1990.

Hunfalvy, Pal. *Magyarorszag Ethnographiaja*. Akademia, 1876.

Hupchick, Dennis. *Concise Historical Atlas of Eastern Europe*. New York: St. Martin, 1996.

"Index to Hungarian-Jewish Records at the Genealogical Society of Utah," *AVOTAYNU* 4, no. 1 (Winter 1988): 11.

Irta, Erenyi Tibor. *Zsidok Totenete Magyarorszagon*. Utmutato, 1996.

Jacobi, Elizabeth. *Hungary, a Kingdom without a King*. Washington: National Geographic, 1932.

Janowsky, Oscar. *People at Bay*. Oxford University Press, 1938.

"Jewish Records in Sopron, Hungary Archives." *AVOTAYNU* 14, no. 2 (Summer 1998): 51.

Kaczer, Illes. *Fear Not, My Servant Jacob*. New York: Metheun, 1947.

Kaczer, Illes. *The Siege*. New York: Dial, 1953.

Kahn, Robert A. *History of the Hapsburg Empire, 1526–1918*. California U. Press, 1974.

Karaly, Bela. *Trianon and East Central Europe*. New York: Columbia University Press, 1995.

Karoly, Antal. *Szombathely Varoskepei-Muemlekei*. Muszaki, 1967.

Karsai, Elek. *Szamjeltavirat Tancsics*. 1969.

Katz, Jacob. *Jewish Emancipation and Self-Emancipation*. Philadelphia: Jewish Publication Society, 1986.

Katzburg, Nathaniel. *Hungary and the Jews 1920–1943*. Ramat Aviv: Bar-Ilan University Press, 1981.

Kaufman, Jonathan. *Hole in the Heart of the World*. New York: Viking, 1997.

Kerner, Robert J. *Czechoslovakia*. University of California, 1949.

Kiraly, Bela K. *Hungary in the Late Eighteenth Century*. New York: Columbia University Press, 1969.

Kiraly, Bela K. *Tolerance and Movements of Religious Dissent*. New York: Columbia University Press, 1975.

Kisch, Guido. *In Search of Freedom*. New York: Bloch, 1949.

Klein, Bernard. *Hungarian Politics and the Jewish Question*. Jewish Social Studies, 1966.

Kobanyai, Janos. *Magyar Siratofal Szepirodalmi-Tevan*. 1990.

Kohn, Samuel. *Heber Kutforrasok es Adatok Magarorszag Torten*. reprint Sorozata, 1990.

Komlos, Aladar Ararat. *Magyar Zsido Evkonyv Orszagas Izr*. Leanyarvahaz, 1944.

Komlos, Aladar Ararat. *Magyar Zsido Evkonyv Orszagas Izr*. (Hungarian Jewish Central Community Annual Book). [Hungarian] Leanyarvahaz, 1943.

Kopeczi, Bela, et al. *History of Transylvania*. Budapest: Akademiai Kiado, 1994.

Kosary, Domini G. *History of Hungary*. Arno Press and New York Times, 1971.

Kovaly, Hedy. *Under a Cruel Star*. New York: Penguin, 1986.

Krausz, Chaim A. *Regi Erdely, 1919–1960*. #9 Krausz Avram, 1993.

Krausz, Chaim A. *Regi Erdely, Arad I. 1717–1993*. Krausz Avram, 1993.

Kurlansky, Mark. *Chosen Few*. Reading, Mass.: Addison Wesleyly, 1995.

Landeszman, Gyorgy. "Holdings of the Hungarian Jews Archives," *AVOTAYNU* 3, no. 2 (Summer 1987): 13.

Landeszman, Gyorgy. "Some Problems of Genealogical Research in Hungary." *AVOTAYNU* 7, no. 3 (Fall 1991): 17.

Lelkes, Gyorgy, ed. *Magyar Helysegnev-Azonosito Szotar* (Hungarian place names past and present and geographical dictionary). [Hungarian] Budapest: Talma, 1998.

Lengyel, Emil. *The Danube*. New York: Random House, 1939.

Lihovay, Eva, ed. *Commemoration 1944/1945*. Budapest: Chosen Tours, 1994.

Lihovay, Eva, ed. *The Historic Ghetto of Pest*. Budapest: Chosen Tours, 1994.

Lihovay, Eva, ed. *Photographic History of Hungarian Jewry*. Budapest: Chosen Tours, 1994.

Lukacs, John. *Budapest 1900*. Budapest: Grove Weidenfeld, 1988.

Lukacs, Lajos. *Chapters on the Hungarian Political Emigration*. Budapest: Akademiai Kiado, 1995.

Macartney, C. A. *Hungary, a Short History*. Edinburgh University, 1962.

Macartney, C. A. *The 1790–1918 Habsburg Empire*. New York: Macmillan, 1969.

Magocsi, Paul Robert. *Historical Atlas of East Central Europe* vol.1. Seattle: University of Washington, 1993.

Magocsi, Paul Robert. *Shaping of a National Identity*. Cambridge, Mass.: Harvard University Press, 1978.

Magocsi, Paul. *Persistence of Regional Cultures*. New York: Columbia University Press, 1993.

Magris, Claudio. *Danube*. London: Collins Harvill, 1989.

Marosan, Gyorgy. *Tenyek es Tanuk Magveto*. 1967.

McCagg, William O. Jr. *Jewish Nobles and Geniuses in Modern Hungary*. New York: Columbia University Press, 1972.

Mendelsohn, Ezra. *The Jews of East Central Europe*. Bloomington: Indiana University Press, 1983.

Moess, Alfred. *Pest Megye es Pest-Buda Zsidosaganak*. Magyar Zsido Hitkoseg, 1968.

Molnar, Miklos. *From Bela Kun to Janos Kadar*. New York: Berg, 1990.

Montgomery, John. *Hungary, the Unwilling Satellite*. Morristown, N.J.: Vista, 1993.

Nanay, Julia. *Transylvania: The Hungarian Minority in Rumania*. Astor, Fla.: Danubian Press, 1976.

Naumann, Friedrich. *Central Europe*. New York: Alfred A. Knopf, 1917.

"New Jewish Records of Hungary and Russia Available at LDS Library," *AVOTAYNU* 13, no. 1 (Spring 1997): 51.

Nyiri, Janos. *Madararorszag*. Budapest: Makkabi, 1990.

Orban, Ferenc. *Magyarorszag Zsido Emlekej*. Panorama, 1991.

Orszagh, Laszlo. *Magyar-Angol and Angol-Magyar Kesziszotar*. Budapest: Akademiai Kiado, 1998.

Orszagh, Laszlo, ed. *English-Hungarian/Hungarian-English Dictionary*. Budapest: Akademiai Kiado, 1970.

Osborne, R.H. *East Central Europe*. London: Chatto and Windus, 1967.

Panchyk, Richard. "Given Names and Hungarian Jews." *AVOTAYNU* 11, no. 2 (Summer 1995): 24.

Panchyk, Richard. "Genealogy and Migration: Jewish Movement in 19th-Century Austro-Hungary." *AVOTAYNU* 12, no. 1 (Spring 1996): 25.

Panchyk, Richard. "Variations and Changes in Hungarian-Jewish Names." *AVOTAYNU* 14, no. 2 (Summer 1998): 41.

Panchyk, Richard. "What Hungarian Censuses Can Tell Us." *AVOTAYNU* 13, no. 3 (Fall 1997): 34.

Pascu, Stefan. *A History of Transylvania*. Detroit: Wayne State University, 1982.

Patai, Joseph. *The Middle Gate*. Philadelphia: Jewish Publication Society, 1994.

Patai, Raphael. *The Jews of Hungary: History, Culture and Psychology*. Detroit: Wayne State University Press, 1996.

Perlman, Robert. "Bar Shaked Plans to Document all of Hungarian Jewry." *AVOTAYNU* 9, no. 2 (Summer 1993): 3.

Perlman, Robert. *Bridging Three Worlds*. Amherst, Mass.: U. of Massachusetts, 1991.

Perlman, Robert. "Searching Your Hungarian Roots." *AVOTAYNU* 3, no. 3 (Fall 1997): 17.

Pecsi, Marton. *The Geography of Hungary*. Budapest: Corvina, 1964.

Peri, Yitzchak. *Toldos Hayehudim B'Hungaria M'Hayomim*. Tarbut, 1993.

"Plans to Document Holdings of Hungarian-Jewish Archives." *AVOTAYNU* 6, no. 3 (Fall 1990): 25.

Puskas, Julianna. *From Hungary to he United States (1880–1914)*. Budapest: Akademiai Kiado, 1982.

Rekai, Miklos. *Munkacsi Zsidok Teritett Asztala*. Osiris, 1997.

Renoff, Richard. *Proceedings on Carpatho-Ruthenian Immigration*. Cambridge: Harvard University Research Institute, 1975.

Riczu, Zoltan. *Zsido Epuletek es Emlekek Nyiregyhazan*. Nyiregyhaza, 1992.

Rossel, Moredechaj. *Frigyszekreny Es Zaszlo*. Nir Ecjon, 1991.

Roth, Joseph. *Zsidok Vandoruton*. Budapest: Makkabi, 1989.

Scheiber, Sandor. *And You Shall Tell Your Son*. Budapest: Corvina Kiado, 1984.

Scheiber, Sandor. *Magyarorszagi Zsido Feliratok Muszaki Vidosa Laszlo*. 1960

Scheiber, Sandor, ed. *Magyar-Zsido Okleveltar* (Hungarian Jewish documents). [Hungarian] Kepviseletnek, 1980.

Scheiber, Sandor, ed. *Magyar-Zsido Okleveltar*. Kepviseletnek, 1974.

Scheiber, Sandor, ed. *Magyar-Zsido Okleveltar*. Kepviseletnek, 1970.

Schonfeld, Louis. "A Report on Selected Hungarian Jewish Cemeteries. *AVOTAYNU* 8, no. 3 (Fall 1993): 18.

Schweitzer, Jozsef. *Pecsi Izraelita Hitkozseg Tortentete Orszagas Kepviseletenek*. 1966.

Schweitzer, Jozsef, ed. *Evkonyv 1985–1991 Rabbikepzo Intezet*. 1991.

Sebok, Laszlo. *Hatarokon Tuli Magyar Helysegnev Szotar Teleki Lazslo Alapotvany*. 1997.

Sebok, Laszlo. *Magyar Neve?* Budapest: Arany, 1990.

Silber, Michael K. ed. *Jews in the Hungarian Economy 1760–1945*. Jerusalem: Magnes Press, 1992.

Sisa, Stephen. *The Spirit of Hungary*. Morristown, N.J.: Vista, 1990.

Smith, Lovina Steward. *Hungary—Land and People*. Budapest: Athenaeum, 1933.

Somogyi, Ferenc. *Faith and Fate*. Cleveland: Karpat, 1976.

Speigel, Dr. Yehuda. *Yahadut Ungvar* (Jewish Hungary). [Hebrew] Tel Aviv: self, 1993.

Stegena, Lajos. *Tudomanyos Terkepezes Karpat-Medenceben*. Budapest: Akademiai Kiado, 1998.

Steiner, Edward. *On the Trail of the Immigrant*. New York: Arno, 1969.

Suess, Jared H. *Handy Guide to Hungarian Genealogical Records*. Salt Lake City: Everton, 1980.

Sugar, Peter Hanak. *History of Hungary*. Bloomington: Indiana University Press, 1994.

Szaploncai, Gyula. *Magyar Belyegek Arjegyzeke–1968*. Magyar Filatelia Vallalat, 1968.

Szikra-Falus, Katalin. *Position and Conditions of Intellectuals*. Budapest: Akadmiai Kiado, 1995.

Tapie, Victor L. *The Rise and Fall of the Habsburg Monarchy*. New York: Praeger, 1971.

Teller, Judd L. *Scapegoat of Revolution*. New York: Scribner, 1954.

Tezla, Albert. *The Hazardous Quest*. Budapest: Corvina, 1993.

Udvary, Andrew. *True Hungary*. Budapest: Corvina, 1965.

Venetianer, Lajos. *Magyar Zsidosag Tortenete*. Konyvertekesito Vallalat, 1986.

Venetianer, Lajos. *Zsido Erkolcs*. Olcso Zsido Konytar, 1998.

Weisl, Dr. Wolfgang. *Juden in Der Armee Osterreich-Ungarns*. Die Olamenu, 1971.

Zsoldos, Jeno. *1848–1849 A Magyar Zsidosag Eleteben*. Mult es Jovo, 1998.

Notes

1. Gates-Coons, Rebecca, *Landed Estates of the Esterhazy Princes*.
2. Conversation with Professor Gyorgy Haraszti, former director of the Hungarian Jewish Archives* in the summer of 1998.
3. Perlman, Robert. *Bridging Three Worlds*.

India

by Sallyann Amdur Sack

Only 6,000 Jews live in India today (out of a population of one billion), but at its peak in 1948, Jews numbered in the tens of thousands. They were comprised of three distinctly different groups, the Bene Israel, the Cochin Jews and the Baghdadis. From the religious point of view, India was always a haven for Jews. Religion was respected and every group formed its own tight social and cultural circle, living in peace alongside others with differing views.

Bene Israel

The Bene Israel form the largest group of Jews from India. Once centered around Bombay, about 20,000 lived in that city in 1948. The majority made *aliyah* (immigration to Israel) after the State of Israel was established in 1948. About 2,000 others settled in Australia, Canada, England and the United States. Perhaps the only Jewish community in the world today that never experienced anti-Semitism, the Bene Israel lived harmoniously with their Indian neighbors for approximately 2,000 years, free to worship as they pleased and to live as a separate community.

Most of the Bene Israel believe that they are descendants of the Ten Lost Tribes, exiled by the Assyrian king in 722 BCE. Others among them believe that their ancestors escaped from Israel by sea in 175 BCE during the reign of Antichous Epiphanes. Their tradition recounts that during the voyage their ancestors were shipwrecked and washed ashore on the Konkan coast south of Bombay. The survivors—reportedly seven men and seven women—buried their dead in a site near the village of Nawgaon which later became the Bene Israel cemetery.

Tradition holds that all holy books were lost in the shipwreck so that over time all Hebrew prayers were forgotten except the *Shema*. The Bene Israel observed the Sabbath, celebrated the major festivals, circumcised their sons and performed 8 of the 11 offerings prescribed in Leviticus and Numbers.

After arrival in India, the survivors decided to settle permanently in the Konkan villages. They adopted Hindu first names similar to their Biblical names, but became known by their "kar" surnames which indicated the village in which they lived. For example, Nawgaonkar would have come from the village of Nawgaon, Penkar from the village of Pen and Wakrulkar from the village of Wakrul. Today they use first names, patronyms or andronyms (husband's patronym and *kar*). More than one hundred such names can be found today among members of the Bene Israel. Under the influence of the Hindu caste system, the Bene Israel villagers were divided into two caste-like groups—white and black, which however, bore no relation to the color of their skin. So-called White Bene Israel claimed descent from the original settlers; Black Bene Israel were the offspring of intermarriage with Hindus. Over time, the distinctions have all but disappeared.

Isolated from the rest of world Jews for 2,000 years, the Bene Israel only made contact with other Jews during the 18th century. Over a period of time, their "religious revival" was guided by a series of other Jewish leaders, mostly Cochin and Baghdadis. Also in the 18th century, the Bene Israel began to move to the recently established port of Bombay where most continued to live.

Originally, many rabbis in Israel did not recognize the Bene Israel as Jews, and they had difficulty marrying other Jews. They were not recognized by the rabbinate as "full" Jews until 1964, after which emigration from India increased. Today more than 25,000 Bene Israel live in Israel.

Cochin Jews

These Jews live in the southwestern India coastal province of Kerala (also known as the Malabar coast). Jewish merchants from Palestine and other areas of the Mediterranean and western Asia settled in South India where they received active encouragement from the local princes. Jewish communities are known to have existed there before the arrival of the first Christians, and almost certainly before the fourth century.

Legend holds that the first immigrants came in the wake of the exiles of Nebuchadnezzar or following the destruction of the second temple in 70 CE. A story still current in the 17th century says that they came in great numbers—15,000 or 20,000—from Majorca and settled in Cranganur (Kdangalur). A Christian tradition holds that a Jewish presence was found in Malabar by a fourth century missionary. Both Benjamin of Tudela in the 12th century and Marco Polo in the 13th century noted the presence of Jews. Today in the village of Chennamangalam, east of Cranganur, outside a deserted synagogue is a tombstone dedicated to the memory of "Sarah, daughter of Israel." The date on the inscription is 1269 CE.

The Jewish community at Cochin probably never numbered more than 2,000, divided between those of full Jewish descent ("White" Jews) and the "Black" offspring of intermarriage with the indigenous population. Dutch rule from 1663 initiated a period of prosperity, but the British rule, starting in 1795, led to a decline in the fortunes of this community. Most emigrated *en masse* to Israel soon after 1948. Today only a handful remain in Jew Town, Cochin.

Baghdadi Jews

Jews from Syria and Iraq began to settle in India in the late 18th century, primarily in the area of Calcutta on the east coast. During an era of peace and economic expansion during the 19th century, Jewish merchants from the Middle East established communities in Bombay and Calcutta. By the mid-

Tomb of David Sasson in Pune, India

among them two marriage registers, a circumcision register and some burial records.

Isaac Saul Sankar, an Israeli with roots in India has written two articles in *Sharsheret Hadorot*. One describes sources he used to trace his Bene Israel family back six generations;[2] the other reports on a research trip he made to India in 1996 with emphasis on cemeteries in specific locations.[3] Sally Solomon has described the old Jewish cemetery in Madras[4] and Shalva Weil has explained how the Bene Israel constructed surnames.[5] Boston HIAS records held by the American Jewish Historical Society in Waltham, Massachusetts,* hold some case files of Jews from India.

Additional information may come only from contact with former Indian Jews living in other countries today. Baghdadi Jews are among the members of Kahal Joseph Congregation* in Los Angeles.

Addresses

American Jewish Historical Society, 160 Herrick Road, Newton Centre, MA; telephone: (617) 559-8880; fax: (617) 559-8881; e-mail: AJHS@AJHS.ORG; website: WWW.AJHS.ORG

Kahal Joseph Congregation, 10505 Santa Monica Boulevard, Los Angeles, CA; telephone: (310) 474-0559; fax: (310) 441-4059

Bibliography

Blady, Ken. *Jewish Communities in Exotic Places*. Northvale, NJ: Jason Aronson, 2000.

Ezra, Esmond. *Turning Back the Pages*. vol. 2. London: Brookside, 1986.

Hyman, Mavis. *Jews of the Raj*. London: Hyman Publishers, 1995.

Flower, Elias and Judith Elias Cooper. *The Jews of Calcutta: the Autobiography of a Community, 1798–1972*. Calcutta: Jewish Association of Calcutta, 1974.

Isenberg, Shirley B. *India's Bene Israel: A Comprehensive Inquiry and Sourcebook*. Berkeley: Magnes Museum, 1988.

Katz, Nathan. "An Annotated Bibliography about Indian Jewry." *Kol Bina*, 1991; supplement 1993–97, *Journal of Indo-Judaic Studies*, 1999.

Katz, Nathan and Ellen Goldberg. *The Last Jews of Cochin*. Columbia, S.C.: University of South Carolina Press, 1993.

Luxembourg, Daniella. *The Jews from the Konkan: The Bene Israel Communities in India*. Tel Aviv: Beth Hatefutsoth, 1981.

Segal, J.B. *A History of the Jews of Cochin*. London: Vallentine Mitchell, 1993.

Strizower, Schifra. *The Bene Israel of Bombay*. New York: Schocken, 1971.

Tahan, Ilana. "Genealogical Resources in the British Library Hebrew Collection." *AVOTAYNU* 18, no. 1 (Spring 2002).

Weil, Shalva. *India's Jewish Heritage: Ritual, Art and Life-cycle*. Bombay: Marg, 2002.

———. "Names and Identity among the Bene Israel," in *Ethnic Groups*, I, 1977.

Notes

1. Tahan, Ilana. "Genealogical Resources in the British Library Hebrew Collection," *AVOTAYNU* 18, no. 1 (Spring 2002).
2. Sankar, Isaac Saul, *Sharsheret Hadorot* 9, no. 2 (May 1995).
3. Sankar, *Sharsheret Hadorot* 10, no. 3 (October 1996).
4. Solomon, Sally. *Shemot* 3, no. 2 (June 1995).
5. Weil, Shalva. *Sharsheret Hadorot* 10, no. 1 (January 1995).

19th century, they had extended their settlement all along the trade routes, primarily in Rangoon, Singapore, Hong Kong and Shanghai. They came from Aleppo, Baghdad and Basra. Most important was David Sassoon who fled Baghdad and arrived in Bombay in 1832. Shalom Cohen from Aleppo was the first Jew from the Middle East to settle in Calcutta in 1798. Other Jews came from Yemen.

Identifying with the attitudes of the British rulers toward the "natives," most of the Baghdadi Jews did not mingle or intermarry with the Bene Israel or the Cochin Jews. After Indian independence from India, most of the Baghdadi Jews emigrated—to England, Australia, Israel, the United States and elsewhere.

Genealogical Resources

Indian Jewry has been the subject of many well-researched scholarly monographs and papers, but little genealogical research has been reported. Although archival records may well exist, none have been reported from India.

The British Library Hebrew collection holds perhaps the most extensive sources described to date, especially for the Bene Israel and the Calcutta Jews.[1] Included in the collection are two extensive burial lists for Calcutta Jews interred in the Narkeldanga cemetery covering the years 1813–1983. The library holds transcripts of burials in Jewish cemeteries at Bhagalpur, Ghazipur and Dinapur as well as a copy of Esmond Ezra's autobiography, volume 2, which is composed solely of genealogical tables. The tables show the relationships among more than 2,500 individuals who formed a substantial portion of Calcutta Jewry—purported the most comprehensive table ever published of any Indian-Jewish family. The most frequently listed name is Cohen. Others are Arakie, Elias, Ezra, Gubay, Jacob and Solomon. Another holding, *The Bene Israel Annual and Year Book for 1919–1920*, holds a wealth of genealogically relevant data including the census of the Jewish population for 1911. A special subset of holdings relate to the Sassoon family,

Iran

by Ephraim Dardashti

Iran, formerly Persia, is a non-Arabic Muslim country approximately three times the size of France. Jews trace their arrival to the land of Aryans and Cyrus to the destruction of the first temple. Dr. Habib Levy in his monumental work, *Tarikhe Yahude Iran*, divides the Iranian-Jewish population into two parts, the remnants of the northern kingdom of Israel who settled in northern and western Iran and the refugees fleeing the downfall of Judea who settled mainly in southern and central Iran. The community began with the deportation of the Israelites by Tilgath Pileser III, king of Assyria, to the Median cities of the Iranian plateau in 722 B.C.E. The original population was augmented by Jews from Babylonia who moved primarily to an area around Hamadan, Isphahan and Shiraz in about 538 B.C.E. The city of Isphahan was founded by Jews and was known as Yahudiyeh. According to the Book of Esther, Jewish settlement in Iran gradually spread to include almost all of the Persian Empire.

Biblical references make it clear that Jews were settled in "the cities of the Medes" as early as 722 B.C.E. (Kings II [17:6]). Certainly, many from the Babylonian exiles of 597 B.C.E. and 586 B.C.E. made their way to the Persian Kingdom where they quickly integrated themselves with the rulers. (Book of Daniel)

The first attempt to destroy the Jews seems to have occurred in the reign of Ahashveros (Artaxerxes II) perhaps 404–361 B.C.E.[1] as we learn from the Book of Esther. The Jewish population of Iran prospered and increased in the early years of the Common Era. The famous medieval Jewish traveler and chronicler, Benjamin of Tudela, reported in the 12th century that more than half a million Jews lived in this land. Conditions worsened dramatically after the Muslim Shi'a creed became the official religion of Iran at the beginning of the 16th century. By the 17th century, the Jewish population was no more than 100,000, a significant decrease since the time of Benjamin of Tudela. Over the centuries, traders crisscrossed Persia, Jews among them. After the Spanish Expulsion, some Ladino-speaking Sephardim found their way to Persia as did a smaller number of Ashkenazim. A few crossed the border from southern Russia after its revolution in 1917.

Religious hostility toward the Jews was a frequent fact of life during the first centuries of the Common Era, as were occasional pogroms and forced conversions. At this time, numerous Jews from Babylonia and Persia fled to India's Malabar Coast. With the conquest of Persia by Arab armies and its subsequent adoption of Islam (in 642 C.E.), Jews were granted *dhimmi* (protected minority) status and forced to pay a special "protection" tax. For the first few hundred years of Islamic rule, however, the Jews suffered no persecution.

From the 6th to 12th centuries, Persian and Babylonian Jews became increasingly isolated from one another, with the Persian Jews losing considerable knowledge of Jewish language and learning. Judeo-Persian developed into a distinct language.

By the 12th century, Jewish leaders in Baghdad had to correspond with Persian communities in the Persian language. The period between the 13th and 18th centuries were hard for Persian Jews with numerous episodes of forced conversions and/or physical attacks. Jewish scholarship and ritual observance suffered as some said that the Persian Jews were the "most ignorant" in the world.[2]

To understand the scarcity of written documents, one need not to go over the long history of the presence of Jews in Iran but rather focus on the events of the early 16th century and the rise to power of the Safavid dynasty and its leader Shah Abbas. The Safavid began to rule Persia in 1502 C.E. and quickly managed to reorganize and refocus their society. They adopted Shiite Islam as the official religion of the country. Shiite Islam and its concept of *najess* (ritual impurity of non-Shiites) was a harbinger of an intellectual downward fall of Persian Jewry. While the rule of the Safavids meant a renaissance for Iran generally, for the Jews it was a social, intellectual, psychological and financial nightmare. Jewish libraries were destroyed and barbaric social restrictions were placed on the Jewish minority. This nightmare outlasted the fall of the Safavids in the 17th century and its dire consequences, as documented by European travelers, scarred the Iranian-Jewish community well into the early 20th century.

Imperial Europe became interested in the economic potential of Persia and the British, French and Russians began negotiating concessions from the Qajar dynasty. Persian Jewry re-established communications with world Jewry; European-Jewish representatives became aware of the conditions of their fellow Jews and lobbied to be allowed to come to the rescue of their downtrodden brethren. In 1858, Jewish organizations began to pressure the British and French ministers in Teheran to intervene on behalf of persecuted located Jews. The renewed contact between the Jews of Europe and the Jews of Iran brought about the introduction of Alliance Israelite Universelle schools throughout the major urban centers, such as Hamadan, Isphahan, Shiraz, Teheran and other cities. Relief organizations sent money and the Alliance Universelle Israelite opened schools beginning in 1898. Missionaries succeeded in converting small numbers of Jews to Christianity while large numbers became Bahais.

Iran's contact with the West alerted the population of its miserable conditions, and in the late 1880s and through the first two decades of the 20th century, new radical thoughts took hold in Iran—radical thoughts such a constitutional monarchy, a critical look at Islam. The Qajar dynasty was overthrown and was replaced by Shah Reza Pahlavi, a modernist. Jews as a whole embraced the new dynasty. Newspapers written in

Farsi with Hebrew (*HaGeullah and Ha Hayim*) characters were published; books dealing with religious thought also were published in the same manner. By the early 1930s, cadres of newly minted Jewish physicians, dentists, engineers and scholars began surfacing throughout Iran. The ghettos were abandoned in favor of living in desegregated neighborhoods. Some Jewish intellectuals also joined the ranks of liberals demanding more political freedom. The leader of one such a liberal movement was "Monsieur" Shmuel Haim who was executed by Reza on charges of treason in 1931.

The flight from the ghettos and the liberation brought about by the introduction of education lead to radical changes in the lives of the Iranian Jews throughout the 20th century. For some though, the new century meant the voluntary abandonment of their ancestors in favor of Bahaism, Islam and even Anglicanism. Several prominent families in Iran today have Jewish roots. Two ayatollahs had Jewish grandparents and the former Anglican bishop of Isphahan who was executed by the Islamic regime was born Jewish.

The Jews of Iran were always urban dwellers, except for a few rural Jews in the Kurdistan region. As a result of massive emigration during the past 25 years, few Jews still live in Iran. Before then, however, they lived in almost every city including Burujerd, Bushehr, Damavand, Firuzabad, Hamadan, Isphahan, Kashan, Kerman, Kermanshah, Merymand, Meshhad, Nahawand, Rasht, Rezayeh, Sanandaj, Shiraz, Tabriz, Teheran, Urmiyeh and Yazd.

Jews with roots in Iran can be found today in three main geographical locations, Israel, the United States and Iran. The vast number of Iranian Jews moved to Israel when the State was declared in 1948. Today, a large concentration of Iranian Jews is found in Bat Yam, Holon, Jerusalem and Rishon L'Tzion. President Moshe Katzav, the president of the State of Israel was born in the Iranian city of Yazd. The minister of defense Shaul Mofaz also was born in Iran; his forefathers had roots in the city of Isphahan.

The second largest number of Iranian Jews moved to the United States, primarily to metropolitan New York (including Long Island) and metropolitan Los Angeles. More than a dozen synagogues have been founded and maintained by Iranian Jews in Los Angeles, as well as day schools and businesses catering to the kosher diet of the Iranian Jews. Most of the Iranian Jews in the United States came after the Islamic revolution in 1979.

An estimated 25,000 Jews are left in Iran, with the largest concentrations in the cities of Isphahan, Shiraz and Teheran.

It is interesting to note that to this day Farsi-speaking Jews refer to all Jews as *Eesrael*, meaning Israelite. Iranian Moslems refer to Jews as *Yahudi, Kalimi* (people of the book) or in harsher moments, as *Johood* (kikes). In the oral tradition of the Jews of Iran, until some 30 or 40 years ago elders of the people would tell their offspring which of the ten tribes of Israel they were from. Dr. Levy recounts that some Iranian Jews trace their lineage to the tribes of Gad, Naphtali, Reuven and Shimon. The Jews of Isphahan identify themselves as remnants of the tribe of Judah.

Genealogical Resources

For the purpose of genealogical research on the Jews of Iran, the most effective current resource remains oral history. Until the advent of the reign of Reza Pahlavi in 1925, vital statistics records were not kept by the government. Records of births, marriages and deaths were kept by individual families (Jewish and Muslim) on the flyleaves of their prayer books. Fixed, hereditary family names were not adopted until approximately 120 years ago. Many adopted names that reflected their occupations; some took geographically based names. A large category of family names end in the suffix *zadeh* which means "son of," or with the suffix *i* meaning "from."

No central archive of Iranian (Persian) Jewry exists anywhere, although this was one of the oldest of Jewish communities in the world. For centuries, Iranian-Jewish history was passed down verbally. Whatever community records may have been kept were left in Iran and are inaccessible today. The lack of records means that genealogical research currently can be done only through contacts with individuals who may know something of a family's history.

To prevent history of their community from being lost totally, the Center for Iranian Jewish Oral History* (CIJOH) was created in Los Angeles in 1995. Its goal is to interview the oldest living Iranian Jews all over the world many of whom are encyclopedias of knowledge. The intent is that they answer questions and tell stories that professors and other academics can research further in the future.

Every year since its creation the Center has hosted a three-day conference that has brought together Iranian Jews from all over the world to interact in a variety of academic and social activities. Papers are presented and discussed by historians and laymen; proceedings are published in a journal. At present, the Center has recorded approximately 100 oral histories. It also has a photograph archive of 700 old photographs, the oldest dating from 1870. Photographs are displayed at the conferences, and many have been identified and the names indexed. The photographs as well as the oral histories are being computerized. To date the CIJOH has published its findings in four volumes, the body of the collection is in Farsi with a short English synopsis provided in the back of the book.

In addition to the Center for Iranian Jewish Oral History,* the best other resources are the synagogues serving Iranian Jews in Israel, Los Angeles* and New York*. An almost complete file of the Judeo-Persian newspaper *Rahamim* (published 1910–14) is held at the Jewish National and University Library in Jerusalem. The Ben-Zvi Institute* in Jerusalem has a publication series called Irano-Judaica that represents serious scholarly research on Iranian studies and touches upon the Jewish experience in that country as well. Schelly Dardashti a seasoned genealogist and writer at the *Jerusalem Post* writes and lectures on Iranian-Jewish genealogy.

Several books in English, while not of direct genealogical value, provide interesting background into the lives of Iranian Jews. Houman Sarshar's fabulous book, *The Children of Esther*, is the most comprehensive book on Iranian-Jewish history published in one volume to date. *Jadid Al_Islam: The Jewish New Moslems of Meshed*, by Raphael Patai, is about the Jews of the northeastern Iran, the Jews of Khorasan who had to hide their ancestry and pretend to have converted to Islam. In his book, *Images of Sephardi and Eastern Jewries in Transition: The Teachers of the Alliance Israelite Universelle, 1860–1939,* Aaron Rodrique opens a window into the work and mindset of the benevolent Alliance teachers in Iran and elsewhere in Islamic lands. Laurence D. Loeb lived among the Jews of Shiraz in southern Iran and published his observations in his book *Outcast: Jewish Life in Southern Iran*, published by Gordon and Breach in New York in 1977. The *Encyclopaedia Judaica* (*Jewish Encyclopedia*) has scholarly sections on the history of the Jews in Iran.

The book, *Irangeles: Iranian in Los Angeles*, edited by Ron Kelley and published by the University of California Press in 1993, provides a snapshot of the Iranian-Jewish population in the Iranian tapestry in Los Angeles. Anton Felton in his book, *Jewish Carpets*, provides a pictorial work on the contribution of the Iranian Jews to the carpet industry in Iran.

For a fuller understanding of the daily conditions the memoirs of most of western travelers to Persia is mandatory reading. A good introduction is the book of Elkan Nathan Adler, titled *Jews in Many Lands*, published by The Jewish Publication Society in 1905. Adler mentions names of Iranian-Jewish notables, and his book is handy for genealogical research.

Dr. Amnon Netzer, an Iranian Jew with roots in Rasht and Isphahan and professor of Iranian studies at Hebrew University of Jerusalem, has written many scholarly and well-documented works on the history of the Jews of Iran. Two of his edited volumes were published by Mazda Publishers and are called: *Padyavand I and II: Judeo-Iranian and Jewish Studies*. Although they are written in Farsi, these works have extensive selections in English. The three-volume work by Dr. Habib Levy, *Tarikhe Yahude Iran* now translated into English, is a must reading.

David Yeroushalmi an Iranian Jew and a professor at Tel Aviv University provides a scholarly work on the Judeo-Persian poet Emrani in his book, *The Judeo-Persian Poet Emrani and His Book of Treasure*, published by E. J. Brill in 1995. Vera Basch Moreen's anthology of Judeo-Persian literature *In Queen Esther's Garden,* Yale University, 2000, is a magnificent volume on the literary side of the Iranian-Jewish experience. Dr. Moreen's earlier work, *Iranian Jewry's Hour of Peril and Heroism*, chronicles a work of the 17th-century Judeo-Persian poet Babai ibn Lutf.

For a romanticized fictional look on the Iranian-Jewish experience the following authors offer their unique points of view. Dora Levi Mossanen in her novel *Harem* writes of a Jewish woman in the ghetto; the setting is very much 18th-century Teheran, but she backdates her story to the Teymurid period.

Gina Barkhordar Nahai has written two works of fiction dealing with Iranian Jewry, *The Cry of the Peacock*, and her latest work, *Moonlight on the Avenue of Faith*. The Iranian-Israeli author Dorit Rabinyan's novel, *Persian Brides*, offers another perspective on life in Iran.

Addresses

Center for Iranian Jewish Oral History, P.O. Box 2543, Beverly Hills, CA 90213; telephone: (310) 472-3012; fax: (310) 472-3043; e-mail: CIJOH@CIJOH.ORG

Ben Zvi Institute, 12 Abravanel Street, Jerusalem 91076, Israel; telephone: 972-2-539-8844; e-mail: MAHONZVI@H2.HUM.HUJI.AC.IL

Jewish National and University Library, Hebrew University, Givat Ram, Jerusalem, Israel; website: HTTP://JNUL.HUJI.AC.IL

Mashadi Jewish Center, 54 Steamboat Road, Great Neck, New York; telephone: (516) 487-3636; fax: (516) 487-3638; e-mail: MOTTIKO@AOL.COM

Nessah Synagogue, 142 South Rexford Drive, Beverly Hills, California, 90212; telephone: (310) 273-2400; fax: 310-276-3800; e-mail: INFO@NESSAH.ORG

Ohr Haemet Synagogue, 1030 South Robertson Boulevard, Los Angeles, California; 90035-1505; telephone: (310)-854-3006

Persian Jewish Center of Brooklyn, 828 Eastern Parkway, Brooklyn, New York

Bibliography

Adler, Elkan Nathan. *Jews in Many Lands*. Philadelphia: Jewish Publication Society, 1905.

Blady, Ken. *Jewish Communities in Exotic Places*. Northvale, N.J.: Jason Aronson, 2000.

Felton, Anton, *Jewish Carpets*. Woodbridge, Suffolk: Antique Collector's Club, 1997.

Levy, Habib. *Tarikhe Yahude Iran* (Comprehensive history of the Jews of Iran). [Farsi; Eng. by George W. Maschke]. Costa Mesa, CA: Mazda, 1999.

Loeb, Laurence. *Outcast: Jewish Life in Southern Iran*. New York, Gordon & Breach, 1977.

Moreen, Vera Basch. *In Queen Esther's Garden*. New Haven: Yale University Press, 2000.

———. *Iranian Jew's Hour of Peril and Heroism*. Philadelphia: American Academy for Jewish Research, 1987.

Mossanen, Dora Levi. *Harem*. New York: Scribner, 2002.

Nahai, Gina Barkhordar. *Moonlight on the Avenue of Faith*. New York: Harcourt Brace, 1997.

———. *The Cry of the Peacock*. New York: Crown, 1991.

Netzer, Amnon. *Padyavad I &II: Judeo-Iranian and Jewish Studies*. [Farsi and English] Costa Mesa, CA: Mazda, 1996.

Patai, Raphael. *Jadid Al-Islam: The Jewish "New Muslims" of Meshhed*. Detroit: Wayne State University Press, 1997.

Rabinyan, Dorit. *Persian Brides*. New York: George Braziller, 1998.

Rodrigue, Aron. *Images of Sephardi and Eastern Jewries in Transition*. Seattle: University of Washington Press, 1993.

Yeroushalmi, David. *The Judeo-Persian Poet Emrani and His Book of Treasure*. Leiden and New York: E.J. Brill, 1995.

Notes

1. Loeb, 275.
2. *op. cit.,* 285.

Iraq

by Sallyann Amdur Sack

Iraq is part of the Fertile Crescent of ancient times where the Tigris and Euphrates Rivers join. Iraq (then Babylonia) is also the place where Judaism began; Abraham was born there in Ur of the Chaldees. Many years later, in 722 BCE, the Assyrian army conquered northern Israel and, over several decades, took thousands of members of the Ten Lost Tribes back to the region of today's northern Iraq and Iran, where they were dispersed. In 586 BCE, the king of Babylonia captured Jerusalem, burned the Temple, and took captive much of the elite of the city—authors, writers, ministers and prophets.

After 50 years, the Jews taken to Babylonia were permitted to return to their homeland; about 40,000 to 50,000 did. Those who remained thrived, and for approximately one thousand years, Babylonia was the world center of Judaism, the center of famous academies and the place where the Babylonian Talmud was written. Hundreds of Jewish agricultural settlements emerged all over Iraq, primarily along the rivers. Remnants of ancient Jewish life can still be found in the names of some communities and in the still extant tombs of Ezra the Scribe and of the prophet Ezekial haNavi, both of which are in southern Iraq.

Throughout history, Jews from other areas came to settle in Iraq, including some from Spain at the time of the Inquisition. After a while, however, life became unpleasant for Jews, and many left. Following the Mongol conquest of Baghdad in 1258, many Jews moved to India, Kurdistan, Persia, and elsewhere including pre-Inquisition Spain. The migration occurred during the 17th, 18th and 19th centuries especially. The chief rabbi of Baghdad moved to India, where he settled first in Bombay and later in Pune. Hundreds of other Jewish families followed him to southeast Asia settling in Bombay and Calcutta. From India, these Babylonian Jews moved to Rangoon, Burma; Singapore; Hong Kong and Shanghai.

During the years of Ottoman rule, Jewish men could be excused from service in the army through the payment of money. Many paid the fee, and registers of these names are in files in Israel today, as are other files created during the years of Turkish rule. Check the Israel State Archives* to see what it holds. Other good resources are Iraqi Jews living in Israel today, contacted (when one knows a family name) simply through the telephone books. Also useful is the magazine, *The Scribe*, published by the Exilarch's Foundation* in London.

Most of the Jews of Iraq made *aliyah* (immigration to Israel) after the establishment of the State of Israel; today, almost none are left in Iraq. Genealogical information is difficult to obtain, but one possible source is the Babylonian Jewish Heritage Center,* a museum and cultural center in the Israeli town of Or Yehuda, about 20 miles east of Tel Aviv. The Center publishes a journal called *Nahal Delah* and has a project to collect genealogical information via questionnaires it circulates, primarily to former Iraqis living in Israel today.

A sizable Iraqi Jewish population lives in Los Angeles today. Eliezer Hamu, Middle East librarian at UCLA, and Victor Ozair, an active member of the Iraqi-Jewish community in Los Angeles, spoke on "Tracing Sephardic and Mizrahi Families in the Land Where Judaism was Born" at the 1998 IAJGS genealogical conference in Los Angeles. Members of this community may be contacted via to synagogues that observe the Baghdadi rite, Kahal Joseph Congregation* and Midrash Od Yosel Hai Synagogue.*

The website THESITE2000.VITUALAVE.NET/IRAQIJEWS is devoted to Jews who left Iraq in the 1960s and 1970s. It has many genealogical queries.

Addresses

Babylonian Jewish Heritage Center, 83 Ben Porat Rd., Or Yehuda, 60251 Israel; telephone: 972-3-533-9278/9; fax: 972-3-533-9936; website: WWW.BABYLONJEWRY.ORG. IL.

Exilarch's Foundation, 20 Queens Gate Terrace; London SW1 5PF, England.

Israel State Archives, 35 Mekor Haim Street, Jerusalem; mailing address: Prime Minister's Office, Kiryat Ben Gurion, 91919 Jerusalem; telephone: 972-2-680-680.

Kahal Joseph Congregation, 10505 Santa Monica Boulevard, Los Angeles, CA 90025.

Midrash Od Yosel Hai Synagogue, 420 North Fairfax Avenue, Los Angeles, CA 90036; mailing address: 427 North Stanley Avenue, Los Angeles, CA 90036.

Note

"Gleanings from the Los Angeles Seminar," AVOTAYNU 14, no. 3, (Fall 1998): 19.

Girls' School of the Alliance Israélite Universelle in Baghdad at the beginning of the 20th century

Ireland

by Len Yodaiken

The first recorded appearance of Jews in Ireland was in the *Annals of Innisfallen*, which state curtly, "Year 1079: Five Jews came over the sea with gifts to Tairdelbach and they were sent back over the sea."[1] Jews continued to come to Ireland throughout medieval times, accompanying the Norman English when they conquered most of eastern Ireland. Presumably they were expelled with the Jews of England in 1290.

After the expulsion of the Jews from Spain in 1492, some trickled into the British Isles under the cover of being converts (*marranos*) or as agents of Jewish merchants in the Netherlands. A 17th-century synagogue thought to belong to *marrano* traders has been excavated in Cork. Oliver Cromwell allowed 12 Jewish families to come to Britain from Holland in 1656 and dispersed them in the British Islands. The Phillips family was the earliest to arrive in Dublin and might have been one of them.

Around 1656, the Cromwellian administration formally permitted Jews to return to Britain, and with the restoration of the monarchy in 1660, Jews came to England and Ireland in greater numbers. A gradual building of a Jewish community in Ireland can be detected from the beginning of the 18th century. Their numbers, which ebbed and flowed with the economic fortunes of the island, averaged about 500 individuals until the arrival of Eastern European Jews beginning in 1882.

Resources

For the period until 1900, one of the best sources of both history and documentation of the Jews is Louis Hyman's *The Jews of Ireland*. In it are the registry of births and deaths kept by the Rev. Julius Sandheim from 1820 to 1879 and lists of officials of the Dublish Hebrew Congregation from 1835 to 1901. The original registers are kept in the Irish Jewish Museum.* Also in Hyman's book is an inventory of tombstone inscriptions, 1777–1885, from the first cemetery acquired by the community at Ballybough, outside of Dublin. This was the only Jewish cemetery in Ireland at the time, and the deceased were often brought for interment from places as far away as Belfast.

Another source of information for this period is Marsh Library,* established in 1701 by Narcissus Marsh, archbishop of Dublin. The first free library in Ireland, it held a very fine collection of Hebrew books and codices (manuscript volumes of a Biblical nature). The library was frequently used by members of the small Jewish community; as a result, here and there the collection has documents relating to members of that community by name.

Promulgation of the anti-Semitic May Laws of 1881 in the Russian Empire caused massive migration of Jews westward, with a resulting flow of Lithuanian Jews into Ireland. One often wonders why particular groups move to specific places; in analyzing the composition of the Irish Jewish community, one can see clearly the *landsmanshaftn* syndrome[2] working with great effect. The core of the Irish-Jewish community came from a village in northwestern Lithuania called Akmijan (today, Akmene). Surrounding them in fairly large numbers were immigrants from other northwestern Lithuanian villages; on the periphery were Jews mainly from other parts of Lithuania and Latvia, with a sprinkling from still other places. Just prior to and in the early years of World War II, it was said that if you did not have an ancestor from Akmijan, you did not belong to "the club."

A number of genealogically important documents are held in the Irish Jewish Museum.* From the last years of the 19th century until 1930, a Jewish midwife, Ada Shillman, kept a journal of all the births in the Dublin community. The section from 1895–1908 is extant and held by the museum. In many cases, Shillman provides names of the child, father and mother, maiden name of mother, and most important, their address. In the middle of this period, in 1901, the British government took a census of the entire British Isles. Censuses are closed for one hundred years in Britain, but since Ireland is not governed by British law, the section for southern Ireland has been made available.[3] Thus, if one consults the census of 1901, or even the census of 1911, armed with addresses from Shillman's journal, one should be able to learn considerable additional details about specific families such as number of family members, ages and places of birth. These censuses were taken when all of Ireland was still part of the United Kingdom and access follows the rules of the United Kingdom. Censuses taken after 1922 are closed for 100 years.

In Dublin, the Jews from Lithuania were concentrated initially in an area on the south side of the city, along the South Circular Road and its side streets. The censuses of 1901 and 1911 can be used to locate a high percentage of the Jewish families in Dublin simply by using the list of streets appearing in the midwife's journal. The concentration of Jews in Cork ran along similar lines; that is, they lived compactly in a specific area of the city. The same is true of the brief period when Jews lived in Limerick.

Jews first settled in Limerick about 1881, and, by 1890, 25 families lived there. In 1902, they purchased a plot to be used as a cemetery at Kilmurry.[4] In 1904, a rabid priest preached that the Jews of Limerick were usurers and bloodsuckers. After some initial stone throwing and slight injuries to the Jews, the priest encouraged a boycott of the community which created such economic difficulties that the emerging community eventually crumbled and dispersed. Although there was no serious bodily harm, this event came to be known as the "Pogrom of Limerick." In his book on Ireland,

Keogh provides considerable detail about this community and the one in Cork and explains exactly where the Jews lived in those towns.[5]

Initially, the incoming Litvak Jews spread out over the countryside, much as they had in Lithuania. They had small groupings in Carlow, Drogheda, Dundalk and Londonderry in addition to Belfast, Cork, Dublin and Limerick. With the outbreak of "the troubles," the period of insurrection against the British leading to Irish independence in 1922, Jews gravitated to the bigger cities for greater security.

During World War I, all aliens that entered Ireland were required to register regularly with the police and to report all changes of address. For every alien and his family, the register includes date of entry into Ireland; surname and "Christian" names; nationality and birthplace; postal address or residence; business, trade or profession; date of arrival in the district; previous place of residence; remarks and

The Adelaide Road Synagogue in Dublin was the principal Synagogue in the city during the 20th century. It was built in 1892 and expanded in the 1920s to accommodate 600 people. Declining attendance forced the membership to sell the structure in 1999.

signature of the alien. The Irish Jewish Museum* holds the Aliens Register for Dublin.

The Jewish Chronicle of London, the weekly newspaper of the Jewish community of Great Britain and Ireland, has published birth, marriage and death notices from 1841 to the present. These include announcements from Ireland. Death notices frequently include a list of mourners, children, grandchildren and, occasionally, great-grandchildren. The *Chronicle* issues as well a *Year Book of Britain* which, until 1922, included the Jews of Ireland. Each year it included the office holders, both religious and civil, of such communities as Belfast, Cork, Dublin and Limerick. A similarly useful publication was *Harfield's Commercial Directory of the Jews of the United Kingdom*, 1894, which had a section on Jewish businesses in Belfast, Cork, Derry, Limerick and Waterford that included the names of owners.

The Public Record Office* at Kew in South London keeps all the naturalization papers of the Jews of Ireland up to 1922. Information includes place of origin of the applicant, parents' names, profession, profession of the father, a list of dependents and their ages. Applications do not include children over the age of 21 who had been naturalized in their own right, but often included are the names of dependent parents.

Prior to 1922, the main repository of Irish vital statistics records was the Customs House in Dublin. It burned in 1922 and a large quantity of documentation was feared lost. As time passed, however, it has become increasingly obvious that local councils had duplicate copies of nearly all vital statistics records. Eventually the duplicate copies were collected into one set that may be found in Joyce House, Dublin.* Also held there are general records such as wills, probates and other legal documents for the years 1864–1999 and non-Catholic records from 1844 to 1922.

The National Archives in Dublin* hold historical archives prior to 1922, copies of the census taken by Britain in 1901 and 1911, wills and probates. The Mormons have microfilmed considerable Irish material, including copies of birth, marriage

The Irish Jewish Museum, located in Dublin, houses many artifacts of the Jewish presence in Ireland. It was once a neighborhood synagogue.

and death registers. Researchers should carefully read the listing for Ireland in the Mormon Family History Library catalogue. (See LDS)

Jewish Communal Records

Various useful Jewish communal records are available to researchers. The office of the Chief Rabbi* has marriage records dating from 1909 and a bar mitzvah book started in 1959. A complete list of burials in the Dolphin's Barn cemetery exists from 1898 and is being computerized. The list is held by the officers of the *chevra kadisha* (Jewish burial society) and by the Jewish Genealogical Society. The Dublin Jewish Progressive Congregation has kept marriage and death records since 1953, while the Irish Jewish Museum* in Dublin holds a death register, with attached death certificates, maintained during the 1930s for the Adelaide Road synagogue.

In Cork, Fred Rosehill, chairman of the now-tiny Jewish community, keeps the Jewish death register for the years 1887–1950 for both the old and the new cemeteries, minute books from the early days of the community and a small number of similar documents. Gerald Goldberg, president of the community and former mayor of Cork, maintains the birth and marriage records from 1887 to 1956.

Almost no documents are known to exist for the small communities in Derry and Waterford. One or two items are housed in the Central Archives for the History of the Jewish People* in Jerusalem, including a minute book of the Dublin Jewish community from 1840 to 1880 and eighteen minute books of the Londonderry community.

The Belfast community* has detailed and accurate records and minute books that have been deposited in bank vaults. To consult them, one must contact the secretary or other official of that community This community has had a cemetery since 1869.

In relation to its size, the Dublin Jewish community has had an almost unbelievably disproportionate number of committees and organizations, most of which have generated publications with some type of genealogical data. The *Jewish Record,* begun in 1935, was a community newspaper for a brief time; *Nachlath Dublin*, begun in 1943, appears twice yearly and describes major events in the community; *HaLapid* begun in 1952–53; the *Jewish Leader*, 1954 to the present; *Hadashot*, in print from 1959–71 and the Dublin *Jewish News* has existed from 1973 to the present. There also are magazines of the Zionist women's organizations, W.I.Z.O, the *Dublin Jewish Daughters of Zion and Ziona*. All include descriptions of events in the community, including the names of participants, marriage and bar mitzvah greetings, tributes and eulogies. The Irish Jewish Museum* has collections of these periodicals.

Many minute books from committees, synagogues, the *chevra kadisha* (burial society), charitable and educational institutions, the zionist organizations and annual reports of synagogues all may be found in the Irish Jewish Museum.* These too offer lists of names and addresses and cover the events of the particular years to which they related.

The Irish Jewish Genealogical Society* headed by Stuart Rosenblatt, holds copies of the following communal files as does this author:

Dublin. Midwife Aida Shillman's birth records 1897–1903
Belfast. Carmon Cemetery
Belfast. City Cemetery
Belfast. Victoria & Annesley Streets Synagogue, marriages
Carmel Beacon membership
Cork. cemetery
Cork. marriage records, 1891–1990
Cork & county mail list, 1950 & 1999
Community list (Brownie records), 1939, 1942, 1959, 1964
Dublin. Adelaide Road Synagogue, marriage records 1893–99
Dublin. Ballybock Dublin cemetery 1810–1908
Dublin. Camden Street Synagogue, marriage records, 1913–16
Dublin. community mail list, 1950s, 1999

Dublin. Dolphin Barn Cemetery

Dublin. Dublin Hebrew Congregation, births 1820–79

Dublin. Greenville Hall building fund and addresses, 1913

Dublin. Greenville Hall Synagogue, marriage records 1916–80

Dublin. Lennox Street Synagogue, marriage records, 1892–1912

Dublin. *Yahrzeit* plaques, Old Age Home

Dublin. Saint Marys Abbey Hebrew Congregation, 1841–1913

Dublin. Terenure Synagogue, marriage records, 1957–98

Dublin. Walworth Road Synagogue, membership list, 1946

Dublin. *Yahrzeit* plaques, Walworth Road Shul (museum)

Dublin. Woodtown Dublin Reform Cemetery

Limerick. cemetery

Police Alien records. 1914–18

Limerick. residences with Jewish names, 1890s.

Addresses

Belfast Synagogue, 49 Somerton Rd., Belfast BT15 3LH, Northern Ireland.

Central Archives for the History of the Jewish People, P.O. Box 1149, Jerusalem, 91010, Israel

Chief Rabbinate, Herzog House, Zion road, Dublin 6, Ireland; telephone: 353-1-492; fax: 353-1-492-4680

Cork City Ancestral Project, c/o Cork County Library, Farranlea Road, Cork City, Ireland; telephone: 353-22- 21778

Cork Community Records, c/o Mr. Fred Rosehill, 10 South Terrace, Cork, Ireland; e-mail: ROSEHILL@IOL.IE

Dublin Jewish Progressive Congregation, 7 Leicester Avenue, Rathgar, Dublin 6, Ireland; telephone: 353-1-285- 6241

Genealogical Office, 2 Kildare Street, Dublin 2, Ireland; telephone: 353-1-661-8811

General Register Office, Joyce House, Archives of Vital Statistics, 8 Lombard Street, East Dublin 2, Ireland; telephone: 353-1-671-1000; fax: 353-1- 678-7116

Irish Jewish Genealogical Society, Stuart Rosenblatt p.c. Irish Jewish Roots, 76 Dame Street, Dublin 2, Ireland; e-mail: MASTER@MEDIANET.IE

Irish Jewish Museum, 3-4 Walworth Road (off Victoria St.), South Circular Road, Dublin 8, Ireland; telephone: 353-1-453-1797

Limerick Archives, The Granary, Michael Street, Limerick, Ireland; telephone: 353-61-410-777; e-mail: OMAHONYC@SHANNON-DEV.IE

Marsh Library, Saint Patrick's Close, Dublin 8, Ireland; telephone and fax: 353-1-454-3511; e-mail: KEEPER @MARSHLIBRARY.IE

National Archives, Bishop Street, Dublin 8, Ireland; telephone: 01-407-2300; fax: 01-478-3650; e-mail: MAIL@NATIONALARCHIVES.IE

Public Records Office, Kew, Richmond, Surrey, TW9 4DU, England; telephone: 41-081-876-3448 for naturalization papers

Northern Ireland Registrars Office, City Hall, Belfast, Northern Ireland

Biography

Abramson-Nurock Family Papers, private collection. Custodian: Maurice Abramson, Dublin.

Benson, Asher. "Jewish Genealogy in Ireland, *Proceedings of the First Irish Genealogical Congress*, 1993: 17–27.

Berman, Hannah. *The Zlotover Story*. Dublin: Healy Thom, 1966.

Bloom, Jesse S. "The Old Days in Dublin." *Commentary*, (July 1952): 21–32.

Briscoe, Robert, and Alden Hatch. *For the Life of Me*. Boston: Little Brown, 1958.

Clein, Michael A. *The Clein Family*. University of Miami: Judaic Studies Program, 1989.

Harfield's Commercial Directory of the Jews in the United Kingdom. London, 1894.

Huhner, Leon. "The Jews of Ireland." *Jewish Encyclopedia*. 1927.

Hyman, Louis. *The Jews of Ireland*. London: Jewish Historical Society of England, 1972.

Irish Jewish Year Book, 1951–1970. Dublin: Chief Rabbinate of Ireland.

Jewish Chronicle. London, 1841 to present.

Jewish Year Book. London: Jewish Chronicle, 1896–1922.

Keogh, Dermot. *Jews in Twentieth-Century Ireland*. Cork: Cork University Press, 1998.

Lipsett, Edward Raphael (HaLitvack). "The Jews of Ireland." *Jewish Chronicle*, December 21, 1906.

MacNiocaill, Gearóid. *Ireland Before the Vikings*. Dublin: Gill and McMillan, 1972.

Marcus, David. *A Land Not Their Own: A Novel of the Jews in Ireland*. London: Corgi.

O'Brian, M.A. *Corpus Genealogiarum Hiberniae*. Dublin, 1962.

Shillman, Bernard. *A Short History of the Jews in Ireland*. Dublin: Eason & Sons, 1945.

Yodaiken, Len. *The Judeikins Family History and Tree*.

Private Edition. Judeikin Publications, 2002.

Notes

1. O'Brian, *Corpus Genealogiarum Hiberniae*
2. Jewish families who appear in the 1858 Revision Lists of Akmene and who settled in Ireland include the following. In brackets are the names used in Ireland: Berenshtayn (Bernstein), Blum (Bloom), Fridman (Freedman), Glaz (Glass), Glezer (Glasser), Goldberg, Goldwasser (Goldwater), Grinspan (Grinspon), Kagan (Kahn), Kleyn (Clein), Kon (Khan), Kristol (Crystal), Markus (Marcus), Medalie (Madolye), Mentsovsky (Menton), Metovsky (Mitovsky), Rok (Rick), Rubinstayn (Rubinstein), Shapira, Shapire (Shapiro), Tsitron (Citron, Zitron), Vayner (Weiner), Veynronk (Weinronk), Vigdor (Wigador), Wolfson and Zaks (Jackson).
3. Until 1922, all of Ireland was an integral part of the United Kingdom of Great Britain. In 1922, the 26 counties of southern Ireland became independent under the name of The Irish Free State. By treaty the northern six counties remained part of the United Kingdom. At that time, Jewish communities existed in Belfast and Londonderry in Northern Ireland. Records for Northern Ireland created since 1921 are kept at the Registration office in Belfast. Those created prior to 1921 are in Dublin except for many that were destroyed in the Customs House fire in 1922.
4. The list of Jews who bought the plot of land at Kilmurry for £150 from the farmer William Nunan of Ballyclough was as follows: Rabbi Elias Levin, Isaac Anonove, Marcus Jacob Blond, David Cropman, Hyman S. Cropman, Louis Clein, Barnet Graff, Hyman Graff, Phillip Griff, Barnet Gould, Julius Greene, Moses Joseph Greenfeld, Benjamin Jaffey, Sydney A Jaffey, Marcus Lionel Jaffe, Solomon Jerome, Harry Levin, Maurice Maissell, Wolf Maissell, Barnett Shockett, Phillip Toohey and Wolf Toohey.
5. Keogh, *Jews in Twentieth Century Ireland*

Israel

by Shalom Bronstein

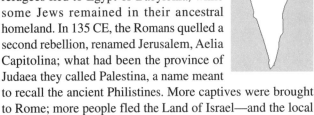

Genealogists examine sources found in the country where their ancestors lived. That is true of all groups, including Jews. But individuals who are tracing their Jewish family history must consider an additional country for investigation—Israel. In the years since the founding of the state on May 14, 1948 (5 Iyar 5708), and the in-gathering of Jews from all over the world, Israel has become the repository of an enormous quantity of information about Jews wherever and whenever they lived. Various archives in the country are dedicated to researching specific communities from which they gather material.

Probably the single most important Israeli resource for Jewish genealogists is Yad Vashem, the Holocaust memorial located in Jerusalem. This is covered in detail in the chapter on Holocaust research.

It is the rare Jew who lives in the same country where his family lived four or five generations ago. Most families were separated and moved to different locations during the mass migrations of the world Jewish population that occurred during the period 1848–1950. Many Jews eventually came to Eretz Yisrael (The Land of Israel, the term used to refer to the area before the establishment of the State of Israel). With Jews from all over the world settling in Israel, it is highly likely that every Jewish genealogist who takes the trouble to search will eventually find branches of his or her families living in Israel.

This chapter is intended to help researchers locate information in Israel that will help them learn as much as possible about their families, both those who have lived in the country and those who have lived elsewhere. More detailed information may be found in *Guide to Jewish Genealogical Research in Israel*.[1]

History[2]

When the Assyrians defeated the Kingdom of Israel in 721 BCE and drove the ten tribes of the northern kingdom into exile, only the Kingdom of Judah remained. The general belief is that the ten northern tribes were assimilated into their new locations, hence, the Ten Lost Tribes. In 587/6 BCE the Kingdom of Judah was defeated and Solomon's Temple destroyed. Numerous prisoners were exiled to Babylonia and others, perhaps a majority, fled to Egypt. Thus began the Diaspora of the Jews.

Cyrus, the Persian king who defeated the Babylonians in 539 BCE, permitted the Jews to return to their ancestral homeland, but few accepted the offer. Many historians believe that even in ancient times, the majority of Jews lived in Diaspora communities. The Land of Israel and especially the Temple in Jerusalem, however, remained central to Jewish life throughout this time. Independence, achieved by the Maccabees, was lost to the Romans a few generations later in 63 BCE. During the Jewish rebellion against their rule, the Romans

destroyed the Second Temple in 70 CE. Contemporary sources tell of the many captives carried to Rome, which already had a functioning Jewish community. Other refugees fled to Egypt or Babylonia, while some Jews remained in their ancestral homeland. In 135 CE, the Romans quelled a second rebellion, renamed Jerusalem, Aelia Capitolina; what had been the province of Judaea they called Palestina, a name meant to recall the ancient Philistines. More captives were brought to Rome; more people fled the Land of Israel—and the local center of Jewish life moved to the Galilee.

A tradition holds that in the small village of Peki'in, in the Upper Galilee not far from Safed, a Jewish family by the name of Zeynati can trace its roots back to this time. Archaeologists have greatly increased our knowledge of life in the Land of Israel during the centuries immediately after the destruction of the Second Temple. Small Jewish communities remained, and there was a continuous Jewish presence in Eretz Yisrael until the first Crusaders conquered the land.

The conquest of Jerusalem on July 15, 1099, by the soldiers of the First Crusade doomed the city's Jewish community. In the early years of Crusader rule, Jews were prohibited from entering Jerusalem. By the middle of the 12th century, however, individual Jews acquired permission to reside in the city when the Crusaders required their skills.[3] Otherwise their presence in Jerusalem was forbidden. In 1210–11, some 300 French and English rabbis settled in Acre, the major Crusader city after Jerusalem. Nachmanides visited Jerusalem in September 1267 and, in a letter to his son, he wrote that he found only two Jews living there. In 1187, when Jerusalem again came under Muslim rule, some Jews returned, but communal life was not restored to its former level.

Old Yishuv. The term "Old Yishuv" refers to the Jewish community that lived in Eretz Yisrael before the first waves of immigration from Eastern Europe beginning in 1880 started a new era in the history of the Land of Israel. Many from the Old Yishuv eschewed contact with the newer arrivals and maintained a separatist existence of piety that others considered to be religious fanaticism.

During the Middle Ages, the cities of Jerusalem, Hebron, Safed and Tiberias, known as the "four holy cities," attracted increasing numbers of Jewish pilgrims. A few of these wayfarers made their permanent home in these cities. The expulsion of the Jews from Spain in 1492 saw some refugees looking to Eretz Yisrael for sanctuary. The conquest of Eretz Yisrael by the Ottoman Turks in 1517 opened new opportunities for settlement. The majority of Spanish Jews who came settled in Safed, and that city soon became the center of Jewish mysticism. Later in the 16th century, the Nasi family, Gracia and her nephew Joseph, prominent members of the Portuguese Jew-

Interior of the Dome of the Rock, the gold-domed mosque that is the best-known edifice in Jerusalem. According to Moslem tradition, the rock shown here is the place where Muhammad is supposed to have ascended into heaven to receive instructions from God. According to Jewish tradition, it is the place where Abraham went to sacrifice Isaac, where Jacob dreamed of a ladder reaching to heaven, and the location of the two Temples of Judaism.

ish community, received permission from the Turkish sultan to rebuild the city of Tiberias, which was then in ruins. They introduced the breeding of silkworms and the wool industry, hoping that many of their fellow Jews fleeing Spain would find refuge there. Their expectations, however, were not realized. Throughout this time, a pious few made their way to the Holy Land to die and be buried on the Mount of Olives in Jerusalem. The majority was of Sephardic origin, with a few Ashkenazim.

In 1699, under the influence of the false messiah Shabbtai Zvi, some 1,300 Jews under the leadership of Rabbi Judah the Pious left Moravia, Hungary and Poland for Eretz Yisrael. A large number of the travelers died along the way, and their leader expired within a week of reaching Jerusalem. Many of these Jews returned to their country of origin. No Ashkenazic community had existed in Jerusalem until the followers of

Shabbtai Zvi came. Initially, they were numerous enough to establish an Ashkenazic community and they began construction of a synagogue, borrowing money from Arabs. In the end, the Ashkenazim were unable to repay their obligation to the Arab moneylenders; many fled to Safed, while a very few remained in Jerusalem, blending into the older, wealthier and more established Sephardic community. For the next century or so, no Ashkenazic Jew could safely come to Jerusalem unless he were disguised as a Sephardi. Eventually the debt was settled and the Ashkenazim built a synagogue. The ruin where they attempted to build a synagogue was called Hurva of Judah Hehasid (Judah the Pious), which is how the Hurva Synagogue got its name.

From the middle of the 18th century onward, interest in living in Eretz Yisrael reawakened in various Eastern European Jewish communities. Rabbi Abraham Gershon of Kutow (today, Kuty, Ukraine), brother-in-law of the Baal Shem Tov, founder of Hasidism, reached Hebron in 1747 before settling in Jerusalem in 1753. Having arrived with Hasidim from Galicia and Volhynia, he was the first who tried to revive the Ashkenazic community in Jerusalem. The first organized attempt of Hasidim to settle in Eretz Yisrael came in 1764. A small but steady wave of Hasidic immigrants started in 1777. Three hundred people, including women and small children, led by Menahem Mendel of Vitebsk and Abraham of Kalisz, settled first in Safed and then in Tiberias. This was the group that revived Jewish life in the Galilee.

Additional Hasidic groups came in 1831 and 1832. Menahem Mendel of Shklov settled in Safed in 1808 before making his home in Jerusalem in 1816. In 1809, 70 families heading by Rabbi Hillel Rivlin of Shklov (Belarus) settled in Jerusalem. They were followers of Rabbi Elijah, the Gaon of Vilna (1720–97), who himself had decided to settle in the Land of Israel and even began his journey. For some unknown reason, he never completed it and returned to Vilna. Additional followers of the Gr"a (acronym for the Gaon Rabbi Elijah of Vilna) joined the first group in 1811. They included Avraham Shlmo Zalman Tzoref whose sons adopted the family name of Solomon. These people formed the basis of the non-Hasidic Ashkenazic community known as the *Perushim*.[4]

Concerned, lest their rivals on the continent gain the upper hand in the weakening Ottoman Empire, the European powers increasingly meddled in the Empire's internal affairs in the Holy Land. Austria was the first in the 18th century, followed by Russia and France in the early 19th century.[5] Over the years, France had become the chief protector of Roman Catholics in the Holy Land. Other powers, taking advantage of the Capitulation Treaties,[6] which gave them extraterritorial authority over their citizens resident in the Land of Israel, were eager to play a more dominant role in the development of events. Ironically, the European powers sought to increase their influence by making former Eastern Europeans living in Eretz Yisrael their protegés. Acquisition of Turkish citizenship was extremely difficult and not always desirable for Jews; increasingly, most Jews looked to the foreign consulates in Jerusalem for protection.

The former Jewish residents of Russia lost their "citizenship" and the protection of that government once they left Russia. R.[7] Isaiah Bardaki (1790–1862), leader of the Ashkenazic Jews in Jerusalem, approached the British consul James Finn in 1849 to request that Finn grant protection to the stateless Russian Jews. The British government in London, was under the growing influence of the Millenarians,[8] who included a number of prominent politicians in their ranks and who took an increasing interest in the possibility of Jewish resettlement in Eretz Yisrael. The government recognized the potential for increasing its political position by adding hundreds of individuals to the list of people for whom they had responsibility and readily agreed. Thus, the British government in London became the patron of most of the former Russian Jews whose own consuls refused them help. Some of the British consular records (covering the years 1849–1914) are held by the Ar-

chives and Manuscript Division of the Jewish National and University Library and are important sources of information about the Jewish community.

The Austrian government realized that with many of its former Jewish residents living in the Land of Israel, it also could gain a presence. R. Isaiah Bardaki also served as the vice-consul of the Austrian government. In the early part of the 19th century, R. Avraham Shlomo Zalman Tzoref served as the Prussian vice-consul. Names of "protected" Jews do not appear in contemporary Turkish records.[10]

In 1827, Moses Montefiore paid the first of seven visits to Jerusalem.[11] During his second visit in 1839, Montefiore had his secretary make an accurate count of every Jew in Eretz Yisrael with the idea of helping to improve his or her condition. Throughout the 19th century, more new arrivals added their stamp to the community. Key personalities in the development of the Jewish community came from Central Europe as well as from Muslim countries. The Sapir family, also disciples of the Gr"a, arrived in 1832. R. Ya'akov Halevi Sapir traveled throughout Eastern European Jewish communities as well as Australia, India, New Zealand and Yemen, raising funds for the community of the Perushim.[12] The Yellin family came from Lomza, Poland, in 1834. Until the middle of the 19th century, however, the Sephardic community was dominant. Some Sephardim were descendants of those who had fled from Spain, while the majority were from families that had come to Jerusalem from other parts of the Ottoman Empire.

Charitable contributions from Jewish communities around the world were the main source of financial support for the Jews of Jerusalem at this time. These funds, called *halukah*, were distributed by organizations that were based primarily on the geographical origin of the recipient. This organization was called a *kolel* (plural, *kolelim*), and unless someone was part of a *kolel*, he or she was not eligible for the subsidy. The largest *kolelim* were those of Austria, Grodno, Habad, H'od (Holland/Deutschland), Hungary, Minsk, Vilna, Volhyn and Warsaw. By the middle of the 19th century, as the Jewish population increased, the various *kolelim* began to split. The main *kolel* of hasidic Jews, that of Volhyn, split into those of Austria and Galicia. By the outbreak of World War I, there were 29 *kolelim*. One very active *kolel* was known as *Kolel America*, most of whose members were originally Jews who had immigrated to the United States and then moved to Eretz Yisrael. Among the *kolel* records which are written in Hebrew, found today in the Jerusalem City Archives* are those of *Kolel* America, Grodno, Habad, Holland/Germany, Minsk, Ungarin (Hungary), Volhyn and Warsaw.

By 1800, Safed, seat of the mystics since the 16th century, had the largest Jewish population of any of the four holy cities. At the same time, Tiberias had 2,000 Jewish residents, but most of the city was destroyed in an earthquake in 1837. Its population was further reduced by cholera outbreaks in 1865 and 1866. The 1837 earthquake also devastated Safed, whose Jewish community had recently been pillaged by competing Arab rulers. Most of the survivors from both cities relocated to Jerusalem, whose Jewish population then reached about 3,000. The Jewish community of Hebron was reestablished in the mid-15th century, but it remained tiny until the 18th century, when it experienced an influx of Sephardic Jews. The first Ashkenazic settlers were Habad Hasidim who arrived in 1820. A branch of the Slobodka Yeshiva of Kovno (today, Kaunas), Lithuania, opened in 1925. This institution also attracted a number of students from the United States, some of whom were murdered in the Arab massacre of August 1929, which brought an end to Hebron's Jewish community. The yeshiva relocated to Jerusalem, where it is now known as the Hebron Yeshiva.[13]

New Yishuv. Moving to the Land of Israel is known as *aliyah*. Historians have identified six major waves of *aliyot* (plural for *aliyah*) and refer to the first five by number. This section discusses each of the six *aliyot*.

The pogroms in Russia that started in 1881 in the wake of the assassination of Czar Alexander II destroyed any hope for the future for most Russian Jews. Sympathy for the nascent Zionist movement became strong, and 1882 saw its concretization with the beginning of the First Aliyah. A group of young people, imbued with the desire to work the Land of Israel, arrived from Europe to join the 30,000 Jews already living there. While the vast majority of Russia's Jews in search of new homes chose the United States, some wanted to build their new lives in the ancestral home of their people. Approximately three percent of the massive Jewish emigration between 1880 and 1914 went to Eretz Yisrael.[14]

The earlier Jewish residents, the "Old Yishuv," were divided among Ashkenazi, Hasidic and Sephardic/Oriental communities. While many kept their distance from the new arrivals, increasing cooperation occurred between segments of the two groups. Changes were already taking place as Jews began to build new Jerusalem neighborhoods outside the city walls.

A group of Jerusalem residents started an agricultural colony called Petah Tikvah. The new group from Russia, called *BILU*, an acronym for their motto: "House of Jacob, let us get up and go" (Isaiah 2:5), established colonies in Rishon LeZion, Rosh Pina and Zikhron Ya'akov. Turkish law did not permit non-Ottoman citizens to purchase land. The new colonies bypassed this law with the assistance of resident Jews that were Ottoman citizens who allowed land to be purchased in their names, thus making the transactions legal and enabling the land to be registered. Alarmed by the new immigrants, the Turkish government issued a decree in 1890 that prohibited the immigration of Austrian, Romanian and Russian Jews. The weakness of the Ottoman Empire, however, precluded enforcement of the decree.

The Second Aliyah covers the years 1904–14. Most of the 40,000 Jews who arrived during that period were young pioneers from Eastern Europe, but they also included a small number of intellectuals. David Ben-Gurion, Yitzhak Ben Zvi and S.Y. Agnon are among the better known members of the Second Aliyah. Many of those who came during this period did not remain but returned to Europe or went on to America. During World War I, the Turkish government, fighting on the side of Germany and Austria-Hungary, expelled some 10,000 Jews living in Eretz Yisrael who were citizens of enemy coun-

tries.[15] Among them were many from England, Russia and the United States. According to published population records, in 1885, 15,674 Jews in the Land of Israel held Ottoman citizenship. By 1912, that number had increased to 35,197 individuals. According to one report:

"...the Jewish population changed its basic characteristics during this period. Instead of a small minority in a precarious situation in a few towns, Jews became, on the eve of World War I, the second largest population group. They constituted the largest population section in Jerusalem; they laid foundations for the first Jewish modern town (Tel Aviv), formed a considerable demographic element in four other towns and had established 47 rural settlements, as compared with 5 such settlements in 1882. (*Encyclopedia Hebraica*, p. 35).

The Jewish population declined from approximately 94,000 in 1914 to 56,000 in 1918 as a result of the upheaval of World War I. In Safed alone, more than half the population died between 1914 and 1918.[16]

The Balfour Declaration of November 2, 1917, issued by Great Britain, assured that a world power now stood behind the Jewish aspirations for Eretz Yisrael. Its implementation, however, had to wait until World War I ended. The Third Aliyah covers the years from the start of the British Mandate in 1919 to 1923. In fighting that went on between October 1917 and September 1918, the British Army defeated the Turks. The victors first instituted a military government which was replaced by a civil administration in 1920. In 1922, the League of Nations issued Great Britain a mandate to administer Palestine. At this time, some 35,000 immigrants, of whom 53 percent were from Russia, 36 percent from Poland and the remainder from Austria, Czechoslovakia, Germany, Hungary, Lithuania and Romania, moved to the Land of Israel.

The Fourth Aliyah, 1924–28, was a movement of a different nature. The Polish finance minister, Ladislas Grabski, who encouraged economic restrictions against the Jews, initiated an economic crisis in Poland. As the same time, the United States imposed severe restrictions on immigration. Thus, a middle class *aliyah* composed mostly of Polish Jews and popularly known at the time as the "Grabski *aliyah*," brought thousands of entrepreneurs to Eretz Yisrael.

The Fifth Aliyah, starting very slowly in 1929, changed momentum with the rise of the Nazis in Germany. Between 1933 and 1936, more than 164,000 Jews arrived.

Those who came on the five legal *aliyot* all had proper and officially authorized documents from the British government. Starting in 1938, however, the number of certificates issued did not meet the demand of refugees fleeing European anti-Semitism. Thus began what is known as *Aliyah Bet*. The second letter of the Hebrew alphabet, *bet,* also indicates "second class." This was a "second class" or illegal *aliyah*, since the immigrants did not have legal documentation. By the beginning of World War II, some 15,000 Jews had come on *Aliyah Bet*. Because these people came with no papers, no central listing exists of all who arrived this way. Some who

Beth Hatefutsoth (Museum of the Diaspora) in Tel Aviv holds the Douglas E. Goldman Jewish Genealogy Center. The museum is a popular tourist attraction because it has exhibits depicting Jewish life throughout the world.

were caught by the British before World War II were exiled to the island of Mauritius. After the war, those who were caught by the British in their blockade of the coast of Eretz Yisrael were exiled to internment camps in Cyprus. During the years 1938 to 1948, an estimated 115,000 "illegal" immigrants made their way to Eretz Yisrael through *Aliyah Bet*.

Researching Family in Israel

Whether you have heard that a relative went directly from Europe to pre-state Palestine, that in Turkish times a relative went to spend his or her last years in Eretz Yisrael, or a survivor of the Holocaust appears on your family tree, best research strategies depend greatly on the time period in which the records were created—Ottoman rule extended up to the end of World War I in 1917, the British Mandate was from 1917 to 1948 or the State of Israel from 1948 on. The resources described in this chapter are categorized by those time periods.

Keep in mind that although Israel has a Freedom of Information Act it is far more restrictive than that in the United States for example. Documents that the researcher may wish to have copied may be considered classified. Some documents are the property of particular government agencies and are not available to the public. Most documents are in Hebrew and, although English is widely spoken and understood, a Hebrew translator

engaged on a professional basis may be necessary to help you obtain exactly what you are seeking. Contact the Israel Genealogical Society for advice about engaging a translator.

Resources for finding family members who live or have lived in Israel are discussed first. Individuals who came to Eretz Yisrael/Israel after World War II often are a good source of information about earlier generations in Europe and elsewhere.

Vital Statistics Records

Records of births, marriages, divorces and deaths are basic genealogical resources. How they were created and their availability to researchers today varies considerably.

Ottoman Empire (Pre-World War I) Records

Birth Records. No official records of birth exist for the Ottoman Period. A person's year of birth or age, if a Turkish citizen, is included in the *Nefus* registers which are in Turkish written in Arabic letters. One *Nefus* register that lists Ashkenazic Jews in Jerusalem from the end of the 19th to the beginning of the 20th century is written in Hebrew. Access to them at the Israel State Archives* in Jerusalem is limited but they have been microfilmed by the LDS (Mormon) Family History Library. Check the British and German consular records held at the Israel State Archives for records of Jews protected by other countries. Such files often include birth, marriage and death information. Records of Jews protected by the American consulate at the U.S. National Archives in Washington, D.C.* are described by Ruth Kark (see Bibliography). A name index is available on microfiche from Avotaynu.*

Marriages. Marriages have always been under the jurisdiction of the couple's religious affiliation. Marriage licenses are kept by the Ministry of Religious Affairs but are not available to the public. Note that the Jerusalem Municipal Archives holds a small register of marriage records for the years 1905–09.

Death Records. Death certificates were not issued in Turkish times. In order to obtain information about a relative who died during this period, the researcher must deal with the *chevra kadisha** (religious burial society) that handled the burial. In Jerusalem especially, *chevrot kadisha* are organized by the country or region of origin of those whose funerals they conduct. Some have computerized or are in the process of computerizing their records, making a search much less difficult, but the more information a researcher can supply, the better. This includes such items of information as the person's name and the name of his or her father, their country and city of origin (if they came from Europe by way of America, mention both), the year of death and date of death. It is essential to supply the correct name; any variations of the name would also be helpful. Other information is also very important, if available, but, if not, the *chevra kadisha* still may be able to search their records and find something, even if some details

Located at Yad Vashem in Jerusalem, the Valley of the Communities commemorates thousands of communities where Jews lived before the Holocaust. This portion remembers the communities of Italy.

are missing. Information received will be in Hebrew. The addresses of these societies are listed at the end of this chapter.

The Tel Aviv situation differs from that found in Jerusalem. None of the cemeteries has a computerized list, but records are complete and information is available (in Hebrew) by telephone. The Tel Aviv *chevra kadisha* is not divided along country-of-origin lines. The oldest cemetery is located in Jaffa. No record exists of the first burial, but it was the original Jewish cemetery in the area and probably dates from the early 19th century. Starting in 1910, burials were in the Trumpeldor Cemetery. Contact the Tel Aviv *chevra kadisha* for information on burials there. Contact the Tel Aviv *chevra kadisha* for information on burials in either the Jaffa or the Trumpeldor Cemeteries. An additional cemetery, Nahalat Yitzhak, opened in 1932. The next cemetery to open was Kiryat Shaul, where burials date from 1949. The Holon and Yarkon cemeteries are also under the jurisdiction of the Tel Aviv *chevra kadisha*, which should be contacted for further information on these cemeteries.

For information about burial societies in other areas of Israel, consult Appendix P in *A Guide to Jewish Genealogical Research in Israel*, pages 211–213.

British Mandate Period (1919–1948) / State of Israel (1948 to present)

The procedure for ordering a Mandate-era birth or death certificate is the same as for ordering ones for events that occurred after the State of Israel was created. The only difference is that photocopies of Mandate-era birth and death certificates are not issued. Instead, one receives a modern Israeli certificate (in Hebrew) with the information contained in the original.

Births. Whatever records exist are on file with the Ministry of the Interior,* but they are incomplete. According to the directors of the Population Registry Office of the Ministry of the Interior and of the ministry archives, records are held for the entire country, but the years covered vary with locality. For example, the Ministry of the Interior holds records from 1918 or 1919 for Jerusalem; for Tel Aviv they hold records beginning only from the mid-1920s.

Israeli residents may request records by completing and submitting a standard request form (in Hebrew) at the Ministry of the Interior. It is also possible that an applicant will be referred to the authorities in the municipality in which the birth (or death) occurred, especially for the early years. The policy of the department is that if a person is deceased, a copy of the birth certificate will not be issued. Non-residents must contact the nearest Israeli consulate or embassy and request an application which they must forward to the Ministry of the Interior. According to the 1991 guide to the Israel State Archives,* this repository holds microfiche of early birth records for several cities. The staff has repeatedly denied, however, that they have such a microfiche. Thus, all requests must be made to the Ministry of Interior which holds the original records and will search them.

Birth certificates include the following information: family name, first name of child, family name of father, paternal grandfather's name, mother's first name, family name of mother's father, gender, identification number, place of birth, name of hospital, date of birth—according to both the Hebrew and the Gregorian calendars, nationality, religion, which office of the Ministry of the Interior issued the document and the date of issuance. No charge is made for either birth or death certificates.

Marriages. Marriages have always been under the jurisdiction of the couple's religious affiliation. Marriage licenses are the sole possession of the Ministry of Religious Affairs. Although the ministry has accurate records and the licenses are on file, they are not available to researchers. One Israeli attorney has suggested that a court order would likely be needed in order for a researcher to obtain a marriage record.

Note that a small file of marriage records for the years 1940–42 are held at the Jerusalem Municipal Archives. Also check British and German consular files held at the Israel State Archives.

Death Certificates. Official death certificates were issued during the British mandate. Residents of Israel should go to the nearest office of the Ministry of the Interior* to complete the application form for the death certificate. The form is in Hebrew and requires the applicant to state their relationship to the deceased.

The application required full name of the deceased and date of death. To obtain the date of death, if unknown, first check with the appropriate *chevra kadisha*. The Ministry of the Interior cannot search its records without a date of death. The name of the deceased's father, if known, also can help.

If a request is successful, the ministry issues a document—which is the same for both the Mandate era and the State of Israel—that has spaces for family name, first name, first name of father, identity number, year, gender, marital status, nationality and date of death according to the Gregorian calendar, date of death according to the Hebrew calendar, place of death and name of hospital, if the death occurred in a hospital. The cause of death is listed only if specifically requested. Some spaces may be left blank if the record does not include all of the requested information. The document also cites the place where the original death certificate is filed.

Non-residents must make application through the nearest Israeli consulate or embassy. If the researcher has a relative who is an Israeli citizen, it may be better for the relative to make the application in Israel.

If someone dies in Israel but is buried abroad, an Israeli death certificate is not issued and the name of the deceased does not appear in the records of the Ministry of the Interior. In place of a death certificate, a document is issued that allows for the transferal of the body to a foreign country for burial. This document is not available to researchers.

Any family member may request a death certificate if more than six months has elapsed since the date of death. Prior to that time, only parents, siblings, children and spouses may have copies. Someone who is not a relative (such as a professional genealogist) may need a Power of Attorney which must be translated into Hebrew and notarized before the Ministry of the Interior will issue the document.

Finding People Who Immigrated to Israel
Search Bureau for Missing Relatives.* Toward the end of World War II, the Jewish Agency in Palestine established its Search Bureau for Missing Relatives. Its purpose was to help reunite families. In the course of its work, the Search Bureau amassed an extensive collection of requests (primarily letters) sent after World War II by individuals seeking information about family lost in the Holocaust. At a minimum, the letters include the name and address of the person initiating the search. In addition, they often include considerable identifying data such as place of birth and parents' names. Answers to the requests form another file. Both files were combined into a computerized, Hebrew-language, database of 1.2 million names. The database can be used to determine quickly if any given family name is in its files. It is also possible to search the database by location, enabling a researcher to acquire the names and addresses of everyone from a given place that has been the subject of an inquiry.

For many years, its director Batya Unterschatz provided invaluable service to genealogists. The Search Bureau closed at the end of 2001. The computerized database and the Search Bureau's records of legal immigration to Palestine/Israel from 1920 onward has been sent to the Central Zionist Archives. Mrs. Unterschatz,* now retired, may be hired to do private research.

Name Changes[17]

A challenge to anyone doing research in Israel is the fact that many people changed their names either upon arrival or when they became citizens. No records exist of name changes during the Ottoman period. During the Mandate era, name changes were recorded in an English-language publication called the *Palestine Gazette* which is available in the Jewish National and University Library (JNUL).* These listings are not alphabetical and are filed by date of name change. In the Microfilm Room of the JNUL is a microfiche arranged alphabetically by both old and new names. Since the establishment of the State of Israel, name changes are published in Hebrew in *Reshumot*. (See Jewish National and University Library below.)

Another important source may be members of your ancestral town's *landsmanschaft*. This unique Yiddish word almost needs a full paragraph to define it. literally, it is an organization whose members are former residents of the same town. During the wave of mass emigration to the United States at the turn of the 20th century, the *landsmanschaft* served the new immigrant in countless ways. It helped the immigrant get settled, obtain a job, find housing and served as a meeting place where he could forget his loneliness in the New World. In larger cities, some of these organizations established their own synagogues. *Landsmanschaftn* often had sections of cemeteries where their members had burial privileges, usually at no extra charge. In the pre-(U.S.)Social Security days, the *landsmanschaft* provided funds to countless widows and orphans. During World War II, when the first news of the Holocaust came to America, many *landsmanschaftn* banded together forming emergency relief committees for those who remained in Europe. After the war, a number published one of our most important sources of study—*yizkor* (remembrance)

Jewish death certificate from 1925, the era of the British Mandate. Records such as this are located in the Israel State Archives.

books where they memorialized and brought back to life—on the books' pages at least—their destroyed birth places. Most of the books, published in the United States in the 1940s were written in Yiddish. Beginning in the 1950s, many *yizkor* books were published jointly with the *landsmanschaft* organizations in Israel; many of these books are written in Hebrew with English summarizations.

Although the *landsmanschaft* organizations have largely disappeared in the United States, many are still active in Israel. A number have experienced a revival as children of the second and third generation of Holocaust survivors have joined their ranks. Their members are potential sources of information both about relatives who lived in Europe up to the Holocaust, as well as more general information about the town and its Jewish residents into the mid-20th century. The 1995 revised edition of *A Guide to Jewish Genealogical Research in Israel* lists telephone numbers and addresses for groups known to exist at that time. Some still have substantial membership but others have only a handful of members. It is best to check with Yad Vashem* (see HOLOCAUST) and with the Israel Genealogical Society* to determine if a *landsmanschaft* of interest is still functioning.

In the wake of the waves of *aliyah* to Israel, a number of groups called *olim* (new immigrants) societies have formed. Like the *landsmanshaftn* of former years, their goal is to help settle into Israeli society those who have come from specific countries. They are listed in the Israel telephone books and often are helpful in locating someone who has come to live in Israel. Among such groups are the British Olim Society and the AACI (Association of Americans and Canadians in Israel).

General Research Resources in Jerusalem
Archives of the Joint Distribution Committee*

The Joint Distribution Committee (JDC) was organized in New York in 1914 to provide emergency war relief to suffering European Jews. During World War I, nearly 15 million dollars was spent aiding Jews in Turkish-controlled Eretz Yisrael, and hundreds of thousands of Jews in Poland received assistance. Social workers supplied to post-World War I Jewish communities helped execute the JDC mission of relief and rescue. After the trauma of World War II, the JDC focused on feeding, clothing and rehabilitating survivors in displaced persons camps throughout Europe. The Joint, as it was commonly known, assumed responsibility for social welfare work in the Cyprus detention camp where the British held more than 50,000 illegal Jewish immigrants.

The Joint archives hold material that will be helpful to advanced researchers. Its large Geneva and Istanbul collections have extensive information on the activities of the Joint in Europe. While some material dates from the 1930s, most deals with the 1940s to the present. Included are numerous Holocaust survivor lists. Agents of the Joint throughout Europe compiled listings of survivors of various DP camps and published them in booklets. Typewritten lists enumerate Auschwitz survivors who were repatriated to France from Odessa after the war, as well as considerable data on people held in the Cyprus internment camps.

The JDC must grant approval before researchers can use its archives. Researchers must complete a form stating the topic and purpose of the research. The request is forwarded to a committee for approval, a process that typically takes a few weeks. Researchers who do not live in Israel may request the form and fax it after completion. They can order material that will be available to them when they arrive in Jerusalem. Because the archives cannot accommodate more than two researchers at a time, advance appointments are essential.

The Joint's policy is that 35 years must have elapsed from the creation of a file before it can be made available to a researcher. Files that deal with financial aid and those containing personal matters are classified as "restricted access" and remain closed beyond the 35-year period. For the present, because of organizational limitations, the collections in the JDC archives are not easily used by researchers but may prove valuable to advanced researchers of the post-World War II era in the future.

Central Archives for the History of the Jewish People

The Central Archives for the History of the Jewish People collects archival material of Jewish communities, organizations, as well as prominent individuals and families from countries throughout the world. Because relatively little original Jewish material survived the Holocaust, the Central Archives also conducts systematic surveys in non-Jewish archives and microfilms selections of the material uncovered.

Today, the Central Archives houses the world's largest and most comprehensive collection of documents and files on Jewish history from the 15th century to the present. The archives of the Vienna Jewish community are the largest single collection. Its French, German and Italian collections are the richest in genealogical material. Microfilm collections for Eastern Europe, especially Poland and Russia, are also extensive, although the amount of genealogical material in them is not as great.[18] Virtually none of the material is in English; finding aids are generally in the language of the documents. A detailed catalogue of the archives Polish holdings has just been published.

Central Zionist Archives

To gain entry to the Central Zionist Archives, visitors must leave their Israeli identity card or passport at the information desk, sign in and receive visitor's pass which must be worn in a visible manner. Before embarking on research, one must arrange an appointment to consult one of the directors regarding the topic. The researcher will be directed to the appropriate sources. After meeting with one of the directors of research, you will fill out request forms for material at the main desk in the reading room; the items will be delivered to you. It is advisable to check the hours when materials are delivered. Requests are taken every hour on the hour beginning at 9 a.m.

The World Zionist Organization, the Jewish Agency, the Jewish National Fund, Keren Hayesod (UJA) and the World Jewish Congress regularly transfer all files deemed worthy of preservation to the Central Zionist Archives. When the Jewish Agency's Search Bureau for Missing Relatives closed at the end of 2001, this archive acquired the Bureau's database of 1.2 million names [in Hebrew] of individuals about whom queries were made from the end of World War II onward. The Search Bureau's list of registered (legal) immigrants from 1920 onward also is here. The Central Zionist Archives has some information and a number of books about *aliyah bet* but most of this information is at the Museum of Illegal Immigration in Atlit.[*]

In addition to these vast collections, other major groups include:

- Territorial Federations. Records of local Zionist organizations wherever they existed. The most complete are those from Great Britain, Holland, South Africa and the United States. Extensive material deals with pre-World War I Eastern European Zionist activity. A small amount of material survives from Muslim countries and from nations overrun by the Nazis during World War II.
- Personal Archives. The Central Zionist Archives holds more than 1,000 personal archives, including the papers of such notable Zionists as Theodor Herzl, Leo Motzkin, Arthur Ruppin, Henrietta Szold and Stephen S. Wise. These archives range in size from one or two to hundreds of files and numerous microfilms.
- Hovevei Zion Societies. Dating from 1882–1917, this collection covers the period of the First and Second *Aliyot*.
- The Yishuv in Eretz Yisrael. Dating from the early 1880s, this material consists of collections of the various organizations that served the Jewish community in pre-State times. Especially rich in pre-World War I material, notable are the Mikveh Israel agricultural school (established in 1870), Baron Rothschild colony administration (1882–99) and Jewish Colonization Association collections.
- Photographic Division. More than one million items reflect the history of the Zionist movement and the *Yishuv*. Included are the collections of a number of well-known photographers of Eretz Yisrael.
- Library and Periodical Collection. More than 100,000 books deal with the history of Eretz Yisrael and the Zionist movement. There is also a vast collection of newspapers of local Zionist organizations from all over the world, mostly in the local language of the country. This section includes rare periodicals and books not found in any other collection.
- Printed Material Collection. Consists of posters, leaflets and pamphlets from various countries and the *Yishuv*.
- Stephen Spielberg Jewish Film Archive. Located on the Mount Scopus campus of Hebrew University, this archive holds more than 9,000 films and is run jointly with the Institute of Contemporary Jewry. It collects and preserves film documentation that relates to all aspects of the Jewish experience in 20th century, with an emphasis on the history of Eretz Yisrael, the Holocaust and Diaspora Jewry.

Israel State Archives[19]

To be admitted to the Archives, researchers must show a passport or an Israeli identity card.

The Israeli State Archives is the repository of official government documents starting with the Ottoman period through the British Mandate to the State of Israel. Of special interest to genealogists are the collections of the Ottoman Agricultural Bank, British consular records (1842–1939), German consular records and various records from the British Mandate, including Palestine naturalization applications [in English]. Since the latter frequently include place of birth (usually in Europe), these documents can be valuable for discovering the name of an European ancestral home.

British consular records include lists of Jewish protegés who enjoyed British protection during the Ottoman period. An alphabetical index lists protegés in Hebron, Jerusalem and Nablus, 1879–1908 and a list of passports granted in 1881. Some birth, marriage and death registers often include age, date or place of birth, date of arrival in Eretz Yisrael and other information. The Jewish National and University Library Manuscripts and Archives Division holds lists and documents of Jewish residents of Acre, Damascus, Haifa, Hebron, Jaffa, Jerusalem, Safed and Tiberias.

German consular records include similar files as well as files dealing with acquisition of real estate, criminal and civil cases (including divorce), legacies, wills, guardianships, passports and citizenship, military serviced as well as Jewish immigration into Eretz Yisrael. A guide to the files located in the Reading Room is written in English and Hebrew.

The archives also holds collections from the private files of well-known personalities in whom the public may have a special interest. The current guideline is that "for the time being, unless 120 years have passed since the birth of the person involved, private material will not be made available to the public unless a declaration has been received from the person concerned or his or her entire family consenting to the opening of these documents at an earlier date."

The State Archives holds a collection of wills, but a court order must to obtained in order to consult any of them. The English-language *Guide to the Archives in Israel* describes in detail the holdings of the Israel State Archives. A copy may be consulted in the reading room.

Jerusalem City Archives

The Jerusalem City Archives collection, covering the Turkish (to 1917), British (1917–48), Jordanian (1948–67) and Israeli administrations, holds some 8,000 meters of material of all kinds, beginning with the establishment of the municipality in 1867 to the present. It includes private as well as public archives of institutions that no longer function. In addition, private archives of individuals whose base of operations was in Jerusalem are part of the collection.

The Archives also holds important genealogical sources dating for the most part from 1870 onward. The following list of these collections was current as of 2002. Additional material is added constantly; a catalogue of holdings is available at the main desk.

Mukhtar **Register Books.** The Archives has both the original and copies of the register books (*pinkasim*) which are written in Hebrew of three of the Ashkenazic *mukhtars* (heads of community): Alter Birnblum, Todros Warshavsky and Aaron Hochstein. These men served as liaisons between their communities and the ruling Ottoman officials. On one hand, they provided information on individuals who were of age to serve in the military, while on the other hand they endeavored to exempt them from being drafted. For this purpose and for that of granting citizenship depositions, these journals, recorded in the *mukhtars'* own handwriting, also included data on Ashkenazic Jewish males who held Turkish citizenship.

Alter Birnblum

- Summary of registry of Ashkenazic males, Turkish citizens, arranged by year of birth, 1883–96
- Register of Turkish naturalizations, based on the Ottoman Turkish register of 1915
- Register of births in 1900
- Lists of males born between 1869–82, based on the census of 1905, arranged according to neighborhoods

Todros Warshavsky

- Register of Ashkenazic families with Turkish citizenship, based on the census of 1905. The register is arranged by neighborhood and contains the following information: full name, name of father and year of birth according to the Turkish calendar.
- Register of Ashkenazic males with Turkish citizenship. Includes name, name of father, date of birth according to the Turkish calendar and membership in which *kolel*.

Aaron Hochstein

- Register of individuals born in 1896. In this registry are individuals born between the years 380–385 (sic); the meaning of the dates for these years is unclear. This register lists the name of the child, the father's name and to which *kolel* they belonged.
- List of American citizens, including name, age, year of *aliyah* or year of naturalization
- List of Ashkenazic Turkish citizens arranged by neighborhood and then by family. These lists include males born approximately 1830–95.

Montefiore Jerusalem Census. Photocopies of the censuses for the years 1855, 1866 and 1875; it includes lists of residents according to their *kolel* and community of origin—full name, name of wife, occupation and number of children

Archives of the Sephardic Community. Includes lists of residents by neighborhood, 1905, 1910 (two lists), 1930, 1940–42; Yemenite residents, 1910 (Kfar Shiloah?);[20] Ashkenazim according to *kolel*, 1910–14; lists of residents according to community of origin (two lists), 1930; lists of members of the Sephardi community, 1930, 1938 (first names, addresses and occupations); list of recipients of assistance, 1920–49; recipients of aid and *matzot*, according to community of origin and occupation, 1928–36; Registry for recording of marriage contracts, 1905–09; 1940–42.

United Home for Aged Men and Women. This is one of the earliest homes for the elderly in Jerusalem. The early records of the Home which still functions, are held here. They include lists of residents, decedents and contributors. Lists of residents (1892–1914) include name, name of father, age, country of origin and year of entry into the home. Occasionally, also includes the name of descendants and addresses, 1892–1914. Lists of deceased (1865–1904) include name of father and date of death; also includes data on Ashkenazic Jewish males who held Turkish citizenship, 1865–1904. The lists of contributors (1930–47), mostly from the United States, include full name and address.

Mandate-Period Registers. The task of registering residents during the British Mandate continued to be the responsibility of the government. These English-language mandatory registers of residents remain the most complete and authoritative source of information concerning the city's population of that period. Within this framework, however, local authorities—the City of Jerusalem, the Jewish City Committee and the Council of the Jewish Community—also continued their activities in this area. These numerous, comprehensive lists are helpful in genealogical research.

Archive of the City Committee (Va'ad) 1918–31. This collection contains a number of lists of Jerusalem residents that were made for the purposes of naturalization and for electing representatives for the City Committee (Va'ad).

Archive of the Council of the Jewish Community, 1932–48. In this collection are lists of individuals eligible to vote for the council of the Jewish communities and the council of elected officials. The lists, arranged alphabetically by family name, include name of the father, address and age. A number of booklets contain voter registration lists for Jerusalem municipal elections.

Archives of Schools That No Longer Exist. Over the years, a number of city schools ceased to function. This repository holds the records (written in Hebrew) of various schools that existed between 1918 and 1998. The student lists are in varying states of preservation. A detailed list of schools is available at the archives. Includes the Lämel School student registers, 1919–60. These registers include information on family name, first name, country of birth, age, country of origin (if the students as born while the family was in transit), father's name, mother's name, ethnic community, occupation of father, address, language spoken in the home, previous places where student was enrolled and other additional material.

State of Israel Voter Registration Lists for the Knesset—Jerusalem. The archives has voter registration books for the years 1955, 1959, 1965, 1973, 1978 and 1993. The books are arranged alphabetically by family name and include information on the name of the father, year of birth and identification card number. They are open to the public.

Leo Baeck Institute

A branch of the Leo Baeck Institute with other locations in New York and London, this library has an extensive collection of material on the Jews in German-speaking countries, a large portion of which dates from the 19th century. Approximately 90 percent of the collection is written in German, with the remainder in Hebrew and/or English. The numerous family trees and its catalogued holdings are available on their website.

Jewish National and University Library

In 1892, the first B'nai Brith lodge in Jerusalem established a public library known as Midrash Abarbanel, which formed the nucleus of the National Library. In 1920, it assumed the function of library to the newly established Hebrew University. The Jewish National and University Library serves a threefold purpose. It is the National Library of the State of Israel, the National Library of the Jewish people and the central library of the Hebrew University. In its capacity as the national library of the State of Israel, it collects all material published in the country. It also attempts to acquire any item published outside of Israel that relates to Israel.

It collects Israeli publications on all subjects, including thousands of periodicals of all types and origins. This includes national and local (including *kibbutz)* newspapers and bulletins issued by any Israeli organization. The library collects any and all information connected with the Jewish people, including art, *belles lettres*, biography, education, folklore, history, philosophy and religion. It collects material in all languages used by Jews, including Hebrew, Ladino, Yiddish and others. It maintains the world's largest collections of Judaica and Hebraica.

More than three million books and periodicals are housed in the library. Many thousands of items are part of special collections. The online catalogue lists all publications received since 1984 and some acquired earlier. The photocopy department serves all readers and fills mail orders as well.

Three bibliographical tools are based on the library's collections: *Kiryat Sefer*, a quarterly bibliography of items published in Israel and of Judaica and Hebraica published throughout the world; *The Index of Articles on Jewish Studies*; and *The Bibliography of the Hebrew Book, 1472–1960*, a retrospective bibliography of books printed in Hebrew, available on a CD-ROM by the same name.

Other Collections of Special Interest to Genealogists

Eran Lior Map Collection. This collection includes antique maps, atlases, travel books and guides with special emphasis on Jerusalem and the Holy Land.

Manuscript and Archives Department. This section has 9,000 Hebrew manuscripts covering all fields of Jewish life and thought. Approximately (for a detailed list see Sack, Guide) 400 personal archives of outstanding Jewish personalities, autographs, historical documents, marriage contracts, pictures and posters.[21] In the collection are microfilms of many *pinkasim* (community registers) from various locations in Europe and Moslem countries.[22] During the British Mandate, name changes, a common occurrence among Jews who moved to Eretz Yisrael, were recorded in the official publication called *The Palestine Gazette*. A microfiche of the entire 27,000 listings of name changes is available at the library. It is alphabetized by both old and new name and has been arranged according to the Daitch-Mokotoff Soundex system. (SEE AVOTAYNU.) Name changes after the state was established in 1948 are found in the official publication *Reshumot*, but this resource has not been alphabetized, microfilmed or translated from Hebrew.

Collections Available Online. The library has separate online files for various collections and databases which can be accessed through *ALEPH*. For access to them from the website, type *LB* and the code of the catalogue you want to reach in any *ALEPH search* screen.

Edelstein Collection. Includes history, medicine, philosophy and technology, with an emphasis on chemistry and textiles. It has a large section on Jews in medicine. Approximately 25 percent of this catalogue is available online.

Gershon Scholem Collection. Includes many rare books, some of significant value to genealogists. The entire collection is online.

Index of Articles on Jewish Studies. This is known as RAMBI and it accessible at JNUL.HUJI.AC.IL/RAMBI. Current periodical index on Israel, Jewish history and Judaism. It has been online since 1985.

Master Films of Jewish Press. A continuously expanding collection of microfilms of Israeli and Jewish newspapers and periodicals. Microfilm copies of non-copyrighted titles can be ordered from the Interlibrary Loan Department. The entire catalogue is online.

Microfilmed Hebrew Manuscripts. Includes 90 percent of the known surviving Hebrew manuscripts gathered from libraries around the world. Approximately 20 percent of the collection is online and is potentially a valuable resource for those fluent in Hebrew who can read the sometimes difficult-to-decipher script of the documents.

Donor Lists.[23] During the 19th century, various societies that collected charitable donations began to publish lists of donors and, sometimes, of recipients. Since such lists usually indicated the place of residence of the donor, potentially they are a useful genealogical tool. The major sources of this type are the published records of donations to the Old Yishuv community of Jerusalem. The JNUL has an incomplete collection of a publication called *Shemesh Tzedakah.* Appearing from 1884 to 1923, it records the grants (*halukah*) distributed by the Va'ad Haklali according to the *kolel* to which an individual belonged—as well as aid provided to other needy Jews.

The yearly report is recorded in two sections, income and expenditure. The income division lists donors. In the reports for some years, they are grouped by city of residence. Included are many locations all over the world, including some very small towns as well as major U.S. cities. The expenditure section lists *halukah* recipients in Eretz Yisrael, usually by town of origin overseas. The two aspects of the lists provide certain cross-sections of communities and can be used to trace individuals living at the time.

Center for the Study of Italian Jewry.[*]
The center's library holds a number of family trees and should be visited by anyone with Italian Jewish ancestry.

Resources Outside of Jerusalem

Each of the major municipalities, such as Tel Aviv and Haifa, have extensive city archives. See *A Guide to Jewish Genealogical Research in Israel* for details of holdings in Beersheva, Haifa and Tel Aviv. Note also that many different immigrant groups have established museums and centers around the country. A few of those likely to have considerable genealogical resources are listed below.

Museum of Illegal Immigration. Before the British established their policy of sending illegal Jewish immigrants to Cyprus, they were often held in detention camps located within Eretz Yisrael, including Atlit. Located just south of Haifa, this museum is located on the site of one such detention camp. Its archives holds testimonies and detailed information about the various ships and their passengers. An entrance fee is charged for the museum.

Babylonian Jewish Heritage Center. Those of Iraqi origin should visit the Babylonian Jewish Heritage Center in Or Yehuda.[*] The museum is a reconstruction of Iraqi Jewish dispersion after the destruction of the First Temple in 500 BCE and its return to Eretz Yisrael in 1948–51. Original documents and photographs held by the Center's library reflect efforts to bring the Jewish population of Iraq to Israel upon establishment of the State. A yearly project of the Center is a publication, *Nehardea, the Journal of the Babylonian Jewry Heritage Center,* published in both Hebrew and English. Most important to genealogists is the project "Families of Iraqi Origin" whose purpose it is to document all Jewish families from Iraq—both those in Israel and those all over the world. Documentation is based primarily upon forms completed by the 120,000 immigrants who came to Palestine/Israel in the years 1930–75. To date, approximately 100,000 forms have been computerized. Members of the community, both in Israel and abroad, are encouraged to submit family trees; these, too, are being computerized.

Archives of the Association of Lithuanian Jews in Israel.[*] This organization holds a wealth of printed information about pre-war Lithuania as well as a photo archive.

LDS (Mormon) Family History Library Microfilms

A small number of Jewish records from the Ottoman and Mandate periods have been microfilmed by the LDS (Mormon) Family History Library and are available for borrowing from their Family History Centers. They include:

- *Mukhtar* registers held at the Jerusalem Municipal Archives[*] described above
- *Nefus* population registers held at the Israel State Archives[*]
- Vital statistics records for the moshav in Rishon le'Zion (1899–1927), plus a minute book from the school in that community
- Passport and legal status records (1916–18)
- List of students in the Lämel School (in German)
- Marriage banns (1880–1911)
- Memorial books (1865–1912) from the United Hebrew Home for the Aged that supply name, city and province from which the resident came, age, date of death if deceased, and (sometimes) names of family members.

One collection written in English includes papers from the British consulate in Jerusalem (1847–1914). Also in English is a book on early Jewish settlement in Israel (1882–1914), with an index of names and places. Six booklets (1901–13) that list transcriptions of tombstones on the Mount of Olives, in the order in which they appear, were filmed at the Jewish National and University Library.*

Addresses

Babylonian Jewish Heritage Center, Rehov Hahagana 83, Or Yehuda, 60251 Israel; website: www.BABYLONJEWRY.ORG.IL; e-mail: BABYLON@BABYLONJEWRY.ORG.IL

Ben Zvi Institute, Rehov Abarbanel 12, P.O. Box 7660, Jerusalem; telephone (main office): 02-539-8888; fax: 02-563-8310; library: 02-539-8811; e-mail: YADBZ@H2.HUM.HUJI.AC.IL; website: www.YBZ.ORG.IL.

Central Archives for the History of the Jewish People, Location: Rehov Jabotinsky 46, Mailing address: P.O. Box 1149, Jerusalem 91010; telephone: 972-2-563-5716; fax: 972-2-566-7686; e-mail: ARCHIVES@VMS.HUJI.AC.IL; website: SITES.HUJI.AC.IL/ARCHIVES

Center for Italian Jewry, Rehov Hillel 27; telephone: 02-624-1610; fax: 02-625-3480; e-mail: JIJA@NETVISION.NET.IL; website: www.ITALCHAM.ORG.IL/MUSEUM; hours: Sunday, Tuesday and Wednesday: 9 a.m. to 5 p.m.; Monday: 9 a.m. to 2 p.m.; Thursday and Friday: 9 a.m. to 1 p.m.; Director: Na'ava Kessler.

Central Zionist Archives, 4 Zalman Shazar Blvd., Mailing address: P.O. Box 92, Jerusalem; telephone: 972-2-620-4800; fax: 02-620-4837; e-mail: CZA@JAZO.ORG.IL; web-site: www.WZO.ORG.IL/CZA/INDEX.HTM

Chevrot Kadisha

Jerusalem. The telephone area code for calls made within Israel is 02; if calling from outside the country, the area code is simply 2. The asterisk indicates those most likely to have information helpful to researchers from the United States.

- General Chevra Kadisha of the Ashkenazic Community,* Pines 14, P.O. Box 1463; telephone: 538-4144
- Habad,* Ein Ya'akov 13; telephone: 627-3498
- Chevra Kadisha of the Hasidim,* Hamabit 17; tele-phone: 538-4518
- Chevra Kadisha of the Iraqi Community, Sha'arey Zedek 1; telephone: 625-2842
- Chevra Kadisha of the Kurdish Community, Beit Ya'akov 11; telephone: 623-4797
- Chevra Kadisha of the Moroccan Community, Mesilsat Yesharim 1; telephone: 625-5504
- Chevra Kadisha of the Persian Community, David Yellin 38; telephone: 538-4589
- Kehilat Yerushalayim;* Elyashar 1; telephone: 625-2281
- United Chevra Kadisha of the Sephardic and Oriental Communities,* Havatzelet 12A; telephone: 625-4371, 622-1073; fax: 623-1827

Tel Aviv. The telephone area code for calls made within Israel is 03; if calling from outside the country, the area code is simply 3.

- Tel Aviv Chevra Kadisha, Rechov Mohilver 33; tele-phone: 03-516-4595; for information about Nahalat Yitzhak, telephone: 732-1873; for Kiryat Shaul cemetery, 647-1405; Holon and Yarkon cemeteries, 516-4595.

Israel State Archives. Location: 35 Mekor Hayim Street, Jerusalem, The Israel State Archives, Office of the Prime Minister, Kiryat Ben Gurion, Jerusalem; telephone: 02-568-0612; 02-568-0662; hours: Sunday—Thursday, 8:00 a.m. to 3:30 p.m.

Jerusalem City Archives; Location: Building 1, Safra Square (City Hall), Jerusalem; telephone: 02-629-7899

Jewish National and University Library, Location: Givat Ram Campus of Hebrew University, P.O. Box 503, Jerusalem 91004; telephone: 02-566-0351; website: JNUL.HUJI.AC.IL. A detailed map in English is available on the Internet at the library's home page.

Joint Distribution Committee. Location: Just before the entrance to the Givat Ram campus of Hebrew University Director; hours by previous appointment only; telephone: 02-655-7250; fax: 02-566-1244 e-mail: SKADOSH@JDC.ORG.IL

Kiryat Shaul Cemetery; Tel Aviv; telephone: 03-647-1405.

Leo Baeck Institute; Location: 33 Bustenai, Jerusalem; telephone and fax: 02-563-3790; e-mail: LEOBAECK@NETVISION.NET.IL; website: www.LEOBAECK.ORG.

Ministry of the Interior and Population Registry Office, 1 Rechov Shlomzion Hamalka, Jerusalem; telephone: 02-629-0231.

Museum of Illegal Immigration, Atlit; telephone: 04-984-1980; fax: 04-984-2814.

Nahalat Yitzhak Cemetery; telephone: 03-732-1873.

Yad Vashem, Har Hazikaron, P.O. Box 3477, Jerusalem 91034; telephone: 02-675-1611; fax: 02-643-3511.

Bibliography

Ben-Arieh, Y. *A City Reflected in Its Times: Jerusalem in the Nineteenth Century—Old City.* Jerusalem: Yad Izhak Ben-Zvi Publications, 1977.

Ben-Zvi, Izhak. *Eretz Yisrael Under Ottoman Rule: Four Centuries of History.* [Hebrew] Jerusalem: Bialik Institute, 1955.

Biachi, Roberto. *The Population of Israel.* Jerusalem: Institute of Contemporary Judaism, the Hebrew University of Jerusalem, 1977.

Clapsaddle, Carol. "Genealogical Useful Records at the Israel Labor Archives." *AVOTAYNU* 9, no. 3 (Fall 1993): 17.

———. "Two Sources for Research on British Palestine." *AVOTAYNU* 8, no. 3 (Fall 1992): 35.

Daitch, Randy. "Research in Israel: Echoes from a Vanished World." *AVOTAYNU* 10, no. 1 (Spring 1994): 19.

"Data Available from Israeli Sources." *AVOTAYNU* 10, no. 1 (Spring 1994): 23.

"Diaspora Research Institute Documenting Carpatho-Russian Jewry." *AVOTAYNU* 12, no. 1 (Spring 1996): 66.

Encyclopedia Hebraica, "Eretz Yisrael," Vol. VI (1), [Hebrew] Encyclopedia Hebraica: Jerusalem, 5753.

Encyclopedia Judaica. "Capitulations." Volume V, Keter: Jerusalem, 1971.

Getz, Mike. "American Consulate." *AVOTAYNU* 10, no. 4 (Winter 1994): 13.

Kark, Ruth. *American Consuls in the Holy Land (1832–1914).* Detroit: Wayne State University Press, Jerusalem: Magnes Press, 1994.

Lederer, Rolf. "Land Claims in Israel." *AVOTAYNU* 14, no. 1 (Spring 1998): 46.

Naftalin, Robin. "Two Genealogical Resources at the Keren Kayemeth. *AVOTAYNU* 10, no. 3 (Fall 1994): 38.

Ramon, Esther. "Central Archives for the History of the Jewish People Filming in Belarus and Negotiations with Lithuanians and Russians, Chinese Jews." *AVOTAYNU* 16, no. 2 (Summer 2000): 47.

———. "Key to the 1939 Census of Palestine." *AVOTAYNU* 9, no. 2 (Summer 1993): 50

———. "Holdings of the Central Archives for the History of the Jewish People." *AVOTAYNU* 13, no. 4 (Winter 1997): 79.

———. "Paul Jacoby Library." *AVOTAYNU* 14, no. 2, (Summer 1998): 47.

———. "Pinchas Lavon Labor Movement Research Institute." *AVOTAYNU* 13, no. 3 (Fall 1997): 49.

———. Printed Books on Jewish Cemeteries in the Jewish National and University Library in Jerusalem: An Annotated Bibliography." *AVOTAYNU* 13, no. 1 (Spring 1997): 39.

———. "Sources for the 1906–1920 Palestine Period." *AVOTAYNU* 9, no. 2 (Summer 1994): 50.

———."The G\1 Collection in Jerusalem's Central Archives for the History." *AVOTAYNU* 11, no. 4 (Winter 1995): 64.

Rappel, Joel ed., *History of Eretz Yisrael: From Prehistory up to 1882.* Vol. II. [Hebrew] Tel Aviv: Ministry of Defense, 1982.

"Records from Burgenland at Central Archives, Israel." *AVOTAYNU* 13, no. 3 (Fall 1997): 54.

"Research Projects at the Diaspora Research Institute." *AVOTAYNU* 10, no. 4 (Winter 1994): 54.

Riley, Gayle Schlissel. "Kollels of Eretz Israel as a Genealogical Treasure." *AVOTAYNU* 14, no. 1 (Spring 1998): 38.

Rosenstein, Neil. "The 19th-Century Montefiore Censuses." *AVOTAYNU* 8, no. 2 (Summer 1992): 25.

Sack, Sallyann Amdur. *A Guide to Jewish Genealogical Research in Israel.* Baltimore: Genealogical Publishing, 1987.

———. "A Genealogical Report on Israel: Fall 1996." *AVOTAYNU* 12, no. 4 (Winter 1996): 17.

———. "Book Review: *American Consuls in the Holy Land, 1832–1914. AVOTAYNU* 10, no. 4 (Winter 1994): 76.

———. "International Tracing Service Records at Yad Vashem." *AVOTAYNU* 10, no. 1 (Spring 1994): 22.

———. "Report on a Return Trip to Israel." *AVOTAYNU* 11, no. 4 (Winter 1995): 21.

———. "The Jewish National and University Library: Another Israeli Resource." *AVOTAYNU* 11, no. 3 (Fall 1995): 19.

Sack, Sallyann Amdur and Israel Genealogical Society. *A Guide to Jewish Genealogical Research in Israel.* rev. ed. Teaneck, N.J.: Avotaynu, 1995.

"Three Important Archives in Israel." *AVOTAYNU* 9, no. 4 (Winter 1993): 17.

Volovici, Hanna. "Polish Sources at the Central Archives for the History of the Jewish People." *AVOTAYNU* 10, no. 2 (Summer 1994): 21.

Weiss, Robert. "Update on Resources in Israel." *AVOTAYNU* 9, no. 2 (Summer 1993): 17.

Winter, Sonia. "Institute for Hebrew Bibliography." *AVOTAYNU* 10, no. 4 (Winter 1994): 19.

Wunder, Rabbi Meir. "The Kollel Galicia Archive." *AVOTAYNU* 6, no. 3 (Fall 1990): 23.

Notes

1. Sallyann Amdur Sack and the Israel Genealogical Society. *A Guide to Jewish Genealogical Research in Israel,* revised edition. Teaneck: Avotaynu, 1995. [Hereafter referred to as *A Guide*].

2. A number of general histories that would help the reader. Among them is the classic: Solomon Grayzel, *A History of the Jews: From the Babylonian Exile to the Establishment of Israel.* Philadelphia: The Jewish Publication Society, 1956; and Chaim Potok, *Wanderings* New York: Alfred A. Knopf, Inc., 1978.

3. Joel Rappel, ed., *History of Eretz Yisrael: From Prehistory up to 1882.* vol. II. [Hebrew] Tel Aviv: Ministry of Defense, 1982. [Hebrew].

4. They utilized this term to differentiate themselves from the other segment of the Ashkenazic community, the Hasidim, to whom they were ideologically opposed. It originally indicated the Pharisees in the time of the Mishna from about 50 BCE to 200 CE.

5. Rappel, p. 520.

6. Treaties dating from the 16th century between the Ottoman Empire and the Christian states of Europe granting extra-territorial rights over each other's subjects when they resided in their respective countries.

7. It is common for the Hebrew letter, *Resh* to appear before a male name in the sources. While it may represent *rabbi,* it could also stand for *reb,* equivalent to Mr.

8. This was an influential group of Christian religious revivalists who believed that the Second Coming of the messiah depended on the ingathering of the Jews to the Holy Land. They were especially active in literary circles and 1848 was the target year for the fulfillment of their vision.

9. *Encyclopedia Judaica.* s.v. "Capitulations."

10. Sack, *A Guide.* These are discussed in length beginning on page 31.

11. The other visits were in 1939, 1848, 1855, 1857, 1866 and 1875.

12. His experiences are recorded in his two volume work, *Even Sapir.* Volume I was printed in Lyck in 1866 and volume II in Mainz in 1874. It was reprinted in Jerusalem by Sifrei Mekorot in 5730/1969.

13. Roberto Biachi, *The Population of Israel.* Jerusalem: Institute of Contemporary Judaism, the Hebrew University of Jerusalem, 1977: 72.

14. *Ibid.*: 87.

15. *Encyclopedia Hebraica,* s.v. "Eretz Yisrael," [Hebrew].

16. *Ibid.*

17. For further information, see *A Guide*: 82–83.

18. An alphabetical listing by family of the genealogical material at the Central Archives for the History of the Jewish People is found in *A Guide*, Appendix F: 133-170.

19. A detailed listing of its holdings is found in *A Guide*: 31-37. A copy is available in the reading room.

20. Although not clearly indicated, it may refer to Kfar Shiloah, which was a Yemenite village near the Shiloah pool, south of the Dung Gate, facing the Southern Wall of Jerusalem. This area was evacuated after being attacked and pillaged during the 1929 Arab riots. Some of the abandoned houses still showed signs of Jewish occupancy after the Six-Day War in 1967.

21. See *A Guide*, for a list of the private archives, family records, family trees and genealogies at the JNUL Appendix J: 181-182.

22. See *A Guide*, for an extensive, albeit partial, list of *pinkasim* as well as register books from a number of European locations: 23-24.

23. This section was originally submitted by Chaim Freedman and is presented here with some revisions.

Italy

by John Colletta, Ruth E. Gruber and Marco R. Soria

The Italian-Jewish community, with its 2,000 years of history, was formed by the merger of several Jewish groups that arrived in Italy at different times. The nucleus was formed by Jews who lived in Italy during the Roman Empire before the destruction of the Second Temple in Jerusalem in 70 C.E. They resided primarily in Rome, throughout the southern Italian peninsula and the island of Sicily. Palestinian Jews arrived in southern Italy during the fourth, fifth and sixth centuries, and later moved north, forming the roots of the Ashkenazic branch of Judaism.

This concentration of Jews in northern Italy grew in the 14th century. Ashkenazic Jews, fleeing Germany because of the Black Plague (1348) and the Crusades, settled in the Piedmont and Veneto regions. French Jews expelled from that country in 1306 and 1394 also went to the Piedmont, and some Jewish-Italian bankers migrated north from Rome.

In 1492, when the Spanish monarchs King Ferdinand and Queen Isabella expelled all Jews who refused to convert to Christianity, the Kingdom of the Two Sicilies was a part of their realm. Many Jews fled Naples and Sicily then and, migrating northward into the Papal States (land governed by the Pope), joined the Jewish community of Rome. Numerous others settled in the northern cities of Florence, Genoa, Leghorn, Milan, Turin and Venice.

At the end of the 15th and during the 16th century, the Spanish Inquisition spurred Sephardic immigration from Spain and Portugal. Directly or via Holland and the Muslim countries, Jews came to Italy. They settled primarily in Rome and in the northern cities of Ferrara, Modena, Reggio Emilia, and especially Livorno (Leghorn).

Finally, some Jews from the Ottoman Empire migrated to Italy from the late 18th through the 19th and early 20th centuries.

Only in Italy did Ashkenazic and Sephardic Jews mingle and marry, and in these prosperous urban centers Italian Jewry enjoyed a Golden Age during the Renaissance. At the same time, however, the first ghetto was established in Venice, followed by others in Rome and in many of the smaller northern towns and villages.

The word "ghetto" is itself of northern Italian origin. Although its precise etymology is "hotly debated by historians and linguists," writes Riccardo Calimani in *The Ghetto of Venice*, "the commonly accepted opinion is that *ghetto* is a Venetian word denoting an enclosed area where the Jews were obliged to live. In earlier times, the site occupied by the ghetto was the site of a foundry, called *geto* in Venetian dialect...."

Many illustrious rabbinical families derive from this Golden Age of Italian-Jewish culture. The Abravanel family, for instance, traces its proud history back to Venice, and the famous Luria family is believed to have taken its name from the northern Italian village of Loria.

Italian Jewry peaked in the 17th century at about 50,000 and has declined steadily ever since. By the end of the Holocaust, most of Italy's Jewish communities had disappeared; today's population is estimated at about 35,000.

Genealogical Resources

Italian genealogical resources are available in a number of ways:

- Searching on-site in person
- Corresponding with Italian repositories
- Examining microfilm copies of records
- Using the Internet
- Hiring a researcher in Italy or (and this is usually the case)
- *All* of the above

However you plan to conduct your research of Italian records, it is essential that you prepare thoroughly. First, you should learn three basic facts about your Italian ancestor: full original name, approximate date of birth and native town.

Full Original Name. Some Jews in Italy adopted hereditary surnames along with their non-Jewish neighbors as early as the 10th and 11th centuries (making them the first in Europe to do so). Normally, they either translated their Hebrew name or assumed the name of their place of origin. Other Italian Jews, however, continued to practice the ancient custom of patronymics, whereby an individual was identified by given name and the given name of the father. In the late 18th century, however, Napoleon decreed that all Jews adopt a fixed surname. At that time, some Italian-Jewish families took as their surname the name of their town or city. Not *all* Jewish surnames, however, will lead directly to an ancestral town.

For pre-18th-century research, therefore, knowing the *given* names of your ancestors becomes vital, because only their given names and patronymics will identify them. Knowing your ancestor's town of birth also becomes especially critical, since only the particular place name following your ancestor's given name and patronymic will distinguish him or her from others with an identical name and patronymic. For instance, the records of a 16th-century notary might include deeds for "Isaac ben Abraham of Turin" and "Isaac ben Abraham of Novara," to distinguish between two Isaac ben Abrahams residing in close proximity.

A useful work, particularly if you are uncertain of the native town of your family, is Samuele Schaert's *I Cognomi degli Ebrei d'Italia* (*Surnames of the Jews of Italy*). This book indicates the place of origin of many Italian-Jewish surnames.

Many Italian surnames, non-Jewish and Jewish alike, have been transformed over the years—translated, transliterated, shortened or changed completely. Nevertheless, to undertake successful research in Italian records, you must first learn what the surname and given names of your ancestor were at the time when he or she left Italy.

Approximate Date of Birth. As a result of both Italian and Jewish customs for naming children, several individuals in virtually every extended family had identical names. Knowing your emigrant ancestor's approximate birth date is one way to distinguish him or her from relatives with the same given name and surname.

Native Town. Genealogical research in Italian records is impossible without knowing the town (*comune*, in Italian) where your emigrant ancestor was born. Most civil and religious records in Italy are kept on the local level, and those that have been removed to a remote repository are still maintained according to *comune*.

Italy as a unified nation is young. Its borders, not established until 1870, have been redrawn as late as 1918. The country encompasses remarkably diverse traditions and dialects. Until recent times, therefore, Italians have identified more strongly with their region, or even their province, than with Italy as a nation. Rather than call themselves *Italiani*, emigrants called themselves *Siciliani* or *Abruzzesi*, for example, after their region, or *Palermitani* or *Genovesi*, after their province. Since the capital of every province has the same name as the province, it is easy to see how an ancestor's birthplace might be mistaken.

Published Materials

Libraries hold a wealth of published material for tracing Jewish families in Italy. The more you know about your ancestor's family, the more productive and successful work in Italian records will be.

Jewish Local History. It is important to learn as much as you can about the Jewish community of your ancestral town. Annie Sacerdoti's *Guida all'Italia Ebraica* (*Guide to Jewish Italy*) surveys, region by region, town by town, all of Italy's Jewish communities—those defunct and those still in existence. Sacerdoti provides a brief historical sketch of each community, followed by a description of its synagogues, cemeteries, museums and libraries or research centers devoted to Jewish history and culture.

There are many works of Italian-Jewish local history. For a bibliographical listing of recent works dealing with the history of Jews in Italy, including works about particular localities and families, consult Aldo Luzzatto's *Biblioteca Italo-Ebraica* (The Italo-Jewish Library) and its supplement to 1995 by Consonni. Substantial histories of individual Jewish communities, such as Riccardo Calimani's *The Ghetto of Venice* or Shlomo Simonsohn's *History of the Jews of the Duchy of Mantua*, for example, are often published in English. They usually include a lengthy bibliography of related works that direct researchers to valuable secondary literature and documentary sources. They are indexed by personal names and some, such as Simonsohn's, by place names and subjects as well.

Italian National Biographies. Other works that are broadly published and readily accessible in libraries are the *Dizionario*

Synagogue in Florence from an early 20th-century photograph

Biografico degli Italiani (*Biographical Dictionary of the Italians*) and the *Enciclopedia Biografica e Bibliografica Italiana* (*Italian Biographical and Bibliographical Encyclopedia*). These multi-volume sets include biographical sketches of thousands of Italians who, from the Middle Ages to the 20th century, distinguished themselves in Italian life, Jews among them.

By noting the places of origin of individuals with your family name, whether or not you can place them on your family tree, you can localize where your surname predominated in Italy and, thereby, define the geographical limits of your research. Family names close to yours may hint at your own surname's original spelling, too.

Maps and Gazetteers. Maps of Italy and gazetteers of Italian towns are essential to consult, because the internal and external boundaries of Italy have been redrawn many times over the centuries, and many Italian towns and villages have the same or similar names. Moreover, these towns and villages often are clustered within a tight geographical area.

Two major gazetteers available in libraries list, in alphabetical order, all of the *comuni* and *frazioni* (villages) of Italy, together with essential data about each one, including its province, current population, postal code, Catholic diocese, and so forth. The *Annuario Generale, Comuni e Frazioni d'Italia* (*General Annual, Towns and Villages of Italy*) is

Map of Italy showing cities and towns where Jews lived

mation about each of the 390 *comuni* of Sicily's nine provinces, and it is available in Italian and English.

In 1870, Austria's southern Tyrol became Italy's region of Trentino-Alto Adige. If your family comes from an alpine town of northeastern Italy, therefore, you may need to consult the gazetteer of the Austro-Hungarian Empire, *Allgemeines Geografisches Statistisches Lexikon aller Osterreicheischen Staaten* (*General Geographical and Statistical Lexicon of All Austrian States*), to determine the town's original name. This 11-volume gazetteer is available on microfilm from the LDS (Mormon) Family History Library (FHL) via any of its thousands of family history centers worldwide. You may also have to pursue your pre-1870 genealogical research in the German-language records of Austria.

Perhaps the most detailed atlas available for Italy is the *Grande Carta Topografica del Regno d'Italia* (*Great Topographical Map of The Kingdom of Italy*) printed by the *Istituto Geografico Militare* (Military Geographical Institute) in Florence beginning in 1882. It comprises the entire Italian peninsula, Sicily and Sardinia in 277 maps at a scale of 1:100,000, all of which were updated and republished periodically into the 20th century. These maps show every topographical feature imaginable, including every hill, valley and river; every tiny cluster of houses; large orchards and vineyards; mines; railroads and railroad stations; all thoroughfares, from surfaced highways to footpaths; all bridges; substantial stone walls enclosing estates, convents and monasteries; ruins from antiquity, and more. Rural churches and cemeteries are marked, and villas in the countryside are often identified by family name. The U. S. Library of Congress* has a complete set of the *Grande Carta Topografica del Regno d'Italia*.

If you want the convenience of owning your own atlas and gazetteer of modern Italy, the best one available is the Euro-Atlas of Italy. Euro-Atlas is a set of volumes comprising all of the countries of Europe; each volume contains the maps of a different country. The maps show not only roads and highways, but topographical features and political divisions, too, and each volume has an extensive alphabetical gazetteer in the back. The Euro-Atlas is printed in Germany and distributed to larger book and map stores around the world. If you plan to travel in Italy, the Euro-Atlas of Italy is indispensable.

Published Genealogies. To exploit fully the resources available in libraries, search to see if a genealogy of your family already has appeared in print. Nello Pavoncello has produced a series of books entitled *Antiche Famiglie Ebraiche Italiane* (*Ancient Italian-Jewish Families*). Volume I, published in 1982, includes the histories of 20 families, reprinted from articles that appeared between 1957 and 1960 in the *Settimanale Israel* (*Israel Weekly*).

Sometimes the genealogy of a Jewish family appears as part of a larger work. For example, Vittore Colorni's *Judaica Minora: Saggi sulla Storia dell'Ebraismo Italiano dall'Antichita all'Eta Moderna* (*Judaica Minora: Essays on The History of Italian Judaism from Antiquity to Modern Times*) includes two essays that trace the prominent Jewish families, Colorni and Finzi, generation by generation, from the 15th century to the present day.

published every five years by the Touring Club Italiano of Milan, and the *Nuovo Dizionario dei Comuni e Frazioni di Comuni* (*New Dictionary of Towns and Villages*) is updated periodically.

Now you may access an Italian gazetteer on the Internet. An effort is currently underway to create a website for every *comune* of Italy. Simply enter the name of your ancestral *comune* into any browser, and chances are good you will find a site containing the town's history, geography, cultural institutions, tourist attractions, administration, and so on. The site will provide address, telephone and fax numbers, e-mail address, and name of the chief of municipal administration (*Segretario comunale)* and the Office for Public Relations (*Ufficio di rapporti con il pubblico*).

Use the facts you gathered from interviewing relatives and examining materials at home to determine which of the towns with the same name is yours. Some had a Jewish population; others did not.

Some websites contain partial gazetteers of Italy. For example, WWW.GENCAMPANIA.COM, a site for researchers of families of Campania (in English), includes a listing of the *comuni* of that region's five provinces with information about each. There are websites for other regions as well, such as SICILIA.INDETTAGLIO.IT/ITA/INDEX.HTML. This site contains infor-

Less detailed Jewish family histories appear in *Parnassim: Le Grand Famiglie Ebraiche Italiane dal Secolo XI al XIX* (*Parnassim: The Great Italian-Jewish Families from the 11th to the 19th Century*) by Franco Pisa. This series of article appears from 1980 through 1984 in the *Annuario di Studi Ebraici* (*Annual of Jewish Studies*).

Telephone directories. Italian telephone directories may be very useful, especially when searching for an ancestor's town, and they are searchable at WWW.VIRGILIO.IT. If you know the region where an ancestor was born, but not the exact province or town, you might consult phone books to see where your family name is concentrated, and then proceed to search the records of that province or town. In Italy, you will find a full set of current telephone books in all airports and major train stations; the FHL has a set on microfilm. Few old telephone directories may be found in libraries, but the largest collection is in the Biblioteca Nazionale Centrale* in Florence.

Business Directories. Business directories, published for some towns since the 1870s, are another valuable library resource.

Genealogical Society Journals. It may also be helpful to read Italian genealogical journals that are not specifically Jewish. In the United States, three organizations help their members research their Italian heritage, and all three have a website and a journal.

The oldest, founded in 1987 and headquartered in Las Vegas, is POINT (Pursuing Our Italian Names Together). Its journal, *POINTers*, is the only American quarterly published nationally that is devoted exclusively to Italian genealogical research. It serves as an informal vehicle for members to exchange information about their experiences with resources and methodologies, both here and in Italy, a kind of "clearing house" of information about Italian-American family research generally. In 1991, POINTers published an article entitled "Researching a Judaic Family in Italy," by Dale Leppart. Leppart relates his surprise at discovering Jewish ancestors. Since the Spanish Inquisition, the Leppart family had guarded the secret of its Jewishness.

The *POINTers* data bank of Italian surnames being researched by members, and the annual seminars POINT sponsors, provide excellent venues for networking with other researchers facing the same challenges you are facing. A cousin of yours in some corner of the United States may already be working on a branch or two of your family tree. Visit POINT's website at HTTP://POINT-POINTERS.NET/HOME.HTM.

The Italian Genealogical Group headquartered in Bethpage, New York, has been helping Italian-Americans of the greater New York City metropolitan area find their ancestors for many years. Its newsletter, published ten times a year, is full of useful information and instructions. Visit IGG's website at WWW.ITALIANGEN.ORG.

The Italian Genealogical Society of America, based in Peabody, Massachusetts, is most active in New England. It strives not only to assist members in their pursuit of ancestors, but also to share and celebrate together in a personal way their "Italian American experience." Visit IGSA's website at WWW.ITALIANROOTS.ORG.

Internet Websites

A number of pertinent Internet websites have already been cited. There are, however, *hundreds* of World Wide Web sites that may be useful for researching your Italian ancestry. It all depends on who your ancestors were, where they resided, and the lives they led. A good place to start is the site of the Italian Genealogical Group, WWW.ITALIANGEN.ORG, then click on the suggested "Links." Or, if you prefer, simply type "Italian genealogy" into any Internet browser and cull through the hundreds of hits one by one. What follows is a representative sampling of six helpful sites.

Family History Library. The LDS (Mormon) Family History Library (FHL) (see LDS) has an extensive collection of resources on microfilm for researching Italian ancestry. Here is a sample of some of the FHL's many useful materials for Italian genealogy.

Instructions and Glossaries. The FHL's website provides excellent instructional materials. A "Research Outline for Italian Genealogy" describes the various types of Italian records that have been created over the centuries. A "Glossary of Italian Words" and "Glossary of Latin Words" contain the terms you are most likely to encounter in genealogical sources, with their English equivalents. Both glossaries will prove indispensable when it comes time to decipher the old Italian records of your ancestors.

Microfilmed Italian Records. The FHL has microfilmed millions of original records of genealogical value in Italian archives. Chances are excellent that at least some of the birth, marriage and death records of your ancestral *comuni* have been filmed. Even if you discover, however, that the FHL has not yet filmed any records of your ancestors' towns, it is still a good idea to borrow and examine several rolls of microfilm for any town in the vicinity. This serves two purposes:

- It familiarizes you with the sources available in that part of Italy, what they look like, what information they contain and so forth
- It introduces you to the script you will encounter when you do eventually access the records of your ancestors (now your training in paleography begins!).

Form Letters. A particularly useful feature of the FHL website, especially if you have little knowledge of Italian, is the form letters for obtaining records from Italian repositories. The letters are in Italian, but blank spaces are left for you to fill in with the pertinent names, dates and places. Correspondence will be discussed further below.

Italian Genealogy Homepage (WWW.ITALIANGENEALOGY. COM). This site contains informative essays in English on various aspects of conducting genealogical research in the records of Italy. The information is useful, and there are sample letters, too; but nowhere near the amount of useful information available at the LDS site..

Windows on Italy (WWW.MI.CNR.IT/WOI/WOIINDEX.HTML). This English-language site contains information provided by the *Istituto Geografico De Agostini* regarding Italy today: historical sketches, administration, geography, population,

Synagogue in Turin from an early 20th-century photograph

economy, tourism and map of every region, and information about major *comuni*. The website of the *Istituto Geografico De Agostini* (www.DEAGOSTINI.IT) is a news magazine in Italian with essays on the history, art, culture, and current events of Italy. This site is *not* genealogical, but provides helpful background information.

In Italy Online (www.INITALY.COM) Owned and operated by Words in Pictures, this site resembles a travel guide for Americans, including practical information about accommodations in Italy, travel tips, weather, customs, transportation, what to do and see in each region, and offers related products for sale, such as maps and guidebooks.

www.NET/CURRENCY is a currency converter that will convert dollars into euros and vice-versa. Very handy!

www.ItalianAncestry.com links to numerous other sites categorized under "Italian Genealogy Web Sites," "Italia in General," "Writing to Italy," "Tool Box," "United States," "Italians in America," "International Italiano," and "General Subjects."

Writing to the Jewish Community

After you have determined your ancestral town, write a letter to the local Jewish community or rabbi to ask about the extent and location of the surviving community records. Use *The Jewish Travel Guide*, published annually by the London *Jewish Chronicle*, to determine if there is still a Jewish community in the town. If there is not (most of the smaller ones have disappeared), write to the nearest surviving community.

Records of birth, marriage and death of many Jewish communities have survived as far back as the 17th century. These usually are kept in local synagogues, but may be part of the town archives. The rabbi will also know if your ancestor's town has a Jewish museum, library of research center. If so, write to them as well.

Civil Record Repositories in Italy

In addition to the civil records described below, town archives (*archivi comunali*) and state archives (*archivi di stato*) often hold a miscellaneous assortment of records relating specifically to Jews. However you conduct your research in Italian records, it is essential for you to be familiar with the country's system of civil archives.

Italy is divided into 20 regions. Tuscany, Lombardy and Campania, for example, are all regions, but no records are kept on the regional level. Each region is composed of one to nine provinces, with a total of 103 provinces in all. The five provinces of Campania, for instance, are Avellino, Benevento, Caserta, Naples and Salerno. Each province has many towns (*comuni*), one of which serves as the provincial capital (*capo luogo*). The name of the province and the name of its capital are the same. The capital of the province of Trapani is the city of Trapani; the capital of the province of Pavia is the city of Pavia, and so forth. Some Italian communities are so small that they do not have their own mayor, but rather fall within the administrative jurisdiction of a nearby *comune*. These are called *frazioni di comuni* or simply *frazioni*, meaning village.

Italy has 104 state archives, one in each provincial capital, plus the *Archivio Centrale dello Stato* (Central State Archives) in Rome. Some state archives have a branch in one or two smaller cities of the province, when the local collections are large enough to warrant such a branch. In addition to the provincial state archives, local town archives are kept in every town hall. Records of genealogical value kept in the state archives generally pre-date 1870, and they have been microfilmed by the LDS (Mormon) Family History Library. Contents of town archives, though, have not been microfilmed, and these generally date since 1870. Genealogical research in Italy, therefore, usually begins in town archives and progresses back into state archives.

The civil records described below vary widely in the amount and type of information they contain, in the accuracy of that information, and in their physical condition. Italy as a modern nation is young; it was unified from numerous independent states during the 1860s, and only became a single country with its capital at Rome in 1870.

Each of Italy's sovereign states experienced different wars and natural disasters and changes in leadership and administration, and each kept its records in its own way. Naturally, therefore, no record description could possibly hold true universally throughout.

It was Napoleon Bonaparte who, during his brief reign as King of Italy from 1806 to 1815, unified the administrative, judicial and legislative system of the entire country into one substantially similar to the one described above. Although Italy was restored to its pre-Napoleonic autonomous states by the Congress of Vienna in 1815, the Emperor's system of *regioni, provincie, comuni* and *frazioni* remained the model for modern-day Italy.

By 1860, King Vittorio Emanuele II of Piedmont had emerged as the champion of Italian unification. Between 1860 and 1865, Garibaldi and his Redshirts, devoted subjects of Vittorio Emanuele, captured Sicily and Naples for their king. In 1866, as a result of war with Austria, the king also gained Venice as part of his realm. Finally, by treaty with the Pope in 1870, Italy as a united country, with Rome as its capital city, was born.

The following descriptions of Italian civil records, therefore, are helpful generalizations. You will discover soon enough in your own search for Italian ancestors just how much these descriptions may vary from the norm in any particular locality and era.

Town Archives. According to Italian law, the registers comprising the town archives may only be searched by an official working in the town hall. Just how much searching and reporting such an official will perform for a foreign genealogist, who either writes or shows up in person, varies widely, not only from one town to another, but from one clerk to another in the same town hall. Some are more cooperative and helpful than others.

On occasion, a researcher who speaks directly to the clerk's superior—the *ufficiale dello stato civile* (official in charge of vital records) or *direttore* (director)—may be allowed to search through the registers himself or herself, one at a time. But this happy scenario is very rare. The more specific and accurate the information you provide, the better the chances you will receive a positive reaction from the clerk. It is good to keep in mind that a town hall is a functioning public office and is neither intended nor staffed to render assistance to historical researchers.

In all of your dealings with the civil servants in your ancestral towns, be mindful to put your best foot forward, show due respect, smile, cooperate, and be patient and considerate and as helpful as you can possibly be. Remember, it is *their* country, *you* are the outsider making requests of them. It is both appropriate and expected that you acquiesce to their way of doing things. Express your appreciation; say "*Grazie tante!*" (Thanks very much!) many times.

There are no published guidebooks to these town archives. They differ vastly from one town to the next, however, one reference work that includes practical information is the *Guida Monaci: Annuario Generale Italiano* (*Monaci Guide: General Italian Annual*). This weighty tome, updated every year, is a directory of all of Italy's governmental offices and agencies. It lists every public archives and library in the country, with its address, phone number and the name of its director. In addition, websites of individual towns (discussed at "Maps and Gazetteers" above) are very helpful.

Birth, marriage and death records, called *stato civile* (vital records), have been kept uniformly throughout Italy since 1870. (Earlier *stato civile* for some regions will be discussed under **State Archives** below.) They are maintained by the *ufficio di stato civile* (office of vital records) in the town hall and are rich in family information.

Birth Records. To create an birth record (*atto di nascita*) the infant had to be presented physically to the town's *ufficiale dello stato civile* (officer of vital records). This was normally the mayor in the town hall. The presenter was usually the father, but sometimes another male relative or the midwife, and the infant was normally less than one day old.

The record contains the date of the presentation; name, age, profession and place of residence of the presenter; maiden name, age and place of residence of the mother; name, age, profession and place of residence of the father; date, hour

Artist's sketch of the ghetto section of Venice. This is the origin of the word "ghetto" which means "iron foundry" in Italian. It was the area in Venice where Jews were forced to live for several hundred years

and place of birth of the infant, and his or her name; and the names, ages, professions and places of residence of two witnesses to the presentation.

The record volumes were printed with blank spaces where the officer of vital records wrote in the particular facts of each birth. Most numbers, including dates, were spelled out in words, rather than using numerals.

Sometimes, when a person married or died in a town other than his or her native town, the officer of vital records would forward the information to the officer of vital records in the town of birth, who in turn would annotate the original birth record. This practice has been observed with varying regularity across the country and across the years.

When an infant was too weak to be carried to the town hall on the day of its birth, or entered the world in the middle of the night, the father might make the presentation a day or two later. If the presenter did not make it clear that the new life was already a day or two old, from force of habit the official would simply insert that the infant was born *lo stesso* (the same day). Many an Italian ancestor was born before the birth date penned into the civil register.

Marriage Records. A marriage record is called an *atto della solenne promessa di celebrare il matrimonio* (record of the solemn promise to celebrate matrimony) because the marriage itself was not contracted at city hall, but rather in the religious ceremony which followed in the synagogue. To create a marriage record, the bride and groom would appear before the officer of vital records with four witnesses.

The record contains the date of the appearance; name, age, birthplace, profession and place of residence of the groom, together with his father's name, age, profession and place of residence, and his mother's maiden name, age and place of residence; name, age, birthplace and place of residence of the bride, together with her father's name, age, profession and place of residence, and her mother's maiden name, age and place of residence; and the names, ages, professions and places of residence of the four witnesses.

If the groom was a widower, or the bride a widow, this will be stated also, sometimes with the name of the former spouse. Those principals who could write signed their names at the end of the record.

An important term used in Italian civil records is "*fu*." Literally, *fu* means "was." It indicates a deceased person. When the parent of an individual named in a record is still living at the time the record is created, the relationship is indicated using *di*. For example, "Leopoldo Sermoneta, figlio *di* Giacomo" means "Leopoldo Sermoneta, son of Giacomo, *who is living*." However, when the parent is deceased at the time the record is created, the relationship is indicated using *del fu* for the father and *della fu* for the mother. For example, "Enrichetta Spizzichino, figlia *della fu* Ester Rosselli" means "Enrichetta Spizzichino, daughter of the *deceased* Ester Rosselli."

But frequently, for expedience, the *del* or *della* would be dropped, and the word *fu* alone was used in place of the word *di* to indicate a deceased parent; for example, Amelia, figlia fu Sergio." This practice may help you find an ancestor's

date of death. For example, if an 1842 marriage record indicates the mother of the bride Paolina as "*di Vittoria*," and the 1844 marriage record of Paolina's sister Anna gives her mother as "*fu Vittoria*," it is evident that Vittoria died sometime between the marriage dates of her two daughters in 1842 and 1844.

Death Records. A death record (*atto di morte*) is as rich in personal information as the birth and marriage record. Besides stating the name and age of the deceased and his or her date and place of death, it usually gives the deceased person's occupation, place of residence, parents' names, as well as the name of the husband or wife, if the deceased was married. If the deceased was a widow or widower, the name of the last spouse is given. A death record may also contain the name of the individual who came to the town hall to report the death. A married woman or widow will appear in the death record under her maiden name, not her husband's name.

The *stato civile* just described are usually kept in volumes by year, and most volumes are indexed alphabetically by surname in the back. Some have ten-year cumulative indexes, too, which normally comprise a complete decade each, such as 1870–80, 1880–90, 1890–1900, and so forth.

Two other types of family records may be requested from your ancestors' town hall. These are *not* original historical records, but rather documents prepared specifically for you from original historical records in the town archives. They are the certificate of family status and the certificate of residency.

Certificate of Family Status. This certificate (*certificato di stato di famiglia*) shows the composition of a family unit, parents and children, including the names, relationships, birth dates and birthplaces of all members, living and deceased. The certificate may also show marriage and death dates in the column headed, *Annotazioni* (Annotations), as well as occupations and occasionally the names of the parents of the father and mother—which is to say, another generation of the family. A certificate of family status is a statistical "snapshot" of a complete family.

You request this certificate from the officer of vital records of your ancestors' town, and it is prepared by a member of the municipal staff from census (*anagrafe*) records. Since it is created from census data, and the first national census to include the name and vital statistics of every person in every household was not taken until 1911 (more about Italian censuses below), most officers of vital records will not prepare a certificate of family status with information pre-dating what is available in the 1911 census.

On rare occasions, however, an officer of vital records may be willing to prepare a certificate of a 19th-century family by using the town's original *stato civile*. Such an undertaking requires considerable searching through the old birth, marriage and death registers, and many town halls simply do not have sufficient staff to offer this service. When they do, it is a potentially expensive proposition for the requester, and the document's completeness and reliability depend on the ability and conscientiousness of the preparer.

When excerpting information from old records, Italian officials always put the family name first, in capital letters, followed by the given name. Writing names this way in official documents is standard procedure in Italy.

Certificate of Residency. The second type of family record you may request from the town hall of your ancestral town is the certificate of residency (*certificato di residenza*). This is secured from the office of the census (*ufficio di anagrafe*), not the office of vital records. A certificate of residency is prepared from census records that document the people living in a particular residence. Those records are updated as changes occur—children born, for example, or persons moved to another town in Italy, or to a foreign country, or residents died. So a certificate of residency might show the exact year when an ancestor of yours emigrated from Italy.

State Archives. After town archives, the record repository of greatest value for genealogical information is the state archives in the capital city of the province where your ancestors lived.

State archives are public archives staffed by archivists and trained clerks who are prepared to help you access the records you seek. The professional staff cannot, however, be expected to conduct research for you, either by correspondence or in person. Limited funds, time and personnel preclude that. They will respond to queries about their repository's holdings, but will not do any searching for you in the collections. That's *your* job.

Access to Italy's state archives for historic purposes is free to all researchers; those working on commercial projects, however, must pay a fee and obtain a written permit. Practically all state archives have their own photocopying and microfilming services, or can provide such services through approved private agencies for a reasonable fee. The bureaucratic obstacle course the researcher must negotiate to access these services, though, may seem maddeningly convoluted and exasperating to non-Italians. But it can be mastered.

Bear in mind as you deal with Italian archivists that you are in *their* archives. They are extending a courtesy to you, a foreigner, and you should follow patiently and cheerfully whatever regulations, formalities and procedures they have put in place to safeguard their own precious patrimony. Show proper deference and exercise proper decorum. The impression *you* make may ease the way for future genealogists.

In the Mezzogiorno (southern Italy and Sicily), state archives may conserve not only the civil records described above, but some of the religious records that will be described later.

There are several ways to familiarize yourself with the organizational structure and documentary holdings of Italy's state archives. First of all, the *Guida Generale degli Archivi di Stato Italiani (General Guide to the Italian State Archives)* is published in four volumes by the Ministero per i Beni Culturali e Ambientali (Ministry of Cultural and Environmental Affairs), the government agency responsible for administration of the archives and libraries of Italy. Taking the state archives in alphabetical order, this guide describes each one's holdings. Every description includes a section titled *Archivi di Famiglie e di Persone* (Individual and Fam-

ily Archives), which are manuscript collections that contain substantial genealogical and biographical information about families of the province.

The Ministero per i Beni Culturali e Ambientali also publishes a set of 20 modest monographs under the colorful title, *Itinerari Archivistici Italiani (Italian Archival Itineraries)*. The first volume—*Organizzazione Archivistica (Archival Organization)*—describes the national archival system. The second—*Archivio Centrale dello Stato*—describes the central archives in Rome. Each of the eighteen others describes the state archives located in each region of Italy (Abruzzo and Molise are combined into one, and there appears to be none, as of this writing, for the Valle D'Aosta). These superbly illustrated little books present a brief overview of the documentary materials in each archives, plus practical information regarding addresses, hours of operation, photocopying services, and so forth.

The online equivalent of these official publications is the beautiful website of the Italian archival system, WWW.ARCHIVI.BENICULTURALI.IT. Here you will find the addresses, phone numbers and hours of operation of all state archives, plus an alphabetical index to each one's collections, which describes very briefly the various records and the years they cover. The site also includes a complete copy of the *Guida Generale* explained above and other finding aids.

In addition, some state archives publish their own guides and indexes, as well as their own website. These provide more detailed information for those archives than does WWW.ARCHIVI.BENICULTURALI.IT.

Birth, Marriage and Death Records. State archives contain *stato civile* kept prior to 1870. It was in 1806 that Napoleon Bonaparte decreed that all births, marriages and deaths be registered with civil authorities throughout the country. In northern Italy, the keeping of *stato civile* was initiated anywhere between 1806 and 1815. After the Congress of Vienna in 1815, however, when Italy reverted to its pre-Napoleonic status, some areas of the north discontinued keeping *stato civile* until 1870. In the central Italian region of Tuscany, the *stato civile* housed in the state archives in Florence is continuous since 1808. In the southern regions of Abruzzo, Molise, Campania, Apulia, Basilicata, Calabria and Sicily—which once comprised the Kingdom of the Two Sicilies—*stato civile* were kept continuously from 1809 on the mainland and from 1820 in Sicily. All of the pre-1870 *stato civile* kept in state archives is similar in form and content to those housed in the town archives described above, and most were microfilmed during the 1980s for the Family History Library.

The northern region of Trentino-Alto Adige, comprised of the provinces of Bolzano and Trento, was under Austrian control prior to Italian unification in 1870. The custom there since the 16th century was for the local priest to serve as the officer of vital records. Pre-1870 *stato civile* for Bolzano and Trento, therefore, may still be found in the custody of local priests, rather than in the state archives. The same applies to some Jewish communities, e.g. that of Livorno (Leghorn), where pre-1870 vital records are kept in the community's archives.

Military Records. Shortly after the unification of Italy, military service became mandatory for all eighteen-year-old males. Since about 1870, therefore, *registri degli Uffici di Leva* (registers of the Offices of Conscription) have been kept. These registers list the name, town of birth, date of birth, parents' names, and physical description of all young men eligible for the draft, together with an explanation of their military status—whether or not they ever served, or deserted, or were exempted, and so forth. The registers are divided into annual *classe di leva* (conscription classes or groups), each of which is indexed by the names of the draftees who composed that *classe di leva*—that is, the names of those men who turned eighteen since the previous *classe di leva*.

Registers of the Offices of Conscription are maintained by the military district (*Distretto Militare*)—a province may contain perhaps five or six military districts—and those created since World War I may still be in the custody of the military district where they were created. But older registers have been deposited in the state archives.

To learn which military district had jurisdiction over your ancestor's town, consult one of the gazetteers discussed in "Maps and Gazetteers." Note, too, that draftee records may sometimes be found on the town level; so you might find a record of your ancestor's military status in the town archives.

Earlier records of military service, dating back sometimes to the late 18th century and containing more or less the same information as the *registri di leva*, are also kept in state archives. These records cover the different Italian states and kingdoms at different periods of history, those of the region of Tuscany being notably plentiful.

Notarial Records. Notaries in Italy have always performed a broad scope of legal services. Italian law requires that marriage contracts and dowries, wills, real and personal property transactions, lawsuits of all kinds, including settlements of heirship and guardianship of orphans, and still other matters be officially registered by a notary. From the Middle Ages through the early 20th century, the notary's professional activity remained substantially unchanged and resulted in three different records of value to genealogists: *minute*, *atti* and *bastardelli*.

When the notary met with his clients, he wrote a rough draft (*minuta*) of the transaction to be recorded, including the names of the principals and the facts of the matter at hand. From his rough draft he prepared the actual deed (*atto*), which is the written record of the transaction. The notary kept his rough draft and a copy of the deed for his own records, but deposited the original deed in the office of the notarial district (*distretto notarile*) where he was licensed. The deed was then considered legally registered.

For his own purposes the notary maintained a chronological list of the deeds he prepared, with a few words defining the parameters of each one. This list—known as "*bastardelli*" because the abstracts were "illegitimate;" that is, they did not constitute a legal document—provided accessibility for the notary to his own work. When a notary retired or died his rough drafts and *bastardelli* were usually passed on to his successor. When the new notary found he had no further need of these, he deposited them in the office of his notarial district.

Notarial records of the past 100 years are still found in the possession of the individual notaries, or in the files of district notarial offices, or in archives—such as the District Notarial Archives of Naples (*Archivio Notarile Distrettuale di Napoli*)—which some populous notarial districts have had to create specifically for that purpose. At the end of 100 years, however, the whole collection of rough drafts, deeds, and *bastardelli* described above is transferred to the state archives. These notarial records in state archives may date back to the fourteenth century and sometimes even earlier.

In the state archives, each notary's archives forms a separate collection, and the *bastardelli* serve as a kind of index to the collection. But remember, the *bastardelli* list the deeds in chronological order and do *not* constitute a name index to the deeds. In addition, the original deeds which were deposited in the district notarial office by all of the notaries licensed in that district—perhaps fifty to eighty notaries—are also gathered into separate collections, one for each notary.

These notarial collections are arranged in chronological order by the registration date of each deed, *not* the date when the transaction occurred, and *not* by the names of the principals or the content of the deed. Therefore, if you do not know the name of the notary engaged by your ancestors to register their legal transactions, or at least an approximate date when any particular record you seek was registered, researching notarial records may be very time-consuming, as a page-by-page search through the collections of all of the notaries of a given district is required.

Depending on your research needs, however, the time may turn out to be wisely spent and may result in a wealth of information about the social and economic status of your ancestors. By their nature, notarial records are full of familial matters, relationships and dates, so that in some cases—when civil or religious records are lacking—they may be the only resource available for establishing a family group.

It is far from an easy task, however, to decipher the content of pre-20th-century notarial records once you have found them! Older deeds were written in a Latin jargon with its own abbreviations in a compact script called notarial gothic (*gotico notarile*). Unless your skills as a paleographer have been finely honed by this time in your research, you will have to hire a professional genealogist to decipher the old notarial records for you.

Fortunately, notary records kept in Jewish communities throughout Italy are currently being edited and published by Shlomo Simonsohn (see Bibliography). A superb example of Simonsohn's efforts is the four-volume set entitled, *The Jews of the Duchy of Milan*. It includes the Jewish notarial records of the area around Milan from the Middle Ages through the 16th century, in English translation with notes.

Censuses. National censuses (*censimenti*) of Italy taken in 1861, 1871, 1881, 1891 and 1901 are available for searching in state archives. Unfortunately, however, these censuses do not name every member of every family. Rather, they list heads of household with only statistical data for the other members of the household.

Later censuses of 1911—considered the first major national census—1921, 1931, 1936, 1951, 1961, 1971, 1981 and 1991 are much more informative. They enumerate the total population of Italy by family unit, including the names and ages of the husband, wife and dependent children, occupation of the head of household, and places of birth of all members of the family. However, these censuses are *not* open to the public. You may request extracts from them, though, by writing to the office of the census (*ufficio di anagrafe*) in the town of your ancestors (as explained under "Certificate of Family Status" and "Certificate of Residency" above). But you must be able to provide sufficient information to make the search feasible, and the census official must be willing to undertake the assignment.

Many state archives also hold an assortment of other censuses taken at various times in various localities. These date back to the middle of the 18th century, and the type and amount of information they show differs a great deal from one area of Italy to another. Special enumerations were often made of Jews. For example, in the state archives in Verona is a manuscript book from 1776 that contains a detailed description of the Jewish ghetto of that city. It includes a map of the ghetto and a house-by-house census listing of the occupants and their occupations.

In addition, censuses were taken in the region of Sardinia in 1848 and 1857. For years prior to about 1750, however, you must turn to tax records for enumerations of family units.

Tax Records. Italians have lived with a wide variety of tax obligations over the centuries, from taxes on land and houses to taxes on livestock and family members, and more. Tax assessment records or lists (*catasti*), therefore, are varied and voluminous. They enumerate property owners—sometimes including the names, or the names and ages, of the property owner's household—and indicate the taxable property and amount of tax assessed on it. They may be civil records or parish tithing records. They may date back as far as the 14th century or be as recent as the 19th century.

Some tax records, called Declarations (*Riveli*), consist of lists of heads of household "declaring" or "revealing" the precise extent and nature of the taxable property they hold, including personal property and real estate. Declarations are particularly useful because they include names of members of each taxpayer's household, however, they are voluminous and require a time-consuming page-by-page search.

Tax records pertaining to the former Papal States—the present-day provinces of Ancona, Ascoli Piceno, Macerata and Pesaro-Urbino (the region of *Marche*), Perugia and Terni (the region of *Umbria*), and Frosinone, Latina, Rieti, Roma and Viterbo (the region of Latium)—are not kept in their respective state archives, but rather in the Secret Archives of the Vatican (*Archivio Segreto del Vaticano*). Unfortunately, access to Vatican archives is not easily obtained. A large portion of Italy's Jewish population has lived for centuries—especially since 1492—in the area that comprised the Papal States.

Tax lists are especially useful sources of information about families that owned land, no matter how little. Ownership of modest pieces of private land was historically much more common north of Naples than in the Mezzogiorno, where most of the land was divided into huge *latifondi* (large estates) owned by a few noble families. As a result of this ancient feudal system, the vast majority of people in the south were landless peasants living and working on their titled landlord's *latifondo*. Nevertheless, persons without real estate could still appear in *catasti* prepared for taxing personal estate, such as a "head tax" on members of the family.

Catasti, unfortunately—like notary records—are a difficult resource to use, since they are multifarious, written in arcane script and unindexed.

Emigration and Passport Records. Of particular interest to non-Italians tracing Italian ancestors, naturally, are records relating to emigration: passport applications and departure lists.

Prior to 1869, permits to emigrate were issued by regional heads of state, such as the King of the Two Sicilies in Naples or the Duke of Tuscany, through a governmental agency. Since the unification of Italy, passport applications have been made at the local police station (*questura*). Registers of Emigration and Passports (*Registri dell'Emigrazione e Passaporti*) from about 1800 through World War I are preserved in state archives, with those dated 1869 and later being among the records of the police (*polizia*) or prefect (*prefettura*). Passport records since World War I are still in the custody of the police station where the application was made. Emigration and passport records usually state the name of each emigrant, town of birth, age or birth date, date when applying to emigrate or date when emigration will be permitted, and the port of departure and destination.

A separate set of records dealing with emigration matters has been kept since 1869 by the Minister of the Interior (*Ministero dell'Interno*) in Rome, where they are maintained today, closed to public inspection. However, requests for genealogical information from these records may be granted if you make clear your relationship to the emigrant and give a reason for the information that the ministry considers satisfactory.

Central State Archives. The Central State Archives (*Archivio Centrale dello Stato*) in Rome is the national repository for the historically valuable records created by the numerous agencies and offices of the Italian government. These records document the official operations of the government and contain little information of genealogical interest. The Central State Archives, therefore, is the *last* civil archives of resort for genealogical research. For specific information about the holdings of the Central State Archives, consult the *Guida Generale degli Archivi di Stato Italiani* discussed above, as well as WWW.ARCHIVI.BENICULTURALI.IT.

Libraries

Italy has a well-organized national system of *biblioteche pubbliche statali* (state public libraries). There is no single "national library" analogous to the Bibliothèque Nationale in Paris or the Library of Congress in Washington, D.C. Rome,

Florence, Bari, Milan, Naples, Potenza, Palermo, Turin and Venice all have a *biblioteca nazionale* (national library). Each one collects and preserves materials relating to its own area within Italy. All house not only published volumes, but many manuscript collections of personal and family papers donated or bequeathed by local families, too.

The libraries of Rome and Florence hold the elevated status of *Biblioteca Nazionale Centrale* (Central National Library), because they serve as depository libraries for all printed matter published in Italy, as well as foreign works pertinent to Italian civilization.

In addition to these national libraries, there are smaller libraries in other provincial capitals called *biblioteche statali* (state libraries), a number of specialized libraries (each one having its own name), and a dozen university libraries (*biblioteche universitarie*). University libraries are located in Bologna, Cagliari, Catania, Genoa, Messina, Modena, Naples, Padua, Pavia, Pisa, Rome and Sassari and are meant to support the research and study needs of the faculty and students there.

The best introduction to Italy's state public libraries is WWW.LIBRARI.BENICULTURALI.IT. Click on *servizi* (services), then click on *biblioteche*. A map of Italy showing the twenty regions will appear. Click on the region of interest to you, and a new screen pops up with a map showing the provinces of that region and a list of the state libraries located there, with each one's city. Click on any library and an informative website will provide the library's designation (national, state, university, etc.), director's name, address, telephone and fax numbers, e-mail address, hours of operation and a detailed history of the library. Some library catalogues may also be searched online.

Besides state libraries, Italy has hundreds of *biblioteche comunali* (local libraries). These are managed by the government of the *comune* and include materials on local history and genealogy.

Two guides, one in Italian, the other in English, are helpful for using Italian libraries. Francesco Marraro's *Repertorio delle Biblioteche Italiane* (*Repertory of Italian Libraries*) is a listing by region, and thereunder by province, of all of Italy's libraries (as of the book's date of publication). It includes the address and hours of each library, as well as the number of volumes and periodicals each one holds. *The Guide to Italian Libraries and Archives*, compiled by Rudolf J. Lewanski and intended specifically for American researchers, offers practical information about Italy's libraries and archives, as well as an overview of the entire national system. The practical information includes rules and regulations governing admission, hours of operation, photocopying, and so forth, which vary from one library to the next throughout Italy.

University Records

Jews have occupied influential and much-respected position in Italian universities. If your ancestor was a scholar, you should consult the *Registri dell'Università* (University Registers) where he or she studied or taught. Such registers may be found either in *archivi di stato* or at the university itself, and they may date back to the 13th century, as do those of Padua and Bologna, two of the oldest universities in the world. (Padua was the first to allow Jews into its medical school.) The registers are generally kept by school, so it is helpful to know not only what university your ancestor may have been associated with, but whether he or she was in the school of medicine, law, theology, history, philosophy, and so forth. Student records tend to be indexed by surname for each freshman class, however, and that makes using them a possible task regardless of how much prior knowledge you bring to the search.

After locating your ancestor in the index, you may consult his or her admission record, which provides the freshman's name, birth date and birthplace, as well as his or her father's name and occupation. When you are certain, based on this information, that you are dealing with the right student, proceed to consult his or her academic file. It will provide complete information about his or her scholarly activities at the university. There are also registers with information about instructors. The genealogical boon of *registri dell'università* is that often, when you find one ancestor, you discover other family members there, too, sometimes for succeeding generations.

An important resource for 19th- and 20th-century research are records kept in libraries that list students and graduates from different universities, for example, the students of the University of Naples (1879–80) or students and graduates of the University of Florence (1924–5) and so forth. These may be obtained via interlibrary loan.

Cemeteries

Jewish cemeteries in Italy are unlike Christian cemeteries. Christian families either own a mausoleum or lease individual graves for 20 or 30 years, after which time the bones are removed to a common ossuary. Jewish custom mandates that graves be maintained in perpetuity. Some of the older cemeteries were destroyed years ago, but many are still maintained. So you may be able to use the names and dates inscribed on cemetery monuments to extend your family tree. In some instances, however, tombstones dating back to the 17th century and earlier bear only the name of the deceased and no date of birth or death.

Guidebooks

Since 1992, the Italian publisher Marsilio has been issuing a series of guidebooks to Jewish heritage in Italy. Each book is a detailed guide to Jewish places, history and art in one of Italy's regions, arranged as a compilation of travel itineraries. The series includes individual books on the regions of Liguria, Marche, Veneto, the city of Venice and its surroundings, Tuscany, Piedmont, Lombardy, and Emilia Romagna. The latest volume, *Jewish Itineraries in Latium*, which appeared in 1997, deals with Rome and its surrounding region.

Several of these books—so far Latium, Tuscany, Venice and Emilia Romagna—are also published in English. Each volume includes a historical overview; schematic maps showing the proposed itineraries; and detailed historical and descriptive presentations of the towns, villages and sights. They describe medieval Jewish quarters, Jewish museums, synagogues, cemeteries and the like, and also provide information on the non-Jewish texture of the various towns and villages.

The texts give fascinating insights into the tenor of Jewish life and the development of Italian Jewry—including the evolution of Jewish surnames, which often were taken from the name of the town where the family originated. Itineraries in individual towns sometimes walk the reader step by step through the old Jewish quarters and surrounding streets. Each book also has an index and a bibliography of source material and suggested further reading. The series is edited by Annie Sacerdoti, Italy's leading expert on local Jewish heritage in Italy (see Bibliography).

In addition to the Regional Itineraries series, the first volume on another Jewish heritage series edited by Sacerdoti has been published by Marsilio. This series will be on Jewish museums in Italy. The first volume is a guide to the Jewish Museum and elaborate synagogue, dating to the early 17th century, in Casale Monferrato, near Milan. At least 70 synagogues stand today in Italy, many of them no longer in use as synagogues. In addition, more than a half dozen Jewish museums showcase thousands of ritual objects and documents relating to Jewish history.

Centers for Jewish Studies

Italy has two centers for Jewish studies, one in Milan, the other in Rome, which are valuable resources for researchers of Italian-Jewish heritage.

Milan's *Centro di Documentazione Ebraica Contemporanea** (Center for Contemporary Jewish Documentation), also known as CDEC, Italy's only institution dedicated to Italian Holocaust research. Founded in 1955, CDEC has a 15,000-volume library of general and specialized books, including monographs on specific Italian-Jewish families and on Jewish communities in specific towns and regions. It also holds collections of 1,550 Italian and foreign periodicals, some dating back to the 19th century, including Jewish communal publications and periodicals on Jewish and Holocaust-related issues.

In addition, CDEC resources include 90 linear meters of historic documents, hundreds of thousands of newspaper clippings and numerous other valuable archival materials that have been reorganized for easier research access over the past two years. Most of CDEC's archival material relates to the 20th-century experience of Italian Jews, with particularly rich collections concerning the Fascist era and World War II. CDEC has published several important works on the experience of Italians during the Holocaust, including the detailed *The Book of Memory: Jews Deported from Italy, 1943–1945*, by Liliana Picciotto Fargion. It also has carried out video interviews with living survivors of these deportations. (These form the basis of a recent documentary film, *Memoria*.)

CDEC staff continue to develop a complete computerized catalogue of its material as well as to draft a definitive catalogue of Italian-Jewish periodicals from the 19th century to the present.

The most useful general Jewish resource institution in Rome is the Centro Bibliografico (Bibliographic Center) of the Union of Italian-Jewish Communities,* which includes an extensive general library as well as archival material and libraries from several small provincial communities.

Both the CDEC in Milan and the Rome Center are useful places to visit before delving into the rich but complex, and often disorganized, world of local town archives or Jewish community archives. For instance, Rome Jewish community archives hold birth and death records dating back to the 18th century, and some archives of other Jewish communities are even older. The Rome Center's resources also include photographs; a collection of *ketubot* (marriage contracts), particularly from the towns of Senigaglia and Ancona; and several family trees of well-known Jewish families. Plans are being made to develop a full-scale guide to Italian-Jewish archives, which will be extremely valuable when completed.

Menorah Bookstore

Another good Jewish resource in Rome is the Menorah* bookstore in the ghetto, around the corner from the main synagogue. Its extensive catalogue is posted on the Internet (see below). Menorah has numerous monographs ranging from pamphlets to lengthy books on Jewish history or Jewish communities in specific Italian cities or regions. Some of these books—many of which have been published in the last 10 years—supply detailed information on individual families. One recent book, for example, *Arte Ebraica a Roma e nel Lazio* (*Jewish Art in Rome and Latium*), provides illustrations of Jewish coats-of-arms, whose symbols often are found on Jewish tombstones and *ketubot*. Two books about the Jewish history of the town of Gorizia include articles with detailed historical background on local Jewish families.

Resources in Israel

Three centers for Jewish studies in Israel hold materials pertaining to Italian Jews.

The Centro di Studi sull'Ebraismo Italiano (27 Hillel Street, Jerusalem), under the direction of Miriam Della Pergola, holds 6,000 books on Italian Jewry and many journals with articles on the Jewish communities of Italy. The center is a part of Jerusalem's Umberto Nahon Museum of Italian Jewish Art (WWW.ITALCHAM.ORG.IL/MUSEUM/ITALINDEX.HTML).

The Manuscript Department at the Jewish National and University Library* and the Central Archives for the History of the Jewish People* (see ISRAEL) hold several manuscripts from Italy. In the Microfilm Department are two *pinkassim* from the Vernadsky collection in Kiev: Milan Jewish birth register, 1792–1831, and from Siena, a *pinkas* of the *chevra kadisha*, late 19th century.

At The Institute for Diaspora Research* (Tel Aviv University, Ramat Aviv, Tel Aviv 69978) Professor Shlomo Simonsohn is devoting himself to publishing a complete documentary history of the Jews in Italy. His books of Milan's notarial records (cited above) constitute part of that project. See the Institute's website at WWW.TAU.AC.IL/HUMANITIES-INDEX.HTML#DIASPORA.

Existing Jewish Communities

The following list gives the names of cities (in alphabetical order) with addresses of local Hebrew congregations as they appear in the *Bollettino della Comunità-ebraica di Milano, Lunario ebraico 5762*. Numbers in parentheses refer to the Jewish population of that city.

Alessandria (few): via Milano 7, 15100 Alessandria; representative: Mr. Silvio Norzi; telephone: 39-0131-262224

Ancona (200): via M. Fanti, 60121 Ancona; secretary: Ms. Cristina Lanternari; telephone and fax: 39-071-202638

Asti (few): via Ottolenghi 8, 14100 Asti; telephone: 39-0141-215526, 39-0141-212566, 39-0141-399206

Bologna (200): via Gombruti 9, 40123 Bologna; secretary: Ms. Sara Saralvo Gatta; telephone: 39-051-232066; fax: 39-051-229474

Casale Monferrato (few): vicolo Salomone Olper 44, 15033 Casale Monferrato (AL); secretary: Ms. Nella Levi Carmi; telephone: 39-0142-71807, 0142-452076, 39-0142-452888; e-mail: CASALEBRAICA@TISCALINET.IT

Cuneo (few): contrada Mondovi' 19, 12100 Cuneo; representative: Mr. Enzo Cavaglion; telephone: 39-0171-690891; fax: 39-0171-693290

Ferrara (100): via Mazzini 95, 44100 Ferrara; president: Ms. Michele Sacerdoti; telephone and fax: 39-0532-247004

Firenze (1,000): via Farini 4, 50121 Firenze; secretary: Mr. Emanuele Viterbo; telephone: 39-055-234-6654; fax: 39-055-241811; e-mail: COMEBRFI@FOL.IT. Of interest is *Taryag*, the Association of English Language Friends of the Hebrew Community of Florence, whose secretary is Nancy Lippmann; telephone: 39-055-475897

Genova (355): via G. Bertora 6, 16122 Genova; president: Mr. Piero Dello Strologo; telephone: 39-010-8391513; fax: 39-010-846-1006; e-mail: COMGENOVA@TIN.IT

Gorizia (few): via Ascoli 19, 34170 Gorizia; telephone: 39-0481-383206, 39-0481-531428; fax: 39-0481-522056

Grosseto (few): representative: Mr. Carlo Tronchi, telephone: 39-0564-408257

Ivrea (few): via San Nazario 22, 10015 Ivrea; representative: Mr. Raffaele Pugliese; telephone: 39-0125-424876

La Spezia (45): via XX settembre 165, 19100 La Spezia; representative: Mr. Alberto Funaro; telephone: 39-0187-20562

Livorno (700): piazza Benamozegh 1, 57123 Livorno; president: Mr. Samuele Zarrugh; telephone and fax: 39-0586-896290

Lucca (18): via dei Garofani 115, 55100 Lucca; representative: Mr. Eugenio Genazzani; telephone: 39-0583-56766

Mantova (110): via G. Govi 13, 46100 Mantova; secretary: Mr. Vittorio Jare'; telephone: 39-0376-321490

Merano (50): via Leopardi 31, 39012 Merano (BZ); president: Mr. Federico Steinhaus; telephone: 39-0473-236127; fax: 39-0473-206210; e-mail: STEINHAUS@TISCALINET.IT

Milano (10,000): via Sally Mayer 2, 20146 Milano; secretary: Mr. Michele Sciama; telephone: 39-02-48302806; fax: 39-02-48304660; e-mail: COMUNITA-EBRAICA@LIBERO.IT

Modena (74): piazza Mazzini 26, 41100 Modena; president: Mr. Felice Crema; telephone and fax: 39-059-223978

Napoli (200): via Cappella Vecchia 31, 80121 Napoli; secretary: Ms. Gabriella Sacerdote Fontana; telephone and fax: 39-081-7643480; e-mail: C.E.NAPOLI@VIRGILIO.IT

Padova (190): via San Martino e Solferino 9, 35122 Padova; president: Mr. Vittorio Sacerdoti; telephone: 39-049-8751106

Parma (few): vicolo Cervi 4, 43100 Parma; president: Ms. Ada Tedeschi Spritzman; telephone and fax: 39-0521-200243; Section in Soragna, telephone: 39-0521-929456

Pisa (85): via Palestro 24, 56100 Pisa; secretary: Mr. Giacomo Schinasi; telephone: 39-050-542580; fax: 39-050-542580; e-mail: COM_EBRAICAPI@TIN.IT

Roma (14,000): lungotevere Cenci, 00186 Roma; secretary: Mr. Emanuele Di Porto; telephone: 39-06-6840061; fax: 3906-6840-0684; e-mail: INFO@ROMACER.ORG

Senigallia (few): via Commercianti 20, 60019 Senigallia (AN); representative: Mr. Hammus Zuare

Siena (80): vicolo delle Scotte 14, 53100 Siena; telephone: 39-0577-284647

Torino (1,070): Piazzetta Primo Levi, 10125 Torino; secretary: Mr. Raffaele Lampronti; telephone: 39-011-6692387, 39-011-658585, 39-011-658586, 39-011-658587; fax: 39-011-669-1173; e-mail: COMEBRATO@LIBERO.IT

Trieste (630): via San Francesco 19, 34133 Trieste; secretary: Mr. Eliahu D. Giorgi; telephone: 39-040-371466; fax: 39-040-371226

Urbino (few): via Stretta 24, 61029 Urbino (PS); representatives: Ms. Maria Luisa Moscati, Ms. Placidia Coen

Venezia (464): Cannaregio 2899, 30121 Venezia; president: Mr. Paolo Gnignati; telephone: 39-041-715012; fax: 39-041-524-1862; e-mail: COM.EBRA.VE@LIBERO.IT

Vercelli (40): via Foa' 56, 13100 Vercelli; president: Mr. Dario Colombo; telephone: 39-0161-252-2958, 39-0161-253-700

Verona (100): via Portici 3, 37121 Verona; secretary: Ms. Ester Silvana Israel; telephone: 39-045-800-7112; fax: 39-045-596627; e-mail: COMEBRAICA@LIBERO.IT

Viareggio (60): via Pacinotti 172/B, 55049 Viareggio; representative: Mr. Joseph Sananes; telephone: 39-0584-961025

Addresses

Centro Bibliografico, Lungotevere Sanzio 5, 00153 Rome, Italy; telephone: 39-6-580k-3690; fax: 39-6-589-9569; open Monday to Thursday.

Centro di Documentazione Ebraica Contemporanea (CDEC), via Eupili 8, 20145 Milan, Italy; telephone: 39-2-316-338; fax: 39-2-336-02728; open mornings five days a week.

Diaspora Research Institute

Menorah Bookstore, via del Tempio 2, 00186 Rome, Italy; telephone: 39-6-687-9297; e-mail: MENORAH@MENORAH.IL

Bibliography

Allgemeines Geografisches Statistisches Lexikon aller Osterreichischen Staaten (*General Geographical and Statistical Dictionary of All Austrian States*). 11 vols. [German].

Annuario Generale, Comuni e Frazioni d'Italia (*General Annual, Towns and Villages of Italy*). [Italian] Milan: Touring Club Italiano, 1968 and later (every five years).

Bondoni, Simonetta. *Cultura Ebraica in Emilia Romagna* (Life of Jews in northern Italy, circa 1300-1860). [Italian] Rimini: Luise, 1987. Many Hebrew manuscripts and documents are catalogued.

Bonomi, Nardo. "The Jews of Livorno, Italy: Archival Sources," *AVOTAYNU* 18, no. 2 (Summer 2002).

Calimani, Riccardo. *Storia del Ghetto di Venezia* (*History of the Ghetto of Venice*). [Italian] Milan: Rusconi Libri, 1985; English translation: Wolfthal, Katherine Silberblatt, *The Ghetto of Venice*. New York: M. Evans, 1987. Extensive bibliography.

Carpi, Daniel, ed. *Shlomo Simonsohn Jubilee Volume: Studies on the History of the Jews in the Middle Ages and Renaissance Period*. Tel Aviv: Tel Aviv University.

Colletta, John P. "Jewish Genealogical Research in Italy." *AVOTAYNU* 8, no. 1 (Spring 1992).

Colorni, Vittore. *Judaica Minora: Saggi sulla Storia dell'Ebraismo Italiano dall'Antichita all'Eta Moderna* (*Judaica Minora: Essays on the History of Italian Jewry from Antiquity to Modern Times*). [Italian] Milan: Dott. A. Giuffre, 1983.

Consonni, Manuela M., ed. *Biblioteca Italo-Ebraica: Bibliografia per la Storia degli Ebraei in Italia, 1986-1995* (*Italian-Jewish Library: Bibliography for the History of Jews in Italy, 1986-1995*). For works published 1974-1985, see Luzzatto (below). [Italian] Rome: Menorah, 1997.

Contributing Editors (France). *AVOTAYNU* 6, no. 3 (Fall 1990).

Contributing Editors (France). *AVOTAYNU* 10, no. 2 (Summer 1994). Includes sources of Venetian Jewish genealogy.

Contributing Editors (France). *AVOTAYNU* 12, no. 4 (Winter 1996). Includes information on Jewish Livorno.

Della Pergola, Sergio. "The Distribution of Italian-Jewish Names," an article in a complete study by Franco Pisa of the great Italian Jewish families from the 11th to 19th century in Pisa, Franco. *Parnassim: Le Grande Famiglie Ebraiche Italiane dal Secolo XI al XIX*. [Italian] See below. Bibliography by town.

Dizionario Biografico degli Italiani (*Biographical Dictionary of the Italians*). [Italian] Rome: Istituto della Enciclopedia Italiana, 1960-present.

Enciclopedia Biografica e Bibliografica Italiana (*Italian Biographical and Bibliographical Encyclopedia*). [Italian] Rome: Istituto Editoriale Italiano, 1941.

Fargion, Liliana Picciotto. *Il Libro della Memoria gli Ebrei Deportati dall'Italia (1943-1945)*. [Italian] Milan: Gruppo Ugo Mursia, 1991.

Filippini, J.P. in *Rivista Italiana di Studi Napoleonici* (*Review of Napoleonic Studies*). Pisa: Giardini, 1982; includes Jewish heads of families from 1809 census.

Guida Generale degli Archivi di Stato Italiani (*General Guide to the Italian State Archives*). 4 vols. [Italian] Rome: Ministero per i Beni Culturali e Ambientali, Ufficio Centrale per i Beni Archivistici, 1986) Describes contents of all state archives of Italy. (See also WWW.ARCHIVI.BENICULTURALI.IT)

Guida Monaci: Annuario Generale Italiano (*Monaci Guide: General Italian Annual*). Rome: Guida Monaci, 1991. 117th ed. (revised annually). Practical guide to all governmental offices and agencies of Italy, including addresses, names of directors and telephone numbers.

Itinerari Archivistici Italiani (*Italian Archival Itineraries*). [Italian] Rome: Ministero per i Beni Culturali e Ambientali.

Lindo, E.H. *A History of the Jews of Spain and Portugal*. New York: Burt Franklin, 1848; reprint, 1970. Provides a short description of Leghorn (*Livorno*) Jewish history.

Lewanski, Rudolf J. *Guide to Italian Libraries and Archives*. New York: Council for European Studies, 1979.

Luzzatto, Aldo. *Biblioteca Italo-Ebraica* (*Italian-Jewish Library*). [Italian] Milan: Franco Angeli Libri, 1989. Extensive bibliography of works published between 1974 and 1985 on Jews in Italy. Includes many works of Jewish local history and works about Jewish families. Indexed by locality, personal names and subjects. For works published 1986-95, see Consonni (above).

Machlin, Edda Servi. *A Classic Cuisine of the Italian Jews*. vol. I. Croton-on-Hudson, New York: Giro Press, 1981. Includes detailed description of the Jews of Pitigliano in Tuscany.

Malka, Jeffrey S. *Sephardic Genealogy: Discovering Your Sephardic Ancestors and Their World*. Bergenfield, NJ: Avotaynu, 2002.

Marraro, Francesco. *Repertorio delle Biblioteche Italiane* (*Repertory of Italian Libraries*). [Italian] Rome: Editoriale Cassia, 1989.

Nuovo Dizionario dei Comuni e Frazioni di Comuni (*New Dictionary of Towns and Villages*). [Italian] Rome: Società Editrice Dizionario Voghera dei Comuni, 1977.

Pavoncello, Nello. *Antiche Famiglie Ebraiche Italiane* (Ancient Italian Jewish families). [Italian] Rome: Carucci Editore, 1982. First volume of a proposed series composed of articles reprinted from the 1957–60 issues of the weekly *Israel*. Gives the histories of 20 Jewish families.

Pisa, Franco. "*Parnassim: Le Grande Famiglie Ebraiche Italiane dal Secolo XI al XIX* (*Parnassim: The Great Italian Jewish Families from the 11th to the 19th Century*). *Annuario di Studi Ebraici* (*Annual of Jewish Studies*). Ariel Toaff, ed. [Italian] Rome: Carucci Editore, 1980–84.

Sarcerdoti, Annie. *Guida all'Italia Ebraica* (*Guide to Jewish Italy*). [Italian] Casale Monferrato: Casa Editrice Marietti, 1986. English editions (with slightly abridged historical information) DeLossa, Richard F. *Guide to Jewish Italy*. Brooklyn: Israelowitz, 1989.

Schaert, Samuele. *I Cognomi degli Ebrei d'Italia* (*Surnames of the Jews of Italy*). [Italian] Florence: Casa Editrice Israel, 1925. Surveys numerous Italian-Jewish family names.

Simonsohn, Shlomo. *History of the Jews in the Duchy of Mantua*. Tel Aviv: Ktav, 1977. Vol. 17 of the Publications of the Diaspora Research Institute. Excellent example of local Jewish history.

———. *The Jews in the Duchy of Milan*. 4 vols. Jerusalem: Israel Academy of Sciences and Humanities, 1986. Part of a proposed complete documentary history of he Jews of Italy.

———. *Jews in Sicily*. Leiden and New York: Brill, 1997.

Tedeschi, Mark. "Genealogy Research by Mail from Australia," *AVOTAYNU* 2, no. 1 (January 1986). Describes research in several Italian cities.

Toaff, Renzo. *La Nazione Ebrea a Livorno e a Pisa (1591–1700)* (*The Hebrew Nation in Livorno and Pisa, 1591–1700*). [Italian] Firenze: Leo S. Olschki, 1992.

Latvia

by Mike Getz

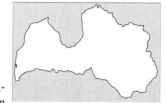

Czarist Russia acquired the Baltic countries, including Latvia, in stages. Table 1 shows Latvia under the Russian Empire, how its regions and major towns related to the Russian administrative system and the implications for archival materials. This status prevailed from 1795 until 1917. Poland controlled Latgale, southeastern Latvia, from 1561 to 1772 and was divided into the *uyezds* (districts) of Daugavpils, Ludza, Rezekne and Vilaka. Latgale came under Russian rule in 1772 as part of Pskov guberniya and was made part of Vitebsk guberniya in 1802. For this reason, many files from Latgale are today in the Central State Historical Archives of Minsk.*

The Duchy of Courland was established in 1561 and absorbed by Russia in 1795. It existed as a separate German-speaking province of the Russian Empire with its capital in Mitau (now Jelgava) from 1795 until 1918. In this region, once ruled by the Teutonic Order, German culture, administration and influence prevailed. Because German was the official language at the beginning of the 19th century when Jews were required to adopt fixed family names, many took names that reflect the German lexicon (e.g., the names end in the German suffix *ovits*, instead of the Russian *ovich*). Archival records were moved to St. Petersburg in 1902 and returned to Riga in 1929. At the end of World War II, the Germans moved some records to Czechoslovakia. Most were returned, but a quarter of the holdings was lost.

Livland was ruled by Poland from 1561 to 1625 and by the Swedes until 1710. Riga and Vidzeme were annexed by Russia in 1710, ushering in 200 years of Russian rule. As northern Latvia, it was a single administrative unit called Riga Province until 1783; in 1796 it became Livland. At that time, most archival records were retained in Riga, but some material was divided between that city and Tartu in Estonia. Livland, with some geographical modification, became the province of Livonia in 1812.

Latvia, as we know it today, became a separate, independent country only after World War I; prior to that time, its provinces had several different rulers. It was briefly independent between the two world wars, but an agreement between Hitler and Stalin ceded Latvia to the Soviet Union in 1940. Latvia was occupied by the Germans in 1941 and returned to Soviet rule in 1945. Latvia regained its independence in 1991. The 19th-century Russian *guberniyas* (provinces) of Livonia, Courland and much of Latgale form today's Latvia.

Jews in Latvian Lands

The Jewish population of Latvian lands was never very large, but references to Jewish tombstones date back to the 14th century. In 1536, a merchant records transactions with "the Jew Jacob."[1] Latvia's Jewry once was among the most urbanized in Eastern Europe. Almost two-thirds of the Jewish population lived in Daugavpils (formerly Dvinsk), Liepaja (Libau) and Riga before the end of the 19th century. Urbanization is a distinguishing feature of Latvian Jewry. Riga and Liepaja, both seaports with rail connections that traversed Lithuania and Russia, advanced this process and spurred mobility.

Latvia's major cities are important to the history and genealogy of Latvian Jewry. Riga is central to the province of Livonia, while Liepaja (Libau) and it environs relate to Courland in more recent times. In Latgale, Latvia's eastern province, Daugavpils (Dvinsk) was a focal center for Jews from neighboring Belarus and Lithuania. The Dvina River in western Latvia was a major artery between Daugavpils and Riga. It was also the *de facto* border between Courland and Latgale. More importantly, Latgale, east of the Dvina, fell within the Pale of Settlement, while Courland to its west did not. Thus, Jekabpils (Yakobshtadt) and Krustpils (Kruizberg), twin cities on the east and west banks of the Dvina, were separated by the Pale. Jewish families and communities developed linkages throughout Latvia, sustained by trade and reinforced by marriage. Jewish migration in this region, frequent during the 18th and especially the 19th centuries, often was based on the pioneering of an earlier generation which moved to an area that offered better economic opportunity. As often, it was driven by hardship and lack of opportunity.

Livonia

A number of accounts date Jewish presence in Riga to 1621 (and earlier). Mendel Bobe writes that Jews were compelled to lodge at the *Juden-Herberge* (Jews' shelter) during their stay in the city. This was documented in 1666, but Jews bringing goods down the Dvina by raft from Russia and Poland to Riga were exempted from this rule.[2] The city came under Russian rule in 1710. Local merchants pressed for measures against their Jewish competitors, but the Jews retained their rights until 1742 when Empress Elizabeth expelled them from Russia. In 1764, under Catherine the Great, a gradually increased Jewish presence was again permitted. By 1822, Jews could stay in five shelters, and in 1842 the first official Jewish community in Riga was established. Livonia, of which Riga was the center, always remained outside the Pale of Settlement. Since Jews were not permitted to leave the Pale legally, Riga and Livonia offered relative freedom of movement and opportunity to those who could manage to live there.

Courland

Courland was created in 1561 from two separate political units, the province of Pilten and the Duchy of Courland. Jewish presence in Pilten, which included the districts of Grobin, Hasenpoth (Aizpute) and Windau (Ventspils), preceded its sale to the king of Denmark in 1559. Because Pilten was near the Baltic Sea, Jewish merchants from Prussia were among the settlers in the 15th century or earlier. German landowners in

Marketplace in Mitau at the beginning of the 20th century where Jews sold their goods. Courtesy of Tomasz Wisniewski.

Pilten promoted the immigration of Jews. Security for the Jews deteriorated after 1635 when discriminatory legislation and taxes were imposed. Expulsions occurred in 1727 and 1738.

In 1750, the Polish *Sejm* (legislature) introduced a system of taxation and granted residence rights to Jews. Civil and general rights were formalized by the Sejm in 1783, and the Jews of Hasenputh (Aizpute) built a synagogue. Jews retained most of their rights when the region was annexed by Russia in 1795.

From 1692 to 1792, discrimination against the Jews was widespread in the Duchy of Courland, fueled by the resentment of merchants and artisans. Aristocrats employed Jews, however, to sell their produce and import goods not produced locally. This made for an uneasy presence in Hasenpoth (Aizpute), Mitau (Jelgava) and Pilten, but in the villages, Jews engaged in trade, innkeeping and distilling. In Mitau (Jelgava), the Jews had a special quarter, the *Judengasse*, and were permitted to buy land for a cemetery in 1710. As in Pilten, Jews suffered threatened expulsions, discriminatory taxes and other uncertainties. In 1760, Duke Charles, son of the king of Poland, required all Jews to leave Courland; many did.

After Duke Charles was overthrown (with Russian help) in 1792, Jews again lived in reasonable security. Conditions improved in 1795 when the Duchy ceased to exist after it merged with Pilten. Courland was excluded from the Pale of Settlement.

Latgale

Poland acquired this region after the decline of the Livonian Order in 1561 and ruled until 1772. Jewish presence is noted after 1650, and almost 3,000 Jews were recorded in 1720. This number had approached 5,000 when it fell under Russian rule in 1792. At that time, Latgale became part of the Polotsk-Vitebsk jurisdiction and was included in the Pale of Settlement with all its restrictions. Latgale was less economically developed than Livonia or Courland, but Daugavpils (Dvinsk), its largest city, was a major regional influence. The Jews of this region typically were of Lithuanian and Belorussian origin, and they embraced both *misnagid* and *hasidic* traditions.

Migration Patterns of Latvian Jewry

Most Eastern European Jewish families, at the end of the 19th century, produced six or eight children. During the massive migration of this population at the turn of the 20th century, Latvian Jews families typically sent two or three siblings to the United States. After 1920, U.S. quota restrictions made South Africa an alternative destination for other siblings. Palestine attracted a relatively high proportion of emigrants because of a strong commitment to Zionism in Latvia. One or two children usually remained in Latvia where they died in the Holocaust. As a result, most families of Latvian origin today have branches in the United States, South Africa and Israel. A number went to Sweden as well.

Affiliations and Traditions

The Jewish community with the longest history in Latvia, probably since 1585, was that of Piltene in Courland. Settlers from Prussia practiced their Jewish orthodoxy in the German tradition, retaining its distinct character. Riga's Jewish community was officially recognized in 1838; it constituted an important element of Jewish life in Riga, leading its institutions and assuming prominence in the city's commercial life. The city reflected the diversity of Latvian Jewry. Business, intellectual and educational interests prominently featured both German and Russian. Jewish life included the *misnagid* tradition of Vilna, the influence of Courland's German Jews and the vibrancy of Lubavich hasidism from White Russia (today Belarus); the Lubavich Shneiersons were in Riga before they went to the United States.

Latvia today has three major provinces. The country is divided by the Dvina River which courses from Riga on the Baltic deep into Belarus. Courland is west of the Dvina and Latgale lies to its east. Riga and the region of Livonia constitute the third province. The present southern border of Latvia divides it from northern Lithuania and Belarus, but it hardly reflects the relationship of Jewish communities of the region in the 18th and early 19th centuries.

The roots and links of a family often reach beyond most borders as we know them. Rather, they are defined by access and common interests. In this context, Jewish identity determines a set of needs and common interests that can be accommodated only among Jews. Well into the 20th century, the practice of Judaism was inseparable from the Jewish way of life for most families. Communities, therefore, required the services of rabbis, cantors, *shochtim* (ritual slaughterers), *mohels* (ritual circumcisers) and teachers. They had pivotal roles in the Jewish life cycle as well as sustaining and maintaining institutions of learning and other communal activities. Communities that were too small or too poor to support their own officials received these services from elsewhere, usually a larger, nearby town.

Latvian Jewry is a part of Jewish migration in Eastern Europe over the centuries, but it also enjoyed a distinctive pattern of its own. German Jews first settled in Courland in the 16th century. Riga attracted Jews from White Russia as well as those of Courland with their Germanic orientation. Dvinsk (today Daugavpils), part of Vitebsk guberniya before the 1917 Russian Revolution, was home to a large Jewish community strongly linked to contemporary Belarus and Lithuania. Libau (today Liepaja), Courland's largest city (and outside the Pale of Settlement), also was a haven for many Litvaks.

In a regional sense, Latvia's three cities, Riga, Libau and Dvinsk, were prized destinations for different reasons and from various locations. Riga, both a cosmopolitan city and a major port, had universal appeal. Dvinsk was perhaps the most Jewish of the cities, second only to Riga in size. Jews in Dvinsk were prominent in a vibrant commercial and industrial sector. Dvinsk, an important Jewish center of opportunity, was in Vitebsk guberniya before the Russian Revolution of 1917. Libau, a major port on Latvia's Baltic seaboard, drew its Jewish population primarily from Courland, but from elsewhere as well.

Significant numbers of Lithuanian Jews entered Courland throughout the 19th century. The general area of Bausk in Latvia was also an important Jewish location in Lithuania, its Latvian status only finalized in 1919. Because Courland had no *yeshivas*, rabbis and teachers increasingly were brought from Lithuania. Wealthy Courlanders sent their sons to the *yeshivas* of Mir and Slobodka and sought husbands for their daughters from among students at these and other Lithuanian *yeshivas*.

Bar-Aron Nurock, chief rabbi of Libau in 1907, came from a well-known rabbinic family in Mitau. His predecessor was Yehuda Leib Kantor, originally from St. Petersburg and later chief rabbi of Riga. Rabbi Abraham Isaac Kook (1865–1935), first chief rabbi of Eretz Yisrael, was born in Griva near Dvinsk and also served in Bausk. He was the pupil of Rabbi Reuvele Dinaburger, himself a major figure. The intellectual rigor of Talmudic study and devotional liturgy that characterized Litvak Jewry blended with the German-Jewish tradition of Courland's Jews.

Dvinsk (today Daugavpils) was the most Jewish of Latvia's cities. It had a developed infrastructure of commerce and industry with Jewish owners and workers both numerous and prominent. Moshe Amir says "the Dvinsk to which memory returns is the famed City and Mother in Israel, teeming with Jews, hospitable beyond belief, bubbling with communal activities."[3] Positioned on the Dvina River between Riga and its course into Belarus, Dvinsk was an important rail, road and river junction. Sons and daughters of the region where the city was pre-emininent traveled from far and wide to work, study and experience the urban life of a Jewish community. Travelers to the city from adjacent Novo-Alexandrovsk passed through three guberniyas—Kovno, Courland and Vitebsk. Not without importance was the availability of education closer to modern ideas and the influence of Haskalah, particularly in Latvia.

Genealogical Resources

Records for Jewish genealogists with roots in contemporary Latvia are extensive, varied and among the most accessible in all of Eastern Europe.

Archival Sources

The Latvian State Historical Archives* was not organized until after Latvia gained independence following World War I, but it has a considerable inventory of value to Jewish genealogists. Fond #5024 holds the birth, marriage, divorce and death records that were maintained by Latvian rabbis acting in an official capacity. The records do not, however, cover every period and location.

Latvia's many masters over the centuries often helped themselves to archival material. Some records are held in the National Archives of Sweden,* while other material is in Moscow. Patricia Kennedy Grimsted in her authoritative *Archives and Manuscript Repositories in the USSR* provides comprehensive details.

The Latvian State Historical Archives* accepts both postal and e-mail requests. The most accessible and comprehensive account of its Jewish holdings may be found on the home page of the Latvia SIG's website WWW.JEWISHGEN.ORG/LATVIA under "Latvian State Archives." The site also details a requirement for a refundable deposit with each request and/or a fee for onsite research. Responses to queries from abroad have included carefully prepared family outlines, often with important supplementary information mentioning extended family. Since Latvia's independence from the former Soviet Union, the Latvian Archives has adopted a market-oriented approach to genealogists. It has not permitted the LDS (Mormon) Family History Library to microfilm any of its collections, nor will it permit local professional genealogists access to vital records for clients (although the professionals may search other records). The Latvian State Historical Archives* holds vital records up to 1906. Records after 1906 are in the Latvian Archives of the Registry Department of the Ministry of Justice* and in the archives of various registry offices (see below).

In addition to the vital records, other primary sources of genealogical data at the state archives include Riga residence books, 1900–40; revision lists (*reviski skazki*), 1772–90 (incomplete); various lists of Jews compiled by the police, 1800–1917; copies of the 1897 Russian Census for some communities; lists of soldiers, 1850–1900; various directories for Riga, Kurland and Livonia 1860–1912. The Latvia SIG website features some of these sources. Its All Latvia Database includes the 1907 Courland Duma Voters List, Jewish inhabitants of Riga (1885/86), the Dvinsk family lists and the 1897 census for Krustpil, Rezekne and other localities. Birth, marriage and death records for the entire country from 1906 to 1921 (and beyond in some cases) are held in the Latvian Archives of the Registry Department.[*] The SIG expects to add databases from the archival project led by Arlene Beare.

A special interest group for Courland led by Martha Lev-Zion and Abraham Lenhoff has paid particular attention to materials and records related to Courland Jewry. Its website is WWW.JEWISHGEN.ORG/COURLAND.

Some important archival holdings were lost during World War II; others were moved and never returned in full. Jurisdictions during the Russian Empire influenced the final location of key records from Latgale which are discussed below. Other records of genealogical value have been filmed by the Mormons; researchers should check the Family History Library catalogue under every community of interest (see LDS).

A set of records called *Kurland Seelenlisten, 1797–1834*, filmed by the Germans in Riga during 1940, were microfilmed by the Mormons at the Herder Institute in Marburg, Germany,[*] and are accessible to researchers. The text is written in German and Russian, and the records include tax, property and tax lists; Jews are included, although not always designated as such. The major cities and towns of Courland are covered, including Mitau (Jelgava), Hasenpoth (Aizpute), Libau (Liepaja), Bausk (Bauske), Dunaburg (Daugavpils), Jacobstsadt (Jekabpils) and Tuckum (Tukums).[4,5]

Jewish Community Records

Records of various types may be found in existing Jewish communities, principally, but not entirely, in the larger cities of Daugavpils, Liepaja and Riga. Obtaining access to them depends on developing relationships with communities and, thus, indicates at least an initial onsite visit.

Daugavpils. Members of the author's family visited this Jewish community in July 1992. We discussed our interest in community records and family histories and inquired about a cemetery register we had heard existed. A few months later, we were sent a copy of the document that listed 50 pages of burials since 1920 with 3,000 names. The document has been transliterated and will be posted on the Latvia SIG website.

Jekabpils. Jekabpils's (Yakobshtadt) well-maintained cemetery is more 150 years old. In addition to a group of family histories, we received family trees and a map showing the locations of Jewish homes and businesses in the town during the 1930s. The map and more comprehensive information about the town, its people and its cemetery appear under "Shtetl Focus" on the Latvia SIG website.

Rezekne. This community maintains a large, 200-year-old cemetery. No burial record exists, but the recently created Rezekne group of the Latvia SIG may help motivate the community to create one.

Subate. Local authorities often have material of various kinds, including property records. Access requires advance planning and communication. Librarians, teachers and older inhabitants can also provide valuable information. For example, in 1992, when this author visited the village of Subate,

northwest of Daugavpils on the Latvian/Lithuanian border, the mayor offered a property record for the years 1936 and 1937 that includes many Jewish names as owners, tenants or heirs. The document is in the possession of this author who will respond to inquiries made through Avotaynu.

Other Locations. Liepaja Jewish cemetery burials, 1909–41, have been compiled by Edward Anders and are posted on the web at WWW.EJ-ANDERS.COM/USERS/XENON2/CEM/CEMINDEX.HTM. Various other documents obtained by Paul Berkay with extensive references to Courland communities, including Jekabpils and Subate, may be viewed online at www.JEWISHGEN.ORG/COURLAND/DATABYSOURCES.HTM. A site about Jewish Latvia today offers some useful insight at WWW.WJC.ORG.IL (go to Communities of Eastern Europe).

Family Histories

A project sponsored by the Jewish Genealogy Society of Greater Washington generated a series of family histories from Daugavpils, Jekabpils and Rezekne. Arrangements for the interviews were made during visits to these communities. A basic questionnaire was provided to guide the interviewer. The project, which focused on interviews with Holocaust survivors, but was not limited to them, yielded 85 family histories, many covering four and five generations and often going back more than a century. Some Holocaust survivor accounts probably are not recorded elsewhere. The interviews were translated from Russian into English. A list of names from the Jekabpils interviews appears under "shtetl focus" for that town on the Latvia SIG web page. The names from Daugavpils and Rezekne will be added to those town pages in the near future. Plans to make the complete record publicly available are under consideration; in the meantime, the author of this chapter will respond to relevant questions directed to him via Avotaynu. Another group of family histories from interviews with Riga survivors is nearly complete and will be featured on the Latvia SIG website and its quarterly newsletter.

Holocaust Project. Professor Ruvin Ferber[*] and Constance Whippman[*] have organized the Latvia Holocaust Names Project: A Memorial List of the Latvian Jewish Community. Its goal is to develop a complete list of Latvian Jewry on the eve of the Holocaust and especially to identify those who were murdered and ensure that their memories are preserved.

Genealogical Resources Outside Latvia

Boundary changes, wars and emigration especially, have caused considerable documentation on Latvian Jewry to be located in many places. Researchers should be aware that Jews of this region emigrated through a variety of routes: Libau to Hull on the east coast of England, from there by train to Liverpool or London; others sailed from Hamburg, while still others may have chosen the little-known route via Copenhagen, Denmark. Genealogists who have not been able to locate emigrant ancestors in the major ports should check the Scandinavian possibility as well as Moscow.

Minsk

The Belarus Historical Archives* in Minsk holds Jewish records from such centers as Dvinsk (Daugavpils), Rezhitsa (Rezekne) and adjoining regions. Fond 1430 covers the period 1797 to 1917 and includes documents that reflect many aspects of Jewish life, including religion, education, trade and pogroms. Fond 2640 includes the 1811 revision lists for Rezhitsa and Lutzin (Lutza). A 1874 family list (a type of census) for Daugavpils, Rezekne and Varklany (Varklan) is held here, too. Many Jewish families are listed.

Estonia

Between 1889 and 1918, some young Jewish men and women studied at the University of Tartu in Estonia. Lists of students, dates of birth, Latvian addresses, faculties and years of study appear in an account entitled *Album Academicum Universitatis Tartuensis 1889–1918* published in 1986.

Israel

Kibbutz Shfayim* is custodian of material that belongs to the Association of Latvian and Estonian Jews (*Igud*). The Igud was founded in 1942 when letters arrived from Latvian Jews exiled to the USSR. From its inception, the Igud collected material on Latvian Jewry, its leaders and communities. In addition to Holocaust accounts; lists of victims, survivors and perpetrators; communal histories and pictures, this archive has 170 personal files on prominent members of the community, including the historian Simon Dubnow (killed in Riga) and Meier

Synagogue in Libau in 1910. Courtesy of Tomasz Wisniewski.

Simcha, the famous *misnagid* rabbi of Dvinsk. Details of records at Shfayim are among the databases on the Latvian SIG website. Contact a curator before making an onsite visit.

Scattered items from Latvian Jewry may be found in various other Israeli repositories, including the Manuscript and the Microfilm Divisions at the Jewish National and University Library,* the Central Archives for the History of the Jewish People* and the Central Zionist Archives.* Yad Vashem has considerable information about the Holocaust era; do not overlook the Pages of Testimony now searchable by locality.

South Africa

Jews of Lithuanian and Latvian origin constitute about 80 percent of South Africa's Jewish community. The Kaplan Centre, University of Cape Town* has records of Jewish arrivals in the 1920s. The handwritten lists were recorded by a representative of the Jewish Board of Deputies as immigrants landed. Details include names, country and town of origin, destination and host in South Africa. Since Jews of Latvian origin had a significant presence in South Africa, a visit to the South African SIG website, WWW.JEWISHGEN.ORG/SAFRICA) could be rewarding. Note, however, that the Kaplan Centre is an academic institution that does not do genealogical research.

South Africa had a number of Latvian *landsmanshaftn* in Cape Town and Johannesburg; those of Dvinsk and Libau were especially prominent from the 1930s until the 1960s. Some mention of South African landsmanshaftn may be found at WWW.JEWISHGEN.ORG/LITVAK/SALANDSREC.HTM. Related and other materials are lodged in libraries of the Jewish community but some remain in private hands. A guide to possible repositories can be viewed on the South African SIG website.

England

At the turn of the 20th century, many Latvian and Lithuanian Jews en route to South Africa used the Poor Jews Temporary Shelter in London as a stopover. Its records include information on Jews who passed through London from the late 1800s until the 1920s. Details are available at WWW.SANSA.UCT.AC.ZA/SHELTER/SHELTER.HTM

United States

The U.S. National Archives,* College Park, Maryland branch, holds Record Groups (RG) 59 and 84. RG 59 deals with records of correspondence from the U.S. Department of State to its consular offices outside the United States. It includes correspondence initiated by U.S. citizens to facilitate the immigration of family members or to transmit funds for those in need in Latvia. Responses or initiatives from the Riga consulate appear in RG 84 which reflects similar correspondence from foreign consulates to the State Department in Washington. These transactions are rich in genealogical content. Records go back to the Russian era in the early 1900s and continue well into the 1930s when Riga was a principal embassy covering the Baltics and Soviet Russia.

YIVO. * Record Group 116, YIVO's Territorial Collection

includes material on the Holocaust in Riga (2.14), names of individuals killed (2.19), events in the Daugavpils ghetto (2.17) and a list of Brith Trumpeldor being instructed to enlist in 1940 (available in English).

United States Holocaust Memorial Museum.[*] This museum has two groups of records important for those tracing Latvian families. The "Extraordinary State Commission to Investigate and Establish War Crimes of the German-Fascist Invaders" was created by the Soviet Union near the end of World War II. Records of Holocaust victims were prepared from investigations involving eye witnesses, neighbors and accused conducted by the NKVD throughout the territories of the USSR. Information about Latvian victims may be viewed on the Latvia SIG website at WWW.JEWISHGEN.ORG/DATABASES/LATVIA. This lists the Latvian towns documented and the number of victims recorded in each location.

Thousands of Jewish victims appear in the records of Stutthof concentration camp. Researchers at the museum have identified Latvian-Jewish victims who were transported to and died in Stutthof. Details include names, date and place of birth, marital status, last place of residence. Occasionally date and cause of death appear.

Landsmanshaftn, Mutual Aid Societies, and Synagogues. Several varieties of extant records document the lives of Jews from Latvia in the United States. YIVO[*] has extensive landsmanshaftn records while two important books linked to Latvian-Jewish communities in the United States are *Bridges to an American City: the Guide to Chicago Landsmanshaftn 1870–1990*, by Sidney Sorkin, and *Jewish Immigrant Associations and American Identity in New York 1880–1939*, by Daniel Soyer.

Chicago had a Kurlander Aid Society, founded in 1911, as well as societies of individuals from Dvinsk, Kraslava, Rezetse (Rezekne) and other locations. The Kurlander Young Men's Mutual Aid Society formed in New York in 1889; its membership records may be viewed on the All Latvia Database at WWW.JEWISHGEN.ORG/LATVIA. It includes valuable information about families, vocations and a way of life. The society's *Historical Review of 1924* mentioned on the site is a fascinating document.

Cemeteries. Several cemeteries have sections for organizations from Latvia. Mount Hebron Cemetery[*] in Flushing, New York, has at least two Kurlander sections. In Baltimore, Maryland, the Rosedale Cemetery[*] has burials with Riga and Kurlander links. and the Dvinsker Progressive Verein in Chicago has a cemetery association.

Addresses

Central Archives for the History of the Jewish People, 46 Jabotinsky Street, P.O. Box 1149, Jerusalem, 91010; telephone: 972-2-563-5716; fax: 972-2-566-7686; e-mail: ARCHIVES@VMS.HUJI.AC.IL; website: SITES.HUJI.AC.IL/ARCHIVES

Central State Historical Archive of Belarus, ulitsa Kozlova, 26, Minsk, Belarus

Central Zionist Archives, 4 Zalman Shazar Blvd., P.O. Box 92, Jerusalem 91920; telephone: 972-2-620-4800; fax: 2-620-4837; e-mail: CZA@JAZO.ORG.IL; website: WWW.WZO.ORG.IL/CZA/INDEX.HTM

Constance Whippman, 33 Dunmore Road, London SW20 8TN; telephone: 44-208-946-8175; e-mail: WHIPPMAN@JEWSLV.ORG

Dvinsker Progressive Verein, 223 North Bisel Street, Chicago, Illinois

Herder Institute Marburg, Gisionenweg 5–7, D-35037 Marburg, Germany; telephone: 49-6421-184-0; fax: 49-6421-180-139; e-mail: AUMANN@MAILER.UNI-MARBURG.DE; website: WWW.UNI-MARBURG.DE./HERDER-INSTITUT/ENGLISH/ALLGEMEIN/INFO.HTML

Jewish Museum, 88 Hatfield Street, Gardens, Cape Town, South Africa; telephone: 27-2721-465-1546; fax: 27-2721-465-0284; e-mail: INFO@SAJEWISHMUSEUM.CO.ZA; website: WWW.SAJEWISHMUSEUM.CO.ZA

Jewish National and University Library, Givat Ram Campus, Hebrew University, P.O.Box 503, Jerusalem 91004; telephone: 972-2-566-0351; website: JNUL.HUJI.AC.IL

Kaplan Center, University of Cape Town, Private Baf, Rondebosch 7701, Cape Town, South Africa; Jewish Studies Library: telephone: 72-21-650-3779; fax: 27-21-650-3062; e-mail: VERONICA@UCTLIB.UCT.AC.ZA; website: WWW.UCT.AC.ZA/DEPTS/KAPLAN

Kibbutz Shfayim, Co-ordinate visits with archivists at 972-9-959-6532 or Association of Latvian & Estonian Jews in Israel 972-3-686-9695

Latvian Archive of the Registry Department, 24 Kalku Street, Riga, Latvia

Latvian State Historical Archives, Slokas iela 16, Riga LV-1007; mail requests to Ms. Irina Veinberga, e-mail: IRINWEIN@LATNET.LV

Mount Hebrew Cemetery, Flushing, New York; telephone: (718) 939-9405

National Archives of Sweden (*Riksarkivet*), Fyrverkarbacken 13-17, postal address: Fack, 100 26 Stockholm, Sweden

Professor Ruvin Ferber, Center for Judaic Studies, University of Latvia, 19 Rainis Blvd., Riga LV-1586; telephone: 371-7-615-703; fax: 371-7-820-113; e-mail: FERBER@JEWSLV.ORG

Rezekne Registry Office, Darza Street 37, Rezekne

Rosedale Cemetery, 6300 Hamilton Avenue, Baltimore, Maryland

United States Holocaust Memorial Museum, 100 Raoul Wallenberg Place SW, Washington, D.C. 20024; telephone: (202) 488-0400; website: WWW.USHMM.ORG

United States National Archives and Record Administration, Archives II, 8601 Adelphi Road, College Park, Maryland; telephone: (301) 713-6800

Yad Vashem, Har Hazikaron, P.O. Box 3477, Jerusalem 91034; telephone: 2-675-1611; fax: 2-643-3511; e-mail: ARCHIVES@YADVASHEM.ORG.IL; website: WWW.YADVASHEM.ORG.IL

YIVO Institute for Jewish Research, Center for Jewish History, 15 West 16th Street, New York, New York

Bibliography

"Additional Latvian Microfilms," *AVOTAYNU* 14, no. 2 (Summer 1998): 24.

Album Academicum Universitatis Tartuensis 1889–1919. Tartu, Estonia: Eesti NSV Ministrite Nõukogu Juures asuv Arhiivide Peavalitsus, 1986.

Anders, Edward and Juris Dubrovskis. *Jews in Liepaja, Latvia 1941–45; A Memorial Book*. Burlingame, CA: Anders Press, 2001.

Beare, Arlene. *A Guide to Jewish Genealogy in Latvia and Estonia*, 2001. Published by the Jewish Genealogy Society of Great Britain.

Bobe, Mendel et al. eds. *The Jews in Latvia*. Tel Aviv: Association of Latvian and Estonian Jews in Israel, 1971. This is probably the most comprehensive English-language work on the subject.

Contributing Editor (Latvia), *AVOTAYNU*, 11, no. 3 (Fall 1995). Reports Jewish vital records in Latvian State Archives.

Daugavpils: History of the Jewish Community. [Russian] Published by the Jewish Community of Daugavpils, 1999.

Feigmanis, Aleksandrs. "Jewish Vital Statistics Records in the Latvian Archives." *AVOTAYNU* 10, no. 1 (Spring 1994): 15–16.

———. "Material from the 1897 All-Empire Russian Census Held by the State Historical Archives of Latvia." *AVOTAYNU* 11, no. 1 (Spring 1995): 15–16.

Flior, Yudel. *Dvinsk: The Rise and Decline of a Town.* [Hebrew; English translation by Bernard Sachs] Johannesburg: Dial, 1965.

Freedman, Chaim. "*Prenumeranten* as a Source for the Jewish Genealogist." *AVOTAYNU* 10, no. 2 (Summer 1994), reports that *Sefer Tzioni* (Vilna, 1874) by Aharon Zelig, rabbi of Lutzin, lists nearly all Jewish males of Lutzin at this time.

Getz, Mike. "Dvinsk, Genealogy and Post-Holocaust Questions." *AVOTAYNU* 8, no. 4 (Winter 1992).

Grimsted, Patricia K. *Archives and Manuscript Repositories in the USSR: Estonia, Latvia, Lithuania and Belorussia.* (Lawrenceville, NJ: Princeton University Press, 1881.

Hundert, Gerson and David Bacon. *The Jews in Poland and Russia: Bibliographical Essays.* Bloomington: Indiana University Press, 1984. The chapter entitled "Local histories: A Bibliographical Gazetteer," lists books on the history of Jews in Latvian towns.

Lande, Peter. "Germany's Finds from Eastern Europe: A Follow-up." *AVOTAYNU* 9, no. 3 (Fall 1993).

Levin, Dov, ed. *Pinkas Hakehilot Latvia and Estonia* (Encyclopedia of Jewish Communities of Latvia and Estonia). [Hebrew] Jerusalem: Yad Vashem, 1988.

"Maps of the Empires of 19th-Century Europe." *AVOTAYNU* 8, no. 4 (Winter 1992): 63.

Mendelsohn, Ezra. *The Jews of East Central Europe Between the World Wars.* Bloomington: Indiana University Press, 1983.

Ovchinsky, Levi ben Duber Yona. *Toldot Hayehudim Bekurland (1561–1923)* (The story of the Jews in Kurland 1561-1923). [Yiddish] Riga: L. Remigolski, 1928. Mentions 47 communities; includes many names of rabbis.

Petrovsky, Yohanan. "Newly Discovered Pinkassim of the Harkavy Collection." *AVOTAYNU* 12, no. 2 (Summer 1996): 32–33. Includes notation of *pinkas* of the *chevra kadisha* of Milau, Courland (now Jelgava, Latvia), 1779–1843.

"Records from Latvia in the LDS Collection Include Jewish Information." *AVOTAYNU* 14, no. 1 (Spring 1998): 23–24.

Schneider, Gertrude. *Muted Voices: Jewish Survivors of Latvia Remember.* New York: Philosophical Library, 1987. Record of life under the Nazis.

Shadevich, Yakov. "New Archival Finds from Lithuania," *AVOTAYNU* 11, no. 2 (Summer 1995). Includes Latvia.

Sorkin, Sidney. *Bridges to an American City: Guide to Chicago Landsmanschaften 1870–1990.* New York: Peter Lang, 1993.

Soyer, Daniel. *Jewish Immigrant Associations and American Identity in New York 1880–1939.* Cambridge, MA: Harvard University, 1997.

Steimanis, Josifs. *History of Latvian Jews, East European Monographs.* New York: Columbia University, 2002. Includes considerable information on Soviet and German occupations.

Valdin, Anton. "Little-Known Sources of Russian-Jewish Data." *AVOTAYNU* 9, no. 1 (Spring 1993).

Valdin, Anton. "Report on Ukrainian and Latvian Archives." *AVOTAYNU* 9, no. 3 (Fall 1993).

Yahadut Latvia. [Hebrew] Tel Aviv, 1953. First post-war attempt to preserve history of Latvian Jewry. Includes members of pre-war Jewish organizations. Biographic material and photographs of rabbis provided.

Zeligman, Yisrael. *Megilat Yuchsin.* A pre-war publication, this includes families in the Latgale region and several towns in Vitebsk guberniya.

Notes

1. Bobe, Mendel, *The Jews in Latvia*: 21.
2. Bobe: 24.
3. Amir, Moshe and Bobe, Mendel, *The Jews in Latvia*: 263
4. "Records from Latvia in LDS Collection Include Jewish Information,": 23–24.
5. "Additional Latvian Microfilms," p. 24.

Libya

by Vivienne R. Roumani-Denn

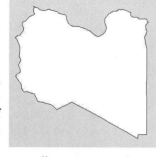

At one time, Libya was part of the Ottoman Empire. Read the chapter entitled OTTOMAN EMPIRE *before starting this section—Ed.*

Until the 20th century, the territory of modern-day Libya consisted of three distinct regions that shared historical traditions with neighboring countries: Cyrenaica, allied with Egypt and the Arab world to the east; Tripolitania, associated with the Maghreb (Algeria, Morocco and Tunisia) to the west; and Fazzan, with ties to Islamic Africa (Chad and Niger) to the south. From antiquity until well after Libya became a united, independent kingdom with federal structure in 1951, these three regions maintained unique characteristics that reflected their separate historical development and cultural traditions. In 1969, the monarchy was overthrown in a military coup that installed Muammar Qaddafi, who still heads the military dictatorship that rules Libya today. United States citizens are forbidden to travel to Libya, and Jews of any nationality are unwelcome. Records of the Jewish community are unavailable. Undocumented reports note that the birth records of the Jewish community in Tripoli were lost in a fire some time after Qaddafi's coup.

Jews resided in Libya since before the third century B.C.E.—at various times under Greek, Roman, Arab, Ottoman, Italian (1911–43) and British rule. Some were descendants of Spanish Jews expelled from Spain in 1492. Approximately 21,000 Jews lived in the country in 1933, the majority of them in Tripoli. Some Jewish families of Tripoli maintained close contact with the Jewish community of Livorno (Leghorn), Italy.

A series of pogroms occurred during the British occupation after World War II. Emigration was illegal at that time, but more than 3,000 Jews managed to leave, many of whom went to Israel. More than 30,000 Jews left when the British permitted emigration in 1949. Nearly all of the remaining 500 Jews were expelled following Qaddafi's coup in 1969. Today the largest communities of former Libyan Jews and their descendants are in Italy and Israel; Israel has an estimated 100,000 Jews of Libyan descent. Some Jews who emigrated to Israel adopted new surnames. The largest communities of Jews of Libyan descent in Italy are in Rome and Milan, while the major communities in Israel are in Netanya, Ashkelon and the Dalton *moshav*. Israel has approximately 18 *moshavim* of Libyan descent.

A few organizations of Libyan Jews in Israel meet regularly. These include Yagdil Torah, Yehudei Benghazi, Or Shalom, World Organization of Libyan Jews and Merkas Moreshet Yehudim Yetzei Luv.

Genealogical Sources

Following emigration, the Jews of Libya who left did not build an organization or develop an organized leadership. The only communal organizations are synagogues. These synagogues can be excellent sources of family names and histories. The American Sephardi Federation[*] website, WWW.ASFONLINE.ORG, lists synagogues known to follow the Libyan *minhag* (tradition of prayer).

Archives of some international organizations and institutions also should be consulted; several institutions sent emissaries to Libya to help financially and educationally, and they have records specific to Libya. Records of the following organizations may be useful: Alliance Israelite Universelle,[*] which provided instruction to the Jews of Libya; American Jewish Joint Distribution Committee,[*] which provided support during the Aliyah of 1948–51; American Sephardi Federation,[*] which has been collecting histories and family trees of Jews from Arab countries; U.S. Library of Congress,[*] which has audio tapes of interviews conducted in 1998 in Italian, Arabic and Hebrew with Jews from Libya residing in Israel (the interviews are listed in the library catalogue under "The Last Jews of Libya"). A copy of the tapes also is catalogued at the Avraham Hartman Institute of Contemporary Jewry at the Hebrew University of Jerusalem.[*] The Ben Zvi Institute[*] in Jerusalem is a center for research and study of Sephardic and Oriental Jewry and holds items pertaining to Libya.

Few publications on or by the Jews of Libya exist. *Ada*, a newsletter published in Israel, is dedicated to the Jews of Libya. The articles are generally in Hebrew, with some proverbs and stories in their original Judeo-Arabic. The contributors are all Jews of Libyan descent. The editor, Pedatzur Benattia, can be reached at Or Shalom.[*] A bibliography on the Jews of North Africa, by Robert Attal, has references to publications on the Jews of Libya that contain family names (see Bibliography below).

Some publications and websites dedicated to Sephardi (Mediterranean and Middle Eastern Jewish) genealogy include an occasional mention of Jewish family names in Libya—but only one unpublished source, a document by Lillo Arbib, president of the Jewish community of Tripoli in 1948, is specifically dedicated to the genealogy of the Libyan-Jewish community. There are future plans to post the full translated text, which includes a list of names with origins and meanings, to the website of the American Sephardi Federation at WWW. ASFONLINE.ORG. Arbib writes in his introduction:

> For the most part Jews did not have a last name, and their heritage was always indicated by their proper name plus the paternal name. Eventually they added "surnames," which, in time, became their true last names. The Italian colonial government, from about 1912, tried to put an end to the anagraphic (i.e., recorded) paternal name, and forced each Jewish family to register its name with the surname that the family gave itself. Note that in my alphabetical listing, families

Interior of a synagogue in Tripoli circa 1965

bearing the same last name [may] have no familial ties to each other.

Many Jewish surnames from Libya are derived from the locations where the families lived (e.g., Arhibi, Bengohar, Castili, Fusati, Gariani, Gramon [from Zerman], Houri, Megidish, Nafusi, Naluti, Sarsucki, Serussi, Zitruk). Guetta is named for a tribe from Garian. Arbib is derived from the word *urbib* (to proliferate).

Different spellings may be used for the same family name, since some names have passed through several languages, using different alphabets, and transliterations are imperfect, (e.g., Roumani is equivalent to Romani and Romano in Hebrew, and all three spellings are used).

Libyan family names can be searched in Jewish encyclopedias under both the family name and the city of residence. For example, the names Roumani, Tesjiba, Youeli, Hakmon, Schima, Touajir and Bedoussa are found under the city Benghazi in *The Jewish Encyclopedia*.

The first name is another useful search vehicle. First names tend to be repeated in families in many cultures, but the Sephardim tend to name a child after a living grandparent, thus allowing for more frequent repetitions of first names within a family than in the Ashkenazi Jewish tradition.

Ultimately, among this generally open, warm, and friendly community with great historical memory, personal contact can be a fruitful exercise in tracing family histories.

It is important to check general genealogical databases and websites, including those that cover the Holocaust, since some Jews of Libya were sent to Bergen-Belsen and Innsbruck. Most of these eventually returned to Libya, weak and diseased, but alive (see HOLOCAUST).

The author maintains a website dedicated to the Jews of Libya with links to family sites at SUNSITE.BERKELEY.EDU/ JEWSOFLIBYA. This may serve as a starting point for research-ing family names and generating discussion with the Jews of Libya and their descendants.

Internet Resources

Jews of Libya: SUNSITE.BERKELEY.EDU/JEWSOFLIBYA.

Addresses

Alliance Israelite Universelle, 45 rue la Bruyere, 75009 Paris, France; website: WWW.AIU.ORG

American Jewish Joint Distribution Committee, 711 Third Avenue, New York, NY 10017; website: WWW.JDC.ORG

American Sephardi Federation, 15 West 16th Street, New York, NY 10011; telephone: (212) 294-8350, e-mail: ASFRECEPTIONIST@ASF. CJH.ORG; website: WWW.ASFONLINE.ORG.

Avraham Hartman Institute of Contemporary Jewry, The Hebrew University of Jerusalem, Mt. Scopus, Jerusalem 91905.

Ben Zvi Institute, P.O. Box 7660, Rehavia, Jerusalem 91076; telephone: 972-02-539-8833; website: SITES.HUJI.AC.IL/YBZ

Or Shalom, P.O. Box 297, Bat Yam, Israel. Editor Pedatzur Benattia can be reached through e-mail at PEDIB@YAHOO.COM.

U.S. Library of Congress, 101 Independence Avenue SE, Washington, D.C. 20540; telephone: (202) 707-5000; website: WWW.LOC.GOV.

Bibliography

Arbib, Lillo. *Nosce te ipsum (Know thyself)* (Names of the Jews of Libya). Trans. by Vivienne Roumani-Denn. Undated.

Attal, Robert. *Les Juifs d'Afrique du Nord: Bibliopgrahie* (Jews of North Africa, a bibliography). [French] Jerusalem: Ben Zvi Institute, 1993.

Benattia, Pedi, ed. *Ada* [Hebrew] Or Shalom, P.O. Box 297, Bat Yam, Israel.

The Jewish Encyclopedia. London: Funk & Wagnalls Company, 1901-06, vol. 3.

Note

Encyclopedia Judaica, vol. II, 1972: 202.

Lithuania

by Harold Rhode

Read the chapter RUSSIAN EMPIRE *before reading this section. Many facts and definitions relevant to Lithuanian research are not repeated here. Read also the section on JRI-Poland (see* JEWISHGEN*). Some portions of contemporary Lithuania once belonged to Poland and are included in that group's activities. Consult also the section on Lithuania in Routes to Roots, Miriam Weiner's* Eastern European Database, *at* WWW.ROUTESTOROOTS.ORG—Ed.

Jewish genealogists who hear that their family was "Litvak" often assume that their ancestors lived on the territory of modern day Lithuania. This is not necessarily true. Because of frequent border changes, not all people whose Jewish ancestors considered themselves Litvaks came from the small area that is modern Lithuania. Lithuania was once much larger.

Litvak is a Yiddish term for the Jewish culture that developed in the Grand Duchy of Lithuania after increasing numbers of Jews moved into that region during the 16th and 17th centuries. The Duchy encompassed much of the territory of contemporary Belarus, Lithuania, Poland and Ukraine. (ref map on pg. 673 in H. H. Ben-Sason) In 1529, the Lithuanian Grand Duchy signed the Treaty of Lublin that created the Polish-Lithuanian Commonwealth. Over the next few centuries, the Grand Duchy of Lithuania shrunk in size until the territory controlled by the Lithuanians was only slightly larger than contemporary Lithuania. It remained under Polish rule until the three partitions of Poland in the late 18th century. By 1795, most of this area had fallen to the Russian Empire, where it remained until the end of World War I. Lithuania was an independent state between the two world wars, but in 1939 it was reconquered by the Soviet Russians, who ruled until the dissolution of the USSR in 1990.

This chapter discusses genealogical resources available for individuals whose forebears resided in a community that is part of contemporary Lithuania.

Litvak Geography

During the 19th century, the Russian *guberniyas* of Kovno and Vilna constituted the heartland of Litvak Jewry. *Guberniyas* were abolished after the 1917 Russian Revolution. Today's Lithuania consists of the territory that was Kovno *guberniya,* a large part of the former Vilna *guberniya* and a small portion of what was Suwalki *guberniya* (southwestern Lithuania).

Initially the czarist Russian government created two entities from the Grand Duchy of Lithuania, Vilna and Slonim *guberniyas*. In 1797, Vilna and Slonim *guberniyas* were consolidated into one entity called Lithuania *guberniya*. In 1801, Lithuania *guberniya* was split into Vilna and Grodno *guberniyas*. Kovno *guberniya* was created in 1842. In 1843, Braslav *uyezd* (later called Novo-Alexandrvosk *uyezd* and today named Zarasai district) became part of Kovno *guberniya*.

After 1842, Vilna *guberniya* was left with seven *uyezds*. As a result of post-World War II border changes, the eastern and southern portion of 19th-century Vilna *guberniya* is now in Belarus. Ceded to Belarus were the districts of Disna, Oshmyany and Vileika, most of Lida district, a considerable portion of Svenciany district and a small portion of Zarasai district.

The Jewish population of Lithuania exploded during the 19th century. Subsequently, many Litvak Jews emigrated to other parts of the Russian Empire, especially to the newly industrialized cities of eastern Poland and to Warsaw. From the mid-19th century, the territory of modern-day Latvia was a favored destination, as well. Others migrated southward to Ukraine, specifically to Odessa. By the late 19th century, large numbers of Litvaks had migrated westward, primarily to the United States. Some went to Great Britain, while still others emigrated to South Africa, where the Jewry ended up being more than 90 percent Litvak.

Beginnings of Litvak Jewry

The first Jews who settled in the Lithuanian Kingdom were traders from southeast Europe who came around the 12th century. Others apparently fled Western Europe because of the Crusades and the pogroms associated with the Black Death. When the Lithuanian Grand Duke Gediminas conquered Volynhia and the area later known as Galicia in the 14th century, he found Jews already settled there. Some moved northward and settled Brisk (today, Brest), Grodno and today's Lithuania.

Most of the original Jewish settlers were traders, and most of the towns established in the Litvak heartland were populated largely by Jews. The non-Jews, mostly Lithuanians, Belarussians, Latvians, Ukrainians and Poles, were farmers who depended on Jews to provide items they did not produce on the land. Jews were largely merchants and artisans. They also became middlemen representing the landed gentry.

The once vibrant Jewish community of Lithuania ceased to exist with the Nazi German invasion during the summer of 1941. Helped by many more-than-eager Lithuanian Christians, almost all Lithuanian Jews had been murdered by the end of the year. The exceptions were the Jews held in the ghettos of Kovno, Siaulaia, Suwalki and Vilna, as well as in some smaller ghettos. Some escaped into Russia proper. The usually accepted percentage of Jews murdered in Lithuania is 94 percent.

Genealogical Resources

Many resources exist for genealogists whose ancestors lived on the territory of modern Lithuania. Because of the extensive 19th and 20th century migration of Litvak Jewry, valuable genealogical information may be found both within and outside of Lithuania. Sources within Lithuania include governmental archives, Jewish cemeteries, the few remaining Jewish residents and the Jewish Museum of Vilnius.* Outside Lithuania, information may be found in such places as the YIVO Institute for Jewish Research* in New York (see YIVO), the Organization of Lithuanian Jews in Israel,* the LDS (Mormon) Family History Library (see LDS) and increasingly on the Internet, especially via LitvakSIG* and its All-Lithuania Database. Also on the Internet, JRI-Poland (see SIGS) is becoming an important source of information about Litvaks who migrated to Poland.

Genealogical Resources in Lithuania

Archival Sources

Prior to the fall of the Soviet Union and the invention of the Internet, Litvak genealogical research was difficult. Researchers were forced to rely on Western resources, mostly vital, census, immigration and naturalization records, and materials available in Western libraries. The resources of the Soviet Union were closed, and genealogists knew little about what documentary evidence actually existed. Most Jewish genealogists believed that, because of the upheavals of World Wars I and II and the Russian Revolution, documentary evidence that had once existed did not survive.

With the dissolution of the Soviet Union and the opening of its archives, researchers discovered that vast numbers of vital, census and communal records actually had survived. Considerable archival material exists for genealogists with roots in modern Lithuania, largely in the state historical archives in the cities of Vilnius (the former Vilna) and in Kaunas (the former Kovno). Moreover, the archives of the newly independent states of Lithuania and Latvia were eager to earn money by supplying excellent genealogical information. Today genealogists may access this archival material by visiting Lithuania and doing onsite research in friendly, well-organized facilities; by writing to the archives for information; by hiring a private researcher; by using the LDS (Mormon) family history centers and by accessing data posted by LitvakSIG (see discussion below) on the Internet.

Archival Documents

The State Historical Archives* in Vilnius, the capital of Lithuania, has one of the largest-known Jewish archival collections in the former Soviet Union. Birth, marriage, death and divorce records are held in two archives. Records from the 1700s until the establishment of the Lithuanian Republic in 1919 are held in the State Historical Archives. Most Jewish vital statistics registers seem to have survived the upheavals of World War I; the wars among the Poles, Lithuanians and communists after World War I; and World War II.

In 1992, all Lithuanian communities were required to send their czarist-period vital records to the Lithuanian State Historical Archives.* Most Jewish records (but not all) were transferred at that time. In January 2002, the Lithuanian Central Civil Register Archives* transferred all pre-1940 vital records to the Lithuanian State Historical Archives.*

Most *reviskie skazki* registers (see RUSSIAN EMPIRE) are kept in the State Historical Archives in Vilnius,* but the Kaunas Archives* has some as well. These registers were compiled for Kovna and Vilna *guberniyas* and other *guberniyas* of the Russian Empire, but were not created for the Kingdom of Poland, an area that included Suwalki *guberniya*. As a result, no revision or family lists exist for this region.

Revision and family lists originally were kept in the capital cities of the *guberniyas* where they were created. For the area of contemporary Lithuania, most have been transferred to the Lithuanian State Historical Archives* in Vilnius. Here are revision lists for areas that were part of Kovna and Vilna *guberniyas* during czarist times. This includes the four eastern *uyezds* (districts) of Vilna *guberniya*—Disna, Lida, Oshamny and Vileyka—that today are part of western Belarus. Also in Vilnius are revision lists for the eastern portion of Novo-Alexandrovsk (Zarasai) *uyezd*, part of Kovna *guberniya* during czarist rule, but today the northwestern section of Belarus.

Communal Documents

The Vilnius and Kaunas archives both hold a vast array of communal documents valuable to Jewish genealogists. They include lists of taxes paid by the Jews, notably the candle and box taxes (see RUSSIAN EMPIRE). Other materials in these archives include abstracts of births and deaths for many communities as well as lists of merchants, artisans and craftsmen; draftees; voters from various synagogues who voted to elect regional rabbis; voters for various Dumas (parliaments); electors of representatives to local municipalities; postal bank records; internal and foreign passports issued; owners of real estate; town dwellers; Jewish farmers; and Jewish taxpayers.

The Kaunas Archives* holds a large number of as-yet-uncatalogued Jewish wills that provide considerable genealogical and financial information, not only about the deceased and his relatives, but also about the executors of the wills. This archive also holds an extremely large collection of police and court records, but because they are unindexed, it is extremely difficult to locate specific records without the date, location and details of an occurrence.

Resources in the Jewish Museum* in Vilnius are related almost entirely to the Holocaust; it also has a collection of photographs of former synagogues.

Few, if any, cemetery records exist in Lithuania. It is mainly gravestones that still exist and are legible that have genealogical value (see CEMETERIES).

Genealogical Resources Outside Lithuania

LitvakSIG

LitvakSIG, an Internet-based special interest group at www.JEWISHGEN.ORG/LITVAK offers a variety of resources to researchers of Jewish families from Lithuania. Begun in 1997, LitvakSIG has focused much of its energy on creating the "All Litvak Database" which includes a database with hundreds of thousands of entries culled from various archival sources, newspapers, and others. A detailed description is at WWW.JEWISHGEN.ORG/LITVAK/ALL.HTM. To search the actual da-

Interior of the Old Synagogue in Vilnius at the beginning of the 20th century.

tabase, go to WWW.JEWISHGEN.ORG/LITVAK/SEARCHALD.HTM. The site includes an online journal WWW.JEWISHGEN.ORG/LITVAK/JOURNAL.HTM and an extensive bibliography of books, articles, and newspapers, videos and periodicals at WWW.JEWISHGEN.ORG/LITVAK/PUBLICATIONS.HTM.

JewishGen also has a large number of additional databases which contain data about Litvaks living both in contemporary Lithuania and in Latvia, Belarus and Poland. See WWW.JEWISHGEN.ORG/DATABASES for a continually updated list of these databases. For a collection of pictures from various Lithuanian towns where Jews lived, see WWW.JEWISHGEN.ORG/LITVAK/PIX.HTM.

Because new documents are continually being discovered in both the Vilnius and Kaunas archives, it is important to revisit periodically WWW.JEWISHGEN.ORG/LITVAK/KAUNASIX.HTM for updates on the Kaunas Archives. For general information about the Lithuanian State Historical Archives,* see www.JEWISHGEN.ORG/LITVAK/FAQS.HTM.

A major problem facing Jewish genealogists is that place names that our ancestors transmitted to their descendants often are impossible to find on maps. This happens because towns were known by different names in the various languages spoken in the area. One town might have a Belarussian,

Lithuanian, Polish, Russian and/or Yiddish name. All of these names are valid, and they all appear in different forms, depending on the language of the document and the time period in question. For those doing Lithuanian research, one of the best ways to navigate this maze is to visit WWW.JEWISHGEN.ORG/LITVAK//SHTETLS/LITHUANIA.HTM on the web, search for and then enter the name of the shtetl spelled as you heard it. Most often you will obtain excellent information on the town for which you are searching. If this does not work, check *Where Once We Walked,* then return to this Internet site for further information about the town. If you are not sure about the name of your *shtetl* but know the name of a nearby town, enter that town name at this website, scroll down, and see if your town is listed in the area. Another approach would be to look up the nearby town in *Where Once We Walked* revised edition, locate its coordinates, and then look up those coordinates in the *WOWW Companion* section which supplies the names of all towns in that vicinity.

YIVO Institute for Jewish Research

YIVO, founded in Vilna in the 1920s, has considerable material in its New York City quarters for researching roots in Lithuania. A large collection of photographs from pre-World War II Lithuania is among the holdings. A good description of the content of YIVO's Lithuanian communities of the interwar period can be found at WWW.JEWISHGEN.ORG/LITVAK/YIVO/HTM..

Association of Lithuanian Jews in Israel

The Association of Lithuanian Jews in Israel,* is an active group that publishes books, organizes lectures and conferences, and helps Jews from Lithuania resettle in Israel. The association has a large archival collection with information and pictures about all aspects of Jewish life in Lithuania. Researchers can use and copy much of this material by visiting the association headquarters in Tel Aviv.

Addresses

Association of Lithuanian Jews in Israel, Derek Ha-Melekh 1, Tel Aviv, telephone: 03-696-4812
Vilna Gaon Jewish State Museum, 12 Pamenkalnios, Vilnius 2001
Lithuanian Central Civil Register Archives, Kalinausko 21, Vilnius 2600
Kaunas Regional Archives, Maironio 28a, Kaunas 3000
Lithuanian State Historical Archives, Gerosios Vilties 10, Vilnius 2009
YIVO Institute for Jewish Research, Center for Jewish History 15 West 16th Street, New York, NY 10011

Bibliography

The most extensive bibliography for Litvak genealogy is on the web at WWW.JEWISHGEN.ORG/LITVAK/PUBLICATIONS.HTM.

The best all-inclusive work about Lithuanian Jewry is Levin, Dov. *Pinkas Hakehillot–Lita.* Jerusalem: Yad Vashem, 1996 (in Hebrew). This book is an encyclopedia of Jewish life in Lithuania from its beginnings until today. After a general description, Levin provides a history of each Jewish community, including the names of many famous individuals.

Eliach, Yaffa. *There Once Was a World: A 900-Year Chronicle of the Shtetl of Eishyshok*. Boston: Little Brown, 1998.

Faitelson, Alex. *Heroism & Bravery in Lithuania, 1941–1945*. Jerusalem: Gefen, 1996.

Fighting Back: Lithuanian Jewry's Armed Resistance to the Holocaust 1941–1945, by Dov Levin with Foreword by Yehuda Bauer. New York, London: Holmes and Meier, 1985, 298 pages; re-issued as a paperback by Holmes and Meier in 1997

Friedlander, Alex. "Jewish Vital Statistic Records in Lithuanian Archives." *AVOTAYNU*, Vol. VI, no. 4 (Winter 1990): 4B12.

Greenbaum, Masha. *The Jews of Lithuania: A History of a Remarkable Community, 1316–1945*. Jerusalem: Gefen, 1995.

Greenblatt, Ada. "Lithuanian Central Civil Register Archives Revisited." *AVOTAYNU*, Vol. XIV, no. 1 (Spring 1998): 22.

Issroff, Saul and Rose Lerer Cohen. *The Holocaust in Lithuania 1941–1945: A Book of Remembrance*. 2002.

Levin, Dov, ed. *The Litvaks*. Jerusalem: Yad Vashem, 2001.

Levin, Dov. *Pinkas Hakehillot: Lita* (Encyclopedia of Jewish Lithuanian Communities from Their Foundation until after the Holocaust), Jerusalem: Yad Vashem, 1996.

Lita [Yiddish], Vol. 1 edited by Mendel Sudarski et. al., New York: Jewish Lithuanian Cultural Society, 1951. Vol 2 edited by Ch. Leikowicz. Tel Aviv, Israel: Peretz Publishing, 1965.

Margol, Howard and Harold Rhode. "Kaunas Archives." *AVOTAYNU*, Vol. XIII, no. 3 (Fall 1997): 25.

Margol, Howard. "Revelations and New Discoveries in the Vilnius Civil Registry Office." *AVOTAYNU*, Vol. XIV, no. 1 (Spring 1998): 21.

Oshry, Rabbi Ephraim. *The Annihilation of Lithuanian Jewry*. Brooklyn, NY: Judaica Press, 1995.

Rhode, Harold and Sallyann Amdur Sack, eds. *Jewish Vital Records, Revision Lists and Other Jewish Holdings in the Lithuanian Archives*. Teaneck, N.J.: Avotaynu, 1996.

Rhode, Harold. "Jewish Revision Lists in Lithuanian Archives." *AVOTAYNU*, Vol. XIII, no. 3 (Fall 1997): 23.

Rudashevski, Yitskhok. *The Diary of the Vilna Ghetto, June 1941–April 1943*. Tel Aviv, Israel: Ghetto Fighters' House, 1973, 192 pages, illustrations.

Schoenburg, Nancy and Stuart Schoenburg. *Lithuanian Jewish Communities*. New York and London: Garland, 1991. Reprinted by Jason Aronson, Northvale, NJ/London

Shadevich, Yakov. "New Archival Finds from Lithuania," *AVOTAYNU*, Vol. XI, no. 2 (Summer 1995): 10–13.

Tautvaisaite, Laima. "Archival Sources in the Lithuanian State Historical Archives." *AVOTAYNU*, Vol. XI, no. 3 (Fall 1995): 3–7.

The Jewish State Museum, Vilnius: The Jewish State Museum, 1996.

Vilniaus Getas (Vilnius Ghetto), Lists of Prisoners, Vols. 1–2. Vilnius: Jewish State Museum of Lithuania, 1996.

Yahudat Lita:

Vol. 1: *Jews of Lithuania to 1918*, editors: N. Goren, L. Garfunkel, et. al. Tel Aviv: Am Hasafer, 1959

Vol. 2: *1918–1941*, editors: R. Hasman, D. Lipec et. al. Tel Aviv: The Association of Lithuanian Jews in Israel, 1972

Vol. 3: *A: People B: Places*, Tel Aviv: Association of Lithuanian Jews in Israel, 1967

Vol. 4: *The Holocaust: 1941–1945*, edited by Leib Garfunkel. Tel Aviv, 1984.

Mexico

by Alejandro Rubinstein

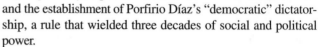

H ome to 100 million inhabitants, including 42,000 Jews, Mexico is a relatively new democracy. Mexico is a country where ethnic origins do not fuse. The child of native Mexican parents whose name or surname does not sound "right" or local will permanently and hopelessly be considered an alien, a stranger, a foreigner. The status of foreigner applies not only to Americans, French, Germans, or Japanese; the Otomi, Tarahumara, Yaqui and Zapoteca peoples also are viewed as foreign. Poverty is the prevailing status, and a good economic situation seldom is enjoyed. In Mexico, with its class-conscious reality, the rich employ the middle class and both are served by the lower classes. This is a country where the yoke of the Spanish conquest is still noticeable.

The Jewish presence in Mexico dates back to the early 16th century, to the period known as "The Colony." In search of a haven following the edict of expulsion proclaimed by Queen Isabella of Castille in 1492, many Jews embarked for the land that later came to be known as America, first on the four voyages made by Columbus and later in the ships of many other travelers.

Their happiness did not last long. The Tribunal of the Holy Inquisition was instituted in Mexico in 1571 as the second of three persecution sites in Latin America.[1] Although the Jews of that time sought to change their life and, of course, their religion, the Church inflicted abuse, insults and vexations that included torture, "relaxation" (public humiliation) and imposing the use of clothing and titles of doubtful honorability such as the *sambenito* (a sort of toga marked with an *X* for the unwilling Jew). They also inflicted the undignified name of "New Christian" that limited the bearer when searching for work, a home or a university that would accept him among the "Old Christians" whose faith was never questioned.

This somber period obliterated the incipient Jewish community that had settled in the area of the Spanish Empire then called the Viceroyalty of New Spain. What remains are the poignantly famous names of the Carvajal family and a handful of Jews who suffered in an exemplary manner the wave of hatred and aggression. Several works have been written on this subject, and it is important to state that some include lists of names, dates and different texts illustrating this black page in history. They are described in the works of Bocanegra and Toro.

Following the conquest of the Aztec people in 1525, the Colony was established in the area that later became Mexico. Until 1810, when Mexico declared its independence, there was hardly a Jewish presence there—perhaps an isolated investor, an unredeemed adventurer or a fugitive. The Jew, as part of a group, did not reach Mexico until the late 19th century, once independence had been instituted and the Republic of Mexico had undergone the convulsions of a newly born

country, including the monarchy imposed by Napoleon III and the establishment of Porfirio Díaz's "democratic" dictatorship, a rule that wielded three decades of social and political power.

Napoleon installed Maximilian of Habsburg in 1864; Benito Juarez executed him in 1867. Following Porfirio Diaz's 34-year rule, the revolution intended to establish a democratic system with a four-year president who could not be re-elected. Partido Revolucionario Institucional (PRI) ruled from its founding in 1929 until 2000. The four-year presidential term extended to six years in 1934, and from 1929 until 2000 every president had to be a member of the PRI.

Despite the ouster of Porfirio Diaz on May 31, 1911, the turmoil of the revolution did not succeed in eliminating strongholds on presidential power. Porfirio ruled for 34 years as a dictator, and the PRI, under various presidents, ruled as a "democratic dictatorship" for 71 years.

Modern Jewish Immigration to Mexico

The first modern Jewish immigration began in the 1890s, based on economic interest. A few American Jews came across Mexico's northern border to do business with the government. Most Jewish immigrants of this period came from France, Germany and Turkey, arriving on steamships at Veracruz and Tamaulipas.

In the great Jewish migration from Central and Eastern Europe at the turn of the 20th century, the United States, Argentina, Canada and even warm, exotic Cuba were the first choices in the Western Hemisphere. Mexico was not considered as an alternative. In Europe, Mexico was believed to be turbulent, as the monarchy had fallen, literally, under the fire of the republican army. They were ruled by a nabob with European tastes, surrounded by ministers and counselors with pompous French or French-sounding surnames. Nevertheless, some Jews reached Mexico, just as many others would later on, simply by accident or due to the exclusion of immigrants from their preferred destinations. Gradually, the families of Jacobo Granat, Levy, Scherer, Tron and others began settling in Mexico. This was not an easy task if one considers the great differences in lifestyles and occupations in their distant continent compared to the difficult conditions they had to confront in a Mexico taking its first steps in the advances of the Industrial Revolution.

Little by little, mispronouncing the Spanish language, but with a highly developed commercial and industrial spirit, the Jewish immigrants became patrons of dozens, and later hundreds, of Mexicans who began to view with "better eyes" these employers who dressed, spoke and ate differently.

The advent of the 20th century brought convulsions to many areas of the planet. Sephardic Jews from Egypt, Greece,

Interior of the Justo Sierra synagogue in Mexico City

Iraq, Lebanon, Morocco, Syria and Turkey, among other exotic places, began to view Mexico as a destination filled with opportunities, instead of just a port of call in their wandering. For this reason, the first organized Jewish community in Mexico originated from the Sephardic world. Ultimately, it became what in Mexico is called the *Shami* community, as most of its population came from Damascus, Syria. This community arose in the middle of the Mexican Revolution—and even today one can find tombstones in the graveyard in the old Mexico City area of Tacuba village inscribed with such epitaphs as "was executed in." A visit to this cemetery is a good way to remember the founders of the Jewish community in Mexico and also constitutes a history lesson, rich with romantic legends and interesting anecdotes.

The Mexican Revolution and the Russian Revolution occurred at virtually the same time, but their effects were completely different. The Mexican Revolution put the country on a path leading toward the possibility of political, social and economic change in an environment with a solid legal structure and good, open relations with other nations. Many Polish and Russian Jews on the other hand, living in an environment that had passed from a corrupt monarchy to a new proletarian corruption, with diminished income and facing physical danger, began to seek a way out.

Mexico became a beacon for many new immigrants during the 1920s and 1930s. It was becoming increasingly difficult to enter the United States; Canada was a cold-climate option, which some people welcomed—yet others let pass. Many Jews had heard of Mexico. They knew that some of their brethren had settled in Guadalajara, Monterrey, Puebla, Saltillo, Tampico, Torreón, Veracruz and Mexico City. They knew that in Mexico people did not speak English, as in the United States or Canada, that in Mexico the weather was gentler than in Havana, and that Mexico was almost virgin territory economically.

The work and efforts of a few to satisfy the needs of many permitted additional Jewish communities to organize. The most solid structure with the best human and technical resources was the Ashkenazi community, known as *La Kehilá Ashkenazí de México.*

Outside Mexico City, concentrations of Jews established themselves in the cities of Guadalajara and Monterrey. The activities of the Mexico City Jewish population included the door-to-door salesman selling ties and handkerchiefs, the established food and clothing businessman, and the small- and medium-scale manufacturer devoted mainly to textiles. There were also professionals—in medicine, law, accounting, civil engineering and dentistry. The first credit and mutual aid financial institutions were formed and operated regularly. Teachers from the old country transmitted their knowledge to children for whom there were no established institutions of Jewish education. The community grew and demanded services. The leaders of the first third of the 20th century created *chevrot kadisha* (burial societies), Jewish cemeteries, synagogues, *mikvah* (ritual baths), *Hilfs Farein* (societies to help the needy), *kashrut* (food services following Jewish dietary laws) and more.

The great Jewish immigration of the 1920s also reflected the support of the Mexican presidents of that period, sympathetic towards Jews and hopeful that their presence would eventually show—as it did—beneficial results for the country's economic development.

The rise to power of President Paul von Hindenburg in Germany and the fateful presence of Hitler also influenced Mexico to some degree. Germans were viewed an example to follow for their ideals of effort, national identity and unity. The Mexican answer to Hitler's "brown shirts" was the "golden shirts." This group vandalized Jewish homes and businesses, harassed Jews verbally and organized public demonstrations, blatantly showing their anti-Semitism during a period when this was an accepted fashion. None of these regretful acts, however, generated enough anxiety among the Jews, individually or as a group, to initiate a new exodus. Instead, they founded a social and welcoming club for immigrants known by its address in the center of Mexico City: Tacuba 15. There, solidarity committees and groups that provided aid and financial support were established in order to attract the largest possible number of European Jews in advance of World War II.

This task was not easy. The Mexican government implemented an immigration quota system based on country of origin. The pressure within and outside Mexico had accomplished its goal. Many people no longer could enter the country, or their admittance was delayed either because they lacked a local affidavit guaranteeing they had a means of support or the necessary connections that could speed up the procedures within the arbitrary network of influence and corruption.

Most Ashkenazic immigration to Mexico occurred during the 1920s and after World War II; most Sephardic immigration occurred primarily at the end of the 19th and beginning of the 20th century.

The Jewish community established an important Jewish school network that currently serves more than 85 percent of

Sample certificate of naturalization

the young Jewish population and includes Zionist and non-Zionist *yeshivot*; schools specializing in English, Hebrew and Yiddish; religious schools; schools for children from different Jewish communities (Maguen David, Monte Sinai or Sephardic—see below); schools that follow traditional methods or the Montessori system; and even includes the *Universidad Hebraica** for professional studies with a high Jewish content.

The Mexican-Jewish community established institutions such as the *Eishel* (assisted living for senior citizens), *OSE* (medical clinic), the *Museo Tuvie Maizel* (Holocaust museum), *Asociación Menorah* (support group for women with breast cancer), *Grupo Retorno* (support and solutions to alcohol and drug abuse problems), *Kadima* (support and rehabilitation for people with disabilities), and *Memoria y Tolerancia* (Tolerance Museum).

The current population of the entire Mexican-Jewish community barely reaches 42,000, yet it has dozens of beautiful, functioning synagogues and several *beit midrash* (religious study houses), groups providing non-formal Jewish studies in the Conservative, Orthodox and Modern Orthodox traditions. For more than 50 years, the community has brought together Jews from all origins and currents in its most popular institution, the *Centro Deportivo Israelita.** Every day, this sports club welcomes thousands of youngsters and adults who use its facilities for sports, cultural, social and entertainment activities.

In 1938, the Jewish community's national political organization was concentrated in the *Comité Central Israelita de Mexico.** This body functions as an assembly, where the presidents of each of the communities, according to origin and organizational tradition, convene and name a president to represent them on issues outside the community and with the country's local and federal authorities. Its communication arm is *Tribuna Israelita,** a body that sometimes acts as the Jewish community's official news agency and currently also analyzes the media and serves as the official spokesperson regarding any event. The community has also created, maintained and promoted social and Zionist youth organizations including *Bnei Akiva, Hanoar Hatzioni, Hashomer Hatzair, Scouts Israelitas* and *Macabi*, among others. As members of these organizations, youngsters receive Zionist and Jewish values according to their interests in a fun and healthy environment.

Many women's organizations provide a network of social services devoted to the welfare of children, schools, underprivileged families and Holocaust survivors. The efforts of Mexican-Jewish women can be seen in *Naamat, Wizo, Federación Femenina* and various committees of women from community centers, communities and schools.

Jewish Mexico maintains close ties with Israel. The local *Keren Hayesod** organizes large drives to raise funds for Israel. The Associations of Friends of various universities, including Bar Ilan, Hebrew University in Jerusalem and Ben Gurion University in the Negev, organize important cultural and scientific exchanges, together with the activities organized by the *Instituto Cultural Mexico Israel.**

Bet El Community is the largest Conservative organization, formed primarily by Ashkenazim in reaction to *Kehila Ashkenazi,* the Orthodox Ashkenazi organization. *Bet Israel* Community was founded primarily by members of Ashkenazi and American origin; in more recent times, it has moved in a more liberal direction, accepting members who are not Jewish in strictly *halachic* terms. The Ashkenazi Community of Mexico includes Orthodox Jews from Central Europe; the *Maguen David* Community serves Orthodox Jews from Aleppo, Syria, also called *halevi*. Members of the *Monte Sinai* Community are Orthodox Jews originally from Damascus, Syria, also known as *shami*; and the Sephardic Community includes Orthodox Jews from Spain, Italy, Greece and Turkey.

Genealogical Resources

The Jewish community has sought to preserve its history, which has been concentrated at the *Centro de Documentación e Investigación** (Documentation and Research Center) of the Ashkenazic community of Mexico (*Consejo Comunitario Ashkenazi**). There, one may find books, periodicals, travel documents, oral histories and many other elements of genealogical value. The Center holds books on Jewish history, literature and philosophy, and collections of publications such as yearbooks, schoolbooks, rabbinic treatises and magazines.

Most importantly, the Center possesses the largest and best documented inventory of foreign population registries, called *Registro Nacional e Extranjeros del Archivo General de la Nacion*. These registers were created under the direction of the *Secretaria de Gobernacion* (Interior Ministry). This ministry is responsible for all foreigners who live in Mexico, as permanent or nonpermanent residents or as immigrants. The registries cover the years 1888 to 1950 and include everyone—Jews and non-Jews. They are an official database of the *Archivio General de la Nacion** (General Archives of Mexico), which makes a copy available at the *Centro*, where it is the most easily accessible copy. The database includes arrival dates, complete name of immigrants and of the persons giving their affidavit, port of entry and other data belonging to 19 groups of countries or population concentrations. This is an invaluable genealogical resource.

The oral histories are a collection of interviews with pioneering immigrants, World War II refugees, Holocaust survivors, community activists and others. In addition to its excellent library, the center also has the largest Spanish-language collection in the Northern Hemisphere about Jews from Eastern Europe, Latin America and North America. A resource area includes encyclopedias in Yiddish, Hebrew, German and Spanish, dictionaries, lexicons, and geographical and historical atlases.

The center's newspaper archive includes yearbooks, bulletins, newspapers and magazines from Mexico and the rest of the world, written in Spanish, English, Yiddish and Hebrew.

The Documentation Center's historical archive receives and classifies valuable documents, including the record groups (called *fondos*) in Table 1.

Table 1. Holdings of Centro's Historical Archives

Record Group	Years
Fondo Ashkenazí	1928–85
Fondo Cámara Israelita de Industria y Comercio	1931–57
Fondo Consejo Mexicano de Mujeres Israelitas	1942–79
Fondo Bnei Brith	1950–69
Fondo Organizaciones Sionistas	1940–71
Fondo Comité Central Israelita	1938–91
Fondo Archivos Incorporados de Particulares (documents and photographs)	Various
Oral History Archive (testimonies)	Various

The Documentation Center is open to any historian, student or genealogist—but any consultation or service must be arranged by previous appointment and with proper identification. To use the library only, a valid identification is needed. For all other facilities and services, the researcher also must present his or her research project for approval.

The Center offers access to computerized databases—documenting 801 Polish refugees who stayed in the Hacienda de Santa Rosa, Guanajuato, during the years 1943–47; about Jewish businesses in Mexico in the years 1948, 1949 and 1950; and a census of the Mexican-Jewish community from 1949. The Center also possesses copies of minutes from meetings of the *Comité Central Israelita** for the years 1938–92.

The *Archivo General de la Nación,** located within what used to be the largest prison in Mexico City, is also the nation's largest resource for information about the Jewish presence in Mexico from the 16th through 19th centuries.

(For events later than the 19th century, the *Centro de Documentacion* is the best place to investigate.) The *Archivo* holds records of Mexico from the time of the 16th-century Spanish colony of Nueva Espana to the present. Books, letters, newspapers, magazines, microfiche and computers are available for consultation and use. Although not easy to access, the wealth of its historical annals is the most important governmental resource in this subject. To do onsite research, always make appointments in advance.

The library of Mexico's National University,* together with its newspaper archive located in Mexico City, also are wonderful facilities in which to do genealogical research. Several works have great genealogical value: *Imágenes de un encuentro*; the six volume work called *"Generaciones judías en México"*; the memory of the Monte Sinai community; yearbooks of the Jewish network schools; the memories of activities from the Centro Deportivo Israelita; the book and compact disk produced by the *Asociación Memoria y Tolerancia* on the memories of Holocaust survivors; and the important testimonial video called *"Un beso a esta tierra"*, based on the arrival and integration into Mexico of several immigrants.

Addresses

Archivo General de la Nacion, Albañiles s/n, Col. Ampliacion Penitenciaria, Mexico, D.F. 15350; telephone: 5789-0864; e-mail: ARGENA@SEGOB.GOB.MX

Centro de Documentacion, Acapulco 70, P.B. Col. Condesa C.P. 06700, Mexico, D.F., Mexico; telephone and fax: 525-5211-5688; e-mail: CDICA@HOTMAIL.COM

Centro Deportivo Israelita: Blvd. Manuel Avila Camacho 620, Col. Lomas de Sotelo Mexico, D.F. 11200

Comite Central Israelita and Tribuna Israelita: Cofre de Perote 115, Col. Loams de Barrilaco Mexico, D.F. 11010

Instituto Cultural Mexico Israel: Republica del Salvador 41, Col. Centro Mexico, D.F. 06080

Kehila Ashkenazi de Mexico (also known as Consejo Comunitario Ashkenazi: Edgar Allan Poe 236, Col. Polanco Mexico, D.F. 11560

Tribuna Israelita, Cofre de Perote 115, Col. Lomas de Barilaco, 11010 Mexico DF

Universidad Hebraica: Av de los Bosques 292 Bis COl. Lomas de Chamizal Cuajimalpa, D.F. 17000

Universidad Nacional Autonoma de Mexico: Domicilio Conocido Col. San Angel Mexico, D.F. 01000

Bibliography

Bocanegra, MatNas de. *Jews and the Inquisition of Mexico; The Great Auto-de-Fe of 1649.*

Elkin, Judith Laikin, and Merkx, Gilbert, W., *The Jewish Presence in Latin America.* Boston: Allen and Unwin, 1987.

Glantz, Margo. *Las Genealogías.* Mexico City: M. Casillas, 1981.

Gojman de Backal, Alicia, ed. *Generaciones Judíos en México: La Kehila Ashkenazi, 1922–1992.* [Spanish]. 7 vols. Mexico City: Comunidad Ashkenazi de México, 1993.

———. La presencia judNa en Mexico, 1987.

Gonzalez Navarro, Moises. *La Colonización en México, 1877–1910,* [Spanish] 1960.

———. *Testimonios de historia oral: Judíos en México.* [Spanish] Jerusalem: Hebrew University Press, 1990.

Hamui de Halabe, Liz, Fredy Charabati et al. *Los Judíios de Alepo en México* with genealogies by Silvia Hamui de Cherem and Liz Sutton Tawil. [Spanish] Mexico City: Maguén David, 1989.

Krause, Corinne A. *The Jews in Mexico: A History with Special Emphasis on the Period from 1857 to 1930.* Mexico City: Universidad Iberoamericana, 1987.

Lesser, Harriet Sara. *A History of the Jewish Community of Mexico, 1912–1970*, New York University, Ph.D. dissertation for PhD, 1972.

Levitz, Jacob. *The Jewish Community in Mexico: Its Life and Education*, Dropsie College, Ph.D. dissertation, 1954.

Liebman, Seymour B. *Guide to Jewish References in the Mexican Colonial Era, 1521–1821.* Philadelphia: University of Pennsylvania, 1964.

———. *Jews and the Inquisition of Mexico: The Great Auto-de-Fe of 1649.* Lawrence, Kan.: Coronado, 1974.

———. *Los judNos en Mexico y America Central*, 1981.

———. *New World Jewry, 1493–1825: Requiem for the Forgotten*, New York: Ktav, 1982.

———. *The Inquisitors and the Jews in the New World: Summaries of Procesos, 1500–1810 and Bibliographical Guide.* Coral Gables, Fla.: University of Miami, 1975.

———. *The Jews in New Spain: Faith, Flame and the Inquisition.* Coral Gables, Fla.: University of Miami, 1970.

Malka, Jeffrey S. *Sephardic Genealogy: Discovering Your Sephardic Ancestors and Their World.* Bergenfield, NJ: Avotaynu, 2002.

Muniz-Huberman, Angelina, comp. *La Lengua Florida* (Flowery language). [Spanish] Mexico City: Fondo de Cultura Economica, 1997.

Nudelstejer, Sergio. *Los Sefaraditas y su Presencia en la Nueva Espana: 500 anos de historia* (Sephardic people and their presence in New Spain: 500 years of history). [Spanish] Mexico City: Editorial Emet, 1992

Patai, Raphael. "The Indios Israelites of Mexico." *Menorah* 38 (1950): 54–67

———. "Venta Prieta Revisited." *Midstream.* 9 (1965): 79–82.

Rischin, Moses, ed. *The Jews of North America.* Detroit: Wayne State, 1987.

de Romano, Graciela. *Orøgines del judaøsmo contemporeneo en Mexico*, 1978.

Toro, Alfonso, comp. *Los Judios en la Nueva Espana* (Jews in New Spain). [Spanish] Mexico City: Fondo de Cultura Economica, 1993.

Zarate Miguel Guadalupe. *México y la Diáspora Judía.* [Spanish] Mexico City: Instituto Nacional de Antropolgia e Historia, 1986.

Note

1. The Tribunal of the Holy Inquisition was instituted in Mexico in 1571 as the second of three in Latin America. The Lima Tribunal in Peru, established in 1569, was the first, and the Barranquilla Tribunal in Colombia in 1618 was the third and last to be instituted.

Moldova

by Vladislav Soshnikov

Read the chapter on the RUSSIAN EMPIRE before reading this section. Important information that applies to Moldova is discussed there and not repeated again in this chapter. Also be sure to read the description of Miriam Weiner's Eastern European Database in the introduction to the chapter POLAND. Information relevant to Moldova is listed there.

The Republic of Moldova, as it exists today, was formed in 1940 on the eve of World War II, when it became the Soviet Republic of Moldova; it has been an independent republic only since 1991. Historically, Moldova was a larger region known as Bessarabia. Bessarabia became part of the Russian Empire in the late 1800s, when all the czarist laws went into effect. For nearly 150 years, it was called Bessarabia guberniya. The contemporary Republic of Moldova is bordered by Ukraine on the north and east and by Romania on the west—where the actual medieval principality of Moldova is situated. Some Jews had lived on this territory for centuries, but population increased considerably in the 19th century when many Jews from the northern guberniyas of the Russian Empire moved south to Bessarabia. Jewish genealogists researching family roots in Podolia and Kherson guberniyas often will find branches in Bessarabia as well. This was an important region for trade. Many Jews came, passed through or stayed—and all left records of their presence.

Genealogical Resources

Archival Resources. Records are concentrated in the National Archives of Moldova* in Kishinev (today Chisinau) and are of the same type as those found throughout the former Russian Empire. The only surviving registry books from Bessarabia are some from the Jewish synagogue in Kishinev: births for 1817 to 1910 and marriages for 1880–96. The valuable 19th-century Jewish *reviskie skazki* have survived and may be found here.

The Mormons (see LDS) have microfilmed almost all surviving Jewish metrical books from Moldova. Researchers should also review the LDS microfilms for the Orthodox Church; in some cases, the Orthodox Church records include Jewish records as well.

Of course, as in every capital city of a guberniya (or in this case, of a region or oblast), many governmental records also survive for the city of Kishinev. Since Jews from smaller communities often went to Kishinev, many registered there (instead of in the smaller communities), and information about them may be found in these government documents.

Jews in Bessarabia, like Jews everywhere, lived mostly in towns. To search for information about them, genealogists should look in record groups of town councils and local governments in every district center of the former Bessarabian region. These districts are Akkerman, Beltsy, Ismail, Khotin,

Kishinev, Oregev and Soroki. Remember that the southern portion of what was Bessarabia-Akkerman and Ismail districts today are part of Odessa *oblast* (region) in Ukraine. So while most of the old Russian Empire records are in Kishinev, some may be found in Ismail or Odessa archives.

Generally, the number of Jews increased in Bessarabian towns, where they often represented a significant part of the population, at the end of the 19th and beginning of the 20th centuries. Bessarabia was settled—especially in the south—primarily by Germans who came at the beginning of the 19th century. Thus, the southern areas are considered to be primarily areas of German settlement. While doing genealogical research for Germans from Russia who live in the U.S., however, I was surprised to find that at least one third of the settlers in the large German agricultural colonies of Bessarabia were Jews who came primarily at the end of the 19th century. For example, lists of tenants in the apartment houses of these "German" colonies were almost all Jewish names. They were the traders, craftsmen and small business owners of these small towns.

In the record group for the Kishinev *duma* (city council) are family lists and taxpayer (revision) lists of Jews dating from the beginning of the 19th century to the Russian Revolution of 1917. Jewish lists were separate and exist for all of the districts: Beltsy, Bendery, Ismail and Kishinev and small towns of the Akkerman, Beltsy, Bendery, Kishinev and Oregev districts—usually for the 1830s and 1850s.

Lists of Jews in towns that are not district centers exist in the same Crown Treasury record group, not as revision lists, but as separate lists of Jewish residents in these cities. Among other records in this fond are lists of Jewish families of Bessarabia subject to the draft in 1852, lists of the Jewish population of Bendery for the year 1874 and lists of merchants of Bessarabia in the 1880s and 1890s. Some Jewish agricultural colonies were established by the czar at the start of the 19th century, mostly by settlers from Belarus and northern Ukrainian guberniyas. In short order, however, most of the settlers moved to towns. Many government reports from the mid-1800s state that Jews who are registered as farmers in one or another colony actually lived in towns, and the colonies existed only on paper. In the face of these facts, the provincial government finally allowed the Jews to resettle officially in towns and enter the rosters of the town communities. By the beginning of the 20th century, almost all of the former colonists lived in towns.

School lists and newspapers held in the National Archives* are other potential sources of genealogical information. The ZAGS archive* holds metrical books and civil registration documents created after 1912.

Bodies of dead Jews murdered during the Kishinev pogrom of 1903. Courtesy of YIVO Institute for Jewish Research.

Conditions for researchers in Kishinev are very good when compared to other archives. The director of the National Archives is professional and friendly, despite an extremely difficult economic situation. There is no genealogical service by mail (although they have promised to organize this), but the regular delivery of files into the reading room is organized properly. I have worked in Kishinev several times since 1998, and the archivists have always been helpful and welcoming. Research requires specific permission from the archives; the fees depend on the number of researched documents. The situation is essentially the same at the ZAGS archives; special permission is required, and fees are charged based upon the number of extracts and hours worked. The National Library in Chisinau* has reference books on the history of the Jews in Moldova and a limited number of old telephone directories.

Jewish Genealogical Resources

Jewish cemeteries, in varying states of disrepair, exist in Balti, Chisinau, Kaminka and Telenesht. In the 1950s, D.N. Groberman photographically recorded many Jewish tombstones that now are destroyed (*Gravestones of the Destroyed Jewish Cemeteries in Moldova*). A small Jewish museum* in Chisinau holds a variety of original documents and ethnographic materials and has staff members who can answer many questions. The U.S. Holocaust Memorial Museum* holds 12,000 microfilmed Holocaust-era documents from Moldova, including records of the Chisinau ghetto.

Research Strategy

The microfilmed records at the LDS Family History Library should be the researcher's first stop. Because most of the available Jewish genealogical resources have not be microfilmed, however, the best results will be obtained by an onsite visit either by the genealogist or a professional genealogical researcher.

Kishinev is a pleasant city, especially in the summer, with many parks and historical buildings, hospitable people and fine vineyards. These factors and an excellent exchange rate make it a good place for a personal research trip. Despite the lack of Jewish vital records registries, I have always been able to compile complete genealogies using additional extant government records.

Addresses

Jewish Museum, 4 Renashterly Avenue, Chisinau 2005, Moldova; 373-2-221-502

Moldova National Archives, 67b Gheorghe Asachi Street, Chisinau 277028, Moldova; 373-273-5827

National Library of Moldova, 78, 31 August Street, Chisinau 2012, Moldova; telephone: 373-222-51-11

Bibliography

Gavis, Ruth R. and Irwin A. Kaufman. "Travel to Bukov-ina and Moldova," *AVOTAYNU* 15, no. 4 (Winter 1999): 42.

Groberman, D.N. *Gravestones of the Destroyed Jewish Cemeteries in Moldova.*

Landau, Luis. "Record Researcher Available in Moldova." *AVOTAYNU* 13, no. 2 (Summer 1997): 67.

Soshnikov, Vladislav. "Jewish Genealogical Research in Moldova." Talk given at 20th-annual conference on Jewish genealogy, Salt Lake City, July 2000, Hobart, Ind.: Repeat Performance.

———. "News from RAGAS." *AVOTAYNU* 15, no. 3 (Fall 1999): 26.

Weiner, Miriam. *Jewish Roots in Ukraine and Moldova; Pages from the Past and Archival Inventories*. Secaucus, N.J: Routes to Roots Foundation, 1999.

Morocco

by Philip Abensur

Morocco, a varied land of plains, plateaus, deserts and mountains situated at the western corner of the North African Mediterranean coast, is an Islamic kingdom that once was home to a sizable Jewish population. Settled primarily by Berbers, it fell under Roman influence in 42 CE and was called Mauritania. Christianity arrived in the 5th century CE and dominated the country until the Arabs conquered it in 688. The *Maghreb*, as the Islamic North African coast was called, was divided into three major Berber kingdoms—primarily the Merinids. Then the various European powers—the Spanish and French especially—began to seize portions during the 19th century. Early in the 20th century, the country was divided into a French protectorate, a Spanish protectorate and some autonomous regions, primarily in the center of the country. Morocco gained independence in 1956.

Jewish Presence in Morocco

The first record of Jewish presence in Morocco dates back to the Roman period, although some legends say that they arrived much earlier. A Jewish community existed in the Roman town of Volubilis, where a Hebrew tombstone and a seven-branched candlestick, dated 2nd century CE, have been found. Jews came to Morocco from other regions in North Africa during this period, some from as far away as Palestine. They were granted rights equal to those of the rest of the country and developed prosperous commercial enterprises. The Jews who lived along the coast were maritime traders with networks all along the Mediterranean. Those who settled inland became almost indistinguishable from the Berber population. This peaceful existence ended when the Christians arrived, and religious persecution prompted many Jews to flee to the mountains.

After the Arab conquest in 688 CE, the local Jews became *dhimmis* (protected nonbelievers), allowed to live in the country, albeit in an inferior status and required to pay a special tax (*jizya*) for the privilege. More Jewish communities developed after the Arab conquest and during the Spanish Golden Age (11th and 12th centuries CE), with many literary and juridical exchanges between Spanish and Moroccan rabbis.[1]

In 1492, after the Spanish Edict of Expulsion, Jews from Spain went in great numbers to Morocco. The number was so great that they added a new community, the *megorashim* (expelled from Spain) to the previous community, the *toshavim* (indigenous).

According to many scholars, Moroccan Jewry generally lived under one of the most oppressive *dhimma* systems in the Islamic world, a system that remained in force throughout Morocco for much of the 19th century and, in some places, well into the 20th century.[2] Exceptions were the mercantile elite, often the Spanish-, English- and French-speaking Jews, who could take advantage of the capitulation treaties and become protected subjects of a European country. *Dhimmi* merchants could travel to French Algeria, Europe and even India, and often returned home as naturalized citizens of another country, safe from the repressive legal system at home. During World War II, the Jewish population was protected by Sultan Mohammed V.

The organization of the Jewish communities depended on the town and the period. For example, only in 1927 did the rabbinical court of Tangier order that every Jew be registered in the Jewish birth, marriage and death community books.

Approximately 150,000 Jews lived in Morocco in the 1930s and more than 200,000 in the 1950s. Most Jews left Morocco after the country gained its independence from France and Spain in 1956. The greatest number went to Israel, where they form a major segment of the population, with many others going to Canada, France and South America, primarily Argentina, Brazil, Peru and Venezuela. A few went to the Cape Verde Islands (see AFRICA).

Although the majority of Jews left Morocco in 1956, that country still has the largest Jewish population left in North Africa, residing primarily in Casablanca, Marakesh and Rabat. Additionally, large groups of Spanish-speaking Jews, descendants of those who fled the Spanish Inquisition (and some French Jews) live in communities along the coast. Morocco is hospitable to Jewish tourists, and it is possible for former Jewish residents to visit their former homeland.

Genealogical Resources

Civil registration began officially at the beginning of the 20th century. Moroccan birth certificates may be obtained from the *Bureau de l'Etat* (municipal government) in each city by former Moroccan nationals born after 1912, including Jews. If the former resident still has a *livret de famille* (family booklet containing identity information about parents and children), he or she may get the birth certificate from the civil authorities with jurisdiction over his or her former place of residence.

Jewish Sources

Because civil registers are largely nonexistent or unavailable, Jewish genealogists with Moroccan background must rely on specifically Jewish sources. One can find Jewish registers such as circumcision, birth, marriage and death registers; ketubot; information in Jewish cemeteries and in some Jewish archives. These various sources are detailed below. Note that the section below on "Jewish registers" includes circumcisions, birth, marriage and death registers.

Jewish Registers. Most Jewish registers date only from the end of the 19th century or the beginning of the 20th century. Typically, they are written in Hebrew, but some documents are in French, Spanish or Judeo-Spanish. Registers usually are kept in the Jewish communities, but

Ketubah (marriage contract) dated the fourth day of Shabat (Wednesday) 28 Shevat 5612 (18 February 1852) at Tetuan, Morocco. The name of the bridegroom is Jacob, son of David (s.t.), son of Joseph (s.t.) AJUELOS. The name of the bride is Donna, daughter of Jacob, son of Samuel (n.e.) HACOHEN. The abbreviation s.t. (samekh-tet, "Sof Tov", let his end be a good one) means that the person is alive, while n.e. (nun-ayin, "Nuho Eden", let he rest in the Paradise) means that the person is dead. Thus it can be assessed that at the time of the marriage, the father, the paternal grandfather of the bridegroom and the father of the bride were alive, while the paternal grandfather of the bride was deceased. From personal collection of the author.

because most Jews have left Morocco, some small towns' archives have been moved to larger cities.

Circumcision Registers. Circumcision registers are held by the *mohel* (ritual circumciser), not by the community. Thus, when they have been preserved, they can be found with the descendants of the rabbi. For example, the circumcision registers of Mogador (Essaouira) are kept by the Bendahan family[*] who now live in London. The Sephardi Museum of Toledo, Spain,[*] holds a circumcision register from Tetuan beginning in 1895. It mentions the dates of birth and of circumcision, the given name and surname of the parents, and the first name of the maternal grandfather.

Birth, Marriage and Death Registers. Birth registers usually include the first name and last name of both parents. Death registers may mention the age at death, the given and surname of the parents, and the place of birth. Marriage registers sometimes also exist in Jewish community archives, but *ketubot* (Jewish marriage contracts) (see below) held by the family may give more information.

Ketubot (Jewish Marriage Contracts). Most existing *ketubot* are held within the families to which they belong. Some *ketubot* are in archives or museums, mainly in Israel, at the Ben Zvi Institute, the Israel Museum and the Jewish National and University Library (JNUL). Most Jewish museums around the world have some collections of *ketubot*. This source can be fascinating and incredibly rich for some Jewish genealogists because of a specifically Moroccan

custom. Before a marriage, the rabbi would ask for the *ketubot* of both sets of parents and would copy onto the new *ketubah* the lineage of the bride's father and the lineage of the groom's father for as many generations as appeared on their *ketubah*. This means that, for each generation, one more name is written down. At the end, one has a huge *ketubot*, sometimes more than ten generations. The Abendanan family has a *ketubah* (held by the family) that extends for 23 generations!

Many other families are documented for more than 10 generations, including Abecassis, Abensur, Abudarham, Attias, Bendelac, Bengualid, Bibas, Buzaglo, Corcos, Coriat, Serero, Serfaty, Taurel, Toledano, and probably many others. The *ketubot* collection held by the Jewish National and University Library in on the Internet at JNUL.HUJI.AC.IL//DL/KETUBBOT.

Cemeteries. The condition ("good" or "poor") of at least 25 Moroccan Jewish cemeteries has been documented, but except for the newest ones, few have written records. The tombstones, however, are generally well preserved. A Moroccan-Jewish tradition holds that only people without descendants have inscriptions on their tombstones, because when people have children, the children can remember where the tombstone is located. Such tombstones do not have the names of the deceased engraved on them. Most tombstones, however, do have inscriptions and those that exist are usually in Hebrew, or in French or Spanish for the recent ones.

Archives of the Alliance Israelite Universelle. The archives of the Alliance Israélite Universelle,[*] located in Paris, are a unique source for the history of Moroccan-Jewish communities since the second half of the 19th century. The first Alliance school opened in Tetuan in 1862. Before 1900, schools opened in Casablanca (1897), Mogador (Essaouira) (1868), Saffi (1868), Tangier (1864) and later in almost 50 other Moroccan cities. Each school director wrote regularly to Paris to report about relationships with local authorities and local Jewish communities. Of genealogical interest are the lists of individuals, such as pupils, local Alliance committee members and people assisted during outbreaks of epidemics. Considerable information also may be found about the life of school teachers, rabbis and Jewish local notables. These archives are difficult to use, however, because the indexes are not detailed. An appointment with the librarian is necessary.

Old Hebrew Manuscripts. Some libraries and private collections hold correspondence between rabbis, responsa (statements made by a rabbi on any everyday life subject) and contracts where the names of the involved persons are mentioned and, thus, may supply some genealogical information. For instance, someone wishing to produce his family tree on the occasion of his daughter's marriage wrote to a rabbi who was a family member and received a response with a great number of details on his family's origin.[3] Researchers with rabbis in the family will find an excellent genealogical source in *Malke Rabbanan*, a compilation of biographies of many Moroccan rabbis. An online index is available at www.SEPHARDICSTUDIES.ORG/M-RAB.HTML.

Consular Archives

Many Moroccan Jews, especially in the north of the country, were protected by the United States or a European country.

Information about them can be found in the corresponding consular archives. Details about the life of rabbis or other Jewish notables and events in which Jews were involved are often related in consular correspondence. In France, The French foreign affairs (Quai d'Orsay)* archives, located in Paris, hold the correspondence sent to France, while the archives of the French consulates can be consulted in the Centre des Archives Diplomatiques,* in Nantes. In Great Britain, all consular archives are kept at the Public Record Office,* in Kew, near London. Much of the catalogue is available on the Internet at CATALOGUE.PRO-GOV.UK. In Spain, consular archives are kept at the Archivo Histórico Nacional,* in Madrid.

Family Names of Moroccan Jews

Extensive literature spanning several centuries demonstrates that Moroccan Jews adopted hereditary surnames well before the (European) Ashkenazim. According to Joseph Toledano:

> Beginning under Berber influence in the 12th century, the custom of carrying a family name in addition to a given one spread to Morocco as well as to Spain. When Jewish exiles from the Spanish Inquisition landed in Morocco in 1492, they brought along with their patrimonial culture the particular sound of their surnames. At the end of the 15th century, the rabbis and registrars in Fez compiled lists of family names to be used for religious purposes, such as composing writs of divorce. The forms these names took then are almost identical today, five centuries later.[4]

According to Abraham I. Laredo[5], the family names of Moroccan Jews can be classified as follows:

- Names coming from a place of origin (primarily Morocco and Spain) represent more than half of the 1,160 recorded names. These include:

  – Names derived from a country name, such as Moghrabi, meaning Moroccan
  – Names derived from old city and tribal names such as Anfawi from Anfa, the name of an old city (destroyed by earthquake in the 18th century) that once stood on the site of modern day Casablanca
  – Names coming from old Berber tribal names such as Eznati from the tribe of Znata
  – Names reflecting tribes or place names such as Tanji from the city of Tangier
  – Names such as Toledano and Castro derived from the names of Spanish cities

- More rarely a name reflects origin in other countries such as Portugal (Ponte and Fonseca), France (Serfati which means French), Italy, Algeria, Tunisia and Palestine.
- Other names come from qualities such as good (Bueno) and benefactor (Hassan), physical peculiarities such as small (Catan), titles such as prince (Razon), occupations such as jeweler (Assayag), feelings such as joy (Sasson), animals such as lion (Saba), plants such as wheat (Trigo and Lezra) and colors such as white (Melul).

Most Moroccan Jewish family names come from the Arabic, Hebrew or Spanish languages.

A study conducted by the Jewish Agency in Israel after the emigration of 160,000 Moroccan Jews between 1961 and 1964 showed that nearly 60 percent of the families carried one of only 40 names. Most of these names were centered in a specific geographical area and are a strong clue to a family origins in Morocco. Several books and articles cited in the reference portion include information about surnames.

Addresses

Note that most local Jewish archives have been transferred to the Jewish communities in the larger cities such as Casablanca

Agadir Jewish Community, Imm. Arsalane Av. Hassan II, Agadir, Morocco; telephone: 8-840-091; fax: 8-822-268

Alliance Israélite Universelle, 45 rue La Bruyère, 75009 Paris, France; e-mail: BIBLIO@AIU.ORG; website: WWW.AIU.ORG

Archives du Quai d'Orsay, 37, quai d'Orsay, 75007 Paris, France; e-mail: LECTURE.ARCHIVES@DIPLOMATIE.FR; website: WWW.FRANCE.DIPLOMATIE.FR/ARCHIVES

Archivo Histórico Nacional, Serrano, 115, Madrid, Spain; telephone: 34-91-561-8001; fax: 34-91-563-1199

Casablanca Jewish Community, rue Abbou Abdallah al Mahassibi, Casablanca, Morocco; telephone: 2-270-976 and 2-222-861; fax: 2-266-953

Centre des Archives Diplomatiques, 17 rue du Casterneau, B.P. 1033, 44036 Nantes cedex 01, France; telephone: 33-51-772-459; fax: 33-51-772-460; e-mail: ARCHIVES.CADN@DIPLOMATIE.FR; website: WWW.FRANCE.DIPLOMATIE.FR/ARCHIVES

El Jadida Jewish Community, P.O. Box 59, El Jadida, Morocco

Essaouira (formerly, Mogador) Jewish Community, 2 rue Ziri Ben Alyah, Essaouira, Morocco

Etsi, Sephardi Genealogical and Historical Society, 77 bd Richard-Lenoir, 75011 Paris, France (only mailing address); website: WWW.GEOCITIES.COM/ETSI-SEFARAD

Fez Jewish Community, rue Dominique Bouchery, Fez, Morocco

GAMT (Genealogy Algeria, Morocco, Tunisia), Maison Maréchal Juin, 29 avenue de Tübingen, 13090 Aix-en-Provence, France; telephone: 33-4-4295-1949; website: GAMT.FREE.FR

Kenitra Jewish Community, 58 rue Sallah Eddine, Kenitra, Morocco

Marrakech Jewish Community, P.O. Box 515, Marrakech, Morocco

Meknes Jewish Community, 5 rue de Ghana, Meknes, Morocco

Museo Sefardi, Sinagoga del Transito, Samuel Levi s/n, 45002 Toledo, Spain; telephone: 34-925-223-665; fax: 34-925-215-831; e-mail: MUSEO.SEFARDI@TLD.SERVICOM.ES; websites: WWW.SERVICOM.ES/MUSEOSEFARDI and WWW.MUSEOSEFARDI.NET

Oujda Jewish Community, Texaco Maroc, 36 boulevard Hasan Loukili, Oujda, Morocco

Public Record Office, Ruskin Avenue, Kew, Surrey TW0 4DU, England; telephone: 44-20-887-634-44; website: CATALOGUE.PRO.GOV.UK

Rabat Jewish Community, 1 rue Boussourni, Rabat, Morocco

Safi Jewish Community, Synagogue Beth El and Mursiand, rue de Rabat, Safi, Morocco

Samuel Bendahan, 77 Sheringham, Queensmead, St. Johns Wood Park, London NW8 6RB, England

Tangier Jewish Community, 1 rue de la Liberté, Tangier, Morocco

Tetuan Jewish Community, 16 rue Moulay Abbas, Tetuan, Morocco

Bibliography

Moroccan Jewish Surnames

Abecassis, José Maria. *Genealogia Hebraica, Portugal e Gibraltar Sécs. XVII a XX* (Portuguese Jewish genealogy from the 17th to the 20th centuries). 5 vols. [Portuguese] Lisbon: Livraria Ferin, 1991.

"Avotaynu Puts Databases on Web," *Avotaynu* 12, no. 3 (Fall 1996).

Benaim, Yosef. *Malke Rabbanan*. Jerusalem, 1931. [Hebrew].

Eisenbeth, Maurice. *Les Juifs de l'Afrique du Nord, Démographie et Onomastique* (The Jews of North Africa, demography and onomastics). [French] Algiers: Imprimerie du Lycée, 1936; Paris: Cercle de Généalogie Juive and Gordes: La Lettre Sépharde, 2000.

Contributing Editors (Brazil). *AVOTAYNU* 4, no. 2 (Summer 1988).

———. *AVOTAYNU* 6, no. 1 (Spring 1990).

———. *AVOTAYNU* 6, no. 4 (Winter 1990).

———. *AVOTAYNU* 9, no. 1 (Spring 1993).

Contributing Editors (England). *AVOTAYNU* 5, no. 3 (Fall 1989).

Contributing Editors (France). *AVOTAYNU* 6, no. 1 (Spring 1990).

———. *AVOTAYNU* 7, no. 2 (Summer 1991).

———. *AVOTAYNU* 8, no. 1 (Spring 1992).

———. *AVOTAYNU* 8, no. 2 (Summer 1992).

———. *AVOTAYNU* 9, no. 2 (Summer 1993).

———. *AVOTAYNU* 9, no. 3 (Fall 1993).

———. *AVOTAYNU* 13, no. 1 (Spring 1997).

Contributing Editors (Israel). *AVOTAYNU* 4, no. 2 (Summer 1988).

———. *AVOTAYNU* 8, no. 2 (Summer 1992).

———. *AVOTAYNU* 11, no. 4 (Winter 1995).

"Family Books in Print" (Toledano). *AVOTAYNU* 15, no. 4 (Winter 1999).

Gaon, Solomon. "Moroccan Jews on the Road to Auschwitz." in Solomon Gaon and M. Mitchell Serels, eds. *Sephardim and the Holocaust*. New York: Yeshiva University, 1987.

"Jews of Livorno, Italy in 1841." *AVOTAYNU* 12, no. 4 (Winter 1996).

Laredo, Abraham I. *Les noms des Juifs du Maroc. Essai d'onomastique judéo-marocaine* (The names of the Jews of Morocco: an essay on Judeo-Moroccan onomastics). [French] Madrid: CSIC, 1978.

Pimienta, Sidney. *"Un échantillon de la population juive de Tanger en 1955 dans le carnet de Isaac Pimienta"* (A sample of the Jewish population of Tangier in 1955 in Isaac Pimienta's notebook). [French, with English summary] *Etsi* 2, no. 7 (1999), 8–11.

Stillman, Norman. *The Jews of Arab Lands. A History and Source Book*. Philadelphia: Jewish Publication Society of America, 1979.

Taïeb Jacques. *"L'onomastique des Juifs du Maghreb et le fait berbère"* (Onomastics of Maghreb Jews and Berber matter). [French, with English summary]. *Etsi* 1, no. 2 (1998): 3–7.

"The 19th Century Montefiore Census." *AVOTAYNU* 8, no. 2 (Summer 1992).

Toledano, Joseph. "An Analysis of Moroccan-Jewish Surnames." *AVOTAYNU* 2, no. 2 (May 1986).

Jewish Communities and Moroccan Jewish History

Abensur, Philip, and Sidney Pimienta. "Sephardic Genealogical Research in Morocco." *AVOTAYNU* 10, no. 3 (Fall 1994): 40–42.

Attal, Robert. *Les Juifs d'Afrique du Nord, Bibliographie* (The Jews of North Africa, bibliography). [French and Hebrew] Jerusalem: Ben Zvi Institute, 1993.

Bennett, Ralph. "About the Jews of Morocco, Algeria and Libya." *AVOTAYNU* 10, no. 3 (Fall 1994).

Chouraqui, André. *Histoire des Juifs en Afrique du Nord* (History of the Jews in North Africa) 2 vols. [French] Paris: Rocher, 1998.

Cohen, Martin A., ed. *Sephardim in America*. Cincinnati: Hebrew Union College and the American Jewish Archives, 1992.

Gerber, Jane S. *Jewish Society in Fez, 1450–1700: Studies in Communal and Economic Life*. Leiden: Brill, 1980.

Hirschberg, Haim-Zeev. *A History of the Jews in North Africa*. 2 vols. Leiden: Brill, 1974, 1981.

"Immigration Records at the National Archives of the Canadian Jewish Congress." *AVOTAYNU* 2, no. 3 (October 1986).

"Index." *AVOTAYNU* 15, no. 1 (Spring 1999).

Laredo, Isaac. *Memorias de un viejo Tangerino*. (Memories of an old Tangerine). [Spanish] Madrid: 1935.

Leibovici, Sarah. *Chronique des Juifs de Tétouan (1860–1896)*. (Chronicle of the Jews of Tetuan [1860–1896]). [French] Paris: Maisonneuve et Larose, 1984.

Les Juifs du Maroc: Images et textes. [French] Paris: Scribe, 1987.

Pariente, Michael. *La Vie Juive au Maroc: Arts et Traditions* (Jewish life in Morocco: art and traditions). [French].

Pimienta, Sidney, transcriber. *Indice del Libro de Actas de la Comunidad Hebrea de Tanger, 1860–1875*. (Index to the minute books of the Hebrew community of Tangier, 1860–1875). [Judeo-Spanish] Paris: S. Pimienta and P. Abensur, 1992.

Proceedings of the 5th International Seminar on Jewish Genealogy. Paris: Cercle de Généalogie Juive, 1998.

"Research Projects at the Diaspora Research Institute." *AVOTAYNU* 10, no. 4 (Winter 1994).

Salafranca Ortega, Jesus F. *La población judía de Melilla (1874–1936)* (The Jewish population of Melilla). [Spanish] Caracas: Centro de Estudios Sefardíes, 1990.

"Sephardic Reference Sources." *AVOTAYNU* 12, no. 3 (Fall 1996).

Serels, Mitchell M. *A History of the Jews of Tangier in the Nineteenth and Twentieth Centuries*. New York: Sepher-Hermon, 1991.

Toledano, Joseph. *La Saga des Familles*. [French] Tel Aviv: Editions Stavit, 1983.

———. *L'esprit du Mellah*. [French]. Jerusalem: Ramtol, 1986.

———. *Le Temps du Mellah*. [French]. Jerusalem: Ramtol, 1982.

Vilar, Juan Bautista. *Tetuan en el resurgimiento judio contemporaneo (1850–1870)* (Tetuan in the contemporary Jewish resurgence). [Spanish] Caracas: Centro de Estudios Sefardíes, 1985.

Zafrani, Haim. *Juifs d'Andalousie et du Maghreb* (The Jews of Andalusia and of North Africa). [French] Paris: Maisonneuve et Larose, 1996.

Published Hebrew Manuscript Catalogues

Aranov, Saul I. *A Descriptive Catalogue of the Bension Collection of Sephardic Manuscripts and Texts*. Edmondon, Alberta: University of Alberta, 1979.

Klagsbald, Victor. *Catalogue des manuscrits marocains de la collection Klagsbald* (Catalogue of the Moroccan manuscripts in the Klagsbald collection). [French] Paris: CNRS, 1980.

Cemeteries

Abensur, Philip. *"Le cimetière juif de Tétouan, hier, aujourd'hui, demain"* (The Jewish cemetery of Tetuan, yesterday, today and tomorrow). [French, with English summary] *Etsi* 1, no. 1 (1998): 4–7.

Zack, Joel. *The Synagogues of Morocco: An Architectural and Preservation Survey*. New York: World Monuments Fund, 1993.

Notes

1. Zafrani, Haim, *Juifs d'Andalousie et du Maghreb*
2. Stillman, Norman, *The Jews of Arab Lands*.
3. Aranov, Saul, *A Descriptive Catalogue*.
4. Toledano, Joseph. *AVOTAYNU* 2, no. 2 (May 1986).
5. Laredo, Abraham, *Les noms des Juifs du Maroc*.

The Netherlands

by Odette Vlessing

Jews began to settle in the Netherlands at the end of the 16th century, coming first to Amsterdam, the largest Dutch city. First to arrive were Portuguese merchants, crypto-Jews (*conversos* or marranos) whose ancestors had been compelled to convert to Christianity, but who probably still observed secretly some Jewish customs.

Recognizing the benefits that *converso* trade and trade relations could bring to the Dutch economy, some of the local Dutch authorities welcomed these merchants. Their economic awareness stimulated a tolerant political climate towards the Portuguese in several mercantile cities, where trade was even more important than religion. This attitude resulted in the marranos' gradual reconversion to Judaism and the establishment of a flourishing Jewish community in Amsterdam. An influx of Ashkenazi Jews from Central and Eastern Europe occurred a few years later.

By the middle of the 17th century, Amsterdam had two important Jewish communities: the Portuguese, which was mighty and rich, and the Ashkenazi, still partly supported by the Portuguese, but which would soon become a prestigious rabbinical seat in Europe. Both communities became important for European Jewry and attracted Jews from the east and the south. Settlements were established elsewhere in Holland—in Rotterdam, The Hague and, by the 18th century, in most of the mercantile cities of Holland.

Between 1795 and 1813, Holland was part of the French Napoleonic Empire, first as a republic—the Batavian Republic, and after 1806, as part of the Napoleonic kingdom—the Kingdom of Holland. French occupation brought change in the political status of the Jews; in 1796 they acquired equal civil rights. From that time onward, the processes of emancipation and integration of the Jew into Dutch society was unstoppable. In November 1813, the princes of Orange-Nassau regained control of the country, and, by March 1814, the federal state was transformed into a monarchy ruled by the House of Orange-Nassau. As a result, the power of the independent cities was abolished and a new constitution implemented. Holland became a constitutional monarchy ruled by an enlightened despot.

The kingdom was extended by adding Belgium to the territory in 1815. While the majority of the Dutch were Protestant, the Belgians were Catholic. When a new constitution was drafted for the Dutch-Belgian kingdom, a balance had to be found between those two religious mainstreams. A constitution committee was appointed consisting of 12 Protestant delegates and 12 Catholics. The king chose a chairman, and the only remaining position was that of a secretary. In order not to be accused of prejudice against either Catholics or Protestants, the king appointed a Jewish lawyer, Jonas Daniel Meijer, who had contacts with the Dutch ruling class. This was the first time that a Jew held a position in Dutch governmental circles.

At the same time, Jews were organized into a National Jewish Council (*Israëlietisch Kerkgenootschap*) that supervised the main synagogues (*Hoofdsynagogen*) in the provincial capitals. The Council itself was under supervision of the Department of Religious Affairs. The constitution was revised a few times, the most important change being the introduction of the ministerial responsibility and the separation of church and state, both in 1848.

Holland became a constitutional monarchy with a combined rule of king, senate and a parliament which was chosen by the wealthiest male inhabitants. In 1917, the right to vote was granted to all Dutch adult male citizens, and in 1922 women were included. The constitutional monarchy became a monarchical democracy. By the end of the 19th century, the Jewish Religious Council had become an independent body. Its only ties to the government dealt with subsidies for religious education. Trustees of the major synagogues controlled the management of their National Council through their delegates to the Council's annual meeting.

By the turn of the 20th century, some Jews had acquired leading positions in Dutch politics. They were a major power behind the trade unions; they were leaders of the Dutch Socialist Movement; but, at the same time, they were important Dutch bankers and innovative entrepreneurs. World War II brought an abrupt change. More than 100,000 of the 140,000 Jews who lived in Holland in the late 1930s were murdered during the war. This traumatic experience for both Jews and Gentiles has left its marks on Dutch society to this day. The history of this war is still one of the most examined periods. The Dutch Institute of War Documentation succeeds time and again in attracting public attention to new studies about War World II and its effects on the Netherlands. Only recently a new institute for Holocaust and Genocide Studies was established. The subject of the first Masters course will be the segregation of Dutch Jews by civil servants during World War II.

Dutch Archival System

The Dutch archival system follows the country's historic development. The National Archive is located at The Hague,* the seat of government. It keeps the historical archives of the States General (the federal government of the Dutch state before 1795, which was run by representatives of the seven constituent independent provinces), of the national trade companies, and of the ministerial departments. The private archives of large business companies and other private bodies whose influence and authority stretches over the entire country also are kept there.

Every province has a provincial archive that is administratively part of the State Archival Services,* and has its seat in the provincial capital. The State Archival Service is run by the National Archives. The archives kept in the provinces emanate from governmental administrations in the region and from other bodies that may choose to deposit their archives there.

Likewise, every major city has its municipal archive, which holds the archives of local councils and of private institutions meaningful to local history. The Amsterdam Municipal Archives* is the largest local archive, storing about 35 linear kilometers of documents. In regional archives, a number of smaller towns and villages have combined their holdings to save funds. The network of archival centers covers the entire country.

The Archives Law of 1995 provides that the country's historical legacy be kept in optimal condition and available to the public, at the same time that it protects the privacy of individual citizens.

How to Find Your Dutch Ancestors

Genealogists should keep in mind that researching one's ancestors does not mean investigating a surname in all sorts of indexes, but trying to trace a family through one individual and consequently digging into the past one step at a time. Each step should be linked to the former, so that the line remains unbroken from the present to the past.

19th- and 20th-Century Resources

Vital Records. The Dutch population administration is meticulously organized. Registrar's offices, established in 1811 under French rule and still in existence today, draft the birth, marriage and death certificates of all the country's legal inhabitants. The records of these deeds originally were kept in books but today are in a computer system. The Dutch term for this system is *Burgerlijke Stand* (civil state). Obviously, copies of these deeds are indispensable for genealogical research.

- Birth certificates include the date of birth, the name and age of the parents, their address and the name and age of the witnesses, as well as their relation to the parents.
- Marriage certificates include the names and ages of bride and groom, their professions, their places of birth, their parents' names and their witnesses' names.
- Death certificates include the date of death, name and age of the deceased, profession, address, name of spouse and sometimes names of the decedent's parents.

The deeds are registered in duplicate. One set of registers is deposited in the local archive (municipal or regional) and one set in the provincial archive. The law determines when the books are transferred from the registrar's office to the archival depot. Birth certificates are usually transferred after at

least 100 years; for deeds of marriage the term is after at least 75 years; and for death certificates, after at least 50 years. Transfer of the documents should occur within 10 years after expiration of the term of privacy. Because of this system, researchers easily know where to expect the deeds one needs.

Currently, the Amsterdam Municipal Archives holds deeds of birth up to 1901, deeds of marriage up to 1926 and death certificates up to 1951. These documents cover all Amsterdam inhabitants between 1811 and the above dates, including Jews. Some local archives have more recent material.

Population registers. Part of the population administration is the Population Register (*Bevolkingsregister*) introduced in 1851 and still in use. The 19th-century registers were arranged by address. All inhabitants of a given house were registered on the same page, and their movements from one address to another were noted as well. In some neighborhoods, people moved so often that one house fills a number of pages. Sometimes, a single page records the inhabitants of just one room (usually in the extremely poor neighborhoods).

Families members are all noted on the same page, with their names, dates and places of birth, professions, civil state (i.e., whether a person is married, single or widowed), dates of moving into and out of the house, and dates of death. Faith is mentioned too: *Ned. Isr.* (*Nederlands Israëlietisch*) for Ashkenazi Jews and *Port. Isr.* (*Portugees Israëlietisch*) for Portuguese Jews. One column is for remarks, such as imprisonment or special police permission for foreigners to settle in town. The first Amsterdam series of these registers running from 1851 to 1853 has been indexed by volunteers, a project initiated and administered by Dave Verdooner. Soon the data will be available on the Internet.

The books were replaced by a card system in the mid-1920s; in Amsterdam, however, the card system began about 1893. Every householder had a registration card (*gezinskaart*) from the moment he or she lived independently. In 1939, a personal card system was introduced for every person above the age of 18 (*persoons-kaart*). These documents were drafted in multiple copies, depending on movement within the country. Each time one moved, an additional card was drafted; this is kept by the local registry office. The cards may be viewed only by the person involved as long as he or she lives. After the person has died, the last set is kept in The Hague in Centraal Bureau voor Genealogie.* After removal to the Central Bureau of Genealogy, the card are publicly available to access for a small fee.

The Amsterdam card system was severely damaged during a sabotage raid by the underground movement in March 1943, intended to prevent special registration and deportation of fellow citizens. The set of cards in The Hague had been meticulously cleared, presumably also by the underground movement, of all cards with Jewish names during the same period. This means that it is sometimes difficult to find data on Jews for the first half of the 20th century. In addition, the Amsterdam Municipal Archives* holds the *Woningkaarten* (residence cards), in which the movements of the city inhab-

Ark of a Sephardic synagogue in Amsterdam at the beginning of the 20th century

itants and their families were registered between the 1920s and the early 1950s. These cards contain less genealogical data than the *Gezinskaarten* and the *Persoonskaarten*. The relevant information for Jewish genealogy is the registration of the date of transportation either to a concentration camp or to Germany and Poland.

Jewish Archives

To fill the gaps in Jewish genealogies, it is sometimes advantageous to research the archives of the Jewish communities themselves. The archives of the larger Dutch communities survived World War II. The municipal archives in Amsterdam,* The Hague,* Utrecht* and Rotterdam* keep large Jewish archives, all of which have been catalogued. Cities, such as Apeldoorn,* Haarlem,* Leeuwarden,* Leiden* and Middelburg,* also keep Jewish archives in their municipal archives, although most are incomplete. These Jewish archives often have 19th- and 20th-century records of membership, marriage and burial. The documents are partly in Dutch and partly in Hebrew. Records of membership contain both Dutch and Jewish names of the members, sometimes their address and their contribution. The marriage records (*ketubot*) include the Hebrew names of bride and bridegroom as well as the first name of the father. Burial records usually have both Dutch and Hebrew names and the age and address of the deceased. The Orthodox Jewish community of Amsterdam has indexed its burial registers, which are stored at the Amsterdam Municipal Archives* and hopefully will publish the index. Some archives contain records of the engravings on the tombstones. Normally the Jewish archives do not have circumcision registers. The *mohel* (ritual circumciser) was expected to keep his own records; as a result, these registers often were not deposited with the community's administration. Today, some of the *mohel* books have reached the book market and are being sold to private collectors instead of being made available to the public in archives or libraries. The Amsterdam Municipal Archives has more than 100 pre-19th century circumcision registers which are now being indexed.

Most Dutch-Jewish genealogies contain a full family line through the 19th century up to 1940, the outbreak of World War II in the Netherlands. The abundance of records allows the genealogist to reconstruct his line, sometimes the collateral lines of the family, and even to gain insight in the economic position of his ancestors. This applies equally to families of Ashkenazic and Sephardic origin.

Register of Surnames

Before 1811 most Ashkenazi Jews did not use a surname in the civil registration. For example, Jacob son of Joseph Kleidersoucher was just Jacob Josephs. The use of a father's name as surname is called *patroniem* in Dutch. A man named Isaac son of Chaim was called Isaac Hijmans. Under Napoleonic rule, Jews were compelled by law to assume a family name. The register of surname adoption (*Register van naamsaanneming*) forms an important link between the detailed registration of the 19th century and the somewhat improvised manner in which 18th-century civil servants recorded names. Most Dutch cities and towns have a register of surname adoptions kept either at the provincial or municipal archives. A general index to these books was published in 1967–70 (see Bibliography). Recently a more extended index was published by the De Nederlandse Kring voor Joodse Genealgie.* The records contain the old civil name, new surname, address, names of the children who assumed the same name and name of their mother. Some deeds even contain the names of grandchildren. The register is incomplete because many Jews failed to appear before the authorities in order to have their surnames registered. Nevertheless, during the 19th century, all Jews eventually assumed a surname. This index is relevant only for Ashkenazi Jews. The Portuguese Jews of Amsterdam had assumed surnames earlier, and these were used on every official occasion in which they were involved.

Ashkenazic Jews rarely used a surname before 1811. When they did, they used one name inside the Jewish community and a different, special civil surname for official civil occasions. For example, the Emmerich family used the name Gompers in the civil records; the Maarssen family used the civil name de Metz; the Rintel family used the civil name De Jongh; and the Wiener family used the civil name De Lemon. An index of Jewish surnames and their Dutch equivalents based on available Amsterdam sources has recently been published (see Bibliography).

17th- and 18th-Century Sources

Dutch-Jewish communities were relatively independent during the 17th and 18th centuries. Jews were allowed to live according to their rites and customs, but, at the same time, were expected to obey the laws of the country and the city in which they lived. The *parnassim* (Jewish governors) were responsible for the community as a whole and represented it in dealings with the civil authorities, who usually did not intervene with the Jewish community's internal affairs.

One of the civil ordinances that Jews were obliged to obey was to register marriages in advance with the civil authorities, so that the Commissioners of Marital Affairs could check whether the intended marriage was allowed, that is, was not bigamous, was consented to by the parents and was not between relatives of a forbidden degree of consanguinity (cousins). No one was exempt from this obligation, although Reformed Protestants were allowed to have this registration done by the clerical authorities.

The most important genealogical source for the 17th and 18th centuries is the civil registration of the intended marriages, the publication of the banns. A couple was required to register about three weeks before the marriage; their names were announced from the terrace of the city hall during the following three Sundays, and finally a solemnization could take place. Even though Jews and Catholics were allowed to marry in their own synagogues and churches, the marriages were not officially recognized without this registration and without the ensuing confirmation of the marriage in city hall. Since the primary religious duty of Jews was to obey the laws of Moses, however, all marriages were consecrated at the synagogue by a rabbi and registered in the books of the communities. During the 17th and early 18th centuries at least, many Jews often neglected to have their marriages registered at the city hall. After many warnings and orders from the civil authorities, more Jewish inhabitants had their marriages additionally solemnized by city officials, especially during the 18th century.

The Amsterdam deeds of publication of the banns include the following data: names of bride and bridegroom, places of birth, ages, addresses, name of witness (usually one of the parents or another relative) and signatures. Those who could not sign in Dutch signed in Hebrew. Some could not write at all and made an "O" as a sign.

In other towns the same deeds usually contain less data than the Amsterdam records; details vary locally. An index to the Amsterdam records has been published, entitled *Trouwen in Mokum; Jewish Marriage in Amsterdam (1598–1811),* by D. Verdooner and H. Snel. The book includes 21 indexes to data in the deeds and, thus, allows the genealogist an excellent opportunity for searching. Indexes to such records are locally available in other archival institutions, too.

Archives of both the Portuguese and Ashkenazi communities hold registers of *ketubot* (Jewish marriage contracts). The documents are in Aramaic and Hebrew and contain the date of the marriage, the names of bride and bridegroom as well as of their fathers and sometimes either a reference to civil records concerning prenuptial arrangements or Jewish prenuptial records (*tena'im rishonim, tena'im aharonim, shetar chalitsa*). The archives of the large Jewish communities in Amsterdam, The Hague, Rotterdam and Utrecht have these documents; they are indexed by name. In Amsterdam, the Portuguese *ketubot* date from 1673, the Ashkenazi from 1725—but with many gaps.

In order to establish a link between the civil and the Jewish records, a dictionary of first names has been published by J. van Straten and H. Snel, entitled: *Joodse voornamen in Amsterdam; Een inventarisatie van Asjkenazische en bijbehorende burgerlijke voornamen tussen 1669 en 1850* (Jewish first names in Amsterdam; an inventory of Ashkenazi and matching civil first names between 1669 and 1850).

Some 17th- and 18th-century Jewish community death records have survived. Registers of the Ashkenazi communities were written in Hebrew and Yiddish; in Portuguese for the Sephardi communities. They cover a long uninterrupted period and, therefore, are a very important source. The Amsterdam Jewish burial registers start in 1614 for the Portuguese community, with a gap between 1646–80. The Portuguese community itself has an ongoing project to catalogue (on index cards) the tombstones in the cemetery at Ouderkerk aan de Amstel.* Its card system (recently computerized) has a compilation of genealogical data collected from a variety of sources. Employees of this community make information available upon request. A supplementary 19th-century index is available at the Amsterdam Municipal Archives.*

The Ashkenazi burial registers start in 1669. An index of burials at Muiderberg Cemetery, covering the period 1669–1811, has been published recently by J. van Straten and H. Snel (see Bibliography). This cemetery was established at 1642 and served the community until 1714 when another cemetery was bought in Zeeburg. The new cemetery, closer to Amsterdam, was established for the burial of the poor, children and those who died on the eve of the Sabbath or a festival. (The children and the poor were included because they were much more numerous than the regular, paying adult members. The community leadership worried about the cemetery of Muiderberg getting full, with no guarantee of being able to buy adjoining land. J. van Straten has published an index of the Zeeburg cemetery entitled *De begraafboeken van Zeeburg* [Burial books of Zeeburg]. The indexes include the name of the deceased, the father's name and sometimes place of birth and profession. Women were registered in their husband's name and, when unmarried, in their father's name. Their given names often remained unregistered. Special events at the time of death such as drowning in the canal, being a victim of a crime or reaching a very old age, sometimes were mentioned as well.

For information about other Jewish cemeteries, one must ask the local or provincial archives at the place of death if the Jewish archives have been preserved. To determine if an index exists, contact the Nederlandse Kring voor Joodse Genealogie* which holds copies of indexes produced by members.

Most of the Jewish community archives have circumcision registers, but the collections of these records are seldom complete. The registers were the property of the circumciser, who sometimes chose to keep their books. Some of the registers are now kept by private collectors. The registers in public collections are usually indexed. The Amsterdam collection contains more than one hundred registers. The lists of babies include the name, the father's name, sometimes the grandfather's name, and sometimes the location of the ceremony. An index of Amsterdam circumcision registers is now in preparation by J. van Straten.

Additional Sources

The sources mentioned thus far are sufficient for the reconstruction of a family tree, but once one starts a genealogical research the desire to know more than names of relatives and their birth, marriage and death dates usually arises. Every person who ever lived somewhere left some traces in the local administration, whether Jewish or not. In the Netherlands, local archives have masses of details concerning local Jews.

If they had served in the army, there are enlistment records; if they attended the local school, that archive has been preserved and one would expect to find their traces as pupils. Even the Jewish schools have had their records. These institutions were subsidized by the Council of Jewish Communities,* and the school board filed reports about the program and achievements. The reports of almost all 19th-century local Jewish schools in the Netherlands—including lists of pupils and names of teachers—have been preserved and kept at the Amsterdam Municipal Archives. They cover the period 1870–1910. Data on Jewish schools before 1870 may be found in the archives of the Department of Religious Affairs in the National Archive at The Hague.*

If one's ancestor was a refugee or held the status of foreigner for some time in the second half of the 19th century or the first half of the 20th century, he or she is likely to be found in the records of the local police under the Foreigners Police, usually kept by the local municipal archives. If a forefather had been a civil servant, the municipal, provincial or state archives would have the records of his office, so that his pension could be secured.

Recently the Amsterdam Municipal Archives put the index to licenses for market-vendors (in the 1920s and 1930s) on the Internet. The index, created by Dave Verdooner, is important because many Amsterdam Jews had a stall on the local markets. License cards often include photographs of the vendors. Some of the younger victims of World War II have, thus, been able to acquire the only tangible memory of their perished relatives. Copies of these cards may be ordered via the Internet.

Notarial and Judicial Records

Jews were somewhat restricted in their professional activities and possibilities during the 17th and 18th centuries. Most were engaged in trade on a large, small or very small scale. Larger traders have left traces in the notarial records. Contracts, agreements, statements about conflicts and demands for payment all were drafted before a notary. Depending on local conditions, these records have survived. In Amsterdam they begin around 1578.

The notarial records of the Portuguese Jews from 1595 onwards have been summarized and published in *Studia Rosenthaliana, Journal for the History, Culture and Heritage of the Jews in the Netherlands*, starting with the first issue in 1967. The project was intended to end with the deeds from 1639, the year in which the Portuguese community Talmud Tora was established. Because the *Studia Rosenthaliana* has switched from being a journal to becoming a yearbook, however, the project will not continue. The deeds up till 1627 have been published. The summaries covering the period up to 1639 (in Dutch) may be used for research at the Amsterdam Archives reading room. A partial index of the notarial records

Title page of a 1679 bible printed in Amsterdam. The bible is located at the Jewish Theological Seminary in New York.

(from 1578 to 1811) can be consulted at the Amsterdam Municipal Archives.* Notarial records in cities such as Rotterdam and The Hague have a better index because the collections are much smaller.

People on the other side of the social ladder have been recorded, too. The 17th- and 18th-century archives of the local judicial authorities include records of Jewish criminals. The circumstances of the poor are recorded in the 19th- and 20th-century archives of the local bodies for poor relief. The Amsterdam municipal archives have files on more than 500,000 families who were dependent on municipal financial support. Among these poor are a few thousand files of the diamond cutters, most of whom were Jews who, during the 1920s and 1930s, became unemployed because of the economic depression. The accessibility of these records is restricted by privacy protection rules.

Records of Emigrants

The most important source on emigrants from Holland is the archives of such shipping companies as the Holland-America

Line held by the Rotterdam municipal archives.* They include passenger lists of the ships that left Rotterdam, the main harbor in Holland. The lists covering the period May 1900-April 1940, are open to researchers. The archive of the Holland America Line has records pertaining to the period until 1972, but these records are restricted by privacy protection legislation and are not available to researchers at this time. The currently available records include the name of the passenger, where he had booked the voyage, destination (mostly New York, Los Angeles or Chicago), the sum he paid and the name of the ship. A chronological name index is available for the periods December 1900-April 1938, January 1947-January 1950 and 1952.

Jews also emigrated to the Dutch colonies. The archives of the Jewish community of Surinam (see CARIBBEAN) are kept by the National Archives* at The Hague and include, for example, the *ketubot* of this community. The archive of the Department of Colonial Affairs (also at the National Archive) holds civil records pertaining to events and people in these areas, such as notarial records and documents emanating from judicial authorities. These records also are kept at the National Archives* in The Hague. Mail inquiries are answered.

Wartime and Recuperation Records

Renewed interest in Dutch victims of World War II and worldwide activities regarding unclaimed property of victims have led to the rediscovery of archives pertaining to the war and the postwar period. In 1995 a list of Dutch victims was published in a book entitled *In Memoriam–Lezecher* (SDU Uitgeverij: The Hague, 1995). There is no author mentioned. The book is based on the publication (1945–50) in the *Staatscourant* (State daily) of lists of murdered Dutch citizens, mostly Jews. The information recovered from various sources and produced by the Red Cross, includes names, birth dates and places and the dates of deaths of more than 100,000 individuals. German refugees who had fled to Holland after 1933 and were murdered on its soil are included in the list.

The National Archive in The Hague has the largest collection of archives concerning recuperation and restitution of properties. Most important is the archive of the *Nederlands Beheersinstituut* (Dutch Control Institute), the office that administered unclaimed properties. A guide to this type of archives has been published as part of the investigation of a state commission into the theft and looting of Jewish properties during and after the war. The guide, by J.M.L. Bockxmeer, P.C.A. Lamboo and H.A.J. van Schie, is entitled *Onderzoeksgids Archieven Joodse Oorlogsgetroffenen* (A research guide to archives on Jewish war victims). (Algemeen Rijksarchief: The Hague 1998). The book may be ordered from the National Archives.*

The Amsterdam Municipal Archives* keep the archives of the Dutch Organization of Jewish Welfare (*Joods Maatschappelijk Werk*). The archives include approximately 30,000 files of war damages claims by Dutch Jews in the 1950s and 1960s. In order to prove their relationships to victims, claimants had to deliver "declarations of heritage" (*Verklaringen van Erfrecht*), notarial deeds containing a genealogical chart with the degree of relationship. To consult these archives, researchers need written permission from either the archivist (for the archives of state institutions) or the owner of the archive (private Jewish organizations).

Other Institutions

In addition to archives, The Netherlands has some specialized libraries in which one may find relevant material for Jewish genealogy. Amsterdam University Library* has a special Judaica library, the *Bibliotheca Rosenthaliana.** This institution collects literature and sometimes also archival material concerning Dutch Jews. Some of the collections, such as the Corwin Collection, are primarily genealogical. The library and its collection can be searched on the Internet at UBA.UVA.NL-ENGELS-COLLECTIONS-BIBLIOTHECAROSENTHALIANA. Collections-Bibliotheca Rosenthaliana. The reading room is open to the public; to borrow books one must obtain a reader's pass, usually available for a fee to students and professional researchers

The library of the Jewish Historical Museum in Amsterdam* (Address: P.O. Box 16737, 1001 RE Amsterdam) also is connected to the Internet at WWW.JHM.NL. Although the library is small, some of its holdings, especially personal documents, may interest genealogists. The majority of the documents are letters and other items related to World War II. Some documents are about Portuguese families.

The archives of the Diamond Cutters Trade Union (ANDB), including its membership administration, are kept at the International Institute of Social History (IISG)* Its website lists an address for inquiries. (Internatinaal Instituut voor Social Geschiedenis, Cruquiusweg 31, 1019 AT Amsterdam; website: WWW.IISG.NL) in Amsterdam. A card index of the members is useful to genealogists.

The *Nederlands Instituut voor Oorlogs-Documentatie* (NIOD),* (Herengracht 380, 1016 CJ Amsterdam; website: WWW.NIOD.NL) is the institute that keeps government and private collections on World War II. They hold the transportation lists of Jewish prisoners from Westerbork concentration camp[1] to Poland; the administration of the Jewish Council (*Joodse Raad*); the administration of Jewish businesses by German agents (*Verwalters*) and others. Researchers who want to know about the fate of relatives during World War II should start there.

The Nederlandse Kring voor Joodse Genealogie* is the Dutch Jewish Genealogical Society . The society has about 500 members and publishes an annual list of members and the genealogies they have produced. The society's quarterly magazine, *Misjpoge,* publishes a list of available indexes on Dutch sources produced by members and sold through the society. Its Internet pages include family trees (www. NLJEWGEN.ORG/FAMILYTREES.HTML) and genealogical sources (WWW.NLJEWGEN.ORG/GENEALOGY.HTML).

How to Get Help

Dutch archives are public institutions. Anyone may write for information; most institutions have professional staff to answer inquiries. Most institutions also are accessible through e-mail and the Internet (see Addresses). For the names of professional genealogists specializing in Jewish genealogy, write either to the Nederlandse Kring voor Joodse Genealogie* or the Centraal Bureau voor Genealogie.* Addresses of other archival institutions in The Netherlands or elsewhere can be found on the site WWW.ARCHIEFNET.NL or on Unesco Archives Portal, WWW.UNESCO.ORG/WEBWORLD/PORTAL archives.

Addresses

Apeldoorn Municipal Archives: Gemeentearchief, Condorweg 5, 7332 AC Apeldoorn, The Netherlands; e-mail: GEMEENTEARCHIEF@APELDOORN.NL

Bibliotheca Rosenthaliana, P.O.Box 19185, 1000 GD Amsterdam

Centraal Bureau voor Genealogie, P.O.Box 11755, 2502 AT Den Haag, The Netherlands; e-mail: WEBMASTER@CBG.NL; website: WWW.CBG.NL

Council of Jewish Communities, P.O. Box 7967, 1008 AD Amsterdam, The Netherlands

De Nederlandse Kring voor Joodse Genealgie (Dutch Circle for Jewish Genealogy), NKvJG, P.O.Box 94703, 1090 GS Amsterdam, The Netherlands; telephone: 0299-644-498; fax: 0299-647-661; website: WWW.NLJEWGEN.ORG/PUBLICS.HTML

Dutch Institute for War Documentation: NIOD, Herengracht 380, 1016 CJ Amsterdam, The Netherlands; e-mail: INFO@NIOD.KNAW.NL; website: WWW.NIOD.NL

Haarlem Municipal Archives: Archiefdienst voor Kennemerland, Jansstraat 40, 2011 RX Haarlem, The Netherlands; e-mail: AVK@HAARLEM.NL; website: WWW.AVK-HAARLEM.NL

The Hague Municipal Archives: Haags Gemeentearchief, Spui 70, 2511 BT Den Haag, The Netherlands; e-mail: POSTBUS.HGA@HGA.DENHAAG.NL; website: WWW.GEMEENTEARCHIEF.DENHAAG.NL.

Leeuwarden Municipal Archives: Historisch Centrum Leeuwarden, Grote Kerkstraat 29, 8911 DZ Leeuwarden, The Netherlands; e-mail: GEMEENTEARCHIEF@LEEUWARDEN.NL; website: WWW.GEMEENTEARCHIEF.NL

Leiden Municipal Archives: Gemeentearchief, P.O.Box 16113, 2301 GC Leiden, The Netherlands; e-mail: INFO@LEIDENARCHIEF.NL; website: WWW.LEIDENARCHIEF.NL

Middelburg Municipal Archives: Zeeuws Archief; P.O. Box 70; 4330 AB Middelburg, The Netherlands; e-mail: INFO@ZEEUWSARCHIEF.NL; website: WWW.ZEEUWSARCHIEF.NL

National Archive: Nationaal Archief, P.O.Box 90520, 2509 LM Den Haag, The Netherlands; e-mail: INFO@NATIONAALARCHIEF.NL; website: WWW.NATIONAALARCHIEF.NL

Ouderkerk aan de Amstel Cemetery, Werkgroep PIB Kerkstraat 7, 1191 JB Ouderkerk a/d Amstel, The Netherlands, c/o Rabbi H. Rodrigues Pereira

Rotterdam Municipal Archives: Gemeentearchief Rotterdam, Hofdijk 651, 3032 CG Rotterdam, The Netherlands; e-mail: INFO@GEMEENTEARCHIEF.ROTTERDAM.NL; website: WWW.GEMEENTEARCHIEF.ROTTERDAM.NL

State Archival Service, Nationaal Archief, P.O. box 90520, 2509 LM Den Haag

Utrecht Municipal Archives: Het Utrechts Archief, Alexander Numankade 199-201, 3572 KW Utrecht, The Netherlands; e-mail: INFO@HETUTRECHTSARCHIEF.NL; website: WWW.HETUTRECHTSARCHIEF.NL

Bibliography

Research Guides

T. Spaans-van der Bijl, *Handleiding joodse genealogie; met bijdragen van Ir. I. B. van Creveld* (Guide for Jewish genealogy,

with contributions by I.B. van Creveld). [Dutch] Voorburg: De Nederlandse Kring voor Joodse Genealgie, 1997. The book was published by the Dutch Circle for Jewish Genealogy on the occasion of its tenth anniversary. It includes a detailed list of publications, mostly indexes pertaining to Dutch Jews.

van Bockxmeer, J.M.L, P.C.A. Lamboo and H.A.J. van Schie. *Onderzoeksgids archieven joodse oorlogsget-roffenen* ('s-Gravenhage 1998) (Research guide of archives concerning Jewish war victims). [Dutch] The Hague: General State Archives, 1998. Published at the request of the state committee investigating the looting and recuperation of Jewish possessions during World War II, the guide can be acquired from The National Archive.

Indexes to Amsterdam Genealogical Sources

van Straten, Jits. *De begraafboeken van Muiderberg 1669–1811: Indexen van personen begraven op de joodse begraafplaats Muiderberg van af 12 januari 1669 tot 21 juli 1811* (Burial books of Muiderberg 1669–1811: indexes of persons buried at the Jewish cemetery Muiderberf from 12 January 1669 until 21 July 1811). [Dutch] Meppel: Stichting Bevordering Onderzoek Joodse Historische Bronnen (Foundation for the Advancement of Research of Jewish Historical Sources), 2000.

———. *De begraafboeken van Zeeburg: Indexen van personen begraven op de joodse begraafplaats Zeeburg tussen 11 oktober 1714 en 21 juni 1811* (Burial books of Zeeberg: indexes of persons buried at the Jewish cemetery Zeeberg between 11 October 1714 and 21 June 1811). [Dutch] Meppel, 1997

van Straten, Jits, Jan Berns, Harmen Snel. *Joodse Achternamen in Amsterdam 1669-1850* (Jewish surnames in Amsterdam 1669–1850). [Dutch] Meppel, 2001

These three volumes can be obtained at: *Stichting bevordering onderzoek joodse historische bronnen,* Hertogenweg 11a, 6721 MJ Bennekom, e-mail: JITS@WORLDONLINE.NL or at the Amsterdam Municipal Archives.*

Nederlands Joods Familiearchief: Register op de akten van aangenomen en behouden familienamen te Amsterdam 1811–1826 en in Nederland (Amsterdam 1967–70), 3 parts.

Verdooner, David and H. Snel, *Trouwen in Mokum; Jewish Marriages in Amsterdam 1598–1811* ('s-Gravenhage [1992]). This is an index of marriages of Jews registered before the civil authorities. The source is the Amsterdam register of publication of the banns. The authors selected only the Jewish couples. This index is available at the Amsterdam Municipal Archives, P.O.Box 51140, 1007 EC Amsterdam; e-mail: SECRETARIAAT@GAAWEB.NL; website: WWW.GEMEENTEARCHIEF.AMSTERDAM.NL

Verdooner, David and H. Snel, *Handleiding bij de index op de ketubot van de Portugees-Israelietische gemeente te Amsterdam 1650–1911* (Guide to the index of ketubot of the Amsterdam Jewish community from 1650–1911).

Note

1. Westerbork was the Dutch concentration camp to which all Dutch Jews were transported between the summer of 1942 and the summer of 1943, and from which each Tuesday a transport of about one thousand Jews was sent to extermination camps in Poland, primarily Auschwitz and Sobibor.

New Zealand

by Claire Bruell

New Zealand is composed of two islands, the North Island and the South Island. The capital is Wellington, at the foot of the North Island; the largest city is Auckland in the north of the North Island. Christchurch and Dunedin are the two major centers in the South Island.

European explorers first came to New Zealand at the end of the 18th century and a steady stream of traders, whalers, sealers and missionaries followed in the early nineteenth century. British rule was formalized by the Treaty of Waitangi signed by both the native Maori and representatives of the Queen of England in 1840. At this time, an estimated 1,200 Europeans lived in the North Island and 200 lived in the South Island. Most of the main cities were founded in the 1840s. A large number of people came in the 1850s and 1860s, when gold was discovered in Coromandel and Thames in the North Island, and in Nelson, Otago and on the west coast in the South Island. In 1861, 14,000 people landed in Dunedin in a single month—all seeking gold.

Jews came along with the others, and there is no doubt that their contribution was greater than their numbers might have suggested. Jewish communities were established in the North Island in Auckland, Wellington; South Island: Christchurch and Dunedin in the early days of the colony. Fledgling communities also developed in Greymouth, Hokitika, Nelson and Westport in the South Island, but they no longer exist. For a time, some Jews lived in Hawke's Bay, Napier and Wanganui in the North Island.

The Auckland community has recently been rejuvenated by South African immigrants and is the largest in New Zealand. Wellington follows close behind. Only a handful of Jews live in Christchurch and Dunedin today. The 2001 census revealed that the total national Jewish population is 7,300 people depending on definition. This is a rise of almost 50 percent over the previous census. The Auckland region registered as the biggest Jewish center with 3,132 individuals. New Zealand's general population is approximately 3.5 million, two thirds of whom live in the North Island; the population of Auckland is more than one million. The major resources for tracing one's Jewish relatives in New Zealand are New Zealand civil records and Jewish records. The Jewish communities have records of congregants; the civil records include birth, marriage, divorce and death records.

Civil Records

Archives New Zealand* (formerly known as National Archives) is the repository for records created by governmental departments considered to be of national importance. Researchers may expect to find such records as noncurrent school registers, shipping records, government employees' records, health and immigration records, and many others. Records are transferred to Archives New Zealand for preservation when they are no longer in use. Access to some records is restricted for 50 or 100 years for privacy reasons. Archives New Zealand has a set of telephone directories dating generally from the early 20th century. Its website* lists a VHS video 16 minutes "A Guide for New Readers" (VHS) available for NZ$35 published 1996. This is an introduction to the reference and research service at Archives New Zealand Head Office in Wellington.

Regional offices in Auckland, Christchurch and Dunedin are repositories for government archives originating within these geographical areas. The head office in Wellington holds records for that region as well as some that originate in other areas.

The publication (1990) "Family History at National Archives" by Bridget Williams describing records held by Archives NZ is now out of print. Since 1990, many records have been transferred to Archives NZ with government restructuring. These changes are reflected in a later (1995) publication, updating the information in the out of print one. This 1995 publication is called *"Beyond the Book: An Outline of Genealogical Sources at National Archives transferred or Identified Since the Preparation of Family History at National Archives"*. This later publication can be ordered from the Archives New Zealand website. The section on "Genealogical Services" will be helpful to researchers who refer to the website.

Alexander Turnbull Library and National Library of New Zealand

Between them, the Alexander Turnbull Library* and the National Library of New Zealand* are the two largest repositories of New Zealand reference material in the country. The Turnbull has compiled a national register of archives and manuscripts in New Zealand. The register may be found in public libraries throughout the country. It is known as NRAM (National Register of Archives and Manuscripts). The Oral History Center at the Turnbull Library will eventually hold copies of the Spielberg Foundation's* interviews with New Zealanders who are Holocaust survivors, as well as the Jewish Oral History Project's interviews with survivors, community personalities and Jewish servicemen who served during World War II—primarily from Auckland.

The Jewish Oral History Project has variously been called The Oral History Project, the Holocaust Oral History Project and a Jewish Oral Archive. It was begun in 1994 by a group in Auckland who decided to interview survivors and individuals displaced by the Holocaust. To date more than 70 people have been interviewed. The interviews, together with photographs, biographical data and transcripts have been deposited with the Oral History Centre at the Turnbull Library. Plans call for copies to be placed at the U.S. Holocaust Memorial Museum in Washington, D.C. and for the oral histories to be held in the archives at the Auckland War Memorial Museum* where they will be available for educational and research purposes.

Public Libraries

Holdings of public libraries throughout New Zealand are many and varied. The Auckland Public Library* has the most comprehensive holdings of any public library in New Zealand. Researchers can peruse directories, almanacs, research by the New Zealand Society of Genealogists,* the *Who's Who* series, family histories, some passenger and shipping arrivals, and local histories rich with genealogical information.

Most public libraries have New Zealand post office directories that are commonly known as Wises. These were published between 1872 and 1961 and contain an alphabetical list of persons and business firms by name. They may be regarded as a combined Yellow Pages and electoral roll and may be used to trace the movement and occupation of a person over an extended period of time.

The Auckland Public Library also holds a copy of "Book of Registry of Births, Deaths and Marriages in Auckland, New Zealand (Auckland Hebrew Congregation) 1842–56," a very slim handwritten, unpublished exercise book, probably donated by someone who discovered it at the synagogue.

Public libraries may hold information on army lists and histories, electoral rolls and newspapers—particularly the older newspapers, which can offer much rich social history. The National Library of New Zealand* holds a major collection of nongovernment archives and manuscripts from the early days of European discovery up to the present.

The Hocken Library* is a library, archive and art museum that focuses on the history and culture of New Zealand and the Pacific. It is administered by the University of Otago in trust for the people of New Zealand. Collections of books, newspapers, pictures, periodicals, archives, photographs and many genealogical sources can be found here. The library is particularly rich in information related to the Otago and Southland areas in the South Island.

Birth, Death and Marriage Records

New Zealand law requires that every birth, death or marriage be registered at the Registrar General's Office,* as well as in local registry offices. The Registry of Births, Deaths and Marriages is a branch of the Department of Internal Affairs.* Civil registration began in 1848, and each birth, death and marriage registration entry is duplicated. One copy is held at the district office where the event was first recorded and another copy is held at the Registrar General's Office. Although Archives New Zealand holds some early registers, mainly from small, closed registry offices, the first place to try is the Registrar General's office that holds the records for the whole country. (See also under "Public Libraries" for early Auckland Jewish records book.)

Records of Foreigners in New Zealand

Matters concerning citizenship were and still are dealt with by the Department of Internal Affairs. As it is a government department, its noncurrent records are held at Archives New Zealand.

When New Zealand became a British Dominion in 1840, anyone born in the country became a British subject by law.

From 1846 to 1866, becoming naturalized required an act of legislation; the lists of naturalizations can be found with other legislation in most public libraries.

In 1866 the Aliens Act instituted a new procedure: An application had to be made giving considerable personal details. The application was to be accompanied by a certificate of good repute and was then published in the official *New Zealand Gazette*, which included reports on decisions of the central government.

Archives New Zealand has much information in its holdings about aliens regarding their registration and the special controls imposed during wartime. During World War I, all enemy aliens were required to report to the nearest police station. A New Zealand Register of Aliens was compiled and published by the Department of Statistics in 1917.

Registration of aliens was introduced again during World War II; the register of the Aliens Tribunal and the records of the Auckland Aliens Authority are at National Archives. The Aliens Tribunal was established in July 1940 to investigate whether aliens should be interned. Later that year, the Aliens Authority was set up in various districts to replace the Tribunal and at the same time an Aliens Appeal Tribunal was set up to hear appeals against decisions of the Authority. By July 1942, the Minister of Justice had received reports on all enemy aliens and almost all non-enemy aliens.

Enemy aliens were those people who had come from countries at war with Britain and her allies. Non-enemy, or so-called "friendly aliens" were so classified because they had originated in countries fighting the Germans and their allies.

The reports are now at Archives New Zealand. Access to alien registration files is restricted until the end of the year 40 years after death, or 100 years from birth, whichever is the sooner. The same is true for the records of the Aliens Tribunal and Authorities. Registration of aliens was undertaken in two systems, first in 1939–48 and again in 1949–77. Archives New Zealand holds indexes to both systems, but only those indexes from the period 1939–45 that were not re-registered into the later system are open for research. The index cards record name, registration number, nationality, sex, marital status, date and place of birth, date of arrival in New Zealand, addresses and dates, and occupation addresses and dates.

The Auckland and Wellington Public Libraries have details of aliens who were naturalized in New Zealand between 1843 and 1916 and registrations of persons granted citizenship

[Alien's Copy.]   [Form Al.—2.
Certificate of Registration of Alien.   Nº   1979

Surname: BRIESS   Forename: Alice
Place of abode: Waverley Hotel : Auckland   Present nationality: Czech
Date and place of application for registration: 6.10.39   Auckland
Date of issue of certificate of registration: 9/10/39   Place of issue of certificate of registration: Auckland

Signature of holder: *Alice Briess*
Signature of Registration Officer: Inspector of Police

PERSONAL DESCRIPTION OF ALIEN.
Sex: Female   Date of birth: 8.7.1912   Place of birth: Brno Czechoslovakia
Height: 5' 5"   Build: Medium   Hair: Brown   Eyes: Green
Distinctive marks, &c.: Nil
IMPORTANT.—Every registered alien who changes his place of abode is required to give notice in writing of the fact within seven days at the police-station nearest his new place of abode.

NEW ZEALAND

Certified Copy of Entry in the Register Book of Deaths

Place of Registration: ____AUCKLAND____

N° 483794

1. When died — —	12 JUNE 1951	
2. Where died — —	"GABLES" PRIVATE HOTEL, 9 ST STEPHENS AVENUE, PARNELL	
3. Usual residence — —	"GABLES" PRIVATE HOTEL, 9 ST STEPHENS AVENUE, PARNELL	
Description of Deceased		
4. Name and surname —	ADELE BRIESS	
5. Profession or occupation —	WIDOW	
6. Sex and age — —	FEMALE 75	
Cause of Death		
7. Causes of death and intervals between onset and death — —	MYOCARDIAL DEGENERATION CARDIAC ENLARGEMENT HYPERTENSION	
8. Medical attendant by whom certified and date last seen alive —	H. KATZ 18 APRIL 1951	
Parents		
9. Name and surname of father	GOTLIEB FRIED	
10. Name and surname of mother	- FRIED	
11. Maiden surname of mother		
12. Profession or occupation of father	FORWARDING AGENT	
Burial		
13. When and where buried —	13 JUNE 1951 WAIKUMETE	
Where Born		
14. Where born and how long in New Zealand	HRADSKE HRADISTE CZECHOSLOVAKIA 5 YEARS	
If Deceased was Married		
15. Where married — —	OLOMOUC, CZECHOSLOVAKIA	
16. At what age married —	55	
17. To whom married —	VITEZSLAV BRIESS	
18. Age of widow — —		
19. Ages and sex of living issue	M. - F.	

I hereby certify that the above is a true copy of the above particulars included in an entry of death in the register book kept in my office.

Dated at ____AUCKLAND____ the ____21st____ day

of ____SEPTEMBER____ 19_67_.

_____
Registrar.

The fee for this certificate is 5s.	CAUTION—Any person who (1) falsifies any of the particulars on this certificate, or (2) uses it as true, knowing it to be false, is liable to prosecution under the Crimes Act 1961.

between 1949 and 1981. Also extant is a register of persons naturalized in New Zealand before 1948 that superseded the Register of Alien Friends published in 1925 by the Department of Internal Affairs. Both registers are held at National Archives. Access to the naturalization files on individuals is restricted to the end of the year following 100 years after the birth of the individual or 40 years after the death, whichever is sooner.

Wills and Probate

Wills of New Zealanders who died before June 16, 1842, were probated in New South Wales, Australia. Copies of the indexes up to 1980 are available at the Auckland Public Library.* The indexes alphabetically list names of the deceased, places of residence and dates of death. Wills are usually probated at the High Court nearest the deceased's residence. Investigation of an individual may lead to the discovery of family relationships; details of children, including their married names; and perhaps names of spouses of family members.

Wills were not filed for probate if the value of the estate was small and if the beneficiaries agreed on distribution. If the deceased owned land, a copy of the will should be with the transfer documents at local land information offices (see Land Records section below). Most probate registers and files have

been transferred to Archives New Zealand. Researchers should first try the appropriate local office and, if unsuccessful, National Archives, Wellington.

Land Records

Land Information New Zealand (LINZ) holds records of transactions relating to land. The Torrens system of land registration provided a government-guaranteed title to land and was implemented with the 1870 Land Transfer Act. LINZ holds certificates of title and other documents relating to land such as leases and mortgages. New Zealand has five land registry districts, in the North Island at Auckland*, Hamilton* and Wellington;* in the South Island at Christchurch* and Dunedin*. Copies of registered documents such as leases, mortgages and transfers are available from the LINZ office in each district.

There is a map on the Web at www.LINZ.GOV.NZ showing the geographic situation of each of the 12 LINZ offices nationwide. The section "Researchers and Historians" is helpful to those seeking information about land ownership. The Skylight Internet Ordering System is aimed at assisting people searching historic land ownership records for genealogical purposes. A researcher who wants to obtain a copy of a land record must know

- The land district to which the search relates
- The record type (certificate of title, lease, other)
- The record number

Record number can be difficult to find unless exact details of ownership are known. Finding old records and record number is not easy. LINZ operates an electronic title and survey system known as Landonline. This is geared for use by land professionals such as attorneys who pay a license fee to use the system. Landonline has had land records only for the past two years and replaces the old Land Title computer system that held the records for approximately 12 years. Predating the Land Title computer system, branch offices kept a card system arranged by owner's name. The maintainance of the card systems varied from office to office and accuracy cannot be assumed. The best way to approach a search for land ownership details is to employ a local "search agent." Such search agents can be located through Yellow Pages.

Census Information

Nationwide census taking began in 1858, but returns prior to 1966 have not been kept. An exception is the local censuses for 1845 and 1849 for the Nelson area (South Island). These records, which include details on occupants, buildings and land use, are held at Archives New Zealand in the Head Office, Wellington. Records from 1966, which have been kept, are not accessible for 100 years.

Electoral Rolls (Voter Registration Lists)

Electoral rolls for all New Zealanders from 1865–1943 are available on microfiche at the Wellington Public Library,* the New Zealand Society of Genealogists Library* and many other public libraries. Records from 1928 to the present are at the Registrar General's Office, Lower Hutt*; some electoral rolls prior to 1900 are held at Archives New Zealand in Wellington. An almost complete set of electoral rolls can be found at the Alexander Turnbull Library in Wellington.*

School Records

The 1877 Education Act provided for a national system of free compulsory education for children. The public school system had been started in 1871, but was not fully functional until 1911. In general, admission registers are held by Archives New Zealand in Auckland, Wellington, Dunedin or Christchurch. Admission registers and class lists, provided they have been fully and correctly completed, should contain the full name and date of birth of the pupil and parent or guardian, previous school attended, pupil's class at time of enrollment, next school to which the pupil transferred, and the reason for the child's removal from the roll. The New Zealand Society of Genealogists* has an ongoing project of indexing and transcribing admission registers. To discover the location of schools, consult Wises Postal Directories, available in most public libraries.

Passenger Ship Arrivals

Ship arrival records are held at Archives New Zealand branch repositories and at Archives New Zealand Head Office in Wellington. The branch of Archives New Zealand that has shipping records for a particular port most likely will be the one that is geographically closest. Records created before 1839 are not available. Lists of passengers up to 1886 are limited to government-assisted immigrants. The lists from the period 1887–1973 are held, with some gaps. The indexes provide reference to the embarkation lists. These sometimes lead to supplementary records containing further information on individual immigrants or shipboard conditions during the voyage to New Zealand. Summaries of some passenger shipping arrivals and departures were published monthly in some newspapers. Newspapers often carried details of arrivals and departures of ships, together with passenger listings and accounts of passage. From the late 1880s lists exist of passengers leaving the country.

Jewish Records

Six Jewish congregations are active in New Zealand today, four of which are in the North Island

- Wellington Hebrew Congregation* has existed for approximately 150 years. A specific list of records held by this congregation is not available, but reportedly, the congregation has a birth register that started in 1876, a death register from 1845, a marriage register from 1863 and a register of converts from the 1940s.
- Wellington Progressive Jewish Congregation Inc.*, was established in 1960.
- Auckland Hebrew Congregation* has existed since 1850.
- The Progressive Jewish Congregation of Auckland*, had its beginnings in 1960.

The New Zealand Jewish Archives* is located at the same address as the Wellington Hebrew Congregation. Between them, the two institutions hold most of Wellington's existing Jewish records. Most records in the archives pertain to the Auckland and Wellington Jewish communities. Included are board minutes of the Wellington Hebrew Congregation from 1885 to the present and ongoing, annual reports, records from various Jewish organizations—Zionist Society, Habonim New Zealand and Jewish Club which seem to be mostly Wellington-based. Archivist Michael Clements claims that the Wellington City Council Cemeteries Department* has a computerized list of those buried at the Karori and Makara cemeteries, but the Jewish burials are not listed separately. Personnel at the Cemeteries Department says that the names are on index cards and they may be manually copied.

The two active Jewish congregations in the South Island are:

- Dunedin Jewish Congregation* was originally a larger and more active community, especially during the gold rushes of the nineteenth century; This community, now with 50 members was established in the decade of the 1840s.

The gravesite of Moss Meyer Levy, who died in 1836, demonstrates that there was Jewish presence in New Zealand even before it formally became a British colony in 1840 with the Treaty of Waitangi between the Crown and the indigenous Maori tribes.

- Canterbury Hebrew Congregation has existed since about 1850 and, like its counterpart in Dunedin, suffers from declining numbers. Canterbury Congregation is situated in the city of Christchurch.

Both the Dunedin and Canterbury congregations hold records for other nineteenth-century South Island communities that have ceased to exist. See "Cemeteries" section for the locations of Jewish burials. These are communities that once had Jewish settlements. Inquiries about records that might be useful to Jewish researchers have elicited responses that range from no response at all to very helpful.

All congregations in New Zealand lack resources and must rely on volunteer help. Most have records that record milestone events, past membership lists and Board of Management minutes. In some cases, records are well-archived and easy to access. Most congregations, however, lack people who are familiar with their records and who have the time available to search for specific information.

Despite these difficulties, the Auckland Hebrew Congregation is prepared to open its archives to any bona fide researcher who visits and who gives advance notice or his or her visit. Other congregations may also be prepared to do this, but in each case, the researcher should write in advance explaining what is desired.

Jewish Publications

Given this situation, the most profitable way to make inquiry of local communities probably would be to place an advertisement in community newsletters or in the monthly *New Zealand Jewish Chronicle**, the only national Jewish newspaper. Back issues of *The Chronicle* and its predecessors *The Jewish Times* and *The Jewish Review* are held at the Alexander Turnbull Library** in Wellington and at the New Zealand Jewish Archives.* (Addresses for all institutions marked with an asterick are given at the end of this chapter.)

Monthly newsletters published by congregations in which researchers might also advertise are:

- Wellington Hebrew Congregation* and Wellington Jewish Social Club* newsletter.
- Wellington Progressive Jewish Congregation.*
- Auckland Hebrew Congregation's *Kesher.* Inquiries may be addressed to the synagogue office.
- Progressive Jewish Congregation of Auckland's *Teruah.* Its editor may be contacted through the congregation office.
- Canterbury Hebrew Congregation's newsletter editor can be reached at the synagogue office.
- *Chadashot* is a community magazine published by the Auckland Zionist Society.* It publishes advertisements.

Cemeteries

Information on the following cemeteries has been compiled by the International Association of Jewish Genealogical Societies (IAJGS)* cemtery project <http://www.jewishgen.org/cemetery>. Sometime in the near future, this project will hold the names of those buried in the cemeteries listed below on a CD available from the International Jewish Cemetery Project which can be contacted through the website. The cemeteries have a number of Jewish graves, even though many of these places no longer have Jewish communities.

Cemeteries in the North Island are:

- Auckland: Karangahape Road cemetery, Waikumete Cemetery, old and new sections
- Dannevirke: Mangatera cemetery, Hamilton cemetery (a few graves only)
- Hawkes Bay: Park Island cemetery
- Napier, Bluff Hill cemetery
- Palmerston North: Kelvin Grove and Old cemeteries
- Wanganui: General cemetery
- Wellington: Bolton Street, Karori and Makara cemeteries

The cemeteries in South Island are:

- Ashburton: old public cemetery
- Christchurch: Linwood cemetery
- Dunedin: Southern cemetery; Naseby cemetery near Dunedin (a few graves only)
- Greymouth: General cemetery
- Hokitika: General cemetery
- Nelson: Wakapuaka cemetery
- Queenstown: General cemetery
- Timaru: General cemetery

In addition, records of burials typically are held at the cemetery itself and in the local council offices. A council is a local body that administers the parks, cemeteries and similar places in every area. For example, no Jewish community exists any longer in Nelson in the South Island but the Nelson community council has records of all burials in the Jewish section of the local cemetery. The New Zealand Society of Genealogists* also has recorded burials in most cemeteries in the country, most of which may be accessed at LDS Family History Centers (see chapter **XX**.) Many public libraries in New Zealand have cemetery records on microfiche.

Addresses

Alexander Turnbull Library, P.O. Box 12-349, Wellington, www. NATLIB.GOVT.NZ/EN/USING/2ATL.HTML

Archives New Zealand Auckland, P.O. Box 91220, Auckland; e-mail: ENQUIRIES@ARCHIVES.GOVT.NZ; AUCKLAND@ARCHIVES.GOVT.NZ

Archives of New Zealand Christchurch, P.O. Box 642, Christchurch; e-mail: CHRISTCHURCH@ARCHIVES.GOVT.NZ

Archives New Zealand, Dunedin, P.O. Box 6183, Dunedin; e-mail: DUNEDIN@ARCHIVES.GOVT.NZ

Archives of New Zealand, Head Office, P.O. Box 6148, Te Aro, Wellington; e-mail: WELLINGTON@ARCHIVES.GOVT.NZ; website: WWW.ARCHIVES.GOVT.NZ

Auckland Hebrew Congregation, 108 Greys Ave., P.O. Box 68-224, Auckland, WWW.AHC.ORG.NZ/

Auckland Institute and Museum Library, Private Bag, Auckland

Auckland Public Library, P.O. Box 4138, Auckland, www. AUCKLANDCITYLIBRARIES.COM

Auckland War Memorial Museum, Private Bag 92018, www. AKMUSEUM.ORG.NZ

Auckland Zionist Society, P.O. Box 315, Auckland; telephone: 649-309-9444; e-mail: AZS@XTRA.CO.NZ

Canterbury Hebrew Congregation, 406 Durham Street, P.O. Box 21-253, Christchurch

Christchurch Public Library, P.O. Box 1466, Christchurch; telephone: 643-941-7923; e-mail: LIBRARY@CCC.GOVT.NZ; website:HTTP://LIBRARY.CHRISTCHURCH.ORG.NZ/HERITAGE/GENEALOGY.ASP

Department of Internal Affairs (Archives), P.O. Box 805, Wellington; telephone: 694-495-7200; website: WWW.DIA.GOVT.NZ

Dunedin Jewish Congregation, corner Dundas and George Streets, Dunedin

Hocken Library, University of Otago, P.O.Box 56, Dunedin; website: WWW.LIBRARY.OTAGO.AC.NZ/LIBS/HOCKEN/INDEX.HTML

Land Information Office, P.O. Box 92016, Auckland; e-mail: AUCKLAND@LINZ.GOVT.NZ

Land Information Office, Private Bag, 3028, Hamilton; e-mail: HAMILTON@LINZ.GOVT.NZ

Land Information Office, P.O. Box 5014 Wellington; e-mail: WELLINGTON@LINZ.GOVT.NZ

Land Information Office, Private Bag 4721, Christchurch; e-mail: CHRISTCHURCH@LINZ.GOVT.NZ

Land Information Office, Private Bag, 90107, Dunedin; e-mail: DUNEDIN@LINZ.GOVT.NZ

National Library of New Zealand, P.O. Box 12-349, Wellington North; telephone: 644-474-300; e-mail: WWW.NATLIB.GOVT.NZ

New Zealand Jewish Archives, 80 Webb St, Wellington, e-mail: CLEMCLAN@IHUG.CO.NZ

New Zealand Jewish Chronicle, P.O. Box 27-156, Wellington; fax: 64-4384-2123; e-mail: EDITOR@RIFKOV.CO.NZ

New Zealand Society of Genealogists, Inc., P.O. Box 8795, Auckland; website: HTTP://WWW.GENEALOGY.ORG.NZ

NRAM (National Registry of Archives and Manuscripts); e-mail: WWW.NRAM.ORG.NZ

Progressive Jewish Congregation of Auckland, 180 Manukau Rd., P.O. Box 26-052, Epsom, Auckland; e-mail: BSHALOM@IHUG.CO.NZ; website: WWW.BETHSHALOM.ORG.NZ

Registrar General of Births, Deaths and Marriages, 131 High Street, P.O. Box 10526, Wellington

Shoah Foundation, P.O. Box 5168, Los Angeles, CA 90078-3168

Wellington City Council Cemetery Department, 101 Wakefield Street, Wellington

Wellington Hebrew Congregation, 80 Webb St., Wellington; website: HTTP://HOMEPAGES.IHUG.CO.NZ/~BETHEL

Wellington Progressive Jewish Congregation, 147 Ghuznee, P.O. Box 27-301, Wellington; e-mail: TEMPLE@ACTRIX.CO.NZ; website: WWW.SINAI.ORG.NZ/INDEX.HTML

Wellington Public Library, 65 Victoria St, P.O. Box 1992, Wellington; telephone: 644-801-4040; e-mail: CENTRAL@WCL.GOVT.NZ; website: WWW.WCL.GOVT.NZ

Bibliography

Beaglehole, Ann. *A Small Price to Pay: Refugees from Hitler in New Zealand, 1936–46*. Wellington: Allen and Unwin, and Historical Branch, Department of Internal Affairs, New Zealand, 1988. Reviewed in AVOTAYNU, IX, no. 1 (Spring 1993).

Beaglehole, Ann. *Facing the Past: Looking Back at Refugee Childhood in New Zealand 1940s–1960s*. Wellington: Allen and Unwin, 1990. Reviewed in AVOTAYNU IX, no.1 (Spring 1993).

Bromell, Anne. *Tracing Family History in New Zealand*, rev. ed. Wellington: GP Publications, 1991.

Gluckman, Ann, ed. *Identity and Involvement: Auckland Jewry: Past and Present, 1840–1990*. Palmerston North, Dunmore Press, 1990. Reviewed in AVOTAYNU, IX, no.1 (Spring 1993).

Goldman, Lazarus Morris. *The History of the Jews in New Zealand*. Wellington: A.H. and A.W. Reed, 1958.

Levine, Stephen, ed. *A Standard for the People: The 150th Anniversary of the Wellington Hebrew Congregation, 1843–1993*. Christchurch: Hazard Press, 1995. Reviewed in AVOTAYNU XII, no.1 (Spring 1996).

National Archives. *Family History at National Archives*. Wellington: Allen and Unwin in association with Archives New Zealand, 1990. *Beyond the Book: An Outline of Genealogical Sources of National Archives Transferred or Identified Since the Preparation of* Family Hiistory at National Archives (now out-of-print)

Rogers, Frank. *Archives in New Zealand*. Auckland: Archives Press, 1984.

Norway

by Carl Henrik Carlsson

Jews were denied residence in Norway until 1851. In 1866, the official number of Jews was 25; in 1890, it was 214; 642 were counted at the turn of the 20th century, and 1,457 were resident in 1920. Most early immigrants came from Denmark, Schleswig-Holstein and Central Europe, but after 1880 the majority came from Eastern Europe, many from Suwalki and adjacent guberniyas. Some had resided in Sweden for many years.

A majority of the immigrants settled in the capital, Christiania (changed to Oslo in 1925), where a congregation was founded in 1892. By 1900, as many as four congregations were functioning in the capital, because of personal rather than religious differences among the Jews. The first Jews in Trondheim settled in the early 1890s, and the congregation which was formally founded in 1905 is reportedly the northernmost Jewish congregation in the world today.

Approximately 1,800 Jews lived in Norway when the Nazis occupied the country on April 9, 1940. Of these, 925 escaped to Sweden and 760 were deported; only 25 of the latter survived. About 100 remained in Norway during the war, most in concentration camps. In 1947–48 more than 500 Jews arrived in Norway from displaced persons camps, but many left soon afterward. In 1950, the official number of Jews in Norway was 836; in 1986 it was approximately 1,200.

Sources

Volume 1 of Oskar Mendelsohn's book about the Jews of Norway is very useful for genealogical purposes, since he names almost all Jews who lived in Norway before 1900, generally with dates and places of birth. The book is indexed. Another, sometimes complementary index of all 80 Jews from Suwalki-Lomza mentioned in the Mendelsohn book was published in *Landsmen*.[1] An article in *AVOTAYNU* lists about half of those buried at the cemetery at Helsfyr in Oslo (begun in 1884) including Hebrew names.[2]

Almost all Jews who lived in Norway in 1940 either escaped to Sweden or were killed by the Germans. Both groups are well documented. Those who perished are listed in *Våre falne,* which consists of short biographies of all Norwegians, both Jews and Gentiles who perished in World War II. In most cases, the information includes birth dates and places, occupation, names of parents and spouses, number of children, details about deportation and fate after deportation.

Norwegian Jews who became refuges in Sweden during World War II are documented in individual files in the Swedish *Riksarkivet* (National Archives) in Stockholm (*Statens Utlänningskommission* [National Board of Aliens—Kanslibyrån, Centraldossiérer]). These files include biographical data as well as information about parents, spouses and children.

Additional genealogical material may be found in the Norwegian *Riksarkivet* (National Archives) in Oslo. Among the sources are:

- Naturalization records, in *Justisdepartementet.* Before 1888, only a declaration was needed.
- Records of real estate purchases by aliens, (*utlendingers erverv av fast eiendom*), 1889.

- Records concerning passports and visas, compulsory since 1917, are filed in the archives of *Sentralpasskontorett* (1917–57), *Statens Utlendingskontor* (1957–88), and *Utlendingsdirektoratet* 1988–).
- Records concerning actions taken against Norwegian Jews during the Nazi occupation, Archives of *Politidepartementet* 1940–1945 *Statespolitiet*; for instance, *Spørreskjema for jøder i Norge,* a questionnaire all Jews were made to complete in February and March 1942.
- Records about individuals whose property was confiscated during the Nazi occupation (*Tillbakeføringskontoret for inddratte formuer 1945–47*).

Norway's eight regional state archives (*statsarkiv*) hold church records, probate records and other genealogically useful documents. Recent probate records concerning individuals living in Oslo, including those killed in German concentration camps, may be found in the archives of Oslo *skifterett.* Additional information is available in the archives of the Jewish communities of Oslo and Trondheim.

Internet Sites

National Archives of Norway: WWW.RIKSARKIVET.NO
National Archives of Norway, free public service for searching transcribed source material: DIGITALARKIVET.NO
JewishGen—Norway: WWW.JEWISHGEN.ORG/SCANDINAVIA/NORWAY.HTM

Addresses

Riksarkivet (National Archives), Pb 4013 Ullevål Stadion, N-0806 Oslo, Norway.
Statsarkivet i Oslo (Regional State Archives of Oslo), same address as above.
Statsarkivet i Trondheim (Regional Archives of Trondheim), Pb 2825 Elgesaeter, N-7432 Trondheim, Norway.
Oslo *skifterett* (Archives of Oslo), Pb 8009 Dep., N-0030 Oslo, Norway.
Det Mosaiske Trossamfunn (Jewish community), Pb 2722, N-0131 Oslo, Norway.
Det Mosaiske Trossamfunn (Jewish community), Pb 2183, N-7 Trondheim, Norway.
Riksarkivet (Swedish National Archives), Box 12541, SE-10229, Stockholm, Sweden.

Bibliography

Mendelsohn, Oskar. *Jødenes historie i Norge gjennom 300 år* (Three hundred years of Jewish history in Norway). [Norwegian] vol. 1, 1660–1940. Oslo, 1969, 1987. vol. 2, 1940–85. Oslo, 1987.
"Norwegian Cemetery Inscriptions." *AVOTAYNU* 6, no. 3 (Fall 1990): 26.
Våre falne 1939–1945 (Our fallen 1939–1945). [Norwegan] Published by the government of Norway in 1949–50.

Notes

1. *Landsmen.* Vol. 2, no. 4 (1992): 54–56.
2. *AVOTAYNU* 6, no. 3 (Fall 1990): 26.

Poland: General Information

During the Middle Ages, the Commonwealth of Poland and Lithuania was the largest country in Europe. It also had the largest Jewish population on that continent. At the end of the 18th century, however, Poland was divided between three hostile neighboring powers, the Austrian Empire, the Prussian Empire and the Russian Empire. It disappeared from the map of the world in 1795 until the 1919 Treaty of Versailles following World War I, when Poland once more was reconstituted as a sovereign nation.

Despite the changes in rulers, Jews never disappeared from its territory, and on the eve of the Holocaust, Poland had Europe's largest Jewish population. More genealogists have Jewish roots in Poland than in any other country. Today, Poland is a single country, but for practical purposes researchers seeking 19th- and early 20th-century Jewish roots must consider it as three countries: Austrian Poland or Galicia, Prussian Poland and Russian Poland. For this reason, Poland is treated in three different chapters because the strategies for genealogical research often differ.

There are some exceptions to this approach. Two major databases apply to all of contemporary Poland, the databases of Jewish Records Indexing-Poland (JRI-P) at www. JRI-POLAND.ORG and the Eastern European Database at Routes to Roots Foundation, www.RTRFOUNDATION.ORG. For additional information about JRI-P see JEWISHGEN; for details about the Eastern European Database, see Miriam Weiner's section on UKRAINE. The third major exception is research into Polish vital statistics records that are less than one hundred years old held in local civil registry offices and their archives. Civil registry offices are described in the section on RUSSIAN POLAND. This description applies to all of modern Poland.

How to Access Records from Home

Birth, Marriage and Death Records
More Than 100 Years Old

- Access JRI-Poland (www.JRI-POLAND.ORG) to see if records you are seeking are indexed. If so, follow directions for obtaining copies.
- Determine if the LDS (Mormon) Family History Library has microfilmed Jewish records from your town for the years you seek. The FHL catalogue is online at www. FAMILYSEARCH.ORG/ENG/LIBRARY/FHLC/FRAMESET_FHLC.ASP. If so, order the film and search for the records.
- Check the Polish State Archives website at BAZA.ARCHIWA. GOV.PL/SEZAM/PRADZIAD.ENG.PHP to see if records for your town exist for the years you seek. If so, determine which regional archive holds the records (addresses are listed) and write to that archive. You can write in your native language, but the response will be in Polish. If you are uncertain about which archive holds a record, send your letter to the head office in Warsaw. If records are indexed

by JRI-Poland, use its ordering procedure to obtain a copy of the record.

- For records from former Galicia that are not in branches of the Polish State Archives (not found at the above sites), check Routes to Roots Foundation website to see what records exist for your town and in what archive they are located (WWW.RTRFOUNDATION.ORG/ SEARCH.ASP). Write to that archive (addresses at www. RTRFOUNDATION.ORG/ARCHDTA6.HTM). See also the Ukraine archives English-language website at WWW.SCARCH.KIEV. US/ENG/ABOUT.PHP.

Birth, Marriage, and Death Records
Less Than 100 Years Old

- Check the Routes to Roots Foundation website (www. RTRFOUNDATION.ORG) to see what records exist for your town and where they are located.
- Write a letter to the Civil Registry Office (USC–Urząd Stanu Cywilnego) for your town. Addresses for Warsaw, Łódź and Kraków are listed below. For small towns, write: Urząd Stanu Cywilnego, [name of town], Poland. (For details, see Russian Poland section under heading "Office of Civil Registration (USC).") Polish Yellow Pages (www.PKT.PL/) may be helpful in finding exact addresses of USCs for a particular town including the Polish postal code. See WWW.RTRFOUNDATION.ORG/ARCHDTA3.HTML for instructions on how to use these pages.
- For Galicia, if records are not listed on JRI-Poland nor on the Routes to Roots Foundation (RTRF) website, write to the Ukrainian Embassy in your country and request specific vital records.

Books of Residents (Księgi Ludności, Karty Meldunkowe, or Rejestry Mieszkańców)
(see RUSSIAN POLAND).

- Look at Routes to Roots Foundation (RTRF) website (WWW.RTRFOUNDATION.ORG) to see what records exist for your town. RTRF calls them census records.
- Order the CD-ROM "Po mieczu i po kądzieli" (On the spear and on the distaff side) from head office of Polish State Archives (PSA) (WWW.ARCHIWA.GOV.PL/INDEX.ENG.HTML). The disk lists all types of population registration documents. (For details, see "New Finding Tools at Polish State Archives" in RUSSIAN POLAND section.)
- Write to the main office of the Polish State Archives. For a fee, staff will search for your family names and send copies from registration books, which list a whole family on one or two pages. If you have found the Fond number on the CD-ROM or on the PSA website, cite it in your letter.

For the current Polish State Archives schedule of fees for genealogical research and copying, consult the Polish State Archives website above.

Visiting Archives in Present-day Poland, Germany, or Ukraine

- Do the necessary research (see above) to determine which archive holds the records you seek.
- Make a list of all records and record groups you wish to see.
- Write to the archive in advance and specify the records

of interest to you to make sure they are available and not housed in another building.

- Verify that the archives will be open at the time you wish to visit; some archive branches close for vacation. Remember also to check local holidays before making a final schedule.
- Arrange for a translator or interpreter if needed.

Poland between World War I and World War II. (From In Their Words Volume 1: Polish *by Jonathan D. Shea and William F. Hoffman.)*

Austrian Poland

by Sallyann Amdur Sack with Alexander Dunai

Read the chapter entitled Austro-Hungarian Empire *before starting this section. Also see the chapter entitled* Ukraine—*Ed.*

Many researchers have heard that their immigrant ancestors came from Austria and were "Galitzianers," but no place called Galicia can be found on any contemporary map. This is because what was called Galicia really was part of Poland until late in the 18th century. When Poland was partitioned for the first time in 1772, the Austrian (Habsburg) Empire acquired the heavily Jewish southeastern section of Poland and named it The Kingdom of Galicia and Lodomeria, although it generally was known just as Galicia.[1]

In 1846, the small, previously independent Republic of Krakow was added to the Austrian holdings. The area remained unchanged and under Habsburg sovereignty from then until the land was returned to reconstituted Poland at the end of World War I. After World War II, the Soviet Union annexed the eastern portion of Galicia, with L'viv as its center; western Galicia remained the southeastern section of contemporary Poland—with Krakow as its center.

During the early Middle Ages, Poland had captured the eastern portion of Galicia from Ukraine and the area became the site of huge estates (*latifundia*) of the Polish magnates. The region remained essentially feudal in nature up to the time of the partitions with serfs, private towns and a premodern economy.

Galicia was the largest, most remote and poorest province in the Austrian (later, Austro-Hungarian) Empire. Initially exploited by the Habsburgs and cut off from its former Polish economic base, Galicia stagnated in the early 19th century at the same time that a huge Austrian bureaucracy harassed the population and forcibly Germanized it. After the formation of the Dual Monarchy in 1867, Galicia was given broad autonomy; the area was returned to Polish culture, Polish became the official language, and the province was ruled by a group of Polish nobles.

Jewish Life in Galicia

Like the Russian Empire, the Austrian Empire acquired a large but unwelcome Jewish population for the first time only after the annexation of Polish land. An Austrian census after partition recorded 171,851 Jews in Galicia and a census in 1785 showed 215,447 Jews, nearly nine percent of the total population. The population was divided between adherents of traditional Orthodoxy and devotees of the Baal Shem Tov (*Hasidim*).

Jews had lived in this region for centuries, some as artisans in the private magnate towns, many managing the estates of the absentee Polish landowners. Trade in alcoholic beverages (*propinacja*) especially was the province of the Jew. This was also the center of the bloody Khmielnitski uprisings of 1648, a major catastrophe for the Jews who, as tax collectors, were the visible symbols of exploiting nobility.[2]

The Polish wars of the 18th century had devastated Galician Jewry economically, and Empress Maria Theresa, whose hatred of Jews bordered on a phobia, made matters even worse. In 1776, her Code of Regulations Concerning the Jews decreed that Jewish beggars be expelled and that only rich Jews be permitted to remain. Jewish artisans were not allowed to work for Christian customers (except where no Christians worked in that trade). Jewish traders could not sell products controlled by state monopoly and heavy new taxes were levied. Until 1830, Austrian law forbade the civil marriage of more than one Jewish male per family.

Maria Theresa's son, Joseph II, tried to supervise all aspects of the lives of his Jewish subjects whom he wished to make into loyal subjects and taxpayers. In keeping with these plans, the Emperor permitted some previously denied professions, opened education and allowed Jews to settled in all cities. At the same time, strenuous efforts were made to end the "separatism" of the Jews. In 1785, Joseph II abolished his mother's decree of 1776 and, in the *Toleranzpatent* of 1789, set forth his plans.

Privileges were granted, but concurrently some restrictions were imposed. Jewish self-government (*kahals*) was abolished, but Jews were still kept in ghettos. They were forbidden to hold leases (*arenda*) on mills, inns, breweries and estates or even to live in rural areas except as artisans or to work on the land—with the result that close to one-third of Galician Jewry lost its livelihood. Jews were made members of the communities in which they lived and required to serve in the army, and also were made to pay special taxes. Because the government wanted to limit the natural increase in the Jewish population, a marriage tax was introduced. A law of 1810 sought to require Jews to pass an examination on German religion before they could marry. Not all of the laws on the books were actually enforced, however.

After the death of Joseph II, most of his laws concerning Jews were abolished. The special government schools were closed, Jews were required to pay an exemption tax in lieu of military service, and the right to vote in municipal elections was sharply restricted. Special Jewish taxes on kosher meat and on candles continued. Jews could not buy land. Some towns prohibited Jewish residence completely while in others they were restricted to ghettos.

For a short time during the revolutions of 1848, Jews acquired new rights and succeeded in eliminating many discriminations. By the end of 1851, however, counter-revolutionary activity canceled these gains. Only in 1867 did the Austrian constitution grant Jews full civil rights, eliminating all feudal restrictions. Only in 1867 were the ghettos of Cracow and Lvov eliminated.

Despite the official rights granted by the constitution, discrimination against Jews did not cease entirely. The

Kingdom of Poland

Sandomierz

Wisła

San River

Kraków • Tarnów • Łańcut
Rzeszów Rawa Ruska
Рава Руська
Wieliczka • Bochnia Pilzno Jarosław Jaworów
Przemyśl Яворів
Biała • Limanowa • Jasło • Krosno
Nowy Sącz Sanok • Dobromil
Lesko Добромиль

•Zamość

Bug River

Żółkiew
Жовква

RUSSIAN EMPIRE

Brody
Броди

Lwów Львів ⊙

Złoczów
Золочів

Tarnopol
Тернопіль

Gródek Jag.
Городок

Sambor
Самбір

Drohobycz
Дрогобич

Turka
Турка

Brzeżany
Бережани

Halicz
Галич

Stryj
Стрий

Dolina
Долина

Kałusz
Калуш

Nadwórna
Надвірна

Kołomyja
Коломия

Śniatyn
Снятин

Kosów
Косів

Trembowla
Теребовля

Buczacz
Бучач

Husiatyn
Гусятин

Dniestr

Czerniowce
Чернівці

Bukowina

AUSTRIA-HUNGARY

Galicia
as of the mid-19th century

━━●━●━ National borders

━ ━ Borders with other Austrian crownlands

From J. Shea and W.F. Hoffman, In Their Words—Volume 2: Russian.

constitution was observed to a greater or lesser extent in different places and at different times. Economic and professional discrimination continued with few Jews in the civil service or on university faculties. In 1910, the introduction of a state salt monopoly meant that hundreds of Jews lost their jobs. A year later they were forbidden to sell alcoholic beverages; this time 15,000 Jewish families lost their livelihoods.

Under the 1867 constitution, Jews were considered a religious group (*religionsgemeinschaft*) rather than a nationality (*Volksstamm*). By a law of 1890, which remained in force until the dissolution of the Austro-Hungarian Empire, the government regulated the *religionsgemeinschaft*. Teachers in Jewish schools were paid by the state, and the curriculum they taught was regulated as well. Every Jew had to belong to such a community. In 1891–93, Galicia had the largest number of Jewish communities in the entire empire (excluding Hungary) with 253; the next largest was Bohemia with 206 communities.

Jews formed the third largest minority (after Poles and Ukrainians) in Galicia, fluctuating between 9 and 11 percent. In some towns, however, they formed a majority, a situation that existed nowhere else in Europe except in the Russian Pale of Settlement. Among the Galician towns with a Jewish majority in 1900 were Brody (71.2 percent), Buszasz (57.1 percent), Rawa Ruska (52.7 percent), Sanok (52.7 percent), Stansilawow (51.2 percent), Gorlice (51.2 percent) and Kolomea (50.8 percent).

Ethnically, Galicia was divided into two sections, one on either side of the San River. Jews constituted only about eight percent of the population in western Galicia which was predominantly Polish, but they accounted for 13.4 percent of the total in the eastern, more Ukrainian section. Most of the Jews of West Galicia concentrated in such towns as Biala, Bochia, Cracow, Gorlice, Jaslo, Krosno, Nowy Sacz, Rzeszow, Tarnow, Wadowice and Wieliczka—the further east, the larger the percentage.

Emigration from Galicia

The Jewish population of Galicia increased considerably throughout most of the 19th century, but the rate of increase started to decrease about 1880 as many Jews emigrated, first to other parts of the Austro-Hungarian Empire and later to the United States and other non-European destinations. Hungary's Jewish population soared in the 19th century, the majority—especially in the easternmost regions—coming from Galicia. Toward the end of the 19th century, increasing numbers moved to Vienna where they accounted for the largest percentage of that city's Jewry—the second largest (after Warsaw) in all of Europe. Others migrated to Germany, Berlin especially. Most of those who remained perished in the Holocaust. On the whole, the Polish-speaking Jews were the most traditional religiously; the German-speaking tended to be more assimilated.

Genealogical Resources

Because the territory that once was called Galicia today is divided between Ukraine and Poland, the first step in tracing Galitzianer roots is to determine the country to which an ancestral town currently belongs. Only then can a researcher know where to look for archival records. Standard archival practice holds that records remain where they were created regardless of which sovereign governs at any given time (the so-called "provenance rule"). For this reason, when Poland was reconstituted after World War I, records created on the territory of Galicia during the years of Austrian (later, Austro-Hungarian) sovereignty were ceded to the Polish archival system. After World War II, the Soviet Union acquired the former eastern Galicia, today western Ukraine. Because of this history, genealogists must know the exact location of an ancestral town of interest. Most records from the Polish area of Galicia are either in Warsaw or in Polish regional archives; records created in the area that is now Ukraine are divided primarily between Warsaw and the Central State Historical Archive of Ukraine in L'viv* with fragmentary documents in Ukrainian regional archives. Various other data may be found scattered in archives and libraries around the world.

Suzan Wynne's book on Galicia[3] and Miriam Weiner's two books, one on Poland[4] and one on Ukraine,[5] include extensive lists of archival holdings relevant to researchers of Jewish genealogy. Kronik also includes holdings from Ukrainian archives.[6] Weiner's website is likely to have the most up-to-date information.[7]

Archival Records

Access to Archival Records: Poland. The LDS (Mormon) Family History Library (FHL) (see MORMON) has extensive microfilms from former western Galicia, but only a scattering include Jewish records. The majority of Jewish records seem to have vanished. Speculations about the fate of the Jewish metrical records include the theory that they were destroyed during or after World War II[8] or that they might have been taken to Germany by the Nazis.[9]

Researchers should first check the FHL catalogue for possible films. Lacking these, researchers should consult the Weiner and Wynne books for addresses and details about archival holdings for towns of interest. The choices then are to write directly to the archives, hire a local researcher or make an onsite research trip. Where records exist, all three methods reportedly have yielded good results.

Access to Archival Records: Ukraine. As always, researchers should first check to see if any Mormon microfilms exist for a town of interest. Although almost none exist as we go to press, the Mormons currently are microfilming in the L'viv archives, and the official word is that the records of all religions ultimately will be filmed. If no microfilms are found, the next step is to determine what, if any, records exist. Compare lists in both Weiner and Wynne. In the case of birth, marriage and death records, determine which are part of the *Zabuzhanski* collection in Warsaw and which are still in L'viv.

Lists of professional researchers may be found in *AVOTAYNU* and in *Gesher Galicia* (see below). Several genealogists report good results with onsite research in L'viv and in Ivano Frankivsk, the location of a regional (*oblast*) archive that holds numerous Jewish record groups from the Galician period.[10] (See UKRAINE for information about obtaining data from civil registry offices [RAHS]).

Beginning in 2001, the Jewish Records Indexing—Poland (JRI-Poland) project (see SIGS) began to index the *Zabuzhanski* records in Warsaw. Check its website (WWW.JEWISHGEN.ORG/ JRI-PL) periodically to see if a town of interest has been computerized. If so, then it will be possible to order copies of records from the archives in Warsaw.*

Census Returns. Although the Austrian and later the Austro-Hungarian Empire took numerous counts of its general and its Jewish population throughout the period that it ruled, almost none have come to light. Reportedly, no Austrian law required that original enumeration documents be preserved after the statistical information in them had been compiled. A former Polish state archivist confirmed some years ago that no regional branch of the Polish archival system that serves the former Galicia area holds a complete set of censuses, but some Jewish genealogists have located fragmentary census returns in local archives. Reports from Ukraine are mixed. One experienced local researcher has failed to find any census returns in the L'viv archives, but two Canadian archivists, George Bolotenko and Lawrence Tapper, visited the same archives in 1993 and were taken by its director to the vault in which Jewish records are preserved. They note:

> Additionally, there are censuses of Galicia from the 18th and 19th centuries. In the basement storage area...We also saw record books dating back several hundreds of years. Many of these books were so bulky and heavy that they require several people to handle them.[10]

Census-like Lists. The Central Archives for the History of the Jewish People* (see ISRAEL) has lists of male members of the Kraków Jewish community eligible to vote in *kehillah* (Jewish community) elections in 1883 and 1929. Although birth dates are not included, these lists resemble a census of Jewish males over the age of 13. Also at the Central Archives* are school lists that indicate the grade a pupil was in for that year as well as lists compiled for tax purposes, among them 1856 and 1895 lists of Jews who lived in small towns near Kraków, such as Balice, Czulice, Górka, Grebalowa, Krzeszowice, Liszki and Mogila among others. The archives holds 20th-century lists of members of five synagogues in Kraków.

In 1996, Fay Bussgang described *Spis Mieszkanców* (list of residents) in the Kraków regional archives.[3] (In Krakow the term used is *Spis Ludnosci*.) Kept by many Polish municipalities, these lists indicate the members of a household, date and place of birth, names of parents, religion and occupation, among other information. Bussgang wrote that the entries seem to have included notations of arrivals, departures, deaths, marriages and other information. The records that Bussgang saw dated from 1921. The Krakow *Spis Ludnosci* are listed on the Polish State Archives websites at BAZA. ARCHIWA.GOV.PL/SEZAM/INDEX.ENG.PHP. Select "Krakow Archive" and enter the word "ludnosci" for the fond. At last count, 54 fonds (for different towns) are listed. Hundreds more are available onsite. For a fee, researchers may obtain information from the *Spis Ludnosci* records by mail. Onsite researchers need only request permission to use the records.

Vital Records. The Austrian government first mandated the maintenance of birth, marriage and death records in 1784.

Jewish quarter of Krakow in the early part of the 20th century. Courtesy of Tomasz Wisniewski.

Records were to be kept in duplicate; initially, the Roman Catholic Church was responsible for maintaining all records, Catholic and non-Catholic, presumably Jews as well. Despite the law, no Jewish records have been found in the Catholic ledgers; neither have any duplicates surfaced.

Judging by what has survived, it appears that various Jewish communities maintained their own records, albeit haphazardly. Some communities have vital statistic records dating from the beginning of the 19th century; for other communities, no records at all have been found.

In 1875, the Habsburgs restructured and standardized the collection of Jewish vital records. A 1877 manual entitled *Führung Der Geburts-, Ehe- und Sterbe-matrikeln für die Israeliten in Galizien*, written by the Austrian ministry of justice, enunciated the official requirements for maintaining Jewish records in Galicia. The manual created 74 record keeping districts, most with subdistricts which were to be administered by official government-employed rabbis who were to oversee the collection of the records. Details of the Jewish record registration law and a complete listing of towns, districts and subdistricts may be found in *Finding Your Jewish Roots in Galicia: A Resource Guide*, by Suzan Wynne.

The new system worked well for birth and death records, but not for marriages. For a variety of reasons, Galician Jews avoided civil registration of their marriages. Until recently, Austrian law had imposed a marriage tax on Jews, only one male per family was permitted to marry and above all, Jews considered marriage a religious, not a secular, function. This also was probably an attempt to avoid military service. The oldest male in a family was exempt from military service.[11] As a consequence, children sometimes (but not always) were registered under the maiden name of the mother. Sometimes the father's name was included but not always. If the father's name was not included, then the children carried their mother's maiden name for life. Genealogists tracing relatives in 19th-century Galicia (and other parts of the Austro-Hungarian Empire) must, therefore, seek the records of ancestors under both the father's name and the mother's maiden name.

At times the father's name was included, perhaps hyphenated with the mother's maiden name. Other times *vel* the Latin word for *also* was included, as in *Spira vel Kahan* which means "Spira also known as Kahan." Sometimes on birth records the father's surname is crossed out on the record and the mother's maiden name inserted with the notation *recte* (meaning *rectified*). Another consequence was that children who officially carried their mother's maiden names often had difficulty claiming inheritances.

Jewish resistance to civil marriages (in addition to religious marriage) began to diminish as emigration increased. The need to prove one's identity and to demonstrate good standing caused many couples to participate in a civil marriage ceremony—often long after their children were grown. When this occurred, the children's birth records generally were amended to include the father's name.

For these reasons, registers from the late 19th century often include marriages performed religiously many years earlier. The presence of grown children and/or the fact that the children carried their mother's maiden name does not indicate illegitimacy.

Records from Eastern Galicia. Despite the intense fighting and widespread massacre of Jews during World War II, large numbers of 19th-century Jewish vital statistics records from eastern Galicia have survived and today are held primarily in the (Ukrainian) Central State Historical Archives* in L'viv. In combination with the *Zabuzanski* collection in Warsaw, (see below) the L'viv collection is probably the largest cache of 19th-century Jewish vital statistics records known to exist in any European archives.

Ivano-Frankivsk, formerly Stanislawów, was once a large Jewish population center; on the eve of World War II, Jews accounted for nearly half of the total population. Today, the capital of a Ukrainian oblast, it is home to a regional state archive with numerous items of genealogical value including an 1857 census of the town, part of an 1880 census of all inhabitants (including Jews), a portion of the 1900 census, list of Jewish-owned real estate and an extensive census of the local population taken in 1939, plus miscellaneous other items.

***Zabuzanski* Collection.** The so-called *Zabuzanski* collection records in Warsaw represent a major exception to the rule that records remain on the territory where they were created. After World War II, in an exchange of archival records with the former USSR, Poland acquired a substantial collection of Jewish birth, marriage and death records from the former eastern Galicia. (*zabuzanski* means "beyond the Bug River," the border between Poland and Ukraine). Records more than 100 years old are held by the Archiwum G»owne Akt Dawnych (AGAD).* Records less than 100 years old are held by Urzad Stanu Cywilnego-Warszawa Srodmiescie, Archiwum Akt Zabuzanskieh.* The USC website, HTTP://BAZA.ARCHIWA.GOV.PL/SEZAM/PRADZIAD.ENG.PHP, indicates that Jewish records for towns formerly in Galicia, now held at the USC in Warsaw are freely accessible to the public.

Records Less Than 100 Years Old in Ukraine. These documents will be in local RAHS (civil registry office). See UKRAINE for information about these repositories and access to them.

Records from Western Galicia. Few records have been found for Jewish districts of the former western Galicia; most seem to have been lost during or soon after World War II. Some scattered 19th-century vital statistics records, primarily from the districts of Kraków and Rzeszów, are available on microfilm from the Mormons; individual researchers have located a sprinkling of other records. Suzan Wynne includes a detailed town-by-town report in her book.[12]

Interior of the Zlota Rosa Synagogue of Lwow in 1931. Courtesy of Tomasz Wisniewski.

Other Genealogically Valuable Archival Records. Genealogists always seek documents in addition to vital statistics records and census returns, but this becomes a necessity in cases where no birth, marriage, death or census information can be found—an all too common situation in the former western Galicia. A wealth of notarial, real estate, school and other similar records are held in the L'viv State Historical Archives* and are well documented by both Weiner and Wynne. Especially important are the Josephine and Franciscan *cadastral* (land holding) records in that archive described by George Bolotenko.[13]

Notarial records can be a useful source of data. In the days before the era of photocopy machines, and other easy methods of duplicating documents, notaries were relied upon to make exact copies. When someone wanted a passport for travel abroad, or needed to prove identity for marriage, school or some other reason, a notary was hired. Notarial records, including real estate documents, for both western and eastern Galicia appeared to be housed in large numbers at the Polish state branch archive in Przemysl.

Various tax, school and other lists pertaining to Jews are held in both Polish and Ukrainian archives and are listed by both Wynne and Weiner. See especially George Bolotenko's detailed report of the Josephine and Franciscan *cadastral* records in the L'viv archives and Ben Solomovitz's description of how a researcher can use an ancestor's former (eastern Galicia) street address as a link connecting different record groups in the L'viv archives.[14]

Jewish Historical Institute*

A valuable, non-archival source in Poland is the Jewish Historical Institute in Warsaw. Most of its Galician holdings come from Kraków and surrounding towns (1701–1942). Scattered other holdings include some doctoral dissertation and masters theses about individual Jewish communities, cemetery records, voter lists and similar community records.

Records Held Outside of Poland and Ukraine

Genealogically relevant records from the former Galicia have been reported in the United States, Israel, Germany and Austria.

Jerusalem. Several valuable items may be found here (see ISRAEL). The Central Archives for the History of the Jewish People* has various historical documents in its holdings that are essentially the equivalent of censuses, including synagogue, taxpayer and voting lists; membership lists of Zionist organizations and others. Occasional vital records are scattered through the collections. Records of the Kollel Galicia* often provide considerable information about individuals still living in Galicia.[15] A copy of the 1875 Montefiore census of Kolel Austria-Galicia held at the Jewish National and University Library* includes an alphabetical list of surnames. (The original is at Jews College, London.) Both the Microfilm Division and the Archives and Manuscript Division of the library have various documents and registers of genealogical value from Jewish communities in Galicia.

Various *landsmanshaftn* and hasidic groups can be excellent first-hand sources of information about life and people from their town of origin. (See Sack, *A Guide to Genealogical Research in Israel* for information about locating representatives of Galician *landsmanshaftn* in Israel.) These individuals usually can also supply names and addresses of parallel *landsmanshaftn* in New York and elsewhere. The personnel at Kollel Galicia probably know which hasidic dynasty was active in specific Galician towns and can refer researchers to representatives of these groups. Many have almost encyclopedic genealogical memories. The computerized Yad Vashem archives and its *Pinkas Hakehillot* series for Galicia also are valuable resources. (See HOLOCAUST for information about *yizkor* memorial books and other sources of Holocaust-era data.)

Leipzig, Germany. Reportedly the *Zentralstelle für Genealogie* in Leipzig holds many birth, marriage and death records for the Jewish communities in Galicia and Ukraine that were captured by the German army during World War II.[16] The Mormons have filmed a collection of Jewish marriage records for the western Galician town of Wadowice (microfilm #127,748) at the Privy State Archives of Prussian Culture in Berlin-Dahlem* raising speculation that additional similar items might also be in that repository.

Vienna. Immigrants from Galicia to Vienna before 1919 may be listed on the register of passports held in Vienna. The records (written in German) have been microfilmed by the Mormons under the title *Wien-Konskription-semt, Passport Registers, 1792–1918*. An index for the years 1792 to 1901 is included. Anyone with a reasonably unusual family name should check these. Military records for the entire Habsburg empire, including Galicia, are in Vienna (see AUSTRIAN EMPIRE).* Numerous Jewish men served in the Austro-Hungarian army during the Franco-Prussian War of 1870 and in World War I.

New York. Large numbers of emigrants from Galicia settled in the New York City area at the end of the 19th century where they founded numerous *landsmanshaftn*. Their ranks were augmented after World War II by Holocaust survivors. YIVO Institute for Jewish Research* has a large collection of papers from defunct *landsmanshaftn* as well as miscellaneous documents of genealogical value.

Addresses

Archiwum Główne Akt Dawnych, ul Długa 7, 00-263 Warsaw, Poland

Central Archives for the History of the Jewish People, Sprinzak Building, Givat Ram Campus, Hebrew University, P.O.B. 1149, Jerusalem 91010, Israel

Jewish Historical Institute (Zydowski Instytut Historyczny w Polsce, 00-900 Warszawa, ul. Tłomackie 3/5, Poland

Jewish National and University Library, P.O.B. 503, Jerusalem 91004, Israel

Kollel Galicia (known as Kollel Hibat Yerusalayim), 120 Mea Shearim Street, Jerusalem, Israel; telephone: 972-2-628-8016, 628-5575

Kraków regional archives, ul. Sienna 15, Kraków, Poland

Privy State Archives of Prussian Culture (Geheimes Staatsarchiv Preussischer Kulturbesitz), Archivstrasse 12-14, 14195 Berlin, Germany

Tsentral'n yi Derzhavnyi Istoryehnyi Archiv u.m. L'viv, 290004 L'viv 4, Ukraine, pl. Vozz'iednannia 3'a

Urzad Stanu Cywilnego-Warszawa Strodmiescie, Urzad Stanu Cywilnego m. st. Warszawy-Archiwum, ul. Smyczkowa 14, 02-678 Warsaw, Poland; telephone: 011-48- 22-847-4821; fax: 22-847-8836; website: WWW.GMINACENTRUM.WAW.PL

YIVO Institute for Jewish Research, Center for Jewish History, 15 West 16th Street, New York, New York 10011

Bibliography

Beider, Alexander. *A Dictionary of Jewish Surnames from the Kingdom of Poland*. Teaneck: Avotaynu, 1996.

Bolotenko, George. "Report on a Recent Trip to Ukrainian Archives." *AVOTAYNU* 10, no. 1 (Spring 1994): 3–7. Describes nature of Josephine and Franciscan *cadastral* records.

Bolotenko, George and Lawrence Tapper. "Canadian Archivists Visit Ukrainian Archives." *AVOTAYNU* 9, no. 4 (Winter 1993): 9–10.

Bussgang, Fay. "Census Records and City Directories in the Krakow Archives." *AVOTAYNU* 12, no. 2 (Summer 1996): 27-28.

Caplan, Sophie. Contributing Editors (Australia). *AVOTAYNU* 5, no. 3 (Fall 1989): 22–23. Discusses *Geschichte der Duisberg Juden* (History of the Jews of Duisberg). 2 vols. Duisberg: Waller Braun. Includes many short biographical sketches of Jewish immigrants from Galicia.

Cymbler, Jeffrey. "Nineteenth- and Twentieth-Century Polish Directories as Resources for Genealogical Information." *AVOTAYNU* 13, no.1 (Spring 1997): 25–33.

Gelles, Edward. "Finding Rabbi Moses Gelles." *AVOTAYNU* 18, no. 1 (Spring 2002): 26–29.

"Kollel Galicia Records." *Sharshert Hadorot* 15, no. 3 (June 2001). Jerusalem: Israel Genealogical Society. Kronik, Alexander and Sallyann Amdur Sack. *Some Archival Sources for Ukrainian-Jewish Genealogy*. Teaneck, N.J.: Avotaynu, 1997.

Luft, Edward D. "German and Polish Archival Holdings in Moscow." *AVOTAYNU* 17, no. 4 (Winter 2001): 11–13.

Pazdziorek, Izabela. "Location of Western Galicia Vital Statistics Records." *AVOTAYNU* 7, no. 2 (Summer 1991): 14–15.

Rosman, Murray J. *The Lord's Jews*. Cambridge, MA: Harvard University Press, 1990.

Sack, Sallyann Amdur and the Israel Genealogical Society, *A Guide to Jewish Genealogical Research in Israel*, rev.ed. Teaneck: Avotaynu, 1995; Sack, Sallyann Amdur. *A Guide to Jewish Genealogical Research in Israel*. (Baltimore: Genealogical Publishing, 1987.

Slomowitz, Benjamin H. "Some Documents in Galician Records." *AVOTAYNU* 13, no. 4 (Winter 1997): 45.

Weiner, Miriam. *Jewish Roots in Poland: Pages from the Past and Archival Inventories*. Secaucus, N.J.: The Miriam Weiner Routes to Roots Foundation and New York: YIVO Institute for Jewish Research, 1997.

Weiner, Miriam. *Jewish Roots in Ukraine and Moldova: Pages from the Past and Archival Inventories*. Secaucus, N.J.: The Miriam Weiner Routes to Roots Foundation and New York: YIVO Institute for Jewish Research, 1999.

Wunder, Meir. "About Galicia." *AVOTAYNU* 2, no. 2 (October 1986): 18–19. Good list of resource books.

Wunder, Meir. "The Kollel Galicia Archive." *AVOTAYNU* 7, no. 3 (Fall 1991): 23–24.

Wynne, Suzan. "Demographic Records of Galicia 1772–1919." *AVOTAYNU* 8, no. 2 (Summer 1992): 7–10.

Wynne, Suzan. *Finding Your Jewish Roots in Galicia: A Resource Guide*. Teaneck, N.J.: Avotaynu, 1998.

Wynne, Suzan. "Highlights of Galician History." *The Galitzianer* 9, no. 2 (February 2002): 20–21.

Wynne, Suzan. "Letter to the Editor." *AVOTAYNU* 7, no. 3 (Fall 1991): 43.

Wynne, Suzan. "Vital Statistics Records from East Galicia Now in Warsaw." *AVOTAYNU* 7, no. 2 (Summer 1992).

Notes

1. The name was taken from the medieval cities of Halych and Vladimir once claimed by Hungary in an attempt to legitimize its sovereignty.
2. Rosman, Moshe. *The Lord's Jews*
3. Wynne, Suzan. *Finding Your Jewish Roots in Galicia*
4. Weiner, Miriam. *Jewish Roots in Poland.*
5. Weiner, Miriam. *Jewish Roots in Ukraine and Moldova*
6. Kronik, Alexander. "Some Archival Sources for Ukrainian-Jewish Genealogy."
7. WWW.RTRFOUNDATION.ORG
8. Wynne, Suzan. *Finding Your Jewish Roots in Galicia.*
9. Luft, Edward D. "German and Polish Archival Holdings in Moscow,": 11-13 .
10. Slomowitz, Ben: 45; Bolotenko, George and Lawrence, Tapper: 9–10.
11. Wunder, Meir. "About Galicia,": 18.
12. Wynne, Suzan. *Finding Your Jewish Roots in Galicia*
13. Bolotenko, George. "Report on a Recent Trip to Ukrainian Archives,": 9–10; Gelles, Edwin, "Finding Rabbi Moses Gelles,": 26–29.
14. Slomovitz, Ben.: 45.
15. Wunder, Meir. "Kollel Galicia."
16. Luft, Edward D.: 11–13.

Prussian Poland
Including East Prussia
by Edward David Luft

After the three partitions of Poland in 1772, 1793 and 1795 and the results of the 1807 Treaty of Tilsit and the Congress of Vienna in 1815, several regions of what had been Poland belonged to Prussia until 1870. From then until 1918, Prussia was part of Germany, and these regions were, therefore, part of Germany until ceded to Poland, with a few minor exceptions, under the Treaty of Versailles. Those regions were again annexed by the Nazis and returned to Poland along with additional areas in 1945. These areas, now in Poland, are what was East Prussia, West Prussia, Posen (today, Great Poland) and some parts of Silesia.

Prussia was, and Poland is, a centralized state whose archives operate along nationally established principles. What is true of one *voivodeship* (province), in principle, was largely true of all others. Since most Jews from the areas of Prussia now in Poland came from Posen, we will concentrate on that region, but the same principles apply to East Prussia, West Prussia, and Polish Silesia as well as the rest of Poland.

Prussia annexed Polish Wielkopolska from Poland in the Partitions of 1772 and 1793.[1] After losing it under Napoleon, it was returned by the Congress of Vienna as the Grand Duchy of Posen (1815–50). In 1850, it became the 17th province of Prussia. Today, most of the former Prussian Posen belongs to the Polish *voivodeship* of Wielkopolska. The northern third, centered on Bydgoszcz, is now in the Polish *voivodeship* of Kujawsko-Pomorskie. The remaining part is today in Zielona Góra *voivodeship*.

The best review of Posen resources for Jewish genealogical research can be found at WWW.JEWISHGEN.ORG/INFOFILES/POSENRESOURCES.HTML. It yields much history and many citations to resources valuable in Posen Jewish genealogical research.

Germanization

The Prussians quickly began to develop their newly acquired territories, starting with the First Partition in 1772. Although Posen had been Poland's oldest and richest province, it was Prussia's poorest. It also came with more Jews than were in all of Prussia's other provinces combined.

Posen became part of the German Empire when the King of Prussia became the Emperor of Germany on Christmas Day, 1870. Prussia quickly tried to co-opt the Jews in an alliance against the majority Poles in the province. It attempted to convince all inhabitants, including the Jews, that German culture was superior to Polish culture. Jews were encouraged to speak, read, and write German to achieve higher objectives. As a result, after 1831, all 19th-century official documents were written in German, rather than Polish.[2] By the early 1880s, this *Kulturkampf* (culture struggle) was an articulated German policy.

In 1812, the Prussian king declared the Jews of Prussia, but not Posen, to be citizens of Prussia for the first time. After 1831, the ruling Prussian party deliberately encouraged Jews to see that their betterment lay with the Prussians rather than the Poles. As a result of uprisings in Posen, encouraged by the example of what was happening in Russian Poland, the Prussians ended the benign administration of Prince Antoni Radziwiłł which followed Polish principles and Polish law and imposed Prussian law and administration under Eduard von Flottwell. In 1833, the King of Prussia, in his capacity as Grand Duke of Posen, declared the Jews could become Jewish citizens of Posen. They were, however, only permitted to vote for their own leaders, although they were obligated to serve in the army, as were all other Prussian subjects.[3] Jewish leaders did not want the Jews exempted from military service as they saw such an exemption as perpetuating stereotypes and keeping the Jews as second class citizens.

Posen Jewry was not economically prosperous. In the period 1793 to 1875, Jews accounted for 75 percent of all bankruptcies in Posen. Jews generally followed higher risk professions than Poles and had fewer choices and opportunities than the generally wealthier Prussian merchants.

Early in the 1840s, as part of its policy to Prussianize Posen, the Prussian monarchy erected tariff barriers to encourage traders (many of them Jews) to abandon their prior natural trading partners to the east and to look west to trade with Berlin, Breslau, Glogau and other German cities. A thriving trade with Silesia had predated Prussian rule, but the Germans greatly increased that trade. The Prussians promoted alliances with Jews against the Poles at every turn, at one point even allowing a converted Jew, Richard Witting, to become Lord Mayor of the city of Posen late in the 19th and into the 20th centuries. The Poles retaliated with greater anti-Semitic feelings, boycotts, and the creation of agricultural cooperatives to bypass the Jews as middlemen.

Not only economics, but culture, played a part in Prussianizing the Jews of Posen. When the Prussians took a census in the Grand Duchy of Posen in 1794, only 8 of the 122 rabbis spoke German. By 1834, all 122 rabbis spoke German. In the intervening years, the Prussians made doing business and keeping accounts only in German a legal and economic necessity.

During the 19th century, some Posen Jews saw conversion as a way to improve their social and economic position. Others saw emigration to Berlin, with or without conversion, as well as emigration to the United States as the solution, especially after crop failures in the mid-19th century. Beginning in the 1860s and accelerating during the next 60 years, the Jewish population of Posen and West Prussia largely emigrated. This was also a period of rising anti-Semitism. Those who remained in Germany overwhelmingly moved to Berlin and Breslau. By the 1920s, after almost all of Posen and most of West Prussia were ceded to the new Polish republic, the two regions had lost more than 95 percent of their Jewish population compared with the peak Jewish population in the early years of the 19th century.

Surname Adoptions

The Edict of March 11, 1812, addressed naturalization of Jews in Prussia. A supplementary order on June 25, 1812, for the provinces that belonged to Prussia before the First Partition of Poland, including Prussian Silesia, dealt with the adoption of family names.[4] All Prussian Jews could initially choose their own surnames. Some Jews selected Polish or Hebrew names, but most chose German surnames. Jews living in the areas of the Ostmark, other than Posen, were required to adopt last names as a result of the promulgation of the *General-judenreglament fur Süd- and Neuostpreußen* (General regulation of the Jews for South and New East Prussia) of April 17, 1797. It also forbid peddling. The earlier *General-judenreglament* of April 17, 1750 applied similar rules to areas then in western Prussia. (The Ostmark was the area of Prussia that today belongs to Poland or Russia.)

In Posen, the royal decree that mandated the keeping of vital records in German and enabled certain Jews to adopt surnames was dated July 30, 1833. Jews in Posen had to prove permanent residence since July 1, 1815, or show proof of state permission to reside in the Grand Duchy, although challenges were very rare.

The Mormons hold records dealing specifically with name adoptions by Jews in either the period just after 1812 for Prussia or just after 1833 for the Grand Duchy of Posen. Other such lists of names are in Warsaw at the Jewish Historical Institute, in Leipzig at the Deutsche Zentralstelle, and in other locations.[5]

Begin Research Close to Home

The LDS (Mormon) Family History Library holds microfilms for many Jewish vital records for the formerly Prussian region of Poland; if possible, researchers should begin with them.[6] In addition, many *landsmanshaftn* records are available in the United States and elsewhere. The Mendel Gottesman Library Rare Book Room at Yeshiva University holds a vast collection of *pinkassim* (register books) and other useful books in the Louis and Daniel Lewin Collection.[7] The Jewish Theological Seminary of America, Rare Book Room,[8] also has a significant collection; however, the largest collections are at the Library of Congress and at the New York Public Library.

The Library of Congress Microform Reading Room, the New York Public Library and the Leo Baeck Institute each hold a microfilmed copy of the *Posener Heimatblätter*.[9] Intended as a popular journal, it is potentially valuable to genealogists since it provides much information about Posen Jews after 1918 and includes many personal names and family histories for the period prior to 1918.

Some data can only be found in repositories in Germany, Poland or at the Central Archives for the History of the Jewish People in Jerusalem.[10] Such research may be done in

Wooden synagogue in Kurnik, Posen, Poland

person, by mail, or through the services of a paid researcher. Check the notices in *AVOTAYNU*, *Stammbaum* and other genealogical publications for advertisers. Some German archives provide names of researchers available to do private research.

Research in Poland

If an archival record sought for Posen or other parts of Poland is not available outside Poland, the appropriate district state archive in Poland is the first place to search. To do onsite research in the Polish archival system, apply to either the local district state archive or to the Main Directorate of the District State Archives in Warsaw for permission to use one or more specific archives in Poland. Permission normally remains valid until the end of the calendar year in which it is granted. A researcher can seek permission in person upon arrival. A letter in English can usually be understood, but one in Polish or German is likely to bring a faster reply, which will be in Polish. For a list of addresses of the Main Directorate of the District State Archives and all Polish district state archives addresses, see WWW.POLISHROOTS.ORG/ARCHIVES_POLISH_POL.HTM, which also gives access to Roman Catholic church archives in Poland.

If you request the archives to do the research (which will be reported in Polish), include as many as possible of the following details about the individual(s) being researched: time period to be searched; town of origin; names of the person(s) to be researched; whether other family members are to be included in the search; dates of birth, marriage, and death; date of emigration; religious titles, such as rabbi or cantor; and any limit on the amount of money to be expended for the search.

Research conducted by mail will utilize essentially the same information but uses the offices of the Polish Main Directorate of the District State Archives rather than one's own knowledge of the system.

Onsite research in Poland takes some ingenuity; time moves more slowly than in countries further west. Most archival workers in Poland are quite dedicated, but the records created between 1772 and 1918 that they must consult usually are written in Gothic German for the portions of Poland that were then under Prussian sovereignty. This is difficult for many archivists to read, so useful information may sometimes not be recognized.

Each archives has a complete index of its available records, and most of these indexes have been published in overview format. If something relevant appears in the indexes, the researcher will be asked to forward $18 to begin the research. Upon receipt of the funds, the district state archive undertakes a more complete search. Whatever is discovered is abstracted or photocopied. Archival staff researchers consult the records for $18 per hour, and charge $10 for each copy made. Archivists sometimes make less expensive photocopies for (US) 50 cents per page. Final results may require up to one year and almost certainly take at least four months.

A researcher who knows the archives in which the desired document is likely to be located may write directly to that archives to save some time. The reply, however, will come from the Main Directorate of the District State Archives.

When the Main Directorate finds an item partially in Hebrew, it can send a photocopy of that item to the Jewish Historical Institute for translation, if necessary. A charge is made for this service, however, and the translation is into Polish. Few, if any, Hebrew documents remain in District State Archives, but some signatures are in Hebrew and, thus, cannot be read unless the name is also written in Latin, German or Polish.

Permission to use a specific archive automatically includes permission to use any sub-archival offices attached to that archive but at a remote location. Permission only extends to the use of archives under the direct control of the Polish government. Researchers must seek permission in other archives from those in control, such as the Jewish Historical Institute archive or Roman Catholic diocesan archives. Permission is seldom denied.

The Main Directorate is across the street from the Archiwum Główne Akt Dawnych w Warszawie [AGAD] (The Central Archives of Historical Records) at ul. Długa 7. Many Jewish items for areas no longer in Poland are at this archive and, most importantly, it holds records shipped by the former Ger-

man Democratic Republic to Poland as a goodwill gesture in violation of international law and custom since that broke up an archival collection in Germany. Among such records are those of Jews in Posen and other areas. There is also an archive for newer records in Warsaw as well as several other specialized archives.

Cities and *voivodeships* in Poland sometimes have separate archives that may be combined with libraries or museums. Since many archives are not open every day and may operate for only a few hours when they do open, always telephone to verify days and hours of operation; they sometimes change seasonally. These archives are not under the control of the Main Directorate of District State Archives, which probably has little information about them.

Every Polish archives has a library, but their size varies considerably. The Main Directorate of the District State Archives has a small but useful library which researchers may consult for indexes of holdings in almost all district state archives in Poland plus many other locations around the world.

A useful but now dated Polish source for which records are available by town is Piechota, Regina, *Miasta Polskie: Dokumentacja Archiwalna.*[11]

A book on archives in Polish describes all Polish district state archives and has an eight-page Introduction in English that explains how to use the book. The description of each archive and sub-archive in Poland has extensive information on holdings, finding aids and other research information, all explained in the English language introduction. The book is organized so that someone who knows no Polish may still be able to derive some benefit from it.[12] This book is especially useful because, although every district state archive in formerly Prussian Poland has published a catalogue of its holdings, some are outdated.[13]

For those who cannot read Polish, a new edition of the standard reference, *Archiwa w Polsce: Informator adresowy*, is a great improvement over earlier editions.[14] The book lists all current state, church, museum, university and private archives plus many other archives in Poland, with address, telephone number and a short list of published inventories for each. Headings at the top of the page are in English on one page and in Polish on the other. The new, longer English translations include "From the Editor," "Archives in Poland: Basic Information," "Abbreviations Used in Book," and "Non-Polish Archives with Holdings of Interest to Poles." This latter chapter is a useful list for seeking records in other countries and includes, for example, the U. S. National Archives.

The difference between the two books is that the latter one is a list of archives around the world of interest to the Poles with only a bare reference, when it exists at all, to a published inventory. The former book confines itself to holdings of the Polish State Archives and provides extensive discussions of holdings, including lists of published inventories. The discussion should be sufficient to enable a researcher to determine the existence of any holdings for a particular town within a given time period. The listing is not the inventory of holdings itself; these can only be found in the published inventories listed in the bibliography for each

Panoramic view of Posen, Poland, in the early 20th century. The domed building to the right is the main synagogue of the city. Courtesy of Tomasz Wisniewski.

archive and each sub-archive. Sometimes, Jewish records are identified as such. A few district state archives may have unpublished inventories of available records.

Go In Person Even If the Records Have Been Filmed

A personal visit to an archive can yield valuable documents; the Mormons have not filmed all Jewish genealogical archival records in Posen. For example, the District State Archive in Leszno holds *Volksbücher* (population lists) for the entire population of Rawitsch for the period 1840–60. This is a house-by-house census of individuals, including married children and grandchildren, dates and places of birth and special notes. The District State Archive in Kalisz holds material on Koschmin and Krotoschin Jews, while the District State Archive in Piła holds a comprehensive census of the Jews of Schönlanke from the 1830s.

District State Archives

From Warsaw, a three-and-a-half hour early morning express train brings one to Poznań, a central point from which to arrange visits to various archives and ancestral towns in western Poland. The city of Poznań is the regional capital of the Polish *voivodeship* that incorporates the largest part of the former Grand Duchy of Posen.

In any relevant town or regional capital, investigate the local library in addition to the library within the archive. Frequently, a city library or museum will hold directories listing all inhabitants of the area, histories of the region and other items, such as local telephone books, that may yield valuable clues. These libraries usually have newspapers, postcard collections and other useful items. Provincial Polish newspapers are not indexed, but ask the librarian to suggest an alternative, such as a printed history of the town, which is likely to give citations to other sources.

The *Archiwum Państwowe w Poznaniu* (Poznań Direct State Archives) is located at ul. 23 Lutego 41/43, 61-744 Poznań. The Main Directorate will have notified the archive in Poznań of your pending arrival if you have obtained permission to use the archive in advance. However, you are no longer required to seek such permission in advance. Reading rooms in most district state archives are small, with as few as eight desks for readers. In many cases, scholars will already have reserved places, especially during the summer months. Furthermore, many archives, such as the one in Poznań, are closed for part of the summer, so it is wise to request in advance a visit for a specific time and specific number of days.

The Poznań District State Archive main office holds a card index for all households in the city dating from about 1860 until about 1931. These cards show date and place of birth, changes of residence, military service, religion, spouses, children, and some other varying bits of information. A similar card index exists for the city of Bydgoszcz (formerly Bromberg), but only archival officials (and not researchers) are allowed to use it.

Some archives, such as the one in Szczecin, have microfilmed records in addition to those of births, marriages and deaths. Copies can be made easily and sent to researchers. All district state archives have the ability to make photocopies and copies from microfilms. Sometimes, however, it is necessary to check branches as well as district state archives main offices since some records for a particular place may be housed in a branch office while other records for that same location may be in the main office of that district state archive. The main regional archive will know what is in all branch offices.

Just because one regional archive holds a given set of records is no reason to assume that an equivalent set of records is in another regional archive. A number of the records in Polish archives, mixed with older German archival records, are in Polish and date from after 1918. Published sources indicate the availability of some such records up through 1950. The researcher should not automatically assume that such records are unavailable.

Especially in archives in more remote areas, persons who speak no Polish should be prepared to converse in German or to bring interpreters with them. Most Poles do not like to speak Russian even if they know it. Educated younger Poles often speak some English while older ones are more likely to speak German or French.

In the district state archives, investigate criminal records, land records and tax records in which the transactions involving both Jews and Christians may appear together. Polish district state archives hold few records of old court cases, but sometimes they have some. These records vary from archive to archive; check each local catalogue. Researchers should also determine if the archive holds police records of fines. Many Jews were peddlers, at times an illegal profession in Prussia and Posen. A check of police records could well turn up a fine or other involvement with the "law" and no listing in other record books. On the other hand, a Jew who was economically more secure was more likely to comply with laws involving registering births, marriages and deaths and might own recorded property or have some other middle class attribute. Thus, a listing in a set of records may also be a clue to economic status.

The local *kehillah* (Jewish community) kept vital records in Posen until October 1, 1874, after which civil record keeping extended to all of the German Empire. All areas of what is today Poland, but was then Germany, were affected by the 1874 law. With some exceptions, the unpublished records in archives that would interest researchers of Jewish families from former Prussian territory now under Polish sovereignty, usually are more than 100 years old. Each district state archive in Poland holds older (pre-1874, for the former Prussian areas) vital statistics records and usually some for later periods as well if more than 100 years old. In Prussian Poland, grandparents' names were not part of the official birth registration, but parents' names do occur in the marriage records. Reportedly, the Jewish tradition in Prussia was to obey the law, so most vital statistics records probably are accurate. Prussian and Posen birth records show the date of birth; names of the parents; profession; location of birth; legitimacy; sex of the child; his or her names; and remarks, such as the birth of twins.

As of October 1, 1874, those parts of Prussia that did not already keep civil registration records were ordered to do so.

The new law included all parts of the German Empire now in Poland and Russia. By law, all Polish vital records more than 100 years old are supposed to be transferred to district state archives. In some cases, however, the Urząd Stanu Cywilnego (local civil record office) may hold records more than 100 years old if they are bound in books that also include records less than 100 years old. The same may be true of any indexes. In the former German areas, all of the records of birth, marriage, divorce, and death for a given year for a given small town are in a single bound volume, which may also contain other years as well.

Because civil record keeping only began in Prussia in 1874 (in most cases), many smaller towns put their records in books that could span 30 years or more. Even those more than 100 years old may not be available in district state archives because of lack of staff to review and catalogue the records. In a few cases, where bound books include records that are both more and less than 100 years old, these books are likely to remain in the local record office until 100 years beyond the newest entry. In fact, most records of birth, marriage and death dating after 1874 for the former Prussian area are no longer held in local registry offices. Each local record office is supposed to retain a list of items sent to the local district state archive; archives usually are about five years behind in processing records turned over to them by local offices.

For Prussian or German records less than 100 years old, one may write directly to the civil registration office (USC) for the town in question or write to the Main Directorate. The Main Directorate will then contact the relevant USC. The Main Directorate will process requests at a slightly higher fee than local offices, but it has the advantage that it can accept payment in dollars and is less difficult to deal with than the local administrations. However, because of the extra steps the response takes longer and is more subject to error.

If a researcher wishes to deal directly with a local authority, for a fee, the registrar will search his records and issue a certificate showing the record of birth, marriage or death of the person. The typescript certificate (generally, no photocopy will be made) includes the date of the event, the name or names of the parties, and the type of record and place. Although the original document contains the address, the typed certificate will not have this information. No special permission is needed to obtain available records from this source as these records are considered current and necessary for public purposes, such as proving date of birth or marriage. These offices continue to record current information. For privacy reasons, documents kept in civil registration offices are not open to public inspection, but most registrars will search, as time permits, if one convinces him or her that the need is genealogical and the person searched for probably is deceased.

Many documents were lost in the two world wars, especially in small towns. This is a problem throughout Poland, not just in the former German areas. Polish authorities have reconstructed some vital records from other sources, such as church records, but this does not help Jews. Avoid wasting time if someone suggests a search in such records. Some-times very old records on Jews are in such church records, but that situation does not normally occur after 1874 when the civil record offices were created.

When other sources fail for pre-1874 records, check the back of the Roman Catholic parish registers of vital records for that town or the next larger location, perhaps in the diocesan archive or perhaps in the district state archive since some Roman Catholic registers were turned over to the State in Communist times. These should have been returned to the Catholic Church, but that may not always have been the case. Some records were seized; others were not. The only way to know is to inquire at the various archives.

Occasionally, early vital records are at the back of the Roman Catholic vital registers. When too few Jews lived in a small village to have their own community, the local Catholic priest was the official agent for keeping Jewish vital records prior to 1874. Some registers may still be in local parish churches. Check this possibility before visiting the Catholic diocesan or archdiocesan archives, where such records are more likely stored. Each bishop and archbishop makes his own rules about accessibility. For example, the bishop of Gniezno speaks some English, has lived in Israel, and pointedly indicates that all persons, regardless of religion, are welcome to use the archive. His staff is too small, however, to answer letters or to do research on behalf of others.

All archives under the control of the Main Directorate must send photocopies or other reproductions to the Main Directorate in Warsaw for transmission to a researcher. The Main Directorate informs a researcher of the charges when it receives the item in Warsaw.

Jewish Historical Institute in Warsaw

Not all manuscript records relating to Jews are held by district state archives. The *Żydowski Instytut Historyczny w Polsce* (Jewish Historical Institute of Poland)* holds a variety of helpful documents. There one can find, for example, a list of Jews not subject to deportation but also not eligible for naturalization in 1834 for the town of Koronowo in Polish, or Deutsch Krone in German, Posen Province. This list is among 122 lists ordered under the decree of June 1, 1833, that granted citizenship to some Jews living in Posen and, so far, is the only list found to have survived. A list of Jews otherwise eligible for naturalization who did not speak German well enough to be naturalized was compiled at that time for Mogilno and its dependent towns. Lists of Jews deported to Austria and Russia in 1834 and 1835 were also compiled. These lists are now at the Jewish Historical Institute in Warsaw.

The staff of the Jewish Historical Institute can read both Hebrew and Yiddish; members of the public are normally permitted to use all records. Personal visits to the archive, library and museum are welcome. No special permission is needed to use the facilities of the Institute, and several employees understand English as well as German. A photocopier is available. The Institute is walking distance from the Main Directorate of the District State Archives.

Libraries in Poland

Many libraries in Poland have special collections housing old books and related records, such as pamphlets. For example, the University Library of Poznań was a depository library when it was the Kaiser Wilhelm II Library before 1918, and many books there date from the time of German administration. A search of the catalogue yielded many useful books including Posen province city directories not available in the West. At least two other good libraries in Poznań hold relevant information. They are the PTPN and Raczyński libraries.[15] Some books belonging to the University Library of Poznań are held at remote sites and must be brought at a later day in the week. The library also holds, for example, published police compilations of persons to be arrested by the Nazis, but few Jews are listed. Only rarely is an address provided since these people were "on the run."

Library use in Poland requires no special permission. The researcher may request photocopies of newer books; these will be made within minutes for a nominal price, but copies of pages of older books, usually those printed prior to 1945, are only photographed at additional cost. Copies of original manuscript documents require special permission. Books printed prior to 1945 may not be exported from Poland without seldom-granted special ministerial permission. A good source for locating Polish libraries and other equivalent institutions is *The World of Learning*, available in most large libraries in the United States and Europe.

Maps Collections in Polish Libraries

As do almost all other archives in the former Prussian areas of Poland, Bydgoszcz has extensive map collections, usually including unpublished manuscript sources, such as very detailed, small scale, land ownership maps available nowhere else.

The best general collection of maps in Poland is in Warsaw at the Zakład Zbiorów Kartograficznych of the Polish National Library. The main library building is located at al. Niepodległości 213, 00-973 Warsaw, far from downtown. The map library has now moved there as well. Many of these maps are available nowhere else. At least one member of the map library staff speaks some English.

Two other good map libraries in Poland are at ul. Narbutta 29, 02-536 Warsaw; telephone 011-48-22-48-07-12; fax: 48-07-28; and ul. Ratajczaka 44 (in the Library of Adam Mickiewicz University), 61-728 Poznań; telephone and fax: 011-48-22-52-27-14.

Poland has released a modern series of maps in both 1:200,000 and 1:100,000 scale for the entire country. Poland has also produced new maps for various cities in which many street names have changed, usually reverting back to the name used in the interwar years. In a few cases, communities have elected to keep the names reflecting the Communist past. The Polish postal system apparently is quite adept at delivering mail regardless of whether one uses the current or former street name.

Cemeteries

The area that was under Prussian/German control from 1772 to 1918 no longer has any significant number of intact Jewish cemeteries. The Nazis systematically destroyed virtually all such locations, although many Jewish cemeteries have survived in other areas of Poland. Agents for the United States Commission for the Preservation of America's Heritage Abroad[16] have surveyed about 1,000 Jewish cemetery locations.[17] Unfortunately, the report does not evaluate all sites, so the location that interests the researcher may not appear in the report. In that case, an onsite visit by a researcher or hired agent is probably the only reliable method of investigation.[18]

Visiting Towns

Having exhausted archival and library sources in Poland, the next step is to visit the town from which the researcher's ancestor came. Many medium-sized towns and all cities in Poland have regional and/or local museums. County towns also hold vital records less than 100 years old. The county town of Flatow, which was in West Prussia and is now Złotów, is an example. The civil record office holds vital records not yet transferred to the archives in Koszalin and will make a typescript extract for a small charge. The researcher must show a blood relationship to the person searched, close enough to satisfy the presiding official or produce a death certificate.

Also in Złotów, one may visit the local museum, *Muzeum Ziemi Złotowskiej*,* where one can find maps of the town and photographs and postcards showing the now-vanished synagogue. The museum even has a list of the last Jewish residents of the town and their spouses, plus original documents showing the signatures and seals of some. Other local museums likely have similar documents and artifacts.

Having exhausted Polish sources, the researcher can always look in Germany for Jewish genealogical information regarding Jews from the former Prussian areas now in Poland.

German Archival Resources

The *Geheimes Staatsarchiv Preußischer Kulturbesitz* (Privy State Archives of Prussian Culture) in Berlin-Dahlem[19] now has all of its holdings in the Berlin area. In 1991, it consolidated two collections that were created with the prior division of Germany. The entire collection comprises 32 linear kilometers (about 20 miles) of records, including a large collection of maps. Many of the records held in this archive that relate to the Jews of the German Ostmark, the area now in Poland, date from the years 1795 to 1815.

The former West German government microfilmed some Jewish vital statistics records held at the Geheimes Staatsarchiv, Berlin-Dahlem. These records are available through the LDS (Mormon) Family History Library. The rest of the Dahlem records include Jewish censuses and a large number of miscellaneous documents. Most of these records have been indexed, but the indexes remain unpublished. Some of the non-microfilmed records are located off site and must be ordered in advance unless ordered early in the day. The Geheimes Staatsarchiv-PK, Berlin-Dahlem holds a very large map collection, about 80 percent hand-drawn or with hand-drawn annotations.

Imperial post office of Schneidemühl (now Piła, Poland) with synagogue on left

Another location to visit in Berlin is the Stiftung Neue Synagoge Berlin-Centrum Judaicum. This center houses the index and files of the Gesamtarchiv der deutschen Juden (Complete Archives of the German Jews). The Gesamtarchiv was compiled by the eminent German-Jewish genealogist Jacob Jacobson, mostly in the 1920s and early 1930s. It includes items dating from approximately 1750 to 1931. Although the Gesamtarchiv was never as complete as its name implies, it does include many important documents, such as naturalization lists and vital statistics records. All of the Berlin holdings of the Gesamtarchiv are now available on microfilm.

The index to the portion of the Gesamtarchiv held at the Stiftung Neue Synagoge Berlin-Centrum Judaicum is generally arranged alphabetically by town. It surveys more than 1,000 documents in the collection from various parts of the pre-1945 German Reich, including areas now in Poland. Most of the documents collected by Jacobson came from Jewish community archives, so the collection contains few official, public records. Some of the original items are in Berlin, some in New York City, and some in Jerusalem.[20]

In Leipzig, Germany, visit the Deutsche Zentalstelle für Genealogie (German Central Office for Genealogy). The Mormons have filmed some, but not all, items concerning Jews in this archive.

To locate additional records for towns in the former German Ostmark, see Jersch-Wenzel, Stefi, and Rürup, Reinhard, *Quellen zur Geschichte der Juden in den Archiven der neuen Bundesländer* (Sources on the history of the Jews in the archives of the new federal states).[21]

Many archival records for areas now in Poland are in German archives as part of larger collections. The records have been inventoried and are available to researchers. Researchers may photocopy any inventory and most records that are not brittle. Typical of some regional archives is the Vorpommersches Landesarchiv Greifswald.[22] It holds vital records for towns in some parts of the former German Ostmark. A marriage record, for example, will contain the names of the newlyweds, the parents' professions, a reference to the local document from which this record was extracted, the date of the marriage, the name of the bride's father, the town of residence of the bride and groom's families, the parties' religion, and the names of the Christian witnesses to the accuracy of the copying of the legal document. Sometimes one finds other records, such as lists of Jews, in separate Jewish census records for the 18th and early 19th centuries.[23]

German Libraries

Many libraries in Germany might be useful to researchers of Ostmark Jewish genealogy. For example, in Munich, the Bayerische Staatsbibliothek holds a printed Program (1895), akin to a yearbook, for the Royal Catholic High School in Ostrowo. It is odd to find this publication in Munich, since Ostrowo was part of Prussia, but Munich never was. The book has a list of 640 graduates of the school, including some who later became rabbis. The first graduate in 1849 and 134 others were Jews, some of whom are listed as having emigrated to the United States. Each is identified by birthdate and birthplace, religion, location, current profession and a description of his father's profession. Using *The Naturalized Jews of the Grand Duchy of Posen in 1834 and 1835*, the researcher may often identify the father as well.

For more detailed information on libraries, see Ellmann-Krüger, Angelika G., *Library Resources for German-Jewish Genealogy*.[24]

Brilling Archives in Frankfurt Museum: An Untapped Resource

When the collection is fully catalogued, the research papers of the late Rabbi Bernhard Brilling will be a major resource for German-Jewish genealogists, especially those with roots in Berlin, Silesia, Westphalia and the former German Ostmark. Donated by his widow to the municipally funded Jüdisches Museum in Frankfurt am Main,[25] this formerly private archive remains largely unknown and unusable today. Brilling was one of the greatest 20th-century researchers of German genealogy. His collection is especially rich in records from Pomerania, Posen, East and West Prussia, Silesia and Westphalia. Brilling lived in Breslau for many years prior to World War II, and his collection of Jewish population, circumcision, cemetery and other Silesian lists is unique.

Using the inventory prepared by the museum and also available at the Leo Baeck Institute in New York and in the library of the Jewish Genealogy Society of Greater Washington, one can find information on such things as the date of an ancestor's Prussian naturalization or an extract of a census record showing the family size, length of residence in the town to that date, the residence of a child not living with the family, and the age of the head of the family.

The collection needs a detailed catalogue for researchers to know what exists. Some of the items listed in the inventory also appear in the museum's computer inventory, but work on computerizing the rest has halted for lack of funds. Eventually, when funds permit, the inventory will be posted online at www.jewishmuseum.de. The inventory itself is far from a complete listing of holdings. Some materials have not been reviewed in depth since Brilling's death. Generally, information of research value is organized by town.

About 50 percent of the 140-meter-long collection, stored in 1,300 boxes, appears to have genealogical data. Among obviously valuable items are those sold by collectors to various archives, such as the source Brilling used for his article "Adoption of Family Names by Jews in Prussia (1804)." (*AVOTAYNU* 1, no. 2 [July 1985]). Another valuable item is a set of copies of tombstone inscriptions from the very old cemetery in Zülz, Silesia, today Biała, Poland.

Currently, using the Brilling collection is difficult. Most of the boxes remain in storage, necessitating an initial visit to the museum to review the inventory unless a copy of the inventory has previously been consulted. Then one must order the desired items. Usually one must wait until the next day for the staff to bring material from storage for use under the curator's supervision.

For a full list of Brilling's writings up to 1968, see "Bibliographie Bernhard Brilling 1928–1968," which has place, name, and subject indexes for 283 entries.[26]

Notes

1. See Lucy H. Dawidowich, *ed.*, *The Golden Tradition: Jewish Life and Thought in Eastern Europe*, New York: Holt, Rinehart and Winston, 1967, 502 pp., with bibliography: 493-95. Contains a four-panel map of the three partitions of Poland and the Kingdom of Poland inside Imperial Russia after the Congress of Vienna: 3. DS135.E8D3 1967. Another edition: Northvale, NJ: J. Aronson, 1989, DS135.E9A13 1989. There are at least four editions. This is an excellent resource, especially for someone who does not know a great deal of the history of the region.

2. For a more general overview, see Richard Wonser Tims, *Germanizing Prussian Poland: The H-K-T Society and the Struggle for the Eastern Marches in the German Empire, 1894–1919.* New York: Columbia University Press, 312 pp., 1941, Library of Congress call number H31.C7, No. 487 and DD337.T5 1941, reprint: DD337.T5 1966.

3. For a fuller discussion of the rights and obligations of the Jews of the Grand Duchy of Posen and a list of the naturalized Jews, see *The Naturalized Jews of the Grand Duchy of Posen in 1834 and 1835*, Decatur, GA: Scholars Press; ©1987, Brown University; 183 pp.; Series "Brown Studies on Jews and their Societies," No. 4.

4. For further details, consult: R. Blumenthal, C. Fraenkel and J. Raba, "Registration of Birth, Deaths and Marriages in European Jewish Communities, in Palestine, and in Israel." *Archivum: Revue internationale des archives*, Paris: Presses Universitaires de France, 1961, Vol. 9, 1959: 101–19. Library of Congress call number CD1.A18. This article lists the dates of name adoptions for all German states. In addition, entries indicate the beginning and ending dates for which each institution, usually the synagogue, kept vital records. For Prussia, see pp. 111–112.

5. Other resources for lists of names are *The Naturalized Jews of the Grand Duchy of Posen in 1834 and 1835*. Decatur, GA: Scholars Press, 1987, and the 1814 lists of Jewish name adoptions for Silesia and West Prussia in the respective *Amtsblatt* (official gazette) for that province, the Silesian list being in Vol. 4, no. 45, Beilage, of the *Amts-Blatt der königlichen Breslauschen Regierung*, JS7.G3 B75; while the West Prussian list being the *General-Verzeichniß sämmtlicher in dem Departement der Königl. Regierung von Westpreußen vorhandenen Juden welchen das Staatsbürger-Recht ertheilet worden* (Complete general index of current Jews whose citizenship rights have been granted in the Department of the Royal Government of West Prussia). No. 19, May 1814, available at the Library of Congress under DS135.P62P6835 1815a Folio; and Microfilm 92/2 (D). (See the online searchable database of the same information at WWW.JEWISHGEN.ORG/DATABASES/WESTPRUSSIA.HTM). The West Prussian list is also at the Leo Baeck Institute and on Later-Day Saints (Mormon) Family History Library microfilm. The Silesian list is *Amts-Blatt der königlichen Breslauschen Regierung*, Vol. 4, 1814, in the supplement to issue No. 45, Library of Congress call number JS7.G3 B75, but scheduled to be microfilmed. Researchers may purchase copies of many microfilms produced at the Library of Congress. In addition, the U.S. Library of Congress holds a microfilm copy of the 1810 West Prussian Census of Jews, along with an indexed list of Jewish concessionaires for the pre-1807 Netze Distrikt (parts of the Bromberg administrative district and West Prussia for the period 1801–1806). This film is also available on loan from the Later-Day Saints (Mormon) Family History Library.

6. See "German Jewish Records at the Genealogical Society of Utah." *Toledot*, Summer 1978: 16–28. This list is less complete than the following *AVOTAYNU* lists and differs slightly from them. "Polish-Jewish Records at the Genealogical Society of Utah." *AVOTAYNU* 2, no. 1 (January 1986): 5–17, and "German-Jewish Records on Microfilm at the Genealogical Society of Utah. *AVOTAYNU* 3, no. 1 (Winter 1987): 3–19. Also worth consulting are the Hamburg Passenger Lists for which a partial index also exists.

7. 2520 Amsterdam Avenue, New York, NY 10033; telephone: (212) 960-5363. Most books are written in Hebrew and German, some in Polish. The collection has more than 500 manuscripts and *pinkassim*, over half of which include genealogical material from the Jewish communities of Posen Province. There are many *mohel* books, death and burial registers from more than 50 communities, including Kempen, Militsch, Myslowitz, Pleschen, Rawitsch and Schrimm. The Library limits access to the collection, which needs to be microfilmed. The Office of the Dean of Libraries requests that a researcher make an advance appointment to use these materials.

8. 3080 Broadway, New York, NY 10027; telephone: (212) 678-8076 or 8973.

9. Edited by Heinrich Kurtzig and published from 1927 until all Jewish publications were banned by the Nazis in November 1938. The U.S. Library of Congress call number is 95/1432 MicRR; at the New York Public Library, it is ZAN-P953; and at the Leo Baeck Institute. Each year is indexed in the last issue of the Hebrew calendrical year.

10. See Central Archives for the History of the Jewish People at SITES.HUJI.AC.IL/ARCHIVES/PAGE3.HTM for such examples as *Poznań*—Community records (1592–1925) including 'Sefer Hazichronot' (1592–1689) and 'Pinkas Haksherim' (1621–1837).

11. Wydanie 1, Warsaw: Państwowe Wydawnictwo Naukowe, 1981, 307 pp. Library of Congress call number CD1757.5A1P53 1981.

12. *Archiwa państwowe w Polsce: przewodnik po zasobach* (The District State Archives of Poland: guide to the holdings). Warsaw: Naczelna Dyrekcja Archiwów Państwowych/Wydawnictwo DiG, 1998, hardcover, 539 pp. plus one page of corrections of telephone numbers; index of Polish archives: 537–39. The ISBNs for the book are 83-86643-17-X and 83-7181-029-6. The Library of Congress call number is CD1740.A825 1998 Poland, in EurRR; also at New York Public Library, R-Slav. Div. 99-5733. For further information, contact the distributor/printer at BIURO@DIG.COM.PL or WWW.DIG.COM.PL. The postal address is Wydawnictwo DiG, Krakowskie Przedmieście 62, 00-322 Warszawa; telephone or fax from the USA: 011-48-

22-828-52-39 or telephone: 011-48-22-828-18-14; 011-48-22-828-64-97; or 011-48-22-828-64-99. The price is 60 Polish zloty, currently about $17.50, plus shipping.

13. For example, the catalogue for the District State Archive in Szczecin indicates that it holds certain Jewish records for Złotów (Flatow, in German). In actuality, that Archives shipped those records to Koszalin (Köslin, in German) in 1989, to the *Archiwum Państwowe w Koszalinie* (District State Archive of Koszalin), 75-950 Koszalin, ul. M. Skłodowskiej-Curie 2, skr. poczt. 149, Poland; telephone: 011-48-94-342-26-22. Only a pencilled notation in the Szczecin Archive's copy of its published catalogue indicated to the public the fact of the transfer. (The Koszalin archive has photocopying facilities and a library.) Holdings for Flatow, now Złotów, date from 1773–1942. Only some of these Koszalin records are in physical condition good enough that the director will make them available for research. The rest need "reconstruction" when funds are available or when donated by someone who wishes to use these records for research in Koszalin.

14. See Konopka, Marek, *ed., Archiwa w Polsce: Informator adresowy: The Archives in Poland: The Archival Directory.* Warsaw: Naczelna Dyrekcja Archiwów Państwowych, Centralny Ośrodek Informacji Archiwalnej, ©1998, softcover, 221 pp., including index of archives by city: 203–05; index of institutions: 207–14; alphabetical index: 215–21. Library of Congress call number CD1740.A83 1998. ISBN: 83-86643-16-1.

15. PTPN Library (Society of the Poznań Friends of Learning): *Wydawnictwo Poznańskiego Towarzystwa Przyjaciól Nauk,* ul. S. Mielzyńskiego 27/29, 61-725 Poznań, telephone: +61 852 74 41; telefax: +61 852 22 05; e-mail: WYDAWNICTWO@PTPN.POZNAN.PL; website: WWW.PTPN.POZNAN.PL; and Raczyński Library: Biblioteka Raczyńskich w Poznaniu, Centrala biblioteki – Plac Wolności 19; telephone: 852-94-42, 852-94-43, with the branch most likely to be of interest to genealogists located a short distance away at ul. Św. Marcin 65; OLD.INFO.POZNAN.PL/KULTURA/LIBRARIES/RACZYNSCY.HTML, partially in English and with a photograph of the main building.

16. 888 Seventeenth Street NW, Suite 1160, Washington, DC 20005, Jeffrey L. Farrow, Executive Director; e-mail: FARROW@HERITAGEABROAD.GOV; telephone: (202) 254-3824

17. A report prepared by Samuel Gruber and Phyllis Myers of the Jewish Heritage Council, World Monuments Fund is entitled *Survey of Historic Jewish Monuments in Poland: a Report to the United States Commission for the Preservation of America's Heritage Abroad.* New York: Jewish Heritage Council, World Monuments Fund, 1995, 109 pp., including 3 appendices. Library of Congress call number DS135.P6G683 1995. The report is also available online at WWW.QUALITYOFLIFE.NET/PLREP.HTML. The report indicates the current state of cemeteries and synagogues in Poland.

18. For further cemetery information, see Kochowska, Wanda, and Wojecki, Mieczysław, *Żydzi w Polsce,* Zielona Góra: Ośrodek Doskonalenia Nauczycieli, 1994, 110 pp., including bibliography: 81-110, + 4 maps. At Biblioteka Narodowa, Warsaw, II 1.736.111 and II 1.815.736A.

19. Archivstraße 12/14, D-14195 Berlin, Germany; 011-49-30-83 20 31; fax: 011-49-30-83 90 180; http://www.GSTA.SPK-BERLIN.DE/FRAMESETS/FRAMESET.PHP

20. For additional information on the three separate locations, see Peter W. Lande, "The Complete Archives of the German Jews." *AVOTAYNU* 9, no. 1 (Spring 1993).

21. Munich; New Providence, NJ: K. G. Saur, 1996. Vol. 1: *Eine Bestandsübersicht* (An overview of the holdings) by Andreas Reinke and Barbara Strenge et al., 602 pp., including index of persons: 549–80; index of places: 581–193; and index of institutions, organizations, and businesses: 595–602, Library of Congress call number DS135.G3Q45 1996. Also at the German Historical Institute, 1607 New Hampshire Avenue, NW, Washington, DC 20009. It lists general descriptions of the holdings on Jews in individual archives in the former German Democratic Republic. Five other volumes have so far appeared, with one more planned. Although the books are in German, because they are a list of archives and holdings, non-German readers can make sense of much of the books. A German-English dictionary should serve to help with the few items that someone who does not read German will need.

22. Martin-Andersen-Nexö-Platz 1, D-17489 Greifswald, Germany. Postal address: Postfach 3323, D-17463 Greifswald, Germany; telephone: 011-49-3834-59-53-14 from the USA; fax: 011-49-3834-59-53-63.

23. See "Records for West Prussia Found in East German Archives," *AVOTAYNU* 15, no. 1 (Spring 1999): 33–34.

24. Teaneck, NJ: Avotaynu, Inc., 1998, 80 pp., including bibliographical references: 79–80. Z6373.G3E55 1998.

25. Unter Main Kai 14-15, D-60311 Frankfurt am Main, Germany; telephone: 011-49-69-212-35000; fax: 49-212-30705.

26. In *Theokratia: Jahrbuch des Institutum Judaicum Delitzschianum (Münster),* Leiden: E. J. Brill, Vol. I, 1967/69. The Brilling article appears in Vol. 2, 1970/72: 263–70. The U.S. Library of Congress call number is DS101.T5.

Bibliography

Bartyś, Julian. "Grand Duchy of Poznań Under Prussian Rule." Leo Baeck Institute *Year Book,* Vol. XVII, 1972: 191–204. Library of Congress call number DS135.G3A262.

Brilling, Bernhard. "Adoption of Family Names by Jews in Prussia (1804)." *AVOTAYNU* 1, no. 2 (July 1985): 23–26. Library of Congress call number DS101.A87. Re: Koźmin, but the source of the list of names is not identified.

Brunck, Wilhelm. *Fest-Schrift zum 110. Stiftungsfest des Königlichen Friedrichs-Gymnasium zu Bromberg 1817–1927* (Festschrift on the 110th Anniversary of the Royal Frederick High School in Bromberg 1817–1927). Berlin, 1929. Library of Congress call number 4LF11. Also at the Leo Baeck Institute. A list of graduates of the school.

Feldstejn, Hermann. *The Poles and the Jews.* Chicago, 1915. Library of Congress call number DS135.P6F4.

Statistisches Landesamt. *Gemeindelexikon für das Königreich Preußen, auf Grund der Materialen der Volkszählung vom 1. Dezember 1905 und anderer amtlicher Quellen* (Gazetteer of the Kingdom of Prussia based upon the 1 December 1905 Census and other local sources). Berlin, 1907–. Vol. 5, Posen. DD308.A2 1905. Vol. 5 also produced for the 1895 census (330 pp.), and 1910 census, Vol. 4, Posen Administrative District (139 pp.), and Vol. 5, Bromberg Administrative District (83 pp.), all three showing the number of Jews in each location in Posen as well as total population and other information. The U.S. Library of Congress has the complete series for each census. The 1887–88 volume for the 1885 census is at the University of Chicago (HA1292.A5 1885a). Although it gives no coordinates, it should help in locating towns and placing the Jews there in context. A very useful guide to how many Jews lived in which locations.

Graetz, Heinrich Hirsch. *History of the Jews.* Philadelphia: Jewish Publication Society of America, 1891–98. Library of Congress call number DS117.G82, 6 volumes. A general history.

Hagen, William W. *Germans, Poles, and Jews: The Nationality Conflict in the Prussian East, 1772–1914.* Chicago: University of Chicago Press, 1980. Library of Congress call number DK4185.P8H33.

Heppner, Rabbi Aaron, and Herzberg, Dr. Isaak. *Aus Vergangenheit und Gegenwart der Juden und der jüdischen Gemeinden in den Posener Landen*. Koschmin-Bromberg, 1904–14, 1921, Breslau, 1927–29, 1034 pp. Library of Congress call number DS135.G4P62. Also available on 17 microfiches, catalogue no. J-23-112/1, from InterDocumentation Company bv, P.O. Box 11205, 2301 EE Leiden, The Netherlands. A major source of information on the subject.

Kössler, Franz. *Verzeichnis von Program-Abhandlungen deutscher, österreicher und schweizerischer Schulen der Jahre 1825-1918, alphabetisch geordnet nach Verfassern, mit ein Vorwort von Hermann Schüling* (Index of High School Annual Lecture Proceedings of German, Austrian and Swiss Students for the Years 1825–1918, Arranged Alphabetically by Author). Vols. 1–5, Munich, New York: K.G. Saur, 1987. *Ergänzungsband, alphabetisch geordnet nach Verfassern* (Supplement, Arranged alphabetically by author, with a foreword by Hermann Schüling), 1991, available in New York from the publisher for about $1,000. Volumes 1–5 are available at the libraries of Harvard, Princeton and the University of Virginia library in Charlottesville, VA, in the United States and at Cambridge University Library in England. The fifth volume picks up items previously missed: Kössler, Franz. *Verzeichnis von Program-Abhandlungen deutscher, ...,*Widener: WID-LC Z2221.K67x 1987 F. Ergänzungsband. Munich: Saur, 1991. 351 pp.

Levine, Hillel. "Gentry, Jews, and Serfs: The Rise of Polish Vodka" *Review-Fernand Braudel Center for the Study of Economies, Historical Systems, and Civilizations*. Binghamton, NY, Vol. IV, No. 2, Fall 1981: 223–50. Library of Congress call number DI.F29a. Discusses *propinatio*, the rights and methods of those brewing spirituous liquors, and the *arenda* system, the rental arrangements of lands in northeastern Europe.

Luft, Edward. *The Naturalized Jews of the Grand Duchy of Posen in 1834 and 1835*. Decatur, GA: Scholars Press, ©1987 Brown University, 183 pp. Library of Congress call number DS135. P62P636 1987. A long list of Jews by name who were granted specific rights. Profession also listed.

Markreich, Max. "Notes on Transformation of Place Names by European Jews" *Jewish Social Studies*. New York: Conference on Jewish Social Studies, Vol. 23, No. 4, 1961: 265–84. Library of Congress call number DS101.J555. Contains a useful appendix of the Hebrew names transliterated and the German name of the same city.

Meynen, Emil. *Amtliche und private Ortsnamenverzeichnisse des Großdeutschen Reiches und der mittel- und osteuropäischen Nachbargebiete 1910–1941*. Leipzig: S. Hirzel, 1942, 162 pp. Library of Congress call number Z2247.G4M4 G&MRR. A bibliography, not a gazetteer. Lists gazetteers of all central and eastern European locations by local name and German name, if different, for the years indicated. Very useful in locating relevant gazetteers.

Piechota, Regina. *Miasta Polskie: Dokumentacja Archiwalna*. Wydanie 1, Warsaw: Państwowe Wydawnictwo Naukowe, 1981, 307 pp. U.S. Library of Congress call number CD1757.5A1P53 1981. A useful, but now outdated, Polish source for what records are available by town.

Rock, Christa Maria (Wiesner). ed., *Das musikalische Juden: Judentum und Musik, mit dem ABC jüdischer und nichtarischer Musikbeflissener* (The Musical Jews: Jewry and Music, with an Alphabetical List of Jews and Non-Aryans with Musical Abilities). Munich: H. Brückner, 1st edition, 1935, 242 pp. Library of Congress call number ML100.R7 1935 Performing Arts; 2nd edition, 1936, 248 pp.; 3rd edition, 1938, 304 pp. plus interleaves and separately bound edition in larger size, both with additional names in typescript. The interleaved 1938 edition is unique. All versions include many names with dates and locations of birth. In the 1938 edition, frequently the letter A appears after an entry. This signifies that the information came from vital statistics records (sometimes from towns whose original records no longer exist). Some name changes also are noted. Library of Congress call number ML100.R7J9 1936 Performing Arts and 1938 Copy 2 Case Performing Arts. The U.S. Library of Congress also has a regular 1938 edition, copy 1. The 1938 edition is marked "Case," which indicates that it is rare. All three editions have approximately 30 names per page with cross references for name changes. The Germans were very thorough, listing virtually anyone "non-Aryan" then alive who had ever given a musical performance or promoted one.

Strauss, Herbert. "Pre-Emancipation Prussian Policies Toward the Jews, 1815–1847." Leo Baeck Institute *Year Book*, Vol. XI, 1966: 107–36. Library of Congress call number DS135.G3A262.

Zarchin, Michael Moses. *Jews in the Province of Posen*. Philadelphia: Jewish Publication Society of America, 1939. Library of Congress call number DS135.G4P69.

Addresses

Bayerische Staatsbibliothek (Bavarian State Library), Ludwigstraße 16, 80539 Munich, Germany; fax: 49-89-286 38293; e-mail: DIR@BIB-BVB.D400.DE; website: WWW.BSB-MUENCHEN.DE/INDEX_E.HTM

Deutsche Zentralstelle für Genealogie (German Central Office for Genealogy), Schongauerstr 1, D-04329 Leipzig; telephone: 011-49-341-255-5551; website: WWW.GENEALOGIENETZ.DE/REG/DEU/DZFG-EN.HTML

Muzeum Ziemi Złotowskiej (Złotów Regional Museum), ul Wojska Polskiego 2a, 77-400 Złotów, Poland

Naczelna Dyrekcja Archiwów Państwowych (Main Directorate of the District State Archives), 00-238 Warszawa, ul. Długa 6, skrytka pocztowa Nr 1005, Poland; website: WWW.ARCHIWA.GOV.PL/INDEX.ENG.HTML

Stiftung Neue Synagoge Berlin-Centrum Judaicum (Foundation for the New Synagogue Berlin—Judaica Center), Oranienburger Straße 28/30, D-10117 Berlin, Germany; telephone: 011-49-30-2801220; fax: 011-49-30-2821176; website: WWW.CJUDAICUM.DE/

University Library of Poznań, ul Ratajczaka 38/40, Poznań, Poland; website: 150.254.35.111/WEBPAC-1.2-BUAMEN/WGBROKER.EXE?NEW+-ACCESS+TOP

Żydowski Instytut Historyczny w Polsce (Jewish Historical Institute of Poland), 00-090 Warsaw, ul. Tłomackie 3/5, Poland; website: WWW.JEWISHINSTITUTE.ORG.PL/OZIHE.HTML

East Prussia

All surviving Jewish records of genealogical interest that were in the Preussische Staatsarchiv Königsberg are now in the Geheimes Staatsarchiv–Preussische Kulturbesitz in Berlin-Dahlem. See Kurt Forstreuter's article, "Das Archiv Königsberg als Quelle für die allgemeine Geschichte" (The Königsberg archives as a source for general history). Much of this material is on microfilm at the LDS (Mormon) Family History Library. The microfilms contain many Jewish vital statistic records, including birth, marriage and death records dating back to 1809 for Königsberg. Presumably these microfilms are from the Berlin holdings, as are records of name changes.

The best book about the Jews of East Prussia and the basic source from which to start is Stefanie Schüler-Springorum's *Die jüdische Minderheit in Königsberg/Preussen, 1871–1945* (The Jewish minority in Königsberg, Prussia, 1871–1945). It includes many references to Jews in Königsberg by name. The *Encyclopedia Judaica* has an article on the city and *Where Once We Walked: A Guide to the Jewish Communities Destroyed in the Holocaust* mentions a *yizkor* book for Königsberg. It also notes that the Central Archives for the History of the Jewish People in Jerusalem has additional records of the city. As reported by Donald Levinsohn, at the Leo Baeck Institute archives, item number III-87 in the Jacob Jacobson Collection, AR-7002, is indexed as the 1812 name adoption list for the Jews of West Prussia. Bound to the back of that document, however, is a handwritten list of Jews living in Königsberg, East Prussia, about 1816. This list is not mentioned under "Königsberg" in the finding aid to the Jacob Jacobson Collection. The list provides the names of the heads of households, the names of wives and children, and either the date of birth in Königsberg or the year that the individual took up residence in that city. The Family History Center (Mormon) catalogue describes microfilm 1184428 as containing birth, marriage and death records for the Jews of Königsberg for the period 1809–71. While the catalogue description is accurate for marriages and deaths, this film includes a German-language index to Jewish births in Königsberg that extends as far back as February 1769, although most of the birth records seem to date from 1779 or later. The index is alphabetical by the first letter of the last name and written in Roman, not Gothic, letters. Births are arranged by the first letter of the father's surname and then chronologically by year and month within each letter. The mother's name is not listed at all. Unfortunately, the microfilmed pages are so dark for several of the earlier letters of the alphabet that they are virtually unreadable even at the highest possible magnification. The birth dates in the LDS indexes, while generally consistent with those in the 1816 list at the Leo Baeck Institute, do not always correspond exactly and, therefore, could not have been the source for that list. For example, the birth date of Markus Mosovius is given as October 28, 1784, in the 1816 list, while the LDS (Mormon) Family History Library microfilm gives it as January 1785. Such minor inconsistencies do not detract from the usefulness of the LDS birth index as a research tool; certainly, it goes back much further than the German-language Jewish vital records available for most locations. In addition, the index nicely bridges the gaps between the 1816 Königsberg list at the Leo Baeck Institute and several earlier lists of Jews in that city, such as the 1785 list printed on pages 1116–1139 of Selma Stern's *Der Preußische Staat und die Juden* (The Prussian State and the Jews) and a list from approximately 1801 that covers Jews in Königsberg and a number of other East Prussian towns in the Jacob Jacobson Collection at the Leo Baeck Institute Archives (item III-118).

Some burials for Königsberg natives appear to have been reported in other cities to which they migrated. A translated excerpt from B. Kagan, *The Jewish Community of Vilkovishk,* reports that this Lithuanian town's history can be documented back to the 1500s, including heavy German (and Enlightenment) influences. Burials from the 18th century include natives from Königsberg. The names of numerous rabbis and civic leaders appear in the book. A source at the U.S. Library of Congress is Jolowicz, H., *Geschichte der Juden in Königsberg i. Pr.: ein Beitrag zur Sittengeschichte des preußischen Staates* (History of the Jews of Königsberg in Prussia: an addition to the moral history of the Prussian state).

Howard Margol, in the Spring 2003 issues of *AVOTAYNU*, discusses records for the period 1796–1966, details where the records are held (in Berlin or in Vilnius) and offers some indication of what a researcher is likely to find in those records. All or most records are in German and cover the period 1796–1944.

Memel was the second largest city in East Prussia and became part of Lithuania after World War I. Some of the records discussed in the article pertain to the city of Königsberg and not to Memel (Klaipeda in Lithuanian).

Bibliography

Brandt, Edward R., and Goertz, Adalbert, Genealogical Guide to East and West Prussia (Ost- und Westpreussen): Records, Sources, Publications & Events / Edward R. Brandt, modified 2003 rev. ed., Minneapolis, MN: E.R. Brandt, 2003, 477 pp., including bibliographical references, index, and 17 appendices. Two chapters on the Jews of the region.

Forstreuter, Kurt. "Das Archiv Königsberg als Quelle für die allgemeine Geschichte" (The Königsberg archives as a source for general history). *Hamburger Mittel- und Ostdeutsche Forschungen*, vol. 6., Hamburg: L. Appel Verlag, 1967: 9–35.

Jolowicz, H., *Geschichte der Juden in Königsberg i. Pr.: ein Beitrag zur Sittengeschichte des preußischen Staates* (History of the Jews of Königsberg in Prussia: an addition to the moral history of the Prussian state). Posen: Verlag von J. Jolowicz, 1867, 210 pp., microfilm: Cambridge, MA: Harvard University Library, 1980, 1 reel, Library of Congress call number 91/8001 (D) MicRR.

Kagan, B. *The Jewish Community of Vilkovishk.* New York: author, 1991.

Levinsohn, Donald. *AVOTAYNU* 11, No. 2 (Summer 1995): 64.

Margol, Howard. *AVOTAYNU* 19, no. 1 (Spring 2003): 19–20.

Schüler-Springorum, Stefanie, *Die jüdische Minderheit in Königsburg/Preussen, 1871–1945* (The Jewish minority in Konigsberg, Prussia, 1871–1945). [German] Göttingen: Vandenbrouck Rupprecht, 1996.

Stern, Selma. *Der Preußische Staat und die Juden* (The Prussian State and the Jews). Part 3, Section 2, Vol. 2.

Russian Poland
by Fay Vogel Bussgang

History

In the late 18th century, Poland's neighbors, Russia, Prussia and Austria, gradually annexed large parts of its lands until the country of Poland ceased to exist. The three successive partitions of 1772, 1793 and 1795 resulted in the people of Poland being divided into three separate regions, each governed by a separate foreign power with different laws, languages and customs. These major political changes, which continued into the 19th and 20th centuries, affected the way our Polish ancestors lived and how records about their lives were kept. The format that was used to record events, the information that was included, the language documents were written in, all depended upon the section of Poland in which one lived. For the purposes of this article, Russian Poland includes the part of Poland that was under Russian domination from 1815 to 1918, even though the material discussed covers the period from the early part of the 19th century until the present time.

Grand Duchy of Warsaw (1807–15)

By the time of the third partition, most of central Poland had been annexed by Prussia. When Napoleon swept across Europe a few years later, he carved out a sizable area from the territory previously annexed by Prussia to create a new entity called the Grand Duchy of Warsaw. Established in January 1807, the Grand Duchy of Warsaw encompassed not only Warsaw but also the areas around Poznań, Bydgoszcz, Kalisz, Łomża and Suwałki. In 1809, Napoleon expanded the Grand Duchy by adding some of the territory originally taken by Austria, including the cities of Kielce, Kraków, Lublin and Zamość and their surroundings. A puppet government with the king of Saxony as its ruler governed the Grand Duchy.

A governmental decree in December 1807 declared that anyone who had been living for ten years in the territory that now belonged to the Grand Duchy of Warsaw and who knew the Polish language would be considered a citizen and could enjoy political rights and equality before the law. Very soon thereafter, however, the king signed several decrees that deprived Jews of their civic and political rights and suspended these rights for a period of 10 years. The rationale was that the Jews were a nation apart, with different customs and a different language, and were not yet ready for citizenship. Occasional exceptions were made, and rights reserved for citizens were granted to individual Jews by the grace of the monarch.

During this time, various reactionary and restrictive decisions were enacted by the government. Jews were to be expelled from villages unless they engaged exclusively in agriculture. They were permitted to settle only in certain towns and then only in restricted areas within those towns. Jews were no longer allowed to engage in the production or sale of alcohol or operate taverns or inns. They also were to be excluded from military service. Special taxes on the Jewish community consisted of a kosher meat tax, a military exemption tax, a tax for permission to contract a Jewish marriage, a stamp duty on all books in Hebrew or Yiddish, and a sojourn tax for any temporary stay in Warsaw.[1] Not all of these restrictions and taxes were systematically enforced.

Kingdom of Poland (1815–1918)

After Napoleon's defeat, the Congress of Vienna, in 1815, established new borders for central Poland that gave the provinces of Poznania and Silesia to Prussia and made Kraków an independent "free" city. The central section of the Duchy of Warsaw was kept together to form the Congress Kingdom of Poland and was made a semi-autonomous region of the Russian Empire. Congress Poland (Kongresówka) was also known as "Russian Poland."

The Congress Kingdom had a constitution, its own parliament (Sejm), state administration and judiciary, a national army and Polish schools. Political rights of citizens were dependent upon property ownership, occupation and education. These rights were granted to the nobility, to burghers who had property in towns and even to some peasants, but no major changes occurred in the status of Jews. The constitution of the Kingdom of Poland stated clearly that only Christians could enjoy civic and political rights.[2]

Legal regulations concerning the Jews often were bypassed, however, under the influence of economic, social and cultural developments. Some assimilated and wealthy Jews began to enter the newly emerging classes of modern society.

In November 1830, the Polish Army in the Congress Kingdom began an insurrection against Russian troops that lasted almost a year. Following the defeat of the insurrection, hundreds of Poles were executed, and 180,000 others were sent to Siberia. The kingdom lost its relative autonomy and, thereafter, was ruled directly by Russia. Polish institutions such as the Polish Army, the Sejm, and the banks were all abolished. In 1841, even Warsaw University was closed and Russian currency introduced. In 1843, the czar reversed his previous position and decreed that military service for Jews would be compulsory.

The restrictions enacted in the Duchy of Warsaw concerning property and civil rights of Jews remained in force in the Kingdom of Poland, but it became easier for individuals to be exempted from the regulations. After 1860, the number of Jews seeking citizenship rights, especially bankers, entrepreneurs and merchants, increased steadily.

In 1861, patriotic demonstrations by the Poles against the Russians took place and many Jews participated, causing their Polish compatriots to view them more favorably. In an attempt to woo peasants and Jews away from the Polish nationalistic cause, several decrees were issued by the czar that increased the rights and privileges of both groups. Gradually, most of the old restrictions for Jews were abolished.

In January 1863, a general uprising of the Polish population began against the Russians. It crumbled after 15 months. Repression, executions, and deportations to Siberia followed. Soon afterwards, the Kingdom of Poland officially (though not in popular terminology) lost its name and its autonomy, and it became the "Vistula Territory" of the Russian Empire.[3] A period of Russification began, and in 1868, Russian became the official language of the government and of instruction in schools. During this period of Russification from 1863 onward, the Catholic Church was persecuted and the Orthodox faith encouraged.

Republic of Poland (1918–39)

When World War I ended on November 11, 1918, Poland once more became an independent country, but its boundaries were not yet stable. With their former occupiers weakened and their patriotism revived, Poles began to expand their country's borders on all fronts. Fighting soon broke out in Lwów between Poles and Ukrainians, ending with Polish control over all of Galicia seven months later. In December 1918, there was a victorious uprising in the German province of Poznań. In the southwest, the Poles and the Czechs fought over the border town of Cieszyn until the allies divided the city, a division that remains in effect to this day. After several months of fighting, the Poles took a part of Upper Silesia from the Germans. In the east, Polish troops engaged the recently turned communist Russians, resulting in Poland taking Wilno (Vilnius) in April and Mińsk in August of 1919[4].

By the time the Treaty of Riga was signed in March 1921 at the end of the Russo-Polish War, the reborn Republic of Poland had within its borders not only the territory from the former Kingdom of Poland but also Galicia, Poznania, West Prussia and parts of the former Russian Pale of Settlement, including Wilno, Grodno, Mińsk and Równo. [See RUSSIAN EMPIRE]. Poland had once again become a multi-ethnic state, with sizable minorities of Lithuanians, Byelorussians, Ukrainians, Germans and Jews. This republic lasted until September 1939, when Poland's western half was overrun by Germany and its eastern half by Russia.

Record Keeping

Following the paper trail of our ancestors leads us to various types of record keeping. The most fruitful for genealogical research in central Poland are civil registration records (vital records) and population registers. Other documents, while less comprehensive, may give facts that supplement the two principal sources or provide at least some information when these major sources are lacking.

Civil Registration Records (Vital Records)

In Poland, civil registration records of births, marriages and deaths were called acts of civil status (*Akta Stanu Cywilnego*). These acts, corresponding to what Americans call vital records, were introduced by Napoleon in the Duchy of Warsaw in 1808. The purpose of civil registration was to aid the state in organizing and controlling the movement of its inhabitants and determining their legal status. To accomplish this goal, it was necessary to ascertain their identity—their given names, surnames and family relationships. Since the legal status of an individual depended primarily on his or her place of birth, marriage and death, the state established a system to obtain and record this data.

According to the Napoleonic Code introduced into the Duchy of Warsaw, the registration of births, marriages and deaths was to be conducted by civil rather than religious authorities. However, because a majority of the population in the Duchy was Roman Catholic and the Church was already involved in recording much of this information for its own use—in what were called *metryki* or metrical records—an 1809 decree named clergy performing parish duties as de facto officials of civil registration.[5] Initially, no separate regulations were made for non-Catholics. Thus, during the period 1808–25, Jewish births, marriages and deaths, if they were recorded at all, were included in records kept by the Catholic Church.

In 1825, the Napoleonic Code was repealed, and in its place was introduced the civil code of the Kingdom of Poland. This law required that the acts of civil status for Christian denominations, both Catholic and non-Catholic, be maintained jointly with church metrical records. These records were to be kept by the head clergymen of parishes, who were thereby considered as officials of the civil registry.

The acts of civil status for non-Christian denominations, however, were to be maintained separately by the mayor or other designated person, and in the city of Warsaw, by separate secular officials of civil registry.[6] Thus, from 1826 on, separate registers were kept for Jewish metrical records.

During the time that Jewish records were kept with Catholic records, between 1808 and 1825, relatively few Jews registered their life events. From 1826 on, however, when provisions were made for Jewish records to be kept separately, the number of Jews who reported these major life events increased markedly.

Starting in 1830, after performing any religious ceremony, the rabbi of a community was responsible for entering the correct information in the acts of civil registry. The entry was to be in the Polish language.[7]

In January 1863, a group of Polish nobility led an unsuccessful uprising against Russian rule. The Russification that followed gradually affected the manner in which government documents were kept. After January 1, 1868, all acts of civil status had to be prepared in Russian. The Russian (Julian) calendar was introduced at the same time. Two dates were entered in all civil registration documents after 1868, the Julian and the Gregorian (e.g., 10/22 June, 1871, or 28 March/9 April 1880). The Gregorian date, used in the rest of Europe, was 12 days later than the Julian date.

In 1875, new regulations required Christian clergymen and rabbis to maintain two copies of registration books in Russian, divided into three parts for births, marriages and deaths. The two books were to be closed each year and placed in the archive of the Registry of Deeds. At the same time, three additional separate books were to be maintained to register births, marriages and deaths. Each of these books

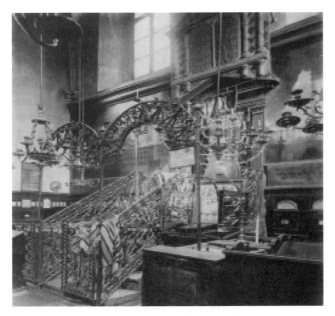

Sketch of the Great Synagogue in Warsaw. Blown up by the Germans during the Holocaust.

was to be used to record the designated life event until the entire book was filled. At that time, divorce and separation were within the jurisdiction of the state prosecutor.[8]

Births had to be recorded within eight days of the event. Acts of marriage required two witnesses. In the case of non-Christian marriages, the rabbi or iman was required to appear with the married couple and the two witnesses at the office of civil registry to register the marriage. Jewish marriages in Russian Poland were thus faithfully entered into the civil record, and there was no problem with legitimacy of children as occurred in Galicia, where a religious wedding was not necessarily followed by civil registration. [See AUSTRIAN POLAND.]

In the Duchy of Warsaw and later in the Kingdom of Poland, all acts of birth, marriage and death were recorded in narrative form following prescribed models. Written by hand, usually in formal and elaborate script, these records are often very difficult to read.

Adoption of Permanent Names

By the time the Grand Duchy of Warsaw was established in 1807, most Jews within the Duchy had already been required to adopt permanent given names and family names. This had occurred on April 17, 1797, in the area formerly ruled by Prussia, and even earlier, on July 23, 1787, in the area formerly ruled by Austria.[9] Since German was the official language in both these areas when permanent names were adopted, most Jews were given German surnames. In small towns and villages where the Prussian or Austrian presence was less strong, surnames were more likely to be Polish.

On March 27, 1821, all Jews in the Kingdom of Poland who had not yet adopted permanent surnames were required to do so and to declare them to the Polish authorities in the Kingdom.[10] Even after this date, however, one occasionally

encounters the same people registering under different surnames or using patronymics (given name of father plus "owicz/ówna," meaning "son/daughter of") on one occasion and their assigned surname on another.[11]

Contents of Civil Registration Documents

Birth Records. Births were not always recorded immediately after they occurred, and sometimes two or more children were registered at one time. In fact, not all births were recorded. Often one finds the death record of a child for whom no birth has been entered. Records of birth (*Akta Urodzeń*) usually included:

Town where the birth was reported

Day, month, year and hour when birth was reported

Name, age, occupation and place of residence of the person, usually the father, appearing with the baby before the registrar (father's name often preceded by *Starozakonny*—person of the Old Faith—to indicate that he was a Jew)

Name, age, occupation and place of residence of two witnesses

Gender of the newborn child

Place of birth (name of town or "at home")

Day, month, year and hour of birth (may say current month and/or year)

Name and age of mother (maiden name, if given, is usually preceded by *z*, which means "from the family of")

Given name or names of newborn (*dwa imiona*, sometimes abbreviated *dw. im.*, means that there are two given names, usually used interchangeably)

Signatures of father and witnesses (often in Hebrew script; Hebrew name may differ from what registrar writes, [e.g., Hebrew: Zvi; Polish: Hersz])

Signature of registrar

(See Frazin for detailed assistance in translating.)

Marriage Records. The actual wording or order of marriage documents (*Akta Małżeństw/Ślubów*) may differ from document to document, but the main elements were the following:

Name of town where marriage was reported

Day, month, year and hour that the report was given to the registrar

Name of the rabbi or his substitute

Date and hour when the religious ceremony occurred

Name, age, occupation and place of residence of two witnesses

Bridegroom's name, status (single, widowed, divorced), age and place of birth

His parents' names, place of residence and occupation

His occupation and/or "living with parents"

Bride's name, status (single, widow, divorced), age and place of birth

Her parents' names, place of residence and occupation

Her occupation or "living with parents"

Statement that marriage banns were posted at the synagogue or town hall on three dates a week apart (at two synagogues or town halls if bride and groom were from different towns)

Statement that there were no objections to the marriage

Statement that oral permission was given by the parents

Statement that there was or was not a prenuptial agreement

Signature of the rabbi, the couple, witnesses and sometimes one parent from each side

Death Records. The information that appears in death records (*Akta Zgonów*) differs widely. Sometimes very little information was given about the person, sometimes a great deal, depending upon the person's age, family circumstances and, of course, how much the persons who reported the death knew about the deceased. Possible elements recorded in death records are:

Name of the town where death was reported

Day, month, year and hour when the report was given

Name, age, occupation and place of residence of the two witnesses attesting to the death

Day, month, year, and hour that the death occurred (usually day before)

Name (maiden name if woman), marital status, occupation and place of residence of deceased

Name, age and occupation of spouse left behind, if applicable

Names and ages of children of deceased, if applicable

Names of parents

Mention of house or property left behind (rarely included)

Finding and Accessing Civil Registration Records

While the original documents of the civil registration records are kept in Polish Offices of Civil Registration or in State Archives, microfilm copies of many documents from the State Archives are available through LDS (Mormon) Family History Libraries. In addition, many of the civil records more than 100 years old have been indexed by the JRI-Poland project (see below), and the indexes are posted on their website in a searchable database.

Office of Civil Registration

Metrical Records that are less than 100 years old are kept in the Office of Civil Registration (*Urząd Stanu Cywilnego*) (USC) in the individual cities and towns in Poland where they were recorded. If the name of the town where one's ancestors lived is known, it is possible to make a request by writing directly to the USC of that town. Usually a specific street address is not needed. Unless it is a major city, the request should be in Polish. (See Frazin or the Polish Genealogical Society of America's website, WWW.PGSA.ORG, for help in composing a letter in Polish. For tips on how to insure receiving a successful answer, see WWW.JEWISHGEN.ORG/INFOFILES/POLAND/WRITING.HTM#NOSUCCESS.

Because of Polish privacy regulations, the relationship of the person making the request to the person whose record is being sought must be stated. If the registration office has the record(s) sought, typically it will notify the Polish ambassador in the capital city of the requestor's country, who will send a letter to the person who made the request asking for payment of as much as $40 per record. Once payment has been made

for the documents one chooses to order, one receives an officially certified abstract of the key data in the record, not a photocopy of the record itself. Researchers are advised to request the long abstract (*odpis zupełny*), which includes names of witnesses, rather than the short abstract (*odpis skrócony*).

To obtain records onsite by going to the town in Poland oneself, some evidence may be needed (depending on the local USC manager or clerk) that the person making the request is related to the person whose record is being sought. To authorize another person to obtain the record, either write a letter of authorization on an official looking letterhead or have a letter of permission notarized—in addition to explaining the relationship. In either case, presenting a family tree may be helpful. Most people who order records by mail have not been required to show proof of relationship; an explanation of relationship has been sufficient. However, this can vary from one clerk or community to another.

Polish State Archives

In 1998, the Polish State Archives (*Archiwa Państwowe*) published for the first time a book listing all birth, marriage and death records—of all denominations—that are housed in Polish archives (see Laszuk). A searchable database called PRADZIAD, which contains these vital records, is now on the website of the Polish State Archives, BAZA.ARCHIWA.GOV.PL/SEZAM/PRADZIAD.ENG.PHP, (must use lowercase letters). A listing of Jewish records can also be found in Weiner's *Jewish Roots in Poland* and on the Routes to Roots Foundation website at WWW.RTRFOUNDATION.ORG.

In general, records more than 100 years old are considered ancient acts and are located in regional branches of the State Archives, which serve as repositories for records from towns within a certain geographical area. Sometimes, however, records more than 100 years old continue to be kept in the local USC office. This is likely to occur if a registration book containing these records covers a span of years and some of the records in it are not yet 100 years old. On the other hand, for a small number of towns, all Jewish vital records, even if less than 100 years old, have been transferred to the State Archives.

At the present time, regional archives exist in the following locations: Białystok, Bydgoszcz, Częstochowa, Elbląg, Malbork, Gdańsk, Kalisz, Katowice, Kielce, Koszalin, Kraków, Leszno, Lublin, Łódź, Olsztyn, Opole, Piotrków Trybunalski, Płock, Poznań, Przemyśl, Radom, Rzeszów, Siedlce, Suwałki, Szczecin, Toruń, Warsaw, Wrocław, Zamość and Zielona Góra. In addition, many of these regional archives have branches in major towns in their district. For addresses of archives and their branches, see the Polish State Archives website at WWW.ARCHIWA.GOV.PL/INDEX.ENG.HTML (must use lowercase letters) and click on "State Archives."

The head office (*Naczelna Dyrekcja*) of the Polish State Archives* is located in Warsaw in the heart of the old city. It is no longer necessary for foreigners to obtain the permission of the head office to view records for genealogical research in the various branches. In such cases, permission is given by the director of the regional branch either in advance or when

Interior of the synagogue in Tykocin. Built in 1642 and restored in the 1970s, it is now a museum. Courtesy of Tomasz Wiśniewski.

one arrives at the archive. However, if there is any doubt as to whether records exist or where a particular record is kept (reorganizations of holdings occur from time to time), it is best to write the head office of the Polish State Archives for information. The head office has a special department that deals with foreigners, so writing in English is acceptable. In compliance with archival rules, however, all replies will be in Polish. (For assistance in understanding replies in Polish, see Frazin or WWW.PGSA.ORG.)

If you plan to do research on site, writing in advance to the archive you wish to visit will greatly expedite matters. Since the books containing the records may need to be brought to the reading room from storage in another building, you should inform the archives before your visit which records you wish to see. There may be a limit to the number of books that can be requested for one day.

If you are searching for vital records, be sure to check the indexes of records posted on JRI-Poland at WWW.JRI-POLAND.ORG. There you may be able to find the correct year and number of the vital record you are seeking, as well as the archive in which it is located. Also, to help focus your research, you can learn in what area or areas a particular surname can be found. Thus, this site can greatly facilitate your search at the archive itself or your request by mail. Order forms for requesting copies from the State Archives of records that have been indexed can be downloaded from the JRI website. (See below for more about JRI-Poland.)

The Church of Jesus Christ of Latter-day Saints (Mormons)

Jewish vital records from many Polish towns have been microfilmed by the Church of Jesus Christ of Latter-day Saints (LDS), known as the Mormons, and are available to the public in local LDS Family History Centers worldwide for a nominal fee. The microfilm numbers for records from these towns are available on the LDS website WWW.FAMILYSEARCH.ORG. [See LDS.]

The LDS website identifies only the film number of the records sought. The records themselves are not available on the web, and the films containing copies of the actual records must be ordered and examined at an LDS Family History Center. However, indexes to thousands of records from LDS microfilms are searchable in the JRI-Poland database.

Jewish Records Indexing-Poland Project

JRI-Poland is an independent volunteer project dedicated to indexing Jewish vital records in Poland. It uses the indexes from LDS microfilms, as well as index pages from branches of the Polish State Archives of later records not yet microfilmed by the Mormons. At the JRI-Poland website, WWW.JRI-POLAND.ORG, one can search through the indexed records for a particular surname in all of Poland, only within a certain town, or only within a certain distance from a particular town. One does not need the exact spelling of the surname or town to do the search. The index includes the reference number of the record (*Akt*), the type of record (birth, marriage, death) and the year the event was registered, as well as the name of the person covered by the record. Information on how to obtain a copy of the original record from the Polish State Archives or from the LDS (Mormon) microfilms is also found at this site. Other material such as marriage supplements and banns, divorce registers, cemetery records and books of residents from some communities are also being indexed and posted.

Finding and Accessing Population Registers

Population Registers in Poland are an extraordinarily rich source of information only now coming to the attention of genealogists. The best known registers are the *Księgi Ludności* (books of residents), but there are also *Karty Meldunkowe* (registration cards) and *Księgi Kontroli Ruchu Ludności* (books for population mobility control). All these books are located in the Polish State Archives' regional facilities.

Books of Residents: History and Purpose

Księgi Ludności, introduced in the 19th century, are huge bound ledgers kept by the authorities in each community as ongoing records. The ledgers spanned a number of years, documenting the comings and goings and life events of the members of the community. Unlike a census, information about the occupants of each household was not taken at a single session or updated only at intervals of 10 or so years; the information was continually modified as changes in the lives of the inhabitants took place. The books of residents did not include the entire population living in a community— only those whose legal residence was in that community.

Books of residents were introduced into the Duchy of Warsaw in 1810, and later, all villages and towns in the Kingdom of Poland were required to keep them.[12] Name, surname, sex, age, place of birth, marital status, previous residence, civil status and occupation were indicated for all members of each household.

Międzyrzec Podlaski school group on Lag B'Omer in 1926. Courtesy of Tomasz Wiśniewski.

The civil registry office, which maintained vital records, was required to report to the keeper of the *Księgi Ludności* all births, marriages and deaths, which then were added to the appropriate family's entry in the ledger.

At the same time that books of residents were mandated, rules were established pertaining to an individual's right to change his or her place of residence. Theoretically, people had the right to live wherever they wished. In reality, however, any person wishing to relocate was required first to secure permission from the authorities in the place where the person wished to settle. In addition, the head of the family needed to get a release from his former place of residence, stating that there were no encumbrances to his move, such as debt.

Over time, the rules became more complex and many documents were required. Because it was so difficult to change one's permanent place of residence, many people kept their official residence in one location, where all notations in the books of residents were made, but actually resided somewhere else. This fact sometimes makes tracing our ancestors more difficult.

Two categories of *księgi*—books of permanent residents (*Księgi Ludności Stałej*) and books of non-permanent residents (*Księgi Ludności Niestałej*)—began in 1886[13] and were maintained until 1932. The first category, kept in duplicate, of which one copy was to be located in the community (*gmina*) office and the second in the office of the appropriate head of the county (*powiat*), recorded only those whose permanent legal residence was in that community. The second category, of which only one copy was kept, in the local *gmina* office, recorded those people who, though living in that community, had legal residence elsewhere. In the city of Warsaw, a third category of books existed for transients, those staying temporarily in the city to visit family or in order

to do business. Most records for non-permanent residents have not survived.

Persons 14 years of age or older were to be supplied by local authorities with an identification booklet (*książeczka legitymacyjna*) verifying that they had been duly recorded in the book of residents.

Starting in 1868, when the official language of the Vistula Territory (Kingdom of Poland) changed from Polish to Russian, all *Księgi Ludności* were kept in Russian. As with civil registration documents, the Russian (Julian) calendar date was used in books of residents along with the Gregorian date. After World War I and the re-establishment of Poland as a country, the books of residents were again kept in Polish.

Books of residents included both Jews and non-Jews and are thus especially valuable for genealogists researching in towns in which purely Jewish records have been destroyed.

Contents of Books of Residents. Books of residents contained, on one or two pages, a list of all persons living in a particular household. Each book covered a different part of the city and was organized by house number or street address, not by family surname. In the beginning, each house in the town received a number. Later, street addresses were used. In most communities, indexes were organized alphabetically by surname (but often only by the first letter of the surname) and accompanied each set of volumes to facilitate location of a particular person. Books of residents displayed columns with the following information about each member of the household, in separate columns for males and females:

Name (maiden name if applicable)
Name of parents, including maiden name of mother
Date and place of birth
Marital status (married, single, divorced, widowed)
Official place of residence

Means of support (often "with husband" for wife, "with parent(s)" for children)

Religion (if Jewish, *mojżeszowa*—i.e., Mosaic religion)

Social status (town dweller or peasant)

For each member of the household, the books of residents contained all the personal data usually seen on a traditional birth certificate. Because the parents' names of each person were listed, it is often possible to learn names not only of everyone who lived in the household, but also names of family members of the previous generation. This information is particularly useful if the maiden name of the mother was given. Listing the parents for each child may seem redundant, but in the case of a second marriage due to the death of a previous spouse, a frequent occurrence, the biological parents of the child are easily seen.

The last column, called *Uwagi* (attention/notes), can be an excellent source of additional information. If the family had moved into the area, the previous place of residence was shown; if they left, the place to which they had moved was indicated. If a child married and moved, the name was crossed out in the first or second column to show that he or she no longer lived in that household, and the number or address of the new household was listed. For a woman, the date and place of her marriage and the name of the person she married was also shown. If someone died, his or her name was crossed out, and the date and place of death was entered. A man's military status was often given—in the army, in the reserves and so forth. Sometimes supporting documents were referenced.

Other Types of Registration Documents

Other types of registration cards or books found in some localities seem to have had a slightly different purpose than the books of residents, but they include much of the same information. They were organized by the surname of a person rather than by house or street number, and the documents kept track of any moves the family made, not only to different towns, but also to different addresses within a city or town. The information was recorded where one actually lived, but the legal place of residence was also noted.

Registration Cards. In the Łódź regional archives, one can find large cards called *Karty Meldunkowe* maintained by the police department in the city of Łódź for the years 1918–20 only. The card used had an alternate German name (*Personnenblatt*), and the spelling of names in some cases was Germanized. For instance, Bursztajn became Burstein.

Data contained in the *Karty Meldunkowe* is only slightly different from that found in the typical *Księgi Ludności*. The information requested for the head of household was:

Name and surname

Name of father (but not of mother)

Occupation

Date and place of birth

Religion (*mojżeszowa*—Mosaic, for Jews)

Nationality (some Polish Jews identified themselves as Polish, others as Jewish)

Place of permanent residence

For the wife and children, only name (including maiden name of wife), date and place of birth were solicited.

A long column at the right of the page listed all changes of address, even if only for a temporary period. A "Notes" column supplied such information as someone's moving out of town, joining the army, or a child coming of age and receiving his or her own card.

Books/Cards for Population Mobility Control. In the period between the two world wars, Poland experienced far greater movement of the population than had existed earlier. Some people were displaced as borders shifted; others moved to areas where work could be found—not an easy matter at the time of the Depression. More modern means of transportation facilitated mobility. The *Księgi Ludności*, which listed people by their official rather than their actual place of residence, became outdated, and they were discontinued in 1932. Authorities instituted in their place a different type of population register called *Księgi/Karty Kontroli Ruchu Ludności* (books/cards for population mobility control), sometimes called *Rejestry Mieszkańców* or *Księgi Meldunkowe*. Like the *Karty Meldunkowe* used in Łódź in 1918, they were organized by name rather than by address.

The information recorded in these books/cards are evidence of a more sophisticated and organized society. For both spouses, the information noted was:

Name and surname (to be written exactly as in the birth record)

Any previous marriages

Names of parents, including maiden name of mother

Date and place of birth

Legal place of residence

Religion

Number on personal identification card, date and place issued

Occupation of husband

Date and place of marriage, identifying number on document, date and place recorded

Army rank and registration number of husband

Nationality, number of document giving evidence, date and place issued

Address where family lived (all changes of address were noted)

For children, only name, date and place of birth were recorded. Children were issued their own cards upon becoming of age.

The fact that legal place of residence was requested indicates that these cards included all the inhabitants of the community rather than only those who had their official residence there. It also shows that the concept of legal residence continued.

New Finding Tools at Polish State Archives

CD-ROM *Po mieczu i po kądzieli* (On the spear and on the distaff side). Until recently, books of residents had not been systematically catalogued, which is perhaps why they are not well known. In 2001, however, the Polish State Archives issued a CD-ROM (for PC only) entitled *Po mieczu i po kądzieli* that lists all registers of population. One can choose English operating instructions, but the names of the documents are in Polish. The program is slow and cumbersome and sometimes crashes, but the information it contains is invaluable.

There are five databases on the disk, but only two are relevant to Jews—registers of population (*Spis Ludności*) and registration of certificates (*Akta Stanu Cywilnego*). The registration of certificates section contains the same list of vital records that is in the Laszuk book (see bibliography), and the PRADZIAD database on the Polish State Archives website. The database for the registers of population includes all records with lists of population (*Ewidencje Ludności*), which in addition to books and registers of residents, includes various lists of Jews, voters, immigrants, military recruits, prisoners, people liable for taxation, people applying for passports and others.

One can search the data on the disk by name of town, type of register, province or archive. If one selects name of town, a list of all towns will be displayed, and one can scroll down to the town of interest or type in the name. All population registers for that town will then be displayed in four columns, showing name of town, type of register, province and dates covered. The list can be sorted on any of these criteria by clicking on the top of the column. Double clicking on a particular listing causes a frame to pop up on the screen that gives details about that register or collection of registers—where located, name of fond (*zespół*), identifying numbers (*sygnatury*) of documents, and number of units within the collection. Clicking on the name of the archive gives the address and telephone number of the archive.

If one chooses "type of register," a list of categories pops up with an explanation in English of each category. If one clicks on "*x*," which stands for Jews, 332 records are displayed, showing name of town, type of register, province and dates covered. One can sort on "town" within this category to organize the records one is seeking. If one clicks on the category "meld" (*księgi meldunkowe*—place of living books and registers), one gets 6,406 records. By clicking on "lst" (*ludności stałej*—permanent population), one gets 9,497 records. There is some overlap between these last two categories. While not all towns are represented, clearly many more population registers exist than was previously thought.

Polish and Israeli Archival Sources. In cooperation with the Museum of the History of Polish Jews in Warsaw now being planned, the Polish State Archives has published a book that lists all documents in both Polish and Israeli archives that have relevance to the history of Jews in Poland, *Źródła archiwalne do dziejów Żydów w Polsce* (Archival sources for the history of Jews in Poland). Both the CD-ROM and the book can be ordered from the head office or purchased at the archive bookstore at ul. Świętojerska 24 (rear of building).

SEZAM. The search tool SEZAM on the Polish State Archives website at www.archiwa.gov.pl/index.eng.html (must use lowercase letters) is based on different categories than the *Po mieczu* CD. While there is some overlap, many records showing up on one system do not show up on the other. Many of the population registers are kept in fonds entitled *Akta Miasta* (town records) of a particular community, and the collections within are not listed individually in the SEZAM system. Thus, searching on SEZAM for *ludnosci* (diacritical marks are not necessary for the search) yields only 54 items, whereas one finds hundreds of population registers on *Po mieczu*. On the other hand, by searching on SEZAM for *Zydow*, records of many more Jewish communities (*gminy żydowskie*) appear than on *Po mieczu*. It is very difficult to cross-reference documents on the two systems, because SEZAM lists the fond number but not its name, and *Po mieczu* lists the name of the fond but not its number.

Kahal, Synagogue and Cemetery Records

Kingdom of Poland Jewish Community Records. Jews had their own form of self-government during the time of the Kingdom of Poland. Each Jewish community (*gmina*) was governed by an administrative body called the *kahal*. *Kahal* records dating from this time are located in the state archives in Warsaw (*Archiwum Główne Akt Dawnych**-AGAD) in the collection called the Central Religious Authorities of the Kingdom of Poland (*Centralne Władze Wyznaniowe Królestwa Polskiego*). Records are concerned primarily with the building and maintaining of synagogues, collecting contributions and electing rabbis. Some records exist of disputes between the rabbi and the *shamas* (synagogue caretaker), or between either or both of them and the congregation. All adult male members and female members, if they had been widowed, voted in elections for rabbis; usually their names are listed along with how they voted. Lists of how much money each member contributed to the *gmina* can also be found here. The size of the contribution that a member was assessed indicated his financial status in the community.

These records may be useful to a genealogist because they place someone in a given community at a given time; a person did not need legal residence to be a member of the Jewish community (*gmina żydowska*).

Republic of Poland Jewish Community Records

These 20th-century records exist for a number of communities. Records for Bromberg/Bydgoszcz, Breslau/Wrocław, Gliwice, Grudziądz, Lublin, Podgórze, Kraków, Poznań, Silesia, Tarnopol, Włocławek and Żychlin can be found in the Jewish Historical Institute,* while records from Biała Podlaska, Chełm, Kalisz, Konin, Lublin, Piotrków Trybunalski, Siedlce, Tarnobrzeg, Zamość and many other communities can be found in Polish regional archives. A list of Jewish community members typically shows not only the names and how much they gave to the community each year, but it also may show the address where they lived. By comparing addresses, one can often see who is related to whom. Ages are not usually given, however, and women are not always mentioned. Sometimes a list of candidates for membership on the Jewish council is included in these records. If so, ages and professions of the candidates may be indicated.

Wooden synagogue in Suchowola. Before the Holocaust there were hundreds of wooden synagogues in Eastern Europe. Courtesy of Tomasz Wiśniewski.

Cemetery Records

Cemetery records exist for a very limited number of communities. Warsaw, Kraków and Łódź are known to have partial lists, maintained by the present-day Jewish community in each city. A 1938 book has information about individuals buried in the old Jewish cemetery in Łódź (*Stary cmentarz żydowski w Łodzi*). Krzysztof Pilarczyk, at the Jagiellonian University in Kraków, has published a book about the Jewish cemetery in Pilica (*Cmentarz żydowski w Pilicy*), documenting what is written on each tombstone. A book by Monika Krajewska, *A Tribe of Stones*, shows photographs of tombstones in many cemeteries and explains the meaning of various images and inscriptions. General information on numerous cemeteries in Poland can be found at WWW.JEWISHGEN.ORG under Hosted Organizations (the IAJGS Cemetery Project) or on the recently established Poland-Jewish Cemeteries Restoration Project website, WWW.PJCRP.ORG. A new project, the JewishGen Online Worldwide Burial Registry, will be a compilation of two databases: a database of burial records linked to a database of information about each particular cemetery. For ongoing developments, see WWW.JEWISHGEN.ORG/DATABASES/CEMETERY.

Business Directories (Address Books)

Address books (*księgi adresowe*) found in Polish regional archives and the libraries of some towns are similar to city directories; they preceded telephone books and list alphabetically most inhabitants of a city along with their addresses. Each edition of *księgi adresowe* found in the archives seems to have slightly different information, but in general they include lists of businesses, lists of individuals by profession, and lists of all heads of households within the city, showing their addresses and professions. Sections in more recent volumes of address books may have telephone numbers, addresses of city offices, schools, institutions and sanitariums, and householders listed by street. (See Bussgang, "Census Records and City Directories" and Cymbler, "Nineteenth- and Twentieth-Century Polish Directories" for a detailed description of particular business directories.)

JRI-Poland volunteers are in the process of indexing town by town all surnames found in the 1929 *Księga Adresowa Polski* (business directory of Poland). This directory covers names and addresses of businesses in current and former areas of Poland, including regions now part of the Vilnius area of Lithuania and the Grodno area of Belarus, as well as East Galicia and the former province of Volhynia, now part of western Ukraine. The business directory database, when completed, will be searchable on the following fields or combinations of fields: surname, given name, surname with given name, industry/business, street/town, *województwo* (province) and *powiat* (county). Individual pages of the directory (more than 2,500) have already been posted as JPEG files. See WWW.JEWISHGEN.ORG/JRI-PL/BIZDIR/START.HTM.

Microfilm copies of the 1895 *Vsia Rossiia* (All of Russia), a Russian language business directory covering all of the Russian Empire including Poland, are available at the U.S. Library of Congress[*] and at the libraries of UCLA,[*] Stanford,[*] and Columbia University.[*] (See Boonin for explanation of organization of *Vsia Rossiia*.)

Calendars

The name of this type of business directory is misleading. Although it is not a calendar, perhaps it derives its name from the fact that it was issued once a year. Found in regional state archives, *kalendarze* list businesses by trade and location and also include advertisements. Because they have not been systematically catalogued in all the archives, it is not yet known exactly what exists where. Information about what is available in a specific archive, however, may be obtained by writing to the main office of the Polish State Archives[*] in Warsaw.

World War II Survivor and Ghetto Lists

Survivor Lists

Jewish Historical Institute. At the end of World War II, Jewish agencies tried to assemble lists of all known survivors to help family members find each other. In orphanages, hospitals, camps, soup kitchens and agency offices in Poland, Germany, Czechoslovakia and Sweden, wherever Polish Jews were likely to be found, lists of thousands of survivors were made. In Poland, these were maintained by the Central Committee of Jews in Poland (*Centralny Komitet Żydów w Polsce*).

The index to many of these records can be found in bound volumes at the Jewish Historical Institute[*] (*Żydowski Instytut Historyczny*) in Warsaw. If all information was filled out, the index includes name, year of birth, names of parents, address before the war and address when registered. Unfortunately, the information is not always complete or accurate.

The cards from which the survivor index was made are stored at the Jewish Historical Institute in boxes and can be accessed on request if an index entry looks promising. One may find additional information on the cards, such as how to get in touch with someone whose name was found on the list, but more often than not, the card has no more information than the index. The survivor index has been microfilmed and is now also at Yad Vashem* and the U.S. Holocaust Memorial Museum* in Washington. Many of these survivors are also listed in *Pinkas ha-nitsolin: Register of Jewish Survivors I*, and *Register of Jewish Survivors II*.

Łódź Ghetto List

Łódź, the second largest city in Poland, had a sizable Jewish population, mainly engaged in the textile business. In addition, the World War II Łódź ghetto included Jews brought there from many other towns. Original lists of Łódź ghetto inhabitants, kept by the Germans during the war and organized by street address, can be found in the regional Polish State Archives in Łódź.* The Organization of Former Lodz Residents in Tel Aviv* took data from these lists, typed it in columns and rearranged it alphabetically by name. These rearranged lists are now available not only at the Tel Aviv office of the former residents, but also at Yad Vashem,* the U.S. Holocaust Memorial Museum in Washington,* the Museum of Jewish Heritage in New York,* Stanford University's Green Library,* University of Notre Dame's Hesburgh Library*, University of Toronto's Robarts Library,* the Bavarian State Library* in Munich, Warsaw University Library,* and the Jewish Holocaust Museum and Research Centre in Melbourne, Australia.* Yad Vashem has already digitized the list and has plans to post it on its website.

Information on the lists includes name, gender, birth date, occupation, current and previous address(es) and notes. The notes column may include address changes, deaths, deportations and sometimes even transport numbers. By comparing addresses of people with the same last name, it is possible to reconstruct family living units. Because the names of the ghetto streets were almost all changed by the Germans, it is important when doing research to consult the list included with the index of names, which shows the original names of streets as well as their German names. For a comprehensive list of changes in street names in Łódź from 1913 to 1990, see WWW.SHTETLINKS.JEWISHGEN.ORG/LODZ/STREETSINDEX1.HTM.

Kennkarten Information

During the war, *Kennkarten* were identification cards issued by the Germans that gave a person the right to work and to receive food rations. In the state archives in Kraków* are files from the Kraków ghetto that contain *Kennkarten* applications, often with photographs. The applications, written in German, included the following information: name of head of family, address, name of applicant, occupation, date and place of birth, nationality, previous address and length of time living in Kraków.

Other Ghetto Information

The Jewish Historical Institute* in Warsaw has information about the inhabitants of ghettos in Białystok, Łódź, Kraków and Warsaw. Some applications exist for *Ausweise*, the identification cards used before *Kennkarten* were instituted. These have similar information to that in the *Kennkarten* ap-

plications and may also contain photographs.

Also at the Jewish Historical Institute* are file boxes with cards documenting the death of Jews in the Warsaw ghetto. The cards list the name of the deceased, date and hour of death, address, place and cause of death, the date and place of birth and names of parents. Copies of various editions of Schindler's list from Kraków are located here and show the names of people employed by Schindler at different times.

The Jewish Historical Institute* is a repository of enormous amounts of information gathered after World War II. Cataloguing and indexing of material continues. Thus far, some lists of pupils, children's homes, and child welfare have been indexed. See Bussgang, "List of Materials in ŻIH Archives".

Other Official Sources of Information

Notary Records. Notaries in Poland recorded wills, drafted contracts for prenuptial agreements and purchases of property, documented loans, verified payments, validated matriculation certificates, issued summons for non-payment of rent or loans, arbitrated disputes and certified the validity of documents needed for traveling abroad. Notary ledgers that are no longer current are considered public documents and are kept in regional state archives. In cities where there were several notaries, each kept his own books, so that many books may need to be searched to find something of relevance. A table of contents usually is located in the back of each book, but there is no index by topic, and books are catalogued in a given archive by name of notary, not content.

Applications for Identity Card, Passports and Medical Licenses. Cards to serve as proof of identity (*Zaświadczenia Tożsamości*) were issued to residents 14 years and older and used as a kind of internal passport. Copies of applications for these cards may be found in regional archives; some include photographs. Applications to permit the practice of certain professions, such as medicine or law, include considerable personal data and may also be found in regional archives. Applications to establish permanent residence and applications for passports (*Świadectwo Kwalifikacyjne*) to travel abroad can also be found here. Old city hall records are stored in regional archives.

To obtain identity cards or passports, a person was required to submit a certified copy (usually copied by hand) of his or her entry in the books of residents. In some cases, the book of residents from which the excerpt came may not have survived, but the certified copy of that person's entry, attached to his or her application for a passport, may still exist in the archive.

Military Records. Military records in Poland have been well maintained and can yield a great deal of data. They include such information as name, rank, birth date, birthplace, names of parents, marital status, maiden name of wife, education, civil occupation, date of joining and leaving the service, decorations and commendations. In the address section below are listed places to write for information, depending on when and where the person served.

Almanacs

During the 1920s and 1930s some larger Jewish communities in Poland published almanacs that gave information about Jewish life in that community or region. Some, like the *Almanach żydowski* (Jewish almanac) published in Lwów in 1937 (Stachel), were a veritable Who's Who of the city and surrounding communities. In addition to describing the organizations that were active, they included photographs and short biographies of Jews prominent in literature, art, music, politics, the professions, business and industry. Copies of the Lwów *Almanach żydowski* can be found in the *Biblioteka Narodowa** (national library) in Warsaw and the Jagiellonian University* library in Kraków. YIVO* in New York has a photocopy.

Various other specialized types of almanacs, such as almanacs of Jews in literature, Jewish schools, Jewish health care organizations, or industry can be found in the *Biblioteka Narodowa*. Non-Jewish almanacs may also yield genealogical data for prominent individuals such as physicians, attorneys, academicians, musicians or literary figures.

Yizkor Books

Yizkor (memorial) books, written by surviving members of destroyed communities, provide a wealth of information about the towns—their history, their religious and political institutions, and their way of life. The articles also often mention names of specific people, and the necrology section lists the names of victims of the Holocaust that were reported by survivors. Almost all the books were originally written in Hebrew and Yiddish and were thus inaccessible to most researchers until recently. Now many are being translated and chapters posted on JewishGen at WWW.JEWISHGEN.ORG/YIZKOR/TRANSLATIONS. HTML#COMMUNITIES. [See JEWISHGEN.]

Other Sources

The availability of research material in Poland is growing, and as Poland prospers and more money becomes available for archives, previously uncatalogued collections are being organized and documented. In addition, great curiosity and interest about the life and history of Jews in Poland has arisen, in part because so few Jews live in Poland today, but also because these topics were suppressed under Communist rule. Much new research has been conducted on minorities in general and Jews in particular.

New research on Polish-Jewish topics by scholars from all over the world is published annually in *POLIN: Studies in Polish Jewry*. Jewish research has also been encouraged in Poland by a competition, every few years—initiated by the Jewish Historical Institute* in cooperation with the Polish-Israeli Friendship Society*—for the best Jewish-related master's thesis or doctoral dissertation. All papers submitted have been collected by the Institute. The list of titles for the first three competitions has been translated into English and can be found in *POLIN*, vols. 9: 236–43 and 11: 386–90.

In 1999, archivists in the city of Włocławek produced a book called *Zapiski Kujawsko-Dobrzyńskie* (Notes about the Kujawy-Dobrzyń region) that includes articles about national minorities in this area. Several of the articles concern Jews—one about Jews in the 1918–39 period, one about Jewish *felczers* (medical practitioners) and doctors in practice there from the 19th century to 1939, two articles on the Holocaust, and another about Jews after the war. The article about doctors and *felczers* not only discusses statistics and generalities but contains names of persons in those professions active in the various communities of the region.

One of the most interesting articles, written by Włocławek head archivist Marianna Gruszczyńska, concerns the first Jewish settlements in Włocławek. It includes the names and addresses of the first 54 settlers, as well as a history of how they came to settle in Włocławek and under what conditions they were allowed to do so. The source materials for this article were found mainly at the regional archives in Włocławek from the collection of records called *Naczelnik Powiatu Włocławskiego z lat 1809–66* (Head of Włocławek County from 1809–66) and from the Central Archive of Old Acts (AGAD) in Warsaw from the collection *Komisja Rządowa Spraw Wewnętrznych," z lat 1815–68* (Government Commission for Internal Affairs from 1815–68), *sygnatury* 2013–34.

Addresses

Bavarian State Library (Bayerische Staatsbibliothek), Dokument-lieferung, Ludwigstrasse 16, Munich 80328, Germany; telephone: 89/28638-2643; fax: 89/2809284; e-mail: INFO@BSB-MUENCHEN. DE; website: WWW.BSB-MUENCHEN.DE/

Columbia University Library, Library Information Office, 201 Butler Library, Columbia University Library, 535 West 114th Street, New York, NY 10027; telephone: (212) 854-2271, e-mail: LIO@COLUMBIA.EDU; website: WWW.COLUMBIA.EDU/CU/LWEB/ (must use lowercase letters)

Jagiellonian University Library (Biblioteka Jagiellońska), al. Mickiewicza 22, 30-059 Kraków, Poland; telephone: 48 (12) 633-6377; website: WWW.BJ.UJ.EDU.PL/

Jewish Historical Institute (Żydowski Instytut Historyczny), ul. Tłomackie 3/5, 00-090 Warsaw, Poland; telephone/fax: 48 (22) 827-83-72; website: WWW.JEWISHINSTITUTE.ORG.PL/

Jewish Holocaust Museum and Research Centre, 13 Selwyn Street, Elsternwick, Melbourne, Australia; telephone: 61 (03) 9528-1985; website: WWW.ARTS.MONASH.EDU.AU/AFFILIATES/HLC/

Library of Congress, Reference Referral Service, 101 Independence Avenue, SE, Washington, DC 20540-4720; website: WWW.LOC.GOV/RR/ASKALIB/ASK-MAIN.HTML (must use lowercase letters.)

Museum of Jewish Heritage, 18 First Place, Battery Park City, New York, NY 10004-1484; telephone: (212) 509-6130; website: WWW.MJHNYC.ORG/

Organization of Former Residents of Lodz in Israel, 158 Dizengoff Street, Tel Aviv 63461, Israel; telephone: 972-(0)3-524-1833; fax: 972-(0)3-523-8126.

Polish-Israeli Friendship Society, Cafe Ejlat, al. Ujazdowskie 47, 00-536 Warsaw, Poland.

Polish National Library (Biblioteka Narodowa), al. Niepodległości 213, 02-086 Warsaw, Poland; telephone: 48 (22) 608-2999; fax: 48 (22) 825-5251, e-mail: BIBLNAR@BN.ORG.PL; website: WWW.BN. ORG.PL/

Polish State Archives Head Office (Naczelna Dyrekcja Archiwów Państwowych), ul. Długa 6, skr. pocztowa 1005, 00-950 Warsaw, Poland; telephone: 48 (22) 831-32-06 to 08; fax: 48 (22) 831-75-63; website: WWW.ARCHIWA.GOV.PL/INDEX.ENG.HTML (must use lowercase letters)

Polish State Archives, Central Archive of Historical Records (AGAD—Archiwum Główne Akt Dawnych), ul. Długa 7, 00-263 Warsaw, Poland; telephone: 48 (22) 831-54-91 to 93; e-mail: ARCHAGAD@POCZTA.ONET.PL; website: WWW.ARCHIWA.GOV.PL/AGAD/ (must use lowercase letters)

Polish State Archives in Kraków, ul. Sienna 16, Kraków, Poland; telephone: 48 (12) 422-40-94; fax: 48 (12) 421-35-44; website: JAZON.HIST.UJ.EDU.PL/AP/GLOWNA.HTM (must use lowercase letters)

Polish State Archives in Łódź, Pl. Wolności 1, Łódź, Poland; telephone: 48 (42) 632-62-01 or 632-62-02; fax: 48 (42) 632-02-11; e-mail: KANCELARIA@ARCHIWUM.LODZ.PL; website: WWW.ARCHPLODZ.INFOCENTRUM. COM/

Stanford Libraries. Databases searchable on website. For privileges, contact Privileges Office, Green Library, Stanford University, Stanford, CA 94305-6004; telephone: (650) 723-1492; fax: (650) 725-6874; e-mail: PRIV@SULMAIL.STANFORD.EDU; website: WWW.SUL.STANFORD.EDU/

UCLA (University of California at Los Angeles) Library, UCLA Library Administration, 11334 Young Research Library, Box 951575, Los Angeles, CA 90095-1575; telephone: (310) 825-1201. Information Service: (310) 825-7143; website: WWW.LIBRARY.UCLA.EDU/

U.S. Holocaust Memorial Museum, 100 Raoul Wallenberg Place, SW Washington, DC, 20024-2126; telephone: (202) 314-7812; fax: (202) 488-2697; website: WWW.USHMM.ORG/

University Libraries of Notre Dame, University of Notre Dame, Notre Dame, IN 46556; telephone: (574) 631-6258. For queries, see HTTP://ASKLIB.ND.EDU/.

University of Toronto Robarts Library, 130 St. George Street, 4th floor, Toronto, Ontario, M5S 1A5, Canada; telephone: (416) 978-2278; fax: (416) 971-3131; website: WWW.LIBRARY.UTORONTO.CA/ROBARTS/ (must use lowercase letters for robarts).

University of Warsaw Library (Biblioteka Uniwersytecka w Warszawie), ul. Dobra 56/66, 00-312, Warsaw, Poland; telephone: 48 (22) 552-5660; fax: 48 (22) 552-5659; e-mail: BUW@MAIL.UW.EDU.PL; website: WWW.BUW.UW.EDU.PL/

Yad Vashem, P.O.B. 3477, Jerusalem 91034, Israel; telephone: 972-2-6443400; fax: 972-2-6443443; website: WWW.YAD-VASHEM.ORG.IL/

YIVO Institute for Jewish Research, The Center for Jewish History, 15 West 16th Street, New York, NY 10011-6301; telephone: (212) 246-6080; fax: (212) 292-1892; e-mail: YIVOMAIL@YIVO.CJH.ORG; website: WWW.YIVOINSTITUTE.ORG/

Addresses to Obtain Polish Military Records

1) Austro-Hungarian Army (including Galicia): Österreich Staatsarchiv/Kriegsarchiv (Austrian State Archives/Military Archives), Nottendorfergasse 2, A-1030 Vienna, Austria; telephone: 43 (1) 79540-0; website: WWW.OESTA.GV.AT/EBESTAND/EKV/EFR1_KV.HTM (must use lowercase letters).

2) Polish Army in the West: (Free Polish Forces, Anders Army [part of British 8th Army], Polish Air Force, units of British Army): Ministry of Defence CS(RM) 2c, Bourne Avenue, Hayes Middlesex UB3 1RF, England; website: WWW.MOD.UK/.

3) Regular Polish Army: Centralne Archiwum Wojskowe (Central Military Archive), ul. Czerwonych Beretów, 00-910 Warsaw-Rembertów, Poland; telephone: 48 (22) 681-45-84; fax: 48 (22) 681-32-02; e-mail: CAW@WP.MIL.PL; website: WWW.CAW.WP. MIL.PL

Bibliography

Archiwum Państwowe we Włocławku (State Archive in Włocławek), Naczelnik Powiatu Włocławskiego (Head of Włocławek County), sygn. 438, 459, 460.

Ascherson, Neal. *The Struggles for Poland*. New York: Random House, 1987.

Beider, Alexander. *A Dictionary of Jewish Surnames from the Kingdom of Poland*. Teaneck, N.J.: Avotaynu, 1996.

Boonin, Harry D., "Russian Business Directories," *AVOTAYNU* 6, no. 4 (Winter 1990): 23–32.

Bussgang, Fay, "Archives of the Jewish Historical Institute in Warsaw," *AVOTAYNU*, 10, no. 1, (Spring 1994): 41–42. Lists materials in the archives.

Bussgang, Fay Vogel, "Census Records and City Directories in the Krakow Archives," *AVOTAYNU* 12, no. 2 (Summer 1996): 27–28.

Bussgang, Fay, "More About Polish Books of Residents Registration," *AVOTAYNU* 16, no. 3 (Fall 2000): 14–15

Bussgang, Julian, "The Polish Concept of Permanent Place of Residence," *AVOTAYNU* 16, no. 3 (Fall 2000): 12–14.

Cymbler, Jeffrey K., "Nineteenth- and Twentieth-Century Polish Directories As Resources for Genealogical Information," *AVOTAYNU* 13, no. 1 (Spring 1997): 25–33. Lists Polish city and business directories available in the U.S.

Davis, Lauren B. Eisenberg. "Alternate Surnames in Russian Poland," *AVOTAYNU* 12, no. 2 (Summer 1996): 15–16.

Eisenbach, Artur. *The Emancipation of the Jews, 1780–1870*. Oxford: Basil Blackwell, 1991.

Frazin, Judith, *A Translation Guide to 19th-Century Polish-Language Civil Registration Documents*. Northbrook, Ill.: JGS of Illinois, 1989. Provides detailed assistance in translating birth, marriage and death records from 1808–67.

Krajewska, Monika. *A Tribe of Stones*. Warsaw: Polish Scientific Publishers, 1993.

Krajewski, Mirosław, ed., *Byli wśród nas—Żydzi we Włocławku*. (They were among us—Jews in Włocławek) [Polish] Włocławek: Włocławskie Towarzystwo Naukowe, 2001. Contains articles about Jews extracted from *Zapiski Kujawsko-Dobrzyńskie,* described below.

Laszuk, Anna. *Księgi metrykalne i stanu cywilnego w archiwach państwowych w Polsce* (Metrical and civil registration ledgers in the state archives in Poland). [Polish] Warsaw: Polish State Archives, 1998.

Okólski, Antoni. *Wykład prawa administracyjnego obowiązującego w Królestwie Polskim* (Exposition of administrative law in force in the Kingdom of Poland). [Polish] Warsaw, 1882, vol. 2: 20–45.

Pilarczyk, Krzysztof. *Cmentarz żydowski w Pilicy* (Jewish cemetery in Pilica). [Polish] Kraków: Judaica Foundation, 1995.

Pinkas ha-nitsolin: Register of Jewish Survivors I, (60,000 names); *Register of Jewish Survivors II* (58,000 names). Jerusalem: Jewish Agency for Palestine, Search Bureau for Missing Persons, 1945. List of Jews rescued in different European countries. Most are Polish Jews.

Polonsky, Antony, ed., *POLIN: A Journal of Polish-Jewish Studies*, vols. 1–7. Oxford: Basil Blackwell, 1986–1992. Volume 3 focuses on Warsaw, volume 6 on Łódź.

Polonsky, Antony, ed., *POLIN: Studies in Polish Jewry*, vols. 8–15, plus a comprehensive index to volumes 1–12. London: Littman Library of Jewish Civilization, 1994–2002. Volume 12 focuses on Galicia, volume 13, on the Holocaust.

Po mieczu i po kądzieli. [CD-ROM]. Warsaw: Naczelna Dyrekcja Archiwów Państwowych, Warsaw, 2001. Catalogue of holdings of Polish State Archives relevant to genealogical research.

Stachel, Herman. *Almanach żydowski* (Jewish almanac). [Polish] Lwów: Culture and Art Publishers, 1937.

Stary cmentarz żydowski w Łodzi (Old Jewish cemetery in Łódź). [Polish] Łódź: Jewish Community of Łódź, 1938.

Weiner, Miriam. *Jewish Roots in Poland: Pages from the Past and Archival Inventories.* New York: YIVO and Secaucus, N.J.: Routes to Roots Foundation, 1997.

Zapiski Kujawsko-Dobrzyńskie: mniejszości narodowe na Kujawach wschodnich i w ziemi dobrzyńskiej, Tom 13 (Notes of the Kujawy-Dobrzyń region: national minorities in eastern Kujawy and Dobrzyń lands, vol. 13). [Polish] Włocławek, Poland: Włocławek Educational Society, 1999.

Źródła archiwalne do dziejów Żydów w Polsce. (Archival sources for the history of Jews in Poland). [Polish with English summaries] Warsaw: Naczelna Dyrekcja Archiwów Państwowych, 2001. Sources for the history of Jews in Poland located in Polish and Israeli archives.

Notes

1. Eisenbach, 143
2. Eisenbach, 153–55
3. Ascherson, 31
4. Ascherson, 56–60
5. Okólski, 38
6. Okólski, 38
7. Laszuk, iv
8. Laszuk, iv
9. Eisenbach, 116, 56
10. Okólski, 40
11. see Davis for examples
12. Okólski, 23
13. Okólski, 24

Romania

by Professor Ladislau Gyémánt

Geography

Romania chose the winning side during World War I, and the Treaty of Versailles doubled its size with annexations from the defunct Austro-Hungarian Empire, Bulgaria and Russia. Romania comprised the historical provinces (described below) of the Banat, Bessarabia, Bukovina, Dobrudja, Maramures, Moldavia, Transylvania and Wallachia. Before 1914, the so-called "Old Kingdom" (the Regat) included only Moldavia and Wallachia with the northern part of Dobrudja.

In 1940, Romania lost Bessarabia and the northern part of Bukovina to the Soviet Union, and the southern portion of Dobrudja was taken back by Bulgaria.

The Old Kingdom (plus Bessarabia and Bukovina)

Moldavia and Wallachia, the eastern and southern part of present-day Romania, were autonomous principalities under Ottoman Turkish rule until 1859, when they united under the name of Romania and gained independence in 1877. Dobrudja, the historical province located between the Danube River and the Black Sea, also became part of Romania after the war of independence against the Ottoman Empire (1877–78). Together these constituted the Regat, or the "Old Kingdom."

Bessarabia, the eastern part of the historical Romanian province of Moldavia, became part of the Russian Empire in 1812. Bukovina, the northern part of Moldavia, fell under Austrian rule in 1775. In 1940, northern Bukovina and Bessarabia were given to the Soviet Union. Today, Bessarabia is the independent state of Moldova with its own specific archival organization. The civil registers of northern Bukovina are in Ukrainian archives; those of Bessarabia are in the Republic of Moldavia.

Transylvania (plus the Banat, and the counties of Arad, Bihor, Maramures and Satu Mare)

Transylvania, the central and western portion of contemporary Romania, is composed of several distinct elements. During the Middle Ages, Transylvania was an autonomous province within the kingdom of Hungary. This kingdom collapsed and disintegrated after the Battle of Mohács in 1526, when the victory of the Ottoman Turks opened the way for Transylvania to establish itself as an autonomous principality, compelled only to pay an annual tribute to the government of the Ottoman Empire.

After 1690, when Transylvania became part of the Austrian Empire, three administrative entities were constituted: the principality (later, the Great Principality of Transylvania), directly subordinate to Vienna; the western districts, including the counties of Arad, Bihor, Maramures and Satu Mare, which became part of Hungary and, in turn, also were subordinated to Vienna; and the so-called Banat in the southwest. The Banat was freed from Turkish rule by the Austrians in 1716 and was an autonomous province within the Austrian

Empire until 1779, when it was divided into the counties of Caras, Timis and Torontal and passed to Hungarian administration.

This administrative system was maintained until 1867, when Transylvania became an integral part of Hungary until 1918. The disintegration of the Austro-Hungarian Empire after World War I united Transylvania and the Banat with Romania.

Between 1940 and 1944, the Nazis returned the northern part of Transylvania (the counties of Bihor, Bistrita, Cluj, Covasna, Harghita, Maramures, Mures, Salaj and Satu Mare) to Hungary. After World War II, all of Transylvania went back to Romania.

History

Some Jews apparently accompanied the Romans to Dacia (as Transylvania was called then) in the first centuries of the Common Era, but not until the Middle Ages do we have written proof of a flourishing Jewish society in Moldavia, Transylvania and Wallachia. Jews came into Romania from the west (Bohemia, Germany and Hungary), the north (Poland) and the south (primarily from the Ottoman Empire where the Sephardim from Spain and Portugal had found refuge). They became intermediaries on the major trade routes; creditors to the political authorities, the gentry and urban and rural communities; and physicians at the courts of the Romanian rulers and Transylvanian princes.

Jews influential in the Ottoman world became directly involved in the political life of the Romanian principalities, supporting and financing pretenders to the throne, or helping Jewish tradesmen integrate themselves into the region, part of an extended system of gathering and transmitting the political, strategic and economic information necessary to the expanding Ottoman Empire.

The attitude of Romanian society, an Orthodox world of Byzantine extraction, toward the increasing economic, social and political role of the Jews has been described as "hostile tolerance."[1] Tolerance refers to unrestricted opportunities to get into, settle, move freely and develop economic activities in the Romanian principalities, even to acquire or lease real estate and to hold public office in Moldavia and Wallachia. But Christians nourished prejudices against Jews inoculated by the Christian church, and with the juridical codification of the 17th century, differences between Jews and Christians were legally sanctioned and conversion to Judaism prohibited. Hostility also was motivated by competition between local and Jewish tradesmen, by the discontent of debtors toward their creditors, and by the image of the Jews as agents of Ottoman power and policy in the Romanian provinces.

Jews in Transylvania

In 1623, the Prince of Transylvania conferred a privilege upon the Jews that became the basic legal document that regulated their social, economic and juridical status until the mid-19th century. Granted as part of a policy to revive the principality's economy through colonization, the privilege enabled Jews to settle and move into the country, to practice their trades freely and to observe their religion without discrimination.

Alba Iulia was the first, and for a long time the only, organized Jewish community in the principality. Its *pinkas* (register)—today lost, but summarized by researchers who had the opportunity to study it—mirrors a system of internal organization led by a rabbi who, in the middle of the 18th century, also became the chief rabbi of all Transylvanian Jewry.[2]

Beginning in 1690, the new Hapsburg regime began periodic censuses. These records are preserved in the Hungarian National Archives in Budapest.[*] The first general census of the Jews in the Great Principality of Transylvania was taken in 1779. A census taken in 1785–86 showed Jews to be slightly more than one-tenth of one percent of the total population. In the western parts of present-day Transylvania (the counties of Arad, Bihor, Caras, Maramures, Satu Mare, Timis and Torontal), which were under Hungarian administration, the Jewish population recorded in the same census was three times larger.

During the first half of the 18th century, official policy towards the Jews alternated between restrictive measures and reiterated renewals of privileges granted in the previous century. During the reign of Maria Theresa (1740–80), a burdensome tolerance tax was levied upon the Jews in the western parts of modern Transylvania. (See below for information about records that still exist.) In 1779–80, the government decided that the entire Jewish population of the Great Principality would be concentrated in Alba Iulia, that all occupations except trade would be prohibited, and that new Jewish immigrants would not be allowed to enter the country. The death of the Empress in 1780 and the accession of Joseph II to the throne prevented implementation of this proposal[3].

In the years just before the 1848 revolution, the Jewish population of Transylvania doubled, and it continued to grow in the years that followed; the Austrian census of 1850–51 registered more than 15,000 Jewish residents. This spectacular growth had come from massive immigration from Bukovina, Galicia and northern Hungary because of more advantageous economic and social conditions offered in Transylvania.

Despite the surge in growth, however, the Jewish population of Transylvania still did not account for even one percent of the total. The Jewish population doubled after civil emancipation in 1867. Before World War I, in the whole territory of present-day Transylvania (including the western counties); the Jewish population amounted to 223,082. The increase in the Jewish population of Transylvania during the 19th century resulted in the creation of new communities with their own rabbis and leaders in addition to the (only) legally recognized community of Alba Iulia.

After the 1848 Hungarian revolution, supporters of institutional and educational reforms requested reorganizations of the communities and the school systems, plus reduction in the influence of the chief rabbi. The proposals were realized after civil emancipation in 1868 when a Congress of Hungarian Jewry was organized within the new Austro-Hungarian dual monarchy. The major result was to create a chasm between the Jewish communities that lasted until after World War II. Those who acknowledged the resolutions of the Congress became the Neolog communities; their opponents declared themselves Orthodox (supporters of the rigorous observance of ritual prescriptions and of full communal authority), or Status Quo Ante (partisans of maintenance of the situation that existed prior to the establishment of the Congress).

Jews in Moldavia and Wallachia

At present, Moldavia is made up of the following counties: Bacau, Botosani, Buzau, Galati, Iasi, Neamt, Suceava, Vaslui and Vrancea. The National Archives has county branches in Bacau, Botosani, Buzau, Focsani (capital of Vrancea county), Galati, Iasi, Piatra Neamt (capital of Neamt county), Suceava and Vaslui.

The first census in Moldavia, organized by the occupying Russian military authorities during a war with the Turks in 1774, recorded 1,300 Jewish families. After Bukovina fell under Austrian rule in 1775, successive censuses revealed a decrease in the number of Jewish families, the result of expulsions ordered by the new rulers.

For two reasons, the Jewish population of Moldavia grew massively from 1803 to 1838: spontaneous immigration from Poland and Russia, countries with a poor economic situation and a restrictive anti-Jewish policy; and a colonization policy initiated by the Romanian rulers, *boyards* (nobility) and church aimed at helping their estates. By 1848, more than 60 small towns and villages with a Jewish majority had been established, including Bucecea, Dorohoi, Falticeni, Mihaileni, Podul Iloaiei and Targul Frumos. Additional factors in the growth of the Jewish population were significant natural growth resulting from early marriage, ritual sanitary and dietary laws, a lower mortality rate than the non-Jewish population and stable family life. As a result, the Jewish population grew to more than 134,100 by 1859–60, of whom 124,897 lived in Moldavia and only 9,234 in Wallachia. In the same period (1856), the Jewish population of Bessarabia numbered 78,751.

Between 1803 and 1899, the Jewish population in Moldavia increased 17 times. At the dawn of the 20th century, it amounted to 200,000 individuals (of a total Jewish population of 260,000 people in the Old Kingdom of Moldavia, Wallachia, and Dobrudja). A 1930 census revealed a total Jewish population of 728,000 in Romania.[4]

In the 18th and 19th centuries, along with massive population growth, significant developments also occurred at the institutional level with resultant consequences for genealogical research. From the mid-18th century onward, in Moldavia and Wallachia, the leader of the Jewish communities was the so-called *hahambasha*. The *hahambasha* had administrative, juridical and fiscal authority as well as the right to nominate rabbis and lay leadership.

Emancipation came late to the Jews in Moldavia and Wallachia. The first ruler of united Romania, Alexandru Ioan Cuza, appointed several Jews to noteworthy public offices,

Synagogue in Cluj as it appears today. Courtesy of David Gordon.

and a communal law of 1864 granted Jews the right to participate, under certain conditions, in municipal elections. After Cuza was deposed in 1866, the public attitude toward Jews changed radically. Adopted under the pressure of street demonstrations, the constitution of 1866 granted the right of citizenship only to Christians.

When, after the Russian-Romanian-Turkish War of 1877–78, the Peace Congress of Berlin traced new political frontiers in the Balkans, the Great Powers made recognition of Romania's newly gained independence conditional upon the granting of civil and political rights irrespective of religion. Revision of the constitution triggered a political storm and a "surrogate solution" offered the possibility of individual naturalization for Jews who had been living in the country for more than ten years. With the single exception of the mass naturalization of the 883 Jewish participants in the War of Independence, (see Carol Iancu) this procedure for gaining civil rights proved utterly impractical and the number of Jews naturalized in the years 1878–1913 was an insignificant 529. Only after World War I, did Jews gain citizenship in Romania under decrees issued in 1919, the Constitution in 1923, and by Romania's acknowledgment of guarantees included in the Treaty of Minorities imposed at the Versailles Peace Conference.[5]

Genealogical Resources

Records Older Than 100 Years
By law, records older than 100 years are held in the county departments of the national archives in every county capital and are available for research. In the same place, the researcher may find inventories, which offer information about the existing registers, classified by year and locality. Generally speaking, the registers were preserved better in southern Transylvania, Moldavia and Wallachia; some records of northern Transylvania and Bukovina were lost during the Holocaust. In the case of Transylvania, the researcher may also find the copies kept at the offices of the county administrative authorities. These records are especially well preserved in Maramures.

Records Less than 100 Years Old
Records newer than 100 years are kept at the registry offices in local town halls, but because they are not intended for re-

search, access is possible only with a special permit. Excerpts from the registers, prepared by registry office personnel, may be obtained upon request by direct relatives. Alphabetical indexes exist for registers kept in some larger localities. Sometimes they are kept according to the given name, rather than the family name.

Former Austro-Hungarian Area
An overview of the sources for Jewish genealogical research in Romania starts with the distinct historical tradition of its constituent provinces, which, introduced at various times, generated different methods of recording the legal status of its inhabitants.

Transylvania and Bukovina (which today is partly in Ukraine) were both part of the Austrian Empire, the former from 1690, the latter from 1775. The first attempts to implement a modern system for recording births, marriages and deaths were part of the Austrian policy of reform instituted in the second half of the 18th century. Emperor Joseph II (1780–90) began a modern system of record keeping for the entire empire, in which the clergy of each religious denomination was responsible for keeping registers of births, marriages and deaths.

In 1812, the Transylvanian government ordered that tables recording the births, marriages and deaths of the Jewish population be forwarded every year to the government offices. In 1813, a law required that in each important locality in Maramures, a clerk be selected from among the Jewish inhabitants to enlist in a register of Jews every birth, death, marriage, number of servants and circulation in and out of the respective locality. In official instructions created in 1837 for the Jewish communities of Arad and Timisoara, the local rabbi was required to update, without remuneration, the register of births, marriages and deaths under his own signature and that of the parents, bride, bridegroom and witnesses. The law stipulated that the register be kept in the archive of the local Jewish community and that a copy be forwarded to the town authorities every year.

Few rabbis complied. Documents in Romanian archives today show that although these laws were implemented—even if not everywhere or regularly—for the entire period of the first half of the 19th century, only fragmentary rabbinical records survive from that period of time, either because the rabbis complied inconsistently with official requirements or because the registers were lost.

The oldest registers of this kind date back to 1794 and come from Arad. They were written in Hebrew until 1832 and in German thereafter. Similar registers may be found in Bihor (in Beius from 1826 on; in Oradea, from 1842 on), in Salaj (in Cehul Silvaniei, from 1823 on; in Nusfalau, from 1841), in Alba (for Vintul de Jos, from 1818).[6]

In Bukovina, rabbinical registers of births in Suceava exist from 1843 and, in Falticeni, for the years 1862 and 1864.

Other Early Records in Transylvania. For the period 1780–1848, although Jewish vital records registers for Transylvania are almost totally nonexistent, researchers may use lists of the periodic fiscal and other censuses of the Jews.

Interior of the synagogue in Brasov. Courtesy of David Gordon.

The most useful censuses date from 1813, 1819, 1835–45 and 1848 for the territory of the Great Principality of Transylvania, which was a distinct administrative unit until 1867.

Many censuses were taken for the purpose of registering people required to pay the tolerance tax. Such censuses exist especially for the counties of Maramures and Satu Mare for the period 1780–1848. They are organized by localities and heads of family. Both counties had large Jewish populations before the Holocaust, but the censuses include only the name of the head of the family and the sum of money paid or owed. These records may be found in the archives of the respective counties; copies are also held at the Dr. Moshe Carmilly Institute of Hebrew and Jewish History of Cluj.

The 1813 fiscal census was taken for the purpose of introducing the tolerance tax for Transylvanian Jews. This levy was a special tax first imposed on Hungarian Jews in the middle of the 18th century. Because of their small numbers and their poverty, Jews who lived in the Principality of Transylvania were originally exempt from the tax, but in approximately 1810, an attempt was made to introduce the tax into Transylvania.

The 1813 census includes the following data, recorded by administrative divisions, localities and families: name of the head of the family; number of family members; cultivated fields, hayfields, vineyards, mills and distilleries, on their own property or under lease; lease paid and income produced by the leased assets; number of shops and the income they produced; tax paid to the state and occupation.

The 1819 census, taken for the same reason, offers the following information: name of the head of the family; number of family members and domestics; cultivated fields, hayfields and vineyards on their property or under lease; number of cattle, sheep, goats and beehives on their property; occupation; income produced by trade, alcohol distillation and leaseholding; taxes on assets and persons; tolerance tax.

The census taken in 1835–45 indicates for each locality name, age, birth place, date of immigration to the respective locality and occupation. The censuses of 1848, drafted according to administrative divisions, localities, families and individuals, give the following data: name and age of the head of the family and of family members, occupation, birthplace, year of settlement in the present residence. Original copies of these censuses, which consist of hundreds of pages, are kept in the Hungarian State Archives in Budapest. Copies are at the Dr. Moshe Carmilly Institute Hebrew and Jewish History of Cluj and in the possession of ROM-SIG.

The 1813 census recorded 3,792 Jews in 21 administrative units; the 1819 census recorded 727 family heads in 16 administrative units. The census taken in 1835–45 recorded 3,629 people in 18 administrative units. For Transylvania, the only data from the 1848 general census of the Jews that still survives is for the Jews of Crasna and Solnocul de Mijloc counties; the census for Caras county is at the Hungarian National Archives in Budapest.[7]

This part of present-day Romania had a significant Jewish population; the population increased from 105,600 individuals in 1869 to more than 230,000 in 1910. According to a 1930 census, the Jews of Transylvania, the Banat, Crisana, and Maramures represented 2.5 percent of the total Jewish population of Romania.

Vital Records in Transylvania and Bukovina after 1850.
After the defeat of the 1848 Hungarian Revolution, the Austrian monarchy introduced an authoritarian regime that strictly imposed compliance with, among other things, the laws providing for registration of the population. After 1850, registers kept by the rabbis exist for almost every community of Transylvania and Bukovina.

In 1850, the Austrian authorities introduced in Transylvania and in Bukovina a generalized and uniform system of recording births, marriages and deaths according to religious denomination. Two identical registers listing Jews were kept in German by local rabbis. One copy was to be kept in the local Jewish community archives; the other was to be forwarded annually to the local administrative authorities. In these registers, each event was written in a line, mentioning the essential data about the newborn and his or her parents; the bride and bridegroom and their parents; and for the deceased, his or her age, occupation and cause of death.

In some places, especially in Maramures (formerly Maramaros County, Hungary), the county office copies are preserved and are more complete than the originals, most of which were lost in the Holocaust. Today these copies are kept in the state archives in the collections of county records or, for records less than 100 years old, in the local offices of vital records, and are available for research. The registers—initially in German and then, after 1867, increasingly in Hungarian (for Transylvania)–include the following data:

Birth registers: name and sex of the newborn; whether legitimate or illegitimate; name, birth date, birth place, residence and occupation of parents; name of midwife. In the case of a boy, the date of circumcision; name of the circumciser and

Tombstones in the Iasi cemetery. Courtesy of David Gordon.

witnesses; in the case of a girl, the date of name giving, given name and the name of the godfather;

Marriage registers: name, age, occupation, residence and birthplace of bride and groom; name, residence and occupation of parents; place and date of the wedding; name of individual who officiated at the ceremony and witnesses.

Death registers: Name, age, occupation, residence of the deceased; cause of death; place and date of death and burial; name of parents (in the case of dead children) or of spouse of the deceased.

Whereas in Bukovina this system of registration lasted until 1918, in Transylvania the situation was different after 1867, upon the establishment of the Austro-Hungarian Monarchy and the separation of the Jewish communities into Orthodox, Neolog and Status-quo-ante. At that time, the registers were written either in Hungarian or German; the three categories of communities each had its own register, each kept by its respective rabbi.

State Registers of Vital Records. In 1895, the civil status of all denominations became the responsibility of the state. From that time onward, civil servants were responsible for the registers. The registers, classified according to religious denomination and written in Hungarian, in Transylvania and German in Bukovina were replaced in 1895 by civil registers kept by the administrative authorities of the state, written in Hungarian and kept in local town halls.

Until 1907, the registers included printed forms that were filled out in handwriting with the pertinent data for each case. After 1907, the authorities reverted to the system of having one line for each recorded event. Beginning in 1920, the registers were kept according to this pattern, but after World War I, following the union of Transylvania and Bukovina with Romania, they were written in Romanian.

Alongside the state registers, the Jewish communities continued to have their own registers kept by rabbis and preserved in the archives of the communities. At present,

those that survived the Holocaust are in the state archives of county capitals. Such registers exist in Baia Mare, Cluj, Oradea, Satu Mare and elsewhere.

Records Older Than 100 Years in Transylvania Today. In contemporary Transylvania, civil registers—the major source for a researcher of Jewish genealogy—are gathered in the county branches of the National Archives: Baia Mare, Maramures County; Satu Mare; Oradea, Bihor county; Arad, Timisoara and Caransebes, Banat county; Zalau, Salaj-Crasna and Solnocul de Mijloc counties; Cluj, Solnocul Interior and Dabaca counties; Alba Iulia, Alba county; Deva, Hunedoara county; Sibiu, Brasov, Targu Mures, the seat of Mures and Tarnava county; Sfantu Gheorghe and Miercurea Ciuc, the Szeckler seats Trei Scaune and Ciuc; Bistrita, the northeastern part of Transylvania.

Maramures County Resources. The Jewish presence in Maramures county, one of the most densely populated areas, has been recorded since the 18th century. The number has increased from 26,000 in 1869 to 65,700 on the eve of World War I, when the Jewish population was more than 18 percent of the total population of the county. After World War I, the part of the former Maramures county south of the Tisza River came to Romania; the portion north of the Tisza River was annexed to sub-Carpathian Ukraine, passed successively under the administration of Czechoslovakia, Hungary, and the USSR, and today is part of western Ukraine. Many of the civil registers, kept separately for each religious denomination, initially in German, and between 1867–1918 in Hungarian, may be found at the state archives in Baia Mare in two copies. One copy is a register of each locality, among which one may find the registers of Sighetu Marmatiei and surrounding areas for the period 1851–1909. The other consists of loose sheets of paper that represented the annual reports of births, marriages, and deaths of each denomination, forwarded to the county authorities in every administrative district during the period 1854–95.

In addition to this fundamental source for genealogical research, the Baia Mare archives also hold a significant collection of censuses of the Jews taken between 1773 and 1843. Most enumerations were related to the tolerance tax, and they mention only the locality, name, and amount paid. Several fiscal censuses taken in 1773, 1784, 1793, 1820/21 supply richer information, including the name(s) of the head of the family, family members and domestic personnel; occupation; economic resources and annual income. Documents from an inquiry conducted by county authorities in 1815 provide numerous details on more than 80 Jewish families that immigrated to the county after 1790. Although only fragments of the portion for Maramures county are preserved, the general census of the Jewish population in Hungary taken in 1848, held in the Hungarian National Archives in Budapest, provides several items of information, including names and ages of heads of family, their birth place, when they settled in each locality and the authorities' notes about their morality and their behavior.

Satu Mare County. The Satu Mare state archives hold the civil registers of the Jews of this important center of Hasidim. The main centers of Jewish population were the town of Satu

Mare and Carei, the first important colonization center of the Jews in the 18th century. In Satu Mare, one finds the rabbinical civil registers of the town and surrounding areas for the years 1850–1921. From 1895 onward, the state civil registers, which record all citizens regardless of denomination, are kept at the registry offices of the town halls in each locality. The registers of the other localities in the county, including Carei, have many gaps, because, at the end of World War II, copies in the community's keeping were moved to Budapest and lost. The 1848 census is well preserved and held in the county archives of Nyiregyhaza, Hungary.

Banat. Civil registers of the Jews of Banat are at the Timis and Caras-Severin county departments of the National Archives in Timisoara and Caransebes. Several censuses of the Jews of Timisoara, taken in 1743, 1744, 1750, 1798/99, 1820, 1821 and 1822, recorded the names of heads of families and of the individual members, ages, welfare standards and fiscal duties. The Jewish community of Timisoara also has a rich archive that includes, among other documents, the census of the Jews of Timisoara taken in 1815 that lists the members of the communities, marriage and divorce papers, and wills. The 1848 census of the Jews of Caras county is at the Hungarian National Archives in Budapest.

Zalau County. The state archives of Zalau hold the civil registers of all religious denominations, including the registers of Jews in Crasna and Solnocul de Mijloc counties. The main centers of Jewish population were Cehul Silvaniei, Nusfalau, Simleul Silvanieli and Zalau. In the archives of Zalau are civil registers for the period 1823–1942, written in Hungarian, with many gaps due to losses during the Holocaust. Civil state registers, begun in 1895, recorded all citizens without regard for religion. Until 1918, they were written in Hungarian; afterwards, in Romanian. They may be consulted at the town halls in each locality.

Cluj County. In the Cluj department of national archives, one may find the civil registers of the Jews of the former counties of Cluj, Dabaca, Solnocul Interior and Turda. The archives in Cluj hold birth registers kept by the Orthodox

Panoramic view of Oradea. The domed building is the synagogue. Courtesy of Tomasz Wisniewski.

congregations for the years 1852–1922, marriages for 1853–1930, and deaths for the period 1852–1902. Neolog registers of births, marriages, and deaths exist for the years 1886–1950. (Other significant Jewish centers, together with the surrounding rural localities whose civil registers also are in Cluj, are Aghires, Dej, Gherla and Turda.) In the archives of the Jewish community of Cluj is a register of burials in the Jewish cemetery for the years 1900–2002.

Alba County. The Alba county archives in the town of Alba Iulia hold the rabbinical civil registers of Alba de Jos county and the town of Alba Iulia, seat of the oldest Jewish community in Transylvania, and until 1848, the only one that was legally recognized. The archives of Alba Iulia hold the civil registers of Alba Iulia, Aiud, Blaj, Ighiu, Ocna Mures, and Vintu de Jos for the years 1850–95; in the case of Alba Iulia, however, the registers continue to 1937. The archive of the Jewish community of Alba Iulia, now at the Federation of Jewish Communities in Bucharest, has not been inventoried yet, but it may turn out to be an extremely valuable source for Jewish genealogists.

Hunedoara County. At the state archives in Deva are the civil registers of Hunedoara county. The registers of this archive come from Orastie and concern the period 1853–1918.

Sibiu and Brasov. County archives in Sibiu and Brasov have registers of the so-called Royal Lands, the areas inhabited and administered by the Transylvanian Saxons, where the Jewish population was much smaller than elsewhere because of the many obstacles they encountered when trying to settle in this region.

In the Szeckler areas of eastern Transylvania, the Jewish presence was more significant in the Seats of Mures and Trei Scaune, especially in Targu Mures and Sfantu Gheorghe. (A Seat is a specific administrative unit of the Szeckler areas.) The civil registers for these areas are in the county branches of the National Archives in Targu Mures (for Mures), Sfantu Gheorghe (for Trei Scaune), and Miercurea Ciuc (for Odorhei).

Bistrita County. The Bistrita county archives has a complete collection of Jewish civil registers for the Jews of northeastern Transylvania. The main Jewish centers were Beclean, Bistrita, Nasaud, and Rodna, all of whose registers for the years 1851–95 are extant.

Sources in Moldavia and Wallachia

A similar system was implemented in Moldavia, where an 1844 document from Iasi mentions a certain Itic sin Marcu who could speak and write Romanian, German and Hebrew, and who was appointed to keep the civil registers (*mitrice*) of the Jewish community.[8] In Moldavia, rabbinical registers exist for Botosani (1849–65), Bucecea (1861 and 1864–65) and Harlau (1860–64). These registers are kept in the state archives of the capital cities of the respective counties.[9]

In Moldavia and Wallachia, the census registers are called *catagrafii*, and they refer either to the entire Jewish population or to Jews called *suditi*, who were under the protection of consulates of the Great Powers (Austria, England, France, Prussia and Russia). In Moldavia, such registers exist for the years 1803, 1808, 1820, 1824–25, 1831, 1832, 1836,

1845 and 1851, but thus far only information about the Jews of Iasi under foreign protection, recorded in 1824–25 (432 families) has been published.[10] Most complete is the register for 1836, which listed the name, place of birth, age, period of immigration, occupation, residence, assets and moral profile of all the Jews in Moldavian administrative units. Although massive numbers of these registers exist, they are extremely difficult to use because they lack supplementary finding aids and are written in a Cyrillic alphabet that is difficult to decipher.

Registration in Moldavia and Wallachia after 1860. Moldavia and Wallachia united under the name Romania in 1859, and the modern system of civil registers was introduced in 1865. Administrative authorities were charged with recording births, marriages and deaths for all religious denominations; the registers were written in Romanian. In larger localities, research is sometimes eased by alphabetical indexes, as is the case for Botosani, Bucharest, Focsani, Iasi and elsewhere. Unfortunately, in most cases, alphabetical order follows the given name and not the family name which makes a researcher's work much more difficult. The following data is recorded:

- Birth registers: Date when the birth was registered; name, sex, religion of the newborn; date and place of birth; name, occupation, residence, age of parents; name, age, occupation and residence of witnesses; name of the registrar.
- Marriage registers: Application for the three announcements of the marriage in the synagogue and in front of the local town hall, certificate attesting to the announcements, birth certificates of bride and groom. If they did not have birth certificates, then documents that proved the date of birth according to five witnesses, similar documents for deceased parents, the agreement of the parents still living, testimony of the witnesses regarding the absence of any impediment to the planned marriage. Sometimes this collection of documents was replaced by a single register page on which the pertinent data about the bride and groom, parents and witnesses was abridged.
- Death registers: Information included the date that the death was recorded, name, sex, age, religion, residence of the deceased, place and date of death, cause of death, witnesses, doctor and registrar.

In the period following 1865, information in the official civil registers was duplicated or supplemented by registers that rabbis of certain Jewish communities continued to keep: the registers of *chevrot kadisha* (burial societies), registers of Jewish cemeteries and the censuses of the Jews of 1941 and 1942. These records may be found in the archives of the Jewish communities in the respective localities, usually in bigger cities.

Jewish Registers in Moldavia

Botosani and Dorohoi Counties. The archives in Botosani keep the civil registers of the former Botosani and Dorohoi counties, areas densely populated with almost 50,000 Jews (25 percent of all Moldavian Jews lived there in 1899). The main Jewish centers were Botosani and Dorohoi. Large Jewish populations lived also in Bucecea, Darabani, Frumusica, Radauti-Prut

and Saveni. Civil registers begin in 1865, and, up to 1900, they may be found in the county archives in Botosani.

Records of births, marriages, and deaths of every religious denomination were kept in a single register written in Romanian. For the town of Botosani, inhabited by nearly one-third of the county's Jewish population, an additional research instrument is an alphabetical index that lists all births and marriages between 1865 and 1939. As valuable as the index can be, some difficulties are associated with using it. The index is alphabetical according to given name, not family name, and it is incomplete; the letters D to J include births only for the years 1865 to 1885, while the list of marriages includes only the letters A to J. The index provides the following data: name(s) of the newborn or married couple, year and number of the document and of the register.

Registers of burials kept by the administrators of the Jewish cemetery of Botosani are a significant additional resource. For the years 1906–86, the registers indicate the name of the deceased, date of death, and location of the grave.

No additional finding aids exist for other localities in the county. Research can be conducted only by going through the registers page by page. For the period 1865–95, in such localities as Darabani and Frumusica, the number of vital events per year varies between 70 and 90.

Before civil registration was introduced in 1865, births, marriages and deaths of each religious denomination were recorded in separate registers called *mitrice*. Few Jewish registers survive from that period. We have some from Botosani (1857–64), Bucecea (1860) and Sulita (1859–65). Research is especially difficult because the records were written in either the Cyrillic alphabet or in a format that represented a mixture of the Cyrillic and the Roman alphabet.

Suceava County. The research situation is more complex in the Suceava county department, where one may find the registers of the former Suceava county and also some sources from Bukovina. Suceava was a part of old Romania. Bukovina, a province in northern Moldavia, was part of the Austrian Empire between 1775 and 1918. Today, the southern part of Bukovina, with Campulung, Gura Humorului, Radauti, Siret, Suceava and Vatra Dornei, belongs to Romania. Northern Bukovina, whose capital is Cernauti, belongs to Ukraine.

Austrian civil registers for the part of Bukovina that is Romania today are at the Suceava county department and are available for research. Each religious denomination is recorded in German in separate registers. The following Jewish registers survive: Burdujeni (1860–61), Campulung (1857–93), Gura Humorului (1857–77), Radauti (1857–87), Suceava (1843–94), and Vatra Dornei (1877–87).

Neamt County. The Neamt county department of the National Archives in Piatra Neamt holds the vital registers for the former Neamt and Roman counties. Major Jewish centers in this area were Piatra Neamt, Roman, and Targu Neamt. Typical of the registers for the years 1890–95 gathered in this archive is the index of names that starts every volume, which considerably facilitates a researcher's work.

For the town of Roman, the archives at Piatra Neamt hold an index of marriages celebrated between 1865 and 1907. An alphabetical (by family name) index of births (1912–44) is held in the registry office of the Roman town hall. The archive of the Jewish community in Roman holds a register of deaths that begins in 1892, but consists only of the letters A–C, as well as two censuses of the Jews of Roman taken in 1941 and 1942. The censuses include name, age, date, and place of birth. The Jewish cemetery of Roman has registers of burials between 1905 and 1990 that record name, date of death, age, and location of the grave.

Bacau County. At the county department of the National Archives in Bacau, one may find the civil registers of the town of Bacau. The main Jewish centers were Bacau proper, Moinesti and Buhusi. Research in the registers for the years 1890–95 is facilitated by the existence of alphabetical and chronological lists of names at the beginning of each register. The archives of the Jewish community* has the register of deaths and burials in the Jewish cemetery of Bacau.

Vrancea County. The most important Jewish centers whose civil registers are kept in the Vrancea county archives in the town of Focsani are those for that city, Tecuci and Panciu. In the case of Focsani, research is aided by the existence of an index of births for the years 1867–99, marriages for 1866–85 and deaths for 1868–75.

County Archives in Buzau, Galati and Vaslui. No additional sources exist in the other county archives of Moldavia (those in Buzau, Galati and Vaslui). Research is limited to a patient perusal of the registers of births, marriages and deaths for the years 1865–95.

Historical Province of Wallachia

Wallachia, the historical province of today's southern Romania, is composed of two distinct elements: Wallachia proper in the west and Oltenia in the east. Except for the capital city of Bucharest, this province was settled by few Jews much later than Moldavia. A Sephardic Jewish community existed in Bucharest as early as the 16th century, but, in 1860, only 9,000 Jews lived in all of Wallachia. Two-thirds of this number lived in Bucharest. A census taken in 1930 recorded 87,500 Jews in Wallachia and Oltenia, representing only 12 percent of the total Jewish population of Greater Romania. General tables from these censuses exist in separate published volumes (in Romanian).

Records in Bucharest

As the statistics indicate, Bucharest was the most significant Jewish center in this part of Romania. Civil registers for the period 1865–95 are in the Bucharest City Archive located on Vacaresti Road. Registers less than 100 years old are at the Registry Office of the City Hall on Kogalniceanu Boulevard. These registers were classified in a specific manner, each section bearing the name of the five former districts, called Red, Yellow, Green, Blue and Black. For each district, we have an index of births, marriages and deaths; for some districts and certain periods of time, the authorities even created two additional sets of records, some according to family name, others by given name. Beginning in 1885, there is a single chronological index for all the districts, arranged by the registration number of the birth, marriage or death.

The Library of the Federation of Jewish Communities in Romania* preserves the most valuable Jewish archive in the country. The Federation has also brought here many community archives from all over the country, among them that of the oldest community in Transylvania, Alba Iulia. Unfortunately, the inventory process is not complete yet, so the genealogical researcher is not able to use this most valuable collection.

A useful source at the Jewish archives is a list of Jewish males born in Bucharest between 1892 and 1906 and registered between 1941 and 1944 in order to be sent to forced labor. In the same archive, one may find a copy of the census of the Jews of Romania taken between 1941 and 1942 and the census of the Jews in northern Transylvania (under Hungarian administration from 1940) taken in 1941.

The Central Office of the National Archives* in Bucharest holds a series of *catagrafii* taken in Wallachia for the years 1831, 1838, 1845 and 1860. The 1838 census provides several details about each Jewish family, including name, age, occupation, domicile, welfare standard, juridical status (local or foreign "suditi" Jews), sanitary condition (vaccinated or not) and moral profile. The general table provided by the *catagrafie* taken in Bucharest is published in the third volume of the collection *Isvoare si marturii referitoare la evreii din Romania* (Sources and testimonies concerning the Jews in Romania). All researchers are permitted to work in this archive.

Civil registers held in other county archives for this part of Romania (Alexandria, Braila, Calarasi Craiova Ploiesti, Pitesti reveal that significant Jewish populations existed in Braila, in Ploiesti and in Craiova (3,300). Unfortunately, the researcher must investigate the registers of these localities without the help of finding aids, except for the archives of Ploiesti, which has an index of births for the periods 1832–65 and 1881–1900—but only for female newborns.

Dobrudja Province

Dobrudja, the historical province located between the Danube River and the Black Sea, became part of Romania after the war of independence from the Ottoman Empire (1877–78). At the two county departments of the National Archives in Tulcea and Constanta, civil registers begin with the year 1879, and one may investigate them up to 1891 in Tulcea and up to 1895 in Constanta. The registers for subsequent years are kept in the registry offices of the respective town halls.

Special Sources

Several categories of special sources exist that might add significant details to those gleaned from civil registers or statistical sources such as censuses and *catagrafii*. The first group are documents issued by educational institutions at all levels. Records of the Universities of Bucharest and of Iasi begin in 1864, and those of the University of Cluj in 1872. They include students' records, including personal data and achievements (grades, scholarships, applications, etc.), and records of the faculties and of the rector offices (including annual statistical data, certificates attesting to the parents' welfare status, correspondence with the Ministry of Education and other institutions).

Documents drafted until 1950 may be consulted at the county departments of the National Archives in Iasi and Cluj, whereas documents of more recent decades may be found in the archives of the respective university. The archive of Iasi University has a good inventory, created in 1982, that describes each file. In Bucharest, the archive is kept in three different buildings; it was not inventoried and was partly destroyed during the two world wars. A portion of the archives concerning the Medical School of Cluj was moved to Targu Mures, where there is a medical school that teaches in Hungarian. At the county department in Oradea, one may peruse the fonds of the former law school that operated during the last century until 1918. Data provided by these archival sources may be supplemented with information supplied by the academic yearbooks, first published in 1891–92. These also include annual lists of students, graduates, scholarships, and doctorates (including the title of the dissertations).

Records of secondary schools also are available. County departments have possession of the archives of the secondary and high schools of their respective county, including lists of pupils, roll books, etc. These are accompanied by yearbooks and commemorative volumes, which published comprehensive lists of pupils, mentioning their religion or nationality, locality of origin and social status. The archives of the elementary schools, including the Jewish ones, also have survived—for example, the archives of the Jewish boys school established in Arad in 1832, whose roll books are in the archives of the Jewish community. The documents issued by the school authorities in the interwar period also offer valuable information, such as lists of Jewish pupils, certificates of ethnic origin, etc.

A second important group, documents issued by military authorities, is deposited in the archives of the Ministry of Defense in Pitesti. Beginning with 1878, this archives hold the record of each recruit, with biographical data, medical records, place where they fulfilled their military service, decorations and punishments, and moral profile and promotions. For the Holocaust period, the source material includes tables, instructions, and reports concerning the status, concentration and deportation of the Jews. A part of this archive was microfilmed and is held by the U.S. Holocaust Memorial Museum in Washington, D.C.

At the county archives in Iasi, researchers may consult documents issued during the period 1900–20 by the courts martial of each army corps throughout the territory of the Old Kingdom. They deal with cases of desertion, espionage or any other offenses committed by enlisted men. The Cluj county department has possession of the police archives, which provide information on the Jews until 1950.

Finally, the Iasi county department has a consistent collection of records of emigration for the years 1895–1913, which supplies information on the organization of Jewish emigration and on financial support for it.

Post-World War I Record Keeping

After 1918, with the establishment of Greater Romania, by the unification of Bessarabia, Bukovina and Transylvania with the Old Kingdom, the system of civil registers was extended throughout the country. The registers were written in Romanian and kept by the registry offices of the town halls for all inhabitants of all denominations. With few exceptions, this system has lasted until today. Northern Transylvania, taken by Hungary in 1940, was returned to Romania after World War II, and surviving registers are, at present, in Romanian archives. Registers of the Ukrainian half of the former Maramaros County are preserved in the state archives at Baia Mare for the period before 1895.

The archives of the Jewish communities in present-day Romania keep documentary material useful for genealogical research especially registers of burials in Jewish cemeteries, lists of members of the communities of the *chevra kadisha* (burial society), etc. These materials are available with the agreement of the community's leadership.

Hungarian Nazis, who assumed control of northern Transylvania in 1940, caused the disappearance and presumed death of 131,633 Jews out of a recorded total of 170,694. A large number of Jews from Bukovina, Bessarabia and Northern Moldova were deported to Transnistria by the Romanian dictator Ion Antonescu in the period 1941–1944. After World War II, the Jewish population of Romania had been reduced in half to 412,312 in 1947. Massive disillusionment with the communist system, concomitant with the establishment of the State of Israel, caused many Romanian Jews to emigrate. As a result, the number of Jews decreased from 146,264 in 1956 to 24,667 by 1977. The latest official census, taken in 2002, shows only about 7,000 Jews in all of Romania today.

Resources Outside of Romania

Except for a few, largely insignificant exceptions in the formerly Hungarian regions, the Mormons have not microfilmed any Romanian archival holdings. Genealogists tracing their Jewish roots in Romania must either hire a private researcher, make an onsite research trip, or look for information outside of the country.

Scattered information exists in various repositories around the world, but no comprehensive listing is known to exist; some are noted in the bibliography below. The ROM-SIG, an online special interest group of Jewish genealogists with roots in Romania, offers the best vehicle for pooling knowledge and resources. Whether one wants to hire a private researcher to work in Romanian archives, hire a guide—essential for any onsite research trip, or make contact with any of the many former Romanians in Israel, ROM-SIG is probably the best place to start. Smaller groups for specific counties or even towns can be investigated through ROM-SIG or the JewishGen discussion group and its archives.

Access to Romanian Archives

Foreign researchers may have access to Romanian archives upon written application to the General Director of the National Archives at least 30 days before arrival. The application may be written in English. The General Director will issue approval sent to the applicant and to the respective county department of the National Archives. Research will begin with the indexes (if they exist), then specific registers may be requested. If the choice is successful, it is possible to order photocopies of the records found.

Addresses

Arhivele Nationale (Romanian National Archives), B-dul M. Kogalniceanu 29, 70602 Bucuresti, Sector 5, Romania; telephone: 0040-213-139-295; e-mail: ArhNat@mi.ro.

Arad Jewish community offices: 10 Tribunul Dobra Street; telephone: 40-257-281-310

Bacau Jewish community offices, 11 Alexandru cel Bun Street; telephone: 40-241-034-714

Botosani Jewish community, 220 Calea Nationala; telephone: 40-231-0315-14-659

Brasov Jewish community offices, 27 Poarta Schei Street; telephone: 40-268-543-532.

Bucharest Jewish community offices, Strada Sf. Vineri 9, Sector 3; telephone: 40-21-313-2538; fax: 40-1-312-0869; e-mail: it&t@phamors.ro

Cluj Napoca Jewish community office: 25 Tipografiei Street; telephone: 40-264-11-667

Constanta Jewish community office: 3 Sarmisagetuza Street; telephone: 40-241-611-598

Dorohoi Jewish community office: 95 Spiru Haret Street; telephone: 40-231-611-797

Galati Jewish community office: 9 Dornei Street; telephone: 40-236-413-662

Iasi Jewish community office: 15 Elena Doamna Street; telephone: 40-232-114-414

Institutul de iudaistica si istorie evreiasca, (Dr. Moshe Carmilly Institute for Hebrew and Jewish History, Babes-Bolyai University) Str. Universitatii 7-9, cam. 61, 40091 Cluj-Napoca, Romania

Library of the Federation of Jewish Communities in Romania, 3 Mamulari Street, Bucharest

Oradea Jewish community office: 4 Mihai Viteazu Street; telephone: 40-259-234-843

Piatra Neamt Jewish community office: 7 Petru Rares Street; telephone: 40-233-623-815

Radauti Jewish community office: 11 Aleea Primaverii, Block 14, apt. 1; telephone: 40-30-461-333

Roman Jewish community office: 131 Sucevei Street

Satu Mare Jewish community office: 4 Decebal Street; telephone: 40-261-743-783

Sighet Jewish community office: 8 Basarabia Street; telephone: 40-262-511-652

Suceava Jewish community office: 8 Armeneasca Street; telephone: 40-230-213-084

Timisoara Jewish community office: 5 Gh. Lazar Street; telephone: 40-256-432-813

Tirgu Mures Jewish community office: 10 Brailei Street; telephone: 40-265-215-001

Vatra Dornei Jewish community office: 54 M. Eminescu Street; telephone: 40-230-371-957

County Departments of the Romanian National Archives

Alba Iulia, Mihai Viteazul Str. 29; telephone: 40-258-810096
Arad, Ceaikovschi Str. 2-6; telephone: 40-257-223-321
Bacau, V. Alecsandri Str. 5; telephone: 40-234-511-686
Baia Mare, Bucuresti Bvd. 26; telephone: 40-243-437-948
Bistrita, Garii Str. 1-3; telephone: 40-263-211-143
Botosani, Luna Str. 7; telephone: 40-231-584-047

Brasov, Gh. Baritiu Str. 34; telephone: 40-268-478-742
Braila, Plevnei Str. 8 bis; telephone: 40-239-613-147
Craiova, Libertatii Str. 34; telephone: 40-251-416-661
Focsani, D. Cantemir Bvd. 19; telephone: 40-237-613-712
Galati, Constructorilor Str. 1; telephone: 40-236-436-114
Iasi, Carol I Str. 26; telephone: 40-232-447-774
Oradea, Ioan de Hunedoara Str. 10; telephone: 40-259-413-876
Piatra Neamt, V.A. Urechea Str. 4-6; telephone: 40-233-211-360
Pitesti, Exercitiului Str. 208; telephone: 40-248-253-144
Ploiesti, Logofat Tautu Str. 3; telephone: 40-244-525-307
Satu Mare, 1 Decembrie Str. 13; telephone: 40-261-711-102
Sibiu, Arhivelor Str. 3; telephone: 40-269-431-356
Suceava, Stefan cel Mare Str. 33; telephone: 40-230-531-572
Timisoara, A. Mocioni Str. 8; telephone: 40-256-493-463
Vaslui, Kogalniceanu Str. 2; telephone: 40-235-311-874
Zalau, T. Vladimirescu Str. 34A; telephone: 40-260-611-016

Bibliography

Clapsaddle, Carol. "Selected Sources on Romania at the Central Archives of the Jewish People," *AVOTAYNU* 6, no. 1 (Spring 1990): 15

Gladstone, Bill. "Discovered: An 1839 Travelogue Through the Jewish World, *AVOTAYNU* 10, no. 3 (Fall 1994)

———. "Romanian Holdings at the Diaspora Research Institute," *AVOTAYNU* 6, no. 2 (Summer 1990)

———. "Beit Maramaros," *AVOTAYNU* 7, no. 2, (Summer 1995)

Goldstein, Irene. "Romanian Records at the Holocaust Memorial Museum: Research Strategies for Records Still Held in Romania," *AVOTAYNU* 9, no. 4 (Winter 1993): 18

Gross, S. Y. and Y. Cohen, eds. *Sefer Maramarosh*. Tel Aviv: Federation of Maramaros Jews, 1983

Gyémánt, L. "Sources of Research for Jewish Genealogists in Transylvania," *AVOTAYNU* 11, no. 2, (Summer 1995): 29

———. "Sources for Jewish Genealogical Research in Romania," *AVOTAYNU* 12, no. 3 (Fall 1996): 8

———. "Sources of Jewish Genealogical Research in the Romanian Archival System," *AVOTAYNU* 14, no. 3 (Fall 1998): 22

———. "Genealogy and History: Sources of Jewish Genealogical Research in Romania (18th-20th Centuries)," *AVOTAYNU* 13, no. 3 (Fall 1997): 42

Luft, Edward D. "Map Resources for the Genealogist at the U.S. Library of Congress," *AVOTAYNU* 7, no. 4 (Winter 1991)

"Material in the [U.S.] National Archives Relating to Romania," pamphlet # 46. Washington: U.S. Government Printing Office

"Nineteenth-Century Montefiore Census," *AVOTAYNU* 8, no. 2 (Summer 1992)

Pascal, Paul. "Researching Jewish Romania on Site," *AVOTAYNU* 11, no. 1 (Spring 1995)

Pascal, Paul "Romania: The Sudits and Other Jewish Discoveries," *AVOTAYNU*, 12, no. 1 (Spring 1996): 29

Pinkas Hakehillot Rumania. Jerusalem: Yad Vashem, Vol. 1, 1969; vol. 2, 1980.

Regenstreif, Daniel. "Origins of the Jews of Romania and Their History to the Basic Rules of 1831–32," *AVOTAYNU* 7, no. 2 (Summer 1992): 19

Robinson, Jacob. *The Holocaust and After: Sources and Literature in English*. Jerusalem: Israel Universities Press, 1973

"Romanian Records in the LDS Family History Library," From Our Mailbox, *AVOTAYNU* 7, no. 3 (Fall 1991)

Sack, Sallyann. *Three Important Archives in Israel, AVOTAYNU* 9, no. 4 (Winter 1993)

———. "Research Projects at the Diaspora Research Institute," *AVOTAYNU* 10, no. 4 (Winter 1994)

Notes

1. Serban Papacostea, "Jews in the Romanian Principalities During the Middle Ages," in *Shvut* (Tel Aviv: 1993): 59–71.

2. Moshe Carmilly-Weinberger, "History of the Jews in Transylvania, (1623–1944);" [Romanian] Bucharest, 1994; in Hungarian, Budapest, 1995; Idem, "Spanish (Sephardi) Communities in Transylvania and Banat in the 17th–19th Century," *Studia Judaica* (Cluj-Napoca: 1991), I: 39–52.

3. Angelica Schaser, "Die Juden Siebenbrgens vom 16. bis zum 18. Jahrhundert," in *Südost-Forschungen*, Munich: 1990: 57–94.

4. Aurel Radutiu, Ladislau Gyemant, *Repertory of the Statistical Sources Concerning Transylvania 1690–1847* [Romanian] Bucharest: 1996; Carol Iancu, *Les Juifs en Roumanie (1866–1919), De l'exclusion a l'emancipation*, [French] Aix-en-Provence, 1978.

5. Carol Iancu, *L'emancipation des Juifs de Roumanie (1913–1919)*, Montpellier, 1992; Beate Welter, *Die Judenpolitik der rumänischen Regierung 1866–1888*, Frankfurt am Main, Bern, New York, Paris, 1989.

6. County Department of Cluj National Archives (hereafter: CD), the Fund of Cluj Town Hall, Register 41/1812, pp. 1111–1112; Baia Mare CD, the Archive of Maramures County, Fund 45, Package XVI, No. 47: 34–39; The Archive of the Arad Community, File 3: 227–228; The Archive of the Timisoara Community, File 2: 132–137.

7. Ladislau Gyémánt, "The Transylvanian Jewish Society in the Age of Emancipation (1790–1867), in *Studia Judaica*, 1996, V: 124–167; idem., *The Jews of Transylvania in the Age of Emancipation, 1790–1867*. Bucharest: Enciclopedica, 2000.

8. Iasi CD, Document no. 1229/1844.

9. *AVOTAYNU* 12, no. 3 (Fall 1996): 8–11.

10. Stela Maries, "Importanta Catagrafiei din anii 1824–1825," in *Studia et Acta Historiae Judaeorum Romaniae*, Iasi, 1996: 51–138.

Russia

by Boris Feldblyum

T*he Russia discussed in this chapter is contemporary, post-Soviet Russia. Most often the country called Russia by our immigrant ancestors circa 1900 was the Imperial Russian Empire, a vastly larger land area. Be sure to read the* RUSSIAN EMPIRE *chapter before reading this chapter; relevant information cited in that chapter is not repeated below.*

The 1917 Russian Revolution abolished the Pale of Settlement, the area where most Jews in the empire had been forced to live under czarist rule. Following the revolution, for the first time Jews were permitted to live anywhere in Russia—and they moved in large numbers to big cities. (Also for the first time, Jews were permitted to change their names to more Russian namesy—and many did. Abraham became Alexander, Boruch changed to Boris, and Velvel re-emerged as Vladimir.) But because of the virtual ban on Jewish residence outside the Pale prior to 1917, most Jews do not have roots in contemporary Russia prior to that date. Records kept in that area before 1917—and after, as explained below—have little to reveal about most Jewish families.

Twentieth-century Russian genealogical research has two unique aspects. First, birth, marriage and death records still are held in the archives of the municipal registry offices (called ZAGS), and the records are not deposited into the governmental archival system until they are 100 years old. The registry books generally are closed to researchers, except, perhaps, to fortunate individuals who make a personal appearance in a specific office and are able to convince a local official to search for precise information on a close, direct relative.

Second, a significant number of Soviet Jews were evacuated or lived beyond the reach of the Nazi extermination machine. This means that it is possible for Jewish genealogists with roots in the former Pale of Settlement to find living relatives in Russia today—an option not often pursued by Jewish genealogists. Those who have followed that path have been rewarded by connecting to families after some 70 to 80 years of separation of the branches.

Looking for people who live in Russia today involves an approach somewhat different from pure archival and library research. The first step is similar—to learn a bit about relevant Jewish history. The next step is to follow the methodology suggested below that is based on personal contact by telephone.

Jewish History in Russia

Russian czars acquired their Jews during the three 18th-century partitions of Poland. Before then, Jews were explicitly forbidden from living in the Russian Empire. At the time of the final partition of Poland in 1795, the Jews lived in the so-called "western lands," the territory of contemporary Belarus,

Lithuania, central Ukraine and eastern Poland. Those areas comprised the Pale of Settlement in the early 19th century. In the more than 200 years since, many events influenced where the descendants of our former Russian relatives may be found today, or at least where one should look for traces of them. Although many emigrated around the turn of the 20th century (see MIGRATIONS), many others remained behind, and while great numbers of the second group were murdered during the Holocaust, many others who lived beyond the reach of the German army escaped. Sizeable numbers of their descendants may still live in Russia today. The timeline describes the internal movement of Russian Jewry.

Date	Event/Conditions
1765–1795	Poland is partitioned three times by Russia, Prussia and Austria.
1795–1915	Russian Jews are required to live within the Pale of Settlement. Exceptions are merchants of the first and second guilds, professionals and retired soldiers.
1820s–1840s	Jews from the Pale of Settlement migrate to the agricultural colonies of Novorossiya (today southern Ukraine and the Crimean Peninsula). From there, many migrate further to such cities as Ekaterinoslav (now Dnipropetrovsk), Nikolaev, Simferopol and others. Odessa, a tax-free zone, is a magnet for many Jews.
1840s	Siberian gold rush. A relatively small number of Jews move east, where they become involved in trade. Many Jews are 1863 as punishment for their participation in the Polish uprising. By 1917, large communities existed in such Siberian cities as Irkutsk, Omsk, Tomsk and others. A page from an Irkutsk Jewish birth register reveals that almost all parents were registered residents of towns in the Pale of Settlement. Kainsk (today Kujbyshev in the Novosibirsk region) was popularly called the Siberian Jerusalem because of its large Jewish population.
1881–1914	First massive wave of Jewish emigration from Russia.
1914–1915	Accused by the czarist government of spying for Germany during World War I, Jews are expelled from the western areas (i.e., from hundreds of towns throughout the Pale of Settlement). Many who settle in southern Ukraine and southern Russia there the war.

1917–1939	The 1917 Russian Revolution abolishes the Pale of Settlement. Jews migrate to big cities in large numbers—not only to Moscow and Leningrad (today St. Petersburg), but to many industrial cities where employment was easier to obtain. Jews with higher education diplomas are assigned to work in factories throughout the Soviet Union.
1917–1920s	Many Jews, primarily from Siberia, emigrate to China, forming large communities in Harbin and elsewhere.
1934	The Jewish Autonomous Region is founded in 1934 in the Khabarovsk region as a "homeland" for Soviet Jews. Thousands migrate at first, but many subsequently return or relocate elsewhere.
1939	Poland is divided, once again, this time between the Soviet Union and Nazi Germany in the early days of World War II. The Soviet Union occupies Western Belarus, Bessarabia, Estonia, Latvia, Lithuania and western Ukraine. Many Jewish professionals, business people, and individuals suspected of less-than-sympathetic attitudes toward the Soviet regime are arrested and deported to Siberia. Many die along the way. Some return in the late 1950s and 1960s. Many Polish Jews who manage to escape east are accused of espionage and sent to the GULAG. (GULAG is a Russian acronym for *Glavnoe Upravlenie Lagerej* or The Main Camp Administration.) Those not arrested often end up in Siberia and Middle Asia.
1941–1945	Soviet Jews and non-Jewish refugees settle throughout Siberia, the Far East and Middle Asia. Many return.
1945–1950s	Jews from the former USSR, primarily those from the Baltic States, go to displaced persons camps and from there to Palestine, the United States and elsewhere in the West. Surviving Jews from small towns move to larger cities.
1945–1946	Jews from Harbin, China, escape to Australia and the United States ahead of the advancing Soviets.
1950s	Soviet Union allows "former citizens of the Polish Republic" to resettle in Socialist Poland. Many Jews from formerly Polish areas of western Ukraine and Belarus, and those from southern Lithuania, as well as some who manage to obtain forged documents, move to Poland. Many go on to Israel and the West. The vast majority of the remaining Polish Jews emigrate in 1968 during the campaign of then-President Gomulka in which Jews were openly accused of being a "fifth column."
1960s	Jewish emigration to Israel in small numbers allowed from the Baltic republics.
1971–1979	Mass Jewish emigration takes place to Israel and, from about 1975, to the United States.

1991–present	Following the demise of the Soviet Union, mass Jewish migration takes place from the former USSR throughout the world.

Methodology

Traditional genealogical methods do not lend themselves to finding relatives living in Russia today for a number of reasons which are described below. The techniques suggested in this chapter, based on establishing personal contacts with living people, reflect the author's personal experience.

Preparation. The steps to take will depend on the researcher's goals and the information possessed. More people are alive today than were alive a hundred years ago, and as much as one might like to subject everyone to a "relative test," it is not feasible. To engage the individuals who are contacted, prepare in advance a concise version of the family tree, one that can be described in little more than 30 seconds.

Suggested Steps. Analyze known information. Extract names, dates and town names from documents gathered about the family. When the Russian names used are unknown, think about names people would have used in the old country. No Russian Jew was ever named Morris Cohen, for example, but the anglicized name Morris Cohen provides clues. Once outside Russia, many Jews adopted names that were more easily spelled or recognizable in their new country. Thus, the Russian version of Morris Cohen might have been Moishe-Leib Kogan or something similar (see GIVEN NAMES).

When the name of the ancestral town is not known, hope to have the good fortune to be searching for an uncommon surname. In such a case, consider contacting every person found with that name.

1. When introducing yourself to these persons, it is a good idea to have an opening phrase such as, "I am looking for descendants of Moishe Kogan who lived in Ovruch near Zhitomir and emigrated in 1910. Is your family from that area?"
2. Learn how to read, write and pronounce the ancestral family name in Russian, Yiddish, Polish, Lithuanian or any other language that might have been used.
3. Gather information on the whereabouts of the surname under investigation. Even if one knows for a fact that an ancestral family lived in Ovruch near Zhitomir, that fact is probably about one hundred years old. The person with whom a researcher today may be trying to establish a link possibly knows of only one other nearby town, Korosten, for example, where family lived after Ovruch.

It is possible to discover where in Russia and/or the Soviet Union an ancestral family name was known to exist. One way is to review old city, business and telephone directories for Russia available in the West (see DIRECTORIES). If, for example, the name Kogan was found in 12 Russian cities and towns before 1917, check Soviet telephone directories for these cities for all years. With luck, such a search will unearth published directories for two or three cities—but telephone directories for a large number of former Soviet cities are available on the Internet today, almost all written in Cyrillic.

Another source is Alexander Beider's *Dictionary of Jewish Surnames from the Russian Empire*. The book is based largely on Russian voter registers of the early 1900s and may include family names not listed in directories.

Still another source is the various indexes available on the Internet, including cemetery lists (see JEWISHGEN.ORG and the indexes posted by JRI-Poland at WWW.JRI-P.ORG, as well as any search engine, such as GOOGLE.COM or ALTAVISTA.COM.) The Ellis Island Data Base (WWW.ELLISISLANDRECORDS.ORG) is a "must" source to consult, but because it includes so many errors, it is necessary to search it creatively. Consult Steven Morse's One-Step program (WWW.STEVEMORSE.ORG) for assistance.

Compile lists of names from the U.S. and other western telephone directories posted on the web. Pay special attention to foreign versions of given names (e.g., Mikhail instead of Michael, or Yelena instead of Helen). Contact the people with foreign spellings first; most likely they emigrated from the former Soviet Union and they speak English. Call them and see where the conversation goes. Typically, people born in the former Soviet Union are less likely to be irritated by an "invasion of privacy" than are many westerners; chances are good that they will be willing to speak with a caller.

4. Prepare a list of family names and cities where the family lived. Compiling a list of specific, family-related questions is premature at this stage.

5. The most productive approach is to ask someone who speaks the appropriate language fluently to conduct the telephone search. Second best is to have an interpreter join the conversations on an extension telephone. Verbal communication is preferable to either e-mail or postal mail. A person is most likely to answer a letter only if the information sent matches almost exactly what he knows—and the letter motivates him to answer. A telephone call is more likely to jolt a person into thinking about what he knows regarding the family. Whether or not he is a "match," the primary goal is to let him talk. He may recall a bit of information that is irrelevant to him—but vital to you (see the discussion of the Morokhovsky search below).

Remember that only about one in ten e-mail messages these days is a real letter; the rest are advertisements. Since most computer users have become proficient at scanning long lists of incoming e-mail and deleting "junk" without reading it, carefully consider what to write in the subject line. It must stand out and be noticed. A suggested subject line might read, "Seeking Kogan (Kagan) family from Zhitomir, Ukraine, area." Avoid too specific a message, because the recipient might not recognize town names and, therefore, delete the message. Be brief, businesslike and formal in the introductory letter. Excessive details may scare the recipient. Address and sign the letter properly. If an old photograph of the Russian family is available, include a scan, about 50–60Kb in size. Ask the recipient to respond briefly, even if he or she does not think a relationship exists. If the e-mail is not answered within a month, send a postal service letter. Make it brief, include a photograph or two, if available, and a self-addressed stamped envelope.

How to Conduct a Conversation To Gain New Knowledge

The first priority is to elicit general information. Remember that the person on the other end of the line may know next to nothing about his or her family's past or may consider her own knowledge insignificant. The main goal is to listen. It is helpful to ask short, probing questions to which the answer is likely to produce a story. For example, rather than asking, "Did you have relatives in Odessa, Minsk, or Vilnius?" inquire about one city at a time. Avoid questions, especially in the beginning of a conversation, that can be answered "yes" or "no." "Did you have relatives ... ?" is one such question. A better version might be, "Do you remember if your parents ever talked about their Odessa relatives?" Although the immediate answer may be "no," the individual's memory will have started working on the subconscious level, and two minutes later he may exclaim, "I just remembered!"

Ask the person for names of parents and grandparents. These may provide clues to the family naming pattern. For example, Sergei Feldman may say that his father was Alexandr Mikhailovich, without realizing that a researcher (simultaneously and analytically) hears the "Abram ben Mikhoel or "Abram ben Moshe" patronymic combination. Patronymics are powerful clues.

Always ask if the person has relatives in the United States and/or other countries. After noting the names, ask whom to call next for more information. Ask who are the eldest relatives. Ask, in a very general manner, if the person has heard of relatives who emigrated from Russia before the Revolution. Most likely everyone had such relatives, even if the knowledge has been lost. In the 1930s, Soviet citizens with relatives abroad often were accused of espionage and imprisoned for 20 years—or even executed. Therefore, such information about relatives abroad was kept from children—who have since became grandparents themselves, often with only a vague notion of their family's past. If the person has a connection to the city of your interest, ask who else from that city emigrated to the West. These people may be related without being aware of it.

When making telephone calls to the former Soviet Union, be aware that the person who answers the telephone may not be the one whose name is listed in the directory. A telephone is a commodity that remains with the apartment, listed under the original name. The apartment may have been exchanged, rented, or sold more than once, while the telephone has remained listed under the original family name.

The first question should be, "Is this the Kogan residence?" The response may vary from "yes" to "no" to "Who are you calling?" to "What do you want?" to "Who are you?"

Take care not to rush the pace of the conversation. The quality of the connection may not be good; conversations often are relayed via satellite, which introduces a few seconds'

Jewish synagogue in Koenigsburg (today Kaliningrad) in the early 20th century

delay and an echo. Moreover, people in the former Soviet Union often answer before you have had a chance to ask your question in full. If you are not satisfied with the answer, blame the poor quality of the connection and ask your question again.

Ask if the person has any family photographs. Do not ask for copies unless he offers. Copying facilities are not as plentiful in Russia as they are in the West, and a seemingly simple task may be a half-day chore.

Ask if the person has access to the Internet and an e-mail address. You may want to establish a special account that is simple to convey over the phone (e.g., 22222@YAHOO.COM) or that consists of letters that also exist in the Cyrillic alphabet (e.g., a, e, k, m). The @ symbol does not exist in Russian and is often called *sobachka* (little doggie).

It is impossible to predict how the conversation will develop after the first question. The primary goal is to establish contact and a relationship with the person.

The following case illustrates some of the techniques described above. It started with an e-mail inquiry from Adrian in Australia:

> I am trying to find out if there are any surviving relatives from my grandmother's family in the former USSR. We know they originated from Dnipropetrovsk in the Ukraine in the early 1900s; several then moved to Moscow around World War II, and nothing has been heard of since. We have names

of about 11 families and addresses of a few. We have some correspondence in old Russian that could help define the spelling of names. We are in Australia.

In response to my willingness to help him, Adrian sent a long list of family names, including Gorodetsky, Boltyansky, Tarnopolsky, Umansky, Volynsky, Morokhovsky and a few others. The list was not promising. With the exception of Morokhovsky from Dnipropetrovsk, the names were too common. Adrian provided details about one uncle Sasha, a doctor, his daughter, Mira, and son, Lyusik—university students in the early 1930s.

The first step was to sample names from U.S. telephone directories. This is preferable to an online search where telephone directory names appear in groups of 10; to copy all of them takes too long. Phone Disc, used at a local library, produced approximately 650 names. Every name was well represented except Morokhovsky. The 150 Gorodetskys and 55 Umanskys were ignored, reasoning that if one Morokhovsky were found, chances were good that he was related. A logical step, but as events later showed, it was wrong.

Next all known online directories on the web were searched for Morokhovsky—they yielded nothing. An unusual source for names was then searched: the Library of Congress catalogue (www.LOC.GOV). (The search feature on the AMAZON.COM website is another good source for finding a person with a given surname.) The Library of Congress catalogue revealed two books, both about the English language and both published in Kiev in the 1970s. One of the authors may have had a Jewish given name; the other almost certainly did not.

Introductions to both books were copied at the Library of Congress. Aside from the obligatory praises to the Communist Party's contribution and its wise guidance in whatever field a book was about, books published in the Soviet Union also included the names of reviewers, editors and other information potentially valuable to genealogists.

The next step was to call Kiev telephone information—but no Morokhovskys were listed. After carefully re-reading the introductions to both books, we called Kiev information again. The operator produced the telephone number of a man listed as a reviewer in one of the books.

The subsequent conversation went as follows. The opening question was, "May I talk to Professor Zhluktenko?" Reply: "He died several years ago. I am his daughter."

"I am trying to help a man who does not speak Russian to find traces of his family." Yes, she had known both Morokhovskys, husband and wife. They also had died, and no, they did not have children. We talked a bit more and she said, "Call me back in half an hour. I will talk to the woman who assumed the chairmanship of the university department when Professor Morokhovsky died."

Half an hour later she said, "You know, they did have a son. Here is his telephone number." After I wondered aloud why I had not gotten the number from information, she replied, "It is probably listed under the previous owner's name." How could I have forgotten! The telephone is a commodity in the former Soviet Union.

After several weeks, I reached Nikolai Morokhovsky—another disappointment. His family had come from Kursk province; his grandfather was a railroad engineer. Kursk province is in the heartland of Russia, outside the Pale of Settlement, and railroad engineer was not exactly a Jewish occupation. We continued to talk, and eventually he said that there was an aunt in Vologda, a city a few hundred miles north of Moscow. "Yes, you can call her. Here is the number. By the way, she spells her name Marakhovsky."

That was a little shocker. I, who preach to others that spellings do not matter, had not thought about other spelling possibilities.

I called Vologda. "I am calling from America to look for relatives." The woman on the other end of the line was delighted to hear from me. "How nice and noble it is. People treat each other like animals, and here you are doing such a nice thing." I probed with my questions. No leads. The family is from Kursk, as Russian as they come. There are no Jews in the family. Well,

actually, one grandfather's brother had married a Jew, and the family excommunicated him; 30 years later they reconciled. Another dead end. We talked a bit more, and she recalled that many years ago in Donetsk (Ukraine), she was surprised to see their family name in the telephone book.

Back to Ukraine. I called information. There is indeed one Morokhovsky listing. The man was polite, but that was about it. No Uncle Sasha, no connections to Dnipropetrovsk. He had a very Russian-sounding name and patronymics, but his manner of speech reminded me a lot of my own uncle, and I did not rush to hang up—or maybe it was because I had no other leads. I kept the conversation going. "Can I talk to anybody else in your family?"

"Well," he answered, "There is a sister." "Is she also in Donetsk?" "No, she lives in Haifa(!)" "Can I call her?" "Sure. Here is the number."

I was elated. He was Jewish! I thanked him and immediately dialed Haifa. His sister was an extremely curious and talkative woman. It turned out that she was not a sister, but a niece. "What do you mean, Uncle Sergei did not know about Dnipropetrovsk connection? They emigrated from there just three years ago; did he forget or what?" Of course, they know the Morokhovskys I am seeking. They were relatives, and Mira Morokhovsky used to visit them frequently. She never married, lived in Dnipropetrovsk. No, she does not remember Mira's address, but I am welcome to call later when the mother is home.

After several more weeks of research, telephone calls and letters to archives, the Jewish community and various individuals revealed that Mira Morokhovsky had died. Her death certificate showed she had died three years before the family emigrated to Haifa. The woman in Haifa had left Dnipropetrovsk only three years earlier, but the timeline of her memory was already skewed. Adrian was happy to establish contact with the family in Haifa and with their help later was successful in searching for other members of his family.

There were several parallel investigations of other Morokhovskys. The most memorable was a short exchange of letters with a college professor found via the Internet. He wrote a sad letter, saying that his father had adopted this family name for unknown reasons. He always had been too busy to talk to his father about the past and the family history, and now the father is dead and he was alone in the world.

This project was the first one in a series of similar searches. Fortunately, most of them were successful, producing a tremendous feeling of satisfaction at being able to reconnect families after so many decades.

Scotland

by Harvey Kaplan

Jewish roots in Scotland do not run deep. Unusual for Europe, no Jewish communities appear to have existed there in medieval times. Although some formerly Jewish converts to Christianity taught at Scottish universities (non-Christians were banned from teaching in universities), the first recorded practicing Jew was David Brown, who lived in Edinburgh in 1691.[1] No substantial number of Jews lived in Scotland until the late 1790s; the first Jewish communities were established in Edinburgh in 1816 and in Glasgow in 1823. Small communities were founded later in the 19th century in Aberdeen and Dundee but, although their synagogues remain, the congregations are minuscule. The even smaller Jewish communities of Ayr, Dunfermline, Falkirk, Greenock and Inverness—all founded in the 1890s and early 1900s–no longer exist.

From the 1880s to the 1920s, many Jews immigrated to Scotland, swelling the existing Jewish communities. Most came from Lithuania. A thriving community grew up in the inner-city Gorbals district of Glasgow, and the city's Jewish population increased from approximately 1,000 in 1879 to 9,000 by 1919. Some 2,000 Jews lived in Edinburgh by the 1930s. These remained the only sizable communities, with Glasgow reaching 14,000 at its peak in the 1930s. Now home to only half that figure, the Glasgow community is nevertheless still vibrant, with six synagogues. The Edinburgh Jewish community now numbers only about 500, with one synagogue.

During the period 1880 to 1920, it often was cheaper to reach the *goldene medine* (golden land) of America by sailing first to Britain, then catching another boat to cross the Atlantic. Many landed at Hull on the east coast of England and crossed by train to take a steamer from Liverpool. A significant number—perhaps thousands—of Jewish emigrants landed at Dundee or Leith on the east coast of Scotland, and crossed over to Glasgow.[2]

Glasgow, at this time, was a major center of commerce, shipbuilding and engineering—the "Second City" of the British Empire. From Glasgow, ships sailed every week to North America, Australia and other immigrant destinations. Many of the transmigrants stayed in Scotland for a few months, or even years, before continuing their journeys; many never actually made it any further.

Civil Records

The public records of Scotland are a rich source for genealogical research.

Vital Records

Civil registration of birth, marriages and deaths began in 1855, and the records are kept in at the General Register Office for Scotland* in New Register House in Edinburgh. Upon payment of a search fee (currently £17.00), one can consult the computerized indexes for the whole of Scotland and then view the actual documents on microfiche or microfilm. For birth, marriage and death certificates, 1855–1926, scanned images are available on computer screens. The "Scots Origin" website at WWW.ORIGINS.NET allows online pay-per-view access to the indexes of births and marriages in Scotland, 1855–1901, and deaths, 1855–1926. It is possible to order copies of documents described in the indexes. The website WWW.SCOTLANDSPEOPLE.GOV.UK offers a fully searchable index of Scottish birth records, 1553–1903; marriage records, 1553–1928; death records, 1855–1953. Copies may be ordered by credit card.

The Strathclyde Area Genealogy Centre in Glasgow offers access to the computer indexes, but holds film or fiche of the certificates only for the west of Scotland which would cover the Jewish communities of Ayr, Glasgow and Greenock. Scottish certificates are often more detailed than those in England. For example, birth certificates give the names of both parents, and the place and date of their marriage (which may point one to an ancestral town). Death certificates provide the names of both parents and the name of the husband or wife.

Censuses

New Register House in Edinburgh* and the Strathclyde Area Genealogy Centre in Glasgow* also hold copies of census records. British censuses are held every 10 years, but are closed for 100 years. Currently, only the censuses for the years 1841 to 1901 are open to public view. Those for 1881, 1891 and 1901 are computer indexed. Microfilms of the censuses for Glasgow and the west of Scotland are available for viewing free at the Mitchell Library* in Glasgow. The scanned images for 1891–1901 can be viewed at New Register House* and also are available through the website WWW.SCOTLANDSPEOPLE. GOV.UK. Future plans call for the 1841–71 censuses to be similarly available online.

The Scottish Jewish Archives Centre* (SJAC) in Glasgow (see also below) has extracted information from the 1891 census on more than 1,000 Jews who lived in the immigrant Gorbals area. The census illustrates clearly how the immigrant Jews moved around the country before settling in one place. Typically, the parents were born in Russia or Germany, while each of the children was born in a different city in England, Ireland or Scotland, before the family finally settled in Glasgow, where the youngest child was born. Records held by the Scottish Jewish Archives Centre may be accessed by post, e-mail (ARCHIVES@SJAC.FSBUSINESS.CO.UK) or website (WWW.SJAC.ORG.UK).

Naturalization Records

If a pre-immigration ancestral town cannot be determined from either the census or the vital records, clues may be found in naturalization files. Indexed naturalization files for all of the British Isles are available in the Public Record Office in Kew,

London. In many cases, the only record of a name change is in these documents. As elsewhere, immigrants often tried to make their names sound less obviously foreign, particularly during World War I. The British royal family took the lead, changing its name from Saxe-Colburg to Windsor, and so in the same way, Baranchik elected to become Brown, Levensteyn became Livingstone, Myerson became Morrison and Fagerson became Ferguson!

SJAC has a list of more than 700 Scottish Jews—only four of them female—who were naturalized in the period from the late 1870s to the early 1920s. About 92 percent of the list were born in either Russia or Germany; 65 percent resided in Glasgow at the time and 25 percent lived in Edinburgh.

During World War I, Glasgow, a major port and center of shipbuilding for the British Navy, was made a prohibited area for aliens. In addition, the accent and names of many Glasgow Jews would have made them conspicuously foreign-born. In 1916, with the cooperation of the local police, the Glasgow Jewish Representative Council undertook to certify than an individual was of Russian nationality (and, thus, a British ally). The Council issued 1,200 copies of a "Declaration of Nationality" signed by a justice of the peace. Many families have preserved this document, which is invaluable genealogically because it states in which town and province of Russia the applicant was born. A variation of this document, which also has sometimes survived, is a letter with the same information issued by the Imperial Russian vice-consulate in Glasgow. Neither the Declaration of Nationality documents or the records of the former Imperial Russian vice-consulate in Glasgow have yet to be found in any list or index.

Finally, Glasgow City Archives has a file of applications from Glasgow Jews of Russian origin who appeared before a special tribunal to claim exemption from military service in 1918 on the grounds of foreign nationality and financial and/ or business hardship.

City Directories

Jewish residents often appear in city directories. *The Post Office Directory* for Glasgow was produced annually from the 1780s until 1978, while *Kelly's Directory* ran from 1924 to 1974. Both have indexes of names; classifications by occupation or trade; and street-by-street lists of shops, businesses and some residents. Similar directories exist for other Scottish cities; all may be found in major reference libraries. Another source for Jewish businessmen and traders is Harfield's *Commercial Directory of the Jews of the United Kingdom*, published in 1894. SJAC has a copy of the Scottish entries from this invaluable book.

Land Records

Libraries in the major cities have valuation rolls, which are annual registers of property. Arranged by street, they provide details of ownership and occupancy of every house and shop with rateable value or amount of rent. Libraries also keep electoral rolls arranged by street within wards. The Glasgow records are held in the Mitchell Library* and cover most years since 1832.

School Records

Glasgow City Archives* (and its counterparts in other cities) holds the records of the schools to which Jewish immigrants sent their children. Gorbals Public School in Glasgow, for example, was two-thirds Jewish in 1912, and the public school log books reveal how the school closed early on Fridays in the winter because of the Jewish Sabbath and how attendance was greatly reduced during Jewish holidays. Because the numbers were smaller, it is not easy to identify schools in other cities to which Jewish immigrants sent their children.

Admission registers for these schools are especially interesting. Not every family had a birth, marriage or death in Scotland. Not everyone was resident in a census year, and only a minority were naturalized, but even if a family was in Scotland for only three months, however, it would have sent the children to school. The registers, which are indexed, usually give date of admission, name and birth date of the pupil, and name and address of their parent or guardian. Many registers state whether the pupil came from a previous school and often mention that they came from another city, or from Poland or Russia. From these records, one may learn the month of arrival from Europe. Similarly, the records state where the pupil went on leaving, which may have been to another school, another city, or sometimes America or Canada (giving a clue to date of departure by ship).

Passenger Lists

Although the passenger lists of the ships leaving Glasgow from 1890 onward are held by the Public Record Office in London* (see England and Wales), the Mitchell Library* in Glasgow has the Wotherspoon Collection, which consists of albums of photographs of ships that carried immigrants across the Atlantic. The Mitchell Library* may be contacted via its website at WWW.MITCHELLLIBRARY.ORG. The *Glasgow Herald* has been the leading Glasgow newspaper since 1783. Back issues carry advertisements for ships leaving Glasgow and also announcements of the ships arriving at their destination in Canada or the United States. In 1898, the journey took 12 days.

Jewish Records

The most important collection of specifically Jewish records is held by the Scottish Jewish Archives Centre* based in Garnethill Synagogue in Glasgow, Scotland's oldest and first purpose-built synagogue (1879). The Centre, which opened in 1987, collects a wide range of material related to all aspects of the history of the Jewish communities of Scotland. The collection's catalogue is computerized and made available to researchers, but as of this writing, is not available online. During most of the year, the Centre, which presents displays on the history of the community, is open one Sunday afternoon per month, otherwise on Friday mornings by appointment.

In addition to the records detailed below, SJAC holds minutes, membership lists, annual reports and yearbooks of synagogues and other communal organizations, all of which can provide information on ancestors who were active in the Jewish community.

Historical Database of Scottish Jewry

The Historical Database of Scottish Jewry, available at SJAC, collates and cross-references some 60 lists and sources, including cemetery records, synagogue registers, naturalizations, charity subscription lists and school administration registers pertaining to Jews in Scotland from the 1700s to the 1940s. The still-growing database includes information on almost 23,000 individuals and is the most comprehensive source for those trying to locate individuals and families during that period.

For each individual, where known, the database records surname, first name(s), father's name, mother's maiden surname, year and place of birth and death, cemetery of burial, date and place of marriage, surname of spouse, occupation and source (but not the names of children).

Vital Records

SJAC has the (incomplete) registers of births, marriages and deaths in the Glasgow (later, Garnethill) Hebrew Congregation from 1855 onwards, as well as a communal directory of Garnethill from 1911 that lists 100 families. It holds the marriage register (1930–81) for the former Pollokshields Hebrew Congregation and copies of registers of circumcisions performed in Edinburgh (and elsewhere) by Moses Joel (1830–60) and Jacob Furst (1879–1905). The circumcision records are indexed in the Historical Database of Scottish Jewry.

Burial Records

SJAC holds records of almost 7,500 burials in Scottish Jewish cemeteries from Aberdeen, Dundee, Edinburgh, Glasgow, Greenock and Inverness. The earliest records date from 1820, when Braid Place cemetery opened in Edinburgh. Other cemetery records are held by the Glasgow Hebrew Burial Society;* these will be copied eventually by SJAC. The financial statement of the Glasgow Hebrew Public Burial Society from 1912–13 includes an invaluable street-by-street list of some 1,000 subscribers; they are not indexed by name.

Garnethill Synagogue* operated a hostel for European Jewish refugees in the 1930s and 1940s; a register from 1938 lists some 250 individuals with age, place of origin and eventual destination.

Publications

The *Jewish Echo*, the community newspaper of Scottish Jewry, was published in Glasgow every week from 1928 until 1992 and succeeded various short-lived Yiddish publications. Back issues provide probably the most comprehensive record of events in the community during this period. Announcements appear for births, bar mitzvahs, engagements, weddings, anniversaries and tombstone consecrations. These back issues are available both at SJAC* and the Mitchell Library,* which also holds back issues of the current newspaper, the *Jewish Telegraph*.

The London *Jewish Chronicle* (established in 1841) has always included coverage of Scottish affairs. Its 19th- century Provincial News column is especially important, because it covers a period of time when there was no Jewish newspaper

in Scotland. Back issues are available at the Mitchell Library* from 1878 onwards.

The *Jewish Yearbook*, published annually from 1896, gives details of all Jewish communities in Britain, including Scotland. The Mitchell Library* has the run of this volume from the 1890s onwards.

Addresses

Aberdeen Synagogue, 74 Dee Street, Aberdeen AB1 2DS

Central Library, George IV Bridge, Edinburgh EH1 1EG

Dundee Synagogue, St. Mary Place, Dundee DD1 5RB

General Register Office for Scotland, New Register House, Edinburgh, EH1 3YT; WWW.OPEN.GOV.UK/GROSHOME.HTM.

Garnethill Synagogue, 2 Hill Street, Glasgow G3 6UB

Glasgow City Archives, Mitchell Library, North Street, Glasgow G3 7DN

Glasgow Department, Mitchell Library, North Street, Glasgow, G3 7DN

Glasgow Hebrew Burial Society, Giffnock Synagogue, Maryville Avenue, Giffnock, Glasgow G46 GUE

New Registry ER House (see General Register Office for Scotland) [Public Records Office]

Public Records Office, 4 Ruskin Avenue, Kew, Richmond, Surrey TW9 4DU, England

Scottish Jewish Archives Centre, Garnethill Synagogue, 129 Hill Street, Glasgow G3 6UB

Strathclyde Area Genealogy Centre, 22 Park Circus, Glasgow G3 6BE

Bibliography

Collins, Kenneth, ed. *Aspects of Scottish Jewry*. Glasgow: Glasgow Jewish Representative Council, 1987.

Collins, Kenneth. *Scotland's Jews: A Guide to the History and Community of the Jews in Glasgow*. Glasgow, Scottish Jewish Archives, 1999.

———. *Second City Jewry: The Jews of Glasgow in the Age of Expansion, 1790-1919*. Glasgow: Scottish Jewish Archives, 1990.

Cory, Kathleen B. Tracing *Your Scottish Ancestry*. Edinburgh: Polygon, 1990.

Hutt, Charlotte and Kaplan, Harvey L., eds. *A Scottish Shtetl: Jewish Life in the Gorbals, 1880-1974*. Glasgow: Gorbals Fair Society, 1984.

James, Alwyn. *Scottish Roots: A Step by Step Guide for Ancestor Hunters in Scotland and Overseas*. Edinburgh: Macdonald, 1981.

Kaplan, Harvey L. "Odyssey," *Shemot*. 1, no. 2 (1993): 5–6.

———. "Passage to America through Scotland." *AVOTAYNU* 5, no. 4 (Winter 1989): 7–8.

———. "Scottish Jewish Cemetery Survey." *AVOTAYNU* 7, no. 4 (Winter 1991): 62–63.

Levy, A. *The Origins of Glasgow Jewry, 1812-1895*. Glasgow: published privately, 1949.

Levy, A. *Origins of Scottish Jewry*. London: Jewish Historical Society of England, 1958.

Phillips, Abel. *A History of the Origins of the First Jewish Community in Scotland: Edinburgh, 1816*. Edinburgh: John Donald, 1979.

Sinclair, Cecil. *Tracing Your Scottish Ancestors: A Guide to Ancestry Research in the Scottish Record Office*. Edinburgh: HMSO, 1990.

Notes

1. *Origins of Scottish Jewry*, 1958: 1.
2. "Passage to America Through Scotland,": 7–8.

Slovak Republic

by Edward David Luft

Read the chapter Austrian-Hungarian Empire before starting this section—Ed.

Slovakia has been part of a succession of other nations for most of the past thousand years. The Slovaks came under Hungarian rule in 906 C.E. where they remained until 1918 when Czechoslovakia was formed out of Bohemia, Moravia, Slovakia, and a portion of Silesia. The Slovaks felt themselves as "poor relations" under the Czechs, until the Germans offered the Slovaks nominal independence during World War II under the pro-Nazi puppet nationalist Father Jozef Tiso. When Germany lost the war, the Slovaks returned to their prior status as part of Czechoslovakia and later became part of a two-nation, nominally federal state under the communists. There they remained until January 1, 1993, when the Slovak Republic declared its independence, with Bratislava as its capital. An eastern region of Slovakia annexed by the Soviet Union after World War II today forms part of Zakarpatskaya Oblast in western Ukraine.

Slovak-Jewish records are held by repositories in the area that today is the Slovak Republic, except for the region ceded to Ukraine. Most of the latter records are in Ukraine today (see Ukraine). The official website of the Ukrainian State Archives is www.archives.ua/eng.

A useful English-language website with a short history of Jews in Slovakia plus considerable information of genealogical value is www.haruth.com/JewsSlovakia.html.

Genealogical Resources

Genealogists with Jewish roots in Slovakia can seek information in a number of different places using a variety of methods. Archival holdings in Slovakia and surrounding territory that once was part of Slovakia survived World War II relatively intact. Research may be done at LDS (Mormon) family history centers, onsite in the archives of Slovakia and Hungary, by mail and by hiring local researchers. Before beginning archival research in Slovakia, consult the website maintained by the U.S. Library of Congress European Reading Room, (www. loc.gov/rr/international/european/slovakia/sk.html. It has extensive information on Jewish genealogy links, libraries and archives in Slovakia.

LDS Family History Library Holdings

The LDS (Mormon) Family History Library has microfilmed most Jewish records held in Slovak archives as well as a number of other useful records that are not specifically Jewish. The only significant records not filmed are those in the regional archives in Bratislava and in Nitra.

Holdings of the LDS (Mormon) Family History Library (see LDS) for former Czechoslovakia now appear in the Library catalogue under Slovakia (and under Czech Republic, for areas now in that country). The lists include film numbers and name changes for the places listed. In Slovakia LDS cameras have filmed a variety of documents, including some of Jewish provenance, such as for the cities of Levoča and Prešov. They may also include records of various kinds in the archives in Bytča and Košice, as well as the heavily Jewish county of Zemplén for 1850–1918, when it straddled the Slovak-Hungarian border.

The LDS Family History Library system has on microfilm Jewish records for, among other places, the towns of Fiľakovo, Lučenec, Prešov, Rusovce (now a suburb of Bratislava), Skalica, Svätý Jur, Trenčin, Trnava, and Vojnice, plus the 1828 Bereg and Szabolcs county land census and the 1848 and 1857 Hungarian Jewish censuses. The 1848 census covers Esztergom, Trencsén and Turocz counties, now part of Slovakia. The especially useful 1848 census lists birth place as well as age and trade.

Archival Resources

Slovak public archives exist at the state, regional, and district level. Researchers cannot be certain that records will be found where they are expected in a given regional archives. Slovak archival authorities are well aware that they must look for records in various places such as archives, libraries, museums and other repositories.

The easiest way to determine the location of vital records is to use the microfiche published by *AVOTAYNU** entitled "Index to Jewish Vital Statistics Records of Slovakia," compiled by Jordan Auslander. (see www.avotaynu.com).

In 1991, the Slovak archives published *Cirkevné matriky na Slovensku zo 16.–19. Storiča* (Slovak parish records for the 16th–19th centuries) by Jana Sarmányová. The book includes a location index and English and German summaries. It lists all available vital records in Slovakia, both Jewish and non-Jewish. The book is arranged by geographical location, type of record, and dates available; these three facts should be submitted in any letter to Slovak archives requesting information for a given location. Categories include Jewish birth, marriage, and death records, and the years held for specific towns and villages. When records are in languages other than Slovak, such as German, Hebrew, or Hungarian, this fact also is noted. Since Jewish records for Slovakia never were centralized, the archive that holds the records for each individual community is noted.

The book's town index does not indicate which town reference denotes records for the Jewish population. Communities with Jewish records are indexed under the name of the towns that served as regional registry depots. Many depots served scores of surrounding communities.

The index created for towns with Jewish records has 3,982 entries. Because of jurisdictional changes, the number of actual

Židovská ulica (Jews Street) in Bratislava

contemporary communities is approximately half that number. Because of differences in years covered, listings have not been combined; towns that were merged or absorbed into adjacent towns and metropolitan areas are referenced by the old and new Slovak names. Parish record books list alphabetically 4,000 towns according to Slovak names. (The Slovak alphabet differs from the English alphabet and includes additional letters—č follows c, ř follows r, š follows s, ž follows z, and ch follows h.) Although the English summary is not written in perfect English, the wording is clear enough for one to understand that Jewish records are always listed last in any entry for a location and that virtually all registers have survived. The locations are listed alphabetically together with a code (explained in the English and German summaries) that identifies which of eight current archival locations holds the indicated records. The summary also provides the addresses of the eight locations, but researchers should check the Slovak National Archives* website to be certain that an address has not changed (CIVIL.GOV.SK/SNARCHIV).

Frequently, records of a small community attached as a satellite to a larger community appear under the name of the larger location, with an indication that these records are included in those of the larger town. To determine the place where records are held for a small original community, consult the index. At the end of the list of locations, the author includes lists of professions written in Latin, Hungarian, and German, with their Slovak equivalent.

Some records from medieval times to about 1750 are held in the Roman Catholic Diocesan Archives (see the Slovak National Archives* for various Roman Catholic archives) for the region of the ancestral town. Some of the oldest records pertaining to Jews are in the National Archives* in Bratislava, but similar records might be in a regional or local archives. It is not unusual for a local archives to hold 18th-century records.[1] Researchers can make photocopies of the documents held at the National Archives* for a nominal fee.

State-owned Jewish archival records, mixed with non-Jewish records, generally are available in regional archives for the geographical area of the town being searched. For example, regional or county archives hold land ownership records and many other records for transactions for which Jews and gentiles had similar rights. An effective search requires that the researcher determine the location to be searched, type of record sought, and the approximate date the record was created. One may do research only on one's own ancestors.

Research by Mail. For research by mail, one may send requests for specific vital statistics (short form) or ask for "long-form research." Long-form research is used if one wants archival research other than simple vital records. In each case, vital records more than 50 years old generally can be searched. Included in the records are date of death, data about parents (such as occupations) on birth records, name of spouse, and names of marriage witnesses in the case of marriage certificates.

Researchers must deposit $15 by cashier's or bank check, not personal check, with the Slovak National Archives* in Bratislava. Domestic postal money orders cannot be processed. The archives suggest that one specify a limit on the amount of money to be spent. Researchers should enclose two international postal reply coupons with each research request. Fees are based upon hours spent and the difficulty of research. Airmail letters to and from Slovakia take from five days to three weeks. Personnel shortages often lead to long waits for a reply. Requests written in Slovak are processed more quickly and accurately. Answers typically are sent by registered mail after the researcher sends a bank check in the amount specified.

Onsite Research. The Slovak National Archives* requires written permission for onsite research. To obtain such permission, write to the Ministry of the Interior, Department of Archives* (CIVIL.GOV.SK/SNARCHVIV). Letters written to Slovak embassies are returned; embassies do not forward requests for genealogical research to the Slovak National Archives*. Write well in advance of a visit and expect long delays in replies. While permission is sometimes granted at the National Archives* upon arrival in person, it is best not to risk a last-minute denial. Regional archives do not have the authority to grant permission to do onsite research.

Research Strategy. After obtaining permission to use the archives for in-person research, researchers should consider beginning their work at the National Archives* in Bratislava even if they already have consulted Sarmányová's book and know that what they want is elsewhere. The National Archives* staff often can ease the way at the regional or local archives with advice and possible contact. Researchers should notify the archives of an impending visit and state their research goals so that the desired record books will be waiting for use. A small fee is charged for each visit; the archives prefers that it be paid in Slovak currency.

An accepted custom is for foreign researchers to ask to speak to the director of the provincial or regional archives when arriving to conduct research. If possible, telephone or write in advance of arrival, because seating is limited. Few older personnel in rural archives understand English, but some understand German. Generally, genealogical research may be done in person or through persons hired by the researcher.

Slovak Geography and Gazetteers

Because records are organized by location, a researcher must know exactly where an ancestor lived. Slovak locality names have changed frequently over the past two centuries. Oral histories or an old record may list a German, Hungarian or Slovak name. Consult a gazetteer to verify the contemporary name. (See references on Slovak geography at the end of this chapter)

From 1867 until the end of World War I, Slovakia was known as Upper Hungary, a part of the Austro-Hungarian Empire. During that time documents were frequently written in Hungarian, German, and Slovak; depending upon the intended audience, a document was written in one, two, or all three languages. Almost all Slovak cities and towns had other names, depending upon the year in question. For example, Bardejov, which was Slovak after the end of World War I, was previously known as Bartfeld in German and Barfó in Hungarian.

Because the Austro-Hungarian Empire was vast and decentralized, people sometimes moved from one part of the Empire to another without a full appreciation of changing jurisdictions. It was not uncommon for people in border areas to confuse the jurisdiction in which they lived. Accordingly, researchers should use a gazetteer to determine the exact location and various names of a given location within the Dual Monarchy.

Many place names changed from German to Hungarian and then (after 1919) to Slovak. Jews sometimes used Yiddish names for locations. Nineteenth-century Jewish vital records were kept in register depots in 138 towns, each depot serving as many as 147 communities. Slovak archivists know the current names for historic locations. Many small towns share names but are distinguished from one another by their river, district or proximity to major towns. Researchers can search the Mormon records or use the Sarmányová book and/or *Where Once We Walked* to obtain the same information.

Bratislava and Košice City Archives

Only Bratislava and Košice have their own municipal archives within the national archives system. Many Jews lived in each town, Bratislava especially. Both towns now have rabbis and Jewish congregations. (see WWW.HARUTH.COM/JEWSSLOVAKIA. HTML). Several persons in the Bratislava city archives speak English. In Bratislava, capital of Slovakia, local record holdings began in 1819, but the Slovak National Archives* holds earlier items of Jewish genealogical interest. The oldest surviving lists of Bratislava Jews are tax lists from 1709 and 1748.[2]

Vital Records

Vital records, called *matrika* in Slovak, were initially filed in the state district office (*Okresny zrad*) for the locality in which the person was born, had married or died. Larger cities, such as Košice and Bratislava, have multiple districts. In some smaller towns, the state district office may be located in the town hall. These state vital records, as distinguished from religious records, remain confidential and inaccessible to anyone but the person involved and close relatives (as determined by the director of the specific state district office) during the entire time that they remain in the state district office, unless the Minister of the Interior* grants special permission for access. See the website of the Slovak National Archives* for details. Legally, when the records are transferred to the regional archives after 50 years, they become open for public inspection. In fact, because of processing time, the actual wait is longer.

Slovak law mandates that records more than 50 years old must be transferred from the local record office that created them to the local archives, unless the item has national relevance, in which case the records go to the National Archives.* Sometimes, however, books, indexes and the associated records remain in the local record office when the records are more than 50 years old because that book or index also includes records less than 50 years old. Thus, if the records sought from the late 19th century are not in the national or local archives, check the local record office to be certain that they are not still there; they might be included with newer records. Although a researcher may not view the book, a local official can search on the researcher's behalf and grant access to the desired records only—probably in the form of an extract or photocopy.

Religious records created prior to 1895 for births, marriages and deaths are held in regional archives because they were the official records of such events. After that date, the state required the keeping of civil *matrika*. Thus, all religious *matrika* created after 1895 are unofficial and typically would not be expected to be held by state archives unless voluntarily submitted in support of some matter dealing with the state. Most such records, however, do not survive. To seek those that do, check with *Židovská Náboženská* (Central Union of Jewish Religious Communities);* it often has this information.

Jewish Vital Records

Some Jewish and vital records exist from the 18th century, but most begin in the middle of the 19th century. Some census records exist as well.[3] Information in register books did not become generally reliable until about 1850 or 1851, when virtually all births, marriages and deaths were recorded accurately. Before that time, conscription and tax considerations, as well as the poverty of the Jewish population and the venality of government officials made it advantageous for Jews of the Austrian Empire (the Austro-Hungarian Empire after 1867) to give inaccurate (or no) information to the authorities. Resistance to authority and the difficulty of travel from outlying regions (to central locations for the purposes of reporting) also may have contributed to lax record keeping. Most records stop in 1943 or 1944, reflecting deportations and the dissolution of Jewish communities in the Holocaust.

This following example illustrates what the researcher may find and the necessity of using ingenuity to find all relevant records. The Regional Archives in Prešov* holds birth, marriage and death records covering the years 1850–95 for the Humenné district. Three ledgers kept by the rabbinate (at that time located in Humenné) hold the vital records for all towns and villages in the region. The Prešov regional archives also holds the files containing the 1939–45 Nazi orders dealing with the Jews of this district. Land and property registers, however, are in the regional archives in Humenné,* where one can obtain a typed abstract of the records of family homestead and land holdings. The years covered are unknown.

Long before the German occupation, the Slovaks had consolidated Jewish communities and their records. In the 1920s, the Slovaks transferred records from very small or abandoned rural areas to larger Jewish communities. In small towns with no Jewish community office but with a Catholic parish office, Jewish births, marriages, divorces and deaths were recorded at the back of the parish registers. Some of these registers may be in the state archives rather than in Catholic parishes or archives. Both possibilities must be checked; check Sarmányová's book to see if an archives controlled by the government holds such records. (Also see Catholic Church records, below.) Other Jewish records have been moved to nearby towns or to the regional archives of the local area. When securing initial permission to do research in archives, be sure to inquire what is where for any given town.

Jewish records of all kinds, including tax lists and vital records, started in the late 1700s, but were not universal until 1895. Jewish records exist for the years 1769–1955, but only some records are available for many places. Reporting of Jewish marriages was constrained by the Jews' wishes to avoid governmental restrictions; male births were routinely left unrecorded to avoid army service. In some cases, Jewish community records augment civil records; sometimes only Jewish records exist. Years for which records exist vary greatly for the same town depending on the registry depot where the records were collected. A repository may have complete marriage records for a given period, but only some—or no—birth records for the same time.

A 1753 decree created religious community districts, with the local rabbi assigned the duty of record keeping. In 1885, another decree established codified Jewish registration of district towns. Official registration districts were established on January 1, 1886. In addition to birth, marriage, divorce, and death registers, conscription and circumcision books also exist. Circumcision books are more likely than official records to provide accurate information about males in a particular location. Many districts changed jurisdiction when a consolidation of local Jewish registration districts occurred in 1895. Thus, a father's record may have been recorded in one location, but because of consolidation of districts, his son's records may be in another place—even though both may have been born in the same house. Nevertheless, if the records still exist, they will be in the same regional archives today—just not necessarily in the same file.

In 1949, all parish records since 1895 were nationalized and subsequently distributed among the then six regional archives in the Slovak archive system based upon the geographical location of the town. Those records remain in what are now seven regional archives. (These records are not in the city archives of Bratislava and Kosice.)

Avotaynu has a set of microfiche entitled *Jewish Vital Statistics Records in Slovakian Archives, Index to Jewish Birth, Marriage and Death Records Located in Archives of Slovakia*. See Archival Resources, above.

Registration of Rabbis

Many regional archives hold files of annual registration required by the Austro-Hungarian Empire for rabbis and other clergy. To find a record, a researcher must know the name of the rabbi and the county in which he served; it is not necessary to know the exact locality within the county. All that is needed then is to determine which regional archives holds the clergy records for the county in question. This can be determined in three ways, from the Mormon index of microfilms, from the National Archives* and from the Sarmányová book.

Use the Mormon catalogue to determine the county of origin of the filmed records. The entry also indicates the county (or other regional area) of the archives (or other repository) in which the filming was done. With this information, search the web for the repository that holds the original records to see what other records are held there. The Mormons do not always film all records of genealogical interest in an archives, All rabbis from 1850/1851 to 1918 (when Czechoslovakia became independent) should appear in the registration records. The records typically are short and provide minimal information, although the exact information recorded varies from entry to entry.

Census Records

From 1850 through the end of the Hapsburg Empire in 1918, and perhaps later, researchers have a fair chance of obtaining

Jewish wedding procession in Stropkov in the 1930s accompanied by gypsy musicians. (From Between Galicia and Hungary: The Jews of Stropkov, by Melody Amsel. Bergenfield, N.J.: Avotaynu, 2002)

census and similar records in regional archives. The 1869 Hungarian census records have been microfilmed by the Mormons and are available through the LDS Family History Centers.[4] Census records generally are not available yet for later periods, but police records showing family movement sometimes are held in the regional archives. For the availability of pre-1850 census records, see Henry Wellisch, "18th-Century Jewish Censuses in Hungary".

Draft Registration

Pre-1919 draft registration records—which are civil, not military records—are available only in Vienna, not in Bratislava, and have been microfilmed by the Mormons.[5]

Holocaust-Era Records

Slovakia has a number of Holocaust-era census records. One collection at the Central State Archives[*] holds the complete 1940 census of the independent Slovak state that existed between 1939 and 1945. This census covers every city, town, and village in Slovakia and includes name; maiden name, where relevant; age; birth place; occupation; year moved to the current locality; religion; description of dwelling and property; and signature of the person supplying the information. Illiterate persons used a thumbprint. The records are not available yet to the public.

The Slovak National Archives[*] holds a February 1942 Jewish census. Contact that archives to determine availability. The Yad Vashem Archives[*] in Jerusalem has the actual deportation lists of May 1942. The lists are organized alphabetically by surname and include only year of birth and place of residence. The February 1942 census is a more comprehensive precursor to the deportation lists and includes birth date, birth place, citizenship status, identification number, and occupation. The Slovak National Archives[*] also has other, more general documents pertaining to Slovak Jewry, but often not

specifically Jewish records. Such documents are many and varied and depend upon time and place. Ask the staff for help with a specific location and time period.

Various regional archives have other record groups pertaining to individuals during the interwar and Holocaust years. In some cases, access to those collections which are more recent or more sensitive may require prior permission from the Ministry of the Interior.[*] Slovak-Jewish records for certain localities created during the Holocaust have been moved to the archives designated to receive all old records of the particular region involved.

Leo Baeck Institute[*] in New York City has a list of the Jewish residents of Liptovský Mikuláš who perished during the Holocaust. Liptovský Mikuláš, an important town in north central Slovakia, had a large Jewish population.

Records in Hungarian Archives

Since Hungary ruled Slovakia for nearly a thousand years, many Hungarian archival and library sources are valuable for Slovak-Jewish genealogical research. To search Hungarian sources, see the U.S. Library of Congress web page on Hungarian libraries and archives which includes Hungarian archives holding Slovak materials (CORC.OCLC.ORG/WEBZ/ XPATHFINDERQUERY?SESSIONID=0:TERM=2047:XID=LCP%20). The website does not specify Slovak holdings, but does list the archives. A researcher must know which archives is relevant.

New borders created following World War I divided some Hungarian counties, such as Zemplén, into districts located in two different countries. The old district seat for Zemplén County was Sátoraljaújhely, today in Hungary, near the Slovak border.

The Hungarian Regional Archives[*] in Sátoraljaújhely holds archival records of the Jews who lived in the northern half of Zemplén County, today in Slovakia. These documents include files from the late 18th and early 19th centuries pertaining to the settlement of specific families in Zemplén County, most of whom came from Galicia across the Polish frontier. It is likely that records, such as the 1869 census for Zemplén County, a microfilm copy of which the LDS (Mormon) Family History Library has in its collection,[4] exist in various other Hungarian archives, especially the National Archives* in Budapest.

In April 1944, Hungary was much larger than it is today. The country included territory from several areas ceded in various political decisions and occupations between 1938 and 1941. Some of these territories are in southern Slovakia today. These administrative areas, under Hungarian rule, were divided into 10 *gendarmerie* areas, one of which, Kassa (Košice) is in Slovakia today.

In early April 1944, all Jews under Hungarian rule registered by command of the *gendarmerie*, a type of rural, provincial police. Jews could leave the place where they resided only by special permission. Thus, registration in the Hungarian National Archives* should include every Jew under Hungarian rule (except those of Budapest, which was under police, rather than *gendarmerie*, administration).

Many Hungarian *gendarmerie* records are available at the Hungarian National Archives* in Budapest. These fonds include records compiled under a 1938 law requiring Jews to obtain certificates of citizenship showing several generations of ancestors. Other fonds hold records of the adoption of family names in 1780. Hungarian censuses taken in 1910 and 1942 are available also (see HUNGARY for archival regulations).

Jewish Sources

Jewish Museum. Slovakia has no specialized Jewish archives, although the Museum of Jewish Culture in Slovakia* in Bratislava has some community records, administered by the Central Union of Jewish Religious Communities.* The Museum forms part of the Slovak National Museum—Museum of History. It also maintains exhibits at SNM-MCJ-Jewish Museum Prešov.* Individuals at the Central Union speak English, German, Hebrew, Hungarian, Russian and Yiddish. Among other records, the museum holds the *pinkassim* (minute books) of the Jewish community of Bratislava. The exact years have not been determined. The Jewish Museum has its own website at WWW.SNM.SK, but only in Slovak; WWW.MUZEUM.SK/ENGLISH/DEFAULT.HTM is partially in English. It is always worthwhile to ask any Jewish museum in Slovakia if it retains archival fonds. Synagogues in Prešov,* Trnava* and Žilina* maintain exhibitions.

Jewish Cemeteries. One of the most important reasons for visiting the Slovak Republic is to inspect gravestones in the remaining Jewish cemeteries. The Slovak government has returned control of some Jewish cemeteries to the Central Union of Jewish Religious Communities,* but it is not known if all Jewish cemetery sites formerly controlled by the Slovak government now belong to the Central Union. The Jewish community office has no inventory of Jewish sites or cemeteries, but has information about specific cemeteries, such as, for example, that a team of volunteers has cleared the

Komárno cemetery. Some Jews apparently requested and received permission to be buried in Christian cemeteries, perhaps because there were no Jewish ones in the area.

The U.S. Commission for the Preservation of America's Heritage Abroad* has completed a survey of Jewish cemeteries in Slovakia. The second printing, *Survey of Historic Jewish Monuments of Slovakia*, may be obtained from the Commission (see CEMETERIES). The Commission also has sent a copy of the report to the JewishGen cemetery project, WWW.JEWISHGEN.ORG/CEMETERY.

It may be useful to visit the local Jewish organizations in Slovakia, if any exist, as these organizations often can provide information on current and prior aspects of Jewish life in the community. Obtain contact information for a local community from the Central Union* in Bratislava.

Holocaust Survivors

Soon after World War II, the American Jewish Congress prepared a book that listed both Hungarian-Jewish survivors of the Holocaust and the registration forms that both Nazi Hungary and the Slovak Nazi state required the Jews to complete.[6] These lists include name, present address, year of birth, name of father and maiden name of mother of all the then-known Slovak-Jewish survivors of the Holocaust. The U.S. Holocaust Memorial Museum* has an offprint in hard copy from a microfilm held by YIVO.* The museum copies are divided into alphabetical registers; the supplements are arranged alphabetically only by the first letter of the last name, A-K and L-Z.

Helpful Organizations

The Genealogical-Heraldic Society* in Martin, Slovakia, which has a designated English-speaking correspondent, publishes a journal with some English-language articles. H-SIG*, the Hungarian-Jewish special interest group WWW.FEEFHS.ORG/JSIG/FRG-HSIG.HTML, includes Slovakia.

Another website of value is FEEFHS.ORG/MASTERI.HTML, the master index page of the Federation of Eastern European Family History Societies (FEEFHS) web page. The website offers an index to many useful links for searching Jewish genealogy topics, including the Slovak Republic and others.

For a list of early Czech and Slovak arrivals in the United States, including Jews, see WWW.JEWISHGEN.ORG/BOHMOR/EARLY_IMMIG.HTML.

Useful Books and Document Collections

Guide Book: Jewish Sights of Bohemia and Moravia, by Jiri Fiedler, is a useful source. Although the title indicates coverage of only Bohemia and Moravia, the author has included (in addition to coverage of Silesia), at the end of the book, similar information for Bratislava, capital of Slovakia. Also included in the book are an easily overlooked explanation of the abbreviations used and an explanation of terms, including Hebrew words. A few bibliographical resources are followed by a place index.

Three other books deserve brief mention. The first uses much the same technique as Fiedler, but is about Slovakia and, unfortunately, seems to be available only there. The book, *Židovské náboženské obce na Slovensku*, by Eugen Barkaný and Ľudovít Dojč, includes a map of Slovakia that identifies several towns. Also included are a table listing towns by Slovak, Hungarian, and German names, and the pages in the book on which descriptions of them appear; a bibliography; and a summary in several languages, including English.

Zeitschrift für die Geschichte der Juden, a quarterly periodical edited by Hugo Gold, contains many articles in German regarding the Jews of the former Austro-Hungarian Empire, especially those of Bratislava.

Narrative of a Mission of Inquiry to the Jews from the Church of Scotland in 1839, by Bonar and McCheyne, Christian missionaries, provides descriptions of and insights into Jewish communities in Central and Eastern Europe, as well as what was then Palestine. The travelers observed Jewish quarters, living conditions, and attitudes. The book is useful for understanding the conditions of the area at the time, but gives no names. The authors traveled through present-day Slovakia, usually staying at inns with Jewish proprietors. They noticed facts as they went but from a Christian missionary viewpoint.

Leo Baeck Institute[*] in New York has a number of books and archival holdings of relevance to German-speaking Jews from Slovakia.[7] For a general overview of the subject, see Artur Görög below.

Researchers may order a Slovak Genealogy Kit designed to assist in recording data and computer matches of participants from the Slovak Genealogy Research Center.[*] Some newsletters that are not specifically Jewish may have useful information. The primary publications are:

- Czech and Slovak Jewish Community Archives,[*] *Phoenix: The Journal of Czech and Slovak Family and Community History*. Although intended as an annual, apparently only one issue appeared. It had genealogical tables and was mostly about Jews.
- *Naše Rodina: Newsletter of the Czech and Slovak Genealogical Society*,[*] includes Silesian, Hungarian, Ruthenian and Jewish interests. The Winter 1990 issue reports that materials from Archives of Czechs and Slovaks Abroad (ACASA) are at the University of Chicago Library.[*]
- *Slovakia: A Slovak Heritage Newsletter*, Helen Cincebeaux, ed.[*]

Geographical Sources

It is helpful to remember a few rules that apply to name changes from Hungarian to Slovak. The prefix *Kis* (little) becomes *Malý*; *Nagy* (big) is *Velký*; and the suffix *falu* becomes *falva* (village, which is *dorf* in German).

The place to start the geographic search is Mokotoff, Gary, and Sallyann Amdur Sack, *Where Once We Walked: A Guide to the Jewish Communities Destroyed in the Holocaust*. Teaneck, NJ: Avotaynu, 1991, rev. ed. 2002. This book enables a researcher to locate all of the towns near a given town using longitude and latitude for a given area in Central and Eastern Europe.

The Slovak State Tourist Bureau, New York City, sells a detailed 1:800,000 scale road map for $3.50. The U.S. Library of Congress and the New York Public Library both have the 1877–1914 and 1896–1944 series of 1:75,000 scale topographic maps of the Austro-Hungarian Empire. Some former German and Hungarian place names are included parenthetically in both map series.

Other useful geographical resources are:

Lelkes, György, *ed.*, *Magyar hélységnév-azonosító szótár* (Place name verification dictionary for Hungary). [Hungarian with introduction in German]. Budapest: Balassi kiadó, 1992. Includes principal towns (administrative seats) for each county in Greater Hungary, a map of each county in Greater Hungary, nationalities in Hungary by location in 1910 and (among others) the Slovak names of locations with the Hungarian equivalent and bibliographical references. The book covers the Kingdom of Hungary as it was in 1913, which includes Slovakia.

Statistische Zentral-Kommission, *Gemeindelexikon der im Reichsräte Vertretenen Königreiche und Länder* (Gazetteer of the Crown Lands and territories represented in the Imperial Council). 14 vols. [German] Vienna, 1903–08. Now available only on microform in the U.S. Library of Congress.

Kendler, Josef von, *Orts- und Verkehrs-Lexikon von Oesterreich-Ungarn: enthaltend sämmtliche Orte und deren politische und gerichtliche Eintheilung, Eisenbahn-, Post, Dampfschiff- und Telegraphen-Stationen mit Bezeichnung der Eisenbahn- und Dampfschiff-Unternehmungen, nebst den wichtigsten Ortschaften von Bosnien und der Herzegowina: ein unentbehrliches Hand- und Nachschlagebuch für Behörden, Aemter, Notäre, Advocaten, Kaufleute, Reisende, etc.* 3rd ed., Vienna: F. Röllinger und Moessmer & Schulda, 1905. Lists every location in the Austro-Hungarian Empire at the time and gives multiple names for each location, where applicable. Copy available at the Austrian Embassy,[*] Washington, D.C., Attention: Cultural Attaché. 3524 International Court, NW, Washington, DC 20008-3035; telephone: (202) 895-6719; fax: (202) 895-6750.

Topographical Lexicon of the Communities of Hungary Compiled Officially in 1773 Published by the Delegation of Peace of Hungary, Budapest: V. Hornyanszky, 1920. This is a reprint of the 1773 book, in Roman type, making it easy to read. The tables are written in Latin along with an introduction in several languages, including English. The book's principal value lies in the fact that it is arranged by Hungarian county and under that the name of each town appears in columns in Latin; then in Hungarian (Magyar); in German; and in another language, depending upon the area of Hungary, such as Croatian or Slovenian. The location is identified as a city, town, or village; also includes main religion, number of schoolteachers, and principal language used in the locality. Indexed.

Magyarország Hélységnévtára, Budapest (LDS Family History Library film 97304), an 1877 Hungarian gazetteer, lists religious population by town and notes where people of the

Findling family of Stropkov proceeding to the deportation center in May, 1942. None survived the Holocaust. (From Between Galicia and Hungary: The Jews of Stropkov, *by Melody Amsel. Bergenfield, N.J.: Avotaynu, 2002)*

town worshiped, which may be a different place. The place of worship is likely to be the location of the cemetery as well. Thus, the 13 Jews of Pravrocz (Pavroc) worshiped at the synagogue in Sztropkó (Stropkov), which had a cemetery. The governmental author is Központi Statisztikai Hivatal, with Hornyanszki V. Nyomdai Müintézet, publishers. Versions after 1921 are limited to Hungary in its then present borders, which included parts of Slovakia during World War II.

Gardiner, Duncan B., *German Towns in Slovakia and Upper Hungary: A Genealogical Gazetteer.* 2nd. ed. Lakewood, Ohio: The Family Historian, 1989.

Addresses

Ministry of the Interior, Department of Archives, 817 01 Bratislava, Drotárska cesta č. 42; 811 04 Bratislava, Slovak Republic; telephone: 07-580-1189; fax: 580 12 47.

Slovak State Archives

Slovak National Archives/Slovenský národný archív, 817 01 Bratislava, Slovakia; Drotárska cesta 42; telephone: 07-421-267-298-111, 628-01178,-81,-83,-85; fax: 421-2 628-012-47; e-mail: SNARCHIV@SNARCHIV.SK; website: WWW.CIVIL.COV.SK/SNARCHIV. The website provides an English-language explanation of the rules for the use of the archives. Normally, the archives will do such research for a fee in response to a written request delivered by mail or in person, but consult the website for a few arcane exceptions. Many employees are fluent in English, and some have been to the United States. For a full list, in both Slovak and English, of Slovak archives controlled by the state or by the Roman Catholic Church, see WWW.CIVIL.GOV.SK/SNARCHIV/TEL99A.HTM, while WWW.CIVIL.GOV.SK/SNARCHIV/UK_WORLD_ARCHIVES. HTM has links to many major public archives, including the Hungarian ones.

Slovenský národný archív, 817 01 Bratislava, Slovakia; Drotárska cesta č. 42; telephone: 07-580 1189; fax: 580 12 47

Provincal Archives (Státný oblastný archív)

For a current list of regional and local archives in Slovakia, use the website HTTP://WWW.CIVIL.GOV.SK/ARCH/ARCHIVY1_03.

HTM. The website lists the current address, the new telephone numbers for each archives, and the current directors. Some other archives are also linked. When sending mail to Slovakia list the ZIP Code and then the town and list those above the street address, underlining the name of the town. The last line should read "Slovak Republic."

The most recent information on written requests made to the Slovak National Archives appears at HTTP://WWW.CIVIL. GOV.SK/SNARCHIV/UK_WRITTEN_REQUESTS.HTM. After opening that website, click on the hyperlink beginning with "Regulations of the Minister of the Interior of the SR no. 9... to obtain application forms. The website will automatically download the forms in Microsoft Word under the filename "opatrenie.doc" in three languages. Use pp. 11–15 for "running accounts" and pp. 16–20 for individual vital records. The document also lists current administrative fees. The 2003 rate of exchange is about 35 Slovak crowns for one United States dollar.

Central Union of Jewish Religious Communities (Židovská Náboženská), ul. Kozia 21, 814 47 Bratislava, Slovak Republic; telephone: 421-7-531-8357; fax: 421-7-531-1106; website: WWW.ANGELFIRE.COM/HI/ZNO/INDEX.HTML.

Czechoslovak Genealogical Society, P.O. Box 18225, St. Paul, MN 55118.

Czech and Slovak Jewish Communities Archive, 86–17 139th Street, Jamaica, NY 11435.

Genealogical-Heraldic Society, nám. J. C. Hronského 1, 036 01 Martin, Slovakia; telephone: 011-421-43-413-1267; fax: 011-421-43-413-3188; website: WWW.GENEALOGY-HERALDRY.SK/ENG/ENG.HTM; e-mail: GENEALOGY@SNK.SK

H-SIG, c/o Louis Schonfeld, P. O. Box 34152, Cleveland, OH 44134-0852; telephone: 1-216-661-3970; e-mail: LMAGYAR@EN.COM; infoFile: HSIG@JEWISHGEN.ORG; newsletter: *Magyar Zsido* [English] published 1993–97. articles: WWW.JEWISHGEN.ORG/HUNGARY/ARTICLES. HTM; website: FEEFHS.ORG/JSIG/FRG-HSIG.HTML

Hungarian National Archives of Hungary, Budapest; postal address: P.O.B. 3, 1250 Budapest, Hungary; street address: Budapest I,

Bécsi kapu tér 2-4; telephone: 011-36-1-356-5811; fax: 011-36-1-212-1619; website: WWW.NATARCH.HU; e-mail: INFO@NATARCH.HU

Leo Baeck Institute, 15 West 16th Street, New York, NY 10011; telephone: 212-744-6400; fax: 212-988-1305; website: WWW.LBI.ORG; catalogue: LBI.CJH.ORG/MCLBIINTERNETMENU.HTM

Ministry of the Interior, Department of Archives, 817 01 Bratislava, Drotárska cesta 42; 811 04 Bratislava, Slovak Republic; telephone: 07-580-1189; fax: 580-12-47

Museum of Jewish Culture in Slovakia, Židovská ulica 17, Bratislava; telephone: 421-2-5934-9111; fax: 421-2-5934-9145; website: WWW.MUSEUM.SK/ENGLISH/DEFAULT.HTM

Slovak Genealogy Research Center, Ray Plutko, director, 16455 East Prentice Place, Aurora, CO 80015

Slovakia: A Slovak Heritage Newsletter, 151 Colebrook Drive, Rochester, NY 14617; telephone: (718) 342-9383; website: www.IARELATIVE.COM/SHFS_QUA.HTM.

SNM-MJC-Jewish Museum Prešov, Orthodox synagogue, Švermova 32, Presov; telephone: 421-51-773-1638; fax: 421-51. See HTTP://WWW.MUZEUM.SK/MUZEUM/DEFAULTE.PHP?CO=ZM_MZK_SNM.

Trnava synagogue, Halenárska ul. č. 2, 917 01 Trnava, Trnava; telephone: 421-33-551-4657.

United States Commission for the Preservation of America's Heritage Abroad, 888 Seventeenth Street NW, Suite 1160, Washington, D.C. 20005; telephone: (202) 254-3824; website: WWW.PRESERVATION COMMISSION.ORG; e-mail FARROW@HERITAGEABROAD.GOV.

University of Chicago Library, 1100 East 57th Street, Chicago, IL 60637; telephone: (312) 702-4685; catalogue: HTTPIPAC.LIB.UCHICAGO. EDU/IPAC20/IPAC.JSP?PROFILE-=UCPUBLIC#FOCUS; website: WWW.USHMM. ORG. The library participates in Electronic Document Delivery, a method of copying articles and delivering them to the requester via computer.

U.S. Holocaust Memorial Museum, 100 Raoul Wallenberg Place, SW, Washington, DC 20024, telephone: (202) 488-4204; website: WWW.USHMM.ORG.

Yad Vashem, P.O. Box 3477, Jerusalem 91034, Israel; website: WWW.YAD-VASHEM.ORG.IL/ABOUT_HOLOCAUST/RECORD_GROUPS/HATIVOT.HTML.

Žilina Little synagogue/Malá synagoga, ul. Dlabacova 15 010 01 Žilina; telephone: 421-41-562-0485.

Bibliography

Auslander, Jordan. *Index to Jewish Vital Statistics Records of Slovakia.* Teaneck, N.J. Avotaynu, 1993.

Bárkány, Eugen and Ľudovít Dojč. *Židovské nábozenské obce na Slovensku.* Bratislava: VESNA, 1991. See WWW.GEOCITIES.COM/DANPOLAK/DATA/BARKANY for a list of the Jewish religious communities in Slovakia shown in this book.

Barnavi, Eli, *ed., Historical Atlas of the Jewish People.* New York: Alfred A. Knopf, 1992. DS117.S8513, 1992.

Bonar, Andrew Alexander, and Robert Murray McCheyne. *Narrative of a Mission of Inquiry to the Jews from the Church of Scotland in 1839.* Edinburgh: William Whyte & Co., London: Hamilton, Adams & Co., and J. Nisbet & Co., 1848.

Braham, Randolph, *ed., Hungarian-Jewish Studies,* 3 vols. New York: World Federation of Hungarian Jews, 1066–1973. DS135.H9H94.

Dawidowicz, Lucy, *The War Against the Jews, 1933–1945.* Ardmore, PA: Seth, 1986.

Fiedler, Jiří. *Guide Book: Jewish Sights of Bohemia and Moravia.* Introduction by Arno Pařík. Drawings, photographs and map. Prague: Sefer, 1991. Available from the U.S. Commission for the Preservation of America's Heritage Abroad

Gold, Hugo, ed. *Die Juden und die Judengemeinde Bratislava in Vergangenheit und Gegenwart: ein Sammelwerk* (The Jews and the Jewish community of Bratislava in the past and the future: An encyclopedia). Brunn: Jüdischer Buchverlag, 1932.

Gold, Hugo, ed. *Zeitschrift für die Geschichte der Juden* (Magazine for the history of the Jews). 11 vols. [German] Tel Aviv, Olamenu, 1964–74.

Görög, Artur. *A kassai zsidóság története és galllériája* (The story of the Jewish community of Košice). [Hungarian, some English, Hebrew and Yiddish] Bné-Brák, Israel: Friedmann Lipe nyomdájában, 1991.

Jews of Czechoslovakia: Historical Studies and Surveys, 3 vols., Philadelphia: Society for the History of Czechoslovak Jews; New York: Jewish Publication Society of America, 1968–84.

Kislin, Mark. *Ungareshe Menchen: A History of the Weisberger Family.* Years covered: 1790–1993. Price: $39.95 plus shipping. Order from: Mark Kislin, 43 North Sherman Street, Wilkes-Barre, PA 18702; telephone: (717) 822-4337. A collection of pictures, documents, maps, anecdotes and information. Family from Zemplén County in present-day Slovakia. Includes many collateral families.

Luft, Edward D. "The 1869 Austro-Hungarian Census," *AVOTAYNU* 17, no. 3 (Fall 2001).

Magyar Zsido: Semi-Annual Publication of the Greater Hungarian SIG, Cleveland, OH: HSIG, Vol. 1, No. 1, Summer 1994. See second unnumbered sheet; the registration forms are on unnumbered sheets 18 and 19. The source for this information appears to be *Register of All Persons Saved from Anti-Jewish Persecution in Slovakia.* 5 vols. Bratislava: American Joint Distribution Committee, October 15, 1945.

Miller, Olga K. *Genealogical Research for Czech and Slovak Americans,* Detroit, Mich.: Gale Research Co., 1978.

Perlman, Robert. *Bridging Three Worlds: Hungarian-Jewish Americans 1848–1914,* Amherst: University of Massachusetts Press, 1991.

Sarmányová, Jana. *Cirkevné, matrikyna Slovensku zo 16–19 Storiba* (Slovak parish registers for the 16th–19th centuries). [Slovak with summaries in English and German] Bratislava: Odbor Archívnictva Ministerstva vnútra SR, 1991. Includes bibliographical references, an index of towns, and an English-language summary with the book's title in English. The work is a list of vital records by town and year and includes Jewish records. A code, explained in the English-language summary, indicates the archives in which the records are held. The book lists Jewish community registers until the end of 1885 when the state assumed responsibility for registration. The book also lists conscription and circumcision registers, the oldest from the 18th century, although these records were kept regularly only after 1850–51. Reviewed by Edward Luft in "Two Guides to the Slovak Archives," *AVOTAYNU* 16, no. 2, (Summer 2000): 65-66.

Schlyter, Daniel. *A Handbook of Czechoslovak Research.* Buffalo Grove, Ill.: Gale Research Co., 1978.

———. "Hungarian Census Returns," typescript booklet at LDS (Mormon) Family History Library. Available on microfiche 6000384. Description of Hungarian census returns at the Genealogical Library of the Church of Jesus Christ of Latter-day Saints with instructions for their use and translation—including a register of microfilm numbers for the 1869 and 1848 censuses of the Jews. Includes areas now in Slovakia.

Wellauer, Maralyn A. *Tracing Your Czech and Slovak Roots.* Milwaukee: self-published, 1980.

Wellisch, Henry. "18th-Century Jewish Censuses in Hungary," *AVOTAYNU* 18, no. 2 (Summer 2002): 8–10. The area covered includes present-day Slovakia where many Jews lived at the time.

Zilbershlag, David Hayim. *Tsadik li-verakhah: Sefer zikaron: Zikhronot, te'udot u-mar'ot mi-yeme shene haye Barukh Hager mi-Sert Viz'nits, Ramat Viz'nits-Hefah: Mosdot Sert Viz'nits be-Erets ha-Kodesh.* 5754-Hebrew calendar (1993 or 1994), Vol. 1 includes genealogical tables.

———. *Sefer zikaron le-rabenu Balal ha-'Mekor Barukh', zatsal.* Many rabbis listed.

Notes

1. For example, the regional archives at Bytča holds Jewish birth, marriage and death records in Matrika, 1771-1852, Židovská obec Trstená-Námestovo (Dolní Kubin), Mikrofilm pôvodnych dokumentov v Štátnom oblastnom archíve v Bytča [Records of Jewish births, marriages and deaths for Trestená and Námestovo, Slovakia, formerly Trsztena and Námesztó, Árva, Hungary. Text in German. Štátny oblastný archív v Bytča: 1165-1166. Narodení 1771-1852 Sobásení 1850-1885. LDS microfilm 2062256, items 7–8.

2. Hugo Gold, ed. *Die Juden und die Judengemeinde Bratislava in Vergangenheit und Gegenwart: ein Sammelwerk.* (The Jews and the Jewish Community of Bratislava in the Past and the Future: An Encyclopedia). [German]. Brunn: Jüdischer Buchverlag, 1932. The book includes two articles by Dr. Max Schay entitled, "Die älteste Steuerliste der Juden in Preßburg" (The oldest tax list of the Jews in Pressburg [now Bratislava]). This list is from the year 1748. "Die älteste Liste der Preßburger Juden" (The oldest list of Pressburg Jews). This list is from 1709. Both are lists of Jewish male taxpayers.

3. See Wellisch, Henry, "18th-Century Jewish Censuses in Hungary," *AVOTAYNU* 18, no. 2 (Summer 2002): 8-10. The area covered includes present-day Slovakia, where many Jews lived at the time.

4. See Luft, Edward, "The 1869 Austro-Hungarian Census," *AVOTAYNU* 17, no. 3 (Fall 2001): 25-27. For a description of Mormon holdings not shown yet in the catalogue but held by the Mormons, see Schlyter, Daniel Martin, "Hungarian Census Returns," [Includes areas now in Slovakia], typescript (photocopy), 21 pp. "Description of Hungarian census returns at the Genealogical Library of the Church of Jesus Christ of Latter-Day Saints with instructions for their use and translation—including a register of microfilm numbers for the 1869 census and the 1848 census of the Jews."—Title page. In English and Hungarian; in booklet form and on LDS microfiche 6000384.

5. Militär-Stammrollen (Conscription lists), 1858–1901, Wien (Niederösterreich). Konskriptionsamt. Microfilm made from manuscripts in the Österreichischen Stadt- und Landesarchiv, Vienna, Austria. Registers of male births for military conscription. Also includes death dates and towns where individuals relocated. Male births start with microfilm 1454455 and continue through microfilm 1505950 and microfilm 1506004. Covers the entire Austrian and Austro-Hungarian Empire.

6. Leo Baeck Institute, Edward Luft Collection, AR 6957, Folder IV-2, Location: S 42/5.

South Africa
Including Countries of Central and Southern Africa
by Saul Issroff

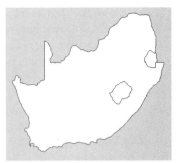

South Africa

This section covers the geographical area of South Africa and the adjacent countries of Zimbabwe (previously Southern Rhodesia), Zambia (previously Northern Rhodesia), Namibia (previously South West Africa) and Mozambique. Each of the countries neighboring South Africa had significant, albeit small, Jewish settlements at various times and all of these communities were closely connected with the Jewish community of South Africa. Some additional information is provided about other sub-Saharan countries, such as Kenya, that have had a significant Jewish presence.

The time period covered is primarily the mid-19th century to the present.

History

South Africa was under Dutch rule from 1652 to 1795 and under the British from 1795 to 1803. Between 1803 and 1806, the colony was ruled by the Batavian Republic. The British ruled the Cape again starting in 1806. In 1836, a group of earlier Dutch settler families started migrating into the interior of the country, the Great Trek that led to the formation of the two Boer republics, the Orange Free State and the Transvaal.

The discovery of diamond fields in 1869 and gold fields in 1886 brought an influx of fortune seekers. After a rebellion culminating in the Anglo-Boer War (1899–1902), four self-governing colonies, Cape Colony, Natal, Orange Free State and Transvaal, existed until the Union of South Africa was formed in 1910. In 1961, South Africa left the British Commonwealth and became a republic.

South African Provinces And Their Capital Cities

The division of South Africa into different administrative regions took place during three distinct periods, of which the first two fade into one another. From the establishment of the Union of South Africa in 1910, the main division was into four provinces. As early as 1913, however, ownership of land by the black majority was restricted to certain areas covering about 13 percent of the country, and from the late 1950s these areas were gradually consolidated into "homelands" (also known as bantustans) to serve as the *de jure* national states of the black population in fulfillment of the white majority government's policy of apartheid. In 1976, the homeland of Transkei was the first to accept independence from South Africa, and although this independence was never acknowl-edged by any other country, three other homelands followed suit. Since 1994, South Africa has been divided into nine provinces. The former homelands were reintegrated into the Republic on the eve of the April 1994 general election which ended minority rule.

Provinces 1910–1994 (with capital cities in parentheses).
- Cape Province (Cape Town)
- Natal (Pietermaritzburg)
- Orange Free State (Bloemfontein)
- Transvaal (Pretoria)

"Independent" Homelands
- Bophutatswana (Mmabatho, declared independent in 1977)
- Ciskei (Bisho, 1981)
- Transkei (Umtata, 1976)
- Venda (Thohoyandou, 1979)

Non-independent Homelands
- Gazankulu
- KaNgwane
- KwaNdebele
- KwaZulu (Ulundi)
- Lebowa
- Qwaqwa

Provinces 1994 to the present
- Eastern Cape (Bisho, other cities: East London, Port Elizabeth)
- Free State (Bloemfontein/Mangaung, other cities: Welcome)
- Gauteng, previously Pretoria (Witwatersrand-Vereeniging-Johannesburg, other cities: Pretoria, Soweto)
- Kwa-Zulu Natal (Ulundi, other city: Durban)
- Mpumalanga, previously Eastern Transvaal (Nelspruit)
- Limpopo, previously Northern Province (Pietersburg, renamed Polokwane in 2002)
- Northern Cape (Kimberley)
- Western Cape (Cape Town)

Jewish links to South Africa started with the Portuguese voyages of exploration around the Cape of Good Hope in 1452. Jews participated in these early voyages as map makers, navigators and sailors. The Portuguese were not interested in permanent settlement in the Cape, but sailed around it to access the profitable trading areas of Asia.

In 1652, the first permanent settlement of Dutch colonists, led by Jan van Riebeck, was established. With his group were at least four Jews, including Samuel Jacobson and David

Hijlbrons, who later converted to Christianity in 1669. Under the control of the Dutch East India Company from 1652 to 1795, only Protestants were permitted to reside at the Cape.

Greater religious freedom, permitted under the short-lived Batavian Republic in 1803, continued after the British took control in 1806. In 1820, the British government gave assisted passage and land grants to people willing to settle in the wilds of the Cape colony. The first group of settlers, including at least five Jewish families, are known as the "1820 settlers;" they represented the first British attempts to provide permanent colonial settlement. By the 1860s, other European Jews had arrived from Germany and Holland.

The first Jewish congregation was founded in 1841 in Cape Town by the English Jew Benjamin Norden, who arrived in the eastern Cape with the 1820 settlers. Most of the early Jewish settler families have totally assimilated and are no longer Jewish.

By 1880, approximately 4,000 Jews lived in South Africa, and Jewish immigration increased rapidly thereafter. The Russian pogroms (1881–84) and other catastrophes (droughts, floods, deportation and fires) were major factors in the emigration. South Africa offered strong potential for economic success—particularly following the discovery of diamond fields in Kimberley (in 1869) and gold fields in the Transvaal (in 1886).

Among early Jews in South Africa were Sammy Marks, from Neustadt in Suwalki guberniya, regarded as the pioneer of Lithuanian emigration to South Africa. He became a friend of South African President Paul Kruger and was highly successful as an industrialist. London-born Barney Barnato was a partner of Cecil John Rhodes in the formation of the De Beers Diamond Company. (Later, with the assistance of the Rothschilds, control of De Beers passed to the German-Jewish family of Ernest Oppenheimer.)

More than 47,000 Jews were counted in the first nationwide census of 1911. Most were "Litvaks" originally from the Russian provinces of Kovno, Vilna, Grodno and (northern) Suwalki and from the Byelorussian provinces of Minsk, Mogilev and Vitebsk.

As an undeveloped country, South Africa offered economic opportunities to early immigrants far greater than they could find in Eastern Europe. The traveling peddler, called *smous*, became an institution in the country's remote rural areas.[1] Many other Jews settled in small towns as shopkeepers and tradesmen. A number of efficient, entrepreneurial farmers and traders were active pioneers in the hides and skin, wool, ostrich feather, potato, maize and citrus farming industries.

Contemporary Jewish Community

Southern African Jewry, with its predominance of Litvaks, had been unusually homogeneous. Recent years, however, have seen substantial emigration to Australia, Britain, Canada, Israel and the United States, with a much smaller influx of Israeli, Russian and Zimbawean Jews.

Zionism is very strong in the South Africa community, and an amalgam of the Anglo-Jewish form and Lithuanian spirit characterize both the lay and religious institutions of the community. The Jewish day school movement is a powerful educational presence, its pupils consistently obtaining excellent scholastic results. Jews have formed part of a privileged white minority that had dominated a multiracial society. At the same time, a number of Jews were prominent in the anti-apartheid and liberation movements.[2]

At various times, attempts were made to limit the influx of Jews, for example, in 1903 by placing them in the same category as Asiatics on the grounds that Yiddish was not a European language. This ruling was successfully challenged and reversed. About 15,000 Jews entered South Africa between 1925 and 1938. In 1930, the Quota Act, without specifically mentioning Jews, was introduced with the effect of limiting the influx to a small number by making "assimilability" a criterion for admission. The rise of Afrikaner nationalism, coupled with its overt Nazi sympathies, led to more severe restrictions on Jewish immigration. Between 1933 and 1936, only 3,600 Jews were permitted to enter; probably fewer than 500 Jews entered during the Holocaust era.

Most Jews lived in Johannesburg (Transvaal) or Cape Town (Cape). Smaller, significant communities existed in Durban (Natal), Pretoria (Transvaal), Port Elizabeth and East London (Cape). More than 1,000 rural towns and small settlements also had a Jewish presence, although most now have a very small or no Jewish presence at all. Today Jews live predominantly in Johannesburg and Cape Town with much smaller communities in Durban, Pretoria, Bloemfontein and Port Elizabeth.

Sources of Genealogical Information

Formal South African resources include the National and Regional Archival Depots, Department of Home Affairs for Vital Records, Master of the Supreme Court and cemeteries. Genealogical information also may be found in commercial, land, military and synagogue records.

More general sources are records held by the Jewish Board of Deputies,* Jewish genealogical societies, LDS (Mormon) family history centers, libraries and museums, the Poor Jews Temporary Shelter (London), the Genealogical Institute of South Africa (GISA) and other associations and societies.

Do not expect a museum, archive, library or institution to do research for you. Government departments will provide copies of certificates and the occasional printout if it is within the scope of their holdings and duties. Most institutions are not able to do any research. Do not expect an academic university department to do research for you either. If you require details or a photograph of a tombstone, be prepared to send a small donation to the organization (e.g., a *chevra kadisha* [burial society]) of whom you are making the request.

Department of Home Affairs

Vital Records

Birth, marriage and death certificates are available from the Department of Home Affairs.* Following are the approximate dates that registration of vital events began in the various provinces:

Provinces	Births	Marr.	Deaths
Cape	1895	1700	1895
Natal	1868	1845	1888
Orange F.S.	1903	1848	1903
Transvaal	1901	1870	1901

These records are not accessible or available to private sector genealogical researchers directly and no publicly available index exists. Within South Africa, applications for copies of birth, marriage and death certificates can be made at any Department of Home Affairs* office. To apply for certificates from outside South Africa one must do so through the nearest South African embassy, consulate or High Commission. The South African National Archives* holds marriage and death registers older than 20 years, but the records may not be copied and the issuance of certificates can only be done by the Department of Home Affairs* which charges a fee for this service.

Birth Certificates. Two types of certificates are available: abridged certificates with limited personal information and full, or unabridged certificates. Limited certificates provide surname, given name, date of birth, district of birth, race and entry number. Full, unabridged certificates include child and father identity number, date of birth, surname, given names, place of birth, the same information for mother plus maiden name. Full certificates are preferable for genealogical purposes.

Marriage Certificates. A full marriage certificate provides the groom's details first: identity number, surname, given names in full, marital status, (population group—probably omitted now), date of birth, permanent residential address. The bride's details are similar: date, place of marriage, consent to marriage (only in the case of a minor), marriage solemnized at. Declaration by the married couple in the presence of witnesses provides the names of witnesses, declaration of the marriage officer, denomination (e.g., Jewish) or magistrate's office.

Death Certificates. These usually are completed by a doctor or a coroner and provide the name, date and cause of death. This is a legal document that then goes to the burial society and is a legal requirement before burial can take place.

Death Notices

Probate or estate files usually include a death notice,[2] a last will and testament and the distribution and liquidation account of the estate. These files are available from the Master of the Supreme Court.* Below are the dates that estate files started to be kept at the various Master's Offices.*

Province	Commencing Dates
Cape	1929 Onward
Grahamstown*	1957 Onward
Natal	1970 Onward
Orange Free State	1930 Onward
Transvaal	1964 Onward

* Eastern Cape Only

Files created before the above dates are kept in the relevant Archives Department (see below). Master's Offices administer the liquidation and distribution of the estates of deceased persons; administer trust property; administer the property of minors and persons under curatorship; administer derelict estates; and regulate the rights of beneficiaries under mutual wills made by two or more individuals.

The Master's Office is not only an office of supervision but also an office of record. In this office, complete information is filed about every estate within the master's jurisdiction. With some exceptions, at any time during office hours, anyone may inspect any document and have a certified copy made of any document upon payment of the relevant fee.

These very important documents give much information about the deceased, including personal details and details about his/her spouse(s), children and other beneficiaries. Addresses often also give clues to the researcher about where to find relatives of the deceased. Not all deceased persons have estate files, since estate files are not opened for those who owned few assets. Many individuals with British citizenship filed their wills in Great Britain. The public does not have access to the files of estates that have not been finalised.

Burials and Cemeteries

Cemetery offices keep records of tombstone inscriptions and burial registers. Burial registers exist for cemeteries within municipal boundaries only and are kept by the respective town council. Burial registers rarely provide more information than the person's full name, date of burial and age at death. The registers are especially valuable when a person is buried in a grave that does not have a headstone.

Many rural or farm cemeteries are outside the jurisdiction of municipalities. The Genealogical Society of South Africa* is documenting headstone inscriptions on all South African cemeteries, including rural farm ones. This information is indexed by cemetery and now is on the National Archives* online database. Copies are available at all archival depositories and at various libraries and institutions. The published indexes provide a quick reference to determine where an individual is buried and, thus, at which provincial archive repository his or her death notice is held. The indexes also indicate when the deceased was born and are particularly helpful in identifying children who died young and for whom there rarely was a death notice.

Jewish Burial Records. One of the unifying movements within the South African-Jewish community was the development of *chevrot kadisha* (burial societies). These societies not only deal with burials but with general aid to the sick and needy. They exist in all major centers of Jewish population, and records from many of the older societies are held at the Jewish Board of Deputies* and the Kaplan Centre.* The Jewishgen Online Worldwide Burial Database* (see CEMETERIES) has records from all Bloemfontein, Johannesburg, Durban and Pretoria, plus some from Cape Town and Bulawayo.

Most Jews are buried in cemeteries in large cities; Johannesburg accounts for an estimated 75 percent of them. Records start in 1887 for Braamfontein cemetery, Brixton in 1914 and West Park in 1942; registers are kept on the pre-

Jews on board ship on arrival at Cape Town docks. Courtesy of South African Jewish Museum.

mises. Occasional burials still occur in the two older cemeteries. The Johannesburg Jewish Helping Hand and Burial Society (*chevra kadisha*) has a database of every burial in West Park, the major cemetery used since 1942. Currently about 600 to 700 burials occur yearly in Johannesburg. In 1980, the LDS (Mormon) Family History Library (see LDS) was granted permission to microfilm the burials records. LDS Film # 1259151 is a record of the Braamfontein cemetery. The Brixton registers were not filmed (see below).

Smaller rural communities largely have vanished and their cemeteries are maintained by the local councils. The LDS (Mormon) microfilms have some details on a few rural cemeteries, but little that is specifically Jewish. The Mormons also have some microfilms that relate to other cemeteries.

Jewish Burials. The spiritual leader of the African Jewish Congress visits many of the rural localities and is responsible for attending to the maintenance and upkeep of the cemeteries.

In all South African cities and towns, the *chevra kadisha* has total responsibility for all burials irrespective of whether the deceased was Orthodox, Reform or any other persuasion. No other groups handled burials. Some people were cremated; if so, this is noted on the death certificate.

National Archives: Archival Sources

Archives repositories exist in Bloemfontein, Cape Town, Durban, Pietermaritzburg and Pretoria. They are responsible for the custody of the archives and other documents relevant to the province in which they are situated. The National Archives in Pretoria* houses the archives of central government departments and the Transvaal Archives Repository. The documents available at an archives repository include correspondence files, registers and other documents of government offices and the offices of the local authorities that are or were located in the province concerned; photographs, maps, microfilms and estate files before the dates listed under the Master of the Supreme Court* for the various provinces. Each repository has a library with books of a

genealogical and historical nature, as well as microfilm readers. In many instances, photocopying restrictions apply to early documents, especially estate files.

Census Records

South Africa is one of the few counties in which census enumeration records are destroyed; only statistics from each census are kept. The sole exception is an 1857 Cape census, (but few Jews were in the country at that time).

The archives in Cape Town have the *Cape Colony Publications* which contain census lists for 1875, 1891, 1904 and 1911 only—but do not specify the names of individuals. Places of birth are mentioned and pertain to the number of people resident in different areas who were born outside of South Africa. *Blue Books* and *Statistical Registers*, part of the archives of the Colonial Office*, cover the period 1821–1909. The *Opgaafrollen* (enumerations) were taken for tax purposes in the Cape and cover the period from 1692 until about 1845.

The Orange Free State has census reports taken March 31, 1880, March 31, 1890, and April 17, 1904. These have information and statistical data on birth places, ages, education, religions occupations, sicknesses and infirmities of the population. No information regarding relationships of individuals is given.

Voter rolls from 1884, 1888, 1889, 1893, 1895, 1896, 1897, 1898, 1899, 1900 and 1907 are available as are some post-1910 rolls. They include surnames, given names, occupations and places of residence. Census and tax registers for the Transvaal are available for 1873, 1890 and 1904. A Johannesburg census was taken on July 15, 1896. Census and tax records for South Africa as a whole are in the Department of Statistics, Pretoria.*

Land Records

Land ownership records (known as title deeds in South Africa) and deeds of transfer are filed with the Deeds Offices* in the relevant district. Land records were started in 1685. Marriage contracts and donations *inter vivos* (a form of prenuptial trust) are also kept at the Deeds Offices. These offices can help locate farms.

Military Records

Military records held by the South African Defence Force Archives* include the archives of the Commander General, Transvaal Republic 1881–99; archives of the Military Governor, Pretoria 1900–02 (Records of the British occupation force which include the names of those who died during the Boer War), and archives recording deaths among the Republican fighting forces and civilians, 1899–1902. The South African Defense Force Archives* are not open to the public; one must write for information. Personal information about all individuals who served in the South African Armed Forces from the time of union in 1910 are available from the South African Defence Force Documentation Centre.*

The person concerned or his eldest living relative must grant permission to obtain information from the records. The Defence Force archives are not open to the public, but they will accept inquiries made by mail. The Commonwealth

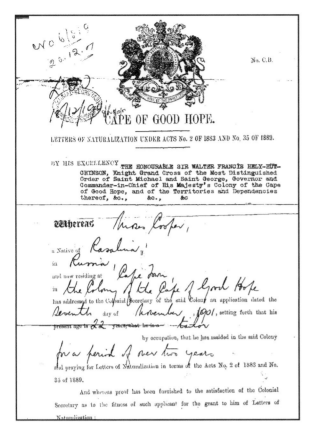

1903 naturalization record shows town of birth as Rasalina, today Rozalimas, Lithuania

War Graves Board* has lists of casualties in South Africa including South African deaths outside the country and British military deaths in South Africa.

South African Jews served and died fighting both for the British and the Boers in the Anglo-Boer Wars. Many Jews served in World War I, and some 120 were killed in action. Most eligible males served in World War II, many in the North African campaigns.

The Commonwealth War Graves Commission* lists all South African military casualties in South Africa, places of burial and related information. Included are all South African deaths overseas and all British troops killed in South Africa. The Commission has a website at http://www.cwgc.org/.

The South African National Museum of Military History* has no personal records but has historical data of various units, including books, Honour Rolls, details of Imperial and war graves and regimental histories.

More than 800 South Africans fought in the 1948 Israeli War of Independence in two volunteer organizations, the Machal and the Nachal.[3] A recent book by Katzew and Woolf lists the names of all volunteers.*

Shipping and Passenger Records

Most immigrants came by ship through Cape Town although the ports of Ports Elizabeth, East London and Durban also were used. Finding immigrant arrival records for South Africa is not as easy as for many other countries such as Australia, New Zealand and the United States. Lists of early settlers who went to South Africa as part of an emigration scheme (such as the 1820 British Settlers) are available.

Lists in England. Researchers may trace shipping and passenger records more easily in the port of departure. Ships' passenger lists at the Public Records Office* in London are stored under reference BT27, Passenger Lists, Outwards 1890–1960. These lists supply the names of all passengers leaving the United Kingdom to ports outside of Europe and the Mediterranean Sea. Few lists prior to those of 1890 have survived.

Post-1890 lists have not been microfilmed; many are in fragile condition and searching them can be extremely time consuming. No indexes have been created, and most lists are not alphabetical. The information given varies, but may include age, occupation, last address and proposed destination. Lists are arranged monthly by port of departure. To use them with any realistic hope of finding a passenger's name, a researcher should know at least the approximate date of departure and the probable port of embarkation.

BT 32 Registers of Passenger Lists from 1906–51 include names of ships for which passenger lists exist in BT 26 and BT 27 (1890–1960). (BT 26 is the record group for ships coming into England.) Entries are not complete; the earliest years have entries for a few ports only and even these have omissions. Generally, the records are of real use only to a researcher who knows the name of the ship on which an individual sailed. They do not include names of passengers or the destination of the ships entered in the registers.

Other Lists. Hamburg is the only European port for which complete passenger lists exist for the years 1850–1934. These lists document more than 5.5 million persons and including sailing to other European ports and to overseas locations—including Africa (see IMMIGRATION).

Jewish Immigration. Jewish immigrants came by ship, most through Cape Town, although a minority entered at Durban, Lourenco Marques (now, Maputo, capital city of Mozambique) and Port Elizabeth. Major waves of migration occurred from 1895 onwards. Shipping agents, Knie and Co. and Spiro and Co., had subagents in Lithuanian shtetls who accepted bookings for passage to South Africa. Many Jews embarked initially at the port of Libau on the Baltic Sea and were transported on small cargo boats to England. A smaller number passed through Hamburg or Bremen. Many came first to Grimsby or London and were taken to the Poor Jews' Temporary Shelter in the East End of London, where they were provided board, lodgings, medical services and travel advice (http://chrysalis.its.uct.ac.za/shelter/shelter.htm). For example, from November 1902 to November 1903, 3,600 of the 4,500 individuals helped by the Poor Jews' Temporary Shelter went to South Africa, most on the Union Castle Line to Cape Town. Many records of the shelter clients are available.[4]

A photographic archive of all Union Castle ships (but no passenger records) exists at the Cape Archives Department, Cape Town.* Similar photographs of ships are kept at the National Maritime Museum* in Greenwich, England.

Naturalization Records

The National Archives holds naturalization records. These files contain copies of naturalization certificates and background papers for the applications. Details of birth place, occupation, age, length of residence in South Africa and addresses are given. Most South African Jews were naturalized in the Cape Colony or Province or in the Transvaal. State archives have copies of the naturalization certificates and background papers of the applications. Photocopies of the certificates and background papers can no longer be obtained by mail because the papers are too fragile, but microfilms are available on order and digital photographs may be taken after personal searches.

Libraries and Museums

Many public libraries have telephone directories, voter rolls, newspapers and much more that can help genealogists. University libraries also contain sections of genealogical interest. Museums, especially specialist museums, hold information pertinent to particular cultures, fashions of the day, historical themes or eras.

The library at the Jewish Board of Deputies* in Johannesburg has an extensive collection of at least 60 years of newspaper items referring to individual Jews. These are indexed and include obituaries. The South African Jewish Yearbooks (South African Jewry and The Jews of South Africa) of 1929, 1943, 1965, 1967/68 and of 1976/7 have brief biographies of many well-known Jews, including their towns of origin.. The library has microfilmed various publications of the South African Jewish press from the turn of the 20th century. A useful potential source of genealogical information are several Yiddish newspapers published in the early 1900s. In the 1920s, the newspapers published on a weekly basis many lists of people in Eastern Europe looking for relatives who had moved to South Africa. The lists are not indexed.

Some *landsmanshaftn* records are also on microfilm. Unfortunately, the records do not appear to be indexed. The Central Archives of the Jewish People* in Jerusalem holds copies of the microfilms, as does the Kaplan Centre for Jewish Studies at the University of Cape Town.* The Kaplan Centre also has records not available elsewhere of small Cape communities. The records of the Cape Jewish orphanage are here, as are some archives of the Zionist movement in South Africa.

Several books have been published on individual Jewish communities in smaller towns. In addition, many general town histories give a story of the local Jewish community. Several recent works listed in the Bibliography have dealt with the economic history of the South African Jews and are useful sources.

Other specialist Jewish libraries are the Gitlin Library* in Cape Town and the library at the Kaplan Centre* in Cape Town, incorporated in the Department of Hebrew and Jewish Studies. The Kaplan Centre seeks to stimulate and promote the field of Jewish studies and research at the University, with a special focus on the South African Jewish community. The Centre is not equipped to undertake genealogical research.

Specialist museums hold information pertinent to particular cultures, fashions of the day, historical themes or eras. The Cape Town Jewish Museum* and the Jewish Pioneers Memorial Museum (old Raleigh St. Synagogue)* have large collections of genealogical interest.

Drawing of Poor Jews Temporary Shelter in London, a stopping point for Eastern European Jews on the way to South Africa

Genealogical Societies

Jewish genealogical societies are active in Johannesburg* and Cape Town.* They do not undertake research on behalf of individual genealogists, but may advise on how to research one's own family. Both societies hold regular meetings, undertake projects and publish newsletters. Also valuable is the web-based South Africa Special Interest Group located at WWW.JEWISHGEN.ORG/SAFRICA and the South Africa SIG Discussion Group.*

The main genealogical society in South Africa is the Genealogical Society of South Africa* which was established in June 1964 and has regional branches. The Society does not undertake research on behalf of individuals but will guide, assist and teach you how to research your own family. The Society and its branches publish quarterly journals. The Genealogical Institute of South Africa* was founded in 1998 and is a private research center accessible to the public at a fee.

South Africa has few professional researchers and no specialists in Jewish genealogy. A central computerized genealogical database exists, however, and researchers may make a request for a listing of a particular name at the reading rooms of the individual regional archives. These listings include data on births, marriages and deaths; legal matters; passport applications; naturalizations; wills and probates. A printout provides direction to where the particular documents are housed. The staff is extremely helpful and responds to postal inquiries.

Documents available at an archives depot include: correspondence files, registers and other documents of government offices and the offices of local authorities that are, or were, located in the provinces concerned; photographs, maps and official publications; microfilms of documents housed in the depot concerned; estate files created before the dates listed under the Master of the Supreme Court* for the various provinces.

Even if preliminary inquiries are unsuccessful, they should be repeated later. Sometimes a second clerk may locate information overlooked in the first search. South African consular representatives abroad are often helpful in forwarding inquiries. They will take payment in local currency.

Newspapers

Jewish newspapers include the *South Africa Jewish Report,* the *Cape Jewish Chronicle, Hashalom* in KwaZulu-Natal and the *Pretoria Jewish Chronicle.* The South African Jewish Board of Deputies* publishes *Jewish Affairs,* which features articles of cultural, historical and communal interest. Some early issues of defunct Jewish newspapers such as the *Zionist Record* and the *Jewish Times* list new immigrants and names of people trying to trace families. The London *Jewish Chronicle* has many entries of South African Jews, such as obituaries and marriage notices.

Der Afrikaner Yiddishe Tzeitung was a Yiddish-language weekly newspaper published in Johannesburg from 1942 to 1971 (HTTP://WWW.JEWISHGEN.ORG/LITVAK/AFRIKANER.HTM). It ran a series of pictures, "A Picture from the Old Home," taken in Lithuanian shtetls before World War II (a few of the last of the series were Polish shtetls). From February 20, 1953, onward, the pictures were accompanied by an article about the shtetl called "There Once Was a Home." The number of people in each picture ranges from just a handful to more than 50; they are identified under each picture. This journal, although unindexed and in Yiddish, also has marriage an-

nouncements, anniversary notices and obituaries in almost every issue. Researchers with family roots in South Africa should check known marriage or death dates of individuals against the appropriate issue to look for family listings. The paper was available all over South Africa; no indexes of individuals or lists of places exist.

Jewish Sources

Specific information about individuals or communities often may be obtained from the South African Jewish Board of Deputies.* The Board controls Jewish cultural, educational, religious and social activities in South Africa and will arrange for publication of a family query in the Jewish press at no charge.

Synagogues and communal records include marriage authorization certificates and copies of *ketubot* (marriage certificates) and *gets* (divorce documents). Marriage records generally supply the full names and family names of both parties, their ages, occupations, marriage authorization certificates, the names of witnesses and of the rabbi. Synagogue minute books are a secondary source, but may have varied genealogical information. Records of many communities that have ceased to exist are kept in the Board of Deputies Library or at the Kaplan Centre* in Cape Town.

The South African Center for Jewish Migration and Genealogy Studies is a center primarily researching the estimated 15,000 core families who migrated to Southern Africa from the Baltic states between 1850–1950. The center is under the umbrella of the Isaac and Jessie Kaplan Center for Jewish Studies at the University of Cape Town and also has a public 'Discovery Centre', located at the South African Jewish Museum in Cape Town. Research focuses on the Eastern European locations where families originated from, patterns of migration to South Africa, places where families first settled, the connections to the broader non-Jewish communities, subsequent movements of Jews, the inter-relationships of families and where they have emigrated to.

This is the first academic center world wide to study Jewish Migration and Genealogy. The aim will be to perform the study at a graduate level. The primary focus will be on South African Jewry and its origins, but close co-operation with other major academic institutes, archives and genealogy interest groups internationally will be sought and maintained.

The project will be integrated in a multi-disciplinary manner within the University of Cape Town and anticipates close collaboration with the Center for Social Research at the same university. Formal courses and certification, including distance learning and the introduction of visiting research fellowships, are envisaged.

Shea Albert is Director of the South African Jewish Museum, Cape Town. Prof. Milton Shain is Director of the Isaac and Jessie Kaplan Centre for Jewish Studies and Research, University of Cape Town, Private Bag Rondebosch 7701, South Africa. Saul Issroff is the project director. E-mail: KAPGEN@HUMANITIES.UCT.AC.ZA.

The office of the chief (Orthodox) rabbi, United Hebrew Congregation* answers written requests for copies of marriage and divorce certificates. Reform communities keep separate records. (Reform is named the United Progressive Jewish

The Star, A Yiddish-language newspaper, published in Johannesburg from 1903–1907, contained announcements from the Hebrew congregations in the area.

Congregation of Johannesburg.*) There is also a strong Lubavich movement and smaller Sephardi and Masorti congregations. Forty-eight Orthodox religious groups are listed in Johannesburg in 2002. No information about accessing their records is available at this time.

LDS (Mormon) Resources for South African Jewish Genealogy Research

This document, compiled by Roy Ogus, Palo Alto, California, summarizes the collection of key records available in the LDS Family History Library (FHL) microfilms that are relevant and useful for Jewish genealogical research in South Africa. Full details of the films can be found in the FHL catalog; the catalog should be consulted before ordering any particular film for review (see LDS). The references are divided here into several categories, and the film numbers of the key films to start research in the particular category are provided.

Estate and Probate Documentation. Estate films typically include the following documents: death notices, wills, and liquidation and distribution accounts. Sometimes other documents are included, such as a pre-nuptial agreements. Both indexes and copies of the actual estate documentation can be found on the microfilms. In the sections below, only the index film numbers are indicated; once the name of interest (together with the estate number) is found in the index, refer to the FHL catalog to determine the film number(s) that should contain the actual documentation.

Cape Province. Complete estate documents, 1834–1950; estate registers (with only date and estate number) available for 1930–89

Estate Index Film numbers:
1834–1912: 1258607 through 1258611
1834–1918: 1367980, 1367981 (alternate films)
1913–1925: 1367987, 1367988
1926–1943: 1367988, 1686870, 1686871, 1686879
1944–1953: 1686879, 1686880, 1670583
Original Wills and Testaments, 1923–28. Documents are sequenced by will number and approximately by estate number.
Film numbers are in the range 1670337 through 1670640, but not all film numbers are used.

Transvaal. Complete estate documents, 1873–1950; Index information, 1873–1958; estate index film numbers: 1873–1910: 0918691 1911–58: 0918692 through 0918699; alternate estate index film numbers: 1873–1956: 1439126, 1439127 1911–58: 1439128, 1439129, 1439131

Natal. Complete estate documents, 1871–1950; Index information available, 1871–1947; Estate index film numbers: 1871–1947: 1295096, 1295409, 1367346, 1367365; Alternate estate index film number: 1840–1956: 1560758.

Orange Free State. Complete estate documents, 1853–1950; Estate index film numbers: 1854–1905: 1367419, 1906–76: 1864338 through 1864341, 1977–92: 1864341 through 1864343.

Naturalization Applications (Cape Colony only)

Available for the period 1883–1911, these documents have considerable genealogical value. They include age information and birth location information, plus details of residence both in the Cape Colony and the British Empire, if applicable.

Documents are filmed in rough alphabetical order. Film numbers:
1883–1911: 1281590, 1281591, 1281592, 1281593, 1281594

Death Certificates

Death certificate documents are available for certain time periods and for selected provinces, as follows. Entries are in rough chronological order, and records are grouped alphabetically by location. No indexes exist. Note: The date of death needs to be known fairly accurately. In order to find a specific certificate, the date of death must be known fairly accurately, but it may be necessary to search before and after the date of death because some certificates were filmed out of order. Consult the FHL catalog to find the precise film numbers for a particular year and location.

National coverage, 1955–65; Film numbers in the range: 1925527 through 1926125 (not all film numbers are used)

Cape Province, 1895–1928; Film numbers in range: 1768645 through 1768970, 1887008 through 1887235, 1925589 through 1926175 (not all film numbers are used)

Transvaal, 1888–1954; Film numbers in range: 1887020 through 1887233, 1925519 through 1925810, 1768631 through 1768968 (not all film numbers are used)

Miscellaneous

These references provide spotty coverage of a few locations and time periods.

Burial, marriage and death information for Cape Town. Interment registers for several Cape Town cemeteries:
1886–1981; indexes are included; 1258779, 1259122 through 1259150

Marriage and death certificates, Cape Town Jewish Congregation:
1851–1989 1560759 through 1560764, 1560773 through 1560775

Jewish Helping Hand and Burial Society (*chevra kadisha*), Jewish cemetery records Johannesburg: Film number: 1259151

City and telephone directories: Rand-Pretoria City directory (covers Pretoria, Johannesburg, and environs): 1942, 0990149;, 1943, 0990150;, 1944, 0990153;, 1945, 0990154;, 1947, 0990163;, 1948, 0990164;, 1949, 0990165;, 1953, 0990166;, 1954, 0990167;, 1960, 0990168;, 1962, 0990169

United Transvaal City directory (covers Johannesburg, Pretoria, and other Transvaal towns): 1925–6 0990143, 0990144; 1934 0990144, 0990145; 1940 0990145, 0990146

Telephone directory: Transvaal; 1951 1441072

Telephone directory: Orange Free State, Northern Cape, Basutoland; 1946 1224502; 1950 1441072

Other

Register of medical practitioners and dentists for the Union of South Africa on January 1, 1945.

Addresses
General Resources

Central Statistical Services, Demographics, Private Bag x44, Pretoria 0001; Contact: Information Officer; telephone: 27-12-310-8911;

fax: 27-12-322-3374; e-mail: ILSEVR@STATSSA.PWV.GOV.ZA; website: WWW.STATSSA.GOV.ZA. Has information about specific individuals, relationships, religion, year of arrival and place of birth.

Home Affairs

Department of Home Affairs (Naturalizations), Private Bag x114, Pretoria 0001, or 242 Struben Street, Pretoria 0001; telephone: 27-12-314-8570; fax: 27-12-323-5955; website: WWW.HOME-AFFAIRS.GOV.ZA/INDEX.ASP. Email: DHA@DBS1.PWV.GOV.ZA.

Genealogical Institute of South Africa (GISA), 115 Banghoek Road, Stellenbosch or P.O. box 3033, Matieland 7602; fax: 2-21-887-5031; website: WWW.SUN.AC.ZA/GISA.

Masters of the Supreme Court (Wills and Probates), Master of the Master of the Supreme Court, Private Bag x20584, Bloemfontein, 9300.

Master of the Supreme Court, Private Bag x9018, Cape Town, 8000.

Master of the Supreme Court, Private Bag x1010, Grahamstown, 6140.

Master of the Supreme Court, Private Bag x9010, Pietermaritzburg, 3200.

Registrar (Births, Marriages and Deaths); Department of Home Affairs; Private Bag x114, Pretoria 0001, or Sentrakor Building, 173 Pretorius Street, Pretoria 0001; telephone: 27-12-314-8911; fax: 27-12-314- 8911.

Supreme Court, Private Bag x60, Pretoria 0001, or Santam Building, Church and Queen Streets, Pretoria 0001; telephone: 27-12-323 - 2404.

Land Registry Records

Registrar of Deeds, Private Bag x9073, Cape Town 8000, or Government Building, Plein Street, Cape Town; telephone: 27-21-45-1037.

Maps

Registrar of Companies, Zanza Buildings, Proes Str., Pretoria 0002; telephone: 27-12-310-8740.

Registrar of Patents, Designs and Trademarks,Zanza Buildings, Proes Str., Pretoria 0002; telephone: 27-12-310-8700.

Surveyor General, Private Bag x9073, Cape Town 8000; telephone: 27-21-45-4711.

National Archives Repositories

Head, National Archives Repository (houses both the Archives of Central Government and of Gauteng, formerly Transvaal Province), Private Bag x236, Pretoria 0001, or 24 Hamilton Street, Arcadia, Pretoria 0001; telephone: 27-12-323-5300; fax: 27-12-323 5287; email: ARG02@ACTS.PWV.GOV.ZA; WWW.NATIONAL.ARCHIVES.GOV.ZA/NAAIRS_CONTENT.HTM.

Chief, Free State Archives Department, Private Bag x20504, Bloemfontein 9300, or 37 Elizabeth Street, Bloemfontein 9301.

Head, Cape Town Archives Repository, Private Bag x9025, Cape Town 8000, or 72 Roeland Street Cape Town 8001; telephone: 27-21-462-4050; fax: 27-21-45-2960.

Head, Durban Archives Repository, Private Bag x22, Greyville 4023, or Nashua Building, 14 Demazenod Road, Greyville 4023; telephone: 27-31-309-5681/4; fax: 27-31-309-5685.

Chief, Natal Archives Depot, Pietermaritzburg Archives Repository, Private Bag x9012, Pietermaritzburg 3200, or 231 Pietermaritz Street, Pietermaritz 3201.

Head, Port Elizabeth Archives Repository, Private Bag x3932, North End 6056, or 1 De Villiers Street, North End, Port Elizabeth 6000; telephone: 27-41-54 6451; fax: 27-41-54-6451.

Military Records

Commonwealth War Graves Commission, website: HTTP://WWW.CWGC.ORG/.

South African National Defence Force Archives, Department of Defence, Documentation Service Directorate, Private Bag x289, Pretoria 0001; telephone: 27-21-322-6350, ext. 227; fax: 27-21-323 5613.

South Africa Defence Force Archives, Private Bag x615, Pretoria 0001.

South African Military History Society, P.O.Box 59227, Kengray, 2100, South Africa; telephone: 27-11-648-2087; fax: 27-11-648-2085; website: RAPIDTTP.COM/MILHIST or RAPIDTTP.CO.ZA/MILHIST.

Chief Archivist (no personal records), South Africa National Museum of Military History, P.O. Box 52090, Saxonwold, 2132 Transvaal; telephone: 27-11-646-5513; fax: 27-11-646-5256.

War Graves Board, 153 Blackwood Street, Pretoria, 0001

Jewish Resources

Durban United Hebrew Congregation, Great Synagogue, 75 Silverton Road, Durban; telephone: 27-31-201-5177.

Johannesburg Jewish Helping Hand and Burial Society (chevra kadisha), postal address: Private Bag X7, Sandringham 2131; telephone: 27-11-532-9600; fax: 27-11-532-9655; e-mail: CHEVRAHGROUP@JHBCHEV.CO.ZA; website: WWW.JHBCHEV.CO.ZA.

South African Jewish Report (weekly newspaper): CARRO@GLOBAL.CO.ZA.

South African Union for Progressive Judaism (SAUPJ), P.O. Box 1190, Houghton, Johannesburg 2041; telephone: 27-11-642-7903; fax: 27-11-64-7904.

Union of Orthodox Synagogues of South Africa (UOS) and Office of the Chief Rabbi, P.O. Box 46559, Orange Grove 2119; telephone: 27-11-485- 4865; fax: 27-11-640-7528; e-mail: JHB@UOS.CO.ZA; website: WWW.UOS.CO.ZA.

Union of Orthodox Synagogues of South Africa and Beth Din, 191 Buitenkant Street, Gardens, Cape Town 8001; P.O. Box 543, Cape Town, 8000; telephone: 27-21-461-6310; fax: 27-21-461-8320; e-mail: UOSCAPE@IAFRICA.COM.

United Chevra Kadisha, Telephone: +27-(0)21-4616310, Fax: +27-(0)21- 4618320.

Burial Societies and Cemeteries

Chevra Kadisha (burial society), Selbourne Road, Durban; telephone: 27-31-201-5177; fax: 27-31-201-1964; e-mail: SHUL@DUHC.ORG.ZA.

Chevra Kadisha (burial society), P.O. Box 2089, Port Elizabeth, 6000, Eastern Cape; telephone: 27-41-581-3529.

Griqualand West Jewish Burial Society, P.O. Box 68, Kimberley 8300; fax: 27-53-181-1281.

Red Hill Cemetery, Durban; telephone: 27-31-564- 5771 or 201-5177.

United Hebrew Institutions of Bloemfontein, P.O. Box 1152, Bloemfontein 9301, Orange Free State; telephone: 27-51-436-2207; fax: 27-51-536-6447.

Museums Libraries of Jewish Interest

Jacob Gitlin Library, 88 Hatfield Street, Gardens, 8001, P.O. Box 4176, Cape Town, 8000; telephone: 27-21-4625088; fax: 27-21-4658671; e-mail: GITLIB@NETACTIVE.CO.ZA.

Israel Aaron Maisels Reference and Lending Library of the SA Zionist Federation, 2 Elray Street, Raedene, Johannesburg 2192, Private Bag X6, Sandringham, 2131; telephone: 27-11-645-2500; fax: 27-11-645-1325.

Jewish Studies Library, University of Cape Town; telephone: 27-21-650-3779; fax: 27-21-650-3062; e-mail: VERONICA@UCTLIB.UCT.AC.ZA; website: WWW.LIB.UCT.AC.ZA/VIRTUAL/1132.HTM.This academic research institute does not do genealogy research.

Jewish Pioneers Memorial Museum (Raleigh St. Synagogue), cnr Raleigh and Edward Street, Port Elizabeth 6001; telephone: 27-41-373-5197; e-mail: EFFIE@IAFRICA.COM.

Kaplan Centre for Jewish Studies, University of Cape Town, Private Bag Rondebosch 7701, Cape Town. Tel: +27-(0)21-6503062; fax: +27-(0)21-6503062. Email: KAPGEN@HUMANITIES.UCT.AC.ZA. Website: WWW.UCT.AC.ZA/DEPTS/KAPLAN/INDEX.HTM.

South Africa Friends of Beit Hatefutsoth (South Africa Country Communities Research Project), Private Bag X6, Sandringham 2131, Johannesburg. fax: 27-11-880-6273; website: WWW.JEWISHDORPS.ORG. Ongoing project to document country Jews.

Malmesbury Museum, 1 Prospect Street, Malmesbury 7300; telephone: 27-22-442-2332. The museum is housed in the synagogue that once served the now-defunct Malmesbury Jewish congregation. Artifacts focus on the Jewish community, 1905–75.

Librarian, South African Jewish Board of Deputies, 2 Elray Street, Raedene, Johannesburg 2192; telephone: 27-11-645-2523; fax: 27-11-645-2559; e-mail: SAJBOD@IAFRICA.COM; website: WWW.SAJBD. ORG.ZA.

South African Jewish Museum, Old Synagogue, 84 Hatfield Street, Gardens, Cape Town 8001; telephone: 27 21 465-1546; fax: 27-21-465-0284; e-mail: INFO@SAJMUSEUM.CO.ZA.

General Libraries and Museums

Africana Library, Du Toitspan Road, P.O. Box 627, Kimberley 8300. Has some local Jewish communal records.

Albany Museum, Somerset Street, Grahamstown, 6140; telephone: 27-46-622-2312; fax: 27-46-622- 2398; e-mail: AMWJ@GIRAFFE.RU.AC.ZA; website: WWW.RU.AC.ZA/DEPARTMENTS/AM/GENERAL. Has a genealogical section relating to the 1820 settlers and some local Jewish communal material.

Cory Library for Historical Research, Grahamstown; telephone: 27-46-603-8436; fax: 27-46-622-3487; e-mail: LBSR@GIRAFFE.RU.AC.ZA; website: WWW.RU.AC.ZA/DEPARTMENTS/LIB/CORY. Has some local Jewish communal records.

Johannesburg Public Library, Market Square, Johannesburg 2000; telephone: 27-11-836-3787; e-mail: JOBURG@MJ.ORG.ZA; website: JOBURG.ORG/ZA/JHLIB. Has newspapers, some Hebraica and Judaica books.

Port Elizabeth City Library, Main St., Port Elizabeth 6000. Holds card index of Jewish notables and country cemetery details.

South African Library Queen Victoria Street, Cape Town 8001; telephone: 27-21-424-6320; fax: 27-21 424-4848; website: ALEPH.SALIB.AC.ZA. National legal repository of all South Africa published material.

State Library of South Africa, P.O. Box 397, Pretoria 0001, or Andries and Vermeulen Street, Pretoria; telephone: 27-12-21-8931; fax: 27-12-32-5594; e-mail: POSTMASTER@STATELIB.PWV-GOV.ZA.

Genealogical Societies, Jewish

Jewish Family History Society of Cape Town, P.O. Box 51985, Waterfront, 8002; telephone: 27 -21-434-4825, 27-21-423-0223.

Jewish Genealogical Society of Johannesburg, P.O. Box 1388, Parklands, 2121; Newsletter: Yichus.

Genealogical Societies – General

Genealogical Institute of South Africa (GISA), P.O. Box 3033, Matieland 7602; telephone: 27-21-887- 5070; fax: 27-21-887-5031; e-mail: GISA@RENET.SUN.AC.ZA; website: WWW.SUN.AC.ZA/GISA/INDEX.HTML. This is a semi-commercial organization.

Genealogical Society of South Africa, Suite 143, Postnet x2600, Houghton 2041; website: WWW.GENWEB.NET~MERCON; research inquiries secretary: Natalie da Silva, e-mail: NATALIE@FUTURE.JHB.CO.ZA; newsletter *Generations*: WWW.RUPERT.NET/~LKOOL.

National Maritime Museum, Romney Road, Greenwich, London SE10 9NF, England; telephone: 44-(0)208-858-4422; website: WWW.NMM.AC.UK.

Public Records Office (PRO) Kew, Richmond, Surrey TW9 4DU, Great Britain; telephone: 44-(0)208-876 3444; fax: 44-(0)208-878-8905; websites: online catalogues: HTTP://WWW.PRO.GOV.UK/. Family Records: WWW.FAMILYRECORDS.GOV.UK/. Moving here: WWW.MOVINGHERE.ORG.UK/.

South Africa Genealogical Societies information: HOME.GLOBAL.CO.ZA~MERCON/INDEX.HTML.

Bibliography

Abrahams, Israel. *The Birth of a Community: a History of Western Province Jewry from Earliest Times to the End of the South African War, 1902.* Cape Town: Cape Town Hebrew Congregation, 1955.

Arkin, Marcus, ed. *South African Jewry: A Contemporary Survey.* Cape Town: Oxford University Press, 1984. (Good review with extensive annotated bibliography).

Belling, Veronica. *Bibliography of South African Jewry.* Kaplan Centre and UCT Libraries: Cape Town, 1997.

Caspar, Rabbi Bernard Moses. *A Decade with South African Jewry.* Cape Town: Howard Timmins, 1972.

Cohen, S. *A History of the Jews of Durban, 1825–1918.* Ph.D. dissertation, University of Natal, Durban, 1982.

Der Afrikaner Yidishe Tzeitung, a Yiddish-language weekly newspaper published in Johannesburg, 1942–71. Microfilm, New York Public Library Jewish Division (Call No. *ZAN-*P49); YIVO (Call No. 64-Y-294-309); U.S. Library of Congress Hebraic Section).

de Saxe, Morris and I.M. Goodman, eds. *South African Jewish Year Book 1929.* Johannesburg: South Africa Jewish Historical Society, 1929.

Dictionary of South African Biography, 5 vols. Pretoria: Human Sciences Research Council. Various dates.

Dubb, Allie A. The Jewish Population of South Africa: The 1991 Sociodemographic Survey. Cape Town: Kaplan Centre, 1994.

Durban United Hebrew Congregation. *Durban United Hebrew Congregation Centenary, 1884–1984: 100 Years.* Durban: D.U.H.C., 1984.

Feldberg, Leon, ed. *South African Jewry: A Survey of the Jewish Community; Its Contributions to South Africa; Directory of Communal Institutions; Who's Who of Leading Personalities 1965.* Johannesburg: Fieldhill, 1965.

———. *South African Jewry: A Survey of the Jewish Community; Its Contributions to South Africa; Directory of Communal Institutions; Who's Who of Leading Personalities,* rev. ed. Johannesburg: Fieldhill, 1968.

———. *South African Jewry 1976/77.* Roodepoort: Alex White, 1977.

These year books have surveys of most aspects of Jewish life in South Africa and very good brief biographies of many prominent individuals.

Feldman, Leibl. *Oudtshoorn: Jerusalem of Africa.* Ed. by Joseph Sherman. Trans. by Lilian Dubb and Sheila Barkusky from Yiddish 1941 ed. Johannesburg: Friends of the Library, University of Witwatersrand, 1989.

———. *Yidn in Dorem Afrika.* Vilna, 1937.

———. *Yidn in Yohannesburg: biz yunion, 31-tn May, 1910.* (Jews of Johannesburg). [Yiddish] Johannesburg: South Africa Yiddish Cultural Federation, 1956.

Gad, Rabbi J. *Sefer Toldot Beit Josef.* 2 vols. Johannesburg: Rabbi J. Gad, 1941. [Hebrew] (Possibly the only *sefer prenumerantn* published in South Africa. Lists about 1,800 subscribers.)

Friedman, S. *Guide to Jewish Research Resources in the Cape Province: Addenda to volumes I, II and III.* Cape Town: Kaplan Centre, University of Cape Town, 1989.

———. "The Jewish Studies Documentary Collection at UCT: An Unexpected Resource for African Studies." *Jagger Journal* 7 (1986/87): 11–13.

Friedman, S. and N. Kagan. *A Guide to Jewish Research Resources in the Cape Province,* 3 vols. Cape Town: Kaplan Centre, UCT, 1984. Vol. 1: Synagogues and Research Institutions of the South-Western Cape; Vol. 2: Jewish Cultural, Educational, Sports, Welfare and Zionist organizations of the South-Western Cape; Vol. 3: The Religious and Communal Organizations of East London, Kimberley, Port Elizabeth and the Cape Country Communities. Review: Vol. 1: Cabo 3(4), 1985: 311; Vol. II: Cabo 4(1), 1986:25]

Gillon, Philip. *Seventy Years of Southern African Aliyah.* Israel: South Africa Zionist Federation-Telfed, Adar Productions, 1992.

Gitlin, Marcia. *The Vision Amazing: The Story of South African Zionism.* Johannesburg: Menorah Book Club, 1950.

Herrman, Louis. *A History of the Jews in South Africa from the Earliest Times to 1895.* London: Victor Gollancz, 1930.

———. *A History of the Jews in South Africa from the Earliest Times to 1895.* rev. South African ed. Johannesburg, Cape Town: South African Jewish Board of Deputies, 1935.

Hoffman, N.D. *Book of Memoirs: Reminiscences of South African Jewry: Contemporary Observations on the Social Environment in the Early Twentieth Century, Collected in the Book "The Jews of South Africa" Published in 1916.* Trans. by Lilian Dubb and Sheila Barkunsky. Cape Town: Jewish Publications, Kaplan Centre, 1996.

———. *Sefer Hazichrones: erinnerungen fun a Litvishen maskil in drey welt-theyin, Europe, Amerike un Afrika* (Jews in South Africa: of all matters concerning Jews and Judaism). Cape Town: N. Hoffman, 1916.

Hoffman, N.D., ed. *Der Soyt-Afrikanisher Yohr-bukh* (South Africa Jewish Year Book). [Yiddish] Cape Town: Beinkenstadt, 1920.

Jewish Affairs, quarterly Journal. Johannesburg: Jewish Board of Deputies of South Africa. Ed Prof. Joseph Sherman. P.O. Box 87557, Houghton 2041; published from 1940s onward.

Jewish Life in the South African Country Communities. Volume 1: The Northern Great Escarpment, The Lowveld, The Northern Highveld, The Bushveld. The South African Friends of Beth Hatefusoth: Johannesburg, 2003. Researched by The South African Friends of Beth Hatefusoth.

Jowell, Phyllis, and Adrienne Folb. *Joe Jowell of Namaqualand: The Story of a Modern Day Pioneer.* Vlaeberg: Fernwood, 1994.

Kaplan, Mendel, and Marian Robertson. *Jewish Roots in the South African Economy.* Cape Town: Struik, 1986.

———. *Founders and Followers: Johannesburg Jewry 1887–1915.* Cape Town: Vlaeberg, 1991. Comprehensive socio-history with very good bibliography.

Katz, Jill, ed. *The Story of the Pretoria Jewish Community up to 1930.* Bophuthatswana: Heer, 1987.

Katzew, Henry. *South Africa's 800: The Story of South African Volunteers in Israel's War of Birth.* Microfilm in the New York Public Library Jewish Division (Call No.*ZAN-*P49), at YIVO (Call No 64-Y-294-309) and in the Library of Congress Hebraic Section.

Kosmin, B.A. *Majuta: A History of the Jewish Community of Zimbabwe.* Gwelo: Mambo, 1980.

Krut, Riva M. *Building a Home and a Community: Jews in Johannesburg. 1886–1914.* Ph.D. dissertation. London: University of London, 1985.

Lombard, R.T.J. *Handbook for Genealogical Research in South Africa.* Pretoria: Human Sciences Research Council, 1990.

Mendelsohn, Richard. *Sammy Marks: The Uncrowned King of the Transvaal.* Cape Town: David Philip; Athens, Ohio: Ohio University Press in association with Jewish Publications, South Africa, 1991.

Mitchell, W.H. and L.A. Sawyer. *The Cape Run: Everything You Need to Know About Ships to the Cape.* Lavenham, England: Terence Dalton, 1984.

Murray, M. *Ships and South Africa.* London: Oxford University Press, 1933.

———. *Union Castle Chronicle 1853–1953.* London: Longmans Green, 1953.

Musiker, Naomi. *Guide to the Manuscript Archives in the South African Jewish Board of Deputies.* Johannesburg: Scarecrow, 2001.

Press, Charles. *The Light of Israel: The Story of the Paarl Jewish Community.* Paarl: Jubilee Publications, 1993.

Redgrave, J.J. *Port Elizabeth in Bygone Days.* Wynberg, Cape: Rustica, 1947: 519–24.

Sachs, Bernard. *The Fordsburg-Mayfair Jewish Community 1893–1964.* Johannesburg: Eagle, 1972.

Saron, Gustav, and Louis Hotz, eds. *The Jews in South Africa from the Earliest Times to 1895.* Cape Town, London, New York: Geoffrey Cumberlege and Oxford University Press, 1955.

Saron, Gustav and Naomi Musiker. *The Jews of South Africa: An Illustrated History to 1953.* Johannesburg: Scarecrow, 2001.

Shain, Milton. *Jewry and Cape Society.* Cape Town: Historical Publication Society, 1983.

Shimoni, Gideon, *Community and Conscience: Jews in Apartheid South Africa.* Hanover and London: University Press of New England, 2003. Also Cape Town: David Philip.

Shimoni, Gideon. *Jews and Zionism: The South African Experience 1910–1967.* Cape Town: Oxford University Press, 1980.

Shimoni, Gideon, ed. *The Jews of South Africa.* Tel Aviv: Beit Hatefutsoth, Nahum Goldmann Museum of the Jewish Diaspora, 1983.

Shur, Chaim. *Shomrim in the Land of Apartheid: The Story of Hashomer Hatzair in South Africa 1935–1970.* Givat Haviva/Havazelet: Yad Yaari-Maarechet, 1998.

Sichel, Frieda ed. *From Refugee to Citizen.* Cape Town, Amsterdam: A.A. Balkema, 1966.

South African Jews in World War II. Johannesburg: South Africa Jewish Board of Deputies, 1950.

Journals & Newsletters Relating to Genealogy in South Africa

FAMILIA: The Quarterly Publication of the GSSA; MDUPREEZ@MWEB.CO.ZA.

Generations: A South African genealogy newsletter. Website: www.RUPERT.NET/~LKOOL. Suite 556, 185-911 Yates Street, Victoria, British Columbia V8V 4Y9, Canada. South African agent: Ms. Z. Castanho, Postnet 17, Private Bage X19, Gardenview, 2047, RSA.

Journal of the Jewish Family History Society of South Africa, P.O. Box 541, Sea Point 8060, South Africa; EWFAMCT@GLOBAL.CO.ZA.

Southern African S.I.G. Newsletter: 5450 Whitley Park Terrace #901 Bethesda MD, 20814 USA; telephone: 1-301-493-5179; fax: 1-301-493-9081; e-mail: MGETZ@EROLS.COM. Printed newsletter of the South African Special Interest Group.

Yichus, the publication of the Jewish Genealogical Society, Johannesburg, P.O. Box 1388, Parklands, Republic of South Africa.

Countries of Central and Southern Africa and Adjacent Islands

Jews settled in many small African countries between 1880 and 1930. Some countries previously were Belgian, British, French, German or Portuguese colonies or protectorates. Most of these communities have dwindled in numbers or even vanished, and information for most is sparse.

An African Jewish Congress, based in Johannesburg, was established in 1994 to attend to the religious needs of the Jews remaining in these areas and to look after Jewish graves and old synagogues. The spiritual leader travels extensively to visit remaining Jews, to photograph cemeteries and old synagogues and to look after areas of Jewish importance. To date he has recorded more than 14,000 tombstones in South Africa and adjacent areas.

The names of some of the South East African and Central African countries have changed. All of the following were once British and, except for Nyasaland, Tanganyika and Uganda, all had significant Jewish communities: Botswana was previously Bechuanaland, Lesotho was Basutoland, Malawi was Nyasaland, Swaziland was Swaziland, Tanzania was a combination of Tanganyika and Zanzibar, Zambia was Northern Rhodesia and Zimbabwe was Southern Rhodesia. Kenya, Tanganyika and Uganda were grouped together as British colonies prior to independence. Mauritius, an island in the Indian ocean, has been French and British. Tanganyika was German East Africa prior to World War I.

German South West Africa, now called Namibia, became a protectorate under the League of Nations and was governed by South Africa until becoming independent in 1990. About 30 Jews live there now, but the Jewish community had approximately 50 families at its peak, and they were very important in commercial development of the country.

Mozambique and Angola were Portuguese colonies, now independent. The old Congo states, French and Belgium, had significant Jewish settlements until independence.

Angola

Jewish cemeteries may be found in at least three Angolan communities. In Benguela, the general cemetery "Campo da Igualdade" has a small Jewish corner. In Catumbela, the general cemetery has 12 Jewish graves; the earliest burial was 1892. In Luanda, the general cemetery of Alto das Cruzes has two Jewish tombstones.

Botswana

A number of Jews were prominent farmers and traders in the 19th and 20th centuries and contributed in many ways to the development of this sparsely populated, vast country. A small community still exists in Gaborone. There, Jews are buried in the cemetery with others.

Cabo Verde (Cape Vert or Cape Verde)

The Republic of Cape Verde consists of 10 islands about 300 miles off the coast of West Africa. From the period of the Spanish and Portuguese Inquisitions until the late 19th century, this predominantly Catholic area had Jewish residents fleeing from religious persecution or searching for greater economic opportunity. During the 19th century, Jews of Spanish descent from Gibraltar and Morocco settled there (see MOROCCO). There are four Jewish cemeteries: Cidade da Praia, Santiago Island, a small, separate Jewish cemetery; Cidade da Ponta do Sol, Santo Antao Island, with a large number of Jewish interburials; Campinas, Penha de Franca, Santo Antao Island, with six Jewish tombstones; and Paul, Santo Antao Island (no details available). Tombstones often list town of origin in Morocco. For more information contact Carol S. Castiel, 1245 4th Street, SW, Suite E202, Washington D.C.; telephone: (202) 484-8283; fax: (202) 554-7794; e-mail: CASTIEL@AOL.COM.

Kenya

Jewish settlement, mainly in Nairobi, dates from around 1900 when the British government offered the Zionists a territory for an autonomous Jewish settlement. Theodore Herzl refused the offer, but shortly thereafter, a few Jews settled in the colony. Later, some Central European refugees settled. Approximately 165 Jewish families currently live in Kenya, including a number of Israelis. Nairobi Hebrew Congregation, established in 1904, can be contacted at P.O. Box 40990 Nairobi; telephone: 254-22-2770. (see Carlebach, Julius. *Jews of Nairobi 1903–1963*. Nairobi: Nairobi Hebrew Congregation, 1962)

Madeira

A Jewish cemetery has existed at Funchal since 1851.

Mauritius

A small Jewish expatriate community exists today. The Jewish cemetery is the site of graves of about 135 refugees denied entry into Palestine and interned by the British on the island during the period 1940–45.

Mozambique

The capital of Mozambique, Maputo, previously called Lourenco Marques, has a Jewish cemetery, Cemiterjo Comunal Israelita, Avenida Latino Coelho. The cemetery, used between 1880 and 1960, has approximately 100 tombstones. Some names are Portuguese, but others are English or East European. Many of those buried here were immigrants from Lithuania to South Africa in the period 1880–1940 and settled in Lourenco Marques rather than in South Africa itself. At least two Jews, Lina Goldstein and Joshua Krongold, are buried in the (non-Jewish) Beira cemetery, in a northern city.

A small community is still active today; a few members are *conversos,* but most are expatriates from all over the world working mainly for non-governmental aid agencies. Address: Jewish Community of Mozambique: P.O. Box 232, Maputo; telephone: 258-494-413.

Namibia

Jews have been present in the capital city of Windhoek since its establishment, but the community which had 170 families in 1965, has dwindled to approximately 30 families today.

Swaziland

A small Jewish community exists, mainly in the capital city of Mbabane. Jews are buried with others.

Zaire

Under Belgian colonial rule (pre-1960), an estimated 2,500 Jews lived in eight communities, centered in Elisabethville. Most of this largely Sephardic community came from Rhodes or Salonika, Greece, and many settled in the Cape Province, South Africa after Zaire gained independence. Now there are about 85 Jews in Kinhasa (Leopoldville) and a few in Lumbasha (Elisabethville) and smaller towns. A number of Israeli expatriates work in Zaire.

Zambia

Approximately 35 Jews now live in the country, mainly in Lusaka. The Zambian "Copperbelt" was an important copper mining and trading area to which many Litvaks emigrated around 1880. For information, contact The Council for Zambia Jewry, Ltd., P.O. Box 30020, Lusaka 10101, Zambia; telephone: 260-22-9190; fax: 260-22 -1428.

Zimbabwe

Daniel Montague Kisch arrived in the country in 1869, long before the British South Africa Company (headed by Cecil John Rhodes) received its charter in 1889. Kisch become the main adviser to the tribal chief, King Lobengula. Many Jewish pioneers of Eastern European origin emigrated to this area beginning in the 1880s, and their efforts were fundamental to the development of the country. Later, some Jews arrived from the South, some walking from the east-coast Portuguese territory of Mozambique. In the 1930s, a small group of German refugees settled mainly in Salisbury (now Harare) and Bulawayo. A community from the Greek island of Rhodes also came to this area in the 1930s.

Approximately 900 Jews now live in Zimbabwe, about 600 in Harare and 300 in Bulawayo. Each community has its own synagogues and Jewish day schools.

Central Africa Genealogy Lists

The following Central Africa countries have web-based genealogy mailing lists. To subscribe send a message to: MAJORDOMO@LISTSERV.NORTHWEST.COM. Put subscribe listname (e.g., "subscribe angola") in the body of the message. Cities with lists are: Angola, Burundi, Cameroon, Central African Republic, Congo, Equatorial Guinea, Gabon, Kenya, Malawi, Rwanda, Somalia, Tanzania, Uganda, Zaire and Zambia.

Addresses

Bulawayo Hebrew Congregation, P.O. Box 337, Bulawayo, Zimbabwe; telephone: 60 829

City of Bulawayo: Athlone Avenue cemetery: Hebrew section
Bulawayo cemetery: Progressive Hebrew section
Harare Hebrew Congregation, P.O. Box 342, Harare, Zimbabwe; telephone: 72 7576
Office of the Registrar, Births, Marriages and Deaths; P.O. Box 7734, Causeway, Harare, Zimbabwe. For vital records, send a letter with the full name, date and place of birth, marriage or death and a bank draft for 10 Zimbabwe dollars to this office.
Sephardi Hebrew Congregation, P.O. Box 1051, Harare, Zimbabwe; telephone: 72 2899
Zimbabwe Jewish Board of Deputies, P.O. Box 1954, Harare, Zimbabwe; telephone: 70 2506 and P.O. Box 1456, Bulawayo, Zimbabwe; telephone: 67-383

Bibliography

Kosmin, B.A. *Majuta: A History of the Jewish Community of Zimbabwe*. Gwelo: Mambo, 1980.

Note

1. smous /sm@Us, smaUs/ n. Also schmous, smaus, smouse. Pl. smouses, smouse /sm@Us@/, rarely schmousen. [S. Afr. Du., hawker, pedlar, transf. use of Du. smous "Jew, usurer, supposed to be the same word as G. dialect schmus talk, patter" (OED); cf. Yiddish s(c)hmooz(e) heart-to-heart talk, fr. Hebrew schmuos "(originally) "things heard"; (in time) "rumors", "idle talk".' (L. Rostein, The joys of Yiddish 1968). <> The obs. spellings "smaus" and "smouse" suggest that /-aU-/ was a common pronunciation in the past.] Esp. during the 19th century: a (Jewish) itinerant trader; a peddler; a hawker; smouch n.; smouser. Also attrib. See also togt-ganger (togt n. sense 1 b). Ref: The Dictionary Unit for South African English (an Associated Institute of Rhodes University, Grahamstown, South Africa).

2. Gideon Shimoni, Community and Conscience. The Jews in Apartheid South Africa. Brandies, UPNE. 2003.

3. Mahal or Machal (Hebrew acronym for volunteers from abroad) was set up by the Jewish Agency in 1948 to supplement the potential Israeli Army formed by Haganah and Palmach. They called on Jewish World War 11 veterans as volunteers in Palestine. There were also a number of non-jewish volunteers. Three thousand South Africans volunteered, 800 were accepted for training.

    Machal volunteers also came from the USA, Britain, Australia and Canada. Proportionally South Africa produced the largest numbers. Nachal (Noar Halutzi Lohem) are Fighting Pioneer Youth, a regular unit of the Israel Defence forces. Soldiers of pioneering youth movements educate their members towards co-operative settlement in Israel with military training and as members of agricultural co-operative settlements. Volunteers came from all over the world.

4. For a more detailed discussion of these and other shipping records, see the article by Professor Aubrey Newman, *SHEMOT* 1 no. 3 (1993). "The Poor Jews' Temporary Shelter the Development of a Database on Jewish Migration, 1896-1914," by Professor Aubrey Newman and Dr. John Graham Smith. HTTP://WWW.LE.AC.UK/HI/TEACHING/PAPERS/JEWSPAP.HTML provides background information about Shelter. Also see HTTP://WWW.SANSA.UCT.AC.ZA/SHELTER/REGISTER.HTML; HTTP://WWW.LE.AC.UK/HI/TEACHING/PAPERS/NEWMAN1.HTM and "Indirect passage from Europe" by Nicholas J. Evans... WWW.JMR.NMM.AC.UK/.../SETTEMPLATE:SINGLE-CONTENT/CONTENTTYPEA/CONJMRARTICLE/CONTENTID/28/PAGEINFO/AUTHORNOTES.

Sweden
by Carl Henrik Carlsson

History

Jews were allowed to settle in Sweden and to observe their religion beginning in the 1770s. The *Judereglemente* (Jewish ordinance) of 1782 gave Jews permission to live only in the cities of Stockholm, Göteborg (Gothenburg), Norrköping and Stockholm, and soon thereafter admitted them to Karlskrona as well. Jews also lived in Marstrand, which was a free port during the period 1775–94.

The *Judereglemente* was abolished in 1838, and, in 1854, Swedish-born Jews were allowed to live in all Swedish cities. In 1860, all Jews who were Swedish citizens, regardless of birth place, were permitted to live anywhere in Sweden—in cities or in the countryside. In 1873, all domicile restrictions for Jews without Swedish citizenship were abolished.

Jewish settlement in Sweden may be divided roughly into the following time periods: 1774–1850, 1850–1917, 1917–1948 and 1948 to the present. In the first period, most Jews came from Germany, primarily from Mecklenburg. In 1850, about 1,000 Jews lived in Sweden, most of them in Stockholm and Göteborg, a few in Norrköping and Karlskrona.

During the second period, most immigrants came from Czarist Russia, including Poland. The official number of Jews rose to about 3,000 in 1880 and to slightly more than 6,000 in 1910. In the first decades of this period, the majority came from Suwalk guberniya in Poland. Later Jews arrived from adjacent guberniyas, such as Kovno, Grodno, Lomza and Vilna; still later they came from other areas of Russia. Some settled in the four cities mentioned above, others in newly established Jewish settlements in Halmstad, Helsingborg, Kalmar, Karlstad, Kristianstad, Landskrona, Lund, Malmö, Oskarshamn, Sölvesborg, Sundsvall, Växjö, Visby, Härnösand, Östersund and other places.

Between 1860 and 1917, immigration to Sweden was largely unregulated; therafter, however, regulations were imposed. The number of Jewish immigrants to Sweden was small during the period between the two world wars. Between 1933 and the outbrook of World War II, slightly more than 2,000 German, Austrian and Czech Jews were allowed to immigrate to Sweden. During the war, more than 7,000 Danish Jews and about 925 Norwegian Jews found asylum in Sweden as well.

Between April and July 1945, 10,000 to 12,000 Jewish internees from concentration camps arrived in Sweden as a result of the rescue actions of the Swedish Red Cross and the United Nations Relief and Rehabilitation Associaiton (UNRRA). The majority eventually emigrated to other countries, but some stayed in Sweden. In 1947 and 1948, roughly 1,000 Jews from German and Polish displaced persons camps arrived. About 600 Jews came from Hungary in 1956, a smaller number from Czechoslovakia in 1968, and approximately 2,500 from Poland in the period 1968–72. In the 1980s and 1990s, 1,000 Russian Jews immigrated. The estimated Jewish population today in Sweden is 17,000, less than 0.2 percent of the total population. Because of intermarriage, a much higher number of Swedes have Jewish roots.

Printed References, Cemeteries and Collections

Many descendants of the Jews who arrived before 1850 are represented in monographs or in Swedish biographical or standard genealogical volumes, such as *Svenska män och kvinnor* (Swedish men and women), *Svenskt biografiskt lexikon* (Dictionary of Swedish biography) and *Svenska släktkalendern* (Swedish family register). Unpublished genealogies can also be found in the Rudolf Simonis Collection at Leo Baeck Institute* in New York. Simonis was a Nazi refugee who did considerable genealogical research for Jewish families in Sweden.

Biographical information, including Hebrew texts of gravestones with translations into Swedish, on almost all the Jews in Stockholm until the mid-1800s and in Norrköping until 1945 can be found in *Gamla Judiska gravplatser i Stockholm* and *Judiska pionjärer och stamfäder*, respectively. All Jews buried in Sundsvall, with additional information, such as place of birth, are listed by Carlsson in *Landsmen* (1998). Lists have been published of all Jews buried in Kalmar until 1973 in Fürstenberg (1980) and in Carlsson (1994–95) and in Gothenburg until 1869 in *Gravskrifter på Göteborgs stads och närgränsande församlingars begrafningsplatser*.

Information about individuals can be found in the following cities: Gothenburg (Jacobowsky, 1955); Kalmar (Fürstenberg, 1980); Lund (Svenson, 1995); Malmö (Siegel, 1946; Rubinstein, 1971); Oskarsham (Hersson-Ringskog, 1995); Växjö (Fürstenberg, 1980); and Visby (Jacobowsky, 1973). Unpublished indexes of the cemeteries of Gothenburg and Malmö and Stockholm are located in the respective Jewish communites.*

Naturalization Applications

One of the most valuable sources for Jewish genealogy in Sweden are the *medborgarrättsansökningar* (naturalization applications). They are filed as *konseljakter* (cabinet acts) in the archives of *Justitiedepartement* (Ministry of Justice), located in *Riksarkivet** (The National Archives) and are indexed by name. The acts often include biographical information about the applicant, his country of birth, including the names of his parents—compulsory since 1925, but common also before then. Many files hold copies and translations of birth documents from Poland or Russia, which, of course, are especialy valuable in those cases where the originals are lost. The acts often also supply information about the applicant's professional and financial situation. Extracts from the national registration (see below) often supply information that provides a key to further research.

Some immigrants applied for naturalization many decades after their arrival, and because many applications were denied, many individuals applied several times. It can be fruitful to look at all applications for an individual, since the amount of information required varied from one act to another.

Applications to Live in Sweden and Operate a Business

An alien who wanted to operate a business in Sweden required special permission called *idka handel*. Until 1880, an alien could apply for such permission only after he had received a permission to *vistas i riket*, which literally means "to stay in the country," a confusing name, since there was no legal restriction against a foreigner settling in Sweden after 1860. For genealogists, the *idka handel* and *vistas i riket* applications may sometimes be as useful as those for naturalization since they often contain the same type of information. *Idka handel* applications for businesses in cities were handled by the *länsstyrelse* (country government board). Records created prior to 1880, are kept in regional archives.* Later applications are kept in the files of the *Civildepartementet** (Ministry of Public Administration) at *Riksarkivet*.

Post-1917 Records in the National Archives

Many genealogically valuable records about aliens and refugees were created after 1917. No privacy restrictions are placed on records more than 50 years old. For more detailed information, see the books (in Swedish) by Reuterswärd (pp.64–66) and Hallberg. See also Guide to Archival Sources on the Holocaust, Holocaustera Assets and Related Issues in the National Archives of Sweden at WWW.RA.SE.

During the years 1918–27, all aliens were required to apply for a residence visa (*uppehållsböcker*). The indexed applications for the entire country are kept in the archives of the *Statens polisbyrå* (State Bureau of Police). Among the questions in the questionnaire are name, birth date, birth place and year of arrival in Sweden; no information is requested about parents. A photograph should also be included. Duplicates may be found in some local police archives at the various regional archives (*landsarkiv*).

Copies of the February 1939 alien registration (*utlänningsräkning*) are kept in the archives of the National Swedish Social Welfare Board (*Socialstyrelsen*). The questions were similar to those in 1918 with some additions (e.g., religion and if the father and/or mother were Jewish). Duplicate records may be found in some local police archives held in various regional archives.

From 1920 onward, labor, residence and other permits for aliens are held in the central files (*Centraldossierer*) of aliens. These records may be found either in the archives of the National Board of Aliens (*utlänningskommissionen*) kept in the National Archives* or in the archives of the Swedish Migration Board (*Migrationsverket*)* in Norrköping. Those records often have considerable genealogically useful information about individuals, such as, for example, names of parents.

Records on former concentration camp prisoners who arrived with the Red Cross and UNRRA transports in 1945 are filed in the archives of National Board of Aliens at the National Archives.* *Inreseviseringsdossierer* (visa files) from 1917–48 are in the archives of the National Board of Aliens. There are also name indexes of aliens who died in Sweden during the years 1939–47, including information about place of death and place of burial.

Post-1917 Records in Other Archives

Some police archives, kept in the various regional archives, hold duplicates of the *uppehållsböcker* (1918–27) and the *utlänningsräkning* (1939) described in the previous section.

The archives of Malmö *läns länsstyrelses civilförsvarssektion*, located in the Regional Archives of Lund* holds approximately 27,000 index cards of the refugees who arrived in the south of Sweden 1944–46 including about 15 boxes with photographs of the refugees. Other records on those refugees may also be found in almost every local police archives in the south of Sweden, which are kept in the Landsarkiv of Lund* as well.

In the archives of the criminal police (*kriminalpolis*) held by the city archives (*Stadsarkiv*)* of Malmö are many records on refugees who arrived through the police district of Malmö. Records concerning refugees can also be found in the archives of the Jewish communities in Gothenburg*, Malmö* and Stockholm*. The printed lists of "Liberated Jews Who Arrived in Sweden 1945 and 1945–46" (see below) are, of course, useful sources. Another book that can help trace Holocaust survivors in Sweden is *Glöm oss inte* (Don't forget us). The book lists approximately 8,300 Jewish Holocaust victims from various countries, honored by surviving relatives living in Sweden. The list includes birth dates and places and death dates and places of the victims, as well as the names of surviving relatives.

National Registration Records

The Lutheran Church was the official state church in Sweden, and until July 1, 1991, its records of birth, marriage and death were the official national registration records. Since that date, local tax offices has been responsible for this registration. Until 1910, however, the records of formal Jewish communities also had the status of official national registration. Many immigrant Jews, were not members of a Jewish community, however, so a Jew may be found either in the records of the Lutheran parish or in those of the Jewish community to which he or she belonged, or maybe in both. Those records sometimes are not as informative as corresponding records in many other countries, but they provide keys to other kinds of resources.

One interesting resource is the *husförhörslängd*, from 1895 called *församlingsbok* (parish registers), a type of resource unique to Sweden and Finland. The registers, arranged geographically, cover a period of five to ten years. Members of the family are grouped together with their names, birth dates and places and other miscellaneous data. The information includes when and from where individuals moved into the parish, and when and to where they moved out, married or died. Through these records an individual can be traced through all changes of addresses from the cradle to the grave. Many of the earliest Jewish immigrants, however, did not appear in the parish registers until after they had been in the country for a number of years. Records of individuals who moved into a parish (*inflyttningslängder*) and those who moved out (*utflyttningslängder*) are good keys to the parish registers.

Another type of useful record is the "in-moving certificate" (*inflyttningsattester*), valuable for researching an immigrant, because the certificates often supply the names of parents in the country of emigration. Sometimes even a copy and translation of the immigrant's birth-record is on file. The years covered vary from parish to parish. Although they should be kept for all years, gaps sometimes exist. Between 1878 and 1926, Stockholm maintained a civil registration called *rotemansarkivet,* copies of which are held in the city archives, Stockholm's *Stadsarkiv.** These records, which are indexed and highly informative, are somewhat difficult to use and will be computerized in the future. Registration from Södermalm, the southern section of Stockholm where most immigrant Jews settled, is computerized and available on a CD-ROM as are CD-ROMS covering the districts of Klara and Gamla Stan (the old city). See reference list for availability.

Records of the Jewish community of Stockholm are on deposit at the National Archives branch of Arninge*. Permission to use them must be obtained from the Jewish community. Included one volume, the so-called *frälingsbok* (records of strangers) for the years 1865–94, which listed Jews who lived in Stockholm and some other places, but who where not members of the community. The records of the Gothenburg Jewish community are kept in the City Archives of Gothenburg,* and the records of Malmö in the City Archives of Malmö.* The records of Karlskrona are kept in the Jewish Museum* in Stockholm, and the records of Norrköping are kept in the city archives of Norrköping*.

The civil records of Göteborg (Gothenburg), started in 1884, are kept in the Regional Archives of Gothenburg.* The

records of Kalmar, Växjö and Oskarshamn are kept in the Regional Archives of Vadstena. The records of Sundsvall are kept in the Regional Archives of Härnösand*. The oldest Lutheran church records are kept in the Regional Archives, and the more recent ones in the local parish offices.

Currently, the national time limit between "old" and "recent" records is in an intermediate stage. Within perhaps 20 years, all records created up to 1991 will be placed in the regional archives. In many cases, this has already been done, but some church records less than 100 years old still are kept in local parish offices. All national registration records after July 1, 1991 are kept in local tax offices. At the tax offices where computers are avaialble, a researcher may search for any individual living in Sweden and obtain information on name, date of birth and address.

Church records up to about 1894 are also available on microfiche and can be bought or borrowed from SVAR,* a department within the National Archives.*

Complete sets of microfiche of all Swedish church records exist in a few places, including the National Archives' branch in Arninge* in the Stockholm area. Most of this material is also available on microfilm through the Mormons (see LDS Church). Jewish communites are not available on microfiche or microfilm, except those of Sundsvall and Oskarshamn.

The archives of *Statistiska centralbyrån* (Statistics Sweden), located in the National Archives' branch in Arninge*, have extracts of all official birth, marriage and death records from 1860–1967 for all parishes, including the Jewish communites. They also have extracts from the parish registers every tenth year between 1860 and 1940, and 1935 and 1945 as well. For people who died 1950–1999, see below (CD-ROM).

Miscellaneous Records

Passport documents can sometimes be found in regional archives. Estate inventories (*bouppteckningar)*, compulsory in Sweden, include names and addresses of all heirs. Records are kept in the archives of the *rådhusrätt* or *tingsrätt* (district or city court) located in the various regional archives.

Because many immigrant Jews were not registred in the parish registers until after they had lived in Sweden for a number of years, a good alternative source is the yearly *mantalslängd* (civil registration for tax purposes), based on personal declarations (*mantalsuppgifter)*. These records may cover a greater percentage of the population but are not as informative as the parish registers and, because they are yearly, usually require more research time. Copies of the *mantalslängd* can be found both in the National Archives* and the various regional archives.

Other valuable sources are various newspaper collections of obituaries and birth, marriage and death announcements and printed registers published in the 19th and 20th century concerning certain professions: physicians, lawyers, dentists, engineers, university teachers, civil servants and others.

Miscellanous Information

Nowadays dates are commonly written in Sweden as "year-month-day" (e.g., 1875–05–31 means May 31, 1875, 1980–04–01

Aron Isaac, "the first Jew in Sweden," from an oil-painting in the possession of the Jewish Community of Stockholm

(or 800401) means April 1, 1980). Every Swede has a unique 10-digit *personnummer* (personal code number), consisting of his or her birthday and a four-digit number. The third digit in the four-digit number indicates gender; an odd number for a male and an even number for a female. Thus, an individual with the *personnummer* 270130-0499 is a male person born January 30, 1927. The *personnummer* may be used, for example, while searching for an individual whose family name is unknown.

The Swedish alphabet is almost the same as the English alphabet with three additional letters. Å,Ä,Ö (å,ä,ö) are located at the end of the alphabet, after Z. The diacritical marks must not be ignored; they are separate letters and just as important as any other letters, a fact that is especially important when searching Swedish indexes.

Research Assistance

Written inquiries may be made to the archives mentioned; they also may be visited in person. Because of the massive quantity of records and language difficulties, genealogists may find it useful to hire a Swedish researcher.

Addresses

Riksarkivet (National Archives):

Riksarkivet, Box 125 41, SE-102 29 Stockholm, Sweden; Web page: WWW.RA.SE. Regional Archives can be located at this site as well.

SVAR/Riksarkivet Box 160, SE-880 40 Ramsele, Sweden.

Regional Archives

- Stockholms Stadsarkiv (City Archives of Stockholm): Kungs-klippan 6, Box 22063 SE-104 22 Stockholm. Regions covered: the city of Stockholm and the province of Stockholm.
- Landsarkivet i Göteborg (Gothenburg) Box 19035, SE-400 12 Göteborg, Sweden. Regions: the län (provinces) of Västra Götaland (formerly Göteborgs och Bohuslän, Älvsborg and Skaraborg)
- Landsarkivet i Härnösand Box 161, SE-871 24 Härnösand, Sweden Regions: the län of Gävleborg, Västernorrland, Väster-botten and Norrbotten
- Landsarkivet i Lund Box 2016, SE-220 02 Lund, Sweden. Regions: the provinces of Halland, Blekinge and Skåne (formerly Malmöhus and Kristianstad) excluding the city of Malmö
- Landsarkivet i Östersund Arkivvägen 1, SE-831 31 Östersund, Sweden Regions: the län of Jämtland
- Landsarkivet i Uppsala Box 135, SE-751 04 Uppsala, Sweden Regions: the län of Uppsala, Västmanland, Örebro, Dalarna (formerly Kopparberg) and Södermanland
- Landsarkivet i Vadstena Box 126, SE-592 23 Vadstena, Sweden. Regions covered: the provinces of Östergötland, Kronoberg, Jönköping and Kalmar
- Landsarkivet i Visby Visborgsgatan 1, SE-621 57 Visby. Region: the province of Gotland
- Värmlandsarkiv/Landsarkiv för Värmlands län Box 475, SE-651 11 Karlstad. Region: the province of Värmland
- Malmö Stadsarkiv (City Archives of Malmö) Norra Varvsgatan 11 N:4, SE-211 19 Malmö, Sweden. Region: the city of Malmö.

Other Archives

- Göteborgs Stadsarkiv (City Archives of Goteborg) Box 2154, SE-403 13, Sweden
- Norrköpings Stadsarkiv (City Archives of Norrköping), Nor-rköpings Kommun, SE-601 81 Norrköping, Sweden.
- Migrationsverket (Swedish Migration Board) Box 6113, SE-600 06 Norrköping, Sweden
- The Jewish communities: Judiska församlingen i Stockholm Box 7427, SE-103 91 Stockholm, Sweden; Judiska församlingen i Göteborg Östra Larmgatan 12, SE-411 07 Göteborg, Sweden; Judiska Församlingen i Malmö Box 4198, SE-202 13 Malmö, Sweden
- The Jewish Genealogical Society of Sweden c/o Gerber, Box 7427, SE-10391 Stockholm, Sweden.

Internet Sites

Complete Swedish telephone directory: HTTP://PRIVATPERSONER.GULASIDORNA.SE

Institute for Jewish Culture (with useful links): WWW.IJK-S.SE

Jewish Genealogy Society of Sweden: WWW.IJK-S.SE/GENEALOGI

National and Regional Archives of Sweden: WWW.RA.SE

Swedish Roots published by Swedish Genealogical Societies: WWW.GENEALOGI.SE

Jewishgen Scandinavia SIG: WWW.JEWISHGEN.ORG/SCANDINAVIA/

Translation of an 1849 birth record from Augustow, Suwalki guberniya, Poland, filed with an application to stay in the country in 1873 (National Archives in Stockholm, The Ministry of Public Administration, Cabinet Act No 4, May 23, 1873). The original Polish record is most likely lost.

References

Carlsson, Carl H. "Raczkiborn Jews who Lived in Sweden," *Landsmen* 7, no. 2–3 (1996–97): 30–31.

———. "Graves in the Sundsvall Jewish cemetery," *Landsmen* 8, no. 3–4 (1998): 17–18.

———. "Jewish Migration from Eastern Europe to Sweden From the 1850s to World War I," *Avotaynu* 14, no. 1 (1998): 39–40.

———. "Jewish Migration from Eastern Europe to Sweden From the 1850s to World War I: Sources in Swedish Archives." *Proceedings of the 5th International Seminar on Jewish Genealogy.* Paris: Cercle de Généalogie Juive, 1998, pages 207–14.

Fürstenberg, Wulff. *Kalmar mosaiska församlings tillkomst och äldsta historia jämte Växjö- och Oskarshamnsförsamlingarnas tillblivelse.* (About the Jews in Kalmar, Växjö and Oskarshamn). [Swedish]. Stockholm, Hillelförlaget, 1980. Index in Carl H. Carlsson. "East European Jews in Kalmar and Vicinity, Sweden," *Landsmen* 5, no. 2–3 (1994–95): 27–33.

Gamla Judiska gravplatser i Stockholm (About the old Jewish cemeteries in Stockholm). [Swedish]. Stockholm: Judiska litteratursamfundet, 1927.

Glöm oss inte (Don't forget us). [Swedish]. Stockholm: Hillelförlaget 1999.

Gravskrifter på Göteborgs stads och närgränsande församlingars begrafningsplatser (About cemeteries in Gothenburg). [Swedish]. Göteborg, 1869; reprinted Göteborg: Göteborgs landsarkiv, 1993.

Göteborgs mosaiska församling 1780–1980 (About the Jews in Gothenburg). [Swedish]. Göteborg, Mosaiska församlingen, 1980.

Hallberg, Lars. *Källor till invandringens historia i. statliga myndigheters arkiv 1840–1990* (Sources on the history of immigration in the state archives, 1840–1990. [Swedish]. Stockholm, Riksarkivet, 2001.

Hersson-Ringskog, Paula. *Oskarshamns mosaiska församling 1888–1938.* (About the Jewish community of Oskarshamn). [Swedish]. Oskarshamn, 1995.

Ivarsson, Martin, and Abraham Brody. *Judiska pionjärer och stamfäder* (About the Jewish community of Norrköping). [Swedish], 1956.

Jacobowsky, C. Vilhelm. *Göteborgs Mosaiska Församling. 1780–1955.* (About the Jewish community in Gothenburg). Göteborg, Mosaiska församlingen, 1955.

———. *Judar på Gotland* (Jews in Gotland). [Swedish]. Visby, 1973. Index (pp. 29–50) in Carlsson, Carl H. "East European Jews in Gotland," *Landsmen* 4, no. 2–3 (1993–94): 30–34.

"Liberated Jews Who Arrived in Sweden in 1945." List no. 1 Lund, Henry Luttrop, 1946.

"Liberated Jews Arrived in Sweden in 1945/46." List no. 2 Lund, Henry Luttrop, 1946.

Reuterswärd, Elisabeth. *Att söka sina utländska rötter* (How to search foreign roots). [Swedish]. Lund, Landsarkivet, 1995.

Rubinstein, Harry ed. *Mosaiska församlingen i Malmö 100 år. 1871–1971* (About the Jews in Malmö). [Swedish]. Malmö, Mosaiska församlingen, 1971.

Selling, Thomas. "Resources for Jewish Genealogy in Sweden." *Avotaynu* 11, no. 2 (1995), 39–40.

Siegel, Walter. *Mosaiska församlingen i Malmö 75 år. 1871–1946.* (About the Jews in Malmö). [Swedish]. Malmö, Mosaiska församlingen, 1946.

Svenska släktkalendern (Swedish family register) 1912–. [Swedish]. Stockholm, Bonniers.

Svenska män och kvinnor (Swedish men and women). vols. 1–8. Stockholm, Bonniers, (1942–55).

Svenskt biografiskt lexikon (Dictionary of Swedish biography). 1917– [Swedish]. Also available on CD-ROM.

Svenson, Anna. *Nöden- en shtetl i Lund* (About the Jews in Lund). [Swedish]. Lund: Föreningen Gamla Lund, 1995.

CD-ROMS

CD-Emigranten 2001. (The CD-emigrant) Göteborgs-Emigranten et. al 2001. The CD includes many different databases, of which *Emihamn* is the most valuable. This is a compilation of all police chamber passenger lists from the main ports of emigration, Göteborg (Gothenburg) 1869–1930, Malmö 1874–1928 and Stockholm 1869–1940, and the minor ports of Norrköping 1859–1922, Helsingborg 1929–1950, and Kalmar 1881–1893. It also covers information from Copenhagen 1868–1908 and Hamburg 1850–1891. In this database will be found the name of the emigrant, age, marital status, hometown, destination, date of emigration and the contract number. It is possible to search on all criteria and also on combinations. This database contains about 1.4 million individuals and is based on the information the emigrants provided the Police chamber before they left port. A majority (ca. 1.1 million) went through Göteborg (Gothenburg). An Amerian version is available and may be ordered at WWW.GOTEBORGS-EMIGRANTEN.COM.

Gamla stan under 740 år [Swedish]. Stockholms stadsarkiv (City Archives of Stockholm), 2002. Contains detailed information on all individuals who lived in Gamla stan (the old city of Stockholm), 1878–1926, based on information in *Rotemansarkivet* (a civil registration described above). A CD and DVD.

Klara-Skivan. [Swedish]. Stockholms stadsarkiv (City Archives of Stockholm), 2000. Contains detailed information on all individuals who lived in the district of Klara, Stockholm, 1878–1926, based on information in *Rotemansarkivet.*

Söder i våra hjärtan. (The South in our hearts). [Swedish]. Stockholm: Stockholms Historiska Databas/Stockholms stadsarkiv (City Archives of Stockholm), 1998. Contains detailed information on all people living 1878–1926 at Södermalm (the southern part of Stockholm), in the years 1878–1926. This area is where a majority of East European Jews settled. It is based on the *rotemansarkivet* (a civil registration). Information includes name, occupation, day and place of birth, day and place of death, date of marriage, family relationship, addresses, day and place of moving in and moving out and more.

Sveriges dödbok 1950-1999. (Deceased in Sweden 1950–1999). Published by Sveriges släktforskarförbund (The Swedish Federation of Genealogical Societies), 2000. Information about all of the slightly more than 4.2 million individuals who died in Sweden during this period. Includes complete names, *personnummer* (birthday plus a four-digit number), place of birth, domicile (parish) at time of death and address are stated, November 1970–1999. Before November 1970, no names are stated, only *personnumer.* Marital status is given for everyone, date of change of marital status is stated for those deceased 1950–51 and 1961–99. A very few persons are not in the database because of security reasons.

Sveriges befolkning 1970 (People living in Sweden 1970). Published by Sveriges släktforskarförbund (The Swedish Federation of Genealogical Societies), 2000. Information about all people living in Sweden November 1970: Name, birth day, exact birth place (if born in Sweden), address etc.

Switzerland

by René Loeb

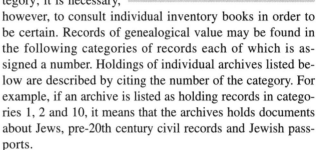

Switzerland is a confederation composed of 26 cantons, each of which has its own local government and corresponding infrastructure. The country has four official languages: German, French, Italian and Romance; the latter is used only in the canton of Grisons. In the year 2001, the Swiss population was approximately 7,123,537; the Jewish population was approximately 18,000, one-third living in the Canton of Zürich and another third in the two cities of Geneva and Basle; and the remainder scattered throughout the country. In all, there are 25 Jewish communities, 18 of which belong to the *Schweizerischer Israelitischer Gemeindebund* (SIG-Swiss Jewish Confederation).

Jews are recorded in Switzerland by the 14th century. In 1420, they were expelled from the country, but until the 17th century, various towns and villages tolerated some Jews. After the 17th century and until the emancipation in 1866, Jews were permitted to live only in the canton of Aargau, and then only in the villages of Endingen and Lengnau. To this day, each village has a synagogue with a cemetery situated between them. Today, the cemetery, opened in 1744, is used occasionally.

Most of the Jews of Endingen and Lengnau came originally from Alsace and Germany. At the end of the 19th century and at the beginning of the 20th century, Jews also came from Poland, Romania and Russia. After World War II, large numbers of Sephardic Jews came from North Africa, Turkey and Persia, settling primarily in the French speaking sections, the western part of the country. Since 2001 *TACHLES,* published in Zürich, has been the only Swiss-Jewish magazine in German; a separate French edition is published weekly for the French-speaking area of the country.

The *Schweizerische Vereinigung für jüdische Genealogie* (Swiss Society of Jewish Genealogy) was founded in spring 1986. It publishes the only German-language Jewish genealogical periodical, the quarterly publication, *MAAJAN-Die Quelle.* For more then five years, *MAAJAN-Die Quelle* has served also as the publication of the only German Jewish Genealogical Society, the *Hamburger Gesellschaft für jüdische Genealogie e.V.* The society has approximately 90 members and, when compared to the Jewish population of Switzerland, is one of the largest Jewish genealogical societies (see ORGANIZED JEWISH GENEALOGY). It has held "Jichus" exhibitions in Basle, Berne and Zürich and, for many years, its monthly roundtable meetings have brought together persons who are interested in a specific family name or a specific region. Members of the governing board attempt to answer the many genealogical queries that arrive yearly from all over the world.

Genealogical Resources

Records about Jews may be found both in public archives and in Jewish repositories. In general, documents about Jews are not segregated from others of the same category; it is necessary, however, to consult individual inventory books in order to be certain. Records of genealogical value may be found in the following categories of records each of which is assigned a number. Holdings of individual archives listed below are described by citing the number of the category. For example, if an archive is listed as holding records in categories 1, 2 and 10, it means that the archives holds documents about Jews, pre-20th century civil records and Jewish passports.

Record Categories

1. Documents about Jews, historical documents, notary records, general documents and specifically Jewish documents
2. Civil documents from before the end of the 19th century
3. Court records
4. Enumerations of inhabitants
5. Community documents
6. Authority documents. Various poll taxes, duty payments, court records, court orders and governmental documents concerning Jews
7. Jewish fascicles. Records of circumcisions, birth, deaths and marriages, plus other varying information in church and community registers
8. Land register documents
9. Person, Body and Protection customs acts. Person (*Personenzoll*) and Body (*Leibzoll*) were expressions used when a person had to pay a tax for permission to enter a town or moved from one village to another. A Protection tax (*Schutzzoll*) was the tax Jews had to pay for permission to stay in a place, open a store, lend money, trade in different merchandise and other activities. The tax was collected by magnates, bishops, cities and all groups of the nobility.
10. Jewish passports

Governmental Archives: Names and Holdings

Schweizerisches Bundesarchiv (Federal Archives)* /1 various, 2 E.21,22, 6 E4300, 4800, 10 E 2001

*Aargau Canton archives** The two major Jewish settlements of Endingen and Lengnau are in Aargau Canton. 1, 2, 3, 4 from mid-19th century 5 from the end of the 18th century, 6, 9; Jewish documents from the Aargau government 1803–77; IA No. 11.15.9

*Basel-Stadt Canton archives** 1 church documents Q 2, 3, 4, 5, 6, 8

*Basel-Land Canton archives** 1 settlement acts A.-F. 2 church documents E.9. 3, 5, 6

*Berne Canton archives** 1, 2, 3, 4, 5, 6, 8

Endingen Community archives* 2 family register 5, 6. Jewish death registers are held by the Jewish community; birth registers after 1875 are held by the municipality. Permission to do research follows the same rules as those for Lengnau (see below).

Fribourg Canton archives*

Geneva Canton archives* Consult *Guides des archives d'Etat de Genève.*

Glarus Canton archives* 2, 3, 4, 6, 8

Graubunden Canton archives* 1 federal minutes 1631–AV IV 1/18, decree books AB IV 4/1–28, minutes of the little council, 1800, 1808, 1809, 1829, CB V 3/1 ff, decrees of the great council 1829 CB II 935–947 CB III 333–357, decrees of the *Standeskommission* 1857 CB II 948–993 CB III 338–343, Acts XIII 22, Police acts 5 b 2, Hawk- and Tadpolice IV 17

Jura Canton archives* none known

Lengnau Community archives* 1, 2, 4, 5, 6. Birth, death and marriage registers since 1823 are in the municipality archives. This archive holds a separate Jewish family register that existed until June 1983. For permission to do genealogical research. it is necessary to write first to the Departement des Innern des Kantons Aargau, Bürgerrecht und Personenstand, CH-5000, Aarau, Switzerland. After receiving permission researchers can go to the Municipality of Lengnau. A copy of a family certificate for direct descendants costs 25 Swiss francs each (approximately US$18). For every additional person the charge is 5 francs per person (approximately US$3.50). The maximum cost is 50 francs (approximately US$35).

Luzern Canton archives* 1 Town Acts 4—compartement 9: SA 5876—SA 5879 1861–71, Archives 2-compartement 7: Box 27/105 B 1807–44, D 1805–12, Box 27/106: A 1813–26, B 1827–35, C 1836–47, D 1801–14 Archives 3—compartment 4 Box 34/89: B 1858–60, C 1861–65 Box 34/90: A 1866–74, B 1866–68, C 1869–70, Box 34/91: A 1871–74 Archives 3—compartement 4 B: Box 34/230: A 1892, B 1893, C 1894, D 1895, Archives 3—compartement 7 Box 37/179: B 1882–99, C 1848–59, Archives 3—compartement 9 Box 39/31: F 1850–92

Neuchâtel Canton archives* 1, 2, 3, 4, 6, 9

St. Gallen Canton archives* 1 HA A 98–1, 98–2, 128–5, 2, 3 G, GA 4 R.91—1c, 91–2 6, 7 R.154, 8

Schaffhausen Canton archives* 1, 2, 3, 4, 5, 6, 8, 9

Solothurn Canton archives* 1 A lff, A 10, 2, 3, 4 BD 21–30, BB 163, 1ff, 5, 5, 8, 9 BB 203, 12

Valais Canton archives* 4, 5, 6, 9

Vaud Canton archives* 2 1875 serie Ed (1821–75) 3, 4, 6, 8 serie G, *communautJ israelite d"avenches:* 1803–63, 1873–85, K XIV 392

Zürich Canton archives* 1 N36, 36a 1842–1919, A–K, 1 *aurochs feud* letter, B VI 192, fol. 287 (1385), B XI 2 E II, E III 3 Y, YY 6 N–U 7 N 2.1 (10) (1838–61) 8 B XI plus four documents: C I 277 (31.01.1329), C I 278 (27.03.1343), C I 280 (21.06.1352), C I 286 (23.02.1354)

Jewish Community Archives

Israelitische Gemeinde Basel* 1, 5, 6, 8

Jüdische Gemeinde Bern* 1, 5 Jewish community after 1848, refugee acts 1933–46

Israelitische Cultusgemeinde Bremarten* 1, 4, 5

Israelitische Kultusgemeinde Endingen* 1, 4, 5

Communaute Israelite Fribourg* 1, 7. See *Les Juifs en pays de Fribourg* for a roll of Jews who lived in the Canton from 1840–1900

Communaute Israelite Vevey* 1, 5, 8

Israelitische Gemeinde Winterthur* Has minutes of the community for the past 100 years

Israelitische Cultusgemeinde Zurich* 1, 5

Other Archives

Jewish Museum of Switzerland, Basel* 1, 7, 9, 10

Florence Guggenheim Archives* 1, 3, 4, 5, 6, 7, 9, 10

See catalogues of the archives, 1974 and additions, 1974–84.

Convent Archives, Sankt Gallen* See bibliography by H. Wartmann.

Convent Archives, Einsiedeln* Record of a Jewish trade from 1798. StiAEins., A. HS (12): Sale of Swiss capitals to Wolf Josef Levi

Addresses

Schweizerisches Bundesarchiv (federal archives), Archivstrasse 24, CH–3003 Berne/Switzerland; telephone: 0041-313-228-989; fax: 0041-313-227-823; e-mail: BUNDESARCHIV@BAR.ADMIN.CH; websites: WWW.BUNDESARCHIV.CH/BAR/ENGINE/SHOWPAGE?

Archives of Canton Aargau, Entfelderstrasse 22, Buchenhof, Postfach, CH-5001 Aarau, Switzerland; telephone: 0041-628-351-290; fax: 0041-628-351-299; e-mail: STAATSARCHIV@AG.CH; website: WWW.AG.CH/STAATSARCHIV

Archives of Canton Basel-Stadt, Martinsgasse 2, Postfach, CH-4001 Basel, Switzerland; telephone: 0041-612-678-601; fax: 0041-612-676-571; e-mail: STABS@BS.CH; website: WWW.BS.CH/STABS/

Archives of Canton Basel-Land, Wiedenhubstrasse 35, Postfach 114, CH-4410 Liestal, Switzerland; telephone: 0041-619-267-676; fax: 0041-619-267-677; e-mail: STAATSARCHIV@LKA.BL.CH; website: WWW.BASELLAND.CH/STAATSARCHIV

Archives of Canton Berne, Falkenplatz 4, CH-3012 Berne, Switzerland; telephone: 0041-316-335-101; fax: 0041-316-335-102; e-mail: none; website: WWW.BE.CH/STAATSARCHIV

Archives of Canton Fribourg, Chemin des Archives 4, CH-1700 Fribourg; telephone: 0041-263-051-270; fax: 0041-263-051-274; e-mail: ARCHIVESETAT@FR.CH; website: WW.FR.CH/AEF/DE or WWW.FR.CH/AEF

Archives of Canton Geneva, Case postale 3964, CH-1211 Genève 31, rue de l'Hôtel-de-Ville, CH-1204 Genève, Switzerland; telephone: 0041-223-193-395; fax: 0041-223-193-365; e-mail: ARCHIVES@ETAT.GE.CH; website: WWW.GE.CH/ARCHIVES

Archives of Canton Glarus, Postgasse 29, Postfach 515, Ch-8750 Glarus, Switzerland; telephone: 0041-556-466-561; fax: 0041-556-466-596; e-mail: LANDESARCHIV@GL.CH; websites: WWW.GL.CH

Archives of Canton Graubünden, Karlihofplatz, CH-7001 Chur, Switzerland; telephone: 0041-812-572-803; fax: 0041-812-572-001; e-mail: STAATSARCHIV@GR.CH; website: WWW.STAATSARCHIV.GR.CH and WWW.LAD-BW.DE/ARGEALP/

Archives of Canton Jura, Hôtel des Halles, Rue Pierre-Péquignat 9, Case postale 64, CH-2900 Porrentruy 2, Switzerland; telephone: 0041-324-657-400; fax: 0041-324-657-499; e-mail: FRANCOIS.NOIRJEAN@JURA.CH; website: WWW.JURA.CH

Archives of Canton Luzern, Schützenstrasse 9, Postfach 7853, CH-6000 Luzern 7, Switzerland; telephone: 0041-412-285-365; fax:

The second Zionist Congress was held in Basel, Switzerland, in August 1898. Theodore Herzl, who called for the Zionist Congresses, can be seen at the podium in the middle of the picture.

0041-412-286-663; e-mail: STAATSARCHIV@LU.CH; website: WWW. STALUZERN.CH

Archives of Canton Neuchâtel, Rue de la Collégiale, Château CH-2001 Neuchâtel, Switzerland; telephone: 0041-328-896-040; fax: 0041-328-896-088; e-mail: SERVICE.ARCHIVESETAT@ACN.ETATNE.CH; website: WWW.NE.CH

Archives of Canton St. Gallen, Regierungsgebaeude. CH-9001 St. Gallen, Switzerland; telephone: 0041-712-293-205; fax: 0041-712-293-805; e-mail: STAATSARCHIV@DIM-STA.SG.CH; website: WW.SG.CH/SGBN/STARCHIV.HTM and WWW.LAD-BW.DE/ARGEALP

Archives of Canton Schaffhausen, Rathausbogen 4, CH-8200 Schaffhausen, Switzerland; telephone: 0041-526-327-368; fax: none; e-mail: STAATSARCHIV@KTSH.CH; website: WWW.SH.CH

Archives of Canton Solothurn, Bielstrasse 41, CH-4509 Solothurn, Switzerland; telephone: 0041-326-270-821; fax: 0041-326-223-487; e-mail: STAATSARCHIV@SK.SO.CH; website: WWW.STAATSARCHIV.SO.CH

Archives of Canton Valais, 7, rue des Vergers, CH-1950 Sion, Switzerland; telephone: 0041-276-064-600; fax: 0041-276-064-604; e-mail: ARCHIVES@VS.ADMIN.CH; website: WWW.VS.CH

Archives of Canton Vaud, Rue de la Mouline 32, CH-1022 Chavannes-près-Renens, Switzerland; telephone: 0041-213-163-711; fax: 0041-213-163-755; e-mail: ARCHIVES.CANTONALES@ACV.VD.CH; website: WWW.DIRE.VD.CH

Archives of Canton Zurich, Winterthurerstrasse 170, CH-8057 Zurich, Switzerland; telephone: 0041-163-56911; fax: 0041-163-569-05; e-mail: STAATSARCHIVZH@JZ.ZH.CH; website: WWW.STAATSARCHIV.ZH.CH

Archives of the Municipality of Endingen, Würenlingerstrasse 11, CH-5304 Endingen, Switzerland; telephone: 0041-562-421-369; fax: 0041-562-421-649; e-mail: GEMEINDEKANZLEI@ENDINGEN.AG.CH; website: WWW.ENDINGEN.CH

Archives of the Municipality of Lengnau/AG, CH-5426 Lengnau-AG, Switzerland; telephone: 0041-562-665-010; fax: 0041-562-665-015; e-mail: GEMEINDEKANZLEI@LENGNAU-AG.CH; website: WWW.LENGNAU-AG.CH

Archiv für Zeitgeschichte (Archives of contemporary history), Hirschengraben 62, ETH-Zentrum, CH-8002 Zürich; telephone: 0041 1 632 40 03; fax: 0041 1 632 13 92; e-mail: AFZ@HISTORY.GESS.ETHZ.CH; website: WWW.AFZ.ETHZ.CH

Israelitische Kultusgemeinde Baden, Parkstrasse 17, Postfach, CH-5400 Baden; telephone: 415-622-294-46; fax: 415-622-294-47; e-mail: JKGB@DPLANET.CH.

Israelitische Gemeinde Basel, Leimenstrasse 24, Postfach, CH-4003 Basel; telephone: 416-127-998-50; fax: 416-127-998-51; e-mail: IGB@IGB.CH; website: WWW.IGB.CH

Israelitische Cultusgemeinde Bremgarten, c/o Werner Meyer, Ringstrasse 37, CH-5620 Bremgarten, Switzerland; telephone: 0041- 566-336-626; fax: 0041-566-336-626

Jüdische Gemeinde Bern, Kapellenstrasse 2, CH-3011 Bern, Switzerland; telephone: 0041-313-814-992; fax: 0041-313-823-861; e-mail: INFO@JGB.CH; website: WWW.JGB.CH

Israelitische Gemeinde Biel, c/o Johanna Molet, Schloessliweg 21, CH-2542 Pieterlen, Switzerland; telephone: 0041-323-773-619

Israelitische Kultusgemeinde Endingen, c/o Jules Bloch, Buckstrasse 2, CH-5304 Endingen, Switzerland; telephone: 0041-124-563-35; fax: 0041-124-566-02; e-mail: BLO@BANK-VON-ERNST.CH

Communauté Israélite Fribourg, Case postale 170, CH-1701 Fribourg, Switzerland; telephone: 0041-264-112-920; fax: 0041-264-114-620; e-mail: C.I.FRIBOURG@BLUEWIN.CH

Communauté Israélite Genève, rue St. Léger 10, CH-1205 Genève, Switzerland; telephone: 0041-223-178-900; fax: 0041-223-178-990; e-mail: SECRETGEN@COMISRA.CH

Communauté Israelite Liberale de Genève, 12, Quai du Seujet, CH-1201 Genève, Switzerland; telephone: 0041-227-323-245; fax:

004-122-738-2852; e-mail: INFOGIL@FREESURF.CH and RAVGARAI@PROLINK.CH

Jüdische Gemeinde Kreuzlingen, c/o Louis Hornung, Schulstrasse 7, CH-8280 Kreuzlingen, Switzerland; telephone: 0041-716-711-630

Jüdische Gemeinde St. Gallen, c/o Dr. Roland Richter, Merkurstrasse 4, CH-9000 St. Gallen, Switzerland, telephone: 0041-712-221-614; fax: 0041-712-225-734; e-mail: R.RICHTER@BLUEWIN.CH

Jüdische Gemeinde Solothurn, Postfach CH-4502 Solothurn, Switzerland; telephone: 0041-326-259-999; fax: 0041-326-259-995

Communauté Israélite Vevey-Montreux, Case postale 200, CH-1800 Vevey 1, Switzerland; telephone: 0041-219-236-009; fax: 0041-219-23 6-023

Israelitische Gemeinde Winterthur, c/o Sylvain Wyler, Moettelistrasse 37, CH-8400 Winterthur, Switzerland; telephone/fax: 0041-522-328-136

Israelitische Cultusgemeinde Zürich, Lavaterstrasse 33, Postfach 282, CH-8027 Zürich, Switzerland; telephone: 0041-120-116-59; fax: 0041-120-222-87; e-mail: INFO@ICZ.ORG; website: WWW.ICZ.ORG

Israelitische Religionsgesellschaft Zürich, Manessestrasse 10, CH-8003 Zürich, Switzerland; telephone: 0041-124-180-57; fax: 0041-124-182-14; e-mail: IRG@BLUEWIN.CH; website: WWW.IRGZ.CH

Jüdische Gemeinde Agudas Achim, Erikastrasse 8, CH-8003 Zürich, Switzerland; telephone: 0041-146-380-33; fax: 0041-146-380-45

Jüdisch Liberale Gemeinde Or Chadasch, Hallwylstrasse 78, CH-8004 Zürich, Switzerland; telephone: 0041-433-220-314; fax: 0041-433-22 0-316; e-mail: INFO@JLG.CH; website: WWW.JLG.CH

Schweizerischer Israelitischer Gemeindebund (Swiss Federation of Jewish Communities), Gotthardstrasse 65, CH-8027 Zürich, Switzerland; telephone: 0041-120-155-83; fax: 0041-120-216-72; e-mail: INFO@SWISSJEWS.ORG; website: WWW.SWISSJEWS.ORG

Florence Guggenheim Archives, c/o Israelitische Cultusgemeinde Zürich (see address above)

Jüdisches Museum der Schweiz (Jewish Museum of Switzerland), Kornhausgasse 8 CH-4051 Basle, Switzerland

Bibliography

Archival References

Agustoni, C., M. Colliard and H. Foerster. "Les Juifs en pays de Fribourg" (Jews in Fribourg). [French] *MAAJAN-Die Quelle,* no. 9, 1988 to no. 17 1990, Zurich.

Merz, W. *Inventory of the State Archives of Aargau,* 2 vols., Aarau, 1935.

Morard, Nicholas and Hubert Foerster. *Das Staatsarchiv Fribourg—Führer durch die Bestände.* Fribourg, 1987.

Stanschi, Catherine. *Guides des Archives d'État en Genève.* (Guide to the state archives in Geneva) [French] Geneva, 1973.

Books and Articles

Boll, Günter. "Die ersten Generationen der Regisheimer Familie Wahl" (The first generations of the family Wahl from Regisheim). *MAAJAN-Die Quelle,* no. 44, Zurich, 1997. Regisheim is a village in Upper Alsace.

Boll, Günther and Daniel Teichman. "Mohelbuch von Schimon ben Naftali Blum" (The Mohel Book of Shimon ben Naftali Blum). *MAAJAN-Die Quelle,* no. 38, 1996 to no. 46, 1998.

Der Judenfriedhof Engingen-Lengnau (The Jewish cemetery Endingen-Lengnau). [German] vols. I, II, III, IV, Baden, 1993 and 1998. Vol. II, Baden, 1993; Vol. III, Baden , 1998; Vol. IV, Baden, 1998

Dreyfus, Emil. "Erinnerungen. Aus den Memoiren eines aus Endingen stammenden israelitischen Schweizers" (Recollections from the memoirs of a Swiss Jew from Endingen) in *Israelitisches Wochenblatt,* nos. 15 to 50, 1924, and nos. 2 to 11, 1925.

Ginsburger, Ernest. *Histoire des Juifs de Carouge, Juifs du Leman et de Genève* (History of the Jews of Carouge, the Jews of Leman and of Geneva). [France] Paris: Librairie Durlacher, 1923.

Gottraux, Yoland. "Die jüdische Gemeinde von Avenches" (The Jewish Community of Avenches). *MAAJAN-Die Quelle,* no. 24, 1992 to no. 27, 1993. Avenches is a village near Lausanne that was of great importance at the time of the Roman Empire.

Guggenheim-Gruenberg, Florence. "Die ältesten jüdischen Familien in Lengnau und Endingen" (The oldest Jewish families of Endingen and Lengnau). *Beiträge zur Geschichte und Volkskunde der Juden in der Schweiz.* [German] Zurich: self-published, 1954

———. "Der Friedhof auf der Judeninsel im Rhein bei Koblenz" (The cemetery on the Jewish Island in the Rhine near Koblenz). *Beiträge zur Geschichte und Volkskunde der Juden in der Schweiz.* vol. 5. [German]. Zurich: self-published, 1956.

———. "Quellen und Probleme jüdischer Familienforschung in der Schweiz" (Sources and problems of Jewish Genealogy in Switzerland). *Schweizer Familienforscher* 36, no. 4 (1969): 23.

———. "Michel Pollag, der Stammvater der Endinger Bollag-Familien" (Michel Pollag, the progenitor of the Endinger Bollag families). *Israelitisches Wochenblatt* 36, September 1964.

———. "Rabbiner, Vorsteher und Gelehrte im Surbtal des 18. Jahrhunderts" (Rabbis, heads and scholars in the Surbtal in the 18th century). *Israelitisches Wochenblatt,* no. 15, 16 and 17, April 1965.

Guth–Dreifuss, Katia. "Das Mohelbuch Levaillant" (The Levaillant *mohel* book). *MAAJAN-Die Quelle,* no. 14, 1990 to no. 24, Zurich, 1992.

Ingold, Denis. "Elsaesser Juden in der Schweiz; Schweizer Juden im Elsass im 17. Jahrhundert" (Jews from Alsace in Switzerland; Swiss Jews in Alsace in the 17th century). *MAAJAN-Die Quelle,* no. 45, Zurich, 1997.

Jung, Raymond. "Kleine Einführung in die Genealogie" (Little introduction to genealogy). *MAAJAN-Die Quelle* no. 1, 1986–no. 27, 1993.

———. "Vom Familienarchiv zur Familienchronik" (From the family archives to the family chronicle). *MAAJAN-Die Quelle,* no.27, 1993 to no. 42, 1997.

———. "Glossar zur jüdischen Familienforschung" (Glossary to the Jewish Genealogy). *MAAJAN-Die Quelle,* no. 44, 1997–no. 49, 1998.

Kahn, Ludwig David. *Die Familie Kahn von Sulzburg/Baden* (The Kahn family of Sulzburg/Baden/Germany). [German] Basel: self-published, 1963.

———. *Die Nachkommen des Nathan Günzburger 1720–1755 aus Uffheim im Elsass* (Descendants of Nathan Günzburger of Uffheim in Alsace 1720–1755). [German] Basel, self-published, 1971.

———. *Die Nachkommen des Simon Guggenheim 1730–1799 von Endingen* (Descendants of Simon Guggenheim of Endingen 1730 to 1799). [German] Basel: self-published, 1969

———. *Die Geschichte der Juden von Sulzburg* (The history of the Jews of Sulzburg). [German] Basel: self-published, 1969

———. *The Loevinger Family of Laupheim; Pioneers in South Dakota.* Basel: self-published, 1967

Purin, Bernard. "Quellen zur jüdischen Familienforschung in Vorarlberg, Oesterreich" (Sources for Jewish genealogy in Vorarlberg, Austria). *MAAJAN-Die Quelle,* no. 21, Zurich, 1991.

Sigg, Otto. "Dokumente zur Geschichte der Juden aus dem Zürcher Staatsarchiv" (Documents on the History of the Jews in the State Archives of Zurich). *MAAJAN-Die Quelle,* no. 9, 1988–no. 12, Zurich, 1989.

Stein, Peter. "Eintagekönig Saul Wahl von Polen und die Wahl von Regisheim" (Saul Wahl, King of Poland for one day and the Wahl family of Regisheim). *MAAJAN-Die Quelle*, no. 44, Zurich, 1997.

Stein, Peter, ed. *Mohelbuch Lazarus Lieber Dreyfuss aus Endingen und seine Familie 65 Beschneidungen von 1827 bis 1863* (Mohel book of Lazarus Lieber Dreyfuss of Endingen and his family; 65 circumcisions from 1827 to 1863). [German] Baden: Israelitische Kultusgemeinde Endingen, 1999.

Teichman, Daniel. "Familien Männlin und Eberlin. Juden in der Schweiz in der 2. Haelfte des 14. Jahrhunderts" (The Männlin and Eberlin families; Jews in Switzerland in the second half of the 4th century). *MAAJAN-Die Quelle*, no. 41, Zurich, 1996.

Teichman, Daniel. "Hochzeitsliste des Naftali ben Schimon Blum" (The marriage lists of Naftali ben Shimon Blum). *MAAJAN-Die Quelle*, no. 48, 1998–no. 63, 2002.

Weingarten, Ralph, "Acht Jahrhunderte schweizerisch-jüdische Geschichte" (Eight centuries of Swiss-Jewish history). *Israelitisches Wochenblatt*, no. 46, November 1991.

Weldler-Steinberg, Augusta and Florence Guggenheim-Gruenberg. *Geschichte der Juden in der Schweiz* (History of the Jews in Switzerland). [German] Zurich: Schweizerischer Israelitischer Gemeindebund, 1966, Vol. I and Vol. II, 1970.

Ymayo Tartakoff, Laura. "L'histoire exeptionelle des Juifs de Carouge" (Special history of the Jews of Carouge). *La Tribune de Genève*, February 24, 1982.

Syria

by H. Daniel Wagner

Jews living in Syria in modern times belonged either to communities dating back to the Old Testament period or to colonies of refugees fleeing the Spanish Inquisition. In Biblical times and later, the Syrian region, Aram, centered around the city-state of Aram-Damascus. The city of Aleppo (or Chaleb) is often recalled as Aram-Zobah. As described by Josephus, the Jewish community in Syria flourished in those times, due to its proximity to the Jewish center in Palestine.

The Byzantine era ended in the 630s C.E. when Syria was conquered by the Muslims. The situation of the Jews was secure; the Umayyad dynasty treated non-Muslims with tolerance. Later, however, struggles between various dynasties caused the condition of the population (including Jews) to decline progressively.

A large number of Jewish immigrants from Iraq settled in Syria during the 10th century. Most Syrian Jews at the time were dyers, tanners and bankers. The period of Shiite Fatimid rule over southern Syria (starting about 969) was a prosperous one for the Jewish communities, with some interruptions until the beginning of the 11th century. The leading communities at that time were located in Aleppo, Damascus and Tyre; smaller groups existed in Baalbek, Baniyas, Judayl, Tripoli and other places. Strong ties existed with the community in Palestine. The Seljuk conquest (in the 1070s) brought disaster to the whole of Syria and Palestine. At the close of the century, the Crusaders arrived in Syria.

The spiritual and religious life of Syrian Jews concentrated around the academy in Damascus, whose leaders were known as *geonim*. The descendants of Babylonian exilarchs, referred to as *nasi*, also played a leading role. During the time of the Kurdish leader Saladin (in the 1170s), the situation of the Jews improved as a result of the economic prosperity of the state.

In 1260, the Mongols invaded Syria, but Jews and Christians suffered less than the Muslims and the two largest Jewish communities—Aleppo and Damascus—remained unharmed. In turn, the Mongols were defeated in 1260 by the Mamluks sultans, who ruled Syria until the beginning of the 16th century.

During the second half of the 14th century, the rulers issued decrees against non-Muslim communities, which caused much suffering. Limitations on clothing were imposed as well as the dismissal of Jews and Christians from government service. At the close of 1400, Tamerlane invaded Syria, and, thereafter, the Jewish population recovered very slowly from the misfortunes of the invasion. Most 15th-century Syrian Jews were craftsmen and small merchants; many lived in poverty and it appears that the Jewish population of Syria numbered no more than approximately 7,000 individuals.

During this period, Spanish exiles gradually began to arrive in Syrian towns, bringing about a decisive change in the composition and nature of the Jewish community. Many came from Italy and Turkey. Their language, customs, way of life and outlook were different from those of native-born Jews (the Mustarabs, or Arabic Jews), which caused considerable difficulties. Problems arose between the two groups in matters regarding the organization of the communities and in the general difficulty of the two groups assimilating harmoniously. Leadership of Syrian Jewry soon passed to the more educated Spanish Jews.

Beginning in the 16th century, the Ottoman Turks ruled Syria for about 400 years. Although they occasionally took discriminatory measures against the Jews on religious pretexts, the Jewish merchants of Aleppo prospered due to extensive trade between Europe and Persia. Ties with India were strong as well. Economic prosperity further increased the immigration of Spanish Jews to Syrian towns. Aleppo was the most important community, economically and culturally. Aside from Aleppo and Damascus, during the 16th century, smaller communities existed in Ayntab and Alexandretta in the north, and Baalbek, Baniyas, Beirut, Hama, Sidon and Tripoli to the west and south.

Famous leaders at the time included Rabbi Meir Anashikon and later Rabbi Samuel Laniado in Aleppo, and Rabbi Hayyim Vital and Rabbi Moses Alsheikh in Damascus. Rabbi Israel Najara was a famous poet in the 1600s. A wealthy class of bankers emerged in Damascus in the second half of the 18th century at the same time that the trade of Aleppo greatly declined. Saul Farhi (and later his son Hayyim) was finance minister to the governor of Damascus. At the end of the 18th century, Rabbi Mordecai Galante and his son were eminent rabbinical authorities.

The Damascus community was the center of Syrian Jewry throughout the 19th century. During the 1830s, the Jewish bankers (*sarrafs*) were led by Raphael Farhi, brother of Hayyim. The Egyptian army, led by Ibrahim Pasha, conquered Syria in 1832. Discriminatory laws against non-Muslims were abolished, but a notorious blood libel occurred in 1840. At the close of the 19th century, the economic situation of the Jews of Damascus declined considerably, primarily as a result of the opening of the Suez Canal and the rerouting of trade patterns. Many Jews from Damascus and elsewhere settled in Beirut, which became an active commercial center. Others emigrated to Egypt, Palestine, North America, Latin America, Great Britain and elsewhere.

Attempts made at the turn of the 20th century to maintain Hebrew schools in Damascus were unsuccessful, but the Orthodox Jews of Aleppo maintained their traditional educational institutions. A Hebrew press was established in Aleppo in 1865. After World War I, in the French protectorates of Syria and Lebanon, large Jewish communities existed in Aleppo,

Beirut and Damascus. Aleppo and Damascus had about 6,000 Jews each, Beirut about 4,000. Another 2,000 Jews lived in smaller communities.

In Qamishli near the Turkish border, most Jews spoke the Kurdish language; in Aleppo, most Jews were descendants of the Spanish expellees, and in Damascus, most were Mustarabs. Although the difference between the communities of Damascus and Aleppo disappeared during the 1950s and 1960s, Damascus Jews and Aleppo Jews still tend to look down upon each other—even after emigrating from Syria.

Approximately 30,000 Jews lived in Syria in the early 1940s, but roughly half emigrated by the end of 1949, many fleeing after anti-Jewish riots in Aleppo in 1947. After the establishment of the State of Israel in 1948, the situation grew worse for the Jews of Syria. Anti-Jewish laws were issued; a prohibition was imposed on the sale of Jewish property (1948); Jewish bank accounts were frozen (1953) and Jews were forbidden to leave the country. In 1964, a decree was enacted that prohibited Jews from traveling more than five kilometers (three miles) beyond the limits of their home towns. Jews were assaulted after the trial of the Israeli intelligence agent Eli Cohen in 1965 and after the Six-Day War in 1967.

Between 1948 and 1961, about 5,000 Syrian Jews reached Israel. In 1972, the number remaining in Syria was estimated at 6,000, and in 1983 only 3,000 were left. Jews of Aleppo developed strong communities in New York, Mexico City, Buenos Aires and Caracas. Another group went from Aleppo to Baghdad, Calcutta and then Shanghai.

In 1992, Jews were allowed to leave Syria, provided their destination was not Israel and that the purpose of their trip was study, tourism or business. Towards the end of 1992, emigration was halted, however, apparently due to the Syrian government's dissatisfaction with the slow pace of the development of Syrian-United States relations. In December 1993, Syria agreed to allow further emigration. About 3,600 Jews went to the United States and 1,200 to Israel. As of 1994, only 230 Jews remained in Syria. By the end of 1995, virtually all Jews who wished to leave had done so.

Genealogical Resources

Because direct access to resources in Syria is impossible at the present time, detailed Jewish-Syrian genealogical investigations are likely to be difficult. Nevertheless, a number of reference works, and at least one direct archival source, are accessible. The following collection of references represents a starting point for Jewish-Syrian genealogical research.

Genealogical Sources

An early and detailed genealogical compilation of about 170 Damascus Jews (including details about themselves and their families) for the years 1540–1640 is included as a separate chapter in a booklet entitled *Lekorot Hayehudim Bedamesek* (History of the Jews in Damascus), by Eliezer and Yosef Yoel Rivlin. (Jerusalem). The booklet is available at the Yad Ben Zvi Institute* in Jerusalem.[1]

Biographies of Aleppo rabbis are described in *Chachamei Aram-Tsoba* (The wise men of Aram-Tsoba) by H. Makover.[2]

(Jerusalem)] The book includes the following surnames: Abadi, Ades, Antebi, Atie, Hadaya, Halevi, Hamawi, Harari-Rafoul, Kaski, Labaton, Laniado, Tawil and Zaafrani.

Kehilat Yehudei Chaleb al-pi Kitvei Hagniza (Jewish community of Chaleb according to the Geniza writings). A master's thesis study by Miriam Frenkel, it includes a chapter on local leaders of Aleppo in the 11th and 12th century.

Shoshana Zonshine's masters thesis on the daily life of the Jewish community of Aleppo, from the middle of the 18th century until the Damascus blood libel includes a list of leaders and rabbis and a genealogical tree of the Laniado family.

A catalogue entitled *Sifrei Rabanei Aram-Tsoba Vekitvei Yadam, Vetoldot Morenu Harva Mordechai Lavton Zets'el* (Books and writings of the rabbis of Aram-Tsoba, and the history of our teacher Harav Mordechai Lavton Zets'el), available from Jerusalem's Haktav Institute,* includes a extensive list of names, and sometimes the year of death, of Aleppo rabbis.

Michpachot Douer-Sakkal-Bnei Kehilat Damesek (Douer-Sakkal families of the Damascus community), published by Yad Tabenkin,* describes the genealogies of the Douer and Sakkal families in Damascus, with roots in Egypt, from the beginning of the 20th century. The book is based on two 1992 family meetings in Yad Tabenkin.

Gdolei Rabanei Suria Vehalebanon (Eminent Rabbis of Syria and Lebanon), by Giora Pozaylov (Jerusalem, 1995). This little booklet in poor shape may be found at the Ben Zvi Institute* in Jerusalem.

The Genealogical Library* in Paris, France, has the following useful sources:

- *Pages Choisies et Index du Livre "Aleppo Chronicles,"* by Joseph D. Sutton, includes a detailed genealogy for many Jewish families who moved from Aleppo and Damascus to Egypt and New York.
- "The Consular Dynasty of the Picciotos," by Alain Bigio. in *Geracoes* 1, no. 2 (1995) [Portuguese].
- A 58-page book entitled *Syrie, Damas, Listes d'Eleves, d'Adherents, d'Ouvrieres (1893–1910)* (Syria, Damascus, list of pupils, members, female workers) which includes handwritten lists of pupils in the boys school and the girls school of Damascus.

The Centre des Archives Diplomatiques de Nantes* has in its possession various archival documents from the French Embassy in Damascus for the years 1824 to 1986 (not all years are covered for all types of documents). Partial data also seem to exist for Aleppo, according to Bierbrier. (see reference below). The Centre holds archives from the French consulate in Beyrouth (Beirut) for the years 1638 to 1978 (including weddings for 1831–81, passports for 1860, relations with Jews in Palestine between 1899 and 1914, information relative to Algerian-French Jews for 1893–1911). Archives for Antioch are mixed with those of Adana, Alexandretta, Ankara, Arsous and Mersine. Arsous and Mersine are towns in the border area between Syria and Turkey.

Also of interest in the Centre are the archives from the French consulate in Buenos Aires for 1833–1970, which include passport registrations of Syrian-Lebanese citizens who emigrated to Argentina. This may be the best (and currently only) direct Syrian-Lebanese resource available.

Morris Bierbrier has intensively researched the pedigrees and history of the Manchester, England, Sephardic community many members of which have origins in Aleppo (see ENGLAND). Several Syrian families came from Livourno and Venice, Italy.

An additional possible source is the Archives of the Alliance Israelite Universelle.

Internet Sites

BSZ.ORG/ASYRIANJEWS.HTM

VIRTUAL.CO.IL/COMMUNITIES/WJCBOOK/SYRIA/INDEX.HTM

WWW.USISRAEL.ORG/JSOURCE/ANTISEMITISM/SYRIANJEWS.HTML

Addresses

American Sephardi Federation, Center for Jewish History, 15 West 16th Street, New York, NY. 10011; telephone: 212-294-8350; fax: 212-294-8348; website: WWW.ASFONLINE.ORG/PORTAL/.

Archives of the Alliance Israelite Universelle, 45 rue de la Bruyere, Paris 75009 France; telephone: 331 5332 8855; fax: 331-4874-5133; e-mail: AIU@IMAGINET.FR.

Association of Syrian Immigrants in Israel, 3 Rosh Pina Street, Tel Aviv 6058, Israel; telephone: 972-3-688-1567, 687-9864.

Centre des Archives Diplomatiques, Ministere des Affaires Etrangers, Direction des Archives et de la Documentation, 17 rue du Casterneau, B.P. 1033, 44036 Nantes, France; telephone: 332-5177-2459; fax: 332-5177-2460.

Genealogical Library, 3 rue de Turbigo, Paris, France

Haktav Institute, P.O. Box 6040, Jerusalem, Israel.

Irgoun Yehudei Suria (Organization of Syrian Jews), Jerusalem, Israel.

Sephardic Magen David Congregation, 7454 Melrose Avenue, Los Angeles, CA 90046.

Syrian Synagogue, Shaare Zion, 2030 Ocean Parkway, Brooklyn, NY 11223.

The American Society of Sephardic Studies, 2815 Ocean Parkway, Brooklyn, NY 11235.

World Center for Aleppo Jews Traditional Culture, Rehov Aaronson 4, Tel-Aviv, Israel.

Yad Ben Zvi Institute, Abravanel 12, Jerusalem, Israel 91076; POB 7660; telephone: 972-2-563 9201/2; fax: 972-2-563 8310; e-mail: MAHONZVI@H2.HUM.HUJI.AC.IL; website SITES.SNUNIT.K12.IL/YBZ/INDEX.HTML.

Yad Tabenkin, Hayasmin Street 1, Ramat Efal, 52960 Israel.

Bibliography-General

Bierbrier, M.L. "The Manchester Sephardi Community and its Sources." Etsi-Sephardi Genealogical and Historical Review 1, no. 3 (Winter 1998): 10–12.

Bierbrier, M.L. "East Meets West: the Altaras Family from Syria to Marseilles." Actes du 5ieme Congress International Genealogie Juive, (Acts of the 5th international congress on Jewish genealogy). Paris: 13–17 Juillet 1997 (1998), 89–96.

Bigio, Alain. "The Consular Dynasty of the Picciotos." [Portuguese] Geracoes 1, no. 2 (1995).

Cardoza, Anne. "Spanish-Jewish `Nobility' of Aleppo, Syria." AVOTAYNU 7, no. 2 (Summer 1991).

———. "Resources for Sephardic Genealogy." AVOTAYNU 8, no. 3 (Fall 1992).

Encyclopedia Judaica, c.f. Syria.

Malka, Jeffrey S. Sephardic Genealogy: Discovering Your Sephardic Ancestors and Their World. Bergenfield, NJ: Avotaynu, 2002.

Rhode, Harold. "The Ottoman Empire and Jewish Genealogy." AVOTAYNU 8, no. 1 (Spring 1992).

Rosanes, Salomon A. Divre Yemei Yisrael be-Togermah (History of the Jews in Turkey and the Levant). [Hebrew] Tel Aviv, 1930. (Available at the U.S. Library of Congress).

Safdie, Abraham. "Family History Without Documents." Sharsheret Hadorot 4, no. 3 (November 1990).

Sinai, Anne, and Pollack, Allen. The Syrian Arab Republic: A Handbook. American Academic Association for Peace in the Middle East, 1976. (See section on the status of Jews, page 65).

Sutton, Joseph D., Aleppo Chronicles (New York: Thayer-Jacoby, 1988). A series of interviews with Syrian Jews, mostly from Aleppo who live in New York or Deal, New Jersey, but who were born in Syria. Mentions many names, often with familial relationships specified. Good background about life in Syria.

Bibliography-Life and Customs of Syrian Jews

Abadi, Moussa. La Reine et le Calligraphe: Mes Juifs de Damas. (The queens and the calligraphy: My Jews of Damascus) [French]. Paris: Christian de Bartillet, 1993.

———. Shimon le Parjure: Mes Juifs de Damas.(Shimon the Perjurer: My Jews of Damascus). [French] Paris: Editions du Lacquet, A.d.

Cohen-Tawil, Abraham. Yahadut Chaleb Be-rei Hadorot (Aleppo Jewry in the mirror of generations).

Shamosh, Amnon. My Sister the Bride. Israel: Massada, 1974.

———. Michel Ezra Safra and Sons. Israel: Massada, 1978.

Steinhorn (Chaluani), Esther. Damesek Iri (Damascus my city). Jerusalem, 1978.

———. Zeakat Yehudei Damesek (Cry of Damascus Jews). Jerusalem, 1982.

Strauss, A. Toldot Hayehudim BeMitsrayim VeSuria (History of the Jews in Egypt and Syria). Jerusalem, 1904.

Sutton, Joseph, A.D. Aleppo in Flatbush. New York, 1979.

———. Aleppo Chronicles. Brooklyn, New York: Thayer-Jacoby, 1988.

Treasures of the Aleppo Community. Jerusalem: The Israel Museum, May 1988. Includes 40 unique photographs of Aleppo taken in 1947 by Sarah Shammah, a native of Aleppo, just before the synagogue was vandalized and desecrated.

Notes

1. Zonshine, Shoshana, Masters Thesis, Department of Islamic Studies, The Hebrew University of Jerusalem (1990). Includes a list of leads and rabbis (p. 48) and a genealogical tree of the Laniado family (pp.45–47).

2. Etsi in AVOTAYNU 15, no. 2 (Summer 1999): 58.

Tunisia

by Sallyann Amdur Sack

Read the chapter entitled OTTOMAN EMPIRE before reading this section. Because Tunisia was once part of the Ottoman Empire, many items discussed in that section apply to this country.—Ed.

This small North African country on the Mediterranean coast, sandwiched between much larger Algeria to the west and Libya to the east, has fewer than 2,000 Jews today. A thousand years ago, it was the largest, most important Jewish community outside of Babylonia (today's Iraq).[1]

Muslim culture flourished between the 9th and 12th centuries in three centers around the Mediterranean basin— Egypt, Ifriqiya (as Tunisia was called then) and Spain, and so did the sizable Jewish populations that found homes among them. A considerable Jewish population had lived in Tunisia earlier, but it is only from this period that we have records. Following is a description of Jewish life during the period from the 9th to 12th centuries.

> Jewish merchants prospered in the generally liberal economic atmosphere of this free-trade zone. The combined factors of general prosperity and official tolerance toward non-Muslims in Fatimid Ifriqiya provided a salubrious climate for the growth and development of a strong and vital Jewish community. The largest concentration of Jews was in Qayrawan, the traditional capital of the province and leading city in all the Maghreb (North Africa). Throughout the greater part of the tenth and eleventh centuries, the Jewish community of Qayrawan was the outstanding major spiritual and intellectual center of Jewry outside of Iraq.[2]

Jewish scholarship especially developed in Tunisia during this time and persisted even after the center of commerce shifted to Egypt.

Jewish life effectively halted in the 12th century as the fanatic Almohad sect, Berbers from the mountains of Morocco, caused the local Jewish community to flee, convert or be killed. Most Jews who left went to Egypt or Syria.[3] After a century of terror, when the Hafsid Berbers took over Tunisia, the Jews enjoyed a period of relative security and tranquility. They paid the *jizya* (Moslem tax on Jews), kept a low profile and adopted the Algerian *minhag* (Jewish prayer ritual).

Significant numbers of Jews fleeing Spain and Portugal settled in Tunisia during the 16th century; in the late 18th century a sizable number of Sephardim came from Livorno, Italy, and together they constituted the majority of Tunisian Jewry. The Livornese came initially as agents for the ransom of Christian slaves captured by North African pirates. Later the Jews became trading agents for their relatives in Italy. The Livornese, called *grana*, had little in common with the native Jews (*touansa*) and maintained themselves as a separate community with their own synagogues, bakeries and even cemeteries. Relationships between the two groups tended to be unfriendly and remained distant up through the 19th century.

Jewish life continued much the same after the Ottoman Turks conquered Tunisia in the 16th century until 1855–59, when civil status reforms for non-Muslims were introduced. At this time, Tunisia was an autonomous tributary state of the Ottoman Empire. Although the special tax paid by Jews was not abolished, the liberalization of laws against the Jews aroused considerable Arab resentment.

Following the Capitulation Treaties (see OTTOMAN EMPIRE chapter) European nations' consular offices offered protection to many Jews, especially those of Spanish, Portuguese or Italian descent. Jews from Livorno tended to prefer Italian protection, while the others opted for French. The Alliance Universelle opened its first schools in 1877, and in 1881, after disturbances on the Tunisia-Algeria border, the French established a protectorate over Tunisia.

Many Jews, especially those whose ancestors were driven from Spain, by reciprocal services or bribery, had succeeded in putting themselves under the protection of the European consulates. This is the reason that "some of the consulates in Tunis count their subjects or proteges by the hundreds, and even thousands, amongst the Tunisian Jews."[4]

The same (non-Jewish) observer claimed that the Jews formed from one-third to one-fifth of the population in the towns along the coast (30,000 in Tunis alone) and in some districts near the Sahara. Because of greater rights enjoyed by virtue of consular protection, they increasingly supplanted the Arabs in trade and industry. Others say, however, that the Jewish population of Tunisia never exceeded 100,000.[5]

Most Jews enthusiastically identified themselves with the French, sent their children to Alliance schools, moved out of the traditional Jewish ghettos into French neighborhoods and generally began a process of modernization, acculturation and assimilation.

But the period of peace and prosperity was short lived. The Germans occupied Tunisia during World War II and pressed Tunisian Jewry into slave labor, although none were deported to European extermination camps. Tunisia gained its independence in 1956, initiating a process of Jewish emigration that became a stampede after the 1967 Six-Days War in Israel. At that time, a mob descended on the Jewish quarter of Tunis, attacked an ancient synagogue and burned a 12th-century Torah from which Rabbi Ibn Ezra (ca. 1089– ca. 1164), the famous poet, philosopher, grammarian and Biblical commentator, had read. Half the Jews emigrated to France at this time; the other half went to Israel—with a tiny number going elsewhere. No more than 2,000 Jews remained in Tunisia.

Genealogical Resources

Tunisia provides no access to its archival holdings at this time, although officials recently have indicated a willingness to discuss the possibility. It is not known whether any genealogically relevant records exist in its archives. No information is available about surviving Jewish cemeteries. Similarly, nothing is known about Jewish cemeteries or records that remained after the mass 20th-century exodus. Genealogical research must focus on people and on records outside of Tunisia today.

Secular Sources

As with other former Ottoman possessions, one potentially excellent source of data may be found in the consular archives of various European powers, especially those of France and Italy. The Archives Departementals de l'Herault* in Montpellier, France, holds French naturalization applications for the years 1830 to 1920. The Centre des Archives Diplomatiques* (Center for Diplomatic Archives) in Nantes, France, holds records of Tunisians granted French consular protection. For Italy, look in the archives of the Italian Foreign Office.*

Two other sources are worth checking for those with an Italian background. Before World War II, many Tunis Jews of Italian background were Freemasons. The archives of the Grande Oriente d'Italia* (Freemasons) in Rome are open to the public and hold considerable information about Jewish Freemasons from Tunis.

GAMT, a genealogical society for individuals with roots in Algeria, Morocco and Tunisia is active in France today. The Cercle de Généalogie Juive (Jewish Genealogical Society)* in Paris maintains good relations with the group; English abstracts of its publications and activities may be found in the *AVOTAYNU* Contributing Editor for France references in the bibliography at the end of this chapter.

Jewish Sources: Documents and Publications

Ketubot (marriage contracts), where they have survived, are prime genealogical treasures. A few from Tunisia are scattered in libraries and museums worldwide. The Portuguese population of Tunisia (including the Jews from Livorno) kept excellent records. Ten *ketubot* dating from 1754 to 1917 are in Jerusalem today; two are in private hands in Paris. The collection of 1,031 *ketubot* has been edited and published (in French) by Robert Attal and Joseph Avivi.[6] The publication is an easy-to-use, indispensable source for Tunisian-Jewish genealogy; microfilms of the documents from which one can read the full text are held at Jerusalem's Central Archives for the History of the Jewish People.* The first volume, covering the years 1788–1824, was brought from Tunis to Paris by Jacob Bouccara, grandson of Rabbi Jacob Bouccara (1843–1941), chief rabbi of Tunis. The second volume, covering the years 1853–78, now is held by Hanna Bouccara (granddaughter of Rabbi Jacob Bouccara) who brought it from Tunis to Paris in 1956. The book for volume 2, missing from the Bouccara family collection, has been found after extraordinary effort. It covers the years 1843–54. All information in the marriage reg-

Tunisian-Jewish men in tradition garb at the beginning of the 20th century.

isters has been transcribed. The transcription presents dates of marriage, names of the betrothed couple and their fathers, names of scribes and witnesses and other facts, such as places of origin and husbands or fathers who were physicians, the amount to be paid in case of death or divorce and miscellaneous information about the couple, such as cases in which the wives were childless widows and, consequently, in need of *levirate* marriage or *halitzah* (release from levirate marriage).

The books also have several indexes—of names, frequency of names, names of places and their frequency, and where they occur. Valuable information about migration patterns within Tunisia, from village to the capital city and important genealogical data on the Jews of Tunis during the 19th century also is presented. Almost as valuable is a publication listing Tunisian rabbis for which Mathilde Tagger has prepared an index of names.[7]

Much has been written about Tunisian Jewry in a variety of languages. Each of the references cited at the end of this chapter includes footnotes and bibliographies leading to other, more detailed, specialized studies. As the primary institution for Sephardic studies, the Ben Zvi Institute* archives holds a variety of items of potential value. Its joint (with Hebrew University) *Oriens Judaicus* project for the Study of Jewish Communities in the East has produced a number of publications about North African Jewry that include items about Tunisia. The Central Archives for the

History of the Jewish People* in Jerusalem holds a few genealogically valuable registers from Tunisia.

Jewish Sources: People

Because Jews from Tunisia emigrated relatively recently and primarily to France and Israel, the Cercle de Généalogie Juive* and genealogical societies in Israel—the Israel Genealogical Society* and the Jewish Family Research Association*—are the most likely resources for person-to-person networking. See especially *AVOTAYNU* references to "contributing editor, France" at the end of this chapter.

Sephardic genealogy forums on the Internet offer additional resources and are especially good places to list interests and to look for others researching a family name. These include:

WWW.HARISSA.COM/ACCUEILENG.HTM
WWW.US-ISRAEL.ORG/SOURCE/ANTI-SEMITISM/TUNISJEWS.HTML
WWW.SEPHARDICSTUDIES.ORG/TUNIS_DEP_FRAN_PDF

In the past few centuries, considerable migration occurred between Livorno and Tunisia, but this movement seems to be the exception, if the list of Portuguese *ketubot* edited by Attal and Avivi are representative. Of the 1,031 documents cited, in only 21 cases did one of the partners live somewhere other than Tunis. Apparently, until the post-1967 mass emigration, Tunisian Jewry was relatively self-contained. For this reason, it may be relatively easy to locate family members if the name can be found in one of the many lists posted on the Web. *[Shalom Bronstein, Elias Boccara and Mathilde Tagger contributed to this chapter.]*

Addresses

Archives Departementals de l'Herault, 2 Avenue de Castelnau, 34001 Montpellier, France; telephone: 4-6714-8214; fax: 4-6702-1528.

Archives Diplomatique d'Outre Mer, 19 rue du Casterneau, 44000 Nantes, France

Association of Former Residents of Tunisia in Israel, 12 Rabbi Meir Street, 93485 Jerusalem; telephone: 972-2-678-2301.

Ben Zvi Institute, mailing address: P.O. Box 7600/7504, Jerusalem 91076; street address: Abarbanel Street, Gan HaKuzari, Rehavia, Jerusalem, Israel

Central Archives for the History of the Jewish People, mailing address: P.O. Box 1149, Jerusalem 91010 Israel; street address: 46 Jabotinsky Street, Jerusalem, Israel

Cercle de Genealogie Juive, 14 rue Saint-Lazare, 75009 Paris, France; telephone/fax: 33-1-4023-0490

Grande Oriente d'Italia, Palazzo Giustiniani, Rome, Italy

Israel Genealogical Society. P.O. Box 4270, Jerusalem 91041, Israel

Jewish Community Center, 15 rue de Cap Vert, Tunis, Tunisia; telephone: 216-1-282-469; 287-153

Jewish Family Research Association, c/o Dardashti, 11 Grinberg #57, Ezorei Chen, Tel Aviv, Israel; telephone: 972 3-699-1693; fax: 972-3-741-1158; e-mail: DARDASHT@BARAK-ONLINE.CO.IL

Ministero degli Affari Esteri, Piazzale della Farnesina, 00194 Rome, Italy

Bibliography

"Al Qabisi (Alkabets) family from Kairowan: The Arabic Portion of the Cairo Genizah at Cambridge." *Jewish Quarterly Review*, 16 (1904), 573-78.

Attal, Robert. *Yahadut Tzafon-Africa: Bibliografich* (Bibliography on the Jewry of North Africa. [Hebrew] Jerusalem: Ben Zvi Institute, 1973. Includes biographies and family histories.

———. *Tunisie*. In *Les Juifs d'Afrique du Nord;* bibliographie. Edition refondue et elargie. Jerusalem, Ben Zvi Institute, 1993. pp. 147-262. Includes: 2,000 bibliographical citations(from item no. 2250 to item no. 4250b). Indexes at the end of the book.

———. *Ketubot d'Afrique du Nord a Jerusalem* (North African marriage contracts in Jerusalem). [French] Jerusalem: Ben Zvi Institute, 1984.

Attal, Robert, and Joseph Avivi. *Registres Matrimoniaux de la Communauté Juive Portugaise de Tunis au XVIIIᵉ et XIXᵉ siecles* (Marriage registers from the Portuguese Jewish community of Tunis in the 18th and 19th centuries). [French] Jerusalem: Ben Zvi Institute, 1989.

Cohen, Benyamin Raphael. *Malkhei Tarshish*. [Hebrew]. Jerusalem, 1986. This is a biographical dictionary of Tunisian rabbis, including those from Djerba.

Contributing editor (Canada). *AVOTAYNU* 7, no. 1 (Spring 1991): 26.

Contributing editor (France). *AVOTAYNU* 11, no. 4 (Winter 1995): 56.

Contributing editor (France). *AVOTAYNU* 14, no. 1 (Spring 1998): 48. Cites *Etre juif au Maghreb a la veille de la colonisation* (Jewish life in North Africa before French colonization), by Jacques Taieb.

Contributing editor (Israel). *AVOTAYNU*, 10, no. 4 (Winter 1994): 65.

Gaon, Solomon and M. Mitchell Serel, eds. *Sephardim and the Holocaust*. New York: Yeshiva University Press, 1987.

Della Pergoli, Sergio. "The Quantitative Aspect of the Distribution of Italian Jewish Names," in *L'annuario di Studi Ebraici*.

Hadad, Moshe David. "*Hagut libi: toldo ha-mehaber vekhen toldot mishpahat hamehaber*" (The family history of the author). *Maamar Ester*. [Hebrew] Djerba, 1946: 1-27.

Hadad, Nissim. "*Toldot ha-mehaber vekhen toldot mishpahat hamehaber*" (The biography of the author and his family history). *Hen tov lemarei nefesh*. [Hebrew] Djerba, 1946: 9-34.

"Jews of Livorno, Italy." *AVOTAYNU*, 12, no. 4 (Winter 1996). Includes names from Tunisia.

Laskier, Michael M. *North African Jewry in the Twentieth Century: The Jews of Morocco, Tunisia and Algeria*. New York: New York University Press, 1994.

Nos martyrs sous la botte Allemand; les ex-travailleurs Juis de Tunisie racontent leur souffrances (Memorial to Jewish laborers under German rule in Tunis; former slave laborers recount their suffering). [Judeo-Arabic, French] Tunis: Gaston Guez, 1946.

"Report on a Return Trip to Israel." *AVOTAYNU* 11, no. 4 (Winter 1995).

Stillman, Norman. *The Jews of Arab Lands: A History and Source Book*. Philadelphia: Jewish Publication Society, 1979.

Tagger, Mathilde. *Maftehot lasefer "Malkhei Tarshish" le-Rab. Benyamin Rafael Cohen*. [Hebrew] Jerusalem: Ben Zvi Institute, 1994. Indexes of the book *Malkhei Tarshish*, by Benyamin Raphael Cohen.

———. "The Jews of Tunisia Under the Nazis." *Memoire de Genocide*. Jerusalem: Le Centre de Documentation Juive Contemporaine. Contributing Editors (France). *AVOTAYNU* 4, no. 1 (Spring 1988).

Notes

1. Stillman; 40–43
2. *op. cit.*: 44
3. *op. cit.*: 61
4. *op. cit.*: 417
5. *op. cit.*: 416, 419
6. Attal and Avivi, *Registres Matrimoniaux*
7. Tagger

Turkey

by Stella Kent

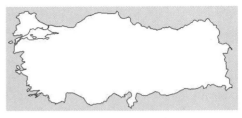

Read the chapter entitled OTTOMAN EMPIRE *before starting this section—Ed.*

Turkey lies between Asia and Europe. Part of the country which is surrounded by the Bosphorous, the Dardanelles and the Aegean Sea in the west, the Black Sea in the north and the Mediterranean Sea in the south, is known as the Anatolian peninsula. Ancient Greeks and Romans referred to western Anatolia as "Asia." Later, the term "Asia Minor" was used to differentiate between Asia and Anatolia. Istanbul, the capital, is a city unique in the world as it falls right between the two continents separated by the Bosphorous. The section that remains in Asia also is called the Anatolian part of Istanbul, while the opposite shore is know as the "European side."

The Genealogical Society of Turkey, known as the "Roots Committee," was established in 1991 under the patronage of the Chief Rabbinate. Its primary function at the beginning was to raise consciousness about Sephardic history, genealogy in general and its importance to Judaism. The group which consisted of non-professional volunteers tried to collect and computerize data, provided the technical information needed to make family trees and helped to organize family reunions. Unfortunately this organization does not exist today and one needs to seek help directly through the Rabbinate or by contacting community leaders.

Diaspora Jewry with ancestry in Turkey has a growing interest in searching its roots as well. The wishes usually are threefold: to obtain vital records of ancestors, to learn about community life and historical events in a certain era and/or from a certain region, and to discover and meet any relatives they may have living in Turkey today.

The Sephardic community, much like the larger Muslim Turkish society, does not have an innate interest in its roots. Individuals are reluctant to kindle memories of the past, of the years of war and their hardships.[1] Community institutions have not done well keeping records of the past either. Demographic changes left settlements without organized communities; synagogues and schools were closed. Most of the archives and paperwork that could be valuable to the genealogist was lost—thrown out or given away without consideration of its historical value. In some cases, fires[2] devastated entire neighborhoods, consuming documentation as well, but anything that could be saved soon will be displayed in The Jewish Museum of Istanbul.* Many other records are hidden away, waiting to be found and classified.

All of these factors have been sizable obstacles to the Roots Committee's efforts to obtain vital records. The group has been more successful in providing factual information and in uniting relatives. More professionalism and community support is need if we are to offer better service, something we hope will occur soon. What follows is a short summary of the past and present of the Jewish communities in Turkey and its existing archives and documents. We list readings about our history with the hope of guiding the reader and telling him or her what to expect.

History

Jewish existence in Anatolia dates back to antiquity. When Alexander the Great (265-323 B.C.E.) invaded Palestine and the concept of "Diaspora" was born, Jews encountered the Hellenistic world. Their geography expanded as Jews migrated to Europe, Asia Minor and North Africa either of their own free will or through forced expulsions as Roman slaves. Asia Minor was one of the major areas of Jewish concentration in the Diaspora. Jews settled in Sinop and Trabzon, Black Sea ports on the ancient trade routes. After the destruction of the Second Temple in 70 C.E., Jews lived in eastern and southern Anatolia in such cities as Antioch and Nusaybin. Historian and writer Avram Galante, one of the major sources of information about Sephardic history in Anatolia, has written about the communities of Ankara, Kayseri, Konya and Tokat in central Anatolia; Baskale, Diyarbakir, Gaziantep, Hakkari, Maras, Mardin Malatya, Urfa and Van in the east and southeast; Adana, Antalya, Fethiye and Mersin on the Mediterranean; Aydýn, Bodrum, Denizli, Manisa, Mugla, Symrna (today, Izmir) and Tire on the Aegean; and Balikesir, Bursa, Canakkale (the Dardanelles), Corlu, Edirne, Kirklarelý and Tekirdað in the Marmara region where Istanbul (formerly Constantinople) is the leading city. Jews lived in commercial centers and on their periphery. Besides the Romaniote (Greek or Byzantium) Jews there also came communities of Ashkenazic Jews fleeing pogroms in Christian Europe.

The Jewish population increased with the settlement of Spanish and Portuguese Jews after the Spanish Edict of Expulsion in 1492 and the subsequent establishment of the Inquisition in both of those countries. The newcomers, numerically and culturally superior, mingled with the older, established Anatolian-Romaniote[3] communities and formed a predominantly Sephardic community.

Ashkenazic Jews came to lands in many waves. During the 14th and 15th centuries, European Jews were under considerable Christian oppression; Ottoman tolerance of non-Muslim subjects was inviting to many. Some arrived in 1470, when the German King Ludwig X expelled Jews of Bavarian, Hungarian, Italian, Polish and Russian origin; the Ottomans settled all of them in Andrianople, thus founding the Ashkenazic community of Turkey. Other Ashkenazic Jews who left Bavaria and other central European states at the time of the Spanish Expulsion were settled in Istanbul, Plevne, Salonika and Sophia by Beyazýd II. Around 1550, at the time of Suleyman the Magnificent, many Ashkenazim who were victimized during the

Turkish invasion of Serbia and Hungary were invited to live in Ottoman lands with an imperial decree known as *Firman de los Almanes* (the German Decree). They settled in Andrianople, Constantinople and Saloniki, as well as Bulgaria, Egypt, Greece, Palestine and Thrace. Ashkenazic emigration to Turkey continued in different periods up to 1920.

In 1934, after the foundation of the Turkish Republic, a law was passed (called *Soyadi Kanunu*) that mandated the adoption of family names for all citizens. In reality, most Turkish Jews already had them. Jews of southern Europe, Venice and today's Italy, had begun to use family names in the 10th and 11th centuries, as did the Jews of Spain in the 13th century. Most Turkish-Jewish families had surnames that referred to their geographic origins, such as "Loya" or "de Toledo." Others had names that were biblical in origin, or derived from their professions or physical appearance. Those of Portuguese *converso* origin had Spanish surnames adopted during their conversion to Catholicism. Many others had ancient names of Arabic origin (Alhadeff), or translated from Hebrew names (Benveniste from Shalom) or Arabic names (Amado or Querido from Habib).

With the passage of the 1934 law, Jews went to census departments to register their names officially, as requested, but not everyone could register the names they wanted. In certain areas, especially in the provinces of Anatolia, Jews were at the mercy of the government official in charge. If, for example, the official decided that too many Kohens, Levi or Behars had already registered, then the next applicant with these names might be required to adopt Ozbahar, Miskohen or Erlev; a mocking officer turned Bahar (spring in Turkish) into Kis which means winter.

Another problem derives from the fact that many Jewish families willingly adopted Turkish names in the hope of avoiding confrontation with the Muslim community. Thus, their line with the past was broken and today we have cases where the younger generation does not know its real Jewish name. Name adoption records do not exist.

Throughout history, Jews have moved all around Anatolia. Earthquakes, epidemics, fires, forced settlements, industrialization, urbanization and wars have forced some movements. Twentieth-century political events and social upheavals such as *varlik*[4] (a tax on wealth) and the so-called "Twenty Classes," forced military service of non-Muslims, and the Thrace upheaval intimidated the Jewish population.[5] These events, plus the creation of the State of Israel, all spurred emigration to Israel.

Today, the Jews of Turkey live primarily in Istanbul where they number approximately 23,000. Other cities that still have an organized Jewish community with functioning synagogues and other communal organizations are Adana, Ankara, Antakya, Bursa, Canakkale-Dardanelles, Gallipoli, Kyklarelýand Edirne-Andrinople. The community of Iskenderum recently disbanded.

Government Records

Registers of Non-Muslim Communities

In the Prime Minister's Archives (*Basbakanlik Arsivi*) in Istanbul and Ankara are registers, *Gayr-I Muslim Cemaatlere Ait Defterler,* pertaining to the non-Muslim communities. During the Ottoman Period, every non-Muslim adult male (*zimmi*) called *dhimmi* (protected by the state) had to pay a tax called *cizye* as a sign of his submission to the dominant religion and as a compensation for the solidarity shown to them despite their inferior status. In return, they also were exempt from military service. Records exist of the collection of these taxes.

There also are inheritance registers (*tereke defterleri*) of Ottoman Jews drawn up in Islamic religious courts. Records about the deceased, created by the court, consist of the date and place of death, list of inheritors and inventory of the goods, property, debts and credits. These provide a glimpse into the life of the individual Jewish family, patterns of the accumulation of wealth and the nature of commercial transactions.

Also extant are expense registers that are detailed account books of the elite Ottoman households covering all household transactions from one month to several years. From them one can glean information on some aspects of Jewish participation in Ottoman society as artisans, physicians, laborers or even as converts.

Jewish Communities in Istanbul

The dominant Jewish community is Sephardic, descendants of Jews expelled from Spain and Portugal. Georgian Jews and Jews from Arabic lands also call themselves Sephardic although this is really not the case. A small Romaniote population descends from Jews who resided in the Greek peninsula, Anatolia, Constantinople and Thrace before Ottoman rule. Some Romaniotes can be traced by family name, but on the whole they cannot be distinguished from the Sephardim who, over time, became culturally and physically dominant. Two other communities are officially represented, the Ashkenazim and the Italian community. Each community has its own separate synagogues, cemeteries, organizations, rituals and community leader, although all are represented by the Sephardic Chief Rabbinate.

Ashkenazic Community. Today the Ashkenazic community is very small in Istanbul. It has a beautifully kept century-old synagogue in Yüksek kaldyrym, a well-known Jewish neighborhood, and a cemetery in Ulus that opened in 1920. Before then, this community primarily used the Balat, Feriköy, Hasköy and Kuzguncuk cemeteries; its records were kept in Yiddish. Records of burials are kept from 1916 to 1999 and are in chronological order; no alphabetical index exists. Birth records (in Yiddish) are available from 1880 and in Turkish from 1917 to 1998. Births of girls are not methodically recorded. Marriage records are available from 1873 onwards, initially in Yiddish but in Turkish from 1923–98. "Mixed" marriages (whether with a Sephardic Jew or a non-Jew) are not recorded. Records of the Ashkenazic community* may be reached through its secretary.

Or Ahayim Hospital in the Balat section of Istanbul at the beginning of the 20th century

Italian Community. The Italian community, founded in 1862 under the protection of the Italian government, consists of Italian Jews and those of nationalities other than Turkish. Although residents of Turkey, they still carry Bulgarian, German, Spanish and other passports. The first record is of August Castro born November 24, 1841. Birth, marriage and death records have all been kept chronologically and alphabetically. The trace of a member is lost, however, if he or she married someone of Turkish nationality. The synagogue at Kuledibi is a magnificent monument, more than 100 years old. The cemetery at Sisli was established by a decree of Sultan Abdulaziz (1830–76) and the first burial was in 1862. Some burial records are available at the community headquarters in Karakoy.*

The Karaite community is very small, but it has a well-kept synagogue and a very old cemetery at Hasköy. Also in Istanbul are Georgian Jews, as well as those of Iranian, Iraqi and Syrian origin who have joined the Sephardic community, but who still maintain their own traditions.

Records of Istanbul

The Neve Shalom Synagogue Foundation* maintains Neve Shalom Synagogue, a relatively new synagogue in Karaköy Büyük Hendek Street, and the biggest in Turkey. It is the place where 23 members were killed at their morning prayer in a terrorist attack on September 6, 1986. Almost all Sephardic weddings and funerals are performed here as well as religious celebrations. The Foundation keeps most of the records of the Sephardi community, especially those of Balat, Galata, Hasköy and Kasimpala. Following are the genealogically useful records held by the Foundation.

Death Records, called *kalamazo* registers are available for the years 1910–50 and are kept alphabetically. All earlier records burned in fires. After 1918, the cemetery and place of death are included in the records. Another register for the years 1910–50 shows burial plots in the *muevo cimiterio* (new cemetery) in the Birinci Ulus district.

Mortuary Records for the years 1930–48 include burials in Hasköy, Kuzguncuk and Ortaköy. Records of burial plots for the years 1921–50 covering location and type of tombstone have been computerized. Two registers, those for the period 1950–74 and from 1974 onward, are available in alphabetical and chronological order. The Ulus cemetery has been used extensively for the past decade and is now completely filled. In 1987, part of the Ashkenazic graveyard in Ulus Etiler was consecrated to the Sephardim; it is now filled also.

Jewish girls in Smyrna (now Izmir) at the beginning of the 20th century

Brit Milah (Circumcision) Records are found in three registers: No. 1 (1915–49), No. 2 (1949–78), No. 3 (1978 to the present). Given name and family names of both parents, birth and circumcision dates, *reşut milah* number are all in both chronological and alphabetical order. (The *resut milah* number is a number given when the Rabbinate grants permission for a bar mitzvah thereby certifying that the boy is totally Jewish.)

Marriage Records. Three registers have been found. The oldest register was for the years 1961–73; it includes ceremonies held in Balat-Ahrida, Kuzguncuk and Zulfaris, the Ashkenazic and Italian synagogues as well as Neve Shalom. A second register (1979–93) is partly in Judeo-Espagnol and the third from 1993 to the present. All provide the given names and family names of both sides, nationalities, status (bachelor, divorced, widow), *kaal* (synagogue—primarily Neve Shalom), address, *aşugar* (dowry as written in the *ketuba*) and date of civil marriage. Everyone must have a civil marriage before the religious one. All records are arranged chronologically.

Records of all Sephardic marriages in Istanbul are kept at the office of the chief rabbi at Tünel. An index exists from 1886 onward, through the family name of the bridegroom. Until April 8, 1963, all information was written in *solitero*, old Jewish writing. Included is the name of the rabbi who performed the ceremony, the name of the synagogue and the information written on the *ketuba*. Up to 1955, the residences are in Balat, Beyoglu, Galata, Hasköy, Haydarpasa, Kadiköy, Kuzguncuk, Ortaköy, Sirkeci, Taksim, Tarlabasi and Tozkoparan. The population consisted primarily of artisans and tradesmen, cloth sellers, glaziers, shoemakers and employees of various sorts. After 1955, places of residence began to change as did occupations. More people lived in Ayazpasa, Kurtulus, Macka, Nisantasi, Osmanbey and Sisli and more people engaged in trade, showing transformations in the society.

Jewish Communities in Istanbul

Hasköy Community. The Hasköy community was a very old and predominantly Jewish residential area on the Golden Horn with more than 17 synagogues; the Hasköy cemetery was allotted to the community at the end of 1582 by edict of the Sultan. Today, however, almost no Jews reside in this area. Maalem, the only synagogue, is kept open by a few old residents. The primary causes of the depopulation were epidemics and major fires that swept whole quarters, such as the one in 1908 which reduced to ashes the Naftali Synagogue, 30 shops and 300 houses, leaving 5,000 people homeless. Most moved to Beyoglu, Galata and areas to the north. The Old People's Home on the former site of the Alliance Israelite School is the only Jewish institution still standing in this neighborhood. The area is very poor and hardly anything remains of its golden days. Hasköy Cemetery has been damaged by road construction and many stones are dislodged. No records exist before the mid-20th century, but Professor Minna Rozen of the Diaspora Research Institute at Tel Aviv University has completed an extensive study of the existing tombstones, recording all legible inscriptions. As of this writing, Rozen's data is not publicly available, although researchers may write for individual information.

Balat Community. The Balat Community is an old community on the opposite side of the Golden Horn from Hasköy where approximately 10,000 Jews lived at the turn of the 20th century. Today, only the Ahrida Synagogue, restored for the Quincentennial, and the Yanbol Synagogue stand witness to the olden days. The Balat Ahrýda Synagogue Foundation is the institution in charge of the old community. Contact The Rabbýnate to acquire permission for a tour.

Ortaköy Community.* The Ortaköy Community is another of the oldest Jewish communities on the European side of Istanbul. It is said to date back to Byzantine times, while documents point to the residence of Jews at least as far back as the 17th century. The monumental resident of the Inquisition-era notable, Don Josef Nasi, Duke of Naxos, was situated in the area called Belevedere. The population here was increased by White Russian immigrants in 1921 and by those fleeing from devastating fires in other neighborhoods, especially one in Bedesten (another neighborhood) in 1618.

Ortaköy also has been the victim of fire. The Kal Kadoş Etz Ahayim Synagogue on the main street, Muallim Nci, was seriously damaged by fire in 1703 and in 1813. The building burned to its foundation on Yom Kippur night in 1941, along with all existing documents and records. Etz Ahayim was rebuilt and again stands side by side with a mosque and a church—a visible sign that non-Muslim communities have coexisted in this area.

Jews lived primarily in Portakal Yokusu, 18 Akaretler-los Dizioco, Taşmerdiven and Karakaş. La Kaleja, is still the Jewish marketplace, but Jews no longer live there. The Duek, Ergas, Hasid, Iile, Kasatoryano, Luzeri, Avram Muppak, Rosales, Rosanes and Celebon Yaep families are known to come from Ortaköy. Currently Sami Kutiyel and Rabbi Pasensya are the oldest Jewish inhabitants left to recount the recent history of this district. At one time, only 20 families were left of the 700 residents in 1936, but recently the area has become popular again, welcoming well-to-do residents. Arnavuköy, Büyükdere, Kuruceşme and Yeniköy are nearby districts with minor Jewish communities.

Ortaköy has been an important religious and cultural center. Rabbi Yaakov Arguete, Rabbi Naftali Akohen and Rabbi Nisim Bitran were renown *Mare de Atra* (chief rabbis) in the late 19th-century theology. Ortaköy had two *yeshivot* and an orphanage, as well as a primary school that closed 40 years ago. Birth records (actually *brit milah*) are available in old Turkish, *Solitero* and Hebrew. They are kept in the synagogue's archives, in the library beside the main building. The Ortaköy cemetery, situated on the hills overlooking the Bosphorous has tombstones that are more than 400 years old, but its records are only of the last decades. People such as the grave digger, Burhan Bey, can be a major source of information.

Kadiköy-Haydarpasa Community.* This community on the Asian side of Istanbul was first established by Ashkenazic Jews fleeing from Europe in the middle of the 19th century. They mingled with those of Daghamam and Sirkeci who came later. Yeldeoirmeni was a major residential area in Kadiköy, at that time in the district of Haydarpasa. The precious Hemdat Israel Synagogue was built more than one hundred years ago in this region. It has a chronological obituaries register begun in 1914 with records of unknown soldiers of war. It also possesses a chronological burial record book begun in 1950 that records name, address, birth date, cause of death, plot number (occasionally). Burial permission slips were issued after 1960. The cemetery is at Acýbadem and is known as the Zeamet; in addition, the community has a separate plot in the Kuzguncuk cemetery. Burial records for the Acibadem-Zeamet cemetery are available for the years 1959 to 1980 in the archives of the community.

Bar mitzvah and wedding application forms have been issued since 1964. Two notebooks exist for weddings (1955–64) and (1964 to the present) as well as three slips of *reşut mila* from July 19, 1924/5715 (Jewish date). Currently, bar mitzvah ceremonies are most frequently held at the Caddebostan Synagogue around which a new and prominent community has formed.

Kuzguncuk Community. The Kuzguncuk community is the only one to survive among those of Baglarbasi, Beykoz, Daghamam, Pasabahce and Selamsiz, minor settlements in the same area. History books write about the existence of a community here in 1625. Wealthy Jews from areas of plight came to live at Daghamam in the hills of Usküdar, but a disastrous fire swept the entire area in 1921 forcing everyone to move to Kuzguncuk and Haydarpasa. Limon Mahalle, Icadiye Street, the Bostan and Virane were preferred regions. Kuzguncuk was and is still a peaceful area with few new buildings, but the prosperous families have left leaving behind the few of lower income. Currently, Yaakov Mizrahi is the oldest inhabitant who can tell about the "here and there" of the district. The newly restored Beth Yaakov Synagogue and the Virane Synagogue are still kept open through the efforts of old residents who go there for Shabbat and holidays. Yaakov Abudara, the community leader of Kuzguncuk, reports that the community possesses burial records for the period July 5, 1939, to August 27, 1943, after which there is a gap until 1980. All records since 1980 have been preserved. The grave digger,

Bayram bey is the major source of information about the cemetery which is in need of upkeep. He can be found either at the cemetery or via synagogue personnel.

Rabbinate Library

The library of the Chief Rabbi has numerous very old books, primarily religious in nature, but it is limited in documents and archives. Many important papers have been lost because of inadequate storage and lack of a computer system during restoration periods. We believe that considerable genealogically relevant information exists in dossiers that have not been examined yet. The Roots Committee had always been in direct contact wýth the Rabbinate and the rabbis are always ready to help those searching their ancestors—especially if notified in advance of onsite visits.

Jewish Settlements in Anatolia

Izmir (formerly Symrna)*

Izmir is the city with the second largest Jewish population in Turkey. Jews have lived in this area for more than 2,400 years through periods of major upheavals. The community became a spiritual center and reached its peak during the 19th century. In 1620, 10,000 Jews lived in Symrna; by the start of the 20th century its population of 50,000 was served by 50 synagogues and *midrashim* (houses of prayer). Economic difficulties between 1908 and 1918 generated massive emigration to the Western hemisphere and a decline in population to 25,000. This was followed by a massive wave of *aliyah* to Israel in the years 1945–50 of those suffering from the effects of World War II, leaving the community with a current population of 2,350 Jews and only 7 synagogues.

In the past, the Jews of Izmir did not live in the city proper, but instead lived in Havra, Ikicesmelik, Sokak and Dikilitas; later in Göztepe, Karantina, Karatas and Karsiyaka. Today, the entire community has come to live in Alsancak, leaving former residences in such areas as Aydýn, Manisa, Milas and Tire. Certain family names were associated with certain localities. Thus, those searching the Saul family should look for earlier roots in Aydin; the Kanyas family had roots in Tire.

Birth and *brit milah*, marriage and death records have been preserved since 1908 with a gap for the war years of 1915–18. Earlier documents are presumed to have burned in the frequent fires of Izmir. *Livro de nasimiyento* (birth records)—for boys only—show the residential *mahalle* (quarter) such as Dikilitas, Efrati, Gaves and HurÕediye. A similar register for girls was started in 1945, but it is incomplete. All of these records can be found in the Rabbinate.

Individual *Livro de Matrimonyo* (marriage records) consist of two pages that provide full information about place and registry of birth, inside and outside of Izmir, profession of the groom, his *situasyon* (situation, i.e., single, divorced or widower), amount of money shown in the *ketuba* and additional family details. Records are not, however, in alphabetical order which creates some difficulties for the researcher. Community leaders can help. The Central Archives for the History of the Jewish People in Jerusalem holds marriage registers

Main synagogue in Smyrna (now Izmir) at the beginning of the 20th century

from 1883 to 1933 (see ISRAEL). *Etsi*, a Sephardic genealogical and historical review, has published—in Roman letters—a statistical and onomastic study of the names using an index prepared by Dov Cohen.[6]

Neither old cemetery at Gürceşme, nor the one in Bornova, have been used since 1934, but Professor Minna Rozen has included the Gürceşme cemetery in her research project. Since February 12, 1934, all burials have been in the Altyndao cemetery. Izak Strugo who works in the community has extracted all Jewish family names presently used in Izmir as well as those that no longer appear. He can be contacted through the Rabbinate. Jews did not, however, live in Izmir proper. Rather, they lived in neighboring areas such as Aydýn, Manisa and Milas. To do research, a genealogist must know exactly where his family resided.

Aydýn once had a Jewish community bigger than that of Izmir. Today, the old Jewish cemetery has become a military zone and the former Alliance school is a Turkish primary school. In Tire, a neighboring district, the *Kehila Grande* (big synagogue) is closed and has been rented to a local businessman. A hospital has been built on the grounds of the old cemetery, and the new cemetery has been transferred since its area has become an industrial site.

Adana

Although Adana had ancient Jewish colonies, an organized community was not established until the end of the 19th century and, at its peak, never exceeded 300 at most. Jozef Amado, the current head of the community, reports that the community shrunk considerably after 1948 and that its records were not kept regularly. The current Jewish population is approximately 50 individuals. Rabbi Gaston Mizrahi was the last rabbi of its only synagogue; the *hazzan* (cantor) Mose Koronado performs services now. The cemetery is within the Muslim graveyard, surrounded by a wall, and is well kept. The community generally was prosperous and composed primarily of businessmen. Jewish family names used were Bahar, Benyeş, Eskenazi, Meşulam, Mizrahi and Termin.

Ankara*

This Jewish community is an old but minor one, never exceeding 1,000 people. Today a single synagogue, one of three, remains open. It has been completely restored, but no minyan remains. The residential area of the community has moved far away, leaving the synagogue in the middle of a Turkish *mahalle* (quarter). The population of about 100 is young and goes to the synagogue only on Rosh Hashanah and Yom Kippur. The remains in the old cemetery of Mamak has been removed to Cebci. The synagogue possesses precious scrolls and documentation, some of which are missing.

Bursa*

Bursa is one of the cities to have an old Anatolian community which flourished during Ottoman times. The population increased after expulsion of the Jews from Spain in 1492 and became predominantly Sephardic. In the first census taken after creation of the Republic in 1923, 1,862 Jews were counted. The number rose to 3,000 Jews in 1950 and then declined drastically when the youth and lower middle class began to emigrate to Israel and to Istanbul. Today, only about 10 to 15 families remain. The old Jewish quarter at *Sakarya Sokaoy* is under the protection of the state. The Mayor Synagogue, built in the 15th century, was in use until 1957. Ezra Venturero, acting head of the community, reports no existing old documents and says that a marriage or bar mitzvah occurs only about once every five years.

Canakkale

Together with the districts of Bayramic, Biga, Ezine, Kemer and Lapseki, Canakkale had Jewish residents before the Ottomans and had an organized community in the 17th century. Canakkale and Gallipoli, situated on either side of the Dardanelles, were strategic points and trade centers. Many Jewish residents acted as consuls and translators to foreigners, but most engaged in commerce. Because Canakkale was a major port, it also was an area of continuous warfare which, in the long run, led to the decline of the community. Many emigrated to the United States or Argentina in pursuit of new opportunities or to avoid interminable military service. This formerly rich community which one had a population of 3,000, is now reduced to fewer than 20.

Of the three synagogues, only the 200-year-old Mekor Hayim still is used. The old cemetery was first divided into two parts following road construction; today, nothing remains. The city expanded and the graveyard was transformed into the Quincentennial Park. Most of the tombstones have been used in building walls and even in toilets in slum areas, while some were moved to a distinctive corner in the new cemetery, a plot within the Muslim burial ground. Mr Yýlmaz Benadrete, a native of Çanakkale who now lives in Istanbul, leads a group of old residents to visit once a year.

Gallipoli

Gallipoli also has lost its Jewish population. Israeli Bensiyon Haliyo, whose father had a grocery story in Gallipoli, reports that at one time in 1934 only two other Jewish families remained: Shemuel Varon, a clothing dealer, and Shion Habip, the goldsmith. Currently, two other Jewish families live in Gallipoli, Salamon Swacy who sells glassware and Robert Kandiyoti. The synagogue is in ruins, and all books and documentation have been lost.

Edirne (Andrinople)

This is one of the major cities of the Ottoman Empire where Jewish culture and theology flourished. Sephardic Jews from Spain and Portugal who settled there in the 16th century established 13 synagogues. The big fire of Edirne in 1835 destroyed three of them. The big Kal Gadol synagogue which accommodated 600 men and 300 women was built in their place. With the drastic decease in population following the disturbances known as the "events of Thrace-Trakya *olaylary*," the *yeshiva* and the Kal Gadol synagogue were closed. These incidents were started by the local authorities at the end of 1934 and were aimed at depopulating Thrace of its Jewish inhabitants.

Turkish law states that synagogues and churches with no followers must be handed over to the *Vakif*—a non-governmental, non-profit, religious foundation. Consequently, the synagogue was placed in the care of the University of Trakya in 1995, to be used for cultural activities. Considerable money is needed, however, for restoration of the facility. The historic cemetery was appropriated by the city council, and most of the tombstones were used for construction. The remaining stones, some of which are 400 years old, were taken under the protection of the university. Many important registers reportedly were illegally stolen by American tourists in the 1960s. Rab Isak Haleva and Abraham Peretz are said to have brought the community archives to the rabbinate in Istanbul.

Kyrklareil

The oldest Jew still living is this city (as of May 2003) is Ryfat Rafeal Haleva who owns a Mobil gasoline station. Rabbi Hayim Vitali Kohen has been there for 50 years, conducting services in the synagogue which is still open, but is in bad shape. The old cemetery is now a Muslim graveyard and the 400-year-old stones have been moved about. The new cemetery has a wall, but no keeper.

Tekirdag

Leon Senegör who left Tekirdag for Israel in 1934 remembers that the Senegörs were a large family. In addition, he recalls families with the names of Abulafya, Abut, AkriÕ, Altaras (another big family), Amon and Ancel.

State Records

National Archives

A special application form exists for those who wish to do research in *Basbakanlik Osmanh Arsivleri*,* the Ottoman archives in Ankara. Items of immediate interest to Jewish genealogists would be non-Muslim community catalogues. They can be invaluable to a researcher who can read old Turkish, but in order to obtain access one must first prove that he can read Ottoman script. (Old Turkish is the Turkish language written in Arabic script instead of the Roman alphabet adopted in 1923.) Jewish culture flourished during the 16th century, and for this period especially, the archives has many valuable documents. Although officially open to researchers, for practical purposes, they are closed to genealogists.

Archives of the period of the Republic (from 1923 onward) are closed to genealogists. Any information retrieved will be about major social events and only of indirect interest.

Census Records

Ottoman poll tax registers are in the *Basbakanlik Istatistik Genel Müdürlügü*,* the government's Department of Statistics in Ankara. They provide only general information about community population and professions. These numbers are kept separate by religion until 1965, after which the census ceased to ask about religion.

Birth Records

These might be found if the exact birth place and the census department (*nüfus dairesi*) in which they are recorded are known. The fact that street names have changed and new settlements have arisen create major problems, but personal relations with governmental clerks and a bit of luck may bring positive results. Knowledge of old Turkish is needed to decipher ancient records.

Jewish Community Records

The **Kizba Organization** in Istanbul collects a tax from almost every Jewish family in Istanbul; it is used to support the community. As a result, it has lists of all of Istanbul's Jewish citizens, invaluable information for the genealogist seeking living relatives. For security and financial reasons, these lists are not publicly available, although it might be possible to make a personal appeal. This is a fairly new system so no old registers exist.

Because Jewish settlement in Turkey goes back to ancient times, many institutions are more than 100 years old. For example, *Or-ahayim*, the Jewish hospital established in 1896, has yearly record books; *Mishne Torah*, founded in 1898 to find work for needy students, has some managerial records that can be useful if one is seeking information on an individual known to have worked in the community.

Schools of the *Alliance Israelite Universelle* were major centers of education for the Jewish population from the end of the 19th century until the creation of the Republic. Many records are in the Alliance archives in Paris; some are at the Central Archives for the History of the Jewish People in Jerusalem.

Archives of the Jewish Press in Turkey: SHALOM* is the only community newspaper which has published (primarily in Turkish with a page or two in Judeo-espagnol) since 1947. It is a weekly that gives national and international news of special concern to Jews, has articles about community and religious events, and has critics and editorials on various subjects. As a result, it is a good source of information and analysis. Publisher Gözlem Gazetecilik Basin ve Yayim A.S. can be reached by e-mail (see below). Gözlem also publishes books of Jewish writers and those about the Jewish world. Copies of all issues—some computerized—may be used by researchers by advance appointment.

Tiryaki is a monthly periodical about the Jewish community society and its history published by Mose Grossman. Grossman, a historian and researcher, has a large collection of Jewish newspapers that are no longer in publication. Among these are *El-Cugeton* (1909–31), edited and published by Elia Karmona; *El Telegrafo* (1872–1930); *El Tiempo, La Boz, La Vera Luz* (1953–72); *Le Journal d'Orient* (1917–71); *Hamenora* (1923–38); *Or Yehuda* (1948) and *La Boz de Türkiye* (1939–49).

Current and Unpublished Research

A Jewish Museum has long been the dream of the Jewish community of Istanbul and the Zulfaris Synagogue-Jewish Museum Project has finally been realized although not quite completed. This museum which is the only one of its kind in Turkey is open to the public. Many of the holdings reflect the long and colorful history of the jews in Turkey, especially the Sephardim.Plans include a library where a variety of publications and documents may be centralized and accessed. Naim Güleryüz, director of the project, is creating maps of old Jewish settlements with their *mahalle* (Jewish quarters). At the same time, he is preparing the second volume of his *The History of Turkish Jews — in the 20th Century*. Naim Guleryuz is one of the most prominant figures a serious researcher of Sephardic Jewry in Turkey, can turn to.

Baruh Pinto soon will publish a dictionary of toponyms concerning the Sephardic Jews of Turkey. His work includes the analysis of family names in five languages and their relationship to names in Spain and Portugal. He also is tracing post-Expulsion emigration routes.

Beki Bahar, a writer and researcher has very recently publíshed her work on her birthplace Ankara, its history and jewish community. Yilmaz Benadrete, a member of the World Sephardi Federation* has unpublished research on Gallipoli and the Dardanelles, as well as a rich library pertaining to Sephardic Jewry. Sibel Franco has done unpublished research on the Jews of Thrace.

Addresses

Ankara Community, Birlik Sokak, Ankara; telephone: 90-312-311-6200

Ashkenazic Community, Yuksekkaldinm Sok. 37, Galata, Istanbul; telephone: 90-212-243-6090/244-2975

Bursa Community, Gerush Synagogue, Kurucesme Caddesi; telephone: 90-224-368-636

Chief Rabbinate of Turkey, Yemenici Sok. 23, Beyoglu, Tünel, Istanbul; telephone: 90-212-293-8794, 8795; fax: 90-212-244-1980; e-mail: JCOMMNTY@ATLAS.NET.TR

Italian Community, Sair Ziya Pasa Yokusu 27, Karaköy, Galata, Istanbul; telephone: 90-212-293-7784

Izmir Community, Azizler Sok.920/44 Guzelyut, Izmir; telephone: 90-232-123-708; fax: 90-232-421-1290

Jewish Museum, Zulfaris Synagogue, Karaköy, Istanbul

Kadiköy-Hadarpasa Community, Hemdat Israel Synagogue, Izettin Sok. 65, Kadiköy, Istanbul; telephone: 90-212-336-5293

Neve Shalom Synagogue, Buyuk Hendek Sok. 61, Galata, Istanbul; telephone: 90-212-293-7566

Ortaköy Community, Etz Ahayim Synagogue, Muallim Naci Cad 40/41, Ortaköy, Istanbul; telephone: 90-212-260-1896

Quincentennial Foundation-Jewish Museum of Turkey-Zulfaris Synagogue; telephone: 90-212-292-63-33; fax: 90-212-244-44-74; e-mail: INFO@MUZE500.COM; website: WWW.MUZE500.COM.

Shalom newspaper, Atiye Sok., Polar Apt. 12/6, Tesvikiye, Istanbul; telephone: 90-212-240-4144, 247-3082; fax: 90-212-231-9283; website: WWW.SALOM.COM.TR; e-mail: SHALOM@TURK.NET

World Sephardi Federation, Nessim D. Gaon, president, 42 Rue du Rhone, 1204 Geneva, Switzerland; telephone: 41-22-311-5622; fax: 41-22-311-1409; website: WWW.WSF.ORG.IL; e-mail: OFFICES@WSF.ORG.IL

Bibliography

Abensur, Hazan Laurence. *Les Pontremoli, deux dynasties rabbinique en Turquie et en Italie* (The Pontremoli, two rabbinical dynasties in Turkey and in Italy). [French] Paris, 1997. Laurence Abensur Hazzan is a founder and current president of Etsi, the Sephardi Historical and Genealogical Society, based in Paris. She is a professional genealogist with extensive resources on Jews from Izmir.

Akar, Ridvan. *Varlik Vergisi* (The Capital Tax; a tax on property). [Turkish] Istanbul: Belge, Matbaasi, 1992. About policy directed against minorities in the time of a single party system in Turkey.

Alok, Ersin-Mitrani Millie. *Anatolian Synagogues*. Istanbul: Ana Basim A.S., 1992. A volume of professional photographs of synagogues and their stories.

Bahar Beki L. *Ordan Burdan Altmis Yilin Ardindan* (From Here and There Remembering 60 Years) [Turkish] Istanbul: Gozlem Basin ve Yayin 2003. The writer's memories of Ankara where she was born, Istanbul and abroad.

Bali, Rifat. *Cumhuriyet Yillarinda Turkiye Yahudkileri: Bir Turklestirme Seruveni (1923-1945)* (The Jews of Turkey in the years of the Republic; An effort to Turkify). [Turkish] Istanbul: Iletisim, 1999.

Barokas, Yakup. *Turkiye'de Yahudi Toplumlari*. (Jewish communities in Turkey). [Turkish] Tel Aviv, 1987.

Behmoras, Liz. *Kimsin Jak Samanon?* (Who are you Jak Samanon?). [Turkish] Istanbul: Sel, Arbas Matbaacilik, 1997. A cross section of Jewish life in Istanbul in the late 19th century, narrated by a granddaughter of the Samanons.

Benbanaste, Nesim. *Orneklerle Türk-Musevi basyryn tarihcesi* (History of the Turkish-Jewish press from the Ottoman Empire to the Republic). [Turkish] Istanbul: Sumbul Basimevi, 1988. In chronological order, includes articles and essays, newspapers, periodicals, the complete works of Nesim Behar, Avram Galante and Jozef Habib Gerez, painter and poet.

Benbassa, Esther. *Haim Nahum, un Grand Rabbin Sepharade en Politique 1892-1923* (Haim Nahum, a Sephardic Chief Rabbi in politics, 1892-1923). [French] Paris: CNRS, 1990; English translation by Miriam Kochan, Tuscaloosa, AL: University of Alabama Press, 1995; Turkish translation by Irfan Yalcin, Milliyet Yayinlari, 1998.

———. *Diaspora Sepharade en Transition (Une) Istanbul XIX-XXeme siecles* (Sephardic Diaspora in transition I., Istanbul 19th–20th centuries). [French] Paris: CERF, 1993.

Benbassa, Esther and Aron Rodrigue. *Sephardi Jewry: A History of the Jewish-Spanish Community, 14th-20th Centuries*. Berkeley, CA: University of California Press, 2000. A thorough synthesis of the Jewish communities in Turkey and the Balkans.

Besalel, Yusuf. *Osmanli ve Turk Yahudileri* (Ottoman and Turkish Jews). [Turkish] Istanbul: Gozlem Gazetecilik, 1999. About Jews, their social life and customs in Turkey; includes bibliographical references.

Besalel, Yusuf. *Osmanli ve Turk Yahudileri* (Ottoman and Turkish Jews). [Turkish] Istanbul: Gozlem Gazetecilik, 2004 (enlarged 2nd.ed.) About Jews, their social life and customs in Turkey. Includes bibliographical references.

Bora, Siren. *Izmir Yahudileri Tarihi* (History of the Jews of Izmir). [Turkish] Istanbul: Gözlem, 1995.

Braude, B. *Christians and Jews in the Ottoman Empire*. New York: Holmes and Meler, 1982.

Deleon, Jak. *Balat ve Cevresi* (Balat and surroundings; A monograph of a neighborhood). [Turkish] Istanbul: Remzi Kitabevi, 1997. Research, including photographs.

———. *Ancient Districts on the Golden Horn*. Istanbul: Gozlem, Rekor Ofset, 1992. Monographs about old Balat, Fener and Hasköy with their different Jewish communities.

Emecan, Feridun M. *Unutulmus Bir cemaat: Manisa Yahudileri*. (A forgotten community: the Jews of Manisa). [Turkish] Istanbul: Eren, 1997.

Epstein, M.A. *Ottoman Documents on Balkan Jews, Sixteenth and Seventeenth Centuries*. Sofia: Centre international de l'information sur les sources de l'histoire balkanique et méditerranéenne, 1990.

Franco, Moise. *Essai sur l'Histroire des Israelites des l'Empire Ottoman* (Essay on the history of the Jews of the Ottoman Empire). [French] Paris: Dularcher, 1897. Essential reading for the genealogist and researcher

Galante, Avram. *Histoire des Juifs de Turquie* (History of the Jews of Turkey). [French] 9 vols. Istanbul Matbaasy: Isis, 1986. Former deputy of Nigde, Turkey, historian and journalist, Professor Galante (1873–1961) is perhaps the most important source for the genealogist and researcher of family roots in Turkey. He devoted his life to recording the history of the Jewish people, its existence on the Anatolian Peninsula beginning in antiquity and continuing through the period of the Ottoman Empire, with primary emphasis on the 19th and early 20th centuries. Every *vilayet* (region) is covered methodically—its communal life and institutions, the synagogues, cemeteries, rabbis, important personalities, intellectual and economic situation, public employees, family names, calamities and other outstanding events. Galante has made extensive use of the works of Salamon Rozanes, the most outstanding historian of Sephardic existence in Anatolia. Because Rozanes wrote only in Hebrew, however, most Diaspora Jews cannot read his essays.

Galante's work include: "Don Joseph Nassi `Duke of Naxos' (1913); "Documents officiels Turcs concernant les Juifs de Turquie" [Official documents concerning the Jews of Turkey] (1931); "Histoire des Juifs de Rhodes, Cio, Cos, etc. (1935); "Don Salamon Aben Yaeche, Duke of Metelin" (1936); "Les Synagogues d'Istanbul" The synagogues of Istanbul) (1937); "Histoire des Juifs d'Anatolie [Les Juifs d'Izmir]" (History of the Jews of Anatolia; the Jews of Izmir) (1937); "Les Juifs de Constantinople sous Byzance" (The Jews of Constantinople under the Byzantines) (1940); "Bodrum Tarihi" (1945); "Ankara Tarihi" (1950). Galante's books and essays have been collected and published in the nine volume *Histoire des Juifs de Turquie*. His most important book in Turkish is *Türkler ve Yahudiler*.

Gerber, J.S. *The Jews of Spain: A History of the Sephardic Experience*. New York: Free Press, 1992.

Grossman, Moshe. *Dr. Marcus (1870-1944) Osmanlidan Cumhuriyete Geciste Turk Yahudilerinden Gorunumler* (Turkish Jews from the Ottoman Empire to the Republic). [Turkish] Istanbul: As Matbaacilik, 1992. The life and works of Rabbi Dr. Markus,

Chief Rabbi of the Ashkenazim of Turkey, one of the founders of the B'nai B'rith and the Jewish high school; translated from German, English, French and Rashi (old Judeo-Spanish) writing. Community life and Jewish institutions of the time.

———. *The History of the Turkish Jews to the Beginning of the Twentieth Century*. Istanbul: Batur Matbaasi, 1992. A concise compilation of historical events, outstanding personalities and families and Jewish life in various communities starting in the Seljuk era (11th century C.E.) and continuing through the different stages of the Ottoman Empire. [Turkish and English]

Güleryüz, Naim. *Istanbul Sinagoglary* (Synagogues of Istanbul). [Turkish] Istanbul: Ajans Class, 1992. A short history with illustrations.

Kalderon, Albert. *Abraham Galante, a Biography*. New York: Sepher Hermon, 1983.

Karabatak, Haluk. *1934 Trakya Olaylary* (The 1934 upheavals in Thrace). [Turkish] No bibliographic information available.

Levy, Avigdor. *Jews of the Ottoman Empire*. Princeton: Darwin, 1994.

———. *The Sephardim in the Ottoman Empire*. Princeton: Darwin, 1999.

Lewis, Bernard. *Istanbul and the Civilization of the Ottoman Empire*. Norman, OK: University of Oklahoma Press, 1989.

———. *The Emergence of Modern Turkey*; Studies in Middle Eastern History. Oxford: Oxford University Press, 2001.

———. *The Jews of Islam*. Princeton, NJ: Princeton University Press, 1984.

Malka, Jeffrey S. *Sephardic Genealogy: Discovering Your Sephardic Ancestors and Their World*. Bergenfield, NJ: Avotaynu, 2002.

Nahum, H. *Juifs de Smyrne XIX-XXe Siecle* (Jews of Smyrna in the 19th and 20th centuries). [French] Paris: Aubier, 1997.

Niyego, Anri, ed. *Haydarpasa'da Gecen 100 Yilimiz* (Our last hundred years in Haydarpasa). [Turkish] Istanbul: Gozlem Gazetecilik, 1999. The untold story of a Jewish community in Istanbul; a rich compilation of names, extensively covered family and community life, biographies and stories.

Or Ahayim Hastanesi Vakfi (Yearbook of the national Jewish hospital Or Ahayim). [Ladino] Istanbul: Almanach, 1923.

Pinto, Baruh B. *What's Behind a Name*. Istanbul: by author: Gözlem Gazetecilil Basin ve Yayin Atiye Sok. Polar Apt. 12/6 Tesvikiye 84200 Istanbul, Turkey; fax: 90 212 231 9283; e-mail: KITABEVI@SALOM.COM.TR.

Pinto, Baruh B. *The Sephardic Onomasticon*. [Turkish, French, Spanish, Judeo-Spanish, Hebrew] Istanbul,Gozlem Basin ve Yayin A.S. 2003. An ethymological research on Sephardic family names of the Jews living in Turkey.

Ragen, Naomi. *The Ghost of Hannah Mendes*. New York: Simon and Schuster, 1998; Griffen Trade Paperback, 2001. A novel that provides insight into the all-powerful Nasi-Mendes family with roots in Turkey.

Rodigue, Aron. *French Jews—Turkish Jews: the Alliance Israelite Universelle in Turkey*. Bloomington, IN: Indiana University Press, 1990.

———. *Ottoman and Turkish Jewry: Community and Leadership*. Bloomington, IN: Indiana University Press, 1992.

———. *Turkiye yahudilerinin Batilasmasi "Alliance Okullari," 1860–1925*. [Turkish] Ankara: Ayra, 1997.

Rosanes, Salamon A. *Divre Yemei Yisrael be-Togermah* (History of the Jews of the Ottoman Empire). [Hebrew] Tel Aviv, 1930. Rosanes is considered the father of all historians of Turkish Jewry. Unfortunately, his works are not widely read because they are only in Hebrew.

———. *Korot ha-Yehudim be-Turkiya ve artsot he-kedem* (The travails of the Jews of Turkey and the ancient countries). [Hebrew] 2 vols. Sofia, 1938/39.

Roth, Cecil. *Dona Gracia of the House of Nasi, Biography*. Philadelphia: Jewish Publication Society, 1992.

———. *The House of Nasi: The Duke of Naxos*. Philadelphia: Jewish Publication Society, 1992. The story of the Nasi family of Spain who ended up wealthy and powerful in Turkey's Constantinople after the expulsion from Spain.

Rozen, Minna. *Hasköy Cemetery: Topology of Stones*. Jerusalem, 1994. Professor Mina Rozen, formerly director of the Diaspora Research Institute at Tel Aviv University and now professor at Haifa University, directed a project to document all extant Jewish cemeteries in Turkey. This first book on the subject largely covers the Hasköy Cemetery, its history, burial caves, techniques and artistry used in the tombstones, as well as the Italian Cemetery at Sisli, those in Bergama, Edirne, Kuzguncuk, Kirklareli, Ortaköy and Tire (in western Anatolia). A large number of synagogues, Jewish neighborhoods and religious objects also were photographed and documented. Between August 1987 and February 1990, 60,000 were recorded.

Salzmann, Ayse Gürsan (text), Laurence Salzmann (photographs). *Anyos Munchos I Buenos* "Good Years and Many More" *Turkey's Sephardim: 1942–1992*. A Blue Flower/Photo Review Book, Philadelphia, 1991. U.S. Library of Congress Catalog #91-714021. The book is accompanied by a film entitled *Turkey's Sephardim* and covers all of Turkey from Edirne to Van, from Bagkale to Bergama.

Saul, E. *Balat'tan Batyam'a*. Istanbul: Iletisim, 1999.

Seni, Nora. *Camondolar-Bir Hanedanin Cokusu* [Turkish] Istanbul: Iletisim, 2000.

Sevilla, Sharon. *Turkiye Yahudileri* (Turkish Jews). [Turkish] Istanbul: Kagil vc Basim I,sleri, 1992.

Shaw, Stanford. *The Jews of the Ottoman Empire and the Turkish Republic*. London: McMillan and New York: New York University Press, 1992.

———. *Turkey and the Holocaust: Turkey's Role in Rescuing Turkish and European Jewry from Nazi Persecution 1933–1945*. London: McMillan and New York: New York University Press, 1993.

Taranto, Roland. "Les noms de famille juifs a Smyrne." *Etsi, Revue de Généalogie et d'Histoire Séfarades*. 5, no. 16 (Mars 2002), pp. 3–9.

Weiker, Walter. *Ottoman Turks and the Jewish Policy*. Lanham, MD: University Press of America, 1992.

Yetkin, Cetin. *Türkiye'nin Devlet Yapaminda Yhudiler* (Jews and the Turkish State). [Turkish] Istanbul: Afa Yayinkary, 1992. A good study of Jewish existence starting with why they chose to settle in the Ottoman land; where they settled; their relations with the state at different stages of the Empire; prominent figures and the period of the Turkish Republic; World War II and its impact on Turkish Jews; the capital (property) tax (*Varlik*) imposed on minorities; the establishment of the State of Israel and its effect on Turkish Jews.

Notes

1. When we speak about the hardships of war, we mean wars that continued for a long time, one after the other. First was World War I, then the War of Independence (1919–23) and, finally, World War II. Although Turkey was not directly involved, the population, and especially the Jewish community felt its effects: scarcities, poverty, a capital tax imposed on non-Muslim subjects, fear and insecurity as a result of Turkey's involvement

with Nazi Germany—all of these factors caused many to make *alyiah* or to emigrate, usually to the United States.

2. Fires were very common in Turkey, especially in the poor areas of old Istanbul. Streets were narrow, wooden buildings stood wall to wall and the fire brigade consisted of people who tried to fight fires with pails of water and primitive hoses. Streets and entire neighborhoods were thus reduced to ashes in a very short time. There are also rumors that *janissaries* (Ottoman infantry) started fires in some areas to create opportunities for pillaging.

3. Byzantine or Romaniote Jews are those who lived in the Balkans, Trace, Constantinople and the islands of Crete, Mora and Rhodes as far back as Roman times. Gallico, Kandiyoti and Politi are examples of these communities.

4. *Varlik*, was an event that deeply affected the lives of non-Muslims in Turkey, especially the Jews. Although Turkey was not directly involved in World War II, its negative effects were deeply felt, especially on the economy. The government of the time, presided over by Sukru Saragoglu, passed certain amendments aiming at decreasing inflation and the government deficit. The most important was a tax imposed on capital, known as *Varlik*. It was aimed at taxing industrialists and tradesmen and having them share the burden of the financial deficit with the working class. In practice, however, things turned out differently. Minorities ended up being heavily overtaxed, largely due to pressure exerted by the Germans. Many people had to sell all their possessions in order to meet the demands of the government.Those who could not pay had to serve in forced labor camps. Although the law referred to all citizens who could not pay, only Armenians, Greeks and above all, Jews, were made to serve. The camps were nothing like those in Germany, there was no molestation or torture, but life was hard and conditions unfavorable. Official records state that 1,400 individuals were sent to the camp, of whom 1,229 were from Istanbul. Twenty-five died of illness or old age; many others never recovered from the psychological effects. Although this racist, uncivilized action was canceled after 16 months, Turkey still suffers from the disgrace it brought.

5. On July 24, 1923, Turkey signed the Lausanne agreement guaranteeing the rights of its minority (non-Muslim) communities and ensuring them the continuity of autonomy as in the Ottoman *millet* system. The new republic, however, aimed to create one people-one language-one state; a single, overriding national identity. The *millet* system was incompatible with this new understanding and the "civil code" passed February 17, 1926, did not allow minorities to live in their own lands. Everyone had to be equal under the same laws. Consequently, non-Muslim communities (the Jews were the first) renounced their rights.

In this period of transition, "Turkizing" (making Turkish) the minorities became a priority—writing and talking in Turkish, taking Turkish names and family names. Cultural assimilation was encouraged and especially intensified in the Jewish community. New measures were taken also in the economic field. For example, at least 50 percent of employees in foreign firms had to be Turkish Muslims instead of Jews and foreigners. Many other similar applications showed that the idea of equality brought by the civil code was left on paper.

Upheavals in Thrace in 1934 against the Jewish population were aimed at ridding the area of its non-Muslim subjects. Certain tragic events showed that only the Muslim Turk was meant when talking about "Turks." The incident of the "Twenty Classes" was one. This took place at the most critical stage of World War II, at a time when the Germans approached the Turkish border. Twenty classes (there is one class for every enlistment period) of Turkish citizens who had already performed their military service and had been discharged—some only a week before—were called back to the army. The disturbing fact was that all these citizens were non-Muslims.

This application started between May 1 and May 15, 1941. Men were seized from wherever they were with no regard for age, status or health and made to join the army. Many could not contact their families. These citizens could not even be called solider because they wore different uniforms and were not given arms. They did not serve in the army, but were made to work in various areas of Anatolia, such as road building. This discriminatory action terrified the Jewish community which feared a similar result as in Germany.

The Twenty Classes were demobilized on July 27, 1942, crippling the community physically and economically. As a matter of fact, these measures had been taken so that Muslims could gain control in trade while the non-Muslim subjects, whom they considered untrustworthy, were under control in case of war, at the same time that they pleased the Nazis.

6. Taranto, "Les noms de famille juifs a Smyrne" (Names of Jewish families in Smyrna): 3–9.

Ukraine

Historical Overview by Sallyann Amdur Sack
Genealogical Resources by Miriam Weiner, CG

Note: Read the chapters on Imperial Russian Empire and the Austro-Hungarian Empire before reading this section. Important information is cited there that is not repeated below. Note especially the description of the Eastern European database on the Routes to Roots Foundation website—Ed.]

Historical Overview
by Sallyann Amdur Sack

Modern Ukraine, a large country with the world's fifth largest Jewish population (after the United States, Israel, Russia, and France), achieved independence from the Soviet Union in 1991. For most of the 20th century, it was known as *the* Ukraine or the Ukrainian Soviet Socialist Republic (SSR).

Jews have lived for more than a millennium on the territory of contemporary Ukraine for varying lengths of time in different regions, not always under the same sovereign. The ancestors of most Jewish genealogists with roots in Ukraine emigrated around the turn of the 20th century, but national boundaries in that part of the world have changed frequently over the past two centuries—and so also have administrative districts within countries. Jewish settlement over the years in the regions that compose contemporary Ukraine is best discussed by geographical area: Austrian area, Little Russia, Novo Rossiia, the Crimea and Odessa. Jewish genealogical research methodology in contemporary Ukraine differs by region. Sometimes the considerations are exceedingly complex.

Austrian Area

Following the three partitions of Poland—in 1772, 1775 and 1795 (see POLAND)—most of the land within the borders of Ukraine today was divided between the Russian Empire and the Austro-Hungarian Empire. Archival collections in contemporary Ukraine reflect this historical division; the country has two state historical archives, one in Kiev (Russian Empire), the other in L'viv (Austro-Hungarian Empire).

Following the partitions of Poland, Austria acquired southeastern Poland, which it named Galicia. The capital of eastern Galicia was called Lemberg when it was part of the Austro-Hungarian Empire, then Lwów when it was part of Poland, L'vov during the Soviet period and today L'viv. After World War I, reconstituted Poland regained the area called Galicia (and historic Podolia). The interwar Polish-Soviet border in this region was drawn about 50 miles west of Zhitomir. In 1939 the Soviet Union occupied the former eastern Galicia and Podolia and annexed that area to the Ukrainian SSR. With the dissolution of the Soviet Union in 1991, all territory within the Ukrainian SSR became the independent country of Ukraine; the former eastern Galicia is now part of western Ukraine.

The 19th-century Austrian province of Bukovina, with its capital at Chernovitsy, was the easternmost province of the Austrian monarchy. From 1786 until 1840, Bukovina was administered as part of Galicia. In 1861, Chernovitsy was made the capital of this province. Today the northernmost portion of the former Bukovina is part of Ukraine; the southern portion belongs to the republic of Moldova.

International archival standards mandate that records be held in the archives of the country that currently governs the land where the records were created. Thus some records created during the 19th century in what was then Austrian Galicia are held today in the Ukrainian State Historical Archives in L'viv, but this convention is not uniformly enforced.

Throughout the 19th century, Czarist Russia was divided into *guberniyas* and *Uezds*. A *guberniya* corresponds roughly to a province, while a *Uezd*, a subdivision of a *guberniya* was similar in size to an American county and frequently is described as a district in English-language publications. *Guberniyas* were abolished after the 1919 Bolshevik Revolution and replaced by a system of *oblasts* and *raions*. An *oblast* may be thought of as akin to one of the 50 states of the United States. The smaller unit, *raion*, is similar in area to an American township and today sometimes is translated as district.

The most recently acquired Ukrainian *oblast* is Zakarpatskaya Oblast, an area that belonged to southeastern Poland and eastern Czechoslovakia before World War II. The USSR annexed this region at the end of the war and called it Western Ukraine. The region became part of Ukraine when that country achieved independence in 1991. Prior to World War I, this heavily Jewish area had belonged to the Austro-Hungarian Empire; part was known as eastern Galicia and part as eastern Hungary. As a result of this history, 19th- and early 20th-century archival records in Zakarpatskaya Oblast reflect the record keeping practices of the Hapsburg monarchy (see AUSTRO-HUNGARIAN EMPIRE).

Little Russia

Jews lived for many centuries in the former Russian *guberniyas* of Kiev, Podolia and Volhynia, together historically called Little Russia. Once part of the Polish kingdom, this area was the territory of the fabled Polish magnate estates and home to many Jews and Jewish towns (see RUSSIAN POLAND). Poland lost the land to the Russian czar after the Ukrainian peasant uprisings in the mid-17th century. This was the time of the infamous Bogdan Chmielnicki massacres, when most Jews of the region were murdered and their communities decimated. A century later, however, Jews had begun to move back into the region and to re-establish their former communities. When the Russian Pale of Settlement was established after the partitions of Poland, the Ukraine was included within it.

Novo Rossiia

The third major region of Jewish settlement in Ukraine was Novo Rossiia (New Russia), the so-called New Territories, an area of southeastern Ukraine that had never belonged to Poland and where the Russian czars historically had forbidden Jews to settle. At the beginning of the 19th century, when the Russian Empire conquered vast territory belonging to the Ottoman Turkish Empire, Jews from the central guberniyas of the Pale of Settlement colonized these new regions. These central *guberniyas* included Grodno, Kovno, Mogilev, Vilna and Vitebsk. At that time, Czar Alexander I (1777–1825) issued a decree to encourage agricultural colonization of Rossiia, territory that extended from the Dneister River in Bessarabia and Moldova in the west to the unpopulated plains (steppes) in the Crimean Peninsula in the south.

For the first time, Jews from the Pale of Settlement were invited to form agricultural colonies. Just as in later migrations to the New World and elsewhere, *landsmen* tended to move together. Typically most (or all) residents of a single agricultural settlement came from the same or neighboring shtetls further north. Archival documents from the 19th century frequently include information on previous (northern) places of residence.

Crimea

Another Ukrainian region where Jews have lived for a long time is the Crimea. Some descended from the Khazarians, inhabitants of the Khazar kingdom along the Sea of Azov, whose king and noble court converted to Judaism in the eighth century C.E. At the beginning of the 10th century C.E., the rabbis report, the three major European Jewish settlements were Prague, the German Rhineland, and (a much smaller enclave) the Crimean region of Ukraine.[1]

Odessa

Special mention must be made of Odessa. This Black Sea port and third largest Russian city became a 19th-century magnet for Jews from all over Central and Eastern Europe, not simply the Russian Empire. In fact, the first Jewish settlers there reportedly came from the Austrian border city of Brody.

Given the varied Jewish history on the land that forms Ukraine today, it is not surprising that few of our ancestors called themselves "Ukrainians" in a manner analogous to the "Litvaks." Rather the term tended to refer simply to the community where they had lived. Even without the geographical name, however, 19th-century Ukrainian Jewry had some distinctive features. Most noticeable was its pronunciation of Yiddish, different from the Litvak/Belarus or the Polish dialects. Thus *kugel* in Lithuania was *kigel* in Ukraine; the *chupah* (marriage canopy) was a *chipah*; and *Yokl* (a variant of Jacob) in Lithuania became *Yukl* further south in Ukraine.

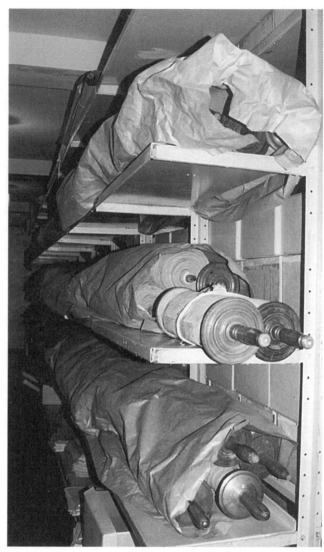

Shelves of Torahs in the Central State Historical Archive in Kiev, 1991. Courtesy of Miriam Weiner.

Culinary differences also existed between Jews who resided in Ukraine and those whose ancestors lived in Lithuania and Belarus. During the 19th century, sugar beets were grown and refined in Ukraine. South of the so-called "sugar-beet line," sugar was a distinctive ingredient in Jewish cooking. Further north sugar was an expensive luxury and noticeably absent. If one's grandmother added sugar to her *kugel/kigel* or *gefilte* fish or *tzimmes*, that in itself may be a clue to residence in Ukraine.

Like most of European Jewry, Ukrainian Jews largely perished in the Holocaust. In early 1941, the Jewish population in Ukraine numbered 2.4 million people; currently the Jewish population is estimated at more than 100,000. With some exceptions most Ukrainian Jews were not transported to extermination camps such as Auschwitz, but were murdered on the spot when the Germans occupied their communities in 1941 (see HOLOCAUST).

Genealogical Resources in Ukraine
by Miriam Weiner, CG

The dozens of archives throughout Ukraine hold millions of documents that together form a documentary history of Jewish life as reflected by the records of individuals, organizations and government institutions. Depending upon the time period and geographical region, these documents were recorded in many languages, including Russian, Ukrainian, German, Polish, Hungarian, Romanian (areas of former Bukovina), Hebrew and Yiddish. Methods for collecting Jewish vital statistics and other archival records varied according to whether the jurisdiction was Russian or Austrian before World War I.

In either case, records that have survived are held today in one of the 24 contemporary *oblast* archives, the State Archive in the Autonomous Republic of Crimea, several branch or division archives (of the *oblast* archives), and two national historical archives. Additional records can be found in the local RAHS (civil registry) archives, oblast RAHS archives, regional museums, and private collections of individuals and Jewish communities.

The Ukrainian archives hold six major types of registration records that constitute an excellent starting place for genealogical research:

- *Kahal* (Jewish community) records
- Poll-tax records (census lists or *reviskiy skaskiy*)
- metrical books
- social estate registration records
- family registers
- recruitment lists

Above all, the state's concern was to ensure the regular collection of taxes and, after 1827, the military conscription of Jews. Unlike registration records, which provide minimal biographical data, invaluable information can be found in archival documents including court, educational and administrative records, which offer rich detail about the daily lives of family members and their communities.

Archival documents for towns currently within Ukraine's borders may be found in many repositories outside of Ukraine, including but not limited to, the Moldova National Archives (SEE MOLDOVA), National Historical Archive of Belarus in Minsk (see MINSK), Russian State Historical Archives (see IMPERIAL RUSSIA), Polish State Archives (AGAD), Urzad Stanu Cywilnego Warsaw Srodmiescie, the Jewish Historical Institute in Warsaw (see POLAND), plus some archives in Northern Romania. The Moldova National Archives has documents from Chernovtsy, Khmelnitskiy, Kherson and Odessa Oblasts.

Main Archival Administration
Under the Cabinet of Ministers of Ukraine

The administrative headquarters of archives in Ukraine (excluding RAHS archives) is located in Kiev, in the same building as the Central State Historical Archive of Ukraine in Kiev. The seven central state archives are the national repositories of valuable archival documentation, organized by certain historical period and by the category of institutions

and documents stored there. Specific archives relevant to Jewish genealogists and historians include:

- Central State Historical Archives of Ukraine in Kiev and in Lviv. Include unique sources that reflect the national history from the 14th century until February 1917 (in Lviv, until 1939).
- Central State Cinema, Phono & Photo Archives of Ukraine. Has videotapes, photographs and audio-visual materials.
- Central State Scientific-Technical Archive of Ukraine, located in Kharkiv. Includes documents that characterize major developments in agriculture, science and technology.
- Central State Archive and the Museum of Literature and Arts of Ukraine. Includes materials on Ukrainian culture.
- State Archives at the Ministry of the Autonomous Republic of Crimea, state regional archives and archives of the cities of Kiev and Sevastopol.[2]

Central State Historical Archive
of Ukraine in Kiev

The Central State Historical Archive of Ukraine in Kiev (TsDIAK) is one of the oldest archival repositories in the country. The foundation of the documentary collection consists of the fonds (record groups) of the Kiev Central Archive of Ancient Acts, Kharkiv Central Archive of the Revolution and the State Archive of Kiev Oblast. The collection in this archive increased substantially upon receipt of documentary materials from a branch of this archive located in Kharkiv that was liquidated in 1971. At present, more than 1,600 fonds and approximately 1.5 million files are kept at the archive in Kiev.

According to Olga Muzychuk, director of TsDIAK, "The most valuable part of the documentary collection in this archive consists of record books of the courts and estate institutions of the right-bank Ukraine (west of the Dnieper River); city, district, and confederate courts (which resolved issues between jurisdictions within the Russian Empire); and city governments. This collection is a priceless resource for studying the history of Ukraine in general and, more specifically, the Jewish history of Ukraine.

"In this archive, the most important resources for studying Jewish genealogy in Ukraine are the metrical books of synagogues of Kiev *guberniya*. These books total approximately 1,500 units dating from the mid-19th century to 1920. If the town was not large enough to have a synagogue, the researcher must locate the nearby larger town that had a synagogue and search the metrical books of this larger town.[3] Unfortunately, many towns were able to preserve only fragments of books (for certain years).

"Some additional archival fonds contain information regarding specific topics. For example, fonds of the administration office of the Board of Education include information about Jewish education and lists of students; fonds of the administration office of governor and governor-general include census information for certain towns and estates; and fonds of police and prison documents include information about pogroms against the Jews (including names of victims and perpetrators)."

РЕВИЗСКАЯ СКАЗКА

Revizskaya Skazka (list of inhabitants) living in Khotin, 1859; No. 45/33 is the family of Duvid Shteinberg, with five generations and 22 names. Courtesy of Moldova National Archives, Kishinev (note that Khotin is within current borders of Ukraine).

This archive is involved in an ongoing computerization project of vital records that will facilitate access to these important documents. More details are available at www.RTRFOUNDATION.ORG.

Central State Historical Archive of Ukraine In Lviv

The largest and most important repository in Western Ukraine is the Central State Historical Archive of Ukraine in Lviv (formerly Lemberg, Lwów and Lvov). The repository is reported to have one of Europe's largest collections of Jewish vital statistics records for towns formerly in Poland and now within the current boundaries of Ukraine. Fond 701 contains 350 registers of religious communities in Galicia for the period 1789–1942, consisting of birth, marriage and death registrations for towns throughout Galicia. The earliest records in this collection date from 1784. These registers (commonly known as metrical books or *kehillah* records) generally are not indexed. One must search page by page and line by line to find specific names. The documents are in Polish, recorded on forms with German column headings.

A source of great value is the book of death registrations in Lviv for 1941–42, which includes the names of more than 6,000 deceased persons. In this book, one may find the date of death, address of deceased and age. In 1941–42, a card index of the inhabitants of the Lviv ghetto was compiled by the Lviv *Judenrat* (Jewish council created by the Nazis). Names, addresses, birth dates and places of work are indicated in this collection of more than 20,000 index cards.[4] Records for the period of German occupation in Western Ukraine are primarilly kept in the State Archive of Lviv Oblast.

Related documents can be found in nearly all the collections of this archive. However, they are scattered, and thus the research is tedious and time consuming. Most of the material is not indexed, so a researcher looking for information based upon specific family names in specific towns must research many different files. To further complicate the matter, these files are arranged not by town name, but by subject matter.

Additionally there are property records (dating back to the late 1700s), school and tax lists (a few), town and local court records, family lists (relating to *kehillah* activities) and Holocaust documents. Very few census lists have survived; most were destroyed by the Austrian government that, by law, kept only the statistical summaries.

A recently published guide to the holdings of this archive provides a comprehensive description of these documents (see Bibliography). The book, *Central State Historical Archive of Ukraine, Lviv: A Guide* (edited by Diana Peltz, archive director), is written in both Polish and Ukrainian and includes illustrations of some documents.

In addition to the historical archive in Lviv, three State oblast archives are located in Western Ukraine: Ternopil, Ivano-Frankivsk and Lviv. Documents in these archives are generally from the 20th century, including Jewish society records and Holocaust documents. Some 19th-century school and property records exist.

For more detailed information about the Central State Historical Archive of Ukraine in Lviv, see the articles at WWW.RTRFOUNDATION.ORG.

Current Inventory of Ukrainian Archive Documents

The archives of Ukraine hold a variety of potentially useful documents in addition to vital records and census lists. The Routes to Roots Foundation (RTRF) website (www.RTRFOUNDATION.ORG) features a town-by-town inventory of archival documents in a consolidated database from archives in Ukraine (and Moldova, Belarus, Poland and Lithuania). The data was collected by Miriam Weiner pursuant to a written agreement and official cooperation between the Routes to Roots Foundation, Inc., and the Ukrainian State Archives (and also archives in Belarus, Lithuania, Poland and Moldova). The project began in Poland in 1989 (and in Ukraine in 1991) and continues. Data has been translated, coded, verified by the relevant archives and entered into the Consolidated Eastern European Archival Database searchable on the website.

The database is continually updated when new material is received from the archives. Postings of new data can be found on the "News Alert" (see the home page of the website). When new information is received from an individual and then verified by the relevant archive, the new information is then added to the database. The website also includes several hundred pages of text consisting of articles by archivists and historians, maps, related websites and other pertinent material for researching Jewish family history.

Access to Documents in the Ukrainian State Archives

Material in the archives may be accessed in one of several ways:

- Write directly to the archives providing current town name and location, original surname, time period of interest, document types of interest, and any other relevant information. It is best to write in Ukrainian. In order not to be surprised and/or disturbed by the cost when the assignment is finished, be sure to inquire about the scope of the search and agree to estimated costs before authorizing the archivists to proceed with the assignment.

- Consult online databases hosted by state archives in Eastern Europe, SIG groups on JewishGen and other databases. Here one may find name indexes to documents along with excerpted information from the documents.

- Hire a professional genealogist/researcher to do the work on one's behalf. Always obtain written references from previous clients *and* be sure to contact the references (see also PROFESSIONAL GENEALOGISTS).[5]

- Travel to the region where the ancestral documents are located and do the research onsite. Keep in mind the substantial costs for travel, visa, translator, car/driver, hotels and incidental expenses. All Ukrainian archives are open to researchers, both resident and foreign. The Ukraine State Archives* has additional information about this subject on its website. See the sections entitled "Genealogy" and "Q&A".

Holocaust Documents in Ukrainian Archives

The Ukrainian State Archives holds numerous Holocaust-related documents. The State Archive of Vinnitsa Oblast, for example, has 275 fonds (comprising 14,000 files) about the

1942 list of Jews who died in the Lviv Jewish Hospital during the Holocaust. Entries include name, age and cause of death. Courtesy of Central State Historical Archive of Ukraine, Lviv.

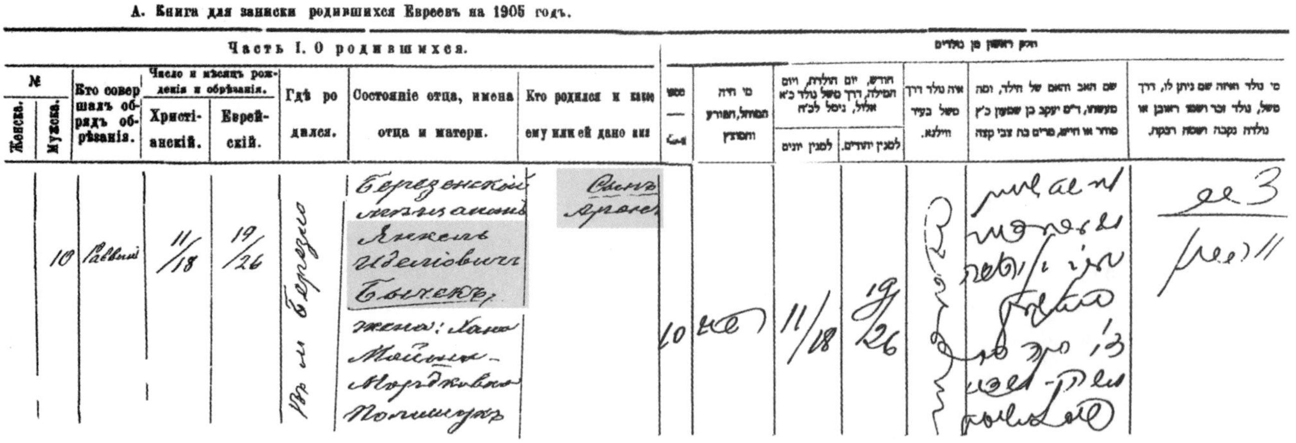

№ Посем. / Мужск.	Кто совершалъ об-рядъ об-рѣзанія.	Число и мѣсяцъ рож-денія и обрѣзанія. Христі-анскій.	Еврей-скій.	Гдѣ ро-дился.	Состояніе отца, имена отца и матери.	Кто родился и какъ ему или ей дано имя						

Часть I. О родившихся.

(Birth record image with handwritten entries)

Birth record of Aron Bichek, born February 11, 1905, in Berezno, Ukraine, son of Yankel Bichek (son of Idel) and Khana Polishuk (daughter of Moishe-Mordko). Courtesy of Rovno RAHS Archive, Ukraine.

persecution and genocide of the Jewish population of the Vinnitsa region from 1941–44.

The historical value of this material lies in the richness of content and unique information, including witness statements, documents and photographs. Records and statements describe the exhumation of graves of people who were executed, the schemes (map plots) of the grave's locations and lists of genocide victims with numerous photographs and testimonies and eyewitness accounts from survivors of the Holocaust. Many of the documents relate to the deportation and living conditions of the Jews from Bukovina and Bessarabia confined to ghettos and concentration camps.[6] Other documents relate to the Jewish partisan detachments and activities of the underground movement in Vinnitsa Oblast.

An ongoing research project headed by Dr. Hennadii Boriak, director of the State Committee on Archives, is surveying "Nazi gold" accumulated in Ukraine during World War II. According to Dr. Boriak, "Within the confines of this project, the concept of Nazi gold includes not only a definition of gold and other confiscated precious metals, but the broad characterization of the process of accumulation of the Third Reich's capital during World War II." Project results to date are published in two volumes entitled *"Nazi Gold" from Ukraine: In Search of Archival Evidence* written in Ukraine with a half-page English summary. The volumes include numerous document examples and summary tables that include names, addresses, and number of items confiscated (monetary value and by weight) with the specific archival source where the document can be found. The state archival system has more than 6,000 "occupation fonds" dating from the period of Nazi occupation (1941–44).

RAHS Archive (formerly ZAGS Archive)

In 1826, the Russian state extended the system of metrical books (communal records of births, deaths, marriages and divorces) to include the Jews and made the state rabbi responsible for record keeping. This system continued through World War I and into the early 1920s. After that, Jewish vital record registrations were included in the general registrations of the town. Throughout Ukraine, vital records were maintained by the *kahal* and stored in Jewish vital registration offices that had their seats in the local administration building. Very small villages were members of a *kahal* in nearby larger towns and their residents registered there. The office that records births, marriages, deaths and divorces is known officially as the RAHS Archive.

The system of RAHS (registration acts of the civil state [formerly known as ZAGS]) state archives is under the jurisdiction of the Ministry of Justice of Ukraine and is based upon the same structure as the state archives system under the State Committee on Archives. Individual RAHS archives exist at the city, district (*raion*) and oblast level, a total of more than 700. The RAHS archives, subsections of the local administrations of justice, exist in each administrative-territorial unit (oblast, district, city) and in the districts of Kiev and Sevastopol.

By law, the RAHS archival system holds records for 75 years, after which all RAHS documents must be transferred to the state archives. As of 2003, the RAHS archives held no records dated earlier than 1925–27. Sometimes an individual register book covers many years; for example, birth records in small towns. For this reason, until the most recent entry in a book is more than 75 years old, the book remains in the RAHS office. This regulation often causes confusion about where documents are kept. In addition, metrical books that by law should be transferred to the state archive often are retained in the RAHS office for various reasons (e.g., insufficient space in the oblast archive or restoration work required on the books prior to their transfer).

Public access to RAHS documents is regulated by law that prohibits onsite access and research by individuals looking for multiple records for genealogical purposes. On the other hand, sometimes a sympathetic clerk in a local RAHS office will cooperate in order to accommodate a visitor. This is a courtesy response, however, and not available upon demand. The amount of payment requested for research is not uniformly established and could vary.

1829	Feldman Mojżesz 1 Salomea	Janowska 36	wł.realn.	400
1830	Feldschuh Adela	Sykstuska 54	wdowa	80
1831	Feldschuh Józef	Lwowska 45	kupiec	50
1832	Feliks Herman	3-go Maja 12	dentysta	16
1833	Dr.Fell Bolesław	Kopernika 14	lekarz	40
1834	Fell Jakób	Ormiańska 30	urzędnik	16
1835	Dr.Fell Marek	Halicka 19	adwokat	50
1836	Feller Arnold Józef	Kotlarska 11	kupiec	6
1837	Feller Henryk	Pasaż Fellerów	wł.realn.	100
1838	Feller Ignacy v.Izak	Teatyńska 11-12a	kupiec	12
1839	Feller Jetti	pl.Strzelecki 1.	restaurat.	6
1840	Feller Józef	Lelewela	malarz pok.	6
1841	Dr.Feller Leon	Legjonów 35	lekarz	450
1842	Feller Luzer 1 żona Bąsia	Lwowska 13	kupiec	24
1843	Feller Majer	Szpitalna 84	wł.realn.	20
1844	Dr.Feller Norbert Ignacy 1 Salomea	Na Skałce 3	lekarz	24
1845	Feller Zygmunt 1 żona Julja	Pordes,Łyczakowska 133,kupiec		12
1846	Fellig Lazar	Rapperta 9	urzędnik	6
1847	Dr.Fels Izrael	Słoneczna 1	lekarz	20
1848	Fels Jakób	Kochanowskiego 4	kapelusznik	6
1849	Fels Joachim	Ossolińskich 14	kierownik	40
1850	Felsenstein Salomon Józef	Słoneczna 14	kupiec	18
1851	Fendrich Herman	Sobieskiego 23	rzeźnik	12
1852	Fenig Róża	Panieńska 20	wł.realn.	16
1853	Fenster Chiel	Nowy Świat	młynarz	40
1854	Ferbel Natan	Kotlarska 12	urzędn.kol.	6
1855	Fenster r.Kordon Jakób	Łyczakowska 22a	restaurat.	6
1856	Ferbel Leon	Kotlarska 12	urzędnik kolj.	6
1857	Färber Izak 1 żona Jüdes	Zamarstynowska 21	kupiec	6
1858	Fern Ire	Krasickich 18	kupiec	12
1859	Hern Jechil	Pasaż Fellerów 3	kupiec	18
1860	Fern Marek	Tarnowskiego 34	urzędnik	100

List of taxpayers in Lviv, including name, address, occupation and amount of taxes paid. This 1936 entry includes three members of the Fern family: Ire, Jechil and Marek. Courtesy of Central State Historical Archive of Ukraine, Lviv.

Researchers may write to Ukrainian consulates and embassies to request a search for a few specific vital records. This search is a time-consuming process; it may take months to receive a response. If the search is successful, a letter is sent to the requestor advising him or her to forward a sum of money to the consulate or embassy. In return, a certified extract of the document (on a typed form) is sent by mail. None of the documents in any RAHS office have been microfilmed, and there are no plans to do so because of privacy restrictions on 20th-century records, To locate the Ukrainian embassy or a consulate in your country, consult WWW.EMBASSYWORLD.COM/EMBASSY/UKRAINE.HTM.

Recordkeeping in the Austro-Hungarian Empire (Galicia)

Because of changing borders and political regimes, archival documents kept in the portion of Ukraine known as Eastern Galicia under the Austro-Hungarian Empire were recorded in several different languages, both on the form itself and in the registration entry (see AUSTRIA-POLAND). Several times during the 19th century, the Austrian government tried to require state-appointed rabbis to maintain civil birth, marriage, divorce and death records, but the attempts often were unsuccessful. Finally in 1875, a law standardized the recording process; with

minor revisions, it remained in effect until the end of Austrian rule in the region following World War I. The time span recorded in each book varied widely with the population and number of events. Forms were printed in German and events were recorded in handwritten Polish. Before 1875, the column headings were printed in Latin.

The 1875 law divided Galicia into 74 major administrative districts, most of which were further subdivided into smaller sub-districts. All but the largest districts incorporated a number of smaller surrounding communities. In this way, all towns where Jews lived were covered for the purposes of registration. All communities designated as administrative districts had at least one officially appointed rabbi whose job was to maintain vital records for the Austrian government. Nevertheless Jews resisted civil registration for two main reasons. Until 1831, Austrian law had limited legal Jewish marriages to the eldest son in a family only, making the populace suspicious of government regulation even many years after that rule had been abolished. Long after Jews had accepted the registration of births and deaths as a matter of state concern, they continued to resist increasing governmental pressure to participate in civil marriages. A child born to a couple married in a religious ceremony only was not supposed to be registered as legitimate. In some cases, the father's name was omitted from the register, or his name was listed in the "Comments" column. Furthermore, a child whose parents' marriage had not been registered with the civil authorities was barred from inheriting his father's property. The civil marriage requirement was enforced with increasing severity in the late 19th and early 20th centuries at which time, some Jews began to have civil marriages. Prior to that time, however, marriage registers are very thin compared to the thick registers of births and deaths.

Records of the towns within a single district usually were combined in separate volumes in the order in which the events occurred. For example, the books of births, marriages and deaths for the town of Brody included records from the sub-district towns of Leszniow (now Leshnev), Podkamien (now Podkamen), Zalozce (now Zalozhtsy), Sokolowka (now Sokolivka), Szczurowice (now Shchurovychi), Stanislawczyk (now Stanislavchik) and Toporow (now Toporiv).

Some large cities had separate registration books: one for the city itself and another for small towns within the district that did not have their own registration books.

Sometimes, as in Brody, the registrations were written in German. Although the forms changed slightly over time, the types of information collected generally included names, house numbers (most of the time), dates of the event, names of parents and witnesses and a wide column on the right for remarks or special circumstances. For various reasons, not all spaces were necessarily filled in for each event. The metrical books were entered in columnar format, and most do not include indexes.

Galician birth records often reveal the names of the grandparents (including both grandmothers' maiden names) and whether the child was legitimate or illegitimate. Jewish children were usually registered as illegitimate, since their parents only infrequently married in a civil ceremony. Birth registrations often were delayed for many years—and then parents decided to register several children at the same time, thereby making it difficult at this time to locate a specific birth by searching for a known birth year.

Death records in Galicia often list the cause of death. Depending upon the time period, the father's name of the deceased appears in the death record. If the deceased were very old, the father's name often was omitted. The age at death is usually included in the death record.

Galician-Jewish marriage records contain both the groom's and the bride's mothers' maiden names, ages of the bride and groom, and, often, the towns of residence with house numbers.

In most cases, vital statistics records (pre-Holocaust) for towns in Western Ukraine are divided among three archives:

- Central State Historical Archive (CSHA) of Ukraine in Lviv (1791–1942)
- Central Archives of Historical Records (AGAD) in Warsaw (1814–1941), but generally mid- to late-19th century)
- Urzad Stanu Cywilnego Warsaw-Srodmiescie (1877–1942, but generally 20th century)

Zabuzanski Collection. During the period 1962–64, as part of a records exchange agreement, the Soviet Union transferred to Warsaw some Jewish birth, marriage and death records for communities in the territory of former eastern Galicia. Collectively these documents are known as the *Zabuzanski* Collection (i.e., "collection from East of the Bug River"). This collection is housed in two repositories, the Central Archives of Historical Records* (AGAD) in Warsaw and the Urzad Stanu Cywilnego (USC) Warszawa-Srodmiescie office.*

Researchers may visit the USC office and request a search for a few documents, which will be done by the staff—if the requestor can provide town name, surnames and exact dates of events. The researcher may be asked to provide proof of relationship to the person named in the document. As of September 2003, none of the three clerks in this office speaks English, and because of time constraints, staff can provide only limited help to onsite visitors. Because this USC office is a vital records office rather than a historical archive, stringent regulations govern access to information.

Limited access is possible via a written request sent directly to the USC office or through Polish embassies and consular offices. Remember, only specific requests for a few documents will be honored. General genealogical research of a town's entire set of books is not allowed. None of the documents in this USC office have been microfilmed; because of 20th-century privacy restrictions, no filming is planned.

All towns listed in the vital records in the Central State Historical Archives of Ukraine in Lviv and the *Zabuzanski* Collection in Warsaw were either district or sub-district collection centers. Vital records for communities within a single district or sub-district were collected in the town that was designated as the collection point for that district. Many smaller Galician towns and villages not listed in either collection had Jewish populations. Records for many of those communities still exist today and may be found in the registrations of the nearby larger registration center.

Researchers who cannot find the name of a town of interest listed in the Lviv archives or the Zabuzanski Collection should assume only that it was not a district or sub-district center. In such case, it is necessary to determine which town was the collection center for the community of interest. To locate the district or sub-district to which a particular community belonged, consult the Galician Town and Administrative Districts microfiche produced by Avotaynu (www.AVOTAYNU.COM) or *Finding your Jewish Roots in Galicia: A Resource Guide*.

The Jewish Records Indexing-Poland Project (JRI-Poland) is collaborating with the Polish State Archives (PSA) to create a name index to documents within the PSA that were not microfilmed by the Family History Library (see POLAND).[7] Some records from towns currently in Western Ukraine are included in the JRI-Poland efforts. Upon locating an entry of interest in the database, a researcher may order photocopies of the document directly from the archives in Poland. Details are available on the JRI-Poland website at WWW.JEWISHGEN.ORG/JRI-PL. For additional information about Jewish genealogical research in former eastern Galicia, subscribe to *Gesher Galicia*, the publication of the Galician Special Interest Group, and monitor its website at WWW.JEWISHGEN.ORG/GALICIA.

Genealogical Documents in the Ukraine State Archives

Ukrainian archival documents may be divided into two categories. One group includes documents created by the Jewish community, including metrical books (birth, death, marriage and divorce registers); Jewish school records and Jewish hospital records; *kahal* documents (including Jewish community and organization records); and *pinkassim* (Jewish register books) and other documents relating to the Jewish community.

The second group consists of documents created by local and district government offices, institutions, and organizations that include birth, death, marriage and divorce records (primarily created after World War I); *reviskiy skaskiy* (poll-tax census lists); family lists (*posemeinyi spisok*); recruit and/or conscription lists (lists of males by household); election and voter lists; documents created during the Holocaust period (including transport lists, lists of people confined in ghettos and concentration camps, and confiscated property lists); emigration records; property records; police files; public school records; name changes; tax lists; bank records; applications for business licenses and occupational lists; notary records; court records; local government records, including wills and transfer of property to and from the Jewish community; social estate registration records and many other related documents.

Documents in the second group include Jewish names integrated with the general population.[8] As a result, documents relating to the Jewish community may be found in virtually every state archive in Ukraine.

As an example, in tracing Jews who once lived in Podolia *guberniya*, a researcher would focus on records in the following archives:

Kamenets Podolskiy City-State Archive. Kamenets Podolskiy was a center of Jewish population from which Jews spread north throughout the Russian Empire. The documents in Kamenets Podolskiy present a graphic and comprehensive picture of Jewish life in the "old country." Zinaida Klimishina, an archivist in Kamenets Podolskiy, states:

> "In Podolia Guberniya, Jews worked primarily in commercial businesses. They rented land and owned mills, inns and shops. Sometimes they were stewards at landowners' estates, plants and factories, or were professionals, such as doctors and lawyers. Often a family was registered in one place, but lived elsewhere. For example, the wife and small children were reported in one locality while the father and older children (usually sons) were registered in another location."

The Kamenets Podolskiy archive holds a substantial collection of *reviskiy skaskiy* lists. Among other documents in this archive are recruit lists, vital records, notary records, school records, court documents, property records and requests to become citizens of the Russian Empire. Thousands of files include Jewish surnames. In virtually every record book of the Podolsk County administration, one can find information about the life of the Jewish community. Note: In April 2003, a tragic fire destroyed thousands of documents in this archive. The archive is now closed to researchers and surviving books were transferred to the State Archive of Khmelnitskiy Oblast where they should be accessible some time in 2004.

State Archives of Khmelnitskiy Oblast. The Kamenets Podolskiy City-State Archive was formerly a branch archive of the State Archives in Khmelnitskiy Oblast. As a result, older documents for towns in Podolia *guberniya* were preserved in Kamenets Podolskiy until the fire. Documents housed in Khmelnitskiy date primarily from the 20th century and include *kahal* documents, voter lists, some property and notary records, school records and Holocaust documents.

State Archives of Vinnitsa Oblast. The State Archives of Vinnitsa Oblast holds documents dating from the 18th century to the present. Due to former administrative-territorial divisions of Vinnitsa Oblast, documents in this archive cover towns from other oblasts (districts) including Cherkassy, Kiev, Zhitomir, Khmelnitskiy, Odessa and Kirovograd, along with some areas of the Republic of Moldova.

More than 600 metrical books of birth registrations by state rabbis contain valuable genealogical material. Most Jewish documents can be found in the general fonds (collections) including:

- Documents of state councils, local authorities, and financial, tax and military service organizations (including revision lists (1795–1858); family lists (1874–1913); tax lists on Jewish property; lists and photographs of men called up for military service; documents about synagogues, schools and home construction; voter records and other miscellaneous documents
- Documents of legal-administrative and notary offices (including regional courts and magistrates), 1796–1872
- Documents of educational establishments (including commercial and Jewish schools)
- Documents of various state and publication organizations; numerous documents about Jewish life for the period 1920–30
- Documents of Jewish agricultural cooperatives
- Documents about Jewish migration to southern Ukraine, Birobijan, Crimea and other regions
- Documents about activities of Jewish national schools and the Pedagogical Technical School
- Massive number of documents on the Holocaust

A few census lists for towns formerly in Podolia *guberniya* may be found in the Moldova National Archives in Kishinev.

Branch Archives (Departments or Divisions)

Ukraine has several branch archives (of *oblast* archives). Formerly called *filials*, these archives now are "departments" or "divisions." Division archives are located in Berdichev, Beregovo, Izmail, Nezhin and Priluki. The division archive in Mukachevo was closed in 2000 and its documents moved to Uzhgorod. Hennadii Boriak, director of the State Committee on Archives of Ukraine notes, "The documents in Beregovo will be moved to the State Archive of Transcarpathian *oblast* in Uzhgorod after the reconstruction of the new archive building is completed. Researchers are requested not to visit this archive during winter months."[9] Unfortunately, a severe storm and flooding in the late 1990s reportedly caused widespread damage to documents in Beregovo.

Division archives generally hold documents from the town where the archive is situated; such holdings can be extensive. For example, documents in the division archive in Priluki

Certification from the Sudilkov town administration that a 300-ruble fine (for evasion of military service) has been paid by Vitla Vinokur, wife of Shmuel-Ber Vinokur, on behalf of her son, Pinkhas, in 1903. Courtesy of Kamyanets-Podolsky City-State Archive, Ukraine.

(formerly in Poltava *guberniya*, now in Chernigov *oblast*) include draft registrations; birth, marriage and death records census and property records; police files; school and tax lists; notary and business license records; court records; and other local government records. Additional vital record books reside in the local RAHS office. For researchers with roots in Priluki, these two repositories are a veritable goldmine.

Jewish Agricultural Communities

To encourage agricultural colonization in the early 19th century, the czarist government permitted Jews to buy or rent land for cultivation in Kherson and Ekaterinoslav *guberniyas* (new provinces) established on these lands. Those who agreed to be colonists were exempt from taxes for 10 years, after which they would be taxed at the same rate as other groups, thereby eliminating the double tax on Jews in force in other parts of the empire at that time. Those who could not afford to buy or rent land were given government land. Although historically most Jews had never been farmers, a substantial number (mostly from Lithuania and the region of contemporary Belarus) accepted the offer. In 1806, colonists from Mogilev and Vitebsk *guberniyas* established the first Jewish agricultural colonies in Kherson *guberniya*.

Traditionally, Jews had lived in towns and engaged in trade, crafts and small business. As a result, they made poor farmers and village dwellers. When resettled in Novo-Rossiia, they soon migrated to major cities in the new *guberniyas*. Eventually the provincial governments allowed most of the Jews to leave the colonies and settle in towns, where they officially registered as part of the town communities. Throughout the 19th century, Jews from more northern regions of the Pale settled in the towns and cities of southern Ukraine and formed a significant proportion of the population in Elizabetgrad (today Dnipropetrovsk), Odessa, Ekaterinoslav (today Kirovograd) and other cities.

Today historical documents for the former Ekaterinoslav *guberniya* are preserved in the archives of Dnipropetrovsk, Donetsk and Zaporozhye. Archives for the former Taurida *guberniya* are in Simferopol and Zaporozhye. Archives for the former Kherson *guberniya* are housed in Kherson, Kirovograd (formerly Elizabetgrad) and Odessa. These holdings have been almost untouched by genealogists.

LDS Family History Library

The Family History Library of the Church of Jesus Christ of Latter-day Saints (Mormons) has microfilmed civil transcripts of church records and Jewish records worldwide, including those from cities and towns in Ukraine (see LDS). Only a small number of Jewish records have been filmed in Ukraine, but the library recently has expanded its microfilming program there to include census lists (*reviskiy skaskiy*). Check the FHL catalogue at www.familysearch.org/Eng/Library/FHLC/frameset_fhlc.asp to determine if microfilms exist for a town of interest.

Jewish vital records have been filmed or were being filmed as of January 2003 in oblast archives in Cherkassy, Chernigov, Sumy, Ternopol, and Zaporozhye and the State Archive of the Autonomous Republic of Crimea in Simferopol. Although the Ukrainian archival administration has imposed no restrictions on filming Jewish records, local archivists make decisions about which records are filmed and in what sequence.

Ukrainian Resources Beyond the Archival System

Some creative researchers have managed to use to good advantage a variety of non-archival sources, including old Jewish newspapers, local regional museums and local historians. Letters written in Russian or Ukrainian and addressed simply "Mayor, town of interest," often have been answered by the local (more or less official) town historian, local newspaper editor, or even from someone in a local museum.[10] Correspondence with these individuals frequently has produced newspaper articles, published articles from books, and other similar sources of information about the town and families in it. Researchers also should check resources in Israel, especially those at the Central Archives for the History of the Jewish People* and those of the Kollel Galicia in Jerusalem. Researchers who can read Russian may find local history studies listed in the U.S. Library of Congress under the heading "USSR, *Krayevedeniye*" to be invaluable.

Regional museums often include Judaica and/or record books among their exhibitions and holdings. For example, the regional museum in Ostrog* holds a significant collection of Yiddish and Hebrew books, more than 50 Torahs, and many civil record books with valuable documents for researchers with roots in Ostrog. Typically, civil record books are housed in the Ukrainian State Archives;* therefore, one would expect to find them in the State Archive of Rovno Oblast in Rovno. Among the documents in the Ostrog Museum are school records, lists of inhabitants and family lists. These books are in relatively good condition and appear to be well preserved. There are no photocopy facilities in this museum, and office space is limited. Access to this material is granted (selectively) by permission of the museum director. In addition, the local Jewish community in Ostrog maintains lists of former residents, Holocaust victims and survivors.

In Ivano-Frankivsk, Rabbi Moishe Leib Kolesnik* has accumulated a sizeable collection of maps, prayer books, vital record books, photographs and documents from a variety of sources, including private collections, copies from archives and other places. Among the items in his collection are passport documents that he rescued from the trash. A town-by-town (partial) inventory of his collection can be seen at www.rtrfoundation.org.

Several special interest groups (SIGs) and community research groups exist for those with roots in contemporary Ukraine. They are listed on the JewishGen website at www.jewishgen.org/listserv.sigs.htm.

Jewish Cemeteries

The U.S. Commission for the Preservation of America's Heritage Abroad* has surveyed the state of surviving Jewish cemeteries in Ukraine. Much (but not all) of its data is posted on the IAJGS/JewishGen Cemetery Project at www.jewishgen. org/cemetery. This site also posts information collected from other sources, including reports made by researchers visiting their ancestral towns.

The Commission has data not posted on the JewishGen site. To be thorough, a researcher should check with the Commission at WWW.ISJM.ORG. Note that only information about the existence and current condition of a cemetery is given; no lists of burials are available. If an old cemetery still exists and if the tombstones are legible, one might be able to find a specific stone, but only by an onsite visit.

Jewish communities slowly are beginning to create lists of individuals buried in their local cemeteries, mostly funded by individuals or Jewish communities outside of Ukraine. Lists of burials have been created in Mogilev Podolskiy (by the local Holocaust survivor community), Tiraspol (the local Jewish community), Brody (by an outside team of Jewish genealogists) and Uzhgorod (the book of burials is now reportedly in Israel with a recent immigrant), among others. At the present time, specific inquiries are best made during a personal visit to the town. *Jewish Roots in Ukraine and Moldova* includes many photographs of Jewish cemeteries in Ukraine.

Pinkassim Collection in the V. Vernadskiy Library in Kiev

Many Jewish communities in Eastern Europe kept internal records that supply considerable historical and genealogical information. The Jewish communities usually created *pinkassim* (register books) or *ksiegi duchowne* (community books) to record births, marriages, deaths, community tax rolls, synagogue-seat ownership, community charitable contributions and other information. Although the majority of these invaluable books were either destroyed in the Holocaust or ritually buried by the community to preserve them from profanation after becoming unusable, many have survived. The Central Archives for the History of the Jewish People in Jerusalem* has one of the largest collections of extant *pinkassim*. The Jewish Theological Seminary Library* and the Jewish National and University Library* also have collections.

The V. Vernadskiy National Library of Ukraine in Kiev (WWW.NBUV.GOV.UA) has an extensive collection of *pinkassim* in the library's Manuscript Department. Among the 100,000 books and 8,000 manuscripts, there are some 100 *pinkassim*, believed to be the largest collection of Eastern European *pinkassim* in the world.[11] The entire collection has been microfilmed for the Microfilm Department of the Jewish National and University Library and may be consulted there. For a locality listing of these books, see: WWW.RTRFOUNDATION.ORG/WEBART/HARKAVYCOLLECT.PDF.

The Sudilkov Synagogue, destroyed during the Holocaust. Courtesy of Miriam Weiner Archives

Addresses

Archives

AGAD (Archives of Ancient Acts), Dluga 6, skr. poczt. 1005, 00-950 Warsaw, Poland; telephone: 48-22-831-5491; fax: 48-22/831-1608; website: WWW.ARCHIWA. GOV.PL/MAPA/CENTRALA.HTML# AGAD

Moldova National Archives, 67b Gheorghe Asachi Street, Kishinev 277028, Republic of Moldova; telephone: 373-4-2273-5827

National Historical Archives of Belarus in Minsk, 55 Kropotkina Street, Minsk 220002, Belarus; telephone: 375-107-268-6522; fax: 268-6520; e-mail: NIAB @ SOLO.BY; website: WWW.PRESIDENT. GOV.BY/ GOSARCHIVES/ EARH/E_NAZ_ ITS.HTM

Polish State Archives, 6, Dluga Street, 00-950 Warsaw, Poland; website: WWW.ARCHIWA.GOV.PL/ INDEX.ENG. HTML

Russian State Historical Archives, Angliiskaia nab. 4, St. Petersburg 190000; telephone: 7-812-311-0925; fax: 7-812-311-2252; e-mail: RGIA@NP7758.SPB.EDU; website: WWW.RUSARCHIVES.RU

State Committee on Archives of Ukraine, 24 Solomians'ka Street 03680, Kyiv, Ukraine; website: http://www.ARCHIVES.GOV.UA/ENG/. Note: Contact information (addresses, telephone, websites and telephone/fax) for all state archives in Ukraine can be found at the foregoing website.

Urzad Stanu Cywilnego Warsaw Srodmiescie; ul. Smyczkowa 14, 02-678 Warsaw, Poland; telephone: 48-22-847-4821; fax: 48-22-847-6062

Institutes, Libraries, Museums, Organizations, and Private Collections

Central Archive for the History of the Jewish People, P.O. Box 1149, Jerusalem 91010, Israel http://SITES.HUJI.AC.IL/ARCHIVES/

Family History Library, 35 North West Temple Street, Salt Lake City, UT 84150; website: WWW.LDS.ORG

Jewish Historical Institute, ul. T umackie 3/5, 00-090 Warszawa, Poland; telephone 827-92-21; fax: 827-8372; e-mail: SECRETARY @ JEWISHINSTITUTE.ORG.PL; website: WWW.JEWISHINSTITUTE.ORG.PL.

Jewish National and University Library, University of Jerusalem, E. Safra Campus, Givat Ram, Jerusalem, Israel; Tel: 972-2-6586780; http://JNUL.HUJI.AC.IL/ENG/

Jewish Theological Seminary, 3080 Broadway, New York, NY 10027; Tel: 212/678-8000; fax: 212/678-8947; http://www.JTSA.EDU/

Ostrog Museum, ul. Academicheskaya 5, 35800 Ostrog, Rovno Oblast, Ukraine

Rabbi Moishe Leib Kolesnik, The Synagogue, 7 Stregeny Street, 76000-490 Ivano-Frankivsk, Ukraine; telephone: 380-3422-2-3029.

Routes to Roots Foundation, Inc., 136 Sandpiper Key, Secaucus, NJ 07094; telephone: (201) 601-9199; fax: (201) 864-9222; email: MWEINER@ROUTESTOROOTS.COM; website: WWW.RTRFOUNDATION.ORG

United States Commission for the Preservation of America's Heritage Abroad, 1101 Fifteenth Street NW, Suite #1040, Washington, DC 20005 http://www.PRESERVATIONCOMMISSION.ORG

V. Vernadskiy National Library of Ukraine, Prospect 40-Richchia Zhotvtnia 3, 03039 Kiev; telephone: 380-44-265-8104; fax: 380-44-264-3398, 264-1770, 265-5602; e-mail: NLU@CSL.FREENET. KIEV.UA, website: WWW.NBUV.GOV.UA

Bibliography

Articles

Beider, Alexander. "The Influence of Migrants from Czech Lands on Jewish Communities in Central and Eastern Europe." *AVOTAYNU* 16, no. 2 (Summer 2000): 19–28.

Bolotenko, George. "Kiev Library Has Wealth of Uncatalogued Judaica," *AVOTAYNU* 8, no. 4 (Winter 1992): 47.

Bolotenko, George, and Lawrence Tapper. "Canadian Archivists Visit Ukrainian Archives." *AVOTAYNU* 9, no.4 (Winter 1993): 9.

Chlenov, Matthew, and Ivan Pichugin. "Documents of the Soviety Evobshestvkom Committee." *AVOTAYNU* 14, no. 1 (Spring 1998): 45.

Contributing Editor (Tapper). "Book Review: Ukrainian Archeographic Year Book." *AVOTAYNU* 10, no. 2 (Summer 1994): 49.

Eastern European Genealogy, 3, no. 4 (1995): 16–18.

Edlund, Thomas K. "The 1st National Census of the Russian Empire." *FEEFHS Journal* 7, nos. 3 & 4 (Fall/Winter 1999): 88–97.

Feldman, Dmitry Z. "Archival Sources for the Genealogy of Jewish Colonists in Southern Russia in the 19th Century." *AVOTAYNU* 15, no. 2 (Summer 1999): 14.

Fox, David. "Records from Northern Bukovina." *AVOTAYNU* 18, no. 3 (Fall 2002): 17.

Grimsted, Patricia Kennedy. "Ukraine: A Guide to East-Central Archives." *Austrian History Yearbook* (Center for Austrian Studies, University of Minnesota), 29, no. 2 (1998): 176-88.

"Jewish Colonists in Ekaterinoslav Guberniya," *AVOTAYNU* 14, no. 2 (Summer 1998): 65.

Kawaler, Foster. "Eastern Galician Records Available from Polish Archives." *AVOTAYNU* 5, no. 2 (Summer 1989): 26.

Khiterer V. "Jewish Documents in the Central State, Historical Archive of Ukraine." *Jews in Eastern Europe* 26, no. 1 (1995): 70–76.

———. "Sources on Jewish History in The Central State Historical Archive of Ukraine." *Shvut: Studies in Russian and East European Jewish History and Culture* 17-18, nos. 1–2 (1995): 393–402.

Klier, John D. "Kiev Archival Materials on East European Jewry." *Soviet Jewish Affairs* 21, no. 2 (Winter 1991): 38–43.

Kotler, Igor. "Crimean Jewish Family Names." *AVOTAYNU* 5, no. 2 (Summer 1989): 5.

Kronick, Katerina. "About Pogroms in Ukrainian Towns in 1919–20." *AVOTAYNU* 10, no. 3 (Fall 1994): 66.

———. "Book Describes Pogroms in Ukrainian Towns in 1919–20." *AVOTAYNU* 10, no. 2 (Summer 1994): 67.

Lozytsky, Volodymyr. "Sources for Jewish Genealogy in the Ukrainian Archives." *AVOTAYNU* 10, no. 2 (Summer 1994): 9–14.

Mehr, Kahlile. "Russian Archival and Historical Terminology." *AVOTAYNU* 12, no. 3 (Fall 1996): 35–36.

———. "Selected Translation of Name Lists and Revisions from the Dnepropetrovsk Archives." *AVOTAYNU* 16, no. 3 (Fall 2000): 28.

Melamed, Efim. "Information for Jewish Genealogists in the State Archive of Zhitomir Oblast." *AVOTAYNU* 12, no. 1 (Spring 1996): 14–18.

———. "In Which Haystack to Search?" *AVOTAYNU* 14, no. 4 (Winter 1998): 16.

Panov, Dmitriy. "Guide to the Jewish Records in the Rovno Oblast State Archives." *AVOTAYNU* 10, no. 4 (Winter 1994): 5.

Petrovsky, Yohanan M. "Newly Discovered Pinkassim of the Harkavy Collection." *AVOTAYNU* 12, no. 2 (Summer 1996): 32–35.

Rodal, Alti. "Bukovina Cemeteries, Archives and Oral History." *AVOTAYNU* 18, no. 3 (Fall 2002): 9.

Rosenbloom, Ruth. "A Trip to Ukraine." *AVOTAYNU* 14, no. 4 (Winter 1998): 51.

Sack, Sallyann Amdur. "A Meeting with Two Officials of the Ukrainian Archives." *AVOTAYNU* 10, no. 2 (Spring 1994): 9.

Shadevich, Yakov "It's a Long Way to Uzhgorod; It's a Long Way to Go." *AVOTAYNU* 12, no. 2 (Summer) 1996: 3.

Soshnikov, Vladislau. "Jewish Agricultural Colonies in New Russia." *AVOTAYNU* 12, no. 3 (Fall 1996): 33–34.

———. "Jewish Genealogical Research in Ukraine." *AVOTAYNU* 14, no. 3 (Fall 1998): 23.

Svarnyk, Ivan. "Ukraine Archivist, Ivan Svarynk Speaks on the Central State Historical Archives in Lviv." *East European Genealogist* 8, no. 4 (Summer 2000): 5–8.

Szumowski, Donald. "Alternative Research Sources in Poland." *AVOTAYNU* 12, no.2 (Fall 1996): 65.

Wrobel, Piotr. "The Jews of Galicia under Austrian-Polish Rule, 1867–1918: Part I." *The Galitizianer* 8, nos. 2 & 3 (May 2001): 15–23; Part II, vol. 8, no. 4 (August 2001): 14–20; Part III, vol. 9, no. 1 (November 2001): 21–24.

Wunder, Rabbi Meir. "The Kollel Galicia Archive." *AVOTAYNU* 6, no. 3 (Fall 1990): 23.

Wynne, Suzan. "Demographic Records of Galicia, 1792–1919." *AVOTAYNU* 8, no. 2 (Summer 1992): 7.

Zelevna, Yulia and Yuliy Lifshits. "Records of the Kiev Board of Craftsmen." *AVOTAYNU* 12, no. 3 (Fall 1996): 41.

Books*

———. *Gosudarstvennij arkhiv Kiyevskoy oblasti* (Guide to the Kiev Oblast State Archives). [Russian] Kiev, 1965.

———. *Iosyfinska [1785–1788] i Frantsiskanska [1819–1820] metryky: pershi pozemelni kadastry Halychyny.*
Pokazchyk naselenykh punktiv [Iosyfinska [1785–1788] i Frantsiskanska [1819–1820], Metric
The First Land Cadastre of Galicia. Kiev: Naukova Dumka, 1965 [Ukrainian]

Boriak, Hennadii, Maryna Dubyk, and Natalia Makovska. *"Nazi Gold" from Ukraine: In Search of Archival Evidence*, Part I. [Ukrainian with short English summary] Kiev, 1998.

Boriak, Hennadii, Maryna Dubyk, Natalia Makovska. *"Nazi Gold" from Ukraine: In Search of Archival Evidence, Part 2: Materials for a Register of Valuables Confiscated from the Population.* [Ukrainian with English summary].Kiev, 2000.

Chapin, David A., and Ben Weinstock. *The Road from Letichev: The History and Culture of a Forgotten Jewish Community in Eastern Europe*, 2 vols. Lincoln, Neb: iUniverse.com, 2000.

Grimsted, Patricia Kennedy. *Archives and Manuscript Repositories in the USSR: Ukraine and Moldova.* Book 1: General Bibliography and Institutional Directory. Princeton: Princeton University Press, 1988.

Himka J.P. Galicia and Bukovina: A Research Handbook About Western Ukraine, Late 19th and 20th Centuries. 1990.

Lukin, V. and V. Khaimovich. *Sto evreiskikh mestecheck Ukrainy*, vol. 1: Podolia (100 Jewish Shtetls in the Ukraine. Vol. 1: Podolia). [Russian/English]. Jerusalem: Izd. "Ezro," 1997.

Lukin, V.M., and B.N. Khaimovich. *Sto evreiskikh mestecheck Ukrainy*, vol. 2: Podolia (100 Jewish Shtetls in the Ukraine. Vol. 2: Podolia). [Russian/English]. Jerusalem: Izd. "Ezro," 2000.

Peltz, Diana, ed. *Central State Historical Archive of Ukraine, Lviv: A Guide*. [Ukrainian/Polish] Lviv/Kiev: State Committee on Archives of Ukraine, 2001.

Weiner, Miriam. *Jewish Roots in Poland: Pages from the Past and Archival Inventories*. Secaucus, N.J./New York: Routes to Roots Foundation, Inc./YIVO Institute for Jewish Research, 1997.

Weiner, Miriam. *Jewish Roots in Ukraine and Moldova: Pages from the Past and Archival Inventories*. Secaucus, N.J./New York: Routes to Roots Foundation, Inc./YIVO Institute for Jewish Research, 1999.

Wynne, Suzan F. *Finding Your Jewish Roots in Galicia: A Resource Guide.* Teaneck, N.J.: *AVOTAYNU*, 1998.

* For comprehensive listing of published inventories by the individual archives in Ukraine, See Appendix I of *Jewish Roots in*

Ukraine and Moldova: Pages from the Past and Archival Inventories. Secaucus, NJ/New York: Routes to Roots Foundation, Inc./YIVO Institute for Jewish Research, 1999. See also: WWW.ARCHIVES.GOV. UA/ENG/GUIDES.PHP and WWW.ARCHIVES.GOV.UA/ENG/ RESOURCES.PHP

Notes

1. Alexander Beider. "The Influence of Migrants from Czech Lands on Jewish Communities in Central and Eastern Europe.": 19.

2. Source: Dr. Hennadii Boriak, director, State Committee on Archives of Ukraine, 2003.

3. Except for towns in Western Ukraine, no source exists for determining which nearby larger town handled registrations for small towns and villages with very small Jewish communities. One can make direct inquiries during an onsite visit to the town or research the Jewish metrical books of the nearest larger town, but this method is time consuming and not always productive.

4. Source: Diana Peltz, director, Central State Historical Archive of Ukraine in Lviv, 2002.

5. Genealogists often receive unsolicited e-mail messages from people purporting to have a research business in another country and offering services. It is wise to be cautious and wary in replying to such solicitations. Many people have requested research from an individual or "company" based in another country and either never received a response after sending money or were told "there are no documents; now send money" without receiving any type of a research report at all.

   When hiring a professional researcher in Ukraine, it is wise to create a written agreement signed by both parties that specifies exactly what is to be researched, time period of the assignment (expected date of completion), costs involved (research time, travel costs, copy costs, etc.), method and terms of payment, what the customer will receive, (e.g., a report that includes a list of documents searched, the years searched, archive numbers [fond/opis/delo in the former Soviet Union; and *zespol/signatura* in Poland]), location and name of archive where search was done, translation of documents (if requested), and document copies (if requested).

6. Interview with Faina A. Vinokurova, vice director, State Archive of Vinnitsa Oblast, 1998.

7. Jewish Records Indexing-Poland (JRI-Poland) is a groundbreaking project to create a computer database of indexes to the 19th-century Jewish vital records of Poland. Launched in 1995, the award-winning JRI-Poland has grown to be the largest fully searchable database of Jewish vital records accessible through the Internet. Teams of volunteers around the world are actively working to expand the database.

8. According to the Russian Statute of 1804, Jews were required to register in one of four social categories: (1) "agriculturalists" (*zemledeltsy*), (2) manufacturers and artisans, (3) merchants (*kuptsy*), and (4) petty townspeople (*meshchane*). The fourth category was a general term that described those outside the three more specific status categories.

9. Interview with Dr. Hennadii Boriak.

10. This writer wrote to the local museum in Priluki and was answered by a Jewish employee who voluntarily researched the family name of Odnopozov in the local RAHS office. The research produced my grandmother's birth record and documents for 11 other family members.

11. Interview with Dr. Irina Sergeyeva, chief, Oriental Department, V. Vernadskiy National Library

Venezuela

by Ignacio Sternberg

Venezuela, with its approximately 24 million inhabitants, is located in the northern part of South America on the Caribbean Sea. It is slightly more than twice the size of California. The country is the largest oil producer in Latin America and one of the main suppliers of oil to the United States. Jews have lived here since the 19th century, primarily in Caracas, the capital.

Columbus came to Venezuela on his third trip to the New World; with him were some individual *conversos* (Crypto-Jews) about whom we have very little information. The first important Jewish group came from Curacao in the Dutch West Indies and settled in Coro, a city in northwest Venezuela, just 35 miles from Curacao.

Jews of Coro

The Jewish community of Coro, in the state of Falcon, began with the immigration of Sephardic Jews from Curacao in the 1820s after Venezuela abolished the Inquisition from its territory. Most Jews came after 1828 and were merchants. In 1830, the Venezuelan government granted foreigners the same personal rights as Venezuelans. Because Curacao was undergoing a major economic depression, many Jews came to settle in Coro.

Some of the first settlers were Isaac Abenatar, Salomon Brandao, Alvarez Correa, Elias Curiel, Isaac Curiel, Jose Curiel, H. Fonseca, David C. Henriquez, M.C. Henriquez, Isaac de Lima, Elias Lopez, Josua Lopez, David Maduro and David Valencia. Other family names among the first settlers are Abensur, Capriles, Chumaceiro, De Castro, De Jongh, Delvalle, De Sola, Jesurun, Lobo, Mendes, Pardo, Salas and Senior. Many of their descendants studied in Europe, became professionals of various kinds and returned to Venezuela, where they practiced their professions. Others were poets and writers, and some held government positions.

This group practiced their religion but with no community organization. The group feared the local authorities and also honored an 1829 legal treaty signed with the Dutch government (who already ruled Curacao, Aruba and Bonaire) whereby religions other than Catholicism must be practiced in private homes. The group maintained close ties with Curacao, where many went to marry. In 1832, they built a Jewish cemetery after having received permission from the local government.

Over time, all these Jews assimilated with the local residents, and many of them, or their descendants, moved to Caracas and other cities. Some became prominent professionals, such as Dr. David Ricardo and S. de Jongh Ricardo, founders and members of the board of directors of the Venezuelan Red Cross in 1895.

In 1855, the Coro cemetery was desecrated, but it was restored in 1858. Since 1970, when a descendant of Jose Curiel was governor of the state of Falcon, the cemetery was designated a national monument. It has 165 graves, the oldest dating from 1832. The last person to be buried was Frida Cirla Szomstein in 1945, an Ashkenazi. Her tombstone is the only one with Hebrew letters in addition to an epitaph.

Jews in Barcelona

By 1844, a small group of Jews of Curacao origin established themselves in Barcelona, a city in northeastern Venezuela, capital of the state of Anzoategui. One of the oldest tombstones in the small cemetery dates from 1891, that of Rebeca Baiz de Moron, born in Saint Thomas in 1820.

Caracas Jewish Community

Jews from North Africa, especially from the Spanish Moroccan cities of Ceuta, Tangier and Tetuan, emigrated to Venezuela during the second half of the 19th century and early 20th century. They began the development of the contemporary Jewish community of Caracas and other smaller Venezuelan cities. The national census of 1891 recorded 247 Jews in the country, but many did not declare their religion; the true number was undoubtedly greater. Among these immigrants' names were Abraham Benaceraff (two of them!), Jacobo Benadi and Jacobo Pariente; other family names were Bendayan, Sananes and Taurel. One Abraham Benacerraf was the father of Baruch Benacerraf, winner of the Nobel Prize in medicine, born in Venezuela but now residing in the United States. Unlike the Jews of Coro, these later immigrants and their descendants have maintained their religious practices until today.

The first organized Sephardic congregation in Caracas was founded in 1907. Called Sociedad Benefica Israelita, it lasted only until 1909. Its president was Enrique B. Levy. At that time, Caracas had fewer than 100,000 inhabitants, including a few hundred Jews. All newcomers received immediate help from Jews who had arrived earlier and were already established.

The first Jewish cemetery in Caracas was Sephardic, built in 1916 with permission of the authorities in a separate section of the Christian cemetery. An important organization created in 1982 is the Centro de Estudios Sefardies de Caracas (Center for Sephardic Studies of Caracas). It publishes a quarterly magazine, *Maguen-Escudo* (Shield). The Asociacion Israelita de Venezuela, organized in 1930, remains the primary Sephardic organization of the country.

After 1956, many immigrants came to Venezuela from Spanish Morocco and other Middle Eastern countries. Because the immigrants already spoke Spanish, they adapted very quickly. In the 1960s and 1970s, many other Sephardim immigrated to Venezuela, primarily from Bulgaria, Egypt and Salonika, Greece. Today they maintain many charitable organizations.

Ashkenazim began to emigrate to Venezuela in the 1920s, mostly from Poland and Romania, including Bessarabia and Bukovina. Some went first to other countries in South

America and from there came to Venezuela. The first Jewish communal organization was founded in 1926 mainly to help newcomers establish themselves. After 1930, the country admitted more immigrants from Poland and Romania and others from Germany, Hungary, Latvia and Russia. The Ashkenazim organized additional community centers in other cities, such as Maracaibo, Maracay, San Cristobal and Valencia.

Some of the principal Jewish pioneers of that time (1920s–30s) were Maximo Freilich, Natalio Glijansky, Bernardo Gutman, Mendel Holder, Isaac Kohn, Manuel Laufer, Haim Itzig Lerner, Kalman Lubowsky, Samul Meiler, Jacobo Mishkin, Isidoro Nash, Moritz Neuman, Eduardo Sonenschein, Leon Sznajderman, Jacobo Zaidman, and Velvel and Haim Zighelboim. Almost all began as house-to-house peddlers (called *clappers* in Yiddish). Initially they were helped by the Sephardi Jews already established in Venezuela, who sold merchandise to the immigrants on credit. Most of the new immigrants were men who came alone, saved money and later sent for their families. As they prospered, they established themselves as merchants and in small textile industries.

Religious life was carried on in private houses where Shabbat services were held. There was no kosher food, but sometimes a *shohet* (kosher slaughterer) came from Colombia to kill their chickens. The immigrants continued to arrive and the community grew. In 1931, the first Ashkenazic Jewish community, Sociedad Israelita Ashkenazi, was established. Initially, the congregation met in rented houses, moving as the membership grew. The type of organizations formed were largely influenced by Poland's Polei Zion, the democratic socialist group.

Jewish life started in the 1930s in other major cities of Venezuela as more immigrants came and established themselves as *clappers* in Barquisimeto, Maracaibo, Maracay, San Cristobal, Valencia and also Coro, where Jews had first settled in the 19th century. Jewish organizations were created in these cities, especially in Maracaibo, the capital of the state of Zulia. It is the second most important city of the country and the state where most Venezuelan oil is produced.

Beginning in 1939, two ships, the *Caribia* and the *Konigstein*, sailed from Hamburg, Germany, carrying Jewish refugees to Venezuela after an ordeal in various countries and ports that would not let the passengers disembark. The *Caribia,* carrying 86 mostly Austrian- Jewish families, was destined for Trinidad which had granted them visas. When the ship arrived, however, the Trinidad government refused to allow them to disembark, arguing that the visas had been canceled. The *Caribia* then sailed to La Guaira, Venezuela, where again the passengers were refused permission to disembark. Immediately the Jewish organization of Venezuela interceded and pleaded with the government to grant asylum to the refugees, explaining that if they were to return to Europe, they would perish.

In the meantime, the ship sailed to Puerto Cabello, another Venezuelan port, and again permission was refused. Next the ship sailed to Curacao with the hope that the passengers would be received there; if not, the captain told the desperate refugees, the ship would go back to Germany. While under sail, the Venezuelan government agreed to allow the ship to return to Puerto Cabello. It arrived on February 3, 1939, at night, and there were no lights in the port. As the news spread, the people of the city lighted all their houses as well as the headlights of their trucks in order to enable the passengers to disembark. When they arrived on shore, a large crowd of Venezuelans received them with joy and food. They were immediately taken in by Jewish families from Valencia and Caracas. After a few days, they received Venezuelan citizenship and permission to remain in the country.

In the meantime, the *Koenigstein* had arrived at Barbados with 165 Jews who had received entry permits for that country while still in Europe. Here, too, they were refused permission to land and were told that the visas had been canceled. Next, the ship went to British Guiana, which reportedly might allow immigration. As soon as the ship arrived in British Guiana, it received a denial. At that moment, the *Koenigstein* heard what had happened to the *Caribia* and decided also to go to La Guaira where, thanks to the efforts of the captain of the ship and the Jewish community, the passengers received permission to disembark. They arrived on February 27, 1939, just 24 days after the *Caribia*.

Jewish life continued to grow during World War II, although the sad news coming from Europe put almost all of the Ashkenazic families in mourning. As soon as the war ended, the community organized to receive refugees from Europe who came after 1945. Many came with visas obtained by their relatives living in Venezuela. At that time, the Venezuelan government had restrictions on granting visas, and it was difficult for European Jews to obtain them. Applicants were asked to state their religion in official documents, and many came listed as Christians, the only way they could obtain a visa to Venezuela.

In 1946, a committee for the establishment of a Jewish state in Palestine was established whose membership included Venezuela Gentiles—politicians, writers, poets and journalists. In 1947, the president of Venezuela was the writer Romulo Gallegos. Under his leadership, Venezuela was one of the first countries to vote in the United Nations for the establishment of the State of Israel.

During the 1950s, an influx of Jewish immigrants came to Venezuela from Argentina, Chile, Colombia and Peru. At that time, Venezuela's government opened immigration, Jews and non-Jews came from Spain, Italy and Portugal, also. This new policy expanded the economy of the country and many Jews living in other Latin American countries also came to Venezuela attracted by the bonanza.

No Venezuelan census gives a precise number of Jews, but the number in Venezuela today is estimated at about 25,000, most residing in Caracas. Jews work in all kinds of occupations—industry, commerce, the professions and as writers. Many professionals of all sorts are second and third generation Venezuelans.

Except for some disturbances organized by extremist groups in the 1960s, Venezuela has seen no major anti-Semitism, only occasional newspaper articles written by individuals. In some former governments, Jews held ministerships and others had important government responsibilities. No Jews are found in today's government, except for a limited number of individuals with minor responsibilities. The Confederation of Jewish Organizations of Venezuela (CAIV) represents the Jewish

Interior of the Union Israelita de Caracas Synagogue, the main Ashkenazi synagogue in Venezuela

community vis-a-vis the Venezuelan government and other institutions.

Jewish Education

Jewish education began in Caracas in the 1940s with the establishment of a *cheder* (religious school) that initially operated only two hours daily. In addition, there was a Shabbat school where most youngsters met, received Hebrew lessons and studied Jewish history. In 1946, a Jewish school, Colegio Moral y Luces Herzl Bialik, was organized by the Ashkenazic community and opened to all Jewish children. The school grew steadily, and today approximately 1,600 elementary and high school students receive both a secular and a Hebrew education. After some years, the Sephardic community joined in the direction and administration of the schools. Some years ago, the Orthodox community founded a small school, the Colegio Cristobal Colon Sinai. There is also a Jewish school in Maracaibo.

In 1968, both organizations (Ashkenazi and Sephardi) joined forces to build a new school and club facilities, the Centro Social y Deportivo Hebraica, for all the Jews of Caracas. All types of sports are practiced there, and it is well recognized by the government sport authorities. Many competitions are celebrated with other clubs and sports organizations.

Cemeteries

The first cemetery in Caracas, built by the Sephardic community, was used also by the Ashkenazim until 1936 when the Ashkenazim organized their own cemetery. Today Caracas has five Jewish cemeteries, three Ashkenazic and two Sephardic. In Caracas, there is Cementerio General del Sur-Panteon de la Union Israelita de Caracas (Israelites Union of Caracas) and Rabinato de Venezuela (Rabbinical Cemetery of Venezuela). Both are located inside the main cemetery of the city and are very well separated from the main cemetery. They are located in the southwest part of the city. Gran Menuja is located in the east part on the way out of Caracas. These are Ashkenazic cemeteries. Others,

Cementerio General del Sur-Panteon de la Asociacion Israelita de Venezuela (Israelite Association of Venezuela) (no longer in use) and Cementerio del Este Asociacion Israelita de Venezuela, are Sephardic cemeteries. To get information, write to the main organizations, Union Israelita de Caracas (Ashkenazic) at WWW.UIC.ORG and Asociacion Israelita de Venezuela at WWW.AIV.ORG.

Religious Life

Most Jews in Venezuela are orthodox. We have also a Lubavitcher organization and synagogue. Caracas has approximately 18 synagogues, most of them small Sephardic organizations that group people from the same country of origin or other groups with similar interests. All of these are under the umbrella of the two major Jewish organizations, Union Israelita de Caracas www.UIC.ORG.VE and Asociacion Israelita de Venezuela WWW.AIV.ORG. Synagogues function also in Maracaibo, Maracay, Margarita Island and Valencia.

A weekly newspaper, *El Nuevo Mundo Israelita* (The New Israelite World), is sent free to all members of the two main Jewish organizations mentioned above. Additional publications with a more restricted circulation are published by special interest groups. *Magen-Escudo* (Shield) is published quarterly by the Asociacion Israelita de Venezuela for its members. *Hagesher* (The Bridge) is published once a year by the Zionist Federation of Venezuela www.UIC.ORG.VE. *Esperanza* (Hope) is published by the Woman's Association Hatikwa once a year. *Rumbo A Mi Judaismo* (Heading to My Judaism) is published by Habad Lubavitcher as a quarterly.

Recently, this author created a Jewish genealogical group, the Asociacion de Genealogia Judia de Venezuela (JGSVENEZUELA@BELLSOUTH.NET), which now has 24 members. A website and publication will begin in the near future, and we offer to help Jewish genealogists all around the world. We thank Howard Margol, former president of the IAJGS, and Paul Armony, president of the Jewish Genealogical Association of Argentina, who helped us form the third Jewish genealogical society in Latin America—after Argentina and Brazil.

Bibliography

Aizenberg, Isidoro. *La Comunidad Judia de Coro, 1824–1900*. Volume 11, Caracas: Biblioteca Popular Sefardi, 1995.

Arbell, Mordechai. *Spanish and Portuguese Jews in the Caribbean and Guiana: A Bibliography*. Providence: edited by The John Carter Brown Library, 1999.

Carciente, Jacob. *Presencia Sefaradi en la Historia de Venezuela* (Sephardic Presence in Venezuela's History). Volume 14, Caracas: Biblioteca Popular Sefardi, 1997.

Emmanuel, Isaac S. *The Jews of Coro-American Jewish Archives on the Cincinnati Campus of the Hebrew Union College–Jewish Institute of Religion*. FHL #987 A1 #2, 1973.

Encyclopaedia Judaica.

Nassi, Mario. *Las Comunidad Ashkenazi de Caracas* (The Jewish Ashkenazi Community of Caracas). Union Israelita de Caracas (Caracas Israelite Union), 1981.

COMISION DE CULTURA UNION ISRAELITA DE CARACAS

Yugoslavia (Former)

by Sallyann Amdur Sack and Harriet Freidenreich

Read the chapters entitled AUSTRO-HUNGARIAN EMPIRE and OTTOMAN EMPIRE before starting this section. The South Slav lands that constituted Yugoslavia in the 20th century were ruled by the Habsburgs and the Ottomans for many centuries prior to that. Knowledge of the history and record keeping practices of the two empires is helpful in understanding research described below—Ed.

European countries altered their borders frequently during the 20th century, no place more than this region. Yugoslavia, created at the end of World War I, lasted until the early 1990s. Prior to that, the Habsburgs and the Ottomans fought over the area for centuries. The warring of the 1990s has yielded to an uneasy cease fire as this is written, and the current world map displays Slovenia, Croatia, Bosnia and Herzegovina and a truncated Yugoslavia composed of Serbia and Montenegro.

For centuries this region has had three different religions and two major ruling powers—one oriental, one European. Slavic tribes migrated to the Balkans in the sixth century. Those that settled in the western portion, the Slovenes and the Croats, became Roman Catholic, while the Serbs affiliated with the eastern Byzantine church. Later, under the Ottoman influence, most of the Bosnians became Muslim.[1]

Sephardic Jews generally lived in the Ottoman territories—primarily Sarajevo, Skoplje, Bitolj (Monastir), Dubrovnik and Split—while the Ashkenazim settled in the Habsburg areas in Zagreb, Osijek, Novi Sad and Subotica. Almost all Yugoslavian Jews lived in urban areas.

Austrian Lands

The Slovenian territories soon became part of the Austrian crownlands; in the 19th century, Dalmatia on the Adriatic, came under Austrian rule after centuries of Venetian domination. Croatia, formerly an independent kingdom, united with Hungary in 1102. Also under the Hungarian crown were the Banat, Backa and Baranja, jointly called the Vojvodina. These Austrian lands north of the Danube were conquered by the Ottomans in the 16th century, but were reclaimed from the Turks in the 17th century. The years of shifting regimes left the area with a mixed population of Germans, Hungarians, Serbs and other ethnic minorities. The final expansion of the Austro-Hungarian Empire into the Balkans was the occupation of Bosnia-Herzegovina in 1878 and the subsequent annexation of these provinces 30 years later.[2]

Ottoman Lands

The Turks had conquered Serbia, Macedonia and the Kingdom of Bosnia by the end of the 15th century. Serbia broke away from the Ottomans in the early 19th century and, by 1881, became a kingdom. Montenegro was never fully conquered by Turkey, but Macedonia remained part of the Ottoman Empire until the Balkan Wars of 1911–13 when it was divided among Bulgaria, Greece and Serbia. The establishment of a single South Slavic nation brought together in one country two distinctly different group of Jews, the Ashkenazim of the Habsburg empire and the Sephardim from the Ottoman area.

Jews in Turkish Lands

Individual Jews had lived in the region since the days of the Greeks and Romans, but they left no records. The first recorded Jewish settlers were those from the Iberian Peninsula following the Spanish and Portuguese expulsions. Ottoman Turkey, at its peak in the 15th and 16th centuries, welcomed the Jews who settled primarily in Constantinople (today Istanbul) and Salonika. From there, they migrated into the hinterlands of the empire, making Sarajevo (in Bosnia) the third major Jewish city of the empire. According to records in local Muslim courts, by 1565 Sarajevo sheltered 10 to 15 Jewish families, merchants who had come from Salonika. Other Jewish communities appeared in Belgrade (in Serbia), Skoplje and Monastir (Bitolj) in Macedonia. Jews settled also in Dubrovnik (Ragusa) and Split (Spalato) on the Dalmatian coast. Greater in number and superior in culture, the Sephardim soon assimilated the scattered indigenous Romaniote Jews to the Sephardic way of life.

The Ottoman Empire was organized into autonomous, religious communities called *millets*, one of which was the Jews. Jews governed themselves according to their laws in matters of family, inheritance, marriage and property. Communal revenues were derived primarily from a religious tax on all Jewish residents. Like all non-Muslims, the Jews also were required to pay a special poll tax, levied on all males above the age of nine years.

Jews in Habsburg Territory

Ashkenazic communities developed late in the Habsburg areas. Until the end of the 18th century, Jews were forbidden to live in Slovenia, Croatia and the military frontier (the military zone on the border area of the Ottoman Empire under Habsburg control), except for Zemun (Semlin, Zimony). During the 19th century, numerous Jews from various parts of the Austro-Hungarian Empire migrated to the South Slav regions under Hungarian control. Major Jewish communities developed in Zagreb (Agram) and Osijek (Essig, Eszek) in Croatia-Slavonia and in Novi Sad (Nesatz, Ujvidek) and Subotica (Szabadka) in the Vojvodina. Genealogically, Ashkenazic roots in the former Yugoslavia are much shallower than those of the Sephardim.

Three Major Cities

During the 19th and 20th centuries, Sarajevo, Bosnia; Belgrade, Serbia; and Zagreb, Croatia; comprised the largest Jewish communities in the South Slav lands. Zagreb Jewry was largely Ashkenazic; Sarajevo was Sephardic; and Belgrade, the capital, was mixed. On the eve of the Holocaust which annihilated 80 percent of Yugoslavian Jewry, the Ashkenazim made up two-thirds of the total Jewish population.

Sarajevo Jewry. Jews engaged in commerce from their earliest years in Bosnia. During the centuries of Ottoman control, Sarajevo Sephardim maintained business contacts with Jews in Belgrade, Dubrovnik, Istanbul, Salonika, Skoplje, Split, Trieste, Venice and even Vienna. Ties were especially close with Salonika, the spiritual center of Balkan Jewry.

The Austro-Hungarian occupation of Bosnia in 1878 profoundly disrupted the Sephardic Jewish community of Sarajevo. The Habsburgs reorganized the internal structure of the established Jewish community in 1882 and, for the first time, the Sephardic community of Sarajevo was subject to state control and interference. According to new regulations, the community "had the right to tax its members for its own use up to 20 percent of the amount of direct state taxes. Membership was compulsory for all Sephardim and a register was to be kept by the communal authorities."[3]

At about the same time, a separate but parallel community of Ashkenazim developed. "The Sephardim and Ashkenazim continued to maintain their separate communities and institutions into the 20th century with relatively little social contact between the two groups."[4]

During the period of Austro-Hungarian rule, the number of Jews living in Sarajevo tripled, in part because of a relatively high Sephardic birth rate and some Sephardic immigration, but also because of numerous Ashkenazim from other parts of Austria-Hungary. An 1885 census showed 2,618 Jews in Sarajevo; most were Sephardim with few Ashkenazim. In 1895, of the 4,058 Jews, 3,159 were Sephardim; by 1910, the count was 4,985 Sephardim and 1,412 Ashkenazim.

In the 1921 census, the Jewish population was 11 percent of the total at 7,458; in 1931 it had dropped to 10 percent (7,615) and by 1939, the Jewish population was estimated at 8,114 of whom 7,054 were Sephardim. During the interwar period, the Sarajevo population remained static with almost no immigration into the city, but with considerable Jewish emigration to Belgrade and Zagreb.

Belgrade. The former capital of Yugoslavia, which always had major strategic and economic importance, is situated on the border between the former Ottoman and Austrian empires. As such, it passed back and forth between them several times during the 17th and 18th centuries. Most of the time it remained primarily under Turkish control until the Serbian independence movement began in the early 19th century.[5]

Nothing is known about Belgrade's earliest Jewish inhabitants and few traces remain of Jewish life there in the Middle Ages. Most Jews arrived after the Turkish conquest. By the mid-16th century, the city had a small Sephardic community. Early marriages were common, families were large and young couples often lived with parents.[6]

During the 17th century, Belgrade became the third center of Jewish learning in the Balkans, after Istanbul and Salonika. A large body of responsa literature in Hebrew and Ladino

Synagogue in Sarajevo, Bosnia, at the beginning of the 20th century

was written by the Belgrade rabbis of this period. This cultural growth was interrupted by the Austrian conquest in 1688.[7] After that, the number of Jews permitted to live in Belgrade was limited. Jews paid a special tolerance tax, could not own real estate or live outside the Jewish quarter. After the treaty of Belgrade of 1739, the Austrians left the town, along with some of the Ashkenazic Jews who moved across the Sava River to Zemun and Novi Sad.

The mid-18th century was a 50-year-period of quiet development and growth for the Sephardic community which was supplemented by new migrations from the south. On the eve of the Austrian-Turkish War of 1788–89, the Jewish population is estimated to have been approximately 800. Most Belgrade Jews, especially the Sephardim, favored Turkish rule over Austrian, but many left the city after Turks returned, fearing reprisals.

"The position of the Jews of Belgrade was not very secure at the turn of the 19th century."[8] In 1861, a decree was passed that allowed a series of expulsions of Jews from rural Serbia over the next few years. By 1865, more than half of the Jews of Serbia lived in Belgrade.[9]

Significant numbers of Ashkenazim began to settle in Belgrade only in the second half of the 19th century. After emancipation in 1888, the Jewish community of Belgrade grew steadily from 2,599 in 1890 to 4,844 in 1921 and to 7,906 ten years later. By 1939, about 10,388 Jews—8,600 of whom were Sephardim—lived in Belgrade.

Zagreb. This capital city of Croatia which managed to escape Turkish domination and remain under Hungarian control, has always been almost entirely Central European in

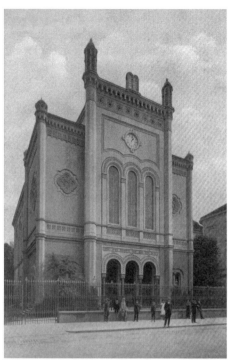
*Synagogue in Zagreb, Croatia, in the 1920s.
Courtesy of Tomasz Wisniewski.*

orientation. The few Jews who lived in Zagreb during the Middle Ages were expelled when the Habsburgs assumed the Hungarian throne in 1526. No Jews lived in northern Croatia until the end of the 18th century. Jews must have filtered back in, however, for in 1729 the Croatian parliament again forbade Jews to live in the region. After 1750, Jews were allowed to attend the annual fair and to remain up to three days for trade purposes. Jews first received permission to live in Zagreb in the 1780s, but they had to obtain a right of residency and pay an annual tolerance tax. As late as 1783 they still were not allowed to settle officially in the city. Not until the end of the 18th century did Jews actually settle openly in Zagreb, and, in 1806, a group of approximately 20 families organized a Jewish community.

The situation was different in Split and Dubrovnik, whose Jewish communities, the oldest in Croatia, were established by Sephardim following their expulsion from Spain and Portugal. Jews in these mercantile cities on the Adriatic coast enjoyed a high level of culture and, overall, suffered less repression and persecution than their co-religionists in the rest of Europe. Jews obtained civil freedom and equality in Split in 1806 and in Dubrovnik in 1808. At the same time, the French military administration in Dalmatia abolished the ghettos and repealed all anti-Jewish laws. In 1814, Dalmatia came under Austrian rule which repealed the democratic French laws. From then on, the Jew of Split and Dubrovnik shared the fate of the other Jews of (mostly northern) Croatia.

The Jews who located in Zagreb were all Ashkenazim from various parts of Central Europe. Most of the early arrivals migrated from Hungary, especially western Hungary and Burgenland; others came from Moravia and Austria and some from Galicia. Throughout the 19th century, the community conducted all of its business in German. Under a 1852 law, all Zagreb Jews were required to constitute a single community with one official rabbi to maintain a register of all births, circumcisions, marriages and burials. On October 21, 1873, the parliament granted civil equality to all the Jews of Croatia, Slavonia and Dalmatia and abolished the requirement of special residency permits.

Under an agreement between Hungary and Croatia in 1868, Zagreb became the capital of the semi-autonomous province of Croatia-Slavonia and Zagreb grew rapidly during the second half of the 19th century. Between World War I and World War II it was the leading industrial, commercial and financial center in Yugoslavia. In the late 19th and early 20th centuries, the Jewish population doubled and redoubled growing from 1,285 in 1880, to 4,233 in 1910 and 8,702 in 1931. By 1925, Zagreb had a small Sephardic settlement of 95 families and in 1939, on the eve of World War II, the Jewish population was estimated at 9,467, 8,712 of whom were Ashkenazim; it constituted approximately five percent of the total population.

Holocaust and Post-Holocaust

The Germans entered Yugoslavia early in 1941 and, by May, Yugoslavia had ceased to exist as a state. Much of its territory was divided among the conquering Axis powers. Almost immediately, the Germans undertook the near total destruction of the existing Jewish community. In October 1941, 4,000 Jewish men were shot. Women and children were sent to a camp in Zemun across the river from Belgrade. During the spring and summer of 1942, more than 6,000 were killed in mobile gas vans. By August 1942 Serbia was *judenrein* (free of Jews). Zagreb Jews remain unconfined until as late as 1944, but then they were interned in torture camps. Those who did not die in the camps were eventually sent to Auschwitz and other death camps.

In March 1943, the Jews in Bulgarian-controlled Macedonia, some 8,000 from Bitolj, Skoplje and other towns, were shipped in three transports to Treblinka where they were almost totally annihilated. A similar fate befell the Jews in Hungarian-occupied areas. In January 1942, bloody massacres erupted in Novi Sad and surrounding towns. Between 1942 and 1944, 4,000 Jewish men were sent in labor battalions to Ukraine and various parts of Hungary. After March 1944, Germans assumed control and began mass roundups, sending the Jews to the newly created Subotica ghetto. Beginning in May 1944, the ghetto was liquidated and the residents sent to Auschwitz.

On the eve of World War II, the Jewish population of Yugoslavia was estimated at 71,342.[10] More than three quarters died in the Holocaust; in 1946, 12,414 Jews lived in Yugoslavia. The government of Marshall Tito permitted Jews to emigrate freely to Israel, and in a series of five *aliyot* (emigrations to Israel), 7,578 Jews departed between 1948 and 1952. A small number of others went to North America. After 1952, Yugoslavia experienced little Jewish emigration or immigration until the civil war of the 1990s. During 1999, hundreds of Yugoslavian Jews emigrated to Israel. Most were well educated and assimilated easily.

Today the Jewish community of Croatia is composed of nine local communities with a total of 2,500 members. In addition to Zagreb, they are Cakovec, Daruvar, Dubrovnik, Osijek, Rijeka, Slavonski Brod, Split and Virovitica. The Co-ordination Committee of Jewish Local Communities in Croatia, headquartered in Zagreb, formed after the disintegration of Yugoslavia and serves as the official body of Croatian Jewry vis-a-vis the Republic of Croatia and various state institutions. A chronology of the history of Zagreb Jewry is found in the Autumn 1998 issue of the *Voice*, the official publication of the Jewish community in this city. A history of the vanished Jewish community of Vukovar appears in the same issue.[11] Histories of the communities of Koprivica, Dubrovnik, Koprivica and Osijek appear in the Autumn 2000 edition of the same publication.

Resources for Jewish Genealogy

Since the break up of Yugoslavia and subsequent civil wars, it has been impossible to maintain previous relationships. To a large extent, it also has been impossible to verify the information given below. Before the current hostilities, considerable efforts were being made to maintain the existing Jewish cemeteries, many—if not most—of which survived World War II.

Bosnia (Sarajevo)

Sarajevo had the oldest Jewish population in all the former Yugoslavia, but, paradoxically, these roots are the hardest to research. At present, fewer records from Sarajevo are known to survive than for Serbia (essentially Belgrade) or Croatia. Also unknown is the current fate of records known to exist prior to the recent civil war. (See OTTOMAN EMPIRE discussion of Ottoman tax and population registers.)

Before World War II, the Sarajevo Jewish community possessed communal minute books dating from 1720 to 1888 with tax lists, data on communal leaders, rabbis and other officials, but the records were destroyed along with many of the community. The only known resource for these records are ones that were translated and included in a 1911 book by Rabbi Morc Levi, *Die Sephardim in Bosnien*. The destroyed records were for the Sephardic community only; no tax records exist for the Ashkenazic community.

Prior to the civil war, birth registers from the late 19th and early 20th centuries were held in the Sarajevo Jewish library separately for both the Sephardic and the Ashkenazic community. The Sephardic records (*maticne knjige rodjenih sefardske opstine jevrejseke, Sarajevo*) covered the years 1894–1941; those for the Ashkenazim (*maticne knjige rodjenih askenaske opstine, Sarajevo*) covered a slightly longer period, 1880–1941. State school records that identify each child by religion existed in the decade before the recent civil war. Nothing is known of the current fate of these records.

If the records have survived and could be accessed, they likely would be extremely helpful. Those who have seen the documents report that the Sephardim of Sarajevo rarely slavicized their last names and had only an unusually small pool of names. Families were easily identifiable. The most common surnames were Altarac, Papo and Levi; Abinun, Albahary, Attias, Danon, Kabiljo, Kamhi and Maestro were not far behind.

With few exceptions, Sephardic first names reflected the same traditional character. Biblical names repeated continuously; it seems that almost all the boys were called Avram, Isak, Jakov, Haim, Salamon, Aser, Aron, Samuel and so forth. Girls names were somewhat more exotic, if not more varied: Simha, Rena, Ora, Buena, Palomba, Mazel-tov, Djentila, Esperanza, Luna, along with Sara, Rifka, Rahel, Mirjam, Debora and Ester.[12]

Within the Ashkenazic community, the range of family names was much greater, but they retained one common characteristic. They were almost all of German-Yiddish or Hungarian origin, with some foreign Slavic (Polish or Czech) admixtures. As a general rule, however, if a first name is Hungarian and a last Germanic, or vice versa, it is a relatively safe guess that the person so designated is probably a Jew, rather than a member of some other ethnic group.

The Ashkenazim in Sarajevo tended to see themselves as Central Europeans and usually did not give identifiably Jewish everyday names to their children. (Other residents of Sarajevo, however, tended to view this group as foreigners.)[13]

Before the civil war, Sarajevo had a state-run Jewish museum for Bosnia and Herzegovina that held documents, artifacts and recordings of Jewish songs and music. No information about the status of the museum is available at present.

Also unknown is the current state of the famous, centuries-old Jewish cemetery. During the recent fighting in this city, the cemetery frequently was the site of fierce gun battles and likely has suffered much destruction.

Belgrade (Current Yugoslavia)

Currently, no archival access is given to foreigners. If the situation changes, genealogists are likely to find substantial resources. The National Archive of Yugoslavia, *Arhiv Jugoslavije*,* is located in Belgrade, but most of its holdings date only from the 20th century and have little value for genealogists. The Archive of Serbia (*Arhiv Srbije*)* was established prior to the creation of Yugoslavia and has many national collections. Most important to genealogists are its many censuses, especially for 1863, 1905 and 1910. The Archiv of Vojvodina (*Arhiv Vojvodine*)* has the 1869 Austrian census for the Novi Sad area as well as a vast collection of parish register transcripts for all religions of the years 1826–95. Of all the Yugoslavian archives, the one in Novi Sad seems to be the most responsive to foreigners.[14]

During World War II, German soldiers confiscated the complete set of birth, marriage and death records belonging to the Jews of Belgrade, Yugoslavia, 1866–1941 and held in the Jewish Museum of Belgrade*. In turn, the records were captured by Soviet soldiers. Today the original documents are held in the Osobyi Archives in Moscow, but the Belgrade Jewish community has a microfilm copy of the entire collection and will answer requests for information from genealogists, according to Jewish community head, Mr. Aca Singer. Requests may be sent in English (or German) to Mr. Singer at 11000 Belgrade, Kralja Petra 71a, third floor, Belgrade, Yugoslavia; telephone: 381 11 624 359; fax: 381 11 626 674; e-mail: SAVEZJEV@INFOSKY.NET. The U.S. Holocaust Memorial Museum[*] has microfilmed other Jewish records from Belgrade held in the Osobyi Archives. These may be freely consulted at the museum.

Currently unknown are the whereabouts of records from other Jewish communities in the Serbian area of Yugoslavia, including Novi Sad and Subotica. One researcher, however, received the following message in March 1998.[15]

> Our archive had documents about Jews in our town in 18 and 19 century, but, during the German occupation of Vojvodina and our town (1941–1945) all these materials were destroyed. We do not know who in our country can help you, because these were local documents.
> [Signed] Milan Djukanov, manager of "the working collective of Historical archive of Zrenjanin."

Zagreb (Croatia)

Jews settled later in Croatia, primarily in Zagreb, than in any other area of Yugoslavia and, by chance, this is the region where genealogists have the best chance of success. Before hostilities ended its activities, the Mormons succeeded in microfilming the Jewish birth, marriage and records for most of Croatia. Films exist for Cakovec, Darda, Drnje, Karlovac, Koprivnica, Ludbreg, Orahovica, Osijek, Prakrac, Slatina, Slavonska Pozega, Varazdin, Virovitica, Vukovar and Zagreb.

The *Hrvatski Drzavni Arhiv*[*] (National Archives of Croatia) is the major depository of old church and synagogue records, although Croatian regional historical archives (*drzavni arhiv*) hold birth and death records before 1860 (and sometimes as late as the 1880s). Regional archives exist in Bjelovar, Dubrovnik, Karlovac, Osijek, Pazin, Rijeka, Sisak, Slavonski Brod, Split, Varazdin and Zadar.

After World War II, all birth, marriage and death records held by religious organizations, including Jewish records, were deposited in city register offices. The 21 Croatian counties (*zupanija*) include 400 municipalities with register offices. Zagreb has many such offices.

One Jewish genealogist reports good results from a letter (written in English) requesting vital records sent to the Varazdin regional archive. The archivist who search the City Book of Inhabitants (1930) and a record of Jews sent to concentration camps (1941), also provided copies of several marriage, death and census records for the years 1879–1930.

Since 1995, the Croatian State Archives[*] has donated to the U.S. Holocaust Memorial Museum and the Jewish community of Zagreb microfilms about Holocaust victims. From materials in its possession, the Croatian archive had created a register with a page for each victim that included personal data about his or her life, work and place and manner of death to the extent that it could be determined. The correct spelling of names was problematic because both given names and surnames appear spelled differently in different documents. In January 1998, the head of the Croatian State Archives[*] presented the president of the Jewish community of Zagreb with 10 rolls of microfilm containing biographies of Zagreb Jews who had perished during the Holocaust. These people either were born, worked or resided for a period of time in Zagreb

and were killed in concentration camps and prisons between April 10, 1941 and May 15, 1945.

In Spring 1996, the Jewish community of Zagreb announced a project to compile and publish a biographical lexicon of Jews in Croatia to include up to 5,000 short biographies of prominent Jews who lived and worked on the territory of contemporary Croatia from Roman times until today, focusing especially on the past 200 years. The Editorial Board of the Jewish Biographical Lexicon[*] is requesting help circulating a questionnaire designed for the purpose.

A non-Jew who lives in London has published an article about researching the roots of his Jewish wife's family from Cakovec (formerly Csaktornya in Zala country, Hungary), Donji Miholjac (misleadingly catalogued as Osijek), Karlovac, Orahovica, Sarajevo Virovitcca, Zagreb.[16] An onsite visit of Osijek revealed that the Jewish community in this city has an unfilmed register of marriages, and the museum in Nasice has a late Jewish register for the years 1929–34. Family names include Altarac (from Bosnia), Breier, Domany, Fischel, Klingenberg, Klinger, Levi/Lowinger, Schlesinger, Schön, Spitzer. Some registers include births and parentages that go back many earlier generations in other communities in Hungary and even Moravia.

Addresses

Archiv Jugoslavije (National Archive of Yugoslavia), Vase Pelagica 33, 11000 Belgrade, Yugoslavia

Archiv Srbije (Archive of Serbia), Karnedzijeva 2, 11000 Belgrade, Yugoslavia

Archiv Vojvodine (Archive of Vojvodina), Dunavska 35, 21000 Novi Sad, Yugoslavia

Archival depository of genealogical information for Vojvodina: Archiv Vojvodine, Bunavska 3s, 21000, Novi Sad, Yugoslavia

Association of Genealogists with Roots in the Banat, Wilfried Nkiesel, Weinbergsweg 2, 6905 Schrieshem, Germany

Association of Immigrants from Yugoslavia, 73 Ibn Gvirol Street, 61162 Tel Aviv, Israel

Drzavni Arhiv Varazdin (Croatian State Archives of Varazdin), Trstenjakova 7, 42000 Varazdin, Croatia

Drzavni Arhiv Zagreb, (Croatian State Archives of Zagreb), Opatica 29, 10000 Zagreb, Croatia

Editorial Board of the Jewish Biogrpahical Lexicon, Palmoticeva 16, 1000 Zagreb, Croatia

Federation of Jewish Communities of Yugoslavia (Savez jevrejskih ops'tina Jugoslavije), ul. 70-og. Jula 71a/III, Belgrade, Yugoslavia

Historical archive of Zrenjanin, Yugoslavia, Trg. Slobode 10, 23000 Zrenjanin, Yugoslavia

Hrvatski Drzavni Arhiv (Central State Archive of Croatia) Marulicev trg 21, 10000 Zagreb, Croatia

Jevreiski Istorijski Musei (Jewish Historical Museum), 7-og Jula 71a/I, POB 841, Belgrade, Yugoslavia

Jewish Community of Belgrade, 7 Kralja Petra Street, 71a/1 1101 Belgrade, Serbia; telephone: 260-11-622-634; fax: 260-11-626-674

Jewish Community of Dubrovnik, Zudioska ul. 3, Dubrovnik, Croatia

Jewish Community of Novi Sad, JNA Street 35, Novi Sad, Yugoslavia

Jewish Community of Sarajevo, Dobrovoljacka ul. 83, Sarajevo, Bosnia

Jewish Community of Skopje, Borka Talevski Street 24, Skopje, Macedonia

Jewish Community of Split, Zidovski prolaz 1, Split, Croatia

Jewish Community of Subotica, ul. dimitrija Tucovic'a 13, Subotica, Serbia

Jewish Community of Zagreb, Jevrejska Opcina, Palmotic'eva Ulica 16, 41001 Zagreb, Croatia

Maticini Ured Centar (a Zagreb city registry office), Ilica 25, 10000 Zagreb, Croatia

Bibliography

"Records of Belgrade Jewry Available" *AVOTAYNU* 16, no. 2 (Summer 2001): 53.

Contributing Editors (Hungary), *AVOTAYNU* 13, no. 4 (Winter 1997).

Domas, Jasminka. *Mishpah—the Family.* Zagreb: Novi Liber and M.S. Freiberger Cultural Society, 1996.

Elazar, Daniel J., Harriet Pass Friedenreich, Baruch Hazzan and Adina Weiss Liberles. *The Balkan Jewish Communities: Yugoslavia, Bulgaria, Greece and Turkey.* Lanham, MD: University Press of America, 1984.

Freidenreich, Harriet Pass. *The Jews of Yugoslavia: a Quest for Community.* Philadelphia: Jewish Publication Society, 1979.

Hardy, Malcolm Scott. "Researching Jewish Family History: Croatia, Slavonia, Hungary." *Voice* no. 3 (Autumn 2000): 63.

Kerem, Yitzchak. "Bibliography of Greek Jewry." *AVOTAYNU* 7, no. 2 (Summer 1992): 40.

Kerem, Yitzchak. "Documentation on Sephardic and Balkan Jewry at the U.S. Holocaust Memorial Museum and U.S. National Archives." *AVOTAYNU* 15, no. 4 (Winter 1999): 20–22.

Kraus, Ognjen. "The Jewish Community in Croatia: History—the Present." *Voice*, No. 1. (Zagreb: Coordination Committee of Jewish Communities in Croatia, Spring 1996).

Malka, Jeffrey S. *Sephardic Genealogy: Discovering Your Sephardic Ancestors and Their World.* Bergenfield, NJ: Avotaynu, 2002.

Mehr, Kahlile. "Yugoslavian Genealogical Sources," *FEEFHS Quarterly* Vol. VI, Nos. 1–4, 1998.

"Moscow's Osobyi Archives: A Genealogical Source at the USHMM," *AVOTAYNU* 12, no. 2 (Summer 1996).

"Research Projects at the Diaspora Research Institute," *AVOTAYNU* 10, no. 4 (Winter 1994).

Romano Jasa. *Jews of Yugoslavia 1941–45: Victims of Genocide and Freedom Fighters.* (Belgrade: Federation of Jewish Communities in Yugoslavia, 1980).

Sack, Sallyann Amdur. "A Genealogical Report on Israel." *AVOTAYNU* 12, no. 3 (Fall 1997): 17–20.

Svob, Melita. *Jews in Croatia: Migration and Changes in the Jewish Population.* [English] Zagreb: Jewish Community of Zagreb and Cultural Society, Miraslav Shalom Freiberger, 1997.

"The Genocide of the Jews in the Independent State of Croatia." *Voice,* no. 1 (Spring 1996). Includes "The Chronology of the Jewish Ordeal."

"The Jews of Vukovar: A Contribution to the History of Vanished Jewish Communities in Croatia," *Voice,* no. 2, Autumn 1998.

Those Who Died in the Jasenovec Death Camp during the Holocaust: Jasenovec, Zrtve Rata Prema Podacimo Statistickog Zavoda Jugoslavije (War victims according to the Yugoslavia Statistical Institute). Zurich and Sarajevo: Bosnjacki Institut, 1998.

Voice of the Jewish Community in Croatia. Palmotićeva 16, 1000 Zagreb, Croatia.

"What Happened to Shmuel and Rebeka during the Holocaust," *AVOTAYNU* 13, no. 4 (Winter 1997).

Zbornik: Studije Arhivska i Memoarska Grada o Istoriji Jevreja u Bralgradu. (Jewish studies: studies, archival and memorial materials about the history of the Jews of Belgrade). Belgrade: Jewish Historical Museum, 1992. [Serb with English summaries]

Notes

1. Friedenreich, 4
2. *Ibid.,* 4
3. *Ibid.,* 15
4. *Ibid.,* 16
5. *Ibid.,* 26
6. *Ibid.,* 27
7. Ibid., 28
8. *Ibid.,* 30
9. *Ibid.,* 33.
10. Elazar, 14
11. *Voice,* No. 1, Autumn 1998
12. Friedenreich, 23
13. *Ibid.,* 24
14. Mehr, 72
15. JewishGen Digest, March 10, 1998
16. *Voice,* No. 3, Autumn 2000

Part V

Appendixes

Appendix A: Alphabets

Deutsch

The German Alphabet

Roman	Fraktur	Cursive
A a	𝕬 𝖆	
B b	𝕭 𝖇	
C c	𝕮 𝖈	
D d	𝕯 𝖉	
E e	𝕰 𝖊	
F f	𝕱 𝖋	
G g	𝕲 𝖌	
H h	𝕳 𝖍	
I i	𝕴 𝖎	
J j	𝕵 𝖏	
K k	𝕶 𝖐	
L l	𝕷 𝖑	
M m	𝕸 𝖒	
N n	𝕹 𝖓	
O o	𝕺 𝖔	
P p	𝕻 𝖕	
Q q	𝕼 𝖖	
R r	𝕽 𝖗	
S s	𝕾 ſ 𝖘	
T t	𝕿 𝖙	
U u	𝖀 𝖚	
V v	𝖁 𝖛	
W w	𝖂 𝖜	
X x	𝖃 𝖝	
Y y	𝖄 𝖞	
Z z	𝖅 𝖟	

Roman	Fraktur	Cursive
Ä ä	𝕬̈ 𝖆̈	
Ö ö	𝕺̈ 𝖔̈	
Ü ü	𝖀̈ 𝖚̈	
ß	ß	
ch	ch	
sch	ſch	
ck	ck	
tz	tz	

The intimidating typeface known as *Fraktur* was generally used in Germany until before World War II, but has since been replaced in common usage by the alphabet familiar to us. A few modified letters used for special sounds in German are listed on the right-hand side of the chart: *ä* (a-umlaut), *ö* (o-umlaut), *ü* (u-umlaut) and *ß* (eszet). The other letter combinations (*ch, sch, ck,* and *tz*) are shown because their printed or cursive forms can be hard to recognize; they are not regarded as separate characters and do not affect alphabetical order. Note also the alternate forms of lower-case *s* in *Fraktur* and cursive: ſ and / are the usual forms, ß and ℓ are used at the end of words or at dividing spots in compound words. We've all seen similar usage in older English-language documents such as the Declaration of Independence, where the letters that look like uncrossed *f*'s are actually *s*'s.

German cursive script can be as intimidating as the printed *Fraktur*. Consider *Gesundheit*, a familiar expression to most Americans; it looks like a series of angular scrawls, but it's *Gesundheit*, what you say when someone sneezes! Any combination of *n (e), c (c), m (m), u (n), ü (u), v (v),* and *w (w)* can be frustrating to decipher, especially if the penmanship is sloppy. The best approach is to identify the easier letters, such as *b, h, a,* and *v*; distinguish / (s) and/or *h* (h) by their extending above and below the other letters; then start counting up-and-down strokes and trying to match them with problem letters. Hints: *ü (u)* should always have that little curve over it, and *v (v)* and *w (w)* end with tailing curves. Your odds improve if you have a limited list of candidate words to compare against; if you've inferred that the word might refer to parents, *Mutter* can suddenly become recognizable as *Mutter,* "mother." So a good dictionary can help a lot with deciphering written words.

עברית # The Hebrew Language — *by Zachary M. Baker*

Printed	Cursive	Rashi	English
א	אc	א	'/silent
ב	ב	ב	b/v
ג	ג	ג	g
ד	ד	ד	d
ה	ה	ה	h
ו	ו	ו	v/u/o
ז	ז	ז	z
ח	ח	ח	ḥ
ט	ט	ט	ṭ
י	י	י	y/i
כ	כ	כ	k/kh
ך	ך	ך	final k
ל	ל	ל	l
מ	מ	מ	m
ם	ם	ם	final m
נ	נ	נ	n
ן	ן	ן	final n
ס	ס	ס	s
ע	ע	ע	'/silent
פ	פ	פ	p/f
ף	ף	ף	final p
צ	צ	צ	ts
ץ	ץ	ץ	final ts
ק	ק	ק	k
ר	ר	ר	r
ש	ש	ש	sh/s
ת	ת	ת	t/s

Hebrew is a Semitic language, closely related to ancient Phoenician and Aramaic, and to classical and modern Arabic. The basic Hebrew alphabet consists of 22 consonants, five of which (כ, מ, נ, פ, צ) possess additional forms used only at the end of words; each is shown in the chart at left as a separate character, in the column immediately below the standard form. There is no distinction between upper- and lower-case forms in Hebrew.

Vowel signs and other diacritical marks ("points" or "dots") are sometimes used above, below, within, and between Hebrew letters. The chart on the next page illustrates their use, using the consonant ה [h] to demonstrate their positioning. Generally the vowels appear below the consonant they follow in pronunciation, as with הַ [ha], but notice the exception הֹ, [ho], with the point above the consonant. "Pointed" texts are largely limited to poems, children's literature, liturgy, and Hebrew Bible editions; otherwise, Hebrew is customarily written or printed without vowel signs. Thus, the pronunciations and meanings of Hebrew words can often be inferred only by context. An authoritative Hebrew-English dictionary, such as those cited below, is an essential tool for reading Hebrew.

Like other languages employing the Hebrew alphabet (such as Yiddish, Ladino, and Judeo-Arabic), Hebrew is written from right to left. Most written documents in Hebrew employ cursive script; printed texts most frequently use "square" letters, though a rounded typeface commonly referred to as "Rashi script" is also found in some religious publications and early Hebrew imprints.

Hebrew words are most often formed on the basis of three-letter consonantal roots. For example, the common stem זמן [zeman] = "time," "date," generates such words as להזמין [le-hazmin] = "to invite," הזמנה [hazmanah] = "invitation," and הזדמנות [hizdamnut] = "chance," "occasion." Hebrew possesses two genders: masculine and feminine. In nouns, the feminine form is frequently signaled by the presence of ה and ת at the end of words.

Over the millennia, Hebrew has evolved from the now-archaic language of the Bible, to Aramaic-tinged rabbinic Hebrew, and most recently, to the revived spoken and written vernacular of the modern State of Israel. Standard Israeli Hebrew follows Sephardic norms of pronunciation; in Eastern Europe, by contrast, the Ashkenazic pronunciation was used. The accompanying alphabet table relies on the Library of Congress standard for the transliteration of Israeli Hebrew, but also includes Ashkenazic pronunciations where these differ from Sephardic. The most striking differences between the two are:

(1) In Sephardic Hebrew most words are stressed on the last syllable, while in Ashkenazic Hebrew they are

stressed on the preceding syllable, e.g.: שבת [shabat] (Sephardic) vs. [shabos] (Ashkenazic) = "Sabbath."

(2) Ashkenazic Hebrew distinguishes between ת [t] and ת [s]; in Sephardic Hebrew both forms of the letter are pronounced [t], as the previous example indicates.

(3) Ashkenazic Hebrew distinguishes between the vowels ָ [o] and ַ [a], while in Sephardic Hebrew both vowels usually are pronounced [a], e. g.: אָמֵן [omein] (Ashkenazic) vs. [amen] (Sephardic) = "Amen."

Four Hebrew letters — shown here in their "pointed" (or "dotted") forms — can represent different consonants in both Ashkenazic and Sephardic Hebrew: בּ [b] vs. ב [v], כּ [k] vs. כ [kh], פּ [p] vs. פ [f], and שׁ [sh] vs. שׂ [s]. The letters ח [ḥ] and כ [kh] are pronounced alike (as in Scottish "loch"), though the Library of Congress transliteration system represents them differently. Similarly, ט and ת are both pronounced [t], and ס and שׂ are both pronounced [s].

Two letters can function as either consonants or vowels: ו [v/o/u] and י [y/i/ei]. There are two variant spelling systems in Hebrew, one of which makes special use of ו and י: "defective" (without vowels) and "plene" (where selected vowels are indicated by the insertion of the letters ו and י), e. g.: ספור ("defective" spelling) vs. סיפור ("plene" spelling), [sipur] = "story."

The letter ה is pronounced [h], except at the end of words, when it is silent. The letter א can either be silent or act in lieu of vowels. The letter ע functions similarly to א, though some Hebrew speakers pronounce it with a guttural inflection, and it is usually transliterated by an inverted apostrophe [ʻ]. The letter ר [r] is pronounced with the soft palate.

Traditional Hebrew texts use letters to represent numbers, including dates. Abbreviations are also frequently encountered in written and printed Hebrew. This example illustrates both concepts: תרס״ד לפ״ק = [5]664 "according to the shortened reckoning" (of the year), or 1903/04 C.E. (תרס״ד adds up to 664, omitting the letter ה׳ [= 5,000], indicating the millennium — see the accompanying chart. לפ״ק is short for לפרט קטן [li-ferat katan] = "according to the shortened reckoning").

Honorifics are also represented in abbreviated forms, of which perhaps the most common is ר׳, short for "rabbi" or "master." Abbreviations and honorifics are

included in authoritative dictionaries; separate lists have also been published.

In pre-World War II Hebrew-language documents and publications, especially those from Europe, personal names of non-Hebrew derivation are often spelled according to their phonetic Yiddish renderings, for example בלומע ראזען [Blume Rozen], rather than בלומה רוזן — the accepted Israeli Hebrew spelling.

Sources:

Alcalay, Reuben. *The Complete Hebrew-English Dictionary.* Tel-Aviv: Massadah, 1963 [and subsequently].

Baltsan, Hayim. *Webster's New World Hebrew Dictionary.* New York: Prentice Hall, 1992.

Hebraica Cataloging: A Guide to ALA/LC Romanization and Descriptive Cataloging. Prepared by Paul Maher. Washington, D.C.: Cataloging Distribution Service, Library of Congress, 1987.

The Numerical Values of Hebrew Letters

Letter	Value	Letter	Value
א	1	ף / פ	80
ב	2	ץ / צ	90
ג	3	ק	100
ד	4	ר	200
ה	5	שׁ	300
ו	6	ת	400
ז	7	תק	500
ח	8	תר	600
ט	9	תש	700
י	10	תת	800
ך / כ	20	תתק	900
ל	30	א׳	1,000
ם / מ	40	ב׳	2,000
ן / נ	50	ג׳	3,000
ס	60	ד׳	4,000
ע	70	ה׳	5,000

A shortcut formula for figuring out the civil calendar (C.E.) equivalent of a Hebrew year, according to the "shortened reckoning": add 1240 to the Hebrew year, e. g., תרס״ד = 664 + 1240 = 1904 C.E. Note: the Hebrew year begins in the autumn of the previous civil calendar year, so 5664 actually began in the autumn of 1903.

Vowel points, using the consonant ה *[h] to illustrate their positioning*	הַ *ha*	הִ *hi*
	הָ *ha/ho*	הוּ *hu*
	הֶ *he*	הְ *hə/h*
	הֵ *he/hei*	הוֹ *ho*

Polski

The Polish Alphabet

Printed	Cursive
A a	*A a*
Ą ą	*Ą ą*
B b	*B b*
C c	*C c*
Ć ć	*Ć ć*
D d	*D d*
E e	*E e*
Ę ę	*Ę ę*
F f	*F f*
G g	*G g*
H h	*H h*
I i	*I i*
J j	*J j*
K k	*K k*
L l	*L l*
Ł ł	*Ł ł*
M m	*M m*
N n	*N n*
Ń ń	*Ń ń*
O o	*O o*
Ó ó	*Ó ó*
P p	*P p*
R r	*R r*
S s	*S s*
Ś ś	*Ś ś*
T t	*T t*

Printed	Cursive	Printed	Cursive
U u	*U u*	Z z	*Z z*
W w	*W w*	Ź ź	*Ź ź*
Y y	*Y y*	Ż ż	*Ż ż*

Polish is one of the Slavic languages that use the Roman alphabet, not the Cyrillic, largely because writing came to the Poles by way of Roman Catholic rather than Greek Orthodox clergy. The letters *q*, *v*, and *x* are not used in Polish, and the distinctly Polish characters *ą*, *ć*, *ę*, *ł*, *ń*, *ó*, *ś*, *ź* and *ż* are considered separate letters of the alphabet, each following its unmodified counterpart (*ą* after *a*, *ć* after *c*, and so on). The *ą*, *ę*, *ń*, and *y* never appear initially and thus are seldom capitalized; but since documents sometimes highlight words by spelling them out in upper-case letters, it seems best to show all upper-case forms, even those rarely seen.

The basic vowels of Polish are much as in the Romance languages: *a* is like the *a* in "father," *e* like that in "let," *i* like that in "machine," *o* somewhat like that in "hot," *u* like the *oo* in "book," and *y* like the short *i* sound in "hit." The vowel *ó* is pronounced exactly the same as Polish *u*, and some words are spelled either way (*Jakób* vs. *Jakub*, for example). The nasal vowel *ą* sounds like English "own" with the *n*-sound never quite finished, but before *b* or *p* it sounds more like *om* in "home." The nasal *ę* is generally pronounced like *en* in "men," again without quite finishing the *n*-sound; before *b* or *p* it sounds more like *em* in "memory," and in some positions it loses its nasal quality. But generally pronouncing *ą* like *on* (*om*) and *ę* like *en* (*em*) will approximate the correct sound. Polish does not distinguish between long and short vowels.

The *i* is special because it often follows consonants as a sign of softening; thus Poles pronounce *ne* as somewhat like "neh," but *nie* more like "nyeh." The consonants *ć*, *ń*, *ś*, and *ź* are spelled that way only when they precede other consonants; before vowels they're spelled *ci*, *ni*, *si*, and *zi*. In either case they are pronounced, respectively, more or less like soft *ch* (as in "cheese"), *ni* (as in "onion"), *sh* (as in "sheep") and the sound of the *s* in "pleasure." In a word like *cicho* (quiet, quietly) the *i* not only softens the *c* to a *ch*-sound, it also supplies the first syllable's vowel.

Many consonants are pronounced much as in English, but the *l* is more like that in "leaf" than that in "hill," and the *r* is lightly trilled, as in Italian. Polish *h* and *ch* are pronounced the same, a little harsher than an initial *h* in English but not quite so guttural as German *ch* in "Bach." Polish *w* sounds like English *v* and Polish *ł* is pronounced like English *w* (all of which explains how "Lech Wałęsa" can come out sounding like "Lekh Vawensa"). The *c* is pronounced like a combined *ts* (e. g., English "knights"), the *g* is always as in "gone" (never as in "gym"), and the *j* is always pronounced like *y* in "yield." The *s* is pronounced as it is in English "soon," and *z* is pronounced as in "zebra" (but remember the softened pronunciation of *ci*, *ni*, *si*, and *zi*).

The *cz*, *rz*, *sz* combinations are similar to *ć*, *ż*, and *ś*, respectively, but are articulated differently; *ż* is pronounced the same as *rz*. The combination *dż* or *dzi* sounds like an English *j* in "jail." In Polish the accent almost always falls on the next-to-last syllable of any given word. Mastering certain sound combinations can be difficult for non-Poles, but once you do master them you'll find Polish words are pronounced exactly as they're spelled!

Русский

The Russian Alphabet

Printed	Cursive	English
А а	*Аа*	a
Б б	*Бб*	b
В в	*Вв*	v
Г г	*Гг*	g
Д д	*Дg*	d
Е е	*Ее*	ye
Ё ё	*Ёё*	yo
Ж ж	*Жж*	zh
З з	*Зз*	z
И и	*Ии*	i
Й й	*Йй*	y
К к	*Кк*	k
Л л	*Лл*	l
М м	*Мм*	m
Н н	*Нн*	n
О о	*Оо*	o
П п	*Пп*	p
Р р	*Рр*	r
С с	*Сс*	s
Т т	*Тт*	t
У у	*Уу*	u
Ф ф	*Фф*	f
Х х	*Хх*	kh
Ц ц	*Цц*	ts
Ч ч	*Чч*	ch

Printed	Cursive	English	Printed	Cursive	English
Ш ш	*Шш*	sh	- ь	*- ь*	—
Щ щ	*Щщ*	shch	Э э	*Ээ*	e
- ъ	*- ъ*	—	Ю ю	*Юю*	yu
- ы	*- ы*	—	Я я	*Яя*	ya

Russian is one of several Slavic languages that use a form of the Cyrillic alphabet (others include Belarussian, Bulgarian, Macedonian, Serbian, and Ukrainian). There are minor variations in the forms of Cyrillic used in the Slavic languages; the version shown here is that used in modern Russian. Pre-1917 Russian documents also used the characters i and ѵ, equivalent to modern и; the character ѣ, equivalent to modern е; and ѳ, equivalent to modern ф.

Even a superficial glance at the Cyrillic alphabet reveals that it is not totally foreign. When St. Cyril (traditionally regarded as the author of this alphabet) undertook devising a way to write Slavic sounds, he borrowed extensively from the Greek alphabet, and also modified some characters to represent distinctively Slavic phonemes. A few sounds were so foreign to Greek that he borrowed characters from other sources, e. g., ש and צ from Hebrew to make ш and ц, representing the *sh* and *ts* sounds.

Besides the printed and cursive forms, italic letters appear in documents. A few italic forms can be puzzling, e. g., *z*, *д*, *т*, but the answer is simple: some italic forms are derived from their cursive equivalents. So *т* = т, *д* = д (*д* and *g* are both acceptable cursive forms of д), *z* = г, and so on. Alternate cursive forms of т or *т* include *у* and what looks like an *i* with a line over it, rather than a dot.

Russian vowels are roughly similar to those of other European languages: а = *a* as in "father," э = *e* as in "let," и = *i* as in "machine," о = a sound somewhere between the *o*'s in "October," and у = *u* as in "rude" — but а, э, ы, о and у follow what are termed "hard" consonants, while the forms я, е, и, ё and ю follow consonants that are "softened" or palatalized. The basic distinction is illustrated by the word нет ("no"), pronounced "nyet" because the *e* vowel follows a palatalized *n* — a word pronounced like English "net," with a hard *n*, would be spelled нэт. This is why one often sees я transcribed as *ya*, ё as *yo*, and so on; the vowels are written differently to reflect the hard or soft quality of the consonants they follow. Standard Russian pronunciation gives full value to the vowel о only in accented syllables, and the farther the vowel is from the stress, the less distinctly it is pronounced: молоко ("milk"), accented on the last syllable, is not pronounced like "mo-lo-ko´" but more like "muh-lah-ko´."

The table at left shows approximate English equivalents of the sounds represented by Russian consonants, but more must be said. The letter г does generally sound like the English *g* in "go," but at the end of words it can sound like *k*, and in the declensional suffixes -ого, -его, and archaic -яго and -аго it sounds like English *v*. The letter ж (often rendered in English as "zh") sounds like *s* in English "pleasure." The ч sounds like the *ch* in "church," the х is pronounced like *ch* in German "Bach" or Scottish "loch," the ш sounds like the *sh* in "sheet," and щ is *sh* and *ch* run together, as in the name "Khrushchev."

Of the letters with no English equivalents given, ъ signifies that the preceding consonant is not softened or palatalized, ь shows that it is softened or palatalized, and ы represents a unique sound somewhat like the *y* in "very."

ייִדיש   The Yiddish Language — *by Zachary M. Baker*

Printed	Cursive	English
א	ן‍c	silent
בּ	ב	b
בֿ	ב̄	v
ג	ל	g
ד	ﭏ	d
ה	ה	h
ו	ו	u
ז	ל	z
ח	ת	kh
ט	ט	t
י	י	y/i
כּ	ﬤ	k
כ	ﬥ	kh
ך	ﬤ	final kh
ל	ﬥ	l

Printed	Cursive	English
מ	א	m
ם	ﬡ	final m
נ	ﬞ	n
ן	ן	final n
ס	ײַ	s
ע	ﬥ	e
פּ	ﬠ	p
פֿ	ﬡ̄	f
ף	ﬤ	final f
צ	ﬤ	ts
ץ	ﬤ	final ts
ק	ﬥ	k
ר	ﬤ	r
שׁ	ﬢ	sh
שׂ	ﬢ	s

Printed	Cursive	English
תּ	ﬠ	t
ת	ﬠ	s

Variants & Combinations

Printed	Cursive	English
אַ	ן‍c	a
אָ	ן‍c	o
וּ	·ו	u
וו	ıı	v
וי	ıı	oy
יִ	:	i
ײ	"	ey
ײַ	"	ay
זש	ﬥﬣ	zh
דזש	ﬥﬣ	dzh
טש	ﬣﬣ	ch

Yiddish, the vernacular of Ashkenazic Jews, uses the Hebrew alphabet in a form adapted to reflect its diverse components. Like other languages employing that alphabet (such as Ladino, Judeo-Arabic, and of course Hebrew), Yiddish is written from right to left. The basic Hebrew alphabet has 22 letters, plus forms of five letters that are used only at the end of words. There is no distinction between upper- and lower-case forms of letters in Yiddish. Most Yiddish written documents employ cursive script, as opposed to the "square" letters found in printed texts.

The underlying structure of Yiddish and most of its vocabulary is Germanic (deriving from Middle High German); Yiddish also contains Romance elements, a substantial Hebrew/Aramaic component, and an extensive Slavic vocabulary. The three principal dialect regions of Yiddish in Eastern Europe are Central ("Polish" and "Galician"), Northeastern ("Lithuanian"), and Southeastern ("Ukrainian"). Standard Yiddish, the basis for the transliterations shown in the accompanying alphabet ta-

ble, largely reflects Northeastern Yiddish pronunciations.

Yiddish employs a spelling system that, in Uriel Weinreich's words, "is based on an integration of two underlying patterns." Words deriving from the non-Hebrew/Aramaic components of the language are rendered phonetically, "in a system with excellent overall correspondence between sounds and letters.... Another part of the vocabulary, of Hebrew-Aramaic derivation, on the whole retains the traditional spelling used in those languages." Because Standard Yiddish Orthography was codified as recently as 1936 (by the YIVO Institute for Jewish Research, in cooperation with the Central Yiddish School Organization in Poland), variant spelling systems will inevitably be encountered in Yiddish texts.

Standard Yiddish Orthography distinguishes between different letters through the use of diacritical marks. Since non-standard Yiddish spelling usually omits diacritics, no distinction is made there between the letters בּ [b] and בֿ [v]; ײ [ey], ײַ [ay], and יִ [yi]; כּ [k] and כ [kh]; פּ [p] and

פ *[f]*; ש *[sh]* and שׂ *[s]*; תּ *[t]* and ת *[s]*. In non-standard Yiddish, therefore, the pronunciation of some letters and letter combinations can be inferred only by context.

In standard Yiddish, the silent א is normally employed only at the beginning of a word (e. g., אין *[in]* = "in"), while in non-standard Yiddish, the silent א will be encountered in other positions as well (e.g., [non-standard] וואו *[vu]* = "where," vs. [standard] וווּ). In non-standard Yiddish, ב *[b]* may sometimes be written בּ; also, ע *[e]* may be inserted before a final ל *[l]* (e.g., [non-standard] זעקעל *[zekel]* vs. [standard] זעקל *[zekl]* = "pouch") or ן *[n]* (e. g., [non-standard] האָבען *[hoben]* vs. [standard] האָבן *[hobn]* = "to have"), and פ used in place of either פּ *[p]* or פֿ *[f]*.

Since Hebrew/Aramaic words in standard Yiddish use traditional, consonantal spellings (i. e., with vowels omitted), their pronunciations can be arrived at only by consulting an authoritative dictionary such as Weinreich's (cited below). Ashkenazic Hebrew — as opposed to Sephardic, or Israeli — serves as the basis for the pronunciation of Yiddish words (including names) deriving from Hebrew and Aramaic, e. g.: אמת *[emes]*, not *[emet]* = "truth"; אדם *[odem]*, not *[adam]* = "Adam." The Hebrew/Aramaic component of Yiddish employs six letters that are not encountered elsewhere in Yiddish: ב *[v]*, ח *[kh]*, כ *[k]*, שׂ *[s]*, תּ *[t]*, ת *[s]*.

(**Note:** In Soviet Yiddish orthography, beginning in the 1920s, these six letters were eliminated and words of Hebrew/Aramaic origin spelled phonetically, e. g.: עמעס *[emes]* = "truth," rather than אמת. Final Hebrew letters were often eliminated in Soviet Yiddish as well, e.g.: לעבנ *[lebn]* = "life," rather than לעבן.)

Yiddish has five basic vowels, pronounced much like those in other European languages. Some letters and letter combinations representing vowels and diphthongs vary in pronunciation, depending on dialect. Examples include: זאָגן *[zogn]* (NE Yiddish) vs. *[zugn]* (C and SE Yiddish) = "to say"; פּוטער *[puter]* (NE Yiddish) vs. *[piter]* (C and SE Yiddish) = "butter"; ברויט *[broyt]* (C and SE Yiddish) vs. *[breyt]* (NE Yiddish) = "bread"; פלייש *[fleysh]* (NE and SE Yiddish) vs. *[flaysh]* (C Yiddish) = "meat."

Yiddish consonants are for the most part similar to those used in English, with the notable exceptions of ח and כ *[kh]*, pronounced as in Scottish "loch," and ר *[r]*, produced with the tip of the tongue or the soft palate.

Yiddish is an inflected language, possessing nominative, accusative, dative, and genitive cases. As with German, Polish, and Russian, three genders are employed in Yiddish: masculine (דער מאַן *[der man]* = "the man"), feminine (די פֿרוי *[di froy]* = "the woman"), and neuter (דאָס קינד *[dos kind]* = "the child"). (All three examples given here are in the nominative case.)

Sources:

Hebraica Cataloging: A Guide to ALA/LC Romanization and Descriptive Cataloging. Prepared by Paul Maher. Washington, D. C.: Cataloging Distribution Service, Library of Congress, 1987.

Weinreich, Max. *History of the Yiddish Language.* Translated by Shlomo Noble, with the assistance of Joshua A. Fishman. Chicago: University of Chicago Press, 1980.

Weinreich, Uriel. *Modern English-Yiddish, Yiddish-English Dictionary.* New York: McGraw-Hill, 1968 [reprinted by Schocken].

Appendix B:
Hiring a Professional Genealogist

by Eileen Polakoff and Gary Mokotoff

Genealogy is thought by most to be merely a hobby, a method of gaining enjoyment by researching one's ancestry. To some, though, it is also a profession, a way to earn a living. Hobbyists may employ professional genealogists for a variety of reasons.

Because of expertise in a particular area, a professional may be able to solve problems that stymie the hobbyist. Some work can be done by a professional in significantly less time than a hobbyist can do it. Those with little time for genealogical pursuits, or for whom speed in gathering information is important, may find hiring a professional a worthwhile expenditure. A professional may have more experience with specific records or repositories and, therefore, is able to do the research much faster. A professional may live closer to the source of records; perhaps he or she may be in a different country. Often, it is less expensive to hire a professional genealogist than to travel to the site of records.

A variety of services are offered by professionals. These include record searching, analysis of problems, compilation of full family histories, computerization, translations, interviews and oral histories, tours of ancestral towns, editing and preparing a family history for publication. The primary services provided are record searching and complete family history research.

Costs vary according to the nature of the work requested. If it is a specific task, such as locating and copying a specific record, the cost may be as low as an hour or two of time at the professional's established rate. If the task is to compile a complete genealogy of a family, which may require hundreds of hours of time, the cost can easily amount to thousands of dollars; it is not unusual to exceed $10,000 and take a year or more.

How a professional works depends on the amount of information provided: no clues versus some clues. It is the responsibility of the person doing the hiring to direct the professional by knowing and communicating exactly what is wanted. When unsure, the client should discuss the problem with the researcher. Most professionals have experience in many areas and will assist in defining goals. In addition, one may reasonably expect an ethical professional genealogist to say if, in his or her professional opinion, that research has gone as far as possible, or that it may be too expensive to realize specific goals.

Usually the professional genealogist charges an hourly rate plus expenses. Most establish a minimum number of hours and require retainers. Hourly fees range from $35 to $100 and depend upon experience, credentials, areas of specialty and services provided. In most cases, one pays for time; a professional genealogist charges for all time used to meet a genealogical request. This includes time to study and analyze the request, execute the research and report the results. In most cases, the customer also pays for travel time and communication with the researcher. By combining jobs and research locations, the active professional researcher saves clients money by pooling travel expenses on more than one job. Time, and therefore money, is saved also because a professional usually works on more than one job at a time in a specific location. Telephone, e-mail, travel and research time are considered billable.

Often a professional researcher is aware of the most current information about new sources in one or more areas of specialty related to genealogical research. A professional may have done research previously in a specific area and, therefore, may recognize names in a family or be able to locate information quickly because of familiarity with records in that locale.

In order to stay current, most professionals read a number of journals and newsletters and attend genealogical conferences where they can learn from other experts. When hiring a professional genealogist to assist you, do not hesitate to ask about conferences attended, whether or not the genealogist lectures or writes about areas of expertise, and how long he or she has been in the profession. The answers to these questions will assist in determining whether or not a specific professional is the best person to accomplish one's research goals.

Each professional has his or her own method of reporting, depending on the agreement with the client. If a researcher specializes in obtaining documents, clients will receive a copy of a document. Other genealogists send a summary of research completed, an analysis of the document, including translation, and suggestions for additional research based upon the information in the document. Customarily, clients are given a list of all sources and repositories consulted in the research, including sources that did not produce results.

When hiring a professional genealogist, supply all known information about the person or branch of the family to be researched and all sources already investigated. The professional genealogist usually does not want to duplicate work already done by the client. Be clear about what is wanted and obtain an explicit statement that the professional will do the requested search or supply other services. Genealogists should not promise delivery of information; rather they indicate that it is a familiar area that he or she researches on a regular basis.

After having obtained the name(s) of a professional genealogist, write a brief letter outlining research goals and some family information applicable to the goal. If any special services are desired, such as translation, travel, or fast

results, make the researcher aware of these needs as soon as possible. Include a self-addressed, stamped envelope (or international postal coupons, if writing outside of your country) with the letter. In the era of the Internet and e-mail, it is not uncommon to contact a professional via website or e-mail. Expect a professional to respond indicating if he or she is prepared to accept the assignment; a summary of services and rates should be included.

No guarantees exist in genealogical research, whether done by an amateur or a professional. No one can be certain that information about a specific family will be found. But time spent by a professional to search for the requested information may produce new details about a family or, if nothing else, a list of sources where no information exists.

Credentials

In North America two recognized organizations dispense credentials to professionals.

The Board of Certification for Genealogists (BCG), founded in 1964, offers the credential "certified" to candidates who meet certain qualifications. The three research categories are Certified Genealogist (CG), Certified Genealogical Records Specialist (CGRS) or Certified Lineage Specialist (CLS). Two teaching categories are Certified Genealogical Instructor (CGI) and Certified Genealogical Lecturer (CGL). Professionals who pass the rigorous tests are entitled to use the letters CG, CGRS, CLS, CGI and/or CGL after their names.

Genealogists also can become Accredited Genealogists through a program administered by the International Com-

mission for the Accreditation of Professional Genealogists (ICAPGen). Professionals who pass a series of tests related to their genealogical research competence in specific geographic regions or subjects of specialization are entitled to use the letters AG after their names.

Other programs exist in Australia, Canada, England, France and Ireland. A list of them may be found at WWW.APGREN.ORG/RESOURCES.

How to Find Information About Professional Genealogists

The Association of Professional Genealogists* (APG) publishes a *Directory of Professional Genealogists*. The APG has open membership (no testing) but requires members to sign and abide by a code of ethics, and the organization offers an arbitration service for consumer protection. The directory, as well as additional information about hiring professional genealogists, can be viewed on its website. The website includes an online directory of members including specialties and areas of research expertise. The directory also may be found in local genealogical libraries. In addition to the member information, the APG website includes consumer information.

The Board for Certification of Genealogists* publishes a *Certification Roster* and offers an arbitration service for consumer protection.

The International Commission for the Accreditation of Professional Genealogists* (ICAPGen) has a downloadable list of accredited genealogists on its website.

For professional genealogists who specialize in Jewish research, locate friends or members of local Jewish genealogical societies and special interest groups who have successfully used a professional's services. Some advertise in *AVOTAYNU*, genealogical society newsletters, genealogical magazines, journals and similar publications.

Addresses

Association for Professional Genealogists, P.O. Box 35098, Westminster, Colorado 80035; telephone: (303) 422-9371; fax: (303) 456-8825; website: WWW.APGEN.ORG.

Board for Certification of Genealogists, P.O.Box 14291, Washington, D.C. 20044; website: WWW.BCGCERTIFICATION.ORG.

International Commission for the Accreditation of Professional Genealogists, P.O. Box 970204, Orem, Utah 84097; website: WWW.ICAPGEN.ORG.

Appendix C
The Importance of Engaging Jewish Children in Family Research

by Ira Wolfman

All italicized quotes come from conversations about genealogy with Jewish youth and Jewish adults who discovered family history when they were children.

I became seriously involved with genealogy when I was 13. It gave me a stronger sense of my identity. It showed me that I was part of a family that had so much history.—Dafna O.

For Jewish children, genealogy can begin at a very early age. Our prayer books are filled with references not just to God, but to the God of Abraham, Isaac and Jacob, and—in some synagogues—also of Sarah, Rebecca, Rachel and Leah.

Our Torah stories, of course, are rich in genealogy. Even though the younger generation is sure to ignore long lists of who begot whom, they still are introduced to many characters by way of ancestry: Joseph, Jacob's eleventh son; Moses, son of Yocheved and Amram (grandson of Levi); Joshua, son of Nun; Solomon, son of David and Bathsheba.

Despite this "Jewish Family History 101," it seems to me that individual Jewish genealogists often neglect to involve their children and/or grandchildren in our genealogical passion. For many, genealogy is a solitary pursuit, one that our offspring can dismiss as "Dad's project" or "Grandma's hobby." Perhaps we're afraid that, with its research and recordkeeping, family history will feel like schoolwork. Of course, there is also the big question: Can we really interest today's teens in the lore and the lives of the long dead?

Yes, in fact, we can, and in growing numbers we are.

Jewish professional genealogists have a growing awareness of the value of encouraging young people to become involved in family history research. The Center for Jewish History in New York recently began offering a summer genealogical workshop for teenagers, called The Samberg Family History Program. In addition, numerous Jewish organizations are developing curricula to bring genealogy into the classroom in fresher ways. There has been an increased awareness of the value of family history at bar and bat mitzvot. As the immigrant experience recedes for many Jewish families, memories of the old ways of life become more precious.

But we can, and should, do more: All Jewish genealogists should make an extra effort to share the excitement of our pastime with the younger generations. Why? Because genealogy has an enormous amount to offer Jewish youth—and they, in turn, have a great deal to offer it, and us.

What Genealogy Gives Our Children

Doing my genealogy showed me that my self was rooted deeper than my personality, [that who I am] is related to the life of every mother and father in my family tree. It is the language my ancestors spoke and the jobs they had, what they stood up for and (what my Jewish ancestors) died for, too.—Jessica P., age 17

I know that young people can be interested in "ancestor-detecting." For one thing, I am the author of a guide to genealogy for young people that has sold more than 150,000 copies—and certainly *some* of those copies were read by the children themselves.

Since the first edition of my book came out in 1991, I have visited dozens of schools, synagogues, and community centers, and talked with hundreds of teens and pre-teens about the rewards of genealogical research. I have seen first-hand how excited youngsters are to learn that information about their great-grandmothers and grandfathers may be located on the children's favorite resource—the Internet. I have noted how amazed they are that their last names might actually tell them something about their ancestors.

Many youngsters today have had at least a taste of genealogy. Family-tree making is a requirement in the Israeli school system. Increasing numbers of American teachers are using family-tree assignments with even very young students: The simple pedigree chart is sent home one day with instructions that it be filled out and returned to school. While this activity may raise confusing, even painful, issues for children in nontraditional families (see discussion below), it also means that by the time they reach age eight or nine, most youngsters will find the concept of a family tree familiar.

Of course, those assignments are mere baby steps into the genealogical world. It is only when they get involved in the nitty-gritty of family research that students begin to reap the many benefits it offers. For example:

- Academic skills are sharpened. When students trace their family history, they develop—without being aware of it—enormously valuable skills, such as organizing, researching, interviewing, weighing of evidence, expository writing, and problem-solving.
- History comes alive. Long-ago family stories often demonstrate to children that the abstractions of world history—immigration, depressions, political movements, wars—directly touched the lives of their ancestors, too. History is transformed into the story of "my family," not just faceless masses.
- Family members talk to each other in new ways. Watch what happens when youngsters get involved in conducting interviews and sharing their discoveries: Suddenly they

interact in new ways with members of the family. Now another acceptable—even interesting—topic is inserted into the family conversational mix. Parents of teenagers may especially appreciate the value of this development!

And while conducting interviews, a child encounters incontrovertible proof that family elders were young once, too, and that they too had dreams and adventures and disappointments.

For Jewish genealogists there is something else, however, something deeper that relates to our children's sense of self and Jewishness. All Jews are linked in an extraordinarily long and resilient chain that reaches back into the mists of history, to the Patriarchs and Matriarchs. In today's world, in which identity is so fluid and can seem tenuous, our Jewish roots are deep and ancient. Genetics are not the issue here. It is simply that every Jewish child is the inheritor of a glorious heritage that has advanced human civilization and thought over thousands of years.

The power of this research is not just about pride in the Jewish people as a whole. It is also about our own ancestors' experiences. By learning about their family history, young Jews discover that their ancestors lived Jewish lives, followed Jewish ritual, stood up for—and sacrificed for—their faith. Learning about the value ancestors placed on Jewish identity can strengthen children's connections and pride in their family—and themselves.

Benefits to You and to Genealogy

Actively involving your children with your genealogical research is not only good for them, but it is also good for you. For one thing, exposing your child to genealogy may actually provide you with a live-in research assistant. That assistant may very well know more about computers than you do (a handy thing!). He or she may also be available when others would not—at odd hours or on family vacations.

In addition, transmitting your enthusiasm for Jewish genealogy to the next generation makes it far more likely that the efforts you've expended on uncovering all those documents and facts will be appreciated in the future. It may even increase the chance that your findings will be appreciated by descendants who value and honor their Jewish tradition.

How to Get the Kids Involved

I started doing genealogy when I was 11 years old. I was a member of the Boy Scouts of America. I've made a lot of progress over the last 15 years, and I look forward to researching for 50 or 60 more years.—Eric A.

All of this good news does not mean that I think your children (or grandchildren) are just waiting for an invitation to become lifelong family-history devotees. As the realistic father of two sons—one a teenager, the other a teen-in-training—I know well that making the genealogical connection is not a simple thing.

Sometimes genealogy drops serendipitously into your child's life. Those school assignments, for example, are a great launching pad for introducing your youngster to your re-search. For Eric (quoted above), the fact that the Boy Scouts offered a genealogy merit badge was enough to initiate him into a lifetime pursuit.

But you don't have to wait for merit badges or family trees to fall from the sky to get your child or grandchild involved. Different ages require different approaches, of course, but—if it is presented appropriately—all children can be turned on to family history. Here are some suggestions:

1. Talk about your family names. An easy way to begin your children's genealogical education—whatever their ages— is to talk about names. Jewish naming traditions often are fascinating and meaningful to children. For example, if you haven't done so already, tell your child the derivation of his or her first name: How did you choose it? What does it mean— and in which language? Is there a family history to the name? If your child was named after someone, talk about why you wanted your child to carry on that person's name. The difference between Sephardic and Ashkenazic traditions is also intriguing, especially if those two types mingle within one family.

Older children may be even more interested in your surname. Is it original? What does it mean? Where does it come from? What about the other surnames in the family? If your child really responds to this approach, pick up a good dictionary of Jewish surnames. If nothing else, your children can look up friends' last names and play a game of "Did you know?" the next time they go to school!

2. Tell family stories. Perhaps no adults—let alone genealogists—need to be encouraged to tell children stories. But the value of relating "When I was a child" tales is great — especially if the stories aren't use to demonstrate how much better things were when you were young. Accounts of colorful relatives, family encounters with famous people, or adventurous sagas of courageous ancestors don't just entertain children. These stories also give them a sense of family heritage and pride, and they whet the child's appetite for learning more.

3. Don't just talk; share sensory memories of the past with your children. All of us have unique family heirlooms— stories, songs, recipes, artifacts and vivid sensory memories of those we were touched by. These are precious bits of your family history and should be shared, in every way you can, with your children.

Telling the story of Great Uncle Louie's escape from Russia is fun. But you can make it even more vivid by bringing out the old photo album that shows him as a young man and by looking at the map of Russia together with the children and find the Eastern European shtetl that he left. Talk about how long the journey was, what you heard about it, and what you have discovered in your research. Sing the songs he used to sing, or tell one of his favorite jokes.

Make the latke recipe of your beloved Aunt Tillie with your child, and use the preparation time—or the munching time—to relate the story of her life, or to talk about how wonderful it felt to celebrate Hanukkah in her home. Another example is when you use the candlesticks that your *bubbe* insisted on carrying all the way from Tarnow, have your kids hold them and feel how heavy they are. Ask them to imagine carrying these heavy items in a satchel across thousands of miles. Ask them what they would have insisted on bringing if they had to leave home.

These activities can have a powerful effect on children. Consider the prototypical example of building memories and creating connections through the use of songs and stories and food: the Passover seder. Doesn't it seem safe to say—given that this well-loved tradition of Jewish holidays has lasted thousands of years—that it works?

4. Invite your children to conduct interviews. Do it even if they are only seven or eight years old. It's a wonderful way to make new connections for your youngsters with older family members. Start by letting your children practice on you. Encourage them to ask about your childhood, how you met your spouse, how each child came into your life. Gently guide them to more interesting and productive areas, but don't try to control the conversation. Teach your kids how to use a tape recorder and make notes, so they become familiar with both. You might also want to have someone run the camcorder.

After they gain experience by talking with immediate family, encourage your children to conduct interviews with elders. Doing an interview opens up a different aspect in a relationship, that of interviewer and interviewee. This role change can bring new understanding and perhaps even greater closeness between two family members. It certainly can help them see that grandma wasn't born at age 70!

Before the interview, you will be a great resource for your child, offering good, simple (and age-appropriate) advice on how to approach this exciting event. But once things are in motion, let them do the interviewing themselves, with no unsolicited help from the resident family expert (you!). The power that comes from being the questioner—and in charge of the conversation—is a great experience for children at any age.

5. Read all about it. A number of excellent books are available to introduce children to the overall topic of genealogy—and to the specific joys and challenges of Jewish genealogy. With photographs, illustrations, charts, and maps, the guides make the subject exciting (see bibliography). There are books for different levels of maturity and reading ability, so you should be able to find one appropriate for engaging your child. Journals and guided-question books (discussed in the next section) are also useful for getting youngsters involved quickly and easily.

Finally, many good-quality children's books describe the time and conditions of life in the old country—wherever your family's old country may be. Historically based fiction, with a protagonist around your children's ages, also can add enormously to the pleasure they will experience learning about their ancestors.

6. Create family-history photo books together. You probably already have scrapbooks or archival-quality tomes filled with family photographs and memorabilia. If your family is anything like mine, you also have tons of old photos and other materials laying in a drawer or shoebox. Here is a chance to do something with them!

For younger children, a scrapbook can be a great rainy-day project. You might decide beforehand which branch of the family you want to focus on. Gather photographs, post-

cards and memorabilia connected to those family members and where they live. Purchase a book that will hold these memorable pictures and other items (ticket stubs, newspaper clippings and other similar items). Be sure to leave empty pages that the children can write or draw on, if they feel so moved. The point here is not to create another grand document; it's to make a family keepsake that may also capture a moment in your child's development.

I know first-hand that even simple versions of this kind of project can work well. I once took my younger son, then nine, to a Family-History Art Workshop at Wave Hill Gardens and Cultural Center in the Bronx, New York. The Center told us to come with a selection of family photographs, so we brought seven or eight photos of siblings and grandparents.

At first, my son was loudly unenthusiastic. But when we arrived, we found a dozen families with kids between age 5 and 12 eagerly at work, making good use of colored construction paper, tissue paper, glue, crayons and markers. They were urged to draw a decorative cover sheet, then fill in a simple family tree chart, and add pages of stories, pictures or drawings of anyone and everyone in their family. My son warmed to the task in this room filled with the sounds of enthusiastic youngsters. And when the pages were assembled into a family book, he was extremely happy with his creation (as were his parents).

Another resource that may inspire some children is the pre-packaged journal. These mostly blank books give pages of questions that they can fill in about themselves, their immediate family, and their ancestors. Despite the allure of the Internet and genealogical software, many children find it comforting to have a small book that they can look at or add to whenever they want. Journals can be filled with the child's handwritten notes, art, photographs and other memorabilia.

7. Tempt a teen with a celebrity genealogical hunt. Older kids might not be very interested in crafts-type projects or someone else's idea of a journal. But you may spark a bit of interest in family history by using a celebrity as bait. Some major genealogy websites include, along with their vital databases and listservs, a bit of famous folk fun. You can find celebrity family trees—from Tom Edison to Tom Cruise—in cyberspace. At GENEALOGY.COM, I stumbled upon the pedigree charts of Muhammad Ali, Ben Franklin, Mary Tyler Moore and Mary, Queen of Scots. Among them I found pedigrees for pop-culture figures who are Jewish, married to Jews, or of Jewish ancestry—including Irving Berlin, Wyatt Earp, Carrie Fisher, Dustin Hoffman and Ben Stiller.

Dafna, quoted at the beginning of this chapter, recalled that she became fascinated with genealogy because of her interest in the family trees of Europe's intertwined royal families. She was amazed to find that her German-Jewish family had roots extending back to the 1770s. While enchantment with royalty appears to have subsided over the last 50 years, celebrities still exert a fascination for many.

The Non-Traditional Family Tree

I always knew that I was adopted as a baby from St. Petersburg, Russia. But when I was assigned to do a family-history

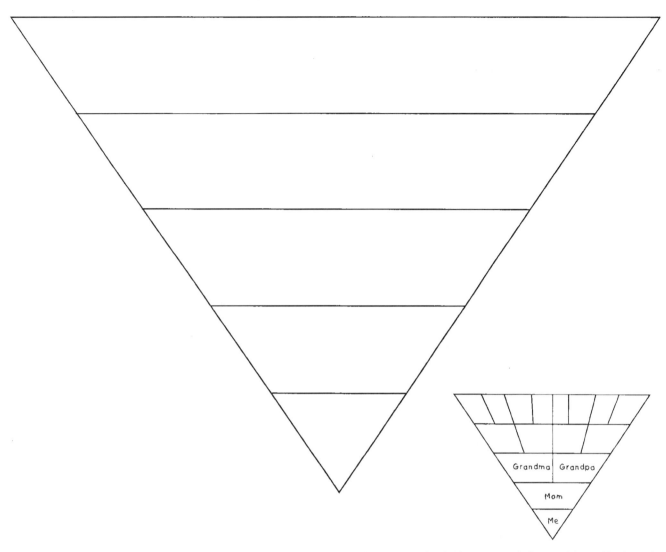

The above Family Pyramid is an easily adaptable form for alternative family trees. Put the child's name (and place and date of birth) in the bottom level. In the levels above, place as many or as few dividers as needed. For example, write one name in the entire space of the next level if the intent is to define a single parent, or divide it in half to name two parents. Another option is to divide the level into three or more parents for parents and stepparents; adoptive and birth parents; etc. Illustration is copyright of Ira Wolfman.

project for my third grade class, I had a problem. The family tree we were given to fill in didn't make sense for me. All my friends had a mother and a father, but I don't. I was adopted by a single mother.—Natasha B, age 9

Family-tree making isn't always a no-stress matter. For some children, the traditional "Mom, Dad, and Me" pedigree chart raises complex issues. Many schools, using a one-size-fits-all approach, completely overlook these concerns and may evoke painful feelings in some children.

If your family doesn't fit the "traditional" mold—because of adoption, divorce, death, remarriage or another issue—inviting your child or grandchild to trace the family tree may bring up sticky questions. How do families formed by adoption handle ancestor questions? How do you handle step-siblings or half-siblings on a standard tree? When someone beloved to a child has died, does the idea of interviewing become a sad reminder of loss? Obviously

these are issues that even practiced Jewish genealogists need to consider. If it is not a concern with your children, it may come up with grandchildren or other family members.

I hadn't given a lot of thought to this issue until I talked with Magda, a Jewish single mom from New York City who had adopted her daughter, Natasha, as a newborn. As a homework assignment, Natasha's teacher had sent home the standard pedigree chart (which actually had been copied from the first edition of my book!). When Natasha sat down with her mom to fill it out, the nine-year-old looked at the "father's side" of the chart and commented that she would leave it blank, saying something to the effect that she had "half a family."

This, of course, deeply upset her mother, who wondered how an enlightened New York City teacher could send home such a rigid document. She and Natasha then began what turned into a long discussion: What is a family? How many people must be in it? Where do people we love, but who aren't related to us biologically, fit in? (Magda later pointed out to me that most families include at least two people who are almost never related biologically: husbands and wives).

The result of this experience, both mother and daughter later told me, was a deep and very useful discussion about families and family trees. Natasha and Magda solved the pedigree chart dilemma by creating a "Family Flower," a form that had Natasha at the center, the people she felt closest to as petals around her, and other friends and family on farther-out petals. On a very large leaf attached to the stem of the flower was the name of Natasha's birth mother, Lyubov.

"Putting together a family tree can be touchy for adoptive families," Magda noted. "But for our family, it opened up a wonderful conversation."

Natasha's family flower didn't include any vital-record data; it's just a graphic representation of the people she loves and the people who have influenced her life. But her mother knew that was exactly what this nine-year-old needed. The original flawed family tree turned out to be a gift in disguise for this family.

As in this case, clearly, family trees can take any shape or form. Whatever your family structure, you can devise charts and pictograms to display it proudly and beautifully. Some adoptive families prefer the Home Chart, in which the different households that created the child are all represented. Other standard options can be modified easily to provide for non-traditional families. I suggest the common fan and pyramid charts (available at WWW.WORKMAN.COM/FAMILYTREE/DOWNLOAD.HTML) which allow for easy insertion of extra names (a step-parent, say) or for a segment with one name (a single-parent family without a known father, for example).

In some ways Natasha's story also is an apt metaphor for this entire discussion of young people and family history. My goal in urging you to invite your children into this rich world is not to create number-spouting, fact-checking, Internet-searching little experts. It is to expose young people to the joys of Jewish genealogy—the thrill of discovery and serendipity and family connections.

For all of us—but especially for children—genealogy ultimately isn't about places and names and numbers and dates. It is about family and history and an appreciation for the lives and struggles of those who came before us. For Jewish genealogists, it is also filled with historical and emotional connections to our faith and our peoplehood. With patience, enthusiasm, and age-appropriate activities, we can pass these gifts on to our children and our children's children—enriching their lives and our own.

Internet Sites for Children

JewishGen. The mother lode for Jewish genealogists of any age is JewishGen at WWW.JEWISHGEN.ORG. Other websites offer Jewish children a bit of fun and easy access to information. My favorites include:

Ellis Island Database. WWW.ELLISISLAND.ORG. You've surely been there, but your offspring may find it fun to explore. Manifests and boat photos are often easy to find, and the "Immigrant Experience" area offers six family stories (including one about a Jewish family from Bohemia) and useful immigration timelines.

Family names. WWW.HAMRICK.COM/NAMES. An engaging way to show kids how common your family name is. Visit this site and click on "all years," and watch the changes in distribution of names across the U.S. from 1850 to 1990. (Only the top 50,000 U.S. names are included.)

WorldGen Web for Kids. WWW.ROOTSWEB.COM/~WGWKIDS/. This site offers non-condescending genealogical information and connections for children and teens. Best for children 8–14 who are curious about genealogy and the countries their families came from.

Climbing Your Family Tree. WWW.WORKMAN.COM/FAMILYTREE. This site was developed from my book, *Climbing Your Family Tree*, and includes quizzes, downloadable forms including non-traditional family trees, child-friendly tips, and more than 100 clickable links.

Bibliography

For the youngest (3–7 years old)
Brown, Deni and Dorling Kindersley Publishing. *Family History: Camera, Activity Book, Record Book, Poster, Stickers.* New York; Dorling Kindersley. 1996
Chorzempa, Rosemary. *My Family Tree Workbook: Genealogy for Beginners.* New York: Dover Publications. 1989.
Leedy, Loren. *Who's Who in My Family?* New York: Holiday House. 1999.

Older Children and Teens (ages 8 and up)
Kurzweil, Arthur. *My Generations: A Course in Jewish Family History.* New York: Behrman House. 1996.
Perl, Lila. *The Great Ancestor Hunt: The Fun of Finding Out Who You Are.* New York: Clarion Press.1996.
Schliefer, Jay. *A Students' Guide to Jewish American Genealogy.* Phoenix. Arizona: Oryx Press. 1996.
Wolfman, Ira. *Climbing Your Family Tree: Online and Offline Genealogy for Kids.* New York: Workman Publishing. 2002.

Appendix D
Daitch-Mokotoff Soundex System

by Gary Mokotoff

What can be more frustrating to a genealogist than to look through an alphabetical index of records and not locate the name being sought—and then to find out later, perhaps years later, that the data was there, but misspelled? How do you locate towns of non-English-speaking immigrant ancestors when the only information available was passed down orally through the generations, and no matter how you try to spell it, you cannot find the town on a map?

A major solution to these problems was provided more than 80 years ago, when Robert C. Russell of Pittsburgh, Pennsylvania, was issued patent number 1,261,167 on April 2, 1918, for having "invented certain new and useful Improvements in Indexes . . . as will enable others skilled in the art to which it appertains to make and use the same."

The idea of indexing information by how it sounds rather than alphabetically was born. It has become known as "soundexing."

Russell Soundex System

Russell noted in his patent the reason for this system:

There are certain sounds which form the nucleus of the English language, and those sounds are inadequately represented merely by the letters of the alphabet, as one sound may sometimes be represented by more than one letter or combination of letters, and one letter or combination of letters may represent two or more sounds. Because of this, a great many names may have two or more different spellings which in an alphabetic index, or an index which separates names according to the sequence of their contained letters in the alphabet, necessitates their filing in widely separate places.

Russell knew that letters of the alphabet were divided phonetically into categories. To each category, he assigned a numerical value. As his patent describes:

1. The vowels (he called them "oral resonants") *a, e, i, o, u, y*
2. The labials and labio-dentals *b, f, p, v*
3. The gutterals and sibilants *c, g, k, q, s, x, z*
4. The dental-mutes *d, t*
5. The palatal-fricative *l*
6. The labio-nasal *m*
7. The dento or lingua-nasal *n*
8. The dental fricative *r*

There were only a few additional rules:

- The initial letter of the word is always kept.
- Two consecutive letters with the same code are considered as a single letter (e.g., *tt* coded the same as *t*.
- The combination *gh* and *s* or *z,* if they end the word, are discarded.

Initial page of patent issued to Robert C. Russell in 1918, which was the genesis of soundex systems

- Only the first occurrence of a vowel (Group 1) is counted.

Thus, Smith and Smyth coded the same because the letters *i* and *y* had the same value, namely 1, even though in a normal alphabetical index, they would be far apart in the list.

A patent exists for two reasons. The first, to give the inventor exclusive rights to his creation; the second, by forcing the inventor to disclose his work publicly, other persons are encouraged to improve on the invention and, thus, create superior products based on the original idea.

Through the years, Russell's system has been improved upon. Persons familiar with the soundex system currently used by the U.S. government will observe that the original system was changed by combining the letters *m* and *n*, dropping vowels altogether unless they are the initial letter of the word, and dropping the rule regarding *gh* and words that end with *s* or *z*.

American Soundex System

The American Soundex code consists of the first letter of the name followed by three digits. These three digits are determined by dropping the letters *a, e, i, o, u, h, w,* and *y* and adding three digits from the remaining letters of the name according to the table below. There are only two additional rules:

1. If two or more consecutive letters have the same code, they are coded as one letter.
2. If there are an insufficient numbers of letters to correspond to three digits, the remaining digits are set to zero.

American Soundex Table

1	b, f, p, v
2	c, g, j, k, q, s, x, z
3	d, t
4	l
5	m, n
6	r

Examples:

Miller	M460
Peterson	P362
Peters	P362
Auerbach	A612
Uhrbach	U612
Moskowitz	M232
Moskovitz	M213

Daitch-Mokotoff Soundex System

The most recent significant improvement to soundexing is the Daitch-Mokotoff Soundex System. In 1985, this author indexed the names of some 28,000 Palestine residents who legally changed their names from 1921 to 1948; most of these individuals were Jews with Germanic or Slavic surnames. It was obvious that numerous spelling variants existed of the same basic surname and that the list should be soundexed. Using the conventional U.S. government system, many Eastern European Jewish names sounded the same, but did not soundex the same. The most prevalent were those names spelled interchangeably with the letter *w* or *v,* for example, the names Moskowitz and Moskovitz.

A modification to the U.S. soundex system was created and published in the first issue of *AVOTAYNU,* the journal of Jewish genealogy, in an article entitled "Proposal for a Jewish Soundex Code." It included the following improvements over the conventional system:

1. The initial letter was encoded just as any other letter within the name. If the initial letter was a vowel, it was given the numerical code 0.
2. Certain double-letter combinations that represent single sounds, namely *ts, tz,* and *tc,* were coded as a single code (the same as the letter *s*).

Just as disclosing a scheme by patenting encourages others to improve on the invention, publishing the article prompted another genealogist, Randy Daitch, to improve on the system. To the above rules, he added:

3. Six (rather than four) significant codes are created. This means that in large databases, names that sound the same initially but differ at the end are coded differently, giving

the researcher a smaller list of data to be searched. For example, Peters and Peterson code identically in the U.S. system, but differently in the new system.

4. Other multiple-letter combinations, in addition to those shown in 2 above, were added, all of Slavic or Germanic origin.
5. If a combination of letters could have two possible sounds, it is coded in both manners. For example, the letters *ch* can have a soft sound, such as in *Chicago,* or a hard sound, as in *Christmas.*

The new scheme was published a year later in *AVOTAYNU* by Daitch under the title "The Jewish Soundex: A Revised Format." This new system has become known as the Daitch-Mokotoff Soundex System. It has been mistakenly called the Jewish Soundex System, the Eastern European Soundex System, and the European Soundex System because of its origins, but its new rules are independent of geographical or ethnic considerations.

The Daitch-Mokotoff system has become the standard of all indexing projects conducted by Jewish genealogical organizations. It has been accepted by the Hebrew Immigrant Aid Society (HIAS), a social welfare organization, as its standard soundex system for retrieving case histories, and it is the standard at the U.S. Holocaust Memorial Museum in Washington, D.C. It is used to search the Ellis Island Data Base of 24 million immigrants at the Stephen P. Morse "Searching the Ellis Island Database in One Step" website.

Daitch-Mokotoff Soundex System Rules

The rules for converting names into Daitch-Mokotoff code numbers are listed below. They are followed by the Coding Chart. Turn to the chart briefly to familiarize yourself with the concept, then return to the specific instructions on this page.

1. Names are coded to six digits, each digit representing a sound listed on the Coding Chart.
2. The letters *a, e, i, o, u, j,* and *y* are always coded at the beginning of a name, as in Augsburg (054795). In any other situation, they are ignored except when two of the letters form a pair and the pair appears before a vowel, as in Breuer (791900) but not Freud (793000). The letter *h* is coded at the beginning of a name, as in Halberstadt (587943), or preceding a vowel, as in Mannheim (665600). Otherwise it is not coded.
3. When adjacent sounds can combine to form a larger sound, they are given the code number of the larger sound, as in Chernowitz, which is *not* coded Chernowi-t-z (496734) but rather Chernowi-tz (496740).
4. When adjacent letters have the same code number, they are coded as one sound, as in Cherkassy, which is not coded Cherka-s-s-y (495440), but rather Cherka-ss-y (495400). Exceptions to this rule are the letter combinations *mn* and *nm,* whose letters are coded separately, as in Kleinman, which is coded 586660, not 586600.

5. When a name consists of more than one word, it is coded as if it were one word, such as Nowy Targ, which is treated as Nowytarg.
6. Several letters and letter combinations pose the problem that they may sound in one of two ways. The letter and letter combinations *ch, ck, c, j,* and *rz* (see Coding Chart below), are assigned two possible code numbers. Be sure to try both possibilities.

7. When a name lacks enough coded sounds to fill the six digits, each of the remaining digits is given the numerical code 0, as in Berlin (798600), which has only four coded sounds (*b-r-l-n*).

Examples:

Ceniow (467000)	Tsenyuv (467000)
Holubica (587400)*	Golubitsa (587400)
Przemysl (746480)*	Pshemeshil (746480)
Rosochowaciec (945744)*	Rosokhovatsets (944744)

* Based on rule 6 above, other code combinations exist for this name.

Daitch-Mokotoff Soundex Coding Chart

Letter	Alternate Letter(s)	Start of A Name	Before A Vowel	All Other
AI	AJ, AY	0	1	N/C
AU		0	7	N/C
A		0		N/C
B				7
CHS		5		54
CH	Try KH (5) and TCH (4)			
CK	Try K (5) and TSK (45)			
CZ	CS, CSZ, CZS			4
C	Try K (5) and TZ (4)			
DRZ	DRS			4
DS	DSH, DSZ			4
DZ	DZH, DZS			4
D	DT			3
EI	EJ, EY	0	1	N/C
EU		1	1	N/C
E		0		N/C
FB				7
F				7
G				5
H		5	5	N/C
IA	IE, IO, IU	1		N/C
I		0		N/C
J	Try Y (1) and DZH (4)			
KS		5		54
KH				5
K				5
L				8
MN				66
M				6
NM				66
N				6
OI	OJ, OY	0	1	N/C
O		0		N/C
P	PF, PH			7
Q				5
RZ, RS	Try RTZ (94) and ZH(4)			
R				9
SCHTSCH, SCHTSH, SCHTCH		2		4
SCH				4

Daitch-Mokotoff Soundex Coding Chart (continued)

Letter	Alternate Letter(s)	Start of A Name	Before A Vowel	All Other
SHTCH	SHCH, SHTSH	2		4
SHT	SCHT, SCHD	2		43
SH				4
STCH	STSCH, SC	2		4
STRZ	STRS, STSH	2		4
ST		2		43
SZCZ	SZCS	2		4
SZT	SHD, SZD, SD	2		43
SZ				4
S				4
TCH	TTCH, TTSCH			4
TH				3
TRZ	TRS			4
TSCH	TSH			4
S	TTS, TTSZ, TC			4
TZ	TTZ, TZS, TSZ, TS			4
T				3
UI	UJ, UY	0	1	N/C
U	UE	0		N/C
V				7
W				7
X		5		54
Y		1		N/C
ZDZ	ZDZH, ZHDZH	2		4
ZD	ZHD	2		43
ZH	ZS, ZSCH, ZSH			4
Z				4

N/C = not coded

Appendix E
Relationship (Cousins) Chart

In order to be related to someone, you must have a common ancestor. To determine the relationship between yourself and the other person, first determine the *column* that shows the relationship between you and the common ancestor. Then determine the *row* that shows the relationship between the other person and the common ancestor. The intersection of the column and row shows the relationship between the two. For example, if you are the great-grand-child of the common ancestor and the other person is also a great-grandchild, then you are second cousins. As a second example, if you are the grandchild of the common ancestor and the other person is the great-grandchild of the common ancestor, then you are first cousins once removed. The term "removed" means "generation(s) removed." In the preceding example, it can be said that you are first cousins one generation removed.

Common Cousin	Child	Grandchild	Great-Grandchild	Great-g Grandchild	G-g-g Grandchild	G-g-g-g Grandchild	G-g-g-g-g Grandchild
Child	Sibling	Niece/ Nephew	Grand Niece/Nephew	Great grand Niece/Nephew	G-g grand Niece/Nephew	G-g-g Niece/Nephew	G-g-g-g Niece/Nephew
Grandchild	Niece/ Nephew	**1st Cousin**	1st Cousin 1 Removed	1st Cousin 2 Removed	1st Cousin 3 Removed	1st Cousin 4 Removed	1st Cousin 5 Removed
Great-Grandchild	Grand Niece/Nephew	1st Cousin 1 Removed	**2nd Cousin**	2nd Cousin 1 Removed	2nd Cousin 2 Removed	2nd Cousin 3 Removed	2nd Cousin 4 Removed
Great-g Grandchild	Great grand Niece/Nephew	1st Cousin 2 Removed	2nd Cousin 1 Removed	**3rd Cousin**	3rd Cousin 1 Removed	3rd Cousin 2 Removed	3rd Cousin 3 Removed
G-g-g Grandchild	G-g grand Niece/Nephew	1st Cousin 3 Removed	2nd Cousin 2 Removed	3rd Cousin 1 Removed	**4th Cousin**	4th Cousin 1 Removed	4th Cousin 2 Removed
G-g-g-g Grandchild	G-g-g Niece/Nephew	1st Cousin 4 Removed	2nd Cousin 3 Removed	3rd Cousin 2 Removed	4th Cousin 1 Removed	**5th Cousin**	5th Cousin 1 Removed
G-g-g-g-g Grandchild	G-g-g-g Niece/Nephew	1st Cousin 5 Removed	2nd Cousin 4 Removed	3rd Cousin 3 Removed	4th Cousin 2 Removed	5th Cousin 1 Removed	**6th Cousin**

Appendix F.
Acknowledgments

The heros and heroines of this book are our 68 authors who painstakingly compiled the wealth of information they have contributed here, and who suffered graciously the seemingly endless questions of a long editing process. We thank them for their patience and good will. Many generously advised us about chapters in addition to their own and contributed valuable suggestions. Eileen Polakoff and Rabbi Shalom Bronstein merit special mention for their unfailing willingness to help.

We greatly appreciate the time, advice and assistance given to us by others who read chapters, shared their knowledge, and provided a variety of good ideas: Dr. Arlene Beare, Carol Clapsaddle, Stanley Diamond, Alexander Dunai, Guilherme Faiguenboim, Professor Zvi Gitelman, Vlasta Kovacs, Howard Margol, Kahlile Mehr, Lolita Nikolovna, Constance Potter, Professor Marsha Rozenblit, Marian Smith, Charles Tucker, Rabbi Meir Wunder and Marlene Zakai.

Thanks and boundless gratitude goes to our professional editor Irene Goldstein for her keen ability to spot ambiguous statements, ask insightful questions, and make any prose ever so much more readable. Ruth Mokotoff did a final reading to minimize grammatical, syntax and spelling errors.

Above all our love, thanks and gratitude go to Ruth Mokotoff and Lawrence Sack who (almost) uncomplainingly endured hours of abandonment from spouses glued to their computers. Larry died a month or so after these words were written, but they remain true nonetheless.

Sallyann Amdur Sack
Gary Mokotoff
July 2003

Tashlich ceremony in Galicia. On Rosh Hashanah, Jews traditionally walk to a natural body of water where they cast breadcrumbs into the water, symbolic of casting away their sins of the previous year. Illustration for *Jewish Encyclopedia* published from 1901–1906.

Appendix G: List of Contributors

PHILIP ABENSUR, MD, is a pediatrician who resides in Paris. Born in Tangier, Morocco, he is a founder of *Etsi* ("my tree" in Hebrew), the Sephardi Genealogical and Historical Society, and serves as editor of its quarterly review. Past president of the *Cercle de Généalogie Juive,* he was chairman of the Paris International Conference on Jewish Genealogy in 1997. Abensur specializes in the Jewish genealogy of northern Morocco and works on the *Alliance Israélite Universelle* archives. He is involved in a worldwide Sephardi *ketubot* recording project. Abensur has edited transcriptions from Solitreo of the index of the first register of the Jewish community of Tangier from 1860 to 1875 by Sidney Pimienta.

MARCEL APSEL was born in Antwerp in 1950 to parents who had hidden in Belgium during World War II. Apsel has served as *AVOTAYNU* contributing editor for Belgium since its first issue, and is a founding member and vice-president of the Jewish Genealogical Society of Belgium. He writes a regular genealogy column in an Antwerp Jewish magazine. Apsel's interest in genealogy began in childhood when he felt envious of friends who had relatives in Antwerp, while he only heard about family members he had never met. During his first visit to Israel in 1967, Apsel realized that he too had family and began his genealogical research. He is a descendant of the Pne Joshua; his wife is a descendant of Rabbi Elimelech of Lizansk.

NANCY LEVIN ARBEITER, CGRS, is a full-time professional genealogist specializing in Jewish family history and immigration research. She has a private research practice and is also the director of genealogy for the American Jewish Historical Society. Arbeiter is author of "A Beginner's Primer in U.S. Jewish Genealogical Research" (*AVOTAYNU* 14, no. 3, Fall 1998) and has the taught beginner's workshop at numerous international Jewish genealogy conferences held worldwide. She has lectured widely on vital, census, immigration, and naturalization records, and, most recently, the Port of New York. She has been featured on the front page of Boston's *Jewish Advocate* newspaper.

PAUL ARMONY is the founder and president of the *Asociacion de Genealogia Judia de Argentina* (Jewish Genealogical Society of Argentina). Established in 1998 with seven members, the membership reached 150 as of Spring 2003. The society has an active program to index Jewish burials all over Argentina, and its newsletter, *Toldot,* received the 2001 IAJGS award for best publication by a Jewish genealogy society. Armony, a retired university professor with a varied subsequent career in the construction and steel business, says that since 1998, "I only live for the genealogical society." Born in Montevideo, Uruguay, Armony emigrated to Buenos Aires, Argentina, when he was a child. Late in 2003 he will emigrate again—this time to Canada—where he and his wife will join their three sons.

JORDAN AUSLANDER has a degree in history that saw practical use in title search, real estate, and other research contracted for various literary projects before he became involved in genealogy. A former urban transportation planner, Auslander is now a New York-based professional genealogist, lecturer and expert witness. He has pursued case research across the United States, Europe, and Israel. Auslander translated, created, and published an index to vital records in the Slovak State Archive system and completed an alphabetized translation of *Magyaroszag Helsegneutara,* a gazetteer of 1877 Hungary.

CHARLES B. BERNSTEIN is a graduate of the University of Chicago and the DePaul University College of Law. He has practiced law in Chicago since 1965, with an emphasis on estate planning and probate. A pioneer in the modern Jewish genealogy movement, he has been doing research for almost 40 years and was one of the 11 founders of the Jewish Genealogical Society, Inc. (New York) in 1977. He has been doing professional genealogical research, consulting, and writing for more than 25 years. The author or coauthor of six family histories, including three commissioned by prominent Chicago Jewish families, and ghostwriter of a 700-page autobiography of a prominent Jewish Chicago industrialist, Bernstein has been a consultant or contributor to five other well-known Jewish genealogy books.

WARREN BLATT is JewishGen's editor-in-chief. He has been pursuing Jewish genealogical research for more than 25 years, doing extensive work with Polish and Russian records. He is author of the "JewishGen FAQ: Frequently Asked Questions about Jewish Genealogy;" dozens of JewishGen InfoFiles; *Resources for Jewish Genealogy in the Boston Area* (1996); and coauthor (with Gary Mokotoff) of *Getting Started in Jewish Genealogy* (1999). He is editor of the *Kielce-Radom SIG Journal* and has written articles for *AVOTAYNU* and other Jewish genealogical publications.

RABBI SHALOM BRONSTEIN, a native of Philadelphia, earned degrees at Gratz College and Temple University and his rabbinic ordination in 1970 from the Jewish Theological Seminary of America. A congregational rabbi for many years, Bronstein moved to Israel with his family in 1986 and now resides in Jerusalem. A member of the Philadelphia Jewish Genealogical Society, the Israel Genealogical Society, Association of Professional Genealogists, and the Rabbinical Assembly, Bronstein has published articles in *AVOTAYNU* and *Sharsheret HaDorot*. He served as president of the Jerusalem branch of the Israel Genealogical Society and is on the editorial staff of *Sharsheret*

HaDorot. An independent researcher, Bronstein specializes in the archival collections of the Central Zionist Archives and Yad Vashem.

CLAIRE BRUELL's family has lived in Auckland, New Zealand, since arriving in that city from Czechoslovakia in 1939. Bruell has been researching family history since 1979. More recently, she has been involved in creating and operating a comprehensive program to tape record interviews with Holocaust survivors in New Zealand. The tapes will form part of the Oral History Archives at both the Alexander Turnbull Library in Wellington and the Auckland Museum research facility. The tapes also will be included in the collection at the U.S. Holocaust Memorial Museum in Washington, D.C. Bruell is actively involved in the Auckland Jewish community. Her interests cover a wide field of language, travel and the arts.

FAY VOGEL BUSSGANG received a B.A. in psychology from Wellesley College, an Ed.D. from Harvard University, and studied child psychology in Geneva, Switzerland, as a Rotary Foundation Fellow. She and her Polish-born husband, Julian, have made ten trips to Poland and have done extensive genealogical research on their families. They also translated into English a collection of wartime accounts of child survivors still living in Poland, *The Last Eyewitnesses: Children of the Holocaust Speak.* Bussgang is author of a number of papers on Jewish genealogy and is active in the JGS of Greater Boston. She served as its co-president from 1998 to 2000.

SOPHIE CAPLAN became interested in genealogy because of the loss of many family members in the *Shoah.* An oral historian and university lecturer on the *Shoah,* Caplan founded the Australian Jewish Genealogical Society in 1991 and served as its president and editor of its publication *Kosher Koala* until 2002. She is *AVOTAYNU'*S contributing editor for Australia, senior vice president of the Australian Jewish Historical Society, and co-author of *With One Voice.* In 1975 Caplan founded the Dr. Hans Kimmel Memorial Essay Competition in Contemporary Jewish History at her children's Jewish high school. This became a compulsory part of the curriculum, and Caplan still judges the essays.

CARL H. CARLSSON, M.A., is a Swedish historian and genealogist with Jewish roots in Suwalki guberniya, Russian Poland. He has been working for many years as one of the editors of *Svenskt biografiskt lexikon* (Dictionary of Swedish biography) and currently is working on his doctoral dissertation, "Eastern Jews and Other Immigrants in Sweden 1860–1920: Citizenship, Liberty to Pursue a Trade and Discrimination" (to be published in 2003). He has published numerous articles on Jewish history and genealogy and has presented lectures at many international conferences. He is president and co-founder of the Jewish Genealogical Society of Sweden. Carlsson is available for professional research consultation.

JOHN PHILIP COLLETTA, PhD, a Washington-based genealogist, teaches at the National Archives, Smithsonian Institute, and area

universities and lectures nationally. His publications include numerous articles, two manuals—*They Came in Ships: A Guide to Finding Your Immigrant Ancestor's Arrival Record* and *Finding Italian Roots: The Complete Guide for Americans*— and a historical narrative—*Only a Few Bones: A True Account of the Rolling Fork Tragedy and Its Aftermath.* Dr. Colletta has appeared on local and national radio and television and is featured in "Ancestors," the PBS television series. His Ph.D. in medieval French is from The Catholic University of America.

CHRISTINE A. CRANDALL is an archivist at the Jacob Rader Marcus Center of the American Jewish Archives in Cincinnati, Ohio. She received her B.A. in history from the University of Florida and M.A. in history and archival/museum sciences from Wright State University in Dayton, Ohio. She currently is head of genealogy collections at the American Jewish Archives and teaches classes, through the Society of Ohio Archivists, on basic archival skills for genealogists and other interested students.

RANDY DAITCH, a professional genealogist and charter member of the Jewish Genealogy Society of Greater Los Angeles, is a coauthor of *AVOTAYNU*'s "Ask the Experts" column. During the past 20 years, he has extensively catalogued maps and gazetteers of Eastern Europe at libraries throughout the United States. In partnership with Gary Mokotoff, he created the Daitch-Mokotoff Soundex, an innovative way of finding place names and surnames by sound instead of spelling. This soundex was incorporated into *Where Once We Walked* and today is one of the main search tools in JewishGen's growing collection of online databases. Daitch is a historical geography researcher at the Survivors of the Shoah Visual History Foundation in Los Angeles.

EPHRIAM DARDASHTI was born in Teheran in 1955, where his primary education was in a French school. He moved to the United States in his teens. Dardashti studied at Temple University, Hebrew University and Rutgers University and has degrees in history and in business administration. He lives in Philadelphia, is married and "blessed with four wonderful children."

DANIEL DRATWA, president of the Association of European Jewish Museums and member of the board of the Council of Brussels Museums, is director of the Jewish Museum of Belgium, which he founded in 1984. He has been president of the Jewish Genealogical Society of Belgium since 1998 and is a founding member of the European Association of Jewish Genealogical Societies. Dratwa has edited numerous catalogues produced by the Jewish Museum and has written articles for, among others, the *Encyclopaedia Judaica* and the *Encyclopedia of Zionism, Revue des etudes Juives,* and *Los Muestros.* He is author of *Repertoire des periodiques juifs de Belgique 1841–1987* and a former assistant researcher at the Institute of Jewish Studies.

BOB DRILSMA is secretary of the Belgian Jewish Genealogical Society and a longtime board member of both B'nai B'rith

Antwerp and the Frechie Foundation, the *chevra kadisha* of Jews of Dutch origin living in Antwerp. As a genealogist, Drilsma specializes in families like his who migrated from Holland to Belgium. He and his wife live in Antwerp and are members of the Shomre Hadas Jewish community.

MICHAEL FELDBERG, executive director of the American Jewish Historical Society since 1991, holds a bachelor's degree from Cornell University and a Ph.D. in history from the University of Rochester. He is author or editor of 11 books in the fields of history and criminal justice, including *Blessings of Freedom: Chapters in American Jewish History,* which is based on his long-running series of articles in the American Jewish press.

BORIS FELDBLYUM is president of FAST Genealogy Service, an organization specializing in archival research in the former Soviet Union. His experience of 20 years includes research and analysis of archival records, search for living relatives and consulting. A speaker at several Jewish genealogical conferences, Feldblyum has published several articles on genealogical archival research and is author of *Russian-Jewish Given Names.* His web presence includes the FAST Genealogy Service page, WWW.AVOTAYNU.COM/FAST.HTML, and his collection of historical photographs from Eastern Europe and throughout the world at WWW.BFCOLLECTION.NET.

DIANNE WEINER FELDMAN, an independent researcher, lives in Davidsonville, Maryland. She is a former employee of the Jewish Museum of Maryland, where she worked for 10 years in the Robert L. Weinberg Family History Center. The archives and art collection of the museum provided Feldman with data that led to the discovery of a forgotten Baltimore congregation and the rediscovery of a Jewish artist. Records of the museum helped her to determine the history and identity of people buried in an abandoned city cemetery. Feldman was the family history coordinator for the museum's exhibit, "We Call This Place Home, Jewish Life in Maryland's Small Towns."

KAREN S. FRANKLIN is director of The Judaica Museum of the Hebrew Home for the Aged at Riverdale and director of the Family Research Program of the Leo Baeck Institute. She also serves as a genealogy consultant to the Jacob Rader Marcus Center of the American Jewish Archives. Franklin is a past chair of the Council of American Jewish Museums and a past president of the International Association of Jewish Genealogical Societies. She currently serves on the board of the American Association of Museums, the first director of a Jewish museum to be elected to this position.

CHAIM FREEDMAN is an author, lecturer and professional researcher on Jewish genealogy. He is author of *Beit Rabbanan,* a reference book for rabbinic genealogical research, and *Eliyahu's Branches,* the genealogy of the descendants of the Vilna Gaon. He has edited *Jewish Personal Names: Their Origin, Derivation and Diminutive Forms,* which represented the efforts of the late Rabbi Shmuel Gorr. He was born in

Melbourne, Australia, to parents of Eastern European origin, and there he received both a traditionally orthodox and secular education. In 1977, he and his wife made *aliyah* and have lived in Israel since. He possesses a large archive and library of genealogical sources and is considered an expert in researching rare Hebrew sources for genealogy.

HARRIET FREIDENREICH is professor of history at Temple University in Philadelphia. A native of Ottawa, Canada, who earned her Ph.D. in Eastern European and Jewish history from Columbia University, she teaches a wide range of courses in women's history, Jewish history and European history. Freidenreich is author of *The Jews of Yugoslavia, Jewish Politics in Vienna*, and *Female, Jewish, and Educated: The Lives of Central European University Women*, as well as articles on Yugoslav and Viennese Jewry and Central European Jewish women in the 20th century.

NORA HELLER FREUND was born in Most, Czechoslovakia, into a family with Jewish Bohemian roots. After escaping from the Nazis with her parents, she grew up in Canada. She earned a degree in hotel management at Cornell University and is married with three children and eight grandchildren. Her husband, a Holocaust survivor, also has roots in the Czech Republic. When their children were adolescents, she became curious about their ancestors, many of whom had died in the Holocaust. Freund began to research the family roots through oral history and, in 1984, produced a family history. In 1989, after the fall of the Iron Curtain, she visited her ancestral home and found that many records still survived. She has been working on a revised edition of her family history ever since.

ALEX E. FRIEDLANDER, an internationally renowned professional genealogist, is an expert on Polish and Lithuanian genealogical documents. He is author of the forthcoming two-volume genealogy *From Suwalki to St. Ignace* and has been acknowledged for his contributions to *Eliyahu's Branches* (Chaim Freedman, 1997) and *The Book of Destiny* (Arthur F. Menton, 1996). He has written articles that have appeared in various publications, including *AVOTAYNU*, and given lectures and presentations at genealogical conferences and seminars. Dr. Friedlander has been a member of the executive council of the Jewish Genealogical Society, Inc., since 1985; editor of its quarterly journal *Dorot* from 1990 to 2001; and president of the society since 2002. He is a member of the Association of Professional Genealogists and the Committee of Professional Jewish Genealogists.

MIKE GETZ was born in Cape Town, South Africa, and moved to the United States in 1992. He was a founding member and president of the Latvia SIG, and vice-president of the Jewish Genealogy Society of Greater Washington. In 1992, he traveled to Latvia with a family group, visiting Daugavpils, Riga, and Subate, the shtetl where his parents were born. In 1997, he revisited these communities as well as Jekabpils, Karsava and Rezekne. His research interests include U.S. State Department records at the National Archives; microfilms of the Soviet Extraordinary Commission at the U.S. Holocaust Memorial Museum; property records of Subate family histories from Daugavpils, Jekabpils, and Rezekne; and various cemetery records.

BASILE GINGER, a retired electronics engineer, was born in Paris to Russian émigrés. He first became interested in genealogy when he was 12 years old and questioned his grandmother about the family roots. Later he joined the *Cercle de Généalogie Juive* and served as the society's treasurer and currently its librarian. His articles have been published in the *Cercle's Revue* and in *AVOTAYNU*. Early in 2002, he wrote a *Guide to Jewish Genealogy in France and Elsewhere* (in French) and is leader of the *Cercle's* Eastern Europe SIG.

BILL GLADSTONE is a longtime contributor to *AVOTAYNU* and many other publications. He is the family historian for the Rubinoff-Naftolin constellation of families in Toronto and elsewhere (originating in Belarus) and globally for all families named Glicenstein and variants (originating in a regional triangle centered around Lodz, Poland). A professional journalist, he lives in Toronto and writes several columns for the *Canadian Jewish News,* including the monthly "Roots and Remembrance" column on Jewish genealogy (under the pseudonym Ze'ev Glicenstein). Gladstone is a past president of the Jewish Genealogical Society of Canada (Toronto).

IRENE SAUNDERS GOLDSTEIN, a professional writer and editor, conducts family history projects among a broad range of other free lance assignments. Her passion is conducting interviews and then publishing heirloom-quality personal histories to mark milestone events. Goldstein has edited most of the major reference books published by *AVOTAYNU*, including the award-winning *Where Once We Walked* (Mokotoff and Sack)*, A Dictionary of Jewish Surnames from the Russian Empire* (Beider), and *Sephardic Genealogy: Discovering Your Sephardic Ancestors and Their World* (Malka). She has served as editor of the *APG Quarterly* and associate editor of *AVOTAYNU*. A member of B'nai B'rith International's Executive Committee and Board of Governors, she also has served as Jewish Roots Committee Chair.

RUTH ELLEN GRUBER is an American writer, photographer and journalist based in Europe for many years. An authority on contemporary Jewish issues in Europe, she has published and lectured widely on the subject, and also has traveled thousands of miles throughout East-Central Europe documenting Jewish heritage sites. Her most recent book is *Virtually Jewish: Reinventing Jewish Culture in Europe* (2002). Other books include *Upon the Doorposts of Thy House: Jewish Life in East-Central Europe, Yesterday and Today* (1994), and *Jewish Heritage Travel: A Guide to East-Central Europe* (1992/94/99). Gruber serves as senior Europe correspondent for the Jewish Telegraphic Agency and has received two Simon Rockower awards for excellence in Jewish journalism.

LADISLAU GYÉMÁNT was born in Oradea, Romania, in 1947. He is professor of Jewish history and European history, director of the Dr. Moshe Carmilly Institute for Hebrew and Jewish Studies, and deputy dean of the Faculty of European Studies of the Babes-Bolyai University in Cluj, Romania. He was editor of the annual review *Studia Judaica*, I–X, Cluj-Napoca, 1991–2001; editor of the series *Bibliotheca Judaica*, I–VII, 1994–2000; and contributing editor for Romania for *AVOTAYNU*. For 30 years, Professor Gyémant has been senior fellow researcher at the Institute of History of the Romanian Academy in Cluj. He is a specialist in 18th- and 19th-century Central European history, the history of Transylvania, the history of Jews in Romania and Romanian Jewish genealogy.

SAUL ISSROFF, is a South African-born, London-based retired dermatologist. A founding member and vice-president of the Jewish Genealogy Society of Great Britain, he co-chaired the 21st International IAJGS Conference, London, 2001. He is project director, The Jewish Migration and Genealogy Centre, Isaac and Jessie Kaplan Centre for Jewish Studies and Research, University of Cape Town; co-founder and president, Southern African Special Interest Group; and editor, Southern Africa website at WWW.JEWISHGEN.ORG/SAFRICA. He is coauthor of *The Holocaust in Lithuania 1941–1945: A Book of Remembrance* (2002) and author of a number of books on Jewish genealogy, including *Jewish Roots,* about Central and Eastern European Jews' migration to the United Kingdom for the "Moving Here" project of the Public Records Office.

ANTHONY JOSEPH is a semi-retired British Midlands general practitioner who has devoted 55 years to pursuing Jewish genealogy. A former president of the Jewish Historical Society of England, he is the first and also current president of the Jewish Genealogical Society of Great Britain. His interests include the Antipodes, and he has been the corresponding member for the United Kingdom of the Australian-Jewish Historical Society since 1966. In 1987, prior to the founding of the Jewish Genealogical Society of Great Britain, Dr. Joseph co-chaired the first Jewish genealogy conference in London. He now serves as a member of the board of directors of the International Association of Jewish Genealogical Societies.

HARVEY L. KAPLAN graduated with an M.A. in history from the University of Glasgow and currently is a civil servant. Founding director of the Scottish Jewish Archives Centre, he has researched widely in the field of Scottish-Jewish family history. He has contributed numerous articles on Scottish Jewish history and genealogy to journals and magazines and has lectured at meetings and conferences. He co-edited "A Scottish Shtetl: Jewish Life in the Gorbals, 1881–1974" (1984) and contributed "Scottish Jewry: Sources and Resources" to *Aspects of Scottish Jewry* (Collins, ed., 1987). He has researched his own family back to early 19th-century Lithuania, Poland and Ukraine and discovered relatives in the U.S., Canada, Israel, South Africa, Australia, Brazil, Costa Rica and elsewhere.

STELLA HAZAN KENT was born in Istanbul, where she was active in Jewish youth activities, co-edited the Jewish youth magazine *Igli*, and headed cultural activities in a Jewish social and youth club. Kent co-founded the genealogical society *Kokler* (Roots) and served as its president. Working under the patronage of the Great Rabbinate, the society did research on Turkish Jewish history, educated the Jewish public about its origins and encouraged family history research. Kent and her family made *aliyah* to Israel in 2003.

YITZCHAK KEREM is a lecturer at Aristotle University in Thessaloniki, Greece; a researcher of Sephardic history at The Hebrew University of Jerusalem; founder and director of the Institute of Hellenic-Jewish Studies at the University of Denver; editor of the monthly Sephardic e-mail publication *Sefarad: The Sephardic Newsletter* since 1992; and author of more than 200 articles on Greek Jewry. He lives in Jerusalem and is a member of the Israel Genealogical Society.

SHARLENE KRANZ is a longtime member and officer of the Jewish Genealogy Society of Greater Washington. She teaches beginner's workshops and edits the society's quarterly newsletter, *Mishpacha*. Her areas of research are Galicia and Russia/Poland. She is author of *Capitol Collections: Jewish Genealogical Research in the Washington, D.C. Area*. When not doing genealogy, she is a law librarian.

ARTHUR KURZWEIL is author of *From Generation to Generation: How to Trace Your Jewish Genealogy and Family History*. First published in 1980, this book has inspired thousands of Jews around the world to pursue Jewish genealogical research. A new edition will be published in 2004 by Jossey-Bass. Kurzweil is also author of *My Generations: A Course in Jewish Family History*, a textbook used in synagogue schools throughout the United States. "How To Trace Your Jewish Roots: A Journey with Arthur Kurzweil" (Ergo Media) is an award-winning video about his genealogical work. He is also a co-founder of *Toledot: The Journal of Jewish Genealogy*, as well as the Jewish Genealogical Society of New York, and is coeditor of *The Encyclopedia of Jewish Genealogy*. Kurzweil has spoken before more than 700 Jewish groups on the subject of Jewish family history and genealogy.

PETER LANDÉ was born in Germany and came to the United States in 1937. As a U.S. State Department Foreign Service Officer, Landé served in New Zealand, Japan, India, Germany, Egypt and Canada, as well as in various assignments at the State Department. He retired in 1988 as economic minister in the United States Embassy in Cairo. He has written and lectured extensively, particularly regarding German-Jewish genealogy and the fate of European Jews in the Holocaust. He received a Lifetime Achievement Award from the International Association of Jewish Genealogical Societies for his work in identifying sources of information on Holocaust victims and survivors. In addition, he has personally computerized and/or proofread about 400,000 names for inclusion in museum and JewishGen databases.

RENE LOEB was born in Basel, Switzerland, in 1939. After World War II he moved with his parents to the Grand Duchy of Luxembourg, where he was educated as a qualified merchant. He returned to Switzerland in 1959. Loeb became interested in genealogy in 1980 and founded the Swiss Society of Jewish Genealogy in 1986. He served as its president until 1999. Loeb also founded and edited the quarterly publication *Majaan-Die Quelle*. Since 1986, he has been *AVOTAYNU*'s contributing editor for Switzerland and has lectured and researched his own genealogy as well as that of others. He is coeditor of the Bernays genealogy in Prof. Dr. Helmut Hirsch's *Freund von Heine, Marx/Engels and Lincoln: Eine Karl Ludwig Bernays-Biografie* (Friend of Heine, Marx/Engels and Lincoln: A Biography of Karl Ludwig Bernays), 2000.

EDWARD DAVID LUFT is a retired attorney and U.S. government employee who lives in Washington, D.C. He is author of *The Naturalized Jews of the Grand Duchy of Posen in 1834 and 1835* (1987) and coauthor with Angelika Ellmann-Krüger of *Library Resources for German-Jewish Genealogy* (1998), as well as author of numerous articles on genealogy and related topics in *AVOTAYNU* and *Stammbaum*. He has delivered a number of lectures in the United States and Europe on genealogy and historical topics.

JEFFREY S. MALKA, MD, born in Sudan, is a U.S. orthopedic surgeon with both Sephardic and Ashkenazi ancestry. He created a large, award-winning Internet website, WWW.ORTHOHELP.COM/GENEAL/SEFARDIM.HTM, devoted to Sephardic genealogy and also developed JewishGen's SefardSig and KahalLinks (Sephardic version of ShtetlLink) websites to provide greater presence and visibility for Sephardic genealogy. Malka is the author of *Sephardic Genealogy: Discovering Your Sephardic Ancestors and Their World* (2002) and recipient of the Association of Jewish Libraries' Reference Book of the Year Award for 2002. The book deals with Sephardic history, country archives, research techniques, and Sephardic languages and scripts, and includes a guide to Sephardic websites and an extensive bibliography.

FRUMA MOHRER is the chief archivist of the YIVO Archives. She is coauthor with Marek Web of the *Guide to the YIVO Archives*, which won the Association of Jewish Libraries Award for the outstanding Judaica reference work published in 1998. Her published translations include *Minutes of the Eldridge Street Synagogue, 1890–1916*, *The Nature of Ghetto Prayer Services in Lodz Ghetto*, and several autobiographies, including one in YIVO's recent publication *Awakening Lives*. Mohrer holds a B.A. in history and a graduate diploma in education from McGill University, as well as a J.D. from New York Law School. She is a member of the New York Bar, the Mid-Atlantic Regional Archives Conference and Archivists' Roundtable of Metropolitan New York.

GARY MOKOTOFF is the first recipient of the Lifetime Achievement Award of the International Association of Jewish Genealogical Societies (IAJGS). He is publisher of *AVOTAYNU* and a past president of IAJGS. He has authored or coauthored a number of books, including the award-winning *Where Once We Walked, How to Document Victims and Locate Survivors of the Holocaust, and Getting Started in Jewish Genealogy.* Mokotoff also is known for his application of computers to genealogy. Among his accomplishments are coauthorship of the Daitch-Mokotoff Soundex code, the JewishGen Family Finder and the Jewish Genealogical People Finder (predecessor to the Family Tree of the Jewish People). He has served on the boards of directors of a number of organizations, including the Federation of Genealogical Societies, Association of Professional Genealogists, JewishGen and the Jewish Book Council.

PETER NASH (formerly Nachemstein) and his immediate family escaped the Holocaust, leaving Berlin in 1939, finding refuge in Shanghai until 1949 and finally emigrating to Australia. Nash has been a keen and successful researcher, tracing family in Germany and in former Prussian provinces, as well as in the United States. Results of some of his researches have been published in *AVOTAYNU* and *Kosher Koala,* the journal of the Australian Jewish Genealogical Society, of which he is a founding member. He has given talks in England, Canada and Australia about his Shanghai experience and resources for China research. Articles on China have been published in *AVOTAYNU, Stammbaum* and *Kosher Koala.* He is an accredited guide of the Sydney Jewish Museum, which is oriented to the Holocaust and Australian Jewish history.

PROFESSOR AUBREY NEWMAN of Leicester University has been responsible for the establishment and development of the database on The Poor Jews' Temporary Shelter of London and has written widely on the migration of Jews from Lithuania to South Africa between 1890 and 1914. Educated in London, Glasgow, and Oxford, he is editor of *Migration and Settlement, Provincial Jewry in Victorian Britain, The Jewish East End 1840–1939,* and (with Stephen Massil) *Patterns of Migration: Impact Upon World Jewry 1850–1914.* Professor Newman has been Samuel Goldstein Distinguished Visiting Professor of Holocaust Studies, Washington University, St. Louis, Missouri; past president of the Jewish Historical Society of England; and council member, World Council of Jewish Studies.

ELSEBETH PAIKIN is vice-president of the Society for Danish-Jewish History, coordinator of JewishGen's Scandinavia Special Interest Group and a member of the board of the Society for Danish Genealogy and Biography. Paikin initiated and served as project coordinator of *Kildeindtastningsprojektet,* a project to computerize historical records, an interdisciplinary and institutional cooperation among members of the Society for Genealogical Computing in Denmark, genealogical societies, local historical archives, the University of Copenhagen, National Archives and Danish Data Archive. She is project coordinator of The Family Tree of the Danish Jews and The Paikin Genealogy Project. Her research project is "Jewish Immigration and Transmigration to/via Denmark in the Beginning of the 20th Century."

PEGGY K. PEARLSTEIN is the area specialist in the Hebraic Section of the Library of Congress. She has an M.A. in Jewish studies from Baltimore Hebrew University, an M.S. in library science from Southern Connecticut State College, and a Ph.D. in American studies from George Washington University. She has contributed to *Jewish Women in America: An Historical Encyclopedia;* to *American Women: A Library of Congress Guide for the Study of Women's History and Culture in the United States;* and to such journals as *AVOTAYNU, Judaica Librarianship,* and *Jewish Political Studies Review.*

EILEEN POLAKOFF is a full-time professional genealogist specializing in Jewish-American family history. Her professional work has involved tracing families back to the early 19th century in Europe and finding long-lost relatives around the world. Based in New York City, her research specialties are New York City (1860–present), Jewish-American research throughout the United States and Jewish family history worldwide. Polakoff is coauthor of *AVOTAYNU*'s "Ask the Experts" column; lectures worldwide on research techniques and methodology; and has published in *AVOTAYNU, Ancestry Magazine* and the *APG Quarterly.* She is a member of the Association of Professional Genealogists (APG), Jewish Genealogical Society, Inc. (New York) and National Genealogical Society. She is a recipient of the APG's Graham T. Smallwood, Jr. Award of Merit (1991) and Certificates of Appreciation (1993, 1997 and 1999).

HAROLD RHODE has been researching his Litvak family roots for more than 30 years. Using vital document analysis and rabbinical texts, he has been able to demonstrate that the Jews were very mobile and that our Eastern European ancestors actually resided in localities that covered large geographical areas, not single communities. A former president of the Jewish Genealogical Society of Greater Washington, Rhode has published several articles in *AVOTAYNU* and is author of *Jewish Vital Records, Revision Lists and Other Jewish Holdings in the Lithuanian Archives.* He holds a Ph.D. in Middle Eastern History and is a foreign affairs analyst at the U.S. Department of Defense.

VIVIENNE ROUMANI-DENN is the national executive director of the American Sephardi Federation (ASF) at the Center for Jewish History in Manhattan. She joined ASF in 1999 as the director of library and archives, where she began building a collection of books, archives and artifacts. Prior to joining ASF, Roumani-Denn was the Judaica librarian at the University of California, Berkeley. She also has held library management positions at Berkeley, the Library of Congress, and the Johns Hopkins University. In addition to her master of library science degree, Vivienne holds a master's degree in administrative science from Johns Hopkins University. Roumani-Denn's current area of scholarship is 20th-century Libyan Jewry.

ALEJANDRO T. RUBINSTEIN has worked for more than six years on the study and compilation of Jewish onomastics. He has given courses and conferences and published studies and articles. His presentations at institutions in Mexico and abroad seek to promote Jewish genealogy and the preservation of Jewish roots. He has concluded several research projects, including a questionnaire in Spanish for genealogical research through interviews, an electronic dictionary of Jewish names and surnames, and a photographic collection of the art of remembrance as seen on Jewish tombstones.

ARLINE SACHS is a retired associate professor of computer information systems. She has served as president of the Jewish Genealogy Society of Greater Washington and secretary of the board of directors of the International Association of Jewish Genealogical Societies. In 1993, Sachs initiated the International Jewish Cemetery Project to find all burial locations of Jews around the world. Sachs co-hosts a bimonthly television show on Jewish genealogy that has produced more than 100 shows. Most recently, she has edited her great-great-grandfather's 54-year (1817–71) diaries, due to be published in 2003 as *Bernhard Cahn, a Man of His Time: Life in Nineteenth-Century Germany* by Avotaynu Foundation.

SALLYANN AMDUR SACK is a recipient of the IAJGS Lifetime Achievement Award, founder and first president of the Jewish Genealogy Society of Greater Washington, editor of *AVOTAYNU* and president of Avotaynu Foundation. Author, lecturer, and consultant, Sack has chaired and co-chaired seven Jewish genealogy conferences and has authored and coauthored *Jewish Genealogical Research in Israel; Where Once We Walked; The Russian Consular Records Index and Catalog; Jewish Vital Records, Revision Lists and Other Jewish Holdings in the Lithuanian Archives;* and *Some Archival Sources for Ukrainian-Jewish Genealogy.* She has served on genealogical advisory boards at the U.S. National Archives and the Douglas E. Goldman Dorot Genealogy Center at Beth Hatefutsoth and is listed in *Jewish Women in America.* Dr. Sack is a clinical psychologist in private practice in Bethesda, Maryland.

LOUIS SCHONFELD is the founder of the Hungarian-Jewish Special Interest Group and former moderator of its online forum. He has traveled extensively to his ancestral communities in Hungary, Slovakia and Subcarpathian Ruthenia, today the southwestern border region of Ukraine. Schonfeld has obtained access and done extensive work in several previously closed archives in Subcarpathian Ruthenia and has escorted individuals and groups on genealogical expeditions to these areas. He is the creator of a *yizkor* website commemorating his primary ancestral town Mukachevo/Munkacs. He continues to travel to Ukraine and other areas in Eastern Europe, recruiting nurses to work for Gemcare Health Systems, a company he founded.

MARCO R. SORIA, MD, earned his medical degree in 1969 at the University of Naples, Italy, and his Ph.D. in 1975 from Harvard University. From 1990 to 2000, he headed the Biotechnology Unit in the Department of Biological and Technological Research at the San Raffaele Research Institute in Milan, Italy. Now professor of biochemistry at the University Magna Graecia in Catanzaro, Italy, he is author of more than 80 publications in peer-reviewed scientific journals. He serves on the editorial board of the *Journal of Drug Targeting,* is chairman of the Section on Applied Genomics of the European Federation of Biotechnology, and is a member of the Life Sciences Working Group of the European Space Agency.

VLADISLAV SOSHNIKOV was an original member of the Russian-American Genealogical Archival Service (RAGAS) in 1991 and served as its director from 1994 until 2000. A graduate of the Institute for History and Archives of the Russian State University for the Humanities in Moscow, he worked with American clients for more than eight years and presented lectures to the Archival Roundtable of New York, the Federation of Eastern European Family History Societies and the 14th Summer Seminar on Jewish Genealogy in Washington, D.C. (1995). Soshnikov lives in Moscow.

IGNACIO STERNBERG is the founder and current president of the *Asociacion de Genealogia Judia de Venezuela,* the Venezuelan Jewish genealogy society. A native of Caracas, where he lives today, Sternberg is a graduate of and former professor at the *Universidad Catolica.* He served as a longtime board member of the *Union Israelita de Caracas* (the Ashkenazi community) and of *Hebraica-Caracas*, the Jewish community center. A certified accountant, Sternberg has worked as a consultant in Israel.

MATHILDE TAGGER holds a master of library and information sciences from the Hebrew University, Jerusalem. Now retired, she was chief librarian in its Atmospheric Sciences Department for 20 years and then scientific advisor at the Ministry of Science and Development for 10 years. She has pursued genealogical research for 17 years, specializing in Sephardim genealogy (including her husband's Bulgarian roots), has published in *Sharsheret HaDorot*, the *Revue* of the *Cercle du Généalogie Juive,* and *Etsi,* and has created more than 30 Internet files on Sephardic genealogy. For the Ben Zvi Institute she prepared *Indexes to Malkhei Rabanan,* a biographical dictionary of Moroccan rabbis by Yosef Ben Naim (Jerusalem, 1931), and *Indexes to Malkhei Yeshurun,* a biographical dictionary of Tunisian rabbis.

LAWRENCE TAPPER is an archivist in the Canadian Archives Branch at the National Archives of Canada in Ottawa. He is responsible for Social Action and Public Policy archives. Tapper was founding president of the Jewish Genealogy Society of Ottawa and currently serves as its director of Research and Special Projects. He is author of *A Biographical Dictionary of Canadian Jewry* (1992). Tapper has written about genealogical resources in Canada in *AVOTAYNU* and has lectured on the topic at Jewish genealogical conferences.

ODETTE VLESSING earned her bachelor's degree in English and history at the Hebrew University in Jerusalem and master's degree in medieval history at the University of Amsterdam. She is certified by the State Archives School as senior archivist.

Vlessing is employed by the Amsterdam Municipal Archives, where she specializes in general cataloguing and in researching the history of Dutch Jews, with emphasis on the Dutch Golden Age (17th century). She has lectured on Dutch-Jewish history all over the world and has published on various topics of her historical research, most recently about the life and excommunication of Baruch Spinoza.

H. DANIEL WAGNER is a professor of materials science at the Weizmann Institute of Science, Rehovot, Israel. He is the author of more than 135 scientific papers and several book chapters. He has been researching his family history since 1995 and has published articles in *AVOTAYNU* (USA), *Sharsheret Hadorot* (Israel), *Toldot* (Argentina), *Regards* (Belgium), and *Genami* (France). His wife, born in Argentina, has Syrian-Lebanese roots. Dr. Wagner is a member of the Israel Genealogical Society and a director of the 2004 Jewish genealogy conference in Jerusalem.

MIRIAM WEINER, CG, author of the award-winning *Jewish Roots in Poland* and *Jewish Roots in Ukraine and Moldova*, is president of Routes to Roots (WWW.ROUTESTOROOTS.COM), a firm offering in-depth archive research services and customized tours in Belarus, Ukraine, Moldova and Poland. Weiner also is president of the Routes to Roots Foundation, Inc., and developer of the Foundation website at WWW.RTRFOUNDATION.ORG. The website includes a town-by-town inventory of archive documents in Poland, Ukraine, Belarus, Moldova and Lithuania, along with several hundred pages of text consisting of articles by archivists and historians, maps, related links and other relevant resource material.

HENRY WELLISCH was born in Vienna in 1922. During World War II, he served with the Jewish Brigade and, in 1948, with the Israeli army. Since 1951, Wellisch has lived in Canada and for many years was a civil engineering technologist. About 18 years ago, he began to research his family background and was able to trace his family back into the middle of the 18th century. Wellisch also has established the fate of numerous relatives who perished in the Holocaust. He is active in various community organizations and was president of the Jewish Genealogical Society of Canada (Toronto) from 1993 to 1998.

IRA WOLFMAN is a writer/editor, publishing consultant and genealogy enthusiast. For ten years, he was Editorial Director of Magazine and School Publishing at Sesame Street, producing award-winning materials for children, parents, and teachers. Wolfman has written four books, including *Climbing Your Family Tree: Online and Off-line Genealogy for Kids* (Workman, 2002) and *Jewish New York: Notable Neighborhoods and Memorable Moments* (Rizzoli, Fall 2003). He discovered the joys of genealogy at the first JGSNY Beginners Workshop in 1987. The proud father of two sons, he lives in New York City.

SUZAN WYNNE has been involved with Jewish genealogy since 1977. She founded Gesher Galicia, the Jewish Genealogical Special Interest Group for persons with Galician ancestry, and is a founding member, past president, and former newsletter editor of the Jewish Genealogical Society of Greater Washington, as well as past vice-president of the Association of Jewish Genealogical Societies. Wynne is author of *Finding Your Jewish Roots in Galicia: A Resource Guide* (1998) and has written and lectured extensively about various aspects of general and Jewish genealogy, including immigration and naturalization, naming patterns, the Lower East Side of Manhattan, Russian consular records and history. Wynne was a professional genealogist for ten years before earning a master's degree in social work in 1993. She currently manages and supervises a large mental health organization in Silver Spring, Maryland.

LEN YODAIKEN was born and educated in Dublin, Ireland. He immigrated to Kibbutz Kfar Hanasai in Israel in 1957, where he ran a fish farm for eight years and later worked in an engineering capacity in the *kibbutz* factory and foundry for almost 30 years. He is married to Shoshana and they have two sons, the elder a mechanical engineer and the younger soon to embark on his studies. In 1968, Yodaiken began to research his family roots and has accumulated 16,000 names of members of his own and his wife's families. Having accumulated a considerable corpus of genealogical knowledge in close to 35 years of research, following his retirement in 1998, he began to work as a professional genealogist. He has authored articles in *AVOTAYNU* and *Sharsheret HaDorot,* the publication of the Israel Genealogical Society.

Appendix H:
List of Advanced Subscribers

Philip Abensur, Paris, France ♦ Tobi D. Adams, Carmel, California ♦ Nancy J. Adelson, Sammamish, Washington ♦ Sheila Kurtz Adler, Highland Heights, Ohio ♦ Norman Agran, Grove End Road, London, England ♦ Barbara Leburg Algaze, Los Angeles, California ♦ Patricia A. Allweiss, Mission Viejo, California ♦ Nolan Altman, Oceanside, New York ♦ Patricia Alexandra Alznauer, San Francisco, California ♦ Dorothy C. Amsden, Los Alamos, New Mexico ♦ Marcel Apsel, Antwerpen, Belgium ♦ Nancy Arbeiter, Needham, Massachusetts ♦ Josef Aretz, Tel Aviv, Israel ♦ Paul Armony, Buenos Aires, Argentina ♦ Jerome W. Atkin, Orange, California ♦ Harold L. Atkins, Setauket, New York ♦ Auckland Hebrew Congregation, Auckland, New Zealand ♦ Jordan Auslander, New York, New York ♦ Richard Allen Avner, Champaign, Illinois

Ralph N. Baer, Washington, D.C. ♦ Carol Davidson Baird, Solana Beach, California ♦ Asher Bar-Zev, Palm Beach, Florida ♦ Paul Baranik, Coconut Creek, Florida ♦ Mary Barkan, Las Vegas, Nevada ♦ Frank C. Barnes, Los Angeles, California ♦ Marlene Barth, East Brunswick, New Jersey ♦ Allan Bass, East Brunswick, New Jersey ♦ Judy Baston, San Francisco, California ♦ Richard Leonard Baum, New York, New York ♦ James J. Becker, Burtonsville, Maryland ♦ Jeffrey D. Beller, Wantagh, New York ♦ Ruth Benny, Hong Kong ♦ Jane Rosen Berenbeim, New York, New York ♦ Jack L. Bergstein, Monessen, Pennsylvania ♦ Berkeley-Richmond JCC, Berkeley, California ♦ Roberta Wagner Berman, La Jolla, California ♦ Anne Feibysowicz Bernhaut, Melbourne, Australia ♦ Charles B. Bernstein, Chicago, Illinois ♦ Jeff Bernstein, Jericho, New York ♦ Deena Berton, Lincoln, Massachusetts ♦ Beth Shalom, Auckland, New Zealand ♦ Warren Blatt, Waltham, Massachusetts ♦ Jean Block, Columbus, Ohio ♦ Lesley Goodman Bloom, Los Angeles, California ♦ James Bloomfield, Bellevue, Washington ♦ Linda A. Brand, Los Angeles, California ♦ Cheryl Braverman, Huntington Beach, California ♦ Debra Braverman, New York, New York ♦ Kenneth A. Bravo, Cleveland, Ohio ♦ Mike Brettschneider, Jefferson City, Missouri ♦ Colin Brockman, Greenwood Village, Colorado ♦ Rabbi Shalom Bronstein, Jerusalem, Israel ♦ Melinda Bronte, Los Angeles, California ♦ Claire Bruell, Auckland, New Zealand ♦ Connie Avner Buchanan, Winston-Salem, North Carolina ♦ Sandy Bursten, Irvine, California ♦ Fay Bussgang, Lexington, Massachusetts ♦ Steven Byars, Sparks, Nevada ♦ Eliot and Michelle Byron, New York, New York ♦ Marcus L. Byruck, Cambridge, Massachusetts

Sophie Caplan, Northbridge, Sydney, NSW, Australia ♦ Carl Henrik Carlsson, Uppsala, Sweden ♦ Deborah Chernin, Berkeley, California ♦ Gerald and Lois Chernoff, Sarasota, Florida ♦ Kelly Christensen, Boise, Idaho ♦ Carol Clapsaddle, Jerusalem, Israel ♦ Rubin Roy Cobb, Atlanta, Georgia ♦ John Philip Colletta, Washington, D.C. ♦ Congregation BethAm, Los Altos Hills, California ♦ Christine Crandall, Cincinnati, Ohio ♦ Leslie S. Culank, Cambridge, England ♦ Ronald Cutler, Valley Stream, New York ♦ Jeffrey Cymbler, Rego Park, New York

Maida Dacher, Sherman Oaks, California ♦ Randy Daitch, Los Angeles, California ♦ Ephraim Dardashti, Merion Station, Pennsylvania ♦ Beverley Davis, Oam, Camberwell, Victoria, Australia ♦ Jacqueline Davis, Ottawa, Ontario, Canada ♦ Moshe Davis, Jerusalem, Israel ♦ Ross De Hovitz, Palo Alto, California ♦ Jeanette Delevie, Toronto, Ontario, Canada ♦ Jerome K. Delson, Palo Alto, California ♦ Linda Desmond, Albany, New York ♦ Mark Deutsch, New York, New York ♦ Donn Devine, Wilmington, Deleware ♦ Michael Diamond, Rowayton, Connecticut ♦ Stanley M. Diamond, Montreal, Quebec, Canada ♦ Ronald Doctor, Portland, Oregon ♦ Daniel Dratwa, Brussels, Belgium ♦ Bob Drilsma, Antwerpen, Belgium ♦ Sylvan M. Dubow, Washington, D.C. ♦ Jonina Duker and Alan David Lichtman, North Bethesda, Maryland

Ivan Elion, Parklands, South Africa ♦ Florence Gotlieb-Nerenberg Elman, Calgary, Alberta, Canada ♦ Paul Epner, Evanston, Illinois ♦ Cissie Eppel, Vancouver, British Columbia, Canada ♦ Rita Fox Esposito, Liverpool, New York ♦ Prof. Gerald L. Esterson, Ra'anana, Israel ♦ Daniel Ewenczyk, Paris, France ♦ Martin Epsztajn Eylat, Strasbourg, France

Phyllis Greenberg Faintich, St. Louis, Missouri ♦ Family History Library, Salt Lake City, Utah ♦ Andrew S. Farber, Terre Haute, Indiana ♦ Michael Feldberg, New York, New York ♦ Boris Feldblyum, Potomac, Maryland ♦ Abel Feldhamer, Cedarhurst, New York ♦ Daniel Feldman, Williamsville, New York ♦ Diane Feldman, Davidsonville, Maryland ♦ William H. Fern, Westport, Connecticut ♦ Gary Fink, Chula Vista, California ♦ Howard Fink, Acton, Massachusetts ♦ Walter G. Firestone, San Anselmo, California ♦ Alvin First, Rydal, Pennsylvania ♦ Judith Anne Raphael Flowers, Santa Rosa, California ♦ Bruce M. Fonoroff, Potomac, Maryland ♦ Judith Koenig Fox, West Bloomfield, Michigan ♦ Janet Reshes Fraidstern, Northampton, Massachusetts ♦ Werner L. Frank, Calabasas, California ♦ Karen Franklin, Yonkers, New York ♦ Chaim Freedman, Petah Tikvah, Israel ♦ Henrietta Little Freedman, Nashua, New Hampshire ♦ Peggy Mosinger Freedman, Atlanta, Georgia ♦ Harriet

Freidenreich, Philadelphia, Pennsylvania ◆ Diane M. Freilich, Farmington Hills, Michigan ◆ Monique Mann Freshman, Menands, New York ◆ Nora Freund, Toronto, Ontario, Canada ◆ Alex E. Friedlander, Brooklyn, New York ◆ Dale Friedman, Berkeley, California ◆ Daniel S. Friedman, Seattle, Washington ◆ Elise R. Friedman, Columbia, Maryland ◆ Thomas Furth, Stockholm, Sweden

Barry Gaines, Albuquerque, New Mexico ◆ Peter Garnick, Eltham North, Victoria, Australia ◆ Marlene Gavens, Suffield, Connecticut ◆ Anne Getlan, Scarsdale, New York ◆ Mike Getz, Bethesda, Maryland ◆ Karen Gilbert, Brooklyn, New York ◆ Marc L. Gilbert, Western Springs, Illinois ◆ Linda Gilmore, Chelmsford, Massachusetts ◆ Basile Ginger, Paris, France ◆ Bill Gladstone, Toronto, Ontario, Canada ◆ Ruth Taubman Glosser, Marina Del Rey, California ◆ Robert J. Glowitz, Mercer Island, Washington ◆ Melba Levitt Gold, Winnetka, Illinois ◆ Nancy J. Goldberg, Los Angeles, California ◆ Loel and Ruth Freund Goldblatt, Simsbury, Connecticut ◆ Milton R. Goldsamt, Silver Spring, Maryland ◆ Susan Goldsmith, Piedmont, California ◆ Irene Saunders Goldstein, Annandale, Virginia ◆ Louise Goldstein, Madison, Wisconsin ◆ Michael Goldstein, Jerusalem, Israel ◆ David Goodtree, Needham, Massachusetts ◆ Deena Yoffa Gordon, Houston, Texas ◆ Elinor Z. Gordon, Largo, Florida ◆ Judith T. Gordon, San Marcos, California ◆ Paul and Rita Gordon, Frederick, Maryland ◆ Glenn A. Gorelick, Sierra Madre, California ◆ Ava Auerbach Gorkin, Bayside, New York ◆ Beryl Greenberg, Winnipeg, Manitoba, Canada ◆ Sandra A. Newberger Greenberg, Denver, Colorado ◆ Judy Kamins Grein, Tampa, Florida ◆ James D. Grey, Bingham Farms, Michigan ◆ Penny Rubinoff Gross, Toronto, Ontario, Canada ◆ Ruth Ellen Gruber, Morre (Tr) Italy ◆ Caroline Guillot, Fresnes, France ◆ Susan Gurman, Lansdale, Pennsylvania ◆ Betty Stein Oppenheimer Guttman, Jerusalem, Israel ◆ Ladislau Gyemant, Cluj-Napoca, Romania

Laurence M. Harris, Pinner, Middlesex, England ◆ Stephen G. Harris, Berkeley, California ◆ Hebrew College Library, Newton Center, Massachusetts ◆ Max Heffler, Houston, Texas ◆ Deborah Levine Herman, Shaker Heights, Ohio ◆ Robert E. Heyman, Silver Spring, Maryland ◆ Harriette Hinderstein, Studio City, California ◆ Eugene M. Hirshberg, Waban, Massachusetts ◆ Jonathan Hodes, London, England ◆ Thea Hodge, Palo Alto, California ◆ John M. Hoenig, Williamsburg, Virginia ◆ Lawrence S. Hofrichter, Highland Park, New Jersey ◆ Robert Hoskinson, Pacific Grove, California ◆ David S. Howard, San Jose, California ◆ Paula Hurwitz, Pasadena, California

Emil H. Isaacson, Palm Harbor, Florida ◆ Saul Issroff, London, England ◆ Joel Ives, Fair Lawn, New Jersey

Betty Ann Jack, Goleta, California ◆ Elizabeth Jackson-Reinhardt, Murfreesboro, Tennessee ◆ Gerald D. Jacobs, Syracuse, Utah ◆ Graham N. Jaffe, London, England ◆ JGS of Canada, Toronto Division, Willowdale, Ontario, Canada ◆ JGS of Greater Boston, Boston, Massachusetts ◆ JGS of Colorado, Denver, Colorado ◆ JGS of Long Island, Plainview, New York ◆ JGS of Michigan, West Bloomfield, Michigan ◆ JGS of Philadelphia, Philadelphia, Pennsylvania ◆ JGS of San Diego, San Diego, California ◆ JGS of San Francisco Bay Area, San Francisco, California ◆ JGS of St. Louis, St. Louis, Missouri ◆ Eden Joachim, Pomona, New York ◆ Anthony P. Joseph, Smethwick, West Midlands, England ◆ Alan S. Josephson, Brooklyn, New York

Harvey L. Kaplan, Glasgow, Scotland ◆ Alex Kapner, Ardmore, Pennsylvania ◆ Jacob and Vicki Karno, Metairie, Louisiana ◆ Norman H. Katz, Monroe Township, New Jersey ◆ Barbara Kaufman, Mount Vernon, New York ◆ Alan F. Kaul, Sharon, Massachusetts ◆ Brian R. Kaye, M.D., Piedmont, California ◆ Louise Kaymen, Lyndeboro, New Hampshire ◆ Jocelyn Keene, Pasadena, California ◆ Gay Lynne Kegan, Palm Desert, California ◆ Joan Keith, Georgetown, Texas ◆ Stella Hazan Kent, Tel Aviv, Israel ◆ Yitzchak Kerem, Jerusalem, Israel ◆ Martin Kesselhaut, New Vernon, New Jersey ◆ Alfred Klayman, Delray Beach, Florida ◆ Harvey Klevit, Portland, Oregon ◆ Ronald Radbill Koegler, Santa Barbara, California ◆ Harvey L. Koizim, New Haven, Connecticut ◆ Don Koller, Rockville, Maryland ◆ Gregory Kolojeski, Winter Springs, Florida ◆ Joan Korin, Oakland, California ◆ Neal Koss, Palos Verdes, California ◆ Marcia R. Kowan, White Plains, New York ◆ Merle Krantzman, Moraga, California ◆ Sharlene Kranz, Washington, D.C. ◆ Samuel Kraus, Rancho Palos Verdes, California ◆ Avrohom Krauss, Saratoga, California ◆ Sandra Stitzer Krisch, Sarasota, Florida ◆ Harold B. Krom, Dallas, Texas ◆ Gladys and Sol Krongelb, Katonah, New York ◆ Harvey M. Krueger, New York, New York ◆ Sharri Rosen Kurpoff, Orlando, Florida ◆ Maurice Kulik, Thornhill, Ontario, Canada ◆ Arthur Kurzweil, Passaic, New Jersey ◆ Gary J. Kushner, Boxboro, Massachusetts

Peter W. Lande, Washington, D.C. ◆ Carol Philipp Landis, Costa Mesa, California ◆ Sheila Landsman, Lexington, Massachusetts ◆ Jack B. Lang, Murphy, North Carolina ◆ Robert M. Langer, Boston, Massachusetts ◆ Shmuel Laufer, Rehovot, Israel ◆ Herbert Irvin Lazerow, San Diego, California ◆ Gene Le Pere, Los Angeles, California ◆ David Lebovitz, Morton Grove, Illinois ◆ Anne Feder Lee, Honolulu, Hawaii ◆ Rosanne D. Leeson, Los Altos, California ◆ David Leon, Norfolk, Virginia ◆ Frances Lerner, Wiliamsburg, New Mexico ◆ Leslie Leven, Potomac, Maryland ◆ Myrna Nadel Levin, McAllen, Texas ◆ Leah Friedman Levine, Cincinnati, Ohio ◆ Barry A. Levitt, Indianapolis, Indiana ◆ Carol Lieberman,

Melville, New York ◆ Roni Seibel Liebowitz, Scarsdale, New York ◆ Alfred Eugene Lipsey, Tucson, Arizona ◆ Logan M. Lockabey, Costa Mesa, California ◆ Rene Loeb, Zurich, Switzerland ◆ Elizabeth Schwartz Lourie, Washington, D.C. ◆ Edward David Luft, Washington, D.C. ◆ Frederick A. Lynn, Scottsdale, Arizona

Peter MacDonald, Hamilton, New York ◆ Thomas J. Magner, Dayton, Ohio ◆ Michael Maidenberg, Grand Forks, North Dakota ◆ David Malinov, Hawley, Pennsylvania ◆ Jeffrey S. Malka, Vienna, Virginia ◆ Robert M. Mandelbaum, New York, New York ◆ Marc D. Manson, Farmington Hills, Michigan ◆ Howard Margol, Atlanta, Georgia ◆ Beverley W. Markowitz, Miami, Florida ◆ Michael Marx, Lexington, Massachusetts ◆ Bette Mas, Miami, Florida ◆ Freya Blitstein Maslov, Morton Grove, Illinois ◆ David, Liz and Talya Masters, London, England ◆ Louise Matz, Santa Barbara, California ◆ Ruth Klawan Hersch Mayo, Mountain View, California ◆ Samuel Mednick, Port Jefferson Station, New York ◆ Phillip Mendel, Temple City, California ◆ Marcia Indianer Meyers, Middletown, Connecticut ◆ Robert A. Michelson, Harrisburg, Pennsylvania ◆ Mid-Continent Public Library, Independence, Missouri ◆ Joanne Mika, Tucson, Arizona ◆ Alan R. Miller, Philadelphia, Pennsylvania ◆ Jeffrey A. Miller, Brookeville, Maryland ◆ Marvin Miller, North York, Ontario, Canada ◆ Rhoda Miller, Babylon, New York ◆ Ronald M. Miller, Dix Hills, New York ◆ Samuel H. Millstone, Farmington Hills, Michigan ◆ Ferne Phillips Mittleman, Williamsville, New York ◆ Kelvin Modlin, Doar Na Bet Shean, Israel ◆ Fruma Mohrer, New York, New York ◆ Gary and Ruth Mokotoff, Northvale, New Jersey ◆ Joel Sisitsky, Boca Raton, Florida ◆ Carole Montello, Las Vegas, Nevada ◆ Giselle Mora, Woodside, New York ◆ Ilene Kanfer Murray, St. Louis, Missouri

Eila D. Nacmias, Brooklyn, New York ◆ Charles B. Nam, Tallahassee, Florida ◆ Richard Narva, West Newton, Massachusetts ◆ Peter and Rieke Nash, Sydney, NSW, Australia ◆ Myron J. Nathan, Miami, Florida ◆ Nancy S. Neschis, New York, New York ◆ Ruth Sragow Newhouse, Bethesda, Maryland ◆ Aubrey Newman, Leicester, England ◆ Norma Neyman, Arvada, Colorado ◆ Fay Nissen, Sydney, Australia ◆ Sylvia Nusinov, Boca Raton, Florida

Gertrude Singer Ogushwitz, Storrs Mansfield, Connecticut ◆ Deborah Olken, Cambridge, Massachusetts ◆ Lewis P. Orans, Houston, Texas ◆ Kevin D. Ossey, Greensboro, North Carolina ◆ Claude M. Oulman, Butte, Montana

Elsebeth Paikin, Copenhagen, Denmark ◆ Gary Palgon, Atlanta, Georgia ◆ Brenda Friedland Pangborn, Bingham Farms, Michigan ◆ Sandra Tidquist Parri, Clearwater, Florida ◆ Gladys Friedman Paulin, Winter Springs, Florida ◆ Peggy K. Pearlstein, Rockville, Maryland ◆ Abraham Peliowski, Edmonton, Alberta, Canada ◆ Lisa Philip, Brooklyn, New York ◆ Harry K. Pick, West Hartford, Connecticut ◆ Wayne L. Pines, Washington, D.C. ◆ Eileen L. Polakoff, New York, New York ◆ Miriam Wolfers Pollak, Lane Cove NSW, Australia ◆ Michael A. Posnick, Minneapolis, Minnesota

Ann Rabinowitz, Miami Beach, Florida ◆ Nathan Radin, Atlanta, Georgia ◆ Lynn Rae, Willowdale, Ontario, Canada ◆ Morris Rapoport, Houston, Texas ◆ Gloria Glickman Rapp, Whitsett, North Carolina ◆ Robert D. Rauch, Bayside, New York ◆ Rita Redlich, Schenectady, New York ◆ Harold Rhode, Potomac, Maryland ◆ Arlene Blank Rich, Highland Heights, Ohio ◆ Edwin Taub Richard, Denver, Colorado ◆ Samuel J. Richelew, Southfield, Michigan ◆ Karen Abrams Rivers, Raleigh, North Carolina ◆ Andrea L. Robinson, Marina Del Rey, California ◆ Morton Rochman, Dix Hills, New York ◆ Lewis Rosen, Claremont, New Hampshire ◆ Roberta Rosen, Long Beach, California ◆ Joel Rosenbloom, Washington, D.C. ◆ Carolyn Rosenstein, Los Angeles, California ◆ Sue M. Rosenstrauch, Bridgewater, Massachusetts ◆ Emma Minkoff Rosow, Wayland, Massachusetts ◆ Robert Roth, Kingston, New York ◆ Vivienne Roumani-Denn, New York, New York ◆ Alejandro T. Rubinstein, Mexico City, Mexico ◆ Gail Stern Rudolph, Toronto, Ontario, Canada ◆ Ruth D. Rush, Gridley, California ◆ Nicki Russler, Knoxville, Tennessee ◆ Mary J. Ryan, Marina Del Rey, California

Arline Sachs, Springfield, Virginia ◆ Sallyann A. Sack, Bethesda, Maryland ◆ Rabbi Richard B. Safran, Tucson, Arizona ◆ Irwin Sagenkahn, Forty Fort, Pennsylvania ◆ Joanne Saltman, Belchertown, Massachusetts ◆ San Antonio Public Library, San Antonio, Texas ◆ Michelle Gail Sandler, Westminster, California ◆ Elias Savada, Bethesda, Maryland ◆ Rabbi Ben-Zion Saydman, Lake Forest, California ◆ Samuel J. Schleman, Malvern, Pennsylvania ◆ Charles M. Schloss, Englewood, Colorado ◆ Jerry Schneider, Burke, Virginia ◆ Benjamin C. Schoenbrun, Arlington, Virginia ◆ Louis Schonfeld, Beachwood, Ohio ◆ Susan Schreiber, Highland Park, Illinois ◆ Sarah Jane Schwarzenberg, Minneapolis, Minnesota ◆ Arthur Seif, Berkeley Heights, New Jersey ◆ Tamara Kleinfeld Selden, Easton, Pennsylvania ◆ Thomas Selling, Bollebygd, Sweden ◆ Murray Shainis, Bayside, New York ◆ Bert Z. Shanas, New York, New York ◆ Paul Shapiro, New York, New York ◆ Steven Shapiro, Mt. Kisco, New York ◆ Lionel Sharpe, Caulfield, Victoria, Australia ◆ Joanne Sher, Duluth, Minnesota ◆ Paula Shifres, Peabody, Massachusetts ◆ Robert Silverstein, Aurora, Colorado ◆ Dov Skiba, Kefar Sava, Israel ◆ Harris J. Sklar, Bala Cynwyd, Pennsylvania ◆ Eva Smith, Toodyay, Western Australia ◆ Norman R. Smith, La Jolla, California ◆ Henry Snyder, St. Paul, Minnesota ◆ Stephen L. Snyder, Reston, Virginia ◆ Deborah B. Somers, Pittsburgh, Pennsylvania ◆ Marco R. Soria, Milano, Italy ◆ David Sperlinger, Kent, England ◆ St. Louis County Library, St. Louis, Missouri ◆ Ethan D. Starr, Washington, D.C. ◆ State Library of Victoria, Melbourne, Australia ◆ Donald W. Stein, Tucson, Arizona ◆ Lewis Stein,

Boynton Beach, Florida ♦ Renee Stern Steinig, Dix Hills, New York ♦ Charles R. Steinman, Port Jefferson, New York ♦ Robert Steinman, San Diego, California ♦ Feige Stern, University Heights, Ohio ♦ Ignacio Sternberg, Caracas, Venezuela ♦ Susan Kaplan Stone, New York, New York ♦ Sara Louise Gulla Sukol, Springfield, Virginia

Mathilde Tagger, Jerusalem, Israel ♦ Lawrence F. Tapper, Ottawa, Ontario, Canada ♦ Victoria Tashman, Los Angeles, California ♦ Ros Tatarka, East St. Kilda, Victoria, Australia ♦ Cleda Taubin, Harrisonburg, Virginia ♦ Gary and Barbara Ludmeyer Teller, Atlanta, Georgia ♦ Don Teter, Baytown, Texas ♦ Arleen Shapiro Tievsky, Washington, D.C. ♦ Teri Tillman, Natchez, Mississippi ♦ Michael R. Tobin, Wellesley, Massachusetts ♦ Philip Trauring, Brookline, Massachusetts ♦ George A. Trief, Roscoe, New York ♦ Greg R. Tuckman, Tempe, Arizona ♦ Sam Turetzky, Ra'anana, Israel ♦ Abner Turk, Weston, Florida

Frances Simon Unger, Chicago, Illinois ♦ U.S. Holocaust Memorial Museum, Survivors Registry, Washington, DC

Peter Van Der Heijden, White Plains, New York ♦ Odette Vlessing, Amsterdam, Holland

Alan Wachtel, Palo Alto, California ♦ H. Daniel Wagner, Rehovot, Israel ♦ David Wallace, North Rocks, NSW, Australia ♦ Kathryn Illoway Wallach, Flushing, New York ♦ Robert S. Walters, Fort Wayne, Indiana ♦ Suzanne S. Waxman, Santa Rosa, California ♦ Miriam Weiner, Secaucus, New Jersey ♦ Susan Weiner, West Newton, Massachusetts ♦ Judith Kloogman Weinstein, Great Neck, New York ♦ Richard Weintraub, Wellesley, Massachusetts ♦ Henry Wellisch, Downsview, Ontario, Canada ♦ Western Reserve Historical Society, Cleveland, Ohio ♦ Jean Wever, Salt Lake City, Utah ♦ Barbara Wiley, Acampo, California ♦ Dorthy Lazelle Williams, Sacramento, California ♦ Barbara Wissoker, Lexington, Massachusetts ♦ Arthur Wolak, Vancouver, British Columbia, Canada ♦ Raymond Wolff, Berlin, Germany ♦ Ira Wolfman, New York, New York ♦ Judith G. Wolkovitch, Los Angeles, California ♦ Alexander Woodle, Groton, Massachusetts ♦ Lynn Wruble, Miami, Florida ♦ Peter S. Wyant, Regina, Saskatchewan, Canada ♦ Suzan Fischer Wynne, Kensington, Maryland

Len Yodaiken, Galil Elyon, Israel ♦ Mary Tonya Young, Albuquerque, New Mexico

Milo Zarakov, Alamo, California ♦ Jerry Zeisler, Leesburg, Virginia ♦ Mary Ann Zeman, Litchfield, Connecticut ♦ Martha Ibanez-Zervoudakis, Southwest Ranches, Florida ♦ Jerry Zevin, Irvine, California ♦ Sandra Zimmerman, Los Angeles, California